SEVENTH EDITION

GUIDE TO NEW ENGLAND MARINAS

Powered by Datastract™

Written by Elizabeth Adams Smith
Edited by Richard Y. Smith

Jerawyn Publishing Inc.

www.AtlanticCruisingClub.com

The Atlantic Cruising Club's Guide to New England Marinas

SEVENTH EDITION

ISBN Number: 0-9664028-3-9
Library of Congress Catalog Number: 2003101452

Cover Photos by Beth Adams Smith & Richard Y. Smith

Front Cover: Camden Harbor, ME
Back Cover: Conanicut Marine, Jamestown, RI
Marina at Rowes Wharf, Boston, MA
Northeast Harbor Marina, Northeast Harbor, ME

Initial Cover Design — Rob Johnson
Executed Cover Design — Jessica Williams, Spark Design
Book Design — Spark Design
Book & CD-ROM Programming — GNG Solutions
Maps — Kasim Khan
Senior Editor — Irina C. Adams
Associate Editor — Kevin Chamberlain

Printed by Edwards Brothers, Ann Arbor, MI.

Atlantic Cruising Club's Guide to New England Marinas
is written, compiled, edited and published by the Atlantic Cruising Club, an imprint of:

Jerawyn Publishing Inc.
PO Box 978; Rye, New York 10580

Table of Contents

To ensure objectivity, ACC neither accepts nor solicits marina advertising and there is absolutely no charge to marinas or boating facilities for their inclusion in the *Atlantic Cruising Club's Guides*. ACC reviewers have visited every Marina included in the Guides at least once — usually multiple times. All ACC reviewers and personnel pay for their dockage and other marina services and, if arriving by boat, do not identify themselves until the conclusion of a marina stay.

Preface

Welcome to the Seventh Edition of the *Atlantic Cruising Club's Guides to Marinas.* This regional volume covers 230 New England marinas from Bar Harbor, ME to Block Island, RI; it's one of 6 regional volumes (describing about 1,300 marinas from Maine to Texas) that will be published over the next year. The other regional volumes cover Long Island Sound (including the New Jersey Coast), The Chesapeake Bay, The Mid-Atlantic (including the ICW and Bermuda), Eastern Florida (including The Keys), and The Gulf Coast. Most of the research for these volumes is complete and they'll be published as quickly as is practical.

- **A Little Background:** To us, cruising is one part fun, one part character building, one part enlightenment, one part food, one part adventure, and one part reading — with a little bit of stress thrown in just to keep us on our toes. So, at the end of the day, we often want to just tie up, kick back and relax in a slip or on a mooring. That usually means we need to find a marina. Easier said than done. A marina stay can be expensive — sometimes as expensive as a nice hotel room — and a lot harder to leave when it's not what you expected.

  After years of trying to guesstimate what we'd find, based on the cruising guides' summary grids and marina ads or by quizzing dockmasters over the phone, we discovered a handy little loose-leaf Marina Guide, covering about 250 East Coast marinas, that was published by the Atlantic Cruising Club. The information was invaluable — it was objective, specific and even included rates along with the ACC Reviews and Ratings. The Guide provided details that weren't available anywhere else and all marinas included had been personally visited by ACC. We acquired the Atlantic Cruising Club in 1996, took it digital, added over a hundred Reports and, a year and a half later, published the first publicly available Atlantic Cruising Club's Guide to East Coat Marinas — Book and CD-ROM. Since then, we've visited more than 1,500 marinas (most of them several times), revised the original Marina Reports, and added more than 1,000 new ones. We've also built a library of well over 10,000 photographs and compiled more than 300 items of information on every significant transient facility along the East and Gulf Coasts.

- **Which Marinas Are Included?** The Guides attempt to include all facilities that can accommodate cruising boats 30 feet or longer and offer transient dockage or moorings. Yacht Clubs, which extend courtesies to all boaters without requiring reciprocity, are also included. Transient accommodations do not need to be dedicated; many of the included facilities welcome transients on a space-available basis. We have given priority in this edition to those facilities in the major cruising grounds or on the most frequented passages. Over time, ACC's reviewers will head farther up the rivers and expand into less visited — but potentially more interesting — areas.

- **Geographic Organization:** The *Guide to New England Marinas* is organized into twelve "sub-regions". Each sub-region corresponds to the gray tabs on the edge of the Guide's pages, to the graphic maps at the beginning of each section, and to the Geographic Marina List that follows this introduction. Within each sub-region, marinas are ordered, generally, from North to South or, for rivers or harbors, from mouth to source. We have attempted to arrange the Reports in the order a boater would encounter the marinas in a cruise from Bar Harbor to Block Island.

- **The Enclosed CD-ROM:** The CD-ROM contains all the Marina Reports included in the print edition plus up to nine full-color photographs of each facility. Users can search over 100 of the information items in the Marina Report, which makes it easy to cull through the roughly 70,000 pieces of data in each volume to find exactly the right marina. Installation is easy — just insert the CD into your computer's CD-ROM drive, and the installation program will begin.

- **The Atlantic Cruising Club's Website:** The Atlantic Cruising Club's new, greatly expanded, website (www.AtlanticCruisingClub.com) will house all the Marina Reports, with updates, a forum for readers to communicate with ACC and with each other, boating and cruising links, and other items of interest to our fellow cruisers. Please check it often for the most current information regarding marinas included in the Guide.

Preparing the Seventh Edition has really been a lot of fun. We've learned a great deal and we're looking forward to expanding ACC's marina coverage with additional volumes. On the drawing board, after the East and Gulf Coasts, are: The Bahamas & The Caribbean, Great Lakes 1 & 2, The Northwest, and The West Coast. We hope that the newly expanded format, the extensive use of photos, and more detailed Marina Reports and Ratings will point you to the right facility, with the most appropriate services and surroundings for your cruising needs. We also hope that you will log-on to the ACC WebSite (or email us) with any changes, inaccuracies, new services or facilities you discover. Finally, we hope that you will share your marina impressions and general experiences with us and with your fellow cruisers.

Fair winds and happy cruising,

Beth and Richard Smith

Beth@AtlanticCruisingClub.com
Richard@AtlanticCruisngClub.com

ACC's *Guide to New England Marinas'* Twelve Sub-Regions

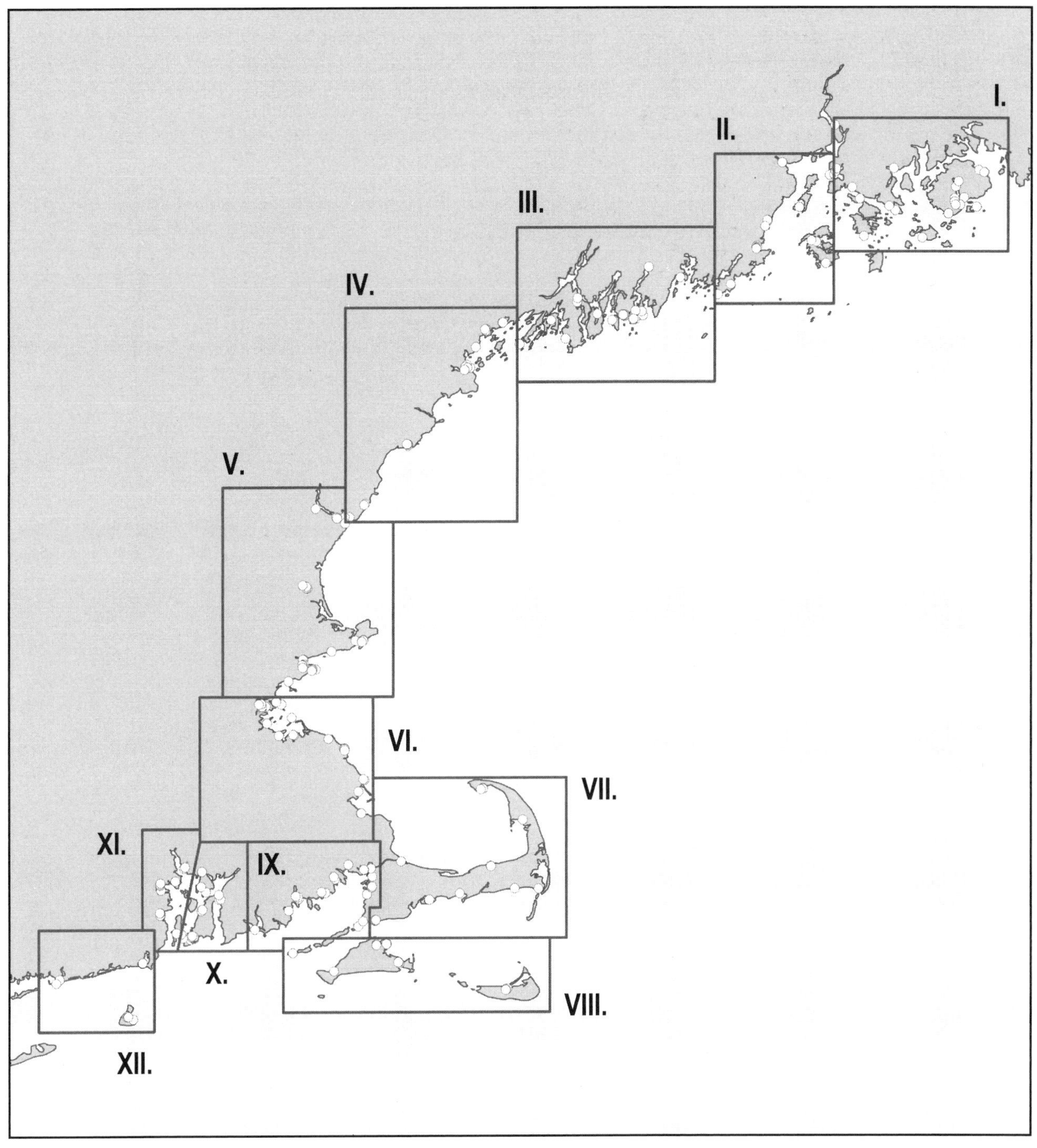

Atlantic Cruising Club's Ratings

The Bell Ratings generally reflect the services and amenities available for the captain and crew rather than the services available for the boat. By their nature, ratings are subjective and may reflect certain biases of the writers, editors and other reviewers. It is important to note that a five-bell marina will not always be a boater's best choice. There tends to be a correlation between higher bell ratings and higher overnight transient rates. Many of the resort-type amenities available at four- and five-bell marinas may be of little interest to boaters arriving late in the day and planning an early start the next morning. Similarly, a facility which has a one- or two-bell rating, good security, convenient transportation and a service-oriented staff, may be the best place to "leave the boat" for a period of time between legs of a longer cruise.

The Boatyard Ratings, on the other hand, are less subjective. They simply indicate the extent of the boatyard services and the size of yachts that the facility can manage. To receive a boatyard rating at all (one-travelift), a facility must have a haul-out mechanism — a travelift or marine railway (or, in some cases, a heavy-duty crane or forklift) plus, at a minimum, a standard array of basic boatyard services. To receive a two-travelift rating, a facility will generally have haul-out capacity in excess of 100 tons and a full complement of all possible boatyard services.

The Sunset Rating is the most subjective of all. This symbol indicates remarkable, special places like a pristine, untouched mooring field with no other facilities in sight, a marina that is, itself, so exquisitely turned out that it is truly beautiful, a skyline or distant vista that is simply breathtaking, or a marina that offers the possibility of a unique experience. A Sunset means that, in our view, there is more here than the first two ratings can convey — and only you can determine if the additional notation is valid for you and your crew. We'd be very interested in hearing your collective views.

The Bell Ratings

Outlined below are some of the facilities and amenities one might generally find at a marina or boating facility within a given Bell-Rating category. Please note that some marinas within a particular category may not have all of the facilities listed here and some may have more. (The word "Marina" is used generically here, and throughout the Guide, to denote all types of marine facilities.)

One Bell: The marina comfortably accommodates vessels well over thirty feet in length, accepts overnight transients at docks or on moorings, and generally has heads. These are the "basic requirements" for ACC inclusion. (Most facilities that are strictly mooring fields with a dinghy dock fall into this category.)

Two Bells: In addition to meeting the basic ACC requirements, the marina generally has a dedicated marina staff, heads, showers and, perhaps, a laundry. It likely has mail-hold and takes phone messages for transients, has an available fax machine, and is served by FedEx, Airborne, UPS, and Express Mail. Often there are dock carts, a picnic area and grills, and limited groceries are onsite or nearby. If this is a "moorings only" facility, there may be a launch service or dinghy loaner.

Three Bells: With attractive and convenient facilities, the marina significantly exceeds basic requirements in many physical and operational categories. In addition to the two-bell services described above, there is a restaurant onsite or very near, a pool, beach or a major recreational amenity onsite or very near, and laundry onsite or easily accessible. The marina usually offers docking assistance and other customer-oriented services, a ships' store, cable TV, some kind of data port accessibility, and, hopefully, a pump-out facility. If there are only moorings, then there is often launch service and/or dinghy loaner.

Four Bells: Worth changing course to visit, the marina significantly exceeds requirements in most physical and operational categories and offers above average service in well-appointed, appealing, and thoughtfully turned-out facilities. In addition to the three-bell services described above, it may offer concierge services, accommodations onsite or very near, golf, tennis or a significant attraction, and historic/scenic sites. If the marina is part of a resort, then a "guest in the marina is a guest of the resort."

Five Bells: A renowned, "destination" facility, the marina is worth a special trip. It has truly superior facilities, services and atmosphere. A five-bell marina is located in a beautiful, luxurious, impeccably maintained environment and provides absolutely everything a cruising boater might reasonably expect. It offers all that is promised in a four-bell marina, plus outstanding quality in every respect.

Bell ratings reflect both subjective judgment and objective criteria. For instance, an ACC bias is discovering interesting and distinctive waterfront destinations or city-center facilities which may not have all the standard marina services, but which provide a unique experience. These may be given ratings higher than their facilities would suggest. Similarly, maritime museums, which most boaters find particularly compelling, are usually given a "Sunset" to indicate that they offer maritime buffs more here than just services. Ratings are also geographically specific and reflect the general level of available services in a given region. In other words, a five-bell marina in Florida (with a year-round season) will usually offer significantly more services and facilities than a five-bell marina in Maine (with a four-month season).

A Tour of a Marina Report

Photo: *One for each marina in the printed Marina Report, up to 9 in full-color on the enclosed CD-ROM. Most were taken by ACC personnel during periodic visits. They are intended to provide a non-commercial, visual sense of each facility.*

Ratings: *Bells (1 - 5) reflect the quality of onsite marina facilities plus location, recreation, dining, lodgings, etc. Travelifts (1 - 2) indicate the extent of the boatyard services. A Sunset notes a particularly beautiful, special, unique, or interesting place.*

Top Section: *Facts, facts and more facts, including VHF channels, phone numbers, e-mail/ website addresses, number of slips, moorings, power options (rates for all), and much more. The format of this section is identical for every Marina Report for easy reference and comparison.*

Wayfarer Marine

ME - MIDCOAST

Navigational Information

Lat: 44°12.547' **Long:** 069°03.641' **Tide:** 10 ft. **Current:** n/a **Chart:** 13305
Rep. Depths (*MLW*): **Entry** 15 ft. **Fuel Dock** 10 ft. **Max Slip/Moor** 13 ft./50 ft.
Access: Past Curtis Island to Camden inner Harbor, first facility to starboard

Marina Facilities *(In Season/Off Season)*

Fuel: *Renneco* - Gasoline, Diesel
Slips: 40 Total, 20 Transient **Max LOA:** 120 ft. **Max Beam:** 30 ft.
Rate *(per ft.)*: **Day** $3.00/Inq.* **Week** n/a **Month** n/a
Power: **30 amp** $10, **50 amp** $20, **100 amp** n/a, **200 amp** n/a
Cable TV: No **Dockside Phone:** No
Dock Type: Wood, Long Fingers, Alongside, Floating, Fixed
Moorings: 59 Total, 54 Transient **Launch:** Yes ($1/pp/1-way), Dinghy Dock
Rate: **Day** $30/35* **Week** $200-230 **Month** Inq.
Heads: 6 Toilet(s), 5 Shower(s)
Laundry: 3 Washer(s), 3 Dryer(s), Book Exchange **Pay Phones:** Yes
Pump-Out: OnSite, Full Service **Fee:** $10 **Closed Heads:** Yes

Marina Operations

Owner/Manager: Wendy Hart **Dockmaster:** Same
In-Season: May-Oct, 8am-5pm **Off-Season:** Nov-Apr, 7am-3:30pm
After-Hours Arrival: Call ahead. Tie up at fuel dock and check in in the am
Reservations: Recommended **Credit Cards:** Visa/MC, Dscvr, Amex
Discounts: None
Pets: Welcome, Dog Walk Area **Handicap Access:** Yes, Heads, Docks

Wayfarer Marine

PO Box 677; Sea Street; Camden, ME 04843

Tel: (207) 236-4378; (800) 229-4378 **VHF:** **Monitor** 71 **Talk** 71
Fax: (207) 236-2371 **Alternate Tel:** (207) 236-4378
Email: info@wayfarermarine.com **Web:** www.wayfarermarine.com
Nearest Town: Camden *(.5 mi.)* **Tourist Info:** (207) 236-4404

Marina Services and Boat Supplies

Services - Docking Assistance, Concierge, Security *(until 10pm)*, Trash Pick-Up, Dock Carts **Communication** - Mail & Package Hold, Phone Messages, Fax in/out *($2/pp)*, Data Ports *(Customer Phone Room)*, FedEx, AirBorne, UPS, Express Mail *(Sat Del)* **Supplies - OnSite:** Ice *(Block, Cube)*, Ships' Store, CNG **Under 1 mi:** Marine Discount Store, Bait/Tackle, Propane *(Willey 236-3256/Farmers Union 236-3266)*

Boatyard Services

OnSite: Engine mechanic *(gas, diesel)*, Travelift *(110T)*, Forklift *(80T, 35T hydraulic trailers)*, Crane *(35T)*, Launching Ramp, Electrical Repairs, Electronic Sales, Electronics Repairs, Hull Repairs, Rigger, Sail Loft, Bottom Cleaning, Brightwork, Air Conditioning, Refrigeration, Compound, Wash & Wax, Interior Cleaning, Propeller Repairs, Woodworking, Life Raft Service, Yacht Interiors, Metal Fabrication, Awlgrip, Yacht Broker, Total Refits **OnCall:** Divers **Dealer for:** Boston Whaler, Westerbeke, Johnson & Evinrude, Mirrocraft, Avon. **Yard Rates:** $35-60/hr., Haul & Launch $12.25-13.50/ft., Power Wash $2/ft., Bottom Paint $9/ft., Member: ABBRA, ABYC, Other Certifications: Nautor's Swan & Oyster Yachts **Storage:** On-Land $35/ft. Inside-$6.75-8.75/sq.ft.

Restaurants and Accommodations

Near: Motel *(River House 236-0500, $150-200)*, Inn/B&B *(Hawthorn 236-8842, $155)* **Under 1 mi:** Restaurant *(Peter Ott's 236-4032, D $16-22)*, *(Whitehall B $8, D $15-23)*, *(Cappys 236-2254, L $7-15, D $10-17)*, Seafood Shack *(Bayview 789-5550, L $3-13, D $3-15)*, Pizzeria *(Camden House 230-2464, L $4-14, D $4-14)*, Inn/B&B *(Whitehall Inn 236-3891, $100-150)*, *(Maine Stay 236-9636, $100-165)*, *(Lord Camden 236-4325, $90-210)*

Recreation and Entertainment

OnSite: Picnic Area, Grills **Near:** Playground, Volleyball, Tennis Courts, Jogging Paths, Boat Rentals, Roller Blade/Bike Paths, Park, Cultural Attract *(Camden Civic Theater 236-2281; Camden Opera House 236-3358)*, Sightseeing **Under 1 mi:** Beach, Movie Theater *(Bay View St. 236-8722)*, Video Rental *(Harbor Video 236-9596)*, Museum *(Conway Homestead, Cramer Mansion)* **1-3 mi:** Heated Pool *(YMCA 236-3375)*, Golf Course *(Goose River 236-8488)*, Fitness Center *(YMCA)*

Provisioning and General Services

OnSite: Provisioning Service *(French & Brawn satellite)*, Wine/Beer **Near:** Gourmet Shop, Lobster Pound, Bank/ATM, Library *(Camden 236-3440)* **Under 1 mi:** Supermarket *(French & Brawn 236-336, Grave's 236-8577)*, Delicatessen *(Camden Deli 236-8343)*, Health Food *(Natures Choice 236-8280)*, Liquor Store *(Rite Aid 236-4546)*, Bakery, Fish Monger, Post Office, Protestant Church, Beauty Salon, Dry Cleaners, Full-Service Laundry, Bookstore, Pharmacy *(Rite Aid 236-4546)*, Hardware Store *(Rankins 236-3275)*, Florist, Department Store *(Remy's)*

Transportation

OnSite: Water Taxi *($1/pp MemDay-LabDay)* **OnCall:** Bikes *(Brown Dog 236-6664 $15/day.)*, Rental Car *(National 594-8424, USave 236-2320)*, Taxi *(Don's Taxi 236-4762)*, Airport Limo *(Schooner Bay 594-5000)* **Near:** Local Bus **Airport:** Rockland/Bangor Int'l. *(12 mi./45 mi.)*

Medical Services

911 Service **OnCall:** Ambulance **Near:** Chiropractor **Under 1 mi:** Doctor, Dentist **Hospital:** Penobscot Bay 596-8000 *(4 mi.)*

Setting -- On the east side of the entrance to protected Camden Harbor, Wayfarer Marine - with its network of well-maintained sheds, docks, facilities, harbor floats, and mooring field - is easily visible. This full-service yachting facility offers its guests breathtaking views of Camden Harbor, the village, and the Camden Hills above, and provides easy access to this picturesque town's extensive services and amenities.

Marina Notes -- *Rates: $3/ft. up to 16 ft. beam, beams greater than 16 ft. $4/ft.; floats: $35/ft., moorings: $30 to 50 ft., $35 over 50 ft. Excellent docks - 20 "alongside" spots, 5 finger slips for trans. Expect to raft up to 3 deep during high season. All moorings are in the outer harbor - marked with a Wayfarer burgee and max. length boat allowed. Launch hours 8am-8pm Jun-Aug. Hauls vessels to 110 tons, with drafts to 14 feet; most comprehensive boatyard in this part of Maine. U.S. Customs & Immigration assistance. Comfortable heads, showers, and laundry room - one full bath, plus men's and women's heads with individual showers. Established in 1963, but the boat building tradition reaches back more than 200 years; there have been seven previous boatyards on this site.

Notable -- Wayfarer is on the "quiet side" of the harbor. Their water taxi ($1/pp) shuttles guests across to the bustling, service-laden side - downtown Camden. Alternatively, one could dinghy to the Town Landing or walk the half mile around the perimeter of the harbor. Seven schooners make their home in Camden; these spectacular vessels offer trips from 2 hours to 6 days and, when in port, are an integral part of the scenery. Labor Day is Windjammer weekend. Edna St. Vincent Millay grew up in Camden and there is much memorabilia here. Camden Hills State Park is 2 mi. Farmers' Market Sat. 9am-noon, Wed 4:30-

PHOTOS ON CD-ROM: 9

CAMDEN HARBOR 31

Sub-Regions: *The New England Edition includes 12 sub-regions. For quick reference, these sub-region tabs are visible on the outside page edges. In each sub-region, Marina Reports are ordered North to South.*

Marina Name: *230 marina and marine facilities included in the New England Edition.*

Middle Section: *What's available, where and how to find it. Marine Services & Boat Supplies, Boatyard Services (including rates), Restaurants and Accommodations, Recreation and Entertainment, Provisioning and General Services, Transportation and Medical Services, all classified by distance — OnSite, Nearby, Within 1 mile, 1-3 miles or beyond. Names, phone numbers, price ranges and more.*

Photos on CD: *Indicates the number of full-color photos of this facility that are on the CD-ROM.*

Bottom Section: The *"Setting" commentary portrays an idea of the marina's surroundings. "Marina Notes" provides important and interesting facts about the marina and its operations that may not have been covered in either of the earlier sections. "Notable" addresses anything the writers/editors feel is noteworthy, from special events and special services to interesting side trips and local lore.*

Harbor: *Harbor or major body of water on which the marina resides.*

The Marina Reports

Individual Marina Reports are presented in a one page, easy-reference format to make the *Guide* as user-friendly as possible.

Each Report provides up to 300 items of information, grouped into the following sections and categories:

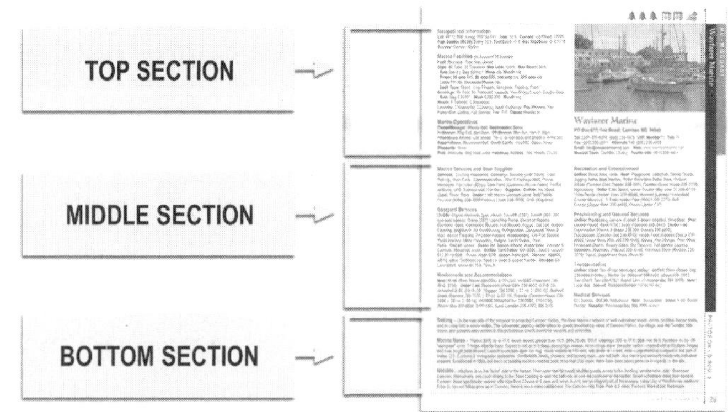

TOP SECTION

Name
Address

Primary & Toll-Free Phone numbers
Alternate Phone — after-hours
Fax number

VHF channels — Talk & Monitor
E-mail address
Web URL

Nearest Town (distance)
Tourist Office Phone

Navigational Information

Harbor (bottom of page)
Latitude/Longitude

Tidal Range & Maximum Current
Chart Number

Access — General Directions
MLW Depths *(Reported by the marinas)*

Entry & Fuel Dock Depths
Deepest Slip/Mooring

Marina Facilities (In Season/Off Season)

Fuel: Availability and Brand
Diesel or Gasoline
Slip-Side or OnCall Fueling
High-Speed Pumps
Maximum Boat LOA & Beam
Slips: Number of Total/Transient
Rates: Daily, Weekly, Monthly
Power (Availability & Rates):
30amp, 50 amp, 100 amp, 200 amp
Cable TV: Availability, Terms, Rates
Dockside Phone: Terms, Rates

Dock Type
Fixed or Floating
Alongside
Short or Long Fingers, Pilings
Dock Material
Wood, Concrete, Vinyl,
Aluminum or Composite
Moorings: Total/Transient
Rates: Daily, Weekly, Monthly
Launch Service — Terms and Fees
Dinghy Dock — Terms and Fees

Heads:
Number of Toilets
Number of Showers
Dressing Rooms
Hair Dryers & Other Amenities
Laundry:
Number of Washers & Dryers
Irons and Ironing Boards
Book Exchange
Pay Phones
Services to Anchored Boats

Pump-out Availability & Fees
OnSite or OnCall
Full Service or Self Service
Number of Central Stations
Number of Portable Stations
In-Slip Dedicated Units
Pump-Out Boats

Closed Head Requirements

The number of transient slips or moorings does not necessarily mean dedicated transient slips or moorings. Many facilities rent open slips and moorings to transient cruisers when their seasonal tenants are not in port. The number of Transient Slips/Moorings indicated is the facility's guesstimate, based on past experience, of the number generally available at any given time. In-Season and Off-Season rates are listed as $2.50/1.75. The parameters of those seasons are outlined in "Marina Operations" — Dates and Hours. If rates are complicated, which is becoming the norm, then the daily rate for a 40-foot boat is selected, followed by an asterisk, and a complete explanation of the rate structure is given in the "Marina Notes" section. The availability of 300 amp, European Voltage and 3-Phase is listed under "Marina Services and Boat Supplies." If there is alongside dockage, rather than individual slips, then the total number of alongside feet is divided by an average boat length of 40 feet and that number is displayed next to the Total/Transient Slips heading — followed by another asterisk. Dock Type is then listed as "Alongside" and the specifics are explained in "Marina Notes." The lack of finger piers — long or short — may signal a "Stern-To, Med-Mooring" approach. Since this can be a critical factor in choosing a marina, this will be highlighted in "Marina Notes." Since Book Exchanges or Lending Libraries, along with Pay Phones, are traditionally in the laundry room, these are itemized in the Laundry section. If there is Launch Services, the hours are usually included in Marina Notes, too.

A discussion of Closed Harbors, Pump-Out Facilities and the current Federal and State Regulations pertaining to Maine, New Hampshire, Massachusetts and Rhode Island can be found in Addendum II.

Marina Operations

Marina Owner/Manager
Harbormaster
Dockmaster
Dates & Hours of Operation

After Hours Arrival Procedure
Reservation Policies
Pets: Welcome?
Dog Walk Area, Kennel

Discount Programs
Boat-US, Nautical Miles, Safe/Sea
Dockage Fuel & Repair Discounts
Handicap Accessibility

Credit Cards Accepted:
Visa, MasterCard, Discover,
Diners Club, American Express

For municipal facilities the Harbormaster is listed under "Marina Owner/Manager" with the designation "(Harbormaster)" following his/her name. Dates and Hours for both in-season and off-season are provided and indicate the requisite time frames for the In-season and Off-season rates. In-season precedes off-season, separated by a (/) slash.

MIDDLE SECTION

Most of the information in this section is classified by "Proximity" — the distance from the marina to the service or facility, as follows:

OnSite — at the marina
OnCall — pick-up, delivery or slipside service
Nearby — up to approximately 4/10 of a mile — a very easy walking distance
Within 1 mile — a reasonable, though more strenuous, walking distance
1 – 3 miles — a comfortable biking distance, a major hike or a cab ride
3+ miles — a taxi, courtesy car or rental car distance — generally included is the approximate distance from the marina

(FYI: In this section, telephone area codes are included only if they are different from the area codes in the marina's contact information.)

Marina Services and Boat Supplies

General Services:
Docking Assistance
Dock Carts
Trash Pick-up
Security — Type & Hours
Concierge Services
Room Service to the Boat

MegaYacht Services:
Additional Power Options:
300 Amps
Three-Phase
European Voltage
Crew Lounge

Communications:
Mail and Package Hold
Courier Services
FedEx. Airborne, UPS
Express Mail, Saturday Delivery
Phone Messages
Fax In and Out — Fees
Internet Access/Data Ports
Type, Location & Fees

Supplies: (Listed by Proximity)
Ice — Block, Cubes, Shaved
Ships' Stores — Local Chandlery
West Marine, Boat-U.S.,
Boaters World,
Other Marine Discount Stores
Bait & Tackle
Live Bait
Propane & CNG

Under Services are additional power options beyond the basic amperage covered in the "Marina Facilities" section. Under Communications, is a list of the couriers that service the Marina's local area. This does not imply that the marina will manage outgoing courier services (unless, of course, they specifically offer concierge services); that process would be up to the individual boater. Communications also covers Internet access and data port availability with additional information provided in "Marina Notes." A brief discussion of Wi-Fi wireless Internet access systems is included in Addendum III. Under Supplies are resources for galley fuel – propane and CNG. As those of you who rely on CNG know, it is becoming harder and harder to find — if you discover any resources that we have not listed, please share them. Note, too, that West Marine has recently purchased all the Boat-U.S. stores. As of our publication date, they are planning to continue to operate them under the Boat-U.S. name — so we have listed them separately.

Boatyard Services

Nearest Boatyard (If not onsite):
Travelift (including tonnage)
Railway
Forklift
Crane
Hydraulic Trailer
Launching Ramp
Engine Mechanics — Gas & Diesel
Electrical Repairs
Electronic Sales
Electronic Repairs
Propeller Repairs

Air Conditioning
Refrigeration
Rigger
Sail Loft
Canvas Work
Upholstery
Yacht Interiors
Brightwork
Painting
Awlgrip (or similar finish)
Woodworking
Hull repairs

Metal Fabrication
Divers
Bottom Cleaning
Compound, Wash & Wax
Inflatable Repairs
Life Raft Service
Interior Cleaning
Yacht Design
Yacht Building
Total Refits
Yacht Broker
Dealer For: (Boats, Engines, Parts)

Yard Rates:
General Hourly Rate
Haul & Launch (Blocking included)
Power Wash
Bottom Paint (Paint included?)
Boat Storage Rates:
On Land (Inside/Outside)
In the Water
Memberships & Certifications:
ABBRA — No. of Cert. Techs.
ABYC — No. of Cert. Techs.
Other Certifications

If the facility does not have a boatyard onsite, then the name and telephone number of the nearest boatyard is provided. In most cases, the services listed as "Nearby" or "Within 1 mile" will be found at that facility. "Dealer For" lists the manufacturers that the Boatyard services and its Authorized Dealerships. "Memberships and Certifications" refers to the two maritime trade organizations (ABBRA — American Boat Builders & Repairers Association & ABYC — American Boat and Yacht Council), which have programs that train and certify boatyard craftspeople and technicians. Several of the other professional maritime organizations and many manufacturers also offer rigorous training and certification on their particular product lines. These are included under "Other Certifications."
A brief description of ABBRA and ABYC, and their certification programs, as well as the other major marine industry organizations is provided in Addendum III.

Restaurants and Accommodations

Restaurants
Seafood Shacks
Raw Bars

Snack Bars
Coffee Shops
Lite Fare

Fast Food
Pizzeria
Hotels

Motels
Inns/B&Bs
Cottages/Condos

Since food is a major component of cruising, considerable attention has been given to both restaurants and provisioning resources. Eateries of all kinds are included (with phone numbers); full-service restaurants are listed simply as Restaurants. If delivery is available it is either noted or the establishment is listed as "OnCall." An attempt has been made to provide a variety of dining options and, whenever possible, to include the meals served Breakfast, Lunch, Dinner, Sunday Brunch (B, L, and/or D), plus the price range for entrées at each meal. If the menu is Prix Fixé (table d'hôte or one-price for 3-4 courses), this is indicated in the commentary. On rare occasion, if a restaurant has received very high marks from a variety of reviewers, that will be noted, too. If we are aware of a children's menu, the listing will indicate "Kids' Menu." Often the hours of onsite restaurants are included in "Marina Notes" or "Notable."

Price ranges have been gathered from menus, websites, site visits, marina notes and phone calls. Although these change over time, the range should give you an idea of the general price point. In large cities, the list generally consists of a handful of the closest restaurants — we expect that you will supplement this with a local restaurant guide. In small towns, the list provided may be "exhaustive" — these may be all there are and they may not be close.

Frequently, the need for local off-boat overnight accommodations arises — either for guests, crew changes, or just because it's time for a real shower or a few more amenities or a bed that doesn't rock. We have attempted to list a variety of local lodgings and, whenever possible, have included the room rate, too. The rates listed generally cover a 12-month range. So, if you are cruising in high season, expect the high end of the range. If the lodgings are part of the marina, then there is often a "package deal" of some sort for marina guests wishing to come ashore. We have asked the question about "package deals" and included the answers in "Marina Notes."

Recreation and Entertainment

Pools (heated or not)
Beach
Picnic Areas & Grills
Children's Playground
Dive Shop
Volleyball
Tennis Courts
Golf Course
Fitness Center
Jogging Paths
Horseback Riding
Roller Blade & Bicycle Paths
Bowling
Sport Fishing Charter
Group Fishing Boat
Movie Theater
Video Rentals
Video Arcade
Park
Museum
Galleries
Cultural Attractions
Sightseeing
Special Events

What there is to do, once you're tied up and cleaned up, is often a driving force in choosing a harbor or a particular marina. If you are choosing a facility to spend a lay-day or escape foul weather, the potential land-based activities become even more important. We have created a list of the possible major types of recreation and entertainment activities and have organized them, again, by proximity; if they are more easily reached by dinghy we note that, too.

A public golf course is almost always listed unless it is farther than 10 miles. Boat Rentals includes kayaks, canoes and small sailboats. Group Fishing Boats are sometimes known as "head boats." Museums covers the gamut from art and maritime to historic houses and districts to anthropological and environmental. Cultural Attractions can range from local craft ateliers to aquaria to live theaters to all manner of musical concerts. Sightseeing can range from whale watching to historical walking tours. Special Events usually covers the major once-a-year local tourist extravaganzas — and almost all require significant advance planning (often these also appear in the "Notable" section). Galleries, both fine art and crafts, are listed under Entertainment rather than General Services since we view them more as opportunities for enlightenment than the shops that they really are. Admission prices are provided for both Adults and Children, when available, and are listed with the Adult price first, followed by the Children's price, i.e. $15/7. Occasionally, there is a family package price, which is also listed. Most entertainment and recreation facilities also offer Student and Senior Citizen pricing and other discounts; unfortunately, we don't have space to note them, but we do provide a phone number, so call and ask.

Provisioning and General Services

Complete Provisioning Service
Convenience Store
Supermarket — usually major chain
Market — smaller, local store
Gourmet Shop
Delicatessen
Health Food Store
Wine/Beer Purveyor
Liquor/Package Store
Bakery
Farmers' Markets
Green Grocer
Fishmonger
Lobster Pound
Meat Market
Bank/ATMs
Post Office
Library
Houses Of Worship
  Catholic Church
  Protestant Church
  Synagogue
  Mosque
Beauty Salon
Barber Shop
Dry Cleaners
Laundry
Bookstore
Pharmacy
Newsstand
Hardware Store
Florist
Retail Shops
Department Store
Copy Shops
Buying Club

As noted above, we think that most boaters travel on their stomachs, so knowing how to find local provisioning resources is very important. In addition, there is a fairly constant need for all kinds of services and supplies. When delivery is available for any of the provisioning resources or services, we've either noted that in the commentary or listed it as "OnCall."

For major provisioning runs, we have tried to identify the closest outlet for a regional supermarket chain. If a smaller, but fairly well supplied, market is close by, we include it as well as the more distant chain supermarket. Most people, we've discovered, really prefer to find interesting, local purveyors, so the presence of a Farmers' Market is notable. Usually these are a one or two-day-a-week events, so the exact days, times and locations are included. To differentiate Farmers' Markets from produce markets and farm stands, these are listed as Green Grocers. We've also tried to locate full Provisioning Services that will "do it all" and deliver dockside. And Fishmonger is just another name for fish sellers — these could be regular fish markets or directly "off-the-boat."

In the "General Services" category, we've included the nearest libraries because they can be wonderful sources of all kinds of "local knowledge," and can provide a welcome port on a foul weather day. They also usually have children's programs during the "season" and, with growing frequency, offer data ports or public Internet access on their own PCs. The Laundry in this section should not to be confused with the washers and dryers at the marina. Laundries are usually combination "do it for you" drop-off and self-service operations — and are frequently near restaurants or recreation or entertainment venues.

Transportation

Courtesy Car or Van
Bikes
Water Taxi
Rental Car — Local and Nat'l
Taxi
Local Bus
Intercity Bus
Rail — Amtrak & Commuter
Ferry Service
Airport Limo
Airport — Regional & Nat'l

Once most cruisers hit land, they are on foot (except for those fortunate souls with sufficient on-board storage to travel with folding bikes). So transportation, in all its guises, becomes a very important consideration. We've divided transportation into two categories — getting around while in port and the longer-range issue of getting to and from the boat. If the marina or boatyard provides some form of courtesy car or van service, it's noted first. These services can include unlimited use of a car (very rare), scheduled use of a car (often 2 hours), an on-demand "chauffeured" van service, a scheduled van service, or a marina manager or employee willing to drive you to "town" at a mutually convenient time. The guests' use of this service is sometimes completely unrestricted; other times, it is reserved exclusively for provisioning or restaurant trips. If the details of this arrangement are simple, they are explained in the commentary; if complicated, they are explained in the "Marina Notes." Courtesy cars and/or vans are one of the most volatile of the marina services so, if this is important to you, call ahead to confirm that it's still available and to ask about the terms.

The Airport Limo services are either individual car services or vans. Rail covers Amtrak as well as commuter services that connect to a city, an Amtrak stop, or an airport. Local Buses also include the seasonal Trolleys that are becoming more common (and extraordinarily useful) in more tourist-oriented ports. Local, regional and inter-city ferry services are listed. Rates, when included, are usually for both Adults and Children, and indicate if one-way or round-trip; they are listed with the Adult price first, followed by the Children's price, i.e. $25/17RT. Note that there are usually Senior Citizen and Student prices but space has precluded their inclusion. Don't forget to ask.

For those of us cruising the coast less than full time, the logistics of going back and forth to the boat is often the stuff of nightmares. Rental cars have a variety of uses — local touring or long distance (back to where you left your car, to the airport or back home). We list local rental car agencies (for day rents), and regional ones (like Enterprise). We tend not to list the national ones (where pick-up and drop-off may be restricted to airports or downtown locations) because these are obvious. Because Enterprise delivers and picks up — remembering that you have to return the driver to his/her office — we always include the nearest Enterprise office, if one exists, as "OnCall." (If another agency advertises pick-up/delivery, that information is included as "OnCall", too).

Note that some franchise auto rentals, because the outlets are locally or regionally owned, seem to have a wide range of "drop-off" policies. Sometimes, if the region is large enough, it is possible to pick the car up at the current marina and drive to the marina where you left your own car, and leave the rental right there. When available, this service is just great. Call and check. The Airport listing often includes both the nearest regional and the nearest international. Because, as noted, long-distance, one-way car rentals are often based at airport locations, a marina's distance from an airport takes on a larger meaning than just catching a plane.

Medical Services

911 Service	Dentist	Holistic Service	Ambulance
Doctor	Chiropractor	Veterinarian	Hospital

The data in this section is provided for informational purposes only and does not imply any recommendation. ACC is simply listing the nearest practitioner in each category. The first listing is the availability of 911 service; this service is surprisingly not ubiquitous — so it is important to know if dialing 911 will "work" in a given area. In the listings for Doctors, preference is given to walk-in clinics, then group practices and then general practitioners or internists. Dentists, Chiropractors, Veterinarians, and Holistic Services are also chosen in a similar fashion. A single practitioner is listed only if a "group" is not nearby. Holistic services will generally list massage therapists, but may also include acupuncturists, energy healers, and yoga classes when we find them. Hospital is usually the nearest major facility; if this is very far away and we are aware of a satellite, that will be noted — especially if there are no physicians nearby.

BOTTOM SECTION

Setting

This section provides a description of the location, environment and ambiance of each marina, boatyard or mooring field, including its views both landside and waterside, and any easily identifiable landmarks.

Marina Notes

Marina-specific information not included in the middle and top sections is detailed here. The source for this data includes interviews with marina staff, marina literature, marina comments provided to ACC, and surveyor/reviewer observations during site visits. If the rate structure is too complicated to detail in the "Facilities" section, a thorough explanation will be included here, preceded by an asterisk. Anything that is noteworthy or interesting about the facility is described in this paragraph. This includes history, background, recent changes, damage, renovations, new facilities, new management, comments on heads and showers (if they are, for instance, below par for the rating or particularly nice) and general marina atmosphere. If there is a restaurant or some form of lodging on-site, it is noted here, including any special deals for marina guests. If the marine services are part of a resort or a private yacht club with extensive recreation facilities, the level of access to those facilities is also detailed here or in "Notable." The facilities and services available to the visiting cruiser are also reflected in the rating.

Notable

This section notes additional items of interest related to the marina itself or the area. Details on special events, nearby attractions, the local community, ways of "getting around", the best beaches, special things to do, or other noteworthy facilities and/or services are listed here. Occasionally, there's also an elaboration of the onsite or nearby restaurants, amenities or accommodations.

The Data Gathering and Review Process

Collecting the data to create the Marina Reports is a multi-step process. A system of checks and balances keeps the information as accurate and as objective as possible. The intention is not to provide a promotional vehicle for marina and boatyard facilities — the intention is to provide a consumers' guide. Reasonable efforts have been made to confirm and corroborate the information. That does not mean that there won't be mistakes. The Marina Reports are a "snapshot in time" and things do change. It is also possible that, despite our best intentions, we just got it wrong. We hope that hasn't happened often, but a vehicle has been provided for you to tell us (and your fellow cruisers) if that is the case. Log-on to the ACC WebSite and add a Cruiser Note to the appropriate Marina Report (or send us an email). The data gathering and review process that ACC follows is outlined below:

- **Questionnaire:** A new marina, which has not been reviewed in an earlier edition, will be asked to fill out a very detailed four-page questionnaire — either before or after ACC's initial site visit and survey. The information provided is entered into ACC's proprietary database.

- **Site Visits:** Every facility included in the *Guide* is visited personally, at least once, by an ACC Reviewer who tours the marina or boatyard, walks the docks, pokes about the sheds, checks out the heads, showers and laundry, inspects the lounges, pool, beach, restaurants and hotel, and interviews the manager and/or dockmaster. The reviewer also takes photographs — one of which is included in each Marina Report in the Book and up to 8 more, in full-color, on the CD-ROM. The information that has been provided by the marinas is reviewed, confirmed, corrected and/or supplemented. If the reviewers arrive by boat, their affiliation with the Atlantic Cruising Club is not disclosed until the end of their stay. If they arrive by car, they introduce themselves before touring the facility. ACC pays in full for all services and refuses any complimentary accommodation, to maintain (both the fact, as well as the perception of) objectivity and impartiality. The ACC writers/editors have personally visited more than 1,500 facilities on the East Coast — to provide a uniform basis for ratings, reviews and commentary. They have visited every facility included in the *Guide* at least once — in most cases, several times.

- **Data Confirmation Report:** After the completion of the Questionnaire and the Site Visit, each facility receives a Data Confirmation Report (DCR) that includes all the information in our database for that facility — up to 300 data points — with a request for updates and corrections. If there are significant changes, a new visit is scheduled as early as is practical.

- **Independent Research:** Information that is included in the final Marina Report is derived from many sources. In addition to the Site Visit, the Questionnaire and the DCR, independent data is also collected. Local tourist offices, chambers of commerce and websites are surveyed and interviewed. Independent researchers are assigned to gather specific data for the "Mid Section" — the "what is where" material. Forty categories have been selected as the most important for cruisers; independent researchers seek out names, phone numbers, rates and distances (from the marinas) for each of these. This data is used to supplement and/or corroborate the information from all the other sources.

- **The Photographs:** About 98% of the photographs in the book and on the CD-ROM have been taken by ACC Reviewers at the time of their site visits (in some cases the photographs will be from more than one visit). In a few cases, marinas have contributed aerial shots which provide a very useful overview. The photographs are not travel or tourism photos or even photojournalistic images. They are "location shots" or "snapshots." The intention is to show you what is there — as accurately as possible. The old saw "a picture is worth a thousand words" certainly applies here. We shoot what you would have seen had you arrived at the same time we did. The quality varies — the weather was not always perfect — but the sense of the place is usually correct.

  We try to provide enough visual information so that you can both make an informed decision and recognize the place when you arrive. There's always a shot of the landside facility, of the view from the docks, and a close-up of a dock to show the quality of the slips and pedestals. And, finally, there are shots of the primary recreation facilities and restaurant, if they exist.

- **The Review and the Ratings:** As noted earlier, the ACC reviewers assign a three-part rating to each facility — A Bell Rating, a Boatyard Rating and a Sunset Rating. Then the Reviewers take all the material that has been gathered, including some subjective impressions, and write the bottom section's three-part Marina Review — "Setting," "Marina Notes" and "Notable."

- **The Draft Marina Report:** All of this material has been input into ACC's proprietary program called Datastract™, developed by the Atlantic Cruising Club's parent company, Jerawyn Publishing Inc. (JPI). The data is captured via a custom-designed multi-table input program which then collates, formats and outputs it as the single-page Marina Report. Every piece of data — including all the graphics and photographs — is placed in its precise position in the Marina Report by Datastract™. A Draft Report is sent to the marina facility for a final review for content accuracy before publication.

- **The Final Marina Report:** Datastract™ creates the final Marina Report, pulling all the corrected data and the photograph from the ACC database, and printing it to an Acrobat PDF file. The completed Marina Reports are then sent to the printer. Datastract™ replaces traditional publishing software resulting in a product that is more accurate and more timely.

- **The CD-ROM:** A very user-friendly version of the marina database resides on the enclosed CD-ROM. The CD-ROM permits users to select up to 100 of the 300 plus possible data points as search criteria for querying the database for suitable marinas. The search engine will return a list of the facilities that meet the requested criteria. A "double-click" on a marina name will generate a color two-page Marina Report — with up to nine full-color photographs each. "Marina Reports" are created "on the fly" and can be viewed on the screen or printed out.

The Digital *Guide* on CD-ROM

The enclosed CD-ROM contains the *Atlantic Cruising Club's Digital Guide to New England Marinas* including all of the data and Marina Reports that are in this print version, but in full color, with more than 1500 color photographs, and searchable on over 100 datafields.

- **Installation**
  Simply insert the enclosed CD-ROM into the CD drive of your computer. The installation program starts automatically. If it doesn't, click Start/ Run and enter "d:\setup.exe" (assuming "d:" is the address of your computer's CD drive). During the installation process, you are asked to choose which of the three ACC Digital Guide components you wish to copy to your hard drive — this affects the amount hard disk space the program uses: Program (2.5 mb), Database (55 mb), and Photos file (530 mb). If you have the hard disk capacity, it is best to install all three components. The program will run somewhat faster and you will not need to have the CD always at hand.

- **The Digital Guide is built around four screens:**

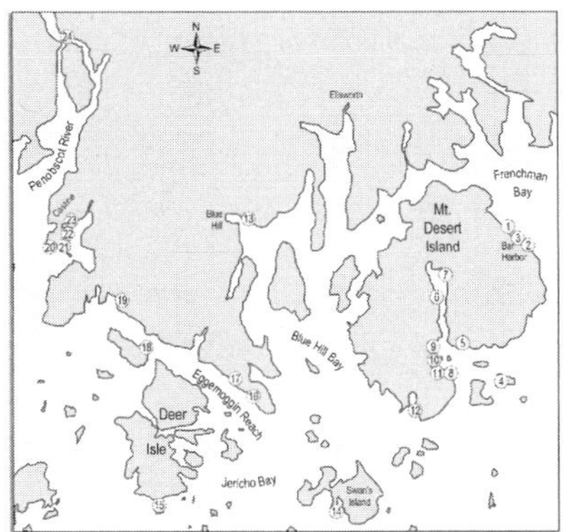

Region and Sub-Region Charts — Click on the "Charts" button to view a chart of the entire New England Region with each of the 12 sub-regions outlined. Click on one of the outlines to access the chart for that particular Sub-Region. The locations of each of the marinas in that geographic area are displayed on the map. The location "points" and the marina names are "hot." Click on them to display the Marina Report for that marina. If you would prefer to add additional criteria to a marina search (or to skip the graphics interface entirely), a button on the New England Regional chart, and on each of the Sub-Region charts, takes you directly to the Marina Search screen.

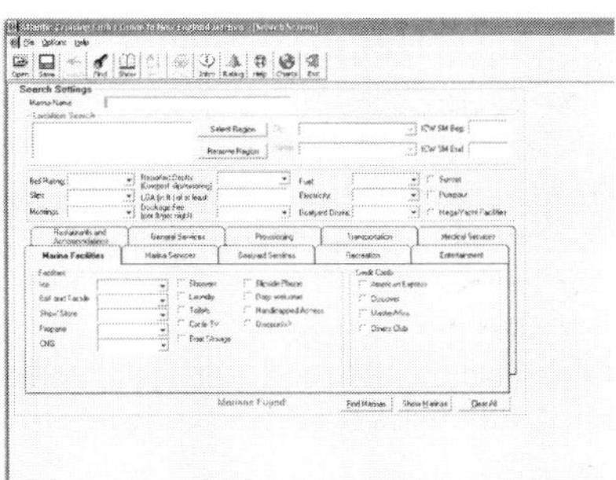

Marina Search Settings — This screen permits the user to enter up to 100 different search criteria—either singly or in combination. You may search for a particular marina by name (or part of name), for all of the marinas in a particular geographic region, city, or body of water, for marinas able to accommodate your vessel's LOA and draft, etc., etc., etc. If you arrived at this screen from one of the Sub-Region charts, then that Sub-Region is already entered in the "Location Search" box. You may add more sub-regions using the "Select Sub-Region" button. Once you have set the criteria for your search, click the "Find Marinas" button at the bottom of the screen (or the "Find" button in the toolbar). The search result (the number of marinas meeting your criteria) is indicated in the "Marinas Found" field. At this point, either refine your search to generate more or fewer marina choices or click the "Show Marinas" button to proceed to the next screen.

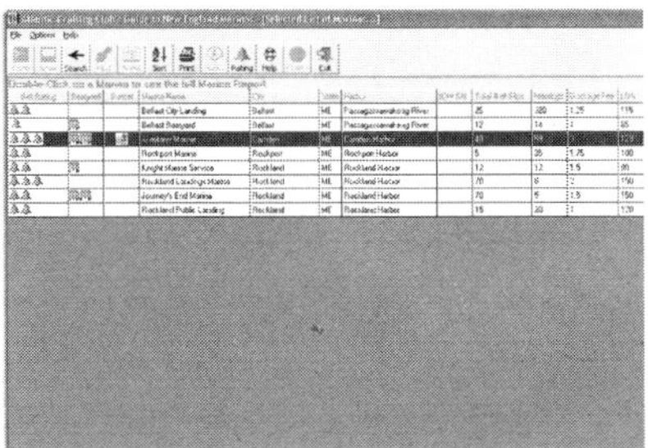

List of Selected Marinas — All of the marinas that meet your criteria are displayed on this screen. Next to each Marina Name are several items of information, including: bell, boatyard, and sunset ratings, city, state, and harbor. If, during the search, you set a criterion for "Slips," "Moorings," "LOA" or "Dockage Fee," a column for each selection also appears in the "List of Selected Marinas." The List may be sorted either geographically (default) or alphabetically. To view a full Marina Report for any of the marinas on the List, simply double-click on its name.

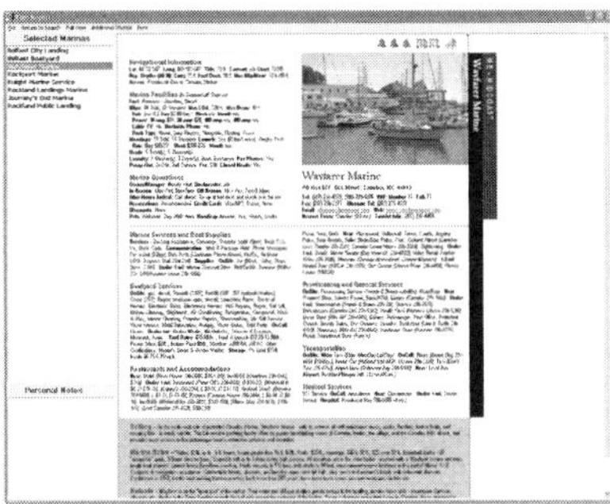

Marina Report — The Marina Reports in *ACC's Digital Guide* are identical to the Marina Reports in this printed version of the *Guide* but with some enhancements: The Reports are in color and each contains from 2 to 8 additional full-color marina photos. The Marina Reports Screen also lists the names of the other marinas that met your most recent search criteria. Clicking on one of those marina names displays its Marina Report. Finally, there is a box in the lower left hand corner of the Marina Report for you to enter your comments and observations about a given marina. This data is stored within the program and becomes part of the record for that marina. You can also print Marina Reports (and your comments, if you wish) using the Print command.

Note: For proper operation of the digital Guide, Internet Explorer 6.0 (or higher) must be installed on your computer.

The Atlantic Cruising Club WebSite

As a reference work, *ACC's Guide to New England Marinas* will be in a constant state of evolution. Its geographic coverage will be expanded as rapidly as time permits and Marina Reports will be modified as facts change and new information is received. As new marinas are added, and as substantive changes are discovered in the facilities of marinas already covered, updates will be posted on the Atlantic Cruising Club's WebSite: www.AtlanticCruisingClub.com

Please visit this site often. It's an easy way to keep your Guide updated and current. You'll also find useful cruising information, a community of cruisers sharing experiences and information, and a forum for your thoughts and comments on the facilities.

- **Cruisers' Comments:** A new section has been added to each on-line Marina Report to provide an opportunity for you to share your experiences and express your opinions. How was your visit at this facility? Is the rating fair or should it be adjusted? How did you find the general staff attitude toward transient boaters? Have the facilities, services, nearby restaurants or area resources changed? Please tell ACC and your fellow cruisers. A compilation of cruisers' comments can add another very useful dimension to the reviews.

  You will find the Cruisers' Comments section divided into the same topic areas as the Marina Reports, so you can easily transfer any notes you may have made in the margins of your Guide into the comparable section on the ACC WebSite.

Acknowledgments

The writers and editors would like to express their deep appreciation to a number of people who have contributed to the compilation and production of past and present editions of the Atlantic Cruising Club's Guides to Marinas:

Senior Editor: Irina C. Adams, for her gentle tenacity and gifted mind combined with her computer expertise, superb management and editing skills and her global understanding of a complex process. **Associate Editor:** Kevin Chamberlain, for his diligence, his computer and language skills, and his continuing commitment to the project; he understands the need to get it right. **Book and Page Design, Cover Execution, Back Cover Design and Execution:** Jessica Williams and Rupert Edson at Spark Design, for a wonderfully elegant book with a little edge — and for working with us all to figure out how to translate that perfectly designed page into 0s and 1s — they were truly the midwives of the Seventh Edition. **Programming:** Girish Ramdas and his team leaders R. Vijayakumar and V.M. Senthil Kumar at GNG Solutions, for their inexhaustible patience, creative code, talented problem solving and tireless determination. **Cover Design:** Rob Johnson, for the original cover design, which we loved at first sight. **Icon Design:** Jennifer Grassmeyer, for the superb, bright and perfect new icons. **Maps/Charts:** Kasim Khan, for his combination of technical expertise and professionalism in developing the maps for both the book and the digital Guide. **Photo Retouching:** Karl Parsons at the Concept Clinic, for making lovely silk purses. **Photo Scanning:** Ian Watt, David Faranda and Michelle Laumeister, for their meticulous focus and computer and graphic expertise. **In-House Research:** Florence Reape, Gabrielle Levin and Kiki Taylor, for managing the fact-checking and data confirmation process. **Proof Reading and Copy Editing:** Lou Anne Osborne, for her pitch-perfect editorial hand and for being a superb "last line of defense."

And our very special thanks to:
Rick and Mary Ellen Adams, for discovering the original Atlantic Cruising Club and giving us our initial membership. We often cruised together and Rick, then the captain of a Wilbur 38, was a fan of "tie up and plug in." Amanda Smith, one of ACC's most discerning and water-resistant reviewers, for her thorough investigations and her deft and perceptive reports. John and Betty Condon, for sharing their insights from their many sails along the Maine to Florida coast in their Tartan 41. John and Sue Scully, who cruise New England, LI Sound and the ICW in their Huckins 44, for their comments and encouragement. Chris Adams, E. Cummings and Jason Smith, for their insights, commentary, support and helpful additions. Rich Scholer of Park Lane Graphics, for sharing his decades of printing expertise — and helping us find the right "house." Original ACC Founder John Curry, and Editors Nancy Schilling and Jennifer Wise, for their impressive groundwork in developing the original Guide and the Sixth Edition Associate Editors Aimee Ganley and Jane Allison Havsey, for helping us take the first step.

The Members of the Atlantic Cruising Club, for their notes and emails describing their marina experiences. And, most important, the facilities' owners, managers and dockmasters who provided enormous quantities of detailed information on their marina and boatyard operations (and reviewed ACC's interpretation at each step along the way) — despite their discomfort with their inability to control the final Marina Report.

GUIDE TO
NEW ENGLAND MARINAS

THE MARINA REPORTS

Geographical Listing of Marinas

I. Maine: Downeast / Acadia

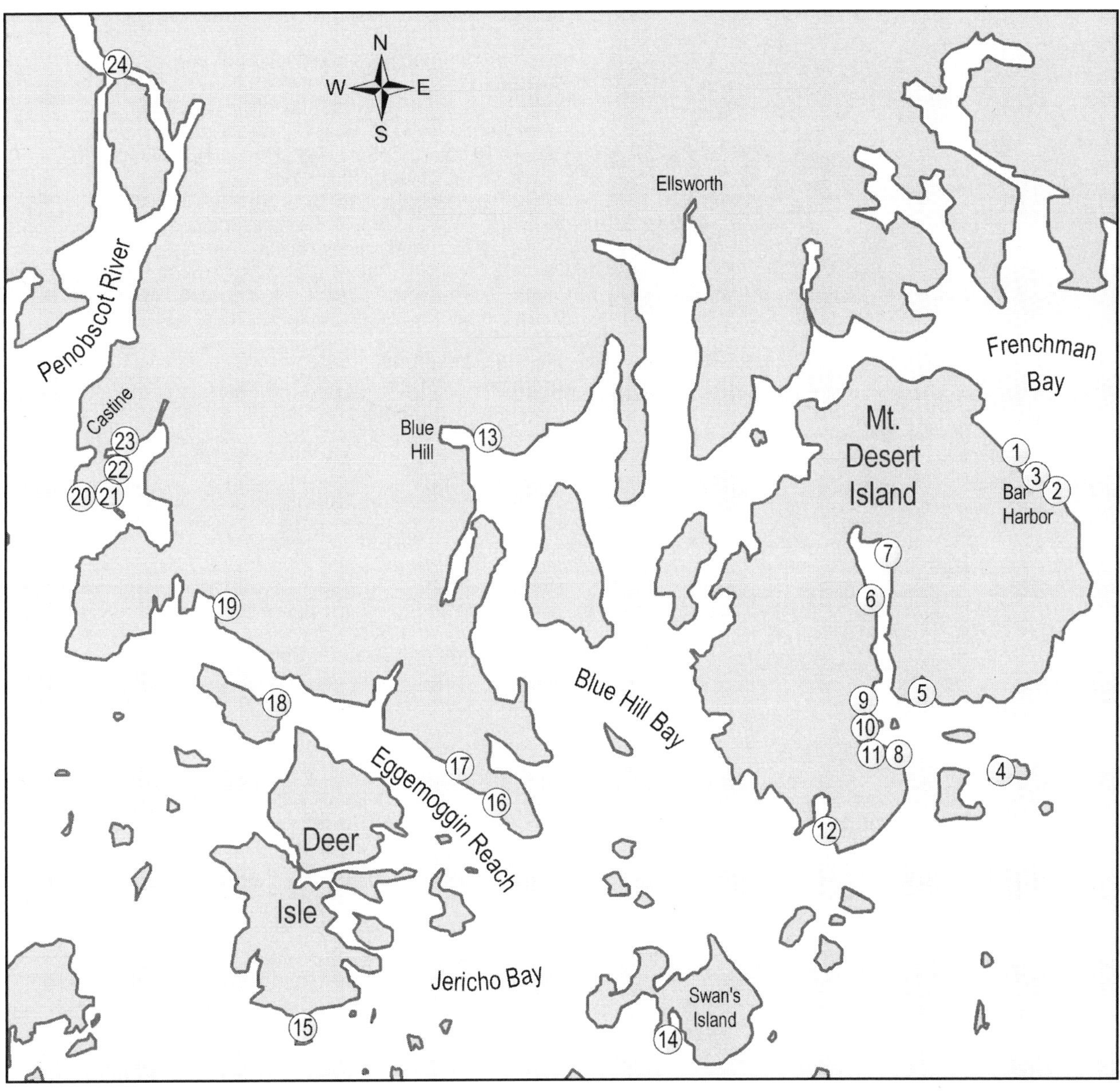

MAP	MARINA	HARBOR	PAGE
1	**Bar Harbor Regency Resort**	*Frenchman Bay*	22
2	**Bar Harbor Municipal Marina**	*Bar Harbor*	23
3	**Harborside Hotel & Marina**	*Bar Harbor*	24
4	**Islesford Dock Restaurant**	*Little Cranberry Is.*	25
5	**Northeast Harbor Marina**	*Northeast Harbor*	26
6	**John M. Williams Company**	*Somes Sound*	27
7	**Henry R. Abel & Co.**	*Somes Sound*	28
8	**Hinckley Service Yacht Yard**	*Southwest Harbor*	29
9	**Beal's Lobster Pier**	*Southwest Harbor*	30
10	**Southwest Boat Marine**	*Southwest Harbor*	31
11	**Dysart's Great Harbor Marina**	*Southwest Harbor*	32
12	**Morris Yachts Inc.**	*Bass Harbor*	33
13	**Kollegewidgwok Yacht Club**	*Blue Hill Bay*	34
14	**Burnt Coat Harbor Moorings**	*Burnt Coat Harbor*	35
15	**Billings Diesel and Marine**	*Deer Is.Thorofare*	36
16	**Wooden Boat School**	*Eggemoggin Reach*	37
17	**Brooklin Boat Yard**	*Eggemoggin Reach*	38
18	**Marina at Eggemoggin Landing**	*Eggemoggin Reach*	39
19	**Buck's Harbor Marine**	*Eggemoggin Reach*	40
20	**Castine Town Dock**	*Bagaduce River*	41
21	**Dennett's Wharf**	*Bagaduce River*	42
22	**Eaton's Boatyard**	*Bagaduce River*	43
23	**Castine Yacht Club**	*Bagaduce River*	44
24	**Bucksport Marina**	*Penobscot River*	45

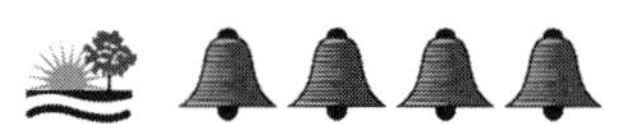

Bar Harbor Regency Sunspree

123 Eden Street; Bar Harbor, ME 04609

Tel: (207) 288-9723; (800) 234-6835 **VHF: Monitor** n/a **Talk** n/a
Fax: (207) 288-3089 **Alternate Tel:** n/a
Email: ebensalvatore@hotmail.com **Web:** www.barharborholidayinn.com
Nearest Town: Bar Harbor *(1.2 mi.)* **Tourist Info:** (207) 288-5103

Navigational Information

Lat: 44°24.003' **Long:** 068°13.514' **Tide:** 13 ft. **Current:** 2 kt. **Chart:** 13302
Rep. Depths (*MLW*): Entry 20 ft. **Fuel Dock** n/a **Max Slip/Moor** 12 ft./12 ft.
Access: North side of the ferry terminal in Frenchman Bay

Marina Facilities *(In Season/Off Season)*

Fuel: No
Slips: 4 Total, 4 Transient **Max LOA:** 200 ft. **Max Beam:** n/a
Rate *(per ft.)*: **Day** $3.00 **Week** Inq. **Month** Inq.
Power: 30 amp Incl., **50 amp** Incl., **100 amp** Incl., **200 amp** n/a
Cable TV: No **Dockside Phone:** No
Dock Type: Wood, Floating
Moorings: 1 Total, 1 Transient **Launch:** None
Rate: Day $50 **Week** n/a **Month** n/a
Heads: 2 Toilet(s), 1 Shower(s) *(with dressing rooms)*, Hair Dryers, Sauna
Laundry: 2 Washer(s), 2 Dryer(s), Iron, Iron Board **Pay Phones:** No
Pump-Out: No **Fee:** n/a **Closed Heads:** No

Marina Operations

Owner/Manager: Debbie Jordan **Dockmaster:** Eben Salvatore
In-Season: MidJun-LateAug **Off-Season:** Sep-May, Closed
After-Hours Arrival: Call ahead, then see front desk at the hotel
Reservations: Required **Credit Cards:** Visa/MC, Dscvr, Din, Amex
Discounts: None
Pets: Welcome **Handicap Access:** Yes, Heads, Docks

Marina Services and Boat Supplies

Services - Docking Assistance, Concierge, Boaters' Lounge **Communication -** Mail & Package Hold, Phone Messages, Fax in/out, Data Ports *(Lobby)*, FedEx, AirBorne, UPS, Express Mail *(Sat Del)* **Supplies - 1-3 mi:** Ice *(Block, Cube)*, Bait/Tackle *(Kyle's Ketch 288-8211)*, Propane *(Clark Coal 288-3309, Burwaldo's 288-5515)*

Boatyard Services

Nearest Yard: Hinckley Yacht Yard, SW Harbor (207) 244-5572

Restaurants and Accommodations

OnSite: Restaurant *(Edenfield 288-9723, B $10, D $8-34)*, Seafood Shack *(Stewmans' Lobster Pound 288-9723, D $15-25)*, Snack Bar *(Tiki Bar L $5-12, at the pool)*, Hotel *(Bar Harbor Regency 288-9723, $150-360)* **Near:** Motel *(Days Inn 288-3321, $99-185)*, *(Bar Harbor Motel 288-3453, $112-125)*, Hotel *(Bayview Hotel 288-5861, $150-250)* **Under 1 mi:** Restaurant *(Rose Garden/Bar Harbor Hotel 288-3348, D $58)*, *(124 Cottage Street 288-4383, D $12-22)* **1-3 mi:** Pizzeria *(Finelli Pizzeria 288-2700)*

Recreation and Entertainment

OnSite: Heated Pool, Spa, Picnic Area, Grills, Playground, Tennis Courts, Fitness Center, Jogging Paths, Roller Blade/Bike Paths **Near:** Museum *(College of the Atlantic's Dorr Museum of Natural History 288-5395, $3.50/1, Mon-Sat 10-5; 1 mi. to: Abbe Native American Museum - 288-4145, 288-2179 & 1904 Ledgelawn 288-4596)*, Galleries *(Blum Art Gallery at COA 288-2015)* **Under 1 mi:** Movie Theater *(Criterion Theatre 288-5829)*, Park *(Acadia National Park 288-3338)* **1-3 mi:** Golf Course *(Kebo Valley Club 288-3000)*, Boat Rentals *(Sea Kayak Tours 800-347-0940)*, Video Rental *(Arnold's TV & Video 288-4145)*, Video Arcade, Cultural Attract *(Bar Harbor Oceanarium & Lobster Hatchery 288-5005)*, Sightseeing *(AtlantiCat Whale Watching 288-9800 - 3 trips/day $43/28/10, $46/30/10, $35/22/8)*

Provisioning and General Services

OnSite: Convenience Store, Lobster Pound, Bank/ATM, Laundry, Newsstand, Clothing Store, Copies Etc. **OnCall:** Florist **Under 1 mi:** Supermarket *(Don's Shop & Save 288-5680)*, Post Office, Catholic Church, Beauty Salon, Barber Shop, Dry Cleaners, Hardware Store *(Bar Harbor Home 288-5567)*, Retail Shops **1-3 mi:** Gourmet Shop *(Butterfields 288-3386)*, Delicatessen *(Cottage Street Bakery & Deli 288-3010)*, Health Food *(Alternative Market 288-8227)*, Wine/Beer, Liquor Store *(Bayside 288-2772)*, Farmers' Market *(Sun 10-1, YMCA)*, Fishmonger *(Maine Lobster & Fish 288-0188)*, Meat Market, Library *(Jesup Memorial 288-4245)*, Bookstore *(Sherman's 288-3161)*, Pharmacy *(Rite Aid 288-2222)*

Transportation

OnSite: Local Bus *(Acadia Island Explorer 288-4573)*, Ferry Service *(The Cat, a high-speed ferry, to Nova Scotia 888-249-7245 - day cruise 8am, $55, also car/passenger longer trips)* **OnCall:** Rental Car *(Enterprise 667-1217)*, Taxi *(O Pooch 288-3898)* **1-3 mi:** Bikes *(Bar Harbor Bicycle Shop 288-3886)* **Airport:** Bar Harbor/Bangor Int'l. *(17 mi./50 mi.)*

Medical Services

911 Service **OnCall:** Ambulance **Under 1 mi:** Veterinarian *(Acadia 288-5733)* **1-3 mi:** Doctor *(Family Health Center 288-5606)*, Dentist *(High Street Dental 288-4754)*, Chiropractor *(Gerrish 288-3980)*, Holistic Services *(Acadia Massage 288-3899)* **Hospital:** M.D.I.Health Center 288-5081 *(1.5 mi.)*

Setting -- Located on Frenchman Bay, the 221-room Regency Sunspree, a Holiday Inn Resort, has well maintained, manicured lawns and gardens and a plethora of resort amenities. There is a single dock with a T-head. The view from there is breathtaking; it's even better from the outdoor hot tub!

Marina Notes -- Emphasis is on the highly-rated resort, but all the facilities are extended to marina guests - including the oceanfront heated pool and hot tub, concierge service, two restaurants, a quaint waterside lobster pound, exercise room, sauna, 2 lighted tennis courts, an oceanfront jogging path, and putting green (bring your own clubs or borrow the resort's). Day/evening child care and a junior program are available. Room service to boats no longer offered. The single head for marina guests is on the lower level, next to the exercise room, and includes a sauna. The dock, at the end of a very long pier, is not well protected and would be uncomfortable in bad weather. Megayacht facilities. An attractive catering facility, with great views, is available for large functions.

Notable -- The College of the Atlantic's waterfront campus is 0.1 mi. and a perfect strolling/picnicking destination. Its Natural History Museum is housed in the original Acadia Nat'l Park headquarters. COA is also home to the Allied Whale Marine Mammal Lab. Acadia Nat'l Park's current Visitors' Center and the Kebo Valley Golf Club are a little over a mile away, as is the town of Bar Harbor. June to Labor Day Acadia Island Explorer's free shuttle stops here, offering easy access to most of Mt. Desert Island, downtown Bar Harbor and 41,000 acre Acadia National Park's hiking trails, carriage roads & beaches. Visitors' Center hours are 8am-6pm Jun-Aug, 4:30pm rest of year. Acadian Whale Adventure's new high speed, state-of-the-art AtlantiCat leaves from the Harborside Hotel.

PHOTOS ON CD-ROM: 9

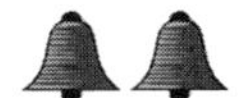

Navigational Information
Lat: 44°23.523' **Long:** 068°12.193' **Tide:** 10 ft. **Current:** 2 kt. **Chart:** 13323
Rep. Depths (*MLW*): Entry 40 ft. **Fuel Dock** 8 ft. **Max Slip/Moor** 12 ft./60 ft.
Access: Frenchman Bay through entrance buoys east of Municipal Pier

Marina Facilities *(In Season/Off Season)*
Fuel: *At Harbor Place* - Slip-Side Fueling, Gasoline, Diesel
Slips: 8 Total, 8* Transient **Max LOA:** 185 ft. **Max Beam:** n/a
Rate *(per ft.)*: **Day** $3.00 **Week** n/a **Month** n/a
Power: 30 amp $5, **50 amp** $10, **100 amp** $20, **200 amp** n/a
Cable TV: No **Dockside Phone:** No
Dock Type: Wood, Alongside, Floating
Moorings: 15 Total, 15 Transient **Launch:** None, Dinghy Dock
Rate: Day $25 **Week** n/a **Month** n/a
Heads: 7 Toilet(s), 3 Shower(s)
Laundry: None **Pay Phones:** Yes
Pump-Out: Full Service *(Next-door)* **Fee:** Free **Closed Heads:** Yes

Marina Operations
Owner/Manager: Charles A. Phippen (Harbormaster) **Dockmaster:** n/a
In-Season: Jul-Aug, 7:30am-9pm **Off-Season:** Sep-Jun, 8am-5pm
After-Hours Arrival: Call before arrival or anchor outside the harbor
Reservations: Preferred, Slips Only **Credit Cards:** Visa/MC
Discounts: None
Pets: Welcome, Dog Walk Area **Handicap Access:** Yes, Heads, Docks

Bar Harbor Municipal Marina

1 Town Pier; Bar Harbor, ME 04609

Tel: (207) 288-5571 **VHF: Monitor** 16 **Talk** 68
Fax: (207) 288-1034 **Alternate Tel:** (207) 288-3391
Email: bhhmaster@acadia.net **Web:** www.BarHarborMaine.com
Nearest Town: Bar Harbor *(0 mi.)* **Tourist Info:** (207) 288-5103

Marina Services and Boat Supplies
Services - Docking Assistance, Security *(24 Hrs., Video)*, Trash Pick-Up, Megayacht Facilities, 3 Phase **Communication -** Mail & Package Hold, Phone Messages, Fax in/out, Data Ports *(Harbormaster's Office)*, FedEx, AirBorne, UPS, Express Mail **Supplies - Near:** Ice *(Cube)*, Bait/Tackle, Propane *(Burwaldo's Texaco/Jordan Everett 288-5515)* **1-3 mi:** Live Bait *(Kyle's Ketch 288-8211)*

Boatyard Services
OnSite: Launching Ramp **OnCall:** Divers

Restaurants and Accommodations
OnSite: Restaurant *(Fish House Grill L $6-10, D $10-18, Lobster $13 'til 6pm)* **Near:** Restaurant *(Reading Room at Bar Harbor Inn 288-3351, B $3-10, L $7-19, D $19-28)*, *(Galyn's 288-9706, D $10-22)*, *(Quarter Deck 288-5292, L $7-12, D $12-22)*, *(Michelle's 288-2138, D $23-30)*, Pizzeria *(Sub & Pizza Shop 288-5853)*, *(Rosalie's 288-5666)*, Hotel *(Bar Harbor Inn 248-8851, $130-350)*, Inn/B&B *(Bass Cottage in the Field 288-3705, $60-100)*, *(Ullikana B&B 288-9552, $140-250)* **Under 1 mi:** Motel *(Quality Inn 288-5403, $70-170)*, Hotel *(Bar Harbor Regency 288-9723)*, Inn/B&B *(Balance Rock 800-753-0494, $95-595)*

Recreation and Entertainment
OnSite: Beach, Picnic Area **Near:** Fitness Center *(YMCA 288-3511)*, Jogging Paths, Boat Rentals *(Aquaterra Sea Kayaks 288-0007)*, Roller Blade/Bike Paths, Fishing Charter *(Dolphin 288-3322)*, Movie Theater *(Criterion 288-5829)*, Video Rental *(Arnold's 288-4145)*, Park, Museum *(Abbe Museum Downtown - Native American 288-2179)*, Cultural Attract *(Bar Harbor Music Fest 288-5744)*, Sightseeing *(Whale Watch 288-2386; Olli's Trolley 288-9899)* **1-3 mi:** Golf Course *(Kebo Valley 288-5000)*

Provisioning and General Services
OnSite: Lobster Pound *(Maine Lobster & Fish Co. 288-0188)* **Near:** Convenience Store *(Burwaldo's 288-3241)*, Supermarket *(Don's Shop & Save 288-5680)*, Gourmet Shop *(Butterfield)*, Delicatessen *(Village Green Bakery 288-9450)*, Health Food *(Alternative 288-8227)*, Wine/Beer *(288-3386)*, Liquor Store *(Bayside 288-2772)*, Bakery *(Village Green)*, Farmers' Market *(Sun 10-1, YMCA)*, Fishmonger *(Bar Harbor 288-0455)*, Bank/ATM, Post Office, Catholic Church, Protestant Church, Library *(Jesup 288-4245)*, Beauty Salon, Barber Shop, Laundry, Bookstore *(Sherman's 288-3161)*, Pharmacy *(West End 288-3318)*, Newsstand, Hardware Store *(True Value 288-4995)*, Florist, Copies Etc. *(Outsource Unlimited 288-0555)*

Transportation
OnSite: Bikes *(Aquaterra 288-0007; Acadia Bike & Canoe 288-9605)*
OnCall: Rental Car *(Enterprise 667-1217 18 mi.)*, Taxi *(AAA 288-3886)*
Near: Local Bus *(Island Explorer 288-4573)*, InterCity Bus *(Concord Trailways)*, Ferry Service *(Southwest Harbor $29.50/18, Cranberry Islands $24/15; 1 mi. - The Cat to Nova Scotia 888-249-7245)* **Airport:** Bar Harbor/Bangor Int'l. *(19 mi./50 mi.)*

Medical Services
911 Service **OnCall:** Ambulance **Near:** Holistic Services *(Women's Massage 288-3402)*, Veterinarian *(Acadia 288-5783)* **Under 1 mi:** Doctor *(Family Health 288-5606)*, Dentist *(High St. 288-4754)* **Hospital:** M.D.I. Health Center 288-5081 *(0.5 mi.)*

Setting -- Sandwiched between Harbor Place, the Bar Harbor Inn, and the main street of Bar Harbor, this municipal facility is a stone's throw away from just about everything. Bar Harbor is a bustling tourist town full of restaurants, shops and activities - with easy access to Acadia National Park. The docks are centrally located, at the bottom of the town's public parking lot, and are home to commercial fishermen, as well as recreational craft. The location at the south end of town, along with the tides, provides a bit of privacy.

Marina Notes -- *Two 96 foot long floating docks, each with gangway. Boats dock along all both sides. Commercial boats are on the opposite side of the pier. Public toilets at dock, 7am-9pm. Showers at Harbor Place no longer available. Nearest showers are at the new YMCA (0.5 mi, $5). There is no launch service - dinghy dockage is on the western side of the pier. Pump out and fuel available next door at Harbor Place; however when cruise ship tenders are in port, they tie up these docks for most of the day. No reservations for moorings -- first come, first served, but slips can be reserved.

Notable -- The Shore Path, with spectacular views of Frenchman Bay, begins here. Nearby Bar Harbor Inn, and its Reading Room restaurant, are both highly regarded. Terrace Grill offers informal al fresco waterfront dining. The 4-masted schooner Margaret Todd departs from the Inn as do the Bar Harbor Ferries to Southwest Harbor and to Little Cranberry Isles 288-2984. The CAT hi-speed ferry to Nova Scotia is 0.7 mi. Many other excursions leave from Harbor Place, including whale and seal watching and lobster trips. Free Acadia Island Explorer (667-5796) stops close by and will take you most places on the island.

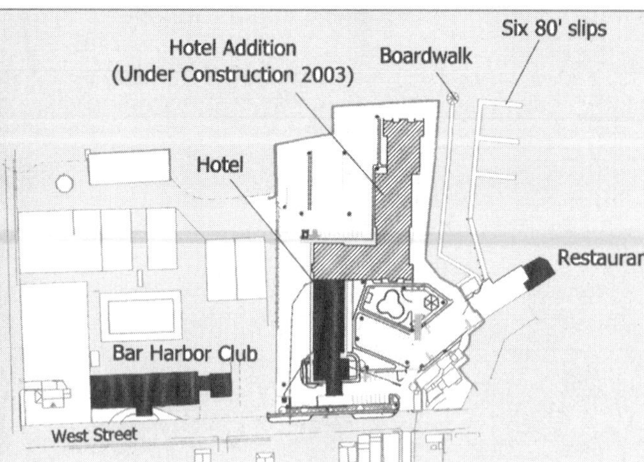

The Harborside Hotel & Marina

55 West Street; Bar Harbor, ME 04609

Tel: (207) 288-5033 **VHF: Monitor** No **Talk** n/a
Fax: (207) 288-3089 **Alternate Tel:** n/a
Email: bhregency@yahoo.com **Web:** www.theharborsidehotel.com
Nearest Town: Bar Harbor *(0 mi.)* **Tourist Info:** (207) 288-5103

Navigational Information

Lat: 44°23.490' **Long:** 068°12.337' **Tide:** 11 ft. **Current:** 0 kt. **Chart:** 13323
Rep. Depths (*MLW*): Entry 8 ft. **Fuel Dock** 8 ft. **Max Slip/Moor** 8 ft./-
Access: Green can 7 into Bar Harbor, then turn to starboard

Marina Facilities *(In Season/Off Season)*

Fuel: Yes
Slips: 10 Total, 10 Transient **Max LOA:** 300 ft. **Max Beam:** 60 ft.
Rate *(per ft.)*: **Day** $3.50 **Week** Inq. **Month** Inq.
Power: 30 amp Inq., **50 amp** Inq., **100 amp** Inq., **200 amp** n/a
Cable TV: No **Dockside Phone:** No
Dock Type: Wood, Floating
Moorings: 0 Total, 0 Transient **Launch:** n/a, Dinghy Dock
Rate: Day n/a **Week** n/a **Month** n/a
Heads: 3 Toilet(s), 3 Shower(s)
Laundry: 6 Washer(s), 6 Dryer(s), Iron, Iron Board **Pay Phones:** Yes
Pump-Out: OnSite **Fee:** n/a **Closed Heads:** Yes

Marina Operations

Owner/Manager: Debbie Jordan **Dockmaster:** Eben Salvatore
In-Season: May-Oct **Off-Season:** n/a
After-Hours Arrival: Call hotel front desk
Reservations: Yes, Preferred **Credit Cards:** Visa/MC, Dscvr, Amex
Discounts: None
Pets: Welcome, Dog Walk Area **Handicap Access:** Yes

Marina Services and Boat Supplies

Services - Docking Assistance, Room Service to the Boat, Security *(Closed ramp)*, Dock Carts, Megayacht Facilities, 3 Phase **Communication -** Mail & Package Hold, Phone Messages, Fax in/out *($1)*, Data Ports *(Business Center)*, FedEx, AirBorne, UPS, Express Mail *(Sat Del)* **Supplies - Near:** Ice *(Block)*, Bait/Tackle, Propane *(Burwaldo's Texaco 288-5515)* **1-3 mi:** Live Bait *(Kyle's Ketch 288-8211)*

Boatyard Services

OnCall: Rigger, Canvas Work, Bottom Cleaning, Divers

Restaurants and Accommodations

OnSite: Restaurant *(Pier Restaurant)*, Hotel *(Harborside Hotel)* **Near:** Restaurant *(Reading Room at Bar Harbor Inn 288-3351, B $3-10, L $7-19, D $19-28)*, *(Havana 288-2822, D $12-28)*, *(George's 288-4505, D $25)*, *(Maggie's Classic Scales 288-9007, D $15-22)*, *(Elaine's 288-3287, D $7-13, vegetarian)*, Lite Fare *(Jordan's 288-3586, B $3-7, L $3-9)*, Hotel *(Bar Harbor Inn 248-8851, $85-350)*, Inn/B&B *(Sunset on West 288-4242, $150-275)*, *(Ivy Manor Inn 288-2138, $95-350)*, *(Maples Inn 288-3443, $60-150)*

Recreation and Entertainment

OnSite: Heated Pool, Spa, Fitness Center, Sightseeing *(Acadian Whale Watch AtlantiCat 289-9800 3 trips/day - $43/28/10, $46/30/10, $35/22/8)* **Near:** Beach, Picnic Area, Jogging Paths, Boat Rentals *(Aquaterra Sea Kayaks 288-0007)*, Roller Blade/Bike Paths, Fishing Charter *(Dolphin 288-3322)*, Movie Theater *(Criterion 288-5829)*, Video Rental *(Arnold's 288-4245)*, Museum *(Abbe Native American 288-2179; College of the Atlantic's Natural History - 1 mi.)*, Cultural Attract *(Bar Harbor Music Fest 288-5744)* **Under 1 mi:** Playground **1-3 mi:** Golf Course *(Kebo Valley 288-5000)*

Provisioning and General Services

Near: Convenience Store *(Burwaldo's 288-3241)*, Supermarket *(Don's Shop & Save 288-5680)*, Gourmet Shop *(Butterfields 288-3386)*, Delicatessen *(Village Green Deli 288-9450)*, Health Food *(Alternative 288-8227)*, Wine/Beer *(Bayside 288-2772)*, Liquor Store, Bakery *(Village Green)*, Farmers' Market *(Sun 10-1, YMCA)*, Fishmonger *(Bar Harbor 288-0455)*, Lobster Pound *(Maine 288-0188)*, Meat Market, Bank/ATM, Post Office, Catholic Church, Protestant Church, Library *(Jesup 288-4245)*, Laundry *(Burwaldo's)*, Bookstore *(Sherman's 288-3161)*, Pharmacy *(West End 288-3318)*, Newsstand, Hardware Store *(Bar Harbor Trustworthy 288-5567; True Value 288-4995)*, Retail Shops, Copies Etc. *(Outsource 288-0555)* **Under 1 mi:** Beauty Salon, Barber Shop, Dry Cleaners, Florist **1-3 mi:** Green Grocer *(Sweet Peas 288-3907)*

Transportation

OnCall: Rental Car *(Enterprise 667-1217)*, Taxi *(AAA 288-3886)* **Near:** Bikes *(Aquaterra 288-0007, Acadia Bike & Canoe 288-9605)*, Local Bus *(Acadia Island Explorer 288-4573)*, InterCity Bus *(Concord Trailways)*, Ferry Service *(Southwest Harbor $29.50/18, Cranberry Islands $24/15, Cat to Nova Scotia)* **Airport:** Bar Harbor *(19 mi.)*

Medical Services

911 Service **OnCall:** Ambulance **Near:** Doctor *(High St. Health Center 288-5119)*, Dentist *(High St. Dental 288-4754)*, Holistic Services *(Women's Massage Center 288-3402)*, Veterinarian *(Acadia 288-5733)* **Hospital:** Mt. Desert Island Health Center 288-5081 *(0.5 mi.)*

PHOTOS ON CD-ROM: 1

Setting -- Once inside Bar Harbor proper, the Harborside Hotel & Marina's docks are the farthest west. Formerly the Golden Anchor, the inn began a multi-year, multi-million dollar renovation in 2001. The reconstruction and new addition were completed in late 2002. The first season for the new docks is Summer 2003. The newly renovated inn is easy to recognize, thanks to its half-timbered, English Tudor architecture and the long, two-storey balconied buildings that line the waterfront. Very convenient in-town location.

Marina Notes -- At the time of publication, the new docks had not been built. The data in this report are provided for informational purposes only. A thorough review and rating of the facility will be developed when the project is complete. Same ownership as the Bar Harbor Regency Sunspree. All hotel services will be available to marina guests. The aptly named Pier Restaurant onsite offers dining inside or topside on the open air deck -- both have beautiful views of the harbor and Frenchman Bay. Currently Harborside has 160 new guest rooms and suites, with balconies overlooking the Bay. 100 more rooms are under construction. New pay phones are to be installed on the pier. Also new for the 2003 season is onsite pump-out and fuel.

Notable -- The Harborside complex traces its heritage to the early 1900's. The site was originally called "Peanut Row" because of its grouping of small shops; the inn was built here during Bar Harbor's restoration period after the fire of 1947. Directly next door, the Victorian Bar Harbor Club is also in the process of a full renovation. At Bridge & West Streets is the path to the Acadia part of Bar Island, a natural wonderland accessible only one hour either side of low tide.

Navigational Information

Lat: 44°15.600' **Long:** 068°14.123' **Tide:** 11 ft. **Current:** n/a **Chart:** 13318
Rep. Depths (*MLW*): Entry 20 ft. **Fuel Dock** 12 ft. **Max Slip/Moor** -/60 ft.
Access: Gilley Thorofare to Cranberry Harbor

Marina Facilities *(In Season/Off Season)*

Fuel: *Fishermen's Co-op* - Gasoline, Diesel
Slips: 0 Total, 0 Transient **Max LOA:** n/a **Max Beam:** n/a
Rate *(per ft.)*: **Day** n/a **Week** n/a **Month** n/a
Power: 30 amp n/a, **50 amp** n/a, **100 amp** n/a, **200 amp** n/a
Cable TV: No **Dockside Phone:** No
Dock Type: Wood, Floating
Moorings: 5 Total, 5 Transient **Launch:** Yes (Free), Dinghy Dock
Rate: Day $15 **Week** Inq. **Month** Inq.
Heads: 4 Toilet(s)
Laundry: None, Book Exchange **Pay Phones:** No
Pump-Out: No **Fee:** n/a **Closed Heads:** Yes

Marina Operations

Owner/Manager: Daniel S. Lief **Dockmaster:** Same
In-Season: MidJun-MidSep, 9am-11pm **Off-Season:** Closed
After-Hours Arrival: Contact restaurant (207) 244-7494
Reservations: No **Credit Cards:** Visa/MC, Dscvr
Discounts: None
Pets: Welcome, Dog Walk Area **Handicap Access:** Yes, Heads

Islesford Dock Restaurant

PO Box 56; Little Cranberry Island; Islesford, ME 04646

Tel: (207) 244-7494 **VHF: Monitor** n/a **Talk** n/a
Fax: n/a **Alternate Tel:** (207) 226-5023
Email: cynthialief@hotmail.com **Web:** www.islesford.com/idr
Nearest Town: Islesford *(1 mi)* **Tourist Info:** (207) 276-5040

Islesford Dock Restaurant & Moorings

ME - DOWNEAST / ACADIA

Marina Services and Boat Supplies

Services - Docking Assistance **Communication -** Fax in/out **Supplies - Near:** Ice *(Cube)* **1-3 mi:** Ships' Store **3+ mi:** Propane *(J.N. Mills 244-3131, 6 mi. on mainland)*, CNG *(Hinckley Co. 244-7100, 7 mi. on mainland)*

Boatyard Services

OnSite: Launching Ramp **Nearest Yard:** Cranberry Island BY, 10 mi. (207) 244-7316

Restaurants and Accommodations

OnSite: Restaurant *(Islesford Dock Restaurant L $7-15, D $7-26, Sunday Brunch $5-$15 - note: high end is for a large lobster)* **Under 1 mi:** Pizzeria *(General Store)*, Inn/B&B *(Islesford Inn)*, *(Braided Rug Inn 244-5943)*

Recreation and Entertainment

OnSite: Beach *(Sand)*, Picnic Area **Near:** Playground, Jogging Paths, Roller Blade/Bike Paths, Park, Museum *(Mt. Desert Islesford Historical Museum 244-9224 - collection that depicts the life and history of the Cranberry Islands and its people -- ship models, nav aids, toys, photos, etc. Open from Jun 15-Sep 9, 10am-4:30pm. Lovely brick Georgian building)*, Cultural Attract, Sightseeing *(Acadia National Park 288-3338)*, Galleries *(Islesford Artists Gallery 244-3145 - MidJun-LabDay 10am-4pm, shows the work of both summer and year-round residents; Islesford Pottery 244-5686)* **1-3 mi:** Tennis Courts

Provisioning and General Services

Near: Market *(Islesford Market 244-7667)*, Wine/Beer, Lobster Pound *(Cranberry Isles Fishermen's Co-op or Thomas Lobster Company 244-5390 www.thomaslobster.com)*, Post Office, Catholic Church, Protestant Church, Library *(Islesford Library 244-9565 - Check out Julie's Garden)*, Hardware Store *(Islesford Lumber)*, Retail Shops *(Winter's Work - www.winterswork.com, a pottery and craft shop - displays include watercolors by Mark Howard and work by author/illustrator Ashley Bryan.)* **Under 1 mi:** Bakery, Bank/ATM

Transportation

OnSite: Water Taxi *(John Dwelley's "Delight" Water Taxi 244-5724 $30-40; MIDI Water Taxi 244-7312)* **Near:** Ferry Service *(NE Harbor, SW Harbor, and Bar Harbor Inn. Beal & Bunker to NE Harbor: $12 RT for adults, $6 for kids, under 3 free; 244-3575. Ferry to Bar Harbor Inn, downtown Bar Harbor $24/$15, 288-2984. Cranberry Cove Boating 244-5882 to SW Harbor $12/8.)* **3+ mi:** Rental Car *(Hertz/Budget at the airport, 18 mi. ferry or water taxi)* **Airport:** Bar Harbor/Bangor Int'l. *(18 mi./55 mi. ferry or water taxi)*

Medical Services

No 911 Service **OnCall:** Ambulance **Under 1 mi:** Doctor **Hospital:** Mount Desert Island 288-8439 *(7 mi. via water & land taxi)*

Setting -- Overlooking two miles of water, the mountains of Acadia National Park and Southwest Harbor, this "on the dock" restaurant-with-moorings is the gateway to an engagingly active and interesting island. The 150-year-old building sits on one of three island docks, next to the Cranberry Isles Fishermen's Cooperative. The sunsets are spectacular. Nearby paths are perfect for long walks or bike rides, with interesting stops along the way.

Marina Notes -- Boats can pull up to the dock while eating at the restaurant (but not for overnight). Overnight moorings available, but no reservations. Facilities are what you would expect to find in a working fishermen's village. Very accommodating staff. Alternative phone numbers: 207 266-2014 or 212 219-9199. Heads in park service building "Blue Duck". Fuel is available at Fishermen's Co-op. The onsite Little Cranberry Yacht Club has 2 moorings. Another dinghy dock is at the Town Dock, on the far side of Fishermen's Co-op. Lobsters are available from the Fishermen's Co-op or Thompson's.

Notable -- From mid-June through early September, The Islesford Dock Restaurant offers local seafood (and fresh vegetables from an onsite greenhouse), inside and deck dining for lunch, dinner, and Sun brunch. Hours: Tue-Sat, 11am-3pm, 5-9pm, Sun 10am-2pm, 5-9pm. Reservations advised. This is a good lunch stop or an overnight destination to escape the summer crowds. Emphasis is on local, organic ingredients with a "kick" - current chefs are Trinidadian Eric Wuppermann and Puerto Rican native Edgardo Ortiz, head chef at Alison on Dominick. Winter's Work is right on the dock, specializing in the "off season" handwork of Islesford's year-round residents. A short and scenic walk inland leads to a well-equipped general store with a snack bar.

PHOTOS ON CD-ROM: 9

Northeast Harbor Marina

PO Box 237; 18 Harbor Drive; Northeast Harbor, ME 04662

Tel: (207) 276-5737 **VHF: Monitor** 9 **Talk** 68
Fax: (207) 276-5741 **Alternate Tel:** n/a
Email: n/a **Web:** n/a
Nearest Town: Northeast Harbor **Tourist Info:** (207) 276-5040

Navigational Information

Lat: 44°17.673' **Long:** 068°17.123' **Tide:** 12 ft. **Current:** n/a **Chart:** 13318
Rep. Depths (*MLW*): Entry 20 ft. **Fuel Dock** 10 ft. **Max Slip/Moor** 10 ft./20 ft.
Access: Gulf of Maine to Eastern Way to Northeast Harbor

Marina Facilities *(In Season/Off Season)*

Fuel: *Clifton Dock - Ch.9* - Gasoline, Diesel
Slips: 60 Total, 15 Transient **Max LOA:** 160 ft. **Max Beam:** n/a
Rate *(per ft.)*: **Day** $1.50 **Week** Inq. **Month** Inq.
Power: 30 amp $3, **50 amp** $10, **100 amp** n/a, **200 amp** n/a
Cable TV: Yes, $5/night **Dockside Phone:** No
Dock Type: Floating
Moorings: 60 Total, 60 Transient **Launch:** None, Dinghy Dock
Rate: Day $15 up to 50', $25 for 50'+ **Week** Inq. **Month** Inq.
Heads: 2 Toilet(s), 2 Shower(s), Hair Dryers
Laundry: 1 Washer(s), 1 Dryer(s) **Pay Phones:** Yes
Pump-Out: OnSite, Full Service, 1 Central **Fee:** Free **Closed Heads:** Yes

Marina Operations

Owner/Manager: Will Boddy (Harbormaster) **Dockmaster:** n/a
In-Season: May 15-Oct 1, 24 hrs. **Off-Season:** Oct-May 14, 8am-4pm
After-Hours Arrival: n/a
Reservations: Recommended* **Credit Cards:** Visa/MC
Discounts: None
Pets: Welcome **Handicap Access:** Yes, Heads

Marina Services and Boat Supplies

Services - Docking Assistance, Dock Carts **Communication -** Mail & Package Hold, Phone Messages, Fax in/out **Supplies - Near:** Ice *(Block, Cube)*, Ships' Store *(F.T. Brown Marine 276-3329; Hodgkins Marine Electronics 276-5090)*, Bait/Tackle **Under 1 mi:** Propane *(Island Plumbing & Heating)* **1-3 mi:** West Marine *(At Dysart's - by water)*, CNG *(Hinckley's 244-7100 - by water)*

Boatyard Services

OnSite: Launching Ramp **OnCall:** Electrical Repairs, Electronics Repairs, Hull Repairs **Nearest Yard:** Mt. Desert Yacht Yard (207) 276-5114

Restaurants and Accommodations

Near: Restaurant *(151 Main St.)*, *(Colonel's Bakery, Deli, Rest. 276-5147, delivers)*, *(Docksider 276-3965, L $3-18, D $3-18)*, *(Asticou Inn Restaurant 276-3344, L $16-22, D $16-22, dinghy landing - no longer requires jacket & tie)*, *(Main Sail 276-5857, L $6-10, D $10-16, overlooks docks)*, Hotel *(Kimball Terrace Inn 276-3883, $130-150)*, Inn/B&B *(Grey Rock 276-9360, $155-375)* **Under 1 mi:** Inn/B&B *(Maison Suisse 276-5423, $135-205)*, *(Asticou 800-258-3373, $250-350, Dinghy Landing)* **1-3 mi:** Restaurant *(Jordan Pond House in Acadia 276-3316, L $7-18, D $14-20, afternoon tea, too $7-8.50)*

Recreation and Entertainment

OnSite: Picnic Area, Tennis Courts *($10/hr. See C. of C. Building)* **Near:** Video Rental *(McGrath Variety 276-5548)*, Park *(Acadia)*, Museum *(Great Harbor Maritime Museum 276-5262)* **Under 1 mi:** Sightseeing *(Acadia Carriage Trails, Thuya & Asticou Gardens, Sea Princess' naturalist-led tours 276-5352, Eliot Mountain Trail from Thuya Garden)* **3+ mi:** Golf Course *(Kebo Valley Club 288-5000, 5.5 mi.)*, Movie Theater *(Criterion 288-5829, 8 mi.)*, Cultural Attract *(Wendell Gilley Museum 244-7555, 4 mi.)*

Provisioning and General Services

OnCall: Provisioning Service *(Pine Tree)*, Dry Cleaners **Near:** Convenience Store, Supermarket *(Pine Tree Market 276-3335 - delivers to docks)*, Gourmet Shop, Delicatessen *(Full Belli Deli 276-4299)*, Wine/Beer *(Pine Tree)*, Liquor Store *(Liquor Locker 244-3788 - delivers)*, Bakery *(The Colonel's 276-5147 bakery, wine, pizza - delivers)*, Bank/ATM, Post Office, Catholic Church, Library *(276-3333)*, Beauty Salon, Laundry *(Shirt Off Your Back 276-5611, Downtown Laundry Cellar)*, Bookstore *(Sherman's 276-3205 & Wikhegan 276-5079)*, Newsstand, Hardware Store *(F.T. Brown 276-3329)* **Under 1 mi:** Farmers' Market *(Thu 9am-Noon Millbrook Rd.)*

Transportation

OnSite: Local Bus *(Island Explorer 288-4573, 667-5796)* **OnCall:** Rental Car *(Enterprise Rent-A-Car 667-1217)*, Taxi *(AAA taxi & limo 288-8294)*, Airport Limo *(Airport and Harbor Car Service 667-5995)* **Near:** Bikes *(NE Harbor Bike 276-5480)*, Water Taxi *(MDI 244-7312 call)*, Ferry Service *(Beal & Bunker's ferry to Cranberry Isles: RT $12 adults, $6 kids, under 3 free 244-3575)* **Airport:** Bar Harbor/Bangor Int'l. *(20 mi./50 mi.)*

Medical Services

No 911 Service **Near:** Doctor *(Northeast Harbor Clinic 276-3311 8:30am-12:15pm)*, Holistic Services *(Greenbaum Massage 276-4057)* **3+ mi:** Chiropractor *(Gerrish 288-3980, 6 mi.)* **Hospital:** M.D.I. 288-8439 *(7 mi.)*

Setting -- Even in the fog, beautiful Northeast Harbor comes very close to delivering that elusive Downeast experience. When the mist lifts, the views across the harbor are of Eliot Mountain and the exquisite Asticou Inn. The quintessential "Old Maine" village is a short walk up the hill from the docks and has good services, a few eateries, provisioning resources, and low key activities that cater to its very private upscale summer residents.

Marina Notes -- *The limited transient slips can be reserved (starting on Jan 1). These are mostly on T-heads, sometimes rafted two or three deep. Moorings cannot be reserved; harbormaster recommends arriving at 11am (check in by VHF once in the harbor). Look for bright green mooring buoys; numbers indicate maximum boat size. Rafting permitted. "Yachtsmen's Building" at the Chamber of Commerce, right next door, has showers ($1- quarters), heads (open 24 hrs.), a reading room, coffee and tea, and an accommodating staff. Public heads in the docks building. No launch service; use the northern-most dinghy docks. Water and electricity available at the floating docks. At harbor entrance, Clifton Fuel Dock Ch.9 or 276-5308 has fuel, ice (50 lb. blocks) and free self-service manual pumpout. Wes Shaw's MDI Water taxi 244-7312 requires advance notice and may also help with moorings that lie outside the harbor.

Notable -- Northeast Harbor is a little out of the tourist bustle, yet the Island Explorer Shuttle makes Acadia National Park and neighboring Southwest Harbor, Bar Harbor, and B.H.Airport easily accessible. The Asticou Terraces, which include Azalea and Thuya Gardens and Thuya Lodge, march up the mountain on the far side of the Harbor; a convenient dinghy dock sits at the base. Dozens of excursions leave from the main docks, including ferries to the Cranberries.

PHOTOS ON CD-ROM: 9

Navigational Information
Lat: 44°20.159' **Long:** 068°19.122' **Tide:** 12 ft. **Current:** 1 kt. **Chart:** 13318
Rep. Depths (*MLW*): Entry 35 ft. **Fuel Dock** n/a **Max Slip/Moor** 35 ft./140 ft.
Access: Southwest Harbor to Somes Sound, two-thirds up on west shore

Marina Facilities *(In Season/Off Season)*
Fuel: No
Slips: 0 Total, 0 Transient **Max LOA:** n/a **Max Beam:** n/a
Rate *(per ft.)*: **Day** n/a **Week** n/a **Month** n/a
Power: 30 amp n/a, **50 amp** n/a, **100 amp** n/a, **200 amp** n/a
Cable TV: No **Dockside Phone:** No
Dock Type: Wood, Floating, Fixed
Moorings: 20 Total, 5 Transient **Launch:** None
Rate: Day $20 **Week** $100 **Month** Inq.
Heads: 1 Toilet(s)
Laundry: None **Pay Phones:** No
Pump-Out: No **Fee:** n/a **Closed Heads:** No

Marina Operations
Owner/Manager: Jock Williams **Dockmaster:** David Munsell
In-Season: Year Round, 8am-4pm **Off-Season:** n/a
After-Hours Arrival: Take any available mooring
Reservations: No **Credit Cards:** Visa/MC, Dscvr, Amex
Discounts: None
Pets: Welcome **Handicap Access:** No

John M. Williams Company

PO Box 80; 17 Shipwright Lane; Mount Desert, ME 04660

Tel: (207) 244-7854 **VHF: Monitor** n/a **Talk** n/a
Fax: (207) 244-9912 **Alternate Tel:** n/a
Email: jmw@acadia.net **Web:** www.stanleyboats.com
Nearest Town: Southwest Harbor *(5 mi.)* **Tourist Info:** (207) 276-5040

Marina Services and Boat Supplies
Services - Docking Assistance, Megayacht Facilities **Communication -** Mail & Package Hold, Phone Messages, Fax in/out, Express Mail **Supplies - 1-3 mi:** Propane *(Somesville One-Stop)* **3+ mi:** West Marine *(5 mi.)*, Bait/Tackle *(5 mi.)*

Boatyard Services
OnSite: Travelift *(30T)*, Crane *(17T)*, Engine mechanic *(gas, diesel)*, Launching Ramp, Electrical Repairs, Hull Repairs, Rigger, Bottom Cleaning, Brightwork, Compound, Wash & Wax, Interior Cleaning, Propeller Repairs, Woodworking, Inflatable Repairs, Metal Fabrication, Painting, Awlgrip, Yacht Design, Yacht Building, Total Refits **OnCall:** Electronic Sales, Life Raft Service **3+ mi:** Sail Loft *(5 mi.)*, Canvas Work *(5 mi.)*. **Member:** ABBRA, ABYC **Yard Rates:** $45/hr., Power Wash $65

Restaurants and Accommodations
1-3 mi: Restaurant *(Café Blackboards 276-4229)*, *(Lighthouse Inn & Restaurant 276-4131)*, Inn/B&B *(Heron House Bed & Breakfast 244-0221)*

Recreation and Entertainment
OnSite: Sightseeing *(Old Quarry - a picturesque "quarry lake" plus the site of an early 20thC quarry that provided exquisite pink granite for national landmark buildings)* **Near:** Boat Rentals *(Canoes at Somes Sound View Campground 244-3890)*, Park *(Acadia National Park 288-3338)* **Under 1 mi:** Beach *(Echo Lake)* **1-3 mi:** Museum *(Mount Desert Island Historical Society, Somesville Museum Tue-Sat 10am-5pm, $1/free)* **3+ mi:** Golf Course *(Causeway Club 244-3780, 4 mi.)*

Provisioning and General Services
1-3 mi: Convenience Store *(Somesville One-Stop - well equipped small market)*, Liquor Store *(in Somesville)*, Bank/ATM, Post Office, Catholic Church, Protestant Church, Library *(Somesville Library Wed 1-6pm, Sat 9am-2pm)*, Bookstore *(Port-in-the-Storm Books 244-4114 Mon-Sat 10am-5:30pm, Sun 1-5pm famous for its maritime collection, local Maine books and also children's books - antique on the outside, contemporary on the inside - spend an afternoon)* **3+ mi:** Supermarket *(Southwest Food Mart, 5 mi.)*, Gourmet Shop *(Sawyers, 5 mi.)*, Wine/Beer *(Sawyers, Liquor Locker, 5 mi.)*, Bakery *(Little Notch, 5 mi.)*, Beauty Salon *(5 mi.)*, Barber Shop *(5 mi.)*, Dry Cleaners *(5 mi.)*, Pharmacy *(5 mi.)*, Newsstand *(5 mi.)*, Hardware Store *(5 mi.)*, Retail Shops *(5 mi.)*

Transportation
OnCall: Taxi *(Happy Harry's 266-1554)* **Near:** Local Bus *(Acadia Island Explorer 288-4573, www.exploreacadia.com)* **Airport:** Bar Harbor/Bangor Int'l. *(20 mi./55 mi.)*

Medical Services
911 Service **OnCall:** Ambulance **1-3 mi:** Doctor *(Mount Desert Seasonal Clinic 276-3331)* **Hospital:** Mount Desert 288-8439 *(10 mi.)*

Setting -- About two-thirds up Somes Sound's western shore, in the shadow of the old Hall Quarry, is the John M. Williams Company. The views from their docks and mooring field are reminiscent of pre-tourist Maine. It's quiet, beautiful, and relatively unspoiled.

Marina Notes -- This is both a full service boatyard and a custom boat builder -- the home of Stanley Yachts, a series of classic pleasure motor yachts and work boats 26 - 44 ft. The yard focuses on combining the best of wood and fiberglass construction. In addition to building yachts, it offers full repair and restoration services plus facilities for indoor and outdoor storage for at least 100 boats. There is also a private float for dockage of large vessels by advance reservation. MDI Water Taxi 244-7312 may also have Somes Sound moorings.

Notable -- Hike to the top of the quarry for a look at the pink granite used in the Franklin Mint and the quarry pool left behind by the excavation. This area of Mt. Desert and Acadia is fairly isolated. There are few services or facilities. However, the free Island Explorer's #7 Southwest Harbor bus stops nearby. It connects Bar Harbor and Southwest Harbor. It also serves Manset, Seawall, Bass Harbor, and Bernard. It makes 9 RTs a day, roughly every 90 min. Also connects with the #6 Brown Mountain bus which links Bar Harbor and Northeast Harbor via the Eagle Lake Road and Route 198 and provides access to carriage roads at Eagle Lake and at the Brown Mountain Gate House. Dinghy (or bus) to Somes Harbor at the head of the Sound; dock on the west side at the town landing (donations welcome). Walk to the main road and turn left for the village and the bookstore, library and museum.

PHOTOS ON CD-ROM: 9

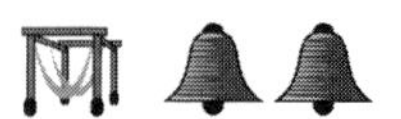

Henry R. Abel & Co. Yacht Yard

P.O.Box 184; Route 198; Mount Desert, ME 04660

Tel: (207) 276-5057 **VHF: Monitor** n/a **Talk** n/a
Fax: (207) 276-9831 **Alternate Tel:** (207) 276-5057
Email: henryr@prexar.com **Web:** n/a
Nearest Town: Somesville *(2 mi.)* **Tourist Info:** (207) 224-9264

Navigational Information

Lat: 44°21.360' **Long:** 068°18.440' **Tide:** 10 ft. **Current:** 3 kt. **Chart:** 13318
Rep. Depths (*MLW*): Entry 60 ft. **Fuel Dock** n/a **Max Slip/Moor** 25 ft./60 ft.
Access: Southwest Harbor to upper Somes Sound, eastern shore

Marina Facilities *(In Season/Off Season)*

Fuel: No
Slips: 9 Total, 3 Transient **Max LOA:** 80 ft. **Max Beam:** 20 ft.
Rate *(per ft.)*: **Day** $1.75/$1.00* **Week** Inq. **Month** Inq.
Power: 30 amp Inq., **50 amp** Inq., **100 amp** n/a, **200 amp** n/a
Cable TV: No **Dockside Phone:** No
Dock Type: Wood, Long Fingers, Floating
Moorings: 28 Total, 10 Transient **Launch:** Yes, Dinghy Dock
Rate: Day $20 **Week** $140 **Month** n/a
Heads: 2 Toilet(s)
Laundry: None **Pay Phones:** No
Pump-Out: OnCall, Full Service, 1 Port **Fee:** n/a **Closed Heads:** No

Marina Operations

Owner/Manager: Frank Gott **Dockmaster:** Same
In-Season: May-Oct 1, 6am-3:30pm **Off-Season:** n/a
After-Hours Arrival: Pick up red ball mooring
Reservations: Yes, Preferred **Credit Cards:** Visa/MC
Discounts: None
Pets: Welcome **Handicap Access:** Yes, Heads

Marina Services and Boat Supplies

Services - Security *(Marina employees)*, Dock Carts **Communication -** Mail & Package Hold, Fax in/out, FedEx, UPS, Express Mail **Supplies - 1-3 mi:** Propane *(Somesville One-Stop)* **3+ mi:** Ships' Store *(5 mi.)*, West Marine *(7 mi.)*, CNG *(Hinckley 244-5525, 7 mi.)*

Boatyard Services

OnSite: Travelift *(50T)*, Forklift, Crane, Engine mechanic *(gas, diesel)*, Hull Repairs, Rigger, Bottom Cleaning, Brightwork, Divers, Compound, Wash & Wax, Interior Cleaning, Woodworking, Yacht Broker **OnCall:** Electrical Repairs, Electronic Sales, Electronics Repairs, Painting, Awlgrip **3+ mi:** Launching Ramp *(Northeast Harbor, 3 mi.)*, Sail Loft *(7 mi.)*, Propeller Repairs *(9 mi.)*. **Yard Rates:** $42/hr., Haul & Launch $180, Power Wash $20/use **Storage:** On-Land Inside $4/sq.ft., Outside $22/ft.

Restaurants and Accommodations

OnSite: Seafood Shack *(Abel's Lobster Pound 276-5827, L $10-14, D $18-40, 7 days 12-9pm Lobster Roll $14, Lobster Dinners $21.50-37, Reef & Beef $43)* **1-3 mi:** Fast Food *(Subway)*

Recreation and Entertainment

OnSite: Beach, Picnic Area **Near:** Jogging Paths, Museum *(Mount Desert Island Historical Society's 1892 Sound School House Museum, Mon-Sat, 10am-5pm)* **Under 1 mi:** Sightseeing *(Acadia's Giant Slide Trail leading to Sargent Mountain)*

Provisioning and General Services

OnSite: Lobster Pound **1-3 mi:** Convenience Store *(Somesville One-Stop - well equipped small market)*, Liquor Store *(in Somesville)*, Bakery, Bank/ATM, Post Office, Library *(Somesville Library Wed 1-6pm, Sat 9am-2pm)*, Beauty Salon, Bookstore *(Port-in-the-Storm Books 244-4114 Mon-Sat, 10am-5:30pm, Sun 1-5pm - famous for its maritime collection, local Maine books and also superb kids' collection - it's worth a special trip)* **3+ mi:** Supermarket *(Shop N Save, 10 mi.)*, Gourmet Shop *(7 mi.)*, Health Food *(7 mi.)*, Dry Cleaners *(7 mi.)*, Laundry *(7 mi.)*, Pharmacy *(7 mi.)*, Hardware Store *(7 mi.)*, Retail Shops *(7 mi.)*

Transportation

OnCall: Taxi *(Happy Harry's 266-1554)* **Near:** Local Bus *(Acadia Island Explorer 288-4573 www.exploreacadia.com)* **Airport:** Bar Harbor/Bangor Int'l. *(20 mi./50 mi.)*

Medical Services

911 Service **OnCall:** Ambulance **Hospital:** Mt. Desert Island *(8 mi.)*

Setting -- On the eastern shore, near the head of Somes Sound, is this very tidy and well maintained boat yard and marina with one of the area's nicest and most attractive lobster pounds/restaurants. This is a quiet part of Mt. Desert and a welcome relief from the hustle and bustle during the season. There are truly beautiful views of the docks and the sound - the only fjord in the northeast.

Marina Notes -- *If you eat at the restaurant, dockage is free during the meal and $1/ft. overnight. Moorings are white, green and orange signifying increasing granite block sizes (up to 15,000 lbs.). The small, onsite boatyard offers extensive facilities and personal service. Abel's Dining Room seatings are a rigid 6pm, 6:30, 8, and 8:30, 7 days. Outside, at the picnic tables under the trees, service is more free-wheeling; you can eat anytime. Advanced restaurant reservations are useful; there's no special treatment for boaters. MDI Water Taxi 244-7312 or Bar Harbor Boating 276-5838 may also have moorings.

Notable -- Most services are about 7 miles away. A 2 mile walk, bus or dinghy ride to Somesville will net the Somesville Museum (Tue-Sat 10am-5pm $1/free), Port-in-the-Storm bookstore, and a library. 0.5 miles in the opposite direction is a small cluster of services - convenience, bakery & liquor stores. There's a town float for tie-up on the west side of Somes Harbor; finding it is a challenge. The free Acadia Explorer provides access to most of Mt. Desert and Acadia Nat'l. Park. Abel's is on the Brown Mountain bus route (#6), which links Bar Harbor and Northeast Harbor via Eagle Lake Road & Rt. 198. There are 7 RT's a day and timed connections with the #7 Southwest Harbor bus in Somesville.

PHOTOS ON CD-ROM: 9

Navigational Information

Lat: 44°16.081' **Long:** 068°18.378' **Tide:** 12 ft. **Current:** n/a **Chart:** 13318
Rep. Depths (*MLW*): Entry 12 ft. **Fuel Dock** 12 ft. **Max Slip/Moor** 40 ft./-
Access: Gulf of Maine to Eastern Way to Southwest Harbor

Marina Facilities *(In Season/Off Season)*

Fuel: Diesel
Slips: 0 Total, 0* Transient **Max LOA:** n/a **Max Beam:** n/a
Rate *(per ft.)*: **Day** n/a **Week** n/a **Month** n/a
Power: 30 amp n/a, **50 amp** n/a, **100 amp** n/a, **200 amp** n/a
Cable TV: No **Dockside Phone:** No
Dock Type: n/a
Moorings: 70 Total, 65 Transient **Launch:** Yes, Dinghy Dock
Rate: Day $30 **Week** $125 **Month** Inq.
Heads: 2 Toilet(s), 3 Shower(s)
Laundry: 2 Washer(s), 2 Dryer(s) **Pay Phones:** Yes
Pump-Out: OnSite, Full Service, 1 Central **Fee:** $15 **Closed Heads:** No

Marina Operations

Owner/Manager: Rusty Bradford **Dockmaster:** Nick Madeira
In-Season: Apr-Nov, 7am-5pm **Off-Season:** Dec-Mar, 9am-4pm
After-Hours Arrival: Pick up a mooring. Hinckley pennant indicates reserved
Reservations: Yes **Credit Cards:** Visa/MC, Amex
Discounts: None
Pets: Welcome **Handicap Access:** No

Hinckley Service Yacht Yard

PO Box 699; 130 Shore Road; Manset, ME 04679

Tel: (207) 244-5572; (888) hin-ckle **VHF: Monitor** 9 **Talk** 9
Fax: (207) 244-9433 **Alternate Tel:** (207) 244-5531
Email: service@hinckleyyachts.com **Web:** n/a
Nearest Town: Southwest Harbor *(1.7 mi.)* **Tourist Info:** (207) 244-9264

Marina Services and Boat Supplies

Services - Docking Assistance, Trash Pick-Up, Dock Carts **Communication -** Mail & Package Hold, Phone Messages, Fax in/out, FedEx, AirBorne, UPS, Express Mail *(Sat Del)* **Supplies - OnSite:** Ice *(Cube)*, Ships' Store, Propane, CNG **Under 1 mi:** West Marine *(at Dysarts)*, Marine Discount Store *(Rockland Boat 244-7870)*

Boatyard Services

OnSite: Travelift *(35, 70 & 160T)*, Forklift, Crane *(20T)*, Engine mechanic *(gas, diesel)*, Electrical Repairs, Electronics Repairs, Hull Repairs, Rigger, Bottom Cleaning, Brightwork, Air Conditioning, Refrigeration, Compound, Wash & Wax, Interior Cleaning, Woodworking, Upholstery, Yacht Interiors, Metal Fabrication, Painting, Awlgrip, Yacht Design, Yacht Broker, Yacht Building, Total Refits **OnCall:** Divers, Inflatable Repairs, Life Raft Service **Yard Rates:** $40-75/hr., Haul & Launch $9-16/ft., Power Wash $2-3/ft., Bottom Paint $48/hr. **Storage:** On-Land Outside $40-45/ft. Inside $75-85/ft.

Restaurants and Accommodations

Near: Restaurant *(XYZ Restaurant & Gallery 244-5221, D $16-18, authentic Mexican)*, *(The Moorings 244-7070, L $4-11, D $13-19)*, *(Seawall Dining Room 244-3020, L $3-18, D $3-18)*, Motel *(Seawall Motel 244-3020)*, *(The Dockside 244-5221, $80-90)*, Inn/B&B *(The Moorings Inn 244-5523, $60-$150, adjacent)*, *(Mansell House 244-5625, $65-150)* **Under 1 mi:** Restaurant *(Preble Grille 244-3034, D $11-27)*, *(Deacon-Seat 244-9229, B $6, L $10, D $12)*, Seafood Shack *(Beal's Lobster Pound 244-3202, dinghy)*, Inn/B&B *(Inn at Southwest 244-3835, $95-150)*

Recreation and Entertainment

Near: Jogging Paths, Video Rental *(Southwest Video 244-9825)*, Park **Under 1 mi:** Cultural Attract *(SW Harbor Oceanarium 244-7330)* **1-3 mi:** Museum *(Wendell Gilley 244-7555)*, Galleries **3+ mi:** Tennis Courts *(Causeway, 4 mi.)*, Golf Course *(Causeway Club 244-3780, 4 mi.)*

Provisioning and General Services

Near: Convenience Store, Gourmet Shop, Delicatessen *(Double J Grocery & Deli 244-5544)* **Under 1 mi:** Protestant Church **1-3 mi:** Provisioning Service, Supermarket *(Gotts Store 244-3431)*, Health Food *(Burdocks 244-0108)*, Wine/Beer, Liquor Store *(Liquor Locker 244-3788)*, Bakery, Fishmonger, Lobster Pound, Meat Market, Bank/ATM, Post Office, Catholic Church, Library *(Southwest Harbor 244-7065)*, Beauty Salon, Dry Cleaners, Laundry *(Village Washtub 244-7228)*, Bookstore *(Rue Cottage Books 244-5542)*, Pharmacy *(Carroll 244-5588)*, Newsstand *(Tom Cat)*, Hardware Store *(McEachern & Hutchins 244-5567)*, Florist, Retail Shops, Copies Etc. *(Downeast Graphics 244-9066)*

Transportation

OnSite: Courtesy Car/Van *(By reservation)* **OnCall:** Rental Car *(Enterprise 667-1217)*, Taxi *(Happy Harry's 244-4314)* **Near:** Water Taxi *(MDI 244-5724 - call)*, Local Bus *(Island Explorer 288-4573)* **1-3 mi:** Bikes *(Southwest Cycle 244-5856)* **Airport:** Bar Harbor/Bangor Int'l. *(23 mi./50 mi.)*

Medical Services

911 Service **Near:** Dentist, Chiropractor, Ambulance **1-3 mi:** Doctor *(SW Harbor Medical 244-5513)* **Hospital:** Mt. Desert Island 288-5081 *(18 mi.)*

Setting -- This is clearly a boatyard, but just as clearly, it's a Hinckley boatyard. Although the "people" amenities are limited, everything is very neat, clean, lovely and "ship shape". The views from the mooring field, usually filled with impeccably maintained, classically designed Hinckleys, are truly inspiring - those made by nature and those made by man. The facility is just under two miles from the town of SW Harbor, so it's more rural and a bit more tranquil.

Marina Notes -- There is very limited dock space, so prepare for a mooring, especially during peak season. Green Hinckley flag on mooring means reserved. Launch runs regularly during business hours; limited on-call after hours. The marina has a dinghy dock and there are loaner dinghies if you arrive by land after hours. Courtesy car available by reservation. The staff is knowledgeable and helpful; the focus here is service. All boatyard services onsite. CNG is available as well as small quantities of gas for outboards. The extensive boatyard services and service staff make this a great place to leave your boat. Ship's Store sells clothing and gifts with the Hinckley name. Inquire about a tour of the boat building sheds: see Hinckleys being built. Seasonal moorings $1,000. SW Harbor's only fuel for big boats is at Beal's. Town of SW Harbor has six additional moorings; contact Gene Thurston, Harbormaster (Ch. 9, 16, 244-7913).

Notable -- The town of Southwest Harbor is still easily accessible by water taxi, your dinghy (across the harbor at Upper Town Dock), by foot (1.7 mi.), or the free Acadia Island Shuttle (which goes to Northeast Harbor and Bar Harbor as well). Also across the harbor is the Southwest Harbor Aquarium with some very fine exhibits and a popular touch tank. Next door is the Moorings Restaurant - with a deck overlooking the mooring field -- and accommodations.

PHOTOS ON CD-ROM: 9

Beal's Lobster Pier

PO Box 225; 182 Clark Point Road; Southwest Harbor, ME 04679

Tel: (207) 244-3202; (800) 245-7178 **VHF: Monitor** 88 **Talk** 88
Fax: (207) 244-9479 **Alternate Tel:** (207) 244-3202
Email: beals@acadia.net **Web:** www.bealslobster.com
Nearest Town: Southwest Harbor *(0.7 mi.)* **Tourist Info:** (207) 224-9264

Navigational Information

Lat: 44°16.536' **Long:** 068°18.835' **Tide:** 10 ft. **Current:** 2 kt. **Chart:** 13318
Rep. Depths (*MLW*): Entry 30 ft. **Fuel Dock** 20 ft. **Max Slip/Moor** -/30 ft.
Access: On the East Shore of Southwest Harbor next to Coast Guard Station

Marina Facilities *(In Season/Off Season)*

Fuel: *Citgo* - Slip-Side Fueling, Gasoline, Diesel, High-Speed Pumps
Slips: 0 Total, 0 Transient **Max LOA:** 100 ft. **Max Beam:** 20 ft.
Rate *(per ft.)*: **Day** n/a **Week** n/a **Month** n/a
Power: 30 amp n/a, **50 amp** n/a, **100 amp** n/a, **200 amp** n/a
Cable TV: No **Dockside Phone:** No
Dock Type: Wood, Floating, Fixed
Moorings: 3 Total, 3 Transient **Launch:** None
Rate: Day $20 **Week** $100 **Month** Inq.
Heads: 4 Toilet(s)
Laundry: None **Pay Phones:** No
Pump-Out: No **Fee:** n/a **Closed Heads:** No

Marina Operations

Owner/Manager: Sam Beal **Dockmaster:** Eugene Thurston III
In-Season: Jun-Sep, 7am-8pm **Off-Season:** Oct-May, 7am-5pm
After-Hours Arrival: n/a
Reservations: No **Credit Cards:** Visa/MC, Dscvr, Amex
Discounts: None
Pets: Welcome **Handicap Access:** Yes, Heads

Marina Services and Boat Supplies

Services - Docking Assistance, Trash Pick-Up **Communication -** Fax in/out *($5)*, FedEx **Supplies - OnSite:** Ice *(Block, Cube, Shaved)* **Near:** Propane *(Mills Oil 244-3131)* **Under 1 mi:** West Marine **1-3 mi:** Ships' Store *(Hinckley 244-7100)*, CNG *(Hinckley)*

Boatyard Services

Near: Railway, Crane, Engine mechanic *(gas, diesel)*, Launching Ramp, Hull Repairs *(Down East Diesel)*, Divers, Woodworking *(Down East)*, Painting *(Down East)*, Awlgrip, Total Refits *(Down East Diesel)*. **Under 1 mi:** Sail Loft, Bottom Cleaning, Brightwork, Interior Cleaning, Yacht Building. **1-3 mi:** Travelift *(50T)*, Electrical Repairs, Rigger, Yacht Broker *(Hinckley)*. **Nearest Yard:** Southwest Boat Corp (207) 244-5525

Restaurants and Accommodations

OnSite: Seafood Shack *(Beal's Lobster Pier)*, Snack Bar *(The Captain's Galley)* **Near:** Restaurant *(Deacon Seat 244-9229, B $6, L $10, D $12)*, *(Eat-A-Pita & Chef Marc 244-4344, B $4-6, L $5-7, D 414-21)*, *(Red Sky D $11-27)*, *(Dry Dock Café 244-3886, B $7, L $6-11, D $10-16)*, Pizzeria *(Little Notch 244-3357)*, Motel *(Harbor View 244-5031, $70)*, Hotel *(Claremont 244-5036, $125-$250)*, Inn/B&B *(Lindenwood Inn 244-5335, $95-255)*, *(Island House 244-5180, $85)* **Under 1 mi:** Restaurant *(Top of the Hill 244-0033)*, *(Fiddler's Green 244-9416, D $19-29)* **1-3 mi:** Condo/Cottage *(Harbor Ridge 244-7000)*

Recreation and Entertainment

OnSite: Picnic Area, Boat Rentals *(Harbor Boat Rentals, 17' Boston Whaler, 22' Mako 244-0557)*, Group Fishing Boat **Near:** Video Rental *(Ya Gotta Love It Videos 244-7700)*, Cultural Attract *(Mt. Desert Oceanarium)* **Under 1 mi:** Beach **1-3 mi:** Tennis Courts *(Causeway Club)*, Golf Course *(Causeway Club 244-3780)*, Museum *(Wendell Gilley 244-7555)*, Sightseeing *(Mt. Desert Island)*

Provisioning and General Services

OnSite: Fishmonger, Lobster Pound **OnCall:** Provisioning Service, Delicatessen *(Double J Grocery & Deli 244-5544)* **Near:** Bank/ATM, Protestant Church, Library *(Southwest Harbor 244-7065)*, Beauty Salon, Bookstore *(Rue Cottage Books 244-5542)*, Pharmacy *(Carroll Drugs 244-5588)*, Newsstand, Retail Shops **Under 1 mi:** Supermarket *(Gott's 244-3431)*, Health Food *(Burdocks 244-0108)*, Wine/Beer, Bakery, Meat Market, Post Office, Barber Shop, Hardware Store *(McEachern & Hutchins 244-7243)*, Copies Etc. *(Downeast Graphics 244-9066)* **1-3 mi:** Liquor Store *(Liquor Locker 244-3788, delivers)*, Laundry *(Village Wash 244-7228)*

Transportation

OnCall: Water Taxi *(MDI 244-7312 call)*, Rental Car *(Enterprise 667-1217)*, Taxi *(Happy Harry's Taxi 244-4314)* **Near:** Bikes *(Southwest Cycle 244-5856)*, Local Bus *(Acadia Island Explorer 288-4573, www.exploreacadia.com)* **Airport:** Bar Harbor/Bangor Int'l. *(21/50 mi.)*

Medical Services

911 Service **Near:** Doctor *(Southwest Harbor Med Center 244-5513)*, Ambulance **Under 1 mi:** Dentist **1-3 mi:** Holistic Services *(Greenbaum Massage 276-4057)*, Veterinarian *(SW Harbor Vet Clinic 244-3336)* **Hospital:** Mount Desert Island 288-5081 *(14 mi.)*

Setting -- Nestled into the eastern shore of Southwest Harbor, next to the U.S. Coast Guard station and Southwest Harbor's town dock, the Beal family facility has been here since 1930, and provides "down-home" atmosphere in a busy, working seaside community. While the amenities are limited, mooring among the fishing fleet is a true down-east experience.

Marina Notes -- This is a restaurant and wholesale lobster operation first and a transient boating facility second. There is a "short stay" dock, which is shared with the lobster fleet, and three moorings (no launch service, bring your dinghy). Overnight slips are not available. There is water, gas, diesel, ice, and some marine hardware. Beal's has been in the same family for over 70 years. A few additional moorings may be available from Southwest Harbor Town Moorings - Town Hall 244-5404 or Harbormaster 244-7913.

Notable -- Enjoy fresh boiled lobster and other seafood specialties at the picnic tables outdoors on the pier. Beal's in-the-rough lobster pound is highly rated by many guides, and serves the crustaceans for B, L, & D, starting at 9am. It is also said that Beal's pier promises an exceptionally cool breeze during the worst of Maine's heat waves. The Southwest Harbor Oceanarium is nearby, just west of the Town Dock, with its own blue lobster boat and enticing touch tanks. All of Mt. Desert is easily reachable on the Acadia Island Explorer that stops nearby. Just under a mile is the Wendell Gilley Museum, which has an extraordinary display of carved birds. There are several inns, restaurants, services, and shops within walking distance.

PHOTOS ON CD-ROM: 9

Navigational Information
Lat: 44°16.565' **Long:** 068°18.827' **Tide:** 10 ft. **Current:** 2 kt. **Chart:** 13318
Rep. Depths (*MLW*): Entry 20 ft. **Fuel Dock** n/a **Max Slip/Moor** 15 ft./20 ft.
Access: Penobscot Bay to Southwest Harbor, eastern shore

Marina Facilities *(In Season/Off Season)*
Fuel: No
Slips: 15 Total, 5 Transient **Max LOA:** 100 ft. **Max Beam:** n/a
Rate *(per ft.)*: **Day** $1.00/Inq. **Week** $5.00 **Month** $15
Power: 30 amp Incl., **50 amp** Incl., **100 amp** n/a, **200 amp** n/a
Cable TV: No **Dockside Phone:** No
Dock Type: Wood, Short Fingers, Pilings, Alongside, Floating, Fixed
Moorings: 3 Total, 3 Transient **Launch:** Yes (Free), Dinghy Dock
Rate: Day $20 **Week** $100 **Month** $250
Heads: 1 Toilet(s), 1 Shower(s)
Laundry: None **Pay Phones:** Yes
Pump-Out: OnSite, Full Service, 1 Central **Fee:** Free **Closed Heads:** No

Marina Operations
Owner/Manager: Jeff Berzinis **Dockmaster:** Same
In-Season: Year-Round, 9am-5pm **Off-Season:** n/a
After-Hours Arrival: Call in advance and then tie up in an available slip
Reservations: Yes, Preferred **Credit Cards:** Visa/MC
Discounts: None
Pets: Welcome **Handicap Access:** No

Southwest Boat Marine Services

PO Box 260; 168 Clark Point Road; Southwest Harbor, ME 04679

Tel: (207) 244-5525 **VHF: Monitor** 16 **Talk** 8
Fax: (207) 667-4013 **Alternate Tel:** (207) 326-8548
Email: n/a **Web:** www.southwestboat.com
Nearest Town: Southwest Harbor *(0.6 mi.)* **Tourist Info:** (207) 244-9264

Marina Services and Boat Supplies
Services - Docking Assistance, Trash Pick-Up, Dock Carts **Communication -** FedEx, AirBorne, UPS, Express Mail **Supplies - OnSite:** Ice *(Shaved)* **Near:** Ships' Store *(Rockland Boat 244-7870)*, West Marine *(at Dysart's)* **Under 1 mi:** Bait/Tackle **1-3 mi:** Propane *(Hinckley's 244-5572)*, CNG *(Hinckley's)*

Boatyard Services
OnSite: Railway *(250 ft.)*, Crane *(25T)*, Bottom Cleaning, Divers *(Underwater hull inspection)*, Metal Fabrication **OnCall:** Engine mechanic *(gas, diesel)*, Electrical Repairs *(Village Electronics 244-7227)*, Electronic Sales *(Village Electronics)*, Rigger, Sail Loft, Air Conditioning, Refrigeration, Compound, Wash & Wax, Interior Cleaning, Propeller Repairs

Restaurants and Accommodations
Near: Restaurant *(Dry Dock Cafe 244-3886, B $7, L $6-11, D $10-16)*, *(Eat-A-Pita & Chef Marc 244-4344, B $4-6, L $5-7, D $14-21)*, Seafood Shack *(Beal's Lobster Pier 244-3202)*, Snack Bar *(The Captain's Galley)*, Pizzeria *(Little Notch 244-3357)*, Motel *(Harbor View Motel & Cottages 244-5031, $70)*, Inn/B&B *(Island House B&B 244-5180, $85)*, *(Clark Point Inn 244-9828)* **Under 1 mi:** Restaurant *(Moorings Restaurant 244-7070, across the harbor)*, *(Top of the Hill 244-0033)*, *(Red Sky)*, *(Fiddler's Green 244-9416, D $19-29)*, Inn/B&B *(Moorings Inn 244-5523, $65-100, by dinghy)*

Recreation and Entertainment
Near: Jogging Paths, Boat Rentals *(Harbor 244-0557)*, Video Rental *(Ya Gotta Love It Videos 244-7700)*, Park, Cultural Attract *(Southwest Oceanarium 244-7330)* **Under 1 mi:** Beach **1-3 mi:** Tennis Courts, Golf Course *(Causeway Club 244-3780)*, Museum *(Wendell Gilley Museum 244-7555)*, Sightseeing *(Acadia National Park 288-3338)* **3+ mi:** Horseback Riding *(Seal Cove Riding Stable 244-7705, 4 mi.)*

Provisioning and General Services
Near: Market *(Sawyers Market 244-3315, Southwest Foodmart 244-5601 both deliver)*, Lobster Pound, Bank/ATM, Protestant Church, Library *(Southwest Harbor PL 244-7065)*, Beauty Salon, Bookstore *(Rue Cottage Books 244-5542)*, Pharmacy *(Carroll Drug Store 244-5588)*, Retail Shops **Under 1 mi:** Convenience Store, Supermarket *(Carroll's IGA; Gotts 244-3931)*, Delicatessen *(Double J Grocery & Deli 244-5544)*, Health Food *(Burdocks 244-0108)*, Wine/Beer, Liquor Store *(Liquor Locker 244-3788, delivers)*, Post Office, Barber Shop, Laundry, Hardware Store *(McEachern & Hutchins 244-7243)*, Copies Etc. *(Downeast Graphics 244-9066)* **1-3 mi:** Florist

Transportation
OnSite: Local Bus *(Island Explorer 288-4573)* **OnCall:** Water Taxi *(MDI 244-7312, 460-3977)*, Rental Car *(Enterprise 667-1217)*, Taxi *(Happy Harry's 244-4314)* **Near:** Bikes *(Southwest Cycle 244-5856)*, Ferry Service *(Cranberry Island)* **Airport:** Bar Harbor/Bangor Int'l. *(21 mi./50 mi.)*

Medical Services
911 Service **OnCall:** Ambulance **Near:** Doctor *(SW Harbor Med Center 244-5513)* **Under 1 mi:** Dentist **1-3 mi:** Holistic Services *(Greenbaum Massage 276-4057)*, Veterinarian *(SW Harbor 244-3336)* **Hospital:** Mt. Desert Island 288-5081 *(14 mi.)*

Setting -- Located near the Coast Guard station, next to Beal's Lobster Pier, Southwest Boat is on the north side of the harbor where most of the working fleet gathers. This venerable recreational and commercial boat yard is convenient to all of Southwest Harbor.

Marina Notes -- Southwest Boat offers year-round dockage and inside storage for vessels up to 100 ft. 25 ton crane and a 250 foot railway. They specialize in steel boat repair; an on-site machine shop can provide welding and metal fabrication. Diver for underwater hull inspections. Towing and salvage. Island 65 foot, 50 ton barge service. They could probably arrange for most repair services, but are limited in what is available onsite. There is no fuel here. One full-size porta-potty. A good place to leave the boat. Additional moorings may be available from Southwest Harbor Town Moorings - Town Hall 244-5404 or Harbormaster 244-7913. Downeast Diesel and Marine (244-5145) is just down the road.

Notable -- Southwest Harbor is beautiful and close to Bar Harbor and Acadia National Park, with endless activities: shopping, restaurants, and local festivals. The free Island Explorer Shuttle runs to Bar Harbor and Acadia. There is a water taxi on-site. About a quarter of a mile walk leads to the Southwest Harbor branch of the Oceanarium, where the touch tanks are a popular attraction. It's right on the water with its own blue lobster boat and a wide range of exhibits on lobstering, fishing and oceanography and offers occasional lectures as well.

PHOTOS ON CD-ROM: 9

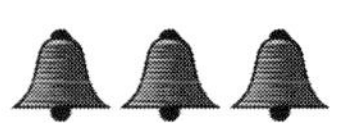

Dysart's Great Harbor Marina

PO Box 1503; 11 Apple Lane; Southwest Harbor, ME 04679

Tel: (207) 244-0117 **VHF: Monitor** 9 **Talk** 8
Fax: (207) 244-7526 **Alternate Tel:** (207) 244-5531
Email: n/a **Web:** www.dysartsmarina.com
Nearest Town: Southwest Harbor *(0.5 mi.)* **Tourist Info:** (207) 244-9264

Navigational Information

Lat: 44°16.487' **Long:** 068°19.381' **Tide:** 12 ft. **Current:** 2 kt. **Chart:** 13318
Rep. Depths (*MLW*): Entry 12 ft. **Fuel Dock** 5 ft. **Max Slip/Moor** 12 ft./-
Access: Gulf of Maine to Eastern Way to Southwest Harbor

Marina Facilities *(In Season/Off Season)*

Fuel: Diesel
Slips: 100 Total, 25 Transient **Max LOA:** 150 ft. **Max Beam:** n/a
Rate *(per ft.)*: **Day** $2.25/Inq.* **Week** Inq. **Month** Inq.
Power: 30 amp $10, **50 amp** $15, **100 amp** $30, **200 amp** n/a
Cable TV: No **Dockside Phone:** No
Dock Type: Concrete, Alongside, Floating
Moorings: 0 Total, 0 Transient **Launch:** n/a
Rate: Day n/a **Week** n/a **Month** n/a
Heads: 14 Toilet(s), 7 Shower(s) *(with dressing rooms)*
Laundry: 2 Washer(s), 2 Dryer(s), Book Exchange **Pay Phones:** Yes, 2
Pump-Out: OnSite, Full Service, 1 Central **Fee:** n/a **Closed Heads:** No

Marina Operations

Owner/Manager: Calvin Anderson **Dockmaster:** Bill McCluskey
In-Season: May-Oct, Dawn-Dusk **Off-Season:** Nov-Apr, 7:30am-4:30pm
After-Hours Arrival: Call ahead for instructions
Reservations: Preferred **Credit Cards:** Visa/MC
Discounts: None
Pets: Welcome **Handicap Access:** Yes, Heads, Docks

Marina Services and Boat Supplies

Services - Docking Assistance, Concierge, Boaters' Lounge, Dock Carts, Megayacht Facilities, 3 Phase **Communication -** Mail & Package Hold, Phone Messages, Fax in/out, Data Ports *(Office)*, FedEx, UPS, Express Mail **Supplies - OnSite:** Ice *(Block, Cube)*, Ships' Store *(also nearby Rockland Boat 244-7870)*, West Marine *(244-0300)*, Propane *(Walls 244-3226)* **Near:** Bait/Tackle **1-3 mi:** CNG *(Hinckley)*

Boatyard Services

OnSite: Forklift, Electronic Sales, Sail Loft, Bottom Cleaning, Brightwork, Divers, Compound, Wash & Wax, Interior Cleaning, Propeller Repairs, Woodworking, Inflatable Repairs **OnCall:** Engine mechanic *(gas, diesel)*, Electrical Repairs, Electronics Repairs, Hull Repairs, Rigger, Air Conditioning, Refrigeration, Upholstery, Yacht Interiors, Metal Fabrication, Painting, Awlgrip, Yacht Design, Yacht Broker **Under 1 mi:** Travelift, Railway, Crane, Launching Ramp, Yacht Building, Total Refits. **Nearest Yard:** Hinckley (207) 244-5572

Restaurants and Accommodations

OnSite: Restaurant *(Deck House 244-5044, D $22, plus $7 for entertainment)* **Near:** Restaurant *(Fiddler's Green 244-9416, D $19-29)*, *(Café Dry Dock 244-3886, L $5-10, D $9-15)*, *(Red Sky)*, *(Eat-A-Pita & Chef Marc B $4-6, L $5-7, D $14-21)*, Seafood Shack *(Head of the Harbor 244-3508, 11am-9pm, $4-18)*, Pizzeria *(Little Notch 244-3357)*, Motel *(Acadia Cabins 244-5388, $80-100)*, Inn/B&B *(Inn at Southwest 244-3835, $65-145)* **Under 1 mi:** Restaurant *(Harbor Cottage Inn 244-5738)*, *(The Claremont 244-5036, D $18-24)*, Inn/B&B *(Lindenwood 244-5335, $75-250)*, *(Lamb's Ear 244-9828, $85-165)*, *(The Kingsleigh 244-5302, $125-220)*

Recreation and Entertainment

OnSite: Picnic Area, Grills, Fishing Charter, Group Fishing Boat, Cultural Attract *(Deck House Cabaret Theater)* **OnCall:** Dive Shop, Boat Rentals *(Kayaks)* **Near:** Pool, Beach, Playground, Tennis Courts, Fitness Center, Video Rental *(Ya Gotta Love It 244-7700)*, Park *(Acadia)* **Under 1 mi:** Golf Course *(Causeway C.C. 244-3780)*, Museum *(Oceanarium 244-7330)*

Provisioning and General Services

OnSite: Bakery *(Little Notch)*, Lobster Pound, Retail Shops **OnCall:** Provisioning Service, Wine/Beer *(Sawyer's Specialties)* **Near:** Convenience Store, Supermarket *(Gotts 244-3431)*, Gourmet Shop, Delicatessen, Health Food *(Burdocks 244-0108)*, Fishmonger, Meat Market, Bank/ATM, Post Office, Protestant Church, Library, Beauty Salon, Barber Shop, Dry Cleaners, Laundry, Bookstore *(Rue Cottage Books 244-5542)*, Pharmacy *(Carroll 244-5588)*, Newsstand, Hardware Store *(McEachern & Hutchins 244-5567)*, Florist, Copies Etc. *(Downeast Graphics 244-9066)* **Under 1 mi:** Liquor Store *(Liquor Locker 244-3788)*

Transportation

OnSite: Water Taxi, Local Bus *(Island Explorer)* **OnCall:** Bikes *(Southwest Cycle 244-5856)*, Rental Car *(Enterprise 667-1217)*, Taxi *(Happy Harry's 266-1554)*, Airport Limo *(Airport Taxi 667-5995)* **Airport:** Bar Harbor/Bangor Int'l. *(21 mi./50 mi.)*

Medical Services

911 Service **Near:** Doctor *(SW Harbor Med. Center 244-5513)*, Dentist, Ambulance **1-3 mi:** Veterinarian *(SW Harbor Vet Clinic 244-3336)*
Hospital: Mt. Desert Island 288-5081 *(14 mi.)*

PHOTOS ON CD-ROM: 9

Setting -- Dysart's sits at the head of Southwest Harbor and just down the hill from "downtown" -- with views up the whole length of the harbor and out to the mouth. It's in a small complex with a cabaret theater, a little bar, a picnic area, and a few nautically-oriented shops. Most other services are an easy walk back "up the hill", including access to Acadia National Park.

Marina Notes -- * Under 50' $2.25; 50-64' $2.50; 65-150' $2.75. Fuel purchases limited to 200 gal min. For smaller quantities, try Beal's. Helpful and friendly staff. There have been continual upgrades and additions since it was built by the Dysart family in 1990. The ownership was formerly a partnership with Hinckley's and was then called Hinckley's Great Harbor. New docks for vessels up to 150 ft. and 3-phase power. Some docakge is stern-to. Courtesy car, concierge services, and customized cruise planning are emblematic of their emphasis on service. Sawyer's Market & Southwest Food both deliver food and wine. Jet skis are prohibited. Off-season, commercial fishing boats dock here.

Notable -- Dysart's is the local center for larger vessels and a popular destination for club cruises, regattas, rendezvous, and other special events. Dysart's hosts cookouts, lobster bakes and, on Saturdays, Caribbean Night with steel drum bands and a potluck supper for all marina guests. Onsite is The Deck House cabaret theater (also available for functions on dark nights). An easy .6 mi. walk out Clarks Point Road is the Mount Desert Oceanarium on the waterfront (Mon-Sat, 9am-5pm, $6.95/4.75, 244-7330). Another .6 mi. walk is Wendell Gilley Museum of Decoys (Tue-Sun, 10am-4pm, $3.25/$1, 244-7555).

Navigational Information

Lat: 44°14.046' **Long:** 068°20.835' **Tide:** 12 ft. **Current:** 1 kt. **Chart:** 13318
Rep. Depths (*MLW*): Entry 20 ft. **Fuel Dock** 20 ft. **Max Slip/Moor** 6 ft./30 ft.
Access: Eastern Blue Hill Bay to Bass Harbor on Mount Desert Island

Marina Facilities *(In Season/Off Season)*

Fuel: *Texaco* - Slip-Side Fueling, Diesel
Slips: 20 Total, 12 Transient **Max LOA:** 50 ft. **Max Beam:** 15 ft.
Rate *(per ft.)*: **Day** $1.50/$1.50 **Week** n/a **Month** n/a
Power: 30 amp Incl., **50 amp** n/a, **100 amp** n/a, **200 amp** n/a
Cable TV: No **Dockside Phone:** No
Dock Type: Wood, Floating
Moorings: 32 Total, 16 Transient **Launch:** None, Dinghy Dock
Rate: Day $30 **Week** $150 **Month** n/a
Heads: 3 Toilet(s), 3 Shower(s) *(with dressing rooms)*
Laundry: 1 Washer(s), 1 Dryer(s), Book Exchange **Pay Phones:** No
Pump-Out: OnSite, 1 Central, 1 Port **Fee:** $20 **Closed Heads:** No

Marina Operations

Owner/Manager: Morris Yachts **Dockmaster:** Dayton Arey
In-Season: Year Round, 9am-5pm **Off-Season:** n/a
After-Hours Arrival: Call ahead
Reservations: Required **Credit Cards:** Visa/MC
Discounts: None
Pets: Welcome, Dog Walk Area **Handicap Access:** No

Morris Yachts Inc.

PO Box 395; Grandville Road; Bass Harbor, ME 04653

Tel: (207) 244-5511 **VHF: Monitor** 9 **Talk** 68
Fax: (207) 244-9726 **Alternate Tel:** n/a
Email: morrisservice@acadia.net **Web:** www.morrisyachts.com
Nearest Town: Southwest Harbor *(3 mi.)* **Tourist Info:** (207) 244-9264

Marina Services and Boat Supplies

Services - Docking Assistance, Boaters' Lounge, Security *(24 Hrs.)* **Communication -** Mail & Package Hold, Phone Messages, Fax in/out, Data Ports *(Office)*, FedEx, AirBorne, UPS, Express Mail *(Sat Del)* **Supplies - OnSite:** Ice *(Block, Cube)* **1-3 mi:** Ships' Store, West Marine *(244-0300)*, Propane *(Hinckley)*, CNG *(Hinckley)*

Boatyard Services

OnSite: Travelift *(35T)*, Engine mechanic *(gas, diesel)*, Electrical Repairs, Electronic Sales, Electronics Repairs, Hull Repairs, Rigger, Bottom Cleaning, Brightwork, Air Conditioning, Refrigeration, Divers, Compound, Wash & Wax, Interior Cleaning, Woodworking, Metal Fabrication, Painting, Awlgrip, Total Refits **Under 1 mi:** Sail Loft, Propeller Repairs, Upholstery. **Dealer for:** Morris, Yanmar, Raytheon, Panda. **Member:** ABBRA, ABYC - 3 Certified Tech(s) **Yard Rates:** $30-70/hr., Haul & Launch $9-12/ft., Power Wash $2-3/ft., Bottom Paint $17/ft. *(paint included)* **Storage:** On-Land Outside $50/ft. Inside $70/ft. Heated $95/ft.

Restaurants and Accommodations

OnCall: Pizzeria *(Little Notch 244-3357)* **Near:** Restaurant *(Maine-Ly Delight 244-3656, B $4-6, L $4-6, D $4-6)*, *(Seafood Ketch 244-7463, L $6-12, D $6-12, 11am-9pm, kids' menu)*, *(The Wharf 244-9101)* **Under 1 mi:** Seafood Shack *(Thurston's Lobster Pound 244-7600, dinghy across the harbor)*, Condo/Cottage *(Bass Harbor Cottages 244-3460, $40-240)* **1-3 mi:** Restaurant *(Seawall Restaurant & Motel 244-3020, L $3-18, D $3-18)*, Snack Bar *(Jumpin Java B $4, L $7)*, Hotel *(Claremont 244-5036)*, Inn/B&B *(Seawall 244-9240)*, *(Lindenwood 244-5330)*, *(Kingsleigh 244-5302)*

Recreation and Entertainment

OnSite: Beach **Near:** Boat Rentals *(Yakman Adventures 244-3333)*, Park *(Acadia Nat'l)* **Under 1 mi:** Jogging Paths, Galleries *(antique shops in Bernard, up the hill is Ravenswood 244-9621 for Ship Models)* **1-3 mi:** Picnic Area, Grills, Playground, Dive Shop, Tennis Courts *(Causeway)*, Golf Course, Fitness Center, Video Rental, Museum, Sightseeing *(Acadia - Seawall Campground)*

Provisioning and General Services

Near: Fishmonger, Lobster Pound **Under 1 mi:** Post Office **1-3 mi:** Provisioning Service *(Sawyers 244-3315)*, Convenience Store, Supermarket *(Sawyers)*, Gourmet Shop, Delicatessen, Health Food, Wine/Beer, Liquor Store, Bakery, Farmers' Market, Green Grocer, Meat Market, Bank/ATM, Catholic Church, Protestant Church, Library, Beauty Salon, Barber Shop, Dry Cleaners, Laundry, Pharmacy *(Carroll Drug 244-0224)*, Newsstand, Hardware Store, Florist, Clothing Store, Copies Etc.

Transportation

OnSite: Courtesy Car/Van **OnCall:** Taxi *(Airport & Harbor Car 667-5995)* **Near:** Local Bus *(Island Explorer)*, Ferry Service *(Swan's Island)* **1-3 mi:** Bikes **3+ mi:** Rental Car *(Hertz 667-5017, delivers, 15 mi.)* **Airport:** Bar Harbor *(15 mi.)*

Medical Services

911 Service **1-3 mi:** Doctor *(Walk-in Clinic 244-5630)*, Dentist, Chiropractor, Holistic Services, Ambulance, Veterinarian *(Southwest Harbor Vet Clinic 244-3336)* **Hospital:** Mount Desert Island 288-5081 *(18 mi.)*

Setting -- The new home of Morris Yachts is the facility just before the ferry landing, in Bass Harbor's Outer Harbor. An attractive complex of nicely restored cottages and antique Maine boatyard buildings along with state-of-the art service sheds line the waterfront and then wind their way up the hill. There is much more here than is apparent from the water. The views are quite spectacular and dramatic.

Marina Notes -- Home of famous custom Morris Yachts. In 1999, Morris purchased Bass Harbor Marine and moved its primary location here from Southwest Harbor. Storage and service capacity were doubled; they now have 38,000 sq. ft. indoor storage, half heated. Parts Dept 7:30am-4pm, 8am-noon on Sat. Three full baths and laundry in a separate building. Mooring field straddles the fairway. No overnight transient docks in the Outer Harbor, but Morris maintains dockage in the Inner Harbor at Up Harbor Marine -- near Thurston's and the town docks. Two spacious full bathrooms (tile floors, beadboard wainscotting) service those docks. Dinghy dockage at Morris as well as at the town dock. Morris's service yard and brokerage is in Bass Harbor, but its production/manufacturing facility is just off the island in Trenton. For additional moorings, check with Bass Harbor harbormaster, Al Price 244-4564, Ch.16.

Notable -- Note that the harbor is wide open at its entrance and some of the moorings could be quite rolly. The ferry to Swan's Island docks next door. A couple of restaurants are within walking or dinghying distance and a convenience store is about a mile and a half toward Southwest Harbor. Sea Kayak rentals $25/day from Yakman Adventures next to the docks. Can tie up at the inner harbor town dock up to two hours for water or to buy lobsters.

PHOTOS ON CD-ROM: 9

Kollegewidgwok Yacht Club

PO Box 368; East Blue Hill Road; Blue Hill, ME 04614

Tel: (207) 374-5581 **VHF: Monitor** 9 **Talk** 78
Fax: n/a **Alternate Tel:** n/a
Email: n/a **Web:** n/a
Nearest Town: Blue Hill *(1.6 mi.)* **Tourist Info:** (207) 374-2281

Navigational Information

Lat: 44°24.453' **Long:** 068°33.723' **Tide:** 10 ft. **Current:** n/a **Chart:** 13316
Rep. Depths (*MLW*): Entry 17 ft. **Fuel Dock** n/a **Max Slip/Moor** 10 ft./24 ft.
Access: R N 6 into Outer Harbor - only facility on eastern shore

Marina Facilities *(In Season/Off Season)*

Fuel: Gasoline, Diesel
Slips: 0 Total, 0 Transient **Max LOA:** n/a **Max Beam:** n/a
Rate *(per ft.)*: **Day** n/a **Week** n/a **Month** n/a
Power: 30 amp n/a, **50 amp** n/a, **100 amp** n/a, **200 amp** n/a
Cable TV: No **Dockside Phone:** No
Dock Type: n/a
Moorings: 30 Total, 6 Transient **Launch:** Yes (Free), Dinghy Dock
Rate: Day $15 **Week** $100 **Month** n/a
Heads: 2 Toilet(s)
Laundry: None, Book Exchange **Pay Phones:** Yes, 1
Pump-Out: No **Fee:** n/a **Closed Heads:** Yes

Marina Operations

Owner/Manager: Sam Vaughn **Dockmaster:** n/a
In-Season: MemDay-ColDay, 8am-6pm **Off-Season:** Closed
After-Hours Arrival: Pick up an open mooring
Reservations: No **Credit Cards:** Cash or Check
Discounts: None
Pets: Welcome **Handicap Access:** No

Marina Services and Boat Supplies

Services - Boaters' Lounge, Dock Carts **Communication -** Data Ports *(At Blue Hill Library 374-5515)* **Supplies - OnSite:** Ice *(Block, Cube)*

Boatyard Services

Under 1 mi: Railway *(and 10T trailer for boats to 30 ft.)*, Engine mechanic *(gas, diesel)*. **Nearest Yard:** Raynes Yacht Yard (207) 374-2877

Restaurants and Accommodations

OnCall: Lite Fare *(Bianco & Rioux 374-5055, D $12-15, Dinner to go Thu & Fri, other days w/24 hrs. notice, delivers)*, Pizzeria *(Merrill & Hinckley 374-2821)* **Under 1 mi:** Seafood Shack *(Fishnet 374-5240, L $5-8, D $9-16)* **1-3 mi:** Restaurant *(Blue Moose at Jonathan's 374-3674, B, L & D, new owner & chef, will pick up)*, *(Jean-Paul's at Fire Pond 374-5852, L $5-9, D $15-18)*, *(Arborvine 374-2119, D $18-24, exquisite fine dining)*, *(Marlintin's Grill L $4-13, D $4-13)*, *(Capt. Issac Merrill D $14-19, B & L, too.)*, *(Hancock's 374-3272, L $5-8, D $11-18)*, Lite Fare *(Ovenworks 374-5775, pizza, subs, pastries, bread, dinners to go)*, *(Blue Hill Co-op 374-8999, L $3-9)*, *(Pain de Famille 374-3839)*, *(The Pantry 374-2229)*, Motel *(Heritage Motor Inn 374-5646, $60-100)*, Inn/B&B *(Blue Hill Farm 374-5166, $90-110)*, *(Capt. Isaac Merrill 374-2555, $95-130)*, *(Blue Hill Inn 374-2844, $140-260, picks up)*, *(First Light 374-5879, $105-175, unconventional faux lighthouse)*

Recreation and Entertainment

OnCall: Boat Rentals *(Rocky Coast Outfitters 374-8866 - kayaks & canoes, free delivery)* **Near:** Jogging Paths, Roller Blade/Bike Paths **1-3 mi:** Beach, Picnic Area *(Blue Hill Town)*, Playground, Fitness Center *(Blue Hill Center for Yoga 374-2004)*, Museum *(Parson Fisher House 374-2339, Mon-Sat 2-5pm $2/free, home of Renaissance man Jonathan Fisher - known as the Thos. Jefferson of Maine; 1815 Holt House 326-8250 houses Blue Hills Historical Society)*, Cultural Attract *(Kneisel Hall Chamber Festival - July-MidAug, Fri eves and Sun afternoons 374-2811, the "Cradle of Chamber Music Teaching in America"; Bagaduce Music Lending Library 374-5454 - one of the largest collections of sheet music in the world)*, Sightseeing *(Blue Hill Tower)*, Special Events *(Blue Hill Fair - Labor Day weekend; Pan New England Steelband Festival - May)*, Galleries *(Artisans)*

Provisioning and General Services

1-3 mi: Supermarket *(Merrill & Hinckley 374-2821 - will deliver - also Tradewinds 0.5 mi. farther)*, Gourmet Shop *(Moveable Feast 374-2441)*, Health Food *(Blue Hill Food Co-op 374-8999)*, Wine/Beer *(Blue Hill Wine Shop 374-2161)*, Liquor Store *(Merrill & Hinckley)*, Bakery *(Pain de Famille 374-3839)*, Farmers' Market *(Sat 9-11:30am at Fairgrounds)*, Fishmonger *(Merrill & Hinckley)*, Bank/ATM, Post Office, Protestant Church, Library *(Blue Hill 374-5515 - internet access)*, Laundry *(Blue Hill Laundry 7am-9pm 374-2777)*, Bookstore *(Blue Hill Books 374-5632, North Light Books 374-5422)*, Pharmacy *(Rite Aid - 0.5 mi. beyond town)*, Hardware Store, Florist *(Fairwinds 374-5621)*, Retail Shops *(Antiques, gifts, crafts)*

Transportation

OnCall: Bikes *(Rocky Coast Outfitters 374-8866 and The Activity Center)*, Airport Limo *(Airport Harbor Taxi 667-5995)* **Airport:** Bangor Int'l. *(40 mi.)*

Medical Services

911 Service **OnCall:** Ambulance **1-3 mi:** Veterinarian *(Maine Coast 374-2385)* **Hospital:** Blue Hill Mem 374-2836 - near dinghy landing *(1.7 mi.)*

Setting -- On the eastern shore of Blue Hill's Outer Harbor, KYC's small, contemporary gray club house and active floats are immediately visible. The mooring field seems to fill the harbor; the surrounding shoreline is unspoiled, quite beautiful and spotted with lovely old, perfectly maintained, Maine "cottages". About a mile and a half by road or dinghy is the charming, picturesque village of Blue Hill - clearly devoted to the arts in all its manifestations.

Marina Notes -- Services include launch service (8am-6pm), a cozy club house (with large fireplace), and 2 knotty pine bathrooms (no showers). KYC, a private club and a Cruising Club of America station, welcomes all visiting boaters. Dearth of taxis limits travel to foot, dinghy, or the kindness of strangers (or restaurants). Town dinghy landing has water 2 hours on each side of high tide. Raynes Marine, in the Inner Harbor, has moorings, limited BY services, but is tricky for bigger boats. Pronunciation? Try KOLL-edg-e-widg-wok. Translations: salt falls, mixed rapids, blue hill on shining green water.

Notable -- A schooner off Blue Hill was the birthplace of The Blue Hill Troupe, a group of very talented amateurs who have been delighting NYC audiences with Gilbert and Sullivan operettas for decades. Blue Hill is home to may artists and artisans, including 3 special pottery studios: Rowantrees 374-5535, Rackliffe's 374-2297, and Mark Bell 374-5881. In 1988, Noel Paul Stookey of Peter, Paul & Mary founded community radio 89.9FM. Thriving musical organizaitons include Kneisel Hall and Bagaduce Music Library. Steel band guru Carl Chase's Flash in the Pans band has ignited an all-age pans explosion here. The foot of Blue Hill trail is about 3 mi. Kids will enjoy the eco-cruises, walks & workshops at MERI Center for Marine Studies (374-2135).

PHOTOS ON CD-ROM: 9

Navigational Information
Lat: 44°08.558' **Long:** 068°26.941' **Tide:** 10 ft. **Current:** n/a **Chart:** 13313
Rep. Depths (*MLW*): Entry 15 ft. **Fuel Dock** 9 ft. **Max Slip/Moor** -/15 ft.
Access: Past Hockamock Head Light, first facility to port

Marina Facilities *(In Season/Off Season)*
Fuel: *at Fishermen's Co-op or Steamboat Wharf* - Gasoline, Diesel
Slips: 0 Total, 0 Transient **Max LOA:** n/a **Max Beam:** n/a
Rate *(per ft.)*: **Day** n/a **Week** n/a **Month** n/a
Power: 30 amp n/a, **50 amp** n/a, **100 amp** n/a, **200 amp** n/a
Cable TV: No **Dockside Phone:** No
Dock Type: n/a
Moorings: 30 Total, 30 Transient **Launch:** None, Dinghy Dock
Rate: Day $20 **Week** Inq. **Month** Inq.
Heads: 2 Toilet(s)
Laundry: None **Pay Phones:** Yes, 1
Pump-Out: No **Fee:** n/a **Closed Heads:** Yes

Marina Operations
Owner/Manager: Kevin Staples **Dockmaster:** Same
In-Season: Jul-Sep, 11am-7pm **Off-Season:** Closed
After-Hours Arrival: Pick up an empty mooring and check-in in the morning
Reservations: No, except for pre-paid groups **Credit Cards:** Cash or check
Discounts: None
Pets: Welcome **Handicap Access:** No

Burnt Coat Harbor Moorings

317 Atlantic Road; Swan's Island, ME 04685

Tel: (207) 526-4201 **VHF: Monitor** 68 **Talk** n/a
Fax: n/a **Alternate Tel:** (207) 526-4323
Email: n/a **Web:** n/a
Nearest Town: Swan's Island Village *(1 mi.)* **Tourist Info:** (207) 244-9624

Marina Services and Boat Supplies
Supplies - Near: Ice *(Block, Cube)*, Ships' Store *(Limited supplies at Fishermen's Co-op)*

Boatyard Services
OnSite: Divers, Propeller Repairs **Near:** Engine mechanic *(gas, diesel)*.

Restaurants and Accommodations
OnCall: Seafood Shack *(The Boathouse 526-4323, L $8-15, D $8-15, 7 days - delivers to boats)* **Near:** Seafood Shack *(Trafton's Wharf 526-4427, prepared lobsters & clams, take-out)*, *(Underwater Taxi 526-4204, L $5.50-$6.75/lb., Lobsters - also fish, steamers, crab & chowders - take out or picnic tables)* **1-3 mi:** Coffee Shop *(Island Bake Shoppe B & L, 7am-2pm Mon-Sat)*, Motel *(Harbor Watch Motel 526-4563, $60-80, 2.5 mi around harbor in Minturn or dinghy across)*, Inn/B&B *(Appletree House B&B 526-4438)*, *(Jeanne's Place 526-4116)*

Recreation and Entertainment
Near: Jogging Paths, Sightseeing *(Walk to the 1872 Lighthouse at Hockamock Head - now part of a Swan's Island park)*, Galleries *(local crafts at The Boathouse)* **Under 1 mi:** Beach *(2 within walking distance or dinghy to Sand Beach in Toothacher Cove or across to Minturn town landing and head inland for the warmer water of Quarry Pond)*, Boat Rentals *(Kayaks from Harbor Watch Motel 526-4563 $35 lesson + tour, $25/half day, $45 Full day incl. lesson - by dinghy)*, Museum *(Swan's Island Library & Museum 526-4330 Mon-Fri, noon-3pm; 3 mi. to S.I. Lobster & Marine Museum 526-4282 - small, but interesting - located just above the Ferry Landing in Mackerel Cove Mon, Wed, Sun 11am-4pm)*, Special Events *(Sweet Chariot Music Festival - a 3-night early August folk festival - in the Harbor & at Oddfellows Hall)* **1-3 mi:** Cultural Attract *(Atlantic Blanket Company 526-4492 - hand-woven woolens from S.I. sheep, 2-5pm Mon-Fri; Saturn Press, a hand-set letter press atelier specializing in cards, near library 526-4000)*

Provisioning and General Services
Near: Gourmet Shop *(Boathouse - limited provisions)*, Fishmonger *(UnderwaterTaxi 526-4204 haddock $5.50, hake $4.25, sole $5.75, crabmeat $13, sea scallops $8.75, Steamers 3.25, lobster chowder $15/qt., seafood/clam chowder $9.75/qt.)*, Lobster Pound *(Swan's Island Steamboat Wharf 526-4186 on western shore soft shell $4, hard shells $5 or Underwater Taxi soft shells $4.50, hard $6.75 + $1 to cook or Tim Trafton's Wharf 526-4427 both on eastern shore)*, Retail Shops *(Gift shop at Boathouse)* **Under 1 mi:** Convenience Store *(Swan's Island General Store in Minturn 526-4200 or dinghy across to town landing)*, Library *(526-4330 Jun-LabDay Mon-Fri, 1-4pm)* **1-3 mi:** Bakery *(Island Bake Shoppe near Ferry Landing)*, Post Office *(526-4194 1.3 mi.)*, Protestant Church, Laundry *(Atlantic Laundromat 526-4478)*

Transportation
1-3 mi: Bikes *(Harbor Watch Motel 526-4563 - $20/day - call ahead, a delivery may be possible - or dinghy across the harbor)* **3+ mi:** Ferry Service *(The Captain Henry Lee Ferry to Bass Harbor in Mackerel Cove, RT $6/3, about 6 trips per day 526-4273 or 244-3254, 3.5 mi.)*

Medical Services
911 Service **OnCall:** Ambulance **1-3 mi:** Holistic Services *(Massage therapist S. Weston 526-4563)* **Hospital:** Mount Desert 288-8439 *(by ferry)*

Setting -- A bit of old Maine, this quintessential working harbor is the perfect antidote to quaint, touristy Maine. Burnt Coat is bounded on the west by Swan's Island village, on the east by Minturn, and on the south by Harbor Island. It is secluded with minimal landside services and an active lobstering fleet.

Marina Notes -- The transient moorings are individually owned by Swan's Island lobstermen and managed by Kevin Staples, a local lobsterman turned entrepreneur. For 5 years, the Staples Family operated the Boathouse Restaurant, the large, natural sided, 2-story building perched on the western shore. When Debbie Staples was promoted to Postmistress, they closed the restaurant and re-opened it as a take-out, call ahead "seafood shack." For small groups, they will deliver to the boat. (Lobsters $12, Lobster + Clams $15, Lobster Roll $10, Crab Roll $8, seafood chowder $8/16oz). The Boathouse also sells local specialties, baked goods, produce, books, and houses an intriguing display of island crafts. On the eastern shore are two take-out places offering limited prepared seafood - lobsters, clams, fish, chowders, plus live/raw seafood, too. Before 1pm, fuel available at Swan's Island Fishermen's Co-op (526-4327), on the west shore below the red buildings, or at Swan's Island Steamboat Wharf, Ch.68, (526-4186) - water, ice, and lobsters, too. Swan's Island is dry, so BYO.

Notable -- The Swan's Island community is working hard at preserving a fragile way of life. But whatever was here last year may not be here the next. The Swan's Island General Store closed in '02 & reopened in '03. The Swan's Island Marine & Lobster Museum (3.5 mi.) is at the Ferry Terminal in Mackerel Cove, past the Island Bake Shoppe. "The Call of the Running Tide: A Portrait of an Island Family" by Nancy Price Graff, 1992, describes life on Swan's Island.

PHOTOS ON CD-ROM: 9

Billings Diesel and Marine

Moose Island Road; Stonington, ME 04681

Tel: (207) 367-2328 **VHF: Monitor** 16 **Talk** 9
Fax: (207) 367-5925 **Alternate Tel:** n/a
Email: billings@acadia.net **Web:** n/a
Nearest Town: Stonington *(1.1 mi.)* **Tourist Info:** (207) 348-6124

Navigational Information
Lat: 44°08.902' **Long:** 068°40.736' **Tide:** 10 ft. **Current:** n/a **Chart:** 13313
Rep. Depths (*MLW*): Entry 20 ft. **Fuel Dock** 12 ft. **Max Slip/Moor** 12 ft./12 ft.
Access: Penobscot Bay to Deer Isle Thorofare to Allen Cove

Marina Facilities *(In Season/Off Season)*
Fuel: Gasoline, Diesel
Slips: 25 Total, 15 Transient **Max LOA:** 150 ft. **Max Beam:** 25 ft.
Rate *(per ft.)*: **Day** $1.00/$1.00 **Week** $7.00 **Month** $30
Power: 30 amp Incl., **50 amp** Incl., **100 amp** Incl., **200 amp** Incl.
Cable TV: No **Dockside Phone:** No
Dock Type: Short Fingers, Pilings, Floating, Fixed
Moorings: 20 Total, 10 Transient **Launch:** None, Dinghy Dock
Rate: Day $15 **Week** $90 **Month** $250
Heads: 2 Toilet(s), 2 Shower(s)
Laundry: 1 Washer(s), 1 Dryer(s) **Pay Phones:** Yes, 2
Pump-Out: OnSite, Full Service **Fee:** Free **Closed Heads:** Yes

Marina Operations
Owner/Manager: Peter Grindle **Dockmaster:** Same
In-Season: Year-Round, 7am-3:30pm **Off-Season:** n/a
After-Hours Arrival: Call ahead for instructions
Reservations: Yes, Preferred **Credit Cards:** Visa/MC
Discounts: None
Pets: Welcome, Dog Walk Area **Handicap Access:** No

Marina Services and Boat Supplies
Services - Docking Assistance, Security *(24 Hrs., watchman)*, Dock Carts, Megayacht Facilities, 3 Phase **Communication -** Mail & Package Hold, Phone Messages, Fax in/out, FedEx, AirBorne, UPS, Express Mail **Supplies - OnSite:** Ice *(Block, Cube)*, Ships' Store *(also New England Marine 367-2692)* **3+ mi:** Propane *(Percy Brown 348-2247, 5.5 mi.)*

Boatyard Services
OnSite: Travelift *(35T)*, Railway *(425T)*, Forklift, Crane, Engine mechanic *(gas, diesel)*, Electrical Repairs *(Blackmore 367-2703)*, Hull Repairs, Rigger, Bottom Cleaning, Brightwork, Air Conditioning, Refrigeration, Compound, Wash & Wax, Propeller Repairs, Woodworking, Metal Fabrication, Painting, Awlgrip, Total Refits **OnCall:** Electronic Sales, Electronics Repairs **Near:** Divers. **Dealer for:** Westerbeke,Caterpiliar, Allison, Cummins, Volvo, Detroit, Z-F, Twin Diesel. **Yard Rates:** $43-75/hr., Haul & Launch $8/ft., Power Wash $43/hr., Bottom Paint $43/hr. + paint **Storage:** In-Water $0.35/sq.ft./mo., On-Land Inside $0.50 sq.ft./mo. Outside $0.30/sq.ft./mo.

Restaurants and Accommodations
Under 1 mi: Restaurant *(Connie's 367-2742)*, *(The Bayview 367-2274)*, *(The Fisherman's Friend 367-2442, L $3-7, D $7-16)*, Seafood Shack *(Café Atlantic 367-6373, D $12-18, currently for sale - call ahead)*, *(Lobster Deck 367-6526)*, Lite Fare *(Harbor Café 367-5099, B $2-5, L $2-10)*, Motel *(Boyce's Motel 367-2421, $50-100)*, Inn/B&B *(Inn on the Harbor 367-2420, $100-140, Free shuttle to/from marina)*, *(Près du Port 367-5007, $85)* **1-3 mi:** Lite Fare *(Lily's Café 367-5936, L $6-11)*

Recreation and Entertainment
Near: Boat Rentals *(Old Quarry Kayak & Canoe 367-8977)* **Under 1 mi:** Park *(Acadia National Park - Isle au Haut Ferry Excursion $14/$5)*, Museum *(Deer Isle Granite Museum 367-6331)*, Cultural Attract *(Opera House Arts 367-2788)*, Sightseeing *(Everett Knowlton's miniature village on East Main St.)*, Special Events *(Deer Isle Jazz Festival - end of July)*, Galleries **3+ mi:** Golf Course *(Island Country Club 348-2379, 10 mi.)*

Provisioning and General Services
OnSite: Lobster Pound *(or North Atlantic)* **Near:** Bank/ATM, Post Office **Under 1 mi:** Convenience Store *(Burnt Cove Market 367-2681)*, Supermarket *(Bartletts Stonington Market 367-2386)*, Gourmet Shop *(Penobscot Bay Provisions 367-5177)*, Health Food *(Nutri Sea 800-732-8072)*, Wine/Beer *(The Clown 367-6348)*, Bakery *(Penobscot Bay Provisions)*, Fishmonger *(North Atlantic Seafood 367-2459)*, Catholic Church, Protestant Church *(Methodist)*, Library *(Stonington PL 367-5926)*, Bookstore *(Dockside 367-2652)*, Pharmacy *(Island Pharmacy 367-6333)*, Hardware Store *(V & South Variety 367-5570)*, Retail Shops

Transportation
OnCall: Local Bus, Airport Limo *(Tranportation Matters 348-2674, $95 to Bangor Airport)* **Under 1 mi:** Ferry Service *(Isle au Haut 367-5193,)* **Airport:** Knox County/Bangor *(30/48 mi.)*

Medical Services
911 Service **OnCall:** Ambulance *(367-2655)* **1-3 mi:** Doctor *(Island Medical Center 367-2311)*, Dentist *(Island Medical Cntr)* **Hospital:** Blue Hill Memorial 374-2836 *(20 mi.)*

Setting -- Billings Diesel is perched on the edge of Moose Head Island, on Deer Isle, with spectacular views up Deer Island Thorofare. Landside, the docks are integrated into a very extensive and well-maintained boatyard. It is a comfortable mile walk from the bustling village of Stonington, a quintessential Maine village with a strong lobster and fishing economy that welcomes, but does not cater to, tourists.

Marina Notes -- Travelift for up to 70,000 lbs, 3 under cover railways capable of 425T, up to 150'. 200 amp dockside service and 3-phase. A network of large sheds house the many yard services, including a full woodworking facility. Services both recreational and commercial vessels (with slightly higher rates for pleasure craft). Harlan Billings offers 24/7 towing $125/hr 367-6559. Very extensive parts inventory and well stocked ships' store. Moorings available daily, weekly, and only very rarely, on a monthly basis. The typical rustic yard heads and cranky dryer are reminders that slips and moorings are not the main focus.

Notable -- Six galleries in town plus a variety of services, restaurants (most BYOB), and B&Bs. The public dock is on the eastern shore below the blue building. Wild and beautiful Isle au Haut, in Acadia National Park, is a 14 mi./45 min. ferry ride from Atlantic Ave Hardware Dock. The ferries go to the town of Isle au Haut (7am, 11am plus after) and even better, to Duck Harbor, which is in the Park (10am, 4:30pm). Rates are complex, roughly $14/7 one way, 367-5193. Or take your "big boat" to Duck Harbor. Home to "Lobster Chronicle" author Linda Greenlaw, the island boasts 500 ft. hills, densely forested shores, and pebble beaches. No services; the only places to stay are five lean-to's or The Keeper's House, a truly unique, off-the-grid experience (367-2261) $294-335 AP.

PHOTOS ON CD-ROM: 9

Wooden Boat School

PO Box 78; Naskeag Point Road; Brooklin, ME 04616

Tel: (207) 359-4651 **VHF: Monitor** n/a **Talk** n/a
Fax: (207) 359-8920 **Alternate Tel:** n/a
Email: rich@woodenboat.com **Web:** www.woodenboat.com
Nearest Town: Brooklin *(1.5 mi.)* **Tourist Info:** (207) 123-4567

Navigational Information

Lat: 44°14.822' **Long:** 068°33.376' **Tide:** 10ft. **Current:** n/a **Chart:** 13316
Rep. Depths (*MLW*): Entry 12 ft. **Fuel Dock** n/a **Max Slip/Moor** -/10 ft.
Access: Eggemoggin Reach to just north of Babson Island

Marina Facilities *(In Season/Off Season)*

Fuel: No
Slips: 0 Total, 0 Transient **Max LOA:** n/a **Max Beam:** n/a
Rate *(per ft.)*: **Day** n/a **Week** n/a **Month** n/a
Power: 30 amp n/a, **50 amp** n/a, **100 amp** n/a, **200 amp** n/a
Cable TV: No **Dockside Phone:** No
Dock Type: n/a
Moorings: 8 Total, 8 Transient **Launch:** None, Dinghy Dock
Rate: Day $10 **Week** $70 **Month** n/a
Heads: 2 Toilet(s)
Laundry: None **Pay Phones:** No
Pump-Out: No **Fee:** n/a **Closed Heads:** No

Marina Operations

Owner/Manager: Jon Wilson, Rich Hilsinger (Director) **Dockmaster:** n/a
In-Season: Jun-Oct, 8am-5pm **Off-Season:** n/a
After-Hours Arrival: Call in advance
Reservations: No **Credit Cards:** n/a
Discounts: None
Pets: Welcome **Handicap Access:** No

Marina Services and Boat Supplies

Supplies - Under 1 mi: Ice *(Block, Cube, Shaved)*, Ships' Store, Propane

Boatyard Services

Nearest Yard: Brooklin Boat Yard (207) 359-2236

Restaurants and Accommodations

1-3 mi: Restaurant *(The Brooklin Inn 359-2777, L $7-10, D $16-29)*, *(Lookout 359-2188)*, *(The Irish Pub Lighter fare at the Brooklin Inn)*, Lite Fare *(Morning Moon Café 359-2373, Tue-Sun, 7am-2pm, also in summer Thu-Sat 5-8pm)*, Inn/B&B *(The Brooklin Inn 5 rooms, semi-private baths)*

Recreation and Entertainment

1-3 mi: Beach *(Naskeag Point)*, Picnic Area **3+ mi:** Golf Course *(Pine Ridge Golf Center 359-6788, 12 mi.)*

Provisioning and General Services

OnSite: Library *(Marine lending library onsite; in town is Friend Memorial 359-2276 - Garden dedicated to Brooklin resident E.B. White)*, Bookstore, Retail Shops **Under 1 mi:** Wine/Beer, Post Office, Protestant Church, Newsstand **1-3 mi:** Convenience Store *(Brooklin General Store 359-8817, 5:30am-7pm 1.5 mi.)* **3+ mi:** Supermarket *(Blue Hill Market 374-5137, 11 mi.)*

Transportation

Airport: Bangor Int'l. *(50 mi.)*

Medical Services

911 Service **OnCall:** Ambulance **3+ mi:** Doctor *(12 mi.)*, Dentist *(12 mi.)*
Hospital: Blue Hill Memorial 374-2836 *(12 mi.)*

Setting -- A 64 acre waterfront estate, with a large white brick restored manor house, overlooks Eggemoggin Reach and is home to the Wooden Boat complex. The old brick stables have been redesigned to house the active school programs. At the water's edge, a stone and shingle two-story boathouse, with green trim, an inviting front porch and a spectacular fieldstone fireplace, sits at the head of the substantial main pier -- with a large dinghy dock at its foot.

Marina Notes -- There are a few moorings, no reservations, and no radio monitoring. A group of picnic tables overlooks the mooring field and Eggemoggin Reach beyond. A bit farther back, a large pavilion shelters many more picnic tables. This is the home of "WoodenBoat Magazine", the quarterly "Maritime Life and Traditions", the journal "Professional Boatbuilder", as well as "Hope Magazine". The book publishing arm specializes in boat building and woodworking titles. They also put on the Wooden Boat Show in Rockland. In the main house is an interesting shop with all manner of useful gifts and nautical necessities, as well as an extensive maritime lending library. All of this was built on the site of an early 20thC fish cannery.

Notable -- Each year, over 600 students, professionals and amateurs, attend the 4-8 concurrent, week-long courses. Costs range from $500-1,000 plus $350 room and board. Visiting the school is fascinating and tours are available - hours are 8am-5pm, Mon-Sat, Jun-Oct. It's a 2.5 mile hike to a small beach with picnic tables at Naskeag Point; a 1.5 mile walk the other way leads to the little town of Brooklin. Noah Publications, publishers of the Calendar of Wooden Boats and many books on wooden boat building, is also in town. Their shop also displays some of owner Benjamin Mendlowitz's spectacular marine photographs.

Brooklin Boat Yard

PO Box 143; Center Harbor Road; Brooklin, ME 04616

Tel: (207) 359-2236 **VHF: Monitor** n/a **Talk** n/a
Fax: (207) 359-8871 **Alternate Tel:** n/a
Email: boatyard@acadia.net **Web:** n/a
Nearest Town: Brooklin *(1.2 mi.)* **Tourist Info:** (207) 123-4567

Navigational Information

Lat: 44°15.781' **Long:** 068°34.790' **Tide:** 12 ft. **Current:** 0 kt. **Chart:** 13316
Rep. Depths (*MLW*): Entry 16 ft. **Fuel Dock** n/a **Max Slip/Moor** 6 ft./25 ft.
Access: Eggemoggin Reach to Center Harbor

Marina Facilities *(In Season/Off Season)*

Fuel: No
Slips: 0 Total, 0 Transient **Max LOA:** 75 ft. **Max Beam:** n/a
Rate *(per ft.)*: **Day** n/a **Week** n/a **Month** n/a
Power: 30 amp n/a, **50 amp** n/a, **100 amp** n/a, **200 amp** n/a
Cable TV: No **Dockside Phone:** No
Dock Type: Long Fingers, Floating
Moorings: 80 Total, 8 Transient **Launch:** n/a, Dinghy Dock (Free)
Rate: Day $20 **Week** $100 **Month** $300
Heads: None
Laundry: None **Pay Phones:** No
Pump-Out: No **Fee:** n/a **Closed Heads:** No

Marina Operations

Owner/Manager: Frank Hull **Dockmaster:** Same
In-Season: Year-Round, 7am-3:30pm Mon-Fri **Off-Season:** n/a
After-Hours Arrival: Call in advance
Reservations: Yes **Credit Cards:** Cash or check only
Discounts: None
Pets: Welcome **Handicap Access:** No

Marina Services and Boat Supplies

Services - Dock Carts **Communication -** Mail & Package Hold, Fax in/out *($1/p)* **Supplies - Under 1 mi:** Ice *(Cube)*, Ships' Store *(Brooklin Marine Supply 359-5030)* **3+ mi:** Propane *(12 mi.)*

Boatyard Services

OnSite: Travelift *(35T)*, Engine mechanic *(gas, diesel)*, Electrical Repairs, Hull Repairs, Rigger, Bottom Cleaning, Brightwork, Air Conditioning, Refrigeration, Compound, Wash & Wax, Propeller Repairs, Woodworking, Metal Fabrication, Painting, Awlgrip, Yacht Design, Yacht Building, Total Refits **Under 1 mi:** Sail Loft. **1-3 mi:** Upholstery. **Dealer for:** Westerbeke. **Member:** ABBRA **Yard Rates:** $43/hr., Haul & Launch $5/ft. *(blocking hourly)*, Power Wash $1/ft., Bottom Paint hourly **Storage:** On-Land $5.50/ft.

Restaurants and Accommodations

1-3 mi: Restaurant *(Morning Moon 359-2573, B $4, L $7, D $12, Also snack bar and pizza - no deliveries)*, *(The Brooklin Inn 359-2777, L $7-10, D $16-29)*, Lite Fare *(The Irish Pub at the Brooklin Inn)*, Inn/B&B *(Brooklin Inn 359-2777, $145-`75)* **3+ mi:** Motel, Inn/B&B *(Heritage Motor Inn 374-5646, $90-150, 12 mi.)*

Recreation and Entertainment

Near: Beach **1-3 mi:** Video Rental, Galleries **3+ mi:** Golf Course *(11 mi.)*

Provisioning and General Services

1-3 mi: Convenience Store *(Brooklin General Store 359-8817, 5:30am-7pm)*, Wine/Beer, Fishmonger *(Brooklin General)*, Post Office, Library *(Friend Memorial 359-2276 - Garden dedicated to Brooklin resident E.B. White)*, Bookstore *(Noah Publications, WoodenBoat School)*, Newsstand **3+ mi:** Supermarket *(11 mi.)*, Delicatessen *(11 mi.)*, Health Food *(11 mi.)*, Bank/ATM *(11 mi.)*

Transportation

Airport: Bangor Int'l. *(50 mi.)*

Medical Services

911 Service **3+ mi:** Doctor *(11 mi.)*, Dentist *(11 mi.)* **Hospital:** Blue Hill Memorial 374-2836 *(11 mi.)*

PHOTOS ON CD-ROM: 9

Setting -- Just off Eggemoggin Reach, Center Harbor is a convenient stop. It also seems to be the spiritual, as well as the actual, home of the contemporary wooden boat movement. The mooring field is filled with the products of Brooklin's boat builders -- from prams to offshore yachts. If you appreciate beautiful vessels, and are enamored with the romance of this ancient craft, then Brooklin moves into the category of destination.

Marina Notes -- This is strictly a boatyard with moorings. No power. No heads. No showers. Brooklin Boat Yard is known world-wide for designing, building, and restoring custom wooden yachts - power and sail. It can also provide most boatyard services. If you can wrangle a tour of the sheds, it's truly an uplifting experience to see these special vessels being built.

Notable -- The tiny village of Brooklin is a 1.2 mi. walk - there you'll find the Brookline Inn, Morning Moon Cafe, library, post office, and the well supplied Brooklin General Store (fish & lobster, too). A couple of miles on the other side of town is The WoodenBoat School (see adjacent Marina Report), which teaches boat building skills and publishes WoodenBoat Magazine. Also in town is marine photographer Benjamin Mendlowitz's Noah Publications which publishes a series of books on wooden boats, including the classic "Wood, Water and Light", and also, for two decades, the famous Calendar of Wooden Boats. Nearby is Wade and Forrest Dow's Bridges Point Boat Yard, builders of the beautiful, classic-looking (although fiberglass) Bridges Point 24 sloop, designed by Joel White.

Navigational Information
Lat: 44°17.458' **Long:** 068°41.718' **Tide:** 11 ft. **Current:** 3 kt. **Chart:** 13309
Rep. Depths (*MLW*): Entry 5 ft. **Fuel Dock** n/a **Max Slip/Moor** -/45 ft.
Access: Eggemoggin Reach just west of the Deer Isle Bridge

Marina Facilities *(In Season/Off Season)*
Fuel: No
Slips: 0 Total, 0 Transient **Max LOA:** 51 ft. **Max Beam:** n/a
Rate *(per ft.)*: **Day** n/a **Week** n/a **Month** n/a
Power: 30 amp n/a, **50 amp** n/a, **100 amp** n/a, **200 amp** n/a
Cable TV: No **Dockside Phone:** No
Dock Type: Floating
Moorings: 10 Total, 4 Transient **Launch:** Yes, Dinghy Dock ($2 per night)
Rate: Day $20 **Week** $125 **Month** $200
Heads: 1 Toilet(s), 1 Shower(s)
Laundry: 1 Washer(s), 1 Dryer(s) **Pay Phones:** Yes, 1
Pump-Out: No **Fee:** n/a **Closed Heads:** No

Marina Operations
Owner/Manager: Show & Rosenquist Families **Dockmaster:** Dick Show
In-Season: Jun-Oct, 9am-9pm **Off-Season:** Closed
After-Hours Arrival: Pick-up pre-arranged mooring
Reservations: Yes, Preferred **Credit Cards:** Visa/MC, Dscvr, Amex
Discounts: None
Pets: Welcome, Dog Walk Area **Handicap Access:** No

Marina at Eggemoggin Landing

PO Box 126; Route 15; Little Deer Isle, ME 04650

Tel: (207) 348-6115 **VHF: Monitor** 9 **Talk** 14
Fax: (207) 348-2738 **Alternate Tel:** (207) 348-6115
Email: eggland@acadia.net **Web:** www.acadia.net/eggland
Nearest Town: Deer Isle *(6 mi.)* **Tourist Info:** (207) 348-6124

Marina Services and Boat Supplies
Services - Docking Assistance, Trash Pick-Up, Dock Carts **Communication -** Phone Messages, Fax in/out *($2)*, Data Ports *(Office, $2)*, FedEx **Supplies - OnSite:** Ice *(Cube)* **1-3 mi:** Propane *(Eggemoggin Country Store)* **3+ mi:** Ships' Store *(8 mi.)*

Boatyard Services
OnSite: Launching Ramp **OnCall:** Engine mechanic *(gas, diesel)*, Electronic Sales, Compound, Wash & Wax **Nearest Yard:** Jericho Bay Boatyard (207) 348-9923

Restaurants and Accommodations
OnSite: Restaurant *(Sisters L $2-9, D $13-20, 7 days L, D, take-out and ice-cream)*, Motel *(Eggemoggin Landing 348-6115, $79-86)* **Near:** Inn/B&B *(Red House B&B 348-5234)*, Condo/Cottage *(Once Upon an Island 348-2258)* **Under 1 mi:** Inn/B&B *(Inn at Ferry Landing 348-7760)* **1-3 mi:** Seafood Shack *(Eaton's Lobster Pool 348-2383)*, Pizzeria *(Country Store 359-2125, no delivery)*

Recreation and Entertainment
OnSite: Beach, Picnic Area, Playground, Boat Rentals *(16' power boats $40/hr., $85/half day, $135/full day. Kayak rentals $30/half day, $45/full day)*, Other *(Day & sunset cruises)* **Near:** Jogging Paths **1-3 mi:** Sightseeing **3+ mi:** Golf Course *(8 mi.)*, Fishing Charter *(12 mi.)*, Video Rental *(3 mi.)*, Museum *(5 mi.)*

Provisioning and General Services
OnSite: Gourmet Shop *(Sisters Gourmet to Go - home-made products, hors d'oeuvres, and basic provisions)*, Wine/Beer *(Beer only)*, Bakery, Lobster Pound **Near:** Post Office **Under 1 mi:** Protestant Church **1-3 mi:** Convenience Store, Liquor Store, Meat Market, Beauty Salon, Barber Shop, Dry Cleaners, Newsstand **3+ mi:** Supermarket *(Tradewinds, 15 mi.)*, Bank/ATM *(5 mi.)*, Library *(5 mi.)*, Laundry *(6 mi.)*, Pharmacy *(10 mi.)*, Hardware Store *(6 mi.)*, Retail Shops *(5-12 mi.)*

Transportation
OnSite: Bikes *($17/day, $12/half day)* **OnCall:** Taxi *(Transportation Matters)*, Airport Limo *(Transportation Matters 348-2674)* **Airport:** Bangor Int'l. *(40 mi.)*

Medical Services
911 Service **OnCall:** Ambulance **3+ mi:** Doctor *(12 mi.)*, Dentist *(12 mi.)*
Hospital: Blue Hill *(20 mi.)*

Setting -- Just west of the Sedgewick-Deer Isle Bridge on Little Deer Isle, this small motel, restaurant and marina complex is an appealingl, peaceful place to relax and watch the parade go by. The laid back quality of island life, coupled with the services and facilities, makes this a superb stop in settled weather.

Marina Notes -- Two dedicated transient moorings and generally 2 more available. The dock is reserved for "dock & dine" customers - for whom there's no charge. Note it can be quite shallow at the dock at low tide. Water is precious on Deer Isle, so any use of water will have a fee: showers currently $3 pp; laundry $4/load (planning to install coin-operated units in near future). Closed MidOct to Jun. Fax charge $2 1st page, $1 additional pages. Email $2. Owned and operated by two families: Carl & Robin Rosenquist and Dick & Patty Show.

Notable -- The onsite Sisters Restaurant (Robin and Patty are sisters) serves a breakfast buffet for guests, sit-down lunch and dinner, 7 days, plus take-out from 11am on ($2-9, Lobster dinner $15) and Gourmet to Go. It has been well reviewed, and Executive Chef Patty Show has been featured on PBS Country Inn Cooking. Will also cater large events. If you need time ashore, the 20 comfortable, family-oriented motel rooms should be most welcome (Discount packages for rooms and moorings). Deer Isle is a haven for authors, artists, and craftspeople. There are galleries, the opera house in Stonington, and the world-famous Haystack Mountain Art School (located at Sunshine on the island's eastern side). There's no public transportation on the island -- so the onsite bike rentals are a great convenience.

PHOTOS ON CD-ROM: 9

Buck's Harbor Marine

PO Box 2; 684 Coastal Road; South Brooksville, ME 04617

Tel: (207) 326-8839 **VHF: Monitor** 9 **Talk** 10
Fax: (207) 348-5254 **Alternate Tel:** (207) 348-5253
Email: bucksharbor@bucksharbor.com **Web:** www.bucksharbor.com
Nearest Town: Blue Hill *(11 mi.)* **Tourist Info:** (207) 244-9625

Navigational Information

Lat: 44°20.014' **Long:** 068°43.602' **Tide:** 14 ft. **Current:** n/a **Chart:** 13309
Rep. Depths (*MLW*): Entry 35 ft. **Fuel Dock** 12 ft. **Max Slip/Moor** -/12 ft.
Access: Penobscot Bay to head of Eggemoggin Reach; use east entrance

Marina Facilities *(In Season/Off Season)*

Fuel: Gasoline, Diesel
Slips: 3 Total, 3 Transient **Max LOA:** 100 ft. **Max Beam:** n/a
Rate *(per ft.)*: **Day** $1.00* **Week** n/a **Month** n/a
Power: 30 amp Incl., **50 amp** Incl., **100 amp** n/a, **200 amp** n/a
Cable TV: No **Dockside Phone:** No
Dock Type: Concrete, Alongside, Floating
Moorings: 26 Total, 26 Transient **Launch:** By arrangement, Dinghy Dock
Rate: Day $27 **Week** $162 **Month** Inq.
Heads: 2 Toilet(s)
Laundry: 1 Washer(s), 1 Dryer(s), Book Exchange **Pay Phones:** Yes
Pump-Out: No **Fee:** n/a **Closed Heads:** Yes

Marina Operations

Owner/Manager: Jerry/Lois Kirschenbaum **Dockmaster:** Jerry/Hope Bates
In-Season: Jul-Aug, 8am-7pm **Off-Season:** Sept-Oct, 9am-5pm
After-Hours Arrival: Call ahead for instructions
Reservations: Yes **Credit Cards:** Visa/MC
Discounts: Fuel - volume **Dockage:** n/a **Fuel:** 100 g **Repair:** n/a
Pets: Welcome **Handicap Access:** No

Marina Services and Boat Supplies

Services - Docking Assistance, Concierge, Trash Pick-Up, Dock Carts **Communication -** Mail & Package Hold, Phone Messages, Fax in/out, FedEx, UPS *(Sat Del)* **Supplies - OnSite:** Ice *(Block, Cube)*, Ships' Store, Bait/Tackle **Near:** Marine Discount Store *(Stone)*

Boatyard Services

OnSite: Crane *(2T)* **OnCall:** Engine mechanic *(gas, diesel)*, Electrical Repairs, Electronic Sales, Electronics Repairs, Rigger, Sail Loft, Bottom Cleaning, Divers, Interior Cleaning, Propeller Repairs **Nearest Yard:** Seal Cove Boat Yard (207) 326-4422

Restaurants and Accommodations

Near: Snack Bar *(Buck's Harbor Market)*, *(Café Outback 326-8683, B, L, D $17-22)*, Pizzeria *(Buck's Harbor Market)* **Under 1 mi:** Inn/B&B *(Buck's Harbor Inn 326-8660)* **1-3 mi:** Restaurant *(Oakland House Restaurant 359-8521)*, Hotel *(Oakland House 359-8521, $145-270; $400-4,000/week, 1907 seaside lodge and 15 cottages)*, Inn/B&B *(Eggemoggin Reach B&B 359-5073, $166-198, waterfront cottages and studios)*

Recreation and Entertainment

OnSite: Boat Rentals, Fishing Charter *(Sail and power bareboat charters and excursions are available - Hunter 40s, smaller sloops and daysailers and lobster boats)* **Near:** Tennis Courts *(Buck's Harbor Yacht Club)*, Video Rental, Special Events *(Flash-in-the-Pan Steel Band plays at the Market alternate Mondays 7:30-9pm.)* **1-3 mi:** Sightseeing *(Tour tiny Sow's Ear Winery 326-4649, 326-4649 Tue-Sat 10am-5pm - for a tasting of wine and cider made from local, organic fruit)* **3+ mi:** Park *(Acadia National Park, 1 hr.)*, Museum *(Searsport Marine Museum; Castine Historical Society 326-4118, 45 min.)*, Cultural Attract *(Wooden Boat School, 30 min.)*

Provisioning and General Services

OnSite: Convenience Store, Wine/Beer, Bakery, Lobster Pound *(lobster pen right under the dock - always available)*, Bookstore **Near:** Market *(Buck's Harbor Market 326-8683, small but has enough of everything)*, Farmers' Market, Fishmonger, Post Office, Protestant Church, Newsstand, Copies Etc. *(Buck's Harbor Market)* **1-3 mi:** Library

Transportation

OnCall: Airport Limo **Airport:** Bar Harbor/Bangor Int'l. *(27mi./33mi.)*

Medical Services

911 Service **OnCall:** Ambulance **Hospital:** Blue Hill Memorial *(12 mi.)*

Setting -- This beautiful, fully protected harbor, on the Eastern shore of Penobscot Bay, at the head of Eggemoggin Reach, offers deep water and attracts some spectacular boats. Buck's Harbor Marine sits on an historic granite pier in the heart of blueberry country near the tiny, interesting town of Brooksville.

Marina Notes -- Groups of up to 60 boats can be accommodated on moorings; boats may be asked to raft. *Very limited dockage and shore power, slips by prior arrangement only. Co-owner Jerry Kirschenbaum is author of "Safe Boat" and other nautical works. Small, helpful, knowledgeable staff. Lobster pound and specialty foods onsite. Limited amenities, but well maintained. Pleasant deck overlooking the water. Marine store has good basic ships' supplies, overnight parts delivery, macramé & fancy knotware gifts, plus books. Mooring balls are green and red and numbered (lime green balls mark the fairway). Fun, enclosed outdoor showers could be a challenge in the rain -- but are still a big draw. Buck's Harbor Yacht Club often has guest moorings (326-9265) - tennis courts, club house, and Thursday night contra dancing. Good hurricane hole, protected through 300 degrees.

Notable -- Buck's Harbor is the setting for Robert McCloskey's well-known children's book "One Morning in Maine" (available onsite) -- a short walk is Condon's Garage (also a Mercury dealer) and some of the other places he describes. Blue Hill Peninsula has also become a serious center for steel bands -- Carl Chase founded Atlantic Clarion Steelband 20 years ago right here in Brooksville. He's been teaching local kids ever since. Seemingly every grade, middle & high school in every town on the Peninsula has a steel band. Flash-in-the-Pans, a 35-member adult community group, plays benefits and area gigs.

PHOTOS ON CD-ROM: 9

Castine Town Dock

PO Box 204; Emerson Hall, Court Street; Castine, ME 04421

Tel: (207) 266-7711 **VHF: Monitor** 16 **Talk** 9
Fax: (207) 326-9465 **Alternate Tel:** (207) 326-4502
Email: n/a **Web:** n/a
Nearest Town: Bucksport *(14 mi.)* **Tourist Info:** (207) 326-8448

Navigational Information

Lat: 44°23.221' **Long:** 068°47.803' **Tide:** 11 ft. **Current:** 3 kt. **Chart:** 13302
Rep. Depths (*MLW*): Entry 50 ft. **Fuel Dock** n/a **Max Slip/Moor** 20 ft./70 ft.
Access: East Penobscot Bay to RW bell "CH". Head 075° up river

Marina Facilities *(In Season/Off Season)*

Fuel: No
Slips: 0 Total, 0 Transient **Max LOA:** 140 ft. **Max Beam:** N/A ft.
Rate *(per ft.)*: **Day** $1.00* **Week** Inq. **Month** Inq.
Power: 30 amp Incl., **50 amp** n/a, **100 amp** n/a, **200 amp** n/a
Cable TV: No **Dockside Phone:** No
Dock Type: Wood, Alongside, Floating
Moorings: 200 Total, 15 Transient **Launch:** None, Dinghy Dock (Free)
Rate: Day Free **Week** n/a **Month** n/a
Heads: 2 Toilet(s)
Laundry: 6 Washer(s), 5 Dryer(s), Book Exchange **Pay Phones:** Yes, 1
Pump-Out: No **Fee:** n/a **Closed Heads:** No

Marina Operations

Owner/Manager: George Plender (Harbormaster) **Dockmaster:** Same
In-Season: Jun 15-Sep 15, 8am-6pm **Off-Season:** On call
After-Hours Arrival: Check with harbormaster in the morning
Reservations: No **Credit Cards:** Check or cash only
Discounts: None
Pets: Welcome, Dog Walk Area **Handicap Access:** Yes, Heads, Docks

Marina Services and Boat Supplies

Services - Docking Assistance, 3 Phase **Communication -** Data Ports *(Castine Library)*, FedEx, UPS, Express Mail *(Sat Del)* **Supplies - Near:** Ice *(Block, Cube)*, Ships' Store *(Four Flags 326-8526)* **1-3 mi:** Live Bait *(South by Northeast 326-2067)* **3+ mi:** Marine Discount Store *(Hamilton Marine, 20 mi.)*, Propane *(Gary's Fuel 326-8808, 6.5 mi.)*

Boatyard Services

OnSite: Launching Ramp **OnCall:** Divers **Near:** Engine mechanic *(gas, diesel)*, Hull Repairs, Rigger, Bottom Cleaning, Brightwork, Compound, Wash & Wax, Interior Cleaning, Propeller Repairs, Woodworking, Inflatable Repairs. **3+ mi:** Yacht Interiors *(20 mi.)*. **Nearest Yard:** Eaton's Boat Yard (207) 326-8579

Restaurants and Accommodations

OnSite: Snack Bar *(The Breeze)* **OnCall:** Pizzeria *(Variety Store 326-8625)* **Near:** Restaurant *(Dennett's Wharf 326-9045, L $6-13, D $12-20)*, *(Castine Inn 326-4365, B $7, D $18-30)*, Lite Fare *(Bah's Bakehouse B $2-7, L $4-7, D $4-7, 7am-7pm)*, *(Variety Store 326-8625, B $3, L $4)*, Inn/B&B *(Village Inn 326-9510, $65-85)*, *(Castine Inn $75-210, Breakfast included)*, *(Pentagoet Inn 326-8616, $100-130, Breakfast included)*, *(Castine Harbor Inn 326-4335, $85-200)* **Under 1 mi:** Restaurant *(Manor Inn 326-4861, D $15-25, Pick up and return to docks)*, Lite Fare *(Pain de Famille 326-4455, L $3-7)*, Inn/B&B *(The Manor Inn 326-4861, $95-195, Picks up at dock; Breakfast included)*, Condo/Cottage *(Castine Cottages 326-8003)*

Recreation and Entertainment

OnSite: Picnic Area, Sightseeing *(State of Maine offers guided tours)* **Near:** Pool *(Maine Maritime Academy 326-4311)*, Playground, Tennis Courts, Roller Blade/Bike Paths, Video Rental, Park *(Ft. Madison, Ft. George, Dyces Head Light,)*, Special Events *(Retired Skippers' Race, Aug)* **Under 1 mi:** Beach *(Backshore Beach)*, Golf Course *(Castine Golf Club 326-8844)*, Museum *(Castine Historical Society 326-4118, Wilson Museum 326-9247, 1665 John Perkins House)*

Provisioning and General Services

Near: Provisioning Service *(Castine Harbor Lodge specializes in megayachts and local ingredients 326-4335)*, Convenience Store *(T & C Grocery 326-4818)*, Wine/Beer, Liquor Store, Bakery *(Bah's Bake House)*, Farmers' Market *(Horsepower Farm Organic Produce, Thu 9-11am at Bah's)*, Lobster Pound *(Eaton's Boatyard)*, Bank/ATM, Post Office, Catholic Church, Protestant Church, Other *(Episcopal, Congregational, Unitarian)*, Library *(Witherle Memorial 326-4375, Internet service)*, Laundry, Bookstore *(Compass Rose 326-9366)*, Newsstand, Retail Shops

Transportation

OnCall: Taxi *(Don's Taxi 236-4762)*, Airport Limo *(Mid-Coast Limo 236-2424)* **Near:** Bikes *(Dennett's rentals: $15/half day, $24/day)*, Water Taxi *(Bagaduce Boating 632-7669, harbor tours and water taxi service)* **Airport:** Bar Harbor/Bangor Int'l. *(29/30 mi.)*

Medical Services

No 911 Service **Near:** Doctor *(Castine Community Health Services 326-4348)*, Dentist *(Ciano 326-9500)*, Ambulance **Hospital:** Blue Hill Memorial 374-2836 *(15 mi.)*

Setting -- As you enter Castine Harbor, from East Penobscot Bay, your view is dominated by the SV State of Maine, the training ship for the Maine Maritime Academy. Just past the ship is the Castine Town Dock which sits at the foot of Main Street, the center of this charming, picturesque historic town.

Marina Notes -- * 39-64 ft. $1.50/ft; 64+ ft. $2.00. There are floating docks at the foot of two gangplanks that peel off from the main wharf. Sections of these floats are used for dinghy docks. Very nice showers are available at Castine Inn 2 blocks north. The Breeze is a snack bar right on the wharf (featuring fried clams, fries, burgers and ice cream) open May through October (326-9034). Data ports at the library. Megayacht dockage and a few moorings are available at the Castine Harbor Lodge 326-4335 - the first dock as you enter the mouth of the river.

Notable -- All of Castine is a don't miss cruising destination and the Town Dock offers a very convenient location. Castine's four hundred years of history permeate the town - it's lived under five "flags": Native American, British, Dutch, French and U.S. Restored houses and commercial buildings line the streets making a walk literally an historic tour (maps are available at the Chamber of Commerce). The 499 foot State of Maine offers free 30-minute guided tours (326-4311, 326-2420). The 4-year Maine Maritime Academy is located a few blocks north (pool open to the public). The Castine Inn has become a "destination" restaurant - classic French training meets exquisite Maine ingredients (a lovely B&B, too).

PHOTOS ON CD-ROM: 9

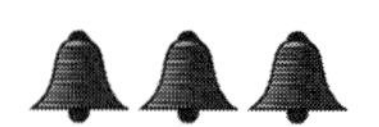

Dennett's Wharf

PO Box 459; 15 Sea Street; Castine, ME 04421

Tel: (207) 326-9045 **VHF: Monitor** 9 **Talk** 72
Fax: (207) 326-9045 **Alternate Tel:** (207) 326-9045
Email: gary@dennettswharf.com **Web:** www.dennettswharf.com
Nearest Town: Bucksport *(14 mi.)* **Tourist Info:** (207) 326-8448

Navigational Information

Lat: 44°23.283' **Long:** 068°47.748' **Tide:** 12 ft. **Current:** 3 kt. **Chart:** 13302
Rep. Depths (*MLW*): Entry 12 ft. **Fuel Dock** n/a **Max Slip/Moor** 10 ft./-
Access: Penobscot Bay to Castine Harbor, look for large yellow awning

Marina Facilities *(In Season/Off Season)*

Fuel: No
Slips: 0 Total, 120' Transient **Max LOA:** 110 ft. **Max Beam:** 15 ft.
Rate *(per ft.)*: **Day** $1.50/Inq.* **Week** Inq. **Month** Inq.
Power: 30 amp Incl., **50 amp** Incl., **100 amp** n/a, **200 amp** n/a
Cable TV: No **Dockside Phone:** Yes
Dock Type: Wood, Alongside, Floating
Moorings: 1 Total, 1 Transient **Launch:** None, Dinghy Dock
Rate: Day $20 **Week** Inq. **Month** Inq.
Heads: 3 Toilet(s), 3 Shower(s)
Laundry: None **Pay Phones:** Yes, 2
Pump-Out: No **Fee:** n/a **Closed Heads:** No

Marina Operations

Owner/Manager: Gary & Carolyn Brouillard **Dockmaster:** Gary Brouillard
In-Season: May 15-Oct 15, 8am-8pm **Off-Season:** n/a
After-Hours Arrival: Tie up, and check in in the morning
Reservations: Yes, Required **Credit Cards:** Visa/MC, Dscvr, Amex
Discounts: None
Pets: Welcome **Handicap Access:** Yes, Heads, Docks

Marina Services and Boat Supplies

Communication - Mail & Package Hold, Data Ports *(Castine Library)*, FedEx, UPS, Express Mail *(Sat Del)* **Supplies - OnSite:** Ice *(Cube)* **Near:** Ice *(Block)*, Ships' Store *(Eaton's 326-4727, Four Flags 326-8526)* **3+ mi:** Bait/Tackle *(South by Northeast 326-2067, 3.5 mi.)*, Propane *(Gary's Fuel 326-8808, 6.5 mi.)*

Boatyard Services

Near: Engine mechanic *(gas, diesel)*, Launching Ramp, Electrical Repairs, Electronic Sales, Electronics Repairs, Hull Repairs, Rigger, Bottom Cleaning, Brightwork, Divers, Compound, Wash & Wax, Interior Cleaning, Propeller Repairs, Woodworking, Inflatable Repairs, Life Raft Service, Upholstery, Yacht Interiors, Yacht Broker, Total Refits. **Nearest Yard:** Eaton's Boatyard (207) 326-8579

Restaurants and Accommodations

OnSite: Restaurant *(Dennett's Wharf 326-9045, L $6-15, D $12-22)* **OnCall:** Pizzeria *(Castine Variety 326-8625)* **Near:** Restaurant *(Castine Inn 326-4365, D $18-30)*, Lite Fare *(Castine Variety B $5, L $5, D $10)*, *(Bah's Bake Shop 326-9510, B $2-7, L $4-7, D $4-7, 7am-7pm)*, Inn/B&B *(Castine Harbor Lodge 326-4335, $80-160)*, *(Castine Inn 326-4365, $75-210)*, *(Pentagoet Inn 326-8616, $100-150)* **Under 1 mi:** Restaurant *(The Manor Inn 326-4861, D $15-25, Picks up at docks and returns after dinner)*, Inn/B&B *(The Manor Inn 326-4861, $100-210)*

Recreation and Entertainment

OnSite: Boat Rentals *(Castine Kayak Adventures tours & rentals 326-9045)* **Near:** Pool *(Maine Maritime Academy 326-4311)*, Picnic Area, Playground, Dive Shop, Tennis Courts, Roller Blade/Bike Paths, Video Rental *(Castine Library 326-4375)*, Cultural Attract *(Castine Historical Society 326-4118)*, Sightseeing *(State of Maine 326-4311 and all of Castine)* **Under 1 mi:** Beach *(Backshore Beach)*, Golf Course *(Castine Golf Club 326-8844)*, Park, Museum *(Wilson Museum 326-8753)*

Provisioning and General Services

Near: Provisioning Service *(Castine Harbor Lodge specializes in megayachts & local ingredients 326-4335)*, Convenience Store *(T & C Grocery 326-4818)*, Gourmet Shop, Delicatessen, Wine/Beer, Liquor Store, Bakery *(Bah's Bakehouse)*, Farmers' Market *(Horsepower Farm Organic Produce, Thu 9-11am at Bah's)*, Lobster Pound *(Eaton's Boatyard 326-4727)*, Bank/ATM, Post Office, Catholic Church, Protestant Church, Library *(Witherle Memorial 326-4375, Internet)*, Bookstore *(Compass Rose 326-9366)*, Newsstand, Retail Shops

Transportation

OnSite: Bikes *(Dennett's Wharf $15-30)* **OnCall:** Rental Car *(Enterprise 800-325-8007)*, Taxi *(Don's Taxi 236-4762)* **Near:** Water Taxi *(Bagaduce Boating 632-7669)* **Airport:** Bar Harbor/Bangor Int'l. *(29mi./30mi.)*

Medical Services

No 911 Service **Near:** Doctor *(Community Health Services 326-4348)*, Dentist *(Ciano 326-9500)*, Ambulance **3+ mi:** Chiropractor **Hospital:** Blue Hill Memorial 374-2836 *(15 mi.)*

Setting -- Just past the Castine Town Docks, Dennett's Wharf is easily identifiable by its bright yellow awning and large decks. This water-side restaurant/wharf/lobster pound, which dates back to the early 1800s, provides easy access to beautiful, picturesque Castine.

Marina Notes -- *120 linear ft. of dock space. Dennett's restaurant has 3 seating areas: indoor (35+ people), outside under an enclosed canopy (65+ people), and an open deck. Lunch $6-16, Dinner $6-26. Interesting assortment of Microbrews. There is a display which shows the history of Dennett's. Live entertainment on weekends. Heads are shared with the restaurant, and there are 2 showers upstairs, through the restaurant - both open until restaurant closes. Mountain bike rentals onsite. Castine Kayak Adventures onsite (326-9045). Half day tour $55, 2 hr. sunset $40. Data ports at the library a few blocks away. Castine Harbor Lodge (326-4335) - the first dock as you enter the river -- provides megayacht dockage.

Notable -- Family-owned Dennett's is rich with history. It was originally a sail and rigging loft but, with the advent of steam vessels, it became a landing wharf for visitors from Boston, Washington and New York. (It was also home to one of the first "9 pin" bowling lanes -- which has been excavated and beautifully restored; it now functions as the bar.) Bagaduce Boating Co., at Eaton's, offers harbor tours and water taxi service $20/hr., $35/2 hrs. pp; children 10-16 half price, under 10 free. State of Maine, the Maine Maritime Academy's training ship, offers tours.

PHOTOS ON CD-ROM: 9

Navigational Information
Lat: 44°23.291' **Long:** 068°47.742' **Tide:** 12 ft. **Current:** 3 kt. **Chart:** 13309
Rep. Depths (*MLW*): Entry 12 ft. **Fuel Dock** 11 ft. **Max Slip/Moor** 11 ft./50 ft.
Access: Penobscot Bay to Castine Harbor, 5th set of docks to port

Marina Facilities *(In Season/Off Season)*
Fuel: Gasoline, Diesel
Slips: 8 Total, 2* Transient **Max LOA:** 200 ft. **Max Beam:** n/a
Rate *(per ft.)*: **Day** $1.25/Inq. **Week** Inq. **Month** Inq.
Power: 30 amp $3, **50 amp** $6, **100 amp** $12, **200 amp** n/a
Cable TV: No **Dockside Phone:** No
Dock Type: Floating
Moorings: 10 Total, 10 Transient **Launch:** n/a
Rate: Day $20 **Week** Inq. **Month** Inq.
Heads: 1 Toilet(s), 1 Shower(s)
Laundry: None **Pay Phones:** Yes, 1
Pump-Out: No **Fee:** n/a **Closed Heads:** No

Marina Operations
Owner/Manager: Kenny Eaton **Dockmaster:** Suzanne Eaton
In-Season: Summer, 6am-Dusk **Off-Season:** Fall-Win-Sprg, 9am-4pm
After-Hours Arrival: Call ahead, then tie up and check in in the morning
Reservations: Yes **Credit Cards:** Visa/MC, Dscvr, Amex
Discounts: None
Pets: Welcome **Handicap Access:** No

Eaton's Boatyard

PO Box 123; Sea Street; Castine, ME 04421

Tel: (207) 326-8579 **VHF: Monitor** 9 **Talk** 9
Fax: (207) 326-4727 **Alternate Tel:** n/a
Email: eatons@hypernet.com **Web:** n/a
Nearest Town: Bucksport *(14 mi.)* **Tourist Info:** (207) 326-8448

Marina Services and Boat Supplies
Services - Docking Assistance, Concierge **Communication -** Mail & Package Hold, Phone Messages, Fax in/out, Data Ports *(Castine Library)*, FedEx, UPS, Express Mail **Supplies - OnSite:** Ice *(Block, Cube)*, Ships' Store **Under 1 mi:** Propane *(Gary's Fuel Service 326-8808)* **3+ mi:** Bait/Tackle *(South by Northeast 326-2067, 3.5 mi.)*

Boatyard Services
OnSite: Forklift *(Hydraulic Trailer 20T, 44 ft.)*, Electrical Repairs, Electronics Repairs, Hull Repairs, Rigger, Bottom Cleaning, Brightwork, Compound, Wash & Wax, Interior Cleaning, Painting, Yacht Broker **OnCall:** Engine mechanic *(gas, diesel)*, Electronic Sales, Refrigeration, Divers, Upholstery, Metal Fabrication **Near:** Launching Ramp. **Yard Rates:** $33/hr., Haul & Launch $6.50/ft. *(blocking incl.)*, Power Wash $1.50, Bottom Paint $33/hr. **Storage:** On-Land Inside $3.50/ft./mo.

Restaurants and Accommodations
OnCall: Pizzeria *(Variety 326-8625)* **Near:** Restaurant *(Dennett's Wharf 326-9045, L $6-15, D $12-22)*, *(The Castine Inn 326-4365, D $20-32)*, Snack Bar *(The Breeze 326-4032)*, Lite Fare *(Bah's Bakehouse 326-9510, B $3-7, L $3-7, D $3-10, 7am-7pm)*, Inn/B&B *(The Castine Inn 326-4365, $75-210)*, *(The Village Inn 326-9510)* **Under 1 mi:** Restaurant *(Manor Inn D $15-26)*, Inn/B&B *(Manor Inn 326-4861, $95-195)*, Condo/Cottage *(Castine Cottages 326-8003)*

Recreation and Entertainment
Near: Tennis Courts, Jogging Paths, Boat Rentals *(Castine Kayak Adventures, Dennett's Wharf 326-9045)*, Roller Blade/Bike Paths, Park, Cultural Attract *(Castine Historical Society 326-4118; John Perkins House)* **Under 1 mi:** Pool *(Maine Maritime Academy 326-4311, also Town Pool)*, Golf Course *(Castine Golf Club 326-8844)*, Video Rental, Museum *(Wilson Museum 326-8753)*, Sightseeing *(The Maine Maritime Academy 464-6565)* **1-3 mi:** Beach *(Backshore Beach)*

Provisioning and General Services
Near: Provisioning Service *(Castine Harbor Lodge 326-4335)*, Convenience Store *(T & C Grocery 326-4818)*, Gourmet Shop, Delicatessen, Wine/Beer, Liquor Store, Farmers' Market *(Horsepower Farm organic produce, Thu 9-11am at Bah's parking lot)*, Lobster Pound, Bank/ATM, Post Office, Library *(Witherle Memorial 326-4375, Internet access)*, Laundry, Bookstore *(Compass Rose 326-9366)*, Newsstand, Florist **Under 1 mi:** Bakery *(Pain de Famille 326-4455)*, Meat Market, Catholic Church **3+ mi:** Supermarket, Pharmacy *(Rite Aid Bucksport, 18 mi.)*

Transportation
OnSite: Courtesy Car/Van, Water Taxi *(Bagaduce)* **OnCall:** Taxi *(Don's Taxi 236-4762)* **Near:** Bikes *(Dennett's 326-9045)* **3+ mi:** Rental Car *(Penguin Auto Rental 338-6111, 14 mi.)* **Airport:** Bar Harbor/Bangor Int'l. *(29 mi./30 mi.)*

Medical Services
No 911 Service **OnCall:** Ambulance **Near:** Doctor *(Castine Community Health Services 326-4348; Olivari 326-4348)*, Dentist *(Ciano 326-9500)* **Hospital:** Blue Hill Memorial 374-2836 *(15 mi.)*

Setting -- Just past Dennett's is this 1927 classic, family-run Maine boatyard, easily identified by its big shingled shed. Four hundred years of history welcome you to this picturesque village filled with intriguing sites and diverse activities. While Eaton's is primarily a boatyard, all the amenities you might need are a short walk into Castine.

Marina Notes -- * 280 running ft. of dock face for transients can accommodate 12-15 boats with rafting. Fuel discounts on volume purchases. The only full-service boatyard in Castine, Eaton's is currently being operated by the fourth generation - father and daughter. There are limited amenities for the boater. A head and shower ($2) are onsite and the lovely Castine Inn, a short walk up the hill, also offers very nice showers for boaters ($5) - just check in at the front desk. If you decide to eat in, Eaton's will provide lobsters, live or cooked. The Manor Inn will pick up and deliver to the docks. Data ports are at the library. On-site 44 ft./20T trailer. 32,000 sq. ft. of inside storage. Megayacht dockage at Castine Harbor Lodge (326-4335).

Notable -- Bagaduce Boating Co. (run by one of the Eaton daughters) offers harbor tours from the dock in a classic 1950's 30-foot boat built right onsite ($20/hr., $35/2 hrs. per person, six passenger limit; children 10-16 half price, under 10 free). Dennett's Wharf is right next door for great people-watching and lunch or dinner. Dennett's also has bike and kayak rentals. A little farther west is the Maine Maritime Academy's 499 ft. State of Maine training ship (tours available). Castine is a walking town with some fascinating history; pick up a copy of the excellent tour map at any local shop.

PHOTOS ON CD-ROM: 9

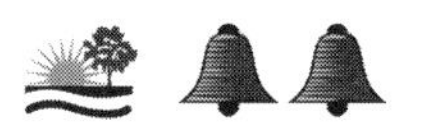

Castine Yacht Club

63 Water Street; Castine, ME 04421

Tel: (207) 326-9231 **VHF: Monitor** 9 **Talk** 10
Fax: n/a **Alternate Tel:** n/a
Email: n/a **Web:** www.prism.net/rogsmu/cyc/
Nearest Town: Bucksport *(14 mi.)* **Tourist Info:** (207) 326-8448

Navigational Information

Lat: 44°23.444' **Long:** 068°47.680' **Tide:** 11 ft. **Current:** 3 kt. **Chart:** 13309
Rep. Depths (*MLW*): Entry 50 ft. **Fuel Dock** n/a **Max Slip/Moor** 15 ft./70 ft.
Access: East Penobscot Bay to Castine Harbor

Marina Facilities *(In Season/Off Season)*

Fuel: No
Slips: 0 Total, 0 Transient **Max LOA:** 90 ft. **Max Beam:** n/a
Rate *(per ft.)*: **Day** n/a **Week** n/a **Month** n/a
Power: 30 amp n/a, **50 amp** n/a, **100 amp** n/a, **200 amp** n/a
Cable TV: No **Dockside Phone:** No
Dock Type: Wood, Floating
Moorings: 20 Total, 5 Transient **Launch:** None, Dinghy Dock
Rate: Day $20 **Week** n/a **Month** n/a
Heads: 2 Toilet(s), 2 Shower(s) *(with dressing rooms)*
Laundry: None **Pay Phones:** Yes
Pump-Out: No **Fee:** n/a **Closed Heads:** No

Marina Operations

Owner/Manager: David Bicks (Commodore) **Dockmaster:** Y.C. Steward
In-Season: Jul-Sep 1, 3 pm-8pm **Off-Season:** n/a
After-Hours Arrival: Sign in book
Reservations: No **Credit Cards:** Cash or check only
Discounts: None
Pets: Welcome **Handicap Access:** No

Marina Services and Boat Supplies

Services - Docking Assistance, Boaters' Lounge, Dock Carts **Communication -** Mail & Package Hold, Data Ports *(Library)*, FedEx, UPS, Express Mail *(Sat Del)* **Supplies - Near:** Ice *(Block, Cube)*, Ships' Store *(Eaton's 326-4727, Four Flags 326-8526)* **3+ mi:** Marine Discount Store *(Hamilton Marine, 20 mi.)*, Propane *(Gary's Fuel 326-2067, 6.5 mi.)*

Boatyard Services

Near: Engine mechanic *(gas, diesel)*, Launching Ramp, Electrical Repairs, Hull Repairs, Rigger, Bottom Cleaning, Brightwork, Divers, Compound, Wash & Wax, Interior Cleaning, Woodworking, Inflatable Repairs, Painting, Yacht Broker *(Eaton's)*. **3+ mi:** Upholstery *(12 mi.)*, Yacht Interiors *(12 mi.)*.
Nearest Yard: Eaton's (207) 326-8579

Restaurants and Accommodations

OnCall: Pizzeria *(Variety Store 326-8625)* **Near:** Restaurant *(Dennett's Wharf 326-9045, L $6-15, D $12-22)*, *(The Reef Restaurant 326-4040)*, Seafood Shack *(The Breeze)*, Coffee Shop *(Bah's Bakehouse 326-9510, B $4, L $7, D $10)*, Inn/B&B *(Pentagoet 326-8616, $80-150)* **Under 1 mi:** Restaurant *(Castine Inn 326-4365, D $18-30)*, *(Pentagoet Inn D $10-20)*, *(Castine Lodge 326-4861)*, Inn/B&B *(Castine Inn 326-4365, $75-210, Breakfast included)*, *(Castine Harbor Inn 326-4335)*, *(Village Inn 326-9510, $65-85, Breakfast included)*, Condo/Cottage *(Castine Cottages 326-8003)* **1-3 mi:** Restaurant *(The Manor Inn 326-4861, D $15-26, Will pick up at club and return)*, Inn/B&B *(The Manor Inn 326-4861)*

Recreation and Entertainment

Near: Playground, Tennis Courts, Boat Rentals *(Castine Kayak Aventures 326-9045)*, Video Rental, Sightseeing *(State of Maine training ship, Castine Historical Society 326-4118)* **Under 1 mi:** Pool *(Maine Maritime Academy 326-4311)*, Beach, Picnic Area, Golf Course *(Castine Golf Club 326-8844)*, Park, Museum *(Wilson Museum 326-9247)*

Provisioning and General Services

Near: Provisioning Service *(Castine Harbor Lodge specializes in megayachts and local ingredients 326-4335)*, Convenience Store *(Tarratine Market 326-4818)*, Health Food, Wine/Beer, Liquor Store, Bakery, Farmers' Market *(Horsepower Farm Organic Produce, Thu 9-11am at Bah's)*, Green Grocer, Lobster Pound, Bank/ATM, Post Office, Catholic Church, Protestant Church, Library *(Witherle Memorial 326-4375)*, Laundry, Bookstore *(Compass Rose 326-9366)*, Newsstand, Retail Shops

Transportation

OnCall: Taxi *(Don's Taxi 236-4762)* **Near:** Bikes *(Dennetts 326-9045)* **3+ mi:** Rental Car *(Penguin Auto Rental 388-6111, 15 mi.)* **Airport:** Bar Harbor/Bangor Int'l. *(29 mi./30 mi.)*

Medical Services

No 911 Service **OnCall:** Ambulance **Near:** Doctor, Dentist *(Ciano 326-9500)* **3+ mi:** Chiropractor *(18 mi.)*, Holistic Services *(18 mi.)* **Hospital:** Blue Hill Memorial 374-2836 *(15 mi.)*

Setting -- The last facility in Castine, on the port side of the Bagaduce River, the lovely, quiet CYC is a short walk from town. Its location makes it the most scenic and residential choice. The 2-story, gray-sided, contemporary clubhouse has an inviting second floor porch, frequently populated by welcoming members enjoying the views: the unspoiled far shore, kids racing their dinghies, or the action down river closer to town.

Marina Notes -- Private yacht club which, as a courtesy, shares its facilities with visitors. Possible overnight dockage on outer float for one or two yachts, weather permitting, and five guest moorings. Active junior sailing club as well as Tuesday night lectures. Bring a dinghy. Heads and showers (with dressing rooms) are onsite. Smith Cove, less than a mile away on the other side of the river, is a good hurricane hole or anchorage area. The Manor Inn will transport you to and from your boat if you stay there or have dinner. The Castine Lodge (326-4861), the first facility on the River, has installed a large floating dock specifically designed for megayachts.

Notable -- Castine is a walking town with lots of history -- it's lived under five flags and was orignally called Ft. Pentagoet. Pick up a copy of the excellent walking tour at any local shops. Kayak and bike rentals at Dennett's are a short walk away, as are the museums, parks, and restored Georgian and Federalist houses. Just two blocks away, off Court Street, is a beautiful square with an inviting library (with data ports) housed in a 19thC building, Abbott and Adams Schools, Whitney House and other early 19thC houses. Wilson Museum (326-8753) features a pre-Revolutionary War house.

PHOTOS ON CD-ROM: 9

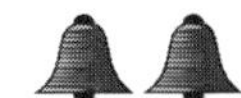

Navigational Information
Lat: 44°34.314' **Long:** 068°47.813' **Tide:** 11 ft. **Current:** 9 kt. **Chart:** 13309
Rep. Depths (*MLW*): Entry 4 ft. **Fuel Dock** 12 ft. **Max Slip/Moor** 26 ft./-
Access: Penobscot River

Marina Facilities *(In Season/Off Season)*
Fuel: Gasoline, On Call Delivery
Slips: 36 Total, 2 Transient **Max LOA:** 45 ft. **Max Beam:** n/a
Rate *(per ft.)*: **Day** $1.25/$1.00* **Week** Inq. **Month** $12/10
Power: 30 amp Incl., **50 amp** Incl., **100 amp** n/a, **200 amp** n/a
Cable TV: No **Dockside Phone:** No
Dock Type: Wood, Floating
Moorings: 0 Total, 0 Transient **Launch:** n/a, Dinghy Dock
Rate: Day n/a **Week** n/a **Month** n/a
Heads: 1 Toilet(s), 1 Shower(s) *(with dressing rooms)*
Laundry: None **Pay Phones:** No
Pump-Out: OnSite **Fee:** n/a **Closed Heads:** No

Marina Operations
Owner/Manager: Steve York **Dockmaster:** Ed Hodgkins
In-Season: May-Aug 30, 9am-6pm **Off-Season:** Sep-Oct 30, 9am-6pm
After-Hours Arrival: Call in advance and pre-pay
Reservations: Preferred **Credit Cards:** Visa/MC, Dscvr, Amex
Discounts: None
Pets: No **Handicap Access:** Yes, Docks

Bucksport Marina

88 Main Street; Bucksport, ME 04416

Tel: (207) 469-5902; (800) 499-5840 **VHF: Monitor** 9 **Talk** n/a
Fax: (207) 989-5842 **Alternate Tel:** (207) 989-5840
Email: n/a **Web:** www.portharbormarine.com
Nearest Town: Bucksport *(0 mi.)* **Tourist Info:** (207) 947-0307

Marina Services and Boat Supplies
Services - Docking Assistance, Security, Dock Carts **Communication -** FedEx, UPS, Express Mail **Supplies - OnSite:** Ice *(Block, Cube, Shaved)*, Ships' Store *(Port Harbor Marine)* **Near:** Bait/Tackle *(also Van Raymond Outfitters 989-6001, 2 mi.)*, Propane *(Hamel Fuels 989-3966)*

Boatyard Services
OnSite: Engine mechanic *(gas, diesel)*, Electrical Repairs, Propeller Repairs, Inflatable Repairs, Total Refits **OnCall:** Rigger, Bottom Cleaning, Brightwork, Divers **Near:** Compound, Wash & Wax, Interior Cleaning, Metal Fabrication. **Nearest Yard:** Port Harbor Marine **Dealer for:** Sea Ray, Grady-White, Whaler. **Member:** ABBRA

Restaurants and Accommodations
OnCall: Pizzeria *(Uncle Jay's 469-3974)* **Near:** Restaurant *(Ming's Chinese Garden)*, *(Riverview Restaurant and Sports Bar 469-7600)*, *(McLeod's Steak House 469-3963, L $5-8, D $10-15)*, Snack Bar *(Dairy Shop ice cream)*, Fast Food *(McDonalds, Subway)*, Lite Fare *(Stewarts 469-2750)*, Motel *(BW Jed Prouty Motor Inn 469-3113, $70-110)*, Inn/B&B *(Riverview 469-3111)* **1-3 mi:** Restaurant *(L'Ermitage 469-3361, D $13-20)*

Recreation and Entertainment
OnSite: Jogging Paths, Roller Blade/Bike Paths, Park *(Chamberlain Freedom Park)*, Special Events **Near:** Movie Theater *(The Alamo 469-6910 across the street - classic and current films, plus those produced by Northeast Historic Film located onsite)*, Museum *(Bucksport Historical Society, Hose 5 Fire Museum 945-3229)*, Sightseeing *(Champion International Paper Mill 469-1700, free tours Mon, Wed, Fri, Jun-Aug, 10am-3pm, 12 yrs & older)* **Under 1 mi:** Picnic Area, Fishing Charter, Video Rental *(Qwik Stop Video 989-7899)*, Video Arcade, Cultural Attract *(Ft. Knox State Park 469-7719 $2/0.50, Daily 9am-Sunset - Civil War encampments last weekend of Jul & Aug)* **1-3 mi:** Golf Course *(Bucksport Golf Club 469-7612)*, Fitness Center *(Isaac Farrar Mansion YWCA 941-2808)*, Bowling *(Bucksport Bowling 469-7902)*

Provisioning and General Services
Near: Convenience Store *(Tozier's Bucksport Variety 469-2753)*, Supermarket *(Hannafords/Shop N Save 469-3282)*, Farmers' Market *(at Post Office Thu 9am-1pm)*, Bank/ATM, Post Office, Catholic Church, Library, Beauty Salon *(Shear Elegance 469-3707)*, Barber Shop, Dry Cleaners, Laundry, Bookstore *(Bookstacks 469-8992)*, Pharmacy *(Community Pharmacy of Bucksport)*, Florist, Retail Shops **Under 1 mi:** Gourmet Shop *(The Vineyard 469-7844)*, Delicatessen, Health Food, Wine/Beer, Liquor Store *(Rite Aid Liquor 469-2925)*, Meat Market, Newsstand, Hardware Store **1-3 mi:** Copies Etc.

Transportation
OnCall: Rental Car *(Enterprise 800-325-8007)*, Taxi *(Port Taxi 469-1155)*, Airport Limo **Under 1 mi:** Bikes **Airport:** Bangor Int'l. *(16 mi.)*

Medical Services
911 Service **OnCall:** Ambulance **Near:** Doctor *(Bucksport Family Medicine)*, Dentist **Under 1 mi:** Chiropractor, Veterinarian *(Bucksport Vet 469-3614)* **1-3 mi:** Holistic Services **Hospital:** Eastern Maine Medical Center 973-8837 *(16 mi.)*

Setting -- Just past the bridge, at a fork in the Penobscot River, is this small, service-oriented facility situated adjacent to a lovely town park and just "feet" from Bucksport's Main Street. The marina offers contemporary docks with recent pedestals, bucolic views down river, views of the large, "unmissable" Fort Knox across the river, and views of a massive papermill up river. There's a new half mile promenade along the restored Bucksport waterfront.

Marina Notes -- Built in 1997. 70 ft. fuel dock, pump-out, and a well-stocked marine store are all onsite. Nicely done full bathroom. Off season monthly rate $10/ft. Note: Pets not welcome. A small town with some nice shops is nearby. Moorings are available from Bucksport Municipal Moorings 469-6300 or fax 469-7429. During winter, mailing address for marina is 23 Main Road, Holden, ME 04429.

Notable -- Built in 1844 to guard approaches to Bangor on the Penobscot River, 125 acre Fort Knox, with its massive 20 foot high granite walls, looks like a 5-sided medieval castle (469-7719). It is the most visited historic site in Maine, with a maze of deep underground tunnels, caves, tours and demonstrations. Kids love it; bring flashlights for the Long Alley tunnel and gun powder room. Chamberlain Freedom Park, on the marina side, also overlooking the river, depicts the Civil War's historic Gettysburg battle at Little Round top and is named for native son Joshua Chamberlain. Penobscot Landing, a $35-50 million project, will revitalize the waterfront over the next ten years with an entertainment district, more boating facilities, a ferry shuttle, a performing arts complex, museums and more recreation facilities. Fort Knox Bay Festival is in late July with a parade and fireworks.

PHOTOS ON CD-ROM: 9

II. Maine: Mid-Coast

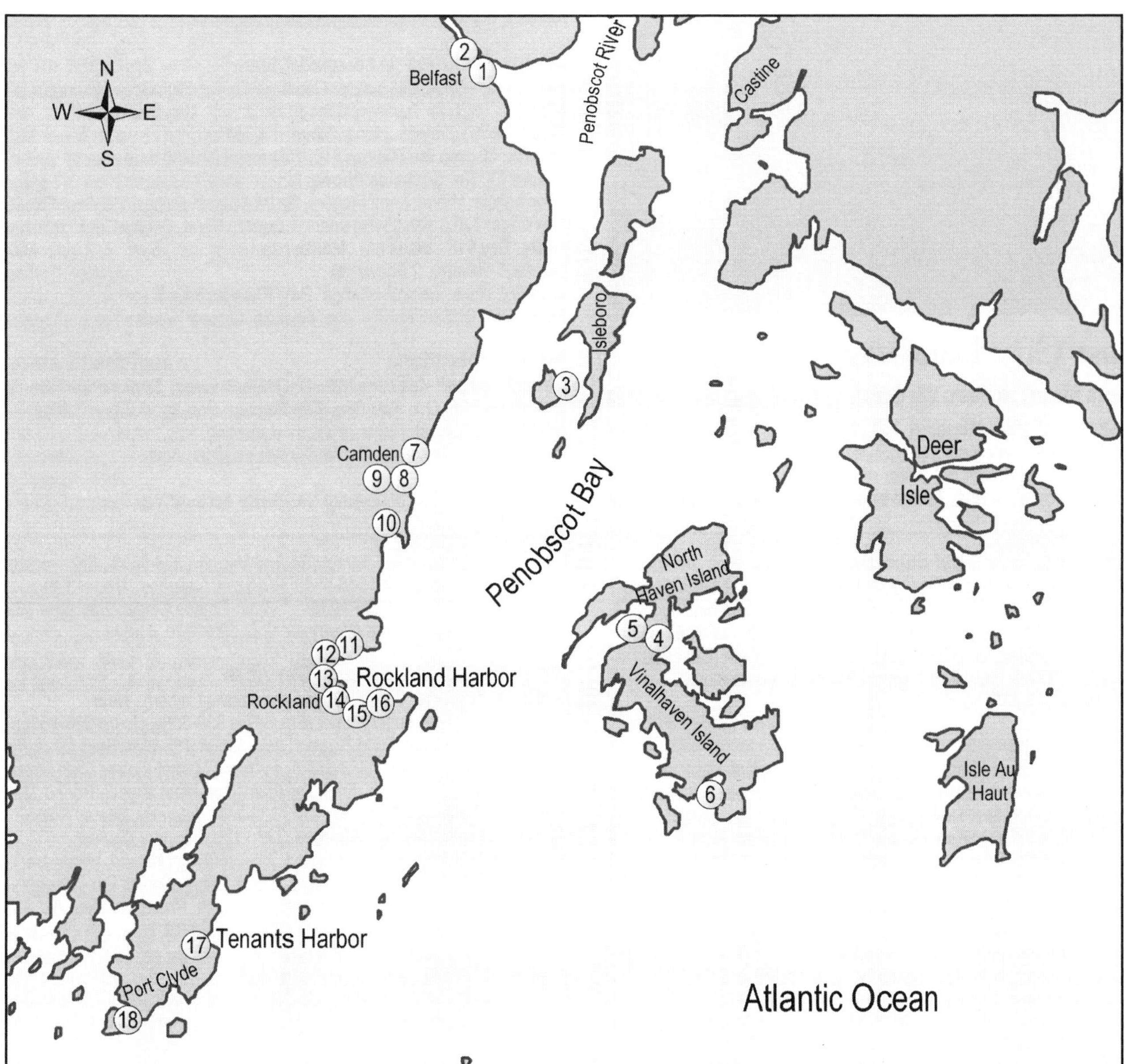

MAP	MARINA	HARBOR	PAGE	MAP	MARINA	HARBOR	PAGE
1	**Belfast City Landing**	*Passagassawakeag R.*	48	10	**Rockport Marine**	*Rockport Harbor*	57
2	**Belfast Boatyard**	*Passagassawakeag R.*	49	11	**Rockland Harbor Boatyard**	*Rockland Harbor*	58
3	**Dark Harbor Boat Yard**	*Gilkey Harbor*	50	12	**Knight Marine Service**	*Rockland Harbor*	59
4	**J.O. Brown & Sons, Inc.**	*Fox Island Thorofare*	51	13	**Beggar's Wharf**	*Rockland Harbor*	60
5	**Thayers Y-Knot Boatyard**	*Southern Harbor*	52	14	**Journey's End Marina**	*Rockland Harbor*	61
6	**Vinalhaven Private Moorings**	*Carvers Harbor*	53	15	**Rockland Landings Marina**	*Rockland Harbor*	62
7	**Wayfarer Marine**	*Camden Harbor*	54	16	**Rockland Public Landing**	*Rockland Harbor*	63
8	**Camden Yacht Club**	*Camden Harbor*	55	17	**Cod End Restaurant & Marina**	*Tenants Harbor*	64
9	**Camden Town Dock**	*Camden Harbor*	56	18	**Port Clyde General Store**	*Port Clyde*	65

Dark Harbor Boat Yard

700 Acre Island*; Islesboro, ME 04848

Tel: (207) 734-2246 **VHF: Monitor** 9 **Talk** 11
Fax: (207) 734-8331 **Alternate Tel:** n/a
Email: darkharbor@acadia.net **Web:** www.darkharborboatyard.com
Nearest Town: Dark Harbor *(3 mi.)* **Tourist Info:** (207) 948-5050

Navigational Information

Lat: 44°15.526' **Long:** 068°56.337' **Tide:** 11 ft. **Current:** n/a **Chart:** 13305
Rep. Depths (*MLW*): Entry 14 ft. **Fuel Dock** 6 ft. **Max Slip/Moor** -/14 ft.
Access: Penobscot Bay to Islesboro to Gilkey Harbor/Cradle Cove

Marina Facilities *(In Season/Off Season)*

Fuel: Gasoline, Diesel
Slips: 0 Total, 0 Transient **Max LOA:** n/a **Max Beam:** n/a
Rate *(per ft.)*: **Day** n/a **Week** n/a **Month** n/a
Power: 30 amp n/a, **50 amp** n/a, **100 amp** n/a, **200 amp** n/a
Cable TV: No **Dockside Phone:** No
Dock Type: n/a
Moorings: 20 Total, 20 Transient **Launch:** None, Dinghy Dock
Rate: Day $20/20 **Week** Inq. **Month** $100
Heads: 1 Toilet(s), 2 Shower(s)
Laundry: 1 Washer(s), 1 Dryer(s) **Pay Phones:** Yes
Pump-Out: No **Fee:** n/a **Closed Heads:** No

Marina Operations

Owner/Manager: John Gorham **Dockmaster:** n/a
In-Season: Jul-Aug, 7am-5pm **Off-Season:** Sep-Jun*, 7am-5pm*
After-Hours Arrival: Call ahead
Reservations: Yes, Preferred **Credit Cards:** Visa/MC
Discounts: None
Pets: Welcome **Handicap Access:** No

Marina Services and Boat Supplies

Supplies - OnSite: Ice *(Block, Cube)*, Ships' Store

Boatyard Services

OnSite: Travelift *(20T)*, Railway, Forklift, Crane, Engine mechanic *(gas, diesel)*, Electrical Repairs, Electronics Repairs **OnCall:** Hull Repairs, Rigger, Bottom Cleaning, Brightwork, Refrigeration

Restaurants and Accommodations

Under 1 mi: Restaurant *(Dark Harbor House 734-6669, by boat, mooring, 6-8:30pm, Mon-Sat)*, *(Latitude 44 734-6543, D $12-20, Wed-Sun 5-Mid, public landing 0.5 mi.)*, Snack Bar *(The Islander 734-2270, by Dinghy)*, Lite Fare *(Longitude 69 734-6543, Pub part of Latitude 44)*, *(The Landing 734-0975, a "gourmet trailer" at the Ferry Landing, Tue-Sat 7am-7pm, Sun 8am-2pm)*, *(Dark Harbor Shop 734-8878, B, L 8am-7pm)*, Inn/B&B *(Dark Harbor House 734-6669, $115-275, 1896 Georgian revival masterpiece, 11 beautiful ensuite rooms, incl. breakfast. Dinner also served, to guests and public. Mooring avail.)*, *(Aunt Laura's 734-8286, $75-135)*, *(Dark Harbor B&B 734-9772, $85-125, public landing 0.5 mi. - call for pick-up)*

Recreation and Entertainment

Near: Beach *(Pendleton Point)*, Tennis Courts *(Tarrantine Tennis Club 734-2241, dinghy)*, Golf Course *(Tarrantine Golf Club 734-6970, dinghy)*, Jogging Paths, Sightseeing *(Dinghy tour of the Dark Harbor "cottages")* **Under 1 mi:** Park *(Warren Island State Park 287-3821)*, Museum *(Islesboro Historical Society 734-6733 Sun-Thu, 12:30-4:30pm; Grindle Pt. Lighthouse & Sailor's Memorial Museum at the Ferry Landing 734-2253 Tue-Sun 9am-4:30pm)*
1-3 mi: Special Events

Provisioning and General Services

1-3 mi: Convenience Store *(Durkee's General Store 734-2201 full grocery inventory, plus take-out)*, Supermarket *(the modest Island Market 734-6672, recently bought by former owners of Blue Heron Rest., "Shake" & "Loony" Mahan; now their famous baked goods, desserts, party platters, picnics, etc., are available again)*, Wine/Beer, Liquor Store *(Durkee's)*, Post Office, Library *(734-2218, plus mini "branch" at ferry landing)*, Beauty Salon, Bookstore *(Island Books 734-6610)*

Transportation

OnCall: Water Taxi *(Capt. McKenzie, Quicksilver 734-8379, Courtney Lane 734-8341 or 557-5350)*, Rental Car *(Enterprise 800-325-8007 to Lincoln Beach)*, Taxi *(on island from dinghy landing)* **Near:** Bikes *(Dark Harbor House 734-6669)*, Ferry Service *(leaves from Grindle Point to Lincolnville Beach, every hour on the half, 7:30am-4:30pm, $4.50/2 RT 734-6935)*, Airport Limo *(on mainland Schooner Bay Limo & Taxi 594-5000)* **Airport:** Bangor Int'l. from Lincoln Beach *(35 mi.)*

Medical Services

No 911 Service **3+ mi:** Doctor *(Thanhauser 338-3995 in Lincolnville, 9 mi.)*
Hospital: Waldo County General 930-2525 - via ferry *(9 mi.)*

Setting -- In Gilkey Harbor's Cradle Cove, just past the eastern tip of Seven Hundred Acre Island, are the moorings and docks of Dark Harbor Boatyard. Known for its classic "cottages", secluded beaches, and great hiking trails, Islesboro has been an exclusive summer resort since the 1890s; some residents are 6th generation. The views are spectacular and the privacy absolute. Note: This private, bridgeless island off Islesboro offers no other public services.

Marina Notes -- Closed Fri-Sun except Jul & Aug. A full-service boatyard with 20T travelift. Tie your dinghy to floats just off the main stone dock. Ashore are a laundry, heads, showers and a fairly complete chandlery. *Mailing Address is: PO Box 25, Lincolnville, ME 04850. There are some interesting restaurants, inns, markets, and sights on Islesboro; the problem is how to get ashore. A long dinghy ride across Gilkey Harbor is Grindle Pt., one of only 2 public landings on Islesboro. Tarrantine Yacht Club docks are open only to members of reciprocal clubs (734-2281). Above distances are almost irrelevant since the key is where you land your dinghy. Pendleton Yacht Yard (734-6728) has 3-5 transient moorings, good BY services, and a dinghy landing dry at low tide.

Notable -- Great place to explore on foot or by dinghy; residents discourage bikes because of the narrow roads. But the area promises serendipitous views and acres of quiet. At the turn of the century, this island was the summer home of Charles Dana Gibson (of Gibson Girl fame). In 1926, he built a miniature Norman castle on the eastern tip for his grandchildren; it's not open to the public but is visible from the water. Opposite Grindle Pt. is spruce covered Warren Island, a state park with a wharf, campsites, shelters, fireplaces, large-group areas and guest moorings (941-4014) - see ranger Charlene "Sunshine" Hood.

PHOTOS ON CD-ROM: 9

Navigational Information
Lat: 44°07.638' **Long:** 068°52.333' **Tide:** 10 ft. **Current:** n/a **Chart:** 13305
Rep. Depths (*MLW*): Entry 15 ft. **Fuel Dock** 6 ft. **Max Slip/Moor** -/30 ft.
Access: Penobscot Bay to Fox IslandsThorofare

Marina Facilities *(In Season/Off Season)*
Fuel: Gasoline, Diesel
Slips: 0 Total, 0 Transient **Max LOA:** 42 ft. **Max Beam:** 13.5 ft.
Rate *(per ft.)*: **Day** n/a **Week** n/a **Month** n/a
Power: 30 amp n/a, **50 amp** n/a, **100 amp** n/a, **200 amp** n/a
Cable TV: No **Dockside Phone:** No
Dock Type: Short Fingers, Concrete, Alongside, Fixed
Moorings: 12 Total, 12 Transient **Launch:** to Vinalhaven ($3), Dinghy Dock
Rate: Day $10 **Week** $70 **Month** Inq.
Heads: 2 Shower(s)
Laundry: 3 Washer(s), 2 Dryer(s) **Pay Phones:** Yes
Pump-Out: No **Fee:** n/a **Closed Heads:** No

Marina Operations
Owner/Manager: Fay W. Brown **Dockmaster:** Same
In-Season: May-Sep 30, 7am-5:30pm **Off-Season:** n/a
After-Hours Arrival: Call ahead; pick up mooring and check-in in the am
Reservations: First come, first served. Be early **Credit Cards:** Visa/MC
Discounts: None
Pets: Welcome **Handicap Access:** No

J.O. Brown & Sons, Inc.

PO Box 525; SeaSide Lane; North Haven, ME 04853

Tel: (207) 867-4621 **VHF: Monitor** 16 **Talk** 9
Fax: (207) 867-4757 **Alternate Tel:** n/a
Email: n/a **Web:** n/a
Nearest Town: Rockland *(2 mi.)* **Tourist Info:** (207) 596-6549

Marina Services and Boat Supplies
Communication - Express Mail **Supplies - OnSite:** Ice *(Cube)*, Ships' Store, Propane *(J.O. Brown)*

Boatyard Services
OnSite: Travelift *(15T)*, Engine mechanic *(gas, diesel)*, Hull Repairs, Bottom Cleaning, Divers **Yard Rates:** Inq.

Restaurants and Accommodations
OnSite: Restaurant *(Brown's Coal Wharf Restaurant 867-4739, D $11-21, 6 days during summer, 6pm-9pm, Fri & Sat 'til Columbus Day. Cash only)* **Near:** Snack Bar *(Coopers Landing 867-2060, Mon-Sat 11am-3:30, 'til 5pm for ice cream)*, *(Burger Shop)* **Under 1 mi:** Inn/B&B *(Our Place Inn 867-4998)* **1-3 mi:** Inn/B&B *(Allen Houses at Bartlett Harbor 867-4822)*

Recreation and Entertainment
OnSite: Sightseeing *(The parade of boats, mostly sail, up and down Fox Islands Thorofare)* **Near:** Tennis Courts *(North Haven Casino 867-4497)*, Golf Course *(North Haven Golf 867-2054)*

Provisioning and General Services
OnSite: Wine/Beer, Fishmonger, Lobster Pound, Post Office **OnCall:** Supermarket *(Shaw's Supermarket in Rockland - 594-8615 & Telford Air - 596-7100 offer a pack-up and delivery service*)* **Near:** Retail Shops *(Galleries, including Calderwood Crafts)* **Under 1 mi:** Catholic Church, Protestant Church *(Episcopal & Baptist services)*, Library *(North Haven Library 867-9797 Irregular hours)*, Laundry, Bookstore *(Paper Store 863-4826)*, Hardware Store **1-3 mi:** Convenience Store *(The Islander General Store 867-4771, near Pulpit Harbor, will deliver large orders)* **3+ mi:** Pharmacy *(Rite Aid in Rockland 596-0036 Phone Orders)*

Transportation
Near: Ferry Service *(to Rockland 596-2202, $26 per car, $9 per person)*
Airport: Knox County/Bangor Int'l. *(17 mi./45 mi.)*

Medical Services
No 911 Service **OnCall:** Doctor, Holistic Services, Ambulance **Hospital:** Penobscot Bay Medical Center 596-8000 *(16 mi. via ferry)*

Setting -- Located on North Haven Island, in the "village", this down-home, classic century-old Maine boatyard is identified by its red shed overhanging the water. It offers moorings, as well as parts and services in this exquisite harbor off the Fox Islands Thorofare. Fifth Generation Browns are still at the helm.

Marina Notes -- Look for the J.O.B. on the mooring balls. Inside there's an incredible array of parts and supplies. A rustic, but nicely maintained bathroom and locked showers are through the blue door to the right of what was formerly Brown's Market. (Note: Brown's Market is now closed.) Laundromat is in the basement of the former Market. There are dinghy landings at J.O. Brown, the Town Landing and the Casino. Launch across to Vinalhaven is $3+ RT. Moorings may also be available from North Haven Casino (marked NHC), a private club, (867-4497) which has a small, appealing facility right in the center of the village. The small building at the end of the dock is the "Casino".

Notable -- Just roaming and dinghying around this delightful island is notable enough - try Perry Creek in Vinalhaven. Golf, sailing lessons and tennis can often be arranged through the Casino down the road. 27 miles of roads for hiking and biking (with your own bikes). In Southern Harbor is the Eric Hopkins gallery and, along the way, a handful of other gift/craft shops and galleries. A passenger/car ferry, to and from Rockland three times a day (596-2202), comes in just down the street. *Fax grocery order to Shaw's at 594-9553 by 11am with telephone, credit card, and Shaw's card numbers. Shaw's will shop and pack up for a fee of $10/1st $100 and $1/each add'l $50. Telford Air will deliver for $7.50 per box. Food is chilled/frozen until picked up.

PHOTOS ON CD-ROM: 7

Thayers Y-Knot Boatyard

668a Main Street; North Haven, ME 04853

Tel: (207) 867-4701 **VHF: Monitor** 9 **Talk** 68
Fax: (207) 867-4702 **Alternate Tel:** (207) 867-4701
Email: thayeryknot@ad.com **Web:** n/a
Nearest Town: Rockland *(2 mi.)* **Tourist Info:** (207) 596-6549

Navigational Information

Lat: 44°07.944' **Long:** 068°53.475' **Tide:** 10 ft. **Current:** 2 kt. **Chart:** 13305
Rep. Depths (*MLW*): Entry 14 ft. **Fuel Dock** n/a **Max Slip/Moor** -/12 ft.
Access: Fox Islands Thorofare to east side of Southern Harbor past the cove

Marina Facilities *(In Season/Off Season)*

Fuel: No
Slips: 0 Total, 0 Transient **Max LOA:** 50 ft. **Max Beam:** 16 ft.
Rate *(per ft.)*: **Day** n/a **Week** n/a **Month** n/a
Power: 30 amp n/a, **50 amp** n/a, **100 amp** n/a, **200 amp** n/a
Cable TV: No **Dockside Phone:** No
Dock Type: Wood, Floating
Moorings: 8 Total, 2 Transient **Launch:** None, Dinghy Dock
Rate: Day $15 **Week** Inq. **Month** Inq.
Heads: None
Laundry: None **Pay Phones:** No
Pump-Out: No **Fee:** n/a **Closed Heads:** No

Marina Operations

Owner/Manager: Collette & Ryan Haskell **Dockmaster:** n/a
In-Season: May-Sep, 7am-5pm **Off-Season:** Oct-Apr, 7am-3:30pm
After-Hours Arrival: n/a
Reservations: Preferred **Credit Cards:** Visa/MC
Discounts: None
Pets: Welcome **Handicap Access:** No

Marina Services and Boat Supplies

Communication - Express Mail **Supplies - OnSite:** Ships' Store **Near:** Ice *(Block, Cube)* **Under 1 mi:** Propane *(Rex Crockett 867-2215)*

Boatyard Services

OnSite: Travelift *(50T)*, Railway, Crane *(20T)*, Engine mechanic *(gas, diesel)*, Launching Ramp, Electrical Repairs, Electronic Sales, Electronics Repairs, Hull Repairs, Rigger, Bottom Cleaning, Brightwork, Air Conditioning, Compound, Wash & Wax, Interior Cleaning, Woodworking, Inflatable Repairs, Metal Fabrication, Awlgrip, Yacht Design, Yacht Building, Total Refits **OnCall:** Divers, Propeller Repairs, Life Raft Service, Upholstery, Yacht Interiors **Dealer for:** Volvo. **Member:** ABBRA, Other Certifications: Diesel Mechanic, Awlgrip Application **Yard Rates:** $40/hr., Haul & Launch $5/ft., Power Wash $25 **Storage:** On-Land Outside/Inside $5-10/ft./mo.

Restaurants and Accommodations

Under 1 mi: Restaurant *(Brown's Coal Wharf Restaurant 867-4739, 6 days during summer, 6pm-9pm, Fri & Sat 'til Columbus Day. Cash only)*, Snack Bar *(Coopers Landing 867-2060, Mon-Sat 11am-3:30, 'til 5pm for ice cream)*, *(Burger Shop)*, Inn/B&B *(Our Place 867-4998)*

Recreation and Entertainment

Near: Jogging Paths, Roller Blade/Bike Paths **Under 1 mi:** Playground, Golf Course *(North Haven Golf 207-867-2054)* **1-3 mi:** Beach, Picnic Area, Tennis Courts *(North Haven Casino 867-4497)*

Provisioning and General Services

OnCall: Supermarket *(Shaw's Supermarket in Rockland 594-8615 & Telford Air 596-7100 offer a pack-up and delivery service*)* **Under 1 mi:** Fishmonger, Lobster Pound *(J.O. Brown 867-4621)*, Post Office, Catholic Church, Protestant Church *(Episcopal & Baptist services)*, Library *(North Haven Library 867-9797 Irregular hours)*, Laundry, Hardware Store **1-3 mi:** Convenience Store *(The Islander General Store, 867-4771, about 3 mi. near Pulpit Harbor - will deliver larger orders)*, Bookstore *(Paper Store 863-4826)*, Pharmacy *(Rockland Rite Aid, on-call or via ferry 596-0036)*, Retail Shops

Transportation

OnCall: Taxi *(867-2076)* **Under 1 mi:** Ferry Service *($26 per car, $9 per person)* **Airport:** Knox County/Bangor Int'l. *(17 mi./46 mi.)*

Medical Services

No 911 Service **OnCall:** Ambulance **Under 1 mi:** Doctor **Hospital:** Penobscot Bay Medical Center 596-8000 *(16 mi. via ferry)*

PHOTOS ON CD-ROM: 3

Setting -- About three quarters of a mile from the village center of picturesque North Haven Island, at the head of Southern Harbor, is this family owned and operated boatyard with rental moorings. Southern Harbor is a quieter, more protected alternative to the main harbor and boasts some exquisite views.

Marina Notes -- Ashore is a full-service boatyard accessible via the dinghy dock, with extensive services for the boat and very few amenities for the visiting cruiser (Note: there are no heads) Marked with red/green stakes, a channel has been dredged to the dock where there is water and electricity. Thayers specializes in high quality repairs and restorations, including repowering and awlgripping. 30 years' experience in boat building and repair. Very protected. Also has some moorings in Pulpit Harbor.

Notable -- 27 miles of roads for hiking and biking (with your own bikes). Southern Harbor is the home of the highly regarded artist Eric Hopkins and his gallery - many of his paintings are of this harbor (867-2229). Between Thayers and the village are a handful of other gift and craft shops, as well as galleries. Please note: Brown's Market is now out of business. * Shaw's and Telford Air have solved the grocery problem. Fax a grocery order to Shaw's at 594-9553 by 11am with telephone, credit card, & Shaw's card numbers. Shaw's will shop and pack up for a fee of $10/1st $100 and $1/each add'l $50. Telford Air will pick up from Shaw's and deliver for $7.50 per box (banana-size box). Shaw's keeps the food appropriately chilled/frozen until called for.

Navigational Information
Lat: 44°02.761' **Long:** 068°50.062' **Tide:** 9 ft. **Current:** n/a **Chart:** 13305
Rep. Depths (*MLW*): Entry 27 ft. **Fuel Dock** n/a **Max Slip/Moor** -/14 ft.
Access: Southern tip of Vinalhaven to Carvers Harbor

Marina Facilities *(In Season/Off Season)*
Fuel: *Fishermen's Co-op -- Emergency only -*
Slips: 0 Total, 0 Transient **Max LOA:** 40 ft. **Max Beam:** n/a
Rate *(per ft.)*: **Day** n/a **Week** n/a **Month** n/a
Power: 30 amp n/a, **50 amp** n/a, **100 amp** n/a, **200 amp** n/a
Cable TV: No **Dockside Phone:** No
Dock Type: n/a
Moorings: 3 Total, 2 Transient **Launch:** No, Dinghy Dock
Rate: Day $20 **Week** n/a **Month** n/a
Heads: None
Laundry: None **Pay Phones:** No
Pump-Out: No **Fee:** n/a **Closed Heads:** Yes

Marina Operations
Owner/Manager: Kevin O'Hearn (Harbormaster) **Dockmaster:** n/a
In-Season: May-Oct 1, 8am-7pm **Off-Season:** Closed
After-Hours Arrival: Call in advance
Reservations: Call harbormaster to reserve **Credit Cards:** Cash only
Discounts: None
Pets: Welcome **Handicap Access:** No

Vinalhaven Private Moorings

Vinalhaven, ME

Tel: (207) 863-9344 **VHF: Monitor** 16 **Talk** 82
Fax: n/a **Alternate Tel:** n/a
Email: VHharbormaster@webtv.net **Web:** n/a
Nearest Town: Vinylhaven *(0 mi.)* **Tourist Info:** (207) 863-4471

Marina Services and Boat Supplies
Supplies - Near: Ships' Store *(Hopkins Boatyard 863-2551)*, Propane *(Vinalhaven Fuel Co. 863-4441)* **Under 1 mi:** Bait/Tackle *(Fisherman's Friend 863-9317, Island Lobster Supply 863-4807)*

Boatyard Services
OnSite: Travelift *(30T)*, Engine mechanic *(gas, diesel)*, Electrical Repairs, Hull Repairs, Propeller Repairs, Woodworking **OnCall:** Divers *(Fox Island Diving 863-4480)* **Near:** Yacht Building *(Jeff Moyer Boats 863-2136)*.

Restaurants and Accommodations
Near: Restaurant *(The Haven 863-4969, dinner only - Tue-Sat 2 seatings 6 & 8:15pm, also casual pub room)*, *(The Islander 863-2028, Mon-Wed, Fri-Sat B, D 5:45 & 7:45pm, BYOB)*, *(The Galley 863-2569)*, *(Candlepin Lodge 863-2730)*, Seafood Shack *(Harbor Gawker 863-9365, to go)*, *(Steaming Kettle B, L in Harbor Wharf)*, Pizzeria *(The Pizza Pit 863-4311)*, Motel *(Tidewater Motel 863-4618, $55-150, built on a bridge overlooking the harbor)*, Inn/B&B *(Fox Island Inn 863-2122, $45-125)*, *(Chatfield House 863-9303)*, *(Candlepin Lodge & Cabins 863-2713, 4 log cabins, on-site restaurant, pool, bowling)*, *(Libby House 863-4696)* **Under 1 mi:** Restaurant *(Gigi's 863-4059)*, *(Surfside 863-2767)*, Inn/B&B *(Payne Homestead 863-9963, $90-145)*

Recreation and Entertainment
OnCall: Boat Rentals *(Canoes & kayaks at Tidewater Motel, $20/day includes delivery)* **Near:** Picnic Area *(Grimes Park)*, Playground *(next to Armbrust Hill Town Park)*, Bowling *(Candlepin Lodge 863-2730)*, Park *(Grimes Park, Armbrust Hill)* **Under 1 mi:** Video Rental *(Boongies Vision Video 863-2510)*, Museum *(Vinalhaven Historical Society 863-4410 11am-3pm, ask for the walking tour brochure)* **1-3 mi:** Beach *(Lawson's Quarry)*, Cultural Attract, Sightseeing *(Granite quarries, Lane's Island seaside nature preserve, Armburst Hill Wildlife Reservation, Carvers Cemetery, Odd-Fellows Hall, The Galamander)*

Provisioning and General Services
Near: Market *(Carvers Harbor Market 863-4319)*, Gourmet Shop *(Frannie's Frills 863-4622)*, Wine/Beer *(Carvers' Harbor)*, Green Grocer *(Downstreet Market)*, Fishmonger *(Vinalhaven Co-op 863-2263 wholesale but sells retail to walk-ins)*, Lobster Pound, Post Office *(863-4620)*, Retail Shops *(Harbor Wharf - galleries, gift shops)* **Under 1 mi:** Liquor Store *(Fisherman's Friend 863-9317)*, Protestant Church, Library *(Vinalhaven Public Library 863-4401)*, Bookstore *(Paper Store 863-4826)*, Newsstand *(Paper Store - out of town papers, gifts, fax & copy machines)*, Hardware Store *(Port O'Call 863-2525)*, Copies Etc. *(Paper Store)*

Transportation
Near: Bikes *(rentals at Tidewater Motel $10/day, delivery possible)*, Rental Car *(Vinalhaven Transportation 863-4501, Tidewater Motel 863-4618)*, Ferry Service *(State Ferry to Rockland, Mon-Sat 7am-4:30pm, Sun 7am-3:15pm 863-4421 $9/4 RT)*

Medical Services
911 Service **OnCall:** Ambulance **Near:** Holistic Services *(Hopewell Massage 549-5676, In Touch Massage 863-2291)* **1-3 mi:** Doctor *(Islands Community Medical Center 863-4341)*, Dentist *(ICMS Dental Services 863-2533)* **Hospital:** Penobscot Bay, Rockport 596-8000 *(20 mi. via ferry)*

Setting -- Commercial Carvers Harbor, and the village on its shore, are part of an active fishing community that sends a large fleet out every morning. It has a long history as a working island -- from the major granite quarry operations of its past to the current lobster and fishing business, and the environs reflect that. The harbor is crowded with working vessels making it not particularly hospitable to pleasure craft. If you can score one of the 2 moorings, it is a fascinating stop nonetheless.

Marina Notes -- No heads, showers, pump-out or laundry. Dinghy dock at town float, located in parking lot across from the grocery store. Tie up to rear or sides, not front. (2 hr. limit on front). Trash barrels at top of ramp. Fuel (emergencies only) at Vinalhaven Co-op - mainly for commercial vessels. Hopkins Boatyard can also manage most emergency repairs and maintains a small ships' store. 13 mile, 75 minute ferry ride to Rockland.

Notable -- 1200 year-round residents (tripling in the summer) make this the most populated island in the state. Many parks and hiking trails populate the island. The Nature Conservancy maintains two islands accessible only by dinghy (729-5181). Vinalhaven Land Trust (863-2543) in Skoog Park has hiking trail maps. There is a growing artist community led by Robert Indiana -- who has restored the curiously interesting 1885 Odd-Fellow's Hall -- and some interesting galleries as a result. Sat morning flea market. SeaEscape Kayak (863-9343) offers guided kayak tours. If you manage to get to the north end of this 7.5 mi. island, then there is a private shuttle that traverses Fox Islands Thorofare to J.O. Brown Boatyard in North Haven.

PHOTOS ON CD-ROM: 9

Navigational Information

Lat: 44°12.547' **Long:** 069°03.641' **Tide:** 10 ft. **Current:** n/a **Chart:** 13305
Rep. Depths (*MLW*): Entry 15 ft. **Fuel Dock** 10 ft. **Max Slip/Moor** 13 ft./50 ft.
Access: Penobscot Bay to Camden Harbor

Marina Facilities *(In Season/Off Season)*

Fuel: *Renneco* - Gasoline, Diesel
Slips: 40 Total, 20 Transient **Max LOA:** 120 ft. **Max Beam:** 30 ft.
Rate *(per ft.)*: **Day** $3.00/Inq.* **Week** n/a **Month** n/a
Power: 30 amp $10, **50 amp** $20, **100 amp** n/a, **200 amp** n/a
Cable TV: No **Dockside Phone:** No
Dock Type: Wood, Long Fingers, Alongside, Floating, Fixed
Moorings: 59 Total, 54 Transient **Launch:** Yes ($1/pp/1-way), Dinghy Dock
Rate: Day $30/35* **Week** $200-230 **Month** Inq.
Heads: 6 Toilet(s), 5 Shower(s)
Laundry: 3 Washer(s), 3 Dryer(s), Book Exchange **Pay Phones:** Yes
Pump-Out: OnSite, Full Service **Fee:** $10 **Closed Heads:** Yes

Wayfarer Marine

PO Box 677; Sea Street; Camden, ME 04843

Tel: (207) 236-4378; (800) 229-4378 **VHF: Monitor** 71 **Talk** 71
Fax: (207) 236-2371 **Alternate Tel:** (207) 236-4378
Email: info@wayfarermarine.com **Web:** www.wayfarermarine.com
Nearest Town: Camden *(0.5 mi.)* **Tourist Info:** (207) 236-4404

Marina Operations

Owner/Manager: Wendy Hart **Dockmaster:** n/a
In-Season: May-Oct, 8am-5pm **Off-Season:** Nov-Apr, 7am-3:30pm
After-Hours Arrival: Call ahead. Tie up at fuel dock and check in in the am
Reservations: Recommended **Credit Cards:** Visa/MC, Dscvr, Amex
Discounts: None
Pets: Welcome, Dog Walk Area **Handicap Access:** Yes, Heads, Docks

Marina Services and Boat Supplies

Services - Docking Assistance, Concierge, Security *(until 10pm)*, Trash Pick-Up, Dock Carts **Communication -** Mail & Package Hold, Phone Messages, Fax in/out *($2/pp)*, Data Ports *(Customer Phone Room)*, FedEx, AirBorne, UPS, Express Mail *(Sat Del)* **Supplies - OnSite:** Ice *(Block, Cube)*, Ships' Store, CNG **Under 1 mi:** Marine Discount Store, Bait/Tackle, Propane *(Willey 236-3256/Farmers Union 236-3266)*

Boatyard Services

OnSite: Travelift *(110T)*, Forklift *(80T, 35T hydraulic trailers)*, Crane *(35T)*, Engine mechanic *(gas, diesel)*, Launching Ramp, Electrical Repairs, Electronic Sales, Electronics Repairs, Hull Repairs, Rigger, Sail Loft, Bottom Cleaning, Brightwork, Air Conditioning, Refrigeration, Compound, Wash & Wax, Interior Cleaning, Propeller Repairs, Woodworking, Life Raft Service, Yacht Interiors, Metal Fabrication, Awlgrip, Yacht Broker, Total Refits **OnCall:** Divers **Dealer for:** Boston Whaler, Westerbeke, Johnson & Evinrude, Mirrocraft, Avon. **Member:** ABBRA, ABYC, Other Certifications: Nautor's Swan & Oyster Yachts **Yard Rates:** $35-60/hr., Haul & Launch $12.25-13.50/ft., Power Wash $2/ft., Bottom Paint $9/ft. **Storage:** On-Land $35/ft. Inside-$6.75-8.75/sq.ft.

Restaurants and Accommodations

Near: Motel *(River House 236-0500, $150-200)*, Inn/B&B *(Hawthorn 236-8842, $155)* **Under 1 mi:** Restaurant *(Peter Ott's 236-4032, D $16-22)*, *(Whitehall B $8, D $15-23)*, *(Cappy's 236-2254, L $7-15, D $10-17)*, Seafood Shack *(Bayview 789-5550, L $3-13, D $3-15)*, Pizzeria *(Camden House 230-2464, L $4-14, D $4-14)*, Inn/B&B *(Whitehall Inn 236-3891, $100-150)*, *(Maine Stay 236-9636, $100-165)*, *(Lord Camden 236-4325, $90-210)*

Recreation and Entertainment

OnSite: Picnic Area, Grills **Near:** Playground, Volleyball, Tennis Courts, Jogging Paths, Boat Rentals, Roller Blade/Bike Paths, Park, Cultural Attract *(Camden Civic Theater 236-2281; Camden Opera House 236-3358)*, Sightseeing **Under 1 mi:** Beach, Movie Theater *(Bay View St. 236-8722)*, Video Rental *(Harbor Video 236-9596)*, Museum *(Conway Homestead, Cramer Mansion 236-2257)* **1-3 mi:** Heated Pool *(YMCA 236-3375)*, Golf Course *(Goose River 236-8488)*, Fitness Center *(YMCA)*

Provisioning and General Services

OnSite: Provisioning Service *(French & Brawn satellite)*, Wine/Beer **Near:** Gourmet Shop, Lobster Pound, Bank/ATM, Library *(Camden 236-3440)* **Under 1 mi:** Supermarket *(French & Brawn 236-3361, Grave's 236-8577)*, Delicatessen *(Camden Deli 236-8343)*, Health Food *(Nature's Choice 236-8280)*, Liquor Store *(Rite Aid 236-4546)*, Bakery, Fishmonger, Post Office, Protestant Church, Beauty Salon, Dry Cleaners, Laundry, Bookstore *(Owl & Turtle 236-4769)*, Pharmacy *(Rite Aid 236-4546)*, Hardware Store *(Rankins 236-3275)*, Florist, Department Store *(Reny's)*

Transportation

OnSite: Water Taxi *($1/pp MemDay-LabDay)* **OnCall:** Bikes *(Brown Dog 236-6664 $15/day.)*, Rental Car *(National 594-8424, USave 236-2320)*, Taxi *(Don's Taxi 236-4762)*, Airport Limo *(Schooner Bay 594-5000)* **Near:** Local Bus **Airport:** Rockland/Bangor Int'l. *(12 mi./45 mi.)*

Medical Services

911 Service **OnCall:** Ambulance **Near:** Chiropractor **Under 1 mi:** Doctor, Dentist **Hospital:** Penobscot Bay 596-8000 *(4 mi.)*

Setting -- On the north east side of protected Camden Harbor, Wayfarer Marine - with its network of well-maintained sheds, docks, facilities, harbor floats, and mooring field - is easily visible. This full-service yachting facility offers its guests breathtaking views of Camden Harbor, the village, and the Camden Hills above, and provides easy access to this picturesque town's extensive services and amenities.

Marina Notes -- *Rates: $3/ft. up to 16 ft. beam, beam greater than 16 ft. $4/ft.; floats: $35/ft., moorings: $30 to 50 ft., $35 over 50 ft. Excellent docks - 20 "alongside" spots, 5 finger slips for trans. Expect to raft up to 3 deep during high season. All moorings are in the outer harbor - marked with a Wayfarer burgee and max. length boat allowed. Launch hours 8am-8pm Jun-Aug. Hauls vessels to 110 tons, with drafts to 14 feet; most comprehensive boatyard in this part of Maine. U.S. Customs & Immigration assistance. Comfortable heads, showers, and laundry room - one full bath, plus men's and women's heads with individual showers. Established in 1963, but the boat building tradition reaches back more than 200 years; there have been seven previous boatyards on this site.

Notable -- Wayfarer is on the "quiet side" of the harbor. Their water taxi ($1/pp) shuttles guests across to the bustling, service-laden side - downtown Camden. Alternatively, dinghy to the Town Landing or walk the half mile around the perimeter of the harbor. Seven schooners make their home in Camden; these spectacular vessels offer trips from 2 hours to 6 days and, when in port, are an integral part of the scenery. Labor Day is Windjammer Weekend. Edna St. Vincent Millay grew up in Camden and there is much memorabilia here. Camden Hills State Park is 2 mi. Farmers' Market Sat 9am-noon, Wed 4:30-6:30pm.

PHOTOS ON CD-ROM: 9

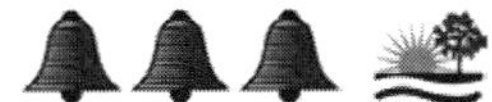

Navigational Information
Lat: 44°12.436' **Long:** 069°03.672' **Tide:** 10 ft. **Current:** n/a **Chart:** 13305
Rep. Depths (*MLW*): Entry 15 ft. **Fuel Dock** n/a **Max Slip/Moor** 8 ft./50 ft.
Access: Past Curtis Island to Camden Inner Harbor, first facility to port

Marina Facilities *(In Season/Off Season)*
Fuel: No
Slips: 2 Total, 2 Transient **Max LOA:** 50 ft. **Max Beam:** n/a
Rate *(per ft.)*: **Day** $30.00 **Week** n/a **Month** n/a
Power: 30 amp n/a, **50 amp** n/a, **100 amp** n/a, **200 amp** n/a
Cable TV: No **Dockside Phone:** No
Dock Type: Wood, Alongside, Floating
Moorings: 2 Total, 2 Transient **Launch:** Yes (Free), Dinghy Dock
Rate: Day $20 **Week** n/a **Month** n/a
Heads: 2 Toilet(s)
Laundry: None **Pay Phones:** No
Pump-Out: OnCall, Self Service **Fee:** n/a **Closed Heads:** Yes

Marina Operations
Owner/Manager: Elaine Booker **Dockmaster:** Patricia Stichman
In-Season: Jul-Aug, 8am-8pm **Off-Season:** May-Jun, Sep-Oct, 8am-4pm
After-Hours Arrival: n/a
Reservations: Yes **Credit Cards:** Cash
Discounts: None
Pets: Welcome **Handicap Access:** No

Camden Yacht Club

PO Box 204; Bayview Street; Camden, ME 04843

Tel: (207) 236-3014 **VHF: Monitor** 68 **Talk** 68
Fax: n/a **Alternate Tel:** n/a
Email: n/a **Web:** n/a
Nearest Town: Camden *(0.4 mi.)* **Tourist Info:** (207) 236-4404

Marina Services and Boat Supplies
Services - Docking Assistance, Dock Carts **Communication -** Mail & Package Hold, FedEx, AirBorne, UPS, Express Mail *(Sat Del)* **Supplies - OnSite:** Ice *(Block, Cube)* **Near:** Ships' Store, Propane *(Farmers' Union 236-3266)*, CNG *(Willey Wharf 236-7969)*

Boatyard Services
Nearest Yard: Wayfarer Marine (207) 236-4378

Restaurants and Accommodations
OnSite: Restaurant *(Camden Y.C. L)* **Near:** Restaurant *(Hartstone Inn 236-4259, D $40 prix fixe, Wed-Sun, 7pm seating, excellent)*, *(Cappy's Chowder 236-2254, L $7-15, D $10-20, 11am-Mid)*, *(Peter Ott's Steakhouse 236-4032, D $16-22)*, *(Cork 236-0533, D $18-26, Table d'hôte $42-60)*, *(The Waterfront 236-3747, L $6-15, D $10-17)*, *(Atlantica 236-6011, L $8-14, D $19-28, also lite menu)*, Seafood Shack *(Bay View Lobster 236-2005, L $3-13, D $3-15, lobster all day)*, Snack Bar *(Scott's Place 236-8751, L $2-6)*, Lite Fare *(Mariner's 236-2647, B $4-6, L $4-12)*, *(Camden Deli 236-8343, B, L, D 6am-10pm great view of falls)*, Hotel *(Camden Harbour Inn 236-4200, $105-255)*, Inn/B&B *(Hartstone Inn $100-190)*, *(Lord Camden 236-4325, $90-210)*, *(Elms B&B 236-7330, $75-125)*, *(The Belmont 236-8053, $85-180)* **Under 1 mi:** Hotel *(Norumbega 236-4646, $130-480)*, Inn/B&B *(Windward House 236-9656, $175-245)* **1-3 mi:** Seafood Shack *(Capt. Andy's Lobsters 236-2312, Take-Out only)*, Motel *(Cedar Crest 236-4859, $100-130, shuttle)*

Recreation and Entertainment
Near: Beach *(Laite Memorial Park)*, Picnic Area *(Dinghy to Curtis Island)*, Grills, Playground, Tennis Courts, Movie Theater *(Bay St. 236-8722)*, Park *(Laite Memorial)*, Cultural Attract *(Camden Civic Theater 236-2281, Camden Opera House 236-3353)*, Sightseeing *(Camden-Rockport Historical Society's 2.5 mi. walking tour from Chamber of Commerce)* **Under 1 mi:** Video Rental *(Harbor Video 236-9596)*, Museum *(1780 Old Homestead incl Conway House/Cramer Museum 236-2257 $5/2 Tue-Fri, 10-4)* **1-3 mi:** Heated Pool *(YMCA 236-3375 moved! Union St., Rockport line $8/4 day)*, Fitness Center *(YMCA)* **3+ mi:** Golf Course *(Goose River 236-8488, 4 mi.)*

Provisioning and General Services
Near: Supermarket *(French & Brawn 236-3611 or taxi to Grave's)*, Delicatessen *(Camden Deli 236-8343)*, Health Food *(Nature's Choice 236-8280)*, Liquor Store *(Rite Aid)*, Bakery *(Cappy's)*, Farmers' Market *(Sat 9am-noon, Wed 4:30-6:30pm on Colcord Ave.)*, Fishmonger *(Angler's)*, Lobster Pound, Bank/ATM, Post Office, Catholic Church, Protestant Church, Library *(236-3440, Internet services)*, Beauty Salon, Barber Shop, Dry Cleaners *(Spotless 236-2530)*, Laundry *(Bishops 236-3339)*, Bookstore *(Owl and Turtle 236-4769)*, Pharmacy *(Rite Aid 236-4546)*, Newsstand, Hardware Store *(Rankins 236-3275)*, Florist, Retail Shops, Copies Etc. *(Kax Office Services)* **Under 1 mi:** Department Store *(Reny's)*

Transportation
OnCall: Bikes *(Brown Dog 236-6664 $15/day)*, Rental Car *(Smith's Garage 236-2320)*, Taxi *(Don's 236-4762)* **Airport:** Rockland/Bangor Int'l. *(12 mi./45 mi.)*

Medical Services
911 Service **Under 1 mi:** Doctor, Dentist, Chiropractor, Holistic Services
3+ mi: Ambulance **Hospital:** Penobscot Bay 596-8000 *(3 mi.)*

Setting -- On the southwest shore of Camden's Inner Harbor, the first facility to port is the lovely Camden Yacht Club. Its deep red, low profile club house is surrounded on three sides by covered patios and by spacious grounds and extensive lawns. This is probably the best spot in the harbor -- its views are just spectacular: north, the Inner Harbor and the Camden Hills, south, the Outer Harbor and Penobscot Bay.

Marina Notes -- Closed MidOct - MidApr. No power on the limited-tie-up docks. Launch service from 8am-8pm. Open to all yachtsmen. Nice heads and showers. Lunch is served in the clubhouse, and guests are welcome. Chef Jason Mulholland also mans the stove at the Cedar Crest Restaurant 236-7722.

Notable -- This side of the harbor is closer to "downtown", and CYC is within easy walking distance of all the delights of Camden. It is a little out of the way of the summer tourist crowds, providing a quieter, more residential ambiance. 6 schooners -- ranging in length from 42 ft. to 123 ft. -- make Camden Harbor their home. The smaller ones offer 2-4 hour harbor cruises and the larger ones 2-6 day excursions. Labor Day is Windjammer Weekend. Camden Hills State Park, 3rd largest in the state, is about 2 miles north $2/.50 - with a wide range of hiking and picnicking possibilities, including a climb to the top of Mt. Battie (1 hr. RT). Camden-Rockport Historical Society publishes a great walking/biking map available at the CofC building, or call 236-2257.

PHOTOS ON CD-ROM: 9

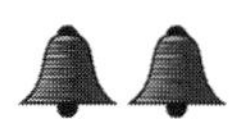

Camden Town Dock

Camden Town Dock

PO Box 1207; Elm Street; Camden, ME 04843

Tel: (207) 236-7969 **VHF: Monitor** 16 **Talk** 11
Fax: n/a **Alternate Tel:** (207) 283-4110
Email: n/a **Web:** n/a
Nearest Town: Camden *(0 mi.)* **Tourist Info:** (207) 236-4404

Navigational Information

Lat: 44°12.549' **Long:** 069°03.792' **Tide:** 10 ft. **Current:** n/a **Chart:** 13305
Rep. Depths (*MLW*): Entry 15 ft. **Fuel Dock** n/a **Max Slip/Moor** 10 ft./-
Access: Penobscot Bay, past Curtis Island to Camden Harbor

Marina Facilities *(In Season/Off Season)*

Fuel: Gasoline, Diesel
Slips: 10 Total, 10 Transient **Max LOA:** 120 ft. **Max Beam:** 30 ft.
Rate *(per ft.)*: **Day** $1.25/Inq. **Week** Inq. **Month** Inq.
Power: 30 amp Inq., **50 amp** Inq., **100 amp** n/a, **200 amp** n/a
Cable TV: No **Dockside Phone:** No
Dock Type: Wood, Alongside, Floating
Moorings: 0 Total, 0 Transient **Launch:** n/a, Dinghy Dock
Rate: Day n/a **Week** n/a **Month** n/a
Heads: 5 Toilet(s), YMCA for showers, $4
Laundry: None **Pay Phones:** Yes, 4
Pump-Out: OnSite, Full Service **Fee:** n/a **Closed Heads:** Yes

Marina Operations

Owner/Manager: Steve Pixley (Harbormaster) **Dockmaster:** n/a
In-Season: Jun 15-Oct 15, 7am-7pm **Off-Season:** Oct 16-Jun 14, 8am-3pm
After-Hours Arrival: Call (207) 236-7969 for instructions
Reservations: Yes, Preferred **Credit Cards:** Cash and check
Discounts: None
Pets: Welcome, Dog Walk Area **Handicap Access:** Yes, Heads

Marina Services and Boat Supplies

Services - Docking Assistance **Communication -** FedEx, AirBorne, UPS, Express Mail *(Sat Del)* **Supplies - Near:** Ice *(Block)*, Ships' Store, Propane *(Farmers Union 236-3266)*, CNG *(Willey Wharf 236-7969)*

Boatyard Services

Near: Travelift *(135T)*, Engine mechanic *(gas, diesel)*, Electrical Repairs, Electronic Sales, Electronics Repairs, Hull Repairs, Rigger, Sail Loft, Bottom Cleaning, Brightwork, Air Conditioning, Refrigeration, Divers, Compound, Wash & Wax, Interior Cleaning, Propeller Repairs, Woodworking, Inflatable Repairs, Life Raft Service, Upholstery, Yacht Interiors, Metal Fabrication, Painting, Awlgrip, Yacht Design, Yacht Building, Total Refits. **Nearest Yard:** Wayfarer (207) 236-4378

Restaurants and Accommodations

OnSite: Restaurant *(Atlantica L $7-14, D $19-28)*, *(Bay View Lobster 236-2005, L $3-$13, D $3-15, lobster all day)*, Snack Bar *(Skips)* **OnCall:** Pizzeria *(Zaddik's 236-6540, L $6-15, D $6-15)* **Near:** Restaurant *(Cappy's Chowder House 236-2254, L $6-15, D $10-20)*, *(Peter Otts Steakhouse 236-4032, D $8-23)*, *(Waterfront 236-3747, L $7-14, D $10-22)*, *(Hartstone Inn 236-4259, D $40 prix fixe, Wed-Sun, 7pm seating, B&B, too)*, Snack Bar *(Bagel Café 236-2661)*, Motel *(Towne 236-3377, $80-130)*, Hotel *(BW Camden River 236-0500, $160-210)*, *(Camden Harbor Inn 236-4200, $105-255)*, Inn/B&B *(Lord Camden 236-4325, $90-210)*, *(Elms B&B 236-7330, $75-125)*, *(Windward House 236-9656, $175-245)*

Recreation and Entertainment

OnSite: Sightseeing **Near:** Beach *(Laite Memorial)*, Picnic Area, Grills, Playground, Tennis Courts, Jogging Paths, Roller Blade/Bike Paths, Movie Theater *(Bay View St. Cinema 236-8722)*, Video Rental *(Harbor Video 236-9596)*, Park *(Laite Memorial)*, Museum, Cultural Attract *(Camden Civic Theater 236-2281, Camden Opera House 236-3353)* **1-3 mi:** Heated Pool *(YMCA 236-3375 Union St., Rockport line $8/4 day pass)*, Fitness Center *(YMCA)* **3+ mi:** Golf Course *(Goose River 236-8488, 4 mi.)*

Provisioning and General Services

Near: Provisioning Service, Supermarket *(French & Brawn 236-3361)*, Gourmet Shop, Delicatessen *(Camden Deli 236-8343)*, Health Food *(Nature's Choice 236-8280)*, Liquor Store *(Rite Aid)*, Bakery *(Cappy's)*, Farmers' Market *(Colcord Ave. Sat 9am-noon, Wed 4:30-6:30pm)*, Fishmonger *(Angler's)*, Lobster Pound, Meat Market, Bank/ATM, Post Office, Catholic Church, Protestant Church, Library *(236-3440, internet service)*, Beauty Salon, Barber Shop, Dry Cleaners, Laundry, Bookstore *(Owl and Turtle 236-4769)*, Pharmacy *(Rite Aid 236-4546)*, Newsstand, Hardware Store *(Rankins 236-3275)*, Florist, Clothing Store, Retail Shops, Department Store *(Reny's)* **Under 1 mi:** Copies Etc. *(Blueprint 236-2387)*

Transportation

OnCall: Bikes *(Brown Dog 236-6664 $15/day)*, Rental Car *(Enterprise 594-9093)*, Taxi *(Mid Coast Limo 236-2424)* **Near:** Water Taxi, InterCity Bus *(Concord Trailways to Boston)* **3+ mi:** Ferry Service *(Islesboro, 4 mi.)*
Airport: Knox County/Bangor Int'l. *(6 mi./45 mi.)*

Medical Services

911 Service **Near:** Doctor, Dentist, Chiropractor *(Johnstone 236-3456)*, Holistic Services, Ambulance **Hospital:** Penobscot Bay 596-8000 *(4 mi.)*

Setting -- Set in the heart of this delightful tourist mecca, the Camden Town Dock is really at the center of the action. Yet it has great views of one of the prettiest harbors on the East Coast, and the Camden Hills. Many, many restaurants, services, shops, attractions, galleries, and activities are available in this good size town. Everything is beautifully maintained, and the town dock is no exception.

Marina Notes -- New in 2003: Pumpout and power on docks. There are public toilets onsite and showers at the YMCA - $4, 6am-9pm (236-3375), now moved to Union St. on Rockport line - or across the harbor at Wayfarer's. Dinghy dock available for all, 2-3 hrs. Fuel is next door at Willey Wharf and at Wayfarer Marine (a full service boatyard). Willey specializes in megayachts and may have available dockage, as well as transient moorings in the outer harbor 236-3256. Note: The flow of boat traffic in harbor is counter-clockwise.

Notable -- Everything is within easy walking distance, with some of the shops and eateries practically sitting on the docks. During the season, Camden is one of the major toursit destinations of Maine, and the Town Dock can feel a bit like Grand Central Station - you are one of the sights. Excursions from 2 hours to 6 days long are available on board 9 schooners in Camden Harbor. If you enjoy hiking, try Camden Hills State Park, 20 minutes away, for a climb to the top of Mt. Battie (1 hr. RT). A walking/biking map published by the Camden-Rockport Historical Society is available at the CofC. Labor Day is Windjammer Weekend.

PHOTOS ON CD-ROM: 9

Navigational Information

Lat: 44°11.200' **Long:** 069°04.333' **Tide:** 9 ft. **Current:** n/a **Chart:** 13305
Rep. Depths (*MLW*): Entry 10 ft. **Fuel Dock** 10 ft. **Max Slip/Moor** 10 ft./65 ft.
Access: Penobscot Bay to the northeast end of Rockport Harbor

Marina Facilities *(In Season/Off Season)*

Fuel: Gasoline, Diesel
Slips: 5 Total, 5 Transient **Max LOA:** 100 ft. **Max Beam:** n/a
Rate *(per ft.)*: **Day** $1.75/Inq. **Week** Inq. **Month** Inq.
Power: 30 amp Incl., **50 amp** Incl., **100 amp** n/a, **200 amp** n/a
Cable TV: No **Dockside Phone:** No
Dock Type: Wood, Long Fingers, Short Fingers, Pilings, Floating
Moorings: 35 Total, 15 Transient **Launch:** n/a, Dinghy Dock
Rate: Day $20 **Week** n/a **Month** $400
Heads: 1 Toilet(s), 1 Shower(s)
Laundry: None **Pay Phones:** Yes, 1
Pump-Out: No **Fee:** n/a **Closed Heads:** No

Marina Operations

Owner/Manager: T. Allen/J. Gelsinger **Dockmaster:** E. Hurlburt/L. Dodge
In-Season: Jun-Sep, 8am-4pm **Off-Season:** May-Oct, 7am-3:30pm
After-Hours Arrival: Help yourself - settle up next morning
Reservations: Yes, Preferred **Credit Cards:** Visa/MC, Amex
Discounts: None
Pets: Welcome, Dog Walk Area **Handicap Access:** No

Rockport Marine

PO Box 203; 1 Main Street; Rockport, ME 04856

Tel: (207) 236-9651 **VHF: Monitor** n/a **Talk** n/a
Fax: (207) 236-0758 **Alternate Tel:** n/a
Email: rockport@tidewater.net **Web:** www.rockportmarine.com
Nearest Town: Rockport *(0 mi.)* **Tourist Info:** (207) 236-4404

Marina Services and Boat Supplies

Services - Docking Assistance, Dock Carts **Communication -** Mail & Package Hold, Phone Messages, Fax in/out, Data Ports *(Library)*, UPS, Express Mail **Supplies - OnSite:** Ice *(Block, Cube)* **Near:** Propane *(Pen-Bay Oil 236-2851)* **1-3 mi:** Ships' Store *(Camden or Rockland)*, CNG *(PG Willey 236-3256)*

Boatyard Services

OnSite: Travelift *(55T)*, Forklift, Crane, Engine mechanic *(gas, diesel)*, Electrical Repairs, Hull Repairs, Rigger, Bottom Cleaning, Brightwork, Divers, Woodworking, Metal Fabrication, Painting, Yacht Building, Total Refits **OnCall:** Refrigeration **Near:** Launching Ramp. **Under 1 mi:** Sail Loft. **1-3 mi:** Yacht Broker. **Member:** ABBRA **Yard Rates:** $42-44/hr., Haul & Launch $5/ft., Power Wash $25-40, Bottom Paint Hourly **Storage:** On-Land In $4/sq.ft./mo. Out $2/sq.ft. wood only

Restaurants and Accommodations

OnCall: Pizzeria *(Dominos 236-6212)* **Near:** Lite Fare *(Rockport Corner Shop B $3-6, L $3-7)*, Motel *(Seven Mountains 236-3276)* **Under 1 mi:** Restaurant *(The Helm 236-4337)*, *(Lotus Chinese 236-2133, L $5-7, D $7-16)*, Coffee Shop *(Cedar Crest 236-7722)* **1-3 mi:** Restaurant *(Marquis D $20-27)*, *(Ingraham's 236-3227, L $7-14, D $16-24, Sun Brunch $7-13)*, Motel *(Cedar Crest 236-4839, $75-135)*, *(Best Western Camden River House 236-0500, $100-210)*, Inn/B&B *(Lord Camden 236-4325, $90-$210)*

Recreation and Entertainment

Near: Park, Cultural Attract *(Bay Chamber Concerts)* **Under 1 mi:** Picnic Area, Playground, Museum **1-3 mi:** Heated Pool *(YMCA 236-3375 Union St., Camden line $8/4 day)*, Golf Course *(Goose River 236-8488)*, Fitness Center *(YMCA)*, Boat Rentals *(Maine Sport 800-722-0826 kayaks $50/day, canoes $35/day)*, Bowling *(Oakland Park 594-7525)*, Movie Theater *(Bay View St. 236-8722)*, Video Rental *(Harbor Video 236-9596)*

Provisioning and General Services

Near: Delicatessen, Lobster Pound, Post Office, Library *(236-3642)* **Under 1 mi:** Convenience Store, Supermarket *(Graves' 236-8577)*, Gourmet Shop *(Market Basket 236-4371)*, Bakery *(Sweet Sensations 230-0955)*, Bank/ATM, Florist **1-3 mi:** Health Food *(Nature's Choice 236-8280)*, Wine/Beer *(Camden Deli 236-8343)*, Liquor Store *(Rite Aid 236-4546)*, Farmers' Market, Catholic Church, Protestant Church, Beauty Salon, Dry Cleaners, Laundry, Bookstore, Pharmacy *(Camden Drug 236-2250)*, Newsstand, Hardware Store *(Rankins 236-3275)*, Copies Etc. *(Elm St. Printing 236-2896)* **3+ mi:** Department Store *(Wal-Mart, 4 mi.)*

Transportation

OnCall: Rental Car *(Enterprise 594-9093, Smith's 236- 2320)*, Taxi *(Don's 236-4762)*, Airport Limo *(Mid-Coast Limousine 236-2424)* **Near:** Water Taxi *(Wildwood 236-6951)* **Under 1 mi:** InterCity Bus *(Concord-Trailways)* **1-3 mi:** Bikes *(Maine Sport Outfitters $15/day 800-722-0826)* **3+ mi:** Ferry Service *(North Haven, Vinalhaven, Islesboro, 5 mi.)* **Airport:** Knox County/Bangor Int'l. *(5 mi./46 mi.)*

Medical Services

911 Service **OnCall:** Ambulance **Near:** Doctor *(Schetky 236-6588)* **1-3 mi:** Dentist *(Zanca 236-4356)*, Chiropractor *(Rockport Family 236-8486)*, Holistic Services **Hospital:** Penobscot Bay 596-8000 *(2 mi.)*

Setting -- Situated at the head of one of the sweetest and most protected working harbors in Maine, Rockport Marine is home to a spectacular collection of classic boats. It is surrounded by lovely homes and beautiful parks, with the Camden Hills in the background. There is a cluster of shops "downtown": galleries, antiques, specialty foods; but most services and supplies are about a mile away - out on Route One - or two miles away in Camden.

Marina Notes -- Known for building and restoring fine wooden yachts, this family-owned business has been open since 1962. The onsite Sail Loft restaurant is closed and has not been replaced (as yet). Moorings ($20 a night) and Marine Park docks ($1.00/ft) without utilities are also available from the Harbormaster 236-0676. Dinghy landings at the Town Dock at the head of the Harbor, at Marine Park on the western side, and onsite at Rockport Marine.

Notable -- Drawn by the natural light and the varied weather conditions, the renowned Maine Photographic Workshop, located here and at a nearby campus, offers professional courses on video, film, photography and digital media. Its store, Resources, overlooks the harbor. Maine Coast Artists' Gallery (236-2875) exhibits contemporary Maine artwork. In nearby Marine Park, there's a statue of André the Seal - for 25 years Rockport's Assistant Harbormaster. A children's book tells his story: "A Seal Called André: The Two Worlds of a Maine Harbor Seal" by Harry Goodridge (former Rockport Harbormaster who trained André) & Lew Dietz. A 1994 Film "André" is also available on video. Marine Park is also home to 3 restored turn of the century lime kilns and the steam locomotive that hauled limestone from the quarries. Picturesque 70-foot windjammer Timberwind moors in the harbor.

PHOTOS ON CD-ROM: 9

Rockland Harbor Boatyard

119 Front Street; Rockland, ME 04841

Tel: (207) 594-1766 **VHF: Monitor** 16 **Talk** 9
Fax: (207) 594-4337 **Alternate Tel:** (207) 785-4975
Email: info@rhby.com **Web:** www.rhby.com
Nearest Town: Rockland *(0.5 mi.)* **Tourist Info:** (207) 596-0376

Navigational Information

Lat: 44°06.718' **Long:** 069°06.239' **Tide:** 9 ft. **Current:** 0.25 kt. **Chart:** 1330
Rep. Depths (*MLW*): Entry 14 ft. **Fuel Dock** 12 ft. **Max Slip/Moor** -/12 ft.
Access: Penobscot Bay to Rockland Lighthouse, 315 deg. to North Channel

Marina Facilities *(In Season/Off Season)*

Fuel: No
Slips: 0 Total, 0 Transient **Max LOA:** 50 ft. **Max Beam:** n/a
Rate *(per ft.)*: **Day** n/a **Week** n/a **Month** n/a
Power: 30 amp free, **50 amp** n/a, **100 amp** n/a, **200 amp** n/a
Cable TV: No **Dockside Phone:** No
Dock Type: Wood, Floating
Moorings: 40 Total, 10 Transient **Launch:** n/a, Dinghy Dock
Rate: Day $30-45* **Week** $100-155 **Month** Inq.
Heads: 1 Toilet(s)
Laundry: None **Pay Phones:** No
Pump-Out: OnSite, Self Service, 1 Port **Fee:** n/a **Closed Heads:** No

Marina Operations

Owner/Manager: Sam Slaymaker **Dockmaster:** Same
In-Season: Year-Round, 8am-5pm **Off-Season:** n/a, 8am-5pm
After-Hours Arrival: Wait 'til morning to pay for mooring
Reservations: Yes, Preferred **Credit Cards:** Cash and check
Discounts: None
Pets: Welcome, Dog Walk Area **Handicap Access:** No

Marina Services and Boat Supplies

Services - Docking Assistance, Dock Carts **Communication -** Mail & Package Hold, Phone Messages, Fax in/out *(free)*, Data Ports *(Office)*, FedEx, AirBorne, UPS, Express Mail **Supplies - OnCall:** Propane, CNG **Near:** Ice *(Block, Cube)*, Ships' Store **Under 1 mi:** Marine Discount Store *(Rockland Boat 594-8181)*

Boatyard Services

OnSite: Travelift *(15T)*, Engine mechanic *(gas, diesel)*, Launching Ramp, Electrical Repairs, Electronic Sales, Electronics Repairs, Hull Repairs, Rigger, Bottom Cleaning, Brightwork, Divers, Compound, Wash & Wax, Interior Cleaning, Propeller Repairs, Woodworking, Inflatable Repairs, Metal Fabrication, Awlgrip, Yacht Design, Yacht Broker **OnCall:** Air Conditioning, Refrigeration, Upholstery **Dealer for:** Beta Marine Diesels. **Yard Rates:** $48/hr., Haul & Launch $4/ft. *(blocking $4/ft.)*, Power Wash $1/ft **Storage:** On-Land $20/ft., Inside $45/ft.

Restaurants and Accommodations

OnCall: Pizzeria *(Snappy's 594-7774)* **Near:** Restaurant *(Thai Kitchen L $8-14, D $8-14)*, Coffee Shop *(Hole in the Wall Bagel L $2-7)*, Motel *(Navigator Motor Inn 594-2131, $55-115)*, Inn/B&B *(Capt. Lindsey House Inn 596-7950, $65-175)* **Under 1 mi:** Restaurant *(Rockland Café 596-7556, L $5-9, D $8-20)*, *(Rockland Landings 596-6573, L $7-11, D $13-25)*, *(Waterworks 596-2753)*, *(Samoset Breakwater D $17-22)*, *(Marcel's D $20-30)*, Motel *(Trade Winds 596-6661, $55-105)*

Recreation and Entertainment

Under 1 mi: Beach, Picnic Area, Playground, Dive Shop, Fitness Center *(Trade Winds)*, Jogging Paths, Boat Rentals, Video Rental *(Mainscreen Video 596-7875)*, Park, Museum *(Farnsworth 596-5789)*, Galleries **1-3 mi:** Golf Course *(Rockland Golf Club 594-9322)*

Provisioning and General Services

Near: Convenience Store, Supermarket *(Hannaford 594-2173, or Shaw's 594-8615, 1.5 mi. - boxes for pick-up - Fax order 594-9553 $10/1st $100, $1/each add'l $50)*, Liquor Store, Bakery *(Willow 596-0564 - 5-10am)*, Lobster Pound, Bank/ATM, Retail Shops **Under 1 mi:** Gourmet Shop, Delicatessen, Health Food, Wine/Beer *(Wine Seller 594-2621)*, Farmers' Market *(Thu 9am-Noon Harbor Park)*, Post Office, Catholic Church, Protestant Church, Synagogue, Library *(Rockland P.L. 596-7532)*, Beauty Salon, Barber Shop, Dry Cleaners, Laundry, Bookstore *(Reading Corner 596-6651; Second Reads 594-4123)*, Pharmacy *(Goodnows 594-5131)*, Newsstand, Hardware Store, Florist, Department Store *(JC Penney, KMart - 1.5 mi)*, Copies Etc. *(Gallery One 594-5441)*

Transportation

OnSite: Bikes *(complimentary)* **OnCall:** Water Taxi *(Two Toots $2.50/pp/1-way Ch.9, 594-2891)*, Rental Car *(Enterprise 594-9093)*, Taxi *(Schooner Bay 594-5000)*, Airport Limo *(Mid-Coast 236-2424)* **Near:** InterCity Bus *(Concord Trailways 800/639-3317)*, Ferry Service *(596-2202 NorthHaven, Vinalhaven, Matinicus)* **Airport:** Owls Head/Bangor Int'l. *(3 mi./52 mi.)*

Medical Services

911 Service **OnCall:** Ambulance **Near:** Chiropractor *(Smith Chiropractic Office 594-2224)* **Under 1 mi:** Dentist, Holistic Services *(Sanctuary)*
Hospital: Penobscot Bay Medical Center *(5 mi.)*

Setting -- This small, seemingly out of the way boatyard at the northern end of the harbor offers terrific views of the large, protected basin and unsuspected convenience. It's just north of the downtown, re-energized Historic District of Rockland. Restaurants, shops, galleries, services, a supermarket, transportation and several museums -- including the Farnsworth and Wyeth Center -- are within a mile.

Marina Notes -- *$30 up to 35 ft., $35 for 35-40 ft., $45 for over 45 ft. boats. Bring a dinghy. Sam and Larrain Slaymaker, the owners/operators of this small, service-oriented family facility, are very accommodating and always happy to help - take advantage of Sam Slaymaker's 20+ years experience as a Maine surveyor. Considering its size, the boatyard offers a surprisingly large array of marine services, specializing in traditional wood and cold molded boatbuilding and fine classic boat restorations. Large inside storage building. Installs block and helix moorings and is exclusive northeastern importer/dealer for Beta Kubota marine diesel auxiliaries.

Notable -- 4-mile Rockland Harbor Trail , which starts at the Samoset, passes here and runs south to Snow Marine Park. Throughout its history, Rockland has been the "Service Depot" for Western Penobscot Bay. It continues to fulfill that mission, but is now doing it with a style and panache that most would have thought impossible only a few years ago - just take a stroll down Main Street. Rockland is homeport to ferries and mailboats heading to the Islands. An enlightening stop is the Island Institute, 386 Main Street (594-9209), which works to preserve Maine's 14 year-round fragile island communities.

PHOTOS ON CD-ROM: 4

Navigational Information
Lat: 44°06.465' **Long:** 069°06.478' **Tide:** 10 ft. **Current:** n/a **Chart:** 13302
Rep. Depths (*MLW*): Entry 15 ft. **Fuel Dock** 11 ft. **Max Slip/Moor** 11 ft./20 ft.
Access: Western Penobscot Bay, past Owls Head to Rockland Harbor

Marina Facilities *(In Season/Off Season)*
Fuel: *Citgo* - Slip-Side Fueling, Gasoline, Diesel
Slips: 12 Total, 10 Transient **Max LOA:** 80 ft. **Max Beam:** n/a
Rate *(per ft.)*: **Day** $1.50/Inq. **Week** $1.50 **Month** $1.50
Power: 30 amp $5, **50 amp** n/a, **100 amp** n/a, **200 amp** n/a
Cable TV: No **Dockside Phone:** No
Dock Type: Wood, Long Fingers, Alongside
Moorings: 12 Total, 10 Transient **Launch:** None, Dinghy Dock
Rate: Day $15 **Week** $100 **Month** $400
Heads: 2 Toilet(s), 2 Shower(s)
Laundry: 4 Washer(s), 2 Dryer(s), Iron **Pay Phones:** No
Pump-Out: No **Fee:** n/a **Closed Heads:** No

Marina Operations
Owner/Manager: Horatio Knight **Dockmaster:** Same
In-Season: Year-Round, 8am-4pm **Off-Season:** n/a
After-Hours Arrival: Call ahead for instructions
Reservations: Yes **Credit Cards:** Visa/MC, Citgo
Discounts: None
Pets: Welcome **Handicap Access:** No

Knight Marine Service

PO Box 443; 525 Main Street; Rockland, ME 04841

Tel: (207) 594-4068 **VHF: Monitor** 16 **Talk** 9
Fax: (207) 594-4068 **Alternate Tel:** (207) 594-9700
Email: knightma@midcoast.com **Web:** www.midcoast.com/~knightma/
Nearest Town: Rockland *(0 mi.)* **Tourist Info:** (207) 596-0376

Marina Services and Boat Supplies
Communication - Mail & Package Hold, Fax in/out, Data Ports, FedEx, AirBorne, UPS, Express Mail *(Sat Del)* **Supplies - OnSite:** Ice *(Block, Cube)*, Ships' Store **Under 1 mi:** Marine Discount Store *(Rockland Boat 594-8181)*, Propane *(Harry French's Garage 594-9866)* **1-3 mi:** Bait/Tackle **3+ mi:** CNG *(Willey Wharf 236-3256, Camden, 8 mi.)*

Boatyard Services
OnSite: Travelift *(2 - 35T)*, Engine mechanic *(gas, diesel)*, Rigger, Bottom Cleaning, Brightwork, Compound, Wash & Wax, Interior Cleaning, Propeller Repairs, Woodworking, Upholstery, Yacht Interiors, Painting, Awlgrip, Total Refits **Near:** Electrical Repairs, Electronic Sales, Electronics Repairs. **Under 1 mi:** Air Conditioning, Refrigeration. **Yard Rates:** $40/hr., Haul & Launch $4/ft., Power Wash $60, Bottom Paint $40/hr. **Storage:** On-Land $208/ft.

Restaurants and Accommodations
OnSite: Snack Bar *(Capt. Hornblower)* **Near:** Restaurant *(Gator)*, Lite Fare *(Brown Bag 596-6372, B&L, also some catering)*, Pizzeria *(North End Sub & Pizza 596-5522)*, Motel *(Navigator 594-2131, $55-115)*, Inn/B&B *(Old Granite Inn 594-9036)* **Under 1 mi:** Restaurant *(Amalfi 596-0012, D $14-23)*, *(Waterworks 596-7950, L $4-9, D $8-15)*, *(Rockland Café 596-7556)*, Hotel *(Trade Winds 596-6661, $55-105)*, Inn/B&B *(Capt. Lindsey House 596-7950, $65-175)* **1-3 mi:** Restaurant *(Primo 596-0770, D $16-30, the best!! Take a cab)*, Fast Food, Hotel *(Samoset Resort 594-2511, $175-365)*

Recreation and Entertainment
Near: Jogging Paths, Video Rental *(Mainescreen 596-7875)*, Museum *(Farnsworth 596-5789)* **Under 1 mi:** Playground, Fitness Center *(Trade Winds)*, Boat Rentals *(Landings)*, Park **1-3 mi:** Beach *(Birch Point State Park)*, Tennis Courts *(Samoset Resort 594-2511)*, Golf Course *(Rockland G.C. 594-9322)*, Movie Theater

Provisioning and General Services
Near: Convenience Store *(Fuller's 594-9744)*, Bakery *(Willow 596-0564 - early am)*, Hardware Store *(Everett Spear 594-7024)*, Florist, Retail Shops, Copies Etc. *(Quepasa 594-6112)* **Under 1 mi:** Supermarket *(Hannaford 594-2173, Shaw's 594-8615 - shops & boxes for pick-up*)*, Gourmet Shop *(Market on Main 594-0015)*, Delicatessen, Health Food *(Good Tern 594-9286)*, Wine/Beer *(Wine Seller 594-2621)*, Liquor Store, Farmers' Market, Fishmonger, Bank/ATM, Post Office, Catholic Church, Protestant Church, Synagogue, Library, Beauty Salon, Barber Shop, Dry Cleaners, Laundry, Bookstore *(Second Reads 594-4123; Reading Corner 596-6651)*, Pharmacy *(Goodnows 594-5131)*

Transportation
OnSite: InterCity Bus *(Concord Trailways Portland, Logan, Boston)*, Ferry Service *(North Haven, Vinalhaven)* **OnCall:** Water Taxi *(Two Toots $2.50/pp/1-way Ch.9, 594-2891)*, Rental Car *(National 594-8424)*, Taxi *(Schooner Bay Limo & Taxi 594-5000)* **3+ mi:** Bikes *(Maine Sport 236-8797 will deliver, 4.5 mi.)* **Airport:** Knox County/Bangor Int'l. *(3 mi./52 mi.)*

Medical Services
911 Service **OnCall:** Ambulance **Near:** Doctor *(Boogusch 594-2609)*, Dentist, Chiropractor *(Bay Chiro 596-6700)*, Holistic Services *(Sanctuary Spa 594-8403)* **Hospital:** Penobscot Bay 596-8000 *(4.5 mi.)*

Setting -- After you pass Rockland Harbor's 7/8 mile granite breakwater, Knight's is on the northern channel -- just past the ferry dock. In fact, it practically shares a dock with the Vinalhaven/North Haven ferries in Lermond's Cove. Located on Main Street, all of Rockland's amenities are a quick walk away. Shops, restaurants, galleries are housed in restored Greek Revival, Colonial, Italianate structures. And, for Wyeth fans, Rockland approaches Nirvana.

Marina Notes -- In business for forty years, Knight Marine has a history of its own. Service focuses on commercial, as well as recreational vessels, so the atmosphere is that of a working yard -- an impeccably maintained working yard. Electricity and water are $5 each. Parking $5 per day. The heads are located in the work area of the main storage shed. Stores over 100 boats in the winter. Knight's workboat, Celia, is so lovingly tended she looks like a picture.

Notable -- More than ten restaurants are within a half-mile radius. The 4 mi. Harbor Trail passes the door. The Lobster Festival's the first week in August and the N.A. Blues Festival and Schooner Days are in late July. Two Toots Water Taxi Ch.9 will transport you around the harbor, $2.50/pp/1-way. Rockland hosts more windjammers than any other port in the East. Walk to the Farnsworth Art Museum and the Wyeth Center, open daily 9am-5pm during the season $9/free. Transportation can be arranged to the Owls Head Transportation Museum - kids love it $6/4. Ferries to North Haven, Vinalhaven and Matinicus $9 RT. www.state.me/us/mdot/opt/ferry/ferry.htm. Harbor Park Farmers' Market Thursday 9am-noon. *Shaw's offers a grocery service: fax order to 594-9553 by 11am with phone & credit card numbers. For $10/1st $100, $1/each add'l $50 they'll shop, box and call you so you can send a taxi to pick-up.

PHOTOS ON CD-ROM: 9

Beggar's Wharf

Beggar's Wharf

9 Wharf Street; Rockland, ME 04841

Tel: (207) 594-8500 **VHF: Monitor** 9, 16 **Talk** 10
Fax: (207) 236-2772 **Alternate Tel:** n/a
Email: moorings@beggarswharf.com **Web:** www.beggarswharf.com
Nearest Town: Rockland **Tourist Info:** (207) 596-0376

Navigational Information

Lat: 44°06.330' **Long:** 069°06.185' **Tide:** 10 ft. **Current:** n/a **Chart:** 13302
Rep. Depths (*MLW*): Entry 12 ft. **Fuel Dock** n/a **Max Slip/Moor** 4 ft./12 ft.
Access: Penobscot Bay, past lighthouse into north channel to G3

Marina Facilities *(In Season/Off Season)*

Fuel: No
Slips: 8 Total, 4 Transient **Max LOA:** 50 ft. **Max Beam:** n/a
Rate *(per ft.)*: **Day** n/a **Week** n/a **Month** n/a
Power: 30 amp n/a, **50 amp** n/a, **100 amp** n/a, **200 amp** n/a
Cable TV: No **Dockside Phone:** No
Dock Type: Short Fingers, Pilings, Floating
Moorings: 40 Total, 35 Transient **Launch:** None, Dinghy Dock ($5)
Rate: Day $30/20 **Week** $150 **Month** $360/150
Heads: 4 Toilet(s), 4 Shower(s)
Laundry: None **Pay Phones:** No
Pump-Out: No **Fee:** n/a **Closed Heads:** No

Marina Operations

Owner/Manager: Charlie Weidman **Dockmaster:** Same
In-Season: Jun 1-Sep 30, 7am-7pm **Off-Season:** Oct 1-May 31, 8am-5pm
After-Hours Arrival: Call for instructions
Reservations: Yes **Credit Cards:** Visa/MC
Discounts: None
Pets: Welcome **Handicap Access:** No

Marina Services and Boat Supplies

Services - Docking Assistance, Concierge, Room Service to the Boat, Trash Pick-Up **Communication -** Mail & Package Hold, Data Ports *(Office)* **Supplies - OnSite:** Ice *(Block, Cube)* **Near:** Ships' Store, Marine Discount Store *(Rockland Boat 594-8181)* **Under 1 mi:** Propane *(Coastal Fuel 594-2268)*

Boatyard Services

OnSite: Bottom Cleaning, Divers **Near:** Travelift, Engine mechanic *(gas, diesel)*, Electrical Repairs, Electronic Sales *(Lew Grant 594-7073, Ocean Pursuits 596-7357)*, Electronics Repairs, Hull Repairs, Rigger *(Pope 596-7293)*, Sail Loft, Canvas Work, Refrigeration, Propeller Repairs. **Under 1 mi:** Launching Ramp. **Nearest Yard:** Journey's End (207) 594-4444

Restaurants and Accommodations

OnCall: Pizzeria *(Dominos 594-9494)* **Near:** Restaurant *(Café Miranda 594-2034, L $3-17, D $11-20), (Black Pearl), (Oceanside Seafood & Steakhouse 594-4583), (Thai Kitchen L $8-14, D $8-14)*, Snack Bar *(Wassa's Hot Dogs & Ice Cream L $1.50-2)*, Lite Fare *(Brown Bag 596-6372, B $4-7, L $4-7)*, Motel *(Navigator 594-2131, $70-110), (Trade Winds 596-6661)*, Inn/B&B *(Capt Lindsey House 596-7950, $65-175), (Lathrop House 594-5771), (Old Granite Inn 594-9036)* **Under 1 mi:** Restaurant *(Park Street Grille 594-4944)* **1-3 mi:** Restaurant *(Primo 596-0770, D $16-30)*

Recreation and Entertainment

Near: Dive Shop, Fitness Center *(Trade Winds - 1/Day $7-20)*, Jogging Paths, Roller Blade/Bike Paths, Video Rental *(Mainescreen 596-7875)*, Museum *(Farnsworth)*, Cultural Attract *(Atlantic Challenge Foundation youth program teaches wooden boatbuilding; inquire about visiting)* **Under 1 mi:** Beach, Playground, Bowling, Special Events *(Lobster Festival - Early Aug, Folk/Blues Festival - Mid July)* **1-3 mi:** Tennis Courts, Golf Course, Movie Theater *(Bay View St. Cinema 236-8722)*

Provisioning and General Services

Near: Provisioning Service, Delicatessen, Wine/Beer *(Wine Seller 594-2621)*, Bank/ATM, Post Office, Library, Barber Shop, Bookstore *(Reading Corner 596-6651; Second Reads 594-4123)*, Pharmacy *(Rite Aid 596-0036)*, Newsstand, Florist, Retail Shops **Under 1 mi:** Supermarket *(Hannaford 594-2173, Shaw's 594-8615 2 mi. fax order & send taxi)*, Health Food *(Good Tern Co-op 594-9286)*, Bakery *(Brown Bag, Willow 596-0564)*, Farmers' Market *(Harbor Park Thu 9am-Noon)*, Fishmonger, Lobster Pound, Catholic Church, Protestant Church, Synagogue, Beauty Salon, Dry Cleaners, Laundry, Hardware Store *(True Value 594-5505)*, Copies Etc. *(Mail Boxes 594-4200)* **1-3 mi:** Liquor Store, Meat Market, Department Store *(JC Penney, Wal-Mart)*

Transportation

OnCall: Water Taxi *(Two Toots Ch.9, 594-2891)*, Rental Car *(Enterprise 594-9093)*, Taxi *(Schooner Bay 594-5000)* **Near:** InterCity Bus *(Concord Trailways 596-6605)* **Under 1 mi:** Ferry Service *(Vinalhaven, No. Haven Ferries)* **Airport:** Knox County/Bangor Int'l. *(3 mi./52 mi.)*

Medical Services

911 Service **Near:** Chiropractor *(Bay 596-6700)*, Holistic Services *(Sanctuary)* **1-3 mi:** Doctor, Dentist, Veterinarian *(Rockland Animal 594-5850)* **Hospital:** Penobscot Bay 596-8000 *(4.5 mi.)*

Setting -- The two Beggar's Wharf mooring fields are on either side of the north channel, just past Journey's End in the vicinity of G3. The landside facility consists of a dock and several as yet unrestored historic wharf buildings. It is located on the largely commercial Tillson Wharf peninsula, dominated by the Coast Guard station and a large seaweed processing plant, that T-bones to the center of town.

Marina Notes -- The newest addition to the Rockland Harbor scene, Beggar's Wharf was launched in 2001, with the goal of providing concierge-like services. It is on the site of the old Rockland Boat Co. property on Wharf Place (Rockland Boat is now at 20 Park Drive). The 3-story building, and its 3 companion structures, sit on a half-acre with 100 feet on the harbor. Docks are re-purposed salmon pens. Scheduled for 2003 is a new bathhouse with a total of 6 toilets and 4 showers. Future plans include launch service, extending the dock another 130 feet, to include 8 slips, and adding more moorings (stay tuned). This is also home to Charlie's Mooring and Dive Services; Charlie Weidman is occasionally in the news for raising and retrieving cars, boats, and wrecks from the harbor and the quarry. Rating is based on current state and will be revised as facilities increase. Check their website, and ACC's, for an update.

Notable -- Beggar's Wharf is very convenient to the gas-lighted Historic District and downtown shops, services and museums. It's just about 0.2 miles off the peninsula to Main Street. It's also in the middle of the Rockland Harbor Trail, a 4 mile public footpath that connects the major waterfront points of interest including Snow Marine Park, Harbor Park, North End wharves, Marie H. Reed Memorial Park, and the 8/10th mile walk to the Breakwater Lighthouse.

Journey's End Marina

Navigational Information
Lat: 44°06.300' **Long:** 069°06.165' **Tide:** 11 ft. **Current:** n/a **Chart:** 13302
Rep. Depths (*MLW*): Entry 15 ft. **Fuel Dock** 10 ft. **Max Slip/Moor** 15 ft./20 ft.
Access: Main channel - marina is on both sides of US Coast Guard station

Marina Facilities *(In Season/Off Season)*
Fuel: *Texaco* - Gasoline, Diesel, High-Speed Pumps
Slips: 70 Total, 8 Transient **Max LOA:** 150 ft. **Max Beam:** n/a
Rate *(per ft.)*: **Day** $1.50/Inq.* **Week** Inq. **Month** Inq.
Power: 30 amp Incl., **50 amp** Incl., **100 amp** n/a, **200 amp** n/a
Cable TV: No **Dockside Phone:** No
Dock Type: Wood, Concrete, Floating
Moorings: 5 Total, 2 Transient **Launch:** None
Rate: Day $20 **Week** $100 **Month** $300
Heads: 6 Toilet(s), 6 Shower(s)
Laundry: None **Pay Phones:** Yes, 1
Pump-Out: OnSite, Self Service, 1 Central **Fee:** $5 **Closed Heads:** No

Marina Operations
Owner/Manager: Scott Donnelly/Stacey Palmer **Dockmaster:** S. Palmer
In-Season: Jul-Sep, 7am-5pm **Off-Season:** Sep-Jul, 8am-5pm
After-Hours Arrival: Call ahead for directions and instructions
Reservations: Preferred **Credit Cards:** Visa/MC, Dscvr
Discounts: Yes **Dockage:** n/a **Fuel:** Vol **Repair:** n/a
Pets: Welcome **Handicap Access:** No

Journey's End Marina
120 Tillson Avenue; Rockland, ME 04841

Tel: (207) 594-4444 **VHF: Monitor** 9 **Talk** 18
Fax: (207) 594-0407 **Alternate Tel:** n/a
Email: oharajem@midcoast.com **Web:** n/a
Nearest Town: Rockland *(0 mi.)* **Tourist Info:** (207) 596-0376

Marina Services and Boat Supplies
Services - Docking Assistance, Security *(Cameras)*, Dock Carts, Megayacht Facilities **Communication -** Mail & Package Hold, Fax in/out *($1.50)*, Data Ports *(Office)* **Supplies - OnSite:** Ice *(Block, Cube)*, Ships' Store **Near:** Marine Discount Store *(Rockland Boat 594-8181)* **1-3 mi:** Propane *(Coastal Fuel 594-2268)* **3+ mi:** CNG *(PG Willey Camden 236-3256, 8 mi.)*

Boatyard Services
OnSite: Travelift *(50T)*, Railway *(2 - 750T & 1200T)*, Forklift *(2 - 30T)*, Crane *(15T)*, Engine mechanic *(gas, diesel)*, Electrical Repairs, Electronic Sales, Electronics Repairs, Hull Repairs, Rigger, Bottom Cleaning, Brightwork, Air Conditioning, Refrigeration, Compound, Wash & Wax, Woodworking, Inflatable Repairs, Metal Fabrication, Painting, Awlgrip, Total Refits **OnCall:** Sail Loft, Divers, Interior Cleaning, Propeller Repairs **Near:** Upholstery. **Under 1 mi:** Launching Ramp. **Dealer for:** Prop Protectors; Yanmar Engines. **Member:** ABBRA **Yard Rates:** $50/hr., Haul & Launch $7.50-8.50/ft., Power Wash $45/hr., Bottom Paint $14/ft. *(paint included)* **Storage:** On-Land $42-64/ft. winter

Restaurants and Accommodations
OnCall: Pizzeria *(Dominos 594-9494)* **Near:** Restaurant *(Amalfi 596-0012, L $3-15, D $14-21)*, *(Café Miranda 594-2034, L $3-17, D $11-20)*, *(Rockland Café 596-7556, L $2-14, D $10-19)*, *(Rockland Landings 596-6573)*, Inn/B&B *(Capt. Lindsey House Inn 596-7950, $65-175)* **Under 1 mi:** Snack Bar *(Hole in the Wall Bagel 594-3600, B $2-8, L $2-8)*, Hotel *(Samoset Resort 594-2511, $195-265)* **1-3 mi:** Restaurant *(Primo 596-0770, D $16-30, One of the best in the Northeast)*, Fast Food

Recreation and Entertainment
OnSite: Boat Rentals **Near:** Picnic Area, Dive Shop, Fitness Center *(Trade Winds)*, Jogging Paths, Video Rental *(Mainescreen 596-7875)*, Museum *(Farnsworth Museum, Owls Head Transportation Museum)*, Special Events *(Lobster Fest early Aug, Folk/Blues Fest Mid July)*, Galleries **Under 1 mi:** Beach, Park **1-3 mi:** Tennis Courts, Golf Course *(Rockland Golf Club 594-9322, Samoset Resort 594-2511)*, Movie Theater *(Bay View St. 236-8722)*

Provisioning and General Services
OnSite: Lobster Pound **OnCall:** Convenience Store **Near:** Gourmet Shop, Delicatessen, Health Food *(Good Tern 594-9286)*, Wine/Beer *(Wine Seller 594-2621)*, Bakery *(Brown Bag, Willow 596-0564)*, Bank/ATM, Bookstore *(Second Reads 594-4123)*, Pharmacy *(Rite Aid 596-0036)*, Newsstand, Hardware Store *(Handle It 594-5333)*, Florist, Retail Shops, Copies Etc. *(Mail Boxes 594-4200)* **Under 1 mi:** Supermarket *(Hannaford 594-2173, Shaw's 594-8615, 2 mi., shopping service*)*, Liquor Store, Farmers' Market *(Harbor Park 9-12)*, Fishmonger, Meat Market, Post Office, Protestant Church, Library, Beauty Salon, Barber Shop, Dry Cleaners, Laundry **1-3 mi:** Catholic Church, Synagogue, Department Store *(Wal-Mart, JC Penney)*

Transportation
OnCall: Water Taxi *(Two Toots Ch.9)*, Rental Car *(Enterprise 594-9093)*, Taxi *(Schooner Bay 594-5000)* **Under 1 mi:** InterCity Bus *(Trailways 596-6605)*, Ferry Service **Airport:** Knox/Bangor Int'l. *(3 mi./52 mi.)*

Medical Services
911 Service **OnSite:** Chiropractor **1-3 mi:** Doctor, Dentist **Hospital:** Pen Bay 596-8000 *(5 mi.)*

Setting -- This working harbor's main channel heads straight for Journey's End, one of the largest and most extensive operations in Mid-Coast Maine. This neat and tidy marina is divided into North and South docks, on either side of very commercial Tillson Avenue wharf and the Coast Guard station. The vibrant, re-energized Rockland downtown is a few blocks away with restaurants, museums, shops, and galleries.

Marina Notes -- * $1.50/ft. under 45', $2.00 over 45'. Once a fish factory, Journey's End is owned and run by the O'Hara Family. Extensive boatyard services and indoor winter storage. The office is in the northern yard - right off the Coast Guard Station -- and the deepest slips are at the southern yard. Be sure to get a map of the marina when you arrive; getting lost would be easy. There are showers inside the office, $2 each, but not after 5pm Mon-Sat, or 3:30pm on Sun. Welcomes cruising clubs - especially mid-week. Large-volume fuel discounts for mega-yachts. Home of Bay Island Sail Maine.

Notable -- The 4-mile Rockland Harbor Trail runs from the Samoset Resort and the North End wharves south to Snow Marine Park. The 5-day Lobster Festival happens every year in early Aug; the three-day Schooner Days and Folk/Blues Festival is the weekend after July 4th. There are many galleries, antique shops, and museums (Farnsworth and Wyeth Center and Shore Village Lighthouse Museum) within walking distance. Pick up an "Arts Walking Tour" map from the CofC. Many schooners make their home here. *Shaw's Supermarket will shop & box your order for pick-up. Fax order, phone and credit card numbers to 594-9553 by 11am. They'll call when ready; you send a taxi for pick-up. Fee: $10/1st $100, $1/each add'l $50. Food kept chilled until pick-up (Judy Robinson).

PHOTOS ON CD-ROM: 8

Rockland Landings Marina

PO Box 1086; 1 Commercial Street; Rockland, ME 04841

Tel: (207) 596-6573 **VHF: Monitor** 9 **Talk** n/a
Fax: (207) 594-4899 **Alternate Tel:** (207) 596-6563
Email: n/a **Web:** n/a
Nearest Town: Rockland *(0 mi.)* **Tourist Info:** (207) 596-0376

Navigational Information

Lat: 44°06.116' **Long:** 069°06.428' **Tide:** 10 ft. **Current:** n/a **Chart:** 13302
Rep. Depths (*MLW*): Entry 12 ft. **Fuel Dock** 10 ft. **Max Slip/Moor** 10 ft./40 ft.
Access: Penobscot Bay to Owls Head past breakwater to South Channel

Marina Facilities *(In Season/Off Season)*

Fuel: Slip-Side Fueling, Gasoline, Diesel
Slips: 70 Total, 25 Transient **Max LOA:** 150 ft. **Max Beam:** n/a
Rate *(per ft.)*: **Day** $2.00/Inq.* **Week** Inq. **Month** Inq.
Power: 30 amp $8, **50 amp** $8+, **100 amp** n/a, **200 amp** n/a
Cable TV: No **Dockside Phone:** Yes
Dock Type: Wood, Floating
Moorings: 8 Total, 6 Transient **Launch:** n/a, Dinghy Dock
Rate: Day $20 **Week** n/a **Month** n/a
Heads: 2 Toilet(s), 4 Shower(s) *(with dressing rooms)*
Laundry: 2 Washer(s), 2 Dryer(s) **Pay Phones:** Yes
Pump-Out: OnSite, Self Service **Fee:** n/a **Closed Heads:** No

Marina Operations

Owner/Manager: Kevin Taylor **Dockmaster:** Jason McKnight
In-Season: May 15-Oct 15, 7am-6pm **Off-Season:** n/a
After-Hours Arrival: Call marina on Ch. 9 or 16
Reservations: Yes, 50% deposit **Credit Cards:** Visa/MC, Dscvr, Amex
Discounts: None
Pets: Welcome, Dog Walk Area **Handicap Access:** Yes, Heads, Docks

Marina Services and Boat Supplies

Services - Docking Assistance, Concierge, Security *(11 Hrs.)*, Dock Carts, Megayacht Facilities **Communication -** Mail & Package Hold, FedEx, AirBorne, UPS, Express Mail *(Sat Del)* **Supplies - OnSite:** Ice *(Block, Cube)* **Near:** Ships' Store, Marine Discount Store *(Rockland Boat 594-8181)*, Bait/Tackle **Under 1 mi:** Propane *(Coastal Fuel)* **3+ mi:** CNG *(Willey's Wharf 236-3256, Camden, 6 mi.)*

Boatyard Services

Near: Travelift, Railway, Forklift, Engine mechanic *(gas, diesel)*, Launching Ramp, Electrical Repairs, Electronic Sales, Electronics Repairs, Hull Repairs, Rigger, Sail Loft, Bottom Cleaning, Brightwork, Air Conditioning, Refrigeration, Divers *(Charlie Weidman-596-dive)*, Compound, Wash & Wax, Interior Cleaning, Propeller Repairs, Woodworking, Inflatable Repairs, Upholstery *(Gemini Marine 596-7705)*, Yacht Interiors *(Gemini)*, Metal Fabrication, Painting, Awlgrip, Yacht Design, Yacht Building, Total Refits.
Nearest Yard: Journey's End (207) 594-4444

Restaurants and Accommodations

OnSite: Restaurant *(Landing's Restaurant L $6-19, D $7-25)* **OnCall:** Pizzeria *(Dominos 594-9494)* **Near:** Restaurant *(Amalfi 596-0012, L $3-15, D $14-21)*, *(Black Pearl re-opened '02)*, *(Waterworks 596-2753, L $4-9, D $8-15)*, *(Trade Winds Oceanside)*, Lite Fare *(Brown Bag B $4-7, L $4-7)*, Motel *(Trade Winds 596-6661, $55-105)*, *(Navigator 594-2131, $55-115)*, Inn/B&B *(Capt. Lindsey House Inn 596-7950, $65-175)* **Under 1 mi:** Inn/B&B *(Berry Manor Inn 596-7696, $80-240)* **1-3 mi:** Restaurant *(Primo 596-0770, D $16-30, for celebrations; advance reservations critical)*

Recreation and Entertainment

OnSite: Boat Rentals **Near:** Dive Shop *(Rockland Boat)*, Fitness Center *(Trade Winds $7-20/day)*, Movie Theater *(Strand Cinema 594-7266)*, Video Rental *(Mainescreen Video 596-7875)*, Park, Museum, Sightseeing **Under 1 mi:** Playground *(MBNA Ocean St.)* **1-3 mi:** Beach *(Birch Point State Park)*, Tennis Courts *(Samoset Resort 594-2511)*, Golf Course *(Samoset)*

Provisioning and General Services

Near: Convenience Store, Gourmet Shop, Delicatessen, Health Food *(Good Tern 594-9286)*, Wine/Beer *(Wine Seller 594-2621)*, Bakery *(Brown Bag, Willow 596-0564)*, Farmers' Market *(Harbor Park Thu 9am-1pm)*, Bank/ATM, Post Office, Catholic Church, Library, Beauty Salon, Barber Shop, Dry Cleaners, Laundry, Bookstore *(Second Reads 594-4123; Reading Corner 596-6651)*, Pharmacy, Newsstand, Clothing Store, Department Store, Copies Etc. *(Lakeside 594-5216)* **Under 1 mi:** Fishmonger, Lobster Pound, Hardware Store, Florist, Retail Shops **1-3 mi:** Supermarket *(Hannaford 594-2173, Shaw's 594-8615 shopping service*)*

Transportation

OnCall: Water Taxi *(Two Toots $2.50/pp/1-way Ch.9, 594-2891)*, Taxi *(Schooner Bay Limo & Taxi 594-5000)* **Near:** Rental Car *(Budget 594-8424, National)*, InterCity Bus **Under 1 mi:** Ferry Service *(Vinalhaven, Matinicus)*
Airport: Knox/Bangor Int'l. *(3 mi./52 mi.)*

Medical Services

911 Service **OnCall:** Ambulance **Near:** Doctor, Chiropractor, Holistic Services *(Sanctuary Day Spa 594-8403)* **1-3 mi:** Dentist **Hospital:** Penobscot Bay Medical Center 596-8000 *(5 mi.)*

Setting -- The first transient facility on the South Channel, well past the Coast Guard Station (but before the Public Landing), this well maintained marina offers beautiful views of the Harbor and the Bay beyond, and includes an onsite restaurant as an added bonus. Just a short walk to bustling, downtown, historic Rockland, which is the commercial and banking center of the region, as well as the supply center for the whole bay.

Marina Notes -- *$2.00 up to 46 ft., $2.25 to 75 ft., $2.50 over 75 ft. Newly renovated heads, showers, and laundry facilities are a short walk up past the restaurant. Reservations require a 50% non-refundable deposit. Marina provides assistance with numerous services for your boat. The Landings Restaurant offers a full menu for eat-in or take-out, featuring a wide range of seafood entrées plus salads, sandwiches and lite fare -- an attractive indoor dining room and an outdoor dining deck overlook the marina. On the 2nd floor, a very nice function room with deck has views of the harbor and accommodates about 60.

Notable -- Home to Breakwater Kayak 596-6895 which offers a variety of tours, including a 3 hr. lighthouse tour, $60. Check out the North Atlantic Blues Festival and Rockland Lobster Festival. Rockland offers plenty of shops, galleries, eateries and activities. Rockland is home to the Farnsworth Museum and the Wyeth Center which houses one of the finest collections of Wyeth artwork anywhere. Owls Head Transportation Museum 594-4418 is 3 mi. from town. Birthplace of Edna St. Vincent Millay (although she grew up in Camden). Rockland boasts the largest fleet of windjammers in the East. *Shaw's will shop & box your order for pick-up. Fax order, phone and credit card numbers to 594-9553 by 11am. Send taxi to pick-up. Fee: $10/1st $100, $1/each add'l $50.

ME - MIDCOAST

PHOTOS ON CD-ROM: 9

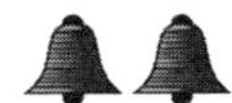

Navigational Information

Lat: 44°06.036' **Long:** 069°06.438' **Tide:** 11 ft. **Current:** .5 kt. **Chart:** 13307
Rep. Depths (*MLW*): Entry 14 ft. **Fuel Dock** n/a **Max Slip/Moor** 10 ft./-
Access: Penobscot Bay to Rockland Harbor to end of South Channel

Marina Facilities *(In Season/Off Season)*

Fuel: No
Slips: 15 Total, 15 Transient **Max LOA:** 120 ft. **Max Beam:** 20 ft.
Rate *(per ft.)*: **Day** $1.00/Inq. **Week** Inq. **Month** Inq.
Power: 30 amp $0.50/ft, **50 amp** $0.50/ft, **100 amp** n/a, **200 amp** n/a
Cable TV: No **Dockside Phone:** No
Dock Type: Wood, Floating
Moorings: 20 Total, 20 Transient **Launch:** n/a, Dinghy Dock ($5/night)
Rate: Day $20 **Week** $100 **Month** n/a
Heads: 2 Toilet(s), 2 Shower(s) *(with dressing rooms)*
Laundry: 1 Washer(s), 1 Dryer(s), Book Exchange **Pay Phones:** Yes, 2
Pump-Out: OnSite, Full Service, 1 Central **Fee:** n/a **Closed Heads:** No

Marina Operations

Owner/Manager: Jon Trumble (Harbormaster) **Dockmaster:** Pete Thibodeau
In-Season: May 15-Oct 15, 8am-5pm* **Off-Season:** n/a
After-Hours Arrival: n/a
Reservations: No. First come, first served **Credit Cards:** Visa/MC
Discounts: None
Pets: Welcome, Dog Walk Area **Handicap Access:** Yes, Heads

Rockland Public Landing

Harbor Park, Main Street; Rockland, ME 04841

Tel: (207) 594-0312 **VHF: Monitor** 9 **Talk** 11
Fax: (207) 596-6549 **Alternate Tel:** n/a
Email: JTrumble@ci.rockland.me.us **Web:** ci.rockland.me.us
Nearest Town: Rockland *(0 mi.)* **Tourist Info:** (207) 596-0376

Marina Services and Boat Supplies

Services - Docking Assistance, Concierge, Dock Carts **Communication -** Mail & Package Hold, Fax in/out *($1/pg)*, Data Ports *(Office)*, FedEx, AirBorne, UPS, Express Mail *(Sat Del)* **Supplies - OnSite:** Ice *(Block, Cube)* **Near:** Ships' Store, Bait/Tackle **Under 1 mi:** Marine Discount Store *(Rockland Boat 594-8181)*, Propane *(Coastal Fuels)*

Boatyard Services

OnCall: Divers, Propeller Repairs **Near:** Electronic Sales, Electronics Repairs, Inflatable Repairs. **Nearest Yard:** Knight's (207) 594-4068

Restaurants and Accommodations

OnCall: Pizzeria *(Domino's 594-9494)* **Near:** Restaurant *(Amalfi 596-0012, L $3-15, D $14-21), (MV Monhegan), (Grapes 594-9050, L $5-9, D $9-15), (Park Street Grille), (The Landings L $6-19, D $7-25)*, Seafood Shack *(Wayfarer lobster in a "basic" environment)*, Lite Fare *(Market On Main L $5-8)* **Under 1 mi:** Restaurant *(Jessica's European Bistro 596-0770, D $11-19)*, Inn/B&B *(Capt Lindsay Inn 596-7950, $65-175), (Berry Manor Inn 596-7696, $80-240)* **1-3 mi:** Restaurant *(Primo 596-0770, D $16-30, If you're looking for a splurge, this is it)*, Fast Food, Motel *(Trade Winds 596-6661, $55-105), (Navigator 594-2131, $55-115)*

Recreation and Entertainment

Near: Beach, Picnic Area, Playground, Dive Shop, Fitness Center *(Trade Winds - day pass $7-20)*, Jogging Paths, Boat Rentals *(Breakwater Kayak 596-6895)*, Roller Blade/Bike Paths, Movie Theater *(Strand Cinema 594-7266)*, Park, Museum *(Farnswoth & Wyeth Center 596-5789 $9/free; Shore Village Lighthouse 594-0311 free)* **Under 1 mi:** Tennis Courts **1-3 mi:** Golf Course *(Rockland Golf Club 594-9322, Samoset Resort 594-2511)*, Bowling, Video Rental *(Mainescreen Video 596-7875)*, Sightseeing *(Owls Head Transportation 594-4418 $6/4)*

Provisioning and General Services

OnSite: Farmers' Market *(Thu 9am-Noon)* **Near:** Convenience Store, Gourmet Shop, Delicatessen, Fishmonger, Lobster Pound, Meat Market, Bank/ATM, Post Office, Barber Shop, Laundry, Bookstore *(Second Reads 594-4123; Reading Corner 596-6651)*, Newsstand, Hardware Store *(Spear 594-4331)*, Florist, Clothing Store, Retail Shops, Copies Etc. *(Good Impressions 596-0707)* **Under 1 mi:** Supermarket *(Hannaford 594-2173, Shaw's 594-8615 1.5 mi.*)*, Health Food *(Good Tern 594-9286)*, Wine/Beer *(Wine Seller 594-2621)*, Bakery *(Brown Bag, Willow 596-0564)*, Catholic Church, Protestant Church, Synagogue, Library *(Rockland PL 596-7532)*, Beauty Salon, Dry Cleaners, Pharmacy *(Goodnows 594-5131)* **1-3 mi:** Liquor Store, Department Store *(Wal-Mart)*

Transportation

OnCall: Water Taxi *(Two Toots $2.50/pp/1-way Ch.9, 594-2891)*, Rental Car *(Enterprise 594-9093)*, Taxi *(Rockland Taxi 596-2575)* **Under 1 mi:** InterCity Bus *(Concord Trailways)*, Ferry Service *(ME State Ferries 596-2202 North Haven, Vinalhaven, Matinicus)* **Airport:** Knox County/Bangor Int'l. *(3 mi./55 mi.)*

Medical Services

911 Service **OnCall:** Holistic Services *(Sanctuary Day Spa)*, Ambulance **Near:** Chiropractor *(Bay Chiropractic Center 596-6700)* **Under 1 mi:** Doctor, Dentist **Hospital:** Pen Bay Medical 596-8000 *(5.5 mi.)*

Setting -- Rockland's public landing is the last facility on the South Channel. During the summer there are lovely southwest prevailing afternoon breezes. From the docks, it's a reasonably quick walk to this renaissance town's substantial array of restaurants, shops, museums, and other activities. This is no longer the industrial port of yesteryear.

Marina Notes -- Two hours free docking. *Open to 7pm weekends. Very helpful dock staff; will assist with carting, tie-ups, ice or water. Floats on the northeast corner of the Public Landing designated 20 min. zones with no services available. The onsite Chamber of Commerce has information on all of Rockland's amenities, including maps and a Harbor Walk guide. It's housed in the white building, just beyond the dinghy docks, in the waterfront park. Heads and showers are located here, too. Note: Mailing address is "270 Pleasant Street".

Notable -- The 4 mi. Harbor Walk begins at the North End and continues to Snow Marine Park. Check out the Farnsworth Museum, the Owl's Head Transportation Museum, and the Wyeth Center. Schooner Days celebration and the North Atlantic Blues Festival are the big events in July, usually the weekend after the fourth. The 5-day Maine Lobster Festival is the main event in early August. Rockland is home to 9 schooners which offer 3-6 day coastal adventures. *Shaw's Supermarket will shop & box your order for pick-up. Fax order, phone and credit card numbers to 594-9553 by 11am. They'll call you when it's ready and you can send a taxi to pick-up. Fee: $10/1st $100, $1/each add'l $50.

Cod End Restaurant & Marina

PO Box 224; Cod End Wharf; Tenants Harbor, ME 04860

Tel: (207) 372-6782 **VHF: Monitor** 16 **Talk** 69
Fax: n/a **Alternate Tel:** (207) 372-8553
Email: codend@midcoast.com **Web:** www.codend.com
Nearest Town: Rockland *(12 mi.)* **Tourist Info:** (207) 596-0376

Navigational Information

Lat: 43°57.940' **Long:** 069°12.550' **Tide:** 12 ft. **Current:** 1 kt. **Chart:** 13302
Rep. Depths (*MLW*): Entry 50 ft. **Fuel Dock** 4 ft. **Max Slip/Moor** -/15 ft.
Access: Gulf of Maine to Tenants Harbor

Marina Facilities *(In Season/Off Season)*

Fuel: Gasoline, Diesel
Slips: 0 Total, 0 Transient **Max LOA:** n/a **Max Beam:** n/a
Rate *(per ft.)*: **Day** n/a **Week** n/a **Month** n/a
Power: 30 amp n/a, **50 amp** n/a, **100 amp** n/a, **200 amp** n/a
Cable TV: No **Dockside Phone:** No
Dock Type: n/a
Moorings: 20 Total, 15 Transient **Launch:** None
Rate: Day $15 **Week** $90 **Month** $350
Heads: 2 Toilet(s)
Laundry: Yes, Book Exchange **Pay Phones:** Yes
Pump-Out: No **Fee:** n/a **Closed Heads:** Yes

Marina Operations

Owner/Manager: Anne W. Miller **Dockmaster:** David Schmanska
In-Season: MidJun-MidSep, 7am-7pm **Off-Season:** Sep-May, 8am-5pm
After-Hours Arrival: Call for instructions.
Reservations: No **Credit Cards:** Visa/MC, Dscvr
Discounts: Boat/US **Dockage:** Inq. **Fuel:** Inq. **Repair:** n/a
Pets: Welcome, Dog Walk Area **Handicap Access:** No

Marina Services and Boat Supplies

Services - Docking Assistance, Trash Pick-Up, Dock Carts **Communication -** Mail & Package Hold, Phone Messages, FedEx, UPS, Express Mail *(Sat Del)* **Supplies - OnSite:** Ice *(Block, Cube)*, Ships' Store *(Also at Tenants Harbor Boatyard)* **1-3 mi:** Bait/Tackle *(St George Marine 372-6308)*

Boatyard Services

Near: Railway, Forklift, Crane, Engine mechanic *(gas, diesel)*, Launching Ramp, Electrical Repairs, Hull Repairs, Rigger, Bottom Cleaning, Brightwork, Compound, Wash & Wax, Woodworking, Inflatable Repairs, Yacht Interiors, Metal Fabrication, Painting, Awlgrip, Yacht Building, Total Refits. **1-3 mi:** Divers. **Nearest Yard:** Tenants Harbor Boatyard (207) 372-8997

Restaurants and Accommodations

OnSite: Restaurant *(Cod End Cookhouse 372-8981, B Cont, L $2-20, D $5-20, PB&J to broiled scallops, will deliver to boat)* **Near:** Restaurant *(East Wind Inn 372-6366, L $13-22, D $13-22, B 7:30-11am, D 5:30-9:30pm, Sun Brunch 11:30am-2pm)*, *(Farmers Restaurant 372-6111, B $5, L $5-16, D $8-16, also delivers, including pizza)*, Lite Fare *(Chandlery L $3-14, 11am-3pm)*, *(Schoolhouse Bakery & Coffee Shop)*, Pizzeria *(Hall's Market)*, Inn/B&B *(East Wind Inn & Meeting House 372-6366, $70-290, next door)*, *(Life is Good 372-2612, $75)* **1-3 mi:** Snack Bar *(Harpoon 372-6304)* **3+ mi:** Inn/B&B *(Ocean House 372-6691, 4 mi.)*, *(Harbor View 372-8162, 4 mi.)*

Recreation and Entertainment

Near: Playground, Volleyball, Jogging Paths, Sightseeing **Under 1 mi:** Dive Shop, Tennis Courts **1-3 mi:** Beach, Museum *(Olson House 354-0102; Marshall Point Lighthouse Museum 372-6450)* **3+ mi:** Video Rental *(Varieties 354-6063, 6 mi.)*

Provisioning and General Services

OnSite: Fishmonger, Lobster Pound **Near:** Convenience Store *(Hall's Market 372-6311)*, Delicatessen, Wine/Beer *(Hall's)*, Bakery *(Schoolhouse)*, Meat Market, Post Office, Protestant Church, Laundry *(also hot showers)*, Bookstore, Newsstand **Under 1 mi:** Farmers' Market **1-3 mi:** Library *(Jackson Memorial 372-8961)* **3+ mi:** Liquor Store *(15 mi.)*, Bank/ATM *(10 mi)*, Pharmacy *(15 mi.)*, Hardware Store *(15 mi.)*, Retail Shops *(15 mi.)*, Department Store *(15 mi.)*

Transportation

OnCall: Rental Car *(Enterprise 594-9093)*, Taxi *(Schooner Bay 594-5000)* **3+ mi:** Ferry Service *(372-8848 Laura B. or Elizabeth Ann to Monhegan Island -- leaves from Port Clyde, 4 mi.)* **Airport:** Knox County/Bangor Int'l. *(12 mi./65 mi.)*

Medical Services

911 Service **OnCall:** Ambulance **3+ mi:** Doctor *(Smith Curtis 273-6400, 11 mi.)*, Dentist *(10 mi.)*, Chiropractor *(Bay Chiropractic 596-6700, 11 mi.)*, Holistic Services *(11 mi.)* **Hospital:** Penobscot Bay 596-8000 *(18 mi.)*

PHOTOS ON CD-ROM: 9

Setting -- Tenants Harbor is the quintessential Maine fishing village -- lobster boats dot the harbor, the streets are lined with clapboard houses, and the views up the harbor and out to sea are classic Maine. Often touted as a refuge from the ubiquitous fog -- but beware of the blanket of lobster traps and fish weirs.

Marina Notes -- Family owned and operated since 1974. Minor repairs and towing available. Look for the yellow/green mooring buoys. Dinghy in to the Cod End Float or the dinghy dock next to the town landing. The onsite Cookhouse Restaurant offers wonderful fresh seafood (lobsters, clams, chowders, pies, ice cream, etc.) in an inviting atmosphere. 7 days, 8am-9pm July & August -- shorter hours Jun, Sep, Oct. Kids' menu and a 10% Senior discount. Will also deliver prepared food to your boat or pack for travel. Lobster deliveries at 6:30pm - you can call orders ahead via radio. Moorings also possible from Jamie Wyeth's Tenants Harbor Boatyard (372-8997) - marked THB, Art's Lobster (372-6265) - green "Rental," Witham's - white balls, or East Wind.

Notable -- Some seasons, a delivery boat plies the harbor with muffins, newspapers, trash pick-up etc. Lovely East Wind Inn (large white house in photo) is adjacent and offers a range of accommodations -- basic but comfortable in the main Inn, higher end rooms and suites in the Meeting House, and the best in the Ginny Wheeler House. Breakfast, dinner and Sunday brunch served at the Inn, along with a "picnic-table" take-out seafood shack on the wharf. Marshall Point Lighthouse Museum is an interesting and scenic stop. Take Monhegan Boat Lines from Port Clyde (372-8848) 9 miles to Monhegan Island ($25/12 RT), home to many artists. Eastern Mussel Farms in Long Cove (372-6317) offers a tour and a great provisioning resource -- mussels and mahogany clams.

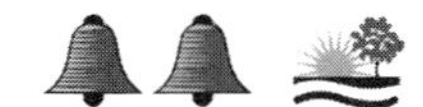

Navigational Information
Lat: 43°55.585' **Long:** 069°15.547' **Tide:** 10 ft. **Current:** n/a **Chart:** 13301
Rep. Depths (*MLW*): Entry 12 ft. **Fuel Dock** 10 ft. **Max Slip/Moor** -/8 ft.
Access: Gulf of Maine to Monhegan Island to Port Clyde

Marina Facilities *(In Season/Off Season)*
Fuel: Gasoline, Diesel
Slips: 0 Total, 0 Transient **Max LOA:** n/a **Max Beam:** n/a
Rate *(per ft.)*: **Day** n/a **Week** n/a **Month** n/a
Power: 30 amp n/a, **50 amp** n/a, **100 amp** n/a, **200 amp** n/a
Cable TV: No **Dockside Phone:** No
Dock Type: Floating
Moorings: 15 Total, 15 Transient **Launch:** None, Dinghy Dock
Rate: Day $20 **Week** $140 **Month** Inq.
Heads: 1 Toilet(s), 1 Shower(s)
Laundry: None **Pay Phones:** No
Pump-Out: No **Fee:** n/a **Closed Heads:** No

Marina Operations
Owner/Manager: Betsy Sherrick **Dockmaster:** Same
In-Season: May 26-Oct 15, 6am-7pm **Off-Season:** Oct 16-May 25, 7am-6pm
After-Hours Arrival: Call early in the day
Reservations: Yes, Preferred **Credit Cards:** Visa/MC, Dscvr, Cash
Discounts: None
Pets: Welcome **Handicap Access:** No

Port Clyde General Store

PO Box 329; 100 Cold Storage Road; Port Clyde, ME 04855

Tel: (207) 372-6543 **VHF: Monitor** n/a **Talk** n/a
Fax: (207) 372-0634 **Alternate Tel:** n/a
Email: n/a **Web:** n/a
Nearest Town: Thomaston *(14 mi.)* **Tourist Info:** (207) 596-0376

Marina Services and Boat Supplies
Services - Trash Pick-Up **Communication -** UPS, Express Mail **Supplies - OnSite:** Ice *(Block, Cube)*, Ships' Store, Propane **Under 1 mi:** Bait/Tackle

Boatyard Services
OnSite: Launching Ramp **OnCall:** Divers **1-3 mi:** Travelift, Engine mechanic *(gas, diesel)*, Electrical Repairs, Bottom Cleaning, Brightwork, Compound, Wash & Wax, Interior Cleaning, Propeller Repairs, Woodworking, Inflatable Repairs, Life Raft Service, Upholstery, Yacht Interiors, Metal Fabrication, Painting, Awlgrip, Total Refits. **Nearest Yard:** Tenants Harbor Boatyard (207) 372-8997

Restaurants and Accommodations
OnSite: Seafood Shack *(Dip Net 372-6543, L $7-24, D $7-24, 11am-7pm - call ahead, open later week-ends during season)* **Near:** Restaurant *(Black Harpoon 372-6304, D 5-9pm)*, *(Ocean House BYO)*, Snack Bar *(Harpoon 372-2630)*, Inn/B&B *(Ocean House 372-6691, $60-90, MAP Add $5 for a single night stay)* **1-3 mi:** Restaurant *(Farmers Restaurant 372-6111, B $5, L $5-16, D $5-16)* **3+ mi:** Restaurant *(East Wind Inn L $13-22, D $13-22, 4.5 mi.)*, *(Cod End Cookhouse 372-6782, B $2-5, L $5-$20, D $5-$20, 4.5 mi.)*, Inn/B&B *(East Wind Inn 372-6366, $70-250, 4.5 mi.)*

Recreation and Entertainment
OnSite: Picnic Area **Near:** Playground, Jogging Paths, Galleries *(Gallery-by-the-Sea 327-8671)* **Under 1 mi:** Beach, Museum *(Marshall Point Lighthouse Museum 372-6450 & The Olson House 354-0102 - 4 mi.)* **1-3 mi:** Cultural Attract *(Port Clyde Arts and Crafts Society 372-0673 Thu-Sun 10am-5pm)* **3+ mi:** Video Rental *(Varieties 354-6063, 10 mi.)*

Provisioning and General Services
OnSite: Convenience Store, Delicatessen, Wine/Beer, Bakery *(Village Ice Cream & Bakery)*, Meat Market, Newsstand, Hardware Store **Near:** Fishmonger, Lobster Pound *(Port Clyde Fishermen's Co-operative & Seafood Market 372-8922)*, Post Office, Protestant Church **1-3 mi:** Supermarket *(Halls 372-6311- a modest market)*, Library *(Jackson Memorial 372-8961)*, Beauty Salon, Barber Shop, Laundry, Florist, Clothing Store, Retail Shops, Copies Etc.

Transportation
OnCall: Rental Car *(Enterprise 594-9093)*, Taxi *(Hit the Road 230-0095)* **Near:** Ferry Service *(to Monhegan Island)* **Airport:** Knox County - Owl's Head/Bangor Int'l. *(17 mi./62 mi.)*

Medical Services
911 Service **OnCall:** Ambulance **3+ mi:** Doctor *(Curtis Smith 273-6400, 13 mi.)*, Chiropractor *(Waldoboro Chiropractic 832-6347, 14 mi.)* **Hospital:** Miles Memorial 563-1234 *(20 mi.)*

Setting -- Located in a small, rural fishing village at the tip of the St. George peninsula, the storied, classic Port Clyde General Store sits right at the water's edge. The tables on the wharf out front invite a relaxing picnic. This is a unique Maine Coast experience. The picturesque little town, known as an artists' colony, offers a lovely afternoon walk with easels at every turn.

Marina Notes -- Although the amenities of a large town are 14 miles away in Thomaston, this waterfront general store provides groceries, deli service, fresh baked goods, as well as fuel and moorings. The store is surprisingly well stocked. The General Store floats are adjacent to the wharf. Dock space is available for a quick stop, moorings and a dinghy dock permit a longer stay. Limited facilities available for boaters. Next door, the Dip Net "seafood shack" turns into a modest little restaurant in the early evening -- and shares the picnic deck overlooking the docks. Town Landing may have dockage. This is a harbor of refuge.

Notable -- Monhegan Boat Line leaves from the General Store's dock and makes the 9-mile trip (372-8848) to famous Monhegan Island $25/12 RT. Monhegan is home to more than 20 artists (including Jamie Wyeth) many of whom open their studios to visitors. The island is also a wildlife sanctuary with more than 600 varieties of wildflowers, 200 species of birds, and 17 miles of hiking trails. Shops and limited eateries are very busy in the season. The Olson House is a draw for Andrew Wyeth fans; he created a series of watercolors and drawings featuring the house and its inhabitants. Marshall Point Lighthouse Museum displays memorabilia from St. George and its lighthouses. Gallery-By-the-Sea has an impressively diverse visual arts collection.

III. Maine: Boothbay Harbor Region

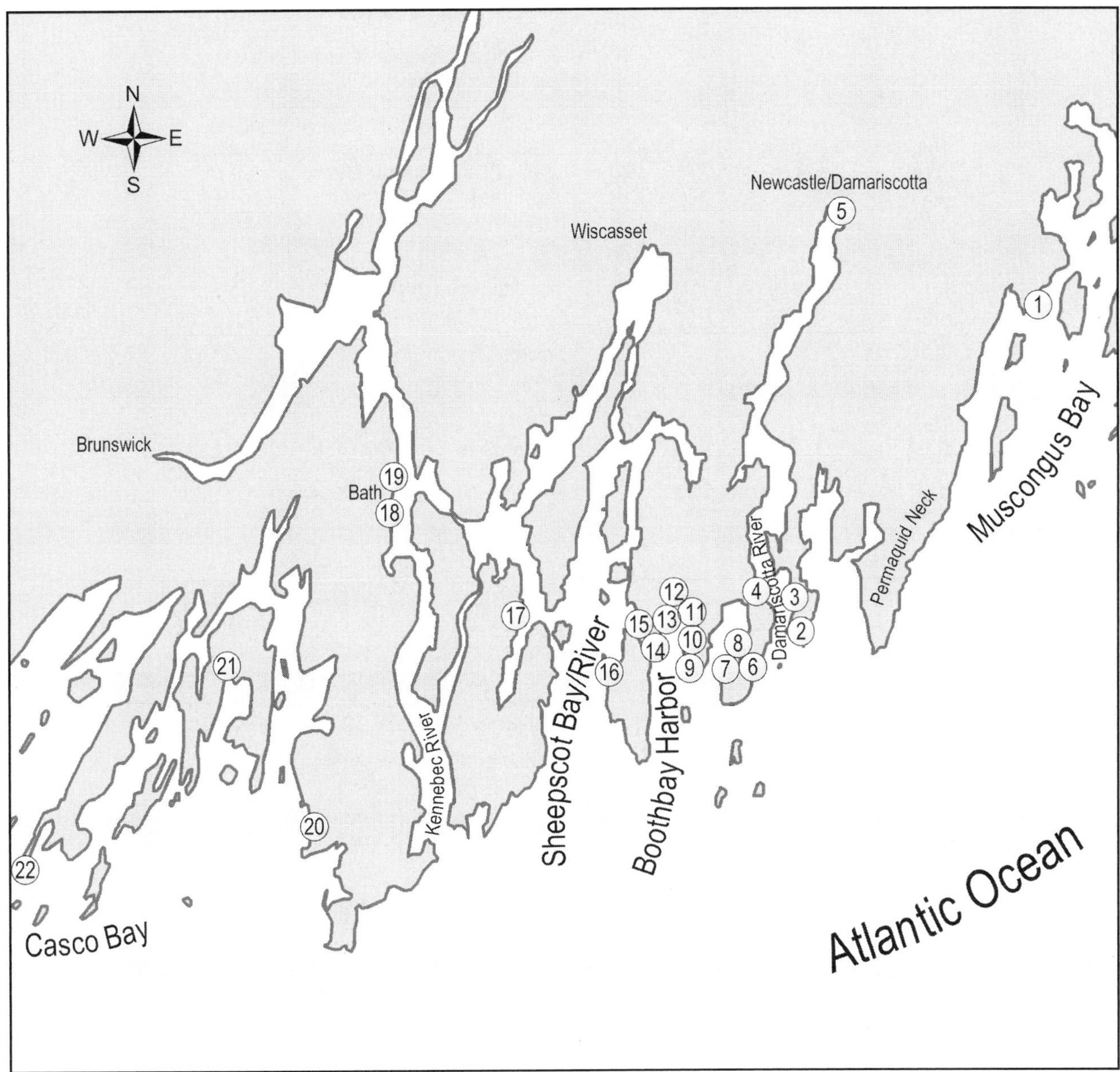

MAP	MARINA	HARBOR	PAGE
1	**Broad Cove Marine Services**	*Medomak River*	68
2	**Coveside Inn & Marina**	*Damariscotta River*	69
3	**Gamage Shipbuilders, Inc.**	*The Gut*	70
4	**Ocean Point Marina**	*Damariscotta River*	71
5	**Schooner Landing**	*Damariscotta River*	72
6	**Spar Shed Marina**	*Little River Harbor*	73
7	**Smuggler's Cove Inn**	*Linekin Bay*	74
8	**Paul E. Luke**	*Linekin Bay*	75
9	**Carousel Marina**	*Boothbay Harbor*	76
10	**Brown's Wharf Marina**	*Boothbay Harbor*	77
11	**Cap'n Fish's Motel & Marina**	*Boothbay Harbor*	78
12	**Boothbay Harbor Marina**	*Boothbay Harbor*	79
13	**Tugboat Inn & Marina**	*Boothbay Harbor*	80
14	**Sample's Shipyard**	*Boothbay Harbor*	81
15	**Signal Point Marina**	*Boothbay Harbor*	82
16	**Boothbay Region Boatyard**	*Sheepscot River*	83
17	**Robinhood Marine Center**	*Sheepscot River*	84
18	**Maine Maritime Museum**	*Kennebec River*	85
19	**Kennebec Tavern & Marina**	*Kennebec River*	86
20	**Sebasco Harbor Resort**	*New Meadows River*	87
21	**Great Island Boat Yard**	*Merriconeag Sound*	88
22	**Dolphin Marina & Restaurant**	*Merriconeag Sound*	89

Broad Cove Marine Services

PO Box 208; Medomak Road; Medomak , ME 04551

Tel: (207) 529-5186 **VHF: Monitor** 9 **Talk** n/a
Fax: (207) 529-4469 **Alternate Tel:** n/a
Email: lbpcms@lincoln.midcoast.com **Web:** n/a
Nearest Town: Damariscotta *(5 mi.)* **Tourist Info:** (207) 563-8340

Navigational Information

Lat: 43°59.549' **Long:** 069°24.466' **Tide:** 9 ft. **Current:** n/a **Chart:** 13301
Rep. Depths (*MLW*): Entry 16 ft. **Fuel Dock** 6 ft. **Max Slip/Moor** 6 ft./30 ft.
Access: Muscongus Sound to Hockomock Channel

Marina Facilities *(In Season/Off Season)*

Fuel: Gasoline, Diesel
Slips: 10 Total, 4 Transient **Max LOA:** 50 ft. **Max Beam:** n/a
Rate *(per ft.)*: **Day** $1.00 **Week** $7 **Month** n/a
Power: 30 amp n/a, **50 amp** n/a, **100 amp** n/a, **200 amp** n/a
Cable TV: No **Dockside Phone:** No
Dock Type: Wood, Floating
Moorings: 6 Total, 6 Transient **Launch:** None, Dinghy Dock
Rate: Day $10 **Week** $70 **Month** Inq.
Heads: 1 Toilet(s)
Laundry: None **Pay Phones:** No
Pump-Out: OnSite, Full Service, 1 Central **Fee:** $10 **Closed Heads:** No

Marina Operations

Owner/Manager: Blair Pyne **Dockmaster:** Same
In-Season: May-Oct, 9am-6pm **Off-Season:** Closed
After-Hours Arrival: Call ahead
Reservations: Yes **Credit Cards:** Visa/MC
Discounts: None
Pets: Welcome **Handicap Access:** No

Marina Services and Boat Supplies

Services - Dock Carts **Communication -** Mail & Package Hold, Phone Messages, Fax in/out *(Free)*, FedEx, AirBorne, UPS, Express Mail **Supplies - OnSite:** Ice *(Block)* **3+ mi:** Ships' Store *(15 mi.)*, Propane *(Columbia Propane 725-4465, 8 mi.)*

Boatyard Services

OnCall: Divers **3+ mi:** Engine mechanic *(gas, diesel)*, Hull Repairs *(6 mi.)*, Bottom Cleaning *(6 mi.)*, Propeller Repairs *(6 mi.)*, Painting *(6 mi.)*, Yacht Design *(6 mi.)*, Yacht Building *(6 mi.)*. **Nearest Yard:** Padebco Custom Boats (207) 529-5106

Restaurants and Accommodations

OnSite: Snack Bar **3+ mi:** Restaurant *(Backstreet Landing 563-5666, L $4-14, D $9-22, 5 mi.)*, *(King Eiders Pub & Restaurant 563-6008, 5 mi.)*, Fast Food *(5 mi.)*, Pizzeria *(Romeo's Pizza 846-1473, 5 mi.)*, Motel *(Oyster Shell Resort 563-3747, $70-150, 5 mi.)*, Inn/B&B *(Brannon-Bunker Inn 563-5941, $70-125, 5 mi.)*

Recreation and Entertainment

Near: Jogging Paths **1-3 mi:** Pool, Beach, Picnic Area, Grills, Playground **3+ mi:** Fitness Center *(YMCA 563-3477, 5 mi.)*, Horseback Riding *(Victorian Stables 563-1991, 6 mi.)*, Video Rental *(Sounds Easy 563-5331, 6 mi.)*, Museum *(Waldoborough Historical Society 832-4725, 6 mi.)*

Provisioning and General Services

OnSite: Lobster Pound **3+ mi:** Supermarket *(Shop N Save 563-8131, 5 mi.)*, Health Food *(Rising Tide Natural Foods 563-5556, 5 mi.)*, Farmers' Market *(Damariscotta Farmers' Market - Fri & Mon 9am-Noon, 5 mi.)*, Bank/ATM *(5 mi.)*, Post Office *(5 mi.)*, Catholic Church *(5 mi.)*, Protestant Church *(5 mi.)*, Beauty Salon *(5 mi.)*, Dry Cleaners *(5 mi.)*, Laundry *(5 mi.)*, Pharmacy *(Rite Aid 563-8489, 5 mi.)*, Hardware Store *(Damariscotta Hardware 563-3428, 5 mi.)*, Copies Etc. *(Supplies Unlimited 563-7010, 5 mi.)*

Transportation

OnCall: Rental Car *(Enterprise 594-9053)* **3+ mi:** Taxi *(Rockland Taxi 596-2575, 17 mi.)* **Airport:** Knox County/Portland Jetport *(23 mi./65 mi.)*

Medical Services

No 911 Service **3+ mi:** Doctor *(Friedland, Goltz & Gold 563-3179, 5 mi.)*, Chiropractor *(Waldoboro Chiropractic 832-6347, 6 mi.)* **Hospital:** Miles Memorial 563-1234 *(6 mi.)*

Setting -- After a tense trip up the Medomak River, the sight of these inviting red and gray buildings, perched on the edge of the Hockomock Channel, is certainly welcome. The surroundings are rural Maine, the views pristine and the "broad cove" beautiful and protected.

Marina Notes -- Down home, customer-oriented Broad Cove services a mix of pleasure and fishing boats with basic but nicely maintained facilities about seven miles from the nearest business center. The staff is knowledgeable and accommodating. Note: there is no power on the docks.

Notable -- There is lobster available and seafood can often be bought directly from the neighboring boats. There is also a modest snack bar onsite that offers steamed lobsters and clams. Broad Cove offers the rare pleasure of nothing. Plan to just relax, eat, read, and enjoy the scenery and the quiet -- there is nowhere to go and nothing to do.

PHOTOS ON CD-ROM: 4

Navigational Information

Lat: 43°50.861' **Long:** 069°33.367' **Tide:** 9 ft. **Current:** n/a **Chart:** 13293
Rep. Depths (*MLW*): Entry 25 ft. **Fuel Dock** 12 ft. **Max Slip/Moor** 12 ft./12 ft.
Access: Damariscotta River to Christmas Cove west shore

Marina Facilities *(In Season/Off Season)*

Fuel: Gasoline, Diesel
Slips: 12 Total, 8 Transient **Max LOA:** 90 ft. **Max Beam:** n/a
Rate *(per ft.)*: **Day** $1.50 **Week** Inq. **Month** Inq.
Power: 30 amp Incl., **50 amp** n/a, **100 amp** n/a, **200 amp** n/a
Cable TV: No **Dockside Phone:** No
Dock Type: Wood, Alongside, Floating
Moorings: 15 Total, 15 Transient **Launch:** Yes (Free), Dinghy Dock
Rate: Day $25 **Week** Inq. **Month** Inq.
Heads: 2 Toilet(s), 2 Shower(s)
Laundry: None **Pay Phones:** Yes
Pump-Out: OnSite, Full Service **Fee:** n/a **Closed Heads:** No

Marina Operations

Owner/Manager: Mike Mitchell **Dockmaster:** John Mitchell
In-Season: MidMay-MidSep **Off-Season:** Closed
After-Hours Arrival: Check in at the Inn desk
Reservations: Yes, Preferred **Credit Cards:** Visa/MC, Amex
Discounts: None
Pets: Welcome **Handicap Access:** No

Coveside Inn & Marina

105 Coveside Road; South Bristol, ME 04568

Tel: (207) 644-8780 **VHF: Monitor** 9 **Talk** 68
Fax: (207) 644-8204 **Alternate Tel:** n/a
Email: coveside@lincoln.midcoast.com **Web:** n/a
Nearest Town: Damariscotta *(12 mi.)* **Tourist Info:** (207) 633-7448

Marina Services and Boat Supplies

Services - Docking Assistance, Dock Carts **Communication -** Mail & Package Hold, Phone Messages, Fax in/out, FedEx, AirBorne, UPS, Express Mail **Supplies - OnSite:** Ice *(Block, Cube)* **Under 1 mi:** Ships' Store *(Osier's Wharf 644-8500)*, Bait/Tackle *(Osier's)*

Boatyard Services

Under 1 mi: Travelift *(25T)*, Forklift, Engine mechanic *(gas, diesel)*, Electrical Repairs, Hull Repairs, Bottom Cleaning, Brightwork, Compound, Wash & Wax, Painting. **Nearest Yard:** Gamage Shipyard (207) 644-8181

Restaurants and Accommodations

OnSite: Restaurant *(Dory Bar & Shorefront Restaurant 644-8282, Lunch & Dinner)*, Inn/B&B *(Coveside Inn 644-8282, $80-105, breakfast incl. 10 shore front and 5 Inn units)* **Under 1 mi:** Restaurant *(Antique Café 644-8400)*, Seafood Shack *(Osier's Wharf 644-8500)*, Snack Bar *(Harborside Grocery & Grill 644-8751)*, *(Bridge House Café)*

Recreation and Entertainment

OnSite: Boat Rentals *(Sailboat Charters - daily, weekly and monthly; Kayak Rentals - Wild Bill Michaud)* **Near:** Beach, Jogging Paths, Roller Blade/Bike Paths **Under 1 mi:** Museum *(The Thompson Ice House 644-8551 Wed, Fri, Sat 1-4pm)* **3+ mi:** Picnic Area *(4 mi.)*, Park *(Pemaquid Beach Park 677-2754, 4 mi.)*

Provisioning and General Services

Under 1 mi: Convenience Store *(Harborside 644-8751, Island Grocery 644-8552)*, Delicatessen *(Osier's Wharf 644-8500)*, Wine/Beer, Fishmonger *(Osier's Wharf)*, Lobster Pound *(South Bristol Fishermen's Co-op 644-8224)*, Bank/ATM, Post Office, Protestant Church, Library

Transportation

OnCall: Rental Car *(Strong Auto Dealer 563-8185)*, Taxi **Airport:** Portland Int'l. *(60 mi.)*

Medical Services

911 Service **OnCall:** Ambulance **Hospital:** Miles Memorial 563-1234 *(11 mi.)*

Setting -- On the shore of Christmas Cove, frequently cited as one of the more beautiful gunkholes in Maine, this multi-building Inn, motel, restaurant and marina complex is easily identified by its barn-red siding and forest green roofs. The marina and the cove, as well as lovely Rutherford Island, are magnets for cruisers and the harbor is often filled with beautiful craft.

Marina Notes -- Family owned and operated since 1968, now two generations of the Mitchell family run the Inn and Marina -- the only commercial facility in the Cove. There are 15 rooms in all: five in the charming 1886 Inn plus 10 shorefront motel units with waterside decks, skylights and private baths -- and unobstructed views of the Cove. The Dory Bar, decorated with yacht club pennants and personal signals, and Shorefront Restaurant -- a well-regarded, 84-seat restaurant with inside and deck dining -- both overlook Christmas Cove and feature fresh local seafood and produce. Coveside is a yacht brokerage and dealer for Pacific Seacraft and Ericsson Yachts. Gamage Shipyard is about 1.5 miles away. Water is limited and for tank refills only.

Notable -- Rich in Maine history, Capt. John Smith discovered Christmas Cove on December 25, 1614. At the turn of the last century, it was a major destination for steamers from Boston and New York. Much quieter now, its intrinsic beauty remains. A little over a mile walk west will take you to the small village of South Bristol, dominated by the swing bridge over The Gut. There is a small group of services including the Island Grocery (which delivers), Osier's Wharf (marine supplies, seafood and groceries), Harborside Café, plus a candy store and ice cream shop. But mostly, this is a place to relax and enjoy the scenery.

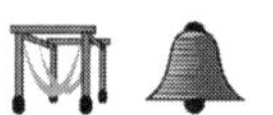

Gamage Shipbuilders, Inc.

6 Gamage Drive; South Bristol, ME 04568

Tel: (207) 644-8181 **VHF: Monitor** 16 **Talk** n/a
Fax: (207) 644-8273 **Alternate Tel:** n/a
Email: linwood@tidewater.net **Web:** n/a
Nearest Town: Damariscotta *(11 mi.)* **Tourist Info:** (207) 633-7448

Navigational Information
Lat: 43°51.752' **Long:** 069°33.622' **Tide:** 8 ft. **Current:** 3 kt. **Chart:** 13293
Rep. Depths (*MLW*): Entry 30 ft. **Fuel Dock** n/a **Max Slip/Moor** 14 ft./80 ft.
Access: Damariscotta River north to R6, to The Gut

Marina Facilities *(In Season/Off Season)*
Fuel: No
Slips: 10 Total, 3 Transient **Max LOA:** 100 ft. **Max Beam:** n/a
Rate *(per ft.)*: **Day** $2.00 **Week** Inq. **Month** Inq.
Power: 30 amp Incl., **50 amp** Incl., **100 amp** n/a, **200 amp** n/a
Cable TV: No **Dockside Phone:** No
Dock Type: Wood, Floating
Moorings: 12 Total, 4 Transient **Launch:** None, Dinghy Dock
Rate: Day $15 **Week** $8.00/ft. **Month** Inq.
Heads: 1 Toilet(s), 1 Shower(s) *(with dressing rooms)*
Laundry: None **Pay Phones:** No
Pump-Out: No **Fee:** n/a **Closed Heads:** No

Marina Operations
Owner/Manager: Linwood Gamage **Dockmaster:** Same
In-Season: Jun-Oct 12, 8am-4:30pm **Off-Season:** Oct 12-May, 8am-4pm
After-Hours Arrival: n/a
Reservations: No. First come, first served **Credit Cards:** Visa/MC
Discounts: None
Pets: Welcome **Handicap Access:** Yes, Docks

Marina Services and Boat Supplies
Services - Docking Assistance, Dock Carts **Communication -** Mail & Package Hold, FedEx, AirBorne, UPS, Express Mail **Supplies - Near:** Ice *(Block, Cube)*

Boatyard Services
OnSite: Travelift *(25T)*, Forklift, Crane, Engine mechanic *(gas, diesel)*, Electronic Sales, Electronics Repairs, Bottom Cleaning, Brightwork, Compound, Wash & Wax **Yard Rates:** $45/hr., Haul & Launch $5/ft., Power Wash $2/ft. **Storage:** On-Land $11/ft. season

Restaurants and Accommodations
Near: Restaurant *(Harborside Café serves pizza)*, Seafood Shack *(Osier's Wharf)*, Snack Bar *(Bridge House Café 644-1449)*, Lite Fare *(Island Grocery & Lunch 644-8500)* **Under 1 mi:** Restaurant *(Coveside Restaurant 644-8540)*, *(Antique Café 644-8400)*, Motel *(Coveside Inn and Motel 644-8282)*

Recreation and Entertainment
Under 1 mi: Museum *(The Thompson Ice House 644-8551 Wed, Fri, Sat 1-4pm)*, Sightseeing *(Witch Island Preserve 781-2330, via dinghy, 1772 Old Walpole Meeting House)*

Provisioning and General Services
Near: Convenience Store *(Island Grocery & Lunch 644-8552, Osier's Wharf 644-8500)*, Wine/Beer *(Island Grocery)*, Fishmonger *(Osier's Wharf, outdoor seaside deck seating)*, Lobster Pound *(South Bristol Fishermen's Co-op 644-8224)*, Bank/ATM, Post Office, Protestant Church, Library **Under 1 mi:** Delicatessen *(Harborside Grocery & Deli 644-8751)*

Transportation
OnCall: Rental Car *(Enterprise 882-8393)* **Airport:** Portland Int'l. *(53 mi.)*

Medical Services
911 Service **OnCall:** Ambulance **Hospital:** Miles Memorial 563-1234 *(11 mi.)*

Setting -- Perched on the northwest side of The Gut, which connects the Damariscotta River and John's Bay, this rustic boatyard offers basic facilities and a perfect place to watch all the small boat and commercial fishing action on this busy stretch of water.

Marina Notes -- Originally noted for its work on wooden boats, Gamage now services all types of vessels. Among the many schooners, research vessels and working boats that were launched here are Hudson River's Clearwater and Cape Cod's Shenandoah. Moorings may also be available from Bittersweet Landing Boatyard (644-8731) and slips from Osier's Wharf (644-8500) -- both on the eastern side of the swing bridge (note there are cables 55 ft. overhead, 6 feet of water, and a significant current). Very active working harbor. The green swing bridge, which crosses the narrow passage known as The Gut, opens and closes frequently to accommodate commercial fishing and lobstering traffic - and takes a considerably long time to do so. Enjoy the scenery.

Notable -- Around the swing bridge is a cluster of services, including an ice cream shop, snack bar, candy store, and a small grocery and fish market. Seafood is often available right off the boats. An easy walk will take you to the beautiful gunkhole, Christmas Cove, and the Coveside Inn and Motel. There you'll also find a bar, deck and a restaurant overlooking the water. Interesting ventures might be the half mile dinghy ride to Maine Audubon's Witch Island Preserve (781-2330), or the 4 mile dinghy ride north (with tide on your side) to Menigawum Preserve on 30 acre Stratton Island - trail maps are available at the preserve.

PHOTOS ON CD-ROM: 4

Navigational Information
Lat: 43°51.900' **Long:** 069°35.070' **Tide:** 9 ft. **Current:** 5 kt. **Chart:** 13293
Rep. Depths (*MLW*): Entry 63 ft. **Fuel Dock** 25 ft. **Max Slip/Moor** 25 ft./63 ft.
Access: Damariscotta River to G7 to East Boothbay

Marina Facilities *(In Season/Off Season)*
Fuel: Slip-Side Fueling, Gasoline, Diesel
Slips: 67 Total, 5 Transient **Max LOA:** 150 ft. **Max Beam:** 50 ft.
Rate *(per ft.)*: **Day** $1.75/$1.00 **Week** $8/4 **Month** $20/10
Power: 30 amp $5, **50 amp** $10, **100 amp** n/a, **200 amp** n/a
Cable TV: Yes, $1 **Dockside Phone:** No
Dock Type: Wood, Long Fingers, Floating
Moorings: 16 Total, 4 Transient **Launch:** Yes, Dinghy Dock
Rate: Day $25/12.50 **Week** $150/75 **Month** $325/150
Heads: 2 Toilet(s), 2 Shower(s)
Laundry: 1 Washer(s), 1 Dryer(s), Book Exchange **Pay Phones:** No
Pump-Out: OnSite, Self Service, 1 Central **Fee:** $5 **Closed Heads:** No

Marina Operations
Owner/Manager: Dan Miller **Dockmaster:** Vicki Corbin
In-Season: May-Oct, 8am-5pm **Off-Season:** Oct-May, 8am-4pm
After-Hours Arrival: Look for slip marked "Transient Available"
Reservations: Preferred **Credit Cards:** Visa/MC, Dscvr
Discounts: Cash **Dockage:** n/a **Fuel:** 0.05 **Repair:** n/a
Pets: Welcome **Handicap Access:** Yes, Heads, Docks

Ocean Point Marina

Route 96; East Boothbay, ME 04544

Tel: (207) 633-0773 **VHF: Monitor** 9 **Talk** 18
Fax: (207) 633-3971 **Alternate Tel:** (207) 633-3673
Email: cbmarina@gwi.net **Web:** www.oceanpointmarina.com
Nearest Town: E. Boothbay *(0 mi.)* **Tourist Info:** (207) 633-7448

Marina Services and Boat Supplies
Services - Docking Assistance, Security *(24 Hrs., Employees onsite)*, Dock Carts, Megayacht Facilities **Communication -** Mail & Package Hold, Phone Messages, Data Ports **Supplies - OnSite:** Ice *(Block, Cube)*, Ships' Store, Bait/Tackle, Live Bait *(Worms)* **1-3 mi:** Propane *(Shore Hill 633-4782)*, CNG *(Shore Hill)*

Boatyard Services
OnSite: Travelift *(35T)*, Crane, Engine mechanic *(gas, diesel)*, Launching Ramp, Electrical Repairs, Electronic Sales *(Coastal 633-7090)*, Electronics Repairs, Hull Repairs, Rigger, Sail Loft *(Wilson 633-5071)*, Bottom Cleaning, Brightwork, Air Conditioning, Divers, Compound, Wash & Wax, Interior Cleaning, Propeller Repairs, Woodworking, Inflatable Repairs, Painting, Awlgrip, Yacht Broker, Total Refits **1-3 mi:** Canvas Work *(Creative Canvas 633-2056)*, Refrigeration, Upholstery, Yacht Interiors, Metal Fabrication *(Mid Coast 633-7553)*. **Dealer for:** Mercury, Mercruiser; Quicksilver Inflatables, Fiberglass dinghies. **Member:** ABBRA, Other Certifications: Mercury **Yard Rates:** $45/hr., Haul & Launch $8.50/ft. *(blocking incl.)*, Power Wash $65, Bottom Paint $6.25/ft. **Storage:** In-Water $27/ft./season, On-Land $3.50/sq.ft./season

Restaurants and Accommodations
Near: Restaurant *(Lobsterman's Wharf 633-3443, L $5-14, D $14-25, 11:30am-Mid)*, Snack Bar *(EB General Store)*, Motel *(Water's Edge Motel & Cottages 633-2505)*, Inn/B&B *(Inn at Lobsterman's Wharf 633-5481)* **Under 1 mi:** Restaurant *(Carriage House 633-6025, D $6-22, also all-you-can-eat fish fry & twofer nites, as well as steak)*, Inn/B&B *(Linekin Bay 633-9900, $85-175)*, *(Five Gables 633-4551, $130-185, moorings for guests)* **1-3 mi:** Restaurant *(1820 House 633-2800, B $6, D $7-18, at Smuggler's Cove)*, Motel *(Smuggler's Cove 633-2800, $70-180)*

Recreation and Entertainment
OnSite: Picnic Area, Grills **Near:** Jogging Paths, Galleries **Under 1 mi:** Fishing Charter **1-3 mi:** Beach, Fitness Center *(YMCA)*, Boat Rentals, Group Fishing Boat, Video Rental *(Boothbay Harbor Framers 633-6509)*, Museum *(Bootbay Railway Museum and Boothbay Region Historical Society 633-0820)*, Sightseeing *(Ocean Point)* **3+ mi:** Golf Course *(Boothbay Country Club 633-6085, 5 mi.)*

Provisioning and General Services
OnSite: Post Office **Near:** Protestant Church *(Methodist)* **Under 1 mi:** Convenience Store *(East Boothbay General 633-4503)*, Wine/Beer **1-3 mi:** Supermarket *(Hannaford 633-6465)*, Gourmet Shop, Delicatessen, Health Food, Liquor Store, Bakery, Farmers' Market *(Boothbay Mini-Mall, Thur. 9am-12 noon)*, Lobster Pound, Bank/ATM, Catholic Church, Library, Beauty Salon, Barber Shop, Dry Cleaners, Laundry, Bookstore, Pharmacy *(Waltz 633-5323)*, Newsstand, Hardware Store *(Poole Brothers 633-4474)*, Florist

Transportation
OnCall: Rental Car *(Enterprise 882-8393)*, Taxi *(Boothbay Harbor Taxi 633-6001)* **Airport:** Portland Int'l. *(50 mi.)*

Medical Services
911 Service **OnCall:** Ambulance **1-3 mi:** Doctor *(Webster 633-3410)*, Dentist, Chiropractor *(Coastal 633-4777)*, Holistic Services *(Massage Therapist 633-6405)* **Hospital:** St. Andrews 633-7820 *(2 mi.)*

Setting -- Situated in a wide, working cove about 4 miles from the Damariscotta's mouth, Ocean Point offers entry to the less touristy village of East Boothbay. The atmosphere is both commercial harbor and downeast tranquility -- a short distance from the bustle of Boothbay Harbor. East Boothbay is an historic wood and steel boatbuilding center. It was, and is, the birthplace of some extraordinary yachts. Maritime history junkies will find this a worthwhile stop.

Marina Notes -- Formerly C&B Marina, ownership changed hands in February 2002. Two floating docks accommodate large craft with full services -- vessels up to 150', 20-50' beam and 18' draft. Roomy, attractive new heads and shower rooms with dressing area. The colorful, extensively inventoried chandlery also offers overnight deliveries. Storage discounts for those who contract for winter work. Seasonal rates $54/ft. For its first 50 years, this site was home to the venerable boatbuilders Goudy & Stevens and Hodgdon Yachts; both have moved nearby. Boothbay Harbor is 3 miles away.

Notable -- A boaters' lounge, with hexagonal picnic tables, coffee dispensary, and a rough-hewn log bar, supplants the now-closed Norma's Pub. Just around the corner, Lobsterman's Wharf Restaurant, (mid May-mid Oct) has waterside tables, inside dining, and a mostly seafood menu. Marine artist Earle Barlow's Studio of Ships, Anderson Studio, and vanHasslet Gallery are walkable. So are East Boothbay General Store, Wee Scottie Antiques, and Five Gables Inn. Hodgdon's Yachts, in East Boothbay since 1816, is now building superyachts using cold-molded wood epoxy and has a convenient ships' store. Goudy & Stevens, builders of notable yachts like America (original winner of the America's Cup), Sea Star and Cassiar, continues to offer traditional boatyard services.

PHOTOS ON CD-ROM: 7

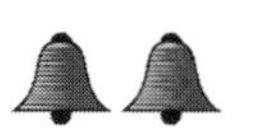

Schooner Landing

PO Box 1473; Main Street; Damariscotta, ME 04543

Tel: (207) 563-7447 **VHF: Monitor** n/a **Talk** n/a
Fax: (207) 563-7447 **Alternate Tel:** n/a
Email: n/a **Web:** n/a
Nearest Town: Damariscotta *(0 mi.)* **Tourist Info:** (207) 563-8340

Navigational Information

Lat: 44°01.955' **Long:** 069°31.974' **Tide:** 9 ft. **Current:** n/a **Chart:** 13293
Rep. Depths (*MLW*): Entry 5 ft. **Fuel Dock** n/a **Max Slip/Moor** 8 ft./-
Access: 14 nm up the Damariscotta River to the Route 1B bridge

Marina Facilities *(In Season/Off Season)*

Fuel: No
Slips: 40 Total, 8 Transient **Max LOA:** 75 ft. **Max Beam:** n/a
Rate *(per ft.)*: **Day** $1.50/Inq. **Week** Inq. **Month** Inq.
Power: 30 amp n/a, **50 amp** n/a, **100 amp** n/a, **200 amp** n/a
Cable TV: No **Dockside Phone:** No
Dock Type: Wood, Short Fingers, Pilings, Floating
Moorings: 0 Total, 0 Transient **Launch:** n/a
Rate: Day n/a **Week** n/a **Month** n/a
Heads: 2 Toilet(s)
Laundry: Yes **Pay Phones:** Yes, 1
Pump-Out: No **Fee:** n/a **Closed Heads:** No

Marina Operations

Owner/Manager: Scott Fulsom / Charlie Herrick **Dockmaster:** Same
In-Season: May 15-Oct 31, 9am-1am **Off-Season:** n/a
After-Hours Arrival: Check in at restaurant
Reservations: Yes, Preferred **Credit Cards:** Visa/MC, Dscvr, Cash
Discounts: None
Pets: Welcome **Handicap Access:** No

Marina Services and Boat Supplies

Services - Docking Assistance **Communication -** FedEx, AirBorne, UPS, Express Mail **Supplies - OnSite:** Ice *(Cube)* **Under 1 mi:** Bait/Tackle, Propane **1-3 mi:** Ships' Store *(Clark Auto Parts 563-8128)*

Boatyard Services

OnCall: Engine mechanic *(gas, diesel)*, Electrical Repairs, Electronic Sales, Electronics Repairs, Hull Repairs, Rigger, Sail Loft, Canvas Work, Bottom Cleaning, Brightwork, Air Conditioning, Refrigeration, Divers, Compound, Wash & Wax, Propeller Repairs, Metal Fabrication, Painting, Awlgrip **Near:** Launching Ramp.

Restaurants and Accommodations

OnSite: Restaurant *(Schooner Landing 563-7447, L $6-15, D $6-15)* **OnCall:** Pizzeria *(Castle Store-All 563-8737)* **Near:** Restaurant *(Backstreet 563-5666, L $4-14, D $9-22)*, *(King Eiders Pub 563-6008, D $10-17, lite fare, too)*, Lite Fare *(Salt Bay Café B $3-4, L $6-9, D $11-20)*, *(Rogue River 563-2992, B,L,D, Sun Brunch 7am-8pm)*, Inn/B&B *(Oak Gables 563-1476, $80-120)*, *(Mandalay 563-2260, $70-150)* **Under 1 mi:** Restaurant *(Thatchers Family Restaurant 563-7171)*, *(New Castle Inn D $45 prix fixe, 4-course, Tue-Sun, 7pm - a Julia Child favorite)*, Motel *(Oyster Shell Resort Condo Motel 563-3747, $70-150)*, Inn/B&B *(Newcastle Inn 563-5685, $100-250)*, *(Flying Cloud 563-2484, $75-120)*

Recreation and Entertainment

OnSite: Boat Rentals *(Sea Spirit Kayaking 563-5732)*, Fishing Charter *(Punky's Comet 567-3684)* **Near:** Movie Theater *(Lincoln Theater - live too)*, Museum *(Chapman-Hall House Tue-Sun 1-5pm $1; W W & F Railway Museum 882-4193 6 mi.)* **Under 1 mi:** Video Rental *(Sounds Easy Video 563-5331)*, Sightseeing *(Salt Bay Preserve Heritage Trail)* **1-3 mi:** Beach, Picnic Area, Grills, Playground, Tennis Courts, Fitness Center *(YMCA 563-3477)*, Jogging Paths, Park *(Whaleback Park and Glidden Point Oyster Mounds)*, Cultural Attract *(Round Top Center for the Arts 563-1507)* **3+ mi:** Golf Course *(Wawenock C. C. 563-3938, 6 mi. or Boothbay Harbor)*

Provisioning and General Services

Near: Convenience Store, Gourmet Shop, Delicatessen, Wine/Beer, Bakery, Fishmonger, Lobster Pound, Bank/ATM, Post Office, Catholic Church, Protestant Church, Library *(Skidompha Library 563-2745)*, Beauty Salon, Barber Shop, Dry Cleaners, Laundry, Bookstore *(Maine Coast Bookshop & Café 563-3207)*, Pharmacy *(Rite Aid 563-8489)*, Newsstand, Hardware Store *(Damariscotta Hardware 563-3428)*, Florist, Retail Shops, Department Store *(Clays)*, Copies Etc. *(Supplies Unlimited 563-7010)* **Under 1 mi:** Health Food *(Rising Tide 563-5556)*, Farmers' Market *(Assembly of God Church 563-1076 Fri & Mon 9am-Noon)*, Meat Market **1-3 mi:** Supermarket *(Hannaford 563-8131)*, Liquor Store

Transportation

OnCall: Rental Car *(Enterprise 882-8393)*, Taxi *(Boothbay Harbor Taxi 633-6001)* **Airport:** Knox County/Portland Int'l. *(30 mi./60 mi.)*

Medical Services

911 Service **OnCall:** Ambulance **Near:** Doctor *(Van Winkle 563-3179)*, Dentist, Chiropractor *(Amato 563-1000)*, Holistic Services *(Therapeutic Massage 563-1441)* **Hospital:** Miles Memorial 563-1234 *(2 mi.)*

Setting -- An integral part of the Schooner Landing Restaurant, this facility is conveniently located in downtown Damariscotta. It's at the head of the Damariscotta River, where it overlooks this beautiful saltwater estuary.

Marina Notes -- The Restaurant offers inside dining, outside dining decks, an outside bar, frequent live music -- and fresh, local seafood. It's run by two self-professed "eligible bachelors" and has a lively, party atmosphere. 7 days 11:30am-9:30pm. Kids' menu. The restaurant is more than 40 years old and the marina about 15 years old. Public dinghy dock next door. Dockage for lunch and dinner. Note: There is no power on the docks, no showers, and heads are shared with the restaurant; laundromat is one block away. Gas and Diesel at Riverside Boat. The current is often very swift, so docking help might be needed.

Notable -- Originally a shipbuilding center, Damariscotta is now the shopping and financial center for nearby resort communities. Everything you might need is within easy reach. The attractive downtown was largely rebuilt after a fire in 1845. Round Top Center for the Arts is a 1.5 mile walk and offers classes, concerts, festivals and arts and crafts exhibits. Mon-Fri 11am-4pm , Sat, Sun noon-4pm. It's an easy walk across the bridge to Newcastle and the trailhead of the Salt Bay Preserve Heritage Trail's 3 mi. loop that skirts around Glidden Point. Or dinghy north under the bridge to the 8 acre Whaleback Park, home to Native American Glidden Point oyster shell mounds. Onsite Sea Spirit Kayak offers rentals and tours, including one going to nearby Dodge Point Wildlife Sanctuary.

Navigational Information
Lat: 43°49.893' **Long:** 069°35.191' **Tide:** 9 ft. **Current:** 2 kt. **Chart:** 13293
Rep. Depths (*MLW*): Entry 6 ft. **Fuel Dock** n/a **Max Slip/Moor** 11 ft./15 ft.
Access: Damariscotta River, Marker 35 to port, and into Little River

Marina Facilities *(In Season/Off Season)*
Fuel: *In Harbor* - Gasoline, Diesel
Slips: 8 Total, 2 Transient **Max LOA:** 52 ft. **Max Beam:** 15 ft.
Rate *(per ft.)*: **Day** $1.50* **Week** $5.00 **Month** $14
Power: 30 amp $2, **50 amp** $3, **100 amp** $4, **200 amp** n/a
Cable TV: No **Dockside Phone:** No
Dock Type: Wood, Alongside, Floating, Fixed
Moorings: 7 Total, 2 Transient **Launch:** n/a, Dinghy Dock
Rate: Day $20 **Week** $120 **Month** $300
Heads: 2 Toilet(s), 2 Shower(s)
Laundry: None **Pay Phones:** No
Pump-Out: No **Fee:** n/a **Closed Heads:** No

Marina Operations
Owner/Manager: George Horn Jr. **Dockmaster:** Tom Sissard
In-Season: May-Sep, 8am-6pm **Off-Season:** Closed
After-Hours Arrival: Pick up mooring or slip and see manager in morning
Reservations: Preferred **Credit Cards:** Cash/check
Discounts: None
Pets: Welcome, Dog Walk Area **Handicap Access:** No

Spar Shed Marina

PO Box 8381; Spar Shed Lane; East Boothbay, ME 04544

Tel: (207) 633-4389 **VHF: Monitor** n/a **Talk** n/a
Fax: (207) 633-4763 **Alternate Tel:** n/a
Email: sparshed@clinic.net **Web:** n/a
Nearest Town: Boothbay *(5 mi.)* **Tourist Info:** (207) 633-7448

Marina Services and Boat Supplies
Services - Docking Assistance, Security *(Manager lives on premises)*, Trash Pick-Up **Communication -** Mail & Package Hold, FedEx, AirBorne, UPS, Express Mail **Supplies - OnCall:** Ice *(Block, Cube)* **1-3 mi:** Ships' Store, West Marine, Bait/Tackle, Propane *(Dead River Oil 633-3144)*, CNG

Boatyard Services
OnSite: Brightwork, Compound, Wash & Wax, Interior Cleaning, Woodworking **OnCall:** Engine mechanic *(gas, diesel)*, Electrical Repairs, Bottom Cleaning, Air Conditioning, Divers, Inflatable Repairs, Upholstery **1-3 mi:** Travelift, Railway, Forklift, Crane, Launching Ramp, Electronic Sales, Hull Repairs, Rigger, Sail Loft, Canvas Work, Metal Fabrication, Yacht Design, Total Refits. **3+ mi:** Painting *(5 mi.)*, Awlgrip *(5 mi.)*. **Nearest Yard:** Ocean Point (207) 633-0773

Restaurants and Accommodations
Near: Restaurant *(1820 Restaurant 633-2800, D $7-18, part of Smuggler's Cove)*, Lite Fare *(Tea by the Sea bakery, sandwiches)*, Motel *(Smuggler's Cove Inn 633-2800, $70-180)* **Under 1 mi:** Restaurant *(Ocean Point Inn 633-4200, D $13-20)*, Hotel *(Ocean Point Inn 633-4200, $82-184)* **1-3 mi:** Restaurant *(Lobsterman's Wharf 633-3443, L $5-12, D $12-19)*, *(Carriage House 633-6025, D $9-20)*, Snack Bar *(East Boothbay General 633-4503)*, Inn/B&B *(Linekin Bay 633-9900, $85-175)*, *(Five Gable Inn 633-4551, $120-185)*

Recreation and Entertainment
Near: Jogging Paths **1-3 mi:** Beach, Tennis Courts **3+ mi:** Golf Course *(Boothbay Country Club 633-6085, 4 mi.)*, Fitness Center *(YMCA, 5 mi.)*, Video Rental *(Boothbay Harbor Framers 633-6509, 4 mi.)*, Museum *(Boothbay Railway Museum, 5 mi.)*

Provisioning and General Services
OnCall: Fishmonger *(Little River Lobster 633-2648)*, Lobster Pound *(Little River Lobster)*, Dry Cleaners *(Pick-up and delivery)* **Near:** Bakery *(Tea by the Sea)* **1-3 mi:** Convenience Store *(East Boothbay General Store)*, Post Office, Catholic Church, Protestant Church **3+ mi:** Supermarket *(Hannaford 366-6465, 5 mi.)*, Wine/Beer *(5 mi.)*, Bank/ATM *(5 mi.)*, Library *(Boothbay Harbor Library 633-3112, 5 mi.)*, Laundry *(5 mi.)*, Pharmacy *(Waltz 633-5323, 5 mi.)*, Hardware Store *(Poole Brothers Lumber 633-4474, 5 mi.)*, Copies Etc. *(Printing Plus 633-5139, 5 mi.)*

Transportation
OnSite: Bikes *(Free)* **OnCall:** Taxi *(Boothbay Harbor Taxi 633-6001)*, Airport Limo *(Mid Coast Limo 800-937-2424)* **Airport:** Portland Int'l. *(60 mi.)*

Medical Services
911 Service **OnCall:** Ambulance **1-3 mi:** Dentist *(Andrews 633-2128)* **3+ mi:** Doctor *(Boothbay Whole Health Medical Center 633-3535, 5 mi.)*, Chiropractor *(Coastal Chiropractic 633-4777, 5 mi.)*, Holistic Services *(Boothbay Whole Health Medical Center; Alt. Health Solutions 633-0072, 5 mi.)* **Hospital:** St. Andrews 633-7820 *(5 mi.)*

Setting -- Right at the mouth of the Damariscotta River, tucked into one of the area's most placid hurricane holes, is this small, photogenic, accommodating marina. It's on the west side of Little River Harbor, just four football fields from the open ocean, and it couldn't be quieter or prettier. A small gray building sits on the dock surrounded by flying flags, tables and chairs with green & white striped umbrellas, and mounds of potted flowers.

Marina Notes -- *Seasonal rental $42/ft. Family-owned and run, very service-oriented. Some basic boatyard services are onsite, others can be contracted for within the area. This facility was originally Little River Lobster Co.'s wholesale lobster pound. That business has now moved to the other side of the river. There is a small separate building that houses the head. Complimentary bicycles (if one assumes all risk) are a welcome perk. Good place to leave the boat; the Horns are happy to watch over it and also oversee any work that needs to be done. Cottage adjoining property available for rent (633-6545).

Notable -- Clearly a green-thumb resides here; the grounds are lovingly tended and there are flowers everywhere. A few restaurants are within a generous hiking or biking distance (along with the tiny, tourist-free village of East Boothbay) and dozens, by taxi, in Boothbay Harbor. Local artists' studios are nearby as is the historic Paul E. Luke boat building company. Most services are about five miles away in Boothbay Harbor. A major dinghy adventure (or big boat lunch stop) might be the Nature Conservancy's Damariscove Island, about 2 miles south. Two miles farther is the Island's harbor; at its head is a dinghy landing and sign-in book.

PHOTOS ON CD-ROM: 9

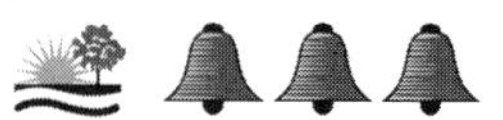

Smuggler's Cove Inn

PO Box 837; Route 96; East Boothbay, ME 04544

Tel: (207) 633-2800; (800) 633-3008 **VHF: Monitor** n/a **Talk** n/a
Fax: (207) 633-5926 **Alternate Tel:** (800) 633-3008
Email: info@smugglerscovemotel.com **Web:** smugglerscovemotel.com
Nearest Town: Boothbay *(4.5 mi.)* **Tourist Info:** (207) 633-7448

Navigational Information

Lat: 43°49.870' **Long:** 069°35.556' **Tide:** 12 ft. **Current:** 1 kt. **Chart:** 13293
Rep. Depths (*MLW*): Entry 30 ft. **Fuel Dock** n/a **Max Slip/Moor** -/50 ft.
Access: Gulf of Maine to Linekin Bay

Marina Facilities *(In Season/Off Season)*

Fuel: No
Slips: 0 Total, 0 Transient **Max LOA:** n/a **Max Beam:** n/a
Rate *(per ft.)*: **Day** n/a **Week** n/a **Month** n/a
Power: 30 amp n/a, **50 amp** n/a, **100 amp** n/a, **200 amp** n/a
Cable TV: No **Dockside Phone:** No
Dock Type: Wood, Floating
Moorings: 7 Total, 4 Transient **Launch:** None, Dinghy Dock
Rate: Day $25/25 **Week** $125 **Month** $600 Max LOA: 60 ft.
Heads: 2 Toilet(s), 2 Shower(s) *(with dressing rooms)*, Hair Dryers
Laundry: None **Pay Phones:** No
Pump-Out: No **Fee:** n/a **Closed Heads:** No

Marina Operations

Owner/Manager: Paul Daniels **Dockmaster:** Same
In-Season: May-Oct, 8am-12mid **Off-Season:** Oct 15-May 25, 8am-10pm
After-Hours Arrival: Call ahead
Reservations: Preferred **Credit Cards:** Visa/MC, Dscvr, Amex
Discounts: None
Pets: Welcome, Dog Walk Area **Handicap Access:** No

Marina Services and Boat Supplies

Services - Boaters' Lounge, Trash Pick-Up **Communication -** Phone Messages, Fax in/out *($2)*, FedEx, AirBorne, UPS, Express Mail **Supplies - OnSite:** Ice *(Cube)* **Under 1 mi:** Ice *(Block)* **1-3 mi:** Ships' Store, Bait/Tackle, Propane *(General Store)*

Boatyard Services

OnCall: Rigger, Sail Loft *(Wilson Sailmaker 633-5071)*, Canvas Work, Refrigeration, Divers **Near:** Electrical Repairs *(Marine Wiring & Electronics 633-3277)*, Electronic Sales, Electronics Repairs *(Coastal Marine 633-7090)*, Propeller Repairs *(Paul Luke)*, Metal Fabrication, Painting. **Under 1 mi:** Travelift, Railway, Forklift, Crane, Engine mechanic *(diesel)*, Launching Ramp. **1-3 mi:** Hull Repairs. **Nearest Yard:** Paul E. Luke (207) 633-4971

Restaurants and Accommodations

OnSite: Restaurant *(1820 House B $4-6, D $7-19, Salads, Sandwiches to Complete Dinners; Sun Brunch $11/7 10am-1pm)*, Motel *(Smuggler's Cove Inn 633-2800, $70-190)* **Under 1 mi:** Restaurant *(Ocean Point Inn 633-4200, D $13-20)* **1-3 mi:** Restaurant *(Carriage House 633-6025, D $9-20)*, *(Lobsterman's Wharf 633-5481, L $5-12, D $12-19)*, Snack Bar *(East Boothbay General)*, Hotel *(Ocean Point Inn 633-4200, $80-185)*, Inn/B&B *(The Inn at Lobsterman's Wharf 633-5481)*, *(Five Gables Inn 633-4551, $130-195)*

Recreation and Entertainment

OnSite: Heated Pool *(84 degrees)*, Beach *(Sandy)*, Boat Rentals *(Windborne Cruises 40' SV Tribute $25/2 hrs., or charter $400/day)* **OnCall:** Group Fishing Boat, Video Rental **Near:** Tennis Courts, Fitness Center **Under 1 mi:** Horseback Riding, Roller Blade/Bike Paths, Fishing Charter **1-3 mi:** Movie Theater, Museum *(Boothbay Region Historical Society 633-0820)*, Sightseeing *(Linekin Preserve Hiking Trails 633-4818)* **3+ mi:** Golf Course *(Boothbay Country Club 633-6085, 4 mi.)*

Provisioning and General Services

Near: Bakery *(Tea by the Sea)* **Under 1 mi:** Newsstand **1-3 mi:** Provisioning Service, Convenience Store *(E Boothbay General)*, Delicatessen *(General Store)*, Wine/Beer, Liquor Store, Bank/ATM, Post Office, Catholic Church, Protestant Church, Library *(Boothbay Harbor 633-3112)*, Beauty Salon, Barber Shop, Dry Cleaners, Laundry, Bookstore, Pharmacy *(Waltz 633-5323)*, Hardware Store *(Poole Brothers Lumber 633-4474)*, Retail Shops, Copies Etc. **3+ mi:** Supermarket *(Hannaford 633-6465, 5 mi.)*

Transportation

OnCall: Rental Car *(Enterprise 882-8393/Strong's)*, Taxi *(Mark's 592-6660)*
Airport: Wiscassett/Portland Int'l. *(20 mi./50 mi.)*

Medical Services

911 Service **OnCall:** Ambulance **1-3 mi:** Doctor *(Boothbay Whole Health Medical Center 633-3535)*, Dentist, Chiropractor *(Coastal Chiropractic 633-4777)*, Holistic Services *(Alt. Health Solutions 633-0072)* **Hospital:** St. Andrews 633-7820 *(8 mi.)*

Setting -- Set in a beautiful, tranquil private cove on Linekin Bay, Smuggler's Cove offers crusiers over 3 acres of attractively landscaped grounds, a private sandy beach, an outdoor heated pool, an onsite restaurant -- and the possibility of getting off the boat for a night or two. There are also spectacular sunsets.

Marina Notes -- Built in 1965 by a health professor from Cornell Medical Center, this family owned and operated complex is now managed by the second generation (with help from the third). The full-service 1820 House Restaurant, in an authentic early 19thC structure, is open May 15-Oct 15. Breakfast 7 days (8-10am, Sun brunch 10am-1pm) and Dinner Tue-Sat 6-9pm. Local artists entertain Fri and Sat. The two story motel has 60 comfortable rooms, all with bay-view balconies. There is a clear commitment to maintenance and service -- the facility seems in a constant state of discreet renovation and upgrade. For now, a motel room bathroom is dedicated to cruisers; in 2003 dedicated heads and showers will be constructed. There are rowboats, a "loaner" dinghy, and a fishing pier. Water's Edge Motel (633-2505) may also have moorings.

Notable -- A 2 mile walk to the quiet little boat-building community of East Boothbay will net a post office, two restaurants, two inns, a general store, and a taste of the non-touristy part of the Maine coast. A walk south leads to the Ocean Point Inn and Restaurant. Just up the road is the historic Paul E. Luke boatyard; an advance call might permit the opportunity to view their small, private "museum" which is housed in a one-room structure -- it displays the yard's history and its current product lines. Farther up the road is 95 acre Linekin Preserve with a 2.3 miles hiking trail along the Damariscotta River.

Navigational Information

Lat: 43°50.025' **Long:** 069°35.532' **Tide:** 8 ft. **Current:** 1 kt. **Chart:** 13293
Rep. Depths (*MLW*): Entry 55 ft. **Fuel Dock** n/a **Max Slip/Moor** 12 ft./80 ft.
Access: Gulf of Maine to Linekin Bay - starboard side

Marina Facilities *(In Season/Off Season)*

Fuel: No
Slips: 0 Total, 0 Transient **Max LOA:** 50 ft. **Max Beam:** n/a
Rate *(per ft.)*: **Day** n/a **Week** n/a **Month** n/a
Power: 30 amp n/a, **50 amp** n/a, **100 amp** n/a, **200 amp** n/a
Cable TV: No **Dockside Phone:** No
Dock Type: Wood, Floating
Moorings: 19 Total, 10 Transient **Launch:** None, Dinghy Dock
Rate: Day $12 **Week** $70.00 **Month** Inq.
Heads: None
Laundry: None **Pay Phones:** No
Pump-Out: No **Fee:** n/a **Closed Heads:** No

Marina Operations

Owner/Manager: The Luke Family **Dockmaster:** Frank Luke
In-Season: Year Round, 9am-5pm **Off-Season:** n/a
After-Hours Arrival: Call in advance
Reservations: Yes **Credit Cards:** Cash only
Discounts: None
Pets: Welcome **Handicap Access:** No

Paul E. Luke

15 Luke's Gulch; East Boothbay, ME 04544

Tel: (207) 633-4971 **VHF: Monitor** n/a **Talk** n/a
Fax: (207) 633-3388 **Alternate Tel:** (207) 633-3487
Email: Frank@peluke.com **Web:** www.peluke.com
Nearest Town: Boothbay Harbor *(5 mi.)* **Tourist Info:** (207) 633-7448

Marina Services and Boat Supplies

Communication - FedEx, AirBorne, UPS, Express Mail **Supplies - 1-3 mi:** Ice *(Cube)*, Propane **3+ mi:** Ships' Store *(5 mi.)*, Bait/Tackle *(5 mi.)*

Boatyard Services

OnSite: Railway *(25T)*, Engine mechanic *(gas, diesel)*, Hull Repairs, Rigger, Brightwork, Compound, Wash & Wax, Propeller Repairs, Woodworking, Metal Fabrication, Painting, Awlgrip, Yacht Design, Yacht Broker **OnCall:** Electrical Repairs, Electronic Sales, Electronics Repairs, Canvas Work, Bottom Cleaning, Air Conditioning, Refrigeration, Divers, Upholstery, Yacht Interiors **1-3 mi:** Launching Ramp, Sail Loft. **Dealer for:** Paul E. Luke two and three blade feathering propellers, soapstone and tile fireplaces, bronze and aluminum ventilators, 12' QT rowboat, Heritage galley stoves, and storm anchors. **Yard Rates:** $45/hr., Haul & Launch $10/ft., Power Wash $35

Restaurants and Accommodations

Near: Restaurant *(1820 House 633-2800, B $6, D $7-18)*, Motel *(Smuggler's Cove Inn 633-2800, $70-180)* **Under 1 mi:** Restaurant *(Ocean Point Inn D $13-20)*, Inn/B&B *(Ocean Point Inn 633-4200, $80-285)* **1-3 mi:** Restaurant *(Carriage House 633-6025, D $9-20)*, *(Lobstermen's Wharf L $5-12, D $12-19)*, Snack Bar *(East Boothbay General Store)*, Inn/B&B *(Inn at Lobstermen's Wharf 633-5481)*, *(Five Gables 633-4551, $130-195)*

Recreation and Entertainment

OnSite: Jogging Paths **OnCall:** Group Fishing Boat, Video Rental **Near:** Tennis Courts, Fitness Center, Boat Rentals **Under 1 mi:** Horseback Riding, Roller Blade/Bike Paths **1-3 mi:** Movie Theater, Museum *(Boothbay Region Historical Society 633-0820)* **3+ mi:** Golf Course *(Boothbay Country Club 633-6085, 4 mi.)*, Park *(3 mi.)*

Provisioning and General Services

Near: Bakery *(Tea by the Sea)* **Under 1 mi:** Newsstand **1-3 mi:** Convenience Store *(East Boothbay General Store)*, Delicatessen *(General Store)*, Wine/Beer, Liquor Store, Lobster Pound, Bank/ATM, Post Office, Catholic Church, Protestant Church, Library *(Boothbay Harbor 633-3112)*, Beauty Salon, Dry Cleaners, Laundry, Bookstore, Pharmacy *(Waltz 633-5323)*, Hardware Store *(Poole Bros Lumber 633-4474)*, Retail Shops, Copies Etc. **3+ mi:** Supermarket *(Hannafords 633-6465, 5 mi.)*

Transportation

OnCall: Rental Car *(Enterprise 882-8393 / Strong's)*, Taxi *(Mark's 592-6660)* **Airport:** Wiscassett/Portland Int'l. *(20 mi./50 mi.)*

Medical Services

911 Service **OnCall:** Ambulance **1-3 mi:** Doctor *(Boothbay Whole Health Med Center 633-3535)*, Dentist, Chiropractor *(Coastal Chiro 633-4777)*, Holistic Services *(Alternative Health Solutions 633-0072)* **Hospital:** St. Andrews 633-7820 *(8 mi.)*

Setting -- On the east side of Linekin Bay, just past Smuggler's Cove Resort in Lewis Cove, are the white sheds and docks of the Paul E. Luke boatyard. The small mooring field has a panoramic view of the Bay and is usually a quiet anchorage.

Marina Notes -- Neither power, launch, nor heads or showers available. Known historically for traditional boat building and ocean racing, and more currently for specialty parts, the Paul E. Luke Yard began its illustrious career in 1939 when it built two 37' cutters for designer Winthrop Warner. It subsequently built dozens of spectacular wooden yachts for well-known designers like Alden, Sparkman & Stephens, Nielsen, etc., and made most of the fittings and parts in-house. Eventually they moved from wood to aluminum construction and established a reputation in that area. In recent years, the yard has focused on its custom, high-end "fittings" and "parts" business: beautiful soapstone, brass and tile boat fireplace stoves, feathering props, 3-piece Luke anchors, galley stoves, dorades, etc. John P. Luke's North Atlantic Industries builds aluminum boats, while Coastal Marine Electronics installs and services electronics. They have also launched a new boat - an elegant 12 ft. rowing dinghy that is absolutely exquisite! Note: the yard and facilities are in serious need of maintenance.

Notable -- Those with interest in maritime history might enjoy Roger Duncan's latest book: "Dorothy Elizabeth: Building a Traditional Wooden Schooner" in which Paul E. Luke is a prominent player. Also, if you call in advance, you might be able to view the private Luke "museum": a small, self-contained building displaying the yard's history as well as its current product lines. Alternatively, a walk south leads to the Ocean Point Inn & Restaurant.

ME - BOOTHBAY HARBOR REGION
PHOTOS ON CD-ROM: 8

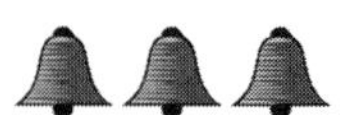

Carousel Marina

P.O.Box 11; 125 Atlantic Avenue; Boothbay Harbor, ME 04538

Tel: (207) 633-2922 **VHF: Monitor** 9 **Talk** 68
Fax: (207) 633-2922 **Alternate Tel:** n/a
Email: carousel1@gwi.net **Web:** n/a
Nearest Town: Boothbay Harbor *(0.5 mi.)* **Tourist Info:** (207) 633-7448

Navigational Information

Lat: 43°50.658' **Long:** 069°37.594' **Tide:** 11 ft. **Current:** 0 kt. **Chart:** 13296
Rep. Depths (*MLW*): Entry 30 ft. **Fuel Dock** 30 ft. **Max Slip/Moor** 40 ft./40 ft.
Access: Just past McKown Point, first facility on western shore

Marina Facilities *(In Season/Off Season)*

Fuel: *Texaco* - Gasoline, Diesel, High-Speed Pumps
Slips: 40 Total, 18 Transient **Max LOA:** 130 ft. **Max Beam:** n/a
Rate *(per ft.)*: **Day** $1.75/1.25* **Week** $8.00 **Month** $24
Power: 30 amp $3.75, **50 amp** $5.75, **100 amp** n/a, **200 amp** n/a
Cable TV: No **Dockside Phone:** No
Dock Type: Wood, Long Fingers, Floating
Moorings: 27 Total, 15 Transient **Launch:** None
Rate: Day $25/20 **Week** $155 **Month** $500
Heads: 4 Toilet(s), 5 Shower(s) *(with dressing rooms)*
Laundry: 2 Washer(s), 2 Dryer(s), Book Exchange **Pay Phones:** Yes
Pump-Out: OnSite, Full Service, 1 Port **Fee:** $25 **Closed Heads:** Yes

Marina Operations

Owner/Manager: Pat Gottlieb **Dockmaster:** Linda Allen
In-Season: Jul & Aug, 8am-6pm **Off-Season:** May-Jun & Sep-Oct, 9am-5pm
After-Hours Arrival: Call ahead for arrangements
Reservations: Yes, Preferred **Credit Cards:** Visa/MC, Dscvr, Amex, Tex
Discounts: 50+ gals fuel **Dockage:** n/a **Fuel:** $0.5 **Repair:** n/a
Pets: Welcome, Dog Walk Area **Handicap Access:** No

Marina Services and Boat Supplies

Services - Docking Assistance, Boaters' Lounge, Trash Pick-Up, Dock Carts **Communication -** Mail & Package Hold, Phone Messages, Fax in/out, Data Ports *(Phone area upstairs)*, FedEx, AirBorne, UPS, Express Mail *(Sat Del)* **Supplies - OnSite:** Ice *(Block, Cube)*, Ships' Store, CNG **1-3 mi:** Bait/Tackle *(White Anchor 633-3788)*, Propane *(Dead River Company 633-3144)*

Boatyard Services

OnSite: Launching Ramp **OnCall:** Bottom Cleaning, Divers **Near:** Engine mechanic *(gas, diesel)*. **Under 1 mi:** Electrical Repairs, Electronics Repairs, Hull Repairs. **1-3 mi:** Rigger, Refrigeration. **Nearest Yard:** Maine Yacht Services (207) 633-6374

Restaurants and Accommodations

OnSite: Restaurant *(Carousel Restaurant 633-6644, L $4-9, D $8-20, 11am-3:30pm, 5-9pm, also a take out menu)*, Coffee Shop **Near:** Restaurant *(Rocktide 633-4470, D $10-22, guest docks)*, *(Talay Thai 633-0025)*, *(Brown's Wharf 633-5540, D $11-19)*, Seafood Shack *(Lobstermen's Co-op 633-4900, L $3-16, D $3-16)*, *(Lobster Dock 633-7120)*, Motel *(Captain Fish's Motel & Marina 633-6605, $55-120)*, Hotel *(Brown's Wharf 633-5440, $80-160)* **Under 1 mi:** Restaurant *(Spruce Point Inn Dining Room 633-4125, D $16-25)*, Hotel *(Spruce Point Inn 633-4151, $155-185)*

Recreation and Entertainment

OnSite: Picnic Area, Grills **Near:** Jogging Paths, Roller Blade/Bike Paths, Bowling, Fishing Charter, Park, Special Events **Under 1 mi:** Boat Rentals, Galleries **1-3 mi:** Playground, Dive Shop, Tennis Courts, Golf Course *(Boothbay Country Club 633-6085)*, Fitness Center, Movie Theater *(Harbor Theatre 633-0438)*, Video Rental *(Video Loft 633-6509)*, Video Arcade *(Harbor Light 633-3799 in Meadow Mall)*, Museum *(Railway Museum 633-4727)*, Cultural Attract *(Carousel Music Theater 633-5297)*

Provisioning and General Services

OnSite: Convenience Store, Laundry *(24 hrs.)*, Newsstand **Near:** Fishmonger *(Sea Pier 633-0627)*, Lobster Pound *(Lobsterman's Co-op 633-4900)*, Catholic Church **Under 1 mi:** Gourmet Shop *(Village Market 633-0944)*, Delicatessen, Wine/Beer, Bank/ATM, Post Office *(633-3090)*, Protestant Church, Beauty Salon, Dry Cleaners, Bookstore *(Sherman's 633-3112)*, Hardware Store *(Grovers 633-2694)*, Florist **1-3 mi:** Supermarket *(Hannaford 633-6465)*, Bakery *(P&P Pastry 633-6511)*, Farmers' Market *(at Mini Mall, Thu 9am-noon)*, Meat Market, Library *(Boothbay Harbor Library 633-3112)*, Pharmacy *(Waltz 633-5323)*, Clothing Store, Retail Shops, Copies Etc. *(Mail Boxes Etc. 633-9991)*

Transportation

OnCall: Rental Car *(Enterprise 882-8393)*, Taxi *(Boothbay Harbor Taxi 633-6001)* **Near:** Bikes, Water Taxi, Local Bus *(Rocktide's & Cap'n Fish's free trolley service 10am-5pm)* **Airport:** Portland Int'l. *(45 mi.)*

Medical Services

911 Service **OnCall:** Ambulance **Near:** Chiropractor *(Coastal Chiropractic 633-4777)* **Under 1 mi:** Doctor *(Whole Health Medical Center 633-3535)*, Dentist *(Family Dental 633-4243)*, Holistic Services *(Orne Massage Therapy 633-6405; Alt. Health Solutions 633-0072)* **1-3 mi:** Veterinarian *(Animal Hosp. 633-3447)* **Hospital:** St. Andrews 633-2121, has dock *(1.5 mi.)*

Setting -- As you enter Boothbay Harbor, Carousel is the first marina on your starboard side on Spruce Point. A gray, two story building with red & white striped awning and a big Texaco sign, it is surrounded by low-rise gray clapboard condos with green & white striped awnings. Stunning views from the docks look outward to the open bay and inward to the bustling harbor. Even though it is near the southern end of the harbor, most services are still an easy walk.

Marina Notes -- *Over 80 ft. $2.25/ft. About 400 ft. of linear dockage. The amenities are graced with a thoughtful, feminine hand; the management has tried to accommodate most cruiser needs. The complimentary Breakfast Galley offers hot beverages, fruit and donuts. The boaters' lounge has cable TV, snacks, "big city" newspapers, a book exchange, and a small kitchen. Phone area upstairs has data ports for computers. Also onsite are dockside picnic tables, a full marine store, and the new Carousel Restaurant (formerly Groovey's) with inside and patio dining -- it's also available for large functions. Both in-house and 24-hour coin-op showers are available -- $2 each (nicely appointed with courtesy supplies). Very dog friendly. Group discounts to yacht clubs.

Notable -- It is a half mile walk from Carousel to the head of the harbor bridge which provides direct access to all of the tourist, retail, and recreational attractions of Boothbay Harbor. Along the way, you will pass restaurants, lobster pounds, inns, motels and other services. Alternatively, there is a free shoppers trolley that stops nearby and goes to the mall and many attractions. Right next door is Brown's Wharf Inn and a 2/3 mile walk the other way (south) will lead to Spruce Point Inn and Restaurant, a sprawling high-end resort with shuttle service. Pick up a copy of the local maps and guides for a complete list.

Navigational Information
Lat: 43°50.684' **Long:** 069°37.555' **Tide:** 11 ft. **Current:** 0 kt. **Chart:** 13296
Rep. Depths (*MLW*): Entry 20 ft. **Fuel Dock** 20 ft. **Max Slip/Moor** 20 ft./20 ft.
Access: Past McKown Point, second facility on eastern shore

Marina Facilities *(In Season/Off Season)*
Fuel: No
Slips: 50 Total, 15 Transient **Max LOA:** 150 ft. **Max Beam:** n/a
Rate *(per ft.)*: **Day** $2.00/Inq.* **Week** Inq. **Month** Inq.
Power: 30 amp $3, **50 amp** $6, **100 amp** n/a, **200 amp** n/a
Cable TV: Yes **Dockside Phone:** No
Dock Type: Wood, Long Fingers, Floating
Moorings: 10 Total, 6 Transient **Launch:** None, Dinghy Dock
Rate: Day $24 **Week** Inq. **Month** Inq.
Heads: 3 Toilet(s), 2 Shower(s)
Laundry: 2 Washer(s), 2 Dryer(s) **Pay Phones:** Yes, 1
Pump-Out: No **Fee:** n/a **Closed Heads:** No

Marina Operations
Owner/Manager: Ken Brown **Dockmaster:** Timothy Brown
In-Season: May 15-Oct 10, 8am-8pm **Off-Season:** Closed
After-Hours Arrival: Call in advance
Reservations: Yes** **Credit Cards:** Visa/MC, Amex
Discounts: None
Pets: Welcome **Handicap Access:** No

Brown's Wharf Marina

PO Box 460; 121 Atlantic Avenue; Boothbay Harbor, ME 04538

Tel: (207) 633-5440; (800) 334-8110 **VHF: Monitor** 9 **Talk** 68
Fax: (207) 633-5440 **Alternate Tel:** (800) 334-8110
Email: Brownswharf@clinic.net **Web:** www.brownswharfinn.com
Nearest Town: Boothbay Harbor *(0.5 mi.)* **Tourist Info:** (207) 633-7448

Marina Services and Boat Supplies
Services - Docking Assistance, Boaters' Lounge, Security *(24 Hrs.)*, Dock Carts **Communication -** Mail & Package Hold, Phone Messages, Fax in/out, Data Ports *(Boaters Lounge)*, FedEx, AirBorne, UPS, Express Mail *(Sat Del)* **Supplies - OnSite:** Ice *(Block, Cube)* **Near:** Ships' Store, CNG *(Carousel Marina next door 633-2922)* **1-3 mi:** Bait/Tackle *(White Anchor 633-3788)*, Propane *(Dead River Co. 633-3144)*

Boatyard Services
OnCall: Divers **Near:** Launching Ramp, Electrical Repairs, Electronics Repairs, Hull Repairs, Rigger, Bottom Cleaning, Brightwork, Refrigeration. **Under 1 mi:** Engine mechanic *(gas, diesel)*. **1-3 mi:** Sail Loft. **Nearest Yard:** Boothbay Region Boatyard 1 mi. (207) 633-2970

Restaurants and Accommodations
OnSite: Restaurant *(Brown's Wharf Restaurant 633-5440, D $11-19)*, Motel *(Brown's Wharf 633-5440, $80-209, 70 rooms, cottages & efficiencies)* **Near:** Restaurant *(Cap'n Fish's 633-6605, B only)*, *(Rocktide Restaurant 633-4455, D $10-22)*, *(Boat House Bistro 633-7300, L $6-14, D $16-30)*, *(Christopher's Boathouse 633-6565, L $6-10, D $16-27)*, *(Carousel Restaurant 633-6644, L $4-9, D $8-20)*, Seafood Shack *(Lobster Dock 633-7120, L $3-15, D $3-15)*, Inn/B&B *(Boothbay Harbor Inn 633-6302, $60-180)* **Under 1 mi:** Restaurant *(Spruce Point Dining Room 633-4152, L $12-20, D $12-20)*, Pizzeria *(Seymour's 633-9707)*, Hotel *(Spruce Point Inn Resort 633-4152, $155-185)*

Recreation and Entertainment
Near: Park, Special Events *(Windjammer Days - mid June)* **Under 1 mi:** Playground, Sightseeing *(Whale Watching)*, Galleries *(Head of the Harbor)* **1-3 mi:** Tennis Courts, Golf Course *(Boothbay Country Club 633-6085)*, Fitness Center *(YMCA)*, Movie Theater *(Harbor Theatre 633-0438)*, Video Rental *(Video Loft 633-6509)*, Video Arcade *(Harbor Light 633-3799)*, Museum *(Aquarium 633-9559, Boothbay Historical Society 633-0820)*, Cultural Attract *(Carousel Music & Dinner Theater 633-5297)*

Provisioning and General Services
Near: Fishmonger *(Sea Pier 633-0627)*, Lobster Pound *(Lobstermen's Co-op)*, Catholic Church **Under 1 mi:** Gourmet Shop *(Village Market 633-0944)*, Delicatessen, Wine/Beer, Bank/ATM, Post Office, Protestant Church, Beauty Salon, Barber Shop, Dry Cleaners, Bookstore *(Sherman's 633-7262)*, Hardware Store *(Grovers 633-2694)*, Florist **1-3 mi:** Supermarket *(Hannaford 633-6465)*, Bakery, Farmers' Market *(Mini Mall, Thu 9am-noon)*, Library *(633-3112)*, Laundry, Pharmacy *(Waltz 633-5323)*, Retail Shops, Copies Etc. *(Mail Boxes Etc. 633-9991)*

Transportation
OnSite: Courtesy Car/Van, Water Taxi, Local Bus *(Free Shoppers Trolleys)* **OnCall:** Rental Car *(Enterprise 882-8393)*, Taxi *(Boothbay Harbor Taxi 633-6001)* **Under 1 mi:** Ferry Service *(Balmy Days II, Monhegan Isl. 633-2284 Daily 9:30am)* **Airport:** Wiscasset/Portland Int'l. *(15 mi./50 mi.)*

Medical Services
911 Service **OnCall:** Ambulance **Under 1 mi:** Doctor *(Boothbay Whole Health Medical Center 633-3535)*, Dentist, Chiropractor *(Coastal Chiropractic 633-4777)*, Holistic Services *(Alt. Health Solutions 633-0072)* **1-3 mi:** Veterinarian **Hospital:** St. Andrews 633-2121, has dock *(1.5 mi.)*

Setting -- Historic Brown's Wharf is picturesque Boothbay Harbor's second marina to starboard. This flower-bedecked, particulary well cared for resort facility is easy to spot -- look for its bold name, flags and the attractive three-story motel facility. Although it is on the "quiet side" of the Harbor, the bustling marina, restaurant and motel complex is a great place to view the action. The docks offer wonderful views of the harbor, the open water, and of delightfully ubiquitous pots of flowers.

Marina Notes -- * Over 60 ft. $2.50/ft. ** Reservations for slips only. Moorings are first come, first served. 3rd generation family management has been here for more than six decades. Many amenities for cruisers. Charles Kuralt's favorite stop. In-season, Breakfast and Dinner are served at the onsite seafood restaurant (the crew will enjoy the large ship models) -- dinner only during the off-season. Try the Old Salt Shed Lounge, too. Heads and showers are inviting, but a bit distant from the dock - $1 for a 10 minute shower. Arriving landside you are greeted by the famous statue of the giant, oil-skinned lobsterman -- and more flowers. Fuel is available from Coastal Marine's fuel boat - at their mooring in the harbor, or delivered dockside for 100 gallons or more.

Notable -- All of Boothbay Harbor is easily accessible whether by foot, dinghy (town dock) or two free trolleys; get a booklet and a map. Whatever your pleasure, you'll likely find it here. Whale watching 633-3244. Friendship Sloop days, third week in July. Windjammer Days in mid-June. The current Boothbay high-end restaurant "faves" are the two "boathouses." There are some first-rate galleries scattered throughout Boothbay; pick up a guide at Head of the Harbor.

PHOTOS ON CD-ROM: 9

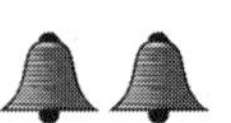

Cap'n Fish's Motel & Marina

PO Box 660; 65 Atlantic Avenue; Boothbay Harbor, ME 04538

Tel: (207) 633-6605; (800) 633-0860 **VHF: Monitor** 9 **Talk** 9
Fax: (207) 633-6239 **Alternate Tel:** n/a
Email: n/a **Web:** www.capnfishmotel.com
Nearest Town: Boothbay Harbor *(0.3 mi.)* **Tourist Info:** (207) 633-7448

Navigational Information
Lat: 43°50.879' **Long:** 069°37.466' **Tide:** 11 ft. **Current:** 0 kt. **Chart:** 13296
Rep. Depths (*MLW*): Entry 15 ft. **Fuel Dock** n/a **Max Slip/Moor** 10 ft./10 ft.
Access: Past G9 on the eastern shore of Boothbay Harbor

Marina Facilities *(In Season/Off Season)*
Fuel: No
Slips: 7 Total, 2 Transient **Max LOA:** 155 ft. **Max Beam:** 29 ft.
Rate *(per ft.)*: **Day** $2.00 **Week** Inq. **Month** Inq.
Power: 30 amp $3, **50 amp** $6, **100 amp** n/a, **200 amp** n/a
Cable TV: No **Dockside Phone:** No
Dock Type: Floating
Moorings: 6 Total, 0 Transient **Launch:** n/a
Rate: Day n/a **Week** n/a **Month** n/a
Heads: 1 Toilet(s)
Laundry: None **Pay Phones:** Yes
Pump-Out: No **Fee:** n/a **Closed Heads:** No

Marina Operations
Owner/Manager: Bob Fish **Dockmaster:** Bob Fish/Ross Maddocks
In-Season: MidMay-MidOct, 7am-11pm **Off-Season:** Closed
After-Hours Arrival: Check in at Motel desk
Reservations: Yes, Preferred **Credit Cards:** Visa/MC, Amex
Discounts: None
Pets: Welcome **Handicap Access:** No

Marina Services and Boat Supplies
Communication - Phone Messages, Fax in/out *($1)*, FedEx, AirBorne, UPS, Express Mail *(Sat Del)* **Supplies - OnSite:** Ice *(Cube)* **Near:** Ships' Store, CNG *(Carousel Marina 633-2922)* **Under 1 mi:** Propane *(Dead River Company 633-3144)* **1-3 mi:** Bait/Tackle *(White Anchor 633-3788)*

Boatyard Services
OnCall: Electrical Repairs **Near:** Engine mechanic *(gas, diesel)*, Bottom Cleaning, Brightwork. **Under 1 mi:** Railway, Forklift, Launching Ramp, Electronic Sales, Hull Repairs, Rigger, Sail Loft, Air Conditioning. **1-3 mi:** Travelift, Crane, Electronics Repairs. **Nearest Yard:** Sample's Shipyard (207) 633-6920

Restaurants and Accommodations
OnSite: Snack Bar *(Dockside Coffee Shop B $3-7)*, Motel *(Cap'n Fish's Motel 633-6605, $65-130)* **Near:** Restaurant *(Brown's Wharf 633-5440, D $11-19)*, *(Boothbay Harbor Inn D.R. B $6-9, D $12-20)*, *(Christopher's Boathouse 633-6565, L $6-10, D $16-27)*, Seafood Shack *(Sea Pier 633-0627, L $2-$16, D $2-16)*, *(Lobster Dock 633-7120, L $12-20, D $12-20)*, Pizzeria *(House of Pizza 633-3468)*, Motel *(Rocktide Inn 633-4455, $82-162, docks for guests)*, Hotel *(Brown's Wharf 633-5440, $80-160)*, Inn/B&B *(Boothbay Harbor Inn 633-6302, $60-180)*, Condo/Cottage *(Griffin Boat House Cottages 633-6300, 2 rustic boathouses perched over the water)* **Under 1 mi:** Restaurant *(Boathouse Bistro 633-7300, L $6-14, D $16-30)*

Recreation and Entertainment
Near: Beach, Boat Rentals *(Tidal Transit Ocean Kayak 633-7140)*, Sightseeing *(Cap'n Fish's Boat Trips)*, Special Events *(Windjammer Days late June)* **Under 1 mi:** Playground, Fishing Charter, Group Fishing Boat, Park **1-3 mi:** Golf Course *(Boothbay Country Club 633-6085)*, Fitness Center *(YMCA)*, Movie Theater *(Harbor Theatre 633-0438)*, Video Rental *(Video Loft 633-6509)*, Video Arcade *(Harbor Light 633-3799 in Meadow Mall)*, Museum *(Boothbay Railway Museum 633-4727)*, Cultural Attract *(Carousel Music Theater 633-5297)*

Provisioning and General Services
Near: Provisioning Service, Convenience Store *(Village Market 633-0944)*, Wine/Beer, Fishmonger *(Sea Pier 633-0627)*, Lobster Pound *(Fishermen's Co-op)*, Catholic Church, Beauty Salon, Bookstore *(Sherman's 633-7262)* **Under 1 mi:** Supermarket *(Hannaford 633-6465)*, Gourmet Shop, Delicatessen, Liquor Store, Bakery *(P&P Pastry 633-6511)*, Farmers' Market *(Thu 9am-noon at Mini Mall)*, Bank/ATM, Post Office *(633-3090)*, Protestant Church, Library *(Boothbay Harbor 633-3112)*, Dry Cleaners, Laundry, Pharmacy *(Waltz 633-5323)*, Hardware Store *(Grovers 633-2694)*, Florist, Clothing Store, Retail Shops, Copies Etc. *(Mail Boxes Etc. 633-9991)*

Transportation
OnSite: Local Bus *(Free shopping trolleys)* **OnCall:** Water Taxi, Rental Car *(Enterprise 882-8393)*, Taxi *(Boothbay Harbor Taxi 633-6001)* **Near:** Bikes *(Rentals in town)* **Airport:** Portland Int'l. *(60 mi.)*

Medical Services
911 Service **OnCall:** Ambulance **Near:** Doctor *(Whole Health Medical Center 633-3535)* **Under 1 mi:** Dentist *(Family Dental 633-4243)*, Chiropractor *(Coastal Chiropractic 633-4777)*, Holistic Services *(Alt. Health Solutions 633-0072)* **Hospital:** St. Andrews 633-2121, has dock *(1.5 mi.)*

Setting -- Just past the Fishermen's Co-op on the town wharf, Cap'n Fish is the third recreational facility to starboard. This low-key facility, with its deep tan buildings and bold sign, offers hospitable, basic wharfage in the most convenient location on the "quiet side" of town. The docks have great views of downtown and are only about an eighth of a mile from the footbridge that crosses into the heart of the action.

Marina Notes -- Founded in 1972, the marina is owned and operated by Boothbay native Captain Bob Fish, who is also the owner of the area's largest fleet of sightseeing boats. Captain Fish originally opened the marina/motel as a comfortable rest-stop for tourists visiting Boothbay. One long floating along-side dock plus a dinghy dock. Special slip rate of $.75/foot if you stay in the motel -- which offers simple but comfortable rooms. There is dockside breakfast every morning; choose from the buffet or an à la carte menu. Keep in mind, there is only one head, shared with the Dockside Coffee Shop, and no showers.

Notable -- Not surprisingly, Cap'n Fish has numerous whale watching trips, scenic nature cruises, a puffin safari, and other boat trips. Call for more info: 800-636-3244 or 207-633-3244/2626, or check at the motel desk. Most leave from Pier One across the harbor, are from 1-3 hours, with rates ranging from $12-25 (kids $6-15). Cap'n Fish also sponsors one of the two free trolley services which provide easy access to the shopping mall, supermarket, and many attractions. There's also a town dock just south of Boothbay Harbor Marina for 3-hr. tie-ups. Railway Village is open 9:30am-5pm, $7/3. Monhegan Island Daytrips on Balmy Days 9:30am, $30/18. There are wonderful art galleries in Boothbay; a favorite is Roger Milinowski's Head-of-the-Harbor.

Navigational Information

Lat: 43°51.042' **Long:** 069°37.592' **Tide:** 11 ft. **Current:** 0 kt. **Chart:** 13296
Rep. Depths (*MLW*): Entry 20 ft. **Fuel Dock** n/a **Max Slip/Moor** 20 ft./-
Access: To the head of Inner Harbor, on port side, 50' before the footbridge

Marina Facilities *(In Season/Off Season)*

Fuel: Yes
Slips: 40 Total, 20 Transient **Max LOA:** 150 ft. **Max Beam:** n/a
Rate *(per ft.)*: **Day** $1.75/Inq.* **Week** $11 **Month** $27
Power: 30 amp $4.75, **50 amp** $6, **100 amp** n/a, **200 amp** n/a
Cable TV: Yes Incl. **Dockside Phone:** No
Dock Type: Wood, Short Fingers, Pilings, Floating
Moorings: 2 Total, 2 Transient **Launch:** n/a, Dinghy Dock
Rate: Day $25 **Week** $160 **Month** $485
Heads: 2 Toilet(s), 2 Shower(s)
Laundry: 2 Washer(s), 2 Dryer(s) **Pay Phones:** Yes, 2
Pump-Out: No **Fee:** n/a **Closed Heads:** No

Marina Operations

Owner/Manager: Judy Engle **Dockmaster:** Same
In-Season: May-Oct, 8am-6pm **Off-Season:** n/a
After-Hours Arrival: Call (207) 633-6003
Reservations: Yes, Preferred **Credit Cards:** Visa/MC
Discounts: None
Pets: Welcome **Handicap Access:** Yes, Docks

Boothbay Harbor Marina

PO Box 524; Pier One; Boothbay Harbor, ME 04538

Tel: (207) 633-6003 **VHF: Monitor** 9 **Talk** 68
Fax: (207) 633-6003 **Alternate Tel:** n/a
Email: jg6003@aol.com **Web:** n/a
Nearest Town: Boothbay Harbor *(0 mi.)* **Tourist Info:** (207) 633-7448

Marina Services and Boat Supplies

Services - Docking Assistance, Security *(6pm-8am Security gate)*, Trash Pick-Up, Dock Carts, Megayacht Facilities **Communication -** Mail & Package Hold, Phone Messages, FedEx, AirBorne, UPS, Express Mail *(Sat Del)* **Supplies - Near:** Ice *(Block, Cube)* **Under 1 mi:** Ships' Store *(Marine Supply 633-0709)*, CNG *(Carousel Marina 633-2922)* **1-3 mi:** Bait/Tackle *(White Anchor Bait and Tackle Shop 633-3788)*

Boatyard Services

OnCall: Divers **Near:** Travelift, Engine mechanic *(gas, diesel)*, Electrical Repairs, Electronic Sales, Electronics Repairs, Hull Repairs, Rigger, Compound, Wash & Wax, Interior Cleaning, Upholstery, Metal Fabrication, Painting. **Nearest Yard:** Sample's Shipyard, 0.25 mi. (207) 633-3171

Restaurants and Accommodations

OnSite: Restaurant *(J.H. Hawk 633-5589, L $5-16, D $6-20, 7 days, live entertainment)*, *(McSeagull's 633-5900, L $6-18, D $11-20)*, *(Gray's Wharf Waterfront 633-5629, L $4-25, D $4-25)* **Near:** Restaurant *(Rocktide 633-4455, D $10-22)*, *(Andrew's Harborside 633-4074, B $3-6, L $4-12, D $10-22)*, *(Boat House Bistro 633-7300, L $6-14, D $16-30)*, *(Talay Thai 633-0025, L $4-11, D $9-15)*, Seafood Shack *(Fisherman's Wharf 633-5090)*, Snack Bar *(King Brud's Hot Dog Cart , McKown & Commercial St., 10am-4pm)*, Motel *(Flagship Motor Inn 633-5094, $75)*, Inn/B&B *(Admiral's Quarters Inn 633-2472, $85-165)*, *(Harborage Inn 633-4640, $65-150)*, *(Harbour Towne 633-4300, $70-300)*, *(Fisherman's Wharf 633-5090)*

Recreation and Entertainment

Near: Boat Rentals, Bowling, Fishing Charter, Special Events *(Windjammer Days - June)*, Galleries *(Many)* **Under 1 mi:** Beach *(Barrett Park)*, Picnic Area *(Barrett Park)*, Grills, Playground, Tennis Courts, Fitness Center *(YMCA 633-2855)*, Movie Theater *(Harbor Light 633-5297)*, Video Rental *(Video Loft 633-6509)*, Park *(Barrett Park)*, Museum *(Boothbay Region Historical Society 633-4727)* **1-3 mi:** Pool *(YMCA 633-2855)*, Golf Course *(Boothbay Country Club 633-6085)*, Cultural Attract *(Carousel Music Theater 633-5279)*, Sightseeing *(Marine Resources Aquarium 633-2741)*

Provisioning and General Services

Near: Convenience Store *(Village Market 633-0944, Eastside Market 633-6465)*, Delicatessen, Wine/Beer *(Eastside)*, Liquor Store, Bakery, Fishmonger, Meat Market, Bank/ATM, Post Office, Protestant Church *(Methodist, Congregational)*, Library, Beauty Salon, Dry Cleaners, Laundry, Bookstore *(Sherman's 633-7262)*, Pharmacy *(Waltz 633-5323)*, Newsstand, Hardware Store, Florist, Retail Shops **Under 1 mi:** Supermarket *(Hannaford 633-6465)*, Farmers' Market *(Thu 9am-noon at Mini Mall)*, Lobster Pound *(Lobstermen's Co-op 633-0627)*, Catholic Church, Copies Etc. *(Mail Boxes, Etc. 633-9991)*

Transportation

OnCall: Rental Car *(Enterprise 882-8393)*, Taxi *(Boothbay Harbor Taxi 633-6001)* **Near:** Bikes, Water Taxi *(Novelty)*, Local Bus *(Free shopping Trolleys)* **Airport:** Portland Int'l. *(60 mi.)*

Medical Services

911 Service **OnCall:** Ambulance **Near:** Doctor *(Harbor Medical Walk-In 633-299)*, Dentist, Holistic Services *(Alt. Health Solutions 633-0072)*
Hospital: St. Andrews 633-2121- has dock *(2 mi.)*

Setting -- Situated on Pier One, right in the heart of Boothbay, this is the closest marina to the downtown action. It is next to the footbridge at the head of the harbor, in the shadow of two bustling restaurants. The views from the outer docks to the mouth of the harbor are simply dazzling.

Marina Notes -- *Over 80 ft. $2.25/ft. J.H. Hawke, Ltd., one of the two onsite restaurants, features live music and dancing every night. Being right on Pier One comes at a price; it is less quiet and less private. The marina is gated, security is quite good and the service accommodating and friendly. Several excursion boats leave from here, starting at 9 am. Off-season rates from May 1 - Jun 30 and Labor Day - Oct. Fuel can be delivered slipside from Coastal Marine (633-3835) 7-9am or 5-7pm or picked-up from their central float from 9am-5pm. Pump-out at Carousel Marina or Tugboat Marina. Dinghy dock. Facilities for megayachts.

Notable -- Surrounded by restaurants, inns, boutiques and gift shops, fudge & ice cream. Two trolleys pick-up nearby for easy access to more distant points, including the supermarket and aquarium. Cap'n Fish's Excursions (633-3244), Balmy Days to Monhegan Island (633-2264), Boothbay Harbor Whalewatch (633-3500). Windjammer Days in late June include tall ships parades, fireworks. Don't miss the galleries; pick up a map from nearby Head-of-the-Harbor. The current Boothbay high-end restaurant picks are the Boat House Bistro (Northern Italian) and Christopher's Boathouse (eclectic inventive).

PHOTOS ON CD-ROM: 5

Tugboat Inn & Marina

PO Box 267; 80 Commercial Street; Boothbay Harbor, ME 04538

Tel: (207) 633-4434; (800) 248-2628 **VHF: Monitor** 9 **Talk** 68
Fax: n/a **Alternate Tel:** (207) 633-4435
Email: n/a **Web:** www.tugboatinn.com
Nearest Town: Boothbay Harbor *(0.2 mi.)* **Tourist Info:** (207) 633-7448

Navigational Information

Lat: 43°50.935' **Long:** 069°37.759' **Tide:** 11 ft. **Current:** 0 kt. **Chart:** 13296
Rep. Depths (*MLW*): Entry 15 ft. **Fuel Dock** n/a **Max Slip/Moor** 15 ft./20 ft.
Access: Past G9 and McFarland Island on the Inner Harbor's western shore

Marina Facilities *(In Season/Off Season)*

Fuel: *Coastal Marine* - Gasoline, Diesel, On Call Delivery
Slips: 30 Total, 15 Transient **Max LOA:** 100 ft. **Max Beam:** n/a
Rate *(per ft.)*: **Day** $1.80/$1.25 **Week** Inq. **Month** Inq.
Power: 30 amp $3, **50 amp** $5, **100 amp** n/a, **200 amp** n/a
Cable TV: Yes Incl. **Dockside Phone:** No
Dock Type: Wood, Short Fingers, Pilings, Alongside, Floating
Moorings: 15 Total, 15 Transient **Launch:** None, Dinghy Dock (Free)
Rate: Day $20/15 **Week** $120 **Month** Inq.
Heads: 3 Toilet(s), 2 Shower(s), Hair Dryers
Laundry: 2 Washer(s), 2 Dryer(s), Iron, Book Exchange **Pay Phones:** Yes, 2
Pump-Out: OnSite, Full Service **Fee:** $10 **Closed Heads:** No

Marina Operations

Owner/Manager: Bonnie Stover **Dockmaster:** Peter Chase
In-Season: Jun-Sep, 7am-7pm **Off-Season:** Oct-May, 7am-4pm
After-Hours Arrival: Check in at hotel office
Reservations: Yes, Recommended **Credit Cards:** Visa/MC, Dscvr, Amex
Discounts: None
Pets: Welcome **Handicap Access:** No

Marina Services and Boat Supplies

Services - Docking Assistance, Dock Carts **Communication -** Mail & Package Hold, FedEx, AirBorne, UPS, Express Mail *(Sat Del)* **Supplies - OnSite:** Ice *(Block, Cube)* **Near:** Ships' Store, CNG *(Dinghy to Carousel Marina)* **Under 1 mi:** Propane *(Carters Propane Service 633-2486)* **1-3 mi:** Bait/Tackle *(White Anchor Bait and Tackle Shop 633-3788)*

Boatyard Services

OnCall: Divers **Near:** Travelift, Forklift, Engine mechanic *(gas, diesel)*, Launching Ramp, Electrical Repairs, Electronic Sales, Electronics Repairs, Hull Repairs, Bottom Cleaning, Brightwork, Propeller Repairs, Metal Fabrication. **1-3 mi:** Crane, Rigger, Sail Loft, Woodworking, Upholstery, Yacht Interiors. **Nearest Yard:** Sample's (207) 633-3171

Restaurants and Accommodations

OnSite: Restaurant *(Tugboat Restaurant 633-4434, L $7-13, D $15-25)*, Hotel *(Tugboat Inn 633-4434, $75-180)* **Near:** Restaurant *(Fisherman's Wharf Inn 633-5090)*, *(Christopher's Boathouse 633-6565, L $6-10, D $15-27)*, Seafood Shack *(Kaler's Crab House 633-5839)*, Snack Bar *(Ebb Tide 633-5692, B $3-6, L $4-13, D $7-13)*, *(Blue Moon Café 633-2349)*, *(King Brud's Hot Dog Cart , McKown & Commercial 10am-4pm)*, Inn/B&B *(1830 Admiral's Quarters 633-2474, $85-165)*, *(Greenleaf Inn 633-7346, $95-160)*, *(Sur la Mer 633-7400, $130-200, moorings for guests)*

Recreation and Entertainment

OnSite: Picnic Area, Boat Rentals, Fishing Charter *(Redhook Charters 633-3807)* **Near:** Bowling, Special Events *(Windjammer Days Mid June)* **Under 1 mi:** Roller Blade/Bike Paths, Movie Theater *(Harbor Light Cinema 633-3799)*, Video Rental *(Video Loft 633-6509)*, Galleries *(Head-of -the-Harbor)* **1-3 mi:** Heated Pool *(YMCA)*, Beach *(Barrett Park)*, Grills, Tennis Courts, Golf Course *(Boothbay Country Club 633-6085)*, Fitness Center, Park *(Barrett Park)*, Cultural Attract *(Carousel Music Theater 633-5297)*, Sightseeing *(Nature and whale watching excursions)*

Provisioning and General Services

Near: Convenience Store *(Village Market 633-0944)*, Delicatessen, Wine/Beer *(Christopher's 633-6565)*, Liquor Store, Bakery, Fishmonger *(Daily Catch)*, Lobster Pound *(Lobstermen's Co-op 633-4900, by dinghy)*, Meat Market, Bank/ATM, Post Office, Protestant Church, Library, Beauty Salon, Barber Shop, Bookstore *(Sherman's 633-7262)*, Pharmacy *(Waltz 633-5323)*, Newsstand, Hardware Store *(Grovers 633-2694)*, Florist, Clothing Store, Retail Shops **Under 1 mi:** Supermarket *(Hannaford 633-6465)*, Farmers' Market *(Mini Mall Thu 9am-noon)*, Green Grocer, Catholic Church, Dry Cleaners, Laundry, Copies Etc. *(Mail Boxes Etc. 633-9991)*

Transportation

OnCall: Water Taxi, Rental Car *(Enterprise 882-8393)*, Taxi *(Boothbay Harbor Taxi 633-6001)* **Near:** Bikes, Local Bus *(Free shopping trolley)*
Airport: Portland Int'l. *(60 mi.)*

Medical Services

911 Service **Under 1 mi:** Doctor *(Harbor Medical Walk-In 633-2999)*, Dentist, Chiropractor *(Coastal Chiropractic 633-4777)*, Holistic Services *(Boothbay Whole Health Medical Center 633-3535; Alt. Health Solutions 633-0072)*, Ambulance **Hospital:** St. Andrews 633-2121, has dock *(1 mi.)*

Setting -- The first facility on the port side of Boothbay Harbor, directly across from Cap'n Fish, Tugboat is a large, picture-perfect, busy marina, restaurant, and inn complex. Look for the two and three-story white buildings with verandas and red roofs. Both the inn and the docks are impeccably maintained and have panoramic views of this active, legendary harbor.

Marina Notes -- Located at the southern edge of downtown, Tugboat is within walking distance of everything. A 3-year, facility-wide renovation was completed in the mid-nineties, which included the new Main Inn. The marina provides extensive, protected dockage snuggled between two wharves. Note there are two new exceptionally nice showers for 30 slips and 15 moorings. Picnic tables are right on the docks. Lovely rooms all have A/C and waterfront verandas. Reservations strongly recommended. Tugboat's moorings balls are red with a "C" and a number. Seasonal Slips $52-55/ft., Seasonal Moorings $690.

Notable -- The Tugboat Inn Restaurant is built into the side of The Maine, a 1917 tugboat, and serves two meals a day -- Lunch - salads, sandwiches, and mostly seafood main courses; Dinner - wide range of house specialties, including seafood pie. The Marina Lounge and Patio Deck offer lighter fare. All activities of Boothbay Harbor are easily accessible. Fishing trips depart daily from here, and nature and whale-watch excursions from nearby docks. Balmy Days Cruises head to Monhegan Island daily at 9:30am (633-2284) and Bay Lady makes a 1.5 hr. harbor cruise in a friendship sloop -- both from Pier 8. Boothbay Whalewatch (633-6300) leaves from Pier 6. For provisioning and lay-day activities, the free trolleys make the shopping center and aquarium easy to reach.

Navigational Information

Lat: 43°50.941' **Long:** 069°37.951' **Tide:** 11 ft. **Current:** 0 kt. **Chart:** 13296
Rep. Depths (*MLW*): Entry 30 ft. **Fuel Dock** n/a **Max Slip/Moor** -/30 ft.
Access: Leave G9 to starboard, to the west of McFarland Island

Marina Facilities *(In Season/Off Season)*

Fuel: *Coastal* - Gasoline, Diesel, On Call Delivery
Slips: 0 Total, 0 Transient **Max LOA:** 100 ft. **Max Beam:** n/a
Rate *(per ft.)*: **Day** n/a **Week** n/a **Month** n/a
Power: 30 amp n/a, **50 amp** n/a, **100 amp** n/a, **200 amp** n/a
Cable TV: No **Dockside Phone:** No
Dock Type: Floating
Moorings: 23 Total, 15 Transient **Launch:** None, Dinghy Dock
Rate: Day $20 **Week** $80 **Month** $210
Heads: None
Laundry: None **Pay Phones:** No
Pump-Out: No **Fee:** n/a **Closed Heads:** No

Marina Operations

Owner/Manager: Bob and Chris Braga **Dockmaster:** n/a
In-Season: Year-Round, 7am-4pm **Off-Season:** n/a
After-Hours Arrival: Pick up a vacant mooring; check in in the morning
Reservations: No **Credit Cards:** Visa/MC
Discounts: None
Pets: Welcome **Handicap Access:** No

Sample's Shipyard

PO Box 462; 120 Commercial St.; Boothbay Harbor, ME 04538

Tel: (207) 633-3171 **VHF: Monitor** 9 **Talk** 68
Fax: (207) 633-3824 **Alternate Tel:** n/a
Email: samples@gw1.net **Web:** n/a
Nearest Town: Boothbay Harbor *(0.5 mi.)* **Tourist Info:** (207) 633-7448

Marina Services and Boat Supplies

Services - Security *(Owner on premises)*, Dock Carts **Communication -** Mail & Package Hold, Fax in/out, FedEx, UPS, Express Mail **Supplies - Near:** Ice *(Cube)*, Ships' Store, Propane *(Dead River Company 633-3144)* **1-3 mi:** Bait/Tackle *(White Anchor Bait and Tackle Shop 633-3788)*, CNG *(Carousel Marina 633-2922)*

Boatyard Services

OnSite: Travelift, Railway *(two)*, Engine mechanic *(gas, diesel)*, Electrical Repairs, Electronic Sales, Electronics Repairs, Hull Repairs, Rigger, Bottom Cleaning, Brightwork, Compound, Wash & Wax, Interior Cleaning, Woodworking, Upholstery, Yacht Interiors, Metal Fabrication, Painting, Total Refits **OnCall:** Sail Loft, Divers **Under 1 mi:** Launching Ramp. **3+ mi:** Propeller Repairs *(3 mi.)*. **Yard Rates:** $40/hr., Haul & Launch $7/ft. *(blocking $40)*, Power Wash $3/ft. **Storage:** On-Land Outside $2.50/ft.

Restaurants and Accommodations

Near: Restaurant *(Tugboat Restaurant 633-4434, L $7-18, D $13-28)*, *(Ebb Tide 633-5692, B $7-13, L $3-13)*, *(Andrew's Harborside 633-4074, B $3-6, L $4-12, D $10-22)*, *(Christopher's Boathouse 633-6565, L $6-10, D $16-27)*, *(Boat House Bistro 633-7300, L $7-14, D $16-30)*, Snack Bar *(Dunton's Doghouse)*, Motel *(Fisherman's Wharf Inn 633-5090)*, Inn/B&B *(Sur la Mer Inn 633-7400, $130-200, moorings for guests)*, *(Anchorwatch B&B 633-7565, $90-160)*, *(1890 Admiral's Quarters 633-2474, $85-165)*

Recreation and Entertainment

Near: Boat Rentals *(Tidal Transit Ocean Kayak 633-7140)*, Bowling, Fishing Charter *(Breakaway Sportfishing 633-6990)*, Sightseeing *(Whalewatching)*, Special Events *(Windjammer Days)* **Under 1 mi:** Tennis Courts, Fitness Center, Group Fishing Boat, Movie Theater *(Harbor Light 633-3799)*, Video Rental *(Video Loft 633-6509)*, Cultural Attract *(Carousel Music Theater 633-5297)*, Galleries *(Head-of-the-Harbor)* **1-3 mi:** Beach *(Barrett Park)*, Picnic Area, Grills, Playground, Golf Course *(Boothbay Country Club 633-6085)*, Park *(Waterfront)*, Museum *(Boothbay Railway Museum 633-4727)*

Provisioning and General Services

Near: Convenience Store *(Village Market 633-0944)*, Wine/Beer *(Christopher's 633-6565)*, Liquor Store, Bakery *(P&P Pastry Shoppe 633-6511)*, Fishmonger, Meat Market, Bank/ATM, Post Office, Protestant Church *(Methodist, Congregational)*, Library, Beauty Salon, Bookstore *(Sherman's 633-7262)*, Pharmacy *(Waltz 633-5323)*, Newsstand, Hardware Store *(Grovers Hardware 633-2694)*, Florist, Clothing Store **Under 1 mi:** Supermarket *(Hannaford 633-6465)*, Farmers' Market *(Mini Mall Thu 9am-noon)*, Catholic Church, Dry Cleaners, Laundry, Copies Etc.

Transportation

OnCall: Water Taxi, Rental Car *(Enterprise 882-8393)* **Near:** Bikes, Local Bus *(Free shopping trolley)* **Under 1 mi:** Taxi *(Boothbay Harbor Taxi 633-6001)* **Airport:** Portland Int'l. *(60 mi.)*

Medical Services

911 Service **OnCall:** Ambulance **Near:** Doctor *(Harbor Medical Walk-In 633-2999)*, Dentist, Chiropractor *(Coastal Chiro 633-4777)*, Holistic Services *(Boothbay Whole Health 633-3535; Alt. Health Solutions 633-0072)*
Hospital: St. Andrews 633-2121- has dock *(1 mi.)*

Setting -- Located just outside the Boothbay Harbor entrance, on the western shore, Sample's offers expansive southern views of open water along with easy access to downtown Boothbay. If you don't require any shoreside services, this combination of peace and quiet and a convenient location makes Sample's an interesting choice.

Marina Notes -- Sample's is the only boatyard in Boothbay capable of managing large yachts and the windjammers. With two marine railways, this full service facility has the ability to haul large vessels up to 140', in addition to providing heavy moorings able to accommodate larger yachts (marked "B"). Fuel can be delivered from Coastal Marine (633-3835) 7-9am and 5-7pm, or use Coastal's central float from 9am-5pm. Pump-out is at Carousel Marina across the harbor or Tugboat Inn just around the point.

Notable -- Boothbay Harbor is overflowing with things to do and Sample's is an easy walk to almost all of the activity: shops, restaurants, museums, sightseeing, etc.. A variety of local festivals take place throughout the year, including the Windjammer Days in June. For entertainment, try the Boothbay Region Playhouse or Carousel Music Theater. Keep an eye out for Brud's Hot Dog cart and Dunton's Doghouse, Boothbay institutions, and quite near Sample's.

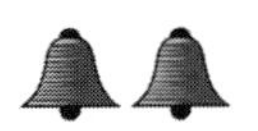

Signal Point Marina

Signal Point Marina

PO Box 446; 45 Commercial Street; Boothbay Harbor, ME 04538

Tel: (207) 633-6920 **VHF: Monitor** 16 **Talk** n/a
Fax: (207) 633-4438 **Alternate Tel:** (207) 633-6920
Email: n/a **Web:** n/a
Nearest Town: Boothbay Harbor *(0.5 mi.)* **Tourist Info:** (207) 633-7448

Navigational Information

Lat: 43°51.025' **Long:** 069°38.135' **Tide:** 11 ft. **Current:** 0 kt. **Chart:** 13296
Rep. Depths (*MLW*): Entry 10 ft. **Fuel Dock** 6 ft. **Max Slip/Moor** 10 ft./-
Access: Outer Boothbay Harbor to McFarland Point

Marina Facilities *(In Season/Off Season)*

Fuel: Gasoline, Diesel
Slips: 47 Total, 20 Transient **Max LOA:** 60 ft. **Max Beam:** 18 ft.
Rate *(per ft.)*: **Day** $1.50 **Week** $9.00 **Month** $30
Power: 30 amp Incl., **50 amp** Incl., **100 amp** n/a, **200 amp** n/a
Cable TV: No **Dockside Phone:** No
Dock Type: Wood, Long Fingers, Floating
Moorings: 0 Total, 0 Transient **Launch:** n/a, Dinghy Dock
Rate: Day n/a **Week** n/a **Month** n/a
Heads: 2 Toilet(s), 2 Shower(s)
Laundry: None **Pay Phones:** No
Pump-Out: No **Fee:** n/a **Closed Heads:** No

Marina Operations

Owner/Manager: Jerry McClure **Dockmaster:** Stan Peterson
In-Season: May 15-Oct 1, 8am-5pm **Off-Season:** Closed
After-Hours Arrival: If you have slip number assigned, proceed to slip
Reservations: Yes, Preferred **Credit Cards:** Check or Cash
Discounts: None
Pets: Welcome, Dog Walk Area **Handicap Access:** No

Marina Services and Boat Supplies

Services - Trash Pick-Up, Dock Carts **Communication -** FedEx, AirBorne, UPS, Express Mail **Supplies - Near:** Ice *(Cube)*, Ships' Store **Under 1 mi:** Propane *(Dead River Company 633-3144)*, CNG *(dinghy to Carousel Marina 633-2922)* **1-3 mi:** Bait/Tackle *(White Anchor Bait and Tackle 633-3788)*

Boatyard Services

OnCall: Sail Loft **Near:** Railway, Engine mechanic *(gas, diesel)*, Electrical Repairs, Electronics Repairs, Hull Repairs, Rigger, Bottom Cleaning, Compound, Wash & Wax, Interior Cleaning, Propeller Repairs, Painting. **Nearest Yard:** Sample's Shipyard (207) 633-3171

Restaurants and Accommodations

Near: Snack Bar *(Dunton's Dogs L $3-$7)*, Inn/B&B *(Greenleaf Inn 633-7346, $100+)*, *(Admiral's Quarters 633-2475, $85-165)* **Under 1 mi:** Restaurant *(Tugboat Inn 633-4434, L $7-18, D $13-28)*, *(No Anchovies 633-9928, L $9-12, D $7-30)*, *(Fisherman's Wharf 633-5090, L $9-13, D $15-30)*, *(Boat House Bistro 633-7300, L $7-14, D $16-30)*, *(Christopher's Boathouse 633-6565, L $6-10, D $17-30)*, *(Andrew's Harborside 633-4074, L $9-22, D $9-22)*, *(Cabbage Island Clambakes 633-7200, L/D $40 Prix Fixe; the Argo leaves from Pier 6 for Cabbage Island)*, Snack Bar *(Blue Moon Café 633-2349, B $3-5, L $4-8)*, Lite Fare *(Upper Deck L $6-10, adjoining Andrew's)*, Pizzeria *(Mario's 633-5586)*, Hotel *(Tugboat Inn 633-4434, $75-180)* **1-3 mi:** Hotel *(Spruce Point 633-4152, $155-185)*

Recreation and Entertainment

Under 1 mi: Jogging Paths, Boat Rentals *(Tidal Transit Kayak 633-7140)*, Bowling *(Romar 633-5721)*, Fishing Charter *(Redhook Charters 633-3807)*, Movie Theater *(Harbor Light 633-3799)*, Video Rental *(Video Loft 633-6509)*, Museum *(Boothbay Region Historical Society 633-0820)*, Sightseeing *(Whale Watch, Lighthouse Tours)*, Special Events *(Clam Bakes, Windjammers - week before July 4, Friendship Sloop Days - 3rd week July)* **1-3 mi:** Beach *(Barrett Park)*, Picnic Area, Grills, Playground, Dive Shop, Tennis Courts, Golf Course *(Boothbay Country Club 633-6085)*, Fitness Center *(YMCA)*, Cultural Attract *(Aquarium 633-9559, Railway Museum 633-4727 $7/3, 9:30am-5pm, Jun-ColDay)*

Provisioning and General Services

Near: Lobster Pound *(Walton Jobs)* **Under 1 mi:** Convenience Store *(Village Market 633-0944)*, Supermarket *(Hannaford 633-6465)*, Gourmet Shop, Delicatessen, Wine/Beer *(Christopher's 933-6565)*, Liquor Store, Bakery, Farmers' Market *(Mini Mall Thu 9am-noon)*, Fishmonger, Meat Market, Bank/ATM, Post Office, Catholic Church, Library, Beauty Salon, Dry Cleaners, Laundry, Bookstore *(Sherman's 633-7262)*, Pharmacy *(Waltz 633-5323)*, Newsstand, Hardware Store *(Grovers 633-2694)*, Florist, Clothing Store, Retail Shops, Copies Etc.

Transportation

OnCall: Rental Car *(Enterprise 882-8393)*, Taxi *(Boothbay Harbor Taxi 633-3003)* **Near:** Local Bus *(Tour & Rocktide Trolleys)* **Under 1 mi:** Bikes *(Harbor Scooters 633-3003)* **Airport:** Portland Int'l. *(60 mi.)*

Medical Services

911 Service **OnCall:** Ambulance **Near:** Chiropractor *(Coastal Chiropractic 633-4777)* **Under 1 mi:** Dentist *(Family Dental 633-4243)*, Holistic Services *(Alt. Health Solutions 633-0072)* **Hospital:** St. Andrews 633-2121 *(1.5 mi.)*

Setting -- Located at the edge of Mill Cove about a half mile west of the entrance to Boothbay's inner harbor, Signal Point's docks are surrounded by a well maintained condominium community. It offers beautiful long views of the outer harbor, first class docks, a very quiet, tranquil environment, and a pleasent 3/4 mile walk past Dunton's Doghouse to the heart of downtown Boothbay.

Marina Notes -- The excellent, easy access docks were built in 1986, along with the condo complex. Convenient showers and heads, located above a lobster pound, are in very good condition. A working lobster dock, right next door, makes staying home for dinner a snap - Walton Jobs 7am-5:30pm, order by 4pm and they'll cook it for you. Consider dinghying to downtown Boothbay; the town float, just south of Pier Six permits 3 hr. tie-ups. In West Harbor, Boothbay Harbor Yacht Club (633-5750, Ch.9) may have moorings with launch service - tennis courts, showers, laundry and dining room.

Notable -- A 0.3 mile walk leads out to the road at the entrance to the condo complex. While in Boothbay check out the local lighthouses, Boothbay Region Playhouse, shipbuilding, and sailmaking around town. Two free Shopping Trolleys (courtesy of Riptide and Cap'n Fish's) leave from McKown and Oak Streets, making all of the outlying sights and services, like the Aquarium, the supermarket and the movie theater, easily accessible. Daily trips to fabled Monhegan Island leave at 9:30am from Pier 8 just north of Tugboat Inn (633-2284). The Railway Museum and replica Village has 27 buildings, a narrow gauge steam train, and more than 50 antique vehicles.

PHOTOS ON CD-ROM: 6

Boothbay Region Boatyard

100 Ebenecook Road; West Southport, ME 04576

Tel: (207) 633-2970 **VHF: Monitor** 9 **Talk** 68
Fax: (207) 633-7144 **Alternate Tel:** n/a
Email: brb@brby.com **Web:** www.brby.com
Nearest Town: Boothbay Harbor *(5 mi.)* **Tourist Info:** (207) 633-7448

Navigational Information

Lat: 43°49.738' **Long:** 069°40.586' **Tide:** 10 ft. **Current:** n/a **Chart:** 13293
Rep. Depths (*MLW*): Entry 10 ft. **Fuel Dock** 8 ft. **Max Slip/Moor** 8 ft./70 ft.
Access: Sheepscot River past Hendrick's Light to Ebenecook Harbor

Marina Facilities *(In Season/Off Season)*

Fuel: *Varies* - Gasoline, Diesel
Slips: 40 Total, 6 Transient **Max LOA:** 80 ft. **Max Beam:** 16 ft.
Rate *(per ft.)*: **Day** $1.40/lnq. **Week** $8.00 **Month** $17.50
Power: 30 amp Incl., **50 amp** Incl., **100 amp** n/a, **200 amp** n/a
Cable TV: No **Dockside Phone:** No
Dock Type: Wood, Short Fingers, Pilings, Floating
Moorings: 40 Total, 6 Transient **Launch:** None, Dinghy Dock ($15)
Rate: Day $15 **Week** $90 **Month** $270
Heads: 2 Toilet(s), 2 Shower(s)
Laundry: 2 Washer(s), 2 Dryer(s), Book Exchange **Pay Phones:** Yes, 1
Pump-Out: Full Service, 1 Central, 8 InSlip **Fee:** $5 **Closed Heads:** Yes

Marina Operations

Owner/Manager: Jeffrey Lowell **Dockmaster:** Lynn Campbell
In-Season: MemDay-ColDay, 7am-5pm **Off-Season:** Oct-May, 7am-3:30pm
After-Hours Arrival: Honor system, no staff
Reservations: Preferred **Credit Cards:** Visa/MC
Discounts: None
Pets: Welcome, Dog Walk Area **Handicap Access:** Yes, Heads, Docks

Marina Services and Boat Supplies

Services - Docking Assistance, Boaters' Lounge, Dock Carts **Communication -** Mail & Package Hold, Phone Messages, FedEx, AirBorne, UPS, Express Mail **Supplies - OnSite:** Ice *(Block, Cube)*, Ships' Store **1-3 mi:** Propane *(Carters Propane Service 633-2486)*, CNG *(Carousel Marina by dinghy 633-2922)* **3+ mi:** Bait/Tackle *(White Anchor Bait and Tackle Shop 633-3788, 5 mi.)*

Boatyard Services

OnSite: Travelift *(55T)*, Forklift *(6T)*, Crane *(15T)*, Engine mechanic *(gas, diesel)*, Electrical Repairs, Electronic Sales, Electronics Repairs, Hull Repairs, Rigger *(Maloney Marine 633-6788)*, Bottom Cleaning, Brightwork, Air Conditioning, Refrigeration, Divers, Compound, Wash & Wax, Interior Cleaning, Woodworking, Painting, Awlgrip, Total Refits **OnCall:** Propeller Repairs, Inflatable Repairs, Life Raft Service, Upholstery, Yacht Interiors, Metal Fabrication, Yacht Design, Yacht Building **Dealer for:** OMC, Westerbeke, Yamaha, Lugger, Yanmar, Mercruiser, Northern Lights. **Member:** ABBRA, ABYC - 3 Certified Tech(s), Other Certifications: Mercruiser **Yard Rates:** $49/hr., Haul & Launch $3/ft., Power Wash $3, Bottom Paint $10/ft. **Storage:** On-Land Inside $6.50/sq.ft. Outside $3 sq.ft.

Restaurants and Accommodations

Near: Lite Fare *(Sweet Dreams Bakery & Café 633-5956)* **Under 1 mi:** Restaurant *(Newagen Colony Inn 633-5242)*, *(Lawnmere Inn Restaurant 633-2522, B $4-7, D $15-22, B 7 days, D Thu-Sun)*, Seafood Shack *(Robinson's Wharf)*, Pizzeria *(Southport General Store 633-6666)*, Hotel *(Newagen Seaside Inn 633-5242)*, *(Oceangate 633-3321, $110-190, 66 room resort)*, Inn/B&B *(Lawnmere Inn 633-2522, $90-230, 32 room waterfront inn)*

Recreation and Entertainment

OnSite: Picnic Area, Grills **Near:** Beach *(half mile walk)*, Playground, Jogging Paths **Under 1 mi:** Museum *(Hendricks Hill Museum 633-1102)* **3+ mi:** Golf Course *(Boothbay Country Club 633-6085, 4.5 mi.)*, Boat Rentals *(5 mi.)*, Bowling *(5 mi.)*, Fishing Charter *(5 mi.)*, Group Fishing Boat *(5 mi.)*, Sightseeing *(Boothbay Harbor, 5 mi.)*

Provisioning and General Services

Near: Convenience Store *(Southport General Store 633-6666)*, Wine/Beer, Bakery *(Sweet Dreams Bakery & Café 633-5956)*, Post Office **Under 1 mi:** Fishmonger, Lobster Pound, Meat Market, Beauty Salon **1-3 mi:** Library **3+ mi:** Supermarket *(Hannaford 633-6465, 5 mi.)*, Bookstore *(Sherman's 633-7262, 5 mi.)*

Transportation

OnCall: Rental Car *(Enterprise 882-8393)*, Taxi *(Boothbay Harbor Taxi 633-6001)* **Airport:** Portland Int'l. *(50 mi.)*

Medical Services

911 Service **OnCall:** Ambulance **Hospital:** St. Andrews 633-2121, has dock *(4 mi.)*

Setting -- A short way from the mouth of the Sheepscot River, tucked into quiet Maddock Cove off Ebenecook Harbor, is this accommodating, full-service boatyard and marina. The surroundings are rural Southport Island, a little less than five miles from the bustle of Boothbay Harbor -- but close enough for an excursion. Landside views are of a nicely maintained boatyard and a bevy of gray-shingled buildings; water views are pristine Maine -- islands, rocks, and a tranquil mooring field.

Marina Notes -- One of the most complete boatyard facilities on this part of the Maine coast. Equipment includes a 55 ton travelift, 15 ton crane, 25 and 45 ton hydraulic trailers, and 6 ton forklift, manned by a staff of over thirty-five full-time craftspeople. Their long-term classic boat renovation projects are always interesting to peek at. Well equipped marine store onsite. A good, safe place to leave the boat. There is a small, comfortable boaters' lounge. Rates are the same year 'round.

Notable -- What BRB has to offer, in addition to good service, is a very busy boatyard in a very quiet place. All the more remarkable since this part of the coast is among the busiest in Maine during the season. A small cluster of services is a little under a half mile and includes the Southport General Store, Sweet Dreams Bakery, and the Post Office. Nearby is one of those rare sandy beaches and less than a mile are some highly regarded resorts and restaurants. If you have bikes on board, this is a good place to haul them ashore. Anything else you might need or want is a 5 mile cab ride into "downtown" Boothbay Harbor.

PHOTOS ON CD-ROM: 6

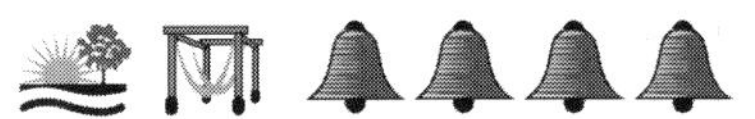

Robinhood Marine Center

340 Robinhood Road; Georgetown, ME 04548

Tel: (207) 371-2525; (800) 443-3625 **VHF: Monitor** 9 **Talk** 71
Fax: (207) 371-2899 **Alternate Tel:** (207) 371-2525
Email: info@robinhoodmarinecenter.com **Web:** robinhoodmarinecenter.com
Nearest Town: Woolwich/Bath *(7 mi.)* **Tourist Info:** (207) 443-9751

Navigational Information

Lat: 43°51.200' **Long:** 069°44.100' **Tide:** 11 ft. **Current:** 2 kt. **Chart:** 13293
Rep. Depths (*MLW*): Entry 70 ft. **Fuel Dock** 10 ft. **Max Slip/Moor** 30 ft./40 ft.
Access: Sheepscot River to Goose Rock Passage

Marina Facilities *(In Season/Off Season)*

Fuel: *Texaco* - Gasoline, Diesel
Slips: 135 Total, 10-20 Transient **Max LOA:** 65 ft. **Max Beam:** n/a
Rate *(per ft.)*: **Day** $1.50/Inq. **Week** $7.00 **Month** $23
Power: 30 amp Incl., **50 amp** n/a, **100 amp** n/a, **200 amp** n/a
Cable TV: No **Dockside Phone:** No
Dock Type: Wood, Long Fingers, Floating
Moorings: 72 Total, 10 Transient **Launch:** None, Dinghy Dock
Rate: Day $20 **Week** $125 **Month** $375
Heads: 2 Toilet(s), 2 Shower(s) *(with dressing rooms)*
Laundry: 1 Washer(s), 1 Dryer(s), Book Exchange **Pay Phones:** Yes, 1
Pump-Out: Full Service, 1 Central **Fee:** Free **Closed Heads:** No

Marina Operations

Owner/Manager: Joe McCarty **Dockmaster:** Same
In-Season: May-Sep, 8am-8pm **Off-Season:** Oct-Apr, 8am-3:30pm
After-Hours Arrival: Choose free mooring or slip - call in morning
Reservations: Yes, Preferred **Credit Cards:** Visa/MC, Dscvr, Tex
Discounts: Boat/US **Dockage:** 10% **Fuel:** n/a **Repair:** n/a
Pets: Welcome, Dog Walk Area **Handicap Access:** Yes, Heads

Marina Services and Boat Supplies

Services - Docking Assistance, Boaters' Lounge, Dock Carts **Communication -** Mail & Package Hold, Phone Messages, Fax in/out *(Free)*, Data Ports *(Library and Gallery)*, FedEx, AirBorne, UPS, Express Mail *(Sat Del)* **Supplies - OnSite:** Ice *(Block, Cube)*, Ships' Store, Propane, CNG **OnCall:** Bait/Tackle

Boatyard Services

OnSite: Travelift *(55T)*, Forklift *(35T Can O Lift)*, Crane *(18T)*, Engine mechanic *(gas, diesel)*, Electrical Repairs, Electronic Sales, Electronics Repairs, Hull Repairs, Rigger, Bottom Cleaning, Brightwork, Air Conditioning, Refrigeration, Compound, Wash & Wax, Interior Cleaning, Propeller Repairs, Woodworking, Inflatable Repairs, Metal Fabrication, Painting, Awlgrip, Yacht Design, Yacht Broker *(David Perry)*, Yacht Building **OnCall:** Divers, Life Raft Service, Upholstery, Yacht Interiors **Dealer for:** Ratheon, Heart, Cruisaire, Seafrost, Robinhood Yachts. 20 man craft and technical team. **Member:** ABBRA, ABYC **Yard Rates:** $48-54/hr., Haul & Launch $4-6/ft., Power Wash $1/ft. **Storage:** In-Water $5.50/sq.ft./mo., On-Land $4/sq.ft./mo.

Restaurants and Accommodations

OnSite: Restaurant *(The Osprey Restaurant 371-2530, D $15-22, Lunch in summer only, Sun brunch. Specializes in seafood)*, Snack Bar *(The Tavern at Riggs Cove 371-2530)* **Near:** Restaurant *(Robinhood Meeting House 371-2188, D $18-30)* **3+ mi:** Hotel *(Holiday Inn $60-140, 7 mi.)*

Recreation and Entertainment

OnSite: Picnic Area, Grills **Near:** Jogging Paths **3+ mi:** Beach *(7 mi.)*, Playground *(7 mi.)*, Tennis Courts *(7 mi.)*, Golf Course *(7 mi.)*, Fitness Center *(7 mi.)*, Horseback Riding *(7 mi.)*, Park *(Reid State Park - 0.5 mi. of beaches, salt marsh, dunes, tidal pools, bath house, fireplaces & picnic tables, 5 mi.)*, Museum *(Maine Maritime Museum 443-1516, $6 adults, $2.50 children, 9am-5:30pm, 7 mi.)*, Cultural Attract *(Chocolate Church Arts Center, 7 mi.)*, Sightseeing *(119 acre Josephine Newman Sanctuary 781-2330, offers 2 mi. of walking trails and an abundance of mosquitoes., 4 mi.)*

Provisioning and General Services

OnSite: Farmers' Market *(Tue 10am)*, Library, Laundry **3+ mi:** Convenience Store *(4 mi.)*, Supermarket *(Shaw's, 7 mi.)*, Bookstore *(Bath Book Shop 443-9338, 7 mi.)*, Pharmacy *(Wilsons Drug Store 442-8786, 7 mi.)*, Hardware Store *(Coastal Hardware of Bath 443-3542, 7 mi.)*

Transportation

OnSite: Courtesy Car/Van *(2 courtesy cars available all hours)* **OnCall:** Rental Car *(Enterprise 882-8393)* **3+ mi:** Taxi *(Kennebec Taxi & Transportation of Bath 443-5108, 7 mi.)* **Airport:** Portland Int'l. *(40 mi.)*

Medical Services

911 Service **OnCall:** Ambulance **3+ mi:** Doctor *(7 mi.)* **Hospital:** Mid-Coast 729-0181 *(15 mi.)*

Setting -- Robinhood sits on the edge of picturesque Riggs Cove, 3 miles from the ocean. This significant site is home to a charming, well thought out, flawlessly landscaped and maintained marina. The landside facilities are a combination of restored 18thC buildings and large boatbuilding "sheds" for the full-service boatyard. Arched footbridges protect the dinghy basin while providing easy access to the docks. A screened gazebo sits at the water's edge. The clear attentlon to detail is evident at every turn.

Marina Notes -- Robinhood sail and power boats built here. Internet/e-mail access and courtesy local calls are available both in the Library and the Gallery, open 24 hrs. Superb customer service provides 2 courtesy cars (for shopping and museum visits), and 2 courtesy boats (a Cape Dory Typhoon Daysailer and a spectacular pulling boat). Gallery has 200 years of articles and photographs of the marina site when it was Riggsville Wharf. The Library is stocked with books, periodicals, and jigsaw puzzles. Onsite Spartan Marine produces high quality marine hardware. Bath is 7 miles away for provisioning and support services.

Notable -- The Osprey Restaurant is a popular choice (from a burger to a seafood entrée). The Tavern at Riggs Cove is another onsite lite-fare food option. A quarter mile walk is the renowned Robinhood Free Meetinghouse where one of Maine's finest chefs, Michael Gagne, presides in a handsomely restored Greek-revival 1855 meeting house; classic American & fusion. Fresh produce boat arrives Tuesday at 10 am. Wednesday is Lecture night; Friday night is Dixieland Jazz in the gazebo.

Navigational Information
Lat: 43°53.871' **Long:** 069°48.889' **Tide:** 7 ft. **Current:** 1 kt. **Chart:** n/a
Rep. Depths (*MLW*): Entry 20 ft. **Fuel Dock** n/a **Max Slip/Moor** 17 ft./30 ft.
Access: 10 miles up the Kennebec River from Gulf of Maine

Marina Facilities *(In Season/Off Season)*
Fuel: *Available on call with advance notice -*
Slips: 1 Total, 1 Transient **Max LOA:** 150 ft. **Max Beam:** n/a
Rate *(per ft.)*: **Day** $1.50/* **Week** n/a **Month** n/a
Power: 30 amp n/a, **50 amp** n/a, **100 amp** n/a, **200 amp** n/a
Cable TV: No **Dockside Phone:** No
Dock Type: Wood, Alongside
Moorings: 8 Total, 6 Transient **Launch:** None, Dinghy Dock
Rate: Day $30 **Week** Inq. **Month** Inq.
Heads: 2 Toilet(s), 2 Shower(s) *(with dressing rooms)*
Laundry: Yes **Pay Phones:** No
Pump-Out: No **Fee:** n/a **Closed Heads:** Yes

Marina Operations
Owner/Manager: Thomas R. Wilcox, Jr. **Dockmaster:** Sue Drumm
In-Season: May-Oct, 8am-5pm **Off-Season:** Closed
After-Hours Arrival: Report in the morning
Reservations: Yes, Preferred **Credit Cards:** Visa/MC, Dscvr
Discounts: Member discount 10% **Dockage:** n/a **Fuel:** n/a **Repair:** n/a
Pets: No **Handicap Access:** Yes, Heads, Docks

Maine Maritime Museum

243 Washington Street; Bath, ME 04530

Tel: (207) 443-1316 **VHF: Monitor** 9 **Talk** n/a
Fax: (207) 443-1665 **Alternate Tel:** n/a
Email: maritime@bathmaine.com **Web:** www.bathmaine.com
Nearest Town: Bath *(1.4 mi.)* **Tourist Info:** (207) 443-9751

Marina Services and Boat Supplies
Communication - FedEx, AirBorne, UPS, Express Mail **Supplies - 1-3 mi:** Ice *(Cube)*, Bait/Tackle *(Kennebec Angler 442-8239)*, Propane *(Propane Gas Association of Maine 443-4200)*

Restaurants and Accommodations
OnCall: Pizzeria *(Little Caesar's 443-1112)* **Under 1 mi:** Restaurant *(Southgate Family Restaurant 442-8185)*, Lite Fare *(The Cabin L $2-10, pizza, pasta, subs)*, Inn/B&B *(Donnell House 443-5324, $85-175)* **1-3 mi:** Restaurant *(Kristina's 442-8577, L $5-9, D $12-17, Sun Brunch, too)*, *(Taste of Maine 443-4554, L $3-25, D $3-25)*, *(J.R. Maxwell's & Co. 443-2014, L $4-9, D $8-18)*, *(Maryellenz Café 442-0960, D $8-20)*, Motel *(New Meadows Inn 443-3921)*, Hotel *(Holiday Inn 442-8281, $60-140)*, *(The Inn at Bath 443-4294, $80-185)*, Inn/B&B *(Galen C. Moses House 442-8771, $110-160)*

Recreation and Entertainment
OnSite: Picnic Area, Playground, Museum *(Maine Maritime Museum's galleries & shipyard - 2 consecutive days: $9.50/6.50, Family $27 for 2 adults & 2 kids - daily 9:30am-5pm)* **Near:** Fitness Center *(Universe Gym 442-0180)*, Jogging Paths, Roller Blade/Bike Paths **Under 1 mi:** Fishing Charter *(Obsession 442-8581)*, Park **1-3 mi:** Tennis Courts, Golf Course *(Bath Golf Club 442-8411)*, Boat Rentals *(H2O Outfitters)*, Video Rental *(Home-Vision Video 442-8689)*, Cultural Attract *(Chocolate Church Arts Center 442-8455, Waterfront Park's Friday night Concerts)*, Sightseeing *(Jet Boat Excursions 538-6786; CofC, 45 Front St, offers 3 walking tour maps -- architectural, historical, botanical)*, Special Events *(Bath Heritage Days - July 4th week)* **3+ mi:** Horseback Riding *(Sable Oak Equestrian Center 443-4006, 4 mi.)*

Provisioning and General Services
OnSite: Bank/ATM, Bookstore **Under 1 mi:** Convenience Store *(The Store)* **1-3 mi:** Supermarket *(Shaw's 443-9179)*, Delicatessen *(Front Street Deli 443-9815)*, Health Food *(Grainery & Morning Glory 442-8012)*, Liquor Store *(New Meadows Super Stop 443-8818)*, Bakery, Farmers' Market *(Waterfront Park Thu & Sat 8:30am-12:30pm)*, Green Grocer, Fishmonger *(Gilmore's)*, Lobster Pound, Post Office, Catholic Church, Protestant Church, Library *(Bath Library 443-5141)*, Beauty Salon, Barber Shop, Dry Cleaners, Laundry, Pharmacy *(CVS 443-9097)*, Newsstand, Hardware Store *(Coastal Hardware 443-3542)*, Florist, Retail Shops *(Hobby Shop 443-4605)*, Department Store *(Reny's)*, Copies Etc. *(Bath Printing 443-3411)*

Transportation
OnSite: Local Bus *(Hourly Bath Trolley & Shuttle Services, $1/pp, connect the museum with the town and outlying shopping center, restaurants, hotels and supermarket.)* **OnCall:** Rental Car *(Enterprise 882-8393)*, Taxi *(Bath Cab 443-4009)*, Airport Limo *(Drew's 443-9166)* **1-3 mi:** Bikes *(Bath Cycle 442-7002 $18/day)*, InterCity Bus *(Concord Trailways)* **3+ mi:** Rail *(Amtrak Portland, 40 mi.)* **Airport:** Portland Int'l. *(38 mi.)*

Medical Services
911 Service **OnCall:** Ambulance **Near:** Chiropractor *(Bath Family Chiro 443-1244)* **Under 1 mi:** Holistic Services *(Massage Therapist)* **1-3 mi:** Doctor *(Mid-Coast Medical Group 442-0048)* **Hospital:** Mid-Coast 729-0181 *(8 mi.)*

Setting -- Set on the banks of the Kennebec River about a mile and a half from the center of Bath, an historic shipbuilding town, is the 40-year-old Maine Maritime Museum. This 20 acre former 19thC shipyard boasts fascinating exhibits, attractive, well maintained grounds, a small mooring field, and beautiful views. The impressive and industrial Bath Iron Works Shipyard is just north of the museum's docks and mooring fields.

Marina Notes -- The MMM is dedicated to preserving and interpreting Maine's maritime heritage and welcomes boaters with a brand new Visiting Yachtsmen's Building (heads, showers and laundry). The wharf was built for the Tall Ships and accommodates yachts *100 feet and larger. A great family destination with constantly changing exhibits, historical boat trips, lobstering dioramas, shipbuilding displays, a children's play ship and a picnic area. The Maritime History building contains displays of life at sea and maritime technology. The Boat Shop teaches traditional boat building techniques. Hour tours of the 19thC Percy & Small Shipyard, builders of large wooden sailing schooners, including the world's largest, "Wyoming" (a "ghost" is slated for Summer '03). Museum boat cruises range from 50-minute river excursions to day-long adventures. The large gift shop boasts an extensive selection of maritime books and products. Attractive, waterfront Long Reach Hall (capacity 125-200), Donnell House and Percy & Small Shipyard all rentable for group functions. No Pets.

Notable -- Historic Bath has been a shipbuilding center since the 1600s. The nearby Bath Iron Works builds nuclear Navy ships and large merchant & commercial vessels. The Chocolate Church Arts Center features year-round cultural events -- concerts, art exhibits, and guided tours of historic buildings.

PHOTOS ON CD-ROM: 6

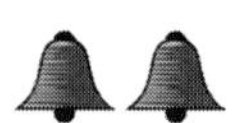

Kennebec Tavern & Marina

119 Commercial Street; Bath, ME 04530

Tel: (207) 442-9636 **VHF: Monitor** n/a **Talk** n/a
Fax: (207) 836-0397 **Alternate Tel:** n/a
Email: kennebectavern@suscom-maine.net **Web:** n/a
Nearest Town: Bath *(0.1 mi.)* **Tourist Info:** (207) 443-9751

Navigational Information

Lat: 43°54.825' **Long:** 069°48.748' **Tide:** 6 ft. **Current:** 5 kt. **Chart:** 13293
Rep. Depths (*MLW*): Entry 41 ft. **Fuel Dock** 20 ft. **Max Slip/Moor** 20 ft./40 ft.
Access: 10 miles up the Kennebec River just north of the Route 1 bridge

Marina Facilities *(In Season/Off Season)*

Fuel: *89/93* - Slip-Side Fueling, Gasoline, On Call Delivery
Slips: 60 Total, 10 Transient **Max LOA:** 32 ft. **Max Beam:** 12 ft.
Rate *(per ft.)*: **Day** $1.50 **Week** $150 **Month** n/a
Power: 30 amp n/a, **50 amp** n/a, **100 amp** n/a, **200 amp** n/a
Cable TV: No **Dockside Phone:** No
Dock Type: Wood, Floating
Moorings: 8 Total, 3 Transient **Launch:** None, Dinghy Dock
Rate: Day $30 **Week** $100 **Month** $200
Heads: 2 Toilet(s)
Laundry: None **Pay Phones:** Yes
Pump-Out: No **Fee:** n/a **Closed Heads:** No

Marina Operations

Owner/Manager: Gene Nygaard **Dockmaster:** Steve Zanco/Jeff Sheires
In-Season: May 15-Oct 15, 8am-8pm **Off-Season:** Oct 15-May 15, 8am-6pm
After-Hours Arrival: Call in advance
Reservations: Yes, Preferred **Credit Cards:** Visa/MC, Dscvr, Din, Amex
Discounts: None
Pets: Welcome **Handicap Access:** Yes, Heads, Docks

Marina Services and Boat Supplies

Services - Docking Assistance, Security *(Locked gate)*, Trash Pick-Up **Communication -** FedEx, AirBorne, UPS, Express Mail *(Sat Del)* **Supplies - OnSite:** Ice *(Block, Cube)* **Near:** Ships' Store, Bait/Tackle *(Kennebec Angler 442-8239)*, Live Bait *(Eels, worms)* **Under 1 mi:** Propane *(Roger's Hardware)*

Boatyard Services

Nearest Yard: BEC Marine (207) 443-3022

Restaurants and Accommodations

OnSite: Restaurant *(Kennebec Tavern D $7-30)* **Near:** Restaurant *(Beale Street Grille 442-9514, D $8-14)*, *(Maryellenz Café 442-0960, D $8-20)*, *(Maxwells 443-2014)*, Pizzeria *(Mario's 443-4126)*, Inn/B&B *(Benjamin F. Packard House 443-6069, $90-130)*, *(The Inn at Bath 443-4294, $80-185)*, *(Galen C. Moses House 442-8771, $110-160)*, *(Pryor House 443-1146)* **Under 1 mi:** Restaurant *(Kristina's 442-8577, L $5-9, D $12-17)*, Lite Fare *(Cabin 443-6224, L $2-10, pastas, pizzas, subs; delivers, too)* **1-3 mi:** Hotel *(Holiday Inn 442-8281, $60-140)*

Recreation and Entertainment

OnSite: Fishing Charter *(Obsession 442-8581)* **Near:** Jogging Paths, Roller Blade/Bike Paths, Other *(Indoor skateboard)*, Park *(Waterfront)*, Cultural Attract *(Chocolate Church Arts Center 442-8455; Waterfront Park's Friday night concerts)*, Sightseeing *(Architectural, Historic, and Botanical walking tours from the Chamber of Commerce 45 Front St.; Jet boat Excursions 538-6786)*, Special Events *(Bath Heritage Days, around July 4)*, Galleries **Under 1 mi:** Playground, Tennis Courts, Fitness Center *(Universe Gym 442-0180)*, Boat Rentals *(H2, Outfitters)* **1-3 mi:** Grills, Golf Course *(Bath Golf Club 442-8411)*, Museum *(Bath Maritime Museum - pass for 2 consecutive days $9.50/6.50, Family $27 - 2 adults & 2 kids)* **3+ mi:** Horseback Riding *(Sable Oak Equestrian Center 443-4006, 4 mi.)*

Provisioning and General Services

Near: Provisioning Service, Convenience Store, Supermarket *(Brackett's, a full service market, just moved across the street)*, Delicatessen *(Front Street Deli 443-9815)*, Health Food *(Grainery & Morning Glory 442-8012)*, Bank/ATM, Post Office, Protestant Church, Library *(Bath 443-5141)*, Beauty Salon, Barber Shop, Dry Cleaners, Laundry, Bookstore *(Bath Book Shop 443-9338)*, Pharmacy *(Rite Aid 442-7771)*, Florist, Retail Shops **Under 1 mi:** Liquor Store *(New Meadows Super Stop 443-8818)*, Catholic Church, Hardware Store *(Coastal Hardware 443-3542)* **1-3 mi:** Fishmonger *(Gilmore's Seafood)*, Department Store *(Reny's Discount)*

Transportation

OnCall: Courtesy Car/Van *(Enterprise 882-8393)*, Taxi *(Bath Cab 443-1244)*, Airport Limo *(Drew's 443-9166)* **Near:** Bikes *(Bath Cycle 442-7002 $18/day)*, Local Bus *(Shuttle and Trolley -- roughly hourly $1/pp. Trolley stops at marina, goes to hotel & grocery store)* **Under 1 mi:** InterCity Bus *(Concord Trailways)* **3+ mi:** Rail *(Portland Amtrak, 40 mi.)* **Airport:** Portland Int'l. *(40 mi.)*

Medical Services

911 Service **OnCall:** Ambulance **Near:** Doctor *(Mid-Coast Medical Group 442-0048)* **Under 1 mi:** Chiropractor *(Bath Family 443-1244)*, Holistic Services *(Massage Therapist)* **Hospital:** Mid-Coast 729-0181 *(8 mi.)*

Setting -- Located right in Bath on the Kennebec River, this small marina and restaurant, just under the highway bridge, is very convenient to the bustling, historically interesting downtown. A short walk yields a number of restaurants, services, resources, and architecturally compelling buildings.

Marina Notes -- The Tavern is a light-filled, casual restaurant with wonderful views of the River. Heads are shared with the marina. The two local shuttle and trolley services make the Maine Maritime Museum, the shopping center out on Route 1 (which includes a Reny's Discount Department Store -- truly a Maine institution), a Shaw's supermarket and the Holiday Inn all easily accessible.

Notable -- The town of Bath has been a shipbuilding center since the 17th century and, as a result, it offers much of interest to the visiting mariner -- including the exceedingly well executed Maine Maritime Museum (about 1.7 miles downriver on the other side of town) and the Hobby Shoppe (443-4605) which houses a wide range of ships' models. The largest employer in the area is Bath Iron Works; the facility looms over the River. Nuclear navy ships and large commercial vessels are currently being built there. It is closed to the public; note the white buoys that create a 400 foot security perimeter. It is reported, however, that BIW ship launches can be observed from the bridge! The Chamber of Commerce offers three self-guided walking tours -- architectural, historical and botanical -- which enhance more plebian excursions. The Chocolate Church Arts Center also offers a wide array of cultural events, from concerts to art exhibits to plays (plus guided tours of the town), and draws its audiences from a very wide geographic area.

PHOTOS ON CD-ROM: 3

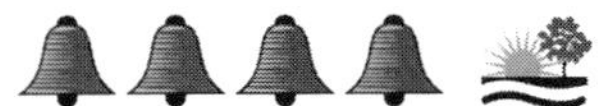

Navigational Information
Lat: 43°45.580' **Long:** 069°51.550' **Tide:** 9 ft. **Current:** 1 kt. **Chart:** 13290
Rep. Depths (*MLW*): Entry 6 ft. **Fuel Dock** 6 ft. **Max Slip/Moor** -/20 ft.
Access: Eastern shore Casco Bay marker by Cupola at Sebasco Harbor

Marina Facilities *(In Season/Off Season)*
Fuel: Gasoline
Slips: 0 Total, 0 Transient **Max LOA:** 60 ft. **Max Beam:** n/a
Rate *(per ft.)*: **Day** n/a **Week** n/a **Month** n/a
Power: 30 amp n/a, **50 amp** n/a, **100 amp** n/a, **200 amp** n/a
Cable TV: No **Dockside Phone:** No
Dock Type: Floating
Moorings: 25 Total, 23 Transient **Launch:** Yes (Free), Dinghy Dock
Rate: Day $25/$15 **Week** $125 **Month** n/a
Heads: 2 Toilet(s), 2 Shower(s)
Laundry: 1 Washer(s), 1 Dryer(s) **Pay Phones:** Yes
Pump-Out: OnSite, Full Service, 1 Central **Fee:** n/a **Closed Heads:** No

Marina Operations
Owner/Manager: Phil Luedee **Dockmaster:** Same
In-Season: Jun-LabDay, 8am-8pm **Off-Season:** n/a
After-Hours Arrival: Pick up mooring ball marked SHR (if available)
Reservations: Yes, Preferred **Credit Cards:** Visa/MC, Dscvr, Amex
Discounts: None
Pets: Welcome, Dog Walk Area **Handicap Access:** No

Sebasco Harbor Resort

PO Box 75; Route 217; Sebasco Estates, ME 04565

Tel: (207) 389-1161; (800) 225-3819 **VHF: Monitor** 9 **Talk** 12
Fax: (207) 389-2004 **Alternate Tel:** n/a
Email: info@sebasco.com **Web:** www.sebasco.com
Nearest Town: Bath *(15 mi.)* **Tourist Info:** (207) 443-9751

Marina Services and Boat Supplies
Services - Trash Pick-Up **Communication -** Data Ports, FedEx, AirBorne, UPS, Express Mail **Supplies - OnSite:** Ice *(Block, Cube)* **Near:** Live Bait *(Purse Line Bait 389-9155)* **3+ mi:** Ships' Store *(15 mi.)*, Bait/Tackle *(15 mi.)*, Propane *(15 mi.)*

Boatyard Services
Under 1 mi: Engine mechanic *(gas, diesel)*, Electrical Repairs, Divers. **3+ mi:** Electronic Sales *(20 mi.)*, Electronics Repairs *(20 mi.)*, Bottom Cleaning *(10 mi.)*, Brightwork *(10 mi.)*, Air Conditioning *(10 mi.)*, Refrigeration *(10 mi.)*, Propeller Repairs *(15 mi.)*, Woodworking *(15 mi.)*. **Nearest Yard:** Brewers Boatyard (207) 389-1388

Restaurants and Accommodations
OnSite: Restaurant *(Pilot House B EP, D $15-24, B 7:30-9am, D 6-8:30pm)*, *(Ledges Pub L $6-12, D $6-15, 1130am-9pm)*, Hotel *(Sebasco Harbor Inn $130-270, EP add $35 for MAP)*, Condo/Cottage *(Sebasco Harbor Cottages $240-1600, EP add $35 for MAP)* **Near:** Inn/B&B *(Rock Gardens Inn 389-1339, $210-296, MAP)* **1-3 mi:** Seafood Shack *(Water's Edge 389-1803, 1.5 mi., at the town landing - eat indoors, on the deck or waterside)*

Recreation and Entertainment
OnSite: Pool, Playground *(Complete children's program - Camp Merritt)*, Tennis Courts *($6/hr.)*, Golf Course *(Shore Acres a newly renovated 9 hole course - par 36/35, 18 holes by 2003. Greens fees $20/day, $99/week)*, Fitness Center, Jogging Paths, Boat Rentals *(Two 14 ft. aluminum w/ 6 hp motors $20/hr.; two 17 ft. O'Days $15/hr.; kayaks, too)*, Roller Blade/Bike Paths, Bowling, Video Rental, Museum *(Ruth Excursion to Adm. Perry's home Eagle Island $22/12)*, Sightseeing *(The Ruth, Sebasco's 38 ft., 1935 Handy, offers many nature excursions and adventures, $10/6 each)* **Near:** Cultural Attract *(Sebasco Art Workshops at Rock Gardens Inn 389-1339)* **3+ mi:** Fishing Charter *(10 mi.)*, Park *(Popham Beach State Park, 10 mi.)*

Provisioning and General Services
OnSite: Beauty Salon **Near:** Liquor Store **Under 1 mi:** Post Office **3+ mi:** Convenience Store *(West Point General Store 389-9113, 5 mi.)*, Supermarket *(Shaw's 443-9179, 15 mi.)*, Health Food *(Grainery 442-8012, 15 mi.)*, Wine/Beer *(5 mi.)*, Bakery *(5 mi.)*, Fishmonger *(15 mi.)*, Lobster Pound *(5 mi.)*, Meat Market *(15 mi.)*, Catholic Church *(15 mi.)*, Protestant Church *(15 mi.)*, Library *(Totman Library 389-2309, 4 mi.)*, Barber Shop *(15 mi.)*, Laundry *(Garden Island 442-7054, also dry cleaning, 15 mi.)*, Bookstore *(Bath Book Shop 443-9338, 15 mi.)*, Pharmacy *(CVS 443-9097, 15 mi.)*, Newsstand *(15 mi.)*, Hardware Store *(Roger's 443-6089, 15 mi.)*, Florist *(15 mi.)*, Retail Shops *(15 mi.)*

Transportation
OnSite: Bikes **OnCall:** Rental Car *(Enterprise 725-1344)*, Taxi **Airport:** Portland Int'l. *(50 mi.)*

Medical Services
911 Service **OnCall:** Ambulance **3+ mi:** Doctor *(15 mi.)*, Dentist *(15 mi.)*, Chiropractor *(15 mi.)*, Holistic Services *(15 mi.)* **Hospital:** Mid-Coast 729-0181 *(15 mi.)*

Setting -- This 600 acre resort sits on the southeast tip of the rocky, pine-treed Phippsburg peninsula. 14,000 feet of water and estuary frontage provide spectacular views of Sebasco Harbor, out to Casco Bay. The wide assortment of 38 buildings, ranging from renovated turn of the century to recent reproductions, promises an upscale step back into old Maine. Seventy-year old Sebasco Harbor Resort offers guests a broad range of activities and services in a low-key, family atmosphere. A guest on a mooring is a guest of the resort.

Marina Notes -- No Dock tie up after hours. Moorings only (2-7 ton granite blocks) with complimentary Launch service (8am-8pm, MemDay-LabDay) & dinghy dock. 115 rooms, many newly renovated, ranging from Inn rooms to 1-6 bedroom cottages. Book a room, the mooring is free. 2 oceanside restaurants: Pilot House & Ledges Pub; interior Cornelius Room (prix fixe for MAP), Jackets suggested at dinner. Special bakes and breakfasts every week. Closest provisioning and services are 5 miles, most are 15 miles in Bath (cabs or occasional courtesy van). Minimal boatyard services available locally at Brewer's Boatyard (not the chain) 389-1388. Harbor can be a little unpleasant in a southerly. All facilities available to those at anchor for $15 per day.

Notable -- An extensive children's program (all-day Mon-Fri, Sat am), child care and special adult activities every night. The resort offers an 18 hole golf course (renovated for '03), tennis courts (rackets & clubs for rent), large saltwater pool, candlepin bowling, scenic boat trips on M/V Ruth, boat and canoe rentals, biking, ocean kayaking, fishing, fitness center, gift shop, pro shop, hiking, lawn bowling, salon & spa services, game room, video rentals, data ports.

Great Island Boat Yard

419 Harpswell Islands Road; Harpswell, ME 04079

Tel: (207) 729-1639 **VHF: Monitor** 9 **Talk** 10
Fax: (207) 729-1139 **Alternate Tel:** n/a
Email: info@greatislandboatyard.com **Web:** www.greatislandboatyard.com
Nearest Town: Brunswick *(7 mi.)* **Tourist Info:** (207) 725-8797

Navigational Information

Lat: 43°49.792' **Long:** 069°54.915' **Tide:** 10 ft. **Current:** 0 kt. **Chart:** 13290
Rep. Depths (*MLW*): Entry 12 ft. **Fuel Dock** 5 ft. **Max Slip/Moor** 12 ft./12 ft.
Access: Casco Bay to Merriconeag Sound to Quahog Bay

Marina Facilities *(In Season/Off Season)*

Fuel: Gasoline, Diesel
Slips: 67 Total, 3 Transient **Max LOA:** 45 ft. **Max Beam:** 12 ft.
Rate *(per ft.)*: **Day** $1.50/Inq. **Week** Inq. **Month** $22
Power: 30 amp Incl., **50 amp** Incl., **100 amp** n/a, **200 amp** n/a
Cable TV: No **Dockside Phone:** No
Dock Type: Wood, Long Fingers, Floating
Moorings: 40 Total, 2 Transient **Launch:** None, Dinghy Dock
Rate: Day $20 **Week** n/a **Month** $200
Heads: 2 Toilet(s), 1 Shower(s)
Laundry: None, Book Exchange **Pay Phones:** Yes
Pump-Out: OnSite, Full Service, 1 Central **Fee:** n/a **Closed Heads:** Yes

Marina Operations

Owner/Manager: Frank & Ellen Kibbe **Dockmaster:** Frank Kibbe
In-Season: May-Nov 1, 8am-5pm **Off-Season:** n/a
After-Hours Arrival: Call in advance
Reservations: Yes, Required **Credit Cards:** Visa/MC
Discounts: None
Pets: Welcome, Dog Walk Area **Handicap Access:** No

Marina Services and Boat Supplies

Services - Docking Assistance, Dock Carts **Communication -** Mail & Package Hold, Phone Messages, FedEx, AirBorne, UPS, Express Mail **Supplies - OnSite:** Ice *(Block, Cube)*, Ships' Store **3+ mi:** Bait/Tackle *(Jim's Live Bait & Bass 725-0440, 7 mi.)*, Propane *(U-Haul 729-8779, 7 mi.)*

Boatyard Services

OnSite: Travelift *(12T)*, Engine mechanic *(gas, diesel)*, Launching Ramp, Electrical Repairs, Hull Repairs, Bottom Cleaning, Brightwork, Air Conditioning, Refrigeration, Divers, Compound, Wash & Wax, Interior Cleaning, Woodworking, Painting, Total Refits **Near:** Yacht Broker *(Stewart Hart)*. **1-3 mi:** Canvas Work, Upholstery. **Yard Rates:** $47/hr., Haul & Launch $2/ft. **Storage:** On-Land Outside $4/sq.ft. Inside $6/sq.ft.

Restaurants and Accommodations

1-3 mi: Restaurant *(Block & Tackle Restaurant 725-5690)*, Inn/B&B *(Bethel Point B&B 725-1115)* **3+ mi:** Restaurant *(Narcissa Stone 725-9898, L $5-11, D $12-23, 7 mi.)*, *(Star Fish Grill 725-7828, D $15-22, 7 mi.)*, Pizzeria *(Sam's Italian Foods 725-4444, 5 mi.)*, Inn/B&B *(Capt. Daniel Stone Inn 725-9898, $105-225, 6 mi.)*

Recreation and Entertainment

Near: Jogging Paths **3+ mi:** Tennis Courts *(Maine Pines Racquet 729-8433, 7 mi.)*, Golf Course *(Brunswick Golf Club 207-725-8224, 7 mi.)*, Bowling *(Yankee Lanes Of Brunswick 725-2963, 7 mi.)*, Video Rental *(Video Galaxy 729-6205, 7 mi.)*, Museum *(Chamberlain Museum 725-6958, 8 mi.)*

Provisioning and General Services

Under 1 mi: Lobster Pound **1-3 mi:** Convenience Store, Bookstore *(Peeka-Book Cottage 833-0006)* **3+ mi:** Supermarket *(Shaw's 725-8751, 7 mi.)*, Gourmet Shop *(Provisions 729-9288, 8 mi.)*, Health Food *(Morning Glory 729-0546, 8 mi.)*, Wine/Beer *(Provisions, 8 mi.)*, Liquor Store *(Maine Package 729-3961, 7 mi.)*, Farmers' Market *(Brunswick Tue & Fri 8am-3pm, 7 mi.)*, Library *(Orrs Island Library 833-7811, 5 mi.)*, Pharmacy *(CVS 729-0414, 7 mi.)*, Hardware Store *(Mariner Lumber 725-5540, 7 mi.)*, Copies Etc. *(Staples 725-2741, 6 mi.)*

Transportation

OnSite: Courtesy Car/Van *(at mutually convenient times, staff will provide rides into town)* **OnCall:** Rental Car *(Enterprise 882-8393)*, Taxi *(Brunswick Taxi 729-3688)*, Airport Limo *(Platinum Plus Limo 442-0155)* **3+ mi:** InterCity Bus *(Concord, 6 mi.)* **Airport:** Portland Int'l. *(40 mi.)*

Medical Services

911 Service **Hospital:** Parkview *(5 mi.)*

Setting -- Up a quiet, isolated, and protected cove off Quahog Bay on Sebascodegan Island (just east of Bailey Island and Orrs Island), the Boat Yard is the only visible sign of development. Views landside are of a modest facility (the big work sheds are discreetly tucked behind trees) and those out to the water are of seemingly untouched nature. Great Island is in a very private, rural setting -- one that is becoming more and more elusive.

Marina Notes -- Full service boatyard with most critical services on site. Established in the early 70's, new owners Frank & Ellen Kibbe took the helm in the summer of 2000. Heads and showers were redone winter 2000-01 - along with new decks. There are new slips (floating docks with fixed fingers) and additional moorings. Sailboats available for charter and a very active brokerage business managed by Stew Hart. Their 4 acres can winter store 168 boats, 18-45 ft. Very service-oriented, accommodating staff. The cove is reputed to be a good hurricane hole, making this a good place to leave the boat. Reservations are a must.

Notable -- There is absolutely nothing to do here except relax, read, swim (the water temperature is reportedly bearable), fish, and enjoy the scenery and the quiet. Quahog Bay promises many protected, pristine coves for dinghy explorations. A lobster pound is within hiking distance. It's seven miles to the city of Brunswick and to Bowdoin College where you'll find several wonderful museums, the professional Maine State Music Theater, a music festival, and free concerts on the mall on Wednesday evenings. Brunswick also has an interesting collection of Federal mansions (reminders of its affluent past), great provisioning and service resources, a 3 star hotel, and a couple of very good restaurants.

Navigational Information
Lat: 43°44.341' **Long:** 070°02.401' **Tide:** 9 ft. **Current:** 2 kt. **Chart:** 13290
Rep. Depths (*MLW*): Entry 40 ft. **Fuel Dock** 15 ft. **Max Slip/Moor** 15 ft./40 ft.
Access: Past Little Birch Island, after Horse Island and Thumb Cap

Marina Facilities *(In Season/Off Season)*
Fuel: Slip-Side Fueling, Gasoline, Diesel
Slips: 6 Total, 6 Transient **Max LOA:** 50 ft. **Max Beam:** 30 ft.
Rate *(per ft.)*: **Day** $1.00/Inq. **Week** Inq. **Month** Inq.
Power: 30 amp Incl., **50 amp** n/a, **100 amp** n/a, **200 amp** n/a
Cable TV: No **Dockside Phone:** No
Dock Type: Wood, Long Fingers, Floating
Moorings: 80 Total, 15 Transient **Launch:** Yes
Rate: Day $10 **Week** $75 **Month** n/a
Heads: 2 Toilet(s)
Laundry: None **Pay Phones:** No
Pump-Out: OnCall, Full Service, 1 Port **Fee:** $5 **Closed Heads:** No

Marina Operations
Owner/Manager: Bill Saxton **Dockmaster:** Chris Saxton
In-Season: Year-Round **Off-Season:** n/a
After-Hours Arrival: Pick up mooring or slip
Reservations: Required **Credit Cards:** Visa/MC
Discounts: None
Pets: Welcome, Dog Walk Area **Handicap Access:** Yes, Heads, Docks

Dolphin Marina & Restaurant

515 Basin Point; Harpswell, ME 04079

Tel: (207) 833-5343 **VHF: Monitor** 9 **Talk** 9
Fax: (207) 833-5671 **Alternate Tel:** (207) 833-6000
Email: n/a **Web:** n/a
Nearest Town: Brunswick *(15 mi.)* **Tourist Info:** (207) 725-8797

Marina Services and Boat Supplies
Services - Docking Assistance, Boaters' Lounge, Security *(7pm - 7am)*, Trash Pick-Up, Dock Carts **Communication -** Mail & Package Hold, Phone Messages, Fax in/out, UPS **Supplies - OnSite:** Ice *(Block, Cube)* **3+ mi:** Propane *(Morse's Market, 5 mi.)*

Boatyard Services
OnSite: Travelift *(35T)*, Engine mechanic *(gas, diesel)*, Launching Ramp, Electrical Repairs, Hull Repairs, Bottom Cleaning, Brightwork, Divers, Compound, Wash & Wax, Propeller Repairs, Woodworking, Metal Fabrication, Total Refits **OnCall:** Air Conditioning, Refrigeration **Member:** ABBRA **Yard Rates:** $52/hr., Haul & Launch $5/ft., Power Wash $1, Bottom Paint $5/ft. *(paint included)* **Storage:** On-Land $20/ft.

Restaurants and Accommodations
OnSite: Restaurant *(Dolphin Marina 833-6000, L $4-9, D $14-20, 11am-8pm - reportedly the best fish chowder in Midcoast Maine)* **Near:** Inn/B&B *(East Wind Inn 372-6366)* **1-3 mi:** Restaurant *(Estes Lobster 833-6340, L $10, D $18-25)*, *(J Hathaway's Restaurant & Tavern 833-5305, D $10-22, 3 mi.)* **3+ mi:** Inn/B&B *(Harpswell Inn 833-5509, $80-200, 6 mi.)*

Recreation and Entertainment
OnSite: Beach, Picnic Area, Grills, Playground **Near:** Jogging Paths **1-3 mi:** Tennis Courts, Sightseeing *(Bailey Island Cribstone Bridge)*, Galleries *(Local Harpswell Craft Guild members mark their studios (mostly along Route 123) with a Blue Heron sign.)*

Provisioning and General Services
1-3 mi: Convenience Store *(Bailey Island General Store 833-6601)*, Post Office, Catholic Church, Protestant Church, Synagogue **3+ mi:** Supermarket *(Shaw's or Hannaford 729-1604, 15 mi.)*, Gourmet Shop *(Store On Orrs 833-2301, 4 mi.)*, Library *(Orrs Island Library 833-7811, 4 mi.)*, Pharmacy *(CVS Brunswick 729-0414, 12 mi.)*

Transportation
OnCall: Rental Car *(Enterprise 725-1344)* **3+ mi:** Taxi *(Brunswick Taxi 729-3688, 15 mi.)* **Airport:** Portland Int'l. *(45 mi.)*

Medical Services
911 Service **3+ mi:** Ambulance *(6 mi.)* **Hospital:** Parkview 373-2000 / Midcoast 729-0181 *(20 mi.)*

Setting -- On surprisingly well protected Potts Harbor, at Basin Point, Dolphin Marine sits at the south end of Harpswell Neck, with wonderful views out to Casco Bay. The small islands that dot the Bay, and the ledges to the south turn this mile-wide bay into a safe harbor. They also offer opportunities for explorations and picnics. Landside, the views are of parking lots, the boatyard, the onsite restaurant, and a generally rural landscape.

Marina Notes -- The Dolphin Marina Restaurant is famous for its delicious fish chowder, lobster stew, and blueberry muffins (from the adjacent blueberry field) - and is well worth a detour. The atmosphere is down-home comfort and well-used varnished wood, with a real mix of customers -- a favorite of local fishermen and Bowdoin professors. They serve lunch and dinner and the restaurant also caters Lobster Bakes for groups. Both dockage and moorings, with launch service (8am-7pm daily) and a dinghy dock. Basic facilities - heads are shared with the restaurant; no showers or laundry. Fuel available slipside but no water. Most expected boatyard services are available onsite, with some additional ones on call.

Notable -- Basin Cove is a great dinghy destination for birdwatching. The 1761 Harpswell Inn, a charming and picturesque three story building, is six miles away. Most provisioning and general services are 15/20 miles away in Brunswick. The nearest taxi has to come from there, too, making a rental car delivered to the marina the only option (and you have to drive the agent back). If you get to Brunswick, Bowdoin College has wonderful museums, a music festival and a professional musical theater; plus the city boasts Federal mansions, great stores and good restaurants.

PHOTOS ON CD-ROM: 4

IV. Maine: Portland & The South Coast

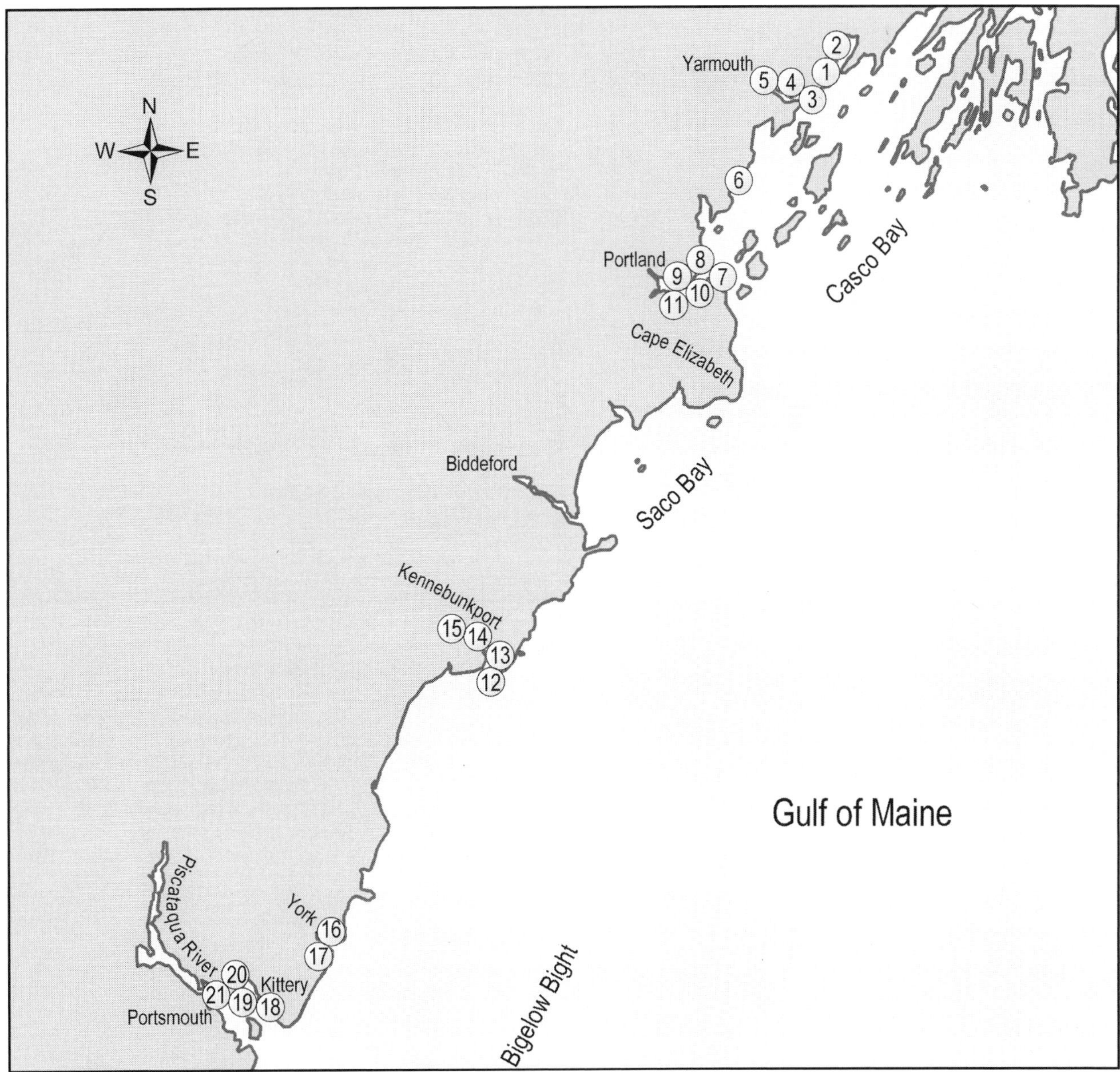

MAP	MARINA	HARBOR	PAGE
1	**Strouts Point Wharf Company**	*Harraseeket River*	92
2	**Brewer South Freeport Marine**	*Harraseeket River*	93
3	**Royal River Boat Yard**	*Royal River*	94
4	**Yankee Marina**	*Royal River*	95
5	**Yarmouth Boat Yard**	*Royal River*	96
6	**Handy Boat Service**	*Falmouth River*	97
7	**Spring Point Marina**	*Portland Harbor*	98
8	**Portland Yacht Services, Inc**	*Portland Harbor*	99
9	**DiMillo's Old Port Marina**	*Portland Harbor*	100
10	**Sunset Marina**	*Portland Harbor*	101
11	**South Port Marine**	*Portland Harbor*	102
12	**Chick's Marina**	*Kennebunk River*	103
13	**Kennebunkport Marina**	*Kennebunk River*	104
14	**Yachtsman Marina**	*Kennebunk River*	105
15	**Performance Marine**	*Kennebunk River*	106
16	**Donnell's Marina**	*York Harbor*	107
17	**York Harbor Marine / Town Moorings**	*York Harbor*	108
18	**Kittery Point Wharf**	*Piscataqua River*	109
19	**Dion's Yacht Yard**	*Piscataqua River*	110
20	**Kittery Landing Marina**	*Piscataqua River*	111
21	**Badgers Island Marina**	*Piscataqua River*	112

Strouts Point Wharf Company

PO Box 95; Main Street; South Freeport, ME 04018

Tel: (207) 865-3899 **VHF: Monitor** 9 **Talk** 9
Fax: (207) 865-4407 **Alternate Tel:** n/a
Email: n/a **Web:** n/a
Nearest Town: Freeport *(2 mi.)* **Tourist Info:** (207) 865-1212

Navigational Information
Lat: 43°49.210' **Long:** 070°06.400' **Tide:** 12ft. **Current:** 3 kt. **Chart:** 13290
Rep. Depths (*MLW*): Entry 20 ft. **Fuel Dock** 18 ft. **Max Slip/Moor** 18 ft./60 ft.
Access: Broad Sound to R6 at Whaleboat Island to G1 to R4

Marina Facilities *(In Season/Off Season)*
Fuel: Gasoline, Diesel
Slips: 100 Total, 2 Transient **Max LOA:** 65 ft. **Max Beam:** 20 ft.
Rate *(per ft.)*: **Day** $1.35 **Week** $8.00 **Month** $16
Power: 30 amp Incl., **50 amp** Incl., **100 amp** n/a, **200 amp** n/a
Cable TV: No **Dockside Phone:** No
Dock Type: Wood, Long Fingers, Floating
Moorings: 15 Total, 3 Transient **Launch:** Brewers Launch
Rate: Day $25 **Week** $125 **Month** $300
Heads: 2 Toilet(s), 2 Shower(s)
Laundry: None **Pay Phones:** No
Pump-Out: OnSite, Full Service **Fee:** $10 **Closed Heads:** Yes

Marina Operations
Owner/Manager: Ted Wengren/Peter Barnes **Dockmaster:** Kelly Rickard
In-Season: May-Oct 31, 8am-7pm **Off-Season:** Nov-Apr, 8am-5pm
After-Hours Arrival: Call ahead for instructions
Reservations: Yes, Preferred **Credit Cards:** Visa/MC
Discounts: None
Pets: Welcome **Handicap Access:** No

Marina Services and Boat Supplies
Services - Docking Assistance, Trash Pick-Up, Dock Carts
Communication - Mail & Package Hold, Phone Messages, Fax in/out, FedEx, UPS, Express Mail **Supplies - OnSite:** Ice *(Cube)*, Ships' Store
1-3 mi: Bait/Tackle *(LL Bean 865-4761)*, Propane

Boatyard Services
OnSite: Travelift *(25T)*, Engine mechanic *(gas, diesel)*, Electrical Repairs, Electronics Repairs, Hull Repairs, Rigger, Bottom Cleaning, Brightwork, Refrigeration

Restaurants and Accommodations
OnCall: Pizzeria *(Dominos 865-6111)* **Near:** Seafood Shack *(Harraseeket Lunch 865-4888, L $5-9, D $9-15, next door)* **Under 1 mi:** Motel *(Super 8 865-1408, $42-130)* **1-3 mi:** Restaurant *(Maine Dining Room 865-9377, L $4-13, D $15-26, in the Harraseeket Inn)*, *(Jameson Tavern 865-4196, L $8-11, D $14-21)*, Fast Food, Motel *(Freeport Inn 865-3106, $60-120)*, Hotel *(Harraseeket Inn 865-9377, $120-275)*, *(Coastline Inn 865-3777, $50-110)*, Inn/B&B *(181 Main Street B&B 865-1226, $85-110)*, *(Kendall Tavern B&B 813-3865, $70-110)*

Recreation and Entertainment
OnCall: Fishing Charter *(Charter fishing 865-1718, $250/6 hr day, $450/12 hr day)* **Near:** Jogging Paths, Roller Blade/Bike Paths, Park *(Wolf Neck Woods - dinghy to eastern shore of the river)*, Sightseeing *(Atlantic Seal Cruises 865-6112, next door at the town wharf 9:30am, 1:30 & 6:00pm)*
1-3 mi: Pool, Beach *(Winslow Memorial Park)*, Picnic Area, Grills, Playground, Tennis Courts, Golf Course *(Freeport Country Club 865-4922)*, Video Rental, Museum *(Harrington House Museum 865-0477)*, Special Events

Provisioning and General Services
Near: Convenience Store *(Village Store)*, Wine/Beer *(Old World Gourmet Deli & Wine Shop 865-4477)*, Liquor Store, Lobster Pound *(Harraseeket)*, Post Office, Protestant Church **1-3 mi:** Supermarket *(Bow Street Market 865-6631, Hannaford, Yarmouth 846-5941)*, Gourmet Shop, Delicatessen, Health Food *(Royal River Natural Foods 865-0046)*, Bakery, Farmers' Market, Meat Market, Bank/ATM, Catholic Church, Library, Beauty Salon, Barber Shop, Dry Cleaners, Laundry, Bookstore, Pharmacy *(Brooks 865-6324)*, Newsstand, Hardware Store *(Freeport Hardware 865-9557)*, Florist, Clothing Store *(LL Beans)*, Retail Shops *(Freeport Factory Outlets)*, Department Store *(Beans)*, Copies Etc.

Transportation
OnCall: Rental Car *(Enterprise 725-1314)*, Taxi *(Classy Taxi 865-0809)*
Near: Ferry Service *(Bustins Island $6/3 each way)* **Under 1 mi:** Bikes *(National Ski & Bike 865-0523)* **Airport:** Portland Int'l. *(18 mi.)*

Medical Services
911 Service **OnCall:** Ambulance **Near:** Chiropractor *(Armstrong 865-3649)* **Under 1 mi:** Holistic Services *(Austen Massage 865-0672)* **1-3 mi:** Doctor *(Donahue 865-2225)*, Dentist **Hospital:** Maine Medical/Mid-Coast 729-0181 *(15 mi.)*

Setting -- Half a mile up the Harraseeket River, this one of a kind full-service boatyard and marina is right next to the Freeport Town Dock and Brewer, in an appealing and very secure Maine harbor. Pristine views of pine-topped islands, Wolf's Neck, and Casco Bay beyond complement the marina's attention to detail, which is reflected in the noteworthy dock designs. Everything is exceptionally well maintained and attests to the staff's woodworking expertise. Quiet South Freeport is seemingly far removed from the bustle of Freeport.

Marina Notes -- Home to Concordia yacht restorers and highly regarded woodworkers, Strouts Point has been family owned for generations. The boatyard specializes in wooden boats. Attractive full baths and half baths. Launch service to the moorings is provided by Brewers South Freeport Marine just up the street. Additional moorings may be located by hailing the harbormaster on Ch.9 or from Ring's Marine (865-6143). Town floats permit 30 minute docking.

Notable -- The Harraseeket River is a snug storm harbor. Harraseeket Lunch and Lobster is a very short walk for lobsters, steamers, crabs, etc. (courtesy dockage at Town Wharf Ch.9). Separate lobster window can minimize the wait. The Village Store is within walking distance and prepares picnic lunches and hot entrées to go. In downtown Freeport, L.L. Bean is open 24 hrs., 7 days (800 341-4341) -- there's the original retail store (with the Dew Drop Inn Café and indoor trout pond), a factory store, and a kids' store (with the "trail of discovery", an indoor climbing wall, fish pond and interactive bike trail). Surrounding Bean are 120 outlet shops, in restored buildings - interspersed with a variety of eateries and lodgings.

PHOTOS ON CD-ROM: 5

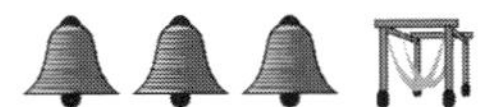

Navigational Information

Lat: 43°49.270' **Long:** 070°06.280' **Tide:** 12 ft. **Current:** 3 kt. **Chart:** 13290
Rep. Depths (*MLW*): Entry 20 ft. **Fuel Dock** 16 ft. **Max Slip/Moor** 16 ft./20 ft.
Access: Broad Sound to R6 at Whaleboat Island to G1 to R4

Marina Facilities *(In Season/Off Season)*

Fuel: Slip-Side Fueling, Gasoline, Diesel
Slips: 90 Total, 4 Transient **Max LOA:** 145 ft. **Max Beam:** n/a
Rate *(per ft.)*: **Day** $2.00* **Week** Inq. **Month** Inq.
Power: 30 amp Incl., **50 amp** Incl., **100 amp** n/a, **200 amp** n/a
Cable TV: No **Dockside Phone:** No
Dock Type: Wood, Long Fingers, Short Fingers, Floating
Moorings: 15 Total, 0-15 Transient **Launch:** Yes ($2/pp)
Rate: Day $25 **Week** $150 **Month** $600
Heads: 3 Toilet(s), 3 Shower(s), lounge
Laundry: 1 Washer(s), 1 Dryer(s), Book Exchange **Pay Phones:** No
Pump-Out: OnSite, Full Service, 1 Central **Fee:** $5 **Closed Heads:** Yes

Marina Operations

Owner/Manager: John S. Brewer **Dockmaster:** Kristin Peterson
In-Season: May-Oct, 8am-6pm **Off-Season:** Oct-May, 8am-4:30pm
After-Hours Arrival: Call ahead for instructions
Reservations: Yes, Required **Credit Cards:** Visa/MC, Dscvr, Amex
Discounts: Brewer Club Members **Dockage:** n/a **Fuel:** n/a **Repair:** n/a
Pets: Welcome, Dog Walk Area **Handicap Access:** No

Brewer South Freeport Marine

PO Box 119; 2 Main Street; South Freeport, ME 04078

Tel: (207) 865-3181 **VHF: Monitor** 9 **Talk** 10
Fax: (207) 865-3183 **Alternate Tel:** n/a
Email: bsf@byy.com **Web:** www.byy.com/freeport
Nearest Town: Freeport *(2 mi.)* **Tourist Info:** (207) 865-1212

Marina Services and Boat Supplies

Services - Docking Assistance, Boaters' Lounge, Trash Pick-Up, Dock Carts **Communication -** Mail & Package Hold, Phone Messages, Fax in/out, Data Ports, FedEx, UPS, Express Mail *(Sat Del)* **Supplies - OnSite:** Ice *(Block, Cube)* **1-3 mi:** Bait/Tackle *(LL Bean 865-4761)*, Propane *(Freeport General Store)* **3+ mi:** Ships' Store *(4 mi.)*, West Marine *(12 mi.)*

Boatyard Services

OnSite: Travelift *(35T)*, Engine mechanic *(gas, diesel)*, Electrical Repairs, Hull Repairs, Rigger, Bottom Cleaning, Brightwork, Divers, Compound, Wash & Wax, Interior Cleaning **OnCall:** Electronics Repairs, Air Conditioning, Refrigeration **Dealer for:** Mercruiser, Yanmar, Westerbeke, Sealand, Yamaha.

Restaurants and Accommodations

Near: Seafood Shack *(Harraseeket Lunch and Lobster 865-4888)*, Snack Bar *(Village Store B $3-10, L $3-10, D $3-10)* **1-3 mi:** Restaurant *(Harraseeket Inn Dining Room 865-9377, L $4-13, D $15-26, Sun Brunch $26)*, *(Gritty Mc Duff's 865-4321, L $4-13, D $4-13)*, Fast Food, Pizzeria *(The Corsican 865-9421)*, Inn/B&B *(Harraseeket Inn 865-9377, $120-285)*, *(Casco Bay Inn 865-4925, $50-99)*, *(Freeport Inn 865-3106, $60-120)*, *(Coastline Inn 865-3777, $50-110)*

Recreation and Entertainment

OnSite: Picnic Area, Grills, Fishing Charter **Near:** Sightseeing *(Atlantic Seal Cruises 865-6112 leave Freeport Town Wharf at 9:30am and 1:30pm, $20)* **Under 1 mi:** Jogging Paths, Park *(Audubon's Mast Landing Sanctuary - dinghy up stream)* **1-3 mi:** Beach *(Winslow Memorial Park)*, Playground, Tennis Courts, Golf Course *(Freeport Country Club 207-865-4922)*, Museum *(Harrington House Museum 865-0477)* **3+ mi:** Video Rental *(4 mi.)*

Provisioning and General Services

Near: Convenience Store, Gourmet Shop, Delicatessen, Wine/Beer *(Village Store)*, Bakery, Lobster Pound, Post Office, Protestant Church **1-3 mi:** Liquor Store *(Bow Street Market)*, Catholic Church, Beauty Salon, Barber Shop, Pharmacy *(Brooks 865-6324)*, Newsstand, Hardware Store *(Freeport Hardware 865-9557)*, Florist, Clothing Store, Retail Shops, Department Store *(LL Bean)* **3+ mi:** Supermarket *(Hannaford - Yarmouth 846-5941, 5 mi.)*, Health Food *(Royal River Natural Foods 865-0046, 4 mi.)*, Library *(4 mi.)*, Dry Cleaners *(4 mi.)*, Bookstore *(4 mi.)*

Transportation

OnSite: Courtesy Car/Van **OnCall:** Rental Car *(Enterprise 725-1344)*, Taxi *(Freeport Taxi 865-9494, Yarmouth Taxi 846-9334)*, Airport Limo *(Outward Express 865-0890)* **Airport:** Portland Int'l. *(12 mi.)*

Medical Services

911 Service **OnCall:** Ambulance **Under 1 mi:** Chiropractor *(Armstrong 865-3649)* **1-3 mi:** Doctor *(Donahue 865-2225)*, Dentist **Hospital:** Maine Medical/Mid-Coast 729-0181 *(15 mi.)*

Setting -- Set in a quiet, protected, deep water tidal harbor a half mile up the Harraseeket River next to Strouts Point Wharf, this exceptionally well maintained boatyard and marina offers a comfortable and secure stop. Brewers is surrounded by active clam flats and lobster docks, with classic Maine views of woodlands and distant islands. Large, recently rebuilt boatyard sheds and other out buildings are on the landside.

Marina Notes -- *Over 50' $2.50/ft. 220 feet of floating face dock makes docking easy (just be sure to watch the 9-12 ft. tidal swing and the 2-3 knots of current). Due to a fire in the late nineties, most of the landside facilities are newly constructed. A complete, full-service boatyard facility, supported by the entire Brewers chain -- all mechanical services as well as Awlgrip, wood and fiberglass finishing, major hull repairs, and interior joinery. New heads, full bathrooms -- and particularly nice, as is the laundry with large folding table. Moorings also available from Harraseeket Yacht Club (865-4949) and Rings (865-6143). Nearby Maine Compass Services (865-6645) for adjustments or refills.

Notable -- The very reasonable Harraseeket Lunch and Lobster is right next door - lobsters, steamers, crabs (live and cooked) - with picnic tables overlooking the town wharf (courtesy dockage on town wharf while eating). The Village Store is a short walk for picnics, entrées to go, ice cream and groceries. L.L. Bean and Freeport's charmingly restored conglomeration of designers' outlets are a taxi or courtesy car ride away. If the fog's rolled in, there's lots to do there. L.L. Bean, open 24 hrs., 7 days (800 341-4341), is truly an experience with the original retail store, a factory store and a kids' store.

PHOTOS ON CD-ROM: 5

Royal River Boat Yard

307 Bayview Street; Yarmouth, ME 04096

Tel: (207) 846-9577 **VHF: Monitor** n/a **Talk** n/a
Fax: (207) 846-6571 **Alternate Tel:** n/a
Email: rrboatyd@nlis.net **Web:** n/a
Nearest Town: Yarmouth *(1.6 mi.)* **Tourist Info:** (207) 846-3984

Navigational Information

Lat: 43°47.722' **Long:** 070°10.131' **Tide:** 9 ft. **Current:** 1 kt. **Chart:** 13290
Rep. Depths (*MLW*): Entry 10 ft. **Fuel Dock** 10 ft. **Max Slip/Moor** 10 ft./-
Access: Cosco Bay to Royal River, follow markers

Marina Facilities *(In Season/Off Season)*

Fuel: Gasoline, Diesel
Slips: 60 Total, 4 Transient **Max LOA:** 50 ft. **Max Beam:** n/a
Rate *(per ft.)*: **Day** $1.25 **Week** $5.50 **Month** n/a
Power: 30 amp Inc., **50 amp** Inc., **100 amp** n/a, **200 amp** n/a
Cable TV: No **Dockside Phone:** No
Dock Type: Wood, Alongside, Floating
Moorings: 0 Total, 0 Transient **Launch:** n/a
Rate: Day n/a **Week** n/a **Month** n/a
Heads: 2 Toilet(s), 1 Shower(s)
Laundry: None **Pay Phones:** No
Pump-Out: No **Fee:** n/a **Closed Heads:** No

Marina Operations

Owner/Manager: Alan J. Dugas **Dockmaster:** n/a
In-Season: May-Oct, 7am-6pm **Off-Season:** Nov-Apr, 7am-5pm
After-Hours Arrival: Call ahead, tie up where instructed
Reservations: Yes **Credit Cards:** Visa/MC, Dscvr, Amex
Discounts: None
Pets: Welcome **Handicap Access:** No

Marina Services and Boat Supplies

Services - Docking Assistance, Trash Pick-Up **Supplies - OnSite:** Ice *(Block, Cube)*, Ships' Store **Under 1 mi:** Marine Discount Store *(Landing Boat Supply 846-3777)* **1-3 mi:** Propane *(Yarmouth Fuel 846-5507)*

Boatyard Services

OnSite: Travelift *(2 -50T)*, Railway *(100T)*, Forklift, Engine mechanic *(gas, diesel)*, Launching Ramp, Electrical Repairs, Electronic Sales, Electronics Repairs, Hull Repairs, Rigger, Sail Loft, Canvas Work, Bottom Cleaning, Brightwork, Air Conditioning, Refrigeration, Compound, Wash & Wax, Interior Cleaning, Propeller Repairs, Woodworking, Inflatable Repairs, Painting, Total Refits **OnCall:** Divers, Metal Fabrication **Dealer for:** Mercury, Yamaha. **Member:** ABYC

Restaurants and Accommodations

Near: Pizzeria *(Pat's Pizza 846-3701)* **Under 1 mi:** Restaurant *(Royal River Grillhouse 846-1226, L $6-12, D $14-24)*, *(233 Grill 846-3633)*, *(Muddy Rudder 846-3082, L $7-10, D $20-25)*, *(Chowderheads 846-4488)* **1-3 mi:** Lite Fare *(Sharon's Breakfast and Lunch 846-4476)*, Motel *(Brookside Motel 846-5512)*

Recreation and Entertainment

Under 1 mi: Video Rental, Museum *(Yarmouth Historical Society 846-6259)* **1-3 mi:** Sightseeing *(DeLorme corporate headquarters 846-7000)*

Provisioning and General Services

1-3 mi: Supermarket *(Hannaford 846-5941)*, Delicatessen *(Old World Gourmet Deli and Wine Shop 865-4477)*, Health Food, Wine/Beer, Liquor Store, Bakery, Fishmonger, Lobster Pound, Bank/ATM, Post Office, Catholic Church, Protestant Church, Library, Beauty Salon, Barber Shop, Dry Cleaners, Laundry, Bookstore, Pharmacy *(Rite Aid 846-1222)*, Newsstand, Hardware Store *(Yarmouth Hardware 846-5932)*, Florist, Retail Shops, Department Store *(Wal-Mart)*, Copies Etc.

Transportation

OnCall: Taxi *(Yarmouth 846-9336)* **Under 1 mi:** Rental Car *(Hometown Rental 846-2470)* **3+ mi:** Rail *(15 mi.)* **Airport:** *(15 mi.)*

Medical Services

911 Service **Near:** Dentist *(Bayview Dental Associates 846-0979)* **Under 1 mi:** Veterinarian *(Yarmouth Vet Center 846-6515)* **1-3 mi:** Chiropractor *(Head to Toes 846-1481)* **Hospital:** Maine Medical 871-0111 *(13 mi.)*

PHOTOS ON CD-ROM: 7

Setting -- About 2 miles from the mouth of the Royal River, this neat and tidy boatyard is the first facility on the starboard side. Two large new buildings dominate its skyline, but otherwise the immediate surroundings are relatively unspoiled. Civilization looms a little upriver on the opposite bank.

Marina Notes -- Royal River is a family operation and now includes the 3rd generation. 2002 saw major upgrades with the addition of two new large work sheds. The town dredges the channel that leads to their docks, so there is usually plenty of depth (last dredging April 2003). Most dockage is "alongside" although there are a few slips. There are extensive dry land storage and commodious inside work and storage areas. One of the new buildings houses the brand new heads - two full baths with showers. Laundry is coming in 2004 - call. Service is available 7 days a week. Bayview Rigging (846-8877) also makes its home onsite.

Notable -- The area is fairly rural. Across and up the river -- just a short dinghy distance -- is the Royal River Grillhouse Restaurant (formerly The Cannery) in the Lower Falls Landing complex (adjacent to Yankee Marina). Yarmouth is famous for its annual Clam Festival which promises, in addition to clams, all manner of river races, a carnival, lots of music and huge, happy crowds. If you can get out to the main highway, Route 1, Yarmouth is also the corporate headquarters for the map-makers DeLorme. Visit the Map Shop and "Eartha", at 42 feet in diameter the world's largest rotating globe (846-7000).

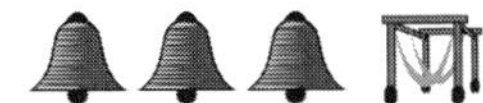

Navigational Information
Lat: 43°47.440' **Long:** 070°10.230' **Tide:** 9 ft. **Current:** 1 kt. **Chart:** 13290
Rep. Depths (*MLW*): Entry 8 ft. **Fuel Dock** n/a **Max Slip/Moor** 9 ft./9 ft.
Access: Casco Bay to the Royal River past R18

Marina Facilities *(In Season/Off Season)*
Fuel: No
Slips: 112 Total, 0 Transient **Max LOA:** 60 ft. **Max Beam:** n/a
Rate *(per ft.)*: **Day** $1.25/$0.75 **Week** n/a **Month** n/a
Power: 30 amp n/a, **50 amp** n/a, **100 amp** n/a, **200 amp** n/a
Cable TV: No **Dockside Phone:** No
Dock Type: Floating
Moorings: 0 Total, 0 Transient **Launch:** n/a
Rate: Day n/a **Week** n/a **Month** n/a
Heads: 2 Toilet(s), 1 Shower(s)
Laundry: None **Pay Phones:** No
Pump-Out: OnSite, Self Service, 1 Central **Fee:** $5 **Closed Heads:** Yes

Marina Operations
Owner/Manager: Ralph Stevens **Dockmaster:** Ben Stevens
In-Season: May-Oct, 7am-5pm **Off-Season:** Nov-Apr, 7am-4pm
After-Hours Arrival: Call in advance
Reservations: Yes, Required **Credit Cards:** Visa/MC, Dscvr
Discounts: None
Pets: Welcome **Handicap Access:** Yes, Heads, Docks

Yankee Marina

PO Box 548; 142 Lafayette Street; Yarmouth, ME 04096

Tel: (207) 846-4328 **VHF: Monitor** 9 **Talk** 9
Fax: (207) 846-4329 **Alternate Tel:** n/a
Email: Yankee@yankeemarina.com **Web:** www.yankeemarina.com
Nearest Town: Yarmouth *(1.3 mi.)* **Tourist Info:** (207) 846-3984

Marina Services and Boat Supplies
Services - Docking Assistance, Security, Trash Pick-Up **Communication -** Mail & Package Hold, Phone Messages, Fax in/out, FedEx, AirBorne, UPS, Express Mail **Supplies - OnSite:** Ice *(Block)*, Ships' Store *(Landing Boat Supply 846-3777)* **Under 1 mi:** Propane *(Downeast Energy)* **1-3 mi:** Bait/Tackle

Boatyard Services
OnSite: Travelift *(15T & 60T)*, Engine mechanic *(gas, diesel)*, Launching Ramp, Electrical Repairs, Electronic Sales, Electronics Repairs, Hull Repairs, Rigger, Bottom Cleaning, Brightwork, Air Conditioning, Refrigeration, Compound, Wash & Wax, Interior Cleaning, Woodworking, Painting, Awlgrip **OnCall:** Divers **Near:** Sail Loft. **Dealer for:** Westerbeke, Espar, Sea Frost, Awlgrip, Interlux, Marine Air, and Grunnert. For East Coast Yacht Sales: commissions Sabre, JBoats, Freedom, Sabreline, Grand Banks. Custom Awlgrip Interlux: Gelcoat repair. **Member:** ABYC - 2 Certified Tech(s), Other Certifications: FCC Licensed

Restaurants and Accommodations
OnSite: Restaurant *(Royal River Grillhouse 846-1226, L $6-12, D $14-24)* **Under 1 mi:** Restaurant *(Muddy Rudder 846-3082, L $7-10, D $20-25)*, *(Down-East Village Restaurant 846-5161, L $6-12, D $10-20)*, Motel *(Down East Village 846-5161, $60-100)* **1-3 mi:** Fast Food, Pizzeria *(De Nuccis 846-8646)*, Motel *(Brookside 846-5512, $50-95)*

Recreation and Entertainment
OnSite: Boat Rentals *(Casco Bay Rowing)* **Near:** Jogging Paths, Park *(Royal River Park, waterfall cascades just past the bridge)*, Museum *(Yarmouth Historical Society 846-6259)*, Cultural Attract *(Wednesday night concerts at R.R. Park)* **Under 1 mi:** Picnic Area, Video Rental **1-3 mi:** Beach, Playground, Golf Course *(Freeport C. C. 865-0711)* **3+ mi:** Horseback Riding *(Equine Estate 829-6056, 4 mi.)*

Provisioning and General Services
Near: Delicatessen **Under 1 mi:** Supermarket *(Hannaford 846-5941)*, Bank/ATM, Post Office, Beauty Salon, Hardware Store *(Goss's Hardware 846-5932)*, Clothing Store, Copies Etc. *(Greetings)* **1-3 mi:** Convenience Store, Gourmet Shop *(Clayton's Gourmet 846-1117)*, Wine/Beer *(Clayton's)*, Liquor Store, Bakery, Farmers' Market, Fishmonger, Lobster Pound, Meat Market, Catholic Church, Library *(Merrill 846-4763)*, Dry Cleaners, Laundry, Bookstore, Pharmacy *(Hannaford)*, Newsstand, Florist, Retail Shops *(Greetings 846-0585)*, Department Store, Buying Club **3+ mi:** Health Food *(Royal River Natural Foods 865-0046, 5 mi.)*

Transportation
OnCall: Taxi *(Yarmouth 846-9336)* **1-3 mi:** Rental Car *(Hometown Rental 846-2470)* **3+ mi:** Water Taxi *(Presumpscot 879-2562, 11 mi.)*, InterCity Bus *(Greyhound 772-6587, 13 mi.)* **Airport:** Portland Int'l. *(15 mi.)*

Medical Services
911 Service **OnSite:** Doctor *(Harborside Medical Practice)* **OnCall:** Ambulance **Under 1 mi:** Dentist, Chiropractor *(French 846-8600)* **1-3 mi:** Holistic Services *(Professional Touch Massage 846-9868)* **Hospital:** Maine Medical Center 871-2381 *(12 mi.)*

Setting -- Almost to the head of the navigable portion of Royal River, just before the I-95 bridge, Yankee Marina is part of Lower Falls Landing. This attractive complex of restored buildings, formerly a fish packing and canning plant, now houses a few services and shops.

Marina Notes -- Owner operated for over 3 decades. One full bath and one half bath. Full service boatyard with lots of room for outside winter storage. Docks only, no moorings. Pay attention to the markers, and the route up river is easy to follow - high banks provide good protection. Storage for 200 boats. Fuel, and additional dockage, available across and a little down river at Royal River Boat Yard 846-9577. Onsite are: Shore Sails (Mon-Fri 8am-4:30pm 846-6400) and Landing Boat Supplies (a large, well-equipped ship's store). Well protected storm port. Casco Bay Rowing Center is headquartered here - shells, sculling lessons, etc. 846-3277.

Notable -- Lower Falls Landing is home to Maine Cottage Furniture and East Coast Yacht Sales (Sabre, Jboats, Freedom and Grand Banks). Note: Royal River Provisions has closed. The onsite Royal River Grillhouse Restaurant offers traditional Maine fare, inside and outside (deck) dining with expansive views of the harbor and marina (7 days). Royal River Falls Park is farther up river. The Yarmouth Clam Festival, held every year the third weekend in July is an easy walk. See the 42 ft. rotating globe "Eartha" at DeLorme Map Company's headquarters, as well as their Map Shop (7 days, 9:30am-6pm, 800 642-0970). It's 4 miles to L.L. Bean & the Freeport Outlets.

PHOTOS ON CD-ROM: 9

Yarmouth Boat Yard

PO Box 214; 72 Lafayette Street; Yarmouth, ME 04096

Tel: (207) 846-9050 **VHF: Monitor** n/a **Talk** n/a
Fax: (207) 846-9050 **Alternate Tel:** n/a
Email: mcdonald@nlis.net **Web:** www.yarmouthboatyard.com
Nearest Town: Yarmouth *(1.2 mi.)* **Tourist Info:** (207) 846-3984

Navigational Information

Lat: 43°47.760' **Long:** 070°10.420' **Tide:** 10 ft. **Current:** 1 kt. **Chart:** 13290
Rep. Depths (*MLW*): Entry 6 ft. **Fuel Dock** 8 ft. **Max Slip/Moor** 6 ft./6 ft.
Access: Casco Bay, up Royal River to the fixed bridge

Marina Facilities *(In Season/Off Season)*

Fuel: No
Slips: 150 Total, 6 Transient **Max LOA:** 35 ft. **Max Beam:** n/a
Rate *(per ft.)*: **Day** $1.00 **Week** $6.00 **Month** n/a
Power: 30 amp n/a, **50 amp** n/a, **100 amp** n/a, **200 amp** n/a
Cable TV: No **Dockside Phone:** No
Dock Type: Floating, Fixed
Moorings: 2 Total, 0 Transient **Launch:** n/a
Rate: Day n/a **Week** n/a **Month** n/a
Heads: 1 Toilet(s)
Laundry: None **Pay Phones:** No
Pump-Out: OnCall, Full Service **Fee:** n/a **Closed Heads:** No

Marina Operations

Owner/Manager: Jock McDonald **Dockmaster:** Same
In-Season: Year-Round, 8am-5pm **Off-Season:** n/a
After-Hours Arrival: Call ahead
Reservations: Yes, Preferred **Credit Cards:** Visa/MC
Discounts: None
Pets: Welcome **Handicap Access:** No

Marina Services and Boat Supplies

Communication - Phone Messages, Fax in/out, FedEx, AirBorne, UPS, Express Mail *(Sat Del)* **Supplies - OnSite:** Ships' Store **Near:** Ice *(Block)* **Under 1 mi:** Propane **3+ mi:** West Marine, Marine Discount Store

Boatyard Services

OnSite: Engine mechanic *(gas)*, Launching Ramp, Electrical Repairs, Electronic Sales, Electronics Repairs, Hull Repairs, Bottom Cleaning, Brightwork, Compound, Wash & Wax, Interior Cleaning **OnCall:** Divers **Near:** Air Conditioning, Refrigeration. **3+ mi:** Forklift *(4T)*.

Restaurants and Accommodations

Near: Restaurant *(Royal River Grillhouse 846-1226, L $6-12, D $14-24)*, Pizzeria *(De Nuccis 846-8646)* **Under 1 mi:** Restaurant *(The Muddy Rudder 846-3082, L $7-10, D $20-25)* **1-3 mi:** Hotel *(Down East Village 846-5161)*, Condo/Cottage **3+ mi:** Motel *(Freeport Inn 864-3106, 5 mi.)*, *(Brookside Motel 846-5512)*

Recreation and Entertainment

Under 1 mi: Video Rental **1-3 mi:** Tennis Courts, Video Arcade, Park, Cultural Attract **3+ mi:** Beach, Picnic Area, Playground, Golf Course *(Val Halla Golf Course 829-2225)*, Movie Theater

Provisioning and General Services

Under 1 mi: Convenience Store, Supermarket *(Hannaford 846-5941)*, Bank/ATM, Post Office, Beauty Salon, Pharmacy *(Hannaford)*, Clothing Store **1-3 mi:** Health Food, Wine/Beer, Liquor Store, Bakery, Farmers' Market, Fishmonger, Lobster Pound, Meat Market, Catholic Church, Protestant Church, Library, Dry Cleaners, Laundry, Bookstore, Newsstand, Hardware Store *(Ace Coastal Hardware 846-6767)*, Florist, Department Store *(Wal-Mart)*, Copies Etc.

Transportation

OnCall: Rental Car *(Enterprise 772-0030, or Hometown Rental 846-2470, 2 mi.)* **Airport:** Portland Int'l. *(10 mi.)*

Medical Services

911 Service **OnCall:** Ambulance **Near:** Doctor *(Harborside Family Practice)* **Under 1 mi:** Dentist, Chiropractor, Holistic Services **Hospital:** Maine Medical Center 871-2381 *(10 mi.)*

PHOTOS ON CD-ROM: 3

Setting -- Hard by the Route 95 bridge, on the port side just past Yankee Marina, this small, very basic facility is within an easy walk of Lower Falls Landing, with its services and restaurant.

Marina Notes -- Smaller boat marina with limited depth and 4 ton forklift haul-out. The head is a Porta-Johnnie. Some dry stack storage. This part of the river is a good hurricane hole.

Notable -- Royal River Park, just north, offers picnic grounds with views of picturesque falls, and paved pathways that encourage strolls. Lower Falls Landing is just south, and includes the Grillhouse Restaurant, Maine Cottage Furniture, Harbor Books (with an extensive marine section) and East Coast Yacht Sales (Sabre, Jboats, Freedom and Grand Banks). The restaurant offers traditional Maine fare - both inside and deck dining, with great views of the harbor (7 days, 800 974-1225). Also within an easy walk is The Yarmouth Clam Festival, held every year the third weekend in July. At the DeLorme Map Company, check out the world's largest globe, "Eartha", and the Map Shop (7 days, 9:30am-6pm, 800 642-0970). The Freeport Outlets and L.L. Bean are a 4 mile drive or cab ride away.

Navigational Information
Lat: 43°43.700' **Long:** 070°12.580' **Tide:** 9 ft. **Current:** 5 kt. **Chart:** 13290
Rep. Depths (*MLW*): Entry 25 ft. **Fuel Dock** 8 ft. **Max Slip/Moor** -/32 ft.
Access: Casco Bay through Hussey Sound

Marina Facilities *(In Season/Off Season)*
Fuel: Gasoline, Diesel
Slips: 40 Total, 20 Transient **Max LOA:** 125 ft. **Max Beam:** n/a
Rate *(per ft.)*: **Day** $2.00* **Week** n/a **Month** n/a
Power: 30 amp Incl., **50 amp** n/a, **100 amp** n/a, **200 amp** n/a
Cable TV: No **Dockside Phone:** No
Dock Type: Wood, Alongside, Floating
Moorings: 300 Total, 20 Transient **Launch:** Yes (Free), Dinghy Dock
Rate: Day $20 **Week** $115 **Month** $460
Heads: 2 Toilet(s)
Laundry: None **Pay Phones:** Yes, 2
Pump-Out: OnSite, Full Service, 1 Central **Fee:** $10 **Closed Heads:** No

Marina Operations
Owner/Manager: Jay Hallett **Dockmaster:** Amy Hagberg
In-Season: Jun-Sep, 8am-9pm **Off-Season:** n/a
After-Hours Arrival: Call in advance
Reservations: Preferred **Credit Cards:** Visa/MC, Dscvr
Discounts: None
Pets: Welcome, Dog Walk Area **Handicap Access:** Yes, Heads, Docks

Handy Boat Service

215 Foreside Road; Falmouth, ME 04105

Tel: (207) 781-5110 **VHF: Monitor** 9 **Talk** 9
Fax: (207) 781-7534 **Alternate Tel:** n/a
Email: handyboat@gwi.net **Web:** www.handyboat.com
Nearest Town: Falmouth *(.5 mi.)* **Tourist Info:** (207) 772-5800

Marina Services and Boat Supplies
Services - Docking Assistance **Communication -** Mail & Package Hold, Phone Messages, Fax in/out *($1.50)*, FedEx, AirBorne, UPS *(Sat Del)* **Supplies - OnSite:** Ice *(Block, Cube)*, Ships' Store *(The Boathouse)*, CNG **Under 1 mi:** Propane *(Shaws)* **3+ mi:** West Marine *(761-7600, 6 mi.)*, Boat/US *(5 mi.)*, Marine Discount Store *(Hamilton Marine 774-1772, 6 mi.)*

Boatyard Services
OnSite: Travelift *(35T)*, Engine mechanic *(gas, diesel)*, Electrical Repairs, Electronic Sales, Electronics Repairs, Hull Repairs, Rigger, Sail Loft *(Hallett Canvas & Sails 781-7070)*, Bottom Cleaning, Brightwork, Air Conditioning, Refrigeration, Divers, Compound, Wash & Wax, Interior Cleaning, Woodworking, Upholstery, Yacht Interiors, Painting, Awlgrip, Yacht Broker, Total Refits **OnCall:** Propeller Repairs, Inflatable Repairs, Life Raft Service, Metal Fabrication **Under 1 mi:** Launching Ramp. **Yard Rates:** $42-48/hr., Haul & Launch $6.25-11.50/ft., Power Wash $2.50/ft., Bottom Paint $9.50-12.25/ft. **Storage:** On-Land $23-56/ft.

Restaurants and Accommodations
OnSite: Restaurant *(Falmouth Sea Grill 781-5658, L $7-15, D $17-25)* **OnCall:** Pizzeria *(Falmouth House of Pizza)* **Under 1 mi:** Restaurant *(Moose Crossing 781-4771, D $8-18)*, Fast Food, Hotel *(Falmouth Inn 781-2120, $45-100)* **1-3 mi:** Restaurant *(Casa Napoli 781-3342, L $10-20, D $14-28)* **3+ mi:** Motel, Inn/B&B, Condo/Cottage

Recreation and Entertainment
Near: Beach, Jogging Paths, Roller Blade/Bike Paths, Sightseeing *(Gisland Farm)* **Under 1 mi:** Movie Theater *(Hoyts 781-5616)*, Video Rental, Park **1-3 mi:** Tennis Courts, Golf Course *(Riverside Municipal 797-3524)*, Fitness Center **3+ mi:** Horseback Riding *(Stonehill Farm 797-0183, 4 mi.)*, Museum *(Yarmouth Historical Society 846-6259; Narrow Gauge Railroad & Museum 828-0814, 4 mi.)*

Provisioning and General Services
OnSite: Bookstore, Retail Shops **Near:** Market *(Town Landing Market 781-2128)* **Under 1 mi:** Catholic Church, Florist **1-3 mi:** Provisioning Service, Supermarket *(Shaw's 781-4520)*, Gourmet Shop, Delicatessen, Health Food, Wine/Beer *(Cork & Barrel 781-7955)*, Liquor Store, Bakery, Fishmonger, Meat Market, Bank/ATM, Post Office, Protestant Church, Library *(Falmouth Memorial 781-2351)*, Beauty Salon, Barber Shop, Dry Cleaners, Pharmacy, Newsstand, Hardware Store, Clothing Store, Department Store *(Wal-Mart)*, Copies Etc. *(Mail Boxes Etc. 781-4866)* **3+ mi:** Farmers' Market *(4 mi.)*, Green Grocer *(4 mi.)*, Lobster Pound *(4 mi.)*, Synagogue *(4 mi.)*, Buying Club *(BJ's, Sams, 5 mi.)*

Transportation
OnCall: Rental Car *(Enterprise 772-0300)*, Taxi *(Mermaid Transport 800-696-2463)* **Airport:** Portland Int'l. *(6 mi.)*

Medical Services
911 Service **OnCall:** Ambulance **1-3 mi:** Chiropractor *(Saulter Chiropractic 781-2003)*, Holistic Services *(Litrocapes Massage 781-8428)* **3+ mi:** Doctor *(Martin's Point Health Care 828-2402, 5 mi.)* **Hospital:** Maine Medical Center 871-2381 *(5 mi.)*

Setting -- Perched on the edge of Casco Bay, this full-service marina, restaurant, boatyard, and sail loft sports attractively landscaped grounds with several well-maintained weathered shingle buildings. Views are of the mooring field and beautiful Casco Bay and many of its 365 islands.

Marina Notes -- Founded in 1934, the current owner has been here for more than 35 years. Moorings for 300 (launch runs from 8am-8pm), land storage for 150. Rarely available slips are $2/ft. Hallett Canvas & Sails, a 5,500 sq. ft. sail loft, specializes in advanced racing sails. The Boathouse, a marine hardware store, and the Chandlery, a retail clothing store are also onsite. Full boatyard services. Parking $5/day, $40/week. Mooring field is exposed from the southwest and the east. Restaurant and Marina share heads. No showers or laundry. Ground transport for provisioning runs when possible. Portland Yacht Club, next door, offers moorings with launch service (Ch.68) to members of reciprocating yacht clubs and includes their laundry, showers, and restaurant.

Notable -- Falmouth Sea Grill Restaurant - a full-service restaurant with pub food and seafood - overlooks the docks and Casco Bay beyond. Open 7 days a week, with inside and inviting outside dining; it was recently voted one of the best seafood restaurants in Portland. Lunch Mon-Thu 11:30am-2pm, Fri-Sun 11:30am-3pm. Piano music Fri, Sat, Sun evenings, and Sunday brunch. Nearby Gisland Farm, home of the Maine Audubon Society, offers 2½ miles of trails through its 60 acres of salt marsh and coastal lowlands along the Presumpscot River. Onsite gift shop has large selection of natural history books 781-2330 Mon-Sat, 9am-4:30pm; Sun 12-5pm.

PHOTOS ON CD-ROM: 6

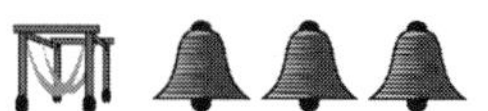

Spring Point Marina

PO Box 2350; 1 Spring Point Drive; South Portland, ME 04106

Tel: (207) 767-3213; (800) 262-8652 **VHF: Monitor** 9 **Talk** 69
Fax: (207) 767-5940 **Alternate Tel:** (207) 767-3254
Email: n/a **Web:** www.portharbormarine.com
Nearest Town: Portland *(3 mi.)* **Tourist Info:** (207) 772-2811

Navigational Information

Lat: 43°39.005' **Long:** 070°13.883' **Tide:** 9 ft. **Current:** 1 kt. **Chart:** 13292
Rep. Depths (*MLW*): Entry 10 ft. **Fuel Dock** 8 ft. **Max Slip/Moor** 10 ft./-
Access: Casco Bay to Portland Harbor east of breakwater

Marina Facilities *(In Season/Off Season)*

Fuel: Gasoline, Diesel
Slips: 250 Total, 30 Transient **Max LOA:** 140 ft. **Max Beam:** n/a
Rate *(per ft.)*: **Day** $1.25/Inq. **Week** $7.50 **Month** $22
Power: 30 amp $3, **50 amp** $5, **100 amp** n/a, **200 amp** n/a
Cable TV: No **Dockside Phone:** No
Dock Type: Wood, Long Fingers, Short Fingers, Floating
Moorings: 0 Total, 0 Transient **Launch:** n/a
Rate: Day n/a **Week** n/a **Month** n/a
Heads: 4 Toilet(s), 4 Shower(s)
Laundry: 2 Washer(s), 2 Dryer(s) **Pay Phones:** Yes
Pump-Out: OnSite, OnCall, Full Service **Fee:** $10 **Closed Heads:** No

Marina Operations

Owner/Manager: Paul Jensen **Dockmaster:** Seth Warner
In-Season: Apr-Oct 1, 8am-8pm **Off-Season:** Oct 1-Apr 1, 8am-4pm
After-Hours Arrival: Call ahead
Reservations: Yes, Preferred **Credit Cards:** Visa/MC, Dscvr, Amex
Discounts: None
Pets: Welcome, Dog Walk Area **Handicap Access:** Yes, Heads, Docks

Marina Services and Boat Supplies

Services - Docking Assistance, Security, Dock Carts **Communication -** Mail & Package Hold, Phone Messages, FedEx, AirBorne, UPS, Express Mail **Supplies - OnSite:** Ice *(Block)*, Ships' Store, Marine Discount Store *(Port Harbor Marine 767-3254)*, Bait/Tackle **1-3 mi:** West Marine *(761-7600)*, Boat/US, Propane *(Yerxas 799-2241)*, CNG *(Yerxas)*

Boatyard Services

OnSite: Travelift *(35T)*, Engine mechanic *(gas, diesel)*, Electrical Repairs, Electronic Sales, Electronics Repairs, Hull Repairs, Rigger, Sail Loft, Bottom Cleaning, Brightwork, Compound, Wash & Wax **OnCall:** Air Conditioning, Refrigeration, Divers, Interior Cleaning **Near:** Launching Ramp.

Restaurants and Accommodations

OnSite: Restaurant *(Joe's Boathouse 741-2780, L $7-10, D $11-19)* **OnCall:** Pizzeria *(Pizza Joint 767-3220)* **Near:** Snack Bar *(Brewed Awakening B & L)*, Lite Fare *(P.A. McKernan Hospitality Center 767-9672, L $6, So. Maine Tech College practice lab)*, Hotel *(So. Maine Tech School 767-9672, $125-155, 8 bay view rooms)*, Condo/Cottage *(Breakwater 799-1549)* **Under 1 mi:** Restaurant *(Snow Squall 799-2232, L $5-12, D $10-23)* **1-3 mi:** Restaurant *(Perfetto 828-0001, L $7-10, D $12-18)*, Motel *(Coastline Inn 772-3838, $40-110)*, Hotel *(Portland Regency 774-4200, $120-270)*, *(Double Tree 774-5611, $120-190)*

Recreation and Entertainment

OnSite: Picnic Area, Grills, Fishing Charter **Near:** Beach, Jogging Paths, Roller Blade/Bike Paths, Park, Museum *(Portland Harbor Museum 799-3862)* **Under 1 mi:** Playground, Tennis Courts, Video Rental *(Show Time Video 767-5658)* **1-3 mi:** Dive Shop, Golf Course *(Sable Oaks 775-6257)*, Fitness Center *(Ocean Fitness 767-1831)*, Movie Theater *(Nickelodeon 772-9751)*, Video Arcade, Cultural Attract, Sightseeing

Provisioning and General Services

Under 1 mi: Convenience Store, Hardware Store *(Drillen 799-4133)* **1-3 mi:** Supermarket *(Hannaford 799-7359)*, Gourmet Shop *(Maines Pantry 228-2028)*, Delicatessen, Wine/Beer *(Clown 756-7399)*, Bakery, Farmers' Market *(Monument Sq. Wed, Deering Oaks Sat)*, Fishmonger, Lobster Pound, Meat Market, Bank/ATM, Post Office, Catholic Church, Protestant Church, Library, Beauty Salon, Barber Shop, Dry Cleaners *(2 days)*, Laundry, Bookstore, Pharmacy *(Rite Aid 799-2261)*, Newsstand, Florist, Retail Shops, Copies Etc. *(Express Copy 775-2444)*

Transportation

OnCall: Rental Car *(Enterprise 772-0030)*, Taxi *(ABC Limo 772-8685)* **Near:** Local Bus *(7 Bus routes 774-0351)* **1-3 mi:** Bikes *(Cycle Mania 774-2933)*, Rail *(Boston-Portland 800-872-7245)*, Ferry Service *(Casco Baylines to local islands 774-2871; Prince of Fundy Cruises to Nova Scotia, 3 mi.)* **3+ mi:** InterCity Bus *(Concord Trailways, 5 mi.)* **Airport:** Portland Int'l. *(5 mi.)*

Medical Services

911 Service **Under 1 mi:** Doctor, Dentist, Chiropractor *(Chiropractic Healing Arts Center 799-0972)* **1-3 mi:** Ambulance **Hospital:** Maine Medical Center 871-0111 *(4 mi.)*

Setting -- Nestled behind Spring Point Light's breakwater is the largest marina in Maine. It's the first facility on the south-east side of the Fore River as you pass the lighthouse (and closest to the ocean). The marina surrounds a long wharf that juts into the bay; most slips to port, fuel dock to starboard. The docks have distant views of Portland and nearer ones of an attractive condominium and seasonal dockominium (Breakwater Marina) complex across the way.

Marina Notes -- With easy access from the Ocean, this full service boatyard boasts more than 250 slips. Port Harbor Marine, a large chandlery, is onsite as is a canvas shop; mechanics are available on Saturdays. Laidback atmosphere set in an historic boatyard (formerly South Portland Shipyard, active in WWII). Marina hosts parties, fishing tournaments and is a rendezvous for many cruising organizations.Onsite are fuel, supplies, and Joe's Boathouse Restaurant -- which offers both inside and outside dining with views of the bay and marina, as well as take-out - they'll even deliver to the boat! (Mon-Sat L 11am-3pm, D 5-9:30pm, Sun Brunch 9am-3pm, D 5-9pm). Casco Bay Baykeeper II pump-out boat answers to Ch. 9 or 776-0136. Moorings may also be available from sleepy, charming Centerboard Yacht Club (Ch.68, 799-7084).

Notable -- It's a long trip to town or services, but walking distance is Spring Point Museum, housed in a former Fort Preble ordnance repair shop next to the lighthouse. There are many exhibits about Casco Bay, maritime history, the clipper ship Snow Squall, and wooden shipbuilding in general (Tue-Sun 1-4pm, $2, 799-6337). Also nearby is the Southern Maine Technical College with two interesting "practice" sites: an 8-room hotel and a lunch-only restaurant.

Navigational Information
Lat: 43°39.690' **Long:** 070°14.656' **Tide:** 11 ft. **Current:** 2 kt. **Chart:** 13290
Rep. Depths (*MLW*): Entry 30 ft. **Fuel Dock** n/a **Max Slip/Moor** 20 ft./40 ft.
Access: North side of Portland Harbor

Marina Facilities *(In Season/Off Season)*
Fuel: No
Slips: 128 Total, 10 Transient **Max LOA:** 120 ft. **Max Beam:** 19 ft.
Rate *(per ft.)*: **Day** $1.00/Inq. **Week** Inq. **Month** Inq.
Power: 30 amp Incl., **50 amp** n/a, **100 amp** n/a, **200 amp** n/a
Cable TV: No **Dockside Phone:** No
Dock Type: Wood, Long Fingers, Short Fingers, Pilings, Alongside, Floating
Moorings: 18 Total, 12 Transient **Launch:** None, Dinghy Dock
Rate: Day $30 **Week** $180 **Month** n/a
Heads: 4 Toilet(s), 1 Shower(s)
Laundry: None **Pay Phones:** No
Pump-Out: OnCall, Full Service **Fee:** $5 **Closed Heads:** No

Marina Operations
Owner/Manager: Dave Tabbutt **Dockmaster:** Mak Sprague
In-Season: May-Oct, 8am-9pm **Off-Season:** Oct-May, 8am-5pm
After-Hours Arrival: Pick up mooring
Reservations: Yes, Preferred **Credit Cards:** Visa/MC
Discounts: None
Pets: Welcome, Dog Walk Area **Handicap Access:** Yes, Docks

Portland Yacht Services, Inc

58 Fore Street; Portland, ME 04101

Tel: (207) 774-1067 **VHF: Monitor** 9 **Talk** 68
Fax: (207) 774-7035 **Alternate Tel:** (207) 775-7308
Email: pys@server.nlbbs.com **Web:** www.PortlandYacht.com
Nearest Town: Portland *(.5 mi.)* **Tourist Info:** (207) 772-2811

Marina Services and Boat Supplies
Services - Docking Assistance, Security, Trash Pick-Up, Dock Carts, Megayacht Facilities **Communication -** Mail & Package Hold, Data Ports *(Office)*, FedEx, UPS **Supplies - OnSite:** Ice *(Block, Cube)* **Near:** Ships' Store, Marine Discount Store *(Hamilton 774-1772)*, Bait/Tackle *(Tackle Shop 773-3474)* **1-3 mi:** West Marine *(761-7600)*, Propane, CNG

Boatyard Services
OnSite: Travelift *(38T)*, Crane, Engine mechanic *(gas, diesel)*, Launching Ramp, Electrical Repairs, Hull Repairs, Rigger, Sail Loft, Bottom Cleaning, Brightwork, Air Conditioning, Refrigeration, Compound, Wash & Wax, Woodworking, Painting, Awlgrip, Yacht Design, Yacht Building, Total Refits **OnCall:** Divers, Interior Cleaning, Propeller Repairs, Inflatable Repairs, Life Raft Service, Upholstery, Yacht Interiors, Metal Fabrication **Near:** Electronic Sales *(Sawyer & Whitten 879-4500)*, Electronics Repairs. **Dealer for:** Crusader, Mercruiser, Nanni, OMC, Perkins, Volvo, Westerbeke, Yanmar, Johnson, Evinrude, Mercury, Suzuki. **Member:** ABBRA, ABYC - 2 Certified Tech(s), Other Certifications: All Outboards **Yard Rates:** $65/hr., Haul & Launch $6.50-8.50/ft. *(blocking incl.)*, Power Wash $2.75, Bottom Paint $10/ft. **Storage:** On-Land $1.50, $4.50, $11/ft./mo.

Restaurants and Accommodations
Near: Restaurant *(Boone's 774-5725, L $6-20, D $9-20)*, *(Village Café 772-5320, L $5-9, D $6-17)*, *(Benkay 773-5555, Japanese)*, Seafood Shack *(Gilbert's Chowder House 871-5636, L $6-20, D $6-20)*, Pizzeria *(Tony Q's 772-2729)* **Under 1 mi:** Restaurant *(Bakehouse Café 773-2217, L $5-10, D $8-16)*, *(Street & Co. 775-0887, D $14-24)*, *(Back Bay Grill 772-8833, D $18-33)*, Hotel *(Regency 774-4200, $120-270)*

Recreation and Entertainment
OnSite: Picnic Area, Grills, Boat Rentals, Museum **Near:** Pool *(Sprint St. "Y" 874-1130)*, Beach, Tennis Courts, Jogging Paths, Roller Blade/Bike Paths, Fishing Charter, Video Arcade, Park *(Fort Allen)*, Sightseeing *(Portland Observatory Tower 774-5661)*, Special Events *(Old Port Fest Jun, Art Show, 3rd Sat Aug)* **Under 1 mi:** Dive Shop, Fitness Center *(Regency 871-7054)*, Movie Theater *(Nickelodeon 772-9751)*, Video Rental *(Videoport 773-1999)* **3+ mi:** Golf Course *(So. Portland 775-0005, 4 mi.)*

Provisioning and General Services
Near: Provisioning Service *(Union Wharf 774-7397)*, Gourmet Shop *(Public Market)*, Delicatessen, Health Food, Wine/Beer *(Clown 756-7399)*, Bakery, Farmers' Market *(Monument Sq., Wed)*, Fishmonger *(775-0251)*, Lobster Pound, Bank/ATM, Post Office, Catholic Church, Protestant Church, Synagogue, Library *(772-4581)*, Beauty Salon, Dry Cleaners, Laundry, Bookstore, Pharmacy *(Rite Aid 774-0344)*, Newsstand, Florist, Clothing Store, Copies Etc. *(Express Copy 775-2444)* **1-3 mi:** Supermarket *(Hannaford 761-5965)*, Liquor Store, Hardware Store

Transportation
OnSite: Water Taxi *(Presumpscot 879-2562)* **OnCall:** Rental Car *(Enterprise 772-0030)*, Taxi *(772-8685)* **Near:** Bikes *(Cycle Mania 774-2933)*, Local Bus *(Explorer 774-9891, Metro 774-0351)*, Ferry Service *(Casco Bay 774-7871)* **1-3 mi:** Rail *(Boston)* **Airport:** Portland Int'l. *(5 mi.)*

Medical Services
911 Service **OnCall:** Ambulance **Under 1 mi:** Doctor, Dentist, Chiropractor, Holistic Services **Hospital:** Maine Medical 871-0111 *(1 mi.)*

Setting -- Portland Yacht is set in a commercial, industrial part of the city. The atmosphere is rustic, urban waterfront with landside views of antique trains, the museum warehouse, and an active big ship dry dock to the west; it's part of the Portland Company Marine Complex. Waterside views of bustling Portland Harbor and Casco Bay. Portland's Harbor Trail runs along the waterfront here.

Marina Notes -- Full-service boatyard with 38T lift. Inside and outside storage. 200 ft. of waterfront. Docks are exposed and can get rolly. Liberty Port with extensive services, including customs and immigration. Heads are in the museum, available to marina guests when the museum is open (Daily 10am-4pm). Also onsite: Marine Computer (871-1575), Traditional Marine Hardware (774-1067), Meissner Winches (761-4554), Stazo Marine Equipment (828-2072), N.E. Fiberglass (773-3537), Sea Tow & Water Taxi (772-6724). Pump-out (Ch. 9 or 776-0136). Home of the March Maine Boatbuilders Show.

Notable -- Reasonable walk to town center, with over 65 restaurants, art museums, sidewalk festivals, micro-breweries, etc. If you have railroad buffs aboard, the onsite Narrow Gauge Railroad Co. & Museum (828-0814) houses a fascinating collection of locomotives and coaches. Daily excursions along Casco Bay, using the museum's exhibits, ($5/3) on the hour, 11am-4pm. The buildings were originally used to build steam locomotives. The Eastern Prom Trail begins nearby - walk, jog, rollerblade, bike - past Ft. Allen Park ending up at East End Beach. Climb the last remaining maritime signal tower at the Observatory for a bird's eye view. Also near is the well-preserved U.S. Customs House and a daily fish auction at Maine State Pier.

PHOTOS ON CD-ROM: 2

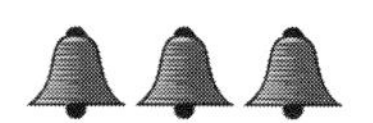

DiMillo's Old Port Marina

Long Wharf; Portland, ME 04101

Tel: (207) 773-7632 **VHF: Monitor** 9 **Talk** 71
Fax: (207) 773-4207 **Alternate Tel:** n/a
Email: marina@dimillos.com **Web:** www.dimillos.com
Nearest Town: Portland *(0 mi.)* **Tourist Info:** (207) 772-2811

Navigational Information

Lat: 43°39.276' **Long:** 070°15.039' **Tide:** 9 ft. **Current:** 1 kt. **Chart:** 13290
Rep. Depths (*MLW*): Entry 30 ft. **Fuel Dock** 30 ft. **Max Slip/Moor** 30 ft./-
Access: Portland Harbor, north side

Marina Facilities *(In Season/Off Season)*

Fuel: Slip-Side Fueling, Gasoline, Diesel
Slips: 120 Total, 10-20 Transient **Max LOA:** 240 ft. **Max Beam:** n/a
Rate *(per ft.)*: **Day** $2.00/$1.00* **Week** Inq. **Month** Inq.
Power: 30 amp $5, **50 amp** $12, **100 amp** $30, **200 amp** n/a
Cable TV: Yes, Incl. **Dockside Phone:** Yes, Inq.
Dock Type: Wood, Long Fingers, Floating, Aluminum
Moorings: 0 Total, 0 Transient **Launch:** n/a
Rate: Day n/a **Week** n/a **Month** n/a
Heads: 2 Toilet(s), 2 Shower(s)
Laundry: 2 Washer(s), 2 Dryer(s) **Pay Phones:** Yes, 2
Pump-Out: OnSite, Self Service **Fee:** $5 **Closed Heads:** No

Marina Operations

Owner/Manager: Sarah Foshay **Dockmaster:** Same
In-Season: Year-Round **Off-Season:** n/a
After-Hours Arrival: n/a
Reservations: Required **Credit Cards:** Visa/MC, Dscvr, Amex
Discounts: None
Pets: Welcome, Dog Walk Area **Handicap Access:** No

Marina Services and Boat Supplies

Services - Docking Assistance, Security, Dock Carts **Communication -** Mail & Package Hold, Phone Messages, Fax in/out, Data Ports *(Office)*, FedEx, AirBorne, UPS *(Sat Del)* **Supplies - OnSite:** Ice *(Block, Cube)* **Near:** Ships' Store *(Chase Leavitt 772-3751, Hamilton Marine 774-1772, Vessel Services 772-5718)*, West Marine *(761-7600)*, Marine Discount Store *(Brown Ship 772-3796)* **Under 1 mi:** Bait/Tackle *(Bait Lady 871-0551)*, Propane

Boatyard Services

OnSite: Engine mechanic *(gas, diesel)*, Brightwork *($19-30/hr.)*, Divers, Yacht Broker **Near:** Travelift, Railway, Forklift, Crane, Launching Ramp, Electrical Repairs, Electronic Sales, Electronics Repairs, Hull Repairs, Rigger, Sail Loft, Bottom Cleaning, Air Conditioning, Refrigeration, Inflatable Repairs. **Nearest Yard:** Gowen Marine (207) 773-1761

Restaurants and Accommodations

OnSite: Restaurant *(DiMillo's Floating Restaurant 772-2216, L $5-9, D $10-19)* **Near:** Restaurant *(Perfetto 828-0001, L $7-10, D $12-18)*, *(Fore Street 775-2717, D $25-30)*, *(Street & Co., 775-0887, D $15-25)*, Seafood Shack *(J's Oyster 772-4828)*, Coffee Shop *(Becky's Diner 773-7070, 4am+)*, Lite Fare *(Bakehouse Café 773-2215, L $8-12)*, Pizzeria *(Bill's 774-6166)*, Hotel *(Portland Harbor 775-9090, $140-330)*, *(Regency 774-4200, $120-270)*

Recreation and Entertainment

OnSite: Boat Rentals, Roller Blade/Bike Paths, Fishing Charter **OnCall:** Dive Shop **Near:** Fitness Center, Jogging Paths, Movie Theater *(Nickelodeon 772-9751)*, Video Rental *(Videoport 773-1999)*, Museum *(Victoria Mansion 772-4841)*, Sightseeing **Under 1 mi:** Beach *(East End Beach)*, Picnic Area *(Eastern Prom)*, Playground, Tennis Courts *(Eastern Prom)*, Park

Provisioning and General Services

OnSite: Lobster Pound, Bank/ATM, Post Office **OnCall:** Dry Cleaners **Near:** Convenience Store *(Union Wharf 774-7397)*, Gourmet Shop *(Maine's Pantry 228-2028, Portland Greengrocer 761-9232)*, Health Food, Wine/Beer *(Clown 756-7399)*, Bakery, Farmers' Market *(Monument Sq. Wed & Deering Oaks Sat)*, Fishmonger *(Harbor Fish 775-0251)*, Meat Market, Catholic Church, Protestant Church, Synagogue, Library, Beauty Salon, Barber Shop, Laundry, Bookstore, Pharmacy *(Rite Aid 774-0344)*, Newsstand, Hardware Store, Florist, Copies Etc. *(Curry 772-5897)* **1-3 mi:** Supermarket *(Hannaford 761-5965)*, Liquor Store **3+ mi:** Department Store *(Maine Mall, Wal-Mart, 6 mi.)*, Buying Club *(Sams, 6 mi.)*

Transportation

OnSite: Courtesy Car/Van **OnCall:** Water Taxi *(Penobscot 329-1087)*, Rental Car *(Enterprise 828-2525)*, Taxi *(Elite 871-7274)* **Near:** Bikes *(Cycle-Mania 774-2933)*, Local Bus *(Portland Explorer 774-9891, Metro 774-0351)*, InterCity Bus *(Concord Trailways/Greyhound)*, Ferry Service *(Casco Bay Ferry)* **1-3 mi:** Rail *(to Boston)* **Airport:** Portland Int'l. *(5 mi.)*

Medical Services

911 Service **OnCall:** Ambulance **Under 1 mi:** Doctor *(Martin's Point Health Care 828-2402)*, Dentist, Chiropractor *(Westgate Chiropractic Clinic 874-222)* **Hospital:** Maine Medical Center 871-2381 *(1 mi.)*

PHOTOS ON CD-ROM: 6

Setting -- On the northern side of Portland Harbor, DiMillo's is right in the heart of the historic Old Port section of Portland -- with its approximately 160 shops, 65 restaurants, and 30 galleries. Landside views are of the charming, restored Old Port; waterviews are of Portland Harbor and South Portland. The marina is dominated by (and surrounds) DiMillo's Floating Restaurant, a stylishly converted 206 foot, 700 ton ferry.

Marina Notes -- *Rates: up to 42' $2.00/ft., 43'+ $2.50/ft. Reservations critical in July & August. This is the only transient marina situated in the Old Port area. A wave fence slows the roll, although not entirely, and provides some protection from the east (the closer you are to the shore, the quieter the ride). Service oriented staff, well-maintained docks, and complimentary shuttle. Many liveaboards. Shore power to 100 amps and megayacht facilities. Heads are nicely appointed full bathrooms. New onsite, self-service pump-out. Ask about construction project.

Notable -- The elegant Portland Regency and new Portland Harbor Hotels are nearby, and so is a sensational provisioning source: the 27,000 sq. ft. Portland Public Market (228-2000). Harbor Fish Market and Lobster Pound is one block away. The onsite, 600 seat restaurant specializes in seafood and Italian (7 days, L 11am-4pm, D 4-11pm); there are two floors of inside dining and two large outside decks that overlook the harbor. Portland is a wonderfully manageable city with constant summertime activities, performances, street festivals, micro-breweries (highest per capita in the U.S.), museums and art galleries - all within walking distance. Oldport Festival is in June, the Art Festival in August.

Navigational Information

Lat: 43°39.030' **Long:** 070°14.560' **Tide:** 10 ft. **Current:** 1 kt. **Chart:** 13292
Rep. Depths (*MLW*): Entry 20 ft. **Fuel Dock** 10 ft. **Max Slip/Moor** 20 ft./-
Access: Casco Bay to Portland Harbor, first facility on port side

Marina Facilities *(In Season/Off Season)*

Fuel: *Super Unleaded* - Gasoline, Diesel, High-Speed Pumps
Slips: 150 Total, 20 Transient **Max LOA:** 250 ft. **Max Beam:** 20 ft.
Rate *(per ft.)*: **Day** $2.00/n/a **Week** 8.00 **Month** 25
Power: 30 amp $2, **50 amp** $5, **100 amp** n/a, **200 amp** n/a
Cable TV: No **Dockside Phone:** No
Dock Type: Wood, Long Fingers, Pilings, Floating
Moorings: 0 Total, 0 Transient **Launch:** Yes (Free), Dinghy Dock
Rate: Day n/a **Week** n/a **Month** n/a
Heads: 2 Toilet(s), 2 Shower(s) *(with dressing rooms)*
Laundry: 2 Washer(s), 2 Dryer(s) **Pay Phones:** Yes, 1
Pump-Out: OnSite, Self Service, 1 Central **Fee:** $5 **Closed Heads:** Yes

Marina Operations

Owner/Manager: Daniel & Elaine Lilley **Dockmaster:** Same
In-Season: Apr-Oct, 8am-8pm **Off-Season:** Nov-Mar, Closed
After-Hours Arrival: Call ahead for instructions
Reservations: Yes **Credit Cards:** Visa/MC, Amex
Discounts: None
Pets: Welcome **Handicap Access:** No

Sunset Marina

231 Front Street; South Portland, ME 04106

Tel: (207) 767-4729 **VHF: Monitor** 9, 16 **Talk** 8
Fax: (207) 767-4721 **Alternate Tel:** (207) 767-4729
Email: sunset@maine.rr.com **Web:** www.sunset-marina.com
Nearest Town: Portland *(1 mi.)* **Tourist Info:** (207) 772-2811

Marina Services and Boat Supplies

Services - Docking Assistance, Security *(24 Hrs., closed circuit)*, Trash Pick-Up, Dock Carts, Megayacht Facilities **Communication -** Mail & Package Hold, Fax in/out *(Free)*, Data Ports, FedEx, AirBorne, UPS, Express Mail *(Sat Del)* **Supplies - OnSite:** Ice *(Block, Cube)*, Ships' Store **OnCall:** Propane *(Yerxas 799-2241)*, CNG **Near:** Bait/Tackle, Live Bait **1-3 mi:** West Marine *(761-7600)*

Boatyard Services

OnSite: Engine mechanic *(gas, diesel)*, Electrical Repairs, Electronics Repairs, Hull Repairs, Bottom Cleaning, Divers **Yard Rates:** $25/hr., Haul & Launch $5/ft. *(blocking incl.)*, Power Wash Incl. **Storage:** In-Water $2/ft., On-Land $25/ft. incl. H&L

Restaurants and Accommodations

OnSite: Restaurant *(Salt Water Grille 799-5400, L $7-13, D $15-22)* **OnCall:** Pizzeria *(Pizza Hut 799-0455)* **Near:** Restaurant *(Old Port Sea Grill and Raw Bar 879-6100), (The Good Table 799-4663), (Barbara's Kitchen 767-6313)* **Under 1 mi:** Restaurant *(Joe's Boathouse 741-2780)*, Hotel *(So. Maine Tech College $125-155)* **1-3 mi:** Hotel *(Regency 774-4200, $120-270), (Holiday Inn 775-2311, $110-170)*, Inn/B&B *(Pomegranate 772-1006, $95-235)*

Recreation and Entertainment

OnSite: Picnic Area, Grills **Near:** Spa, Playground, Dive Shop *(721-2110)*, Fitness Center *(Ocean 767-1831)*, Jogging Paths *(Green Belt)*, Roller Blade/Bike Paths, Video Rental *(Blockbuster 741-2713)* **Under 1 mi:** Beach *(Willard)*, Boat Rentals, Fishing Charter, Movie Theater *(Nickelodeon 772-9751)*, Museum *(Museum of Art 775-6148 $8/2; Children's Museum 828-1234 $5/5; Victoria Mansion 772-4841 $7/3)*, Cultural Attract *(Merrill Auditorium 874-8200; Portland Opera 767-0773)*, Sightseeing **1-3 mi:** Tennis Courts *(Eastern Prom)*, Golf Course *(So. Portland 775-0005)*

Provisioning and General Services

OnSite: Convenience Store, Newsstand **Near:** Bakery *(Mr. Bagel)*, Lobster Pound, Bank/ATM, Post Office, Catholic Church, Beauty Salon **Under 1 mi:** Supermarket *(Shaw's, Hannaford 799-7359)*, Gourmet Shop *(Browne 775-3118)*, Delicatessen *(Smaha's 799-3374)*, Health Food *(Whole Grocer)*, Wine/Beer, Liquor Store *(Di Pietros)*, Green Grocer *(Portland Greengrocer 761-9232)*, Fishmonger, Protestant Church, Library *(767-7660)*, Dry Cleaners, Bookstore *(799-2659)*, Pharmacy *(Rite Aid 799-2261)*, Hardware Store *(Drillen 799-4133)*, Retail Shops, Copies Etc. *(Mailboxes Etc 767-1826)* **1-3 mi:** Farmers' Market *(Monument Sq. Wed, Deering Oaks Sat)*, Synagogue, Department Store *(Maine Mall)*, Buying Club *(Sam's)*

Transportation

OnSite: Courtesy Car/Van *(for provisioning)*, Water Taxi *(Comp. to/from Portland, or Presumpscot 879-2562)* **OnCall:** Rental Car *(Enterprise 772-0030)*, Taxi *(ABC 772-8685)* **Near:** Local Bus *(Explorer 774-0351)* **Under 1 mi:** Bikes *(Back Bay 773-6906)* **1-3 mi:** InterCity Bus *(Concord 828-1151)*, Rail *(Boston 780-1000)* **Airport:** Portland Int'l.

Medical Services

911 Service **OnCall:** Ambulance **Under 1 mi:** Doctor, Dentist, Chiropractor, Holistic Services, Veterinarian *(Cape Vet Clinic 799-2788)*
Hospital: Maine Medical 871-2381 *(1 mi.)*

Setting -- On the east shore of the Fore River, Sunset sits directly across Portland Harbor from the historic Old Port district. Spectacular Portland skyline views (and sunsets); landside views are of the attractive marina building, the South Portland "storage tank farm" and an inactive commercial wharf.

Marina Notes -- Originally called Channel Crossing, the marina was bought by the Lilleys in 1998. On-demand complimentary shuttle boat to/from Portland's Old Port (to the Casco Bay Ferry Wharf) for shopping and sightseeing (until 8pm), and a courtesy car for provisioning are emblematic of the commitment to customer service. Mark Loring's highly-rated Salt Water Grille, onsite, shares the stunning harbor and skyline views - from the cathedraled dining room, wicker-furnished screened porch or wide, umbrellaed front deck - 5-9:30pm 7 days. Laundry facilities, limited groceries and provisions onsite.

Notable -- The "Green Belt", a pedestrian walk along the South Portland waterfront, provides a shortcut to two large shopping malls putting them within walking distance. Between the two malls -- and the Old Port -- almost all major provisioning, entertainment and other service needs can be met. Portland Public Market (a version of Seattle's Pike Place) is worth a trip even if you don't need provisions (228-2000). The Portland Explorer (774-9891) connects Casco Bay Ferry Terminal (where the Sunset Shuttle docks) with the Jetport, Bus/Train station, Scotia Prince, and a couple of hotels $3/trip or $7/day. Portland Metro (774-0351) connects the Transport Center with the Jetport, downtown hotels & the Maine Mall $1. So. Maine Tech College has 8 bay-front rooms for student hospitality practice. The Old Port & the Congress St. Downtown Arts District make for great sightseeing.

PHOTOS ON CD-ROM: 6

South Port Marine

14 Ocean Street; Portland, ME 04106

Tel: (207) 799-8191 **VHF: Monitor** 9 **Talk** n/a
Fax: (207) 767-5937 **Alternate Tel:** n/a
Email: southport@ime.net **Web:** www.southportmarine.com
Nearest Town: Portland *(0.25 mi.)* **Tourist Info:** (207) 772-2811

Navigational Information

Lat: 43°38.555' **Long:** 070°15.219' **Tide:** 9 ft. **Current:** 1 kt. **Chart:** 13292
Rep. Depths (*MLW*): Entry 8 ft. **Fuel Dock** 8 ft. **Max Slip/Moor** 13 ft./-
Access: Inner harbor by Casco Bay Bridge South Portland

Marina Facilities *(In Season/Off Season)*

Fuel: *Irving* - Gasoline, Diesel
Slips: 140 Total, 10 Transient **Max LOA:** 100 ft. **Max Beam:** 25 ft.
Rate *(per ft.)*: **Day** $1.25/Inq.* **Week** $7.50 **Month** $15.50
Power: 30 amp Incl., **50 amp** Extra charge, **100 amp** n/a, **200 amp** n/a
Cable TV: Yes, $33 Per month **Dockside Phone:** Yes by arrangement
Dock Type: Wood, Long Fingers, Short Fingers, Floating
Moorings: 1 Total, 1 Transient **Launch:** None
Rate: Day n/a **Week** n/a **Month** n/a
Heads: 2 Toilet(s), 2 Shower(s) *(with dressing rooms)*
Laundry: 2 Washer(s), 2 Dryer(s) **Pay Phones:** Yes
Pump-Out: OnCall, Full Service **Fee:** $5 **Closed Heads:** No

Marina Operations

Owner/Manager: Kip Reynolds **Dockmaster:** Michelle Haynes
In-Season: Apr 15-Oct 15, 8am-5:30pm **Off-Season:** Oct -Apr, 8am-4pm
After-Hours Arrival: Call in advance
Reservations: Yes, Preferred **Credit Cards:** Visa/MC, Dscvr, Amex
Discounts: Boat/US **Dockage:** 10% **Fuel:** n/a **Repair:** n/a
Pets: Welcome, Dog Walk Area **Handicap Access:** Yes, Heads, Docks

Marina Services and Boat Supplies

Services - Docking Assistance, Security *(Police and TV monitor)*, Dock Carts, 3 Phase **Communication -** Mail & Package Hold, Fax in/out, Data Ports *(by arrangement)*, FedEx, AirBorne, UPS, Express Mail *(Sat Del)* **Supplies - OnSite:** Ice *(Block, Cube)*, Ships' Store *(Yacht Connection)* **OnCall:** Propane *(Yerxas 799-2241)*, CNG **Near:** Ice *(Shaved)*, Live Bait **1-3 mi:** West Marine *(761-7600)*, Boat/US, Marine Discount Store *(Hamilton Marine)*, Bait/Tackle **3+ mi:** Boater's World *(774-0027, 5 mi.)*

Boatyard Services

OnSite: Travelift *(20T/35T)*, Forklift, Crane, Engine mechanic *(gas, diesel)*, Launching Ramp, Electrical Repairs, Electronic Sales, Electronics Repairs, Hull Repairs, Rigger, Bottom Cleaning, Brightwork, Air Conditioning, Refrigeration, Divers, Compound, Wash & Wax, Interior Cleaning, Yacht Interiors, Metal Fabrication, Awlgrip, Yacht Broker, Total Refits **OnCall:** Sail Loft, Propeller Repairs, Woodworking, Inflatable Repairs, Life Raft Service, Yacht Design **Dealer for:** Mercury, Mercruiser, Smoker Craft, Quicksilver Inflatables. **Member:** ABBRA, ABYC **Yard Rates:** $60/hr., Haul & Launch $8/ft., Power Wash $0.75/ft., Bottom Paint $10/ft. **Storage:** In-Water $74/ft.

Restaurants and Accommodations

OnSite: Restaurant *(Snow Squall 799-2232, L $5-12, D $10-23)* **OnCall:** Pizzeria *(Pizza Hut 799-0455)* **Near:** Restaurant *(Bridgeway 799-5418, L $4-8, D $4-12)*, *(Newick's Seafood 799-3090, L $6-19, D $6-19)*, Fast Food, Pizzeria *(Papa Mios)* **Under 1 mi:** Restaurant *(DiMillo's 772-2216, L $5-9, D $10-19, Dinghy)*, Hotel *(Regency 774-4200, $120-270)*, *(Holiday Inn 775-2311, $110-170)*

Recreation and Entertainment

OnSite: Picnic Area, Grills **Near:** Playground, Dive Shop, Fitness Center *(Ocean Fitness 767-1831)*, Jogging Paths, Roller Blade/Bike Paths, Video Rental *(Home-Vision 799-4411)*, Park **Under 1 mi:** Volleyball, Fishing Charter, Movie Theater *(Nickelodeon 772-9751)*, Museum *(Victoria Mansion 772-4841, Museum of African Tribal Art 871-7188)*, Cultural Attract **1-3 mi:** Pool, Beach, Tennis Courts *(Eastern Promenade)*, Golf Course *(So. Portland 775-0005)*, Boat Rentals, Video Arcade

Provisioning and General Services

OnSite: Convenience Store, Wine/Beer, Lobster Pound, Beauty Salon, Newsstand **Near:** Supermarket *(Shaw's, Hannaford 799-7359)*, Delicatessen, Health Food, Bakery, Meat Market, Bank/ATM, Post Office, Catholic Church, Dry Cleaners, Bookstore, Pharmacy *(Rite Aid 799-2261)*, Hardware Store *(Rufus Deering 772-6505)*, Florist, Retail Shops **Under 1 mi:** Gourmet Shop *(Aurora 871-9060)*, Green Grocer, Fishmonger, Protestant Church, Library *(767-7660)*, Copies Etc. **1-3 mi:** Farmers' Market, Synagogue, Department Store, Buying Club *(Sam's)*

Transportation

OnCall: Water Taxi *(Presumpscot 879-2562)*, Rental Car *(Enterprise 772-0030)*, Taxi *(South Portland Taxi 767-5200)* **Near:** Local Bus **1-3 mi:** InterCity Bus *(Concord Trailways 828-1151)*, Rail *(Portland-Boston)*, Ferry Service *(Casco Bay)* **Airport:** Portland Int'l. *(4 mi.)*

Medical Services

911 Service **OnCall:** Ambulance **Near:** Doctor, Dentist, Holistic Services **Under 1 mi:** Chiropractor **Hospital:** Maine Medical *(0.5 mi.)*

Setting -- This attractively landscaped facility is in a very quiet, protected basin off the southside of Portland Harbor just west of the Coast Guard station. Views are of Portland Harbor, the skyline and of the high banks that protect the basin.

Marina Notes -- Inner harbor location limits surges on passing wakes. Depths vary, call to confirm. Telephone, cable TV (monthly only). New showers and laundry. Full-service boatyard, including travelift, welding, fiberglass repair, painting, and a chandlery with a small convenience store. 10% discount on fuel and repairs for commercial boats. Next to The Anchorage condominium complex. Good, protected place to leave the boat. Casco Bay Baykeeper II pump-out boat answers to Ch.9, 776-0136.

Notable -- Onsite is the Snow Squall Restaurant with views of Portland Harbor (11:30am-10pm, Sat from 5pm - Light menu in lounge plus Sunday Brunch. Dinner theater Thursday night ($35). Many other restaurants are an 1/8 mile walk. Quite near is the South Portland "Waterfront Market", making all support services, provisioning resources and shops readily available - including the Mill Creek Shopping Center which can be a major provisioning and services stop. Also fairly near is the South Portland end of the Casco Bay Bridge which leads to downtown Portland and the Old Port district - with many dozens of restaurants, shops and galleries. Beaches, resorts and landmarks are easy biking distance. Local bus - Portland Transit nearby. Farmers' Market at Monument Sq. on Wed, Deering Oaks Sat. 1st week in June is Old Port Festival.

PHOTOS ON CD-ROM: 7

Navigational Information
Lat: 43°21.180' **Long:** 070°28.440' **Tide:** 9 ft. **Current:** 5 kt. **Chart:** 13286
Rep. Depths (*MLW*): Entry 5 ft. **Fuel Dock** 6 ft. **Max Slip/Moor** 6 ft./-
Access: 0.5 mi. from Kennebunk R. entrance jetty, just off G13 to starboard

Marina Facilities *(In Season/Off Season)*
Fuel: *Unbrand* - Slip-Side Fueling, Gasoline, Diesel
Slips: 50 Total, 10 Transient **Max LOA:** 140 ft. **Max Beam:** n/a
Rate *(per ft.)*: **Day** $3.50* **Week** n/a **Month** n/a
Power: 30 amp $7.50, **50 amp** $14, **100 amp** $35, **200 amp** n/a
Cable TV: Yes, $7 **Dockside Phone:** No
Dock Type: Floating
Moorings: 0 Total, 0 Transient **Launch:** n/a
Rate: Day n/a **Week** n/a **Month** n/a
Heads: 2 Toilet(s), 3 Shower(s)
Laundry: 1 Washer(s), 1 Dryer(s), Book Exchange **Pay Phones:** Yes, 1
Pump-Out: OnSite **Fee:** Yes **Closed Heads:** No

Marina Operations
Owner/Manager: Lillian Fox **Dockmaster:** Same
In-Season: Jul-Sep, 8am-6pm **Off-Season:** Oct-Jun, 8am-4pm
After-Hours Arrival: Call first
Reservations: Yes, Preferred **Credit Cards:** Visa/MC
Discounts: None
Pets: Welcome, Dog Walk Area **Handicap Access:** No

Chick's Marina

PO Box 2758; 75 Ocean Avenue; Kennebunkport, ME 04046

Tel: (207) 967-2782 **VHF: Monitor** 9 **Talk** 68
Fax: (207) 967-2034 **Alternate Tel:** n/a
Email: chicksmarina@mypowerlink.net **Web:** www.chicksmarina.com
Nearest Town: Kennebunkport *(0.4 mi.)* **Tourist Info:** (207) 967-8600

Marina Services and Boat Supplies
Services - Docking Assistance, Concierge, Security, Trash Pick-Up, Dock Carts, Megayacht Facilities **Communication -** Mail & Package Hold, Phone Messages, Fax in/out, FedEx *(Sat Del)* **Supplies - OnSite:** Ice *(Block, Cube)*, Ships' Store **1-3 mi:** Propane *(Champagnes Propane & Oil 283-1518)*

Boatyard Services
OnSite: Engine mechanic *(gas, diesel)*, Launching Ramp, Electrical Repairs, Electronic Sales, Hull Repairs *(minor)*, Bottom Cleaning, Brightwork, Compound, Wash & Wax, Interior Cleaning, Woodworking, Inflatable Repairs **OnCall:** Sail Loft, Air Conditioning, Refrigeration, Divers, Propeller Repairs **Near:** Travelift. **1-3 mi:** Forklift.

Restaurants and Accommodations
OnCall: Pizzeria *(Atlantic Pizza 967-0333)* **Near:** Restaurant *(Mabel's Lobster Claw 967-2562, L $8-16, D $14-28)*, *(Nonantum Dining Room D $12-23)*, Seafood Shack *(Port Lobster Co. 967-2081)*, Motel *(Yachtsman Lodge 967-2511, $170-250)*, Hotel *(Nonantum Resort 967-4050, $110-260)*, Inn/B&B *(Schooners Inn 967-5333, $105-295)*, *(Breakwater Inn 967-3118, $125-175)* **Under 1 mi:** Restaurant *(Grissini 967-2211, $16-22 dinner)* **1-3 mi:** Restaurant *(White Barn Inn 967-2321, D $78)*

Recreation and Entertainment
OnSite: Picnic Area, Grills **Near:** Jogging Paths, Fishing Charter, Cultural Attract, Sightseeing *(Whale watch 967-0707)* **Under 1 mi:** Beach *(Gooch's Beach - Trolley)*, Tennis Courts, Golf Course *(Cape Arundel 967-3494)* **1-3 mi:** Playground, Fitness Center, Horseback Riding *(Rockin' Horse Stables 967-4288)*, Video Rental, Museum *(Seashore Trolley Museum 967-2800 $7.25/4.75, Maritime Museum 967-4195)* **3+ mi:** Movie Theater *(Hoyts Biddeford 282-5995, 5 mi.)*

Provisioning and General Services
OnSite: Newsstand **Near:** Convenience Store, Gourmet Shop, Delicatessen, Wine/Beer, Bakery, Green Grocer, Fishmonger, Lobster Pound *(Port Lobster Co.)*, Bank/ATM, Post Office, Protestant Church, Bookstore, Pharmacy *(Colonial 967-4442)*, Clothing Store, Retail Shops **Under 1 mi:** Farmers' Market *(Sat 8am-1pm, Wed 12-3pm, Grove St. & Rt.1 behind Kennebunk Inn)*, Catholic Church, Library *(Graves Memorial 967-2778)*, Beauty Salon, Barber Shop, Hardware Store, Florist, Copies Etc. *(Ocean Exposure 967-0500)* **1-3 mi:** Provisioning Service, Liquor Store, Dry Cleaners, Laundry **3+ mi:** Supermarket *(Garden Street Market 985-2081, 5 mi.)*, Health Food *(New Morning, 8 mi.)*

Transportation
OnCall: Taxi *(John's 985-6291)*, Airport Limo *(Mermaid 800-696-2463)* **Near:** Local Bus *(In Town Trolley 967-3686)* **1-3 mi:** Bikes *(Cape-Able 967-4382 $15/day)* **3+ mi:** Rental Car *(Arundel Ford 985-7171, 5 mi.)*, Rail *(Wells-Boston, 8 mi.)* **Airport:** Portland Int'l. *(25 mi.)*

Medical Services
911 Service **OnCall:** Ambulance **1-3 mi:** Doctor *(Kennebunk Walk-in Clinic 985-3726)*, Dentist, Chiropractor *(Kennebunk Chiro 985-2900)*, Holistic Services **Hospital:** Southern Maine Medical Center 283-7000 *(12 mi.)*

Setting -- An attractive, contemporary shingled building greets cruisers as they wend their way a half mile up the Kennebunk River. Views from the docks are of the heavily wooded Franciscan Monastery across the river or of the attractive deck and buildings that overlook the marina. Street side is Ocean Avenue, the major thorofare of Kennebunkport and home to some wonderfully renovated historic houses - now resorts, inns and restaurants.

Marina Notes -- *50-69' $4/ft., over 70' $4.50/ft. Able to manage larger yachts to 140 feet. Private heads and showers. Laundry. Service oriented with dock hands and concierge support. Ships' store onsite. Limited onsite boatyard services including a hydraulic trailer; others available on call or nearby. Founded over thirty years ago by Booth Chick, a well-known local boat builder and fisherman.

Notable -- Dock Square, with galleries and shops, is a half mile away. Village Cove Inn is a short walk away, as is its Changing Tide Restaurant and Jaxson's Grille (B 8:30-11:30am; D Thu 5:30-8pm, Fri-Sat 5:30-9pm). Visit Kennebunkport Maritime Museum, weekdays 10am-3pm, weekends 11am-4pm, closed Wednesday. Walking tours of the historic village available from Kennebunkport Historical Society (967-2751). In Town Trolley service passes the door from 10am-5pm (Day Pass $8/4); it follows the rocky shore of Cape Arundel - watch for the waterspout near Walker's Point - and heads out to the beaches.

PHOTOS ON CD-ROM: 4

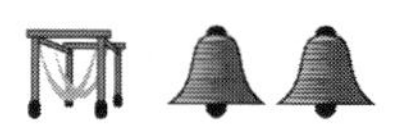

Kennebunkport Marina

PO Box 2734; 67 Ocean Avenue; Kennebunkport, ME 04046

Tel: (207) 967-3411 **VHF: Monitor** 9 **Talk** 71
Fax: (207) 967-9808 **Alternate Tel:** (207) 590-0634
Email: n/a **Web:** n/a
Nearest Town: Kennebunkport *(0.3 mi.)* **Tourist Info:** (207) 967-8600

Navigational Information

Lat: 43°21.455' **Long:** 070°28.470' **Tide:** 9 ft. **Current:** 5 kt. **Chart:** 13286
Rep. Depths (*MLW*): Entry 6 ft. **Fuel Dock** n/a **Max Slip/Moor** 8 ft./-
Access: 0.7 miles from the mouth of the Kennebunk River on east side

Marina Facilities *(In Season/Off Season)*

Fuel: No
Slips: 41 Total, 2 Transient **Max LOA:** 65 ft. **Max Beam:** n/a
Rate *(per ft.)*: **Day** $2.75/Inq. **Week** $13.50 **Month** $73
Power: 30 amp Yes, **50 amp** Yes, **100 amp** n/a, **200 amp** n/a
Cable TV: No **Dockside Phone:** No
Dock Type: Wood, Long Fingers, Short Fingers, Pilings, Floating
Moorings: 0 Total, 0 Transient **Launch:** n/a, Dinghy Dock
Rate: Day n/a **Week** n/a **Month** n/a
Heads: 2 Toilet(s), 2 Shower(s)
Laundry: 1 Washer(s), 1 Dryer(s) **Pay Phones:** No
Pump-Out: OnSite, Full Service **Fee:** $40 **Closed Heads:** Yes

Marina Operations

Owner/Manager: Gary Martin **Dockmaster:** Dave Emmons
In-Season: Apr 15-Oct 15, 8am-5pm **Off-Season:** n/a
After-Hours Arrival: Call during business hours to arrange
Reservations: Yes, Preferred **Credit Cards:** Visa/MC, Dscvr, Amex
Discounts: None
Pets: Welcome, Dog Walk Area **Handicap Access:** No

Marina Services and Boat Supplies

Services - Docking Assistance, Boaters' Lounge, Trash Pick-Up, Dock Carts **Communication -** Phone Messages, Fax in/out *($1)*, FedEx, AirBorne, UPS, Express Mail **Supplies - OnSite:** Ice *(Block, Cube)*, Ships' Store, Marine Discount Store, Bait/Tackle, Propane

Boatyard Services

OnSite: Engine mechanic *(gas, diesel)*, Launching Ramp, Electrical Repairs, Electronic Sales, Bottom Cleaning, Brightwork, Divers, Compound, Wash & Wax, Interior Cleaning, Woodworking, Inflatable Repairs, Painting **OnCall:** Propeller Repairs **1-3 mi:** Hull Repairs. **Yard Rates:** $55/hr., Haul & Launch $6/ft., ($5 commercial), Power Wash $2.75, Bottom Paint $5.50/ft. **Storage:** In-Water $13.50/ft/mo., On-Land $30/ft. incl. H&L

Restaurants and Accommodations

OnSite: Condo/Cottage *(Marina Cottage 967-3411)* **OnCall:** Pizzeria *(Atlantic Pizza 967-0033)* **Near:** Restaurant *(Arundel Wharf 967-3444, L $3-12, D $14-30)*, *(Alisson's 967-4841, L $5-14, D $11-17)*, Seafood Shack *(Port Lobster)*, Snack Bar *(Old Salt Pantry)*, Hotel *(Nonantum Resort 967-4050, $110-260)*, Inn/B&B *(Maine Stay Inn and Cottages 967-2117, $170-275)* **1-3 mi:** Restaurant *(White Barn Inn 967-1100, D $78 prix fixe, 4 course, reservations a must)*, Motel *(Rhumb Line 967-5457, $80-160, B incl.)*, Inn/B&B *(White Barn Inn $330-700, across the River)*

Recreation and Entertainment

OnSite: Picnic Area, Grills, Boat Rentals, Sightseeing *(Whale Watching)* **Near:** Beach *(Gooch's Beach/Colony)*, Roller Blade/Bike Paths *(on streets)*, Park **Under 1 mi:** Museum *(Kennebunkport Historical Society 967-2751, Nott House Tue-Fri 1-4pm, Sat 10am-1pm $5/2)* **1-3 mi:** Pool, Playground, Tennis Courts *(Edgcomb Tennis Club 967-5791)*, Golf Course *(Cape Arundel 967-3494)*, Jogging Paths, Horseback Riding *(Rockin' Horse Stables 967-4288)*, Video Rental *(Arundel Video 985-5555)* **3+ mi:** Movie Theater *(5 mi.)*, Cultural Attract *(Arundel Theater, 5 mi.)*

Provisioning and General Services

Near: Lobster Pound *(Port Lobster 967-4620)*, Bank/ATM, Bookstore, Pharmacy *(Colonial 967-4442)*, Newsstand, Clothing Store, Retail Shops **Under 1 mi:** Convenience Store, Delicatessen *(Nathan's 967-8383)*, Wine/Beer, Liquor Store, Bakery, Farmers' Market *(Sat 8am-1pm, Wed 12-3pm, Grove St. & Rt.1 behind Kennebunk Inn)*, Fishmonger *(Clam Shack 967-3321)*, Post Office, Library, Beauty Salon, Florist, Copies Etc. *(Ocean Exposure 967-0500)* **1-3 mi:** Gourmet Shop, Meat Market, Protestant Church, Barber Shop, Dry Cleaners, Laundry, Hardware Store *(Cape Hardware 967-2021)* **3+ mi:** Supermarket *(Garden Street Market 985-3343, 5 mi.)*, Health Food *(New Morning 985-6774, 5 mi.)*

Transportation

Near: Bikes *(Cape-Able 967-4382 $15/day)*, InterCity Bus *(Trolley - Day Pass: $8/4)* **3+ mi:** Rental Car *(Dupuis 985-9055, 5 mi.)*, Rail *(Boston-Wells, 8 mi.)* **Airport:** Portland Intl *(25 mi.)*

Medical Services

911 Service **OnCall:** Ambulance **1-3 mi:** Chiropractor, Holistic Services **3+ mi:** Doctor *(5 mi.)*, Dentist *(5 mi.)* **Hospital:** Southern Maine Medical Center 283-7000 *(9 mi.)*

Setting -- Situated on the east side of the Kennebunk River about 2/3 mi. from the mouth, the docks at this perfect spot deliver pristine views of the pine woods across the river. Landside, the small, attractive, well maintained Kennebunkport Marina sits on picturesque Ocean Avenue - with its restored mansions, many of which are now restaurants and inns. It's just a short half mile from bustling Dock Square.

Marina Notes -- A very nicely appointed Captain's Lounge and picnic area overlook the marina. Well supplied marine store, plus canoe and kayak rentals onsite. Most boatyard services are also onsite, including engine mechanics, electronic sales, bottom cleaning, brightwork, and electrical. Over Road hydraulic trailer also available. Winter weekly storage rates are $13.50 per foot. Note: pump-out fee is $40. Arundel Yacht Club may also have slips (967-3060).

Notable -- Many restaurants are an easy walk. Take a tour aboard one of the nearby sloops (Bellatrix $15/hr. pp, 967-8685, Edna $30 pp, 2 hrs., 967-8809). Or stroll Parson's Way out to Porpoise Point, passing Walker's Point, St. Ann's Church, and trails to the mid-tide natural phenomena: blowing cave and spouting rock. Seashore Trolley Museum, daily 10am-5:30pm, $8/age 6-16 $4.50 (967-2800). Kennebunkport Maritime Museum, weekdays 10am-3pm, weekends 11am-4pm, closed Wed, 967-4195. Narrated Trolley service passes the door from 10am-5pm, $8/4 - 45 min loop. Natural products Tom's of Maine headquarters are here and the Natural Living Store (985-3874) is their local outlet. Factory tours also possible - 775-2388 - reservations essential.

PHOTOS ON CD-ROM: 5

Navigational Information
Lat: 43°21.550' **Long:** 070°28.586' **Tide:** 9 ft. **Current:** 5 kt. **Chart:** 13286
Rep. Depths (*MLW*): Entry 6 ft. **Fuel Dock** n/a **Max Slip/Moor** 6 ft./-
Access: .75 mi. from Kennebunk River entrance on the east side

Marina Facilities *(In Season/Off Season)*
Fuel: Gasoline, Diesel
Slips: 54 Total, 4 Transient **Max LOA:** 100 ft. **Max Beam:** 20 ft.
Rate *(per ft.)*: **Day** $3.50* **Week** n/a **Month** n/a
Power: 30 amp Incl., **50 amp** Incl., **100 amp** n/a, **200 amp** n/a
Cable TV: No **Dockside Phone:** No
Dock Type: Wood, Alongside, Floating
Moorings: 0 Total, 0 Transient **Launch:** n/a, Dinghy Dock
Rate: Day n/a **Week** n/a **Month** n/a
Heads: 2 Toilet(s), 2 Shower(s) *(with dressing rooms)*, Towels
Laundry: None **Pay Phones:** No
Pump-Out: No **Fee:** n/a **Closed Heads:** Yes

Marina Operations
Owner/Manager: John M. Webster **Dockmaster:** Same
In-Season: May 15-Oct 15, 7am-9pm **Off-Season:** Closed
After-Hours Arrival: No after hours arrival
Reservations: Required **Credit Cards:** Visa/MC, Amex
Discounts: None
Pets: Welcome **Handicap Access:** No

Yachtsman Marina

PO Box 2609; Ocean Avenue; Kennebunkport, ME 04046

Tel: (207) 967-2511; (800) 992-2487 **VHF: Monitor** n/a **Talk** n/a
Fax: (207) 967-5056 **Alternate Tel:** (207) 967-2321
Email: Innkeeper@yachtsmanlodge.com **Web:** www.yachtsmanlodge.com
Nearest Town: Kennebunkport *(0.25 mi)* **Tourist Info:** (207) 967-8600

Marina Services and Boat Supplies
Services - Docking Assistance, Concierge, Dock Carts **Communication -** Fax in/out, FedEx, AirBorne, UPS, Express Mail *(Sat Del)* **Supplies - OnSite:** Ice *(Cube)* **Near:** Ships' Store **3+ mi:** Bait/Tackle *(Northeast Angler 967-5889, 4 mi.)*, Propane *(Downeast Energy 985-3154, 4 mi.)*

Boatyard Services
OnCall: Engine mechanic *(gas, diesel)* **Nearest Yard:** Chick's Marina (207) 967-2782

Restaurants and Accommodations
OnSite: Motel *(Yachtsman Lodge 967-2511, 170-250)* **Near:** Restaurant *(Breakwater 967-3118, D $14)*, *(Nonantum Restaurant D $12-23)*, *(Kennebunkport Inn 967-2621, D $17-32)*, Snack Bar *(La Crêperie 967-5115)*, Pizzeria *(Atlantic Pizza 967-0033)*, Inn/B&B *(Nonantum Resort 967-4050, $110-260)*, *(Captain Lord 967-3141, $200-450)*, *(1802 House B&B 967-5632, $170-380)* **Under 1 mi:** Restaurant *(Mabel's Lobster Claw 967-2562, L $8-16, D $14-28, near Walker Point)* **1-3 mi:** Restaurant *(White Barn Inn 967-2321, D $78 prix fixe, 4 courses - across river)*, Inn/B&B *(White Barn Inn 967-2321, $330-700, across river)*

Recreation and Entertainment
OnSite: Fishing Charter **Near:** Tennis Courts *(Edgcomb Club 967-5791)*, Jogging Paths, Museum *(Kennebunkport Historical Society 967-2751)*, Sightseeing *(Nautilus Whale Watching 967-0707 leaves Kennebunkport Marina; daily, narrated excursions 10am and 4pm)* **Under 1 mi:** Beach, Horseback Riding *(Rockin' Horse Stables 967-4288)*, Boat Rentals **1-3 mi:** Golf Course *(Cape Arundel 967-3494)*, Roller Blade/Bike Paths, Video Rental *(Arundel Video 985-5555)*, Park, Cultural Attract **3+ mi:** Fitness Center *(Living Fit 985-8778, 5 mi.)*, Bowling, Movie Theater *(Hoyts Biddeford 282-5995, 9 mi.)*

Provisioning and General Services
Near: Delicatessen, Bakery, Green Grocer, Bank/ATM, Post Office, Pharmacy *(Colonial 967-4442)*, Newsstand, Clothing Store, Retail Shops **Under 1 mi:** Convenience Store, Gourmet Shop *(Stonehouse Port & Cheese 967-9764)*, Wine/Beer *(Stonehouse Port & Cheese)*, Farmers' Market *(Old Schoolhouse Farm 967-8018)*, Fishmonger, Lobster Pound *(Port Lobster 967-2081)*, Meat Market, Catholic Church, Protestant Church, Library, Bookstore, Hardware Store *(Cape Hardware 967-2021)*, Florist, Copies Etc. *(Ocean Exposure 967-0500)* **1-3 mi:** Synagogue, Beauty Salon, Barber Shop, Dry Cleaners, Laundry **3+ mi:** Supermarket *(Garden Street Market, 5 mi.)*, Health Food *(New Morning 985-6774, 5 mi.)*, Liquor Store *(Garden St., 5 mi.)*

Transportation
OnCall: Taxi *(John's 985-6291)*, Airport Limo *(Lilley's Limo 773-5765)* **Near:** Bikes *(Cape-Able 967-4382)*, Local Bus *(InTown Trolley)* **1-3 mi:** Rental Car *(Arundel Ford 985-7171)* **3+ mi:** Water Taxi *(Presumpscot 879-2562, 25 mi.)*, Rail *(Wells, 8 mi.)* **Airport:** Portland Int'l. *(25 mi.)*

Medical Services
911 Service **OnCall:** Ambulance **Under 1 mi:** Dentist, Holistic Services **3+ mi:** Doctor *(Schill 985-7176, 4 mi.)*, Chiropractor *(Natural Way 985-3055, 5 mi.)* **Hospital:** So. Maine Medical Center 283-7979 *(8 mi.)*

Setting -- An impeccably maintained, exquisitely landscaped marina and "motel," the Yachtsman complex sits on the starboard side of the Kennebunk River. It's about 3/4 mile from the mouth and 1/4 mile from Kennebunkport's Dock Square. Perennial and annual flower beds, punctuated by contemporary sculpture, soften the edges of the buildings, patios and decks. Views are of the river, the dense woods on the far side and the beautiful grounds.

Marina Notes -- *In Season night rates range from $3.50-5.50/ft. No dedicated transient slips, but slips frequently available. Reservations are a must for both marina and lodgings. The heads are exceptional - private rooms with raised tile showers, sinks and toilets, and complimentary towel service. 29 beautifully appointed "yacht-like" rooms fan out along the marina. Don't be fooled; amenities, attention to detail, and views of the river and marina raise these rooms way beyond the motel category - they're four-diamond rated. For a special evening, consider the White Barn Inn, dinner 5-9pm, 4-course prix fixe $78, across the river - under the same ownership (jackets required). Grissini Trattoria ($12-20) in Kennebunk is also owned by the same group.

Notable -- Close by is the Nonatum Resort and the Nonatum Riverside Restaurant. Seashore Trolley Museum has 200 antique streetcars - the largest collection in the world - daily 10am-5:30pm, $8/age 6-16 $4 (967-2800). The nearby Nott House, an 1853 Greek Revival house with original wallpaper and furnishings, is open to the public (967-2751). InTown Trolley to Colony Beach, Goose Rocks Beach, and the museums, offers on-going narration. Secret Service boats are frequently seen here along with the senior Bush's boat and a small fleet of Hinckley picnic boats.

PHOTOS ON CD-ROM: 5

Performance Marine

PO Box 1039; 4 Western Avenue; Kennebunkport, ME 04043

Tel: (207) 967-5550 **VHF: Monitor** 9 **Talk** 17
Fax: (207) 967-5519 **Alternate Tel:** n/a
Email: n/a **Web:** n/a
Nearest Town: Kennebunkport *(0 mi.)* **Tourist Info:** (207) 967-8600

Navigational Information

Lat: 43°21.580' **Long:** 070°28.722' **Tide:** 9 ft. **Current:** 5 kt. **Chart:** 13286
Rep. Depths (*MLW*): Entry 6 ft. **Fuel Dock** n/a **Max Slip/Moor** 6 ft./-
Access: 1 mi. from mouth of Kennebunk River on west side before bridge

Marina Facilities *(In Season/Off Season)*

Fuel: Gasoline, Diesel
Slips: 20 Total, 2 Transient **Max LOA:** 70 ft. **Max Beam:** 20 ft.
Rate *(per ft.)*: **Day** $2.00/Inq. **Week** Inq. **Month** Inq.
Power: 30 amp Inc., **50 amp** Incl, **100 amp** n/a, **200 amp** n/a
Cable TV: No **Dockside Phone:** No
Dock Type: Wood, Floating
Moorings: 0 Total, 0 Transient **Launch:** n/a, Dinghy Dock
Rate: Day n/a **Week** n/a **Month** n/a
Heads: 1 Toilet(s)
Laundry: None **Pay Phones:** Yes, 1
Pump-Out: OnSite, Full Service, 1 Central **Fee:** n/a **Closed Heads:** No

Marina Operations

Owner/Manager: Dwight Raymond **Dockmaster:** Same
In-Season: May-Oct, 8am-8pm **Off-Season:** Nov-Apr, 8am-5pm
After-Hours Arrival: Pull up to fuel dock
Reservations: Required **Credit Cards:** Visa/MC
Discounts: None
Pets: Welcome **Handicap Access:** Yes, Docks

Marina Services and Boat Supplies

Services - Docking Assistance **Communication -** FedEx, UPS, Express Mail **Supplies - OnSite:** Ice *(Block, Cube)*, Ships' Store **Near:** Bait/Tackle **Under 1 mi:** Propane

Boatyard Services

OnSite: Travelift, Crane *(10T)*, Engine mechanic *(gas, diesel)*, Electrical Repairs, Hull Repairs, Bottom Cleaning, Brightwork, Divers, Compound, Wash & Wax, Interior Cleaning, Woodworking, Metal Fabrication, Painting, Awlgrip, Yacht Design, Yacht Building, Total Refits **OnCall:** Propeller Repairs **Under 1 mi:** Launching Ramp. **3+ mi:** Inflatable Repairs *(20 mi.)*, Life Raft Service *(20 mi.)*. **Yard Rates:** $60/hr., Haul & Launch $7.50/ft., Power Wash $2, Bottom Paint $10/ft. *(paint included)* **Storage:** In-Water $14/ft. winter, On-Land $24/ft.

Restaurants and Accommodations

OnSite: Restaurant *(Pilot House Restaurant 967-9961, L $5, D $8-20)* **Near:** Restaurant *(Federal Jacks 967-4322, L $4-15, D $6-20)*, *(Alisson's 967-4841, L $5-14, D $10-17)*, *(Kennebunkport Inn 967-2621, D $17-32)*, *(Grissini 967-2211, D $16-22)*, *(Windows on the Water 967-3313)*, Seafood Shack *(Clam Shack 967-3321)*, Snack Bar *(Dock Sq. Coffee House)*, Pizzeria *(Atlantic Pizza 967-0033)*, Inn/B&B *(Village Cove Inn 967-3993, $70-210)*, *(The Kennebunkport Inn 967-5425, $80-325)*, *(Maine Stay Inn & Cottages 967-2117, $170-275)* **Under 1 mi:** Restaurant *(White Barn Inn 967-2321, D $78 prix fixe, 4 courses, jacket required)*

Recreation and Entertainment

OnSite: Boat Rentals, Fishing Charter, Other *(whale watch/scenic cruises)* **Near:** Playground, Jogging Paths, Sightseeing *(Narrated Trolley 967-3686)* **Under 1 mi:** Beach *(Gooch's Beach - Trolley)* **1-3 mi:** Tennis Courts *(Edgcomb Tennis Club 967-5791)*, Golf Course *(Cape Arundel 967-3494)*, Video Rental *(Arundel Video 985-5555)*, Museum *(Kennebunkport Maritime Museum 967-4195, Seashore Trolley)* **3+ mi:** Movie Theater *(10 mi.)*

Provisioning and General Services

Near: Convenience Store, Delicatessen *(Nathan's 967-8383)*, Liquor Store, Bakery, Fishmonger, Lobster Pound *(Clam Shack Seafoods 967-3321)*, Bank/ATM, Post Office, Protestant Church, Library, Beauty Salon, Barber Shop, Dry Cleaners, Laundry, Bookstore, Pharmacy *(Colonial Pharmacy 967-4442)*, Newsstand, Florist, Clothing Store, Retail Shops, Copies Etc. *(Ocean Exposure)* **Under 1 mi:** Gourmet Shop, Farmers' Market *(Old Schoolhouse Farm 967-8018)* **1-3 mi:** Wine/Beer, Hardware Store *(Cape Hardware 967-2021)* **3+ mi:** Supermarket *(Garden Street Market 985-3343, 5 mi.)*, Catholic Church *(5 mi.)*

Transportation

OnCall: Taxi *(John's 985-6291)*, Airport Limo *(Lilley's Limo 773-5765)*
Near: Bikes *(Cape-Able 967-4382 $15/day)*, Local Bus *(Trolley 967-3686)*
3+ mi: Rail *(Boston-Wells, 8 mi.)* **Airport:** Portland Int'l. *(25 mi.)*

Medical Services

911 Service **OnCall:** Ambulance **1-3 mi:** Doctor *(Skill Med. Group 985-7174)*, Dentist *(Kennebunk Family Dental 985-7944)*, Chiropractor *(Family Chiropractic 967-8888)*, Holistic Services *(Northern Lights 967-9850)*
Hospital: So. Maine Medical Center 283-7979 *(6 mi.)*

Setting -- Located right in the heart of the picturesque and carefully manicured seaside town of Kennebunkport, Performance Marine offers the benefit of convenience and location. It is just across the drawbridge from Dock Square, the busy town center with its boutiques, galleries, restaurants, crafts shops, and T-shirt emporiums. There are few facilities for cruisers; just very well located docks and extensive boatyard services. Views are of the docks and the town.

Marina Notes -- Full service boatyard facilities and services. Just one head, no showers or laundry. Don't expect dock carts, message services or email access. Here it is all about the boat. The only marina service Performance offers is docking assistance, but with its location, a cruiser may not feel the need for anything else.

Notable -- Virtually onsite is the Pilot House Restaurant, located in the contemporary "mall" building adjacent to the marina, with views of the river and the town. Parson's Way is a wonderful walkway beginning at Dock Square and passing Walker's Point, home to former President George Bush. Seashore Trolley Museum, daily 10am-5:30pm, $8/age 6-16 $4.50 (967-2800). Kennebunkport Maritime Museum is open weekdays 10am-3pm, weekends 11am-4pm, closed Wednesday (967-4195). Trolley service makes 9 loops throughout Kennebunkport - including the beaches - from 10am-5pm; day pass: $8/4, under 6 free. Most convenient marina to the White Barn Inn, an extraordinary restaurant on the western side of the River.

Navigational Information

Lat: 43°07.980' **Long:** 070°38.550' **Tide:** 8 ft. **Current:** 4 kt. **Chart:** 13283
Rep. Depths (*MLW*): Entry 10 ft. **Fuel Dock** 10 ft. **Max Slip/Moor** 10 ft./-
Access: Up River beyond Stage Neck on the northeast side

Marina Facilities *(In Season/Off Season)*

Fuel: No
Slips: 6 Total, 6 Transient **Max LOA:** 135 ft. **Max Beam:** n/a
Rate *(per ft.)*: **Day** $1.00/Inq.* **Week** Inq. **Month** Inq.
Power: 30 amp $3, **50 amp** $8, **100 amp** $10, **200 amp** n/a
Cable TV: No **Dockside Phone:** No
Dock Type: Floating
Moorings: 0 Total, 0 Transient **Launch:** n/a
Rate: Day n/a **Week** n/a **Month** n/a
Heads: None
Laundry: None **Pay Phones:** No
Pump-Out: No **Fee:** n/a **Closed Heads:** Yes

Marina Operations

Owner/Manager: Mary Coite **Dockmaster:** Mary Coite / Dan Donnell
In-Season: May-Oct 30, 7am-8pm **Off-Season:** n/a
After-Hours Arrival: Call ahead
Reservations: Yes **Credit Cards:** personal check or cash
Discounts: None
Pets: Welcome, Dog Walk Area **Handicap Access:** No

Donnell's Marina

PO Box 472; 39 Varrell Lane; York Harbor, ME 03911

Tel: (207) 363-5324 **VHF: Monitor** n/a **Talk** n/a
Fax: n/a **Alternate Tel:** (207) 363-4308
Email: n/a **Web:** n/a
Nearest Town: York Village **Tourist Info:** (207) 363-4422

Marina Services and Boat Supplies

Services - Docking Assistance, Trash Pick-Up **Communication -** Phone Messages, FedEx, AirBorne, UPS, Express Mail **Supplies - Near:** Bait/Tackle **Under 1 mi:** Propane *(Downeast Energy 363-4331)* **3+ mi:** West Marine *(603-436-8300, 12 mi.)*

Boatyard Services

OnSite: Launching Ramp **Near:** Travelift, Engine mechanic *(gas, diesel)*, Electrical Repairs, Electronic Sales, Electronics Repairs, Hull Repairs, Bottom Cleaning. **Nearest Yard:** York Harbor Marine Services (207) 363-3602

Restaurants and Accommodations

Near: Restaurant *(Fazio's 363-1718, D $5-18)*, *(Harbor Porches at Stageneck Inn B $8, L $8-23, D $18-30, formal)*, *(York Harbor Inn B $8, L 6-15, D $19-28, Cellar Pub Grill has lite fare)*, Seafood Shack *(Fosters Downeast Clambake 363-3255, L $6-24, D $8-24)*, Lite Fare *(Sandpiper Grill at Stageneck L $8-23, D $8-23, casual, L & D 2pm on, serves Harbor Porches lunch menu)*, Pizzeria *(York House of Pizza 363-6171)*, Inn/B&B *(Stage Neck Inn 363-3850, $135-325)*, *(York Harbor Inn 363-5119, $110-280)*, *(Edwards Harborside Inn 363-3037, $50-270, also has some dockage)*, *(Tanglewood Hall 351-1075, $115-215)* **Under 1 mi:** Condo/Cottage *(Kingsbury Cottages 363-5688)*

Recreation and Entertainment

OnSite: Fishing Charter **Near:** Beach, Jogging Paths, Park, Sightseeing *(Harbor Adventures 363-8466)* **Under 1 mi:** Dive Shop, Video Rental *(Stop N Go Video 363-4762)*, Museum *(Old York Historical Society 363-4974 7 building tour $7/3 www.oldyork.org; Sayward-Wheeler House)* **1-3 mi:** Volleyball, Tennis Courts, Golf Course *(Ledges Golf Course 351-3000)*, Fitness Center, Horseback Riding *(Beltane Farm 363-5559)*, Movie Theater *(York Cinema 363-2074 8pm, Rainy Day matinée at 2pm)*, Cultural Attract *(York's Wild Kingdom zoo + rides 363-4911 $15.25/11.75)*

Provisioning and General Services

OnSite: Lobster Pound **Near:** Gourmet Shop *(Country Gourmet 363-7454)*, Newsstand **Under 1 mi:** Supermarket *(Dave's York Village IGA 363-3171)*, Delicatessen *(Munchies)*, Wine/Beer, Bakery, Meat Market, Bank/ATM, Catholic Church, Protestant Church, Library, Barber Shop, Dry Cleaners, Laundry, Pharmacy *(Rite Aid 363-4312)*, Hardware Store *(Cooks Hardware 363-2242)*, Florist, Retail Shops **1-3 mi:** Health Food *(Ascending Health 363-1663)*, Copies Etc. *(Watermark Printing 363-6618)*

Transportation

OnSite: Courtesy Car/Van *(for grocery shopping)*, Local Bus *(Summer Trolley Service - 400' top of street)* **OnCall:** Airport Limo *(Coastal Limo 363-5151)* **Near:** Bikes *(Bergers Bike Shop 363-4070)*, Taxi *(Sunshine Taxi 363-7600)* **3+ mi:** Rental Car *(National 636-8355, 4 mi.)* **Airport:** Portland Int'l. *(47 mi.)*

Medical Services

911 Service **OnCall:** Ambulance **Near:** Dentist **Under 1 mi:** Doctor **1-3 mi:** Chiropractor *(Chiropractic Works 363-5966)* **Hospital:** York *(1 mi.)*

Setting -- On the convenient, northeast side of York Harbor, Donnell's upholds generations of family tradition with rustic charm and downeast grace. There are minimal services and facilities, but that is more than compensated for by the personal service and great location. Views from the docks are of the shingled buildings on both sides of the river and all the activity in this busy, fashionable, recreational harbor - that still maintains a touch of its 18C roots.

Marina Notes -- *$1/ft. up to 50', $1.30/ft. for 50'+. Very well protected. Good hurricane hole. There are no heads or showers. Family owned and operated, with two sets of docks - those pictured are run by second generation Mary Donnell Coite (363-5324) and those next door by her father, Daniel Donnell (363-4308). 50 amp/100 amp service. Docks were new in 1998. The York Trolley (May 31-Labor Day) stops nearby for easy access to provisioning, shops and other services. Owners will also take guests grocery shopping.

Notable -- Quarter mile to Harbor Beach. Beautiful walkway along the river and through the woods leads to the restored Wiggley Steel Suspension Bridge. The Stage Neck Inn resort is an easy walk as are its three restaurants: Harbor Porches, Sandpiper Bar and Grille, and the Outdoor Terrace. Take the trolley to Old York Historical Society's seven different restored buildings (June-Columbus Day, Tue-Sat 10am-5pm, Sun 1-5pm) or a cab to the mile-long Kittery Outlet Center. York Harbor Days are 10 days from Late July - Early August.

PHOTOS ON CD-ROM: 5

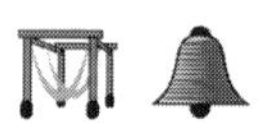

York Harbor Marine/Moorings

PO Box 578; Route 103; York Harbor, ME 03911

Tel: (207) 363-3602 **VHF: Monitor** 16 **Talk** 10
Fax: n/a **Alternate Tel:** (207) 363-1010
Email: service@yorkharbormarine.com **Web:** www.yorkharbormarine.com
Nearest Town: York Harbor *(1 mi.)* **Tourist Info:** (207) 363-4422

Navigational Information
Lat: 43°07.760' **Long:** 070°38.767' **Tide:** 10 ft. **Current:** 6 kt. **Chart:** 13283
Rep. Depths (*MLW*): Entry 20 ft. **Fuel Dock** 10 ft. **Max Slip/Moor** 10 ft./20 ft.
Access: York River just beyond Stage Neck on west shore

Marina Facilities *(In Season/Off Season)*
Fuel: Gasoline, Diesel
Slips: 50 Total, 0 Transient **Max LOA:** 40 ft. **Max Beam:** n/a
Rate *(per ft.)*: **Day** n/a **Week** n/a **Month** n/a
Power: 30 amp Incl., **50 amp** Incl., **100 amp** n/a, **200 amp** n/a
Cable TV: No **Dockside Phone:** No
Dock Type: Long Fingers, Floating, Composition
Moorings: 10 Total, 6 Transient **Launch:** None, Dinghy Dock
Rate: Day $25 **Week** n/a **Month** n/a
Heads: 1 Toilet(s), 1 Shower(s) *(with dressing rooms)*
Laundry: 1 Washer(s), 1 Dryer(s), Book Exchange **Pay Phones:** No
Pump-Out: No **Fee:** n/a **Closed Heads:** No

Marina Operations
Owner/Manager: Fred Muehl **Dockmaster:** Gordon Parry (Harbormaster)
In-Season: May-Nov, 8am-5pm **Off-Season:** Dec-Apr, 8am-4:30pm
After-Hours Arrival: n/a
Reservations: No **Credit Cards:** n/a
Discounts: None
Pets: Welcome, Dog Walk Area **Handicap Access:** No

Marina Services and Boat Supplies
Services - Trash Pick-Up **Communication -** FedEx, AirBorne, UPS, Express Mail **Supplies - OnSite:** Ships' Store, West Marine **Near:** Bait/Tackle **Under 1 mi:** Propane *(Downeast Energy 363-4331)* **3+ mi:** Boat/US *(15 mi.)*, Marine Discount Store *(15 mi.)*

Boatyard Services
OnSite: Railway *(60T)*, Forklift, Crane, Engine mechanic *(gas, diesel)*, Electrical Repairs, Hull Repairs, Rigger, Bottom Cleaning, Brightwork, Compound, Wash & Wax, Interior Cleaning, Yacht Broker *(Rick Bennet)*, Total Refits **OnCall:** Electronics Repairs, Air Conditioning, Refrigeration, Divers, Propeller Repairs, Woodworking, Upholstery, Yacht Interiors, Metal Fabrication **Under 1 mi:** Launching Ramp. **Dealer for:** Honda, OMC, Boston Whaler, Mercruiser. **Member:** Other Certifications: OMC, Honda, Mercruiser **Yard Rates:** $52/hr., Haul & Launch $8.50/ft., Power Wash $3.50

Restaurants and Accommodations
Near: Restaurant *(The Restaurant at Dockside 363-2722, L $7-11, D $11-23, Tue-Sun, inside a screened porch dining)*, *(York Harbor 363-5119, L $15-23, D $19-28)*, Inn/B&B *(Dockside Guest Quarters 363-2868, $90-220, dockage for guests)* **Under 1 mi:** Seafood Shack *(Fosters Downeast Clambake 363-3255, L $6-24, D $8-24)*, Pizzeria *(York House of Pizza 363-6171)*, Hotel *(York Harbor Inn 363-5119, $110-280)* **1-3 mi:** Restaurant *(Harbor Porches at Stageneck Inn B $8, L $8-23, D $18-28, formal)*, Lite Fare *(Sandpiper Grill at Stageneck L $8-23, D $8-23, casual - from 2pm on Harbor Porches lunch menu served)*, Hotel *(Stage Neck Inn 363-2221, $135-325, walk around harbor or just dinghy across)*

Recreation and Entertainment
Near: Beach, Fishing Charter **Under 1 mi:** Video Rental *(York Stop N Go Video 363-4762)*, Park, Museum *(Old York Museum Shop 351-3298; Old York Historical Society 363-4974)*, Sightseeing *(Lobstering Trips)* **1-3 mi:** Dive Shop, Tennis Courts, Golf Course *(Ledges Golf Club 351-3000)*, Fitness Center *(York Fitness 363-4090)*, Horseback Riding, Group Fishing Boat, Movie Theater, Video Arcade

Provisioning and General Services
Near: Gourmet Shop *(Country Gourmet 363-7454)*, Lobster Pound *(Donnell's or Finestkind Fish Market 363-5000)*, Bank/ATM, Post Office, Catholic Church, Protestant Church, Beauty Salon, Barber Shop, Dry Cleaners **Under 1 mi:** Convenience Store *(Cumberland Farms)*, Delicatessen, Wine/Beer, Bakery, Fishmonger, Meat Market, Library, Laundry **1-3 mi:** Supermarket *(Dave's IGA 363-3171)*, Health Food *(Ascending Health 363-1663)*, Pharmacy *(Rite Aid 363-4312)*, Newsstand, Hardware Store *(Cooks Hardware 363-2242)*, Florist, Retail Shops, Copies Etc. *(Watermark Printing 363-6618)* **3+ mi:** Liquor Store

Transportation
OnCall: Taxi *(Sunshine Cab 363-7600)*, Airport Limo *(Coastal Limo 363-5151)* **Under 1 mi:** Bikes *(Bergers Bike Shop 363-4070)*, Local Bus *(Summer Trolley Service)* **3+ mi:** Rental Car *(National 36-38355, 5 mi.)*
Airport: Portland Int'l. *(48 mi.)*

Medical Services
911 Service **OnCall:** Ambulance **Under 1 mi:** Doctor, Dentist **1-3 mi:** Chiropractor *(Gallant)* **Hospital:** York 351-2118 *(1 mi.)*

Setting -- On the west side of snug, upscale York Harbor, this long-established Harris Island boatyard facility provides services to the moorings located off its docks, as well as to other cruising boats. The ambiance is clearly that of a working boatyard; the views are of a harbor filled with downeast boats and the not too distant opposite shore.

Marina Notes -- To reserve one of the six transient moorings, contact the York Harbormaster (363-4445). York Harbor Marine may have a rare available slip; the docks at Dockside Guest Quarter next door (888 769-3047) are also managed by YHM, and may be available as well. There are heads, showers and laundry facilities available to mooring guests for a fee. This is a full service boatyard, staffed with factory certified technicians, offering almost all services onsite. A well equipped ships' store is also onsite. Their 50 slips are seasonal only, and there's an active drystack storage operation. Excellent hurricane hole. Pump-out service coming soon.

Notable -- "Downtown" York Harbor is within walking distance and Dockside Guest Quarters lodgings and Restaurant - overlooking the harbor - are practically next door (Tue-Sun, L 11:30am-2pm, D 5:30-9pm). Dinghy across the narrow harbor entrance to the Stage Neck Resort. Beaches are an easy walk. Several cruises leave from the harbor (Finestkind). The 120 store Kittery Outlet Center is a cab ride away and there is a trolley that operates within the shops once you get there.

Kittery Point Wharf

PO Box 808; Pepperell Road; Kittery, ME 03904

Tel: (207) 439-0912; (207) 438-9714 **VHF: Monitor** 16 **Talk** n/a
Fax: n/a **Alternate Tel:** (207) 439-1638
Email: n/a **Web:** n/a
Nearest Town: Kittery *(3 mi.)* **Tourist Info:** (207) 439-7545

Navigational Information
Lat: 43°04.946' **Long:** 070°42.212' **Tide:** 10 ft. **Current:** 4 kt. **Chart:** 13278
Rep. Depths (*MLW*): Entry 12 ft. **Fuel Dock** 12 ft. **Max Slip/Moor** -/30 ft.
Access: Piscataqua River to Pepperell Cove

Marina Facilities *(In Season/Off Season)*
Fuel: *Varvej* - Gasoline, Diesel
Slips: 0 Total, 0 Transient **Max LOA:** 60 ft. **Max Beam:** n/a
Rate *(per ft.)*: **Day** n/a **Week** n/a **Month** n/a
Power: 30 amp n/a, **50 amp** n/a, **100 amp** n/a, **200 amp** n/a
Cable TV: No **Dockside Phone:** No
Dock Type: n/a
Moorings: 20 Total, 9 Transient **Launch:** None, Dinghy Dock
Rate: Day $10 **Week** $70 **Month** Inq.
Heads: 1 Toilet(s)
Laundry: None **Pay Phones:** Yes
Pump-Out: No **Fee:** n/a **Closed Heads:** Yes

Marina Operations
Owner/Manager: John V. McCollett (Harbormaster) **Dockmaster:** n/a
In-Season: n/a, 24 hrs. **Off-Season:** On Call
After-Hours Arrival: n/a
Reservations: No **Credit Cards:** Cash only
Discounts: None
Pets: Welcome **Handicap Access:** Yes, Heads, Docks

Marina Services and Boat Supplies
Supplies - OnSite: Ice *(Cube)* **Under 1 mi:** Ships' Store *(Dion's Yacht Yard 439-9582)*, Propane *(Proulx 439-3881)* **1-3 mi:** Bait/Tackle **3+ mi:** West Marine *(436-8300, 13 mi.)*, Marine Discount Store *(Jacksons Hardware & Marine 439-1133, 8 mi.)*

Boatyard Services
OnSite: Launching Ramp, Bottom Cleaning, Divers, Life Raft Service **Under 1 mi:** Travelift, Engine mechanic *(gas, diesel)*, Electronic Sales, Electronics Repairs, Hull Repairs, Rigger, Compound, Wash & Wax, Interior Cleaning, Total Refits. **1-3 mi:** Sail Loft. **Nearest Yard:** Dion's Yacht Yard (207) 439-9582

Restaurants and Accommodations
OnSite: Restaurant *(Captain Simeon's 439-3655, L $7-11, D $7-15)* **OnCall:** Pizzeria *(Town Pizza 439-1265)* **Near:** Seafood Shack *(Chauncey Creek 439-1030, BYO - by dinghy)*, Inn/B&B *(Enchanted Nights B& B 439-2489, $42-150)* **3+ mi:** Restaurant *(Warren's Lobster House 439-1630, L $5-8, D $10-15, 4 mi.)*, *(Quarterdeck 439-5198, L $5-10$10-15, 4 mi.)*, Motel *(Charter House 439-2000, 4 mi.)*, Hotel *(Coachman Inn 439-4434, $60-110, 4 mi.)*, *(Gundalow Inn 439-4040, 4 mi.)*, Inn/B&B *(Inn at Portsmouth Harbor 439-4040, $95-175, 4 mi.)*

Recreation and Entertainment
Near: Beach, Picnic Area *(Ft. McClary)*, Grills, Playground, Jogging Paths **3+ mi:** Golf Course *(Pease Golf Course - Great Bay Golf Course 603 433-1331, 4 mi.)*, Fitness Center *(Danish Health Club 439-7188 , 4 mi.)*, Video Rental *(Five Star Video 439-0010 , 4 mi.)*, Museum *(Kittery Historical and Naval Museum 439-3080, 4 mi.)*, Sightseeing *(Fort McClary, 4 mi.)*

Provisioning and General Services
OnSite: Convenience Store *(Frisbee's Supermarket 439-0014)*, Wine/Beer **Near:** Beauty Salon, Dry Cleaners **Under 1 mi:** Bank/ATM, Post Office, Protestant Church **3+ mi:** Supermarket *(Christy's Market 439-5767, 4 mi.)*, Health Food *(Rising Tide 439-8898, 4 mi.)*, Liquor Store *(Maine Liquor Outlet 439-2332, 4 mi.)*, Green Grocer *(Golden Harvest 439-2113, 4 mi.)*, Lobster Pound *(Seaview, 4 mi.)*, Catholic Church *(4 mi.)*, Synagogue *(4 mi.)*, Library *(Rice Library 439-1553, 4 mi.)*, Barber Shop *(4 mi.)*, Laundry *(4 mi.)*, Bookstore *(4 mi.)*, Pharmacy *(Osco Drug 439-1966, 4 mi.)*, Hardware Store *(Shaw & Son 439-4150, 4 mi.)*, Florist *(4 mi.)*, Retail Shops *(Kittery Outlet Center, 4 mi.)*, Copies Etc. *(Kittery Pack & Ship 439-5704, 4 mi.)*

Transportation
OnCall: Rental Car *(Enterprise 603-433-1177)*, Taxi *(Jeff's Taxi 603-431-2345)* **Airport:** Portland Int'l. *(50 mi.)*

Medical Services
911 Service **OnCall:** Ambulance **3+ mi:** Doctor *(Kittery Family Practice 439-4430, 4 mi.)*, Chiropractor *(Natural Care 439-7246, 4 mi.)* **Hospital:** York 351-2118 *(8 mi.)*

Setting -- Set in a classic Maine harbor, the Town Wharf offers spectacular views and easy access to the charm of Kittery Point. The kaleidoscope of dinghies that surround the Wharf speaks to the diversity of the harbor's inhabitants and adds to the quaintness of the surroundings.

Marina Notes -- This is strictly a mooring field; the dinghy dock and one basic head are the full extent of the amenities. The town has 2 transient moorings, Cap'n Simeon has 2 moorings, and Pepperell Cove Yacht Club 5, ($20/night incl. launch service). Cap'n Simeon's Galley, above the yacht club, is practically onsite and serves lunch, dinner (11am-9pm) and Sun brunch (10am-2pm); its down-home atmosphere is perfect for enjoying a well-prepared lobster, with a spectacular view of the harbor. Modest Frisbee's "Supermarket", claiming the distinction as the oldest supermarket in the country, also manages the gas/diesel dock. While many places across the river in Portsmouth can theoretically be reached by dinghy or "big boat", go at slack tide; the current can be very swift.

Notable -- Browsing Kittery's cobbled streets, with its charming old houses and antiques shops, is a good excursion. Possible destinations include Fort McClary (439-2845) by foot or by dinghy (which boasts a picnic area & memorial) and then on to Lady Pepperell's Mansion on Rt. 103 (a privately owned example of early American Palladian-style architecture). Or dinghy up Chauncey Creek to Fort Foster (439-2182) with a stop for lobster in the rough. Famous Kittery Outlets - with its mile of 120 designer shops -- is a short cab ride away (call either Sunshine in York 363-7600 or Jeff's Taxi in Portsmouth 603 431-2345). A Trolley provides transportation within and among the various outlet centers.

PHOTOS ON CD-ROM: 4

Dion's Yacht Yard

PO Box 838; 48 Bowen Road; Kittery, ME 03904

Tel: (207) 439-9582 **VHF: Monitor** 69 **Talk** 8
Fax: (207) 439-4298 **Alternate Tel:** n/a
Email: info@dionsyachtyard.com **Web:** www.dionsyachtyard.com
Nearest Town: Kittery *(2 mi.)* **Tourist Info:** (207) 439-7545

Navigational Information
Lat: 43°04.970' **Long:** 070°43.340' **Tide:** 10 ft. **Current:** 4 kt. **Chart:** 13278
Rep. Depths (*MLW*): Entry 24 ft. **Fuel Dock** n/a **Max Slip/Moor** 24 ft./24 ft.
Access: Portsmouth Harbor Kittery Beach Channel no Bridge

Marina Facilities *(In Season/Off Season)*
Fuel: No
Slips: 12 Total, 8 Transient **Max LOA:** 110 ft. **Max Beam:** n/a
Rate *(per ft.)*: **Day** $2.00/Inq. **Week** Inq. **Month** Inq.
Power: 30 amp n/a, **50 amp** $5, **100 amp** n/a, **200 amp** n/a
Cable TV: No **Dockside Phone:** No
Dock Type: Wood, Floating
Moorings: 42 Total, 12 Transient **Launch:** None, Dinghy Dock
Rate: Day $30 **Week** $180 **Month** Inq.
Heads: 1 Toilet(s), 1 Shower(s)
Laundry: None **Pay Phones:** Yes
Pump-Out: No **Fee:** n/a **Closed Heads:** No

Marina Operations
Owner/Manager: John Glessner **Dockmaster:** Same
In-Season: Year-Round, 7:30am-5pm, Sat. 8am-12pm **Off-Season:** n/a
After-Hours Arrival: Call on the VHF for instructions
Reservations: Required **Credit Cards:** Visa/MC, Amex
Discounts: None
Pets: No **Handicap Access:** No

Marina Services and Boat Supplies
Services - Docking Assistance, Trash Pick-Up, Dock Carts, Megayacht Facilities **Communication -** Mail & Package Hold, Phone Messages, FedEx, AirBorne, UPS, Express Mail **Supplies - OnSite:** Ice *(Block, Cube)* **1-3 mi:** Ships' Store, Bait/Tackle *(Kittery Trading Post 439-2700)* **3+ mi:** West Marine *(Portsmouth 603-436-8300, 4 mi.)*

Boatyard Services
OnSite: Railway *(100T)*, Engine mechanic *(gas, diesel)*, Electrical Repairs, Electronic Sales, Electronics Repairs, Hull Repairs, Rigger, Bottom Cleaning, Brightwork, Air Conditioning, Refrigeration, Compound, Wash & Wax, Interior Cleaning, Propeller Repairs, Woodworking, Painting, Total Refits **OnCall:** Divers, Inflatable Repairs, Life Raft Service, Upholstery, Yacht Interiors, Metal Fabrication **1-3 mi:** Launching Ramp. **Member:** ABBRA **Yard Rates:** $60/hr., Haul & Launch $5.50/ft., Power Wash $2/ft.

Restaurants and Accommodations
OnCall: Pizzeria *(Dominos 207-439-1300)* **Under 1 mi:** Inn/B&B *(Deep Water 439-0824)* **1-3 mi:** Restaurant *(Warren's Lobster House 439-1630, L $5-8, D $10-15)*, *(Ship's Quarter Deck 439-5198, L $5-10, D $10-15)*, Snack Bar *(Bagel House)*, Fast Food, Motel *(Days Inn 439-5555, $90-100)*, *(Charter House 439-2000)*, *(Coachman 439-4434, $60-110)*

Recreation and Entertainment
OnCall: Boat Rentals, Fishing Charter **Near:** Picnic Area, Grills, Jogging Paths, Park, Sightseeing *(Fort McClary)* **Under 1 mi:** Group Fishing Boat, Museum *(Kittery Historical and Naval Museum 439-3080 Tue-Sat 10am-4pm)* **1-3 mi:** Beach, Golf Course, Fitness Center *(Danish Health Club 439-7188)*, Movie Theater, Video Rental *(Atlantic Video 431-2331)* **3+ mi:** Bowling *(Bowl O Rama 436-0504, 5 mi.)*

Provisioning and General Services
Under 1 mi: Convenience Store *(Osco, Frisbee's 439-0014)*, Bakery, Fishmonger, Lobster Pound, Post Office, Catholic Church, Beauty Salon, Barber Shop, Laundry, Pharmacy *(Osco Drug 439-1966)*, Hardware Store *(Ace 439-4150)*, Florist **1-3 mi:** Supermarket *(Puffin-Stop 439-6713)*, Delicatessen, Health Food *(Rising Tide Natural Foods 439-8898)*, Wine/Beer, Liquor Store *(Maine Liquor Outlet 439-2332)*, Farmers' Market, Meat Market, Bank/ATM, Library, Dry Cleaners, Clothing Store, Retail Shops, Department Store, Copies Etc. *(Kittery Business Center 439-5704)*

Transportation
OnCall: Water Taxi *(603-431-6687)* **1-3 mi:** Taxi *(John's Coastal Taxi 985-6291)* **3+ mi:** Rental Car *(Enterprise 603-433-1177, 4 mi.)* **Airport:** Portland Int'l. *(55 mi.)*

Medical Services
911 Service **OnCall:** Ambulance **Near:** Doctor **Under 1 mi:** Dentist, Chiropractor **1-3 mi:** Holistic Services **Hospital:** Portsmouth Regional 603 436-6262 *(5 mi.)*

Setting -- Snugged well up into Portsmouth Harbor's "Back Channel", past Pepperell Cove, north of Seavey Island, Dion's is located in the quiet, residential part of charming and picturesque Kittery. The atmosphere is very much well-maintained down-east boatyard with limited cruiser services. At Dion's, it is all about the boat.

Marina Notes -- A family business since 1963, Dion's was bought in 1999 by Manchester Marine. 100 ton railway, two hydraulic trailers, full services from major rebuilding to Awlgrip to rigging to bow thruster and stabilizer installations. Boat transportation and deliveries, Brownell air ride trailers, DOT and ICC authorized. More than two dozen craftsmen with decades of experience are employed year 'round. Well equipped Bosun's Locker ships' store is onsite. Heads and shower available during business hours only. Note: Pets are not allowed.

Notable -- Nearby are Fort McClary's 27 acre historic site (7 days 9am-dusk, $1/free) and Portsmouth Naval Shipyard Museum (by appointment only 438-5550). Five miles away in Portsmouth, NH, Isles of Shoals Steamship Co. (800 441-4620) and Portsmouth Harbor Cruises (800 776-0915 $7.50-15) offer cruises, whale watching and tours of Star Island. The 120 store Kittery Outlet Center is a few miles - either take a taxi (Sunshine 363-7600) or call the Outlet, with at least 24 hrs. notice (888 KITTERY), and they'll send the Trolley for you.

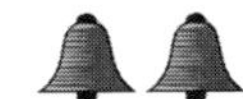

Navigational Information
Lat: 43°04.900' **Long:** 070°45.080' **Tide:** 10 ft. **Current:** 4 kt. **Chart:** 13278
Rep. Depths (*MLW*): Entry 34 ft. **Fuel Dock** n/a **Max Slip/Moor** 12 ft./-
Access: Piscataqua River, past Portsmouth Navy Yard, on starbord side

Marina Facilities *(In Season/Off Season)*
Fuel: No
Slips: 30 Total, 2 Transient **Max LOA:** 120 ft. **Max Beam:** n/a
Rate *(per ft.)*: **Day** $1.50/Inq. **Week** $9.45 **Month** Inq.
Power: 30 amp Incl., **50 amp** Incl., **100 amp** n/a, **200 amp** n/a
Cable TV: Yes **Dockside Phone:** No
Dock Type: Long Fingers, Concrete, Pilings, Floating, Aluminum
Moorings: 0 Total, 0 Transient **Launch:** n/a
Rate: Day n/a **Week** n/a **Month** n/a
Heads: 2 Toilet(s), 2 Shower(s)
Laundry: 1 Washer(s), 1 Dryer(s) **Pay Phones:** No
Pump-Out: OnCall, 1 Central **Fee:** n/a **Closed Heads:** No

Marina Operations
Owner/Manager: Sky Mar **Dockmaster:** Same
In-Season: May-Oct 31, 9am-5pm **Off-Season:** n/a
After-Hours Arrival: Take end dock
Reservations: Preferred **Credit Cards:** Cash or Traveler's Checks
Discounts: None
Pets: Welcome **Handicap Access:** Yes, Heads

Kittery Landing Marina

4 Island Avenue; Kittery, ME 03904

Tel: (207) 439-1661 **VHF: Monitor** 9 **Talk** 68
Fax: (603) 431-9557 **Alternate Tel:** n/a
Email: n/a **Web:** n/a
Nearest Town: Portsmouth, NH *(0.5 mi.)* **Tourist Info:** (207) 439-7545

Marina Services and Boat Supplies
Services - Trash Pick-Up **Communication -** FedEx, AirBorne, UPS, Express Mail **Supplies - OnSite:** Ice *(Block)* **Near:** Ice *(Cube)*, Boat/US, Marine Discount Store, Live Bait, CNG **Under 1 mi:** Propane *(Sea 3 603-431-5990)* **1-3 mi:** Ships' Store *(Dion's Yacht Yard 439-9582)*, West Marine *(603-436-8300)*, Bait/Tackle *(Kittery Trading Post 439-2700)*

Boatyard Services
OnCall: Divers **Near:** Engine mechanic *(gas, diesel)*, Launching Ramp, Electrical Repairs, Electronic Sales, Electronics Repairs, Bottom Cleaning, Brightwork, Compound, Wash & Wax, Interior Cleaning, Propeller Repairs, Woodworking. **1-3 mi:** Railway, Hull Repairs, Rigger, Air Conditioning, Refrigeration, Metal Fabrication, Painting, Awlgrip, Total Refits. **Nearest Yard:** Island Marine Services (207) 439-3810

Restaurants and Accommodations
Near: Restaurant *(Warren's Lobster House 439-1630, L $5-8, D $10-15)*, *(Rosa 603-436-9715, L $4-10, D $7-18)*, *(Weathervane Seafood 439-0330, L $3-8, D $5-18)*, Seafood Shack *(Morrison's Lobster 439-2501)*, Pizzeria *(Kittery House of Pizza 439-4989)*, Hotel *(Inn at Portsmouth Harbor 439-4040, $95-175)*, Inn/B&B *(Gundalow Inn 439-4040)* **Under 1 mi:** Hotel *(Sheraton Harborside 603-431-2300, $135-450)*, Inn/B&B *(Inn at Strawberry Banke 603-436-7242, $85-150)* **1-3 mi:** Inn/B&B *(Coachman Inn 439-4434, $110-135)*

Recreation and Entertainment
Near: Park *(Prescott Park, Portsmouth)*, Museum *(Kittery Historical - Naval Museum)*, Cultural Attract *(Prescott Park Arts Festival 436-2848)*, Sightseeing *(Strawbery Banke, Portsmouth Historical District 603-433-1100)*, Special Events *(Prescott Park Arts Festival)* **1-3 mi:** Bowling *(Bowl USA 603-431-4292)*, Video Rental *(Atlantic Video 603-431-2331)* **3+ mi:** Golf Course *(Pease Golf Course - Great Bay Golf Course 603-433-1331)*

Provisioning and General Services
Near: Gourmet Shop *(Buon Giorno 603-430-0002)*, Lobster Pound *(Sea Hags Seafood)* **Under 1 mi:** Health Food *(Portsmouth Health Food 603-436-1722)*, Wine/Beer *(Ceres Street Wine Merchants 603-431-2640)*, Liquor Store *(Garys Beverages 603-436-5854)*, Bakery, Green Grocer *(Golden Harvest 439-2113)*, Library, Hardware Store *(Peaveys Hardware 603-436-1123)*, Copies Etc. *(Johnson Printing 439-2567)* **1-3 mi:** Supermarket *(Puffin-Stop 439-6713)*, Fishmonger *(Olde Mill 603-436-4568)*, Post Office, Protestant Church *(North Church)*, Synagogue, Pharmacy *(Osco Drug 439-1966)*, Retail Shops *(Kittery Outlet Stores)*

Transportation
OnCall: Taxi *(Sunshine 363-7600)* **Under 1 mi:** Rental Car *(Budget 603-436-2588)*, InterCity Bus *(Greyhound 603-436-0163)* **Airport:** Portland Int'l. *(55 mi.)*

Medical Services
911 Service **OnCall:** Ambulance **Under 1 mi:** Doctor, Chiropractor, Holistic Services **1-3 mi:** Dentist **Hospital:** Portsmouth Regional 603-436-5110 *(4 mi.)*

Setting -- This small, mostly seasonal, marina is situated on the Kittery side of the Piscataqua River, directly across from Prescott Park. It offers attractive, secure, relatively new, nicely landscaped dockage with views of the Portsmouth waterfront. The facility, part of a remarkably well-maintained condominium complex, is snuggled up next to the Route One bridge directly across from Portsmouth's Strawberry Banke Museum.

Marina Notes -- Limited transient dockage -- call ahead for reservations (the office keeps bankers' hours). New ownership 2000. There are heads, showers and laundry -- all very inviting -- on the first floor of the condo complex. Pump-out is available with advance notice. There is a strong current; take care when approaching and expect some roll. Most services are an easy walk over the bridge in Portsmouth, NH. Warren's Lobster House, a local institution, is down the block - optional outside waterfront dining (Sun-Thu 11:30am-9pm, Fri-Sat 11:30am-10pm).

Notable -- Kittery Outlets, 2.5 miles north, is home to 4 outlet malls - a total of 120 designer outlet stores, plus the Kittery Trading Post and Weathervane Seafood Restaurant. Either take a taxi or call the Outlet, with at least 24 hrs. notice (888 KITTERY), and they'll send their internal Trolley for you. Just across the Route One Bridge is the historic section of Portsmouth, Strawbery Banke Museum, and Prescott Park. Pick up a copy of the Harbor Trail Walking Guide. On the Kittery side, Kittery Historical and Naval Museum is about a mile away (10am-4pm, June-Oct, $3/$1.50).

PHOTOS ON CD-ROM: 9

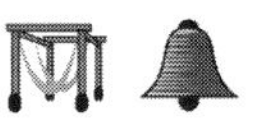

Badger's Island Marina

27 Badgers Island West ; Kittery, ME 03904

Tel: (207) 439-3810 **VHF: Monitor** 9 **Talk** 68
Fax: (603) 431-9557 **Alternate Tel:** n/a
Email: n/a **Web:** n/a
Nearest Town: Portsmouth *(0.5 mi.)* **Tourist Info:** (207) 439-7545

Navigational Information

Lat: 43°04.890' **Long:** 070°45.310' **Tide:** 10 ft. **Current:** 4 kt. **Chart:** 13278
Rep. Depths (*MLW*): Entry 40 ft. **Fuel Dock** n/a **Max Slip/Moor** 40 ft./-
Access: Piscataqua River, past Navy Yard, under bridge - starbord side

Marina Facilities *(In Season/Off Season)*

Fuel: No
Slips: 27 Total, 3 Transient **Max LOA:** 100 ft. **Max Beam:** n/a
Rate *(per ft.)*: **Day** $1.50/Inq. **Week** $8.75 **Month** Inq.
Power: 30 amp Incl., **50 amp** Incl., **100 amp** n/a, **200 amp** n/a
Cable TV: No **Dockside Phone:** No
Dock Type: Long Fingers, Short Fingers, Concrete, Pilings, Floating
Moorings: 0 Total, 0 Transient **Launch:** n/a
Rate: Day n/a **Week** n/a **Month** n/a
Heads: 2 Toilet(s), 2 Shower(s)
Laundry: 1 Washer(s), 1 Dryer(s) **Pay Phones:** No
Pump-Out: OnCall *(Local EPA boat)* **Fee:** n/a **Closed Heads:** No

Marina Operations

Owner/Manager: Darren Lapierre **Dockmaster:** n/a
In-Season: May-Oct 31, 9am-5pm **Off-Season:** n/a
After-Hours Arrival: Take end dock
Reservations: Preferred **Credit Cards:** Cash or Traveler's Checks
Discounts: None
Pets: Welcome **Handicap Access:** Yes, Heads

Marina Services and Boat Supplies

Services - Trash Pick-Up **Communication -** FedEx, AirBorne, UPS, Express Mail **Supplies - OnSite:** Ice *(Block, Cube)*, Ships' Store **Under 1 mi:** Bait/Tackle *(Kittery Trading Post 439-2700)* **1-3 mi:** West Marine *(603-436-8300)*, Marine Discount Store *(Dion's Yacht Yard 439-9582)*

Boatyard Services

OnSite: Railway *(80T)*, Engine mechanic *(gas, diesel)*, Launching Ramp *(by appointment)*, Electrical Repairs, Hull Repairs, Bottom Cleaning, Brightwork, Propeller Repairs **OnCall:** Divers **Near:** Electronic Sales, Electronics Repairs, Compound, Wash & Wax, Yacht Broker. **1-3 mi:** Rigger, Air Conditioning, Refrigeration, Woodworking, Metal Fabrication, Painting, Awlgrip, Total Refits. **Nearest Yard:** Badgers Island Marine Service (207) 439-3810

Restaurants and Accommodations

Near: Restaurant *(Dolphin Striker 603-431-5222, L $7-15, D $15-23)*, *(Porto Bello 603-431-2989, L $9-13, D $12-22)*, *(Weathervane 439-0335, L $3-8, D $5-18)*, *(Warren's Lobster House 439-1630, L $5-8, D $10-15)*, Seafood Shack *(Morrison's Lobsters 439-2501)*, Pizzeria *(Kittery House of Pizza 439-4989)*, Motel *(Gundalow Inn 439-4040)*, Hotel *(Sheraton Harborside 603-431-2300, $175-245)*, Inn/B&B *(Inn at Portsmouth Harbor 439-4040, $95-175)* **Under 1 mi:** Inn/B&B *(Inn at Strawbery Banke 603-436-7242, $85-150)*, *(Sise Inn 603-433-1200, $120-240)*

Recreation and Entertainment

Near: Jogging Paths, Boat Rentals, Sightseeing *(Seafari Charters 439-5068, Port City Lady to Isles of Shoals 439-5070)* **1-3 mi:** Picnic Area *(Ft. McClary)*, Grills, Bowling *(Bowl USA 603-431-4292)*, Museum *(Strawbery Banke, Colonial Dames House 603-430-7968)*, Cultural Attract *(Seacoast Repertory 603-433-4422)* **3+ mi:** Golf Course *(Breakfast Hill Golf Club 603-431-5005, 7 mi.)*

Provisioning and General Services

Near: Gourmet Shop *(Buon Giorno 603-430-0002)*, Health Food, Lobster Pound *(Sea Hags Seafood)*, Library, Hardware Store *(Peavey's Hardware 603-436-1123)*, Copies Etc. *(Johnson Printing 439-2567)* **Under 1 mi:** Wine/Beer *(Ceres Street Wine 603-431-2640)*, Liquor Store *(Gary's Beverages 603-436-5854)*, Fishmonger, Beauty Salon, Dry Cleaners, Bookstore, Pharmacy *(Osco Drug 439-1966)* **1-3 mi:** Supermarket *(Puffin-Stop 439-6713)*, Bank/ATM, Post Office, Protestant Church, Synagogue *(Temple Israel)*, Retail Shops *(Kittery Outlets)*

Transportation

OnCall: Rental Car *(Enterprise 603-433-1177)* **1-3 mi:** Bikes *(Banagans 603-436-0660)* **Airport:** Portland Int'l. *(55 mi.)*

Medical Services

911 Service **OnCall:** Ambulance **Under 1 mi:** Doctor, Chiropractor **1-3 mi:** Dentist, Holistic Services **Hospital:** Portsmouth Regional 603-436-5110 *(3 mi.)*

Setting -- Its location, on Badgers Island in the middle of the Piscataqua River, directly across from the Portsmouth waterfront, puts this marina about equidistant between Kittery, Maine and Portsmouth, New Hampshire. It's surrounded by the shingled, neo-Victorian Badgers Island West condos and the attractive corporate headquarters of Weathervane Seafood restaurants.

Marina Notes -- Limited transient dockage. Dockmaster is off on Mondays and Tuesdays. Currently offices and amenities are in a large floating barge. Warren's Lobster House is a reasonably short walk. Most services are in Portsmouth - an easy walk, south, over the bridge or a more difficult dinghy ride. Big boat and dinghy dockage is available in Portsmouth at the Prescott Park Municipal Docks, part of a lovely park with formal gardens, and home to the famous Prescott Park Arts Festival. Pump-out provided by the local EPA Service.

Notable -- The Strawbery Banke "Museum", a ten-acre restoration of one of Portsmouth's first settlements includes about 45 buildings, from 1695-1850's, and is just over the bridge. Three blocks farther south is the hands-on Children's Museum of Portsmouth (Mon-Sat 10am-5pm, Sun 1-5pm, closed Mon except summer - $4). Isles of Shoals Steamship Co. (800 441-4620) and Portsmouth Harbor Cruises (800 776-0915 $7.50-$15) offer whale watching and tours of Star Island. The 120 store Kittery Outlet Center is about 2.5 miles north - either take a taxi or call the Outlet, with at least 24 hrs. notice (888 KITTERY), and they'll send the Trolley for you.

V. New Hampshire / Massachusetts: The North Shore

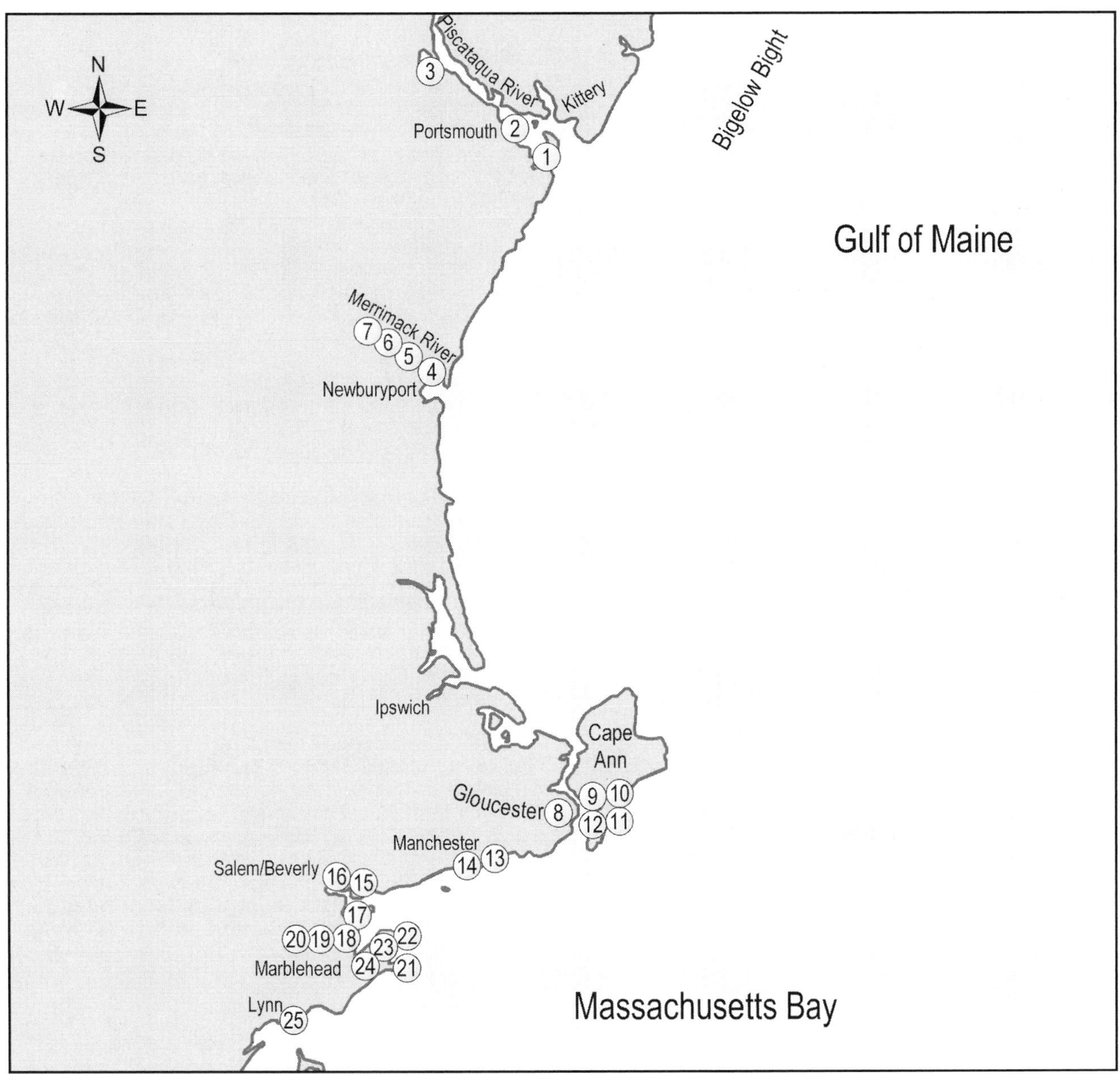

MAP	MARINA	HARBOR	PAGE	MAP	MARINA	HARBOR	PAGE
1	**Wentworth by the Sea Marina**	*Little Harbor*	114	14	**Manchester Marine Corp.**	*Manchester Harbor*	127
2	**Prescott Park Municipal Dock**	*Piscataqua River*	115	15	**Beverly Port Marina**	*Danvers River*	128
3	**Great Bay Marine**	*Piscataqua River*	116	16	**Glover Wharf Municipal Marina**	*Danvers River*	129
4	**Newburyport Waterfront Park Marina**	*Merrimack River*	117	17	**Hawthorne Cove Marina**	*Salem Harbor*	130
5	**Windward Yacht Yard**	*Merrimack River*	118	18	**Pickering Wharf Marina**	*Salem Harbor*	131
6	**Cove Marina**	*Merrimack River*	119	19	**Salem Water Taxi**	*Salem Harbor*	132
7	**Merri-Mar Yacht Basin**	*Merrimack River*	120	20	**Fred J. Dion Yacht Yard**	*Salem Harbor*	133
8	**Cape Ann's Marina Resort**	*Annisquam River*	121	21	**Corinthian Yacht Club**	*Marblehead Harbor*	134
9	**Gloucester Town Landing**	*Gloucester Harbor*	122	22	**Tucker's Wharf Municipal Docks**	*Marblehead Harbor*	135
10	**Pier 7/Enos Marine**	*Gloucester Harbor*	123	23	**Boston Yacht Club**	*Marblehead Harbor*	136
11	**Brown's Yacht Yard, Inc.**	*Gloucester Harbor*	124	24	**Dolphin Yacht Club**	*Marblehead Harbor*	137
12	**Madfish Grille & The Studio**	*Gloucester Harbor*	125	25	**Seaport Landing Marina**	*Lynn Harbor*	138
13	**Crocker's Boat Yard**	*Manchester Harbor*	126				

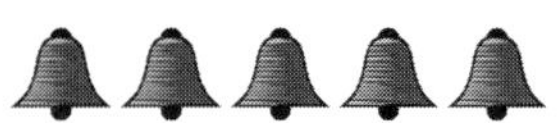

Wentworth by the Sea Marina

PO Box 2079; 116 Morgans Way; New Castle, NH 03854

Tel: (603) 433-5050 **VHF: Monitor** 71 **Talk** 71
Fax: (603) 427-1092 **Alternate Tel:** n/a
Email: Info@wentworthmarina.com **Web:** www.wentworthmarina.com
Nearest Town: Portsmouth *(3 mi.)* **Tourist Info:** (603) 436-1118

Navigational Information

Lat: 43°03.518' **Long:** 070°43.261' **Tide:** 9 ft. **Current:** 2 kt. **Chart:** 13278
Rep. Depths (*MLW*): Entry 10 ft. **Fuel Dock** 12 ft. **Max Slip/Moor** 12 ft./10 ft.
Access: From R "2KR" at Portsmouth Harbor entrance steer 300 degrees

Marina Facilities *(In Season/Off Season)*

Fuel: *Inpep* - Gasoline, Diesel, High-Speed Pumps
Slips: 170 Total, 25 Transient **Max LOA:** 250 ft. **Max Beam:** n/a
Rate *(per ft.)*: **Day** $2.75/$2.50* **Week** $2.50 **Month** Inq.
Power: 30 amp $6, **50 amp** $12, **100 amp** $38, **200 amp** n/a
Cable TV: Yes, $6 Basic package **Dockside Phone:** Yes, $8 Dial 9
Dock Type: Long Fingers, Floating
Moorings: 2 Total, 0 Transient **Launch:** Yes, Dinghy Dock
Rate: Day n/a **Week** n/a **Month** n/a
Heads: 8 Toilet(s), 8 Shower(s) *(with dressing rooms)*, Hair Dryers
Laundry: 5 Washer(s), 5 Dryer(s), Iron, Iron Board **Pay Phones:** Yes, 2
Pump-Out: OnSite, Self Service, 1 Central **Fee:** Free **Closed Heads:** Yes

Marina Operations

Owner/Manager: Pat Kelley **Dockmaster:** Cheryl Strong
In-Season: Jul-Sep 15, 8am-8pm **Off-Season:** Oct-Jun, 8am-5pm
After-Hours Arrival: Contact Security on Ch. 71
Reservations: Preferred **Credit Cards:** Visa/MC, Amex
Discounts: None
Pets: Welcome, Dog Walk Area **Handicap Access:** Yes, Heads, Docks

Marina Services and Boat Supplies

Services - Docking Assistance, Concierge, Room Service to the Boat, Security, Trash Pick-Up, Dock Carts, Megayacht Facilities, 3 Phase **Communication -** Mail & Package Hold, Phone Messages, Fax in/out, FedEx, AirBorne, UPS, Express Mail *(Sat Del)* **Supplies - OnSite:** Ice *(Cube)*, Ships' Store **1-3 mi:** West Marine *(436-8300)*, Marine Discount Store *(Jackson's Hardware & Marine 439-1133)*, Bait/Tackle *(Kittery Trading Post 439-2700)*, Propane, CNG *(H And H 363-1213)*

Boatyard Services

OnSite: Bottom Cleaning, Brightwork, Air Conditioning, Refrigeration, Divers, Compound, Wash & Wax, Interior Cleaning **Near:** Yacht Broker. **Under 1 mi:** Launching Ramp. **1-3 mi:** Travelift, Engine mechanic *(gas, diesel)*, Electrical Repairs, Electronics Repairs, Hull Repairs, Rigger, Propeller Repairs. **Nearest Yard:** Dion's Yacht Yard (207) 439-9582

Restaurants and Accommodations

OnSite: Restaurant *(Joseph's 436-1661, D $19-32, Tue-Sun 5-10pm)*, Seafood Shack *(Shore Bites 431-8699, L $3-10, D $4-10)*, Hotel *(Wentworth-by-The-Sea Marriott opened spring 2003)* **Near:** Snack Bar *(Ice House L $2-9, D $2-9)* **Under 1 mi:** Restaurant *(BG's Boathouse 431-1074, dockage for dinghies)* **1-3 mi:** Restaurant *(Dolphin Striker 431-5222, L $7-15, D $15-23)*, *(Dunfey's 433-3111, L $5-15, D $18-35)*, Motel *(Comfort Inn 433-3338, $50-140)*, *(Anchorage 431-8111, $55-150)*, Hotel *(Sheraton 431-2300, $175-245)*, Inn/B&B *(Sise Inn 433-1200, $120-240)*

Recreation and Entertainment

OnSite: Heated Pool, Picnic Area, Grills, Tennis Courts *(complimentary)*, Jogging Paths, Fishing Charter, Video Rental **Near:** Beach *(via dinghy)*, Golf Course *(Wentworth by the Sea Country Club, private; public courses nearby)*, Roller Blade/Bike Paths **Under 1 mi:** Dive Shop, Volleyball, Fitness Center, Boat Rentals *(Kayaks)*, Video Arcade, Park, Sightseeing *(Odiorne Point State Park - Seacoast Science Center 436-8043)* **1-3 mi:** Playground, Movie Theater *(Hoyts 436-3456)*, Museum *(Wentworth Coolidge Historic Mansion 436-6607)* **3+ mi:** Cultural Attract *(Portsmouth, 5 mi.)*

Provisioning and General Services

OnSite: Laundry, Newsstand **OnCall:** Beauty Salon, Retail Shops **Under 1 mi:** Convenience Store, Meat Market, Post Office, Dry Cleaners, Bookstore *(Gulliver's Travel 431-5556)*, Florist **1-3 mi:** Gourmet Shop *(Buon Giorno 430-0002)*, Delicatessen *(Bread Box 436-1631)*, Bakery, Farmers' Market *(Sat 8am-1pm)*, Bank/ATM, Catholic Church, Protestant Church, Synagogue, Library *(431-6773)*, Barber Shop, Pharmacy *(Green's 436-0010)*, Hardware Store, Clothing Store **3+ mi:** Supermarket *(Market Basket 430-2160 or Hannaford 436-6669 4 mi., 4 mi.)*, Wine/Beer *(South Street and Vine 430-9342 , 5 mi.)*, Fishmonger *(5 mi.)*, Buying Club *(BJ's, 5 mi.)*, Copies Etc. *(Mail Boxes Etc. 433-2050, 4 mi.)*

Transportation

OnSite: Courtesy Car/Van *(2 cars, 1 van)*, Rental Car *(Enterprise 433-1177)*, Taxi *(Coastal Limo 436-5151)* **Near:** Local Bus *(Seacoast Trolley)* **1-3 mi:** Rail, Ferry Service *(Isle of Shoals)* **Airport:** Pease/Logan Int'l. *(5 mi./55 mi.)*

Medical Services

911 Service **Under 1 mi:** Ambulance **1-3 mi:** Doctor, Dentist, Chiropractor, Holistic Services **Hospital:** Portsmouth 436-5110 *(6 mi.)*

PHOTOS ON CD-ROM: 9

Setting -- In Little Harbor, just at the mouth of the Piscataqua River, is this impeccably managed and maintained facility. Located in the quaint village of New Castle, it's surrounded by an attractive high end development. Looming above the marina is the venerable 1890 Wentworth-by-the-Sea Hotel, one of the most recognizable images on the New Hampshire coast, now the Marriott Wentworth-by-the-Sea Grand Hotel and Spa. Historic Portsmouth is minutes away.

Marina Notes -- *5 nights+ $2.50/ft.. 51'+ $3.50/ft., 5 nights+ $3.25. Off season $2.50/2.25, 51' $3.25/3.00. 100 amp 3 phase. Moorings no longer available for transients. 15 passenger courtesy van shuttles guests to Portsmouth, plus 2 courtesy cars. Highly service oriented: concierge service, dock hands, guide boats greet and escort incoming vessels. Book exchange, courtesy phone, wireless internet to boats - available for a fee. Shore Bites on boardwalk, all home-made: B 7:30-11am, L 11am-3pm. Joseph's also onsite for waterfront high-end dining - Sunset Prix fixe Supper 4-5:30pm, $14-19; D 6-10pm, $19-32. Bar menu $4-11. (Joseph's will be renamed in Summer 2003.) Tent on Boardwalk for large groups. 2002 new marble & granite heads, power posts & fuel line.

Notable -- Pool, tennis, restaurants. Annual bluefish, striped bass, tuna tournaments. All of New Castle and Portsmouth (including beaches) accessible on the Seacoast Trolley - stops at the marina half past every hour, 10am-5pm, and makes a 17 mi. loop of the area ($5/2.50 for the day) Mid June-Lab Day. Strawbery Banke, Prescott Park. New Castle Island is good biking country. The new 170 room Marriott Wentworth-by-the-Sea Grand Hotel opened in May 2003. It offers a full 6,000 sq. ft. spa, plus two new restaurants and two bars. Expect some construction during 2003 season - hotel and condo developments.

Navigational Information

Lat: 43°04.658' **Long:** 070°45.121' **Tide:** 6 ft. **Current:** 9 kt. **Chart:** 13278
Rep. Depths (*MLW*): Entry 10 ft. **Fuel Dock** n/a **Max Slip/Moor** 10 ft./-
Access: Piscataqua River past Goat Island, just east of the Memorial Bridge

Marina Facilities *(In Season/Off Season)*

Fuel: *Fishermen's Co-op, nearby* - Diesel
Slips: 16 Total, 16 Transient **Max LOA:** 55 ft. **Max Beam:** 16 ft.
Rate *(per ft.)*: **Day** $1.00* **Week** n/a **Month** n/a
Power: 30 amp Inq., **50 amp** n/a, **100 amp** n/a, **200 amp** n/a
Cable TV: No **Dockside Phone:** No
Dock Type: Wood, Long Fingers, Concrete, Floating
Moorings: 0 Total, 0 Transient **Launch:** n/a
Rate: Day n/a **Week** n/a **Month** n/a
Heads: 7 Toilet(s)
Laundry: None **Pay Phones:** Yes
Pump-Out: No **Fee:** n/a **Closed Heads:** No

Marina Operations

Owner/Manager: Michael Warhurst **Dockmaster:** Joan Diemer
In-Season: May-Oct, 9am-5pm **Off-Season:** Oct-May, Closed
After-Hours Arrival: n/a
Reservations: Yes, Preferred **Credit Cards:** None. Cash or advance check
Discounts: None
Pets: No **Handicap Access:** Yes, Heads, Docks

Prescott Park Municipal Dock

PO Box 1103; Shaw Bldg., Marcy Street; Portsmouth, NH 03802

Tel: (603) 431-8748 **VHF: Monitor** 9 **Talk** n/a
Fax: (603) 436-1034 **Alternate Tel:** n/a
Email: n/a **Web:** www.portsmouthnh.com
Nearest Town: Portsmouth *(0 mi.)* **Tourist Info:** (603) 436-1118

Marina Services and Boat Supplies

Services - Docking Assistance, Trash Pick-Up **Supplies - Near:** Ice *(Block, Cube)* **Under 1 mi:** Ships' Store *(Navtronics 436-2544)*, Propane *(Sea 3 431-5990)* **1-3 mi:** West Marine *(436-8300)*, Boat/US, Bait/Tackle *(Kittery Trading Post 207-439-2700)*

Boatyard Services

Under 1 mi: Electronic Sales, Electronics Repairs. **1-3 mi:** Railway, Engine mechanic *(gas, diesel)*, Electrical Repairs, Rigger, Brightwork, Air Conditioning, Refrigeration. **Nearest Yard:** Dion's (207) 439-9582

Restaurants and Accommodations

Near: Restaurant *(Library Restaurant 431-5202, L $6-12, D $12-25, Rockingham House)*, *(Metro American Bistro 436-0521, L $6-11, D $12-24, live jazz Fri & Sat)*, *(Café Mediterrano 427-5563, L $5-13, D $8-19)*, *(Poco's Cantina 431-5967, L $8-20, D $8-20)*, *(Chiangmai 433-1289, L $7-16, D $7-16)*, Lite Fare *(Geno's Chowder & Sandwich 427-2070)*, Inn/B&B *(Sise Inn 433-1200, $120-240)*, *(Governor's House 427-5140)*, *(Inn at Strawbery Banke 436-7242, $135-150)*, *(Bow Street Inn 433-2680, $130-175)* **Under 1 mi:** Restaurant *(Dolphin Striker 431-5222, L $7-15, D $15-23)*, Pizzeria *(Joe's New York Pizza 431-1200)*, Hotel *(Harbors Edge 431-2300)*, *(Sheraton Harborside 559-2600, $135-245)*

Recreation and Entertainment

OnSite: Playground, Special Events *(Prescott Park Arts Festival 436-2848)* **Near:** Jogging Paths, Fishing Charter *(Sushi Hunter 231-4662)*, Video Rental *(Atlantic Video 431-2331)*, Museum *(Strawbery Banke 433-1100, Star Island, Children's Museum 436-3853 - engagingly illuminates the area's maritime history)*, Cultural Attract *(Seacoast Repertory Theatre 433-4472)*, Sightseeing *(Isles of Shoals Steamship Co. 800-441-4620, 431-5500)* **Under 1 mi:** Picnic Area, Bowling *(Bowl O Rama 436-0504)*, Park *(Albacore, Portsmouth's Maritime Museum - centerpiece is U.S.S. Albacore - a 205 ft. decommissioned '53 submarine)* **1-3 mi:** Movie Theater *(Hoyts 436-3456)*

Provisioning and General Services

Near: Gourmet Shop *(Stonewall Kitchen 422-7303)*, Delicatessen, Health Food *(Portsmouth Health Food 436-1722)*, Liquor Store, Bakery, Bank/ATM, Post Office, Catholic Church, Protestant Church, Library *(427-1540, Internet)*, Beauty Salon *(Ceres 436-6518)*, Bookstore, Pharmacy *(CVS 431-0231)*, Newsstand, Hardware Store *(Peavey's 436-1123)*, Clothing Store, Retail Shops, Copies Etc. *(Jiffy Copy Center 436-8286)* **Under 1 mi:** Supermarket *(Hannaford 436-6669)*, Wine/Beer *(Ceres Street 431-2640)*, Farmers' Market *(8am-1pm Sat Pleasant St. & Junkins Ave.)*, Fishmonger *(Olde Mill 436-4568)*, Lobster Pound, Synagogue, Dry Cleaners, Florist

Transportation

OnCall: Taxi *(Blue Star Taxi 436-2774)* **Near:** Local Bus *(Coast Trolley 743-5777)*, InterCity Bus *(Trailways 800-258-7111, Greyhound-Vermont Transit 436-0163)* **Under 1 mi:** Bikes *(Papa Wheelies 427-2060)*, Rental Car *(Budget 436-2588)* **Airport:** Pease/Logan Int'l. *(4 mi./55 mi.)*

Medical Services

911 Service **OnCall:** Ambulance **Near:** Chiropractor *(Grazier Chiropractic)* **Under 1 mi:** Holistic Services **1-3 mi:** Doctor *(Seapoint Family Practice 207-439-2007)*, Dentist, Veterinarian **Hospital:** Portsmouth Regional 436-5110 *(3.5 mi.)*

Setting -- Situated in the heart of historic, picturesque downtown Portsmouth, in Prescott Park - a lovely promenade with formal gardens, fountains, and more than 500 varieties of annuals - promising unrestrained color. It's an ideally located base for touring this fascinating, enlightened "big" small city. Prescott Park is adjacent to the Strawbery Banke Restoration and within easy walking distance of shops, services, charming Bow Street, and Market Square. The docks sit right on the fast moving Piscataqua River with views of the Portsmouth Navy Shipyard and Kittery Landing. Dozens of restaurants, cruises, and tours are nearby.

Marina Notes -- *Dockage is flat-rate: under 20' $20, 21-30' $25, 31-40' $30, 41-50' $40, over 51' $50. No boats larger than 55 feet, and only 2 spots this size. 72-hour limit on stays. Reservation must be paid in advance by check or cash. Hourly tie-up during day: 20' $1, 21-30' $2, 31-40' $3, 41-50' $4, over 50' $5. Second set of docks 2002. New 30 amp pedestals on both sets. Wide open to the river and the fast-moving current; bring extra fenders. Only heads are those in the park - open dawn to dusk. No pets in the Park. Post 9/11, the Navy Yard has enforced speed restrictions reducing wake wash (and rolling).

Notable -- Adjacent Strawbery Banke "Museum", a ten-acre restoration of one of Portsmouth's first settlements, includes 45 buildings, from 1695-1850's -- nine of which are restored with period furniture. It offers many activities, tours and special events (April-Nov, 7 days, 10am-5pm - 2 days $12/8, family $28). Onsite Prescott Park Arts Festival is a summer-long celebration of the arts featuring outdoor theatre, music, dance, children's performances, and special events -- Jazz, Folk and Chowder and Chili Festivals. The hands-on Children's Museum (Mon-Sat 10am-5pm, Sun 1-5pm, $4/3) is 3 blocks east.

PHOTOS ON CD-ROM: 9

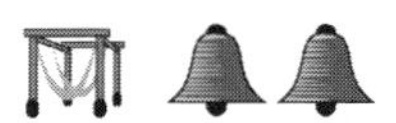

Great Bay Marine

61 Beane Lane; Portsmouth, NH 03801

Tel: (603) 436-5299 **VHF: Monitor** 16 **Talk** n/a
Fax: (603) 436-9834 **Alternate Tel:** n/a
Email: email@greatbaymarine.com **Web:** www.greatbaymarine.com
Nearest Town: Portsmouth *(5 mi.)* **Tourist Info:** (603) 436-1118

Navigational Information

Lat: 43°06.930' **Long:** 070°50.113' **Tide:** 6 ft. **Current:** 9 kt. **Chart:** 13283
Rep. Depths (*MLW*): Entry 30 ft. **Fuel Dock** n/a **Max Slip/Moor** 6 ft./-
Access: About 6 miles from mouth of the Piscataqua River

Marina Facilities *(In Season/Off Season)*

Fuel: *93 Octane* - Gasoline, Diesel
Slips: 125 Total, 9 Transient **Max LOA:** 50 ft. **Max Beam:** n/a
Rate *(per ft.)*: **Day** $2.00* **Week** Inq. **Month** n/a
Power: 30 amp Incl., **50 amp** Incl., **100 amp** n/a, **200 amp** n/a
Cable TV: No **Dockside Phone:** No
Dock Type: Wood, Long Fingers, Pilings, Alongside, Floating, Fixed
Moorings: 90 Total, 10 Transient **Launch:** n/a, Dinghy Dock (Yes)
Rate: Day $15. **Week** Inq. **Month** Inq.
Heads: 8 Toilet(s), 4 Shower(s) *(with dressing rooms)*
Laundry: 2 Washer(s), 2 Dryer(s) **Pay Phones:** Yes, 2
Pump-Out: OnSite, Self Service, 1 Central **Fee:** n/a **Closed Heads:** No

Marina Operations

Owner/Manager: Sandy Hislop **Dockmaster:** n/a
In-Season: May-Nov 11, 8am-4:30pm **Off-Season:** Nov-May, 8am-4:30pm
After-Hours Arrival: Call ahead
Reservations: Yes, Preferred **Credit Cards:** Visa/MC, Dscvr
Discounts: None
Pets: Welcome **Handicap Access:** Yes, Heads, Docks

Marina Services and Boat Supplies

Services - Docking Assistance, Security *(24 Hrs., Live onsite)*, Trash Pick-Up, Dock Carts **Communication -** Mail & Package Hold, Phone Messages, FedEx, AirBorne, UPS, Express Mail *(Sat Del)* **Supplies - OnSite:** Ice *(Block, Cube)*, Ships' Store **Under 1 mi:** Propane **1-3 mi:** Bait/Tackle **3+ mi:** West Marine *(436-8300)*, Boat/US *(12 mi.)*

Boatyard Services

OnSite: Travelift *(36T)*, Forklift *(15T)*, Crane, Engine mechanic *(gas, diesel)*, Launching Ramp *(Fully paved)*, Electrical Repairs, Electronic Sales, Electronics Repairs, Hull Repairs, Rigger, Bottom Cleaning, Brightwork, Air Conditioning, Refrigeration, Divers, Compound, Wash & Wax, Interior Cleaning, Propeller Repairs, Woodworking, Inflatable Repairs, Painting, Awlgrip, Total Refits **OnCall:** Life Raft Service, Metal Fabrication **Dealer for:** Avon, Honda, Yanmar, Westerbeke, Volvo, Mercruiser. **Member:** ABBRA, ABYC - 3 Certified Tech(s), Other Certifications: Honda, DMC, Mercruiser, Yanmar **Yard Rates:** $40-60/hr., Haul & Launch $5/ft each way *(blocking incl.)*, Power Wash $3/ft., Bottom Paint $15-16/ft. *(paint included)* **Storage:** On-Land Outside $27/ft. Inside $55/ft.*

Restaurants and Accommodations

OnSite: Restaurant *(Currants Café & Grille 430-8565, award winning small café; everything is home-made)* **1-3 mi:** Inn/B&B *(The Inn at Newington 431-0777)* **3+ mi:** Restaurant *(Redhook Ale Brewery 430-8600, 3 mi.)*, *(Bugaboo Creek Steak House 422-0921, 3 mi.)*, *(Plum Crazy 422-7586, 3 mi.)*, Motel *(Hampton Inn 431-6111, 3 mi.)*, Hotel *(Courtyard Portsmouth 436-2121, 4 mi.)*

Recreation and Entertainment

OnSite: Picnic Area, Grills, Group Fishing Boat **Under 1 mi:** Fitness Center, Jogging Paths, Horseback Riding, Video Rental, Park **1-3 mi:** Beach, Dive Shop, Movie Theater *(Hoyts 431-4200)* **3+ mi:** Golf Course *(Pease Golf Course, Great Bay Golf Course 433-1331, 5 mi.)*, Special Events *(Portsmouth Jazz Festival, 5 mi.)*

Provisioning and General Services

Near: Catholic Church **Under 1 mi:** Convenience Store, Wine/Beer, Fishmonger, Bank/ATM, Newsstand **1-3 mi:** Delicatessen, Liquor Store, Bakery, Post Office, Protestant Church, Synagogue, Beauty Salon, Barber Shop, Dry Cleaners, Laundry, Pharmacy *(Wal-Mart Pharmacy 433-6129)*, Florist, Clothing Store, Retail Shops, Department Store *(Wal-Mart)* **3+ mi:** Supermarket *(Hannaford 436-6669, 5 mi.)*, Library *(427-1540, Internet access, 6 mi.)*, Bookstore *(Barnes & Noble 422-7733, 4 mi.)*, Hardware Store *(Home Depot 422-0855, 4 mi.)*, Copies Etc. *(OfficeMax 431-2920, 4 mi.)*

Transportation

OnCall: Rental Car *(Enterprise 433-1177, National 334-6000 3 mi.)*, Taxi *(Sunshine 431-4555)* **Airport:** Pease/Logan Int'l. *(2mi./55mi.)*

Medical Services

911 Service **1-3 mi:** Doctor, Dentist, Chiropractor, Holistic Services, Ambulance **Hospital:** Portsmouth Regional 436-5110 *(1-3 mi)*

PHOTOS ON CD-ROM: 5

Setting -- As the Piscataqua makes a westerly bend, the fixed General Sullivan Bridge, with a 46-foot vertical clearance, spans the river. Great Bay Marine is a quarter mile west, surrounded by the unspoiled vistas of pristine Great Bay, a well regarded fishing and birding destination. The waterside views from the docks are of the islands, the bridge, and Durham in the distance. Many shops and malls are within a couple of miles.

Marina Notes -- Originally used as a source of gravel for the J.P. Griffin Construction Company. In 1956, the Griffin Family converted the site to Great Bay Marine and still owns and operates it. Dedicated, fully enclosed fiberglass and paint shops. One of the largest Avon Inflatables dealers. Specializes in engine repowering. Pump-out & recycling. 34 acres of boat storage. *Storage prices include haul, launch and bottom wash. Onsite is the popular little café - Currants - mostly vegetarian, all home-made, with tables inside and outside, overlooking the docks. Summer hours: B Mon-Sat 7:30-11am, Sun 7:30am-2pm; L Mon-Sat 11am-3pm (cash only).

Notable -- On the eastern shore is the Great Bay National Wildlife Refuge, home to an abundance of wildlife, including some endangered species such as the American Bald Eagle, Peregrine Falcon and the Osprey -- providing perfect opportunities for hiking, birding and picnicking. The warm waters of Great Bay make for very good fishing. The lanes and byways of residential, picturesque 19thC Newington village are good for walks or runs. Historic and charming Portsmouth, with all its restaurants, services, activities, cultural attractions and tourist sites, is a short cab ride away.

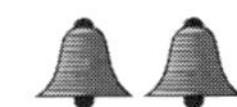

Navigational Information

Lat: 42°48.754' **Long:** 070°52.125' **Tide:** 10 ft. **Current:** 6 kt. **Chart:** 13274
Rep. Depths (*MLW*): Entry n/a **Fuel Dock** n/a **Max Slip/Moor** 20 ft./20 ft.
Access: Merrimack River, first facility to port, about 3 nm from the mouth

Marina Facilities *(In Season/Off Season)*

Fuel: No
Slips: 15 Total, 15 Transient **Max LOA:** 100 ft. **Max Beam:** n/a
Rate *(per ft.)*: **Day** $0.50* **Week** n/a **Month** n/a
Power: 30 amp n/a, **50 amp** n/a, **100 amp** n/a, **200 amp** n/a
Cable TV: No **Dockside Phone:** No
Dock Type: Alongside, Floating
Moorings: 4 Total, 4 Transient **Launch:** None
Rate: Day $15 **Week** n/a **Month** n/a
Heads: 1 Toilet(s)
Laundry: None **Pay Phones:** Yes
Pump-Out: Full Service, Self Service, 1 Port **Fee:** Free **Closed Heads:** Yes

Marina Operations

Owner/Manager: Ralph Steele (Harbormaster) **Dockmaster:** A. Chaisson
In-Season: Mem-LabDay, 9am-6pm **Off-Season:** MidJun-ColDay
After-Hours Arrival: n/a
Reservations: First come, first served **Credit Cards:** Cash
Discounts: None
Pets: Welcome **Handicap Access:** No

Newburyport Waterfront Park

Merrimac Street; Newburyport, MA 01950

Tel: (978) 462-3476 **VHF: Monitor** 12 **Talk** 12
Fax: n/a **Alternate Tel:** n/a
Email: harbormaster@cityofnewburyport.com **Web:** n/a
Nearest Town: Newburyport *(0 mi.)* **Tourist Info:** (978) 462-6680

Marina Services and Boat Supplies

Supplies - Under 1 mi: Bait/Tackle *(Bridge Rd Bait & Tackle 465-3221)*, Propane *(Lunt True Value)* **1-3 mi:** Marine Discount Store *(Diamond Marine 463-0440)* **3+ mi:** Boat/US *(603-474-7170 , 6 mi.)*

Boatyard Services

Nearest Yard: Windward Yacht Yard (978) 462-6500

Restaurants and Accommodations

Near: Restaurant *(Ten Center Street 462-6255, L $6-15, D $7-23)*, *(Grog 465-3811, L $6-15, D $6-15)*, *(Glenn's 465-2555, D $18-23)*, *(Purple Onion 465-9600)*, *(Aquatini 463-8266)*, *(The Rockfish 465-6601, D $6-18)*, *(Ciro's 463-3335, L $7-13)*, Inn/B&B *(Essex Street Inn 465-3148, $90-130)*, *(Clark Currier Inn 465-8363, $95-160)*, *(Windsor House 462-3778, $130-150)*, *(Garrison Inn 499-8500, $105-120)* **Under 1 mi:** Restaurant *(Rossi's 499-0240)*, *(Tannery 463-9797)* **1-3 mi:** Hotel *(Fairfield Inn by Marriott 388-3400)*

Recreation and Entertainment

OnSite: Fishing Charter, Group Fishing Boat, Park *(Waterfront Park)*, Sightseeing *(Newburyport Whale Watch 499-0832; Yankee Clipper Tours 462-9316)*, Special Events *(Yankee Homecoming - late July)* **OnCall:** Roller Blade/Bike Paths **Near:** Video Rental *(Express Video 463-3066)*, Museum *(Custom House Maritime Museum 462-8681$3/2, Cushing House Museum 462-2681 $4/1.50, a 21 room Federalist Mansion)* **Under 1 mi:** Beach, Fitness Center *(Fitness Factory 465-2546)*, Boat Rentals *(Adventure Learning Kayaks 800-649-9728 at Plum Island)* **1-3 mi:** Horseback Riding *(Maudslay Park)*, Movie Theater *(Screening Room 462-3456)*, Cultural Attract *(Theater in the Open)* **3+ mi:** Golf Course *(Amesbury Golf & Country Club 388-5153, 5 mi.)*

Provisioning and General Services

Near: Gourmet Shop *(Gourmet Pantry 462-1646)*, Post Office, Catholic Church, Protestant Church, Synagogue, Retail Shops *(The Tannery)* **Under 1 mi:** Convenience Store *(White Hen Pantry 463-3057)*, Delicatessen *(Fruit Basket 462-9164)*, Liquor Store *(New England Wine & Spirits 462-2131)*, Library *(465-4428)*, Bookstore *(Eureka 465-9359)*, Pharmacy *(Lynch 462-2232)*, Hardware Store *(Lunt True Value 465-6650)* **3+ mi:** Supermarket *(Shaw's 462-7121, 4 mi.)*

Transportation

OnCall: Rental Car *(Enterprise 499-0021)*, Taxi *(Walkeys Livery 462-7722)* **Under 1 mi:** Bikes *(Northeast Bikes 465-8099)*, InterCity Bus *(Trailways)*, Rail *(commuter link to Boston)* **Airport:** Pease/Logan Int'l. *(20 mi./55 mi.)*

Medical Services

911 Service **OnCall:** Ambulance **Under 1 mi:** Doctor *(Lydia 463-7420)*, Dentist **Hospital:** Anna Jacques 463-1000 *(1 mi.)*

Setting -- The first facility to port as the Merrimack River approaches Newburyport. The municipal city marina is directly in the center of this restored and picturesque early Federalist town - just east of the Park, where you can find a convenient Information Booth.

Marina Notes -- *NOTE: The $0.50/ft. overnight dockage rate is only for 7pm-7am. The City has separate fees for daytime, 7am-7pm: 21-40' $2/hr., 41-60' $3/hr., over 60' $5/hr. Overnight transients must pay the appropriate daytime fees in addition to the overnight rate. There is also a maximum 72 hour tie-up. New docks built during the 2002 season, including new pedestals. Yellow moorings. Dinghy dock is in a deep rectangular basin that cuts right into the Waterfront Park. Free pump-out available onsite, week-ends only. For fuel, see Hilton's or Windward Yacht Yard up the river. All distances are measured from the main docks rather than from the dinghy dock.

Notable -- A newly constructed, attractive waterfront boardwalk makes the city easily accessible to boaters and the harbor front to the citizenry. The charming downtown shopping district is a couple of short blocks away. About a dozen restaurants are within easy reach. The 1835 Custom House Maritime Museum is virtually onsite. The Information Booth can provide a walking tour of Historic Newburyport, which boasts the largest stock of American Federalist brick buildings in the state. Particularly interesting are the houses along High Street, built by early sea captains and ship owners. 4662-acre Parker River Wildlife Refuge on Plum Island (at the mouth of the river) offers extraordinary bird watching as well as a wide range of habitats.

PHOTOS ON CD-ROM: 9

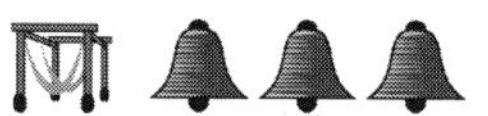

Windward Yacht Yard, Inc.

McKay's Wharf; Newburyport, MA 01950

Tel: (978) 462-6500 **VHF: Monitor** 9 **Talk** 11
Fax: (978) 462-3484 **Alternate Tel:** n/a
Email: n/a **Web:** n/a
Nearest Town: Newburyport *(0.25 mi.)* **Tourist Info:** (978) 462-6680

Navigational Information

Lat: 42°48.817' **Long:** 070°52.412' **Tide:** 9 ft. **Current:** 3 kt. **Chart:** 13274
Rep. Depths (*MLW*): Entry 10 ft. **Fuel Dock** 12 ft. **Max Slip/Moor** 12 ft./12 ft.
Access: 2nd docks after City Landing; to port just before bascule bridge

Marina Facilities *(In Season/Off Season)*

Fuel: Gasoline, Diesel
Slips: 150 Total, 5 Transient **Max LOA:** 65 ft. **Max Beam:** 25 ft.
Rate *(per ft.)*: **Day** $1.50 **Week** n/a **Month** n/a
Power: 30 amp $12, **50 amp** $20, **100 amp** n/a, **200 amp** n/a
Cable TV: Yes Some **Dockside Phone:** No
Dock Type: Composition, Fixed
Moorings: 15 Total, 2 Transient **Launch:** n/a, Dinghy Dock
Rate: Day $20 **Week** n/a **Month** n/a
Heads: 9 Toilet(s), Shower(s)
Laundry: 1 Washer(s), 1 Dryer(s) **Pay Phones:** No
Pump-Out: OnCall **Fee:** n/a **Closed Heads:** Yes

Marina Operations

Owner/Manager: Butch Frangipane **Dockmaster:** Fletcher Wasson
In-Season: May-Oct 15, 9am-5pm **Off-Season:** Oct 15-May 1, 9am-5pm
After-Hours Arrival: Call in advance
Reservations: Yes, Preferred **Credit Cards:** Cash or check
Discounts: None
Pets: Welcome, Dog Walk Area **Handicap Access:** Yes, Heads, Docks

Marina Services and Boat Supplies

Services - Docking Assistance, Concierge, Security, Trash Pick-Up, Dock Carts **Communication -** Mail & Package Hold, Phone Messages, Fax in/out, FedEx, AirBorne, UPS, Express Mail *(Sat Del)* **Supplies - OnSite:** Ice *(Block, Cube)* **Near:** Ships' Store, Bait/Tackle **Under 1 mi:** Propane *(Lunt & Kellys 465-6650)* **3+ mi:** Boat/US *(603-474-7170, 7 mi.)*, CNG

Boatyard Services

OnSite: Travelift *(25/80T)*, Engine mechanic *(gas, diesel)*, Electrical Repairs, Electronic Sales, Electronics Repairs, Hull Repairs, Canvas Work, Bottom Cleaning, Brightwork, Divers, Compound, Wash & Wax, Woodworking, Upholstery, Awlgrip, Yacht Design, Total Refits **OnCall:** Rigger, Sail Loft, Interior Cleaning, Propeller Repairs, Inflatable Repairs, Life Raft Service, Yacht Building **Near:** Air Conditioning, Refrigeration. **Yard Rates:** $50/hr., Haul & Launch $5/ft. *(blocking $2/ft.)*, Power Wash $2/ft., Bottom Paint $5/ft.

Restaurants and Accommodations

OnSite: Restaurant *(Michael's Harborside 462-7785, L $6-12, D $7-17)*, *(Black Cow 499-8811)* **Near:** Restaurant *(Scandia 462-6271, L $5-8, D $14-24)*, *(The Purple Onion 465-9600)*, *(Bluewater Café 462-1088)*, *(Chef's Harvest 463-1775)*, *(Glenn's Galley 465-3811, D $18-23)*, *(Mr. India 465-8600, L $7-12, D $7-12)*, Pizzeria *(Nicks 465-9853)*, Motel *(Garrison Inn 499-8500, $100-195)*, *(Country Garden Motel 948-7773)*, *(Michael's Oceanfront 465-6202)* **Under 1 mi:** Inn/B&B *(Essex St. Inn 465-3148, $85-175)*

Recreation and Entertainment

OnSite: Picnic Area **Near:** Fitness Center, Jogging Paths, Boat Rentals, Roller Blade/Bike Paths, Video Rental, Cultural Attract *(Firehouse Center 462-7336 $12-22)* **Under 1 mi:** Tennis Courts, Fishing Charter *(Atlantis Charters 463-7765)*, Sightseeing *(Newburyport Whale Watch 499-0832)*, Special Events **1-3 mi:** Beach *(Plum Island by dinghy)*, Movie Theater, Video Arcade, Museum *(Custom House Museum 462-8681 $3/2, Cushing House 462-2681 $4/1)* **3+ mi:** Dive Shop, Golf Course *(Amesbury Golf & Country Club 388-5153 , 5 mi.)*, Bowling *(Leos Super Bowl 388-2010, 5 mi.)*

Provisioning and General Services

Near: Convenience Store *(White Hen Pantry 463-3057)*, Gourmet Shop, Delicatessen, Health Food, Wine/Beer *(Leary's 462-4451)*, Farmers' Market, Fishmonger, Lobster Pound, Meat Market, Bank/ATM, Post Office, Catholic Church, Protestant Church, Synagogue, Library *(465-4428)*, Beauty Salon, Barber Shop, Dry Cleaners, Laundry, Bookstore *(Eureka 465-9359)*, Pharmacy *(Lynch 462-2232, CVS)*, Newsstand, Florist, Retail Shops, Department Store, Copies Etc. **Under 1 mi:** Liquor Store *(New England 462-2131)*, Bakery, Hardware Store *(Lunt True Value 462-2951)* **3+ mi:** Supermarket *(Shaw's 462-7121, 6 mi.)*

Transportation

OnCall: Rental Car *(Enterprise 499-0021)*, Taxi *(Port Taxi 465-2333)* **Near:** Local Bus, InterCity Bus **Under 1 mi:** Rail *(Commuter link to Boston)* **Airport:** Pease/Logan Int'l. *(20 mi./50 mi.)*

Medical Services

911 Service **OnCall:** Ambulance **Near:** Doctor, Dentist, Chiropractor, Holistic Services **Hospital:** Anna Jacques 463-1000 *(1 mi.)*

Setting -- Just past the town docks, on the port side, Windward is the closest full-service facility to the center of the historic, restored seaport town of Newburyport. It is on the "ocean-side" of the bascule bridge. Landside views are of an attractive, well-maintained marina; waterside views are across and down the river.

Marina Notes -- Under the same ownership for 28 years. Full service yacht yard can haul up to 80T and 100 ft. Almost any service you'll need is right here. Michael's Harborside Restaurant, onsite, offers seafood in a casual atmosphere -- inside or on the deck; almost onsite is the Black Cow Tap & Grill for fine dining overlooking the harbor. Nice heads, showers, and laundry. Very good docks, also moorings.

Notable -- It's a very short walk to the city riverfront boardwalk and to downtown Newburyport with all its restaurants, historic sites, and retail shops. Walking tours of High Street and the historic district are available from the Tourist Info kiosk at the edge of Waterfront Park. Whale Watch trips, group fishing boats, and harbor cruises are all nearby on the "boardwalk". In addition to the shops on Pleasant, Inn and State Streets, there is an indoor mall located in The Tannery, the site of an old mill (Independent & Water Sts.). Newburyport is the birthplace of the U.S. Coastguard. Maudslay Art Center - theater in the open - is in Maudslay Park.

Navigational Information

Lat: 42°49.144' **Long:** 070°52.356' **Tide:** 9 ft. **Current:** 3 kt. **Chart:** 13274
Rep. Depths (*MLW*): Entry 17 ft. **Fuel Dock** n/a **Max Slip/Moor** 15 ft./-
Access: Merrimack River, under the bascule bridge, first marina to starboard

Marina Facilities *(In Season/Off Season)*

Fuel: No
Slips: 142 Total, 2 Transient **Max LOA:** 50 ft. **Max Beam:** 16 ft.
Rate *(per ft.)*: **Day** $1.50 **Week** 7.50 **Month** n/a
Power: 30 amp Yes, **50 amp** Yes, **100 amp** n/a, **200 amp** n/a
Cable TV: No **Dockside Phone:** No
Dock Type: Floating
Moorings: 14 Total, 0 Transient **Launch:** n/a
Rate: Day n/a **Week** n/a **Month** n/a
Heads: 4 Toilet(s), 2 Shower(s)
Laundry: 1 Washer(s), 1 Dryer(s) **Pay Phones:** No
Pump-Out: No **Fee:** n/a **Closed Heads:** No

Marina Operations

Owner/Manager: Brian Mullen **Dockmaster:** Same
In-Season: May 15-Oct 15, 8am-8 pm **Off-Season:** n/a
After-Hours Arrival: Call in advance
Reservations: Yes, Preferred **Credit Cards:** Cash or check
Discounts: None
Pets: Welcome, Dog Walk Area **Handicap Access:** Yes, Heads, Docks

Cove Marina

8 Friedenfels Street; Salisbury, MA 01952

Tel: (978) 462-4998 **VHF: Monitor** 10 **Talk** n/a
Fax: n/a **Alternate Tel:** n/a
Email: n/a **Web:** n/a
Nearest Town: Newburyport *(0.5 mi.)* **Tourist Info:** (978) 462-6680

Marina Services and Boat Supplies

Services - Docking Assistance, Dock Carts **Supplies - OnSite:** Ice *(Block, Cube)* **Near:** Ships' Store, Bait/Tackle **Under 1 mi:** Propane *(Lunt True Value 462-2951)* **3+ mi:** West Marine, Boat/US *(603-474-7170, 6 mi.)*

Boatyard Services

OnSite: Forklift, Engine mechanic *(gas)*, Electrical Repairs, Divers **OnCall:** Propeller Repairs **Near:** Travelift. **Under 1 mi:** Launching Ramp, Electronic Sales, Electronics Repairs, Hull Repairs, Rigger, Canvas Work, Bottom Cleaning, Brightwork, Woodworking, Painting, Awlgrip. **Nearest Yard:** Bridge Marina (978) 462-2294

Restaurants and Accommodations

Near: Restaurant *(Stripers Grille 499-0400)*, *(Fishtale Diner 465-1674)*, *(Marsh View Café 465-1199)* **Under 1 mi:** Restaurant *(Black Cow 499-8811)*, *(Thirsty Whale 465-6191)*, *(Park Lunch 465-9817)*, *(Michael's Harborside 462-7785, L $6-12, D $7-17)*, Pizzeria *(Angelinas 462-9696)*, Motel *(Country Garden 948-7773)*, *(Michael's Oceanfront 465-6202)*, Inn/B&B *(Garrison Inn 499-8500, $100-140)*, *(Clark Currier Inn 465-8363, $100-150)*, *(Windsor House 462-3778, $100-145)*

Recreation and Entertainment

OnSite: Picnic Area, Grills, Playground **Near:** Fishing Charter **Under 1 mi:** Video Rental **1-3 mi:** Beach *(Salisbury Beach by dinghy)*, Movie Theater *(Screening Room 462-3456)*, Museum *(Custom House Maritime Museum 462-8681$3/2, Cushing House Museum 462-2681 $4/1.50)*, Cultural Attract **3+ mi:** Dive Shop, Golf Course *(Amesbury Golf & Country Club 388-5153, 4 mi.)*, Boat Rentals, Bowling *(Lafayette Lanes 388-4338, 5 mi.)*

Provisioning and General Services

Under 1 mi: Wine/Beer *(Leary's 462-4451)*, Liquor Store *(Mike's Package Store 465-3103)*, Fishmonger, Lobster Pound, Pharmacy *(Lynch 462-2232)*, Hardware Store *(Lunt True Value 462-2951)* **1-3 mi:** Convenience Store, Delicatessen *(Fruit Basket 462-9164)*, Meat Market, Post Office, Catholic Church, Protestant Church, Library *(465-4428)*, Beauty Salon, Barber Shop, Dry Cleaners, Laundry, Bookstore *(Eureka 465-9359)*, Newsstand, Florist, Retail Shops, Copies Etc.

Transportation

OnCall: Rental Car *(Enterprise 499-0021)*, Taxi *(Port Taxi 465-2333)*, Airport Limo *(Cassidy Limo)* **Airport:** Pease/Logan Int'l. *(20 mi./50 mi.)*

Medical Services

911 Service **OnCall:** Ambulance **1-3 mi:** Doctor **Hospital:** Anna Jacques 463-1000 *(2 mi.)*

Setting -- Just past the bridge, on the starboard side, is this small, immaculate, family operated marina. The two story building houses the necessary facilities and sports views up and across the River. The charming, picturesque village of Newburyport is just across the bridge. The area around the marina is residential and a bit rural.

Marina Notes -- Dockhands are on duty 8am-8pm, 7 days. The mostly seasonal slip holders create a friendly, helpful atmosphere and the staff focuses on service; they couldn't be more accommodating and are available to help. Good, fiberglass docks. Port Taxi will pick up groceries or take cruisers to the store, train station or Logan Airport. See Hilton Yacht Yard across the river for fuel.

Notable -- Just under the bridge is Stripers Grille, and directly across the bridge are Michael's Harborside (casual seafood -- inside or on the deck) and Black Cow Tap & Grill (fine dining overlooking the harbor). A short walk farther is the beginning of the city boardwalk which runs along the river to "downtown" Newburyport with its many restaurants, historic sites, and retail shops. Walking tours of High Street and the Federal-era historic district are available from the Tourist Info kiosk at the edge of Waterfront Park. Whale Watch trips, group fishing boats, and harbor cruises are all also on the "boardwalk".

PHOTOS ON CD-ROM: 8

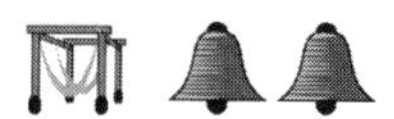

Merri-Mar Yacht Basin

364 Merrimac Street; Newburyport, MA 01950

Tel: (978) 465-3022 **VHF: Monitor** 16 **Talk** 10
Fax: (978) 465-1443 **Alternate Tel:** n/a
Email: mmyb@newburyport.net **Web:** n/a
Nearest Town: Newburyport *(1 mi.)* **Tourist Info:** (978) 462-6680

Navigational Information

Lat: 42°49.463' **Long:** 070°53.272' **Tide:** 9 ft. **Current:** 3 kt. **Chart:** 13274
Rep. Depths (*MLW*): Entry 20 ft. **Fuel Dock** n/a **Max Slip/Moor** 27 ft./50 ft.
Access: Ipswich Bay to Merrimack River, 3.2 nm on port side

Marina Facilities *(In Season/Off Season)*

Fuel: No
Slips: 50 Total, 5 Transient **Max LOA:** 100 ft. **Max Beam:** 25 ft.
Rate *(per ft.)*: **Day** $1.50 **Week** n/a **Month** n/a
Power: 30 amp Inq., **50 amp** Inq., **100 amp** n/a, **200 amp** n/a
Cable TV: No **Dockside Phone:** No
Dock Type: Alongside, Floating
Moorings: 30 Total, 5 Transient **Launch:** Yes (Free), Dinghy Dock
Rate: Day $30 **Week** n/a **Month** n/a
Heads: Toilet(s)
Laundry: None **Pay Phones:** No
Pump-Out: OnCall, Full Service **Fee:** n/a **Closed Heads:** No

Marina Operations

Owner/Manager: W. Jay Lesynski, Jr. **Dockmaster:** Same
In-Season: Year round, 7 am-7 pm **Off-Season:** n/a
After-Hours Arrival: Dock attendant will meet you
Reservations: Yes, Preferred **Credit Cards:** Visa/MC, Amex
Discounts: None
Pets: Welcome, Dog Walk Area **Handicap Access:** Yes, Docks

Marina Services and Boat Supplies

Services - Docking Assistance, Boaters' Lounge, Security, Trash Pick-Up, Dock Carts **Communication -** Mail & Package Hold, Phone Messages, Fax in/out, Data Ports *(Marina)*, Express Mail *(Sat Del)* **Supplies - OnSite:** Ice *(Block, Cube)*, Ships' Store **Near:** Bait/Tackle **Under 1 mi:** Propane *(Lunt 465-6650)* **3+ mi:** Boat/US *(603-474-7170, 6 mi.)*

Boatyard Services

OnSite: Travelift *(35T)*, Engine mechanic *(gas, diesel)*, Electrical Repairs, Electronic Sales, Electronics Repairs, Hull Repairs, Rigger, Sail Loft, Canvas Work, Bottom Cleaning, Brightwork, Air Conditioning, Refrigeration, Divers, Compound, Wash & Wax, Interior Cleaning, Propeller Repairs, Woodworking, Inflatable Repairs, Metal Fabrication, Painting, Awlgrip, Total Refits **OnCall:** Life Raft Service, Upholstery, Yacht Interiors **Near:** Launching Ramp. **Dealer for:** Yanmar, Mercruiser, Cummins, Hohler, Northern Lights, Crusader. **Yard Rates:** $65/hr., Haul & Launch $3 *(blocking $1.50)*, Power Wash $1.50

Restaurants and Accommodations

Near: Lite Fare *(Kathy Ann's Bakery 462-7415)*, Inn/B&B *(Newburyport B&B 463-4637)* **Under 1 mi:** Restaurant *(Finest Kind 462-9131, D $15-25)*, *(Glenn's Restaurant and Cool Bar 465-3811, D $17-30, live piano music Wed, Fri, & Sun night)*, *(Rim 462-8077)*, *(Michael's Harborside 462-7785, L $6-12, D $7-17)*, *(Black Cow 499-8811)*, *(Scandia D $15-24)*, Fast Food, Lite Fare *(Park Lunch 465-9817)*, Pizzeria *(Famous Pizza 462-9644)*, Motel *(Country Garden 948-7773)* **1-3 mi:** Motel *(Garrison Inn 499-8500, $10-150)*, *(Michael's Oceanfront 465-6202)*

Recreation and Entertainment

OnSite: Picnic Area, Grills, Fishing Charter **Near:** Jogging Paths, Boat Rentals **Under 1 mi:** Playground, Tennis Courts, Fitness Center, Roller Blade/Bike Paths, Park **1-3 mi:** Beach, Dive Shop, Golf Course *(Amesbury Golf & Country Club 388-5153)*, Movie Theater, Video Rental *(Blockbuster 463-3741)*, Video Arcade, Museum *(Custom House Maritime Museum 462-8681 $3/2)* **3+ mi:** Bowling *(Lafayette Lanes 388-4338, 4 mi.)*

Provisioning and General Services

Near: Health Food, Post Office, Beauty Salon, Barber Shop **Under 1 mi:** Convenience Store *(Bumblebee Market 499-2337)*, Supermarket *(White Hen Pantry 465-6507)*, Gourmet Shop, Delicatessen, Bakery, Meat Market, Catholic Church, Protestant Church, Synagogue, Library *(465-4428)*, Dry Cleaners, Laundry *(near Maritime Museum)*, Pharmacy *(Brooks 462-5084)*, Newsstand, Florist, Retail Shops **1-3 mi:** Liquor Store *(Mike's 465-3103)*, Farmers' Market, Fishmonger, Lobster Pound, Bookstore *(Eureka 465-9359)*, Hardware Store *(Lunt True Value 465-6650)*, Copies Etc.

Transportation

OnSite: Courtesy Car/Van **OnCall:** Rental Car *(Enterprise 499-0021)*, Taxi *(A American 499-9346)*, Airport Limo *(Port Taxi 465-2333)* **Near:** Local Bus **Under 1 mi:** Rail *(Commuter Link to Boston $5)* **Airport:** Pease/Logan Int'l. *(20 mi./50 mi.)*

Medical Services

911 Service **OnCall:** Ambulance **Near:** Chiropractor *(Newburyport Chiropractic 463-3361)* **Under 1 mi:** Doctor, Dentist **Hospital:** Anna Jacques 463-1000 *(1 mi.)*

Setting -- Once past downtown Newburyport and the bascule bridge, Merri-Mar is the fourth facility to port. Its extensive network of docks makes it easy to spot. This part of the river is quiet and safe, and the environs are very residential. It's a long walk or dinghy ride back to the center of delightful Newburyport.

Marina Notes -- Founded in 1952, this service-oriented family business now includes three generations. It's open 7 days and takes exceptional personal care of its seasonal customers and transient visitors. There's a welcome courtesy car for quick trips downtown or out to the supermarkets. The staff is full-time, well-trained and year-round. There is no longer a restaurant onsite (but the space is there so one may return.) Heads are those that were part of the restaurant operation and one must access them through the closed facility. Specializes in the repair and refit of sail and power vessels. Well-equipped ships' store onsite. The facility could use a little sprucing up. See Hilton or Windward Yacht Yard for fuel.

Notable -- Downtown Newburyport, with its brick streets and enormous stock of Federalist buildings, is charming, picturesque, and filled with things to do, places to eat, and shops of all descriptions. The new waterfront park (wtih dinghy dock) and the Boardwalk make the River easily accessible (stop at the Tourist Office for a walking tour map and brochures). There are special events practically evey weekend from Labor Day to Memorial Day. The Firehouse Center for the Performing and Visual Arts (462-7336) is within 1 mile, and a little farther is the Maudslay State Park, with its immense stands of laurel, panoramic river views and exquisitely landscaped grounds.

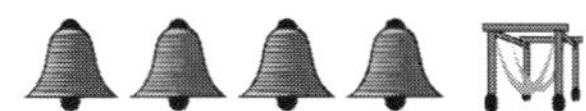

Navigational Information

Lat: 42°36.743' **Long:** 070°40.815' **Tide:** 9 ft. **Current:** 5 kt. **Chart:** 13281
Rep. Depths (*MLW*): Entry 10 ft. **Fuel Dock** 7 ft. **Max Slip/Moor** 7 ft./-
Access: Gloucester Harbor to Blynman Canal, far side on port side

Marina Facilities *(In Season/Off Season)*

Fuel: *Varies* - Gasoline
Slips: 275 Total, 10 Transient **Max LOA:** 100 ft. **Max Beam:** n/a
Rate *(per ft.)*: **Day** $2.75/$2.00 **Week** Inq. **Month** Inq.
Power: 30 amp $5, **50 amp** $5, **100 amp** n/a, **200 amp** n/a
Cable TV: No **Dockside Phone:** No
Dock Type: Wood, Long Fingers, Alongside, Floating
Moorings: 0 Total, 0 Transient **Launch:** n/a
Rate: Day n/a **Week** n/a **Month** n/a
Heads: 4 Toilet(s), 2 Shower(s) *(with dressing rooms)*
Laundry: 2 Washer(s), 2 Dryer(s) **Pay Phones:** Yes, 4
Pump-Out: Full Service, 1 Central, 1 Port **Fee:** Free **Closed Heads:** No

Marina Operations

Owner/Manager: Andrew & Tobin Dominick **Dockmaster:** Peter Favazza
In-Season: May-Oct 15, 8am-6pm **Off-Season:** Oct 16-Apr 30, 8am-4pm
After-Hours Arrival: Call in advance
Reservations: Yes, Preferred **Credit Cards:** Visa/MC, Dscvr, Din, Amex
Discounts: Boat/US; Parts 10% **Dockage:** n/a **Fuel:** 2.2% **Repair:** n/a
Pets: Welcome, Dog Walk Area **Handicap Access:** Yes, Heads, Docks

Cape Ann's Marina Resort

75 Essex Avenue; Gloucester, MA 01930

Tel: (978) 283-2112 **VHF: Monitor** 10 **Talk** 10
Fax: (978) 283-2116 **Alternate Tel:** (978) 283-2116
Email: camoffice@capeannmarina.com **Web:** www.capeannmarina.com
Nearest Town: Gloucester *(1 mi.)* **Tourist Info:** (978) 283-1601

Marina Services and Boat Supplies

Services - Docking Assistance, Concierge, Boaters' Lounge, Crew Lounge, Security *(24 Hrs.)* **Communication -** Mail & Package Hold, Fax in/out, FedEx, AirBorne, UPS, Express Mail *(Sat Del)* **Supplies - OnSite:** Ice *(Block, Cube)*, Ships' Store, Bait/Tackle, Live Bait *(Worms)* **1-3 mi:** Marine Discount Store *(3 Lanterns 281-2080)*, Propane *(Fosters 283-1131)*

Boatyard Services

OnSite: Travelift *(70T)*, Forklift, Crane, Engine mechanic *(gas, diesel)*, Electrical Repairs, Electronic Sales, Electronics Repairs, Hull Repairs, Bottom Cleaning, Brightwork, Air Conditioning, Refrigeration, Compound, Wash & Wax, Painting, Awlgrip, Total Refits **OnCall:** Divers, Interior Cleaning, Propeller Repairs, Woodworking, Inflatable Repairs, Life Raft Service, Upholstery, Yacht Interiors, Metal Fabrication **Under 1 mi:** Launching Ramp. **Dealer for:** Suzuki, Interlux, Towmaster, Mercury, Yanmar, Westerbeke. **Yard Rates:** Haul & Launch $7.20/ft. *(blocking $2.10/ft.)*, Power Wash $2.75

Restaurants and Accommodations

OnSite: Restaurant *(Gull 283-6565, B $4-6, L $5-9, D $19-32)*, Motel *(Cape Ann's Marina Resort 283-2116, $60-130)* **Near:** Snack Bar *(Cupboard in Stage Fort Park 281-1908)*, Lite Fare *(The Causeway)*, Hotel *(Manor Inn 283-0674, $75-145)*, Inn/B&B *(Harborview Inn 283-2277)*, *(Inn at Babson Court 281-4469, $125-210)* **Under 1 mi:** Restaurant *(McT's Lobster House 282-0950, L $6-18, D $6-18)*, *(Blackburn Tavern 282-1919, L $5-13, D $5-13, live blues & rock Thu-Sat)*, *(Pilot House BBQ 283-0131)*, *(White Rainbow 281-0017, D $27-39)*, Pizzeria *(Sebastian's 283-4407)*

Recreation and Entertainment

OnSite: Pool, Spa, Picnic Area, Grills, Group Fishing Boat, Video Arcade, Sightseeing **Near:** Tennis Courts, Movie Theater, Park **Under 1 mi:** Beach, Playground, Fitness Center *(Streamline 281-5347)*, Roller Blade/Bike Paths, Bowling *(Cape Ann Bowling 283-9753)*, Video Rental *(West Coast 283-8606)* **1-3 mi:** Dive Shop, Boat Rentals, Museum *(Hammond Castle 283-7673 $6.50/4.50 - monument to the great American inventor; Sargent House 281-2432)* **3+ mi:** Golf Course *(Cape Ann 768-7544, 7 mi.)*

Provisioning and General Services

OnSite: Bank/ATM, Newsstand **Near:** Convenience Store, Wine/Beer **Under 1 mi:** Protestant Church, Synagogue, Library *(Sawyer 281-9763)*, Pharmacy *(CVS 283-8489)*, Copies Etc. *(Black & Blueprints 283-1900)* **1-3 mi:** Supermarket *(Stop & Shop, Shaw's)*, Gourmet Shop *(Grange Gourmet 283-2639)*, Delicatessen, Health Food *(Common Crow 283-1665)*, Liquor Store *(Railroad Ave. 283-9392)*, Green Grocer, Fishmonger, Lobster Pound, Post Office, Catholic Church, Beauty Salon, Laundry, Bookstore *(The Bookstore 281-1548)*, Hardware Store, Retail Shops

Transportation

OnSite: Local Bus *(CATA around harbor, peninsula, and beaches)* **OnCall:** Rental Car *(Enterprise 281-3288)* **Under 1 mi:** Bikes *(Joes 283-3638)*, Rail *(MBTA to Boston)*, Ferry Service *(Provincetown)* **1-3 mi:** Taxi *(Atlantic 381-5550)* **Airport:** Logan Int'l. *(32 mi.)*

Medical Services

911 Service **Under 1 mi:** Chiropractor **1-3 mi:** Doctor, Dentist, Holistic Services, Ambulance **Hospital:** Addison Gilbert 283-4000 *(1 mi.)*

Setting -- Tucked into a protected basin on the picturesque Blynman Canal lies this full-service, conveniently located, resort. To get there, you have to pass through the busiest drawbridge on the East Coast. Cape Ann Marina's extensive dockage offers northwestern views of the pristine Annisquam River and Marsh, and surrounds a large complex of accommodations, restaurants, and facilities.

Marina Notes -- Complete boatyard onsite (including 3 travelifts, 15, 20 & 70T), with 24/7 security and onsite personnel. Amenities here include indoor pool with jacuzzi (7:30am-9:30pm), game room with video games, conference center, laundry (7am-9:30pm), and complimentary coffee. Tent area for 20-300 people. Clam bake and bar area. Attractive brick picnic and grill area overlooks marina. Significant tackle shop and large, well-equipped ships' store. Whale watching and a number of party fishing and sport fishing boats also onsite. (Yankee Deep Sea Fishing 283-0313). Heads are tile, but aging, as are the wood docks with full-finger piers.

Notable -- The active and busy facilities and 52 waterview rooms are comfortable, although not luxurious, and well maintained. The large windows of the airy, upbeat, contemporary Gull Restaurant look out on the docks; seafood is their strong suit - lobster rolls to clambakes - 7 days, 4am-10pm. Will cook your catch, too. Movie theater across the street. 5 minutes to Fisherman's Monument, Pavilion Beach, concerts, tennis, playground, and a walking/jogging esplanade. 1.5 miles to most services. Gloucester Maritime Trail's "Settler's Walk" begins nearby (Visitors' Center 281-8865).

Gloucester Town Landing

19 Harbor Loop; Gloucester, MA 01930

Tel: (978) 282-3012 **VHF: Monitor** 16 **Talk** n/a
Fax: (978) 281-4188 **Alternate Tel:** n/a
Email: jcaulkett@ci.gloucester.ma.us **Web:** n/a
Nearest Town: Gloucester *(0.2 mi.)* **Tourist Info:** (978) 283-1601

Navigational Information

Lat: 42°36.655' **Long:** 070°39.347' **Tide:** 9 ft. **Current:** n/a **Chart:** 13281
Rep. Depths (*MLW*): Entry 25 ft. **Fuel Dock** n/a **Max Slip/Moor** -/16 ft.
Access: Gloucester Harbor Channel to Inner Harbor

Marina Facilities *(In Season/Off Season)*

Fuel: No
Slips: 0 Total, 0 Transient **Max LOA:** n/a **Max Beam:** n/a
Rate *(per ft.)*: **Day** n/a **Week** n/a **Month** n/a
Power: 30 amp n/a, **50 amp** n/a, **100 amp** n/a, **200 amp** n/a
Cable TV: No **Dockside Phone:** No
Dock Type: n/a
Moorings: 29 Total, 29 Transient **Launch:** None - Water Taxi ($5/pp)
Rate: Day $25 **Week** n/a **Month** n/a
Heads: 2 Toilet(s)
Laundry: None **Pay Phones:** No
Pump-Out: OnCall, Full Service, 1 Port **Fee:** Free **Closed Heads:** Yes

Marina Operations

Owner/Manager: James Caulkett (Harbormaster) **Dockmaster:** n/a
In-Season: Year Round, 8am-6pm **Off-Season:** n/a
After-Hours Arrival: Pick up any available mooring, check-in next morning
Reservations: Yes **Credit Cards:** Cash
Discounts: None
Pets: Welcome **Handicap Access:** No

Marina Services and Boat Supplies

Supplies - Under 1 mi: Ice *(Block, Cube)*, Ships' Store *(Rose's Marine 283-3334, 3 Lanterns 281-2080)*, Bait/Tackle *(D&B Bait 281-1866)* **1-3 mi:** Propane *(Fosters BBQ 283-1131)*

Boatyard Services

Nearest Yard: Brown's Yacht Yard (978) 281-3200

Restaurants and Accommodations

Near: Restaurant *(Savory Skillet 281-4042)*, *(Halibut Point 281-1900, L $5-13, D $5-13)*, *(Schooners 281-1962)*, *(McT's Lobster House 282-0950, L $6-18, D $6-18)*, *(White Rainbow 281-0017, D $27-39)*, *(Jalapenos 283-8228, D $11-17)*, Lite Fare *(Sunny Day Café 281-3997)*, Pizzeria *(Leonardo's 281-7882)*, Inn/B&B *(Inn at Babson Court 281-4469, $100-225)* **Under 1 mi:** Motel *(Cape Ann's Marina 281-4905)*, *(Crows Nest 281-2965)*, Inn/B&B *(Julietta House 281-2300, $75-118)* **1-3 mi:** Inn/B&B *(Harbor View B&B)*

Recreation and Entertainment

Near: Beach *(Pavilion)*, Jogging Paths, Roller Blade/Bike Paths, Park *(St. Peter's)*, Museum *(Gloucester Maritime Heritage Center 281-0470, Gloucester Fishermens Museum, Cape Ann Historical Museum 283-0455 $3.50/2 single largest collecton of works by Gloucester native and marine artist Fitz Hugh Lane)*, Sightseeing *(Moby Duck Amphibious Tour 281-3825 $14/12; Cape Ann Whale Watch 283-5110, from Rose's Wharf; Seven Seas Whale Watch 283-1776, from Rogers St.; Capt. Bill's Whale Watch 283-6995, from Capt. Carlos Seafood Mkt.; Yankee Fleet Whale Watch 283-0313, from Cape Ann's Marina - all 4 $28/16)*, Special Events *(St. Peter's Fiesta - blessing of the fleet, late Jun weekend)*
Under 1 mi: Pool *(Cape Ann Resort)*, Playground, Tennis Courts *(Stage Fort Park)*, Group Fishing Boat *(Yankee Fleet, Capt. Bill's)*, Movie Theater *(Essex Ave.)*, Cultural Attract *(North Shore Arts Association - dinghy across the harbor; Gloucester Stage Co. 281-4099)* **1-3 mi:** Bowling *(Cape Ann Bowling 283-9753)* **3+ mi:** Golf Course *(Cape Ann Golf, 7mi.)*

Provisioning and General Services

Near: Liquor Store *(Liquor Locker 283-0630)*, Bank/ATM, Catholic Church, Protestant Church, Library *(Sawyer 281-9763)*, Beauty Salon, Barber Shop, Laundry *(Home Style 281-4805)*, Bookstore *(Bookends 281-2053, The Bookstore 281-1548)*, Pharmacy *(CVS 281-2450)*, Retail Shops, Copies Etc. *(Office Center 283-5020)* **Under 1 mi:** Gourmet Shop *(Grange Gourmet 283-2639)*, Health Food *(Common Crow 283-1665)*, Fishmonger, Hardware Store *(Building Center 283-3060)* **1-3 mi:** Supermarket *(Stop & Shop 283-4405, Shaw's)*

Transportation

OnCall: Water Taxi *(281-5268/Ch 16, 8am-10pm. Mooring field to facility $5/one way)*, Rental Car *(Enterprise 281-3288)*, Taxi *(Atlantic Taxi 281-5550)* **Near:** Bikes *(Harborside Cycle 281-7744)*, Local Bus *(CATA Trolley - circles harbor, Cape Ann peninsula, and beaches)*, Rail *(MBTA to Boston)*
Under 1 mi: Ferry Service *(Provincetown)* **Airport:** Logan Int'l. *(32 mi.)*

Medical Services

911 Service **OnCall:** Ambulance **Near:** Chiropractor *(Atlantic Family Chiropractic 282-4994)* **1-3 mi:** Doctor *(Workwell Health Services 283-4000)* **Hospital:** Addison Gilbert 283-4000 *(2 mi.)*

Setting -- At the head of Harbor Cove lies the Town Landing in St. Peter's Park. Its dinghy docks sit at the foot of the Harbormaster's Office. This facility services all the Gloucester City moorings in Southeast Harbor and Inner Harbor. Moorings in the Inner Harbor occupy a prime spot in the center of this busy, historic, working harbor. Those in Southeast Harbor are about 1 mile inside the breakwater.

Marina Notes -- The 14 moorings in the Southeast Harbor and 15 in the Inner Harbor are identifed by orange balls. Transient mooring dinghy docks are on the back side of the float in Harbor Cove, designated by bright yellow combing. Additional public landings at: Solomon Jacob Landing, Cripple Cove Landing, Bickford Marina, Dunfudgin Landing. Cape Ann Boating Services' Harbor Dog runs a launch/water taxi service 8am-10pm - $5/1-way, discounts for groups 804-9575, 804-9578, Ch.16 & 6. They will take boaters to Town Landings and restaurants. Salty Dog 281-5268 also has a water shuttle, $10/RT or $50/tix pass. Gas and diesel at North Shore Fishing Dock (283-6880) which may also have dockage; try Beacon Marine (283-2380) for dockage & moorings, too.

Notable -- If you're ready to let someone else do the driving, there's Salty Dog Harbor Tours 281-5268 $10 adults/5 children or Harbor Tours, 283-1979 narrated tours and lobstering trips, $20/10. Four whale watch boats leave from various parts of town and tour Stellwagen Bank. Nearby Cape Ann Chamber of Commerce publishes a "Perfect Storm" Landmarks map. (Sebastian Unger's "Perfect Storm" documents the Oct '91 storm of the century and the loss of the crew of Gloucester-based swordfish trawler Andrea Gail.) www.capeannvacations.com. The CATA Trolley puts everything within easy reach.

PHOTOS ON CD-ROM: 5

Navigational Information

Lat: 42°36.890' **Long:** 070°38.966' **Tide:** 9 ft. **Current:** n/a **Chart:** 13281
Rep. Depths (*MLW*): Entry 20 ft. **Fuel Dock** n/a **Max Slip/Moor** 30 ft./-
Access: Main channel to Inner Harbor, then South Channel

Marina Facilities *(In Season/Off Season)*

Fuel: No
Slips: 40 Total, 3 Transient **Max LOA:** 60 ft. **Max Beam:** 18 ft.
Rate *(per ft.)*: **Day** $2.00/Inq. **Week** Inq. **Month** n/a
Power: 30 amp Inq., **50 amp** n/a, **100 amp** n/a, **200 amp** n/a
Cable TV: Yes **Dockside Phone:** No
Dock Type: Wood, Long Fingers, Floating
Moorings: 10 Total, 3 Transient **Launch:** None
Rate: Day $25 **Week** n/a **Month** n/a
Heads: 2 Toilet(s), 2 Shower(s)
Laundry: None **Pay Phones:** No
Pump-Out: OnCall, Full Service, 1 Port **Fee:** Free **Closed Heads:** Yes

Marina Operations

Owner/Manager: Jay & Diane Enos **Dockmaster:** Jay Enos
In-Season: Apr-Oct, 8am-6pm **Off-Season:** Nov-Apr, 9am-5pm
After-Hours Arrival: Call in advance
Reservations: Yes, Preferred **Credit Cards:** Visa/MC
Discounts: None
Pets: Welcome **Handicap Access:** Yes, Docks

Pier 7/Enos Marine

51 Parker Street; Gloucester, MA 01930

Tel: (978) 281-1935 **VHF: Monitor** n/a **Talk** n/a
Fax: (978) 281-4107 **Alternate Tel:** n/a
Email: Jay@enosmarine.com **Web:** www.enosmarine.com
Nearest Town: Gloucester *(0.5 mi.)* **Tourist Info:** (978) 283-1601

Marina Services and Boat Supplies

Services - Boaters' Lounge, Trash Pick-Up **Communication -** FedEx, AirBorne, UPS, Express Mail **Supplies - OnSite:** Ice *(Block, Cube)*, Ships' Store **Near:** Bait/Tackle *(New England Marine 281-2080)*, Propane *(Fosters BBQ 283-1131)*

Boatyard Services

OnSite: Engine mechanic *(gas)* **Near:** Travelift, Launching Ramp.
Nearest Yard: Brown's Yacht Yard (978) 281-3200

Restaurants and Accommodations

Near: Restaurant *(Captain Vito's 283-3626)*, *(L'Amante 282-4426, D $17-22)*, *(Halibut Point 281-1900, L $5-13, D $5-13)*, Coffee Shop *(Cathy's Coffee 283-6445)*, Lite Fare *(Crow's Nest 281-2965, Perfect Storm hang-out)* **Under 1 mi:** Restaurant *(Dockside 281-4554)*, Pizzeria *(Leonardo's 281-7882)*, Inn/B&B *(Julietta House B&B 281-2300, $100-200)*, *(Gray Manor Inn 283-5409, $60-80)*, *(Colonial Inn 281-1953)*, *(Williams Guest House 283-4931, $50-75)* **1-3 mi:** Motel *(Cape Ann Motor Inn 281-2900, $70-130)*

Recreation and Entertainment

Near: Beach *(Good Harbor)*, Picnic Area, Playground *(Cripple Cove)*, Dive Shop, Jogging Paths, Boat Rentals, Roller Blade/Bike Paths, Fishing Charter, Movie Theater, Video Arcade, Park *(Gordon Thomas)*, Special Events *(St. Peter's Fiesta - last weekend in June)* **Under 1 mi:** Bowling, Group Fishing Boat *(Yankee Fleet, Capt. Bill's)*, Video Rental *(Blockbuster 283-6210)*, Sightseeing *(Moby Duck Amphibious Tour 281-3825 $14/12; Whale Watching tours: Cape Ann 283-5110; Capt. Bill's 283-6995; Seven Seas 283-1776; Yankee Fleet 283-0313 - all 4 $28/16)* **1-3 mi:** Fitness Center *(Fitness Zone 281-5761)*, Museum *(Gloucester Maritime Heritage Center 281-0470, Gloucester Fishermen's Museum 281-1820, Cape Ann Historical Museum 283-0455 $3.50/2)*, Cultural Attract *(Gloucester Stage Co. 281-4099 $15-30 classic & contemporary works, plus Israel Horovitz's)* **3+ mi:** Golf Course *(Cape Ann Golf 768-7544, 8 mi.)*

Provisioning and General Services

Near: Convenience Store, Delicatessen, Liquor Store *(Liquor Locker 283-0630)*, Farmers' Market, Fishmonger, Bank/ATM, Post Office, Catholic Church, Protestant Church, Beauty Salon, Barber Shop, Dry Cleaners, Bookstore *(Bookends 281-2053, The Bookstore 281-1548)*, Newsstand, Florist, Retail Shops, Department Store, Buying Club, Copies Etc. **Under 1 mi:** Supermarket *(Shaw's 281-4844, Stop & Shop 283-4405)*, Health Food *(Common Crow 283-1665)*, Bakery *(Virgilio's 282-9798)*, Library *(Sawyer 281-9763)*, Laundry *(Home Style 281-4805)*, Pharmacy *(Walgreens 283-1344)*, Hardware Store *(Harbor Loop Building Center 283-3060)* **1-3 mi:** Gourmet Shop *(Grange Gourmet 283-2639)*

Transportation

OnCall: Rental Car *(Enterprise 281-3288)*, Taxi *(Atlantic Taxi 281-5550)*, Airport Limo *(A1 Airport Livery 281-8121)* **Near:** Local Bus *(CATA around harbor)* **Under 1 mi:** Bikes *(Harborside Cycle 281-7744)*, Rail *(MBTA to Boston)*, Ferry Service *(Provincetown)* **Airport:** Logan Int'l. *(32 mi.)*

Medical Services

911 Service **Under 1 mi:** Dentist, Chiropractor *(Gloucester Chiropractic 281-0049)* **1-3 mi:** Holistic Services, Veterinarian *(North Shore Vet Hosp. 283-0214)* **Hospital:** Addison Gilbert 283-4000 *(2 mi.)*

Setting -- Snugly sited, right at the head of the Inner Harbor's South Channel, this exemplary facility -- with its gray-sided, restored New England clubhouse -- has panoramic views out to the main harbor. Carefully preserved original floors and fish-house detail enhance the funky and charming wood-sided main room -- filled with maritime memorabilia, a fish tank, comfortable chairs and sofas, and a kitchen. Umbrella tables and chairs populate the front deck.

Marina Notes -- Very personal, service-oriented facility. Family owned and managed -- the Enoses live onsite. Jay Enos' father managed part of Cape Ann Resort's marina. Jay grew up in the marina business and is also an engine mechanic. The new docks are extraordinarily nice and boast screwed-down beveled, wood planks and good pedestals. Dealer for Honda, AB Inflatables and Maritime Skiff. To the west is Lighthouse Marina; to the east is the Cripple Cove Public Landing. This is a stop for Cape Ann Boating Services' Harbor Dog water taxi service - $5/each way - discount for groups (804-9575, 804-9578, Ch.16 & 6), 8am-10pm. They'll take boaters to all the Town Landings and to restaurants.

Notable -- Cape Ann Chamber of Commerce - www.capeannvacations.com. - publishes the Gloucester Maritime Trail Map and Perfect Storm Landmarks map. (Sebastian Unger's "Perfect Storm" documents the Oct '91 storm of the century and the loss of the crew of Gloucester-based swordfish trawler Andrea Gail.) The Vessels View portion of the Maritime Trail goes past the door. Within an easy walk is new 8 acre Jodrey State Fish Pier for working vessels. Rocky Neck Art Colony is a short dinghy ride across the harbor - public landing at Bickford Marina. Bass Rocks Golf Course, private, is 0.6 miles away (283-7571).

PHOTOS ON CD-ROM: 8

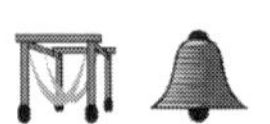

Brown's Yacht Yard, Inc.

Brown's Yacht Yard, Inc.

Rear 139 East Main Street; Gloucester, MA 01930

Tel: (978) 281-3200 **VHF: Monitor** 9 **Talk** 19
Fax: (978) 281-3201 **Alternate Tel:** n/a
Email: info@brownsyy.com **Web:** www.brownsyy.com
Nearest Town: Gloucester *(1.5 mi.)* **Tourist Info:** (978) 283-1601

Navigational Information

Lat: 42°36.717' **Long:** 070°38.991' **Tide:** 9 ft. **Current:** n/a **Chart:** 13281
Rep. Depths (*MLW*): Entry 12 ft. **Fuel Dock** 12 ft. **Max Slip/Moor** 12 ft./22 ft.
Access: South Channel of Gloucester Harbor

Marina Facilities *(In Season/Off Season)*

Fuel: *Gulf* - Slip-Side Fueling, Gasoline, Diesel
Slips: 15 Total, 6 Transient **Max LOA:** 70 ft. **Max Beam:** 14 ft.
Rate *(per ft.)*: **Day** $1.75/$1.25 **Week** Inq. **Month** Inq.
Power: 30 amp incl, **50 amp** incl., **100 amp** n/a, **200 amp** n/a
Cable TV: No **Dockside Phone:** No
Dock Type: Wood, Long Fingers, Floating
Moorings: 3 Total, 3 Transient **Launch:** None, Dinghy Dock
Rate: Day $25 **Week** $120 **Month** Inq.
Heads: 4 Toilet(s), 3 Shower(s)
Laundry: None **Pay Phones:** Yes, 1
Pump-Out: OnCall, Full Service **Fee:** Free **Closed Heads:** Yes

Marina Operations

Owner/Manager: Greg Porter **Dockmaster:** Same
In-Season: May-Oct, 8am-5pm **Off-Season:** Inq.
After-Hours Arrival: Call for info
Reservations: Yes, Preferred **Credit Cards:** Visa/MC, Dscvr, Amex, Gulf
Discounts: None
Pets: Welcome **Handicap Access:** No

Marina Services and Boat Supplies

Communication - Mail & Package Hold, Phone Messages, Fax in/out, FedEx, AirBorne, UPS, Express Mail *(Sat Del)* **Supplies - OnSite:** Ice *(Block, Cube)*, Ships' Store **Near:** Bait/Tackle *(Winchester 281-1619)* **Under 1 mi:** Marine Discount Store *(Rose's 283-3334, 3 Lanterns 281-2080)* **1-3 mi:** Propane *(Foster's 283-1131)*

Boatyard Services

OnSite: Travelift *(35T)*, Forklift, Engine mechanic *(gas, diesel)*, Hull Repairs, Rigger, Bottom Cleaning, Brightwork, Compound, Wash & Wax, Interior Cleaning, Woodworking, Inflatable Repairs, Yacht Broker *(David Zingg)* **OnCall:** Propeller Repairs **Under 1 mi:** Electronic Sales, Electronics Repairs, Divers. **Dealer for:** Zodiac, Dyer, Evinrude, Johnson, Vanguard. **Member:** ABBRA, Other Certifications: Zodiac, Dyer **Yard Rates:** $40-60/hr., Haul & Launch $6/ft. *(blocking $4/ft.)*, Power Wash $3/ft., Bottom Paint $35 *(paint included)* **Storage:** In-Water $8/ft. mast in/out, On-Land $40/ft./season

Restaurants and Accommodations

Near: Restaurant *(Catfish Grille 281-7212)*, *(El-Souk 281-0169)*, *(Jalapenos Mexican 283-8228, D $7-11)*, Pizzeria *(Sebastian's 283-4407)* **Under 1 mi:** Restaurant *(Madfish Grille 281-4554, L $7-10, D $16-27)*, *(Ristorante L'Amante 282-4426, D $17-22)*, *(The Rudder 283-7967, L $7-11, D $16-25)*, Motel *(Vista Motel 281-3910, $110-130, Good Harbor Beach)*, Inn/B&B *(Williams Guest House 283-4931, $55-75, $600/week)* **1-3 mi:** Restaurant *(Gloucester House 283-1812, L $6-12, D $9-25, water taxi)*, *(McT's Lobster House 282-0950, L $6-18, D $6-18)*, Seafood Shack *(Capt Carlos Seafood 283-6342)*, Hotel *(Bass Rocks Ocean Inn 283-7600)*

Recreation and Entertainment

Near: Fitness Center *(Streamline Strength 281-5347)*, Bowling *(Cape Ann Bowl 283-9753)* **Under 1 mi:** Playground, Dive Shop *(Cape Ann Divers)*, Fishing Charter, Video Rental *(Videosmith 283-8606)*, Cultural Attract *(Rocky Neck)* **1-3 mi:** Pool *(Cape Ann Marina)*, Beach, Picnic Area, Grills, Tennis Courts, Jogging Paths, Museum *(Hammond Castle 283-7673, Sargent House 281-2432)* **3+ mi:** Golf Course *(Cape Ann 768-7544, 7 mi.)*

Provisioning and General Services

Near: Convenience Store, Wine/Beer, Bank/ATM, Laundry *(Laundry Agencies 282-4340)* **Under 1 mi:** Gourmet Shop *(Grange Gourmet 283-2639)*, Liquor Store *(Liquor Locker 283-0630)*, Catholic Church **1-3 mi:** Supermarket *(Stop & Shop 283-4405, Shaw's)*, Health Food *(Common Crow 283-1665)*, Bakery, Fishmonger, Post Office, Protestant Church, Synagogue, Library *(281-9763)*, Barber Shop, Dry Cleaners, Bookstore *(Bookends 281-2053)*, Pharmacy *(CVS 283-8489)*, Newsstand, Florist, Retail Shops, Copies Etc. *(Black/Blueprints 283-1900)*

Transportation

OnCall: Rental Car *(Enterprise 281-3288)*, Taxi *(Atlantic 281-5550)* **Near:** Bikes *(Joes 283-3638)*, Water Taxi, Local Bus *(CATA around harbor, peninsula, & to beaches)* **Under 1 mi:** Ferry Service *(Provincetown/ Nantucket)* **1-3 mi:** Rail *(MBTA)* **Airport:** Logan Int'l. *(35 mi.)*

Medical Services

911 Service **OnCall:** Ambulance **Under 1 mi:** Dentist **1-3 mi:** Doctor, Chiropractor *(Gloucester Chiro 281-0049)* **Hospital:** Addison Gilbert 283-4000 *(4 mi.)*

Setting -- Tucked along the eastern shore of well-protected Inner Harbor's Cripple Cove, Brown's is a rustic working boatyard with a great location. Although it is home to mostly recreational vessels, the views are of working boats in a working harbor.

Marina Notes -- Open 7 days a week Memorial Day to Columbus Day. Very well supplied ships' store onsite. Docks are in good repair but aging. Commuter rail (MBTA) to Boston is nearby. Sail and Power Yacht Brokerage onsite since 1976 - David Zingg (281-3200). Dealer for Vanguard Sailboats, Dyer Dinghies, Zodiac Inflatables and Evinrude/Johnson outboards. At the outer edge of the harbor, Eastern Point Yacht Club (283-3520) has transient moorings ($25) with launch service.

Notable -- It's a short walk to the 80 year-old North Shore Arts Association, which will provide you with maps of the Painters Path, (one of the four Maritime Trails) where many great American artists -- past and present -- have found inspiration. Just follow the red line to visit Rocky Neck with more than 2 dozen active galleries and a handful of restaurants. Water shuttle stops here, too. A longer walk in the other direction you will find harbor cruises (281-1700 or 283-1979), whale watch trips (Cape Ann 283-5110, Captain Bill's 283-6995, Yankee 283-0313 $25/15, or 7 Seas 283-1776 $28/16 8:30am & 1:30pm), walking tours (283-4194) and the Gloucester to Provincetown Express (leave 9am, return 6pm 283-5110). Special events: St. Peter's Fiesta (End of June) Schooner Festival (Labor Day Weekend).

PHOTOS ON CD-ROM: 6

Navigational Information

Lat: 42°36.476' **Long:** 070°39.352' **Tide:** 9 ft. **Current:** n/a **Chart:** 13281
Rep. Depths (*MLW*): Entry 15 ft. **Fuel Dock** n/a **Max Slip/Moor** 11 ft./-
Access: Massachusetts Bay to Gloucester Harbor to Smith Cove

Marina Facilities *(In Season/Off Season)*

Fuel: No
Slips: 8 Total, 8 Transient **Max LOA:** 140 ft. **Max Beam:** n/a
Rate *(per ft.)*: **Day** $2.50 **Week** Inq. **Month** n/a
Power: 30 amp Incl., **50 amp** Incl., **100 amp** n/a, **200 amp** n/a
Cable TV: Yes **Dockside Phone:** No
Dock Type: Wood, Alongside, Fixed
Moorings: 0 Total, 0 Transient **Launch:** n/a
Rate: Day n/a **Week** n/a **Month** n/a
Heads: 2 Toilet(s)
Laundry: None **Pay Phones:** Yes
Pump-Out: OnCall, Self Service **Fee:** n/a **Closed Heads:** Yes

Marina Operations

Owner/Manager: Frank Ahearn **Dockmaster:** Same
In-Season: Apr-Oct, 10am-Mid **Off-Season:** n/a
After-Hours Arrival: Call ahead/check in at restaurant
Reservations: Yes, Required **Credit Cards:** Visa/MC, Dscvr, Din, Amex
Discounts: None
Pets: Welcome **Handicap Access:** No

Madfish Grille & The Studio

PO Box 630; 79/51 Rocky Neck Avenue; Gloucester, MA 01930

Tel: (978) 281-4554 **VHF: Monitor** n/a **Talk** n/a
Fax: n/a **Alternate Tel:** (978) 283-4123
Email: n/a **Web:** n/a
Nearest Town: Gloucester *(2.5 mi.)* **Tourist Info:** (978) 283-1601

Marina Services and Boat Supplies

Services - Docking Assistance, Trash Pick-Up, Megayacht Facilities **Communication -** Mail & Package Hold, Phone Messages, Express Mail *(Sat Del)* **Supplies - OnSite:** Ice *(Block, Cube)* **Near:** Ships' Store *(Boat Shop 281-0328)* **Under 1 mi:** Propane *(Foster 283-1131)* **1-3 mi:** Marine Discount Store *(Three Lanterns 281-2080)*, Bait/Tackle

Boatyard Services

Near: Engine mechanic *(gas)*, Launching Ramp, Electrical Repairs, Electronic Sales, Electronics Repairs, Hull Repairs, Rigger, Bottom Cleaning, Brightwork, Divers, Compound, Wash & Wax, Inflatable Repairs, Metal Fabrication, Painting, Awlgrip, Total Refits. **Under 1 mi:** Travelift, Railway, Forklift, Crane, Sail Loft, Air Conditioning, Refrigeration, Interior Cleaning, Propeller Repairs, Life Raft Service. **3+ mi:** Upholstery, Yacht Interiors. **Nearest Yard:** Beacon Marine (978) 283-2380

Restaurants and Accommodations

OnSite: Restaurant *(Madfish Grille 281-4554, L $7-10, D $16-27, free dining dockage)*, *(Studio Restaurant 283-4123, D $17-21, free dining dockage)* **Near:** Restaurant *(Rudder Restaurant 283-7967, L $7-11, D $16-25, Gloucester's oldest restaurant, impromptu staff entertainment)*, Inn/B&B *(Colonial Inn 381-1953)* **Under 1 mi:** Pizzeria *(Espresso 283-0600)* **1-3 mi:** Motel *(Atlantis Oceanfront Motor Inn 283-0014, $150)*, Hotel *(Ocean View Resort 283-6200, $190)*, *(BW Bass Rocks 283-7600, $125-250)*

Recreation and Entertainment

OnSite: Sightseeing *(Rocky Neck Art Colony)* **Near:** Beach *(Niles Beach)*, Picnic Area, Grills, Playground, Jogging Paths, Boat Rentals, Roller Blade/Bike Paths, Fishing Charter, Video Rental *(Parkhursts Video 283-0034)*, Park, Museum *(Beauport Sleeper McCann House)*, Cultural Attract *(Gloucester Stage Co.)*, Special Events *(St. Peter's Blessing of the Fleet)* **Under 1 mi:** Fitness Center **1-3 mi:** Pool, Dive Shop, Tennis Courts, Bowling *(Cape Ann Bowling 283-9753)*, Movie Theater, Video Arcade **3+ mi:** Golf Course *(Cape Ann Golf 768-7544, 9 mi.)*

Provisioning and General Services

Near: Bank/ATM, Catholic Church, Protestant Church **Under 1 mi:** Health Food *(Common Crow 283-1665)*, Wine/Beer, Liquor Store *(Liquor Locker 283-0630)*, Pharmacy *(CVS 281-2450)*, Copies Etc. *(Office Center 283-5020)* **1-3 mi:** Convenience Store, Supermarket *(Stop & Shop 283-4405)*, Gourmet Shop *(Grange Gourmet 283-2639)*, Delicatessen, Bakery *(Virgilio's 283-5295)*, Green Grocer, Post Office, Synagogue, Library *(Sawyer 281-9763)*, Beauty Salon, Barber Shop, Dry Cleaners, Laundry, Bookstore *(Bookends 281-2053)*, Newsstand, Florist, Clothing Store, Retail Shops **3+ mi:** Hardware Store *(Smith Hardware 546-6518, 4 mi.)*

Transportation

OnCall: Rental Car *(Enterprise 281-3288, Rent-A-Wreck 282-7478)* **Near:** Water Taxi, Local Bus *(CATA around harbor, to beaches)* **Under 1 mi:** Bikes *(Harborside Cycle 281-7744)* **1-3 mi:** Rail *(MBTA Commuter)*, Ferry Service *(Gloucester-Nantucket)* **Airport:** Logan Int'l. *(35 mi.)*

Medical Services

911 Service **OnCall:** Ambulance **Near:** Dentist **1-3 mi:** Doctor, Chiropractor *(Cape Ann Chiropractic 281-4800)*, Holistic Services *(Massage Therapy 282-1125)* **Hospital:** Addison Gilbert 283-4000 *(5 mi.)*

Setting -- The Studio and Mad Fish Restaurants are located on the back side of Gloucester Harbor inside Smith Cove. They are in the heart of the famous Artists' Colony of Rocky Neck. Landside the atmosphere is funky and off beat, and the views from the docks are of the restaurants or their pilings - depending on the tide. Seaside, there are short views of Smith Cove across to East Gloucester. There is limited but well protected dockage.

Marina Notes -- The restaurants - which are less than a block apart -- offer overnight dockage just outside their waterside tables. There are few services or amenities for the cruiser or for the boat (just restaurant heads). Courtyards of potted flowers provide welcoming streetside entrances to the restaurants - and to the galleries. The Studio can accommodate boats up to 100 ft. and Madfish is a regular stop for yachts up to 130 ft. Two 100 amp service plus 3 phase; there's usually a megayacht at Madfish; 2 at The Studio, along with smaller vessels. Both restaurants are charming, inviting, comfortable with great views of the harbor and indoor & deck dining, fireplaces for chilly nights. Madfish is known for its nightly entertainment - Fri & Sat mainstream rock cover bands, Sun reggae.

Notable -- Rocky Neck is the oldest artists' colony in the U.S.; among its alumni are Winslow Homer and Edward Hopper. Each year, it becomes more charming and more gentrified. The two dozen artist-owned galleries are usually open from 10am-10pm - traditional and modern art, photography, jewelry, quilts and antiques. "Painters Path" is a tour marked in red; it begins nearby and ends at the International North Shore Arts Assoc (283-1857). Mon-Sat 10am-5pm, Sun 12-5pm. Whale Watching and Deep Sea fishing excursions: Captain Bill's (283-6995); Cape Ann Whale Watch (283-5110); Yankee Fishing (283-0313).

PHOTOS ON CD-ROM: 9

Crocker's Boat Yard

PO Box 268; 15 Ashland Avenue; Manchester, MA 01944

Tel: (978) 526-1971; (888) 332-6004 **VHF: Monitor** 78 **Talk** 78
Fax: (978) 526-7625 **Alternate Tel:** n/a
Email: sam@crockersboatyard.com **Web:** www.crockersboatyard.com
Nearest Town: Manchester *(0.3 mi.)* **Tourist Info:** (781) 631-2868

Navigational Information

Lat: 42°34.289' **Long:** 070°46.475' **Tide:** 10 ft. **Current:** n/a **Chart:** 13274
Rep. Depths (*MLW*): Entry 8 ft. **Fuel Dock** n/a **Max Slip/Moor** 7 ft./15 ft.
Access: Straight into Manchester Harbor -- on west side

Marina Facilities *(In Season/Off Season)*

Fuel: No
Slips: 16 Total, 2 Transient **Max LOA:** 50 ft. **Max Beam:** 16 ft.
Rate *(per ft.)*: **Day** $2.00/Inq. **Week** Inq. **Month** Inq.
Power: 30 amp n/a, **50 amp** n/a, **100 amp** n/a, **200 amp** n/a
Cable TV: No **Dockside Phone:** No
Dock Type: Wood, Floating
Moorings: 0 Total, 0 Transient **Launch:** n/a
Rate: Day n/a **Week** n/a **Month** n/a
Heads: 2 Toilet(s)
Laundry: None **Pay Phones:** No
Pump-Out: No **Fee:** n/a **Closed Heads:** No

Marina Operations

Owner/Manager: Sam Crocker **Dockmaster:** Kitty Crocker
In-Season: Apr-Jul 1, 7am-4:30pm **Off-Season:** Jul 1- Mar 31, 7am-3:30pm
After-Hours Arrival: n/a
Reservations: No **Credit Cards:** Visa/MC, Cash/check
Discounts: None
Pets: Welcome **Handicap Access:** No

Marina Services and Boat Supplies

Communication - FedEx, AirBorne, UPS, Express Mail **Supplies - OnSite:** Ships' Store **OnCall:** Propane, CNG **Near:** Ice *(Cube)*, Bait/Tackle *(First Light Anglers 526-4477)* **3+ mi:** Marine Discount Store *(Lynn Marine Supply 781-631-1305, 7 mi.)*

Boatyard Services

OnSite: Travelift *(30T)*, Crane *(7T)*, Engine mechanic *(gas, diesel)*, Hull Repairs, Rigger, Bottom Cleaning, Brightwork, Air Conditioning, Refrigeration, Divers, Compound, Wash & Wax, Interior Cleaning, Propeller Repairs, Woodworking, Painting, Awlgrip, Yacht Design, Yacht Building, Total Refits **OnCall:** Electrical Repairs, Electronics Repairs, Inflatable Repairs, Life Raft Service, Upholstery, Yacht Interiors, Metal Fabrication **Under 1 mi:** Electronic Sales. **3+ mi:** Sail Loft *(4 mi.)*. **Member:** ABBRA, ABYC - 1 Certified Tech(s), Other Certifications: ABBRA Crane and travelift
Yard Rates: $65/hr., Haul & Launch $7-7.50/ft., Power Wash $2.50

Restaurants and Accommodations

OnCall: Pizzeria *(Harry's Pizza & Deli 921-4777)* **Near:** Restaurant *(7 Central Publick House 526-7494, L $6-10, D $15-20, Kid's menu, Pub menu)*, *(Harbour House 526-8542)*, Snack Bar *(Beach Street Café)*, Inn/B&B *(Old Corner Inn 526-4996, $90-175, weekly rates, too)* **1-3 mi:** Restaurant *(KC's 927-3368)*, *(Yanks 232-9898)*, Inn/B&B *(Vine & Ivy 927-2917)*

Recreation and Entertainment

Near: Beach *(Singing Beach)*, Park, Museum *(Trask House 526-7230)*, Cultural Attract *(Music in Masconomo Park Tue 6-8pm)* **Under 1 mi:** Horseback Riding *(Winthrop Farm 526-1273)*, Video Rental *(Video Viewpoint 526-4126)* **1-3 mi:** Picnic Area *(Misery Islands - $3 fee)*, Grills, Playground, Fitness Center *(Manchester Athletic Club 526-4610)*, Jogging Paths, Roller Blade/Bike Paths, Fishing Charter, Sightseeing **3+ mi:** Dive Shop *(4 mi.)*, Tennis Courts *(Beverly Golf & Tennis 922-9127, 8 mi.)*, Golf Course *(Cape Ann Golf 768-7544, 4 mi.)*, Bowling *(Bowl-O-Mat 922-1140, 8 mi.)*, Movie Theater *(Cabot Street Cinema 927-3677, 8 mi.)*

Provisioning and General Services

Near: Convenience Store, Supermarket *(Crosby's Marketplace 526-4444 - delivers to the boat)*, Delicatessen, Wine/Beer *(Harrigans Wine and Spirits 526-8440)*, Liquor Store, Fishmonger, Lobster Pound, Meat Market *(Michael's Meat Market 526-4955)*, Bank/ATM, Post Office, Protestant Church, Library *(526-7711 Internet access)*, Beauty Salon, Barber Shop, Dry Cleaners, Laundry, Pharmacy *(Allens 526-1321)*, Newsstand, Hardware Store, Florist, Clothing Store **Under 1 mi:** Catholic Church **1-3 mi:** Health Food *(Wild Oats 921-0411)*, Bakery, Farmers' Market, Bookstore *(Book Shop of Beverly Farms 927-2122)*, Copies Etc. *(Daily Printing 927-4630)* **3+ mi:** Department Store *(10 mi.)*

Transportation

OnCall: Rental Car *(Enterprise 524-9555)* **Near:** Bikes *(Seaside Cycle 526-1200)*, Rail *(MBTA commuter to Boston)* **3+ mi:** Taxi *(Patriot Taxi 781-284-2222, 19 mi.)* **Airport:** Logan Int'l. *(25 mi.)*

Medical Services

911 Service **Near:** Dentist, Ambulance **Under 1 mi:** Doctor **Hospital:** Beverly 922-3000 *(5 mi.)*

Setting -- After passing Manchester Yacht Club and the first set of Town Floats on Tucks Point, the next facility to port, deep in the Manchester Inner Harbor, is Crocker's Boat Yard. The small, seaside village of Manchester-by-the-Sea is an easy walk or dinghy ride away. Views are of the boatyard landside and the picturesque harbor populated by beautiful boats.

Marina Notes -- Manchester is one of the best protected harbors on the East Coast. Moorings only, and a dinghy dock. Family owned and operated. Third generation is at helm; established in 1946 by Sturgis Crocker, son of the internationally known yacht designer, Samuel Crocker. Full service boatyard, specializing in wood and fiberglass repairs and restorations; gas and diesel mechanics and repowerings. Manchester Y.C. 526-4595 may have moorings.

Notable -- Elegant Manchester-By-The-Sea, in the heart of the North Shore, was a fashionable summer colony in the mid 19thC and is now a very lovely commuter suburb. Walking this charming town, with its stock of beautiful Colonial and Federal style houses, is a delightful way to spend the afternoon. Misery Islands is a good picnic & beach spot -- $3 fee to ranger, moorings also available (921-6059). Dinghy to the second set of Town Floats at the head of the harbor - Masconomo Park hosts free concerts Tuesdays, 6-8pm, from early July to late August. The Library, at 15 Union Street, has T1/256K Internet access (526-7711). Singing Beach, so called for the sound your feet make on the sand, is easily walkable; there are lifeguards, food stands, and rest rooms.

Navigational Information
Lat: 42°34.289' **Long:** 070°46.430' **Tide:** 10 ft. **Current:** n/a **Chart:** 13274
Rep. Depths (*MLW*): Entry 8 ft. **Fuel Dock** 8 ft. **Max Slip/Moor** 8 ft./10 ft.
Access: Manchester Channel past Norton's Point

Marina Facilities *(In Season/Off Season)*
Fuel: *Texaco* - Gasoline, Diesel
Slips: 30 Total, 1 Transient **Max LOA:** 60 ft. **Max Beam:** 16 ft.
Rate *(per ft.)*: **Day** $2.00/$2.00 **Week** $12/12 **Month** Inq.
Power: 30 amp Incl., **50 amp** Incl., **100 amp** n/a, **200 amp** n/a
Cable TV: No **Dockside Phone:** Yes, 5 line(s)
Dock Type: Long Fingers, Fixed
Moorings: 2 Total, 2 Transient **Launch:** Yes ($4/pp/1-way), Dinghy Dock
Rate: Day $30/30 **Week** $180/180 **Month** n/a
Heads: 2 Toilet(s), 2 Shower(s)
Laundry: None **Pay Phones:** No
Pump-Out: Full Service, 1 Central, 1 Port **Fee:** Free **Closed Heads:** No

Marina Operations
Owner/Manager: Rob Hoyle **Dockmaster:** n/a
In-Season: May 15-Oct 15, 7am-3:30pm **Off-Season:** n/a
After-Hours Arrival: Call ahead for instruction
Reservations: Yes, Required **Credit Cards:** Visa/MC, Amex, Tex
Discounts: None
Pets: Welcome **Handicap Access:** No

Manchester Marine

PO Box 1469; 17 Ashland Avenue; Manchester, MA 01944

Tel: (978) 526-7911 **VHF: Monitor** 72 **Talk** 72
Fax: (978) 526-8638 **Alternate Tel:** n/a
Email: info@manchestermarine.com **Web:** www.manchestermarine.com
Nearest Town: Manchester *(0.2 mi.)* **Tourist Info:** (781) 631-2868

Marina Services and Boat Supplies
Services - Docking Assistance, Dock Carts **Communication -** Mail & Package Hold, Phone Messages, Fax in/out, FedEx, AirBorne, UPS, Express Mail **Supplies - OnSite:** Ice *(Block, Cube)*, Bait/Tackle *(First Light Anglers 526-4477)*, Propane, CNG **3+ mi:** Ships' Store *(Lynn Marine Supply 781-631-1305, 7 mi.)*, West Marine *(8 mi.)*, Boat/US *(6 mi.)*

Boatyard Services
OnSite: Travelift *(30T)*, Engine mechanic *(gas, diesel)*, Electrical Repairs, Electronic Sales, Electronics Repairs, Hull Repairs, Rigger, Bottom Cleaning, Brightwork, Air Conditioning, Refrigeration, Divers, Compound, Wash & Wax, Interior Cleaning, Woodworking, Metal Fabrication, Painting, Awlgrip, Yacht Design, Yacht Building, Total Refits **OnCall:** Sail Loft, Propeller Repairs, Inflatable Repairs, Life Raft Service, Upholstery, Yacht Interiors **Dealer for:** Cat, Yanmar, Northernlight, Sabre. **Member:** ABBRA, ABYC - 6 Certified Tech(s), Other Certifications: Nema **Yard Rates:** $40-70/hr., Haul & Launch $7/ft., Power Wash $2.50, Bottom Paint $55 **Storage:** On-Land Outside $4/sq.ft. Inside $7.50 sq.ft

Restaurants and Accommodations
Near: Restaurant *(7 Central Publick House 526-7494, L $6-10, D $15-20, Kid's menu, Pub menu, Brunch 11:30am-2pm)*, *(Coffee Cup B $5, L $5, D $8-12)*, *(Harbour House 526-8542)*, Snack Bar *(Beach St. B $5, L $5-10)*, Inn/B&B *(Old Corner Inn 526-4996, $90-175)* **Under 1 mi:** Hotel *(Mountain View Resort 526-4464)* **1-3 mi:** Restaurant *(Yanks 232-9898)*, Pizzeria *(Harry's Pizza & Deli 921-4777)*, Motel *(Vine & Ivy 927-2917)* **3+ mi:** Inn/B&B *(Essex River House 768-6800, 4 mi.)*

Recreation and Entertainment
OnSite: Picnic Area, Grills, Fishing Charter *(Light Tackle Charter/Guide Service)*, Special Events *(Flyfishing clinics and seminars)* **Near:** Beach *(Singing Beach)*, Playground, Park **Under 1 mi:** Horseback Riding *(Winthrop Farm 526-1273)*, Video Rental *(Video Viewpoint 526-4126)*, Cultural Attract *(Music in Masconomo Park - Tue, 6-8pm)* **1-3 mi:** Fitness Center *(Manchester Athletic 526-4610)*, Group Fishing Boat *(Gloucester)* **3+ mi:** Golf Course *(Cape Ann Golf 768-7544, 4 mi.)*, Museum *(Essex Ship Building Museum 768-7541, 4 mi.)*

Provisioning and General Services
Near: Convenience Store *(Richdale)*, Supermarket *(Crosby's Marketplace 526-4444 - delivers to the boat)*, Gourmet Shop *(Kitchen Witch 526-9995)*, Wine/Beer *(Harrigan's 526-8440, Crosby's)*, Liquor Store *(Magnolia Beverage 526-4242)*, Bakery *(DeFuscos Bakery & Cafe)*, Fishmonger *(Go fish)*, Meat Market *(Michael's 526-4955)*, Bank/ATM, Post Office, Catholic Church, Protestant Church *(Baptist, Congregational)*, Library *(526-7711 Internet service)*, Beauty Salon, Barber Shop, Dry Cleaners, Laundry, Pharmacy *(Allens 526-1321)*, Newsstand, Hardware Store, Florist, Clothing Store, Retail Shops **1-3 mi:** Health Food *(Wild Oats 921-0411)*

Transportation
OnCall: Rental Car *(Enterprise 524-9555)* **Near:** Bikes *(Seaside Cycle 526-1200)*, Rail *(MBTA commuter)* **Airport:** Logan Int'l. *(25 mi.)*

Medical Services
911 Service **OnSite:** Ambulance **Near:** Doctor, Dentist **Under 1 mi:** Holistic Services *(Healing Arts 526-4400)* **Hospital:** Essex 768-9004 *(4 mi.)*

Setting -- An impeccable boatyard marina, tucked into very protected, picturesque Manchester Harbor, Manchester Marine is just past Crocker's, and about a half mile walk (or dinghy ride) to the charming town of Manchester-by-the-Sea.

Marina Notes -- Very service-oriented staff. Both slips and moorings, with launch service and a dinghy dock. Reservations required, very limited space. Heads and showers onsite. Full service boatyard with a crew of over 40 craftspeople available year 'round, 7 days a week. Very impressive facilities (many new after a 1989 fire): 26,000 sq. ft. indoor storage (10,000 of it heated); large rigging loft and 2,500 sq. ft. temperature controlled finish bay. Fly fishing seminars and supplies at First Anglers store onsite. Also Yacht Brokerage and dealer for Sabre Yachts, Edgewater, Albermarle Boats, and Aerodyne.

Notable -- The docks, and the harbor beyond, are home to some truly exquisite yachts - which may make the best sightseeing of all. Singing Beach is within walking distance. Dinghy to the nearby Misery Islands for a picnic - $3 fee to ranger. Stroll the town with its impeccably restored 19thC houses, as well as supermarket, laundry, and a good selection of other resources and services. Internet access at the Public Library on Union Street (256-7711). Summer concerts at Masconomo Park Tuesdays, 6-8pm, early July to late August - one of the Town Floats is right there.

PHOTOS ON CD-ROM: 4

Beverly Port Marina

43 Water Street; Beverly, MA 01915

Tel: (978) 232-3300 **VHF: Monitor** 79 **Talk** 79
Fax: (978) 232-3329 **Alternate Tel:** (978) 232-3306
Email: n/a **Web:** www.beverlyportmarina.com
Nearest Town: Beverly *(0.2 mi.)* **Tourist Info:** (978) 744-0004

Navigational Information

Lat: 42°32.440' **Long:** 070°53.042' **Tide:** 8 ft. **Current:** 3 kt. **Chart:** 13275
Rep. Depths (*MLW*): Entry 27 ft. **Fuel Dock** 27 ft. **Max Slip/Moor** 26 ft./-
Access: Beverly Harbor Channel past Tuck Point

Marina Facilities *(In Season/Off Season)*

Fuel: Gasoline, Diesel, High-Speed Pumps
Slips: 180 Total, 10 Transient **Max LOA:** 100 ft. **Max Beam:** n/a
Rate *(per ft.)*: **Day** $2.00/$1 **Week** Inq. **Month** Inq.
Power: 30 amp Incl., **50 amp** Incl., **100 amp** n/a, **200 amp** n/a
Cable TV: No **Dockside Phone:** No
Dock Type: Wood, Long Fingers, Floating
Moorings: 0 Total, 0 Transient **Launch:** n/a, Dinghy Dock
Rate: Day n/a **Week** n/a **Month** n/a
Heads: 4 Toilet(s), 4 Shower(s)
Laundry: 2 Washer(s), 2 Dryer(s) **Pay Phones:** No
Pump-Out: OnCall, Full Service, 1 Port **Fee:** n/a **Closed Heads:** No

Marina Operations

Owner/Manager: Frank and Sue Kinzie **Dockmaster:** Sue Kinzie
In-Season: May 15-Oct 15, 8am-8pm **Off-Season:** Oct 15-May 15, 8am-6pm
After-Hours Arrival: Call and leave message
Reservations: Preferred **Credit Cards:** Visa/MC, Dscvr
Discounts: None
Pets: Welcome **Handicap Access:** No

Marina Services and Boat Supplies

Services - Docking Assistance, Trash Pick-Up **Communication -** Mail & Package Hold, Fax in/out *(Free)*, Data Ports *(Office)*, FedEx, AirBorne, UPS *(Sat Del)* **Supplies - OnSite:** Ice *(Block, Cube)*, Ships' Store **OnCall:** Propane **Under 1 mi:** Bait/Tackle *(Als 927-3312)* **3+ mi:** West Marine *(535-7332, 7 mi.)*, Boat/US *(777-5940, 4 mi.)*

Boatyard Services

OnSite: Travelift *(2-35Ts)*, Forklift, Engine mechanic *(gas, diesel)*, Electrical Repairs, Electronic Sales, Electronics Repairs, Hull Repairs, Rigger, Bottom Cleaning, Brightwork, Divers, Compound, Wash & Wax, Interior Cleaning, Propeller Repairs, Inflatable Repairs, Life Raft Service **OnCall:** Air Conditioning **1-3 mi:** Sail Loft. **Dealer for:** Formula, Pro-Line, Monterey, Lund, Quintrex, Avon, Volvo, Yamaha, Merc. **Yard Rates:** $75/hr., Haul & Launch $6.50/ft. *(blocking incl.)*, Power Wash $4/ft., Bottom Paint $15/ft. *(paint included)* **Storage:** In-Water $45/ft/mo., On-Land Inside $102/ft., Outside $45/ft.

Restaurants and Accommodations

OnCall: Pizzeria *(Beverly House of Pizza 922-8400)* **Near:** Restaurant *(Stromberg's 744-1863, over the bridge)*, Snack Bar *(Variety & Deli B $2, L $5, D $7)* **1-3 mi:** Restaurant *(Beverly Depot 927-5402, D $14-24)*, *(Casablanca)*, Motel *(Motel 6 744-4045)*, *(Lakeview 922-7535, $70-110)*, Inn/B&B *(Salem Inn 741-0680, $130-290)*, *(Clipper Ship 745-5503)*

Recreation and Entertainment

Near: Picnic Area, Grills, Dive Shop, Museum *(Beverly Historical Society 922-1186)*, Special Events *(Beverly in Bloom, Beverly Homecoming)* **Under 1 mi:** Beach, Playground, Bowling *(Bowl-O-Mat 922-1140)*, Movie Theater *(Cabot St. Cinema 927-3677 a restored 1920s art deco "palace")*, Park, Cultural Attract *(Cabot St. Theatre Magic Show 927-3677 $15)* **1-3 mi:** Tennis Courts *(Beverly Golf & Tennis 922-9127)*, Golf Course *(Beverly G&T)*, Fitness Center *(All American 927-6888)*, Jogging Paths, Fishing Charter, Video Rental, Video Arcade, Sightseeing *(Pickering Wharf)*

Provisioning and General Services

OnSite: Newsstand **Near:** Convenience Store, Delicatessen, Wine/Beer, Lobster Pound, Laundry *(Home Style Laundry 927-6460)*, Hardware Store *(Hansbury General Store 927-3145)*, Copies Etc. *(Best Press 921-0456)* **Under 1 mi:** Health Food *(New Leaf 927-5955)*, Liquor Store *(Cosgroves 744-4000)*, Bank/ATM, Post Office, Beauty Salon, Dry Cleaners, Pharmacy *(Brooks 921-4550)* **1-3 mi:** Supermarket *(Stop & Shop)*, Bakery, Meat Market, Catholic Church, Protestant Church, Library *(Salem Athenaeum 744-2540)*, Barber Shop, Bookstore *(Derby Square 745-8804)*, Florist, Retail Shops

Transportation

OnSite: Courtesy Car/Van *(Yes, if pre-arranged)* **OnCall:** Rental Car *(Enterprise 524-9555)*, Taxi **Near:** Bikes *(Bay Road Bikes 468-1301)* **Under 1 mi:** Rail *(MBTA Commuter to Boston)* **1-3 mi:** Ferry Service *(Boston/Salem Ferry)* **Airport:** Logan Int'l. *(20 mi.)*

Medical Services

911 Service **Near:** Chiropractor *(Beverly Chiropractic Center 927-9181)* **Under 1 mi:** Doctor *(Taylor 468-7381)* **1-3 mi:** Dentist, Holistic Services, Ambulance **Hospital:** Beverly 922-3000 *(2 mi.)*

Setting -- Beverly Harbor is easily and quickly accessible from the ocean and Massachusetts Bay. Well protected from the northeast, it has deep water at all tides. Beverly Port Marina is on the north (starbord) side just before the municipal marina at the swing bridge; the views from the docks are of Salem across the channel, and of an active, nicely maintained boatyard and drystack operation landside.

Marina Notes -- Family owned and operated. Boatyard has four lifts - two 35 ton travelifts and 2 forklifts (for boats up to 42 ft). One of the largest marinas in Massachusetts, it can handle as many as 400 boats and up to 100 feet in length. Mechanics and other service personnel on duty seven days during summer. Hi-speed fuel dock open 8am-8pm. Boat Valet will ready boat in morning and clean up at night. Only indoor rack storage in Boston area. Good tiled heads, showers with private dressing rooms, laundry. Dive shop, sail rigger onsite. Cable TV and phone for long term only.

Notable -- Nearby Beverly is known as the Garden City because of the magnificent summer homes and gardens built here by wealthy Bostonians. Many are open during the Beverly in Bloom Festival - last weekend in June. Beverly Historical Society offers guided tours of three historic residences - 1636 Balch House, 18thC John Cabot House, and 1695 John Hale House - Tue-Fri, 10am-4pm, Sat noon-4, each $4. For entertainment, try Le Grand David and His Own Spectacular Magic Company at Cabot St. Theatre, Sun 3pm (Mid-September through July) - it really is spectacular; or summer stock at the 1800 seat North Shore Musical Theatre (922-8500). The Salem Historical District is also a short ride by big boat or dinghy, as is the Peabody Museum.

PHOTOS ON CD-ROM: 9

Navigational Information

Lat: 42°32.417' **Long:** 070°53.181' **Tide:** 8 ft. **Current:** 3 kt. **Chart:** 13275
Rep. Depths (*MLW*): Entry 23 ft. **Fuel Dock** n/a **Max Slip/Moor** 12 ft./24 ft.
Access: Beverly Harbor Channel, last facility before bridge

Marina Facilities *(In Season/Off Season)*

Fuel: No
Slips: 28 Total, 1* Transient **Max LOA:** 50 ft. **Max Beam:** n/a
Rate *(per ft.)*: **Day** $2.00 **Week** Inq. **Month** Inq.
Power: 30 amp Metered, **50 amp** n/a, **100 amp** n/a, **200 amp** n/a
Cable TV: Yes Seasonal only **Dockside Phone:** No
Dock Type: Wood, Floating
Moorings: 12 Total, 12 Transient **Launch:** None, Dinghy Dock
Rate: Day $5 **Week** $35 **Month** $150
Heads: 2 Toilet(s)
Laundry: None **Pay Phones:** No
Pump-Out: OnCall, Full Service, 1 Port **Fee:** free **Closed Heads:** Yes

Marina Operations

Owner/Manager: Daniel G. McPherson (Harbormaster) **Dockmaster:** n/a
In-Season: May-Sep, 8am-Mid **Off-Season:** Oct-Apr, 8am-6pm
After-Hours Arrival: Call in advance
Reservations: Yes **Credit Cards:** Cash or Checks
Discounts: None
Pets: Welcome **Handicap Access:** No

Glover Wharf Municipal Marina

PO Box 211; 1 Water Street; Beverly, MA 01915

Tel: (978) 921-6059 **VHF: Monitor** 16 **Talk** 12
Fax: (978) 921-8592 **Alternate Tel:** n/a
Email: dmcpherson@ci.beverly.ma.us **Web:** harbormasters.org/beverly
Nearest Town: Beverly *(1.5 mi.)* **Tourist Info:** (978) 232-9559

Marina Services and Boat Supplies

Services - Security *(8am-Mid)* **Communication -** FedEx, AirBorne, UPS, Express Mail **Supplies - OnCall:** Propane **Near:** Ice *(Block, Cube)*, Ships' Store *(Beverly Port Marina)* **Under 1 mi:** Bait/Tackle *(Al's 927-3312)* **3+ mi:** West Marine *(535-7332, 7 mi.)*, Boat/US *(777-5940, 4 mi.)*

Boatyard Services

OnCall: Bottom Cleaning, Refrigeration **Near:** Travelift, Engine mechanic *(gas, diesel)*, Electrical Repairs, Electronics Repairs, Hull Repairs, Rigger, Brightwork, Compound, Wash & Wax, Propeller Repairs. **Under 1 mi:** Launching Ramp. **Nearest Yard:** Beverly Port Marina (978) 232-3300

Restaurants and Accommodations

OnCall: Pizzeria *(Beverly House of Pizza 922-8400)* **Near:** Restaurant *(Siam Delight 922-8514, L $7-14, D $7-14)*, *(Café Salerno 927-1979)*, *(Goat Hill Grille 927-9263)*, *(1886 House 922-1995)*, *(Casa DeLucca 922-1760)*, Snack Bar *(Variety Deli B $2, L $5, D $7)* **Under 1 mi:** Restaurant *(Stromberg's 744-1863, across the bridge)* **1-3 mi:** Restaurant *(Beverly Depot 927-5402, D $14-24)*, *(Casablanca)*, Motel *(Lakeview Motor Lodge 922-7535, $85-100)*, Inn/B&B *(Clipper Ship 745-5503)*, *(Salem Inn 741-0680, $130-290)*

Recreation and Entertainment

OnSite: Picnic Area, Park **Near:** Grills, Dive Shop, Jogging Paths **Under 1 mi:** Beach, Playground, Bowling *(Bowl-O-Mat 922-1140)*, Movie Theater *(Cabot Street Cinema 927-3677)*, Cultural Attract *(Cabot Street Theatre Magic Show 927-3677)* **1-3 mi:** Tennis Courts *(Beverly Golf & Tennis 922-9127)*, Golf Course *(Beverly G&T)*, Fitness Center *(All American 927-6888)*, Fishing Charter, Video Rental, Museum *(Peabody and Customs House)*, Sightseeing *(all of Salem and Pickering Wharf)*

Provisioning and General Services

Near: Convenience Store, Delicatessen, Wine/Beer, Lobster Pound, Laundry *(Home Style Laundry 927-6460)*, Newsstand, Hardware Store *(Hansbury General Store 927-3145)*, Copies Etc. *(Best Press 921-0456)* **Under 1 mi:** Health Food *(New Leaf 927-5955)*, Liquor Store *(Cosgroves 744-4000)*, Bank/ATM, Beauty Salon, Dry Cleaners, Pharmacy *(Brooks 921-4550)* **1-3 mi:** Supermarket *(Stop & Shop)*, Bakery, Catholic Church, Protestant Church, Library *(Salem Athenaeum 744-2540)*, Barber Shop, Bookstore *(Derby Square 745-8804)*, Florist, Clothing Store, Retail Shops

Transportation

OnCall: Rental Car *(Enterprise 524-9555)*, Taxi *(City Taxi of Beverly 921-1111)* **Near:** Bikes *(Bay Road Bikes 468-1301)* **Under 1 mi:** Rail *(MBTA Commuter to Boston)* **1-3 mi:** Ferry Service *(Boston-Salem Ferry)* **Airport:** Logan Int'l. *(20 mi.)*

Medical Services

911 Service **OnCall:** Ambulance **Near:** Chiropractor *(Beverly Chiro Center 927-9181)* **Under 1 mi:** Doctor *(Taylor 468-7381)* **1-3 mi:** Dentist, Holistic Services **Hospital:** Beverly 922-3000 *(2 mi.)*

Setting -- Off Beverly Harbor, Glover Wharf is the fourth facility to starboard up the Danvers River. It is hard by the Salem Bridge, just past Beverly Port Marina. Carpozza Pier, a single long public wharf, is on the site of historic Old Ferryway Landing. The pier divides this municipal facility into working boat docks on the west and recreational boating to the east and is also a popular fishing spot as well as the public landing for the municipal moorings.

Marina Notes -- Beverly offers 4 moorings in the inner harbor off the Old Ferryway Public Landing, as well as 8 moorings in the coves of Misery and Little Misery Islands. The Moorings are handled by the Harbormaster's Office - Harbormaster Daniel McPherson (921-6059). *In addition, on rare occasion, there is dockage available. Note that there are no dedicated transient slips -- only those temporarily vacated by seasonal tenants; these are managed by a separate office: The Harbor Authority (921-8561) - Operations Manager is Louis Bochynski. Rates are $2/ft. with metered electricity. Seasonal moorings are $4/ft. for residents and $6/ft. for non-residents. Seasonal dockage for residents $89/ft. Well maintained docks. Tight security. One acceptable full bath.

Notable -- Public picnic area and comfortable benches sit on a concrete boardwalk that overlooks the docks and the river. The onsite "no-longer-operational" McDonald's building has been painted brown to blend in with the weathered shingled marina building. With 355 years of history, The Olde Public Ferryway is one of the oldest "still in use" Common Landing places in the U.S. Beverly, it is believed, is also one of the birthplaces of the American Navy.

PHOTOS ON CD-ROM: 9

Hawthorne Cove Marina

Hawthorne Cove Marina

10 White Street; Salem, MA 01970

Tel: (978) 740-9890 **VHF: Monitor** 9 **Talk** 8
Fax: (978) 740-9994 **Alternate Tel:** (978) 745-8710
Email: info@hawthornecove.com **Web:** www.hawthornecove.com
Nearest Town: Salem *(0 mi.)* **Tourist Info:** (978) 740-0004

Navigational Information

Lat: 42°31.316' **Long:** 070°52.945' **Tide:** 9 ft. **Current:** n/a **Chart:** 13275
Rep. Depths (*MLW*): Entry 10 ft. **Fuel Dock** n/a **Max Slip/Moor** 8 ft./10 ft.
Access: Massachusetts Bay to Salem Channel to Salem Harbor

Marina Facilities *(In Season/Off Season)*

Fuel: No
Slips: 110 Total, 30 Transient **Max LOA:** 65 ft. **Max Beam:** 15 ft.
Rate *(per ft.)*: **Day** $2.00/Inq. **Week** $9.00 **Month** $25
Power: 30 amp $3, **50 amp** $5, **100 amp** n/a, **200 amp** n/a
Cable TV: Yes Seasonal **Dockside Phone:** Yes Seasonal
Dock Type: Wood, Long Fingers, Floating
Moorings: 135 Total, 10 Transient **Launch:** Yes (Free), Dinghy Dock
Rate: Day $35 **Week** $125 **Month** n/a
Heads: 4 Toilet(s), 8 Shower(s)
Laundry: 2 Washer(s), 2 Dryer(s), Book Exchange **Pay Phones:** Yes, 1
Pump-Out: OnSite, OnCall, 1 Port **Fee:** Free **Closed Heads:** No

Marina Operations

Owner/Manager: Russ Vickers **Dockmaster:** Mike Bunyar
In-Season: May-Oct, 7am-8pm **Off-Season:** Nov-Apr, 7am-5pm
After-Hours Arrival: Call in advance
Reservations: Yes, Preferred **Credit Cards:** Visa/MC
Discounts: None
Pets: Welcome, Dog Walk Area **Handicap Access:** No

Marina Services and Boat Supplies

Services - Docking Assistance, Concierge, Security *(24 Hrs., Key entry gate)*, Trash Pick-Up, Dock Carts **Communication -** Mail & Package Hold, Phone Messages, Fax in/out, FedEx, AirBorne, UPS, Express Mail *(Sat Del)* **Supplies - OnSite:** Ice *(Block, Cube)*, Ships' Store **Under 1 mi:** Bait/Tackle *(Jerrys 744-1547)*, Propane *(U-Haul)* **3+ mi:** West Marine *(535-7332, 7 mi.)*, Boat/US *(777-5940, 4 mi.)*

Boatyard Services

OnSite: Travelift *(35T)*, Engine mechanic *(gas, diesel)*, Hull Repairs, Rigger, Bottom Cleaning, Divers, Compound, Wash & Wax, Woodworking, Yacht Design, Yacht Building, Total Refits **Near:** Electrical Repairs, Electronic Sales, Electronics Repairs *(Mass Marine)*, Propeller Repairs *(H&H Propeller)*. **1-3 mi:** Metal Fabrication. **Member:** Other Certifications: IMI member **Yard Rates:** $55/hr., Haul & Launch $4/ft., Power Wash $3.25, Bottom Paint $13/ft. *(paint included)* **Storage:** On-Land $10/ft./mo.

Restaurants and Accommodations

OnCall: Pizzeria *(Engine House 745-1744)* **Near:** Restaurant *(Nathaniel's 825-4311, L $6-19, D $17-38, piano Thu-Sat, Sun Jazz Brunch, Tavern menu $8-19)*, *(In a Pig's Eye 741-4436, L $8, D $12)*, Seafood Shack *(Derby Fish & Lobster 745-2064, L $6-15, D $6-15)*, Fast Food, Hotel *(Hawthorne Hotel 744-4080, $120-310)*, Inn/B&B *(Daniels House 744-5709, $100-150)*, *(Morning Glory B&B 741-1703, $110-160)* **Under 1 mi:** Restaurant *(Red Raven's 745-8558, D $15-25)*, Motel *(Salem Inn 741-0680, $130-300)*

Recreation and Entertainment

OnSite: Picnic Area, Grills **Near:** Playground, Video Arcade, Park, Museum *(Peabody & Essex Museum 745-9500 $10/Free, Pirate Museum 741-2800)*, Sightseeing *(House of The Seven Gables 744-0991)*, Special Events *(Annual Seaport Festival - late May 740-1650)* **Under 1 mi:** Pool, Beach, Video Rental *(Superstar Video 740-4455)* **1-3 mi:** Dive Shop, Tennis Courts *(Beverly Golf & Tennis 922-9127)*, Golf Course *(Olde Salem Green 744-2149)*, Fitness Center *(Healthworks 745-7390)*, Bowling *(Bowl-O-Mat 922-1140)*, Movie Theater *(Museum Place 744-3700)*

Provisioning and General Services

Near: Convenience Store, Delicatessen, Liquor Store *(Bung Hole 744-2251)*, Bakery, Fishmonger, Bank/ATM, Post Office, Dry Cleaners, Laundry, Newsstand, Florist, Retail Shops **Under 1 mi:** Supermarket *(Shaw's 741-8660)*, Health Food *(Nature's Gate 741-3859)*, Catholic Church, Protestant Church, Beauty Salon, Pharmacy *(CVS 744-2224)*, Hardware Store *(Winer Bros 744-0780)*, Copies Etc. *(Deschamps 744-215)* **1-3 mi:** Gourmet Shop, Meat Market, Library *(Athenaeum 744-2540)*, Department Store *(Liberty Tree Mall)*, Buying Club *(BJ's, Costco)*

Transportation

OnSite: Bikes *(Courtesy)* **OnCall:** Water Taxi *($5 1way)*, Rental Car *(Enterprise 740-5666)*, Airport Limo *(George 777-3377)* **Near:** Local Bus *(Trolley)*, InterCity Bus *(MBTA 800 392-6100)*, Rail *(MBTA Commuter Rail)*
Airport: Logan Int'l. *(17 mi.)*

Medical Services

911 Service **OnCall:** Ambulance **Under 1 mi:** Holistic Services *(Body Work Shop 745-2900)* **1-3 mi:** Doctor, Dentist, Chiropractor **Hospital:** North Shore - Salem 745-9000 *(1-3 mi)*

Setting -- The first facility to starboard as you enter protected Salem Harbor, this large, private family marina is located in the heart of the Salem Historic District and right down the street from the House of Seven Gables Historic Site. Landside views are of the boatyard and factory; waterviews are of the wide, attractive, boat laden harbor. There is an extensive network of docks, a large mooring field, a dinghy dock and a small seating area overlooking the docks.

Marina Notes -- Full service yard with 35 ton lift. Pump-out. 110 slips, 135 moorings, launch service and dinghy dock. Good, up-to-date docks and services juxtaposed to old boatyard wharf. Complimentary bicycles. Basic, aging heads. Spare, but pleasant, seating area, just outside the laundry, overlooks the marina. Complimentary coffee, newspapers & donuts accompanied by live harp music on Sunday mornings. Sea Tow onsite. Salem Water Taxi also berths here and shares the facilities. Harbormaster: 741-0098.

Notable -- All of Salem's 200 attractions are within a mile. The setting for Nathaniel Hawthorne's classic novel "The House of Seven Gables", as well as his birthplace, is a block away - there are guided tours, an AV show, shops and a café - open daily 10am-5pm (744-0991). Peabody Essex Museum, which includes 30 galleries and 11 historic houses, including East India Marine Society's 1824 home, and Salem Maritime National Historic Site (740-1660) are within walking distance -- good places to begin. Home of the Nautical Flea Market, Salem Maritime Festival. Haunted Happening begins weekend before Halloween.

PHOTOS ON CD-ROM: 9

Navigational Information
Lat: 42°31.165' **Long:** 070°53.279' **Tide:** 9 ft. **Current:** n/a **Chart:** 13275
Rep. Depths (*MLW*): Entry 10 ft. **Fuel Dock** n/a **Max Slip/Moor** 7 ft./-
Access: Mass. Bay to Salem Channel to Salem Harbor to South River

Marina Facilities *(In Season/Off Season)*
Fuel: No
Slips: 100 Total, 3 Transient **Max LOA:** 120 ft. **Max Beam:** n/a
Rate *(per ft.)*: **Day** $2.00/Inq.* **Week** $12 **Month** Inq.
Power: 30 amp $3, **50 amp** $5, **100 amp** n/a, **200 amp** n/a
Cable TV: No **Dockside Phone:** No
Dock Type: Floating
Moorings: 0 Total, 0 Transient **Launch:** n/a, Dinghy Dock
Rate: Day n/a **Week** n/a **Month** n/a
Heads: 2 Toilet(s), 2 Shower(s)
Laundry: 1 Washer(s), 1 Dryer(s), Book Exchange **Pay Phones:** Yes
Pump-Out: OnCall, Full Service, 1 Port **Fee:** n/a **Closed Heads:** No

Marina Operations
Owner/Manager: Rick Rocket **Dockmaster:** Timothy Pickering
In-Season: May-Oct 31, 7:30am-10pm **Off-Season:** Nov-Apr 30, 8am-4pm
After-Hours Arrival: Call in advance
Reservations: Preferred **Credit Cards:** Visa/MC
Discounts: None
Pets: Welcome, Dog Walk Area **Handicap Access:** No

Pickering Wharf Marina

23 Congress Street; Salem, MA 01970

Tel: (978) 744-2727 **VHF: Monitor** 9 **Talk** 8
Fax: (978) 740-6728 **Alternate Tel:** n/a
Email: tpickering@pickeringwharf.com **Web:** www.pickeringwharf.com
Nearest Town: Salem *(0 mi.)* **Tourist Info:** (978) 744-0004

Marina Services and Boat Supplies
Services - Docking Assistance, Trash Pick-Up, Dock Carts
Communication - Mail & Package Hold, Phone Messages, Fax in/out, Data Ports *(Office)*, FedEx, AirBorne, UPS, Express Mail **Supplies - OnSite:** Ice *(Cube)* **1-3 mi:** Marine Discount Store, Bait/Tackle *(Petes Bait & Tackle 744-9000)*, Propane *(U-Haul)* **3+ mi:** West Marine *(535-7332, 8 mi.)*, Boat/US *(777-5940, 4 mi.)*

Boatyard Services
OnCall: Bottom Cleaning, Divers, Compound, Wash & Wax, Interior Cleaning, Woodworking, Inflatable Repairs, Life Raft Service, Upholstery, Yacht Interiors, Metal Fabrication **Near:** Engine mechanic *(gas)*. **Under 1 mi:** Travelift, Launching Ramp, Propeller Repairs. **1-3 mi:** Sail Loft.
Nearest Yard: Dion's Boat Yard (978) 744-0844

Restaurants and Accommodations
OnSite: Restaurant *(The Essex Room)*, *(Victoria Station 745-3400, L $6-10, D $11-21)*, *(Rockmore Dry Dock 740-1001)*, *(Bella Luna Café 744-5555, D $25-30)*, *(Finz Seafood 744-8485, L $6-12, D $16-25)*, *(The Grapevine 745-9335, D $14-22)*, Hotel *(Pickering Wharf 100 room hotel opening soon)*
OnCall: Pizzeria *(Dominos 744-4040)* **Near:** Restaurant *(Nathaniel's 825-4311, L $6-19, D $17-38, live piano Thu-Sat, Tavern Menu $8-19, Sun Jazz Brunch)*, Hotel *(Hawthorne Hotel 744-4080, $130-300)*, Inn/B&B *(The Salem Inn 741-0680, $110-190, 28 rooms in 3 restored historic buildings)*, *(Inn at Seven Winter Street 745-9520)*, *(Amelia Payson 944-8304)*

Recreation and Entertainment
Near: Beach, Playground, Park, Museum *(Peabody-Essex 745-1876, $10/Free; House of The Seven Gables 744-0991)*, Sightseeing *(Moby Duck tours 741-4386)*, Special Events *(Seaport Fest - May, Maritime Fest - July)*
Under 1 mi: Golf Course *(Olde Salem Green 744-2149)*, Fitness Center *(Healthworks 745-7390)*, Jogging Paths, Movie Theater *(Museum Place 744-3700)*, Video Rental *(Superstar 740-4455)* **1-3 mi:** Tennis Courts *(Beverly Golf & Tennis 922-9127)*, Bowling *(Bowl-O-Mat 922-1140)*

Provisioning and General Services
Near: Convenience Store, Delicatessen *(Red's Sandwich Shop 745-3527)*, Liquor Store *(Bung Hole Liquor 744-2251)*, Bakery, Bank/ATM, Bookstore *(Pyramid Books 745-7171)*, Newsstand, Hardware Store *(Winer Bros 744-0780)*, Florist, Retail Shops **Under 1 mi:** Supermarket *(Stop & Shop)*, Health Food *(Nature's Gate 741-3859)*, Post Office, Library *(Athenaeum 744-2540)*, Barber Shop, Pharmacy *(CVS 744-2224)*, Copies Etc. *(Mail Boxes Etc 745-9191)* **1-3 mi:** Beauty Salon, Dry Cleaners, Laundry, Clothing Store **3+ mi:** Buying Club *(Costco, BJ's, 6 mi.)*

Transportation
OnCall: Water Taxi *(Salem Water Taxi $5 1-Way)*, Airport Limo *(George 777-3377)* **Near:** Local Bus *(Salem Trolley)*, InterCity Bus *(MBTA)*, Rail *(Commuter Rail to Boston)* **Under 1 mi:** Taxi *(Adventure Limo 774-2112)*
3+ mi: Rental Car *(Hertz 745-5275/ Enterprise 740-5666, 1 mi./2 mi.)*
Airport: Logan Int'l. *(16 mi.)*

Medical Services
911 Service **OnCall:** Ambulance **1-3 mi:** Doctor *(Lydia Pinkham Memorial Clinic 744-3288)*, Dentist, Chiropractor, Holistic Services **Hospital:** North Shore - Salem 741-1215 *(1.5 mi.)*

Setting -- Tucked deeply into Salem Harbor, on the far side of Derby Wharf, the docks surround the attractive Pickering Wharf complex, a six acre commercial and residential village. Views are of the colorful restaurants, shops, the nicely landscaped promenades, some large commercial buildings, and the adjacent Salem National Maritime Historic Site.

Marina Notes -- * $1.75/ft. up to 50', $2/ft. over 50'. Weekly slips (and an occasional nightly slip, with dinghy dock). Accommodating dock staff. Heads, showers and laundry located in the complex. Onsite are four restaurants: Victoria Station on the wharf, 2nd floor Rockmore Drydock overlooking the harbor, FINZ Seafood (all serve lunch 11:30am-4pm and dinner 5:30pm on) and Bella Luna (dinner only). Many shops and galleries to explore.

Notable -- All of Salem's many, many attractions are within walking distance; start at the Visitor Center, 10 Liberty St. Nine acre Salem Maritime Site has five restored buildings, including the Custom House on Derby Wharf, all open daily 9am-5pm (740-1660). Nearby is the marvelous Peabody Essex Museum complex (notable is the Maritime Art & History Exhibit), the oldest private museum in the U.S. and one of the most compelling maritime museums in New England, daily 10am-5pm (745-9500). Farther out is the Pioneer Village living history museum - Salem, 1630, the Massachusetts Bay Colony capital. Stroll Chestnut Street to enjoy the magnificent houses. Salem is steeped in Witch kitsch: Salem Witch Museum, daily 10am-5pm, open 'til 7pm in July and Aug, $6/4 (740-9229), Witch Dungeon (741-3570), and Witch House just scratch the surface. Haunted Happenings, Halloween Salem-style, lasts for three weeks.

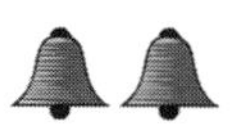

Salem Water Taxi

10 White Street; Salem, MA 01970

Tel: (978) 745-6070 **VHF: Monitor** 68 **Talk** 68
Fax: (978) 740-9994 **Alternate Tel:** n/a
Email: info@salemwatertaxi.com **Web:** www.salemwatertaxi.com
Nearest Town: Salem *(0 mi.)* **Tourist Info:** (978) 744-0004

Navigational Information

Lat: 42°31.137' **Long:** 070°53.362' **Tide:** 9 ft. **Current:** n/a **Chart:** 13275
Rep. Depths (*MLW*): Entry 15 ft. **Fuel Dock** n/a **Max Slip/Moor** 10 ft./15 ft.
Access: Salem Channel to Salem Harbor mooring field

Marina Facilities *(In Season/Off Season)*

Fuel: No
Slips: 0 Total, 0 Transient **Max LOA:** 60 ft. **Max Beam:** 20 ft.
Rate *(per ft.)*: **Day** n/a **Week** n/a **Month** n/a
Power: 30 amp n/a, **50 amp** n/a, **100 amp** n/a, **200 amp** n/a
Cable TV: No **Dockside Phone:** No
Dock Type: n/a
Moorings: 130 Total, 10 Transient **Launch:** Yes (Free), Dinghy Dock
Rate: Day $30 **Week** $150 **Month** $300
Heads: 4 Toilet(s), 4 Shower(s) *(with dressing rooms)*
Laundry: 2 Washer(s), 2 Dryer(s), Book Exchange **Pay Phones:** No
Pump-Out: OnCall, Full Service, 1 Central **Fee:** n/a **Closed Heads:** No

Marina Operations

Owner/Manager: Russ Vickers **Dockmaster:** Todd Dochner
In-Season: May-Oct, 8 am-10 pm **Off-Season:** Nov-Apr 30, Closed
After-Hours Arrival: Call in advance for assignment
Reservations: Preferred **Credit Cards:** Visa/MC, Amex
Discounts: None
Pets: Welcome **Handicap Access:** No

Marina Services and Boat Supplies

Supplies - OnSite: Ice *(Block, Cube)* **Under 1 mi:** Propane *(U-Haul 744-6030)* **1-3 mi:** Ships' Store, Bait/Tackle *(Petes Bait & Tackle 744-9000)* **3+ mi:** West Marine *(535-7332, 7 mi.)*, Boat/US *(777-5940, 4 mi.)*

Boatyard Services

Nearest Yard: Fred J. Dion Yacht Yard (978) 744-0844

Restaurants and Accommodations

Near: Restaurant *(Victoria Station 745-3400, D $8-24)*, *(The Grapevine 745-9335, D $14-22)*, *(Finz 744-8485, L $6-12, D $16-25)*, *(Rockmore Dry Dock 740-1001)*, *(Bella Luna 744-5555, D $25-30)*, Seafood Shack *(Derby Fish & Lobster 745-2065)*, Inn/B&B *(Morning Glory 741-1703)*, *(Inn on Washington Square 741-4997)* **Under 1 mi:** Restaurant *(Nathaniels 744-4080, L $6-19, D $17-38, at the Hawthorne Hotel, live piano Thu-Sat, Tavern Menu $8-19, Sun Jazz Brunch)*, Hotel *(Hawthorne Hotel 744-4080, $120-310)*, *(Lafayette 745-5503)*, Inn/B&B *(Stepping Stone Inn 741-8900, $80-130)*, *(Salem Inn 741-8900, $130-300, 3 restored 19thC buildings)*

Recreation and Entertainment

Under 1 mi: Video Rental *(West Coast Video 978-745-4005)*, Museum *(Peabody Essex 745-1876 $10/Free - the oldest private museum in the country, with one of the finest Maritime collecitons; New England Pirate Museum 741-2800, Salem Witch Museum 744-1692)*, Cultural Attract *(Salem Maritime National Historic Site 740-1660 daily 9am-5pm Free)*, Sightseeing *(Salem 1630: Pioneer Village 744-0991)* **1-3 mi:** Beach, Golf Course *(Olde Salem Green 978-744-2149)*, Fitness Center, Jogging Paths, Roller Blade/Bike Paths, Bowling *(Bowl O Mat 978-922-1140)*, Fishing Charter *(China Sea Charters 603-580-1238)*, Movie Theater *(Museum Place Cinemas 978-744-3700)*, Video Arcade, Park

Provisioning and General Services

Near: Convenience Store *(Brother's Café & Mini Mart)*, Wine/Beer, Liquor Store *(Bung Hole Liquor 744-2251)*, Fishmonger, Lobster Pound, Bank/ATM, Catholic Church, Newsstand, Retail Shops, Copies Etc. **Under 1 mi:** Gourmet Shop, Delicatessen *(Polonus Deli & Ice Cream 740-3203)*, Health Food *(Natures Gate 741-3859)*, Meat Market, Post Office, Protestant Church, Synagogue, Beauty Salon, Barber Shop, Dry Cleaners, Laundry, Bookstore *(Pyramid Books 745-7171)*, Pharmacy *(CVS 744-2224)*, Hardware Store *(Winer Bros 744-0780)*, Florist **1-3 mi:** Supermarket *(Shaw's 741-8660)*, Library, Department Store *(Kmart 741-5239)* **3+ mi:** Buying Club *(Costco, BJ's, 5 mi.)*

Transportation

OnSite: Water Taxi **OnCall:** Taxi *(Tri-City Taxi 744-4772)*, Airport Limo *(George 777-3377)* **Under 1 mi:** Bikes *(Salem Cycle 741-2222)*, Rail *(MBTA to Boston)* **3+ mi:** Rental Car *(Enterprise 740-5666/Hertz 745-5275, on call/2 mi.)* **Airport:** Logan Int'l. *(20 mi.)*

Medical Services

911 Service **Under 1 mi:** Doctor *(Lydia Pinkham Memorial Clinic 744-3288)*, Chiropractor *(Salem Chiropractic 741-9416)* **Hospital:** North Shore - Salem 741-1215 *(1.5 mi.)*

PHOTOS ON CD-ROM: 7

Setting -- Tucked up the channel behind Pickering Wharf is the little, bright yellow house which is the main base for Salem Water Taxi (also known as Barnegat Marine Launch). It manages the moorings in the center of Salem Harbor. Their bright yellow launches are easy to spot as they ply the harbor.

Marina Notes -- Under same ownership as Hawthorne Cove Marina. Landside services, which include wash-down dock, showers, laundry and loaner dinghies, are available at Hawthorne Cove. It is the Hawthorne Cove launch that will pick you up to use the facilities -- included in the mooring fee. Also included is unlimited use of Salem Water Taxi Launch, which delivers you to the back side of Pickering Wharf, at the foot of the Congress St. bridge. Just up the block is Brothers Café and Mini Mart, an ATM, as well as all of Pickering Wharf . Pickering Wharf Hotel being built next door. Derby Fish and Lobster 1 block. 2 blocks to Friendship of Salem schooner. Additional moorings on the Marblehead side of Salem Harbor available from Mid-Harbor Marine 741-8141, Ch.9 or West Shore Marine 639-1290 -- includes launch service to either side of the Harbor. Above address is for the Office near Hawthorne Cove, not the Landing.

Notable -- The launch dock is conveniently located for most of Salem's attractions. A couple of blocks' walk is the Maritime National Historic Site's Orientation Center, a good jumping off point for a nautically flavored Salem visit. The 1824 Peabody Essex Museum has over 700 ship models and other artifacts, many from Salem's maritime heritage. Rockmore Dry Dock Floating Restaurant is in the middle of the harbor -- dinghy over or take their red launch from Pickering Wharf. Salem 1630 is a 17thC outdoor living history museum, a recreation of the original English colony - Mon-Sat 10am-5pm, Sun 12-5pm.

Navigational Information

Lat: 42°30.579' **Long:** 070°53.269' **Tide:** 9 ft. **Current:** 1 kt. **Chart:** 13275
Rep. Depths (*MLW*): Entry 8 ft. **Fuel Dock** n/a **Max Slip/Moor** 8 ft./8 ft.
Access: Salem Harbor main Channel to G3 then private Channel

Marina Facilities *(In Season/Off Season)*

Fuel: Diesel, On Call Delivery
Slips: 18 Total, 10 Transient **Max LOA:** 100 ft. **Max Beam:** n/a
Rate *(per ft.)*: **Day** $2.00/Inq. **Week** Inq. **Month** Inq.
Power: 30 amp Yes, **50 amp** Yes, **100 amp** n/a, **200 amp** n/a
Cable TV: No **Dockside Phone:** No
Dock Type: Wood, Alongside, Floating
Moorings: 13 Total, 6 Transient **Launch:** Yes (Free)
Rate: Day $25 **Week** Inq. **Month** Inq.
Heads: 1 Toilet(s), 1 Shower(s)
Laundry: None **Pay Phones:** No
Pump-Out: OnCall, Full Service, 1 Central **Fee:** Free **Closed Heads:** No

Marina Operations

Owner/Manager: Fred Atkins **Dockmaster:** n/a
In-Season: May-Nov, 7am-4pm **Off-Season:** n/a
After-Hours Arrival: Prior arrangement.
Reservations: Yes, Required **Credit Cards:** Visa/MC, Amex
Discounts: None
Pets: Welcome **Handicap Access:** No

Fred J. Dion Yacht Yard

23 Glendale Street; Salem, MA 01970

Tel: (978) 744-0844 **VHF: Monitor** 9 **Talk** n/a
Fax: (978) 745-7258 **Alternate Tel:** n/a
Email: fjdions@msn.com **Web:** n/a
Nearest Town: Salem *(1 mi.)* **Tourist Info:** (978) 744-0004

Marina Services and Boat Supplies

Communication - Phone Messages, Fax in/out, FedEx, AirBorne, UPS, Express Mail **Supplies - OnSite:** Ice *(Block, Cube)*, CNG **Near:** Ships' Store **Under 1 mi:** Propane *(Salem Moving & Storage 744-6030)* **1-3 mi:** Bait/Tackle *(Jerrys 744-1547)* **3+ mi:** West Marine *(535-7332, 8 mi.)*, Boat/US *(777-5940, 4.5 mi.)*

Boatyard Services

OnSite: Travelift *(50T)*, Engine mechanic *(gas, diesel)*, Electrical Repairs, Hull Repairs, Rigger, Sail Loft, Bottom Cleaning, Brightwork, Air Conditioning, Refrigeration, Compound, Wash & Wax, Interior Cleaning, Woodworking, Metal Fabrication, Painting, Awlgrip, Yacht Design, Yacht Building, Total Refits **Under 1 mi:** Divers *(Salem Mooring Services 745-0059)*, Propeller Repairs. **1-3 mi:** Upholstery. **Dealer for:** Westerbeke, Cummins, Universal, Edson, Fischer Panda, Grunert, Sea Frost. **Yard Rates:** $60/hr., Haul & Launch $6/ft., Power Wash $1.70 **Storage:** On-Land $50/ft.

Restaurants and Accommodations

OnCall: Pizzeria *(Engine House 745-1744)* **Near:** Restaurant *(Salem Jade 744-3360)*, Lite Fare *(Yellow Dog Café 745-6443)* **Under 1 mi:** Restaurant *(The Grapevine 745-9335, D $13-24)*, *(Bertini's 744-1436)*, *(Nathaniel's 744-4080, L $6-19, D $17-38, live piano Thu-Sat, Tavern Menu $8-19, Sun Jazz Brunch)*, *(Lyceum 745-7665, L $6-11, D $14-20)*, *(Red Raven Love Noodle 745-8558)*, Seafood Shack *(Derby Fish & Lobster 745-2064, L $6-15, D $6-15)*, Hotel *(Hawthorne Hotel 744-4080, $120-310)*, *(Lafayette 745-5503)*, Inn/B&B *(Coach House 744-4092, $95-185)*, *(Salem Inn 741-8022, $130-290)* **1-3 mi:** Inn/B&B *(Clipper Ship Inn 745-8022, $95-140)*

Recreation and Entertainment

Near: Beach, Picnic Area, Grills, Playground, Tennis Courts, Jogging Paths, Roller Blade/Bike Paths, Park **Under 1 mi:** Bowling *(Candlepin 744-3954)*, Fishing Charter, Movie Theater, Video Rental *(Superstar Video 740-4455)*, Museum *(Peabody Essex 745-9500, House of the Seven Gables 744-0991)*, Cultural Attract, Sightseeing **1-3 mi:** Dive Shop, Golf Course *(Olde Salem Green 744-2149)*, Fitness Center *(Healthworks 745-7390)*

Provisioning and General Services

Near: Wine/Beer, Liquor Store *(Salem Liquors 744-2335)*, Synagogue, Beauty Salon, Barber Shop, Laundry, Florist **Under 1 mi:** Convenience Store *(Kwik Shop 740-9955)*, Health Food *(Nature's Gate 741-3859)*, Post Office, Catholic Church, Protestant Church, Library *(Athenaeum 744-2540)*, Dry Cleaners, Bookstore *(Open A Book 745-4334)*, Pharmacy *(CVS 744-2224)*, Newsstand, Hardware Store *(Winer Bros 744-0780)*, Retail Shops, Copies Etc. *(Mail Boxes Etc. 745-9191)* **1-3 mi:** Supermarket *(Stop & Shop)*, Gourmet Shop *(Brandis 781-631-5040)*, Fishmonger, Lobster Pound, Bank/ATM **3+ mi:** Buying Club *(Costco, BJ's, 4 mi.)*

Transportation

OnSite: Water Taxi **OnCall:** Rental Car *(Hertz 745-5275/ Enterprise 740-5666)*, Taxi *(Tri-City 744-4772)*, Airport Limo *(Adventure Limo 774-2112)* **Near:** Local Bus *(Salem Trolley)* **Under 1 mi:** Bikes *(Pure Bicycle 745-5558)* **1-3 mi:** Rail *(MBTA to Boston)* **Airport:** Logan Int'l. *(15 mi.)*

Medical Services

911 Service **OnCall:** Ambulance **Near:** Chiropractor **Under 1 mi:** Doctor, Dentist, Holistic Services **Hospital:** North Shore - Salem 745-1215 *(2 mi.)*

Setting -- Tucked way up at the head of Salem Harbor, in a residential area, this small historic boatyard doesn't pretend to be anything else. The ambiance is pure old-time working yard. There are two docks that stretch out into the harbor; each accommodates about five boats "alongisde", and there are moorings in the harbor.

Marina Notes -- A full service boatyard. Family owned and operated since 1914. Year 'round, full-time professional staff. Repair, restoration and storage of sail and power boats. Can haul yachts to 75 ft. and transport, overland, yachts up to 45 ft. The Salem Trolley makes most of the community easily available.

Notable -- It's a about a mile to the historic area of "downtown" Salem -- where the activity choices range from witch kitsch to truly superb maritime and historic sites. For a nautically flavored visit, at which Salem truly excels, begin at the Maritime National Historic Site's Orientation Center, which offers a free overview film (740-1660). The 2-block 1824 Peabody Essex Museum, which added 5 new galleries in the summer of 2003, has, among its many exhibits, over 700 ship models and other artifacts from Salem's maritime heritage. Moby Duck amphibious vessel tours are also a fun way to see the sites (741-4386). Salem special events include: Seaport Fest (Late May), Maritime Fest (July), Heritage Days (August) and Haunted Happenings (3 weeks in October).

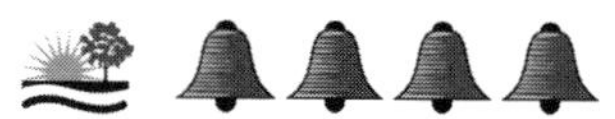

Corinthian Yacht Club

PO Box 401; 1 Nahant Street; Marblehead, MA 01945

Tel: (781) 631-0005 **VHF: Monitor** 69 **Talk** 69
Fax: (781) 631-4968 **Alternate Tel:** n/a
Email: n/a **Web:** www.corinthianyc.org
Nearest Town: Marblehead *(2 mi.)* **Tourist Info:** (781) 631-2868

Navigational Information

Lat: 42°30.205' **Long:** 070°50.160' **Tide:** 10 ft. **Current:** 0.5 kt. **Chart:** n/a
Rep. Depths (*MLW*): Entry 30 ft. **Fuel Dock** n/a **Max Slip/Moor** -/30 ft.
Access: Just inside the harbor, beyond Marblehead Light, directly to port

Marina Facilities *(In Season/Off Season)*

Fuel: No
Slips: 0 Total, 0 Transient **Max LOA:** n/a **Max Beam:** n/a
Rate *(per ft.)*: **Day** n/a **Week** n/a **Month** n/a
Power: 30 amp n/a, **50 amp** n/a, **100 amp** n/a, **200 amp** n/a
Cable TV: No **Dockside Phone:** No
Dock Type: n/a
Moorings: 350 Total, 4-10 Transient **Launch:** Yes (Free), Dinghy Dock
Rate: Day $25 **Week** n/a **Month** n/a
Heads: 6 Toilet(s), 6 Shower(s)
Laundry: 1 Washer(s), 1 Dryer(s) **Pay Phones:** Yes
Pump-Out: No **Fee:** n/a **Closed Heads:** No

Marina Operations

Owner/Manager: Jack Carney **Dockmaster:** Same
In-Season: June-Sep 1, 8am-11pm **Off-Season:** May & Sep, 9am-6pm
After-Hours Arrival: Call in advance
Reservations: Yes **Credit Cards:** Visa/MC
Discounts: None
Pets: Welcome **Handicap Access:** No

Marina Services and Boat Supplies

Services - Docking Assistance, Dock Carts **Communication -** Phone Messages, Fax in/out *(Free)*, AirBorne, UPS, Express Mail **Supplies - OnSite:** Ice *(Block, Cube)* **1-3 mi:** Ships' Store *(The Forepeak 639-0029, Lynne Marine Supplies 631-1305, Woods Nautical 631-0221)*, Bait/Tackle *(Boat Shop 631-5348)* **3+ mi:** West Marine *(978/535-7332, 10 mi.)*, Boat/US *(978-777-5940, 4 mi.)*

Boatyard Services

OnSite: Launching Ramp **1-3 mi:** Travelift *(Marblehead Trading)*, Electrical Repairs *(Boatworks Marine Electronics 631-7565)*, Electronic Sales *(Boatworks)*, Electronics Repairs, Sail Loft *(Doyle Sailmakers, town dock)*. **3+ mi:** Propeller Repairs *(Haskell & Hall, 5 mi.)*. **Nearest Yard:** Marblehead Trading Co. (781) 639-0029

Restaurants and Accommodations

OnSite: Restaurant *(Corinthian Y.C. Dining Room L $15, D $20)*, Snack Bar *(continental breakfast, sandwiches and burgers)*, Lite Fare *(Corinthian Grille pub food, sandwiches to light entrées)* **Near:** Inn/B&B *(Seagull Inn 631-1893, $125-250)* **1-3 mi:** Restaurant *(Pellino's 631-3344, D $18-33, by launch, highly rated)*, *(Maddie's Sail Loft 631-9824, L $5-16, D $9-18, burgers, fish & chips, beer)*, *(The Barnacle 631-4236, L $5-9, D $10-14)*, Snack Bar *(Muffin Shop 631-8223, B $2-7, L $2-7)*, Inn/B&B *(Harborside House 631-1032, $70-95)*, *(Harbor Light Inn 631-2186, $105-275)*

Recreation and Entertainment

OnSite: Pool, Heated Pool, Tennis Courts, Jogging Paths **Near:** Beach, Park *(Chandler Hovey Park at eastern end of Neck, Castle Rock across the Neck)*, Sightseeing *(The mansions of Marblehead Neck and directly across the harbor - Fort Sewall)* **Under 1 mi:** Cultural Attract *(Audubon Bird Sanctuary, free; Marblehead Little Theatre 631-9697)*

Provisioning and General Services

Under 1 mi: Bakery *(Bowman's 744-5200)* **1-3 mi:** Convenience Store *(Little Store 631-0477)*, Gourmet Shop *(Crosby's delivers)*, Delicatessen, Wine/Beer, Liquor Store *(Shubie's Liquors & Market Place 631-0149)*, Fishmonger, Bank/ATM, Post Office, Catholic Church, Protestant Church, Synagogue, Library *(Town of Marblehead 631-1480)*, Beauty Salon, Barber Shop, Dry Cleaners, Laundry *(Home Style Laundry 631-6491)*, Bookstore *(The Spirit of '76 631-7199)*, Pharmacy *(CVS 639-1412)*, Newsstand, Hardware Store, Florist, Retail Shops, Department Store, Buying Club, Copies Etc. **3+ mi:** Supermarket *(Shaw's 639-9700, 4 mi.)*

Transportation

OnSite: Water Taxi *(Launch to town)* **OnCall:** Rental Car *(Enterprise 978/740-5666)*, Taxi *(Tri-City 639-2488)*, Airport Limo *(Dependable 639-1020)* **1-3 mi:** Bikes *(Marblehead Bike 631-1570)*, Rail *(MBTA commuter train to Boston)* **Airport:** Logan Int'l. *(15 mi.)*

Medical Services

911 Service **OnCall:** Ambulance **1-3 mi:** Doctor, Dentist, Chiropractor *(Marblehead Chiro 639-0808)*, Holistic Services *(Marblehead Massage 639-8444)* **Hospital:** North Shore - Salem 978-745-9000 *(4 mi.)*

PHOTOS ON CD-ROM: 9

Setting -- This beautiful, hospitable and very gracious private club sits on Jack's Point on the eastern shore at the mouth of Marblehead Harbor. The facilities, the services and the amenities are wonderful, topped only by the spectacular views. Perched on a rocky ledge, the club house, with its verandas, porches and newly renovated dining and living rooms, has 180 degree panoramic vistas across the yacht-filled harbor, out to the South Channel and beyond.

Marina Notes -- The club facilities are open to all visiting boaters. It is located on the residential side of Marblehead Harbor, so downtown is most easily accessed by either dinghy or the club launch. A major renovation was begun in Fall 2002 and will continue into 2003. This includes a new dining room and fairly massive renewal of an already very lovely facility. Please observe the dress code: Dining Room: collared shirt, slacks, shoes for men; comparable attire for women. Jackets & ties after 6pm on Saturdays. Porch: collared shirt, slacks, shoes for men; comparable attire for women. Sailing attire with pants/shorts and tennis whites also acceptable. (No tank tops, torn jeans, or cutoffs are allowed anywhere.) Function facilities (accommodating 60-180) available to other YCs.

Notable -- The picture-perfect streets of Marblehead Neck are lined with turn of the century "cottages", spectacular mansions and even a stone castle. There are views at every turn, and a couple of facilities -- the Seagull Inn and Oceanside. Note: All distances above are "driving distance" around the harbor. Utilizing the club launch (or your dinghy) to theTucker's Wharf town landing puts all the historic old town section "nearby". See "Tucker's Wharf" for those distances.

Navigational Information

Lat: 42°30.248' **Long:** 070°50.833' **Tide:** 10 ft. **Current:** 1 kt. **Chart:** 13275
Rep. Depths (*MLW*): Entry 20 ft. **Fuel Dock** n/a **Max Slip/Moor** 20 ft./20 ft.
Access: Marblehead Harbor, follow fairway along western shore

Marina Facilities *(In Season/Off Season)*

Fuel: *Marblehead Trading* - Gasoline, Diesel
Slips: 6 Total, 6* Transient **Max LOA:** 100 ft. **Max Beam:** n/a
Rate *(per ft.)*: **Day** $1.50/n/a **Week** n/a **Month** n/a
Power: 30 amp $15, **50 amp** $25, **100 amp** n/a, **200 amp** n/a
Cable TV: No **Dockside Phone:** No
Dock Type: Wood, Alongside, Floating
Moorings: 0 Total, 0 Transient **Launch:** n/a, Dinghy Dock
Rate: Day n/a **Week** n/a **Month** n/a
Heads: 4 Toilet(s)
Laundry: None **Pay Phones:** Yes
Pump-Out: Self Service, 1 Central **Fee:** Free **Closed Heads:** Yes

Marina Operations

Owner/Manager: Warner Hazell (Harbormaster) **Dockmaster:** n/a
In-Season: May 16-Oct, 7:30am-3pm **Off-Season:** Nov-May 15, 7:30-3pm
After-Hours Arrival: Take any open slip, check in in the morning
Reservations: Yes **Credit Cards:** Visa/MC
Discounts: None
Pets: Welcome **Handicap Access:** No

Tucker's Wharf Municipal Docks

Tucker's Wharf; Marblehead, MA 01945

Tel: (781) 631-2386 **VHF: Monitor** 16 **Talk** 14
Fax: n/a **Alternate Tel:** n/a
Email: n/a **Web:** n/a
Nearest Town: Marblehead *(0.5 mi.)* **Tourist Info:** (781) 639-8469

Marina Services and Boat Supplies

Services - Megayacht Facilities **Communication -** FedEx, AirBorne, UPS, Express Mail **Supplies - Near:** Ice *(Block, Cube)*, Ships' Store *(Forepeak Ship's 631-7184)* **Under 1 mi:** Bait/Tackle *(Boat Shop 631-5348)*

Boatyard Services

Near: Travelift, Railway, Crane, Engine mechanic *(gas, diesel)*, Electrical Repairs, Electronics Repairs, Hull Repairs, Rigger, Sail Loft, Canvas Work, Bottom Cleaning, Brightwork, Air Conditioning, Refrigeration, Propeller Repairs, Woodworking, Painting, Awlgrip. **Nearest Yard:** Marblehead Trading (781) 639-0029

Restaurants and Accommodations

OnSite: Restaurant *(The Landing 632-3218, L $8-18, D $18-38, overlooking docks & harbor, lunch menu in Pub evenings, Sun brunch $7-14, kids' menu)* **Near:** Restaurant *(126 Washington 631-3900, D $10-20, Tue-Sun Contemp American - beneath the Muffin Shop)*, *(Maddie's Sail Loft 631-9824, L $5-16, D $9-18)*, *(Driftwood 631-1145, B&L, opens 5:30am)*, *(The Barnacle 631-4236, L $5-9, D $10-14)*, Snack Bar *(Muffin Shop 631-8223, L $2-6)*, Inn/B&B *(Harbor Light Inn 631-2186, $125-295)*, *(Brimblecomb Hill 631-3172, $85-130)* **Under 1 mi:** Pizzeria *(Village Pizza & Subs 693-8588)*, Inn/B&B *(Marblehead Inn 631-9999, $120-170)*

Recreation and Entertainment

Near: Beach *(Crocker Park and a mi. to Gas House Beach)*, Picnic Area *(west to Crocker Park or farther east to Fort Sewall)*, Museum *(Marblehead Historical Society 631-1768; 1768 Jeremiah Lee Mansion 631-1069 $5/Free; King Hooper Mansion 631-2608 Free)*, Cultural Attract *(Summer Jazz 631-1528 Unitarian Church)*, Sightseeing *(Historic District)*, Special Events *(Marblehead Race Week late July, Arts Festival early July)*

Provisioning and General Services

Near: Gourmet Shop *(Crosbys Market 631-1741)*, Liquor Store *(Haley's Package 631-0169)*, Bakery *(Ladycakes 631-1284)*, Bank/ATM, Protestant Church, Library *(Marblehead Library 631-1480)*, Hardware Store *(Flag Hanger 631-7137)*, Florist *(Flores Mantilla 631-9483)*, Retail Shops, Copies Etc. *(Litchmans 631-0175)* **Under 1 mi:** Convenience Store *(7-Eleven)*, Wine/Beer *(Village Liquors 631-0570)*, Farmers' Market *(Sat am Village St. 631-2868)*, Fishmonger *(Marblehead Lobster 631-0787)*, Laundry *(Home Style Laundry 631-6491)*, Bookstore *(Spirit of '76 631-7199)*, Pharmacy *(CVS 639-1412)* **1-3 mi:** Supermarket *(Shaw's 639-9700)*, Catholic Church

Transportation

OnCall: Taxi *(Tri-City 639-2488)*, Airport Limo *(Dependable 639-1020)*
Near: Rail *("T" to Boston)* **Under 1 mi:** Bikes *(Marblehead Bike 631-1570)*
1-3 mi: Rental Car *(Hertz 745-5275)* **Airport:** Logan Int'l. *(15 mi.)*

Medical Services

911 Service **OnCall:** Ambulance **Under 1 mi:** Doctor, Chiropractor *(Marblehead Chiro 639-0808)*, Holistic Services *(Marblehead Massage 639-8444)* **Hospital:** North Shore -Salem 978-745-9000 *(5 mi.)*

Setting -- Right in the heart of spectacular Marblehead, Tucker's Wharf is maintained by the town and managed by the Harbormaster's office. Waterside views are of the picturesque harbor, awash in beautiful boats. Landside is little Phillip T. Clark Public Landing park, Marblehead Trading's facility and The Landings Restaurant -- all surrounded by the historic district.

Marina Notes -- * 218 ft. of alongside transient dockage. Dinghy dock is at State Street Park. Harbormaster's office is more than a mile from the docks -- address: 6B Cliff Street; Marblehead, MA 01945 (and is right next to Marblehead Trading's second facility). Any package would have to be shipped to that address and guests would have to get to the office to pick it up. There are public rest rooms in Phillip Clark Park. Marblehead Trading may have transient dockage (639-0029); they also have 3 yards and complete BY services - rates $45-70/hr. Inside storage $6/ft., outside $4.10/ft . Haul & launch RT $5.50/ft.

Notable -- Take a walking tour up the historic district's narrow, winding roads lined with 18th & 19thC houses (booklet available at most shops). A number of restaurants, extensive chandleries, nautical gift shops, and modest provisioning possibilities are within easy reach. The 1,400 moorings in Marblehead Harbor are permitted to individuals. Harbormaster's office has interested transients contact the individual yacht clubs. Larger vessel moorings at the mouth of the Harbor are shared by all 5 yacht clubs and can be accessed through any of them. 15 year wait list for permanent moorings. Marblehead shares with Beverly the claim to birthplace of the American Navy.

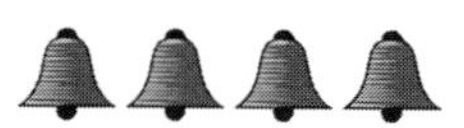

Boston Yacht Club

One Front Street; Marblehead, MA 01945

Tel: (617) 631-3100 **VHF: Monitor** 16 **Talk** 78
Fax: n/a **Alternate Tel:** n/a
Email: n/a **Web:** www.bostonyc.org/
Nearest Town: Marblehead *(0.2 mi.)* **Tourist Info:** (781) 631-2868

Navigational Information

Lat: 42°30.126' **Long:** 070°51.002' **Tide:** 10 ft. **Current:** .5 kt. **Chart:** 13275
Rep. Depths (*MLW*): Entry 20 ft. **Fuel Dock** n/a **Max Slip/Moor** -/20 ft.
Access: Marblehead Harbor about half way, 3rd facility on Western shore

Marina Facilities *(In Season/Off Season)*

Fuel: *Private* - Gasoline, Diesel
Slips: 0 Total, 0 Transient **Max LOA:** 50 ft. **Max Beam:** n/a
Rate *(per ft.)*: **Day** n/a **Week** n/a **Month** n/a
Power: 30 amp n/a, **50 amp** n/a, **100 amp** n/a, **200 amp** n/a
Cable TV: No **Dockside Phone:** No
Dock Type: n/a
Moorings: 200 Total, 5 Transient **Launch:** Yes (Free), Dinghy Dock
Rate: Day $35 **Week** n/a **Month** n/a
Heads: 4 Toilet(s), 4 Shower(s)
Laundry: None **Pay Phones:** Yes, 1
Pump-Out: OnCall, Full Service, 1 Port **Fee:** Free **Closed Heads:** Yes

Marina Operations

Owner/Manager: n/a **Dockmaster:** Roger Hastings
In-Season: May-Oct 31, 8am-11pm **Off-Season:** n/a
After-Hours Arrival: n/a
Reservations: No **Credit Cards:** Visa/MC, Amex
Discounts: None
Pets: Welcome **Handicap Access:** Yes, Heads, Docks

Marina Services and Boat Supplies

Communication - Mail & Package Hold, FedEx, AirBorne, UPS, Express Mail *(Sat Del)* **Supplies - Near:** Ships' Store *(Lynn Marine 631-1305 7 days)*, CNG *(Forepeak 781-631-7184)* **1-3 mi:** Propane *(Salem Moving & Storage 978-744-6030)* **3+ mi:** West Marine *(978-535-7332, 10 mi.)*, Boat/US *(978-777-5940, 7 mi.)*

Boatyard Services

Nearest Yard: Marblehead Trading (781) 639-0029

Restaurants and Accommodations

OnSite: Restaurant *(Boston Y.C. Dining Room)*, Hotel *(Boston Yacht Club $70-170)* **OnCall:** Pizzeria *(House of Pizza 1-631-4898)* **Near:** Restaurant *(126 Washington 631-3900, D $10-20)*, *(The Landing 639-1266, L $8-16, D $16-27, lunch menu in pub at night, Sun brunch)*, *(Pellino's Italian 631-3344, D $18-33)*, Coffee Shop *(Driftwood 631-4236, B $2-6, L $2-8, 5:30am-2pm breakfast all day)*, Inn/B&B *(Harbor Light Inn 631-2186, $125-295)*, *(Herreshoff Castle 631-1950, $185, 2-night min.)*, *(Hollyhock House & Cottage 631-8220, $165-300)*, *(Captain's Loft 639-9051, $115)* **Under 1 mi:** Snack Bar *(Flynnies at the Beach 639-3035, L $1.50-11, D $1.50-11, seasonal)*, Inn/B&B *(Marblehead Inn 639-9999, $120-220)*

Recreation and Entertainment

Near: Picnic Area, Video Rental *(Videoscope 781-631-7867)*, Park *(Crocker Park)*, Museum *(Jeremiah Lee Mansion 631-1768 Jun-Oct)*, Cultural Attract *(Marblehead Arts Assoc in the King Hooper Mansion)*, Sightseeing *(Historic District)*, Special Events *(Marblehead Race Week, late July)* **Under 1 mi:** Beach *(Devereaux Beach)*, Fitness Center *(Energy Works 631-7030)* **3+ mi:** Tennis Courts *(Beverly Golf & Tennis 978/922-9127, 5 mi.)*, Golf Course *(Olde Salem Green 978/744-2149, 5 mi.)*, Bowling *(Candlepin Lanes 978/744-3954, 5 mi.)*

Provisioning and General Services

Near: Supermarket *(Shaw's 639-9700)*, Liquor Store *(Haley's Package 631-0169)*, Bakery *(Ladycakes 631-1284, Muffin Shop)*, Bank/ATM, Protestant Church, Library *(Marblehead 631-1480)*, Pharmacy *(CVS 639-1466)*, Hardware Store *(Marblehead Hardware 639-2257)*, Florist, Retail Shops, Copies Etc. *(Mail Boxes Etc. 631-1669)* **Under 1 mi:** Gourmet Shop *(Crosby's 631-1741)*, Health Food *(Body & Soul 781/631-7286)*, Wine/Beer *(Village 631-0570)*, Farmers' Market *(Sat 9am-noon Village Street)*, Lobster Pound *(Marblehead Lobster 631-0787)*, Bookstore *(Spirit of '76 631-7199)* **1-3 mi:** Catholic Church, Laundry

Transportation

OnCall: Rental Car *(Enterprise 978-740-5666)*, Taxi *(Boston Sedan 631-1011)*, Airport Limo *(Dependable 639-1020)* **Near:** Bikes *(Marblehead Bike 631-1570)* **Under 1 mi:** Rail *(MBTA commuter train to Boston)* **Airport:** Logan Int'l. *(15 mi.)*

Medical Services

911 Service **OnCall:** Ambulance **Under 1 mi:** Doctor, Chiropractor *(Marblehead Chiropractic 781-639-0808)*, Holistic Services *(Marblehead Massage 781-639-8444)* **Hospital:** North Shore - Salem 978-745-9000 *(4 mi.)*

Setting -- Nestled in the historic "Old Town" section of Marblehead, this is the only club in the central harbor area. Boston Yacht Club is a beautiful, full-service facility, including hotel - with luxurious and impeccably maintained quarters - that literally overlooks the harbor. The Clubhouse sits right at the water's edge and the porches overhang the water.

Marina Notes -- Mooring guests have full use of the launch, heads, and showers. Those with membership in a reciprocal yacht club -- that would permit charging through BYC to his/her home account -- can make reservations in the dining room, and also have the option of coming ashore for a night in one of the club's 20+ rooms (some with shared and some with private baths). BYC is the third oldest yacht club in the country, and the oldest club in New England. It's played a leading role in the America's Cup races of the last century, the founding of the U.S. Power Squadrons in 1912, and held the first world women's sailing championship in 1924 (and led the USSA to do the same). In 1939, BYC formalized the biennial Marblehead-to-Halifax Ocean Race and hosted the first World Disabled Sailing Championship held in North America.

Notable -- All of charming, historic Marblehead is within easy walking distance. There is a fairly wide range of dining options, many nautically-oriented galleries and shops, chandleries and yacht services, and a nice selection of delightful B&Bs and Inns. Pick up a copy of the historic walking tour from any shopkeeper. More extensive services are in the commercial section of Marblehead on Atlantic and Pleasant Streets, about one mile distant.

PHOTOS ON CD-ROM: 9

Navigational Information
Lat: 42°29.912' **Long:** 070°51.061' **Tide:** 10 ft. **Current:** 1 kt. **Chart:** 13275
Rep. Depths (*MLW*): Entry 22 ft. **Fuel Dock** n/a **Max Slip/Moor** -/15 ft.
Access: Marblehead Harbor almost to head, 4th facility to starboard

Marina Facilities *(In Season/Off Season)*
Fuel: No
Slips: 0 Total, 0 Transient **Max LOA:** n/a **Max Beam:** n/a
Rate *(per ft.)*: **Day** n/a **Week** n/a **Month** n/a
Power: 30 amp n/a, **50 amp** n/a, **100 amp** n/a, **200 amp** n/a
Cable TV: No **Dockside Phone:** No
Dock Type: n/a
Moorings: 200 Total, 5 Transient **Launch:** Yes (Free), Dinghy Dock
Rate: Day $25 **Week** Inq. **Month** Inq.
Heads: 2 Toilet(s), 1 Shower(s)
Laundry: None **Pay Phones:** No
Pump-Out: OnCall, Full Service, 1 Port **Fee:** Free **Closed Heads:** Yes

Marina Operations
Owner/Manager: Patti Cohen (Commodore) **Dockmaster:** n/a
In-Season: MemDay-LabDay, 8am-8pm **Off-Season:** Sep-Nov, Apr-May*
After-Hours Arrival: Call in advance
Reservations: Yes **Credit Cards:** Visa/MC, Cash, Check
Discounts: None
Pets: Welcome **Handicap Access:** No

Dolphin Yacht Club

PO Box 905; 17 Allerton Place; Marblehead, MA 01945

Tel: (781) 631-8000 **VHF: Monitor** 16 **Talk** 68
Fax: n/a **Alternate Tel:** (781) 639-6399
Email: n/a **Web:** www.dolphinyachtclub.tripod.com
Nearest Town: Marblehead *(1 mi.)* **Tourist Info:** (781) 639-8469

Marina Services and Boat Supplies
Services - Trash Pick-Up, Dock Carts **Communication -** Mail & Package Hold, FedEx, AirBorne, UPS, Express Mail **Supplies - OnSite:** Ice *(Block, Cube)* **Near:** Ships' Store *(The Forepeak 639-0029, Lynne Marine Supplies 631-1305, Woods Nautical 631-0221)* **1-3 mi:** Propane *(Salem Storage 978/744-6030)* **3+ mi:** West Marine *(978/535-7332, 10 mi.)*, Boat/US *(978-777-5940, 7 mi.)*

Boatyard Services
Near: Travelift, Engine mechanic *(gas, diesel)*, Electronic Sales *(Boatworks 639-7565)*, Sail Loft *(Doyle 639-1490)*. **Nearest Yard:** Marblehead Trading (781) 639-0029

Restaurants and Accommodations
OnSite: Restaurant *("The View" - Dolphin Y.C. Dining Room L $8-14, D $8-23, Kids' menu $6)* **Near:** Restaurant *(Flynnie's on the Avenue 639-2100, L $6-15, D $6-16, Sun Brunch $6-10)*, *(Mino's Roast Beef 631-7228, Middle Eastern)*, *(Rio Grand Café 639-1828, L & D)*, *(Roxanne's 631-1687, L & D)*, Inn/B&B *(Darci's Parkside 631-5733, $95-200)*, *(Pheasant Hill 639-3949)*, *(53 Beach Street 631-7484, $75-90)* **Under 1 mi:** Seafood Shack *(Flynnie's at the Beach 639-3035, L $1.50-$11, D $1.50-11, seasonal only)*, Inn/B&B *(Stowaway Suites 639-1003, $110-125)* **1-3 mi:** Inn/B&B *(Spray Cliff on the Ocean 631-6789, $200-250)*

Recreation and Entertainment
Near: Picnic Area *(Crocker Park)*, Playground, Jogging Paths, Boat Rentals *(Kayak Learning Center 922-5322)*, Video Rental *(Videoscope 631-7867)*, Park *(Seaside Park)*, Cultural Attract *(King Hooper Mansion, Marblehead Streets Assoc. 631-2608 Free)*, Sightseeing *(Marblehead Old Town Historic District Walking Tour)*, Special Events *(Race Week - late July)* **Under 1 mi:** Beach *(Devereaux Beach 631-3551)*, Museum *(Jeremiah Lee Mansion 631-1768 $5/Free)* **1-3 mi:** Bowling *(Candlepin Lanes 978/744-3954)* **3+ mi:** Golf Course *(Olde Salem Green 978/744-2149, 5 mi.)*

Provisioning and General Services
Near: Gourmet Shop *(Crosby's Market 631-1741)*, Delicatessen, Bakery *(Ladycakes 631-1284, Muffin Shop)*, Farmers' Market *(Village St. Sat am)*, Fishmonger, Lobster Pound *(Marblehead Lobster 631-0787)*, Bank/ATM, Protestant Church, Pharmacy *(CVS 639-1412)*, Hardware Store *(Marblehead Hardware 639-2257)*, Florist, Retail Shops, Copies Etc. *(Litchman's 631-0175)* **Under 1 mi:** Convenience Store *(7-Eleven)*, Health Food *(Body and Soul 631-7286)*, Wine/Beer *(Village 631-0570)*, Laundry, Bookstore *(Spirit of '76 631-7199)* **1-3 mi:** Supermarket *(Shaw's 639-9700)*, Catholic Church, Library *(Marblehead 631-1480)*

Transportation
OnCall: Rental Car *(Enterprise 978/740-5666)*, Taxi *(Tri-City 639-2488)*, Airport Limo *(Dependable 639-1020)* **Under 1 mi:** Bikes *(Marblehead Bike 631-1570)*, Rail *(MBTA Commuter to Boston)* **Airport:** Logan Int'l. *(15 mi.)*

Medical Services
911 Service **OnCall:** Ambulance **Under 1 mi:** Doctor, Chiropractor *(Marblehead Chiro 639-0808)*, Holistic Services *(Marblehead Massage 639-8444)* **Hospital:** North Shore - Salem 978-745-9000 *(4 mi.)*

Setting -- This perfectly charming, hospitable small club sits near the head of Marblehead Harbor. Perched on a promontory, it has expansive views of one of the most tightly packed and most beautiful mooring fields in the East. The rolling lawn tumbles down to the very ship-shape launch and dinghy dock. The landside environs are residential.

Marina Notes -- *Off season open 9am-5pm. A mooring guest is a guest of the Club. Services include launch, dining room, heads and showers, and use of the porch. Founded in 1951, the DYC has recently remodeled its Dining Room and added a new Bar and a new outdoor deck on the second floor. Lunch and a full-service Dinner are served in the dining room -- inside or outside on the deck -- overlooking the harbor. Called "The View", it's open 7 days and managed by Patty Johnson of Sylvan Street Grille. Specialty nights include Thursday fajita & margaritas ($12+$6), Wednesday raw bar & seafood, Tuesday kids' movies, Mondays buffalo wings. A $6 children's menu is also available. Check with club regarding proper attire. Dining room available for private functions.

Notable -- Dolphin is outside the Old Town historic district, a little closer to the beaches -- on the other side of the narrow causeway that forms the head of Marblehead Harbor. Seaside Park and Riverhead, Devereaux and Tucker Beaches are all within walking distance. The commercial "downtown" is also a little closer and more convenient.

PHOTOS ON CD-ROM: 6

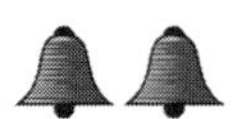

Seaport Landing Marina

154 Lynnway; Lynn, MA 01902

Tel: (781) 592-5821 **VHF: Monitor** 9 **Talk** 16
Fax: n/a **Alternate Tel:** n/a
Email: jperry5821@aol.com **Web:** n/a
Nearest Town: Lynn *(0.25 mi.)* **Tourist Info:** (781) 592-2900

Navigational Information

Lat: 42°27.496' **Long:** 070°56.631' **Tide:** 9 ft. **Current:** 2 kt. **Chart:** 13275
Rep. Depths (*MLW*): Entry 20 ft. **Fuel Dock** 20 ft. **Max Slip/Moor** 20 ft./15 ft.
Access: Massachusetts Bay to Flip Rock Buoy to Lynn Channel R2

Marina Facilities *(In Season/Off Season)*

Fuel: *Private* - Gasoline, Diesel
Slips: 200 Total, 20 Transient **Max LOA:** 300 ft. **Max Beam:** 50 ft.
Rate *(per ft.)*: **Day** $2.00/$1.00 **Week** n/a **Month** n/a
Power: 30 amp Incl., **50 amp** Incl., **100 amp** n/a, **200 amp** n/a
Cable TV: Yes monthly only **Dockside Phone:** Yes monthly only
Dock Type: Long Fingers, Concrete, Pilings, Floating
Moorings: 400 Total, 0 Transient **Launch:** n/a
Rate: Day n/a **Week** n/a **Month** n/a
Heads: 2 Toilet(s), 2 Shower(s)
Laundry: 1 Washer(s), 1 Dryer(s) **Pay Phones:** Yes, 2
Pump-Out: OnSite, Self Service, 1 Central **Fee:** Free **Closed Heads:** No

Marina Operations

Owner/Manager: James Perry (Harbormaster) **Dockmaster:** Brian LeBlanc
In-Season: Apr 15-Nov 1, 7am-7pm **Off-Season:** Nov 2-Apr 14, 9am-5 pm
After-Hours Arrival: Call ahead on channels 9 or 16
Reservations: Preferred **Credit Cards:** Visa/MC, Amex
Discounts: None
Pets: Welcome **Handicap Access:** No

Marina Services and Boat Supplies

Services - Docking Assistance, Concierge, Security *(Security guard)*, Dock Carts **Communication -** Mail & Package Hold, Phone Messages, FedEx, AirBorne, UPS, Express Mail *(Sat Del)* **Supplies - OnSite:** Ice *(Block, Cube)*, Ships' Store *(Will order anything needed for overnight delivery)* **Under 1 mi:** Bait/Tackle *(10 min by boat)*, Propane

Boatyard Services

OnCall: Engine mechanic *(gas, diesel)*, Electrical Repairs, Electronics Repairs, Canvas Work **Near:** Travelift, Rigger, Divers, Compound, Wash & Wax, Interior Cleaning, Propeller Repairs. **Under 1 mi:** Launching Ramp. **Nearest Yard:** Lynn Yacht Club (781) 595-9825

Restaurants and Accommodations

OnCall: Pizzeria *(Mandy's 599-0600)* **Near:** Restaurant *(The Porthole 595-7733, L $5-13, D $5-15, right next door)*, *(Celines 581-0054)*, *(Christie's 598-1122)*, *(Kevin's Bar & Grille 596-3072)*, Coffee Shop *(Capital Diner 595-5314)*, Hotel *(Hotel Edison 595-1500)* **Under 1 mi:** Fast Food *(Dunkin Donuts, Wendy's, McDonald's, KFC)*, Inn/B&B *(Diamond District B&B 595-4770, $90-270)* **1-3 mi:** Inn/B&B *(Oceanview 598-6388, $100-125)*, *(Capt. Jack's 595-7910)*

Recreation and Entertainment

OnSite: Special Events *(Bluefish Tournament - Aug, Lynn Harbor Monster Day - Childrens' Fest - 2nd Sat in Aug)* **OnCall:** Fishing Charter *(Walsh's Deep Sea Fishing 592-9505)* **Near:** Beach *(Lynn & Nahant Beaches -- 3 mile sand crescent)*, Picnic Area, Playground, Tennis Courts, Jogging Paths, Roller Blade/Bike Paths, Park *(Lynn Heritage State Park - elegantly renovated shoe factory is visitors' center which includes an early 1800s shoe shop plus a 4 acre oceanfront promenade)*, Sightseeing *(walking tour of some original shoe factories - brochure at Lynn Historical Society)* **Under 1 mi:** Museum *(City of Lynn Historical Society 592-2465 $4 - restored 1836 house shelters a diverse collection and an extensive research library)* **1-3 mi:** Golf Course *(Kelley Greens 581-0840)*

Provisioning and General Services

Near: Convenience Store *(Johnnie's Market)*, Supermarket *(Star Market 599-8473)*, Liquor Store *(Santo Domingo 598-3272)*, Bank/ATM, Post Office, Catholic Church **Under 1 mi:** Gourmet Shop, Delicatessen *(Junction Deli 595-9827)*, Wine/Beer, Farmers' Market *(Olympia Square, Thu 11am-3pm, 586-6764)*, Fishmonger *(Seafood America 581-5180)*, Library, Beauty Salon, Dry Cleaners, Laundry, Pharmacy *(Walgreens 593-1230)*, Newsstand, Hardware Store, Florist, Department Store *(Wal-Mart)*, Copies Etc.

Transportation

OnCall: Rental Car *(Enterprise 581-5000)*, Taxi *(Tom's 595-0049)*, Airport Limo *(All-City 598-8760)* **Near:** Local Bus **Under 1 mi:** Rail *("T" to Boston; Boston Amtrak 8 mi.)* **Airport:** Logan Int'l. *(6 mi.)*

Medical Services

911 Service **OnSite:** Chiropractor *(Rosella Lent)* **OnCall:** Ambulance **Under 1 mi:** Doctor, Dentist **Hospital:** Union Hospital 581-9200 *(4 mi.)*

PHOTOS ON CD-ROM: 9

Setting -- A municipal facility, Seaport Landing shares this small basin with the Lynn and Volunteer Yacht Clubs. It sits seaward of a modest apartment and professional offices complex and is surrounded by a boardwalk. Farther inland, Lynn offers some fascinating attractions that trace its history as an early center of "invisibly stitched" women's shoe manufacturing and design.

Marina Notes -- Owned and operated by the City of Lynn since 1987. 24 hour security and locked piers. Very friendly and accommodating staff. Concrete floating docks provide good protection. Free afternoon tie-up for casino boat. Jim Perry is also Lynn Harbormaster. Boatyard services are provided by the neighboring yacht clubs. Starting to show its age. Basic, usable municipal heads and laundry. Substantial seasonal occupancy and few liveaboards.

Notable -- An impressive nine panel mosaic, which lines the exterior wall of one of the onsite buildings, depicts the history of Lynn, including its prominence as the birthplace of the U.S. shoe industry. Onsite mailboxes, UPS and FedEx boxes, and newspaper vending machines. The Porthole, right next door, is an inviting seafood-oriented restaurant with views over its parking lot to the marina docks (7 days, L 11:30am-4pm, D 4-9:30pm. Live entertainment on weekends). The Historical Society's Museum is about half a mile. Founded in 1897, it tells the city's story with a broad collection -- one focus is the shoe business ($4, Mon-Sat 1-4pm - all day for research). About a mile walk is Lynn's Diamond Historical District, an enclave of architecturally important 19thC mansions -- many built by Lynn shoe manufacturers. Horizon's Edge Casino Cruise is a dinghy or cab ride away. Nearby Nahant Beach is a favorite of boardsailers.

VI. Massachusetts: Boston & The South Shore

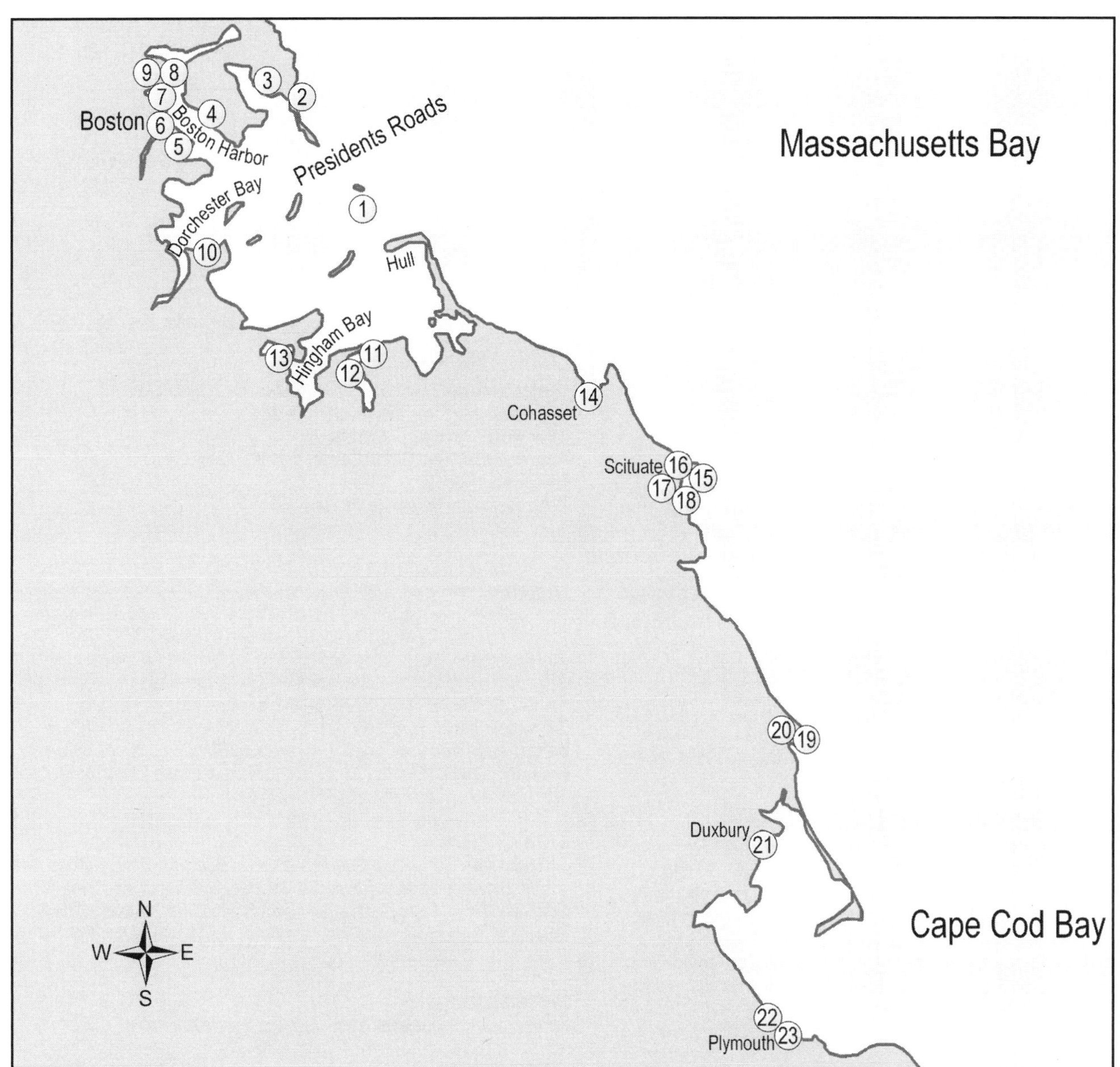

MAP	MARINA	HARBOR	PAGE	MAP	MARINA	HARBOR	PAGE
1	**Boston Harbor Island Moorings**	*Boston Outer Harbor*	140	13	**Captain's Cove Marina**	*Town River Bay*	152
2	**Crystal Cove Marina**	*President Roads*	141	14	**Cohasset Harbor Marina**	*Cohasset Cove*	153
3	**Atlantis Marina**	*President Roads*	142	15	**Scituate Harbor Yacht Club**	*Scituate Harbor*	154
4	**Boston Harbor Shipyard & Marina**	*Boston Harbor*	143	16	**Scituate Harbor Marina**	*Scituate Harbor*	155
5	**The Marina at Rowes Wharf**	*Boston Harbor*	144	17	**Scituate Launch "Cedar Point"**	*Scituate Harbor*	156
6	**Boston Waterboat Marina**	*Boston Harbor*	145	18	**Cole Parkway**	*Scituate Harbor*	157
7	**Boston Yacht Haven**	*Boston Harbor*	146	19	**Taylor Marine**	*Green Harbor River*	158
8	**Shipyard Quarters Marina**	*Boston Harbor*	147	20	**Green Harbor Marina**	*Green Harbor River*	159
9	**Constitution Marina**	*Boston Harbor*	148	21	**Duxbury Town Pier**	*Duxbury Bay*	160
10	**Marina Bay**	*Dorchester Bay*	149	22	**Brewer Plymouth Marine**	*Plymouth Bay*	161
11	**Hewitts Cove Marina**	*Weymouth Back River*	150	23	**Plymouth Yacht Club**	*Plymouth Bay*	162
12	**Tern Harbor Marina**	*Weymouth Back River*	151				

Boston Harbor Island Moorings

28 Constitution Road; Boston, MA 02124

Tel: (617) 241-9640 **VHF: Monitor** 69 **Talk** 69
Fax: (617) 242-3013 **Alternate Tel:** (617) 223-8666
Email: cm@bosport.com **Web:** www.bostonislands.org
Nearest Town: Boston *(7 mi.)* **Tourist Info:** (617) 227-4500

Navigational Information

Lat: 42°19.268' **Long:** 070°55.864' **Tide:** 10 ft. **Current:** 2 kt. **Chart:** 13272
Rep. Depths (*MLW*): Entry 30 ft. **Fuel Dock** n/a **Max Slip/Moor** -/20 ft.
Access: Outer Harbor to Gallops, George's, Long Island, Rainford, Peddocks

Marina Facilities *(In Season/Off Season)*

Fuel: No
Slips: 0 Total, 0 Transient **Max LOA:** 80 ft. **Max Beam:** 20 ft.
Rate *(per ft.)*: **Day** n/a **Week** n/a **Month** n/a
Power: 30 amp n/a, **50 amp** n/a, **100 amp** n/a, **200 amp** n/a
Cable TV: No **Dockside Phone:** No
Dock Type: n/a
Moorings: 50 Total, 50 Transient **Launch:** None
Rate: Day $25 **Week** $175 **Month** n/a
Heads: 6 Toilet(s)
Laundry: None **Pay Phones:** No
Pump-Out: OnCall, 1 Port **Fee:** Free **Closed Heads:** Yes

Marina Operations

Owner/Manager: Tom Cox **Dockmaster:** Keith McClearn
In-Season: May-Oct **Off-Season:** Closed
After-Hours Arrival: Call in advance
Reservations: Yes **Credit Cards:** Visa/MC, Dscvr, Amex
Discounts: None
Pets: Welcome **Handicap Access:** No

Marina Services and Boat Supplies

Services - Trash Pick-Up **Supplies - OnSite:** Ice *(Block, Cube)*

Boatyard Services

Nearest Yard: Boston Harbor Shipyard (617) 561-1400

Restaurants and Accommodations

OnSite: Lite Fare *(George's Island B $2-5, L $5-12, D $5-18, only food service on the islands, outdoor grill with nearby picnic tables, lobster bake 11am-7pm)*

Recreation and Entertainment

OnSite: Park *(George's is one of the eight islands that form the Harbor Islands State Park)*, Museum *(explore the Civil War era National Historic Landmark Fort Warren on 28 acre George's Island - also picnic grounds, open fields, paved walkways, parade grounds and a gravel beach)* **Near:** Beach *(Lovells' supervised swimming beach with dunes, Gallops' sand beach with ocean views, Bumpkin & Grape)*, Picnic Area *(on George's and most other islands, plus berry picking, rasberries, blackberries and wild rose hips, on Grape)*, Grills *(Beach fires below the high-tide line; designated fire pits)*, Dive Shop *(Harbor Island Divers 284-5300)*, Jogging Paths *(Deer Island, actually a peninsula attached to Winthrop, has 4.6 mi. of trails around perimeter of Treatment Plant and 2 mi. of interior hill trails in 60 acre park - dogs permitted here 539-4248; Peddock's has trails around Ft. Andrews)*, Cultural Attract *(157 acre Thompson, home to Willauer School & an Outward Bound program, tours Sat by app't 328-3900; rentable for special events 275-1641)*, Sightseeing *(Little Brewster Island's last "manned" lighthouse - Fri, Sat, Sun 12:30-3pm 223-8666; take a nature walk on Peddocks, see the 2nd largest Waste Treatment plant is on Deer Island, search for fabled buried treasure on Lovell, pick wildflowers on Bumpkin or roses on Great Brewster)*, Special Events *("wild edibles" tours of Grape Island; occasional concerts; Gallops Island Apple Fest - late Sep)*

Transportation

OnSite: Water Taxi *(From George's Island to Bumpkin, Deer, Gallops, Great & Little Brewster, Lovells, Peddocks, Spectacles, & Thompson 9am-Sundown, Free)*, Ferry Service *(George's Island to Boston/Long Wharf, Hingham/Hingham Shipyard, Hewetts Cove, Hull at Pemberton Point - $10/RT 223-8666)* **Airport:** Logan Int'l. *(5 mi.)*

Medical Services

No 911 Service **Hospital:** Mass. General 248-1926 *(7 mi.)*

PHOTOS ON CD-ROM: 9

Setting -- Of the 30 Boston Harbor Islands, situated just 7 mi. from downtown Boston, currently 10 can be visited. 50 moorings are located in quiet, protected anchorages off 5 of the islands: Long Island, Peddocks, George's, Bumpkin, and Rainsford. (Gallops is temporarily closed). The archipelago promises skyline and oceanviews, spectacular sunsets, hiking trails, historic sights, inter-island water shuttles, and beaches made usable by the Boston Harbor cleanup.

Marina Notes -- Managed by Constitution Marina - takes reservations, sends a boat twice daily to collect fees, and generally trouble-shoots (tel. or VHF). 1200 lb. mushrooms, numbered with tel. number and VHF 69. Rafting permitted, but all pay full mooring fee. $25, or $10 "lunch hook". No Water. Landing on most islands usually permitted only during daylight hours. Free daytime-only dockage at George's available for dinghies and boats 30+ feet (stern-to). At Bumpkin, Grape, Little Brewster, Lovells, & Peddocks boats may offload /load at the floats, then anchor offshore (loaner dinghies). Public heads on Geroge's, compost toilets others. Overnight camping (Grape, Bumpkin, Peddocks & Lovells) with permit. On-island Picnic and Event Services available (568-9100).

Notable -- Part of the National Park area established in 1996, the 30 islands are managed by the Island Alliance, a unique, 13 member Partnership which includes the National Park Service and other public & private organizations. This is truly a special and remarkable experience -- explore the islands, have a picnic, walk along the beaches, take the inter-island shuttle or the ferry into Boston. Hiking, wildlife, views on all islands. Quiet and peaceful except when the Boston ferries bring school/camp day-trips -- but they all leave at sundown. Island Moorings (241-9640) pumps out, picks up trash, and brings Sunday papers.

Navigational Information
Lat: 42°22.262' **Long:** 070°58.275' **Tide:** 10 ft. **Current:** n/a **Chart:** 13270
Rep. Depths (*MLW*): Entry 15 ft. **Fuel Dock** n/a **Max Slip/Moor** 7 ft./-
Access: President Roads to G3, follow channel past Winthrop YC

Marina Facilities *(In Season/Off Season)*
Fuel: Gasoline, Diesel, High-Speed Pumps
Slips: 120 Total, 5 Transient **Max LOA:** 75 ft. **Max Beam:** n/a
Rate *(per ft.)*: **Day** $2.75/Inq. **Week** $8 **Month** $29
Power: 30 amp Incl., **50 amp** Incl., **100 amp** n/a, **200 amp** n/a
Cable TV: No **Dockside Phone:** No
Dock Type: Wood, Floating
Moorings: 0 Total, 0 Transient **Launch:** n/a, Dinghy Dock
Rate: Day n/a **Week** n/a **Month** n/a
Heads: 4 Toilet(s), 4 Shower(s)
Laundry: 12 Washer(s), 12 Dryer(s) **Pay Phones:** No
Pump-Out: OnCall, Full Service, 1 Port **Fee:** Free **Closed Heads:** No

Marina Operations
Owner/Manager: Ron Deveau **Dockmaster:** Same
In-Season: Mar-Dec, 8am-5pm **Off-Season:** Jan-Feb, 8am-4pm
After-Hours Arrival: Pre-arranged
Reservations: Yes, Required **Credit Cards:** Visa/MC
Discounts: None
Pets: Welcome **Handicap Access:** Yes, Heads

Crystal Cove Marina

529 Shirley Street; Winthrop, MA 02152

Tel: (617) 846-7245 **VHF: Monitor** 10 **Talk** 10
Fax: (617) 846-4301 **Alternate Tel:** n/a
Email: CurtinAssociates@aol.com **Web:** n/a
Nearest Town: Winthrop *(1 mi.)* **Tourist Info:** (617) 846-9898

Marina Services and Boat Supplies
Services - Security *(Video surveillance)*, Trash Pick-Up **Communication -** FedEx, AirBorne, UPS, Express Mail **Supplies - OnSite:** Ice *(Cube)* **Under 1 mi:** Ships' Store *(Vista Ward Marine 846-1421)*, Bait/Tackle, Live Bait **3+ mi:** Marine Discount Store *(CG Edwards 268-4111, 7 mi.)*

Boatyard Services
OnSite: Forklift *(20T)*, Crane, Engine mechanic *(gas, diesel)*, Launching Ramp, Electrical Repairs, Electronic Sales, Hull Repairs, Rigger, Bottom Cleaning, Brightwork, Compound, Wash & Wax, Interior Cleaning, Woodworking, Painting, Awlgrip **OnCall:** Divers **Near:** Electronics Repairs. **Under 1 mi:** Air Conditioning, Refrigeration. **Nearest Yard:** Action Mobil Marine (617) 539-1425

Restaurants and Accommodations
OnSite: Pizzeria *(Dominos)* **Near:** Restaurant *(Lucky Garden 846-8560, L $4-6, D $4-12, Szechuan, Hong Kong & Thai food, right across the street)*, *(Papa Luigi 846-8801)*, *(Taste Buds 539-3400)*, *(Crystal Cove Café 539-3424)*, *(Sole E Mare 846-0400)*, *(Tony & Angel's 567-9671)*, *(Trattoria di Parma 846-5867)*, Snack Bar *(Quick Food)*, Motel *(Ocean Spray Inn 539-3487)*, Inn/B&B *(Inn at Crystal Cove 846-9217)* **Under 1 mi:** Hotel *(Winthrop Arms Hotel 846-4000)* **1-3 mi:** Motel *(Castle-Mar 781-286-0586)*

Recreation and Entertainment
OnSite: Fishing Charter **Near:** Beach *(Winthrop Beach, Yirrell Beach 727-5114)*, Picnic Area, Playground, Roller Blade/Bike Paths, Video Rental, Park, Special Events *(July 4th at Point Shirley)* **Under 1 mi:** Tennis Courts, Golf Course *(Winthrop Golf Course 846-9775)* **3+ mi:** Bowling *(Central Park Lanes 567-7073, 5 mi.)*

Provisioning and General Services
OnSite: Convenience Store **Near:** Wine/Beer, Liquor Store *(Williams Package Store 846-3030)*, Bakery, Laundry, Hardware Store *(Dave's Hardware 846-2050; Shirley Hardware)* **Under 1 mi:** Delicatessen *(The Eatery Deli & Ice Cream 846-4577)*, Beauty Salon, Barber Shop, Dry Cleaners, Pharmacy *(CVS 846-9155)*, Newsstand, Florist, Retail Shops, Copies Etc. *(Shirley Hardware)* **1-3 mi:** Bank/ATM, Post Office, Catholic Church, Protestant Church, Synagogue, Library, Bookstore *(Winthrop Book Depot 846-3099)* **3+ mi:** Supermarket *(Stop & Shop 781-284-7373, 5 mi.)*

Transportation
OnSite: Local Bus **OnCall:** Rental Car *(Enterprise 781-289-4002 or Hertz 561-3000, 4 mi.)*, Taxi *(Patriot 781-284-2222)* **Airport:** Logan Int'l. *(6 mi.)*

Medical Services
911 Service **OnCall:** Ambulance **Hospital:** Quigley Memorial, Chelsea 884-5660 *(5 mi.)*

Setting -- Snugged into a well protected dead-end basin that was created by a large man-made jetty, just past the Winthrop Yacht Club. Seaside are views of the mooring fields, Logan Airport, and the Boston skyline beyond. Landside is rustic boatyard, a small strip-mall complex, and, farther afield, a mixed commercial/residential seaside neighborhood on a small peninsula.

Marina Notes -- Proximity to Boston's Logan International Airport makes this a very interesting choice for "leaving the boat". Winthrop maintains a town pump-out boat -- hail on Channel 9. Boatyard services are onsite and part of the facility but are managed by a separate entity - Action Mobile Marine. Onsite, too, is a commercial laundromat so the number of washers/dryers refers to that. The decent but aging docks have pedestals with 30 amp service. There are a few 50 amp pedestals; specify if that's important. Heads are institutional and pretty basic. Fuel dock. Onsite are: Bobby Lee's fiberglass repair 697-4232, Dominos Pizza 539-3344, laundromat, and the above mentioned Action Mobile Marine Services 539-1425.

Notable -- The whole town is only about 1.5 square miles and offers panoramic views of the water and the Boston skyline at every turn -- so the most interesting activity might be to take a walk. Across the street is a modest antiques gallery, a Thai/Chinese restaurant, a liquor store and pet groomer (Benjio's 846-777). It's a short, couple blocks' walk to a lovely public beach with life-guard on duty. It is wide, sandy, and protected by a series of breakwaters. On your approach to the marina, you'll see Deer Island to starboard, home to a huge sewage treatment plant - it's hard to miss.

Atlantis Marina

Atlantis Marina

550 Pleasant Street; Winthrop, MA 02152

Tel: (617) 846-5262 **VHF: Monitor** 14 **Talk** n/a
Fax: (617) 846-3454 **Alternate Tel:** n/a
Email: atlantismarina-ma@verizon.net **Web:** www.atlantismarina.com
Nearest Town: Winthrop *(1 mi.)* **Tourist Info:** (617) 846-9898

Navigational Information

Lat: 42°22.827' **Long:** 070°59.536' **Tide:** 10 ft. **Current:** 5 kts **Chart:** 13270
Rep. Depths (*MLW*): Entry 35 ft. **Fuel Dock** 35 ft. **Max Slip/Moor** 30 ft./35 ft.
Access: Winthrop Channel; bear left at Winthrop Light

Marina Facilities *(In Season/Off Season)*

Fuel: No
Slips: 91 Total, 3 Transient **Max LOA:** n/a **Max Beam:** n/a
Rate *(per ft.)*: **Day** $35.00 **Week** n/a **Month** n/a/95
Power: 30 amp Incl., **50 amp** n/a, **100 amp** n/a, **200 amp** n/a
Cable TV: Yes **Dockside Phone:** Yes
Dock Type: Wood, Long Fingers, Short Fingers, Floating
Moorings: 0 Total, 0 Transient **Launch:** n/a, Dinghy Dock
Rate: Day n/a **Week** n/a **Month** n/a
Heads: 2 Toilet(s), 2 Shower(s) *(with dressing rooms)*
Laundry: None **Pay Phones:** No
Pump-Out: OnCall, 1 Port **Fee:** Free **Closed Heads:** No

Marina Operations

Owner/Manager: David Christopher **Dockmaster:** Same
In-Season: Year Round **Off-Season:** n/a
After-Hours Arrival: n/a
Reservations: Yes, Preferred **Credit Cards:** Visa/MC, Dscvr
Discounts: Boat/US **Dockage:** n/a **Fuel:** n/a **Repair:** 10%
Pets: Welcome, Dog Walk Area **Handicap Access:** Yes

Marina Services and Boat Supplies

Services - Security *(24 Hrs., Live on-site)*, Dock Carts **Communication -** Mail & Package Hold, Express Mail *(Sat Del)* **Supplies - OnSite:** Ice *(Cube)* **Near:** Bait/Tackle *(Bob's Bait Shack 846-5896)* **1-3 mi:** Ships' Store *(Ward Marine 846-1421)*

Boatyard Services

OnCall: Engine mechanic *(gas, diesel)*, Electrical Repairs, Hull Repairs, Rigger, Canvas Work, Bottom Cleaning, Brightwork, Air Conditioning, Refrigeration, Divers, Compound, Wash & Wax, Interior Cleaning, Propeller Repairs, Woodworking, Inflatable Repairs, Life Raft Service, Upholstery, Yacht Interiors, Metal Fabrication, Painting, Awlgrip, Yacht Design, Yacht Broker, Yacht Building, Total Refits **Near:** Travelift *(30T)*, Launching Ramp. **Nearest Yard:** Mullins Marine (617) 846-1551

Restaurants and Accommodations

Near: Restaurant *(Odyssey Grill 846-7200, subs, gyros, delivers)* **Under 1 mi:** Restaurant *(Café Delite 539-1535)*, *(Hong Kong Dragon 539-0012)*, *(Center Bistro 539-4484)*, Lite Fare *(Rhonda's Place 846-6411)* **1-3 mi:** Inn/B&B *(Inn At Crystal Cove 846-9217, $90-130)*, *(Ocean Spray Inn 539-3487, $80-130)*

Recreation and Entertainment

Near: Jogging Paths, Roller Blade/Bike Paths, Park, Sightseeing, Special Events *(Fourth of July)* **Under 1 mi:** Fitness Center *(Kathy's Place 846-6868)*, Video Rental *(Superstar Video 846-5577)* **1-3 mi:** Bowling *(Central Park Lanes 567-7073)* **3+ mi:** Golf Course *(Mt. Hood G. C. 665-8139, 8 mi.)*, Horseback Riding *(Revere-Saugus Riding Academy 322-7788, 6 mi.)*, Museum *(Paul Revere House 523-2338, 4.5 mi.)*

Provisioning and General Services

Near: Convenience Store, Delicatessen *(Lunch Box 846-3755)*, Wine/Beer, Liquor Store *(Swetts 846-0005)*, Bakery, Bank/ATM, Post Office, Beauty Salon, Barber Shop, Laundry, Pharmacy *(CVS 846-9474)*, Newsstand, Hardware Store *(Ace Woodside 846-2141)*, Florist, Retail Shops, Copies Etc. **Under 1 mi:** Library *(Orient Heights 567-2516)*, Bookstore *(Winthrop Book Depot 846-3099)* **1-3 mi:** Supermarket *(Stop & Shop 781-485-0015)*, Catholic Church, Protestant Church, Synagogue, Dry Cleaners

Transportation

OnCall: Rental Car *(Enterprise 561-7895)*, Taxi *(Suffolk 846-9999, Viking 846-6000)* **Near:** Local Bus **Airport:** Logan Int'l. *(4 mi.)*

Medical Services

911 Service **OnCall:** Ambulance **Near:** Dentist *(Smiles Winthrop 846-1280)* **Under 1 mi:** Chiropractor *(Boston Sports Chiro 846-3502)*, Veterinarian *(East Boston 617-567-0101)* **1-3 mi:** Doctor *(Medical Center 781-286-3000)* **Hospital:** Quigley Memorial 884-5660 *(3 mi.)*

Setting -- Access to this extremely well protected basin is through a narrow channel that cuts between a runway arm of Logan Airport and the Winthrop peninsula. This down home, rustic facility is tucked into its virtually enclosed basin along with several other similar facilities. The immediate landside neighborhood is a bit industrial, but a few blocks away is a pretty, gentrified residential neighborhood chock a block with early 20thC houses. The view seaward is of the Airport directly across the harbor with the spectacular Boston skyline in the background.

Marina Notes -- A small, service oriented-staff manages a basic marina with solid wooden docks, heads (2 full baths), minimal facilities, right in the flight pattern -- all practically at the airport. This adds up to an interesting place to leave the boat. It's a flat 10 min. to Logan and the staff will give you a ride if mutually convenient. Fuel right next door. Handles boats 30-50ft. Winthrop Harbormaster has pump-out boat which will come to you. Manager lives onsite.

Notable -- Harbormaster docks here. Large, full service laundry right down the street. It's a reasonable walk across the Winthrop peninsula to the beaches on the other side -- Winthrop Beach is well protected by a jetty, and has services and a life-guard; a little farther south is Yirrell Beach, with opportunities for ocean swimming. The major and successful Boston Harbor cleanup has made these beaches swimmable (check on current conditions at 727-5114).

PHOTOS ON CD-ROM: 7

Boston Harbor Shipyard & Marina

256 Marginal Street; East Boston, MA 02128

Tel: (617) 561-1400 **VHF: Monitor** 9 **Talk** 8
Fax: (617) 561-9539 **Alternate Tel:** n/a
Email: pgately@seachain.com **Web:** www.bhmarina.com
Nearest Town: Boston *(1 mi. by water)* **Tourist Info:** (617) 227-4500

Navigational Information

Lat: 42°21.837' **Long:** 071°02.027' **Tide:** 10 ft. **Current:** 2 kt. **Chart:** 13272
Rep. Depths (*MLW*): Entry 30 ft. **Fuel Dock** 30 ft. **Max Slip/Moor** 30 ft./-
Access: Boston Harbor main channel, past Logan, first facility to starboard

Marina Facilities *(In Season/Off Season)*

Fuel: *Valvtect* - Gasoline, Diesel
Slips: 180 Total, 20 Transient **Max LOA:** 250 ft. **Max Beam:** n/a
Rate *(per ft.)*: **Day** $2.50/$1.50 **Week** $10 **Month** $35
Power: 30 amp $5, **50 amp** $10, **100 amp** Metered, **200 amp** n/a
Cable TV: Yes Monthly **Dockside Phone:** Yes Monthly
Dock Type: Long Fingers, Floating
Moorings: 0 Total, 0 Transient **Launch:** n/a
Rate: Day n/a **Week** n/a **Month** n/a
Heads: 2 Toilet(s), 2 Shower(s) *(with dressing rooms)*
Laundry: 2 Washer(s), 2 Dryer(s), Book Exchange **Pay Phones:** Yes
Pump-Out: OnSite, Full Service, 1 Central **Fee:** Free **Closed Heads:** No

Marina Operations

Owner/Manager: Pat Gately **Dockmaster:** n/a
In-Season: May-Oct 31, 8am-8pm **Off-Season:** Nov-Apr 30, 8am-4pm
After-Hours Arrival: Call in advance
Reservations: Yes, Required **Credit Cards:** Visa/MC, Dscvr, Amex
Discounts: Seatow **Dockage:** n/a **Fuel:** $0.10 **Repair:** n/a
Pets: Welcome, Dog Walk Area **Handicap Access:** Yes, Heads

Marina Services and Boat Supplies

Services - Docking Assistance, Room Service to the Boat, Security *(24 Hrs., Guard)*, Trash Pick-Up, Dock Carts **Communication -** Mail & Package Hold, Phone Messages, Fax in/out, Data Ports *(Office)*, FedEx, AirBorne, UPS, Express Mail *(Sat Del)* **Supplies - OnSite:** Ice *(Block, Cube, Shaved)* **Under 1 mi:** Ships' Store **1-3 mi:** Bait/Tackle **3+ mi:** Marine Discount Store *(CG Edwards 268-4111, 3 mi)*, Propane *(U-Haul 625-2789)*

Boatyard Services

OnSite: Travelift *(50T)*, Forklift, Crane, Engine mechanic *(gas, diesel)*, Electrical Repairs, Hull Repairs, Rigger, Bottom Cleaning, Brightwork, Divers, Compound, Wash & Wax, Interior Cleaning, Propeller Repairs, Woodworking, Upholstery, Yacht Interiors, Metal Fabrication, Awlgrip, Yacht Design, Yacht Building, Total Refits **OnCall:** Electronics Repairs, Canvas Work **Near:** Inflatable Repairs, Life Raft Service. **Dealer for:** Onsite vendor Boston Boatworks 617-561-9111. **Member:** ABBRA, ABYC - 2 Certified Tech(s), Other Certifications: Mercruiser **Yard Rates:** Haul & Launch $3.50/ft *(blocking incl.)*, Power Wash $3.75/ft., Bottom Paint $16/ft. **Storage:** In-Water $35/ft., On-Land $74/ft

Restaurants and Accommodations

OnCall: Seafood Shack *(Barking Crab 426-2722)* **Near:** Lite Fare *(American Ice Cream & Sandwich 569-0137)* **Under 1 mi:** Restaurant *(Rostiria Cancun 567-5808)*, *(Side St. Café 569-7000)*, *(Barneys 567-7170)*, Seafood Shack *(Angelos 567-2500)*, Hotel *(Hyatt 568-1234)* **1-3 mi:** Restaurant *(Anthony's Pier 4 482-6262)*, Hotel *(Marriott 227-0800)*, *(Boston Harbor 439-7000)*, Inn/B&B *(Faneuil Hall 720-3540)*

Recreation and Entertainment

OnSite: Picnic Area, Playground, Park **Near:** Video Rental *(Maverick 561-3993)*, Cultural Attract, Sightseeing **Under 1 mi:** Beach, Fishing Charter, Group Fishing Boat **1-3 mi:** Horseback Riding, Bowling *(Central Park Lanes 567-7073)*, Movie Theater *(Hoyts 247-0587)*, Museum *(Paul Revere House 523-1676, Boston Fire Museum 482-1344)*

Provisioning and General Services

OnSite: Provisioning Service *(Silver Platters 568-9100)* **Near:** Convenience Store, Delicatessen, Bakery *(A & L 569-7597)*, Farmers' Market, Green Grocer, Fishmonger, Bank/ATM, Post Office, Catholic Church, Beauty Salon, Barber Shop, Dry Cleaners, Laundry, Newsstand, Florist **Under 1 mi:** Supermarket *(Shaw's 567-4116)*, Gourmet Shop *(White Hen 569-7069)*, Health Food, Wine/Beer, Liquor Store *(Cappy's)*, Protestant Church, Synagogue, Library *(569-0271)*, Bookstore *(Brattle 542-0210)*, Pharmacy *(Brooks 561-0610)* **1-3 mi:** Hardware Store *(Boston 523-1683)*

Transportation

OnSite: Courtesy Car/Van *(Airport & local mkts)*, Water Taxi *($5/1-way to downtown Boston)* **OnCall:** Rental Car *(Enterprise 423-3352)*, Taxi *(East Boston Tunnel 567-2700)*, Airport Limo *(A & A 567-0070)* **Near:** Local Bus *(T line)* **1-3 mi:** Rail *(South Station)* **Airport:** Logan *(1 mi.)*

Medical Services

911 Service **OnCall:** Ambulance **Near:** Doctor **Under 1 mi:** Dentist *(E. Boston Dental Associates 569-7300)*, Holistic Services **1-3 mi:** Chiropractor *(Backworks 451-2225)*, Veterinarian *(So. Boston Animal Hospital 269-0610)* **Hospital:** Mass. General 248-1926 *(5 mi.)*

Setting -- Located at the historic Bethlehem Steel Shipyard in East Boston, this marina/boatyard has the unique advantage of truly spectacular views of the Boston skyline -- with relatively easy access to the city centers. It is directly across the Harbor from Rowes Wharf. In addition, its neighbor is the award-winning East Boston Piers Park.

Marina Notes -- Built in 1989, BHSYM currently has 180 deep-water slips. Megayachts are easily accommodated with electrical connections for extended stays. Marina also houses a 256' by 44' graving dock, which can accommodate vessels up to 16,500 long tons -- permitting servicing of virtually every type of vessel ---- tugs, excursion and commuter boats, barges and scows, fishing and pleasure boats. Also a 50T travelift and onsite repair and refit services - specializes in custom composite construction - performance fairing. 10-cent per gallon fuel discount to Seatow members. Complimentary continental breakfast on weekend mornings in season. Catering available onsite for that impromptu gathering. Free shuttle service to/from Logan and local markets during normal business hours. BHSYM is one of the Sea Chain Marinas.

Notable -- Guests can enjoy a private sunset gathering on the marina rooftop. Nearby is 6.5 acre East Boston Piers Park which offers 2 large pavilions with Boston skyline views, a 600 ft. waterside promenade, with 4 smaller pavilions, a wonderful playground, 32 varieties of trees, an amphitheater, a fitness trail system and a sailing center. 3-mile ride to downtown Boston by land -- taxi or public transportation, 1-mile ride by water.

PHOTOS ON CD-ROM: 9

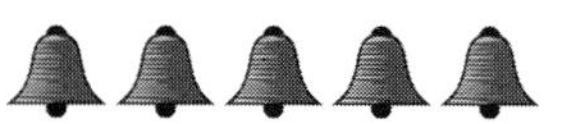

The Marina at Rowes Wharf

50 Rowes Wharf, Suite 200; Boston, MA 02110

Tel: (617) 439-3131 **VHF: Monitor** 9 **Talk** 67
Fax: (617) 204-1145 **Alternate Tel:** (617) 425-7500
Email: n/a **Web:** n/a
Nearest Town: Boston *(0 mi.)* **Tourist Info:** (617) 227-4500

Navigational Information

Lat: 42°21.419' **Long:** 071°02.952' **Tide:** 10 ft. **Current:** 2 kt. **Chart:** 13272
Rep. Depths (*MLW*): Entry 30 ft. **Fuel Dock** n/a **Max Slip/Moor** 30 ft./-
Access: Cape Cod Bay to Boston Harbor, first facility on port side

Marina Facilities *(In Season/Off Season)*

Fuel: No
Slips: 30 Total, 20 Transient **Max LOA:** 280 ft. **Max Beam:** n/a
Rate *(per ft.)*: **Day** $3.00/Inq.* **Week** n/a **Month** n/a
Power: 30 amp $12, **50 amp** $16, **100 amp** $25, **200 amp** n/a
Cable TV: Yes **Dockside Phone:** Yes Local
Dock Type: Wood, Floating
Moorings: 0 Total, 0 Transient **Launch:** n/a
Rate: Day n/a **Week** n/a **Month** n/a
Heads: 2 Toilet(s), 2 Shower(s), Hair Dryers
Laundry: 1 Washer(s), 1 Dryer(s) **Pay Phones:** Yes
Pump-Out: OnSite **Fee:** n/a **Closed Heads:** No

Marina Operations

Owner/Manager: Marisa Brennan **Dockmaster:** John Reardon
In-Season: May-Oct, 9am-9pm **Off-Season:** Nov-Apr, 9am-5pm
After-Hours Arrival: Call in advance
Reservations: Required **Credit Cards:** Visa/MC, Dscvr, Din, Amex
Discounts: None
Pets: Welcome **Handicap Access:** No

Marina Services and Boat Supplies

Services - Docking Assistance, Concierge, Room Service to the Boat, Security *(24 hrs.)*, Trash Pick-Up, Dock Carts **Communication -** Mail & Package Hold, Phone Messages, Fax in/out, Data Ports *(Business Center)*, FedEx, AirBorne, UPS, Express Mail *(Sat Del)* **Supplies - OnSite:** Ice *(Cube)* **OnCall:** Propane **Under 1 mi:** Bait/Tackle *(Firefly 423-3474, Orvis 742-0288)* **1-3 mi:** Ships' Store *(CG Edwards 268-4111)*

Boatyard Services

OnSite: Bottom Cleaning **OnCall:** Interior Cleaning **Under 1 mi:** Travelift, Railway, Forklift, Launching Ramp, Electrical Repairs, Electronics Repairs, Hull Repairs, Rigger, Brightwork, Refrigeration. **1-3 mi:** Crane, Engine mechanic *(gas, diesel)*, Electronic Sales, Divers, Compound, Wash & Wax, Inflatable Repairs.

Restaurants and Accommodations

OnSite: Restaurant *(Intrigue Café 856-7744, B $5-11, L $9-16, D $9-16, tea)*, *(Meritage 439-3995, D $14-28, Sun Brunch $45, Kids' menu $20)*, Lite Fare *(Rowes Wharf Bar, Pub food, 4pm on)*, Hotel *(Boston Harbor 439-7000, $225-2000)* **Near:** Restaurant *(Legal Seafood 227-3115, L $8-15, D $15-25)*, *(Nara 338-5935)*, Pizzeria *(Al Capone 227-2692)*, Hotel *(Harborside Inn 723-7500, $145-310)*, *(Wyndham 556-0006, $240-380)*, *(Marriott Long Wharf 422-0392, $160-600)*

Recreation and Entertainment

OnSite: Pool, Spa, Fitness Center *(Rowes Wharf Health Club & Spa 439-3914)*, Jogging Paths, Roller Blade/Bike Paths **Near:** Playground, Park, Museum *(Paul Revere House 523-1676, Children's Museum 426-8855 $7/6/2)*, Cultural Attract *(New England Aquarium $13/7)*, Sightseeing *(Freedom Trail - follow the red line)* **Under 1 mi:** Dive Shop, Movie Theater, Video Rental *(Video Cinema 248-6860)* **1-3 mi:** Golf Course *(Harmon Club 242-1449)*, Bowling *(So. Boston Candlepin 464-4858)* **3+ mi:** Tennis Courts *(Sportsmen's Tennis Club 288-9092, 6 mi.)*

Provisioning and General Services

OnSite: Delicatessen, Bank/ATM, Beauty Salon, Laundry, Newsstand, Florist, Copies Etc. *(Business Center)* **Near:** Convenience Store, Supermarket *(Christy's Markets 227-9534)*, Bakery, Farmers' Market, Fishmonger, Meat Market, Post Office, Catholic Church, Barber Shop, Dry Cleaners, Hardware Store *(Hardware Outlet 426-0326)*, Clothing Store, Retail Shops, Department Store **Under 1 mi:** Wine/Beer *(Federal Wine & Spirits 367-8605)*, Liquor Store *(Cirace Liquor 227-3193)*, Bookstore *(Borders 557-7188)*, Pharmacy *(CVS 426-8964)* **1-3 mi:** Gourmet Shop *(Le Saucier 227-9649)*, Library, Buying Club

Transportation

OnSite: Water Taxi *(951-0255, 422-0392 Boston Harbor, Logan)*, Rental Car *(Enterprise 261-7447, Hertz 434-6885)*, Taxi, Ferry Service *(Hingham, Logan)* **Under 1 mi:** InterCity Bus *(Greyhound 526-1800)* **1-3 mi:** Bikes *(Federicos 269-1309)* **3+ mi:** Rail *(Boston South Station, 10 min.)* **Airport:** Logan Int'l. *(3 mi.)*

Medical Services

911 Service **OnSite:** Holistic Services *(massage services)* **OnCall:** Doctor, Ambulance **Under 1 mi:** Chiropractor *(Backworks 728-7246)* **Hospital:** Mass. General 248-1926 *(1 mi.)*

Setting -- An integral part of the impressive $193 million Rowes Wharf complex, the marina, the first on your port side as you enter the inner harbor, is located in the heart of downtown Boston's financial district. It sits at the foot of Boston Harbor Hotel, one of the city's finest, with views across the water to East Boston. Landside views, at high tide, are of the hotel, town houses, the commercial ferries and tour boats, and the outdoor café. Pilings appear at low tide.

Marina Notes -- * Over 60' $3.50/ft. 24-hour room service to boats. Designed in the shape of an "E", with the wharves extending into the water. The Boston Harbor Hotel offers 230 rooms, function rooms, florist, ATM, and car rental. Access to the very handsome health club, spa & fitness center with pool is included with dockage. Onsite restaurants: considered one of the best in Boston, Chef Daniel Bruce's spectacular, contemporary Meritage offers an abundance of choices as either small ($14) or large plates ($28), each dish paired with a wine, Sun-Thu 5:30-10pm, Fri-Sat 'til 11pm, Sun Brunch10:30-2; Intrigue Bistro Café has a wonderful terrace overlooking the docks, Sun-Thu 6am-9pm, Fri-Sat 'til 10pm; Rowes Wharf Bar serves pub food form 4pm 'til? Docks can be a bit exposed to the constant wakes. The southern docks are home to many commercial vessels; recreational docks are on the quieter, more sheltered, north side.

Notable -- Commuter ferry to Hingham & South Shore (RT $10/5 6am-8:30pm, 227-4321); Logan Airport water shuttle (7 min. $10). Three blocks to New England Aquarium, Boston Children's Museum, Faneuil Hall/Quincy Marketplace (125 shops and 21 restaurants). Odyssey offers lunch, brunch, dinner and moonlight harbor cruises $29-86, 888 741-0281. Boston Harbor Whale Watch 345-9866. Boston Harbor Sailing Club operates its program from Rowes Wharf.

PHOTOS ON CD-ROM: 9

Navigational Information
Lat: 42°21.670' **Long:** 071°02.922' **Tide:** 10 ft. **Current:** 2 kt. **Chart:** 13272
Rep. Depths (*MLW*): Entry 15 ft. **Fuel Dock** n/a **Max Slip/Moor** 14 ft./35 ft.
Access: Follow Harbor channel to Inner Harbor, 3rd facility on port side

Marina Facilities *(In Season/Off Season)*
Fuel: No
Slips: 36 Total, 20 Transient **Max LOA:** 200 ft. **Max Beam:** n/a
Rate *(per ft.)*: **Day** $2.75* **Week** $16.50 **Month** n/a
Power: 30 amp $7.50, **50 amp** $15, **100 amp** $30, **200 amp** n/a
Cable TV: No **Dockside Phone:** No
Dock Type: Long Fingers, Floating
Moorings: 7 Total, 7 Transient **Launch:** None, Dinghy Dock
Rate: Day $35-45 **Week** $210-270 **Month** n/a
Heads: 2 Toilet(s), 2 Shower(s)
Laundry: 1 Washer(s), 1 Dryer(s) **Pay Phones:** Yes
Pump-Out: Full Service, 1 Central, 2 Port **Fee:** n/a **Closed Heads:** No

Marina Operations
Owner/Manager: Larry Cannon **Dockmaster:** Alex Markhoff
In-Season: May-Nov 1, 8am-6pm **Off-Season:** Closed
After-Hours Arrival: Call during office hours
Reservations: Yes **Credit Cards:** Visa/MC, Amex
Discounts: None
Pets: Welcome, Dog Walk Area **Handicap Access:** No

Boston Waterboat Marina

66 Long Wharf; Boston, MA 02110

Tel: (617) 523-1027 **VHF: Monitor** 9 **Talk** n/a
Fax: (617) 523-1215 **Alternate Tel:** n/a
Email: n/a **Web:** n/a
Nearest Town: Boston *(0 mi.)* **Tourist Info:** (617) 227-4500

Marina Services and Boat Supplies
Services - Docking Assistance, Security *(24 Hrs.)*, Dock Carts **Communication -** Mail & Package Hold, Fax in/out, Data Ports *(Office)*, FedEx, AirBorne, UPS, Express Mail *(Sat Del)* **Supplies - OnSite:** Ice *(Cube)* **Under 1 mi:** Bait/Tackle *(Orvis 742-0288)*, Propane *(Perfection Propane 928-4133)* **1-3 mi:** Ships' Store, Marine Discount Store *(CG Edwards 268-4111)*

Boatyard Services
OnSite: Engine mechanic *(gas, diesel)*, Bottom Cleaning, Brightwork, Divers, Compound, Wash & Wax **Near:** Total Refits. **1-3 mi:** Inflatable Repairs, Life Raft Service. **Nearest Yard:** Marina Bay (617) 847-1800

Restaurants and Accommodations
OnSite: Restaurant *(Chart House 227-1576)*, *(Oceana 227-0800, D $17-35, B, L & D)*, Lite Fare *(Waves L $9-16, D $9-16, on the deck)*, Hotel *(Marriott Long Wharf 227-0800, $160-600)* **Near:** Restaurant *(Rowes Wharf 439-3995, B $6-11, L $11-17, D $14-28, Sun Brunch)*, *(Legal Seafoods 227-3115, L $8-15, D $15-25, doz oysters $20)*, *(Tias on the Waterfront 227-0828)*, *(Intrigue Café 856-7744, L $9-16, D $9-16)*, *(Meritage 439-3995, Sun Brunch)*, Hotel *(Boston Harbor 439-7000, $400-2000)*, *(Regal Bostonian 523-3600, $245-625)*, *(Harborside Inn 723-7500, $145-310)*

Recreation and Entertainment
OnSite: Sightseeing *(Liberty Tall Ships noon-2, 3-5, 6-8 $30/18)* **Near:** Pool, Playground *(playscape at Columbus Park)*, Tennis Courts, Fitness Center *(Rowes Wharf Health Club & Spa 439-3914)*, Fishing Charter, Movie Theater, Video Arcade, Park *(Christopher Columbus Park at the foot of Long Wharf)*, Cultural Attract *(Boston Aquarium $13/7, with Imax/Whale Watch $22 573-9200)* **Under 1 mi:** Jogging Paths, Video Rental *(Video Cinema 248-6860)*, Museum *(Children's 426-8855 $7/6/2 Boston Tea Party Ship 269-7150 $8/4, Paul Revere House 523-1676)* **1-3 mi:** Golf Course *(Harmon Club 242-1449)*, Bowling *(So. Boston Candlepin 464-4858)*

Provisioning and General Services
Near: Provisioning Service, Convenience Store, Supermarket *(Christys Markets 227-9534)*, Delicatessen, Bakery *(Quincy Market/Faneuil Hall)*, Farmers' Market *(City Hall Plaza 781-893-8222 Mon & Wed 11am-6pm)*, Fishmonger *(Quincy)*, Meat Market, Bank/ATM, Post Office, Catholic Church, Library, Beauty Salon, Barber Shop, Dry Cleaners, Laundry, Bookstore, Pharmacy *(Southworths Market 951-0312)*, Newsstand, Florist, Clothing Store, Retail Shops, Department Store, Copies Etc. *(Boston Business Printing 482-3122)* **Under 1 mi:** Gourmet Shop *(Le Saucier 227-9649)*, Wine/Beer *(Federal Wine & Spirits 367-8605)*, Liquor Store *(Cirace Liquor 227-3193)*, Hardware Store *(Boston Hardware 523-1683)*

Transportation
OnSite: Water Taxi *(MBTA 422-0392)*, Taxi *(Cap's Limo 523-0727)*, Ferry Service *(Fast Ferry to Provincetown 9am ret 4pm daily $45/35 RT, Logan water shuttle at Rowes Wharf)* **OnCall:** Rental Car *(Enterprise 261-7447, Hertz 434-6885)* **Under 1 mi:** Rail **1-3 mi:** Bikes *(Federico's Bike 269-1309)* **Airport:** Logan Int'l. *(3 mi.)*

Medical Services
911 Service **OnCall:** Ambulance **Under 1 mi:** Chiropractor *(Backworks 728-7246)* **Hospital:** Mass. General/Boston Medical Cntr. 638-8000 *(1 mi.)*

Setting -- In the heart of historic downtown Boston, is this delightfully unexpected, home-grown, perfect city marina -- just a short walk to famous Quincy Market/Faneuil Hall and the New England Aquarium. This low-key, ideally situated facility is the third set of docks on your port side as you enter the inner harbor. It's on Long Wharf, tucked among renovated warehouses which house nautical enterprises, tours, restaurants, and the Marriott Long Wharf Hotel.

Marina Notes -- *Over 45' $3/ft., Sat only $3.50-4/ft. $10/hr. during day. Weekly rate $16.50-17.50/ft. In the same family for three generations, now run by a Boston harbor pilot who lives onsite. Reasonably well-protected, slips are aligned into the prevailing swell - rather than across. Nice heads, showers and laundry on its own barge. A few liveaboards. Trans-Ocean station onsite. Onsite chain eateries: Oceana (and its Waves Deck) and Boston Chart House (Mon-Fri 5-10pm, Weekends 4-10pm), in the 1760's four-story brick Gardiner Building, the oldest building still in use on the Boston waterfront -- formerly John Hancock's counting house. For location, charm, and determined saltiness, this is surely Boston's "best pick."

Notable -- Columbus Park at the foot of the wharf has a wonderful children's playground and a dog run. Home of the Liberty Fleet of Tall Ships. Offering daily sails, charters and adventure sail vacations in Boston 742-0333. 125' Schooner Liberty Clipper goes out three times daily during the summer $30/18. Antique boat Show in September. The MBTA Boston-By-Boat runs a shuttle ($5/4 for the day) to most of the waterside museums, including world class Children's 426-8855 $7/6/2 and Boston Tea Party Ship 269-7150 $8/4. Ferry and/or sightseeing cruise to Charlestown Navy Yard and/or Quincy 227-4321.

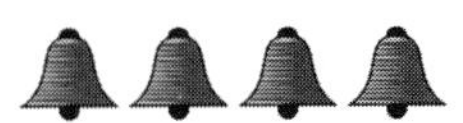

Boston Yacht Haven

87 Commercial Wharf; Boston, MA 02110

Tel: (617) 523-7352 **VHF: Monitor** 9 **Talk** 8
Fax: (617) 523-2270 **Alternate Tel:** (617) 523-7352
Email: pdanaher@moderncontinental.com **Web:** bostonyachthaven.com
Nearest Town: Boston *(0 mi.)* **Tourist Info:** (617) 227-4500

Navigational Information

Lat: 42°21.703' **Long:** 071°02.923' **Tide:** 10 ft. **Current:** 2 kt. **Chart:** 13272
Rep. Depths (*MLW*): Entry 35 ft. **Fuel Dock** n/a **Max Slip/Moor** 35 ft./-
Access: Cape Cod Bay to Boston Inner Harbor, 4th facility on port side

Marina Facilities *(In Season/Off Season)*

Fuel: No
Slips: 70 Total, Inq. Transient **Max LOA:** 300 ft. **Max Beam:** 40 ft.
Rate *(per ft.)*: **Day** $3.25/Inq.* **Week** $10 **Month** $35
Power: 30 amp $15, **50 amp** $20, **100 amp** $35, **200 amp** n/a
Cable TV: Yes Satellite **Dockside Phone:** Yes, 2 line(s)
Dock Type: Floating
Moorings: 0 Total, 0 Transient **Launch:** n/a
Rate: Day n/a **Week** n/a **Month** n/a
Heads: 6 Toilet(s), 4 Shower(s)
Laundry: 2 Washer(s), 2 Dryer(s) **Pay Phones:** Yes
Pump-Out: No **Fee:** n/a **Closed Heads:** No

Marina Operations

Owner/Manager: Patrick Danaher **Dockmaster:** Same
In-Season: May-Oct 31, 8am-Mid **Off-Season:** Nov 1-Apr 30, 9am-4pm
After-Hours Arrival: Call in advance
Reservations: Preferred **Credit Cards:** Visa/MC, Dscvr, Din, Amex
Discounts: None
Pets: Welcome **Handicap Access:** Yes, Heads, Docks

Marina Services and Boat Supplies

Services - Docking Assistance, Security *(24 Hrs., guard at gate, CCT/cards)*, Dock Carts, Megayacht Facilities, 3 Phase **Communication -** Mail & Package Hold, Phone Messages, Fax in/out, FedEx, AirBorne, UPS, Express Mail *(Sat Del)* **Supplies - OnSite:** Ice *(Cube)* **Near:** Ice *(Block)* **Under 1 mi:** Ships' Store, Bait/Tackle *(Orvis 742-0288)*, Propane *(Perfection Propane 928-4133)* **1-3 mi:** Marine Discount Store *(CG Edwards 268-4111)*

Boatyard Services

Under 1 mi: Travelift, Railway, Forklift, Crane, Engine mechanic *(gas, diesel)*, Launching Ramp, Electrical Repairs, Electronic Sales, Electronics Repairs, Hull Repairs, Rigger, Sail Loft, Yacht Design *(John Alden Yachts)*, Yacht Broker *(Alden)*, Yacht Building *(Alden)*. **Nearest Yard:** Boston Boat Yard (617) 531-1400

Restaurants and Accommodations

OnSite: Hotel *(Boston Yacht Haven Rooms & Suites 523-7352, $175-275, 10 waterfront rooms)* **Near:** Restaurant *(Sel de la terre 720-1300, L $7-14, D $8-21)*, *(Union Oyster House 227-2750, L $7-16, D $15-25)*, *(Seasons 523-3600, B $8-16, L $10-24, D $26-37)*, *(Durgin Park 227-2038, L $5-17, D $6-17)*, *(Tavern on the Water 242-4280, L $6-10, D $10-16)*, Hotel *(Boston Harbor Hotel 439-7000, $400-2000)*, *(Marriott Long Wharf 227-0800, $425-600)*, *(Harborside Inn 723-7500, $160-330)*

Recreation and Entertainment

Near: Playground, Fitness Center *(Beacon Hill Athletic Club 742-0055)*, Park, Cultural Attract *(Aquarium)*, Sightseeing *(Faneuil Hall, Duck Tours)* **Under 1 mi:** Jogging Paths, Roller Blade/Bike Paths, Video Rental *(North End Video 367-3533)*, Video Arcade, Museum *(Boston Tea Party Ship 269-7150 $8/4, Paul Revere House 523-1676)* **1-3 mi:** Beach, Bowling *(So. Boston Candlepin 464-4858)*, Fishing Charter, Movie Theater **3+ mi:** Tennis Courts *(Sportsmen's Tennis Club 288-9092, 6 mi.)*, Golf Course *(Franklin Park 265-4084, 6 mi.)*

Provisioning and General Services

Near: Convenience Store *(Christys Market 227-9534)*, Gourmet Shop *(Quincy Market)*, Delicatessen, Bakery *(Quincy)*, Green Grocer *(Faneuil Hall Market)*, Fishmonger *(Quincy)*, Meat Market, Bank/ATM, Beauty Salon, Barber Shop, Dry Cleaners, Newsstand, Clothing Store, Retail Shops **Under 1 mi:** Supermarket *(Stop & Shop 742-6094)*, Health Food, Wine/Beer *(Wine Bottega 227-6607)*, Liquor Store *(Cirace & Sons 227-3193)*, Farmers' Market *(City Hall Plaza Mon & Wed 11am-6pm)*, Post Office, Laundry, Bookstore *(Borders 557-7188)*, Pharmacy *(Green Cross 227-3728)*, Hardware Store *(Boston Hware 523-1683)*, Florist, Department Store *(Macy's, JC Penney)*, Copies Etc. *(Harborside Copy 367-4345)*

Transportation

OnCall: Rental Car *(Enterprise 261-7447, Hertz 434-6885)* **Near:** Water Taxi *(422-0392)*, Ferry Service *(to Logan)* **Under 1 mi:** Taxi *(Caps 523-0727)*, Local Bus *(MBTA)*, InterCity Bus, Rail *(South Station)* **1-3 mi:** Bikes *(Federico's Bike 269-1309)* **Airport:** Logan Int'l. *(3 mi.)*

Medical Services

911 Service **OnCall:** Dentist, Ambulance **Near:** Doctor, Chiropractor **Under 1 mi:** Holistic Services *(Backworks 728-7246)* **Hospital:** Mass. General 248-1926 *(1 mi.)*

Setting -- The fourth facility to port in the inner harbor, on Commercial Wharf, Boston Yacht Haven is just in front of the Boston Waterfront Park. Conveniently located, this newly renovated and enlarged, luxurious, high-end facility could not be more comfortable. The views are of the New England style boathouse that is the centerpiece of the marina, the Boston skyline and the harbor.

Marina Notes -- *Up to 30' $3/ft., 50-100' $3.25/ft; 100'+ $3.50/ft. Stern-to berthing $2.50/ft. Day $10/hr. A 25% deposit, non-refundable, is required with reservations. Marina has deluxe guest accommodations onsite as well as new, high-end marble heads and showers, and particularly attractive public rooms. Luxurious facility that can handle megayachts: large slips, electric hookups - 100 amp single and 3-phase. Concierge service available to all guests. The docks are protected by a Radisson Wave Attenuating floating dock system that helps ensure a comfortable night's sleep. Part of the Modern Continental Group.

Notable -- Ten very attractive, well-appointed waterfront rooms, each with its own deck, are on the second and third floors of the main building ($175-275/nt.). All of Boston is within easy reach. There are literally hundreds of restaurants and historic sights within an easy walk. Tavern on the Water at the beginning of the pier will prepare take-out. The water taxi stops nearby, as do land taxis, the "T", and the "ferry" to Logan airport. A short walk is Quincy Market, the New England Aquarium and Boston's financial center. The MBTA's Boston-By-Boat shuttle stops at all waterside museums - including the world class Children's Museum (426-8855) $7/6/2.

PHOTOS ON CD-ROM: 9

Navigational Information
Lat: 42°22.404' **Long:** 071°03.021' **Tide:** 10 ft. **Current:** n/a **Chart:** 13272
Rep. Depths (*MLW*): Entry 30 ft. **Fuel Dock** n/a **Max Slip/Moor** 45 ft./-
Access: Inner Harbor, past Coast Guard, straight to Pier 6 & 8 in Navy Yard

Marina Facilities *(In Season/Off Season)*
Fuel: No
Slips: 300 Total, 100 Transient **Max LOA:** 300 ft. **Max Beam:** n/a
Rate *(per ft.)*: **Day** $2.25/$1.00* **Week** Inq. **Month** $25 per foot
Power: 30 amp $5, **50 amp** $10, **100 amp** $16, **200 amp** n/a
Cable TV: Yes **Dockside Phone:** Yes
Dock Type: Wood, Long Fingers, Pilings, Floating
Moorings: 0 Total, 0 Transient **Launch:** n/a
Rate: Day n/a **Week** n/a **Month** n/a
Heads: 10 Toilet(s), 8 Shower(s), Hair Dryers
Laundry: 6 Washer(s), 8 Dryer(s) **Pay Phones:** Yes
Pump-Out: OnSite, Full Service, 1 Central **Fee:** n/a **Closed Heads:** No

Marina Operations
Owner/Manager: n/a **Dockmaster:** Catherine E. MacAlpine
In-Season: May-Oct 31, 8am-8pm **Off-Season:** Nov-Apr 30, 9am-5pm
After-Hours Arrival: Call in advance
Reservations: Recommended **Credit Cards:** Visa/MC, Dscvr
Discounts: Groups 5+ boats **Dockage:** n/a **Fuel:** n/a **Repair:** n/a
Pets: Welcome, Dog Walk Area **Handicap Access:** No

Shipyard Quarters Marina

1 Pier Eight; Charlestown, MA 02129

Tel: (617) 242-2020 **VHF: Monitor** 9 **Talk** 71
Fax: (617) 242-5246 **Alternate Tel:** (617) 242-2070
Email: sqmarina@aol.com **Web:** www.shipyardquartersmarina.com
Nearest Town: Boston *(0.25 mi.)* **Tourist Info:** (617) 227-4500

Marina Services and Boat Supplies
Services - Docking Assistance, Concierge, Trash Pick-Up, Dock Carts, 3-Phase **Communication -** Mail & Package Hold, Phone Messages, Fax in/out *($1)*, FedEx, AirBorne, UPS, Express Mail *(Sat Del)* **Supplies - OnSite:** Ice *(Cube)* **1-3 mi:** Ships' Store *(McLellan Bros 389-5508)*, Bait/Tackle, Propane *(Perfection Propane 928-4133)* **3+ mi:** Marine Discount Store *(CG Edwards 268-4111, 3.5 mi.)*

Boatyard Services
OnCall: Engine mechanic *(gas, diesel)*, Electrical Repairs, Electronics Repairs, Hull Repairs, Rigger, Bottom Cleaning, Brightwork, Refrigeration, Divers **Nearest Yard:** Hewitts Cove Marina (781) 749-6647

Restaurants and Accommodations
OnSite: Restaurant *(Tavern on the Water 242-8040, L $6.50-17, D $6.50-17, Sun brunch $5.50-13)*, Snack Bar **Near:** Restaurant *(Jumbo Seafood 542-2823)*, *(New Shanghai 338-6688)*, *(Ironside Grille 242-1384)*, Inn/B&B *(Constitution Inn 241-8400)* **Under 1 mi:** Pizzeria *(Kipos 242-4141)*, Hotel *(Boston Marriott 422-0392)* **1-3 mi:** Hotel *(Regal Bostonian 526-3600, $245-625)*, *(Holiday Inn 742-7630, $150-330)*

Recreation and Entertainment
OnSite: Picnic Area, Grills, Jogging Paths, Roller Blade/Bike Paths, Park, Sightseeing *(Tea Party Ship and Museum 338-1773)* **Near:** Pool, Playground, Dive Shop, Cultural Attract **Under 1 mi:** Golf Course *(Harmon Club 242-1449)*, Fitness Center *(YMCA 482-1122)*, Movie Theater, Video Rental *(Blockbuster 242-9893)*, Museum *(USS Constitution 242-5670)* **1-3 mi:** Bowling *(Central Park Lanes 567-7073)* **3+ mi:** Tennis Courts *(Badminton & Tennis Club 247-8748, 3.5 mi.)*, Horseback Riding *(Revere Saugus Riding Academy 781-322-7788, 6 mi.)*

Provisioning and General Services
OnSite: Bakery, Dry Cleaners **OnCall:** Wine/Beer **Near:** Convenience Store, Delicatessen, Liquor Store *(Mc Carthy Bros 242-4877)*, Farmers' Market *(Thompson Square - Main & Austin 241-8866 Wed 2-7pm)*, Meat Market, Bank/ATM, Post Office, Catholic Church, Beauty Salon, Laundry *(Mary Ann's 242-9386)*, Newsstand **Under 1 mi:** Supermarket *(Foodmaster 660-1372, Shaw's 567-4116)*, Fishmonger, Library *(Boston 242-1248)*, Bookstore, Pharmacy *(High Pharmacy 242-0415)*, Hardware Store *(Boston Hardware 523-1683)*, Copies Etc. *(Copy Cop 367-3370)* **1-3 mi:** Gourmet Shop *(Le Saucier 227-9649)*, Health Food *(Springwell Market 723-9828)*, Department Store

Transportation
OnSite: Water Taxi *(422-0392 or MBTA's water shuttle)*, Local Bus, Ferry Service *(Rowes Wharf 227-4321)* **OnCall:** Rental Car *(Avis 534-1400, Enterprise 261-7447)* **Near:** Bikes **Under 1 mi:** Taxi *(After Hours Limousine 242-2666)* **1-3 mi:** InterCity Bus *(Coach 887-2200)*, Rail *(Boston 268-9000)* **Airport:** Logan Int'l. *(5 mi.)*

Medical Services
911 Service **OnCall:** Ambulance **Under 1 mi:** Doctor, Dentist, Chiropractor *(Broadway Chiropractic Clinic 685-7775)*, Holistic Services *(Boston's Best Waterfront Massage 367-6996)* **Hospital:** Mass. General 248-1926 *(1 mi.)*

Setting -- In the heart of the retired and historic 63 acre Charlestown Navy Yard, with parks, jogging paths and tourists, this multimillion dollar marina complex includes retail shops, a boardwalk, a restaurant and dockage for 350 boats - runabouts to megayachts. It's in two sections, each a wharf with docks on both sides. The first, Pier Six, is recognizable by the bright blue canvas awnings and the two-story Tavern on the Water Restaurant. The second, Pier Eight, has a low-country style contemporary clubhouse, with a pale green shed roof, as its centerpiece.

Marina Notes -- * Over 60' $3/ft. Pier Eight, protected by an 800-foot floating breakwater, is a bit more private with its own set of heads and showers plus laundry room in a restored building off the parking lot. Pier Six has better views of Boston (at high tide), a bit more roll and an onsite restaurant (hours: 11:30am-10:30pm Mon-Fri, 10:30am-10:30pm Sat-Sun; entertainment Wed night). State of the art, well-maintained docks permit four way tie-ups. 24 hr. security (CCTV/Card Access). Complimentary courtesy van. 100 amp 1 and 3-phase electric; Boston's largest dock staff works at being accommodating.

Notable -- The Charlestown Navy Yard is part of the Boston National Historical Park, and home of USS Constitution, USS Constitution Museum and Bunker Hill Monument. A stop on the 2.5 mi. historic Freedom Trail. Paul Revere's House and Kings Chapel are also near. Fleet Center is easily accessible. Ferry from Charlestown Navy Yard to Long Wharf downtown every 15 min weekdays 6am - 8:10pm (from 10am on weekends, every 30 min). $2.50/1.50. Water taxi ($10) or TA's Water Shuttle ($5/4 for all-day) from Pier 4 to downtown.

PHOTOS ON CD-ROM: 9

Constitution Marina

28 Constitution Road; Charlestown, MA 02129

Tel: (617) 241-9640 **VHF: Monitor** 9 **Talk** 69
Fax: (617) 242-3013 **Alternate Tel:** n/a
Email: tom@bosport.com **Web:** www.constitutionmarina.com
Nearest Town: Boston *(0.25 mi.)* **Tourist Info:** (617) 227-4500

Navigational Information

Lat: 42°22.260' **Long:** 071°03.600' **Tide:** 10 ft. **Current:** n/a **Chart:** 13272
Rep. Depths (*MLW*): Entry 30 ft. **Fuel Dock** n/a **Max Slip/Moor** 40 ft./40 ft.
Access: Charles River, turn to port at Coast Guard, on starboard

Marina Facilities *(In Season/Off Season)*

Fuel: No
Slips: 265 Total, 30 Transient **Max LOA:** 150 ft. **Max Beam:** 30 ft.
Rate *(per ft.)*: **Day** $2.75/$1.00* **Week** $14-17 **Month** $45-50
Power: 30 amp Incl., **50 amp** $5, **100 amp** $25, **200 amp** n/a
Cable TV: Yes **Dockside Phone:** Yes
Dock Type: Wood, Long Fingers, Alongside, Floating, Composition
Moorings: 9 Total, 9 Transient **Launch:** None, Dinghy Dock (Free)
Rate: Day $35 **Week** n/a **Month** n/a
Heads: 5 Toilet(s), 7 Shower(s) *(with dressing rooms)*
Laundry: 3 Washer(s), 4 Dryer(s), Book Exchange **Pay Phones:** Yes, 3
Pump-Out: Full Service, 1 Central, 1 Port **Fee:** Free **Closed Heads:** Yes

Marina Operations

Owner/Manager: Tom Cox **Dockmaster:** Keith McClearn
In-Season: Mar-Nov, 8am-8pm **Off-Season:** Dec-Apr, 9am-5pm
After-Hours Arrival: Call ahead.
Reservations: Yes, Preferred **Credit Cards:** Visa/MC, Dscvr, Amex
Discounts: Boat/US; Restrictions **Dockage:** 25% **Fuel:** n/a **Repair:** n/a
Pets: Welcome, Dog Walk Area **Handicap Access:** Yes, Heads

Marina Services and Boat Supplies

Services - Docking Assistance, Concierge, Room Service to the Boat, Boaters' Lounge, Security, Dock Carts, Megayacht Facilities **Communication -** Mail & Package Hold, Phone Messages, Fax in/out *($1)*, Data Ports *(Office)*, FedEx, AirBorne, UPS, Express Mail *(Sat Del)* **Supplies - OnSite:** Ice *(Block, Cube)* **1-3 mi:** Marine Discount Store *(CG Edwards 268-4111)*, Propane *(Perfection Propane 928-4133)*

Boatyard Services

OnSite: Crane, Engine mechanic *(gas, diesel)*, Electrical Repairs, Electronics Repairs, Hull Repairs, Rigger, Bottom Cleaning, Brightwork, Refrigeration, Divers, Yacht Broker **OnCall:** Air Conditioning, Compound, Wash & Wax, Interior Cleaning, Propeller Repairs, Woodworking, Upholstery, Yacht Interiors **1-3 mi:** Sail Loft, Inflatable Repairs, Life Raft Service, Metal Fabrication, Painting, Awlgrip, Yacht Design, Yacht Building.

Restaurants and Accommodations

OnSite: Restaurant *(Olives 242-1999, D $22-28)*, *(Ironside Grille 242-1384)*, Inn/B&B *(B&B Afloat 241-9640, $165-390, on yachts at marina)* **OnCall:** Pizzeria *(Pizza In Piazza 742-4142)* **Near:** Restaurant *(Jumbo Seafood 542-2823)*, *(Warren Tavern 241-8142)*, Lite Fare *(Sorrell Bakery Café 242-2125, B & L $5)*, Hotel *(Marriott 227-0800)* **Under 1 mi:** Motel *(Shawmut Inn 720-5544)*, Hotel *(Regal Bostonian 523-3600, $245-625)*, *(Holiday Inn 742-7630, $200-260)*

Recreation and Entertainment

OnSite: Heated Pool, Picnic Area, Grills, Playground, Jogging Paths, Boat Rentals, Roller Blade/Bike Paths, Fishing Charter, Group Fishing Boat **Near:** Volleyball, Tennis Courts, Movie Theater, Park, Museum *(1797 USS Constitution, 426-1812 Free; USS Cassin Young, a WWII destroyer)*, Sightseeing *(Freedom Trail)*, Special Events *(Fleet Center, 5 min walk.)* **Under 1 mi:** Golf Course *(Harmon Club 242-1449)*, Fitness Center *(YMCA 482-1122)*, Video Rental *(Blockbuster 242-9893)* **1-3 mi:** Beach, Bowling *(Central Park 567-7073)*

Provisioning and General Services

OnCall: Provisioning Service **Near:** Convenience Store, Delicatessen, Farmers' Market *(Thompson Square - Main & Austin 241-8866 Wed 2-7pm)*, Fishmonger, Lobster Pound, Bank/ATM, Post Office, Catholic Church, Beauty Salon, Dry Cleaners, Laundry, Pharmacy *(High Pharm. 242-0415)*, Newsstand, Florist **Under 1 mi:** Supermarket *(Foodmaster 660-1372, Shaw's 567-4116)*, Wine/Beer *(Wine Bottega 227-6607)*, Library *(Boston 242-1248)*, Hardware Store *(Boston Hware 523-1683)*, Copies Etc. *(Copy Cop 367-3370)* **1-3 mi:** Gourmet Shop *(Le Saucier 227-9649)*, Bookstore *(Barnes & Noble 426-5502)*, Department Store

Transportation

OnSite: Courtesy Car/Van, Water Taxi *(442-0392 $5/4 all day)*, Local Bus *(MBTA)*, Ferry Service *(to Logan)* **OnCall:** Rental Car *(Avis 534-1400, Enterprise 261-7447)* **Near:** InterCity Bus **Under 1 mi:** Taxi *(After Hours 242-2666)* **1-3 mi:** Bikes *(Community Bike 542-8623)*, Rail *(Boston 268-9000)* **Airport:** Logan Int'l. *(5 mi.)*

Medical Services

911 Service **OnCall:** Ambulance **Near:** Doctor, Dentist **1-3 mi:** Chiropractor **Hospital:** Mass. General 248-1926 *(1 mi.)*

Setting -- Located "in the shadow" of Old Ironsides (the USS Constitution), the marina is in a quiet, protected section of the Harbor -- on the seaward side of the Charles River locks. This well run, service-oriented, inviting facility promises an engaging combination of family atmosphere and spectacular views of the downtown Boston skyline and the active harbor front. Adjacent to the historic Charlestown Navy Yard and all its attractions.

Marina Notes -- *Over 55' $3.25/ft., $17/ft. weekly; May/Oct $25/ft., Jun/Sep $35/ft. Add $5/ft. for over 55'. Add $0.50/ft. to all rates Jul 1-7. Power: 1st 30 amp cord is free, 2nd is $5; 1st 50 amp cord $5, 2nd $15. 100 amp $25. This is a well maintained marina with good services, megayacht facilities, attentive staff, and inner docks well protected from swells. 5 very nice full, private bathrooms are off the laundry area in the main building (right off the pool). Limited, but high-quality facilities. Boat/U.S. cooperating marina. Concierge services for all yachts from 10' - 140'. Manages the Harbor Island Moorings.

Notable -- A heated pool, open year-round, overlooks the docks and harbor. A water taxi ($10) or nearby TA's Water Shuttle ($5/4 all day) will take you to Rowe's Wharf and many other downtown stops. Events every weekend. Group discounts available. Adjacent USS Constitution (242-5670) is one of the 16 stops on the 2.5 mi. Freedom Trail - 227-8800 or www.freedomtrail.org for an annotated map. The Sports Museum Of New England (787-7678) is also nearby. Hundreds of restaurants are within easy reach, as is all that Boston has to offer. Live-aboards and long term guests encouraged. Charter boats onsite.

PHOTOS ON CD-ROM: 9

Navigational Information

Lat: 42°17.970' **Long:** 071°01.700' **Tide:** 9 ft. **Current:** n/a **Chart:** 13270
Rep. Depths (*MLW*): Entry 13 ft. **Fuel Dock** 13 ft. **Max Slip/Moor** 13 ft./-
Access: Dorchester Bay; Rainbow tank to starboard, to Squantum Channel

Marina Facilities *(In Season/Off Season)*

Fuel: *Gulf* - Gasoline, Diesel
Slips: 685 Total, 60 Transient **Max LOA:** 210 ft. **Max Beam:** n/a
Rate *(per ft.)*: **Day** $2.50/$1.25* **Week** $10.50 ($12 over 60') **Month** $32
Power: 30 amp $6, **50 amp** $12, **100 amp** $40, **200 amp** n/a
Cable TV: No **Dockside Phone:** No
Dock Type: Wood, Concrete, Pilings, Alongside, Floating
Moorings: 0 Total, 0 Transient **Launch:** n/a
Rate: Day n/a **Week** n/a **Month** n/a
Heads: 4 Toilet(s), 7 Shower(s)
Laundry: 3 Washer(s), 3 Dryer(s) **Pay Phones:** Yes, 4
Pump-Out: OnSite, Self Service, 2 Central **Fee:** Free **Closed Heads:** No

Marina Operations

Owner/Manager: Clark Goebel **Dockmaster:** Craig Parkhurst
In-Season: Apr 15-Oct 31, 7am-Dusk **Off-Season:** Nov-Apr 14, 7:30am-5pm
After-Hours Arrival: Call security on Ch. 10
Reservations: Yes **Credit Cards:** Visa/MC, Amex
Discounts: None
Pets: Welcome, Dog Walk Area **Handicap Access:** No

Marina Bay

333 Victory Road; North Quincy, MA 02171

Tel: (617) 847-1800 **VHF: Monitor** 10 **Talk** n/a
Fax: (617) 847-1840 **Alternate Tel:** n/a
Email: MarinaBay@marinasintl.com **Web:** www.MarinaBayMarina.com
Nearest Town: Boston *(7 mi.)* **Tourist Info:** (617) 227-4500

Marina Services and Boat Supplies

Services - Docking Assistance, Concierge, Security, Trash Pick-Up, Dock Carts **Communication -** Mail & Package Hold, Phone Messages, Fax in/out, FedEx, AirBorne, UPS, Express Mail *(Sat Del)* **Supplies - OnSite:** Ice *(Cube)*, Ships' Store **Under 1 mi:** Live Bait, Propane *(Neponset Circle Car Wash 288-1581)* **1-3 mi:** West Marine *(356-2100)*, Bait/Tackle *(Neponset Circle Fishing 436-9231)*

Boatyard Services

OnSite: Travelift *(35T)*, Forklift, Crane, Engine mechanic *(gas, diesel)*, Electrical Repairs, Electronic Sales, Electronics Repairs, Hull Repairs, Rigger, Bottom Cleaning, Brightwork, Refrigeration, Divers, Compound, Wash & Wax, Interior Cleaning, Woodworking, Upholstery, Painting, Awlgrip, Yacht Broker, Total Refits **OnCall:** Sail Loft, Propeller Repairs **1-3 mi:** Launching Ramp. **Dealer for:** Northern Lights, Kohler, Yanmar, Kellog, Manset. **Yard Rates:** $60/hr., Haul & Launch $4.50/ft. *(blocking $1.50/ft.)*, Power Wash $3.50 **Storage:** In-Water $35/ft., On-Land $35/ft.

Restaurants and Accommodations

OnSite: Restaurant *(Siro's 472-4500, L $8-13, D $15-25, 11:30-4pm, 5-10pm, Fri & Sat to 11pm)*, *(Captain Fishbones 471-3511, L $4-12, D $6-20, kids' menu)*, *(Gina's 770-9355)*, Seafood Shack *(Chantey Seafood 770-4121)*, *(Oyster Bar 328-5564, L $6-15, D $6-18)*, Snack Bar *(Amelia's 471-1453)*, Coffee Shop *(Cream & Sugar)*, Lite Fare *(Waterclub 328-6500, D $5, hors d'oeuvres only - a club)* **Near:** Restaurant *(Tavern 786-9600)*, *(Waterworks 689-0600)* **Under 1 mi:** Pizzeria *(Pizano 288-4040)*, Hotel *(W. B. Adams Inn 328-1500, $130-160)* **1-3 mi:** Motel *(Ramada Inn 287-9100, $150-190)*, *(Howard Johnson 287-9200, $175-219)*

Recreation and Entertainment

OnSite: Spa *(Aria Salon)*, Picnic Area, Grills, Jogging Paths, Boat Rentals, Roller Blade/Bike Paths, Fishing Charter **Near:** Beach, Volleyball, Park **Under 1 mi:** Playground **1-3 mi:** Golf Course *(Presidents 328-3444)*, Fitness Center *(Fitcorp 472-8746)*, Bowling *(First Boston Tenpin 825-3800)*, Movie Theater *(Wollaston Theatre 773-4600)*, Video Rental *(Hollywood 786-9604)*, Museum *(Josiah Quincy House 227-3956)*

Provisioning and General Services

OnSite: Delicatessen, Bank/ATM, Beauty Salon, Dry Cleaners, Newsstand, Retail Shops **Near:** Catholic Church, Copies Etc. *(Highland 665-9000)* **Under 1 mi:** Liquor Store *(Alexander's 436-3815 free delivery)*, Post Office, Library *(Crane 376-1320)*, Laundry, Pharmacy *(CVS 471-0041)* **1-3 mi:** Supermarket *(Stop & Shop 287-9193)*, Health Food, Bakery *(Regal Beagle 328-3530)*, Farmers' Market, Fishmonger *(Sousa Seafood)*, Meat Market, Bookstore, Hardware Store *(O'Malley Ace 773-0808)*, Florist, Clothing Store, Department Store

Transportation

OnSite: Ferry Service *(to Boston)* **OnCall:** Rental Car *(Enterprise 261-7447, Verc 770-0007)*, Taxi *(Wings 695-6818)* **Near:** Water Taxi *(MBTA Shuttle)*, Local Bus **1-3 mi:** Bikes *(Codman Cycle 282-5585)* **3+ mi:** Rail *(Boston 268-9000, 4 mi.)* **Airport:** Logan Int'l. *(6 mi.)*

Medical Services

911 Service **OnSite:** Dentist **OnCall:** Ambulance **Near:** Doctor **Under 1 mi:** Chiropractor *(South Bay Chiropractic 328-6300)* **Hospital:** Carney 296-3114 *(3.5 mi.)*

Setting -- Marina Bay is the centerpiece of New England's largest waterfront office/residential/retail complex - with nine waterfront restaurants, a Nantucket-style boardwalk, and views of Boston's skyline. It is located on the Squantum Peninsula in Quincy.

Marina Notes -- *Monthly rate: 30 days can be used over length of the season. Docks are protected by a continuous breakwater. Service-oriented, professional operation -- and one of the most popular Boston summer destinations. Well stocked ships' store. Onsite laundry and heads open 24 hrs. Controlled access to docks. Free parking. Boat World brokerage onsite. In Logan Airport's landing pattern. Charter fishing trips onsite. Boatyard with extensive services. Megayacht facilities. Catering available to the boats. 3 annual fishing tournaments. Convenience store closed as of publication.

Notable -- Most of the onsite eateries have al fresco options. The Oyster Bar serves lunch & dinner under a tent overlooking the docks and Boston skyline. Siro's offers more upscale dining. Captain Fishbones is a good family place - with kids' menu. Amelia's has sandwiches, salads and munchies. The Chantey has fish & chips to go. Summerhouse can accommodate large private groups. Waterworks, an outdoor entertainment complex, includes a nightclub, live music, dancing and 18 billiard tables. One of the Nantucket Light Ships is moored next door and open to the public. Antique Boat & Auto Festival in mid-July, plus many other activities. Across Dorchester Bay is the Kennedy Library with 21 exhibits and a dock that it shares with UMass (929-4523).

PHOTOS ON CD-ROM: 9

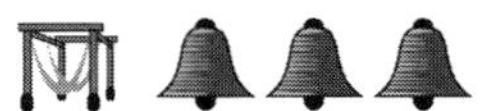

Hewitts Cove Marina

349 Lincoln Street, Route 3A; Hingham, MA 02043

Tel: (781) 749-6647 **VHF: Monitor** 9 **Talk** 9
Fax: (781) 740-0700 **Alternate Tel:** n/a
Email: hcm@seachain.com **Web:** www.seachain.com
Nearest Town: Hingham *(2 mi.)* **Tourist Info:** (781) 925-9980

Navigational Information

Lat: 42°15.210' **Long:** 070°55.290' **Tide:** 10 ft. **Current:** 5 kt. **Chart:** 13270
Rep. Depths (*MLW*): Entry 15 ft. **Fuel Dock** 19 ft. **Max Slip/Moor** 12 ft./-
Access: Hingham Bay to Weymouth Back River, south side

Marina Facilities *(In Season/Off Season)*

Fuel: *Texaco* - Gasoline, Diesel
Slips: 365 Total, 10 Transient **Max LOA:** 125 ft. **Max Beam:** n/a
Rate *(per ft.)*: **Day** $2.25/Inq.* **Week** Inq. **Month** Inq.
Power: 30 amp add'l, **50 amp** add'l, **100 amp** n/a, **200 amp** n/a
Cable TV: No **Dockside Phone:** Yes
Dock Type: Concrete, Alongside, Floating
Moorings: 100 Total, 10-20 Transient **Launch:** Yes ($5), Dinghy Dock
Rate: Day $20 **Week** Inq. **Month** Inq.
Heads: 8 Toilet(s), 8 Shower(s)
Laundry: 1 Washer(s), 1 Dryer(s) **Pay Phones:** Yes, 1
Pump-Out: OnSite, Full Service, 1 Central **Fee:** Free **Closed Heads:** Yes

Marina Operations

Owner/Manager: n/a **Dockmaster:** Sue Slattery
In-Season: Summer, 7am-10pm **Off-Season:** Winter, 8am-5pm*
After-Hours Arrival: See Security
Reservations: Yes **Credit Cards:** Visa/MC, Dscvr, Din, Amex, Tex
Discounts: Boat/US; Parts 10% **Dockage:** n/a **Fuel:** $.10g **Repair:** n/a
Pets: Welcome, Dog Walk Area **Handicap Access:** Yes, Heads, Docks

Marina Services and Boat Supplies

Services - Docking Assistance, Room Service to the Boat, Security *(24 Hrs.)*, Dock Carts **Communication -** Mail & Package Hold, Phone Messages, Fax in/out *(Free)*, FedEx, AirBorne, UPS, Express Mail *(Sat Del)* **Supplies - OnSite:** Ice *(Block, Cube)*, Ships' Store, Bait/Tackle **Near:** Ice *(Shaved)*, Marine Discount Store *(Foster 749-7390)* **1-3 mi:** Propane *(Boc Gases 340-6735)* **3+ mi:** West Marine *(356-2100, 8 mi.)*

Boatyard Services

OnSite: Travelift *(35T)*, Forklift, Crane, Engine mechanic *(gas, diesel)*, Electrical Repairs, Electronics Repairs, Hull Repairs, Rigger, Bottom Cleaning, Brightwork, Air Conditioning, Refrigeration, Compound, Wash & Wax, Interior Cleaning, Propeller Repairs, Woodworking, Inflatable Repairs, Upholstery, Yacht Interiors, Metal Fabrication, Painting, Awlgrip, Yacht Broker, Total Refits **OnCall:** Sail Loft, Divers **Under 1 mi:** Launching Ramp. **Dealer for:** Wellcraft, Mako. **Yard Rates:** $65/hr., Haul & Launch $3.50/ft. *(blocking $2.50/ft.)*, Power Wash $2/ft., Bottom Paint $12/ft. **Storage:** In-Water $28/ft., On-Land $33/ft.

Restaurants and Accommodations

OnSite: Restaurant *(Hingham Bay Club 740-8200, L $10-12, D $14-19, 11:30am-11pm 7days)*, Snack Bar *(Galley at Hewitts Cove 749-4755, 8am-6pm, closed Tue)* **OnCall:** Restaurant *(China Coast 740-9797)*, Pizzeria *(Dominos 331-8700)* **Near:** Restaurant *(Ninety Nine 740-8599)*, *(Ocean Kai 749-6300)*, Fast Food **Under 1 mi:** Restaurant *(Applebees 331-8550)* **1-3 mi:** Restaurant *(Tosca 740-0800, D $18-27)*, Motel *(Arbor Inn 337-8070)*

Recreation and Entertainment

OnSite: Picnic Area, Grills, Fishing Charter *(First Light 925-3616)*, Sightseeing *(First Light Harbor Island/Lighthouse Tours 925-3616)* **Near:** Jogging Paths, Roller Blade/Bike Paths **Under 1 mi:** Beach, Boat Rentals, Movie Theater, Video Rental *(One Stop 617-332-1212)*, Park, Special Events *(Historic Homes tour - late May)* **1-3 mi:** Golf Course *(So. Shore Country Club 749-1747)*, Fitness Center *(Bay Shore 331-3410)*, Bowling *(Country Club Lanes 749-8400)*, Museum *(Old Ordinary Museum 749-0013 17thC tavern now a museum of Hingham history $3/1)*

Provisioning and General Services

OnSite: Lobster Pound *(So. Shore Lobster 749-2213)*, Copies Etc. **Near:** Convenience Store, Gourmet Shop, Delicatessen, Bakery, Fishmonger, Meat Market, Bank/ATM, Post Office, Catholic Church, Beauty Salon, Barber Shop, Dry Cleaners, Newsstand **Under 1 mi:** Florist, Retail Shops **1-3 mi:** Supermarket *(Tedeschi 749-4248)*, Liquor Store *(Macys 335-1330)*, Farmers' Market *(749-3444 Station St. Sat 10am-2pm)*, Bookstore *(Buck A Book 335-5819)*, Pharmacy *(Brooks 749-0572)*, Hardware Store *(Cazeault 335-4000)*

Transportation

OnSite: Water Taxi, Ferry Service *(Rowes Wharf, Boston Harbor Islands)* **OnCall:** Rental Car *(Enterprise 617-261-7447)*, Taxi *(Hingham Taxi 749-7070)* **Near:** Local Bus **3+ mi:** Bikes *(Bicycle Link 337-7125, 4 mi.)*, Rail *(Boston 617-268-9000, 13 mi.)* **Airport:** Logan Int'l. *(13 mi.)*

Medical Services

911 Service **Near:** Doctor, Dentist, Ambulance **1-3 mi:** Chiropractor *(So. Shore Family 335-7671)* **Hospital:** South Shore 340-4090 *(4.5 mi.)*

Setting -- This full-service boatyard and marina sits at the mouth of Weymouth Back River two miles from the lovely town of Hingham. Views are out to the mouth of the river and to the industrial shoreline. The well protected river location coupled with easy access to Boston makes this an interesting spot as a sightseeing base or to leave the boat. The lovely Hingham Bay Club restaurant, with views of the docks and river beyond, is also right onsite.

Marina Notes -- *Rates: $2/ft. weekdays, $2.50/ft. weekends, $3/ft. holidays. A full-service boatyard. Affiliated with Tern Harbor Marina, Bass River Marina & Cohasset Harbor Marina. Member of the Sea Chain group. Concrete docks. Wave attenuator minimizes the roll from wakes. Boat/U.S. cooperating marina. Snack bar is located in the well-equipped ships' store. Launch service from 7am - 10pm, ($5 RT/Boatload)

Notable -- Hewitts Cove is on the site of the Hingham Shipyard, which employed more than 24,000 people during WWII, turning out six ships per month -- more than 275 vessels in all. See the Old Ordinary (749-0013), a 14-room 17thC structure, and the Old Ship Meeting House (749-1679), a 17thC church about 2 miles away. Commuter boat to Rowes Wharf in downtown Boston (near Faneuil Hall/Quincy Market) and the Harbor Islands leaves from next door 740-1253 - frequent service from 6am-8:30pm weekdays $5/1-way. About 4 miles is World's End, a 249-acre reservation designed by Fredrick Law Olmstead, with views of Boston's skyline - $4/Free; it's a possible dinghy destination. Boston Harbor Islands are also nearby for day or overnight trips - moorings $10 for lunch, $25 overnight. A hike into Hingham would net a stroll along Main Street with a wonderful assortment of restored antique houses spanning three centuries.

PHOTOS ON CD-ROM: 9

Navigational Information
Lat: 42°15.322' **Long:** 070°55.530' **Tide:** 9 ft. **Current:** n/a **Chart:** 13270
Rep. Depths (*MLW*): Entry 14 ft. **Fuel Dock** n/a **Max Slip/Moor** 15 ft./-
Access: Hingham Bay to Weymouth Back River, north side

Marina Facilities *(In Season/Off Season)*
Fuel: No
Slips: 134 Total, 10 Transient **Max LOA:** 275 ft. **Max Beam:** n/a
Rate *(per ft.)*: **Day** $2.00* **Week** Inq. **Month** Inq.
Power: 30 amp $5, **50 amp** $10, **100 amp** n/a, **200 amp** n/a
Cable TV: No **Dockside Phone:** No
Dock Type: Wood, Long Fingers, Concrete, Floating
Moorings: 15 Total, 0 Transient **Launch:** n/a, Dinghy Dock
Rate: Day n/a **Week** n/a **Month** n/a
Heads: 2 Toilet(s), Shower(s)
Laundry: None **Pay Phones:** Yes
Pump-Out: OnCall, 1 Port **Fee:** n/a **Closed Heads:** No

Marina Operations
Owner/Manager: Bob Dawley **Dockmaster:** Same
In-Season: Year-Round, 8am-5pm **Off-Season:** n/a
After-Hours Arrival: Call ahead
Reservations: Yes **Credit Cards:** Visa/MC, Dscvr, Amex
Discounts: Boat/US; Restrictions **Dockage:** 25% **Fuel:** n/a **Repair:** n/a
Pets: Welcome **Handicap Access:** Yes, Heads

Tern Harbor Marina

275 River Street; North Weymouth, MA 02191

Tel: (781) 337-1964 **VHF: Monitor** 9 **Talk** n/a
Fax: (781) 337-3718 **Alternate Tel:** n/a
Email: n/a **Web:** www.seachain.com
Nearest Town: Quincy *(3 mi.)* **Tourist Info:** (617) 846-9898

Marina Services and Boat Supplies
Services - Docking Assistance, Security *(24 Hrs., Night watchman)*, Trash Pick-Up, Dock Carts **Communication -** FedEx, AirBorne, UPS, Express Mail **Supplies - OnSite:** Ice *(Block, Cube)*, Ships' Store *(Limited)* **Under 1 mi:** Bait/Tackle *(Landfall Marine 749-1255)* **1-3 mi:** Propane *(Boc Gases 340-6735)* **3+ mi:** West Marine *(356-2100, 8mi.)*

Boatyard Services
OnSite: Travelift *(35T)*, Forklift, Bottom Cleaning, Compound, Wash & Wax, Interior Cleaning, Propeller Repairs **OnCall:** Engine mechanic *(gas, diesel)*, Electrical Repairs, Brightwork **Near:** Electronic Sales, Hull Repairs, Rigger. **Under 1 mi:** Launching Ramp. **Dealer for:** Wellcraft, Sabreline, Mercury. **Yard Rates:** $65/hr., Haul & Launch $9/ft. *(blocking $2/ft.)*, Power Wash $2.50/ft., Bottom Paint $14/ft. **Storage:** On-Land $1/ft./day

Restaurants and Accommodations
OnCall: Pizzeria *(Dominos 740-4131)* **Near:** Restaurant *(Hingham Bay Club 740-8200, L $10-12, D $14-19, by dinghy)*, *(Galley at Hewitts Cove 749-4755, by dinghy)* **Under 1 mi:** Restaurant *(Applebees 331-8550)*, Fast Food **1-3 mi:** Restaurant *(Kelly's Landing 335-9899)*, *(Cliff Hanger Pub 335-9607)*, Snack Bar *(Michele's Ice Cream & Sandwich 331-2988)*, Motel *(Arbor Inn 337-8070)* **3+ mi:** Motel *(Boston Motel 337-5200, 4 mi.)*

Recreation and Entertainment
OnSite: Fishing Charter **Near:** Park **Under 1 mi:** Beach *(Wessagussett Beach)*, Picnic Area *(Webb Memorial Park)*, Grills, Jogging Paths, Roller Blade/Bike Paths, Video Rental *(One Stop Video 332-1212)*, Sightseeing *(Webb Memorial State Park)* **1-3 mi:** Golf Course *(So. Shore Country Club 749-1747)*, Fitness Center *(Bay Shore Athletic Club 331-3410)*, Boat Rentals, Bowling *(Country Club Lanes 749-8400)*, Movie Theater, Museum *(US Naval Ship Building Museum 617-479-7900)*, Cultural Attract *(No Wey Café 337-1020, comedy club)*

Provisioning and General Services
Under 1 mi: Convenience Store, Gourmet Shop, Delicatessen, Wine/Beer, Bakery, Green Grocer, Fishmonger, Lobster Pound, Meat Market, Beauty Salon, Barber Shop, Dry Cleaners, Laundry, Newsstand, Florist, Clothing Store, Retail Shops, Department Store, Copies Etc. *(Flinn Printing 749-4677)* **1-3 mi:** Supermarket *(Stop & Shop 331-9565)*, Liquor Store *(Macys Beachway Liquors 335-1330)*, Farmers' Market *(749-3444 Station Street Sat 10am-2pm)*, Bank/ATM, Post Office, Catholic Church, Bookstore *(Buck A Book 335-5819)*, Pharmacy *(Brooks 749-0572)*, Hardware Store *(Cazeault & Sons 335-4000)* **3+ mi:** Health Food *(The Good Earth 925-2402, 6 mi.)*

Transportation
OnCall: Rental Car *(Verc Rentals 740-2965, Enterprise 261-7447)*, Taxi *(North Weymouth Cab 335-3633)* **Near:** Ferry Service *(Fast Ferry to Rowes Wharf, Boston - Dinghy across river)* **Under 1 mi:** Water Taxi **1-3 mi:** InterCity Bus *(A & B Coach Line 617-770-3566; P & B 746-0378 to Boston)* **3+ mi:** Bikes *(Bicycle Link 337-7125, 4 mi.)*, Rail *(Boston 268-9000, 12 mi.)* **Airport:** Logan Int'l. *(12 mi.)*

Medical Services
911 Service **OnCall:** Ambulance **1-3 mi:** Chiropractor *(So. Shore Family Chiropractic 335-7671)* **Hospital:** South Shore 340-4090 *(4.5 mi.)*

Setting -- This down-home, low-key marina is on your starboard side just past Hewitts Cove, on the Weymouth Back River - a small river off the southern end of Hingham Bay that offers protected dockage and interesting explorations. Views are of the river banks and the tall condo complex next door. The landside is largely residential.

Marina Notes -- *Rates: $2.25/ft. weekends, $2/ft. weekdays, $3/ft. holidays. The 120 slips accommodate boats up to 45 ft. and have a maximum draft of 9 ft. MLW. The face dock accommodates yachts up to 275 ft. with 14 ft. MLW. Office is open 8am-5pm Mon-Fri, Sat 9am-4pm, Sun 10am-2pm. No laundry. Owned by Sea Chain Marine. Sabreline dealer.

Notable -- A short walk to inviting Wessagussett Beach with a view of the Boston skyline and access to William K. Webb Park. Abigail Smith Adams' Birthplace (335-4205), a restored 17thC house, is a couple of miles away, $1. Across the river at Hewitts Cove is the fast ferry to Rowes Wharf in Boston's downtown (Faneuil Hall/Quincy Market) - Mon-Fri, 6am-8:30pm, $5. The many Boston Harbor Islands are a short cruise for either a day trip or an overnight stay ($10 lunch-time mooring, $25 overnight).

Captain's Cove Marina

PO Box 6903; 100 Cove Way; Quincy, MA 02269

Tel: (617) 479-2424 **VHF: Monitor** n/a **Talk** n/a
Fax: (617) 773-3840 **Alternate Tel:** (617) 328-3331
Email: CaptsCoveMarina@aol.com **Web:** n/a
Nearest Town: n/a **Tourist Info:** (617) 479-1111

Navigational Information

Lat: 42°15.157' **Long:** 070°58.870' **Tide:** n/a **Current:** n/a **Chart:** 13270
Rep. Depths (*MLW*): Entry n/a **Fuel Dock** n/a **Max Slip/Moor** -/-
Access: Weymouth Fore River to Hole Point reach entrance channel

Marina Facilities *(In Season/Off Season)*

Fuel: No
Slips: 222 Total, 17 Transient **Max LOA:** 65 ft. **Max Beam:** 20 ft.
Rate *(per ft.)*: **Day** $2.00/$1.00 **Week** $10 **Month** $30
Power: 30 amp Incl., **50 amp** $0.50, **100 amp** $1, **200 amp** n/a
Cable TV: No **Dockside Phone:** No
Dock Type: Floating, Aluminium
Moorings: 0 Total, 0 Transient **Launch:** n/a, Dinghy Dock
Rate: Day n/a **Week** n/a **Month** n/a
Heads: 2 Toilet(s), 2 Shower(s)
Laundry: None **Pay Phones:** No
Pump-Out: OnSite, Self Service **Fee:** Free **Closed Heads:** No

Marina Operations

Owner/Manager: Capt. Steve Rodri **Dockmaster:** Same
In-Season: Apr-Nov 30, 9am-5pm **Off-Season:** Dec-Mar, 9am-5pm
After-Hours Arrival: Proceed to assigned slip. Prior registration required
Reservations: Required **Credit Cards:** Visa/MC
Discounts: None
Pets: Welcome, Dog Walk Area **Handicap Access:** Yes, Heads, Docks

Marina Services and Boat Supplies

Services - Security *(Video surveillance)*, Dock Carts **Supplies - OnSite:** Ice *(Block, Cube)* **Under 1 mi:** Bait/Tackle *(Sportsman's Den 770-3884)* **1-3 mi:** Ships' Store, Marine Discount Store *(Monahan's 335-2746)*, Propane **3+ mi:** West Marine *(781-356-2100, 4 mi.)*

Boatyard Services

OnCall: Bottom Cleaning, Brightwork, Divers, Interior Cleaning, Inflatable Repairs, Life Raft Service **Near:** Engine mechanic *(gas)*, Launching Ramp. **1-3 mi:** Sail Loft *(DiMattia)*, Metal Fabrication *(CMI)*. **3+ mi:** Rigger *(Hewitts Cove)*. **Nearest Yard:** Town River Marina (617) 745-9813

Restaurants and Accommodations

OnCall: Pizzeria *(5 Star 971-5555)* **Near:** Restaurant *(Brigadoons 786-7777)*, *(Inn at Bay Pointe 472-3200)*, *(Punjab Café 472-4860, reportedly wonderful Indian food)*, *(Inn at Bay Pointe 472-3200, L $6-16, D $9-16, Mon-Thu 11:30am-9:30pm, Fri-Sun 'til 10:30pm)*, Fast Food, Inn/B&B *(Atlantic House 770-9660)* **Under 1 mi:** Restaurant *(Bickfords 479-3561, B $2-5, L $5, D $8)*, Inn/B&B *(Presidents City Inn 479-6500, $95)* **1-3 mi:** Restaurant *(Grumpy White's 770-2835, L $4, D $10)*, *(Quincy Ships 376-2221, Brewing Co.)*, Raw Bar *(Tony's Clam Shop 773-5090)*, Motel *(Best Western Adams Inn 328-1500, $120)*, Hotel *(Marriott 472-1000, $200)*

Recreation and Entertainment

OnSite: Picnic Area, Grills, Tennis Courts, Fishing Charter **OnCall:** Group Fishing Boat **Near:** Park **Under 1 mi:** Dive Shop *(South Shore)*, Video Rental *(Massive Video 773-0552)*, Video Arcade, Museum *(US Naval Ship Building Museum 479-7900 $6/4)* **1-3 mi:** Fitness Center *(YMCA-South Shore 479-8500)*, Bowling *(Quincy Ave. Lanes 472-3597)*, Movie Theater *(Showcase Cinemas 773-5700)*, Cultural Attract *(Adams National Historical Site 773-1177, Apr-Nov)* **3+ mi:** Golf Course *(Presidents Golf Course 328-3444, 4 mi.)*

Provisioning and General Services

Near: Supermarket *(Stop & Shop 380-8200)*, Liquor Store *(Artery 773-8251)*, Catholic Church, Pharmacy *(Baxter 773-7733)*, Newsstand, Florist **Under 1 mi:** Protestant Church, Synagogue, Library *(Thomas Crane 376-1320)*, Beauty Salon, Barber Shop, Dry Cleaners, Laundry, Retail Shops, Buying Club **1-3 mi:** Convenience Store, Delicatessen, Post Office, Bookstore *(Buck A Book 328-4719)*, Hardware Store *(Curry Ace Hardware 781-843-1616)*, Department Store **3+ mi:** Bakery *(Montillios 472-5500, 3 mi.)*

Transportation

OnCall: Taxi *(Quincy Cab 471-8294, $5 - downtown/subway)* **Near:** Rental Car *(Hertz 786-0660)* **Under 1 mi:** Ferry Service *(Harbor Express)* **1-3 mi:** Local Bus *(T line)*, Rail *(T to Boston)* **Airport:** Logan Int'l. *(12 mi.)*

Medical Services

911 Service **Under 1 mi:** Dentist *(Quincy Dental 471-4449)*, Chiropractor *(Family Practice of Chiropractic 472-4220)*, Holistic Services **1-3 mi:** Doctor **3+ mi:** Veterinarian *(VCA Animal Hospital 773-8247, 3 mi.)*
Hospital: Quincy Medical Center 773-6100 *(3 mi.)*

Setting -- Tucked way up Hole Point Reach entrance channel in Town River Bay (off Weymouth Fore River), is this 200 slip deep-water marina -- shadowed by a 10-story apartment complex at its back and Sprague's large green storage tanks to its north.

Marina Notes -- Office address: 218 Willard Street, Quincy, MA 02169 (617) 479-2440. Heads and showers in cinder block building that is part of pool entrance (pool is not available to marina guests). Large range of boat sizes and types. Manager lives onsite. Small group of helpful liveaboards. Good security. Bridge-free access. Free pump-out. Good parking.

Notable -- If services are an issue, this is a convenient spot. A short distance through the apartment complex's parking lots is Southern Artery, one of the main drags of industrial/commercial/residential Quincy. Many services are within an easy, if not particularly lovely, walk -- Inn at Bay Point, Garden Café, Punjab Café, only half a mile to Stop and Shop, restaurants, Hertz, CVS and many other services. Less than a mile away is the U.S. Naval and Shipbuilding Museum, located on the site of abadoned Fore River Shipyard, builder of navy vessels for more than 60 years. The Museum is open Sat and Sun 10am-4pm, and offers guided and self-guided tours of the 700 foot cruiser USS Salem.

MA - BOSTON & THE SOUTH SHORE

PHOTOS ON CD-ROM: 6

Navigational Information

Lat: 42°14.337' **Long:** 070°47.200' **Tide:** n/a **Current:** n/a **Chart:** 13270
Rep. Depths (*MLW*): Entry 5 ft. **Fuel Dock** n/a **Max Slip/Moor** -/-
Access: Cohasset Harbor to Cohasset Cove, on far Southeast side

Marina Facilities *(In Season/Off Season)*

Fuel: No
Slips: 75 Total, 3 Transient **Max LOA:** 42 ft. **Max Beam:** 12 ft.
Rate *(per ft.)*: **Day** $2.00 **Week** n/a **Month** n/a
Power: 30 amp Inq., **50 amp** Inq., **100 amp** n/a, **200 amp** n/a
Cable TV: No **Dockside Phone:** No
Dock Type: Floating
Moorings: 0 Total, 0 Transient **Launch:** n/a
Rate: Day n/a **Week** n/a **Month** n/a
Heads: Toilet(s)
Laundry: None **Pay Phones:** No
Pump-Out: OnCall, 1 Port **Fee:** Free **Closed Heads:** No

Marina Operations

Owner/Manager: Joe Sugar **Dockmaster:** Bill Jackson
In-Season: May 15-Oct 15, 7:30am-5pm Mon-Thu* **Off-Season:** n/a
After-Hours Arrival: Call in advance
Reservations: Yes, Required **Credit Cards:** n/a
Discounts: None
Pets: Welcome **Handicap Access:** No

Cohasset Harbor Marina

33 Parker Avenue; Cohasset, MA 02025

Tel: (781) 383-1504 **VHF: Monitor** n/a **Talk** n/a
Fax: (781) 740-0700 **Alternate Tel:** n/a
Email: n/a **Web:** www.seachain.com
Nearest Town: Boston *(16 mi.)* **Tourist Info:** (781) 383-1010

Marina Services and Boat Supplies

Supplies - 1-3 mi: Bait/Tackle *(Trask Tackle 545-4228)* **3+ mi:** Propane *(Good Sport 383-6550, 5 mi.)*

Boatyard Services

Near: Launching Ramp. **Nearest Yard:** Mill River Marine Railways (781) 383-1207

Restaurants and Accommodations

OnCall: Pizzeria *(Really Great Pizza 383-0464)* **Near:** Restaurant *(Atlantica 383-0900, D $14-39)*, *(Olde Salt House 383-2203, L $8-20, D $8-20)*, Inn/B&B *(Kimball's Cohasset Harbor Inn 383-6550, $110-210)* **Under 1 mi:** Restaurant *(Red Lion Inn 383-1704)*, *(Bernard's 383-8300, D $12-21)*, Lite Fare *(Chez Jean-Claude Bakery & Café at Red Lion Inn)*, *(Strawberry Parfait 383-9681, mostly take-out, some picnic tables)*, Inn/B&B *(Red Lion Inn 383-1704, $175-375)*, *(Saltmarsh Farm 383-6205, $75-100)* **1-3 mi:** Inn/B&B *(Konohassett Lodge 383-1815)*, *(Minot Inn 545-2170)*

Recreation and Entertainment

Near: Spa *(at Cohasset Harbor Inn)* **Under 1 mi:** Beach *(Bassing's Beach)*, Park *(Cohasset Common)*, Museum *(Cohasset Historical Society's Maritime Museum 383-1434 - explains Minot's Light - one of three buildings, each worth a stop 383-1434)*, Cultural Attract *(South Shore Arts Center 383-2787)*, Special Events *(Carillon Concerts 6pm, Sunday afternoon at St. Stephen's Church 383-1083 featuring their 57 bell carillon; Cohasset Arts Festival on the Common)* **1-3 mi:** Tennis Courts *(Hatherly Country Club 545-9891)*, Video Rental *(Blockbuster 383-6735)* **3+ mi:** Golf Course *(Widows Walk 544-7777, 6 mi.)*, Bowling *(Satuit Bowlaway 545-9726 , 6 mi.)*, Fishing Charter *(Capt. Mac Charters 544-0301 , 4 mi.)*, Movie Theater *(Patriot Cinemas, Hingham 749-1400, 7 mi.)*

Provisioning and General Services

Under 1 mi: Convenience Store *(Cohasset News 383-6127)*, Delicatessen *(Village Butcher Shop & Deli 383-8181)*, Bakery *(French Memories 383-2216)*, Farmers' Market *(Cohasset Common 545-6063 Thu 2:30-6:30pm)*, Library *(Paul Pratt Mem. 383-1348)*, Newsstand **1-3 mi:** Supermarket *(Shaw's 383-2315)*, Liquor Store *(Village Wine and Spirits 383-8886)*, Post Office *(383-0318)*, Bookstore *(Buttonwood Books & Toys 383-2665)*, Pharmacy *(Walgreens 383-1773)* **3+ mi:** Hardware Store *(Satuit Hardware 545-8370, 5 mi.)*

Transportation

OnCall: Rental Car *(Enterprise 383-2966)*, Taxi *(EZ Rider 545-1195/Cohasset Limousine 545-6600)* **Airport:** Logan Int'l. *(16 mi.)*

Medical Services

911 Service **OnCall:** Ambulance **Under 1 mi:** Doctor *(Goldenson 383-1155)*, Dentist *(Thompson 383-1450)* **1-3 mi:** Chiropractor *(Chiropractic & Family Wellness 383-1330)* **Hospital:** South Shore 340-8352 *(12 mi.)*

Setting -- The only transient facility in protected, private Cohasset Harbor, this small, mostly seasonal, marina provides a secluded venue. Views out to the harbor mouth are of pristine marsh and sea. Views toward the picturesque inner harbor include the replica of the top of Minot's Light at the Cohasset Sailing Club next door. Strolls through the area will pass beautiful estates and lovely old houses.

Marina Notes -- *Hours: Mon-Thu 7:30am - 5pm, Fri-Sat 8am - 7pm, Sun 8am - 5pm. Member of the Sea Chain group. Heads are in their own building; cold water only; although there is a tub and shower, they are not available for use at this time. Very good security. Three charter skippers onsite - Peter Flaherty 20' Mako (383-2035), Mike Bartlett 20' Hydrosport (293-9443 - fly fishing), Bill Jackson 20' Grady-White (335-5082). Mill River Marine Railways may also have a slip or mooring available 383-1207. Legend says that the Minot Light's 1-4-3 flash means I Love You. The harbor is very popular with kayakers.

Notable -- A boardwalk across the marsh leads to Government Island (the Harbormaster's Office), then it's a very short walk to Atlantica Restaurant (its attractive dining room overlooks the harbor) and more casual Olde Salt House (with limited inside seating and an upscale, very inviting deck right on the water), and to their "parent" resort - Cohasset Harbor Inn, also called Kimball's. Then on to the Red Lion Inn. A pleasant one-mile walk leads to the charming village of Cohasset -- a couple of blocks lined with eateries (with sidewalk tables), galleries, gift shops, a convenience store and a hardware store - plus a true New England town green replete with duck pond. For a quick trip into town, the Cohasset town Landing permits 30 minute tie-ups and is quite a bit closer to town.

PHOTOS ON CD-ROM: 7

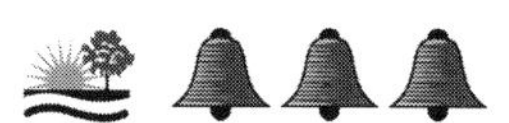

Scituate Harbor Yacht Club

PO Box 275; 84 Jericho Road; Scituate, MA 02066

Tel: (781) 545-0372 **VHF: Monitor** 9 **Talk** 9
Fax: (781) 545-2612 **Alternate Tel:** n/a
Email: manager@shyc.net **Web:** www.shyc.net
Nearest Town: Scituate *(0.5 mi.)* **Tourist Info:** (781) 545-4000

Navigational Information

Lat: 42°12.169' **Long:** 070°43.442' **Tide:** 9 ft. **Current:** n/a **Chart:** 13269
Rep. Depths (*MLW*): Entry 10 ft. **Fuel Dock** n/a **Max Slip/Moor** -/8 ft.
Access: Cape Cod Bay to Scituate Harbor RW "SA", 1st facility to starboard

Marina Facilities *(In Season/Off Season)*

Fuel: No
Slips: 0 Total, 0 Transient **Max LOA:** 50 ft. **Max Beam:** n/a
Rate *(per ft.)*: **Day** n/a **Week** n/a **Month** n/a
Power: 30 amp n/a, **50 amp** n/a, **100 amp** n/a, **200 amp** n/a
Cable TV: No **Dockside Phone:** No
Dock Type: n/a
Moorings: 40 Total, 15 Transient **Launch:** Yes (Free)
Rate: Day $25 **Week** $175 **Month** $750
Heads: 2 Toilet(s), 3 Shower(s)
Laundry: None **Pay Phones:** Yes
Pump-Out: OnCall, 1 Port **Fee:** Free **Closed Heads:** Yes

Marina Operations

Owner/Manager: n/a **Dockmaster:** Nancy Anderson
In-Season: LateMay-MidOct, 8am-11pm **Off-Season:** Closed
After-Hours Arrival: Call first and pick up mooring.
Reservations: No. First come, first served **Credit Cards:** Cash or check
Discounts: None
Pets: Welcome, Dog Walk Area **Handicap Access:** No

Marina Services and Boat Supplies

Services - Concierge, Dock Carts **Communication -** Mail & Package Hold, Phone Messages, FedEx, AirBorne, UPS, Express Mail *(Sat Del)* **Supplies - OnSite:** Ice *(Block, Cube)* **Under 1 mi:** Ships' Store, Bait/Tackle **3+ mi:** Marine Discount Store *(Erickson Marine 837-2687, 5 mi.)*, Propane *(Good Sport 383-6550, 8 mi.)*

Boatyard Services

OnSite: Engine mechanic *(gas, diesel)* **OnCall:** Electrical Repairs, Electronics Repairs, Bottom Cleaning, Brightwork, Divers **Near:** Launching Ramp. **1-3 mi:** Hull Repairs. **Nearest Yard:** Simms Brothers (781) 834-6070

Restaurants and Accommodations

OnSite: Restaurant *(Scituate Harbor YC Dining Room D $14-22, Wed-Sun, kids' menu)*, Snack Bar **Near:** Restaurant *(Pier 44 545-4700, L $8-16, D $8-16)*, *(Barker Tavern 545-6533, D $18-32, built 1634, Tue-Sat 6-10pm, Sun 1-10pm)*, Lite Fare *(Satuit Tavern L $4-14, D $4-14, also take-out & pizza)*, Motel *(Inn at Scituate Harbor 545-5550)*, Inn/B&B *(Oceanside Inn 544-0002, $90-240, all rooms have waterfront balconies)*, *(Sophie's Place)* **Under 1 mi:** Restaurant *(TK O'Malley Sports Café 545-4012, L $5-13, D $5-14)*, *(Mill Wharf Rest. & Chesters 545-3999, L $7-14, D $14-25)*, Coffee Shop *(Atlantic Bagel 545-1331)*, Pizzeria *(Harbor House Pizza 545-5407)*

Recreation and Entertainment

Near: Dive Shop, Movie Theater *(Scituate Playhouse - 4 screens 545-0045)*, Video Rental *(Hennessy News 545-6940)*, Park, Sightseeing *(Scituate Lighthouse, Lawson Water Tower 545-1083)* **Under 1 mi:** Beach *(Peggoty Beach)*, Bowling *(Satuit Bowlaway 545-9726)* **1-3 mi:** Tennis Courts *(Scituate Tennis Club 545-1184)*, Golf Course *(Widows Walk Golf Course 544-7777)*, Fitness Center *(Bay State Athletic Club 545-2249)*, Horseback Riding *(Longmeadow Farms 545-8153)*, Museum *(Maritime Museum 545-5565)*, Special Events

Provisioning and General Services

Near: Convenience Store *(Silent Chef)*, Supermarket *(Scituate Marketplace 545-4896)*, Bakery, Bank/ATM, Post Office, Catholic Church, Beauty Salon, Barber Shop, Dry Cleaners, Laundry, Newsstand, Florist, Clothing Store, Copies Etc. *(Thompson Business)* **Under 1 mi:** Delicatessen *(Maria's Submarine 545-2323)*, Wine/Beer *(Bailey's)*, Liquor Store *(Bailey's Package Store 545-0620)*, Fishmonger *(Coastal Fish & Lobster)*, Lobster Pound, Library *(Scituate 545-8727)*, Bookstore *(Front Street Book Shop 545-5011)*, Pharmacy *(CVS 545-1531)*, Hardware Store *(Satuit Hardware 545-8370)* **1-3 mi:** Protestant Church **3+ mi:** Gourmet Shop *(Bo Tes Imports 659-9888, 6 mi.)*

Transportation

OnCall: Water Taxi *($10.00)*, Rental Car *(Enterprise 617-261-7447)* **Near:** Local Bus **1-3 mi:** Bikes *(Seacoast Cycle & Sports 545-7000)*, InterCity Bus *(P&B 746-0378 to Boston)*, Ferry Service **3+ mi:** Rail *(Boston 617-268-9000, 30 mi.)* **Airport:** Logan Int'l. *(27 mi.)*

Medical Services

911 Service **OnCall:** Ambulance **Near:** Dentist *(Bortnick 545-0339)* **1-3 mi:** Doctor *(Harbor Medical 545-5225)*, Chiropractor *(Scituate Chiropractic 545-7388)* **Hospital:** South Shore, Weymouth 340-4090 *(15 mi.)*

Setting -- This engagingly landscaped and well cared for private club sits on a low bluff with panoramic views of the outer harbor. Its docks radiate from a long, raised, boardwalk-like pier. Restaurants and extensive services are within easy walking distance, in the classic New England beach town of Scituate.

Marina Notes -- The club welcomes all cruising boaters and has a special affinity for sailors. Mooring fee includes launch service (7 days during Jul & Aug), club heads and showers, and use of the club dining room (Dinner Wed-Sun, $14-22 -- jackets and ties required). The "mostly windows" dining room offers spectacular views of the mooring field and the breakwater beyond. Note: Club pool and tennis courts not available to transients. Complimentary Pump-out boat will call at the moorings. Additional moorings may be available from the Satuit Boat Club next door (545-9752).

Notable -- The town of Scituate offers a surprisingly complete assortment of services, entertainment options, restaurants and destinations. A very short walk toward town will yield the Pier 44 Restaurant and just up the hill (in the other direction) is well-known Barker Tavern. Historic Scituate Lighthouse played a key role in the War of 1812 (545-1083, by appointment). The Maritime and Irish Mossing Museum, The Driftway, has artifacts from the wreck of the steamship Pinthis. Heritage Days in early August are always a major event. Occasional Friday night concerts at the band shell in the town park.

Navigational Information
Lat: 42°12.070' **Long:** 070°43.540' **Tide:** 9 ft. **Current:** n/a **Chart:** 13269
Rep. Depths (*MLW*): Entry 12 ft. **Fuel Dock** 12 ft. **Max Slip/Moor** 12 ft./-
Access: Cape Cod Bay to Scituate Harbor RW "SA", 3rd facility to starboard

Marina Facilities *(In Season/Off Season)*
Fuel: *Gulf* - Gasoline, Diesel
Slips: 90 Total, 5 Transient **Max LOA:** 75 ft. **Max Beam:** n/a
Rate *(per ft.)*: **Day** $2.50/Inq. **Week** Inq. **Month** Inq.
Power: 30 amp Incl., **50 amp** Incl., **100 amp** n/a, **200 amp** n/a
Cable TV: Yes, $1 **Dockside Phone:** Yes
Dock Type: Long Fingers, Floating
Moorings: 0 Total, 0 Transient **Launch:** n/a
Rate: Day n/a **Week** n/a **Month** n/a
Heads: 1 Toilet(s)
Laundry: None **Pay Phones:** Yes
Pump-Out: OnCall, Full Service **Fee:** Free **Closed Heads:** Yes

Marina Operations
Owner/Manager: Dobber Reynolds **Dockmaster:** Same
In-Season: Jun-Oct 10, 8am-7pm* **Off-Season:** Oct-Jun 1, 9am-6pm
After-Hours Arrival: Tie up at fuel dock.
Reservations: Yes **Credit Cards:** Visa/MC, Dscvr, Din, Amex, Gulf
Discounts: None
Pets: Welcome, Dog Walk Area **Handicap Access:** No

Scituate Harbor Marina

Scituate Harbor Marina

PO Box 295; 48 Jericho Road; Scituate, MA 02066

Tel: (781) 545-2165 **VHF: Monitor** 9 **Talk** 12
Fax: (781) 545-6754 **Alternate Tel:** n/a
Email: dobshm@attbi.com **Web:** www.scituateharbor.com
Nearest Town: Scituate *(0.4 mi.)* **Tourist Info:** (781) 545-4000

MA - BOSTON & THE SOUTH SHORE

Marina Services and Boat Supplies
Services - Docking Assistance, Security *(24 Hrs., Gate and cameras)*, Trash Pick-Up, Dock Carts **Communication -** Phone Messages, FedEx, AirBorne, UPS, Express Mail **Supplies - OnSite:** Ice *(Block, Cube)* **Near:** Ships' Store, Bait/Tackle, Propane **3+ mi:** Marine Discount Store *(Erickson Marine 837-2687, 5 mi.)*

Boatyard Services
OnSite: Launching Ramp, Electrical Repairs **Near:** Electronics Repairs, Hull Repairs, Rigger, Bottom Cleaning, Brightwork, Refrigeration, Divers.
Nearest Yard: Youngs (781) 545-0440

Restaurants and Accommodations
OnSite: Restaurant *(Pier 44 Restaurant 545-4700, L $4-13, D $8-16)* **OnCall:** Pizzeria *(Harbor House 545-5407)* **Near:** Restaurant *(Barker Tavern 545-6533, D $18-32)*, *(Mill Wharf 545-3999, L $7-14, D $14-25)*, Lite Fare *(Satuit Tavern 545-2500, L $4-14, D $4-14)*, Inn/B&B *(Inn at Scituate Harbor/Clipper Ship Lodge 545-5550)*, *(Allen House 545-8221, $80-215)* **Under 1 mi:** Restaurant *(Flounder Inn 545-7756)*, Coffee Shop *(Atlantic Bagel 545-1331)*, Hotel *(Oceanside Inn 544-0002, $90-240, private waterfront balconies)*, Inn/B&B *(Well Feathered Nest 545-5591, $75-135)*

Recreation and Entertainment
Near: Beach, Playground, Jogging Paths, Boat Rentals, Roller Blade/Bike Paths, Fishing Charter, Movie Theater *(Scituate Playhouse - 4 screens 545-0045)*, Park, Sightseeing *(Scituate Lightouse, Lawson water tower 545-1083)*, Special Events *(Heritage Days)* **Under 1 mi:** Bowling *(Satuit Bowlaway 545-9726)*, Video Rental *(Hennessy News 545-6940)*

1-3 mi: Tennis Courts *(Scituate Tennis Club 545-1184)*, Golf Course *(Widows Walk Golf Course 544-7777)*, Fitness Center *(Bay State Athletic Club 545-2249)*, Horseback Riding *(Longmeadow Farms 545-8153)*, Museum *(Maritime Museum 545-5565)* **3+ mi:** Dive Shop *(5 mi.)*

Provisioning and General Services
Near: Convenience Store, Supermarket *(Scituate Marketplace 545-4896 or Shaw's Cohasset 383-2315, 6 mi.)*, Gourmet Shop, Delicatessen, Wine/Beer, Liquor Store *(Bailey's Package Store 781-545-0620)*, Bakery, Green Grocer, Fishmonger, Lobster Pound *(Coastal Fish & Lobster)*, Meat Market, Bank/ATM, Post Office, Catholic Church, Protestant Church, Library *(Scituate 545-8727)*, Beauty Salon, Barber Shop, Dry Cleaners, Laundry, Bookstore *(Front Street Book Shop 545-5011)*, Newsstand, Florist, Retail Shops, Copies Etc. **Under 1 mi:** Pharmacy *(CVS 545-0240)*, Hardware Store *(Satuit Hardware 545-8370)*

Transportation
OnSite: Water Taxi *(Easy Rider 545-1195 , Waterline Launch Ch.9)* **OnCall:** Rental Car *(Enterprise 617-261-7447)*, Taxi *(Scituate Taxi 545-5222)*, Airport Limo *(Abbey Rd. Limo 545-5726)* **Near:** Local Bus **1-3 mi:** Bikes *(Seacoast Cycle & Sports 545-7000)*, InterCity Bus *(P&B 746-0378 to Boston)* **3+ mi:** Rail *(Boston 617-268-9000, 27 mi.)* **Airport:** Logan Int'l. *(27 mi.)*

Medical Services
911 Service **OnCall:** Ambulance **Near:** Dentist *(Bortnick 545-0339)* **1-3 mi:** Doctor *(Harbor Medical 545-5225)*, Chiropractor *(Scituate Harbor Chiropractic 545-7388)* **Hospital:** South Shore 340-4090 *(15 mi.)*

Setting -- This low-key, modest facility offers good dockage, open views and convenient access to the restaurants and services in the engaging New England seacoast town of Scituate Harbor. It is the third facility in the harbor, past the Yacht Club and Satuit Boat Club -- look for the floating red building.

Marina Notes -- *Office is closed weekdays Sep 1-Oct 10. New docks at 75 percent of the slips in 1996. Docks are moored at the end of 125' fixed pier. Head is no longer located on the floating dock, but is now a full-size porta-potty at the top of the ramp. The marina has been operational since the '60's (originally as O'Neil's or The Lobster House). The current owner, Dobber Reynolds, after working at the marina from age 12 onward, first managed, then leased and finally purchased the facility in 1993. Caters to sport fishing boats.

Notable -- Directly adjacent to the marina is Pier 44, a large, casual restaurant specializing in Italian seafood and local lobster -- with views of Scituate Harbor; it also has an extensive catering and take-out menu, as well as a kids' menu. Across the street is the casual Satuit Tavern. The highly regarded, elegant 1634 Barker Tavern Restaurant, the oldest original inn in the country, is a 5 minute walk (many come just for the swordfish). The services, amusements and restaurants of Scituate Harbor are an easy stroll away - town begins 0.2 miles away.

PHOTOS ON CD-ROM: 9

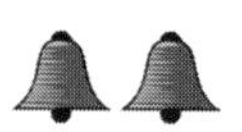

Scituate Launch "Cedar Point"

PO Box 35; 79 Cole Parkway; Scituate, MA 02066

Tel: (781) 545-4154; (800) 256-6667 **VHF: Monitor** 9 **Talk** 9
Fax: (781) 545-4881 **Alternate Tel:** (781) 597-5535
Email: scituateharbor@attbi.com **Web:** n/a
Nearest Town: Scituate *(0 mi.)* **Tourist Info:** (781) 545-4000

Navigational Information

Lat: 42°12.020' **Long:** 070°43.390' **Tide:** 9 ft. **Current:** n/a **Chart:** 13269
Rep. Depths (*MLW*): Entry 10 ft. **Fuel Dock** 9 ft. **Max Slip/Moor** 10 ft./12 ft.
Access: Cape Cod Bay to Scituate Harbor RW "SA" to mooring field

Marina Facilities *(In Season/Off Season)*

Fuel: *Texaco* - Slip-Side Fueling, Gasoline, Diesel, On Call Delivery
Slips: 0 Total, 0 Transient **Max LOA:** 50 ft. **Max Beam:** 15 ft.
Rate *(per ft.)*: **Day** n/a **Week** n/a **Month** n/a
Power: 30 amp n/a, **50 amp** n/a, **100 amp** n/a, **200 amp** n/a
Cable TV: No **Dockside Phone:** No
Dock Type: n/a
Moorings: 100 Total, 25 Transient **Launch:** Yes (Free), Dinghy Dock (Free)
Rate: Day $25 **Week** Inq. **Month** Inq.
Heads: 4 Toilet(s), 4 Shower(s)
Laundry: Yes **Pay Phones:** Yes, 3
Pump-Out: OnCall, Full Service **Fee:** Free **Closed Heads:** No

Marina Operations

Owner/Manager: Fran McMillen **Dockmaster:** n/a
In-Season: May-Oct, 8am-10pm **Off-Season:** Closed
After-Hours Arrival: Pager 781-597-5535
Reservations: Preferred **Credit Cards:** n/a
Discounts: None
Pets: Welcome, Dog Walk Area **Handicap Access:** No

Marina Services and Boat Supplies

Services - Concierge, Room Service to the Boat, Security *(24 Hrs., Harbormaster patrol)*, Trash Pick-Up, Dock Carts **Communication -** Mail & Package Hold, Phone Messages, Fax in/out, Data Ports *(5 min.)*, FedEx, UPS, Express Mail *(Sat Del)* **Supplies - OnCall:** Ice *(Block, Cube)* **Near:** Ships' Store, Bait/Tackle, Live Bait, Propane, CNG **3+ mi:** Marine Discount Store *(Erickson Marine 837-2687, 5 mi.)*

Boatyard Services

OnSite: Launching Ramp, Bottom Cleaning, Divers, Propeller Repairs **OnCall:** Engine mechanic *(gas, diesel)*, Electrical Repairs, Electronics Repairs, Hull Repairs *(Emergency)*, Rigger, Sail Loft, Brightwork, Air Conditioning, Refrigeration, Compound, Wash & Wax, Interior Cleaning, Woodworking, Inflatable Repairs, Metal Fabrication **Nearest Yard:** North River Marine (781) 545-7811

Restaurants and Accommodations

OnCall: Pizzeria *(Harbor House 545-5407, delivers)* **Near:** Restaurant *(Riva B $10, D $12)*, *(Mill Wharf & Chesters 545-3999, L $7-14, D $14-25)*, *(TK O'Malley's Sports Café 545-4012, L $5-13, D $5-15)*, Snack Bar *(Atlantic B $5, L $5)*, Coffee Shop *(Café Morada 544-3144, B $3-10, L $3-10, breakfast & desserts 5am-10pm)*, Inn/B&B *(Inn at Scituate Harbor 545-5550)*, *(Allen House 545-8222, $80-215)* **Under 1 mi:** Inn/B&B *(Well-Feathered Nest 545-5591, $75-135)*, *(Oceanside Inn 544-0002, $90-240)*

Recreation and Entertainment

OnSite: Fishing Charter **Near:** Beach, Jogging Paths, Bowling *(Bowlaway 545-9726)*, Movie Theater *(Scituate Playhouse - 4 screens 545-0045)*, Video Rental, Special Events *(Heritage Days, early Aug)* **1-3 mi:** Tennis Courts *(Scituate Tennis Club 545-1184)*, Golf Course *(Widows Walk Golf Course 544-7777)*, Museum *(Maritime 545-5565)*, Sightseeing *(Beaches, Salt marshes)*

Provisioning and General Services

Near: Convenience Store, Supermarket *(Scituate Marketplace 545-4896)*, Wine/Beer, Liquor Store *(Harborside Wine and Spirits 545-0059)*, Bakery, Fishmonger *(Coastal Fish & Lobster 545-7650)*, Lobster Pound, Meat Market, Bank/ATM, Catholic Church, Protestant Church, Library *(Scituate 545-8727)*, Beauty Salon, Dry Cleaners, Laundry *(Super Wash 545-7445)*, Bookstore *(Front Street Book Shop 545-5011)*, Pharmacy *(CVS 545-1531)*, Newsstand, Hardware Store *(Satuit Hardware 545-8370)*, Retail Shops, Copies Etc. *(Thompsons Business Services 545-4470)* **Under 1 mi:** Delicatessen *(Flynn's Grocery & Deli 545-4580)*, Post Office

Transportation

OnCall: Rental Car *(Enterprise 383-2966)*, Taxi *(Scituate Taxi 545-5222)* **Under 1 mi:** Ferry Service *(Harbor Express - airport)* **1-3 mi:** Bikes *(Seacoast Cycle & Sports 545-7000)* **3+ mi:** Rail *(Boston, 15 mi.)* **Airport:** Logan Int'l. *(15 mi.)*

Medical Services

911 Service **OnCall:** Ambulance **Near:** Doctor *(Harbor Medical 545-5225)*, Dentist *(Bortnick 545-0339)*, Chiropractor *(Scituate Harbor Chiropractic 545-7388)* **Hospital:** South Shore 340-4090 *(15 mi.)*

PHOTOS ON CD-ROM: 9

Setting -- Cedar Point Launch's moorings are sprinkled throughout the Outer and Inner Scituate Harbors. This is the largest mooring/launch provider and makes the Cole Parkway Municipal Marina, in the Inner Harbor, its centrally located home port.

Marina Notes -- Closed Nov 1 - Apr 25. Alternative phone number is a pager. Also called Waterline. Has arranged with Cole Parkway Town Marina to provide access to the heads and showers in the Harbormaster's building for its mooring/launch customers. Very service-oriented management and staff - just ask. Complimentary Sunday morning coffee, donuts and NY Times or Boston Globe for overnight mooring customers. "Room-service" provisions to boat on request and "Dinner on board" restaurant service. Will take trash. Discount for repeat customers or extended stay. Runs pump-out boat in harbor. Immaculate, club-quality launches.

Notable -- Four groups maintain and manage the moorings in Scituate Harbor (and generally have transient ones available): Scituate Launch Cedar Point, EZ Rider (545-1195), Satuit Boat Club (545-9752) and Scituate Harbor Yacht Club (545-0372) - each offers different amenities. Heritage Days: town streets are closed, shops move into the streets. Music performances live all weekend (Bach to rock) - early August. Alternate Friday night concerts in Band Shell. All of Scituate is within easy walking distance of the launch dock at Cole Parkway.

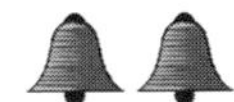

Cole Parkway Municipal Marina

100 Cole Parkway; Scituate, MA 02066

Tel: (781) 545-8724 **VHF: Monitor** 9 **Talk** 14
Fax: (781) 545-8704 **Alternate Tel:** n/a
Email: n/a **Web:** n/a
Nearest Town: Scituate *(0 mi.)* **Tourist Info:** (781) 545-4000

Navigational Information

Lat: 42°11.697' **Long:** 070°43.392' **Tide:** n/a **Current:** n/a **Chart:** 13267
Rep. Depths (*MLW*): Entry 12 ft. **Fuel Dock** 8 ft. **Max Slip/Moor** 10 ft./12 ft.
Access: Cape Cod Bay to Scituate Inner Harbor

Marina Facilities *(In Season/Off Season)*

Fuel: Gasoline, Diesel
Slips: 199 Total, 6-10 Transient **Max LOA:** 40 ft. **Max Beam:** 15 ft.
Rate *(per ft.)*: **Day** $2.00 **Week** n/a **Month** n/a
Power: 30 amp Incl., **50 amp** n/a, **100 amp** n/a, **200 amp** n/a
Cable TV: No **Dockside Phone:** No
Dock Type: Wood, Long Fingers, Floating
Moorings: 0 Total, 0 Transient **Launch:** n/a, Dinghy Dock (Free)
Rate: Day n/a **Week** n/a **Month** n/a
Heads: 8 Toilet(s), 4 Shower(s)
Laundry: Yes **Pay Phones:** Yes
Pump-Out: Full Service, 1 Central, 1 Port **Fee:** Free **Closed Heads:** No

Marina Operations

Owner/Manager: Elmer E. Pooler (Hrbrmstr) **Dockmaster:** Mark Patterson
In-Season: n/a, 8:30am-4:30pm **Off-Season:** n/a, 8:30am-4:30pm Mon-Fri
After-Hours Arrival: Please call ahead
Reservations: Preferred **Credit Cards:** Cash or Check
Discounts: None
Pets: Welcome **Handicap Access:** Yes, Heads

Marina Services and Boat Supplies

Services - Docking Assistance, Security *(24 Hrs., Guard and patrol boat)*, Trash Pick-Up, Dock Carts **Supplies - OnSite:** Ice *(Block, Cube)* **1-3 mi:** Marine Discount Store *(North River Marina)*, Bait/Tackle *(Belsan Bait and Tackle 545-9400)*, Propane *(U-Haul 545-7335)*

Boatyard Services

OnSite: Bottom Cleaning, Divers, Compound, Wash & Wax **OnCall:** Propeller Repairs, Life Raft Service **Near:** Engine mechanic *(gas)*. **1-3 mi:** Hull Repairs. **Nearest Yard:** Young's Boatyard (781) 545-0440

Restaurants and Accommodations

Near: Restaurant *(Chester's & Mill Wharf 545-3999, L $7-14, D $14-25)*, *(TK O'Malley's 545-4012, L $5-13, D $5-14)*, *(Riva 545-5881)*, Coffee Shop *(Morada Café 544-3144, B $3-10, L $3-10, breakfast, desserts)*, Pizzeria *(Marias 545-2323, no delivery)*, Inn/B&B *(Inn at Scituate Harbor 545-5550, $80-215)*, *(Allen House 545-8229)*, *(Clipper Ship Lodge 545-5550)* **Under 1 mi:** Restaurant *(Pier 44 545-4700, L $4-13, D $12-17)*, *(Blue Mooring 545-5144)*, Inn/B&B *(Well-Feathered Nest 545-5591)*

Recreation and Entertainment

OnSite: Fishing Charter *(Quality Time)*, Cultural Attract *(Band concerts)*, Special Events *(Heritage Days 1st weekend in Aug)* **Near:** Bowling *(Satuit Bowlaway 545-9726)*, Movie Theater *(Scituate Playhouse - 4 screens 545-0045)*, Video Rental *(Hennessy News)* **1-3 mi:** Beach *(Cedar Point or Pegotty Beaches - dinghy)*, Tennis Courts *(Scituate Tennis Club 545-1184)*, Golf Course *(Widows Walk 544-7777)*, Fitness Center *(Bay State Athletic Club 545-2249)*, Jogging Paths, Park, Museum *(Lawson Tower 545-1083, built by a copper magnate in 15thC Roman-style to camouflage a water tower; it now houses carillon bells)*

Provisioning and General Services

Near: Convenience Store, Supermarket *(Village Market 545-4896)*, Delicatessen *(Maria's Submarine 545-2323)*, Wine/Beer, Liquor Store *(Scituate Package 545-0620, Harborside Wine and Spirits 545-0059)*, Bakery, Fishmonger *(Coastal Fish & Lobster 545-7650)*, Lobster Pound, Bank/ATM, Protestant Church, Library *(Scituate 545-8727)*, Beauty Salon, Barber Shop, Dry Cleaners, Laundry *(Super Wash 545-7445, next door)*, Bookstore *(Front Street Book Shop 545-5011)*, Pharmacy *(CVS 545-1531)*, Newsstand *(Hennessy News 545-6940)*, Hardware Store *(Satuit Hardware 545-8370)*, Florist, Retail Shops, Copies Etc. *(Thompsons Business Services 545-4470)* **Under 1 mi:** Post Office **1-3 mi:** Green Grocer

Transportation

OnCall: Rental Car *(Enterprise 383-2966)*, Taxi *(EZ Rider 545-1195/ Cohasset Limousine 545-6600)* **1-3 mi:** Bikes *(Seacoast Cycle & Sports 545-7000)* **Airport:** Logan Int'l. *(20 mi.)*

Medical Services

911 Service **OnCall:** Ambulance **Near:** Doctor *(Harbor Medical 545-5225)*, Dentist *(Parsons 545-0039)*, Chiropractor *(Scituate Harbor Chiropractic 545-7388)* **Hospital:** South Shore 340-8000 *(15 mi.)*

Setting -- Past the commercial town docks, tucked behind the breakwater, municipal marina Cole Parkway is the only facility in the well protected and extremely convenient inner harbor. The docks spread out along the town park and share the basin with a modest mooring field. Walking barely one block inland, through the parking lot, is the center of appealing "downtown" Scituate.

Marina Notes -- Onsite stationary pump-out, plus an on-call pump-out boat managed by Waterline (545-4154). Better than average municipal heads and showers are in the well-manned and active Harbormaster's Building -- that sits at the top of the ramp to the docks. Staff works long days and is very accommodating and helpful. Two mooring/launch services make their home here: Scituate Launch Cedar Point (545-4154, Ch.9) and E-Z Rider (545-1195, Ch.9).

Notable -- Occasional Friday night concerts are held at the band shell overlooking the marina. Just about everything you might need is within a quick walk of the town docks; a variety of eateries, services, supplies, gifts, and provisioning line Scituate's Front Street -- including a very handy supermarket. Next door is the Mill Wharf Restaurant and Chester's at Mill Wharf (lite fare upstairs for lunch; downstairs becomes Chester's for more upscale dinner dining -- all overlooking the harbor -- 11:30am-10pm, Sun 10:30am-9pm).

PHOTOS ON CD-ROM: 8

Taylor Marine

95 Central Avenue; Green Harbor, MA 02041

Tel: (781) 837-9617 **VHF: Monitor** n/a **Talk** n/a
Fax: n/a **Alternate Tel:** n/a
Email: n/a **Web:** n/a
Nearest Town: Green Harbor *(0.7 mi.)* **Tourist Info:** (508) 872-1620

Navigational Information

Lat: 42°04.927' **Long:** 070°38.722' **Tide:** 9 ft. **Current:** 5 kt. **Chart:** 13252
Rep. Depths (*MLW*): Entry 9 ft. **Fuel Dock** n/a **Max Slip/Moor** 6 ft./-
Access: Green Harbor River, first facility to starboard

Marina Facilities *(In Season/Off Season)*

Fuel: Gasoline, Diesel
Slips: 140 Total, 4 Transient **Max LOA:** 45 ft. **Max Beam:** n/a
Rate *(per ft.)*: **Day** $1.50/Inq. **Week** n/a **Month** n/a
Power: 30 amp Incl., **50 amp** n/a, **100 amp** n/a, **200 amp** n/a
Cable TV: No **Dockside Phone:** No
Dock Type: Wood, Short Fingers, Floating
Moorings: 0 Total, 0 Transient **Launch:** n/a
Rate: Day n/a **Week** n/a **Month** n/a
Heads: 2 Toilet(s)
Laundry: None **Pay Phones:** No
Pump-Out: OnSite, Full Service, 1 Central **Fee:** $5 **Closed Heads:** Yes

Marina Operations

Owner/Manager: John Taylor **Dockmaster:** Ben Stevens
In-Season: Apr-Nov, 9am-6pm **Off-Season:** n/a
After-Hours Arrival: Call in advance
Reservations: Yes **Credit Cards:** Visa/MC
Discounts: None
Pets: Welcome **Handicap Access:** No

Marina Services and Boat Supplies

Services - Docking Assistance, Trash Pick-Up, Dock Carts **Communication -** Mail & Package Hold, FedEx, AirBorne, UPS, Express Mail *(Sat Del)* **Supplies - OnSite:** Ice *(Block, Cube)* **Near:** Ships' Store *(New England Marine & Industrial)* **Under 1 mi:** Bait/Tackle *(Fisherman's Outfitter)* **3+ mi:** Propane *(Hearth & Yard 837-5333, 3 mi.)*

Boatyard Services

Nearest Yard: Green Harbor Marine (781) 837-1181

Restaurants and Accommodations

Near: Restaurant *(Compass Rose 837-6591, L $5-9, D $5-17)*, *(Haddad's Ocean Café 837-2722)*, *(Venus II Pizza, too)*, *(The Lobster Tale 834-3333)*, Lite Fare *(Arthur & Pat's 834-9755, B $4-12, L $4-15)*, *(Cosmos Café 837-4247, B&L)* **Under 1 mi:** Seafood Shack *(Charlie's on the Ocean)* **1-3 mi:** Motel *(Ocean Village Motor Inn 837-9901)*, Inn/B&B *(Powder Point B&B 934-7727)*

Recreation and Entertainment

Near: Beach *(Sunrise Beach)*, Playground, Dive Shop, Tennis Courts, Jogging Paths, Fishing Charter *(Green Harbor)*, Movie Theater, Video Rental **Under 1 mi:** Sightseeing *(Massachusetts Audubon Society's wildlife sanctuaries 575-1552)*, Special Events *(Marshfield Fair in Aug 834-6629)* **1-3 mi:** Museum *(Winslow Mansion, Daniel Webster's Study 837-5753 $3/1)* **3+ mi:** Golf Course *(Green Harbor G.C. 834-7303, 4 mi.)*

Provisioning and General Services

Near: Convenience Store *(Brant Rock Market 837-8839, small supermarket)*, Gourmet Shop, Health Food, Green Grocer, Fishmonger *(Brant Rock Fish 834-6231)*, Bank/ATM, Post Office, Catholic Church, Beauty Salon, Barber Shop, Laundry *(Brant Rock Laundromat)*, Newsstand, Retail Shops *(Brant Rock Variety)* **1-3 mi:** Farmers' Market, Library, Hardware Store *(Patriot Supply 934-8713)*, Florist **3+ mi:** Pharmacy *(CVS 837-5105, 4 mi.)*

Transportation

OnCall: Rental Car *(Enterprise 585-4218; Hertz)*, Taxi *(Green Harbor Taxi 834-3300)* **Near:** InterCity Bus *(Cape Cod to Boston)* **Airport:** Marshfield/Logan Int'l. *(3 mi./30 mi.)*

Medical Services

911 Service **OnCall:** Ambulance **Under 1 mi:** Chiropractor *(McDonough Chiro.)* **1-3 mi:** Doctor *(PMG Assoc. 934-6227)*, Veterinarian *(Kaczoroswski & Maas 837-5611)* **Hospital:** Jordan 746-2000 *(9 mi.)*

Setting -- Well protected Green Harbor River provides easy access to and from Stellwagen Bank for sport fishing and whale watching -- and offers a safe port in a storm. Landside the narrow, pretty river has four facilities - laid back Taylor Marine to starboard, followed by the town pier, and then, to port, Green Harbor Yacht Club followed by Green Harbor Marina.

Marina Notes -- Constant shoaling at the mouth is managed on a regular basis by the corps of engineers; call ahead for current conditions. Onsite restaurant is closed and has been replaced by a catering operation. The only heads are those in the restaurant building. Note: Green Harbor is a designated "no discharge zone".

Notable -- Brant Rock Beach, a stretch of ocean sand, and all of the village services, restaurants and facilities of Brant Rock/Green Harbor -- an old fashioned, modest beach town-- are an easy half mile walk to the edge of town. The Audubon Society's four sanctuaries are within reach. It'll take a cab to get to the 1699 Winslow Mansion, now owned by the grandson of Plymouth Colony Governor Edward Winslow, to Daniel Webster's law offices, and a coach museum, Wed-Sun 11am-3pm (837-5753, $3/1).

Navigational Information
Lat: 42°05.100' **Long:** 070°39.000' **Tide:** 9 ft. **Current:** 5 kt. **Chart:** 13253
Rep. Depths (*MLW*): Entry 9 ft. **Fuel Dock** 7 ft. **Max Slip/Moor** 8 ft./-
Access: Green Harbor River, second facility to port

Marina Facilities *(In Season/Off Season)*
Fuel: Gasoline, Diesel
Slips: 181 Total, 8 Transient **Max LOA:** 55 ft. **Max Beam:** n/a
Rate *(per ft.)*: **Day** $2.00/Inq. **Week** Inq. **Month** n/a
Power: 30 amp Incl., **50 amp** Incl., **100 amp** n/a, **200 amp** n/a
Cable TV: No **Dockside Phone:** No
Dock Type: Wood, Short Fingers, Pilings, Floating
Moorings: 0 Total, 0 Transient **Launch:** n/a
Rate: Day n/a **Week** n/a **Month** n/a
Heads: 4 Toilet(s), 4 Shower(s)
Laundry: None **Pay Phones:** No
Pump-Out: OnSite, 1 Central **Fee:** $5 **Closed Heads:** Yes

Marina Operations
Owner/Manager: Dan Vigneau **Dockmaster:** Ray Stauff
In-Season: Apr-Nov, 8am-5pm **Off-Season:** n/a
After-Hours Arrival: Call VHF 65 - will direct you to slip
Reservations: Yes **Credit Cards:** Visa/MC, Amex
Discounts: None
Pets: Welcome **Handicap Access:** No

Green Harbor Marina

PO Box 338; 239 Dyke Road; Green Harbor, MA 02041

Tel: (781) 837-1181 **VHF: Monitor** 65 **Talk** n/a
Fax: (781) 834-0163 **Alternate Tel:** n/a
Email: n/a **Web:** n/a
Nearest Town: Green Harbor *(.5 mi.)* **Tourist Info:** (508) 872-1620

Marina Services and Boat Supplies
Services - Docking Assistance, Boaters' Lounge, Dock Carts **Communication -** Mail & Package Hold, Phone Messages, Fax in/out, FedEx, AirBorne, UPS, Express Mail *(Sat Del)* **Supplies - OnSite:** Ice *(Cube)*, Ships' Store, Bait/Tackle *(Fisherman's Outfitter 834-3750)* **3+ mi:** Propane *(Hearth & Yard 837-5333, 3 mi.)*

Boatyard Services
OnSite: Travelift *(30T)*, Engine mechanic *(gas, diesel)*, Launching Ramp, Electrical Repairs, Electronic Sales, Electronics Repairs, Hull Repairs, Bottom Cleaning, Brightwork, Compound, Wash & Wax, Interior Cleaning, Propeller Repairs **OnCall:** Canvas Work, Air Conditioning, Refrigeration, Woodworking, Life Raft Service, Upholstery, Yacht Interiors, Metal Fabrication, Painting, Awlgrip **Member:** ABBRA **Yard Rates:** $60/hr., Haul & Launch $6/ft. *(blocking $1.50/ft.)*, Power Wash $2/ft., Bottom Paint $15/ft.

Restaurants and Accommodations
OnSite: Restaurant *(Compass Rose 837-6591, L $5-9, D $5-17, kids' menu, pizza)* **Near:** Restaurant *(Hung's Chinese 837-4441, take-out, too)*, Snack Bar *(The Coffee Shop 5am-6pm, smoothies, pastries, newspapers)* **Under 1 mi:** Restaurant *(Venus II - pizza, too)*, *(Haddad's Ocean Café 837-2722)*, *(The Lobster Tale 834-3333)*, Snack Bar *(Brant Rock Variety)*, Lite Fare *(Arthur & Pat's 834-9755, B $4-12, L $4-15, famous breakfasts)* **1-3 mi:** Motel *(Ocean Village Motor Inn 837-9901)*, *(Sunrise Beach Oceanfront B&B 837-6269)*

Recreation and Entertainment
OnSite: Picnic Area, Grills, Fishing Charter **Near:** Playground, Dive Shop, Tennis Courts, Jogging Paths, Bowling, Movie Theater, Video Rental **Under 1 mi:** Beach *(Brant Rock Beach)*, Sightseeing *(Massachusetts Audubon Society's wildlife sanctuaries 575-1552)*, Special Events *(Marshfield Fair - Aug 834-6629)* **1-3 mi:** Museum *(Winslow Mansion, Daniel Webster's Study 837-5753 $3/1)* **3+ mi:** Golf Course *(Green Harbor 834-7303, 4 mi.)*

Provisioning and General Services
Near: Convenience Store, Supermarket *(Brant Rock Market 837-8839 - small)*, Gourmet Shop, Health Food, Wine/Beer, Liquor Store, Bakery, Green Grocer, Meat Market, Bank/ATM, Post Office, Catholic Church, Beauty Salon, Barber Shop, Newsstand **Under 1 mi:** Fishmonger *(Brant Rock Fish 834-6231)*, Laundry *(Brant Rock Laundromat)* **1-3 mi:** Farmers' Market, Library, Florist, Retail Shops, Copies Etc. **3+ mi:** Pharmacy *(CVS 837-5105, 4 mi.)*, Hardware Store *(Patriot Supply 934-8713, 3 mi.)*

Transportation
OnCall: Taxi *(Green Harbor Taxi 834-3300)* **Near:** Local Bus **3+ mi:** Rental Car *(Enterprise 585-4318/Hertz 585-3385, on call/8 mi.)* **Airport:** Marshfield/Logan Int'l. *(3 mi./30 mi.)*

Medical Services
911 Service **Under 1 mi:** Chiropractor *(McDonough Chiropractic)* **1-3 mi:** Doctor *(Healthstop Marshfield 837-6561)* **Hospital:** Highland Medical Center 848-6040 *(6 mi.)*

Setting -- On the west side of Green Harbor River, just past the yacht club, this sport fishing facility is home port to many of the recreational boats that fish the Stellwagen Bank. Views waterside are of the marsh and out to the mouth of the river; landside views are of the imposing 2-story Compass Rose restaurant and the marina's support services.

Marina Notes -- Very service-oriented. Caters to sport fishermen. A tuna processor right onsite is available for immediate ice-down of the fish and to manage transfers and sales. Nice heads and showers. 60T travelift and well-equipped ships' store onsite. Regular shoaling at the river's mouth is periodically dredged by the Army Corps of Engineers; marina dredges slip area regularly. Green Harbor is a no discharge zone.

Notable -- Number of sport fishing charter boats live here as does the venerable Green Harbor Tuna Club, which hosts a wide variety of tournaments and friendly competitions. Compass Rose has a couple of comfortable second floor dining rooms with expansive views of the marina and river. Food ranges from sandwiches & pizza to a full-service menu, Italian, seafood, etc. L 11:30am-4pm, D 4:30-10pm, 7 days, kids' menu. Indoor, live "easy listening" entertainment Fri, Sat, Sun. It's a half mile to the edge of the quirky Green Harbor/Brant Rock beachside village, which has an interesting range of services, supplies, and eateries -- plus a beach.

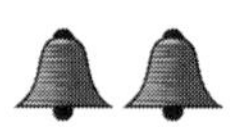

Duxbury Town Pier

Washington Street & Mattakeesett Court *; Duxbury, MA 02332

Tel: (781) 934-2866 **VHF: Monitor** 16 **Talk** 9
Fax: (781) 934-9011 **Alternate Tel:** (781) 858-7447
Email: n/a **Web:** www.duxburyharbormaster.org
Nearest Town: Duxbury *(0.1 mi.)* **Tourist Info:** (508) 830-1620

Navigational Information

Lat: 42°02.312' **Long:** 070°40.178' **Tide:** 9 ft. **Current:** n/a **Chart:** 13253
Rep. Depths (*MLW*): Entry 9 ft. **Fuel Dock** n/a **Max Slip/Moor** -/8 ft.
Access: Duxbury Bay, turn to port at G11, follow channel to end

Marina Facilities *(In Season/Off Season)*

Fuel: No
Slips: 0 Total, 0 Transient **Max LOA:** n/a **Max Beam:** n/a
Rate *(per ft.)*: **Day** n/a **Week** n/a **Month** n/a
Power: 30 amp n/a, **50 amp** n/a, **100 amp** n/a, **200 amp** n/a
Cable TV: No **Dockside Phone:** No
Dock Type: n/a
Moorings: 150 Total, 5 Transient **Launch:** Yes ($10-15)
Rate: Day $10 **Week** n/a **Month** n/a
Heads: 2 Toilet(s)
Laundry: None **Pay Phones:** Yes, 1
Pump-Out: Full Service, 1 Central, 1 Port **Fee:** Free **Closed Heads:** No

Marina Operations

Owner/Manager: Donald Beers (HM) **Dockmaster:** Denis Pearse (Ex.Off.)
In-Season: May-Oct, 8am-8pm **Off-Season:** Nov-Apr, 9am-5pm
After-Hours Arrival: Call in advance
Reservations: Yes **Credit Cards:** n/a
Discounts: None
Pets: Welcome **Handicap Access:** No

Marina Services and Boat Supplies

Services - Security **Communication -** Mail & Package Hold, UPS, Express Mail **Supplies - Near:** Ice *(Cube)*, Ships' Store *(Bayside Marine 934-0561)* **3+ mi:** Bait/Tackle *(Rod Builders Workshop 582-1015, 5 mi.)*, Propane *(Chandlers 834-7387, 4 mi.)*

Boatyard Services

OnSite: Engine mechanic *(gas, diesel)*, Electrical Repairs, Electronics Repairs, Hull Repairs, Rigger, Sail Loft, Propeller Repairs **Nearest Yard:** Snug Harbor Boatworks (781) 934-1366

Restaurants and Accommodations

Near: Restaurant *(La Maison du Vin 934-6393)*, Seafood Shack *(Snug Harbor Fish Co. 934-8167, L $6-17, Take-Out only)* **Under 1 mi:** Restaurant *(Winsor House 934-0991)*, Inn/B&B *(Winsor House Inn 934-0991)*, *(Powder Point 934-7727)* **1-3 mi:** Restaurant *(The Milepost 934-6801)*, *(Wildflower Café 934-7814, B $4, L $6, D $10-22, Sun Brunch, Early bird break $4 before 9am, Dinner Thu-Sat 4-6pm $11, Box lunch to-go $6)*, *(Tsang's Café 934-8222)*, Snack Bar *(Dunkin Donuts 934-5225)*, Pizzeria *(Duxbury Pizza 934-6568)*, *(Joe's Pizzeria and Deli 829-1055)*

Recreation and Entertainment

Near: Jogging Paths, Boat Rentals *(Schooner Charter Aries 789-7245)*, Sightseeing *(stroll the lanes of nearby neighborhoods)* **Under 1 mi:** Beach *(Duxbury Beach - a prime spot for boardsailing)*, Museum *(Alden House 934-9092 $2.50/1)* **1-3 mi:** Golf Course *(North Hill Golf Course 934-3249)*, Fitness Center *(Gymnastics With Flair 934-5145)*, Bowling *(Executive Lanes 585-5151)*, Video Rental *(Video Scene 934-2591)*, Cultural Attract *(Art Complex Museum 934-6634 Wed-Sun, 1-4pm)* **3+ mi:** Movie Theater *(Hoyts Cinema 582-2000, 3.5 mi.)*

Provisioning and General Services

Near: Gourmet Shop *(Gourmet's Pantry 934-2567)*, Wine/Beer *(La Maison Du Vin 934-6393)*, Bakery *(French Memories)*, Fishmonger *(Snug Harbor Fish Co. 934-8167)*, Lobster Pound, Post Office, Protestant Church, Florist *(Petals 934-5855)*, Retail Shops **Under 1 mi:** Convenience Store *(Millbrook Market 934-2921)*, Library *(934-2721)*, Beauty Salon, Bookstore *(Once Upon A Time 934-9788; Westwind in So. Duxbury 934-2128)* **1-3 mi:** Supermarket *(A&P 934-0113)*, Delicatessen *(The Deli 934-2875)*, Liquor Store *(Wine Depot 934-6171)*, Dry Cleaners, Pharmacy *(Brooks 934-0694)*, Hardware Store *(Goodrich Lumber 934-5611)* **3+ mi:** Bank/ATM *(Fleet 800/841-4000, 3.5 mi.)*, Catholic Church *(4 mi.)*

Transportation

OnCall: Rental Car *(Enterprise 747-1212)*, Taxi *(Green Harbor 837-1234)*, Airport Limo *(Aerobus 837-1234)* **Under 1 mi:** InterCity Bus *(P&B 746-0378 Ptown to Boston)* **Airport:** Plymouth/Logan Int'l. *(5 mi./30 mi.)*

Medical Services

911 Service **OnCall:** Ambulance **Under 1 mi:** Dentist *(Pellegrini 934-2311)* **1-3 mi:** Doctor *(Physician Associates 934-6227)*, Chiropractor *(Karr 934-2268)* **Hospital:** Jordan 746-2000 *(7 mi.)*

Setting -- Tucked into Snug Harbor, the Harbormaster's Office at the Duxbury Town Pier is the first stop for visiting boaters -- they control all of the transient moorings and manage most of them. Views are of the historic and picturesque waterfront and the energetic activities of the Duxbury Bay Maritime School.

Marina Notes -- Inner basin moorings up to 45 ft.; 1 mile out, 2-Rock moorings for up to 80 ft. Dinghy dock & two launch services: Bay Rider (Ch.10, 225-5934) & Bayside Marine (Ch.9) $10/Basin, $15/2-Rock. MidMay-MidJun 8am-6pm, MidJun-LabDay 8am-8pm, LabDay-MidOct, 8am-Sunset. Max 30 min tie-up at Town Dock. Town Tender Finger Float at Town Pier. Heads are in the building at the back of the property. No showers (except outdoor one). All moorings privately owned - available only when owners are away. Stationary, self-serve pump-out on pier, plus pump-out boat on-call. Annual moorings $3.25-4.50/ft. *Mailing Address: 878 Tremont St. Moorings/Launch also available from Duxbury Yacht Club (Ch.11, 934-5815) for reciprocating YC members. Slips might be available from virtually onsite Snug Harbor Boat Yard. About 1.8 mi. south on Washington St., in So. Duxbury, are several eateries, retail shops, and an A&P.

Notable -- Onsite non-profit Duxbury Bay Maritime School (934-7555) has sailing and racing programs for kids & adults, plus summer ecology and shore programs in boat building, model making, piloting, navigation & safety. A cab ride to Duxbury Art Complex for contemporary regional exhibits, Oriental, Shaker furniture, tea ceremonies (last Sun of month). Duxbury was founded in 1628 by Myles Standish & John Alden as a Plymouth outpost; it was a shipbuilding center until the mid-19thC when ships became too large for the shallow bay. Many historic, restored houses from Pilgrim and shipbuilding eras.

Navigational Information

Lat: 41°57.370' **Long:** 070°39.597' **Tide:** 10 ft. **Current:** 0 kt. **Chart:** 13253
Rep. Depths (*MLW*): Entry 9 ft. **Fuel Dock** 12 ft. **Max Slip/Moor** 12 ft./-
Access: Duxbury Pier Light, Plymouth Harbor Channel, to port at G 9

Marina Facilities *(In Season/Off Season)*

Fuel: *Texaco* - Gasoline, Diesel, On Call Delivery
Slips: 110 Total, 40 Transient **Max LOA:** 150 ft. **Max Beam:** n/a
Rate *(per ft.)*: **Day** $2.50/$1.25 **Week** $1.75 **Month** Inq.
Power: 30 amp Yes, **50 amp** Yes, **100 amp** n/a, **200 amp** n/a
Cable TV: Yes **Dockside Phone:** No
Dock Type: Concrete, Floating
Moorings: 0 Total, 0 Transient **Launch:** n/a
Rate: Day n/a **Week** n/a **Month** n/a
Heads: 6 Toilet(s), 6 Shower(s)
Laundry: 2 Washer(s), 3 Dryer(s), Book Exchange **Pay Phones:** Yes
Pump-Out: OnSite, Full Service **Fee:** $5 **Closed Heads:** Yes

Marina Operations

Owner/Manager: Tim Moll **Dockmaster:** Same
In-Season: Summer, 7am-7pm **Off-Season:** Fall-Win-Sprg, 7am-5pm
After-Hours Arrival: Check in the next morning
Reservations: Yes **Credit Cards:** Visa/MC, Dscvr, Amex
Discounts: Brewer Customer Club **Dockage:** n/a **Fuel:** n/a **Repair:** n/a
Pets: Welcome, Dog Walk Area **Handicap Access:** No

Brewer Plymouth Marine

14 Union Street; Plymouth, MA 02360

Tel: (508) 746-4500 **VHF: Monitor** 9 **Talk** 72
Fax: (508) 746-2883 **Alternate Tel:** n/a
Email: byybpm@aol.com **Web:** www.byy.com/Plymouth
Nearest Town: Plymouth *(0.2 mi.)* **Tourist Info:** (508) 747-7525

Marina Services and Boat Supplies

Services - Docking Assistance, Security, Dock Carts, Megayacht Facilities **Communication -** Mail & Package Hold, Phone Messages, Fax in/out, FedEx, AirBorne, UPS, Express Mail *(Sat Del)* **Supplies - OnSite:** Ice *(Block, Cube)*, Boater's World *(747-5774)* **1-3 mi:** Bait/Tackle *(Tackle Shop 746-7429)*, Propane *(Sunoco 746-2009)*

Boatyard Services

OnSite: Travelift *(2, 60T each)*, Forklift *(20,000 lb.)*, Crane *(for spars to 70 ft.)*, Engine mechanic *(gas, diesel)*, Electrical Repairs, Electronics Repairs, Hull Repairs, Rigger, Bottom Cleaning, Brightwork, Refrigeration, Compound, Wash & Wax, Awlgrip, Yacht Broker *(Brewer)*, Total Refits **OnCall:** Divers **Near:** Launching Ramp, Propeller Repairs. **3+ mi:** Sail Loft *(10 mi.)*. **Dealer for:** Cummins, Caterpillar, Volvo, Dedham Sportsman Sea Ray, Cat, Westerbeke, Yanmar. **Member:** ABBRA, ABYC - 6 Certified Tech (s) **Yard Rates:** $60/hr., Haul & Launch $8/ft. to 40', $10/ft. to 50' *(blocking $12/ft. 50'+)*, Bottom Paint $10/ft. **Storage:** On-Land $28/ft.

Restaurants and Accommodations

OnSite: Restaurant *(Mayflower 747-4503, D $14-22, overlooks Plymouth Rock)*, Lite Fare *(Deck at 1620 Café 747-4503, L $6-10, D $6-17, seasonal)* **OnCall:** Pizzeria *(House Of Pizza 746-0444)* **Near:** Restaurant *(Hearth and Kettle 747-7405, L $4-11, D $9-16)*, *(Isaac's on the Water 830-0001, L $6-10, D $10-15)*, *(Sam Diego's Mexican 747-0048)*, Fast Food, Motel *(Blue Anchor 746-9551)*, *(Governor Bradford 746-6200, $70-165)*, Inn/B&B *(John Carver Inn 746-7100, $90-250)* **Under 1 mi:** Restaurant *(Weathervane 746-4195)*, Seafood Shack *(Lobster Hut 746-2270)*, *(Wood's Seafood 746-0261, L $7-18, D $7-18)*

Recreation and Entertainment

OnSite: Grills **Near:** Beach *(Nelson Field/Stephens Field)*, Picnic Area, Tennis Courts, Boat Rentals, Museum *(Pilgrim Hall 746-1620, Plimoth Plantation)*, Cultural Attract, Sightseeing *(Plymouth Rock, Mayflower II 746-1622)*, Special Events **Under 1 mi:** Fishing Charter, Group Fishing Boat **1-3 mi:** Playground, Dive Shop, Fitness Center *(Fitness Plymouth 746-7448)*, Movie Theater, Video Rental *(Massive Video 747-3200)*

Provisioning and General Services

Near: Convenience Store, Gourmet Shop, Delicatessen, Health Food *(Common Sense 732-0427)*, Bakery, Lobster Pound *(Woods 746-0261)*, Meat Market, Bank/ATM, Post Office, Catholic Church, Synagogue, Beauty Salon, Dry Cleaners, Laundry, Bookstore *(Wing and A Prayer Books & Toys 747-1301)*, Newsstand, Florist, Clothing Store, Retail Shops **Under 1 mi:** Liquor Store *(Richards 747-3311)*, Library *(830-4250)*, Pharmacy *(Medicine Shoppe 747-1247)*, Hardware Store *(Holmes Pt. Supply 830-9407)*, Copies Etc. *(Ocean Printing 746-2266)* **1-3 mi:** Supermarket *(Shaw's 747-2325)*, Farmers' Market, Fishmonger *(Wayne's 747-7700)*

Transportation

OnCall: Rental Car *(Hertz 585-3385, Enterprise 747-1212)*, Taxi *(Mayflower 746-7887)* **Near:** Local Bus *(Trolley)*, InterCity Bus *(P&B 746-0378 Ptown to Boston)*, Ferry Service *(Ptown 747-2400)* **1-3 mi:** Bikes *(Martha's 746-2109)* **Airport:** Plymouth *(6 mi.)*

Medical Services

911 Service **OnCall:** Ambulance **Near:** Doctor, Dentist **Hospital:** Jordan 746-2000 *(1.5 mi.)*

Setting -- Located in historic Plymouth Harbor, the marina has beautiful views of the harbor and, beyond, to Plymouth Beach, a narrow barrier peninsula dotted with old summer homes. Mayflower II, a couple of blocks away, is clearly visible from the slips.

Marina Notes -- 325 feet of dockage. Recent dredging project increased depths to 12 ft. at face dock and 8-10 ft. throughout the basin (MLW). Showers have attached dressing rooms; fresh flowers in the heads. Winter storage for 200 vessels, rack storage for 40. Founded in 1947 as Plymouth Marine railways. Present facility built in 1981, purchased and rebuilt by Brewer in 1992. Good service techs with strong mechanical background.

Notable -- Within easy walking distance of museums, restaurants, beaches and parks. Follow Pilgrim Path, a 20-site self-guided tour. Visit First House and 1627 House, plus the Pilgrim Hall Museum - the nation's oldest public museum, the original Pilgrim Fort, Burial Hill, and the Plimoth Plantation. The Mayflower II, Plymouth's popular Pilgrim vessel replica, berths at the State Pier, just north of the marina. Within walking distance are Plymouth Rock, the downtown Harbor District, and historical sites dating back to the 1620s when the Pilgrims first landed. The Plymouth trolley also circles the historic sites. Good restaurants and a growing assortment of antique shops along Main Street. For shopping, go to Ropewalk factory outlets.

Plymouth Yacht Club

34 Union Street; Plymouth, MA 02360

Tel: (508) 746-7207 **VHF: Monitor** 8 **Talk** 8
Fax: (508) 747-2015 **Alternate Tel:** n/a
Email: pyc@capecod.net **Web:** www.plymouthyacthclub.org
Nearest Town: Plymouth *(0.2 mi.)* **Tourist Info:** (508) 747-7525

Navigational Information

Lat: 41°57.332' **Long:** 070°39.476' **Tide:** 10 ft. **Current:** 0 kt. **Chart:** 13253
Rep. Depths (*MLW*): Entry 10 ft. **Fuel Dock** n/a **Max Slip/Moor** -/8 ft.
Access: Duxbury Pier Light, to port at G9, to Plymouth Harbor Channel

Marina Facilities *(In Season/Off Season)*

Fuel: No
Slips: 0 Total, 0 Transient **Max LOA:** 40 ft. **Max Beam:** n/a
Rate *(per ft.)*: **Day** n/a **Week** n/a **Month** n/a
Power: 30 amp n/a, **50 amp** n/a, **100 amp** n/a, **200 amp** n/a
Cable TV: No **Dockside Phone:** No
Dock Type: n/a
Moorings: 647 Total, 25 Transient **Launch:** Yes (Free), Dinghy Dock
Rate: Day $40* **Week** n/a **Month** n/a
Heads: Toilet(s), Shower(s)
Laundry: 1 Washer(s), 1 Dryer(s) **Pay Phones:** No
Pump-Out: OnCall *(MemDay-LabDay)* **Fee:** n/a **Closed Heads:** Yes

Marina Operations

Owner/Manager: Rebecca Darsch **Dockmaster:** n/a
In-Season: May-Oct, 7am-10pm **Off-Season:** Nov-Apr, 8am-8pm
After-Hours Arrival: Call in advance
Reservations: No **Credit Cards:** n/a
Discounts: None
Pets: Welcome **Handicap Access:** No

Marina Services and Boat Supplies

Services - Docking Assistance, Boaters' Lounge, Dock Carts **Supplies - OnSite:** Ice *(Block, Cube)* **Near:** Boater's World *(747-5774)* **1-3 mi:** Bait/Tackle *(Tackle Shop 746-7429)*, Propane *(Sunoco 746-2009)*

Boatyard Services

Nearest Yard: Brewer Plymouth Marine (508) 746-4500

Restaurants and Accommodations

OnCall: Pizzeria *(House Of Pizza 746-0444)* **Near:** Restaurant *(Mayflower 747-4503, D $14-22)*, *(Hearth and Kettle 747-4705, L $4-11, D $9-16)*, *(Tropical Grill 747-9559)*, *(Colonial Restaurant 746-0838)*, Inn/B&B *(Blue Anchor 746-9551)*, *(Governor Bradford 746-6200, $70-165)*, *(Oceanside B&B 747-2669)* **Under 1 mi:** Restaurant *(Riptides Grill & Bar 747-8337)*, Seafood Shack *(Wood's Seafood 746-0261, L $7-18, D $7-18)*, *(Lobster Hut 746-2270)*, Hotel *(Plymouth Sheraton 747-4900, $120-190)*, Inn/B&B *(John Carver Inn 746-7100, $90-250)*

Recreation and Entertainment

Near: Beach *(Nelson Field/Stephens Field)*, Museum *(Pilgrim Hall, $5/3; Mayflower Society $4/1)*, Cultural Attract *(Mayflower II; Cranberry World 747-2350)*, Special Events *(Aug Fridays parade from Plymouth Rock through town)* **Under 1 mi:** Fishing Charter, Group Fishing Boat *(Wavelength 746-6749)*, Sightseeing *(Capt John Whale Watch $28/17; Splashdown Amphibious Tours 800-225-4000)* **1-3 mi:** Fitness Center *(Fitness Plymouth 746-7448)*, Movie Theater, Video Rental *(Massive Video 747-3200)* **3+ mi:** Golf Course *(Squirrel Run Country Club 746-5001, 5 mi.)*

Provisioning and General Services

Near: Convenience Store *(Tedeschi 746-9304)*, Delicatessen *(Paulie's Deli and Bakery 746-9363)*, Health Food *(Common Sense Wholesome Food Market 732-0427)*, Bakery, Lobster Pound *(Woods 746-0261)*, Bank/ATM, Post Office, Catholic Church, Synagogue, Beauty Salon, Dry Cleaners, Laundry, Bookstore *(Wing and A Prayer Books & Toys 747-1301)*, Newsstand, Florist, Retail Shops **Under 1 mi:** Liquor Store *(Richards 747-3311)*, Library *(Plymouth PL 830-4250 high-speed Internet access)*, Pharmacy *(Medicine Shoppe 747-1247)*, Hardware Store *(Holmes Pt. Supply 830-9407)*, Copies Etc. *(Ocean Printing 746-2266)* **1-3 mi:** Supermarket *(Shaw's 747-2325)*, Fishmonger *(Wayne's 747-7700)*

Transportation

OnCall: Rental Car *(Hertz 585-3385, Enterprise 747-1212)*, Taxi *(Mayflower 746-7887)* **Near:** Local Bus *(Plymouth Rock Trolley)*, InterCity Bus *(P&B 746-0378 Ptown to Boston)*, Ferry Service *(Plymouth-Provincetown 747-2400, 10am $28/18)* **1-3 mi:** Bikes *(Martha's 746-2109)* **Airport:** Plymouth *(6 mi.)*

Medical Services

911 Service **OnCall:** Ambulance **Near:** Doctor, Dentist, Chiropractor *(Wholehealth New England 830-1201)* **Hospital:** Jordan 746-2000 *(1.5 mi.)*

Setting -- Right next to Brewer's, the small, attractive Plymouth Yacht Club offers a convenient location with spectacular views of Plymouth, the Mayflower II, and the harbor -- from its mooring field, its front lawn, and from its first and second floor decks.

Marina Notes -- Call Harbormaster Joe Ritz (830-4182) in advance for accomodations for vessles over 40 ft. *Mooring is technically free, the fee is for use of the Club's launch and its other facilities. Launch hours: Jul & Aug 7:30am-10pm Sun-Thu, 7:30am-11pm Fri, Sat; shoulder season 8am-10pm. Pump-out boat MemDay-LabDay 7 days, Ch.9. The two-story clubhouse has decks with tables and chairs, nice heads and showers, a club room on the second floor, and a lovely main floor room overlooking the harbor, which can accommodate 150 for a special event. The Topside Bar is open 4-10pm Tue-Thu, 4-11pm Fri, 2-10pm Sat & Sun. Burgers and Dogs on the Lawn Wed 6-7pm, Sat 4-7:30pm; Steak/Chicken Thu 6-8pm, Friday Night Specials at 7pm, Sun Barbecue 4-7:30pm.

Notable -- Everything in this historic town is within an easy walk -- 0.7 mi. to the main wharf. 0.3 mi. to Plymouth Rock, Park & the Mayflower II (9am-5pm, $7/4.50). Plymouth Rock Trolley passes 40 sites, including the yacht club and marina (747-3419, all-day pass $8/4). The Pilgrim Path includes more than 20 sites (maps at Info Center 130 Water St.). Plimoth Plantation, 3 mi., is a living history museum: costumed villagers go about 17thC lives amid thatched roof cottages, tending authentic plants and livestock (746-1622 $17/9.50; comb with Mayflower $19/11). Capt John's Plymouth-Provincetown Ferry leaves State Pier (Mayflower dock) 10am, returns 4:30pm.

PHOTOS ON CD-ROM: 9

VII. Massachusetts: Cape Cod

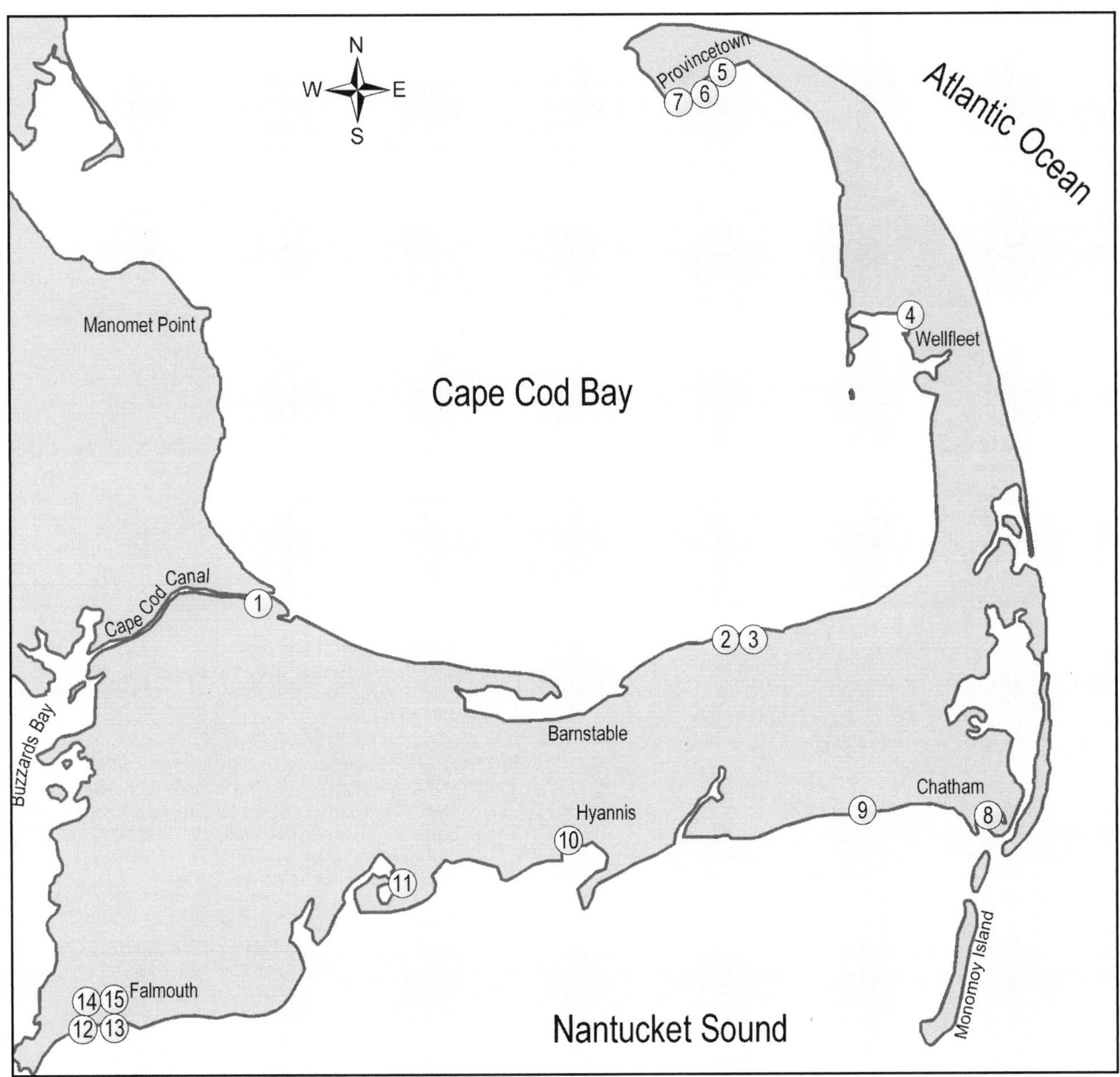

MAP	MARINA	HARBOR	PAGE
1	**Sandwich Marina**	*Cape Cod Canal*	164
2	**Northside Marina**	*Sesuit Harbor*	165
3	**Town of Dennis Municipal Marina**	*Sesuit Harbor*	166
4	**Town of Wellfleet Marina**	*Wellfleet Harbor*	167
5	**Provincetown Yacht Marina**	*Provincetown Harbor*	168
6	**Provincetown Marina**	*Provincetown Harbor*	169
7	**Flyer's Boat Rental**	*Provincetown Harbor*	170
8	**Stage Harbor Marine**	*Stage Harbor*	171
9	**Saquatucket Harbor Marina**	*Saquatucket Harbor*	172
10	**Hyannis Marina**	*Hyannis Harbor*	173
11	**Crosby Yacht Yard**	*Crosby Basin*	174
12	**Falmouth Marine & Yachting Center**	*Falmouth Harbor*	175
13	**MacDougalls' Cape Cod Marine**	*Falmouth Harbor*	176
14	**Falmouth Harbor Town Marina**	*Falmouth Harbor*	177
15	**East Marine**	*Falmouth Harbor*	178

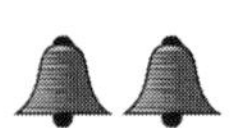

Sandwich Marina

PO Box 1393; 25 Ed Moffitt Drive; Sandwich, MA 02563

Tel: (508) 833-0808 **VHF: Monitor** 9/16 **Talk** 8
Fax: (508) 833-8026 **Alternate Tel:** n/a
Email: ebbasin@townofsandwich.net **Web:** www.sandwichmarina.com
Nearest Town: Sandwich *(1mi.)* **Tourist Info:** (508) 759-6000

Navigational Information

Lat: 41°46.295' **Long:** 070°30.104' **Tide:** 11 ft. **Current:** n/a **Chart:** 13246
Rep. Depths (*MLW*): Entry 11 ft. **Fuel Dock** 11 ft. **Max Slip/Moor** 11 ft./-
Access: Buzzard's Bay/Cape Cod Bay to Cape Cod Canal

Marina Facilities *(In Season/Off Season)*

Fuel: *Citgo Premium* - Gasoline, Diesel, High-Speed Pumps
Slips: 200 Total, 25 Transient **Max LOA:** 110 ft. **Max Beam:** 25 ft.
Rate *(per ft.)*: **Day** $1.50/$1.25 **Week** n/a **Month** n/a
Power: 30 amp $7, **50 amp** $10, **100 amp** n/a, **200 amp** n/a
Cable TV: No **Dockside Phone:** No
Dock Type: Wood, Long Fingers, Concrete, Floating
Moorings: 0 Total, 0 Transient **Launch:** n/a
Rate: Day n/a **Week** n/a **Month** n/a
Heads: 4 Toilet(s), 2 Shower(s)
Laundry: None **Pay Phones:** Yes
Pump-Out: OnCall, Full Service, 1 Central **Fee:** $5 **Closed Heads:** No

Marina Operations

Owner/Manager: Gregory E. Fayne **Dockmaster:** Same
In-Season: Year-Round, 24 hrs. **Off-Season:** n/a
After-Hours Arrival: Call in advance Ch. 9 or 16
Reservations: Yes, Preferred **Credit Cards:** Visa/MC, Dscvr, Amex, Citgo
Discounts: None
Pets: Welcome **Handicap Access:** No

Marina Services and Boat Supplies

Services - Docking Assistance **Communication -** Mail & Package Hold, Phone Messages, Fax in/out, Data Ports *(Office)*, FedEx, UPS **Supplies - OnSite:** Ice *(Block, Cube)* **Near:** Ships' Store *(Sandwich Ship Supply 888-0200)*, Bait/Tackle *(Canal Marine Fisheries 888-0096)*, Propane

Boatyard Services

OnSite: Launching Ramp, Divers **OnCall:** Engine mechanic *(gas, diesel)*, Air Conditioning, Refrigeration **Nearest Yard:** Brewer Plymouth Marine (508) 746-4500

Restaurants and Accommodations

OnSite: Restaurant *(Aqua Grille 888-8889, L $7-14, D $10-20)* **OnCall:** Pizzeria *(Sandwich Pizza 888-3109)* **Near:** Restaurant *(Capt. Scott's 888-1675, L $5, D $5)*, *(Horizons on Cape Cod Bay 888-6166, L $5-14, D $10-20)*, Seafood Shack *(Sea Food Sam's 888-4629)*, Snack Bar *(Bobby Byrne's Pub 888-6088, L $6-10, D $6-10, next to Stop & Shop)*, Motel *(Sandwich Motor Lodge 888-9716, $55-160)*, *(Shady Nook Inn 888-0409, $65-200)* **Under 1 mi:** Restaurant *(Daniel Webster Inn L $6-12, D $17-26)*, Motel *(Country Acres 888-2878, $50-100)*, Inn/B&B *(Daniel Webster Inn 888-3622, $120-350)*, *(Isaiah Jones Homestead 888-9115, $100-185)*

Recreation and Entertainment

OnSite: Picnic Area, Playground, Jogging Paths, Roller Blade/Bike Paths *(14 mi. loop alongside canal)*, Fishing Charter **Near:** Beach *(Sandy Neck 362-8300)*, Dive Shop, Video Rental **Under 1 mi:** Museum *(Sandwich Glass Museum 888-0251, Thornton Burgess Museum 888-6870)* **1-3 mi:** Cultural Attract *(Heritage Plantation 888-3300)* **3+ mi:** Golf Course *(Sandwich Hollows Golf Club 888-3384, 6 mi.)*, Fitness Center *(Rma Nautilus Racquetball & Fitness 759-7111, 3.5 mi.)*, Sightseeing *(Green Briar Nature Center, 4 mi.)*

Provisioning and General Services

OnSite: Fishmonger, Lobster Pound *(Joe's Lobster Market)* **Near:** Convenience Store, Supermarket *(Stop & Shop 833-1302)*, Delicatessen *(Sandwich Mart & Spirits 888-3362)*, Bank/ATM, Post Office **Under 1 mi:** Gourmet Shop *(Gourmet Pantry 888-4773)*, Health Food *(Healthy Body & Soul 888-8600)*, Wine/Beer, Liquor Store *(Paradise Wines & Spirits 888-8810)*, Protestant Church, Library *(Sandwich PL 888-0625)*, Beauty Salon, Barber Shop, Dry Cleaners, Laundry, Newsstand, Florist, Clothing Store, Retail Shops, Copies Etc. *(Copy To Copy 888-0078)* **1-3 mi:** Catholic Church, Bookstore *(Titcomb's Book Shop 888-2331)*, Pharmacy *(CVS 888-4335)*, Hardware Store *(Aubuchon Hardware 888-3011)*

Transportation

OnCall: Rental Car *(Thrifty 888-8333, Enterprise 759-2299)*, Taxi *(Sandwich Taxi 888-7174)* **Under 1 mi:** Bikes *(Cape Cod Bike Rental 833-2453)* **1-3 mi:** Local Bus, InterCity Bus *(P&B 746-0378 Provincetown to Boston)*, Rail *(Cape Cod Central-Hyannis 771-3800 $12/8)* **3+ mi:** Ferry Service *(Barnstable-Falmouth, 9 mi.)* **Airport:** Barnstable 775-2020 *(18 mi.)*

Medical Services

911 Service **Under 1 mi:** Chiropractor *(Back In Motion 833-0433)* **1-3 mi:** Doctor *(Sandwich Adult Urgent Care 833-4950)*, Dentist, Holistic Services, Ambulance **Hospital:** Cape Cod 778-0505 *(10 mi.)*

Setting -- Strategically located at the east (Cape Cod Bay) end of the Cape Cod Canal, just north of the power station, this facility is well sheltered, convenient, functional and makes a good jumping-off point. Sandwich, established in 1639, is the oldest town on the Cape and is the quintessential New England village. Many of its interesting sights and diversions are within a mile walk of the marina.

Marina Notes -- Operated by the Town of Sandwich since 1989; its recreational, commercial and transient slips fill all of the East Boat Basin. The Harbormaster is on duty 24/7. Fuel Dock: 7 days 7:30am-8pm, Pump-out: 7 days 8am-4pm. Winter storage $12/ft. Basic heads. The adjacent bistro-style American restaurant Aqua Grille overlooks the canal with inside and outside dining. Joe's Lobster Market is a welcome convenience.

Notable -- The canal is lined with walking/biking paths (part of the 7 mile Cap Cod Canal Bike Path) and is so brightly lit at night, it is close to daylight. A variety of restaurants are within walking distance as is the small Stop & Shop Plaza. Town Neck Beach is at the canal's eastern entrance. Sandwich was the site of one of the largest glass factories in the U.S. The Sandwich Glass Museum is about a mile walk 9:30am-5pm, $3.50/1. Close to it, the Thornton Burgess Museum, is a memorial to the well-known naturalist and children's author ("Peter Cottontail", etc.), housed in a 1756 house. 4 miles out of town is the Green Briar Nature Center with a 1-mile Old Briar Patch Nature Trail and Green Briar Jam Kitchen. About 2 miles away is the 76 acre Heritage Plantation with early American exhibits, 35 historic autos, military museum, folk art, restored 1912 carousel, a café and occasional concerts. 9am-5pm, $9/4.50.

Navigational Information
Lat: 41°45.227' **Long:** 070°09.177' **Tide:** 10 ft. **Current:** 1 kt. **Chart:** 13246
Rep. Depths (*MLW*): Entry 6 ft. **Fuel Dock** 4 ft. **Max Slip/Moor** 6 ft./-
Access: Cape Cod Bay due south of the G "1S" buoy

Marina Facilities *(In Season/Off Season)*
Fuel: *Un Branded* - Gasoline, Diesel, High-Speed Pumps, On Call Delivery
Slips: 120 Total, 5 Transient **Max LOA:** 70 ft. **Max Beam:** 20 ft.
Rate *(per ft.)*: **Day** $2.00/$1.00 **Week** $2.00/1.00 **Month** Inq.
Power: 30 amp Incl., **50 amp** Incl., **100 amp** n/a, **200 amp** n/a
Cable TV: Yes, Call Comp. **Dockside Phone:** Yes, Call Comp.
Dock Type: Wood, Floating
Moorings: 0 Total, 0 Transient **Launch:** n/a
Rate: Day n/a **Week** n/a **Month** n/a
Heads: 2 Toilet(s), 1 Shower(s) *(with dressing rooms)*, Hair Dryers
Laundry: None **Pay Phones:** Yes, 1
Pump-Out: OnSite, Self Service, 1 Central **Fee:** n/a **Closed Heads:** No

Marina Operations
Owner/Manager: n/a **Dockmaster:** n/a
In-Season: May 15-Oct 15, 8am-5pm **Off-Season:** Oct 15-May 15, Mon-Fri*
After-Hours Arrival: Call the day before
Reservations: Yes, Preferred **Credit Cards:** Visa/MC
Discounts: None
Pets: Welcome, Dog Walk Area **Handicap Access:** Yes, Heads, Docks

Northside Marina

PO Box 1415; 357 Sesuit Neck Road; South Dennis, MA 02660

Tel: (508) 385-3936 **VHF: Monitor** 7/9 **Talk** 7
Fax: (508) 385-3938 **Alternate Tel:** n/a
Email: n/a **Web:** n/a
Nearest Town: Brewster *(2 mi.)* **Tourist Info:** (508) 398-3568

Marina Services and Boat Supplies
Services - Docking Assistance, Boaters' Lounge, Crew Lounge, Dock Carts **Communication -** Mail & Package Hold, Phone Messages, Fax in/out *(Free)*, FedEx, AirBorne, UPS, Express Mail *(Sat Del)* **Supplies - OnSite:** Ice *(Block, Cube)*, Ships' Store, Marine Discount Store **Near:** Bait/Tackle **3+ mi:** West Marine *(Hyannis 862-2700, 11 mi.)*, Propane *(Eastern Propane 760-2778, 4 mi.)*

Boatyard Services
OnSite: Travelift *(35T)*, Forklift, Engine mechanic *(gas, diesel)*, Launching Ramp, Electrical Repairs, Electronic Sales, Electronics Repairs, Hull Repairs, Rigger, Canvas Work, Bottom Cleaning, Brightwork, Air Conditioning, Refrigeration, Divers, Compound, Wash & Wax, Interior Cleaning, Propeller Repairs, Woodworking, Inflatable Repairs, Life Raft Service, Upholstery, Yacht Interiors, Painting, Awlgrip, Total Refits **3+ mi:** Sail Loft *(5 mi.)*, Metal Fabrication *(10 mi.)*. **Dealer for:** Mercruiser, Yamaha, Sailfish, Formula, Sea Ray, SeaCraft . **Yard Rates:** $65/hr., Power Wash $4, Bottom Paint $10/ft. *(paint included)* **Storage:** In-Water $35/ft., On-Land $25/ft.

Restaurants and Accommodations
OnSite: Snack Bar *(Sesuit Harbor Café 385-6134, 385-6134)* **Under 1 mi:** Restaurant *(Red Pheasant 385-2133, D $15-27)*, *(Scargo Café 385-8200, L $4-12, D $10-18)*, *(Grumpys 385-2911)*, *(Marshside 385-4010, B $3-6, L $5-10, D $7-15)*, Motel *(Sesuit Harbor Motel 385-3326, $100)*, Inn/B&B *(Captain Judah Paddock 385-9959)* **1-3 mi:** Seafood Shack *(Capt. Frosty's)*, Motel *(Briarcliffe 385-3464)*, Inn/B&B *(Isaiah Hall B&B 385-9928, $110-$165)*

Recreation and Entertainment
OnSite: Picnic Area, Grills, Playground, Fishing Charter *(Blue Fish 385-7265; First Light 385-1648)* **Near:** Beach *(Harborview Beach - about a block)*, Tennis Courts *(Sesuit Tennis 385-2200)* **1-3 mi:** Golf Course *(Dennis Highlands 347)*, Fitness Center *(Fitness Connection 385-2166)*, Horseback Riding *(Paradise Stables 398-5679)*, Movie Theater *(Cape Cinema 385-2503, an extraordinary 300 seat theatre $7/4)*, Video Rental *(Entertainment & More 385-7666)*, Museum *(Cape Museum Of Fine Arts 385-4477)*, Cultural Attract *(Cape Playhouse 385-3911 $15-35/6)*

Provisioning and General Services
Under 1 mi: Convenience Store *(Tedeschi 385-4858)*, Delicatessen, Wine/Beer, Liquor Store *(East Dennis Bottled Liquors 385-2222)*, Bank/ATM, Post Office, Newsstand **1-3 mi:** Supermarket *(Dennis Public Market 385-3215, Super Foodmart 394-1240, Waldbaums 398-0783)*, Library *(Dennis Memorial 385-2255)*, Bookstore *(Armchair Bookstore 385-0900)*, Pharmacy *(CVS 394-0926)*, Hardware Store *(Just Ask Rental True Value 385-3666)*, Copies Etc. *(Mail Boxes & More 398-4400)*

Transportation
OnSite: Bikes *($10/day)* **OnCall:** Rental Car *(Enterprise 398-4555)* **1-3 mi:** InterCity Bus *(P&B 746-0378 Provincetown to Boston at Players Plaza)* **Airport:** Chatham/Provincetown *(14 mi./24 mi.)*

Medical Services
No 911 Service **Under 1 mi:** Doctor *(Walker 385-2211)*, Chiropractor *(Dixon 385-9895)* **Hospital:** Cape Cod 778-0505 *(11 mi.)*

Setting -- This full-service boatyard and marina is tucked into a basin accessed through a narrow, picturesque channel just off Cape Cod Bay. It is the first facility on the starboard side, just past the fuel docks. The views within the basin are largely of facilities and boats (depending on the tide), but walk to the edge of the incoming channel and there are spectacular views of the marsh, the jetties and the Bay beyond.

Marina Notes -- *Off season hours: Mon-Fri 9am-5pm, Closed Sat & Sun. The channel tends to shoal and can be quite shallow at low tide; call ahead for local knowledge. Full service boatyard has a moderately active dry stack facility as well as a 35T travelift and two forklifts. A few very well-placed picnic tables overlook the incoming channel and the Bay. Northside rents bikes for $10/day -- a great convenience. There are also some sport fishing charters, a canvas shop and Karl Anderson's sail loft (432-4488) onsite.

Notable -- Onsite is the Sesuit Harbor Café, a very low-key seafood shack and snack bar. Very near is the really lovely Harborview Beach that serves the quiet surrounding residential neighborhood. About three quarters of a mile inland, there is a small strip mall with a restaurant, Marshside, and a convenience store, Tedeschi. A mile farther is famous Captain Frosty's roadside clam shack - 385-8548 $3-13 - reputed to be one of the best.

PHOTOS ON CD-ROM: 4

Town of Dennis Marina

PO Box 1419; 351 Sesuit Neck Road; South Dennis, MA 02660

Tel: (508) 385-5555 **VHF: Monitor** 9 **Talk** 66
Fax: (508) 394-8309 **Alternate Tel:** (508) 760-6159
Email: denis@cape.com **Web:** www.vsj.cape.com/~dennis
Nearest Town: East Dennis **Tourist Info:** (508) 896-3500

Navigational Information

Lat: 41°45.136' **Long:** 070°09.121' **Tide:** 10 ft. **Current:** 1 kt. **Chart:** 13246
Rep. Depths (*MLW*): Entry 4 ft. **Fuel Dock** n/a **Max Slip/Moor** 6 ft./-
Access: Due south of the G "1S" buoy, past Northside docks

Marina Facilities *(In Season/Off Season)*

Fuel: No
Slips: 250 Total, 5 Transient **Max LOA:** 50 ft. **Max Beam:** n/a
Rate *(per ft.)*: **Day** $1.50/$1.00* **Week** Inq. **Month** n/a
Power: 30 amp $5, **50 amp** $5, **100 amp** n/a, **200 amp** n/a
Cable TV: No **Dockside Phone:** No
Dock Type: Wood, Long Fingers, Pilings, Floating
Moorings: 0 Total, 0 Transient **Launch:** n/a, Dinghy Dock
Rate: Day n/a **Week** n/a **Month** n/a
Heads: 2 Toilet(s), 2 Shower(s)
Laundry: None **Pay Phones:** No
Pump-Out: No **Fee:** n/a **Closed Heads:** No

Marina Operations

Owner/Manager: Ed Goggin, Jr. **Dockmaster:** Same
In-Season: May-Nov 1 **Off-Season:** Closed
After-Hours Arrival: Call ahead
Reservations: Yes, Preferred **Credit Cards:** Check or cash only
Discounts: None
Pets: Welcome **Handicap Access:** Yes, Heads, Docks

Marina Services and Boat Supplies

Supplies - Near: Ice *(Block, Cube, Shaved)*, Ships' Store, Live Bait **3+ mi:** West Marine *(15 mi.)*, Marine Discount Store *(Edwards Boatyard 540-9149, 7 mi.)*, Bait/Tackle *(Bass River Bait & Tackle 394-8666, 7 mi.)*, Propane *(Eastern Propane Gas 760-2778, 5 mi.)*

Boatyard Services

OnSite: Launching Ramp **Near:** Travelift *(20T)*, Engine mechanic *(gas, diesel)*, Electrical Repairs, Hull Repairs, Canvas Work, Bottom Cleaning, Brightwork, Divers, Compound, Wash & Wax. **3+ mi:** Electronic Sales *(7 mi.)*, Electronics Repairs *(7 mi.)*, Air Conditioning *(10 mi.)*, Refrigeration *(10 mi.)*, Interior Cleaning *(10 mi.)*, Propeller Repairs *(25 mi.)*. **Nearest Yard:** Northside Marina (508) 385-3936

Restaurants and Accommodations

Near: Snack Bar *(Sesuit Harbor Café 385-6134)* **Under 1 mi:** Restaurant *(Grumpys 385-2911)*, *(Marshside 385-4010, B $3-6, L $5-10, D $7-15, Overlooks Sesuit Creek)*, Snack Bar *(Lost Dog Public 385-6177)*, Motel *(Sesuit Harbor Motel 385-3326, $100)* **1-3 mi:** Seafood Shack *(Captain Frosty's Roadside Clam Shack 385-8548, L $3-13)*, Motel *(Briarcliffe Motel 385-3464)*, Inn/B&B *(Isaiah Hall B&B 385-9928, $110-165)*

Recreation and Entertainment

OnSite: Jogging Paths, Fishing Charter *(Lad-Nav 385-8150; Prime Rate 385-4626; Jeanie B 790-7820)*, Group Fishing Boat *(Albatross 835-3244 $25/18 half day)* **Near:** Beach *(Harborview Beach)* **Under 1 mi:** Tennis Courts *(Sesuit Tennis 385-2200)* **1-3 mi:** Golf Course *(Dennis Pines Golf Course 385-8347)*, Fitness Center *(Fitness Connection 385-2166)*, Horseback Riding *(Paradise Stables 398-5679)*, Movie Theater *(Cape Cinema 385-2503, 300 seat theater $7/4)*, Video Rental *(Entertainment & More 385-7666)*, Museum *(Cape Museum Of Fine Arts, 3.2 mi 385-4477, New England Fire And History Museum, 4.5 mi. 896-5711)* **3+ mi:** Bowling *(Ryan Amusement Co. 394-5644, 8 mi.)*, Park *(7 mi.)*

Provisioning and General Services

Near: Convenience Store *(Tedeschi 385-4858)* **Under 1 mi:** Wine/Beer *(East Dennis Bottled Liquors 385-2222)*, Fishmonger, Lobster Pound, Library *(East Dennis 385-8151)* **1-3 mi:** Supermarket *(Dennis Public Market 385-3215, Stop & Shop, 7 mi.)*, Bookstore *(Armchair Bookstore 385-0900)*, Pharmacy *(CVS 394-0926)*, Hardware Store *(Just Ask Rental True Value 385-3666)*, Copies Etc. *(Mail Boxes & More 398-4400)* **3+ mi:** Health Food *(Dennisport Natural Market 760-3043, 7 mi.)*, Liquor Store *(Seven Gs 385-9550, 4 mi.)*, Meat Market *(5 mi.)*, Catholic Church *(4 mi.)*, Barber Shop *(5 mi.)*, Dry Cleaners *(7 mi.)*

Transportation

OnCall: Rental Car *(Enterprise 398-4555)*, Taxi *(Admirality Of Cape Cod 760-1100)* **Under 1 mi:** InterCity Bus *(P&B 746-0378 Provincetown to Boston at Players Plaza)* **1-3 mi:** Bikes *(Barbara's 760-4723)* **Airport:** Barnstable/Chatham *(12 mi./14 mi.)*

Medical Services

No 911 Service **Under 1 mi:** Doctor *(Walker 385-2211)* **1-3 mi:** Chiropractor *(Dixon 385-9895)* **3+ mi:** Holistic Services *(Yarmouthport Massage Therapy 362-7101, 4 mi.)* **Hospital:** Cape Cod 778-0505 *(12 mi.)*

Setting -- This very large municipal facility completely fills the quiet, protected basin that is Sesuit Harbor. After passing the breakwater and traveling through the narrow, scenic channel, the water widens. Immediately to starboard is the fuel dock for Northside, then the Northside boatyard and docks. The remaining docks belong to the Town Marina.

Marina Notes -- *Summer $1.50/ft., Spring/Fall $1/ft., Late Fall, Winter, Early Spring $0.50/ft. The town facility includes about 250 slips that are divided between the east and west sides of the harbor. There is very little maneuvering room (turning radius is barely sufficient for a 40 ft. vessel), and limited services and facilities -- but good docks, water, power and impeccable protection. The basin narrows down to Sesuit Creek which offers an interesting dinghy ride. At the head, a small dock at the bridge base makes Tedeschi and Marshside quite convenient.

Notable -- Beautiful Harborview Beach is a short walk from the west side docks. If you are on the east side, there is another beach there, just at the breakwater. Neither has services; both are lovely and quiet. The Marshside restaurant and the convenience store are on the east side of Sesuit Creek, but a longer walk from the east side docks than the west ones because of road accessibility. Almost anything else will necessitate a taxi or bike rental. Cape Cinema is a real 1930's movie theater - The Wizard of Oz premiered here - a fine arts film house, worth a look. Cape Playhouse 385-3838 is a full equity theater with shows daily and a children's theater Friday morning.

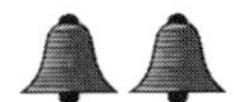

Town of Wellfleet Marina

300 Main Street; Wellfleet, MA 02667

Tel: (508) 349-0320 **VHF: Monitor** 9 **Talk** 16
Fax: (508) 349-0320 **Alternate Tel:** n/a
Email: marina98@gis.net **Web:** www.townofwellfleetmarina.com
Nearest Town: Wellfleet *(0.25 mi.)* **Tourist Info:** (508) 349-2510

Navigational Information

Lat: 41°55.789' **Long:** 070°01.697' **Tide:** 10 ft. **Current:** 1 kt. **Chart:** 13250
Rep. Depths (*MLW*): Entry 6 ft. **Fuel Dock** 6 ft. **Max Slip/Moor** 6 ft./6 ft.
Access: Cape Cod Bay to G1, follow channel into Wellfleet Harbor

Marina Facilities *(In Season/Off Season)*

Fuel: Gasoline, Diesel
Slips: 185 Total, 5 Transient **Max LOA:** 55 ft. **Max Beam:** 16 ft.
Rate *(per ft.)*: **Day** $2.15* **Week** n/a **Month** n/a
Power: 30 amp Incl., **50 amp** n/a, **100 amp** n/a, **200 amp** n/a
Cable TV: No **Dockside Phone:** No
Dock Type: Wood, Concrete, Floating
Moorings: 200 Total, 15 Transient **Launch:** Yes (Free), Dinghy Dock
Rate: Day $25/20 **Week** Inq. **Month** n/a
Heads: Toilet(s), 2 Shower(s)
Laundry: None **Pay Phones:** Yes, 2
Pump-Out: OnCall, Full Service **Fee:** n/a **Closed Heads:** Yes

Marina Operations

Owner/Manager: Michael Flanagan (Harbormaster) **Dockmaster:** n/a
In-Season: May 15-Oct 15, 24 hrs. **Off-Season:** Oct 16-May 14, 8am-5pm
After-Hours Arrival: Call in advance
Reservations: Yes **Credit Cards:** Cash or check
Discounts: None
Pets: Welcome **Handicap Access:** Yes, Heads, Docks

Marina Services and Boat Supplies

Services - Trash Pick-Up **Supplies - OnSite:** Ice *(Block, Cube)*, Ships' Store *(Wellfleet Marine 349-6417)*, Bait/Tackle, Live Bait **3+ mi:** Propane *(Maurice's Market 349-9245, 5 mi.)*

Boatyard Services

OnSite: Engine mechanic *(gas, diesel)*, Launching Ramp **Under 1 mi:** Hull Repairs.

Restaurants and Accommodations

OnSite: Restaurant *(Capt Higgins Seafood 349-6027, L $4-11, D $13-20)*, Seafood Shack *(Mac's Seafood 349-0404, D $10-15, 7 days 10am-8pm)*, Snack Bar *(Harbor Grill 349-9611, L $3-10, 11am-4pm takeout)* **OnCall:** Pizzeria *(High Toss Pizza 349-0005)* **Near:** Restaurant *(Book Store & Restaurant 349-3154, seafood grill)*, *(Flying Fish Café 349-3100, B $4-7, D $11-19)*, Seafood Shack *(Bayside Lobster Hutt 349-6055, BYOB)*, Snack Bar *(Uncle Frank's early am breakfast)*, Inn/B&B *(Blue Gateways 349-7530, $90-120)* **Under 1 mi:** Restaurant *(Aesop's Tables 349-6450, L $7-16, D $15-25)*, Seafood Shack *(Moby Dick's 349-9795, L $8-19, D $8-19, kids' menu)*, Motel *(Duck Creeke Inn 349-9333, $65-95)* **1-3 mi:** Motel *(Southfleet Motor Inn 349-3580, $62-150)*, Inn/B&B *(Holden Inn 349-3450, $55-150)*

Recreation and Entertainment

OnSite: Beach *(or hike to Cahoon Hollow for surf 349-6055)*, Boat Rentals *(Wellfleet Marine 349-2233)*, Fishing Charter *(Jac's 225-2978, Snoop 349-6113)*, Group Fishing Boat *(Naviator 349-6003)*, Sightseeing *(2 hr. cruise to 1,000 acre Wellfleet Bay Wildlife Sanctuary 349-2615)*, Special Events *(Square Dance, Wed 7pm, free; youth concerts Fri)* **Near:** Playground, Museum *(Wellfleet Historical Soc Museum 349-9157; Marconi Site)*, Galleries *(Wellfleet Gallery Crawl Sat eves in Summer- more than a dozen galleries)* **Under 1 mi:** Roller Blade/Bike Paths *(Rail Trail 896-3491 25 mi. to So. Dennis)*, Cultural Attract *(Wellfleet Harbor Actors Theater 349-6835 $18)* **1-3 mi:** Tennis Courts *(Oliver Tennis Courts 349-3330)*, Golf Course *(Chequessett C C 349-3704)*, Movie Theater *(Wellfleet Drive-In & Wellfleet Cinema 349-7176)*, Video Rental *(Video Stuga 349-9253)*

Provisioning and General Services

OnSite: Fishmonger *(Mac's Seafood - sushi, takeout 349-9611)* **Near:** Delicatessen *(Flying Fish Café & Deli 349-3100)*, Bakery, Green Grocer, Lobster Pound, Bank/ATM, Catholic Church, Protestant Church, Library *(Wellfleet PL 349-0310 Internet access)*, Newsstand, Hardware Store *(Mid-Cape Home Centers 349-3734)*, Florist, Retail Shops **Under 1 mi:** Convenience Store, Supermarket *(Lema's 349-3156)*, Gourmet Shop, Post Office **1-3 mi:** Wine/Beer *(Wellfleet Wine Cellar 349-6880)*, Liquor Store *(Wellfleet Spirits 349-3731)*, Beauty Salon, Barber Shop **3+ mi:** Pharmacy *(Ptown or Orleans)*

Transportation

OnCall: Rental Car *(Enterprise 255-2997)* **Near:** Bikes *(Wellfleet Cycles 349-9322)*, InterCity Bus *(P&B 746-0378 Provincetown to Boston at Town Hall)* **3+ mi:** Taxi *(Vintage Limousine 349-0934, 5 mi.)* **Airport:** Provincetown *(15 mi.)*

Medical Services

911 Service **Under 1 mi:** Doctor *(Outer Cape Health 349-3131)*, Dentist, Ambulance **Hospital:** Cape Cod, Hyannis 778-0505 *(30 mi.)*

Setting -- Tucked into picturesque Wellfleet Harbor, behind Shirttail Point, this is one of the most easily accessible marinas on the Cape's northern shore, and one of the most protected. The harbor is a comfortable mix of working boats and pleasure craft, and still hosts an active fishing industry. The small, quiet town of Wellfleet is known for its art galleries, beaches and resorts.

Marina Notes -- *Rate is actually a flat $35 for the first 30 feet and additional $2/ft. over that. Dockage is stern-to, no finger piers. Note: the harbor has recently been dredged and is now accessible throughout all the tides. All moorings are now town operated, but owned by Bay Sails and Wellfleet Marina. Launch service 7 days 8am-7pm included in fee - loaner dinghies provided to row at other times. Assistant Harbormaster is Paul Lindberg. Pump-out Boat 349-0320. Onsite Captain Higgins restaurant overlooks the docks and offers a varied seafood menu and inside and outside dining; Mac's Seafood, Harbor Grill and Uncle Frank's also onsite.

Notable -- Wellfleet dominated the oyster business in the 19thC. Today you can harvest shellfish from the waters with a permit - office onsite. Flea Market at the Wellfleet Drive-in Sat, Sun, Wed, Thu. Audubon's Society's Wildlife Sanctuary offers over 5 mi. of hiking trails as well as field walks, cruises and guided tours (7 days, 8am-8pm, $3/2). Marconi Station area of the Cape Cod Nat'l. Sea Shore (home to the first transatlantic broadcast) is a bit of a hike. Mayo Beach onsite; closest Nat'l. Sea Shore beach is about 2.5 mi. About the same to head of Cape Cod Rail Trail - extended here in mid 90's.

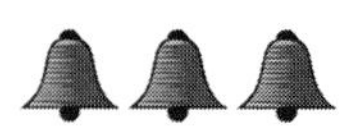

Provincetown Yacht Marina

PO Box 493; 16 MacMillan Wharf; Provincetown, MA 02657

Tel: (508) 487-4602 **VHF: Monitor** 9 **Talk** 12
Fax: n/a **Alternate Tel:** (508) 487-8899
Email: n/a **Web:** n/a
Nearest Town: Provincetown **Tourist Info:** (508) 487-3424

Navigational Information
Lat: 42°03.000' **Long:** 070°10.967' **Tide:** 12 ft. **Current:** 1 kt. **Chart:** 13249
Rep. Depths (*MLW*): Entry 20 ft. **Fuel Dock** n/a **Max Slip/Moor** 15 ft./-
Access: Cape Cod Bay to Long Point; inside breakwater to east docks

Marina Facilities *(In Season/Off Season)*
Fuel: No
Slips: 14 Total, 6 Transient **Max LOA:** 120 ft. **Max Beam:** 35 ft.
Rate *(per ft.)*: **Day** $4.00/Inq. **Week** $3 **Month** n/a
Power: 30 amp $5, **50 amp** $10, **100 amp** $15, **200 amp** n/a
Cable TV: No **Dockside Phone:** No
Dock Type: Long Fingers, Concrete, Floating
Moorings: 0 Total, 0 Transient **Launch:** n/a
Rate: Day n/a **Week** n/a **Month** n/a
Heads: 1 Toilet(s), 1 Shower(s) *(with dressing rooms)*
Laundry: None **Pay Phones:** No
Pump-Out: OnCall, Full Service, 1 Port **Fee:** Free **Closed Heads:** No

Marina Operations
Owner/Manager: Ken Kincor **Dockmaster:** Same
In-Season: May 15-Nov 1 **Off-Season:** n/a
After-Hours Arrival: Call in advance
Reservations: Yes, Required **Credit Cards:** Visa/MC
Discounts: $1 less for long slip **Dockage:** n/a **Fuel:** n/a **Repair:** n/a
Pets: Welcome **Handicap Access:** Yes, Heads, Docks

Marina Services and Boat Supplies
Services - Docking Assistance **Communication -** FedEx, AirBorne, UPS, Express Mail *(Sat Del)* **Supplies - OnSite:** Ice *(Block, Cube)* **Near:** Ships' Store, Bait/Tackle *(Nelsons Bait & Tackle 487-0034)*, Propane *(Days FA & Sons 487-0041)*

Boatyard Services
OnSite: Divers **OnCall:** Engine mechanic *(gas, diesel)*, Electrical Repairs, Electronic Sales, Electronics Repairs, Hull Repairs, Bottom Cleaning, Brightwork, Propeller Repairs, Metal Fabrication **Near:** Travelift, Launching Ramp, Rigger. **1-3 mi:** Sail Loft, Canvas Work.

Restaurants and Accommodations
OnSite: Restaurant *(The Surf Restaurant 487-1367, L $5-10, D $5-$16, very casual, at the foot of MacMillan Pier)* **Near:** Restaurant *(Napis 487-1145, D $13-25)*, *(Ciro & Sal's 487-6444, D $14-26)*, *(Stormy Harbor 487-1680)*, *(The Lobster Pot 487-0842, L $7-12, D $10-18)*, *(Red Inn 487-0050, D $19-25)*, Pizzeria *(George's 487-3744)*, Motel *(Best Inn 487-1711, $75-170)*, Inn/B&B *(Anchor Inn Beach House 487-0432, $95-375)*, *(Crowne Point Historic Inn 487-6767, $185-395)*

Recreation and Entertainment
OnSite: Fishing Charter *(Ginny G 246-3656)*, Group Fishing Boat *(CeeJay 487-4330)*, Sightseeing *(Expedition Whydah Sea Lab 487-8899 $5/3.50; Whale watching cruises - BHC, Dolphin Fleet)* **Near:** Fitness Center *(Ptown Gym 487-2776)*, Jogging Paths, Boat Rentals, Roller Blade/Bike Paths, Movie Theater *(New Art 487-9222)* **Under 1 mi:** Beach *(Race Point Beach - "non-denominational" 487-1256)*, Video Rental *(City Video 487-4493)*, Park, Museum *(Pilgrim Monument & Provincetown Museum 487-1310)* **1-3 mi:** Tennis Courts *(Ptown Tennis 487-9574)*, Horseback Riding *(Bayberry Hollow Farm 487-6584)* **3+ mi:** Golf Course *(Highland G. C. 487-9201, 5 mi.)*

Provisioning and General Services
OnSite: Fishmonger **Near:** Convenience Store, Health Food *(Lembas-Health Foods 487-9784)*, Wine/Beer *(Perry's Liquors 487-0140)*, Liquor Store, Bank/ATM, Post Office, Laundry *(Mama's Cleaners 487-4941)*, Hardware Store *(Lands End Marine Supply 487-0784)* **Under 1 mi:** Supermarket *(A&P 487-4903, Super Foodmart 487-4903, Stop & Shop)*, Gourmet Shop, Delicatessen, Bakery, Lobster Pound, Meat Market, Catholic Church, Library *(Provincetown 487-7094)*, Beauty Salon, Barber Shop, Dry Cleaners, Bookstore *(Provincetown Bookshop 487-0964)*, Pharmacy *(A&P Pharmacy 487-3738)*, Newsstand, Florist, Retail Shops, Copies Etc. *(Mail Spot 487-6650)*

Transportation
OnSite: Bikes *($15/day)*, InterCity Bus *(P&B to Boston 746-0378 $45 RT)*, Ferry Service *(to Boston: Bay State 487-9284, fast & slow; Boston Harbor Cruises 617-227-4321, fast ferry $30-40 RT; Capt John to Plymouth $27 RT)* **OnCall:** Rental Car *(Rod's Auto 487-1539, Enterprise 487-0009)*, Taxi *(Mercedes Cab 487-3333, Provincetown Taxi 487-8294)* **Near:** Local Bus *(The Shuttle 385-8326 $1/.50)* **Airport:** Provincetown *(2 mi.)*

Medical Services
911 Service **OnCall:** Ambulance **Near:** Doctor *(Outer Cape Health 487-9395)*, Holistic Services **Under 1 mi:** Dentist, Chiropractor *(Provincetown Chiropractor 487-3800)* **Hospital:** Cape Cod 778-0505 *(31 mi.)*

Setting -- In the heart of Provincetown, this small big-boat marina makes all of this amazing seaside "village" easily accessible. An attractive shingle-sided building sits at the end of the recently refurbished MacMillan Pier and the docks surround it. The facility is far out on the pier affording spectacular views of both Provincetown and the harbor. This is also home to Provincetown's fishing fleet so you can watch the unloading of the catch.

Marina Notes -- Reservations canceled 48 hours prior get full refund, 24 hours prior half refund. Facilities are limited, but the location makes up for it. A full service laundry is about a quarter of a mile walk. Bike rentals are onsite. The shingled "headquarters" also houses the Expedition Whydah Pirate Museum, SeaLab and Learning Center 487-8899 -- home to the worlds' only pirate shipwreck treasure: 1717 Whydah. This is a National Geographic "Special Event" archeological mission (7 days in season 10am-8pm). Harbormaster: 487-7030.

Notable -- Three whale-watching trips leave from MacMillan Wharf: Cape Cod Whale Watch, 3 hrs, Adventurer, 10am, 1:30, 5pm $19/12 487-4079. Dolphin Fleet, 3-4 hrs, $19-20/16-17 800-826-9300. Portuguese Princess offers 3.5 hr. naturalist-conducted excursions 487-2651. Pilgrim Monument and Provincetown Museum are very close 7 days, 9am-7pm, $6/3 487-1310. Shuttle to Long Point leaves Slip 2 at half past hour 10am-6pm $10RT (487-0898). The spectacular National Seashore Herring Cove Beach is easily accessible via the Provincetown Shuttle 385-8326.

PHOTOS ON CD-ROM: 6

Navigational Information
Lat: 42°02.930' **Long:** 070°10.971' **Tide:** 12 ft. **Current:** 1 kt. **Chart:** 13249
Rep. Depths (*MLW*): Entry 13 ft. **Fuel Dock** 5 ft. **Max Slip/Moor** 14 ft./30 ft.
Access: Cape Cod Bay to Long Point; inside breakwater to west docks

Marina Facilities *(In Season/Off Season)*
Fuel: *Citgo* - Gasoline, Diesel
Slips: 30 Total, 30 Transient **Max LOA:** 75 ft. **Max Beam:** 20 ft.
Rate *(per ft.)*: **Day** $2.00/Inq.* **Week** Inq. **Month** Inq.
Power: 30 amp Incl., **50 amp** Incl., **100 amp** n/a, **200 amp** n/a
Cable TV: No **Dockside Phone:** No
Dock Type: Long Fingers, Concrete
Moorings: 100 Total, 50 Transient **Launch:** Yes (Free), Dinghy Dock
Rate: Day $35-50* **Week** $300/week **Month** $200/week
Heads: 6 Toilet(s), 6 Shower(s)
Laundry: None **Pay Phones:** Yes
Pump-Out: OnCall, Full Service, 1 Port **Fee:** Free **Closed Heads:** No

Marina Operations
Owner/Manager: Beth Townsend **Dockmaster:** n/a
In-Season: MemDay-ColDay, 24 hrs. **Off-Season:** Closed
After-Hours Arrival: Call in advance
Reservations: Yes, Preferred **Credit Cards:** Visa/MC
Discounts: None
Pets: Welcome **Handicap Access:** Yes, Heads, Docks

Provincetown Marina

PO Box 1042; Ryder Street Ext.; Provincetown, MA 02657

Tel: (508) 487-0571 **VHF: Monitor** 9 **Talk** 8
Fax: (508) 487-0571 **Alternate Tel:** n/a
Email: n/a **Web:** n/a
Nearest Town: Provincetown *(0 mi.)* **Tourist Info:** (508) 487-3424

Marina Services and Boat Supplies
Services - Docking Assistance, Security *(24 Hrs., Night watch)* **Communication -** Mail & Package Hold, FedEx, UPS **Supplies - OnSite:** Ice *(Cube)* **Near:** Ships' Store *(Lands End Marine Supply 487-0784)*, Bait/Tackle *(Nelsons Bait & Tackle 487-0034)* **Under 1 mi:** Propane *(National Propane 487-0855)*

Boatyard Services
OnSite: Divers **OnCall:** Engine mechanic *(gas, diesel)*, Air Conditioning, Refrigeration **Near:** Travelift. **Under 1 mi:** Launching Ramp.

Restaurants and Accommodations
Near: Restaurant *(Napis 487-1145, D $13-25)*, *(Front Street 487-9715, L $10-15, D $15-25)*, *(Dancing Lobster 487-0900, L $7-15, D $15-35)*, *(Lobster Pot 487-0842, L $7-12, D $10-18)*, Pizzeria *(George's Pizza 487-3744)*, Motel *(Best Western Chateau 487-1286, $100-220)*, Inn/B&B *(White Wind Inn 487-1526, $75-225)*, *(Somerset House 487-0383, $75-130)*, *(Crown & Anchor Inn 487-1430)*, *(Crown Pointe Historic Inn 487-6767, $115-400)*

Recreation and Entertainment
Near: Pool *(Ptown Inn 487-9500)*, Jogging Paths, Boat Rentals, Roller Blade/Bike Paths *(Province Lands)*, Fishing Charter, Group Fishing Boat, Movie Theater *(New Art Cinema 487-9222; Best Inn 487-1711 - free movies every night)*, Museum *(Pilgrim Monument 487-1077, Provincetown Museum 487-1310 7days, 9am-7pm)*, Special Events *(Portuguese Fest, Jun)* **Under 1 mi:** Beach *(Race Point 487-1256 - "universal")*, Fitness Center *(Ptown Gym 487-2776)*, Video Rental *(City Video 487-4493)*, Sightseeing *(Trolley/Sand dune tours, Whale watching tours)* **1-3 mi:** Tennis Courts *(Bissell Tennis Courts 487-9512)*, Horseback Riding *(Bayberry Hollow Farm 487-6584)*, Park **3+ mi:** Golf Course *(5 mi.)*

Provisioning and General Services
Near: Convenience Store *(Provincetown General Store 487-0300)*, Gourmet Shop, Delicatessen *(Nelson's Market & Deli 487-4335)*, Health Food *(Lembas Health Foods 487-9784)*, Wine/Beer *(Yardarm Liquors 487-0700)*, Liquor Store *(Big Vins 487-0635)*, Bakery, Meat Market, Bank/ATM, Post Office, Catholic Church, Protestant Church, Library *(Provincetown 487-7094)*, Beauty Salon, Barber Shop, Bookstore *(Provincetown Bookshop 487-0964)*, Pharmacy *(Adams Pharmacy 487-0069)*, Newsstand, Hardware Store *(Conwell Lumber 487-0150)*, Florist, Retail Shops, Copies Etc. *(Advantage Print & Mail 487-1709)* **Under 1 mi:** Supermarket *(A&P 487-4903)*, Fishmonger, Lobster Pound

Transportation
OnSite: Bikes, Water Taxi, InterCity Bus *(P&B 746-0378 Provincetown to Boston)* **OnCall:** Rental Car *(Enterprise 747-1212, Thrifty 487-9418)*, Taxi *(Atlantic Sam's Taxi 487-7777, Cape Cab 487-2222)* **Near:** Local Bus *(The Shuttle 385-8326)*, Ferry Service *(Boston Harbor Cruises 617-227-4321 $30-40 RT; Boston Bay State 487-9284 $28/20 1-Way; Plymouth via Capt John 747-2400)* **Airport:** Provincetown *(2 mi.)*

Medical Services
911 Service **Near:** Holistic Services, Ambulance **Under 1 mi:** Doctor *(Outer Cape Health 487-9395)*, Dentist *(Provincetown Dental Assoc. 487-9936)*, Chiropractor *(Provincetown Chiropractor 487-3800)* **Hospital:** Cape Cod 778-0505 *(32 mi.)*

Setting -- Provincetown's largest and most complete marina facility is stretched along Fisherman's Wharf in the center of the village. There are two piers that reach out into Provincetown Harbor from "downtown": Fisherman's Wharf, the more western of the two, and MacMillan Wharf, which parallels it to the east. Provincetown Marina's mooring fields are to the south and to the west. From either the docks or the moorings, there are spectacular vistas of this timeless village and beautiful harbor -- especially at sunset.

Marina Notes -- *Slips are $2/ft. but there is an $80 minimum. Moorings are $35/night, $200/wk up to 50', $50/night, $300/wk over 50'. Launch service is provided and included in the fee -- Weekdays 8am-11pm, Sat & Sun 8am-Mid, Jun - LabDay. The heads and shower stalls are wooden but nicely maintained. Docks are half wood and half cement, with a mix of older and newer pedestals. The Fast Ferry to Boston's Rowes Wharf leaves from here (while convenient, it is also people heavy).

Notable -- The National Seashore is about a mile on the other side of the peninsula -- easily accessible by bike, trolley, shuttle or on foot, and the beaches are really wonderful - extensive biking, hiking and riding trails. Three whale-watching trips leave from MacMillan Wharf next door: Cape Cod Whale Watch, 3 hrs.; Adventurer, 10am, 1:30, 5pm $19/12 487-4079; Dolphin Fleet, 3-4 hrs, $19-20/16-17 800-826-9300. Or try the 3.5 hrs. naturalist-conducted excursions onboard the Portuguese Princess 487-2651. Province Lands - 8 miles of bike paths through 4,000 diverse acres - starts in less than 1 mile.

PHOTOS ON CD-ROM: 5

Flyer's Boat Rental

PO Box 561; 131A Commercial Street; Provincetown, MA 02657

Tel: (508) 487-0898; (800) 750-0898 **VHF: Monitor** 9 **Talk** 11
Fax: (508) 487-3875 **Alternate Tel:** (508) 487-0898
Email: flyers@capecod.net **Web:** www.flyersrentals.com
Nearest Town: Provincetown *(0.25 mi.)* **Tourist Info:** (508) 487-3424

Navigational Information

Lat: 42°02.734' **Long:** 070°11.460' **Tide:** 10 ft. **Current:** 1 kt. **Chart:** 13249
Rep. Depths (*MLW*): Entry 18 ft. **Fuel Dock** n/a **Max Slip/Moor** -/15 ft.
Access: Long Point, cross harbor bearing WNW, 1.4 miles to inner harbor

Marina Facilities *(In Season/Off Season)*

Fuel: No
Slips: 0 Total, 0 Transient **Max LOA:** n/a **Max Beam:** n/a
Rate *(per ft.)*: **Day** n/a **Week** n/a **Month** n/a
Power: 30 amp n/a, **50 amp** n/a, **100 amp** n/a, **200 amp** n/a
Cable TV: No **Dockside Phone:** No
Dock Type: n/a
Moorings: 50 Total, 18 Transient **Launch:** Yes (Free), Dinghy Dock
Rate: Day $40 **Week** $200 **Month** Inq.
Heads: 3 Toilet(s), 2 Shower(s) *(with dressing rooms)*
Laundry: 1 Washer(s), 1 Dryer(s) **Pay Phones:** Yes, 1
Pump-Out: OnCall, Full Service, 1 Central **Fee:** n/a **Closed Heads:** No

Marina Operations

Owner/Manager: Ann Colbourn **Dockmaster:** Rex McKinsey
In-Season: May 15-Oct 15, 8am-6 pm **Off-Season:** n/a, 9am-4pm
After-Hours Arrival: Pick-up mooring by Coast Guard piers - look for sign
Reservations: Yes, Preferred **Credit Cards:** Debit Cards or Cash
Discounts: None
Pets: Welcome **Handicap Access:** Yes, Heads

Marina Services and Boat Supplies

Services - Docking Assistance **Communication -** Mail & Package Hold, Phone Messages, Fax in/out, Data Ports *(Office)*, FedEx, AirBorne, UPS, Express Mail *(Sat Del)* **Supplies - OnSite:** Ice *(Block)* **Near:** Bait/Tackle *(Nelson's Bait 487-0034)*, Propane *(Days & Sons 487-0041)*

Boatyard Services

OnSite: Railway, Forklift, Engine mechanic *(gas, diesel)*, Electrical Repairs, Electronic Sales, Electronics Repairs, Hull Repairs, Rigger, Bottom Cleaning, Brightwork, Divers, Compound, Wash & Wax, Interior Cleaning, Propeller Repairs, Woodworking, Inflatable Repairs, Painting, Awlgrip, Total Refits **Near:** Launching Ramp. **Dealer for:** Evinrude, Johnson.

Restaurants and Accommodations

Near: Restaurant *(Sal's by the Sea 487-1279, D $13-22, Italian)*, *(Martin House 487-1327, D $14-28)*, *(Red Inn Restaurant 487-0050, D $19-25)*, *(Gallerani's Café 487-4433, D $12-25)*, *(The Moors 487-0840, D $12-22)*, Seafood Shack *(Silva's 487-1574, D $5-14)*, Motel *(BW Chateau 487-1286, $140-220)*, *(Masthead 487-0523, $65-355, variety of accommodations, plus moorings and launch)*, Inn/B&B *(Provincetown Inn 487-9500, $140-330)*

Recreation and Entertainment

OnSite: Beach, Boat Rentals *(Kayaks singles $40/day, doubles $50; rowboats & canoes $40)* **Near:** Tennis Courts *(Bissell 487-9512)*, Fitness Center *(Mussel Beach 487-0001)*, Jogging Paths, Horseback Riding *(Bayberry Hollow Farm 487-6584)*, Group Fishing Boat, Special Events *(Portuguese Days, June)* **Under 1 mi:** Movie Theater, Video Rental *(City Video 487-4493)*, Park, Museum *(Pilgrim Monument & Provincetown Museum 487-1310)*, Cultural Attract *(Provincetown Art Association & Museum, Campus Provincetown)* **1-3 mi:** Picnic Area, Golf Course *(Highland G. C. 487-9201)*, Sightseeing *(National Seashore self-guided nature trails 487-1256)*

Provisioning and General Services

Near: Convenience Store *(Provincetown General Store 487-0300)*, Delicatessen *(Cheese Market and Deli 487-3032)*, Bakery, Fishmonger, Lobster Pound, Newsstand **Under 1 mi:** Supermarket *(A&P 487-4903)*, Liquor Store *(Perrys Liquors 487-0140)*, Farmers' Market, Post Office, Catholic Church, Protestant Church, Library *(Provincetown 487-7094)*, Beauty Salon, Barber Shop, Dry Cleaners, Laundry, Bookstore *(Provincetown Bookshop 487-0964)*, Pharmacy *(A&P Pharmacy 487-3738)*, Hardware Store *(Lands End Marine Supply 487-0784)*, Copies Etc. *(The Mail Spot 487-6650)* **1-3 mi:** Health Food *(Lembas-Health Foods 487-9784)*

Transportation

OnSite: Water Taxi *($5 min/$2pp)* **OnCall:** Rental Car *(Enterprise 487-0009, Thrifty 487-9418)*, Taxi *(Mercedes Cab 487-3333)* **Near:** Bikes *(Beach Market Bike Rentals 487-4849)*, Local Bus *(Ptown Trolley or Shuttle)* **Under 1 mi:** InterCity Bus *(P&B 746-0378 Provincetown to Boston)*, Ferry Service *(Boston-Plymouth & Gloucester)* **Airport:** Provincetown/Barnstable *(1 mi./30 mi.)*

Medical Services

911 Service **OnCall:** Ambulance **Under 1 mi:** Doctor *(Alberts 487-9395)*, Dentist, Chiropractor *(Provincetown Chiropractor 487-3800)* **Hospital:** Cape Cod 778-0505 *(30 mi.)*

Setting -- For over fifty years, this unique, service-oriented establishment -- on the western edge of the Provincetown waterfront just east of the Coast Guard Station -- has been providing a wide variety of marine services. Its mooring field offers great views of Provincetown and Long Point.

Marina Notes -- Seasonal and Transient moorings with launch and a dinghy dock. Call ahead as mooring field is often full. The launch will deliver guests to either their dock or to MacMillan Wharf in the heart of the village. Harbor launch service is also available to anchored boats. Onsite Sailing School - Beginner to Bare Boat. Ships' store has a complete line of OMC parts; also onsite marine mechanic, emergency assistance - towing, battery boost, etc. Heads and showers are complete new bathrooms.

Notable -- There is an onsite shuttle, in a large pontoon boat, to Long Point (the tip of the Cape) $12 RT -- good beach walk or day-long picnic excursion. Weekly rentals of onsite 3-4 bedroom apartment with harbor views 487-3064. Boat rentals also onsite -- variety of sailboats 10-20 ft. $50-100/day, sea kayaks and rowboats $40/day, power boats, 16-17 ft. $90+/day. All of Provincetown is easily available from here and Herring Cove Beach is a reasonable walk -- or take the P-Town shuttle, which stops a block away. Tour the Stellwagen Bank Marine Sanctuary. Bike Province Land's trails through 4,000 acres of dunes, bogs, and to the beaches.

PHOTOS ON CD-ROM: 4

Navigational Information

Lat: 41°39.994' **Long:** 069°58.011' **Tide:** 4 ft. **Current:** n/a **Chart:** 13229
Rep. Depths (*MLW*): Entry 10 ft. **Fuel Dock** 6 ft. **Max Slip/Moor** 8 ft./12 ft.
Access: Chatham Roads to G1/R2, follow the Stage Harbor Channel

Marina Facilities *(In Season/Off Season)*

Fuel: Gasoline, Diesel
Slips: 30 Total, 3 Transient **Max LOA:** 115 ft. **Max Beam:** n/a
Rate *(per ft.)*: **Day** $2.00/$1.50 **Week** Inq. **Month** Inq.
Power: 30 amp Incl., **50 amp** n/a, **100 amp** n/a, **200 amp** n/a
Cable TV: No **Dockside Phone:** No
Dock Type: Wood, Short Fingers, Pilings, Alongside, Floating
Moorings: 44 Total, 10 Transient **Launch:** Yes (Free), Dinghy Dock
Rate: Day $35/25 **Week** $190/150 **Month** n/a
Heads: 2 Toilet(s)
Laundry: None **Pay Phones:** Yes
Pump-Out: OnCall, Full Service, 1 Central **Fee:** n/a **Closed Heads:** No

Marina Operations

Owner/Manager: Andrew Meincke **Dockmaster:** n/a
In-Season: Year-Round, 8am-5pm **Off-Season:** n/a
After-Hours Arrival: Call in advance
Reservations: Preferred **Credit Cards:** Visa/MC, Amex
Discounts: None
Pets: Welcome **Handicap Access:** No

Stage Harbor Marine

PO Box 646; 80 Bridge Street; Chatham, MA 02633

Tel: (508) 945-1860 **VHF: Monitor** 9 **Talk** 8
Fax: (508) 945-2522 **Alternate Tel:** n/a
Email: andy@stageharbormarine.com **Web:** www.stageharbormarine.com
Nearest Town: Chatham *(1 mi.)* **Tourist Info:** (805) 945-5199

Marina Services and Boat Supplies

Services - Docking Assistance, Trash Pick-Up, Dock Carts **Communication -** Phone Messages, Fax in/out *(Free)*, FedEx, AirBorne, UPS, Express Mail **Supplies - OnSite:** Ice *(Block, Cube)*, Ships' Store **Under 1 mi:** Bait/Tackle **1-3 mi:** Propane *(Cape Cod 945-7516)*

Boatyard Services

OnSite: Engine mechanic *(gas)*, Launching Ramp, Electronic Sales, Hull Repairs, Rigger, Bottom Cleaning, Brightwork, Divers, Compound, Wash & Wax, Interior Cleaning, Woodworking, Painting **OnCall:** Engine mechanic *(diesel)*, Electrical Repairs, Canvas Work, Propeller Repairs, Inflatable Repairs, Life Raft Service **Under 1 mi:** Upholstery, Yacht Interiors, Awlgrip. **1-3 mi:** Electronics Repairs, Metal Fabrication. **Dealer for:** Stamas Yachts, Cobra, Beacon Boats, Edgewater, Mercury. **Yard Rates:** $60/hr., Haul & Launch $5/ft., Power Wash $4, Bottom Paint $12/ft. *(paint included)* **Storage:** On-Land $19/ft.

Restaurants and Accommodations

Under 1 mi: Restaurant *(Dogfish Café 945-6100)*, *(Chatham Squire 945-0942, L $5-12, D $10-22)*, *(Impudent Oyster 945-3545, L $6-12, D $14-25)*, *(Christian's 945-3362, D $8-22)*, *(Chatham Bars Inn 945-0096, B $15, D $20-34)*, *(Sosumi 945-0300, D $15-24, Asian, sushi bar)*, Motel *(Wayside 945-5550, $95-365)*, *(Town House Inn 945-2180, $165-425)*, Inn/B&B *(Chatham Bars Inn 800-527-4884, $150-400)*, *(Bradford Inn 945-1030, $105-425)*

Recreation and Entertainment

OnSite: Fishing Charter **OnCall:** Sightseeing *(Beach Comber Seal Watch 945-5265)* **Near:** Jogging Paths **Under 1 mi:** Beach *(Dinghy)*, Picnic Area, Grills, Playground, Fitness Center *(Allez Fitness & Spa 945-5595)*, Boat Rentals, Park, Museum *(Atwood House 945-2493 $3)* **1-3 mi:** Pool, Tennis Courts *(Queen Anne Tennis 945-4726)*, Golf Course *(Seaside Links 945-4774)*, Horseback Riding *(Hidden Valley Stables 945-1283)*, Roller Blade/Bike Paths, Group Fishing Boat, Movie Theater, Cultural Attract *(Monomoy Theater Ohio U Players 945-1589)*

Provisioning and General Services

Under 1 mi: Convenience Store, Supermarket *(A&P 945-2993)*, Delicatessen *(Amaras 945-5777)*, Meat Market, Bank/ATM, Post Office, Beauty Salon, Laundry, Bookstore *(Yellow Umbrella 945-0144)*, Pharmacy *(CVS 945-4340)*, Newsstand, Florist **1-3 mi:** Gourmet Shop *(Pampered Palate 945-3663)*, Health Food *(Natural Foods 945-4139)*, Wine/Beer, Liquor Store *(Light Liquors 945-2826)*, Bakery, Farmers' Market *(Veterans Park Tue 8am-noon)*, Fishmonger, Lobster Pound, Catholic Church, Library *(Eldredge 945-5170)*, Dry Cleaners, Copies Etc. *(Madison Printing 982-1911)* **3+ mi:** Hardware Store *(Chatham 945-0107, 4 mi.)*

Transportation

OnSite: Water Taxi *($10/pp)* **Under 1 mi:** Taxi *(Chatham Taxi 945-0068)*, InterCity Bus *(H2O Hyannis-Orleans, stops at rotary in town)* **1-3 mi:** Bikes *(Bikes & Blades 945-7600)* **3+ mi:** Rental Car *(Thrifty 945-5891 2 mi./Enterprise 759-2299)* **Airport:** Hyannis/Barnstable *(20 mi./25 mi.)*

Medical Services

911 Service **OnCall:** Ambulance **Under 1 mi:** Dentist *(Chatham Dental 945-0207)*, Holistic Services **1-3 mi:** Doctor *(Gaunya Group 945-4101)*, Chiropractor *(Chatham 945-3131)* **Hospital:** Cape Cod 771-6776 *(24 mi.)*

Setting -- Situated at the head of protected Stage Harbor near the Mitchell River Bridge, this full service marina & boatyard provides a good base for offshore fishing or runs up the outside. A little off the beaten path, the harbor is a nice mix of pleasure and working craft; it's home to active scallop draggers and trap fishers. The surrounding town of Chatham is quintessential classic, elegant and charming Cape Cod - and a destination in itself.

Marina Notes -- Very well-supplied ships' store onsite and full service boatyard. Hauling up to 45 feet with inside and outside storage. Dealer for Stamas Yachts, Cobia, Beacon Boats, Edgewater, Mercury Motors. Dinghy further up the Mitchell River into Mill Pond to get closer to services and provisioning resources. There's a convenient, often filled, town landing. Internet access at Eldridge Library. Harbormaster: 945-5185

Notable -- Beachcomber Seal Watching picks up here for a look at pinheads in their natural habitat, as well as excursions to area beaches and wildlife habitats 10am-4pm, $18/12 (945-5265). Also 4-7 hr. naturalist-led tours (896-3867). Stage Harbor provides water taxi service to 9 mi. long Monomoy Island, part of the 2,500 acre Monomoy National Wildlife Refuge 945-0594. Many other great beaches nearby. Check out the view from nearby Chatham Light 945-5199. Cape Cod Flying Circus at Chatham Airport (945-9000) offers sightseeing flights $80-150. Commercial fishermen offload their catch at nearby pier on Shore Road. Reportedly great bass and bluefish fishing. Main Street is lined with upscale shops - many with a maritime flair, restaurants, inns, and wonderful houses; ask about the bow-shaped roofs. Band Concerts Fri at Kate Gould Park 945-5199.

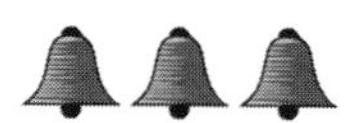

Saquatucket Harbor Marina

PO Box 207; 715 Main Street; Harwich, MA 02645

Tel: (508) 430-7532 **VHF: Monitor** 16 **Talk** 68
Fax: (508) 432-5039 **Alternate Tel:** (508) 430-7541
Email: harbor@capecod.net **Web:** www.vsv.cape.com/~harharb/saq.html
Nearest Town: Harwich Port *(1 mi.)* **Tourist Info:** (508) 432-1600

Navigational Information

Lat: 41°40.100' **Long:** 070°03.600' **Tide:** 4 ft. **Current:** n/a **Chart:** 13237
Rep. Depths (*MLW*): Entry 6 ft. **Fuel Dock** 5 ft. **Max Slip/Moor** 14 ft./6 ft.
Access: Nantucket Sound, follow channel straight ahead through breakwater

Marina Facilities *(In Season/Off Season)*

Fuel: *Mobil* - Gasoline, Diesel, On Call Delivery
Slips: 195 Total, 12 Transient **Max LOA:** 65 ft. **Max Beam:** 16 ft.
Rate *(per ft.)*: **Day** $1.52/$0.53* **Week** Inq. **Month** Inq.
Power: 30 amp $4.20, **50 amp** n/a, **100 amp** n/a, **200 amp** n/a
Cable TV: No **Dockside Phone:** No
Dock Type: Wood, Long Fingers, Pilings, Floating
Moorings: 0 Total, 0 Transient **Launch:** n/a, Dinghy Dock
Rate: Day n/a **Week** n/a **Month** n/a
Heads: 8 Toilet(s), 4 Shower(s)
Laundry: 1 Washer(s), 1 Dryer(s) **Pay Phones:** No
Pump-Out: 1 Central, 3 Port, 2 InSlip **Fee:** n/a **Closed Heads:** Yes

Marina Operations

Owner/Manager: Thomas Leach **Dockmaster:** Same
In-Season: Jun-Oct 15, 24 hrs. **Off-Season:** Oct 16-May, 8:30am-4pm
After-Hours Arrival: Call 68 see desk
Reservations: Yes **Credit Cards:** Cash or Checks
Discounts: None
Pets: Welcome, Dog Walk Area **Handicap Access:** Yes, Heads, Docks

Marina Services and Boat Supplies

Services - Security *(24 Hrs., Watchman)*, Trash Pick-Up, Dock Carts **Communication -** Mail & Package Hold, Phone Messages, FedEx, AirBorne, UPS, Express Mail *(Sat Del)* **Supplies - OnSite:** Ice *(Cube)* **Under 1 mi:** Ships' Store **1-3 mi:** Bait/Tackle, Live Bait, Propane *(Speedway 432-8729, Snow's 255-0158)* **3+ mi:** West Marine *(15 mi.)*, Boat/US *(15 mi.)*

Boatyard Services

OnSite: Launching Ramp **OnCall:** Divers *(432-9035)* **Near:** Engine mechanic *(gas, diesel)*. **1-3 mi:** Electronic Sales, Electronics Repairs, Hull Repairs, Rigger, Sail Loft, Canvas Work, Bottom Cleaning, Brightwork, Air Conditioning, Refrigeration, Compound, Wash & Wax, Interior Cleaning, Woodworking, Upholstery, Yacht Interiors, Metal Fabrication, Painting, Awlgrip, Total Refits. **Yard Rates:** $59/hr.

Restaurants and Accommodations

OnSite: Restaurant *(Brax Landing L $7-10, D $13-19)* **Near:** Restaurant *(Ay Caramba 432-9800, L $6-12, D $6-12)*, *(Alouette 430-0405, D $17-27)* **Under 1 mi:** Restaurant *(Dino's Harwichport Grill 432-0700)*, *(New Moon Bar & Grille 432-9911)*, Pizzeria *(George's 432-3144)*, Motel *(Coachman 432-0707, $98-110)*, *(Country Inn 432-2769, $90)*, *(Stone Horse 430-2998)*, Inn/B&B *(Barry Preston B&B 432-1675)* **1-3 mi:** Restaurant *(Depot Restaurant & Oyster Bar 432-6900)*, Inn/B&B *(Dunscroft by the Sea 432-4345, $185-375)*

Recreation and Entertainment

OnSite: Picnic Area, Boat Rentals *(Sailing charters Jubilee 432-3416, Sabbatical 896-2730)*, Fishing Charter *(Magellan 430-7437, Striper 432-4025, SUE-Z 432-3294, Arlie eX 432-1145, Pauly 430-0053, Fishtale 432-3783, Take It E-Z 432-277)*, Group Fishing Boat *(Yankee 432-2520, daily 8am & 12:30pm, Sun 1pm $20)* **1-3 mi:** Tennis Courts *(Manning's 432-3958)*, Golf Course *(Cranberry Valley G. C. 430-7560)*, Roller Blade/Bike Paths, Movie Theater, Park, Museum *(Brooks Academy 432-8089)*, Special Events *(Cranberry harvest, Sep)*

Provisioning and General Services

Near: Supermarket *(Lambert's Market 432-5415)*, Wine/Beer, Bakery, Green Grocer, Fishmonger, Lobster Pound, Meat Market **1-3 mi:** Health Food *(Wild Oats Natural Foods 430-2507)*, Liquor Store *(Harvest Fine Wines & Spirits 432-0100)*, Post Office, Catholic Church, Protestant Church, Library *(Harwich 430-7562)*, Beauty Salon, Barber Shop, Dry Cleaners, Laundry, Bookstore *(Wychmere Book & Coffee Shop 432-7868)*, Pharmacy *(CVS 430-0512)*, Newsstand, Hardware Store *(True Value 432-1113)*, Florist, Retail Shops, Department Store, Copies Etc. *(Red River Print Shop 432-3000)*

Transportation

OnSite: Ferry Service *(Freedom to Nantucket 432-8999)* **OnCall:** Rental Car *(Enterprise 398-4555)*, Taxi *(Skip's 432-0935)* **Under 1 mi:** Local Bus *(H2O 385-8326)* **3+ mi:** InterCity Bus *(Plymouth Brocktow 771-6191, 4 mi.)* **Airport:** Hyannis/Barnstable *(15 mi./20 mi.)*

Medical Services

911 Service **OnCall:** Ambulance **1-3 mi:** Doctor *(Crossroads Medical 432-1400)* **Hospital:** Cape Cod 771-6776 *(15 mi.)*

Setting -- Located on Nantucket Sound, this well protected, full-service municipal marina is up a narrow channel in a really lovely cove, virtually filled with dockage. Once inside there is a comfortable mix of pleasure craft, working vessels, and charter boats. Harwich Port provides great strolling opportunities.

Marina Notes -- *$1.52/ft. with a $30.40 minimum. Off season Mid Sep-Mid Oct $.90/ft, Mid Oct-Mid Nov and May-Mid Jun $0.53/ft/nt, $2.68/ft/week, $7.35/ft/mo, plus daily power charge of $4.20. 3-night minimum and two-week maximum (but ask about flexibility). Transient moorings no longer available. Developed in 1969, it was the last marina built in a salt marsh. Operated by the Harwich Harbormaster's Office, but the Channel is maintained by the Army Corps of Engineers - to a depth of six feet at low tide. Nicely maintained handicapped accessible bathrooms, showers, and laundry facilities for guests. Paved two-lane boat ramp. Open May 1-Nov 15 for recreational boaters. Harbormaster: 430-7532.

Notable -- Freedom ferry to Nantucket (432-8999) leaves from a nearby dock at 8am, 11:30am, 5:45pm during the season RT $43/36, 90 minute trip. Brax Landing Restaurant is perched on a hill overlooking the marina, with both inside and inviting terrace dining. Mostly seafood; kids' menu and great Sunday brunch 10am-2pm, $12/7. Tiny Mexican Ay! Caramba Café is equally convenient and very inexpensive. Across the street, the fabulous Lambert's Farm Market -- housed in a delightful blue awninged, shingled structure -- should satisfy every possible provisioning need - groceries, produce, bakery, seafood, meat, deli, beer, wine, etc. Plus a café!

MA - CAPE COD

PHOTOS ON CD-ROM: 6

Navigational Information

Lat: 41°38.992' **Long:** 070°16.438' **Tide:** 3 ft. **Current:** 1 kt. **Chart:** 13229
Rep. Depths (*MLW*): Entry 16 ft. **Fuel Dock** 13 ft. **Max Slip/Moor** 13 ft./-
Access: Hyannis Harbor to Lewis Bay to just inside the Inner Harbor

Marina Facilities *(In Season/Off Season)*

Fuel: *Texaco* - Slip-Side Fueling, High-Speed Pumps
Slips: 180 Total, 25 Transient **Max LOA:** 200 ft. **Max Beam:** 40 ft.
Rate *(per ft.)*: **Day** $3.25/Inq.* **Week** Inq. **Month** Inq.
Power: 30 amp $8, **50 amp** $16, **100 amp** Metered, **200 amp** n/a
Cable TV: Yes Incl. **Dockside Phone:** Yes Incl.
Dock Type: Wood, Long Fingers, Concrete, Floating, Fixed
Moorings: 0 Total, 0 Transient **Launch:** n/a
Rate: Day n/a **Week** n/a **Month** n/a
Heads: 12 Toilet(s), Shower(s)Private
Laundry: 4 Washer(s), 4 Dryer(s) **Pay Phones:** Yes, 2
Pump-Out: OnCall, Self Service, 3 Port **Fee:** Free **Closed Heads:** Yes

Marina Operations

Owner/Manager: Wayne Kurker **Dockmaster:** Carla A. Sullivan
In-Season: May-Oct, 8am-8pm **Off-Season:** Nov-Apr, 8am-5pm
After-Hours Arrival: See security guard, onsite 24 hrs.
Reservations: Strongly recommended **Credit Cards:** Visa/MC, Tex
Discounts: Yes **Dockage:** n/a **Fuel:** Volume **Repair:** n/a
Pets: Welcome, Dog Walk Area **Handicap Access:** Yes, Heads, Docks

Hyannis Marina

1 Willow Street; Hyannis, MA 02601

Tel: (508) 790-4000 **VHF: Monitor** 9 **Talk** n/a
Fax: (508) 775-0851 **Alternate Tel:** n/a
Email: docks@hyannismarina.com **Web:** www.hyannismarina.com
Nearest Town: Hyannis *(0.5 mi.)* **Tourist Info:** (508) 362-5230

Marina Services and Boat Supplies

Services - Docking Assistance, Concierge, Security *(24 Hrs., Gate, guard on duty)*, Trash Pick-Up, Dock Carts, Megayacht Facilities, 3 Phase, European Voltage **Communication -** Mail & Package Hold, Phone Messages, Fax in/out *(Free)*, Data Ports *(Wireless, dockside)*, FedEx, AirBorne, UPS *(Sat Del)* **Supplies - OnSite:** Ice *(Block, Cube)*, Ships' Store **OnCall:** Live Bait, CNG **Near:** Bait/Tackle *(Hy Line 771-2551)* **1-3 mi:** West Marine *(862-2700)*, Boater's World *(862-2756)*, Propane *(Amerigas 775-0686)*

Boatyard Services

OnSite: Travelift *(35T)*, Forklift, Engine mechanic *(gas, diesel)*, Launching Ramp, Electrical Repairs, Electronic Sales, Electronics Repairs, Hull Repairs, Rigger, Sail Loft, Canvas Work, Bottom Cleaning, Brightwork, Air Conditioning, Refrigeration, Compound, Wash & Wax, Interior Cleaning, Woodworking, Inflatable Repairs, Upholstery, Yacht Interiors, Metal Fabrication, Painting, Awlgrip, Yacht Broker **OnCall:** Divers, Propeller Repairs, Life Raft Service

Restaurants and Accommodations

OnSite: Restaurant *(Tugboats 775-6433, L $7-11, D $12-17)*, Raw Bar *(Beazer's)*, Snack Bar *(Trader Ed's 790-8686, B $2-7, L $6-13, D $6-13)* **Near:** Restaurant *(Baxter's Boat House 775-7040, L $10-17, D $10-17)*, *(Black Cat 778-1233, L $6-13, D $14-22)*, *(Eclectic Café 771-7187)*, *(Roobar 778-6515, D $14-20)*, Seafood Shack *(Steamers 778-0818)*, Motel *(Anchor In 775-0357, $45-180)*, *(Hyannis Holiday 775-1639)* **Under 1 mi:** Restaurant *(Penguins Seagrill 775-2023, D $16-22)*, Pizzeria *(Pappa Bello 790-9399)*, Motel *(Harbor House 771-1880)*, Inn/B&B *(Mansfield House 771-9455, $75-95)* **1-3 mi:** Hotel *(Sheraton Resort 775-7775, $110-250)*

Recreation and Entertainment

OnSite: Pool, Picnic Area, Grills, Playground **Near:** Jogging Paths, Video Rental *(Video Tech 775-7366)*, Cultural Attract *(Ocean Quest maritime lectures 778-1782)* **Under 1 mi:** Beach, Fitness Center *(Gold's 790-4477)*, Bowling *(Cape Bowling 775-3411)*, Museum *(Hibel Museum of Art 778-7877)* **1-3 mi:** Dive Shop, Tennis Courts *(Vineyard 696-8000)*, Golf Course *(Hyannis Resort 775-7775)*, Movie Theater *(Hoyts 771-7460)*, Park

Provisioning and General Services

OnCall: Liquor Store *(Hyannis Package 775-1205)*, Dry Cleaners, Laundry, Florist **Near:** Copies Etc. *(Minuteman 778-0220)* **Under 1 mi:** Convenience Store *(Willow Tree 790-1177)*, Gourmet Shop *(Nantucket Trading 790-3933)*, Delicatessen *(Cape 771-9955)*, Health Food *(Nutrition Corner 775-5697)*, Library *(775-2280)*, Hardware Store *(Ace 775-0620)* **1-3 mi:** Supermarket *(Star Markets 775-7611)*, Lobster Pound, Post Office, Bookstore *(Annie's Book Shop 775-5056)*, Pharmacy *(Osco 771-6511)*

Transportation

OnSite: Courtesy Car/Van *(3)*, Local Bus *(HAT Shuttle 385-8326)* **OnCall:** Rental Car *(Enterprise 778-2205)*, Taxi *(Cape Cod Limo 771-2640)* **Near:** Bikes *(Emma's Cycle 778-7245)*, InterCity Bus *(H2O Woods Hole/Orleans, Sealine & Villager 385-8326; 1-3 mi. to P&B 778-9767, Bonanza 775-6502 to Ptown/Boston)*, Ferry Service *(Nantucket, Oak Bluffs 778-2600)* **Airport:** Barnstable/Chatham *(2 mi./22 mi.)*

Medical Services

911 Service **OnCall:** Ambulance **Near:** Doctor, Dentist, Chiropractor, Holistic Services **Hospital:** Cape Cod 771-6776, behind marina *(0.1 mi.)*

Setting -- Hyannis is the only natural deep harbor on the Cape, and Hyannis Marina has created a large, first class, service-oriented facility that takes full advantage of that. The marina and boatyard sit on the east side of the harbor with views of, and easy access to, the bustling tourist haven on the opposite shore. The inviting pool looks to the water and to a well-designed, shingled building that houses many of the facilities. Hyannis caters to a wide range of vessels; it understands the particular needs of each and delivers.

Marina Notes -- *Over 90' $4/ft. Family owned and operated for more than 2 dozen yrs. Pristine, private showers and heads, harborside pool, 3 courtesy cars, playground, complimentary dockside phone and cable TV, internet access, phone messages delivered to boat. Extra tall pilings, high speed Texaco refueling, and discount marine store. Accommodates deep draft vessels up to 200 ft. long. Megayacht facilities and special attention to sport fish boats. Sea Ray dealership.

Notable -- Onsite eateries: Trader Ed's is a poolside snack bar open Jul-Aug 8am-late 7 days, May-ColDay 11:30am on, weekends only; also a raw bar here. Tugboats, a full-service restaurant on the second floor of the marina, overlooks the docks and the harbor - inside or outside dining, 7 days 11:30am-10pm, closed Mon in off-season. Giant bluefin tuna season in fall. Cape Cod Guild Of Fine Arts (775-0900), John F. Kennedy Museum (790-3077 $3/Free), and Town Green Concerts within 3 mi. Boston Pops by the sea in Aug. Hyannis is the heart and transportation hub of the Cape; it is easy to get anywhere from here.

PHOTOS ON CD-ROM: 9

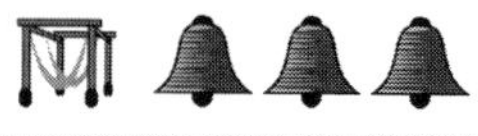

Crosby Yacht Yard

72 Crosby Circle; Osterville, MA 02655

Tel: (508) 428-6900 **VHF: Monitor** 9 **Talk** 68
Fax: (508) 428-0323 **Alternate Tel:** n/a
Email: contact@crosbyyacht.com **Web:** www.crosbyyacht.com
Nearest Town: Osterville *(0.7 mi.)* **Tourist Info:** (508) 790-3077

Navigational Information

Lat: 41°37.541' **Long:** 070°23.601' **Tide:** 3 ft. **Current:** 1 kt. **Chart:** 13229
Rep. Depths (*MLW*): Entry 6 ft. **Fuel Dock** 10 ft. **Max Slip/Moor** 10 ft./9 ft.
Access: Nantucket Sound, through West Bay, through bascule bridge

Marina Facilities *(In Season/Off Season)*

Fuel: Gasoline, Diesel, High-Speed Pumps
Slips: 125 Total, 15 Transient **Max LOA:** 120 ft. **Max Beam:** n/a
Rate *(per ft.)*: **Day** n/a **Week** n/a **Month** n/a
Power: 30 amp Yes, **50 amp** Yes, **100 amp** n/a, **200 amp** n/a
Cable TV: No **Dockside Phone:** No
Dock Type: Wood, Long Fingers, Fixed
Moorings: 150 Total, 25 Transient **Launch:** n/a
Rate: Day n/a **Week** n/a **Month** n/a
Heads: 4 Toilet(s)
Laundry: 2 Washer(s), 2 Dryer(s) **Pay Phones:** Yes
Pump-Out: OnCall, Full Service, 2 Port **Fee:** n/a **Closed Heads:** No

Marina Operations

Owner/Manager: Greg Egan (VP) **Dockmaster:** n/a
In-Season: Year-Round **Off-Season:** n/a
After-Hours Arrival: Call in advance
Reservations: Yes, Required **Credit Cards:** Visa/MC
Discounts: None
Pets: No **Handicap Access:** No

Marina Services and Boat Supplies

Services - Docking Assistance, Dock Carts **Communication -** Phone Messages, AirBorne, UPS, Express Mail **Supplies - OnSite:** Ice *(Block, Cube)*, Ships' Store **Under 1 mi:** Bait/Tackle *(Sporting Life 539-0007)*, Propane *(Botello 477-3084)* **3+ mi:** West Marine *(862-2700)*

Boatyard Services

OnSite: Travelift *(70T)*, Railway, Forklift *(2)*, Engine mechanic *(gas, diesel)*, Electrical Repairs, Electronic Sales, Electronics Repairs, Hull Repairs, Rigger, Canvas Work, Bottom Cleaning, Brightwork, Air Conditioning, Refrigeration, Divers, Compound, Wash & Wax, Interior Cleaning, Propeller Repairs, Woodworking, Inflatable Repairs, Upholstery, Yacht Interiors, Metal Fabrication, Painting, Awlgrip, Yacht Design, Yacht Building, Total Refits **Dealer for:** Sealine, Scout Boats, Uniesse. **Member:** ABBRA, Other Certifications: MMTA, CCMTA, YBAA

Restaurants and Accommodations

OnSite: Restaurant *(Harborside Café 428-0222, B $2-5, L $5-9.50, D $7-16)*, *(Keepers 428-6719)* **Near:** Restaurant *(Five Bays Bistro 420-3854)* **Under 1 mi:** Restaurant *(La Petite Maison 420-2700)*, Coffee Shop *(Breaking Grounds Café 420-1311, B $3-6, L $3-6, 7 days 6:30am-2pm)*, Pizzeria *(Sweet Tomatoes 420-1717, 7 days, 11am-9pm)* **1-3 mi:** Restaurant *(Mills 428-9814)*, *(Regatta of Cotuit 428-5715, D $23-36, 3-course early bird $25-28)*, Motel *(Centerville Corners Motor Lodge 775-7223, $70-150)*, *(Ocean View 775-1962)*, *(Suni Sands 775-7646)*

Recreation and Entertainment

Near: Jogging Paths **Under 1 mi:** Beach *(Dowses Beach - Seaview & Wianno Aves. or Wianno Beach)*, Picnic Area, Tennis Courts *(Osterville Bay School 428-8538)*, Cultural Attract *(Audubon Bird Sanctuary - on port side as you enter West Bay)*, Special Events *(Village Day 3rd weekend July, Fall Fest late Sep)* **1-3 mi:** Golf Course *(New Seabury 477-9400)*, Fitness Center *(Osterville Fitness 428-3775)*, Roller Blade/Bike Paths, Video Rental *(Box Office 428-8848)*, Museum *(Osterville Historical Soc. 428-5861, Centerville Historical M. 775-0331)* **3+ mi:** Movie Theater *(Hoyts, 5 mi.)*

Provisioning and General Services

Near: Convenience Store *(Country Store 428-2097)*, Gourmet Shop *(Fancy's 428-6954, Osterville Cheese 428-9085)*, Fishmonger *(PY's Seafood 428-6300)*, Bank/ATM, Post Office, Catholic Church, Protestant Church, Library *(Osterville 428-5757)*, Bookstore *(Baker Books 428-4635)*, Pharmacy *(Brooks 428-3525)*, Newsstand, Hardware Store *(House & Garden 428-6911)*, Florist, Retail Shops **Under 1 mi:** Delicatessen *(Cheese & Sandwich Shop 428-9085)*, Health Food *(Earthly Delights 420-2206)*, Wine/Beer *(Osterville Package Store 428-6327)*, Liquor Store **1-3 mi:** Supermarket *(Shaw's, Stop & Shop 428-1278)*, Copies Etc. *(Aztec Repro 420-1880)*

Transportation

Under 1 mi: Taxi *(Kon Limousine 945-2941)*, InterCity Bus *(CCRTA Woods Hole, Orleans, Hyannis)* **3+ mi:** Rental Car *(Budget 790-1614, Avis 775-2888, 8 mi.)* **Airport:** Barnstable 775-2020 *(9 mi.)*

Medical Services

911 Service **OnCall:** Ambulance **Under 1 mi:** Doctor, Dentist *(Bober Chirprctr 420-0495)*, Holistic Services *(Glaser 420-9266)* **Hospital:** Cape Cod 539-2144 *(1 mi.)*

Setting -- From West Bay, follow the narrow channel, through the bascule bridge, into lovely North Bay's Crosby Basin. Rimmed with docks, it is home to several marine facilities. On the eastern shore, the second set of well protected dockage, belongs to the venerable Crosby Yacht Yard.

Marina Notes -- Boatbuilding began on this site in the 1700's and a boatyard was formally established in 1850 -- making this the oldest continuously operating boatyard. In the mid 19thC, it was the original designer and builder of the world-famous Crosby Catboat, Wianno Senior, Crosby Striper, Canyon, Hawk. Today, it offers full service restorations, and still builds a complete line of Tugs and custom boats. Crosby's also manages the moorings in Contuit Bay, which use the Contuit Pier dinghy dock and Contuit Launch - these moorings are included in the total number. Fuel dock open 7 days Apr-Oct. Nauticus Marina (428-4537, Ch.9), next door, may have transient slips and is worth a stop just to appreciate the exquisite facility. Harbormaster: 790-6237.

Notable -- Onsite Keeper's Restaurant, overlooking the basin, serves breakfast, lunch and dinner, 7 days, 7am-9pm from May-Sep. It is less than a mile stroll through the classic and exceptionally affluent surrounding community of Osterville, on the east side of the bascule bridge. Main Street promises an interesting mix of upscale restaurants, galleries and shops. On the west side is Osterville Grand Island. If you have a deep draft boat, consider circumnavigating Grand Island and Little Island in the dinghy -- the exquisite houses (many actually mansions) add to the experience. You might come ashore on the Dead Neck side of Seapuit River and walk across to the long barrier beach. Reportedly this is the best crabbing on the Cape. Regatta Restaurant is worth the trip.

PHOTOS ON CD-ROM: 9

Navigational Information
Lat: 41°32.777' **Long:** 070°36.304' **Tide:** 2 ft. **Current:** 2 kt. **Chart:** 13229
Rep. Depths (*MLW*): Entry 8 ft. **Fuel Dock** 8 ft. **Max Slip/Moor** 8 ft./10 ft.
Access: Vineyard Sound to Falmouth Harbor to Inner Harbor, port side

Marina Facilities *(In Season/Off Season)*
Fuel: *Mobil* - Slip-Side Fueling, Gasoline, Diesel
Slips: 15 Total, 15 Transient **Max LOA:** 70 ft. **Max Beam:** 22 ft.
Rate *(per ft.)*: **Day** $2.50/Inq. **Week** Inq. **Month** Inq.
Power: 30 amp $8, **50 amp** $10, **100 amp** n/a, **200 amp** n/a
Cable TV: Yes If available **Dockside Phone:** No
Dock Type: Wood, Long Fingers, Pilings, Alongside, Floating, Fixed
Moorings: 15 Total, 15 Transient **Launch:** None, Dinghy Dock
Rate: Day $35/15 **Week** n/a **Month** n/a
Heads: 4 Toilet(s), Shower(s)
Laundry: None **Pay Phones:** No
Pump-Out: OnSite, OnCall, Full Service **Fee:** Free **Closed Heads:** Yes

Marina Operations
Owner/Manager: Jack Erikson **Dockmaster:** Deborah Selleck
In-Season: May 15-Oct 15, 7:30am-7:30pm **Off-Season:** Oct 15-May 15*
After-Hours Arrival: Call ahead
Reservations: Yes, 24 hrs. in advance **Credit Cards:** Visa/MC, Mobil, Exon
Discounts: None
Pets: Welcome, Dog Walk Area **Handicap Access:** No

Falmouth Marine & Yachting

278 Scranton Avenue; Falmouth, MA 02540

Tel: (508) 548-4600 **VHF: Monitor** 9 **Talk** 68
Fax: (508) 540-0297 **Alternate Tel:** n/a
Email: n/a **Web:** n/a
Nearest Town: Falmouth *(1mi.)* **Tourist Info:** (800) 526-8532

Marina Services and Boat Supplies
Services - Docking Assistance, Trash Pick-Up, Dock Carts **Communication -** Phone Messages, Fax in/out, UPS, Express Mail *(Sat Del)* **Supplies - OnSite:** Ice *(Block, Cube)*, Ships' Store **Near:** West Marine *(457-6500)*, Live Bait **Under 1 mi:** Bait/Tackle *(Harborside 548-0143)* **1-3 mi:** Propane *(Advanced Propane 548-0077)*

Boatyard Services
OnSite: Travelift *(70T)*, Crane, Engine mechanic *(gas, diesel)*, Hull Repairs, Rigger, Sail Loft, Bottom Cleaning, Brightwork, Compound, Wash & Wax, Interior Cleaning, Propeller Repairs, Woodworking, Painting, Awlgrip, Yacht Broker *(Chris Herb)*, Total Refits **OnCall:** Divers, Inflatable Repairs, Life Raft Service, Upholstery, Yacht Interiors **Near:** Electrical Repairs, Electronic Sales, Electronics Repairs, Air Conditioning, Refrigeration. **Yard Rates:** $65/hr., Haul & Launch $3.50/ft. *(blocking $6.50/ft.)*, Power Wash $2.50, Bottom Paint $25-55/ft. **Storage:** In-Water $20/ft., On-Land Inside $65/ft., Outside $28/ft.

Restaurants and Accommodations
OnCall: Pizzeria *(Steve's 459-9454)* **Near:** Restaurant *(Flying Bridge 548-2700, L $6-26, D $6-26)*, *(Boathouse 548-7800, L $6-10, D $10-23)*, Seafood Shack *(Clam Shack 540-7758, L $5-10, D $5-10)*, Motel *(Marina Tradewinds 548-4300, $80-165)*, Inn/B&B *(La Maison Cappellari 548-3786, $195-240)* **Under 1 mi:** Restaurant *(British Beer 540-9600)*, Hotel *(Ramada 457-0606, $80-500)*, Inn/B&B *(Palmer House 548-1230, $85-195)*

Recreation and Entertainment
Near: Beach, Picnic Area, Fishing Charter *(Patriot)*, Park *(Marine)*, Special Events **Under 1 mi:** Bowling *(Trade Center Bowl 548-7000)*, Video Rental *(Video Paradise 457-1388)*, Museum *(Museums on the Green 548-4857 $5/Free)*, Sightseeing *(Trolley tours 548-4857 $12/8)* **1-3 mi:** Playground, Tennis Courts *(Falmouth Tennis 548-4370)*, Golf Course *(Woodbriar 495-5500)*, Fitness Center *(Falmouth Sports 548-7384)*, Jogging Paths, Boat Rentals, Roller Blade/Bike Paths *(Shining Sea to Woods Hole)*, Movie Theater *(Falmouth Mall 540-2169)*, Video Arcade, Cultural Attract *(College Light Opera 548-0668)*

Provisioning and General Services
Near: Wine/Beer *(Palmer Av. 548-4824)*, Bakery, Farmers' Market, Meat Market, Dry Cleaners, Laundry, Copies Etc. *(Mail Boxes Etc. 540-1900)* **Under 1 mi:** Provisioning Service, Convenience Store, Supermarket *(Star Mkts 548-4033)*, Delicatessen *(Windfall 548-0099)*, Health Food *(Amber Waves 540-3538)*, Bank/ATM, Library *(457-2555)*, Bookstore *(Booksmith 540-6064)*, Pharmacy *(Brooks 495-2931)* **1-3 mi:** Fishmonger, Post Office, Hardware Store *(Eastman's 548-0407)*, Department Store

Transportation
OnSite: Ferry Service *(to MV)* **OnCall:** Courtesy Car/Van, Rental Car *(Enterprise 540-7784)* **Near:** Water Taxi **Under 1 mi:** Bikes *(Holiday Cycles 540-3549)*, Local Bus *(Sea-Line Woods Hole & Falmouth-to-Mashpee, WOOSH trolley Woods Hole Falmouth 352-7155)* **1-3 mi:** InterCity Bus *(Bonanza 548-7588)* **Airport:** Barnstable *(25 mi.)*

Medical Services
911 Service **Near:** Doctor, Dentist **1-3 mi:** Ambulance *(Fire Dept. 548-2323)* **Hospital:** Falmouth 457-9700 *(2 mi.)*

Setting -- The second facility on the port side as you enter the Inner Harbor, just past the Patriot Party Boats, this attractive, esteemed institution's slips and alongside dockage line the bulkhead. Flower baskets and picket fences add to the charm. Located on the "Village" side of the Harbor, it's a good base of operations for enjoying Falmouth, a year-round resort rich in seafaring history, with an historic village press, six golf courses and many beaches.

Marina Notes -- *Oct 15-May 15 open 7:30am-4:30pm, closed on weekends. Founded in 1939, Falmouth Marine was established as a yard capable of handing the requirements of the magnificent yachts which cruised the coast in that era, and still has a reputation as a complete yacht service. Offers a 70T travelift, yacht carpentry, engine repair, fiberglass, machine shop, paint and awlgrip, props, shafts, electronics, and rigging services. Excellent staff members skilled in every phase of yacht care. Hassle-free ferry to Edgartown leaves from here daily May-Oct, 60 min. trip, 548-9400. Harbormaster: 457-2550.

Notable -- Flying Bridge Restaurant is next door. The Island Queen to Oak Bluffs leaves from across the harbor 6 times a day, 35 min. trip, 548-4800. Patriot Fishing and Sightseeing Cruises is nearby at the mouth of the Harbor. Nearest Beach is Surf Drive a few blocks away. Part of the historic district is a couple of blocks' walk and makes an interesting mile plus stroll, ending at the Village Green and the Museums on the Green. At the head of the harbor is the Harbor Band Shell in Marina Park, Concerts Thu, 8pm Jul & Aug. In Noonan Park on Fridays at 6pm. Access to the 4 mile Shining Sea bike Path, from Ice Arena to Steamship Authority, is less than a mile. Falmouth Road Race takes place in Aug. Falmouth Historical Society 548-4857.

PHOTOS ON CD-ROM: 6

MacDougalls' Cape Cod Marine

145 Falmouth Heights; Falmouth, MA 02540

Tel: (508) 548-3146 **VHF: Monitor** 9 **Talk** 71
Fax: (508) 548-7262 **Alternate Tel:** n/a
Email: ccmarine1@capecod.net **Web:** www.macdougalls.com
Nearest Town: Falmouth **Tourist Info:** (508) 548-8500

Navigational Information

Lat: 41°32.815' **Long:** 070°36.126' **Tide:** 2 ft. **Current:** 2 kt. **Chart:** 13229
Rep. Depths (*MLW*): Entry 9 ft. **Fuel Dock** 10 ft. **Max Slip/Moor** 10 ft./10 ft.
Access: Falmouth Harbor R16 to G1 light into Falmouth Inner Harbor

Marina Facilities *(In Season/Off Season)*

Fuel: *Texaco* - Gasoline, Diesel, High-Speed Pumps
Slips: 100 Total, 25 Transient **Max LOA:** 100 ft. **Max Beam:** n/a
Rate *(per ft.)*: **Day** $2.50/Inq. **Week** Inq. **Month** Inq.
Power: 30 amp $6, **50 amp** $12, **100 amp** n/a, **200 amp** n/a
Cable TV: Yes Incl. **Dockside Phone:** No
Dock Type: Wood, Alongside, Floating, Fixed
Moorings: 8 Total, 2 Transient **Launch:** None, Dinghy Dock
Rate: Day $40 **Week** Inq. **Month** Inq.
Heads: 4 Toilet(s), 4 Shower(s)
Laundry: 3 Washer(s), 2 Dryer(s) **Pay Phones:** Yes, 2
Pump-Out: OnSite, Full Service, 1 Central **Fee:** n/a **Closed Heads:** Yes

Marina Operations

Owner/Manager: Thomas Stainton **Dockmaster:** n/a
In-Season: Summer, 7:30am-7:30pm **Off-Season:** Fall/Sprg, 7:30am-5pm
After-Hours Arrival: n/a
Reservations: No **Credit Cards:** Visa/MC, Amex, Tex, Debit Cards
Discounts: None
Pets: Welcome **Handicap Access:** No

Marina Services and Boat Supplies

Services - Docking Assistance, Dock Carts **Communication -** Mail & Package Hold, Phone Messages, Fax in/out, FedEx, AirBorne, UPS, Express Mail **Supplies - OnSite:** Ice *(Block, Cube)*, Ships' Store, CNG **OnCall:** Propane **Under 1 mi:** West Marine *(457-6500)*, Bait/Tackle *(Harborside 548-0143)*

Boatyard Services

OnSite: Travelift *(50T)*, Forklift, Crane, Engine mechanic *(gas, diesel)*, Electrical Repairs, Electronic Sales, Electronics Repairs, Hull Repairs, Rigger, Sail Loft, Bottom Cleaning, Brightwork, Air Conditioning, Refrigeration, Compound, Wash & Wax, Interior Cleaning, Propeller Repairs, Woodworking, Upholstery, Metal Fabrication, Painting, Awlgrip, Yacht Broker, Total Refits **OnCall:** Divers, Inflatable Repairs

Restaurants and Accommodations

Near: Snack Bar *(Food Buoy 540-0080, take out)*, Lite Fare *(Box Lunch Deli 457-7657)*, Pizzeria *(Paul's 548-5838)*, Motel *(Falmouth Heights 548-3623, $80-155)*, *(Seaside Inn 540-4120, $50-220)*, *(Tradewinds 548-4300, $80-165)*, Inn/B&B *(Bailey's 548-5748, $135-300)*, *(Grafton Inn 540-8688, $125-260)* **Under 1 mi:** Restaurant *(The Boathouse 548-7800, dinghy)*, *(Flying Bridge 548-2700, across bridge)*, Seafood Shack *(Clam Shack 540-7758)*

Recreation and Entertainment

OnSite: Picnic Area, Grills **Near:** Beach, Group Fishing Boat *(Patriot Party Boats across the harbor 548-2626 $25/17)* **Under 1 mi:** Roller Blade/Bike Paths *(Shining Sea Bike Path to Woods Hole)*, Fishing Charter, Video Rental *(Video Paradise 457-1388)*, Park *(Central)*, Sightseeing *(Whalewatching)* **1-3 mi:** Tennis Courts *(Falmouth Tennis 548-4370)*, Golf Course *(Woodbriar 495-5500)*, Fitness Center *(Falmouth Sports Center 548-7384)*, Bowling *(Trade Center Bowl 548-7000)*, Movie Theater *(Falmouth Mall 540-2169)*, Video Arcade, Museum *(Falmouth Historical Society 548-4857, Children's Museum 539-8788)*, Cultural Attract *(College Light Opera 548-0668)*

Provisioning and General Services

Near: Wine/Beer *(John's 548-2287)* **Under 1 mi:** Convenience Store, Supermarket *(Windfall 548-0099)*, Delicatessen, Health Food *(Amber Waves 540-3538)*, Liquor Store, Bakery, Green Grocer *(Andrew's 548-4717)*, Fishmonger, Lobster Pound, Bank/ATM, Post Office, Catholic Church, Protestant Church, Library *(Falmouth 457-2555)*, Beauty Salon, Barber Shop, Dry Cleaners, Laundry, Bookstore *(Booksmith 540-6064)*, Pharmacy *(Brooks 495-2931)*, Newsstand, Florist, Clothing Store, Retail Shops, Copies Etc. *(Mail Boxes Etc. 540-1900)* **1-3 mi:** Hardware Store *(Eastman's 548-0407)*

Transportation

OnCall: Rental Car *(Enterprise 540-7784)*, Taxi *(Falmouth Taxi 548-3100, Kennedy Limo 548-1066)* **Near:** Bikes *(Holiday Cycles 540-3549, across the street)*, Local Bus *(Sea-Line Woods Hole & Falmouth-to-Mashpee, WOOSH Woods Hole Trollley 352-7155)*, Ferry Service *(to Edgartown & Oak Bluffs)* **Under 1 mi:** InterCity Bus *(Bonanza 888-751-8800, SeaLine 385-8326)* **Airport:** Barnstable *(26 mi.)*

Medical Services

911 Service **OnCall:** Ambulance **Under 1 mi:** Doctor, Dentist, Chiropractor **Hospital:** Falmouth 457-9700 *(2 mi.)*

Setting -- The first major facility on the starboard side as you enter the well protected Falmouth Harbor, (just past Falmouth Yacht Club) MacDougalls' Marine spreads out along the eastern shore. Its large work sheds are easily visible from the Harbor's mouth. This marina promises (and delivers) extremely well maintained, first class facilities, along with handsome, newish docks and pedestals. Historic Falmouth Heights are out the "back door".

Marina Notes -- In business since 1938, MacDougalls' caters to cruising yachts, sport fishermen, and racing sailboats. A large, extensive, working yard offers just about every service for all types of boats. Very service-oriented, this is the most complete facility in the Inner Harbor. Marine electronics, yacht interiors, engine services, electrical/plumbing, canvas shop, air conditioning/refrigeration, paint/fiberglass repair, carpentry, rigging, sail loft, re-powers, awlgrip. Dealers for Detroit Diesel, Yanmar, Westerbeke, Caterpillar, Raytheon, EZ2CY Enclosures, & Furuno. Weekly discounts available. Harbormaster: 457-2550.

Notable -- Falmouth Heights Beach is an easy walk. Falmouth Harbor is a good provisioning stop -- everything for the boat and crew is within reasonable walking distance. Daily ferry to Martha's Vineyard: Island Queen to Oak Bluffs 548-4800 is nearby, and directly across the harbor is the Falmouth Ferry to Edgartown 548-9400. Relatively easy transportation from here: Bonanza Bus to NY, Boston, TF Green, New Bedford, etc. RTA's SeaLine to Hyannis and Woods Hole. WHOOSH Trolley for local sprints. Bike the Shining Sea Trail to Woods Hole - four miles along the water, bus back.

PHOTOS ON CD-ROM: 5

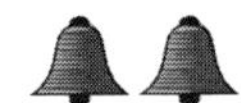

Navigational Information
Lat: 41°32.947' **Long:** 070°36.207' **Tide:** 2 ft. **Current:** 2 kt. **Chart:** 13229
Rep. Depths (*MLW*): Entry 6 ft. **Fuel Dock** 6 ft. **Max Slip/Moor** 6 ft./6 ft.
Access: Falmouth Harbor R16 to G1 light to Falmouth Inner Harbor

Marina Facilities *(In Season/Off Season)*
Fuel: No
Slips: 60 Total, 10 Transient **Max LOA:** 165 ft. **Max Beam:** 21 ft.
Rate *(per ft.)*: **Day** $1.50/1.00 **Week** n/a **Month** n/a
Power: 30 amp n/a, **50 amp** n/a, **100 amp** n/a, **200 amp** n/a
Cable TV: Yes **Dockside Phone:** No
Dock Type: Wood, Long Fingers, Fixed
Moorings: 0 Total, 0 Transient **Launch:** n/a, Dinghy Dock (Free)
Rate: Day n/a **Week** n/a **Month** n/a
Heads: Toilet(s), Shower(s)
Laundry: None **Pay Phones:** No
Pump-Out: OnCall, Full Service, 1 Port **Fee:** n/a **Closed Heads:** Yes

Marina Operations
Owner/Manager: Gregg P. Fraser (Harbormaster) **Dockmaster:** n/a
In-Season: Apr-Oct 31, 8am-6pm **Off-Season:** Closed
After-Hours Arrival: Call in advance
Reservations: Yes, Preferred **Credit Cards:** Visa/MC, Check/Cash
Discounts: None
Pets: Welcome **Handicap Access:** Yes, Docks

Falmouth Harbor Town Marina

180 Scranton Avenue; Falmouth, MA 02540

Tel: (508) 457-2550 **VHF: Monitor** 16 **Talk** 12
Fax: (508) 457-2525 **Alternate Tel:** n/a
Email: n/a **Web:** www.falmouth-capecod.com/boating.html
Nearest Town: Falmouth *(1 mi.)* **Tourist Info:** (508) 548-8500

Marina Services and Boat Supplies
Services - Docking Assistance **Communication -** FedEx, UPS, Express Mail **Supplies - OnCall:** Marine Discount Store *(Stem To Stern Mobile Marine Service 563-6553)* **Near:** Ice *(Cube)*, Ships' Store, West Marine *(457-6500)*, Bait/Tackle *(Harborside 548-0143)* **1-3 mi:** Propane *(Advanced Propane 548-0077)*

Boatyard Services
Near: Travelift, Engine mechanic *(gas, diesel)*, Electrical Repairs, Electronic Sales, Electronics Repairs, Hull Repairs, Rigger, Sail Loft, Bottom Cleaning, Brightwork, Air Conditioning, Refrigeration.

Restaurants and Accommodations
OnCall: Pizzeria *(Pizza 1 & Subs 2 457-1212)* **Near:** Restaurant *(Flying Bridge 548-2700, L $6-26, D $6-26, literally next door)*, *(The Boathouse 548-7800, L $6-10, D $10-24)*, *(Food Buoy 540-0080)*, Motel *(Falmouth Marina Trade Winds 548-4300, $80-165)*, Inn/B&B *(La Maison Cappellari 548-3786, $195-240, 2-3 day min)*, *(Inn at One Main 540-7469)* **Under 1 mi:** Restaurant *(Quarterdeck 548-9900, L $7-12, D $12-22)*, *(Laureen's 540-9104)*, Seafood Shack *(Clam Shack 540-7758, L $5-10, D $5-10)*, Fast Food, Inn/B&B *(Palmer House Inn 548-1230, $85-195)* **1-3 mi:** Restaurant *(Coonamessett 548-2300, D $15-30)*

Recreation and Entertainment
OnSite: Fishing Charter **Near:** Picnic Area, Group Fishing Boat *(Patriot Party Boats 548-2626 $25/17)*, Park *(Marine)*, Special Events *(Band Concerts)* **Under 1 mi:** Beach, Fitness Center *(Falmouth Sports Center 548-7384)*, Video Rental *(Video Paradise 457-1388)*, Museum *(Falmouth Historical Society 548-4857)*, Sightseeing *(Historic Section)* **1-3 mi:** Tennis Courts *(Falmouth Tennis 548-4370)*, Golf Course *(Ballymeade 540-4005)*, Horseback Riding *(Fieldcrest Farm 540-0626)*, Roller Blade/Bike Paths *(Shining Sea to Woods Hole)*, Bowling *(Trade Center Bowl & Amusements 548-7000)*, Movie Theater *(Falmouth Mall 540-2169)*, Cultural Attract *(College Light Opera 548-0668)*

Provisioning and General Services
Near: Convenience Store *(Windfall 548-0099)*, Health Food *(Amber Waves 540-3538)*, Bakery *(Mary Ellen's 540-9696)*, Green Grocer *(Andrew's 548-4717)*, Bank/ATM, Dry Cleaners, Laundry, Bookstore *(Booksmith 540-6064)*, Pharmacy *(Brooks 495-2931)*, Newsstand **Under 1 mi:** Gourmet Shop *(Nantucket Trading 548-5881)*, Liquor Store *(Kappy's 548-2600)* **1-3 mi:** Supermarket *(Star Markets 548-4033)*, Fishmonger, Lobster Pound, Post Office, Catholic Church, Protestant Church, Library *(Falmouth 457-2555)*, Beauty Salon, Hardware Store *(Eastmans 548-0407)*, Copies Etc. *(Mail Boxes Etc. 540-1900)*

Transportation
Near: Bikes *(Holiday Cycles 540-3549)*, Local Bus *(SeaLine Woods Hole & Falmouth-to-Mashpee, WOOSH Woods Hole to Falmouth Trollley 352-7155)* **Under 1 mi:** Rental Car *(Enterprise 540-7784)*, Taxi *(Kennedy Limo 548-1066)* **1-3 mi:** InterCity Bus *(Bonanza 548-7588)* **Airport:** Barnstable *(26 mi.)*

Medical Services
No 911 Service **Near:** Doctor **Under 1 mi:** Holistic Services *(Massage 495-9911)* **1-3 mi:** Chiropractor **Hospital:** Falmouth 457-9700 *(1.5 mi.)*

Setting -- The fourth facility on your port side, just past Falmouth Marine, after you enter the Inner Harbor, this municipal marina's docks are strung along the bulkhead, stern-to. Its shingled landside base provides an easy landmark.

Marina Notes -- Heads and showers are in the Harbormaster's office. Just up the street is the Windfall Market for gourmet/deli items and groceries, a laundromat, bait and tackle, and a liquor store. A little farther is the charming, picturesque "downtown" of Falmouth Village -- the street is lined with shops, restaurants, galleries, services and ends at the Village Green with its Historical Society and restored 18thC sea captains' houses. Harbormaster: 457-2550. Bonanza bus leaves from Woods Hole for Boston. The seasonal CCRTA WHOOSH and Falmouth-to-Mashpee trolleys provide transport to both malls, sights, and connect to the main bus and ferry lines.

Notable -- Nearest beach is Surf Drive, a few blocks away. The Island Queen to Oak Bluffs leaves from across the harbor 6 times a day, 35 min. trip, 548-4800. Falmouth-Edgartown ferry leaves from Falmouth Marine down the harbor, May-Oct daily service, 60 min. trip, 548-9400. Patriot Fishing and Sightseeing cruises is nearby at the mouth of the Harbor. A part of the historic district is a couple of blocks' walk and makes an interesting mile-long stroll, past the library, Town Hall Square, to the Historical Society. Down the block is the Harbor Band Shell in Marina Park - concerts Thu, 8pm Jul & Aug. Access to the 4 mile Shining Sea bike path, from Ice Arena to Steamship Authority, is less than a mile.

PHOTOS ON CD-ROM: 5

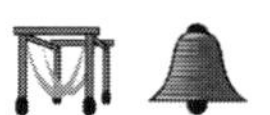

East Marine

PO Box 610; 84 Falmouth Mts. Road; Falmouth, MA 02541

Tel: (508) 540-3611; (800) 54d-ocks **VHF: Monitor** 16 **Talk** n/a
Fax: (508) 540-2385 **Alternate Tel:** (508) 548-2704
Email: n/a **Web:** www.eastmarine.com
Nearest Town: Falmouth *(1 mi.)* **Tourist Info:** (508) 548-8500

Navigational Information

Lat: 41°32.949' **Long:** 070°36.064' **Tide:** 2 ft. **Current:** 2 kt. **Chart:** 13229
Rep. Depths (*MLW*): Entry 10 ft. **Fuel Dock** 10 ft. **Max Slip/Moor** 8 ft./-
Access: Falmouth Harbor R16 to G1 light to Falmouth Inner Harbor

Marina Facilities *(In Season/Off Season)*

Fuel: *Texaco* - Gasoline, Diesel, High-Speed Pumps
Slips: 30 Total, 3 Transient **Max LOA:** 70 ft. **Max Beam:** n/a
Rate *(per ft.)*: **Day** $2.50/Inq. **Week** Inq. **Month** Inq.
Power: 30 amp n/a, **50 amp** n/a, **100 amp** n/a, **200 amp** n/a
Cable TV: No **Dockside Phone:** No
Dock Type: Wood, Short Fingers, Alongside, Fixed
Moorings: 0 Total, 0 Transient **Launch:** n/a
Rate: Day n/a **Week** n/a **Month** n/a
Heads: None
Laundry: None **Pay Phones:** No
Pump-Out: OnCall, Full Service **Fee:** Free **Closed Heads:** Yes

Marina Operations

Owner/Manager: F. Phillips Wormelle **Dockmaster:** Same
In-Season: n/a, 8am-5pm **Off-Season:** n/a
After-Hours Arrival: Call (508) 548-2704
Reservations: Yes, Preferred **Credit Cards:** Visa/MC, Dscvr, Amex, Tex
Discounts: None
Pets: No **Handicap Access:** No

Marina Services and Boat Supplies

Services - Docking Assistance, Security **Supplies - OnSite:** Ice *(Block, Cube)* **Near:** Ships' Store **1-3 mi:** West Marine *(457-6500)*, Bait/Tackle *(Harborside 548-0143)* **3+ mi:** Propane *(Advanced Propane 548-0077, 4 mi.)*

Boatyard Services

OnSite: Travelift *(35T)* **OnCall:** Divers, Inflatable Repairs, Life Raft Service **Near:** Engine mechanic *(gas, diesel)*, Launching Ramp, Electrical Repairs, Electronic Sales, Electronics Repairs, Hull Repairs, Rigger, Sail Loft, Bottom Cleaning, Brightwork, Air Conditioning, Refrigeration, Compound, Wash & Wax, Interior Cleaning, Propeller Repairs, Metal Fabrication, Painting, Yacht Broker.

Restaurants and Accommodations

OnCall: Pizzeria *(Dominos 540-8004)* **Near:** Snack Bar *(Food Buoy 540-0080, take-out)*, Motel *(Red Horse Inn 548-0053, $120-180)*, Inn/B&B *(Moorings Lodge 540-2370, $125-165)*, *(Beach House 457-0310, $100-225)* **Under 1 mi:** Restaurant *(Golden Swan 540-6080, D $15-22)*, *(Seafood Sam's 540-7877, L $5-11, D $5-11)*, *(Hearth 'n Kettle 548-6115, L $4-11, D $9-16)*, *(Flying Bridge 548-2700, L $6-26, D $6-26, by dinghy)*, *(Eli's Tavern D $7-15)*, Motel *(BW Trade Winds 548-4300, $80-225)* **1-3 mi:** Restaurant *(Coonamessett 548-2300, D $15-30)*

Recreation and Entertainment

Near: Pool, Beach, Picnic Area, Grills, Playground, Dive Shop, Jogging Paths, Horseback Riding, Boat Rentals, Fishing Charter, Group Fishing Boat *(Patriot Party Boats across the harbor 548-2626)*, Sightseeing *(Martha's Vineyard)* **Under 1 mi:** Roller Blade/Bike Paths *(Shining Sea to Woods Hole)*, Park *(Marina)* **1-3 mi:** Tennis Courts *(Falmouth Tennis 548-4370)*, Golf Course *(Woodbriar 495-5500)*, Fitness Center *(Falmouth Sports Center 548-7384)*, Bowling *(Trade Center Bowl 548-7000)*, Movie Theater *(Falmouth Mall 540-2169)*, Video Rental *(Video Paradise 457-1388)*, Museum *(Falmouth Historical Society 548-4857)*, Cultural Attract *(College Light Opera 548-0668)*

Provisioning and General Services

Near: Bakery *(Mary Ellen's 540-9696)*, Bank/ATM, Catholic Church, Beauty Salon, Barber Shop, Dry Cleaners, Laundry, Newsstand **Under 1 mi:** Liquor Store *(Kappy's 548-2600)*, Farmers' Market *(Andrew's 548-4717)*, Post Office, Protestant Church, Bookstore *(Booksmith 540-6064)*, Pharmacy *(Brooks 495-2931)*, Hardware Store *(Eastman's 548-0407)*, Clothing Store **1-3 mi:** Supermarket *(Star Markets 548-4033)*, Gourmet Shop *(Bean and Cod 548-8840)*, Health Food *(Amber Waves 540-3538)*, Library *(Falmouth 457-2555)*, Copies Etc. *(Mail Boxes Etc. 540-1900)*

Transportation

OnCall: Rental Car *(Thrifty 540-9942, Enterprise 540-7784)*, Taxi *(All Village 540-7200)* **Near:** Local Bus *(Sea-Line Woods Hole & Falmouth-to-Mashpee, WOOSH Woods Hole Falmouth Trolley 352-7155)*, Ferry Service *(to Edgartown and Nantucket)* **1-3 mi:** Bikes *(Holiday Cycles 540-3549)*
Airport: Barnstable 775-2020 *(26 mi.)*

Medical Services

911 Service **OnCall:** Ambulance **1-3 mi:** Doctor *(Falmouth Medical Center 540-6790)* **Hospital:** Falmouth 457-9700 *(2 mi.)*

Setting -- East Marine is the second facility on your starboard side, just past MacDougall's, as you enter the Inner Harbor. It's the quintessential New England boatyard - not fancy, but solid and professional. Look for the curved roof of its landside facility.

Marina Notes -- Fast pumps for marine diesel and 87-89-93 octane gasoline. Extensive winter boat storage. Basic services in a good, protected location. Work on your own boat is permitted here, but full service also available. This is really a boatyard with docks; there are no heads, showers or laundry facilities. Note: Pets not welcome. Harbormaster: 457-2550.

Notable -- Falmouth Heights Beach is an easy walk. Walk less than a mile to Main Street to find many restaurants, services, and Falmouth Plaza. Across the harbor is the Harbor Band Shell in Marina Park, Concerts 8pm Thursdays, Jul & Aug; also in Noonan Park in the Village, 6pm on Fridays. The Island Queen to Oak Bluffs leaves from farther up the harbor, 35 min. trip, 6 times a day (548-4800). Falmouth-Edgartown ferry leaves from Falmouth Marine, daily service May-Oct, 60 min. trip, 548-9400. Patriot Fishing and Sightseeing cruises are located at the mouth of the Harbor on the western shore. Falmouth Heights, behind the marina, is an historic district with many wonderfully restored houses, some of them Inns and B&Bs. Blessing of the Fleet is at Falmouth Heights Beach, July 4th. Arts and Crafts Fair Mid July. Falmouth Road Race Mid August.

VIII. Massachusetts: The Islands

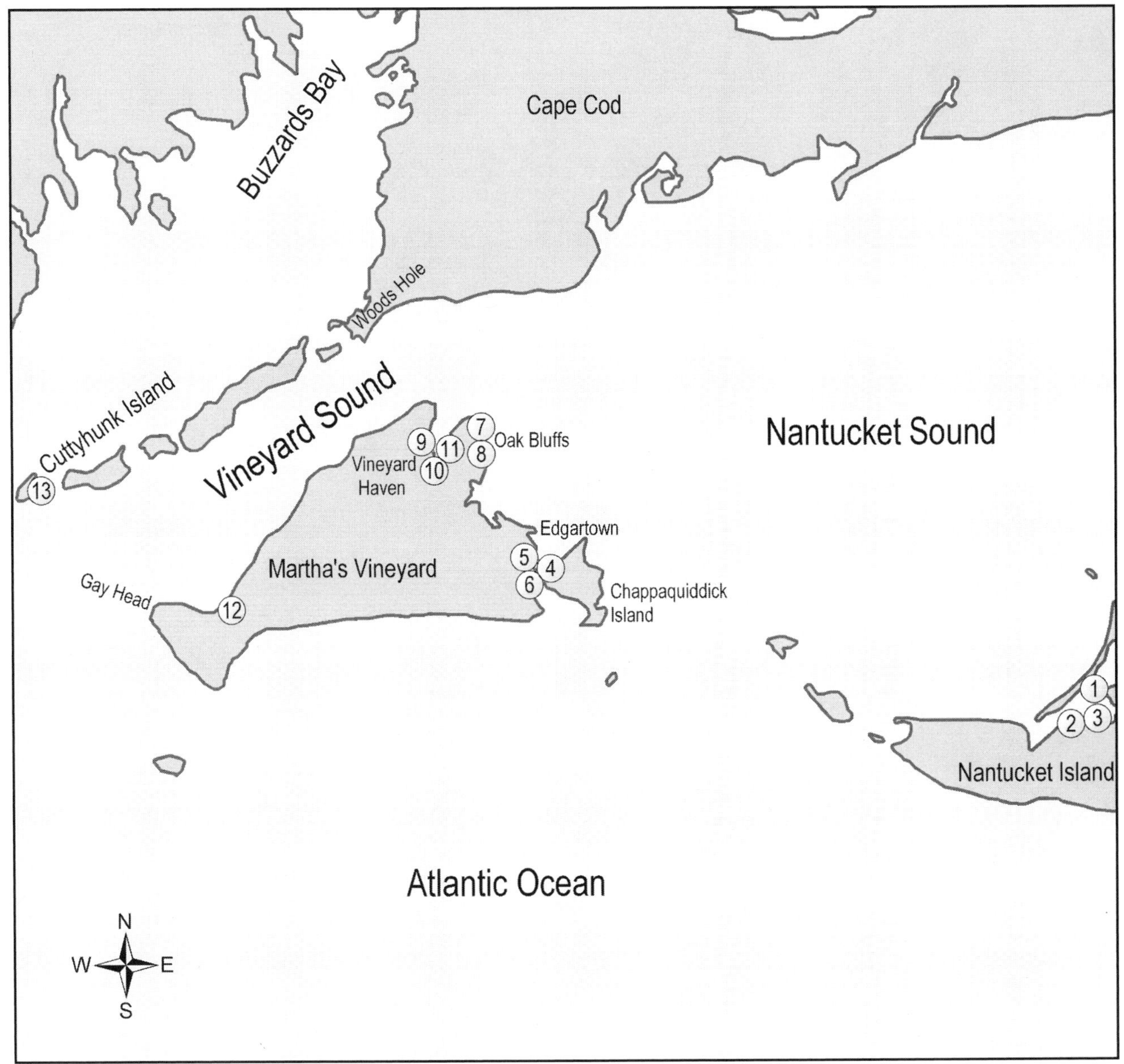

MAP	MARINA	HARBOR	PAGE
1	**Nantucket Moorings**	*Nantucket Harbor*	180
2	**Nantucket Boat Basin**	*Nantucket Harbor*	181
3	**Nantucket Town Pier & Dinghy Dock**	*Nantucket Harbor*	182
4	**North Wharf/Edgartown Moorings**	*Edgartown Harbor*	183
5	**Mad Max Marina**	*Edgartown Harbor*	184
6	**Harborside Inn**	*Edgartown Harbor*	185
7	**Dockside Market Place & Marina**	*Oak Bluffs Harbor*	186
8	**Oak Bluffs Marina**	*Oak Bluffs Harbor*	187
9	**Owen Park Town Dock & Moorings**	*Vineyard Haven Harbor*	188
10	**Vineyard Haven Maritime Wharf**	*Vinyard Haven Harbor*	189
11	**Vineyard Haven Marina**	*Vineyard Haven Harbor*	190
12	**Menemsha Harbor**	*Menemsha Harbor*	191
13	**Cuttyhunk Town Marina**	*Cuttyhunk Island*	192

Nantucket Moorings

85 Bartlett Road; Nantucket, MA 02554

Tel: (508) 228-4472 **VHF: Monitor** 68 **Talk** 68
Fax: (508) 228-7441 **Alternate Tel:** n/a
Email: moorings@nantucket.net **Web:** www.nantucketmoorings.com
Nearest Town: Nantucket *(0.1 mi.)* **Tourist Info:** (508) 228-0925

Navigational Information

Lat: 41°17.164' **Long:** 070°05.339' **Tide:** 3 ft. **Current:** n/a **Chart:** 13242
Rep. Depths (*MLW*): Entry 20 ft. **Fuel Dock** n/a **Max Slip/Moor** 15 ft./100 ft.
Access: Nantucket Sound to Nantucket Harbor

Marina Facilities *(In Season/Off Season)*

Fuel: *at Lady Grey Marine -*
Slips: 0 Total, 0 Transient **Max LOA:** 15 ft. **Max Beam:** 100 ft.
Rate *(per ft.)*: **Day** n/a **Week** n/a **Month** n/a
Power: 30 amp n/a, **50 amp** n/a, **100 amp** n/a, **200 amp** n/a
Cable TV: No **Dockside Phone:** No
Dock Type: n/a
Moorings: 125 Total, 125 Transient **Launch:** Yes ($4/pp/1-way, discounts)
Rate: Day $55 **Week** n/a **Month** n/a
Heads: 2 Toilet(s), 2 Shower(s)
Laundry: Yes **Pay Phones:** Yes
Pump-Out: OnSite, Full Service, 2 Port **Fee:** Free **Closed Heads:** Yes

Marina Operations

Owner/Manager: Dennis & Wendy Metcalfe **Dockmaster:** Same
In-Season: May-Oct **Off-Season:** Closed
After-Hours Arrival: Call in advance Ch. 68 or by phone
Reservations: Yes **Credit Cards:** Visa/MC, Amex
Discounts: May/Sep - Inq. **Dockage:** n/a **Fuel:** n/a **Repair:** n/a
Pets: Welcome, Dog Walk Area **Handicap Access:** No

Marina Services and Boat Supplies

Services - Docking Assistance **Communication -** Mail & Package Hold, Data Ports *(Internet Café 228-9165)*, FedEx, AirBorne, UPS, Express Mail *(Sat Del)* **Supplies - OnCall:** Ice *(Cube)* **Near:** Ships' Store *(228-6244 Brant Point Marine)*, Bait/Tackle *(Nantucket Tackle 228-4081; Cross Rip Outfitters 228-4900)* **Under 1 mi:** Marine Discount Store *(Nantucket Ship Chandlery 228-2300)*, Propane *(Nantucket Gas 228-0655)*

Boatyard Services

Near: Travelift *(20T)*, Launching Ramp, Electrical Repairs, Electronics Repairs, Hull Repairs, Rigger, Bottom Cleaning, Brightwork. **Nearest Yard:** Grey Lady Marine (508) 228-6525

Restaurants and Accommodations

Near: Restaurant *(Cap'n Tobey's 228-0836, L $6-10, D $13-28)*, *(American Bounty 228-3886, B $4-8, D $14-28)*, *(Woodbox 228-0587, D $16-$30)*, *(Atlantic Café 228-0570, L $5-11, D $7-20)*, *(Pearl 228-9701, D $30-46)*, Seafood Shack *(Sayle's 228-4599)*, Pizzeria *(Steamboat Wharf 228-1131)*, Hotel *(White Elephant 228-2500, $350-700)*, *(Jared Coffin House 228-2400, $325)*, Inn/B&B *(Carlisle House 228-0720, $95-200)*, *(Tuckernuck Inn 228-4886, $80-250)*, *(Pineapple 228-3577, $170-325)*

Recreation and Entertainment

Near: Picnic Area, Playground *(dinghy to Children's Beach)*, Dive Shop, Boat Rentals *(Nantucket Kayak 325-6900)*, Roller Blade/Bike Paths *(5 major "road-separated" paths - 25 mi.)*, Fishing Charter *(Topspin Fishing 228-7724)*, Movie Theater *(Gaslight Theatre 228-4435)*, Video Rental *(Nantucket Video 228-0101)*, Park, Museum *(Nantucket Whaling Museum; Nantucket Historical Association 228-1894)*, Cultural Attract *(Maria Mitchell Aquarium 228-5387)*, Sightseeing *(Whale Watch Trips)* **Under 1 mi:** Beach *(Jetties Beach or dinghy to Coatue)*, Jogging Paths **1-3 mi:** Tennis Courts *(Brant Point Racquet Club 228-3700)*, Fitness Center *(Nantucket Health Club 228-4750)* **3+ mi:** Golf Course *(Siasconset Golf Club 257-6596 , 9 mi.)*

Provisioning and General Services

Near: Convenience Store, Supermarket *(Stop & Shop 228-2178, A&P 228-9756)*, Gourmet Shop *(Nantucket Gourmet 228-6447)*, Delicatessen, Health Food *(Annye's Whole Foods)*, Liquor Store *(Island Spirits 228-4484)*, Bakery, Farmers' Market, Fishmonger *(Straight Wharf Fish 228-1095)*, Bank/ATM, Post Office, Catholic Church, Protestant Church, Library, Beauty Salon, Laundry *(Swain's Wharf)*, Bookstore *(Nantucket Bookworks 228-4000)*, Pharmacy *(Nantucket Pharm. 228-0180)*, Newsstand, Hardware Store *(Marine Home Center 228-0900)* **Under 1 mi:** Dry Cleaners

Transportation

OnCall: Rental Car *(Nantucket Windmill 228-1227, Affordable 228-3501, Nantucket Car 228-7474)*, Taxi *(Independent Taxi 228-5035)* **Near:** Bikes *(Wheel Happy 627-5928)*, Local Bus *(NRTA 228-7025, MemDay-Oct 1, 7am-11:30pm)*, Ferry Service *(Hyline Cruises & Steamship Authority to Boston, Chatham, Harwich, Hyannis, MV, Ptown)* **Airport:** Nantucket - service to Boston, NY, Hyannis, Barnstable and MV. *(3 mi.)*

Medical Services

911 Service **OnCall:** Holistic Services *(Spa to Go 228-5574)*, Ambulance **Near:** Doctor **Under 1 mi:** Dentist, Chiropractor **Hospital:** Nantucket Cottage 228-9788 *(0.5 mi.)*

Setting -- This beautiful island was once the whaling capital of the world. Thanks to its spectacular harbor, it's now one of the premier ports of call on the East Coast. The only transient mooring field, 125 strong, is located in the center of the harbor - across the channel from Nantucket Boat Basin - with unparalleled views of picturesque, historic Nantucket Town. Access to the Island is by launch or dinghy. Most services, restaurants and inns are within a few blocks.

Marina Notes -- *Up to 60' $55, 60-79' $65, over 80' $75. Established 1978. Minimum 2 night stay. Prepayment of 2 nights (3 on holiday week-ends) required with reservation and is non-refundable (but can be changed with 24 hrs. notice). Reservations beginning April 1. Check in after 2 pm; check out by noon. Escort to mooring. The landing for Harbor Launch is at the foot of Main St. in the heart of town 325-1350 ($4 pp/1-way, multi-trip discounts available). Two free dinghy docks, water, garbage, ice, and free pump-out are at the Town Pier (9 ft. depths), a short walk from town center. Or call the Pump-out Boat on Ch.9/14. Free heads & showers at Town Pier and Straight Wharf. Fuel at Grey Lady Marine and Nantucket Boat Basin.

Notable -- The 18th & 19thC buildings comprise one of the country's best historic districts. Self-guided tours from any of the 12 properties operated by the Historical Association ($10 pass) 7 days MemDay-ColDay. The Whaling Museum and Peter Foulger Museum are both on Broad St. 5 bike paths provide access to beaches and moors. NRTA Shuttle makes most of Nantucket accessible and intersects with bicycle routes. Catch it in town at Salem & Washington Sts., to beaches on Broad St. The Allserve boat, Ch.69, still plies the harbor with coffee, newspapers, food and drinks (this was the beginning of Nantucket Nectars).

Navigational Information

Lat: 41°17.036' **Long:** 070°05.639' **Tide:** 3 ft. **Current:** n/a **Chart:** 13242
Rep. Depths (*MLW*): Entry 12 ft. **Fuel Dock** 12 ft. **Max Slip/Moor** 15 ft./-
Access: Nantucket Sound to Nantucket Harbor

Marina Facilities *(In Season/Off Season)*

Fuel: *Mobil* - Gasoline, Diesel, High-Speed Pumps
Slips: 242 Total, 100 Transient **Max LOA:** 400 ft. **Max Beam:** n/a
Rate *(per ft.)*: **Day** $4.00/$2.50* **Week** Inq. **Month** Inq.
Power: 30 amp $10, **50 amp** $22.50, **100 amp** $45, **200 amp** n/a
Cable TV: Yes, $8 **Dockside Phone:** Yes, $6, up to 8 line(s)
Dock Type: Wood, Long Fingers, Pilings, Fixed
Moorings: 0 Total, 0 Transient **Launch:** n/a, Dinghy Dock
Rate: Day n/a **Week** n/a **Month** n/a
Heads: 18 Toilet(s), 18 Shower(s)
Laundry: 9 Washer(s), 9 Dryer(s) **Pay Phones:** Yes, 3
Pump-Out: OnSite, OnCall, Full Service **Fee:** Free **Closed Heads:** Yes

Marina Operations

Owner/Manager: George H. Bassett Jr. **Dockmaster:** Christina S. Martin
In-Season: Jun 21-LabDay, 7am-7pm **Off-Season:** LabDay-Jun, 8am-5pm
After-Hours Arrival: Call ahead
Reservations: Yes **Credit Cards:** Visa/MC, Dscvr, Din, Amex, Mobil
Discounts: None
Pets: Welcome, Dog Walk Area **Handicap Access:** No

Nantucket Boat Basin

PO Box 1139; Swain's Wharf; Nantucket, MA 02554

Tel: (508) 325-1350; (800) 626-2628 **VHF: Monitor** 9 **Talk** 11
Fax: (508) 228-8941 **Alternate Tel:** n/a
Email: n/a **Web:** www. nantucketboatbasin.com
Nearest Town: Nantucket *(0 mi.)* **Tourist Info:** (508) 228-0925

Marina Services and Boat Supplies

Services - Docking Assistance, Concierge, Security *(7pm-8am)*, Trash Pick-Up, Dock Carts, Megayacht Facilities **Communication -** Mail & Package Hold, Phone Messages, Fax in/out, FedEx, AirBorne, UPS, Express Mail **Supplies - OnSite:** Ice *(Block, Cube)*, Ships' Store *(Nantucket Ship 228-2300)* **OnCall:** Propane **Near:** Bait/Tackle *(Cross Rip 228-4900)*

Boatyard Services

Near: Launching Ramp, Electrical Repairs, Electronics Repairs, Hull Repairs, Rigger, Bottom Cleaning, Brightwork, Refrigeration. **Nearest Yard:** Grey Lady Marine (508) 228-6525

Restaurants and Accommodations

OnSite: Restaurant *(Ropewalk 228-8886, L $7-14, D $15-27, Kids' menu)*, *(Straight Wharf 228-4499, D $30-40)*, Lite Fare *(Provisions 228-3258, 8am-5:30pm)*, Condo/Cottage *(The Wharf Cottages 228-4620, $200-600)* **OnCall:** Restaurant *(Toppers at the Wauwinet 228-0145, L $20-25, D $34-52, guests picked up by boat)* **Near:** Restaurant *(Bosun's Bistro 228-7774, B $6-9, L $7-15, D $19-28)*, *(Cioppino's 228-4622, L $8-14, D $18-38)*, *(Le Languedoc 228-2552, L $7-19, D $23-36)*, Seafood Shack *(Lobster Trap 228-4200)*, Hotel *(White Elephant 228-2500, $350-700)*, Inn/B&B *(7 Sea St. $175-295)*, Condo/Cottage *(Old North Wharf Cottages 228-6071, $1,000-5,800/wk)* **3+ mi:** Hotel *(The Wauwinet 228-0145, $600-1000, 9 mi.)*

Recreation and Entertainment

OnSite: Picnic Area, Grills, Boat Rentals *(Nantucket Boat Rental 325-1001)*, Fishing Charter *(Topspin 228-7724;)*, Sightseeing *(Natural history & seal cruises 228-7037 $50-70; Nant. Whalewatch 800-322-0013 $85/45 7 hrs.)* **Near:** Playground *(Children's Beach)*, Dive Shop, Jogging Paths, Roller Blade/Bike Paths *(to Madaket or Surfside)*, Movie Theater *(Gaslight 228-4435)*, Video Rental *(Nantucket Video 228-0101)*, Park, Museum *(Nantucket Historical Society 228-1894, Nantucket Whaling Museum)*, Cultural Attract, Galleries **Under 1 mi:** Beach *(Jetties Beach)*, Tennis Courts *(Brant Point Racquet Club 228-3700)* **1-3 mi:** Golf Course *(Miacomet Golf Club, private 325-0335)*, Fitness Center

Provisioning and General Services

OnSite: Convenience Store, Fishmonger *(Sayle's 228-4599)* **OnCall:** Dry Cleaners **Near:** Supermarket *(A&P 228-9756, Stop & Shop 228-2178)*, Gourmet Shop *(Nant. Gourmet 228-4353)*, Health Food *(Light Generation 228-4554)*, Liquor Store *(Island Spirits 228-4484)*, Green Grocer, Bank/ATM, Post Office, Catholic Church, Library *(Atheneum 228-1110)*, Beauty Salon, Bookstore *(Bookworks 228-4000)*, Pharmacy *(Congdon's 228-0020)*, Newsstand **Under 1 mi:** Hardware Store *(Marine Home Center 228-0900)*

Transportation

OnSite: Bikes *(Nantucket Bikes 228-1999)* **OnCall:** Rental Car *(Nantucket Car Rental 228-7474)*, Taxi *(Poppy's 228-7874)* **Near:** Water Taxi, Local Bus *(NRTA - all around the island)*, Ferry Service *(Hyline Cruises & Steamship Authority to Boston, Chatham, Harwich, Hyannis, MV, Provincetown)* **Airport:** Nantucket Memorial *(3 mi.)*

Medical Services

911 Service **OnCall:** Ambulance **Near:** Doctor *(Butterworth 228-3200)*, Dentist, Chiropractor *(Nantucket Family Chiro 325-4777)* **Hospital:** Nantucket Cottage 228-1200 *(0.5 mi.)*

Setting -- Located right in the heart of historic Nantucket Town, the 242 slips of this world-class facility are gracefully woven along three wharfs. The docks sit among charming flower decked cottages and gray shingled buildings. Views are mostly of the town, the docks and the megayachts lining the outer piers.

Marina Notes -- *35-59' $4/ft., 60-99' $5/ft.,100-124' $5.50/ft., 125' + $6/ft. 35 ft. minimum. Call for off-season & long-term rates. 2-night minimum. Single night dockage, space available only. 3-night minimum deposit required. Arrival after 1pm, departure 11am. Reservations highly recommended! 15% surcharge for special slip requests. Dock staff moves ladders to line-up with life-line openings. Federal No-Discharge Zone. Free dockside pumpouts. Supply own power, telephone, cable cords. Caryn Carlson takes service very seriously; there are three concierge "desks" -- one on each wharf -- open 8am-6pm; this service is free 325-1360. Owned by Nantucket Island Resorts, owners of The Wharf Cottages, Harbor House, White Elephant, The Breakers and The Wauwinet.

Notable -- All of Nantucket Town, with its 18 &19C buildings, cobblestone streets and narrow lanes, is a sightseeing destination and has been designated a national historic site. Wander the side streets to see restored whaling merchants' homes. Self-guided tour maps available from the Historical Assoc. 25 miles of bicycle paths criss-cross the island. NRTA seasonal shuttles cover the Island and have bike racks ($0.50-2). 50 sq. mi. of moors and beaches accessible by dinghy, bike or shuttle. Dog park as well as children's beach nearby. 792 acre Coskata-Coatue Wildlife Refuge. Twenty-two cottages that overlook the marina are available for rent 228-4260. Many Inns/B&Bs nearby. Green Market daily (except Sun) 9am - 1pm at Main & Federal Sts. Many megayachts stop here.

PHOTOS ON CD-ROM: 9

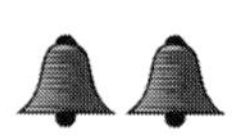

Nantucket Town Pier

34 Washington Street; Nantucket, MA 02554

Tel: (508) 228-7261 **VHF: Monitor** 9 **Talk** 14
Fax: (508) 325-5388 **Alternate Tel:** n/a
Email: marine@nantucket.net **Web:** www.nantucket.net*
Nearest Town: Nantucket *(0.25 mi.)* **Tourist Info:** (508) 228-1700

Navigational Information

Lat: 41°16.887' **Long:** 070°05.705' **Tide:** 3 ft. **Current:** n/a **Chart:** 13242
Rep. Depths (*MLW*): Entry 12 ft. **Fuel Dock** n/a **Max Slip/Moor** 9 ft./-
Access: Past Nantucket Boat Basin, next set of docks

Marina Facilities *(In Season/Off Season)*

Fuel: No
Slips: 150 Total, 10 Transient **Max LOA:** 30 ft. **Max Beam:** 10 ft.
Rate *(per ft.)*: **Day** $100.00 **Week** n/a **Month** n/a
Power: 30 amp Incl., **50 amp** n/a, **100 amp** n/a, **200 amp** n/a
Cable TV: No **Dockside Phone:** No
Dock Type: Wood, Floating, Fixed
Moorings: 0 Total, 0 Transient **Launch:** n/a, Dinghy Dock
Rate: Day n/a **Week** n/a **Month** n/a
Heads: 6 Toilet(s), 4 Shower(s)
Laundry: None **Pay Phones:** Yes
Pump-Out: OnCall, Full Service, 2 Central **Fee:** n/a **Closed Heads:** Yes

Marina Operations

Owner/Manager: n/a **Dockmaster:** D. F. Fronzuto
In-Season: Jul-Sep 1, 8am-10pm **Off-Season:** n/a, 8am-4pm
After-Hours Arrival: n/a
Reservations: No **Credit Cards:** Visa/MC, Cash
Discounts: None
Pets: Welcome, Dog Walk Area **Handicap Access:** Yes, Heads, Docks

Marina Services and Boat Supplies

Services - Docking Assistance, Security *(police 10pm-3am)*, Trash Pick-Up, Dock Carts **Communication -** Mail & Package Hold, Phone Messages, FedEx, UPS, Express Mail *(Sat Del)* **Supplies - OnSite:** Ice *(Block, Cube)* **Near:** Bait/Tackle *(Cross Rip 228-4900)* **Under 1 mi:** Ships' Store *(Nantucket Ship Chandlery 228-2300)*, Propane

Boatyard Services

OnCall: Engine mechanic *(gas, diesel)* **Near:** Travelift, Launching Ramp, Electrical Repairs, Electronic Sales, Electronics Repairs, Hull Repairs, Rigger, Sail Loft, Canvas Work, Bottom Cleaning, Brightwork, Air Conditioning, Refrigeration, Divers, Compound, Wash & Wax, Interior Cleaning, Propeller Repairs, Inflatable Repairs, Metal Fabrication, Awlgrip. **Nearest Yard:** Grey Lady Marine (508) 228-6525

Restaurants and Accommodations

Near: Restaurant *(Captain Tobey's 228-0836, L $20, D $25)*, *(Club Car 228-1101, D $30-40)*, *(Cioppino's 228-4622, L $9-14, D $19-32)*, *(Vincent's Italian 228-0189, L $7-12, D $10-23, pizza, too)*, *(American Seasons 228-7111, D $25-33)*, *(Jared's 228-2400, B $7-10, D $25-34, Wed & Sun Seafood Buffet $27)*, Pizzeria *(Steamboat Wharf 228-1131)*, Hotel *(White Elephant 228-2500, $350-700)*, Inn/B&B *(Woodbox Inn 228-0587, $165-300)*, *(Pineapple Inn 228-9992, $110-300)*, Condo/Cottage *(Harbor Cottages 228-4485, $120-185)* **Under 1 mi:** Inn/B&B *(Brant Point Inn 228-5442, $150-200)*

Recreation and Entertainment

Near: Pool, Movie Theater, Video Rental *(Camera Shop & Video 228-0101)*, Museum *(Whaling Museum, Nantucket Lightship Baskets 228-1177)* **Under 1 mi:** Heated Pool, Beach *(Jetties Beach)*, Special Events *(4th of July/Boston Pops)* **1-3 mi:** Spa, Picnic Area, Grills, Playground, Dive Shop, Volleyball, Tennis Courts *(Brant Point Racquet Club 228-3700)*, Fitness Center *(Nantucket Health Club 228-4750)*, Jogging Paths, Horseback Riding, Boat Rentals, Roller Blade/Bike Paths, Bowling, Fishing Charter, Group Fishing Boat **3+ mi:** Golf Course *(Siasconset G.C.257-6596, 10 mi.)*

Provisioning and General Services

Near: Convenience Store, Supermarket *(A&P 228-9756)*, Gourmet Shop *(Nantucket Gourmet 228-6447)*, Delicatessen, Health Food *(Light Generation 228-4554)*, Liquor Store *(Island Spirits 228-4484)*, Bakery *(Bake Shop 228-2797)*, Farmers' Market *(Main & Federal St. Mon-Sat)*, Fishmonger, Lobster Pound, Meat Market, Bank/ATM, Post Office, Catholic Church, Protestant Church, Synagogue *(228-6785)*, Library *(Atheneum 228-1110)*, Beauty Salon, Barber Shop, Dry Cleaners, Laundry, Bookstore *(Bookworks 228-4000)*, Pharmacy *(Nantucket 228-0180)*, Newsstand, Hardware Store, Florist, Retail Shops, Copies Etc.

Transportation

OnCall: Rental Car *(Nantucket Windmill 228-1227)* **Near:** Bikes *(Wheel Happy 627-5928)*, Water Taxi, Taxi *(Independent 228-5035)*, Local Bus *(NBTA Shuttle 228-7025)*, InterCity Bus, Ferry Service *(Hyannis, MV, Harwich)* **Airport:** Nantucket Memorial 945-9000 *(3 mi.)*

Medical Services

911 Service **Under 1 mi:** Doctor *(Butterworth 228-3200)*, Dentist, Chiropractor *(Ranney 228-2200)*, Holistic Services *(Nantucket Therapy 257-6832)*, Ambulance **Hospital:** Nantucket Cottage 825-9165 *(1 mi.)*

Setting -- Just beyond the extensive docks of the Nantucket Boat Basin, this recently upgraded municipal facility serves as a landing spot and service center for the 125 moorings and anchorage out in the Harbor. The dockage is primarily for local, smaller boats; but the dinghy docks are open to all.

Marina Notes -- Dockage $100 flat rate. Up to 10 transient spots available for boats under 30 feet -- but, note, sleeping aboard is not permitted!! New floating docks. All the landside services -- heads, showers, pump-out, mail hold, etc. -- are available, free of charge, to transients who are moored or anchored in the harbor. Several large dinghy docks. Shellfish harvesting and fishing licenses. *On the Web at www.nantucket.net/marineandcoastalresources.

Notable -- Charming, exquisite Nantucket Town, declared a National Historic Landmark in 1966, is a short walk away. Cobblestone streets and brick sidewalks are lined with 800 pre-1850 buildings and electrified "gas" lights. Teeming with tourists from July through Labor Day, it is, nonetheless, one of the premier cruising destinations on the east coast (Jun & Sep are great). Just about any provisioning or service need can be accommodated within a short walk -- including a full-size supermarket. Most sites are within a mile. Wonderful, world-class restaurants -- from seafood shacks to top tier, gastronomic adventures -- are a short walk, bike or cab ride away. B&Bs and beautifully restored Inns are equally plentiful and convenient. MBTA Shuttle busses make the whole island, including its spectacular public beaches, easily accessible (7am-11:30pm $.50-1 per trip or $15 week pass. Don't miss Sconset's rose-covered cottages. Visit the Tourist Office at 45 Federal St. or one of the kiosks at Steamboat or Straight Wharf. Internet access at InterNet Café 228-9165 - 2 Union St. $10/hr.

Navigational Information
Lat: 41°23.065' **Long:** 070°30.463' **Tide:** 2 ft. **Current:** 1kt. **Chart:** 13238
Rep. Depths (*MLW*): Entry 19 ft. **Fuel Dock** 20 ft. **Max Slip/Moor** 20 ft./20 ft.
Access: First commercial dock on starboard side

Marina Facilities *(In Season/Off Season)*
Fuel: *Texaco* - Gasoline, Diesel, On Call Delivery
Slips: 33 Total, 4 Transient **Max LOA:** 300 ft. **Max Beam:** 27 ft.
Rate *(per ft.)*: **Day** $4.00/$2.00 **Week** n/a **Month** n/a
Power: 30 amp Incl., **50 amp** Incl., **100 amp** n/a, **200 amp** n/a
Cable TV: No **Dockside Phone:** No
Dock Type: Wood, Long Fingers, Alongside, Floating, Fixed
Moorings: 100 Total, 75 Transient **Launch:** Yes ($2/pp/1-way), Dinghy Dock
Rate: Day $35/10 **Week** n/a **Month** n/a
Heads: 2 Toilet(s), 3 Shower(s)
Laundry: None **Pay Phones:** No
Pump-Out: OnSite, OnCall, Full Service **Fee:** Free **Closed Heads:** Yes

Marina Operations
Owner/Manager: n/a **Dockmaster:** Charles Blair
In-Season: May-Nov, 7am-9pm **Off-Season:** Dec-Apr, Closed
After-Hours Arrival: Call VHF 74
Reservations: Yes, Preferred **Credit Cards:** Visa/MC, Dscvr, Amex, Tex
Discounts: None
Pets: Welcome **Handicap Access:** Yes, Heads, Docks

North Wharf & Moorings

PO Box 739; 1 Morse Street; Edgartown, MA 02539

Tel: (508) 627-4746 **VHF: Monitor** 9 **Talk** 74
Fax: (508) 627-6123 **Alternate Tel:** n/a
Email: edgh@vineyard.net **Web:** n/a
Nearest Town: Edgartown *(0 mi.)* **Tourist Info:** (508) 693-0085

Marina Services and Boat Supplies
Services - Docking Assistance, Security *(20 Hrs., Patrol)*, Trash Pick-Up, Megayacht Facilities **Communication -** Mail & Package Hold, FedEx, UPS, Express Mail **Supplies - OnSite:** Ice *(Block, Cube)*, Ships' Store *(Edgartown Marine 627-4388)*, Bait/Tackle, Live Bait *(Eels)* **Near:** Propane *(Vineyard Propane 627-5080)*

Boatyard Services
OnSite: Travelift *(36T)*, Engine mechanic *(gas, diesel)*, Electronic Sales **OnCall:** Bottom Cleaning, Divers *(Fathom Divers 627-9667)*, Compound, Wash & Wax, Interior Cleaning, Propeller Repairs **Near:** Launching Ramp, Rigger. **Under 1 mi:** Electrical Repairs, Electronics Repairs, Hull Repairs, Air Conditioning, Refrigeration, Woodworking, Yacht Interiors, Painting, Yacht Broker, Total Refits. **1-3 mi:** Forklift, Brightwork.

Restaurants and Accommodations
Near: Restaurant *(Seafood Shanty 627-8622)*, *(Chesca's 627-1234, D $25)*, *(Black Bean 627-6655)*, *(L'Etoile Restaurant 627-5187)*, Hotel *(Harbor View 627-7000, $115-775)*, Inn/B&B *(Colonial Inn of Martha's Vineyard 627-4711, $110-375)*, *(Edgartown Inn 627-4794, $150-210)*, *(Daggett House 627-4600, $115-550)* **Under 1 mi:** Restaurant *(David Ryan's 627-4100, L $6-13, D $12-26)*, Snack Bar *(Dock Street 627-5232, B $5, L $5)*, Pizzeria *(Island Pizza)*, Hotel *(Charlotte Inn $$275-$850)*

Recreation and Entertainment
Near: Beach *(Lighthouse or dinghy to East Beach on Chappaquiddick)*, Roller Blade/Bike Paths *(to Oak Bluffs)*, Fishing Charter *(Big Eye Charters 627-3649)*, Movie Theater *(Entertainment Cinemas 627-8008)*, Museum *(North Water Street's 19thC sea captains' homes)*, Cultural Attract *(Old Sculpin Gallery)* **Under 1 mi:** Playground, Fitness Center, Jogging Paths, Boat Rentals *(Kasoon Kayak 627-2553)*, Video Rental *(Hollywood Video 627-3533)*, Galleries **1-3 mi:** Tennis Courts *(Mattakesett Island 627-9506)*, Horseback Riding *(Katama Stables 627-8367)*, Park, Sightseeing *(Felix Neck Sanctuary 627-4850f)* **3+ mi:** Golf Course *(TVGC 696-3163, 5 mi.)*

Provisioning and General Services
OnCall: Dry Cleaners, Laundry *(Airport Laundromat 693-5005)* **Near:** Convenience Store, Gourmet Shop *(Great Harbour Gourmet)*, Delicatessen *(Winter St. Sandwich 627-9144)*, Liquor Store, Bakery, Bank/ATM, Post Office, Catholic Church, Library *(Edgartown PL 627-1373)*, Beauty Salon, Bookstore *(Bickerton & Ripley Books 627-8463)*, Newsstand, Hardware Store *(Granite Ace 696-3999)*, Clothing Store, Retail Shops **Under 1 mi:** Health Food, Fishmonger *(Edgartown Seafood Market 627-3791)*, Meat Market, Protestant Church, Barber Shop **1-3 mi:** Supermarket *(A&P 627-9522)*, Farmers' Market, Pharmacy *(Triangle 627-4351)*, Florist

Transportation
OnCall: Taxi *(Accurate Cab 627-9798)* **Near:** Bikes *(Edgartown Bike Rentals 627-4052)*, Water Taxi *($2/pp 1/Way)*, Local Bus *(South Beach & Edgartown Trolleys 627-7448)*, InterCity Bus *(MVTA to all towns)* **Under 1 mi:** Ferry Service *(Edgartown to Falmouth or Chappaquiddick)* **1-3 mi:** Rental Car *(Budget 693-1911)* **Airport:** Martha's Vineyard *(8 mi.)*

Medical Services
911 Service **OnCall:** Ambulance **Near:** Holistic Services **Under 1 mi:** Doctor, Dentist, Chiropractor **Hospital:** Martha's Vineyard 693-0410 *(7 mi.)*

Setting -- Boats of all sizes intermingle in the mooring field that is spread out along narrow Edgartown Harbor. They all share spectacular views of this classic, elegant town, with its old whaling captains' homes set high on the steep hill. The lovely yachts that line the waterfront confirm Edgartown's boast as the sailing capital of the world. The North Wharf land base, with its full-service dockage, is on the north end of the Edgartown historic district.

Marina Notes -- North Wharf is a municipal facility with two mooring fields managed by the Edgartown Harbormaster - North has 25 blue balls, is unreserved, closer to town and fills by 1pm. South has 50 yellow balls and is by reservation. Onsite dinghy dockage. Oldport Marine provides launch service -- Ch.68 -- launch docks at North Wharf and just north of Edgartown YC. Public dinghy docks are just south of the EYC in front of Navigator Restaurant. Edgartown Marine maintains an onsite chandlery, travelift, and 9 acres of boat storage. Two large docks separated by a hauling slip. Face slips take up to 130 ft. vessels. Two interslips up to 90 ft., the fuel dock up to 150 ft. Water at Memorial Wharf with pump out, at North Wharf while fueling, or the Water Barge in front of North Wharf. Free pump-out at Memorial Wharf or from Harbormaster's pump-out boat 9am-4pm Ch.74. Heads and showers at North Wharf.

Notable -- The Lighthouse Beach is an easy walk as are all of the restored buildings and houses. Pick up a map and start on North Water Street with its exquisite 19C Greek Revival and Federal style houses built by whaling and China trade captains. There are rambling bicycle paths, one-of-a-kind shops, boutiques, art galleries, and local historical museums -- all within a short distance of the North Wharf, the dinghy docks or Launch Landing.

MA - THE ISLANDS

PHOTOS ON CD-ROM: 9

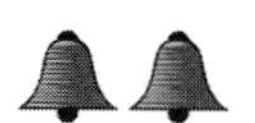

Mad Max Marina

PO Box 2821; 25 Dock Street; Edgartown, MA 02539

Tel: (508) 627-7400 **VHF: Monitor** 9 **Talk** 71
Fax: (508) 627-7245 **Alternate Tel:** n/a
Email: n/a **Web:** n/a
Nearest Town: Edgartown *(0 mi.)* **Tourist Info:** (508) 693-0085

Navigational Information

Lat: 41°23.330' **Long:** 070°30.671' **Tide:** 2 ft. **Current:** 1 kt. **Chart:** 13238
Rep. Depths (*MLW*): Entry 15 ft. **Fuel Dock** n/a **Max Slip/Moor** 15 ft./-
Access: Head South from R2 bell located in Nantucket Sound

Marina Facilities *(In Season/Off Season)*

Fuel: No
Slips: 9 Total, 9 Transient **Max LOA:** 150 ft. **Max Beam:** 30 ft.
Rate *(per ft.)*: **Day** $200.00/Inq.* **Week** Inq. **Month** Inq.
Power: 30 amp $10, **50 amp** $20, **100 amp** n/a, **200 amp** n/a
Cable TV: No **Dockside Phone:** No
Dock Type: Wood, Short Fingers, Pilings, Fixed
Moorings: 0 Total, 0 Transient **Launch:** n/a
Rate: Day n/a **Week** n/a **Month** n/a
Heads: None
Laundry: None **Pay Phones:** No
Pump-Out: OnCall, Full Service, 2 Port **Fee:** Free **Closed Heads:** Yes

Marina Operations

Owner/Manager: Robert Colacray **Dockmaster:** Seasonal
In-Season: May 25-Oct 10, 9am-6pm **Off-Season:** Oct 10-May 25, Closed
After-Hours Arrival: Call (508) 627-7400 for instructions
Reservations: Yes, Required **Credit Cards:** Visa/MC
Discounts: None
Pets: Welcome **Handicap Access:** No

Marina Services and Boat Supplies

Services - Docking Assistance, Trash Pick-Up **Communication -** FedEx, UPS, Express Mail **Supplies - OnSite:** Ice *(Block, Cube)* **Near:** Ships' Store *(Edgartown Marine Services 627-7752)*, Bait/Tackle *(Captain Porky's 627-7177)* **1-3 mi:** Propane *(Vineyard Propane 693-5080)*, CNG

Boatyard Services

Near: Travelift *(75T)*, Railway, Forklift, Crane, Engine mechanic *(gas, diesel)*, Launching Ramp, Hull Repairs, Bottom Cleaning, Brightwork, Divers. **1-3 mi:** Electronic Sales, Electronics Repairs, Sail Loft. **Nearest Yard:** North Wharf (508) 627-4746

Restaurants and Accommodations

Near: Restaurant *(Chesca's 627-1234, D $15-25)*, *(L'Etoile Restaurant 627-5187)*, *(Savoir Fare 627-9864, D $24-35)*, *(Seafood Shanty 627-8622, L & D overlooking Mad Max)*, *(David Ryans 627-4100, L $6-13, D $12-26, kids' menu)*, *(The Coach House 627-7000, B $6-12, L $8-15, D $24-35)*, Snack Bar *(Dock Street 627-5232, B $5, L $5)*, Lite Fare *(Bagel Authority 627-5366)*, Hotel *(Harbor View Hotel 627-7000, $115-775)*, Inn/B&B *(Colonial Inn of Martha's Vineyard 627-4711, $110-375)*, *(Daggett House 627-4600, $100-575)*, *(Edgartown Inn 627-4794, $75-210)*, *(Kelley House 627-7900, $160-775)*, *(Hobknob 627-9510, $200-525)*

Recreation and Entertainment

Near: Beach *(walk to Lighthouse or dinghy to East Beach)*, Boat Rentals *(Gold Coast Parasail, Jetski & Kayak 693-3330)*, Fishing Charter *(Great Harbor 627-3122)*, Movie Theater *(Entertainment Cinemas 627-8008)*, Galleries **Under 1 mi:** Playground, Jogging Paths, Roller Blade/Bike Paths *(to Oak Bluffs)*, Park, Museum *(Vineyard Museum, Lighthouse Tours 627-4441)*, Sightseeing **1-3 mi:** Tennis Courts *(Mattakesett Island Club 627-9506)*, Fitness Center, Horseback Riding *(Katama Stables 627-8367)*, Bowling, Video Rental *(Hollywood Video 627-3533)* **3+ mi:** Golf Course *(TVGC 696-3163, 5 mi.)*

Provisioning and General Services

Near: Convenience Store, Delicatessen *(Winter St. Sandwich Shoppe 627-9144)*, Wine/Beer, Bakery, Bank/ATM, Catholic Church, Protestant Church, Library *(Edgartown PL 627-1373)*, Beauty Salon, Barber Shop, Newsstand, Florist, Clothing Store, Retail Shops **Under 1 mi:** Supermarket *(A&P 627-4144)*, Gourmet Shop *(Great Harbour Gourmet 627-4390)*, Green Grocer, Post Office, Bookstore *(Bickerton & Ripley Books 627-8463)*, Copies Etc. **1-3 mi:** Liquor Store *(Al's Package Store 627-4347)*, Dry Cleaners, Pharmacy *(Triangle 627-4351)*, Hardware Store *(Granite Ace 696-3999)*

Transportation

OnCall: Taxi *(John's Taxi 627-4677)* **Near:** Bikes *(Cutler Bike 627-4052)*, Water Taxi *(Oldport Launch)*, Rental Car *(Island Auto Rental 627-6800)*, Local Bus *(MVTA 15 major routes cover the island)*, Ferry Service *(to Chappaquiddick - Falmouth)* **Airport:** Martha's Vineyard *(8 mi.)*

Medical Services

911 Service **OnCall:** Ambulance **Under 1 mi:** Doctor *(Hoak 627-1044)*, Holistic Services *(Therapeutic Massage 627-6633)* **1-3 mi:** Dentist
Hospital: Martha's Vineyard 693-0410 *(6 mi.)*

Setting -- Edgartown was once a prosperous whaling center. Stately white Greek revival houses, built by ships' captains, line its narrow streets and brick sidewalks. Over a hundred years ago, it reinvented itself as an elegant, passionate yachting center. Occupying a prime location in this beautiful harbor, Mad Max is easily identifiable by the bright red catamaran with the Mad Max logo. It is just after the Memorial Town Dock and before the Edgartown Yacht Club.

Marina Notes -- *Slips are a flat rate starting at $200 per night plus electric. Please call for precise rates. No discharge harbor. Free pump-out boat Ch.74 or go to Memorial Wharf - both 9am-4pm. Mad Max Adventure cruises set sail from here and travel through the harbor in the red catamaran 2 hrs. $45/35. There is a small store onsite that sells Mad Max memorabilia. Mad Max is strictly dockage in a really great location -- there are no heads, showers, laundry or other services.Two chandlers are within walking distance. Showers at Edgartown Community Center.

Notable -- Carefully restored Vincent House, circa 1672, is the oldest known house on the island (Jun-Oct, 7days, Noon-3pm $3). Walk up to North Water Street for a view of some of the most perfectly preserved 18th & 19thC houses anywhere; they make this seaport village a museum-piece community. The 1834 Old Whaling Church has become a performing arts center. Beaches abound - Katma for surf, nearby Lighthouse for calm water and views. Take the On Time Ferry to Chappaquiddick Island (every 5 min, 7am-Mid) and visit East Beach, bike the Wasque Reservation $3 (5 mi. from ferry landing), take a naturalist-led tour of Cape Pogue Wildlife Refuge - 6 mi. of wilderness, or visit My Toi Preserve, a Japanese garden.

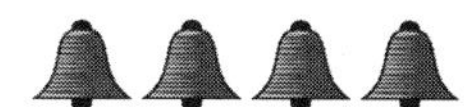

Navigational Information
Lat: 41°23.322' **Long:** 070°30.761' **Tide:** 2 ft. **Current:** 1 kt. **Chart:** 13238
Rep. Depths (*MLW*): Entry 21 ft. **Fuel Dock** n/a **Max Slip/Moor** 6 ft./-
Access: Past Chappaquiddick Point, the last set of docks to starboard

Marina Facilities *(In Season/Off Season)*
Fuel: No
Slips: 15 Total, 15 Transient **Max LOA:** 125 ft. **Max Beam:** n/a
Rate *(per ft.)*: **Day** $4.00* **Week** $28 **Month** n/a
Power: 30 amp n/a, **50 amp** n/a, **100 amp** n/a, **200 amp** n/a
Cable TV: No **Dockside Phone:** No
Dock Type: Wood
Moorings: 0 Total, 0 Transient **Launch:** n/a, Dinghy Dock
Rate: Day n/a **Week** n/a **Month** n/a
Heads: 2 Toilet(s)
Laundry: None **Pay Phones:** No
Pump-Out: OnCall, Full Service, 1 Port **Fee:** Free **Closed Heads:** Yes

Marina Operations
Owner/Manager: Joseph D. Badot **Dockmaster:** n/a
In-Season: MidApr-MidNov **Off-Season:** n/a
After-Hours Arrival: Please call ahead
Reservations: Yes, Necessary **Credit Cards:** Visa/MC, Amex
Discounts: None
Pets: No **Handicap Access:** No

Harborside Inn

PO Box 67; 3 South Water Street; Edgartown, MA 02539

Tel: (508) 627-4321 **VHF: Monitor** 9 **Talk** 9
Fax: (508) 627-7631 **Alternate Tel:** n/a
Email: harbside@vineyard.net **Web:** www.TheHarborsideInn.com
Nearest Town: Edgartown *(0.1 mi.)* **Tourist Info:** (508) 693-0085

Marina Services and Boat Supplies
Services - Docking Assistance, Trash Pick-Up **Communication -** Fax in/out, FedEx, UPS, Express Mail **Supplies - Near:** Ice *(Block, Cube)*, Ships' Store *(Edgartown Marine Services 627-7752)*, Bait/Tackle *(Coop's 627-3909)* **1-3 mi:** Propane *(Vineyard Propane 693-5080)*

Boatyard Services
Under 1 mi: Travelift *(75T)*, Engine mechanic *(gas, diesel)*, Hull Repairs, Bottom Cleaning, Brightwork. **Nearest Yard:** North Wharf (508) 627-4746

Restaurants and Accommodations
OnSite: Hotel *(Harborside Inn $85-375)* **Near:** Restaurant *(Navigator Restaurant 627-4320, L $7-12, D $20-29, kids' menu)*, *(L'Etoile Restaurant 627-5187)*, *(Chesca's 627-1234, D $15-25)*, *(Daggett House 627-4600)*, *(David Ryan's 627-4100, L $6-13, D $12-26)*, *(Black Bean 627-6655)*, Lite Fare *(Bagel Authority 627-5366)*, Inn/B&B *(Edgartown Inn 627-4794, $75-220)*, *(Point Way Inn 627-8633, $155-335)*, *(Colonial Inn of Martha's Vineyard 627-4711, $110-375)*, *(Hobknob Inn 627-9510, $200-525)*

Recreation and Entertainment
OnSite: Heated Pool, Spa **Near:** Beach *(Lighthouse or dinghy to East Beaches)*, Jogging Paths, Boat Rentals *(Gold Coast Jet Ski & Kayak 693-3330)*, Roller Blade/Bike Paths *(to Oak Bluffs)*, Fishing Charter *(Great Harbor 627-3122)* **Under 1 mi:** Playground, Fitness Center, Movie Theater *(Entertainment Cinemas 627-8008)*, Park, Museum *(Vincent House noon-3pm $3)*, Cultural Attract *(1834 Old Whaling Church Performing Arts Center)*, Sightseeing *(North Water Street's 19thC Sea Captains' homes, MV Historical Society's Lighthouse Tours)*, Galleries *(Old Sculpin Gallery)* **1-3 mi:** Tennis Courts *(Mattakesett Island 627-9506)*, Horseback Riding *(Katama Stables 627-8367)*, Video Rental *(Hollywood Video 627-3533)*

Provisioning and General Services
Near: Convenience Store, Delicatessen *(Winter St. Sandwich Shoppe 627-9144)*, Bank/ATM, Catholic Church, Protestant Church, Library *(Edgartown PL 627-1373)*, Beauty Salon, Florist, Clothing Store **Under 1 mi:** Supermarket *(A&P 627-4144)*, Gourmet Shop *(Great Harbour Gourmet 627-4390)*, Farmers' Market, Green Grocer, Fishmonger *(Edgartown Seafood Market 627-3791)*, Post Office, Bookstore *(Bickerton & Ripley Books 627-8463)*, Copies Etc. **1-3 mi:** Liquor Store *(Al's Package 627-4347)*, Dry Cleaners, Pharmacy *(Triangle 627-4351)*, Hardware Store *(Granite Ace 696-3999)*

Transportation
OnCall: Water Taxi *(Oldport Launch Ch.68, $2 pp/ 1-way)*, Taxi *(Accurate 627-9798)* **Near:** Bikes *(Cutler's 627-4052, Edgartown Bike 627-4052)*, Rental Car *(Island Auto Rental 627-6800)*, Local Bus *(MVTA - 15 routes cover the island)*, Ferry Service *(to Chappaquiddick 627-9794, Falmouth 548-9400, Woods Hole 477-8600)* **Airport:** Martha's Vineyard *(8 mi.)*

Medical Services
911 Service **OnCall:** Ambulance **Under 1 mi:** Doctor, Holistic Services *(Almost Heaven Massage 696 8400)* **1-3 mi:** Dentist *(Schaeffer 696-8426)*
Hospital: Martha's Vineyard 693-0410 *(7 mi.)*

Setting -- Tucked into its own basin, just south of the Edgartown Yacht Club, Harborside is centrally located in historic Edgartown, near the town's prime attractions. The Inn, a full-service waterfront resort with dockage, is a charming collection of seven buildings, many of them 19th century whaling captains' homes. An inviting kidney-shaped pool overlooks the docks, rose beds line brick walks, and the views across the harbor are spectacular.

Marina Notes -- *$144 per night minimum. 2 night minimum stay, 3 nights holiday weekends. Last-minute 4 hr. lunch stop also possible; fee approx. $40. Note: Harborside does not have power on the docks, only water, and requires that all transient vessels have both a marine head and a generator on board. Reservations, particularly for larger boats or groups, should be made far in advance. Onsite is an 89 room hotel; many of its rooms face the harbor and have verandas. All rooms have cable TV, A/C and refrigerators. Hotel and the docks are part of a "sold-out" time-share resort; the management rents both when not occupied by owners. Pool and whirlpool available to overnight dockage guests (but grills and laundry are not). Children are very welcome, but pets not allowed in resort and may not leave their boats. Pump-out provided by the Harbormaster's office - Ch.74 9am-4pm or at Memorial Wharf 9am-4pm.

Notable -- All of Edgartown is a very short walk away. Or walk/bike half a mile to Lighthouse Beach which promises calm water, or out to Katama for surf. Just two blocks from the Pied Piper Ferry and the On Time Ferry to Chappaquiddick (every 5 min. 7am-Mid) -- home to some wonderful beaches, especially East, and to the Wasque Reservation $3, 5 miles from ferry landing.

PHOTOS ON CD-ROM: 9

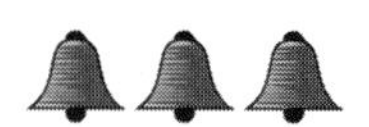

Dockside Market Place & Marina

PO Box 1386; 12 Circuit Avenue Ext; Oak Bluffs, MA 02557

Tel: (508) 693-3392 **VHF: Monitor** 9 **Talk** n/a
Fax: (508) 693-1001 **Alternate Tel:** n/a
Email: n/a **Web:** n/a
Nearest Town: Oak Bluffs *(0 mi.)* **Tourist Info:** (508) 693-0085

Navigational Information

Lat: 41°27.527' **Long:** 070°33.505' **Tide:** 3 ft. **Current:** 1 kt. **Chart:** 13238
Rep. Depths (*MLW*): Entry n/a **Fuel Dock** 12 ft. **Max Slip/Moor** 8 ft./-
Access: Nantucket Sound to port side of Oak Bluffs Harbor

Marina Facilities *(In Season/Off Season)*

Fuel: *Texaco* - Gasoline, Diesel
Slips: 10 Total, 10 Transient **Max LOA:** 60 ft. **Max Beam:** 16 ft.
Rate *(per ft.)*: **Day** $2.50 **Week** n/a **Month** n/a
Power: 30 amp $5, **50 amp** $10, **100 amp** n/a, **200 amp** n/a
Cable TV: Yes Incl. **Dockside Phone:** No
Dock Type: Wood, Long Fingers, Fixed
Moorings: 0 Total, 0 Transient **Launch:** Yes, Dinghy Dock
Rate: Day $25 **Week** Inq. **Month** Inq.
Heads: 6 Toilet(s), 6 Shower(s)
Laundry: None **Pay Phones:** Yes, 2
Pump-Out: OnCall, Full Service, 1 Port **Fee:** Free **Closed Heads:** Yes

Marina Operations

Owner/Manager: Terry McCarthy **Dockmaster:** n/a
In-Season: May 20-Oct 29, 7am-8pm **Off-Season:** Oct 30-May 19
After-Hours Arrival: Call ahead
Reservations: Yes, Preferred **Credit Cards:** Visa/MC
Discounts: None
Pets: Welcome **Handicap Access:** Yes, Heads, Docks

Marina Services and Boat Supplies

Services - Docking Assistance, Security *(16 Hrs., On duty dock)*, Trash Pick-Up **Communication -** FedEx, UPS, Express Mail **Supplies - OnCall:** Propane *(De Bettencourt 693-0751)* **Near:** Ice *(Cube)*, Ships' Store, Bait/Tackle *(Dick's Bait & Tackle 693-7669)* **1-3 mi:** CNG *(Martha's Vineyard Shipyard 693-0400)*

Boatyard Services

OnSite: Divers **OnCall:** Electronics Repairs **Near:** Launching Ramp, Electrical Repairs, Hull Repairs, Rigger, Brightwork, Refrigeration. **1-3 mi:** Travelift, Engine mechanic *(gas, diesel)*, Electronic Sales, Sail Loft, Compound, Wash & Wax, Propeller Repairs, Woodworking, Inflatable Repairs, Metal Fabrication, Painting, Awlgrip. **Nearest Yard:** Maciel Marine (508) 693-0751

Restaurants and Accommodations

OnSite: Restaurant *(Fishbones 696-8227)*, Seafood Shack *(Coop DeVille 693-3420, L $6-22, D $6-22)*, Snack Bar *(Bubba's)*, Inn/B&B *(Dockside Inn 693-2966, $75-350)* **Near:** Restaurant *(Sweet Life 696-0200, D $24-37)*, Pizzeria *(Giordano's 693-0184, L $8-16, D $8-16)*, Inn/B&B *(Wesley House 693-6611, $105-175)*, *(Oak House Inn 693-7171, $110-275)* **Under 1 mi:** Restaurant *(Lola's 693-5007, D $20-35)*

Recreation and Entertainment

OnSite: Boat Rentals *(Martha's Vineyard Watersports 693-8476)*, Fishing Charter *(Banjo Charters 693-3154, Fly Fishing 696-7551)* **Near:** Beach *(Oak Bluffs Town Beach)*, Fitness Center, Roller Blade/Bike Paths *(to Edgartown)*, Movie Theater *(Island Theater 696-8300)*, Video Rental *(Jaba's 696-1996)*, Video Arcade, Park *(Ocean Park)*, Museum *(The Oak Bluffs Wesleyan Grove Campground)*, Cultural Attract *(Trinity Park Tabernacle Concerts)* **Under 1 mi:** Playground, Tennis Courts *(Niantic Park 693-6535)*, Golf Course *(Farm Neck 693-3057)*, Galleries

Provisioning and General Services

OnSite: Clothing Store, Retail Shops **Near:** Convenience Store, Supermarket *(Reliable 693-1102)*, Gourmet Shop, Delicatessen, Wine/Beer *(Vineyard Wine & Cheese Shop 693-0943)*, Liquor Store *(Jim's Package Store 693-0236)*, Bakery, Fishmonger *(Moby Dick's 693-0748)*, Meat Market, Bank/ATM *(Edgartown National Bank 627-1110)*, Post Office, Catholic Church, Protestant Church, Beauty Salon, Barber Shop, Newsstand, Hardware Store *(Phillips Hardware 693-0377)*, Copies Etc. *(Good Impressions 693-7682)* **Under 1 mi:** Library *(Oak Bluffs PL 693-9433)* **1-3 mi:** Health Food, Synagogue, Bookstore, Pharmacy *(Medicine Shoppe 693-7979)*, Florist, Department Store *(Brickman's)*

Transportation

OnSite: Rental Car *(Budget Rental)*, Ferry Service *(HiLine to Hyannis or Nantucket 778-2600; Island Queen to Falmouth 548-4800)* **OnCall:** Taxi *(Martha's Vineyard Taxi 693-8660)* **Near:** Bikes *(King's 693-1887)*, Local Bus *(MVTA buses cover the island)* **Airport:** Martha's Vineyard *(7 mi.)*

Medical Services

911 Service **OnCall:** Ambulance **Under 1 mi:** Doctor *(Miller 693-2400)*, Holistic Services *(Vineyard Massage & Spa 693-7331)* **1-3 mi:** Dentist
Hospital: Martha's Vineyard 693-0410 *(1 mi.)*

Setting -- On the east side of placid, protected, picturesque -- but crowded -- Oak Bluffs Harbor, Dockside has two piers with slips which book-end a long face dock. The face dock lies alongside the Oak Bluffs Harbor Boardwalk -- known as The Strip -- which is lined with a series of restaurants, pubs and shops. Views are across the boat-filled harbor to the residential shore beyond.

Marina Notes -- Oak Bluffs Marina and Dockside share heads and showers, which are located in the northwest corner of the harbor -- a fairly long walk from the docks. Safe and protected facility. Closed head harbor. Free Pump-out Boat on call Ch.71.

Notable -- Docking here puts you squarely in the "action" and is convenient to all of Oak Bluffs. During the season, there is a variety of live entertainment at diverse establishments along the harbor, creating a festive party atmosphere. Bicycle and moped rentals abound. Nearby is the 34 acre landmark Oak Bluffs Campground, with more than 300 brightly painted, gingerbread-trimmed, Carpenter Gothic Victorian cottages surrounding Wesleyan Grove and 1879 Trinity Park Tabernacle. This has been the site of Methodist Summer Camp meetings since 1835. The 1876 Flying Horses Carousel (693-9481) is the oldest operating carousel in the U.S. The harbor was created by cutting through a narrow stretch of beach that separated what was then Lake Anthony from the Sound.

PHOTOS ON CD-ROM: 5

Navigational Information

Lat: 41°27.453' **Long:** 070°33.555' **Tide:** 3 ft. **Current:** n/a **Chart:** 13238
Rep. Depths (*MLW*): Entry 7 ft. **Fuel Dock** 12 ft. **Max Slip/Moor** 12 ft./12 ft.
Access: Nantucket Sound to Oak Bluffs Harbor

Marina Facilities *(In Season/Off Season)*

Fuel: Gasoline, Diesel
Slips: 80 Total, 75 Transient **Max LOA:** 135 ft. **Max Beam:** n/a
Rate *(per ft.)*: **Day** $2.50/$1.50* **Week** Inq. **Month** Inq.
Power: 30 amp $5, **50 amp** $10, **100 amp** n/a, **200 amp** n/a
Cable TV: No **Dockside Phone:** No
Dock Type: Long Fingers, Short Fingers, Pilings, Alongside, Fixed
Moorings: 50 Total, 50 Transient **Launch:** None
Rate: Day $30/20 **Week** Inq. **Month** Inq.
Heads: 6 Toilet(s), 6 Shower(s)
Laundry: None **Pay Phones:** Yes
Pump-Out: OnSite, 1 Port **Fee:** Free **Closed Heads:** Yes

Marina Operations

Owner/Manager: Joshua Williams **Dockmaster:** Todd Alexander (HM)
In-Season: Jun 15-Sep 2, 7am-9pm **Off-Season:** May-Jun 15, Sep-Oct 15**
After-Hours Arrival: Call in advance
Reservations: Yes **Credit Cards:** Visa/MC
Discounts: None
Pets: Welcome, Dog Walk Area **Handicap Access:** Yes

Oak Bluffs Marina

PO Box 2676; 310 Circuit Ave. Extension; Oak Bluffs, MA 02557

Tel: (508) 693-7402 **VHF: Monitor** 9 **Talk** 71
Fax: (508) 696-7736 **Alternate Tel:** n/a
Email: obmarina@vineyard.net **Web:** www.oakbluffsharbor@vineyard.net
Nearest Town: Oak Bluffs *(0 mi.)* **Tourist Info:** (508) 693-0085

Marina Services and Boat Supplies

Services - Docking Assistance, Megayacht Facilities **Communication -** Mail & Package Hold, Phone Messages, Fax in/out *(Ask)*, FedEx, AirBorne, UPS, Express Mail *(Sat Del)* **Supplies - Near:** Ice *(Cube)*, Bait/Tackle *(Dick's Bait & Tackle 693-7669)*, Propane *(De Bettencourt 693-0751)* **1-3 mi:** Ships' Store, CNG *(Martha's Vineyard Shipyard 693-0400)*

Boatyard Services

OnSite: Launching Ramp, Electrical Repairs, Bottom Cleaning **OnCall:** Electronics Repairs, Divers **Near:** Hull Repairs, Rigger, Brightwork, Refrigeration. **1-3 mi:** Travelift *(MV Shipyard)*, Engine mechanic *(gas, diesel)*, Sail Loft, Propeller Repairs, Inflatable Repairs, Life Raft Service, Painting, Awlgrip, Yacht Broker, Total Refits. **Nearest Yard:** Martha's Vineyard Shipyard (508) 693-0400

Restaurants and Accommodations

Near: Restaurant *(Zapotec Southwestern 693-6800, L $8-17, D $12-17)*, *(Sweet Life Café 696-0200, D $24-37)*, *(Island House 693-4516, D $8-24)*, *(Giordano's 693-0184, L $7-13, D $13-18)*, *(Linda Jean's 693-4093, B $4-6, L $3-18)*, *(Lola's 693-5007, D $20-35, Pub $7-15, Sun Brunch $12-14)*, Snack Bar *(Bubba's Hot Dogs)*, Hotel *(Island House 693-8343, $90-135)*, *(Pequot 693-5087, $65-225)*, *(Dockside Inn 693-2966, $75-350)*, Inn/B&B *(Narragansett House 693-3627, $85-275)*

Recreation and Entertainment

OnSite: Beach *(Oak Bluffs Town Beach)*, Jogging Paths, Boat Rentals *(Dockside Watersports 693-1300)* **Near:** Picnic Area, Playground, Tennis Courts *(Farm Neck)*, Golf Course *(Farm Neck Golf Club 693-9728)*, Roller Blade/Bike Paths *(to Edgartown)*, Fishing Charter *(Party Boat Skipper 693-1238)*, Other *(Flying Horses Carousel 693-9481)*, Movie Theater *(Island Theater 696-8300)*, Video Rental *(Jabas 696-1996)*, Park *(Ocean Park)*, Museum *(Cottage Museum 693-7784, donation)*, Cultural Attract *(Tabernacle Community Sing - Wed nights)*, Sightseeing *(Gay Head 693-1555 $14/6, Wesleyan Grove walking tour)*, Special Events *(Fireworks Aug 22)*

Provisioning and General Services

Near: Convenience Store, Supermarket *(Reliable 693-1102)*, Gourmet Shop, Delicatessen, Wine/Beer *(Vineyard Wine & Cheese Shop 693-0943)*, Liquor Store *(Tony's Market 693-4799)*, Bakery, Farmers' Market, Fishmonger *(Moby Dick's 693-0748)*, Meat Market, Bank/ATM *(Edgartown National Bank 627-1110)*, Post Office, Catholic Church, Beauty Salon, Dry Cleaners, Laundry, Bookstore, Hardware Store *(Phillips Hardware 693-0377)*, Copies Etc. *(Good Impressions 693-7682)* **Under 1 mi:** Library *(Oak Bluffs 693-9433)* **1-3 mi:** Pharmacy *(Leslie's 693-1010)*

Transportation

OnSite: Ferry Service *(to Falmouth 548-4800 and Hyannis 778-2600)* **OnCall:** Rental Car *(Sun 'n Fun 693-5457)*, Taxi *(Marlene's 693-0037)* **Near:** Courtesy Car/Van, Bikes *(Anderson's 693-9346)*, Local Bus *(MVTA buses criss cross the island. Buses have bike racks)* **Airport:** Martha's Vineyard *(6 mi.)*

Medical Services

911 Service **OnCall:** Ambulance **Near:** Doctor *(Miller 693-2400)*, Dentist, Holistic Services *(Vineyard Massage & Spa 693-7331)* **Hospital:** Martha's Vineyard 693-0410 *(1 mi.)*

Setting -- Right in the heart of quaint, funky, high energy Oak Bluffs, 60 moorings sit in the midst of placid St. Anthony's "Lake" and 80 transient berths rim the head of the harbor. This is the most crowded of the Vineyard harbors, and it offers the most facilities. Oak Bluffs municipal facility is the largest marina on MV.

Marina Notes -- *30-69' $2.50/1.50; 70-99' $3.50/2.50; over 100' $4.00/3.00. 2-night min. on weekends, 30 ft. min. charge. Reservations necessary for slips, especially for electricity. Moorings first come first served, up to four boats per mooring. Check-in Noon, check-out 11am. Have a bridle for the moorings. Rafting encouraged and often required. **Off-season hours 10am - 2pm. Launch Ch.71, Jun 29-LabDay, 8am-10pm + weekends in shoulder season $4pp/RT. Dinghy dock for 100 tenders. Slips are med-mooring (stern-to) style with a cement combing and ladders at each berth. Pedestals serve two slips, so bring extension cords. Caters to Megayachts up to 90 ft. in slips. Can med-moor yachts to 140 ft. Accommodates and encourages groups, offering special services.

Notable -- The town boasts blocks of gingerbread houses, parks, nightlife, and events all season long -- and within an easy walk. The 1876 Flying Horses Carousel in the center of town is the oldest in the country, 10am-10pm $1. 1879 Trinity Park Tabernacle is surrounded by Wesleyan Grove and rows of over 300 brightly colored gingerbread cottages. About 15 bus routes which intersect with bike paths make the whole Island accessible. Local stops at the Steamship Authority. Tournaments throughout the summer. Oak Bluffs Campground Illumination Night at the end of the season. Big Game Fish Tournament Mid-Aug.

PHOTOS ON CD-ROM: 8

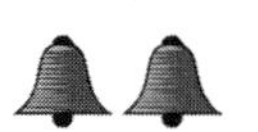

Owen Park Town Dock

PO Box 1239; 51 Spring Street; Vineyard Haven, MA 02568

Tel: (508) 696-4249 **VHF: Monitor** 9 **Talk** 69
Fax: (508) 693-5876 **Alternate Tel:** n/a
Email: n/a **Web:** www.ci.tisbury.ma.us
Nearest Town: Vineyard Haven *(0 mi.)* **Tourist Info:** (508) 693-0085

Navigational Information

Lat: 41°27.439' **Long:** 070°35.940' **Tide:** 2 ft. **Current:** 1 kt. **Chart:** 13238
Rep. Depths (*MLW*): Entry 12 ft. **Fuel Dock** n/a **Max Slip/Moor** 6 ft./12 ft.
Access: Vineyard Harbor past breakwater, starboard into mooring field

Marina Facilities *(In Season/Off Season)*

Fuel: No
Slips: 10 Total, 10 Transient **Max LOA:** 55 ft. **Max Beam:** 16 ft.
Rate *(per ft.)*: **Day** $1.00/Inq.* **Week** Inq. **Month** Inq.
Power: 30 amp n/a, **50 amp** n/a, **100 amp** n/a, **200 amp** n/a
Cable TV: No **Dockside Phone:** No
Dock Type: Wood, Fixed
Moorings: 30 Total, 30 Transient **Launch:** Yes ($2), Dinghy Dock
Rate: Day $30/25 shoulder season **Week** n/a **Month** n/a
Heads: 2 Toilet(s), 2 Shower(s)
Laundry: None **Pay Phones:** Yes, 1
Pump-Out: OnCall, Full Service, 1 Port **Fee:** n/a **Closed Heads:** Yes

Marina Operations

Owner/Manager: Jay Wilbur (Harbormaster) **Dockmaster:** n/a
In-Season: Jun 15-Sep 15, 7:30am-7:30pm **Off-Season:** Varies
After-Hours Arrival: VHF or pick up empty mooring/dock in alongside space
Reservations: No **Credit Cards:** Cash or Check
Discounts: None
Pets: Welcome, Dog Walk Area **Handicap Access:** No

Marina Services and Boat Supplies

Services - Docking Assistance, Trash Pick-Up, Dock Carts **Communication -** FedEx, UPS, Express Mail **Supplies - OnCall:** Ice *(Block)*, Ships' Store **1-3 mi:** Marine Discount Store *(Island Marine Supply 696-7502)*, Propane *(Ipi Island Propane 696-6122)* **3+ mi:** Bait/Tackle *(Dick's Bait & Tackle 693-7669, 4 mi.)*

Boatyard Services

OnCall: Travelift, Engine mechanic *(gas)*, Electronic Sales **Under 1 mi:** Launching Ramp, Hull Repairs, Rigger, Sail Loft, Bottom Cleaning, Brightwork, Air Conditioning, Refrigeration, Divers, Compound, Wash & Wax, Interior Cleaning, Propeller Repairs, Woodworking, Inflatable Repairs, Painting, Awlgrip, Yacht Design, Yacht Broker, Total Refits. **Nearest Yard:** Martha's Vineyard Shipyard (508) 693-6400

Restaurants and Accommodations

Near: Restaurant *(Zephrus at the Tisbury Inn 693-3416, L $6-15, D $18-30)*, *(Black Dog 693-9223, B $5-9, L $6-13, D $12-26)*, *(Le Grenier 693-4906, D $22-30, French bistro)*, *(Chestnut House 696-6735)*, Pizzeria *(Bob's 693-8266, L $5-6, D $5-8)*, Inn/B&B *(Hanover House 693-1066, $128-315)*, *(Twin Oaks 693-8633, $85-225)*, *(The Look 693-6893, $90-125)*

Recreation and Entertainment

OnSite: Beach, Picnic Area, Playground, Park **OnCall:** Sightseeing *(Island Transport 693-0058)* **Near:** Fitness Center *(Tisbury Inn)*, Jogging Paths, Fishing Charter, Movie Theater *(Capawock)*, Museum *(Old Schoolhouse Museum)*, Cultural Attract *(The Vineyard Playhouse 693-6450)* **Under 1 mi:** Pool, Video Rental *(Island Entertainment 693-7441)* **1-3 mi:** Tennis Courts *(Farm Neck Golf Club 693-9728)*, Golf Course *(Mink Meadows Golf Club 693-0600)*, Roller Blade/Bike Paths

Provisioning and General Services

OnCall: Liquor Store *(Our Market 627-4000)*, Laundry **Near:** Convenience Store, Supermarket *(A&P 693-8339)*, Delicatessen, Bakery *(Black Dog)*, Green Grocer, Fishmonger, Lobster Pound, Bank/ATM, Post Office, Catholic Church, Protestant Church, Synagogue, Library *(696-4211)*, Beauty Salon, Barber Shop, Bookstore *(Bunch of Grapes 693-2291)*, Newsstand, Clothing Store, Retail Shops **Under 1 mi:** Dry Cleaners, Pharmacy *(Medicine Shoppe 693-7979)*, Florist, Copies Etc. *(Da Rosas Printing 693-0110)* **1-3 mi:** Gourmet Shop *(Vineyard Gourmet 693-5181)*, Health Food *(Super Natural 696-0773)*, Wine/Beer, Hardware Store *(Hinckley & Sons Ace 693-0075)* **3+ mi:** Farmers' Market *(5 mi.)*

Transportation

Near: Bikes *(MV Strictly Bikes 693-0782)*, Water Taxi, Rental Car *(AAA Island Rental 696-5300, Bayside Auto Rental 693-4777)*, Taxi, Local Bus *(Tisbury Shuttle Bus $0.25)*, InterCity Bus *(MTA & ITA to all island destinations 693-1589)*, Ferry Service *(Woods Hole, New London & Glen Cove 860-437-6928; New Bedford 997-1688 $19/11)* **Airport:** Martha's Vineyard *(5 mi.)*

Medical Services

911 Service **OnSite:** Ambulance **Near:** Dentist *(Island Dentistry 696-8426)*, Chiropractor *(Berger 693-4668)*, Holistic Services **Under 1 mi:** Doctor *(Fudem 696-7416)*, Veterinarian *(My Pet's Vet 693-4040)* **Hospital:** Martha's Vineyard 693-0410 *(3.5 mi.)*

Setting -- Tucked safely into the western portion of V-shaped Vineyard Haven Harbor, this municipal facility and mooring field is bounded on the north by the breakwater, on the south by a wide swath of sand beach, and on the east by the very active ferry channel.

Marina Notes -- From 10am-4pm, the dock is intended for temporary tie-ups. 1st 15 min. free, $5/hr. thereafter. 4pm -10am, $1.00/ft. only after all private marinas are full. Mooring rows run parallel to the breakwater and "lettering" begins there. Over 40' A-E, under 40' F & higher. Look for pale blue & black balls. Rafting up to 3 boats permitted. No power. Fuel available from Vineyard Haven Marina and Tisbury Wharf Co. Dinghy dock at Owen Park Town Dock or Steamship Dock, both on north side of pier. Dinghies may also be beached just north of Town Dock. Launch $2pp/1-way, Ch.72. No trash service at Steamship Authority Dock; use dumpster located at Owen Park. Sealed heads required! Free pump-out boat Ch.9/71, 7 days, 9am-5pm.

Notable -- Very nice showers, sauna, hot tub, pool and gym are available, for a fee, at the Health Club at the Tisbury Inn (693-7400). Rates begin at $10/7 pp/day, longer term packages and group discounts available. (See www.tisburyinn.com for more info.) Laundry at airport (45 min bus ride) 693-5005. Road Runner may pickup/deliver 696-8013. William St. Historic District has some fine, old captains' houses that were untouched by the 1883 fire. Concerts in Owen Park band stand alternate Sundays. Wooden boat building and preservation at Gannon & Benjamin. VTA & ITI buses and shuttles make all of MV accessible. Vineyard Haven is dry, BYOB to most restaurants. Watch out for the ferries!

PHOTOS ON CD-ROM: 7

Navigational Information
Lat: 41°27.263' **Long:** 070°35.988' **Tide:** 2 ft. **Current:** n/a **Chart:** 13238
Rep. Depths (*MLW*): Entry 12 ft. **Fuel Dock** n/a **Max Slip/Moor** 10 ft./17 ft.
Access: Past breakwater to east side of the Ferry Terminal

Marina Facilities *(In Season/Off Season)*
Fuel: No
Slips: 18 Total, 18 Transient **Max LOA:** 60 ft. **Max Beam:** 16 ft.
Rate *(per ft.)*: **Day** $2.50/$1.75 **Week** $17.50/12.25 **Month** Inq.
Power: 30 amp Incl., **50 amp** Incl., **100 amp** n/a, **200 amp** n/a
Cable TV: No **Dockside Phone:** No
Dock Type: Wood, Pilings, Alongside, Fixed
Moorings: 22 Total, 22 Transient **Launch:** Yes ($2)
Rate: Day $30 **Week** n/a **Month** n/a
Heads: 2 Toilet(s), 2 Shower(s)
Laundry: 2 Washer(s), 2 Dryer(s) **Pay Phones:** Yes, 2
Pump-Out: OnSite, Full Service, 1 Central **Fee:** Free **Closed Heads:** Yes

Marina Operations
Owner/Manager: Capt. Robert S. Douglas **Dockmaster:** Shawn Ahearn
In-Season: Jun 20-Sep 5, 8am-7pm **Off-Season:** LabDay-Jun 19, 9am-4pm
After-Hours Arrival: Call for instructions
Reservations: Yes, Required **Credit Cards:** Visa/MC
Discounts: None
Pets: Welcome, Dog Walk Area **Handicap Access:** No

Vineyard Haven Maritime Wharf

PO Box 429; 1 Beach Street Ext.; Vineyard Haven, MA 02568

Tel: (508) 693-3854 **VHF: Monitor** 72 **Talk** 72
Fax: (508) 693-7030 **Alternate Tel:** n/a
Email: n/a **Web:** www.CoastwisePacket.com
Nearest Town: Vineyard Haven *(0.1 mi.)* **Tourist Info:** (508) 693-0085

Marina Services and Boat Supplies
Services - Docking Assistance, Trash Pick-Up **Communication -** Phone Messages, FedEx, UPS, Express Mail **Supplies - OnSite:** Ice *(Block, Cube)* **Near:** Ships' Store **1-3 mi:** Marine Discount Store *(Island Marine 696-7502)*, Bait/Tackle *(Dick's 693-7669)*, Propane *(Ipi Propane 696-6122)*

Boatyard Services
Near: Travelift, Railway, Forklift, Crane, Engine mechanic *(gas, diesel)*, Launching Ramp, Electrical Repairs, Electronic Sales, Electronics Repairs, Hull Repairs, Rigger, Sail Loft, Bottom Cleaning, Brightwork, Divers, Compound, Wash & Wax, Interior Cleaning, Propeller Repairs, Woodworking, Inflatable Repairs, Life Raft Service, Upholstery, Yacht Interiors, Metal Fabrication, Painting, Awlgrip, Yacht Design, Yacht Building, Total Refits. **Nearest Yard:** Martha's Vineyard Shipyard (508) 693-0400

Restaurants and Accommodations
OnSite: Restaurant *(Black Dog 693-9223, B $5-5, L $6-13, D $12-26, no reservations)* **Near:** Restaurant *(Zephrus at the Tisbury Inn 693-3416, L $6-15, D $18-30)*, *(Le Grenier 693-4906, D $21-30)*, *(Ipanema 693-8383, D $17-27)*, Snack Bar *(E&E Deli 693-2223, L $3-9)*, Pizzeria *(Bob's Pizza 693-8266, L $3-7)*, Inn/B&B *(Twin Oaks 693-8633, $85-225)*, *(The Tisbury Inn 693-2200, $75-325, Health Club)*, *(Captain Dexter's House 693-6564, $100-275)* **Under 1 mi:** Snack Bar *(Louis Tisbury Café 693-3255, L $6-18, D $6-18, take-out, too)*, Inn/B&B *(The Look 693-6893, $90-125)*

Recreation and Entertainment
OnSite: Beach, Picnic Area, Grills, Playground **Near:** Dive Shop, Tennis Courts, Jogging Paths, Boat Rentals *(MV's Parasailing, Waterskiing and Jetskiing 693-2838)*, Roller Blade/Bike Paths, Movie Theater *(Capawock)*, Park, Museum, Cultural Attract *(The Vineyard Playhouse 693-6450)*, Special Events *(Tisbury Street Fair)* **Under 1 mi:** Golf Course *(Mink Meadows 693-0600)*, Fitness Center *(Fitness Firm 693-5533)* **1-3 mi:** Fishing Charter, Video Rental *(Island Entertainment -693-7441)*, Sightseeing *(Long Point Refuge 693-7392)*

Provisioning and General Services
Near: Convenience Store, Supermarket *(A&P 693-9845)*, Gourmet Shop *(Vineyard Gourmet 693-5181)*, Delicatessen, Bakery, Fishmonger *(John's)*, Lobster Pound, Meat Market, Bank/ATM, Post Office, Catholic Church, Protestant Church, Synagogue, Library *(963-4211)*, Beauty Salon, Barber Shop, Pharmacy *(Medicine Shoppe 693-7979)*, Newsstand, Florist, Clothing Store, Retail Shops **Under 1 mi:** Health Food *(Super Natural 696-0773)*, Bookstore *(Bunch of Grapes 693-2291)*, Hardware Store *(Hinckley & Sons Ace 693-0075)*, Copies Etc. *(Tisbury Printer 693-7068)* **1-3 mi:** Liquor Store *(Jim's 693-0236)*, Farmers' Market, Dry Cleaners

Transportation
OnCall: Taxi *(Adam Cab 693-3332)* **Near:** Bikes *(Cycle Works 693-6966)*, Rental Car *(Thrifty 693-1959, Bayside Auto Rental 693-4777)*, Local Bus *(Tisbury's Shuttle)*, InterCity Bus *(MTA's 15 bus lines 693-1589)*, Ferry Service *(Woods Hole, New Bedford)* **Airport:** Martha's Vineyard *(5 mi.)*

Medical Services
911 Service **OnCall:** Ambulance **Near:** Holistic Services *(Therapeutic Massage 693-8020)* **Under 1 mi:** Doctor *(Walk-in Med 693-4400)*, Dentist, Chiropractor **Hospital:** Martha's Vineyard 693-0410 *(2 mi.)*

Setting -- Just south-east of the Steamship Authority Ferry Dock, this small, professional facility is right in the center of Vineyard Haven. Landside a brick walk leads past the Black Dog complex through the porch of a small, weathered shingle building, to the docks beyond. Those docks are home to many beautifully restored wooden boats -- from schooners to day-sailers.

Marina Notes -- Alongside and "stern-to" med-moor dockage. Rafting quite possible. One power cord included in fee, extra 30 amp $5, extra 50 amp $10/nt. Temporary dockage 1-3 hrs, $10/hr. Shower, bathroom, ice, and laundry facilities (with $50 refundable key deposit). Complimentary Black Dog coffee and doughnuts every morning around 8am. 2 washers, 2 commercial dryers, 2 heads with water-saver compressed air toilets and 2 simple showers with private dressing rooms. Launch to the moorings makes its home here. On-call Pump-out Boat. Additional moorings from Vineyard Haven Launch Co. which runs 20-passenger launch Ch.72 693-7030. FYI: Transient boats cannot be left unattended for a period of time in any harbor on the island.

Notable -- Coastwise (the Boatyard part of this operation) and its neighbor, Gannon & Benjamin, have rejuvenated wooden boat restoration in VH - there are more wooden boats here than in any comparable harbor in the North East. Coastwise is home to Shenandoah (108' sq. topsail) and Alabama (90' ex-pilot schooner) which are available for charter, weekend or week cruises, or all-kids cruises; next door is the 80' schooner When and If. This is a "dry" town with BYOB restaurants; come prepared. In the event of a Nor'Easter, the marina will insist that all boats leave and there isn't any place to go on the island.

PHOTOS ON CD-ROM: 6

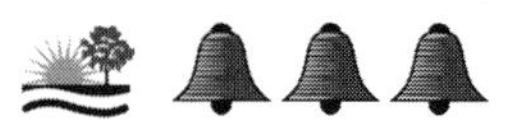

Vineyard Haven Marina

PO Box 4203; 52 Beach Road; Vineyard Haven, MA 02568

Tel: (508) 693-0720; (508) 693-7377 **VHF: Monitor** 9 **Talk** 10
Fax: (508) 696-9341 **Alternate Tel:** (978) 771-7133
Email: mvhm@sne.1.com **Web:** www.vineyardhavenmarina.com
Nearest Town: Vineyard Haven *(0.1 mi.)* **Tourist Info:** (508) 693-0085

Navigational Information

Lat: 41°27.215' **Long:** 070°35.934' **Tide:** 2 ft. **Current:** n/a **Chart:** 13238
Rep. Depths (*MLW*): Entry 20 ft. **Fuel Dock** 10 ft. **Max Slip/Moor** 12 ft./35 ft.
Access: Past the breakwater to 2nd set of docks east of of Ferry Terminal

Marina Facilities *(In Season/Off Season)*

Fuel: *Mobil* - Gasoline, Diesel, High-Speed Pumps
Slips: 40 Total, 40 Transient **Max LOA:** 200 ft. **Max Beam:** 40 ft.
Rate *(per ft.)*: **Day** $4.00* **Week** Inq. **Month** n/a
Power: 30 amp Incl, **50 amp** Incl, **100 amp** Incl, **200 amp** Incl
Cable TV: Yes **Dockside Phone:** Yes
Dock Type: Wood, Alongside, Fixed
Moorings: 20 Total, 20 Transient **Launch:** None, Dinghy Dock
Rate: Day $30/25 **Week** Inq. **Month** Inq.
Heads: 8 Toilet(s), 4 Shower(s) *(with dressing rooms)*, Hair Dryers
Laundry: 2 Washer(s), 2 Dryer(s), Iron, Iron Board **Pay Phones:** Yes, 2
Pump-Out: OnSite, Full Service, 1 Central **Fee:** Free **Closed Heads:** Yes

Marina Operations

Owner/Manager: Liz Wild **Dockmaster:** Jo Wild
In-Season: Jun-Sep, 7am-12am **Off-Season:** Oct-May, 7am-12mid
After-Hours Arrival: Call 978-771-7133
Reservations: Yes, Required **Credit Cards:** Visa/MC, Amex
Discounts: None
Pets: Welcome **Handicap Access:** Yes, Heads, Docks

Marina Services and Boat Supplies

Services - Docking Assistance, Concierge, Room Service to the Boat, Boaters' Lounge, Crew Lounge, Security *(24 Hrs.)*, Trash Pick-Up, Dock Carts, Megayacht Facilities, 300 amps **Communication -** Mail & Package Hold, Phone Messages, Fax in/out, Data Ports *(Slips)*, FedEx, UPS, Express Mail *(Sat Del)* **Supplies - OnSite:** Ice *(Block, Cube)* **Near:** West Marine **Under 1 mi:** Marine Discount Store *(Island Marine 696-7502)*, Live Bait, Propane *(Ipi 696-6122)* **1-3 mi:** Bait/Tackle *(Dick's 693-7669)*

Boatyard Services

OnCall: Electronic Sales, Electronics Repairs, Divers, Life Raft Service **Near:** Railway *(45T)*, Engine mechanic *(gas, diesel)*, Launching Ramp, Electrical Repairs, Hull Repairs *(wood only)*, Rigger, Sail Loft, Bottom Cleaning, Brightwork, Compound, Wash & Wax, Interior Cleaning, Propeller Repairs, Woodworking, Inflatable Repairs, Painting, Awlgrip, Yacht Design, Yacht Building, Total Refits. **Yard Rates:** $48/hr., Haul & Launch $8/ft.

Restaurants and Accommodations

OnSite: Restaurant *(Ipanema 693-8383, D $17-26, Brazilian)*, Seafood Shack *(Pilot House)*, Motel *(Vineyard Harbor 693-4300, $80-190, 3 night min.)* **OnCall:** Restaurant *(Island Indulgence 693-4130)*, Pizzeria *(Island 693-1125)* **Near:** Restaurant *(Café Moxie 693-1484, D $22-28)*, *(Black Dog 693-9223, B $5-9, L $6-13, D $12-26)*, Seafood Shack *(Net Result 693-6071)*, Inn/B&B *(1720 House 693-6407, $200)*, *(Martha's Place 693-0253, $200-425)* **Under 1 mi:** Restaurant *(Zephrus at the Tisbury Inn 693-3416, L $6-15, D $18-30)*, Inn/B&B *(Twin Oaks 693-8633, $85-225)*, *(The Look 693-6893, $90-125)*

Recreation and Entertainment

OnSite: Beach, Picnic Area, Grills, Boat Rentals **OnCall:** Sightseeing **Near:** Pool, Heated Pool, Spa, Playground, Volleyball, Tennis Courts, Fitness Center *(Fitness Firm 693-5533)*, Jogging Paths, Movie Theater *(Capawock Theater 696-9200)* **Under 1 mi:** Dive Shop, Golf Course *(Mink Meadows 693-0600)*, Roller Blade/Bike Paths, Fishing Charter, Park, Cultural Attract *(Vineyard Playhouse)* **1-3 mi:** Bowling, Video Rental *(Island Entertainment 693-7441)*, Video Arcade

Provisioning and General Services

OnSite: Laundry **OnCall:** Convenience Store, Liquor Store *(Our Market 627-4000)*, Newsstand **Near:** Supermarket *(A&P 693-9845)*, Gourmet Shop *(Vineyard Gourmet 693-5181)*, Delicatessen *(E&E 693-2223)*, Bakery, Farmers' Market, Fishmonger *(John's 693-1220)*, Lobster Pound, Bank/ATM, Post Office **Under 1 mi:** Health Food *(Super Natural 696-0773)*, Catholic Church, Synagogue, Library *(696-4211)*, Beauty Salon, Dry Cleaners, Bookstore *(Bunch of Grapes 693-2291)*, Pharmacy *(Medicine Shoppe 693-7979)*, Hardware Store *(Shirley's)*, Copies Etc. *(Tisbury Printer 693-7068)*

Transportation

OnCall: Taxi *(Atlantic Cab 693-7110)* **Near:** Bikes *(Martha's Bicycle Rental 693-6593)*, Rental Car *(AAA Rental 696-5300, Bayside 693-4777)*, Local Bus *(ITI Shuttle)*, InterCity Bus *(MTA buses 693-1580)*, Ferry Service *(Woods Hole, New Bedford)* **Airport:** Martha's Vineyard *(5 mi.)*

Medical Services

911 Service **OnCall:** Ambulance **Near:** Dentist **Under 1 mi:** Doctor, Chiropractor, Holistic Services **Hospital:** Martha's Vineyard *(2 mi.)*

Setting -- This diminutive, well-maintained marina has a two-story primary facility at the end of its main dock. It's run like a small hotel, and offers concierge services, an attractive lounge, a tiny onsite beach (another within easy walking distance), restaurants and a responsive staff. Views are right across the harbor, and out the back door it's an easy walk to shops, restaurants, art galleries, and all the amenities of the bustling, charming community of Vineyard Haven.

Marina Notes -- *Over 100' $5/ft. Moorings $25/night in shoulder season. Inside/outside dining upstairs overlooking the harbor. First floor porch and lounge. Casual personal service, privacy and numerous amenities. Off-season, the marina caters to special events for yachts, boat clubs, rendezvous, etc. 30, 50 & 100 amp service. Fuel, pump-out, barbecues, liquor service, rental cars, jeeps, scooters. Can accommodate vessels up to 200 ft. dockside or on deep water moorings. Additional moorings from Vineyard Haven Launch Company which runs 20-passenger launch Ch.72, 693-7030.

Notable -- Bike rentals down the street ($10-15) along with several restaurants, hotels, B&Bs, markets, deli, and a bakery. Local shuttle buses and inter-village buses make the whole island very easily accessible. Bus routes intersect with bike paths and buses have bike racks. Vineyard Haven is "dry", most restaurants are BYOB - call in advance. Look for the dozen wooden schooners and hundred other restored craft in the main mooring field. Gannon & Benjamin Shipyard and Coastwise Packet are part of Vineyard Haven's burgeoning shipwright and preservationist industry. Gay Head tours, on call, 693-1555. FYI: Maciel Marina rents moorings in the center of Lagoon Pond, max 3-days or for season. Bascule bridge opens 5 times daily; dinghy dock at Maciel.

PHOTOS ON CD-ROM: 6

Navigational Information

Lat: 41°21.215' **Long:** 070°45.960' **Tide:** 4 ft. **Current:** 5 kt. **Chart:** 13218
Rep. Depths (*MLW*): Entry 7 ft. **Fuel Dock** 7 ft. **Max Slip/Moor** 7 ft./7 ft.
Access: 100 yards past entrance, turn left into basin

Marina Facilities *(In Season/Off Season)*

Fuel: *Texaco* - Slip-Side Fueling, Gasoline, Diesel
Slips: 100 Total, 20 Transient **Max LOA:** 55 ft. **Max Beam:** n/a
Rate *(per ft.)*: **Day** $2.25/Inq.* **Week** $14 **Month** n/a
Power: 30 amp $5, **50 amp** $10, **100 amp** n/a, **200 amp** n/a
Cable TV: No **Dockside Phone:** No
Dock Type: Wood, Long Fingers
Moorings: 10 Total, 5 Transient **Launch:** None, Dinghy Dock (Free)
Rate: Day $30 **Week** $175 **Month** Inq.
Heads: 2 Toilet(s), 2 Shower(s) *(with dressing rooms)*
Laundry: None **Pay Phones:** No
Pump-Out: OnSite, OnCall, Full Service **Fee:** Free **Closed Heads:** Yes

Marina Operations

Owner/Manager: Dennis Jason **Dockmaster:** Same
In-Season: Jun-Nov 1, 7am-9pm **Off-Season:** n/a
After-Hours Arrival: Call on VHF Ch 9
Reservations: Only after 8am of arrival day **Credit Cards:** Cash only
Discounts: None
Pets: Welcome **Handicap Access:** No

Menemsha Harbor

PO Box 119; 401 Middle Road; Chilmark, MA 02535

Tel: (508) 645-2846 **VHF: Monitor** 9 **Talk** 8
Fax: (508) 645-2846 **Alternate Tel:** n/a
Email: n/a **Web:** n/a
Nearest Town: Chilmark *(2 mi.)* **Tourist Info:** (508) 693-0085

Marina Services and Boat Supplies

Services - Docking Assistance **Supplies - OnSite:** Ice *(Block, Cube)*
Near: Ships' Store, Bait/Tackle

Boatyard Services

Nearest Yard: Martha's Vineyard Shipyard (508) 693-0400

Restaurants and Accommodations

Near: Restaurant *(Feast Of Chilmark 645-3553)*, *(Beach Plum 645-9454, D $30-40 or Prix fixe $48, Rated best on MV)*, Seafood Shack *(Home Port 645-2675)*, Snack Bar *(The Bite 645-9239)*, Inn/B&B *(Beach Plum Inn & Restaurant 645-9454, $150-400)*, *(Menemsha Inn & Cottages 645-2521)* **1-3 mi:** Restaurant *(Theo's Restaurant 645-3322, D Prix fixe $45)*, Inn/B&B *(Inn at Blueberry Hill 645-3322, $154-700)*, *(Duck Inn 645-9018, $75-175)* **3+ mi:** Restaurant *(Outermost Inn D Prix fixe $65, 4 mi., includes beverages)*, Inn/B&B *(Outermost Inn 645-3511, $210-340, 4 mi.)*

Recreation and Entertainment

OnSite: Fishing Charter *(The Island Lure/Glory B II 645-9026 Half Day $350)*, Group Fishing Boat, Video Rental **OnCall:** Boat Rentals *(Kayaks - MV Kayak 627-0151)* **Near:** Beach *(or Gay Head/Aquinnah Beach)*, Picnic Area, Jogging Paths **Under 1 mi:** Roller Blade/Bike Paths *(Gay Head to Chilmark)*, Park **1-3 mi:** Sightseeing *(Cranberry Lands, Squibnocket Herring Run, Gay Head Cliffs & Lighthouse)* **3+ mi:** Golf Course *(TVGC 696-3163, 15 mi.)*, Horseback Riding *(Arrowhead Farm 693-8831, 8 mi.)*

Provisioning and General Services

OnSite: Convenience Store, Fishmonger *(Larsen's Fish Market 645-2680)*, Lobster Pound *(Poole's Fish 645-2282)* **Near:** Delicatessen *(Menemsha Deli 645-9902)*, Clothing Store, Retail Shops **1-3 mi:** Supermarket *(Menemsha Market & Post Office 645-3501)*, Bakery, Post Office *(Beetlebung Corner)*, Catholic Church, Protestant Church, Library *(Aquinnah 645-2314, Chilmark 645-3360)*, Copies Etc. *(Educomp 693-0803)* **3+ mi:** Farmers' Market *(Solviva Organic Farm 693-3733, 8 mi.)*

Transportation

OnSite: Local Bus *(MTA buses 693-1589)* **OnCall:** Taxi *(Up Island 645-3000)* **3+ mi:** Rental Car *(All-Island Rent A Car 693-6868, 8 mi.)*, Ferry Service *(Hugh Taylor's Bike Ferry across Menemsha Creek to Lobsterville Beach & Aquinnah $7/RT, 13 mi.)* **Airport:** Martha's Vineyard *(8 mi.)*

Medical Services

911 Service **OnCall:** Ambulance **3+ mi:** Doctor *(Dr. Quinn's Walk In 693-7100, 6 mi.)* **Hospital:** Martha's Vineyard 693-0410 *(16 mi.)*

Setting -- Located just inside the narrow entrance to Menemsha Pond. On the Vineyard's western end, Menemsha Harbor, a real fishing village, offers a low-key, laid-back alternative to the bustle of the eastern harbors. It is also a gateway to Chilmark with its rolling hills, stone fences, and breathtaking coastline, as well as dramatic Aquinnah (Gay Head) with the mile-long, 150 ft. colorful clay bluffs.

Marina Notes -- Reservations only on the day of arrival beginning at 8am. Max stay 2 weeks. Transient slips provide full services with either med moor (stern-to) or alongside dockage. Turn left 100 yds into the basin. Menemsha Beach is just on the other side of the parking lot. Coast Guard Station also onsite. A bike ferry crosses at the mouth of the Pond. "Jaws" was shot here. As in all of Matha's Vineyard, this is a closed head harbor.

Notable -- Spectacular sunsets, with an occasional fabled green flash! Menemsha Pond is both an active working harbor and a recreational destination. The draggers and lobstermen arrive with their catch -- which can sometimes be purchased right off the boats and cooked on the spot (along with anything you catch, too). Famous for its swordfish. Most of the catch goes to Larsen's Fish Market or Poole's. Couple of picnic tables overlook the harbor for on-the-spot eating. 1.5 mile walk to Beetlebung Corner - post office, library and a few shops. MV's extensive bus system makes the rest of the island quite accessible -- about 30 min. to either Edgartown, Vineyard Haven or Oak Bluffs ($1.50, bikes and kids free). Nearest bike rental is Vineyard Haven. Many fishing charters leave from here: Capt. Jennifer Clarke 645-2440, Book-A-Boat 645-2400, Menemsha Blues 645-3778, etc. Chilmark is "dry", so BYOB to restaurants - call first.

Cuttyhunk Town Marina

PO Box 28; 28 Tower Hill Road; Cuttyhunk, MA 02713

Tel: (508) 996-9292 **VHF: Monitor** 9 **Talk** 10
Fax: (508) 990-3318 **Alternate Tel:** (508) 993-6490
Email: n/a **Web:** n/a
Nearest Town: New Bedford *(14 mi.)* **Tourist Info:** (508) 999-5231

Navigational Information

Lat: 41°25.453' **Long:** 070°55.685' **Tide:** 3 ft. **Current:** n/a **Chart:** 13229
Rep. Depths (*MLW*): Entry 12 ft. **Fuel Dock** 12 ft. **Max Slip/Moor** 6 ft./6 ft.
Access: Buzzard's Bay or Vineyard Sound. Follow channel!

Marina Facilities *(In Season/Off Season)*

Fuel: *At Ferry Dock* - Slip-Side Fueling, Gasoline, Diesel
Slips: 99 Total, 50 Transient **Max LOA:** 100 ft. **Max Beam:** n/a
Rate *(per ft.)*: **Day** $1.65/Inq. **Week** Inq. **Month** Inq.
Power: 30 amp $4, **50 amp** $6, **100 amp** n/a, **200 amp** n/a
Cable TV: No **Dockside Phone:** No
Dock Type: Wood, Floating, Fixed
Moorings: 46 Total, 46 Transient **Launch:** No, Dinghy Dock
Rate: Day $25 **Week** n/a **Month** n/a
Heads: 4 Toilet(s)
Laundry: None **Pay Phones:** Yes
Pump-Out: No **Fee:** n/a **Closed Heads:** Yes

Marina Operations

Owner/Manager: Asa Lombard (Harbormaster) **Dockmaster:** n/a
In-Season: Jul-Sep 10, 8am-6pm **Off-Season:** Sep 11-Oct 15, 8am-3pm
After-Hours Arrival: Call VHF Ch. 9 or 508 993-6490
Reservations: Yes, for slips only **Credit Cards:** Cash only
Discounts: None
Pets: Welcome **Handicap Access:** No

Marina Services and Boat Supplies

Services - Docking Assistance **Supplies - Near:** Ice *(Block, Cube, Shaved)*, Ships' Store, Propane

Boatyard Services

Near: Engine mechanic *(gas, diesel)*, Launching Ramp, Electrical Repairs, Hull Repairs, Bottom Cleaning, Divers.

Restaurants and Accommodations

OnSite: Snack Bar *(Vedeer's Bakery & Ice Cream Shop B 8-9am, L 11am-1:30pm, D 7-8:30pm)* **OnCall:** Raw Bar *(The Garfield's Cuttyhunk Shellfish & Raw Bar Ch.72. 11am-1:30pm, 3-7pm clams $12 doz, oysters $14 doz, shrimps $15 doz, chowder too)*, Pizzeria *(Alicia's)* **Near:** Restaurant *(Bart's Place L $5-11, D $10-22, MemDay-LabDay, 11:30am-2:30pm, 5:30-8:30pm)*, *(Cuttyhunk Fishing Club 992-5585, B $5-8, 7-11am)*, Snack Bar *(Island Market B $2, L $5, take-out)*, *(Smooth Temptations smoothies and coffee - MemDay-LabDay Mon-Fri 1-5pm, 7-9pm, Sat & Sun 10am-5pm, 7-9pm)*, Inn/B&B *(Cuttyhunk Fishing Club B&B 992-5585, $135-330)*, *(Pete's Place 992-5131, $700-2500 wk, 2 night min, also has laundry)*, *(Cuttyhunk B&B 992-6490)*

Recreation and Entertainment

OnSite: Fishing Charter *(See the Cuttyhunk Fish Dock)* **Near:** Beach *(Barges & Churches Beaches)*, Picnic Area, Jogging Paths, Movie Theater *(Town Hall, Fridays, 6:30 & 8:45pm $1)*, Video Rental, Museum *(Historical Society Museum Sun 10am-4pm, Tue, Fri, Sat 10:30am-12:30pm & 2-4pm, Thu 10:30am-12:30pm)*, Sightseeing *(Bird and Wildlife Sanctuary)*, Special Events *(Jul 4th Parade, Clam Bakes)*

Provisioning and General Services

OnSite: Fishmonger *(Capt. Borges Old Squaw on Dock - lobsters & fish 2-6pm)* **OnCall:** Liquor Store *(Cordoza's Liquor in New Bedford 992-4477)* **Near:** Convenience Store *(Island Market 993-6490)*, Bakery *(Vineyard View Bakery)*, Lobster Pound *(Peg Leg)*, Meat Market *(Island Market)*, Bank/ATM *(at Corner Store)*, Post Office, Catholic Church, Protestant Church *(The Methodist Church also holds Roman Catholic and Episcopal services during the summer)*, Library, Laundry *(up the hill at Pete's Place - get tokens from office)*, Newsstand, Hardware Store, Retail Shops, Copies Etc. *(Smooth Temptations - fax, copies, typing)*

Transportation

Near: Water Taxi *(Sea Horse 993-5754 to and from Cuttyhunk, delivers groceries, liquor, etc.)*, Ferry Service *(Alert II to New Bedford 992-1432 in Summer 1 trip Mon-Thu, 2 trips Fri-Sun $20/13 RT, less frequent during off-season)* **Airport:** Bayside Air Seaplanes 636-3762 *(0.5 mi.)*

Medical Services

911 Service **OnCall:** Doctor *(At Town Clinic - call Harbormaster)* **Hospital:** Town Clinic *(0.5 mi.)*

Setting -- This once "stopped in time" 500-acre island (the largest of the 16 Elizabeth Islands) has seen significant changes in the last decade. However, it remains true to its character - quiet, uncommercial, unspoiled, and still delightfully backward. Views from the harbor are of the hills, seemingly "stuck" with haphazardly perched houses. Almost all of Cuttyhunk, except the wharf area, is privately owned. Hike to the top of Lookout Hill for spectacular views.

Marina Notes -- Slips can be reserved, but moorings in the Inner Habor cannot - call for availability. Mooring balls marked "City of Gosnold" - beware of the many private stake moorings in the harbor. No launch. Dinghy dock south of marina slips next to the seaplane dock. 2-boat raft permitted in good weather. 40 Moorings in the Outer Harbor available from two independent companies: Frog Pond (orange) 992-7530 and Jenkins' (blue stripe) 996-9294. Pick up empty mooring; boat will be by to collect fee. Town dinghy dock available to all. Fuel at the ferry dock. Sealed heads required, but there is no pump-out on the island. Suggest arriving with empty holding tank since public heads are marginal at best. Trash collection $1 small, $2 large bag. Cuttyhunk is "dry" so BYO.

Notable -- There is delightfully little to do here - beachcomb, bird watch, swim, relax. Some services and provisioning right on the dock. The inviting Pete's Place Restaurant, Alicia's Pizza next door, and Corner Store Gifts are a short walk inland. Around the harbor toward the ferry dock are a couple of small shops - Sweet Temptations and Island Market (closed at noon to meet the ferry). The library, museum, church, town hall, and post office are a bit of a hike, halfway up the hill. Around the other side is the very special 19th Cuttyhunk Fishing Club B&B - a great early morning hike ending in a breakfast with views and history.

IX. Massachusetts: Buzzards Bay

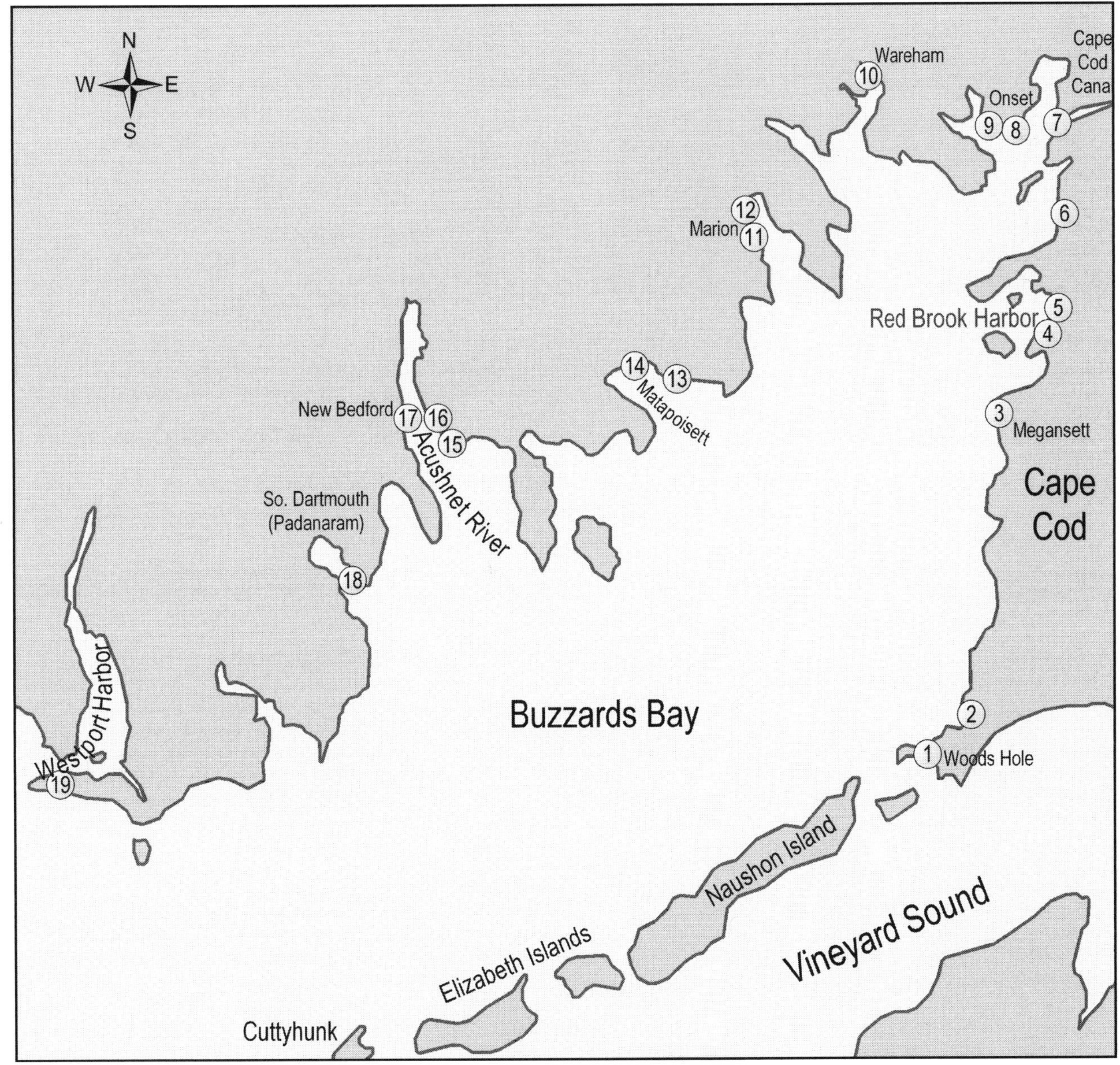

MAP	MARINA	HARBOR	PAGE
1	**Woods Hole Marine**	*Eel Pond/Woods Hole*	194
2	**Quissett Harbor Boatyard**	*Quissett Harbor*	195
3	**Brewer Fiddler's Cove Marina**	*Megansett Harbor*	196
4	**Parker's Boat Yard**	*Red Brook Harbor*	197
5	**Kingman Yacht Center**	*Red Brook Harbor*	198
6	**Monument Beach Marina**	*Phinneys Harbor*	199
7	**Bourne Marina**	*Cohassset Narrows*	200
8	**Onset Bay Marina**	*Onset Bay*	201
9	**Point Independence Yacht Club**	*Onset Bay*	202
10	**Warr's Marina**	*Wareham River*	203
11	**Barden's Boat Yard**	*Sippican Harbor*	204
12	**Burr Bros. Boats, Inc.**	*Sippican Harbor*	205
13	**Mattapoisett Boatyard**	*Mattapoisett Harbor*	206
14	**Brownell Boatyard**	*Mattapoisett Harbor*	207
15	**Fairhaven Shipyard & Marina**	*Acushnet River*	208
16	**D.N. Kelley & Son Shipyard**	*Acushnet River*	209
17	**Pope's Island Marina**	*Acushnet River*	210
18	**New Bedford Yacht Club**	*Apponagansett Harbor*	211
19	**F. L. Tripp & Sons, Inc.**	*Westport Harbor*	212

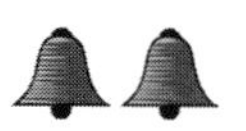

Woods Hole Marine

PO Box 746; 91A Water Street; Woods Hole, MA 02543

Tel: (508) 540-2402 **VHF: Monitor** 9 **Talk** 72
Fax: (508) 540-7927 **Alternate Tel:** n/a
Email: n/a **Web:** n/a
Nearest Town: Falmouth *(4 mi.)* **Tourist Info:** (508) 487-3424

Navigational Information

Lat: 41°31.478' **Long:** 070°40.232' **Tide:** 1.5 ft. **Current:** n/a **Chart:** 13235
Rep. Depths (*MLW*): Entry 10 ft. **Fuel Dock** n/a **Max Slip/Moor** 10 ft./20 ft.
Access: Woods Hole Passage to Great Harbor, through bridge into Eel Pond

Marina Facilities *(In Season/Off Season)*

Fuel: No
Slips: 22 Total, 1 Transient **Max LOA:** 55 ft. **Max Beam:** 18 ft.
Rate *(per ft.)*: **Day** $1.75/Inq. **Week** Inq. **Month** Inq.
Power: 30 amp Incl., **50 amp** n/a, **100 amp** n/a, **200 amp** n/a
Cable TV: No **Dockside Phone:** No
Dock Type: Short Fingers, Pilings, Fixed
Moorings: 37 Total, 1 Transient **Launch:** None, Dinghy Dock
Rate: Day $45 **Week** Inq. **Month** Inq.
Heads: 3 Toilet(s), 1 Shower(s)
Laundry: None **Pay Phones:** Yes
Pump-Out: No **Fee:** n/a **Closed Heads:** No

Marina Operations

Owner/Manager: Buzz Harvey **Dockmaster:** n/a
In-Season: Jun-Sep 1, 8am-7pm **Off-Season:** Nov-May 31, 10am-2pm
After-Hours Arrival: Call in advance
Reservations: Yes, Preferred **Credit Cards:** Visa/MC, Amex
Discounts: None
Pets: No **Handicap Access:** Yes, Heads, Docks

Marina Services and Boat Supplies

Services - Trash Pick-Up **Communication -** FedEx, UPS, Express Mail **Supplies - Near:** Ice *(Cube)* **3+ mi:** West Marine *(457-6500, 5 mi.)*, Bait/Tackle *(Eastman's Sport 548-6900, 5 mi.)*, Propane *(Fay's, 4 mi.)*

Boatyard Services

OnSite: Bottom Cleaning, Divers **Nearest Yard:** Falmouth Marine/East Marine (508) 548-4600

Restaurants and Accommodations

OnSite: Restaurant *(Black Duck 548-9165, B $4, L $5-14, D $5-19, overlooks Eel Pond)*, *(Shuckers 548-3850, L $6-9, D $10-20, overlooks Eel Pond and the drawbridge)* **Near:** Restaurant *(Captain Kidd 548-9206, L $7-16, D $16-25)*, *(Landfall 548-1758, L $6-9, D $11-20)*, *(Fishmonger's 548-9148, L $6-13, D $8-22)*, *(Naked Lobster 540-4848)*, *(Leeside 548-9744, L $5-12, D $5-12)*, Motel *(Nautilus Motor Inn 548-1525, $65-165, swimming pool, tennis courts)*, *(Sands of Time 548-6300, $80-180)*, Inn/B&B *(Woods Hole Inn 495-0248)* **Under 1 mi:** Restaurant *(Dome 548-0800, D $9-20, designed by Buckminster Fuller)*, Motel *(Sleepy Hollow 548-1986, $75-125)* **1-3 mi:** Inn/B&B *(Marlborough Capeside Cottages 548-8628, $85-135)*

Recreation and Entertainment

OnSite: Fishing Charter *(Susan Jean 548-6901; Ocean Quest 457-0508 - family-oriented marine education)* **Near:** Beach *(by dinghy)*, Playground, Jogging Paths, Roller Blade/Bike Paths, Park *(Mary Gardens)*, Museum *(Bradley House - Woods Hole Historical Museum 548-7270)*, Sightseeing *(Guided walking tour of village)* **3+ mi:** Tennis Courts *(Falmouth Sports Center 548-7433, 5 mi.)*, Golf Course *(Woodbriar 495-5500, 6 mi.)*, Fitness Center *(Falmouth Sports Center, 5 mi.)*, Horseback Riding *(Fieldcrest Farm 540-0626, 5 mi.)*, Bowling *(Leary Amusements 540-4877, 5 mi.)*

Provisioning and General Services

Near: Convenience Store *(Food Buoy 540-4792)*, Delicatessen, Bakery *(Pie in the Sky 540-5475 - sandwiches, too)*, Bank/ATM, Post Office, Catholic Church, Library *(Woods Hole 548-8961)*, Pharmacy, Newsstand, Clothing Store **Under 1 mi:** Wine/Beer, Liquor Store *(Old Barn Package Store 548-4855)* **1-3 mi:** Copies Etc. *(Stone Printing 548-3662)* **3+ mi:** Supermarket *(Tedeschi 457-1191, 4 mi.)*, Gourmet Shop *(Bean And Cod Gourmet 548-8840, 4 mi.)*, Health Food *(Harvest Abundant 540-5598, 5 mi.)*, Hardware Store *(Eastman's Hardware 548-0407, 5 mi.)*

Transportation

OnCall: Rental Car *(National 548-1303, Enterprise 540-7784)*, Taxi *(Kennedy Limo 548-1066, All Village Taxi 540-7200)* **Near:** Local Bus *(Seasonal Trolley to Falmouth, Mashpee, Hyannis 385-8326/548-8500)*, InterCity Bus *(Bonanza to Boston, Providence, NY & airports 888-751-8800)*, Ferry Service *(to Vineyard Haven, 17 times/day in season, 45 min, $5/2; to Oak Bluffs 7 times/day, 45 min, $5/2. 477-8600)* **Airport:** Barnstable 775-2020 *(28 mi.)*

Medical Services

911 Service **OnCall:** Ambulance **Hospital:** Falmouth 457-1200 *(5 mi.)*

Setting -- Tucked into placid, protected Eel Pond, behind the draw bridge, Woods Hole Marine's dockage and moorings provide gorgeous views and an unbeatable location. Walk down a small cobblestone alley and you are in the heart of tiny, busy, interesting Woods Hole. There are seven restaurants within a couple of blocks, and all the services of Falmouth are only 4 miles away.

Marina Notes -- Note: Pets not allowed. Minimal amenities for boaters: no laundry, only one shower. Note, too, there is no longer launch service. The boats, usually an assortment of very attractive ones, provide scenery for the diners at the two onsite restaurants: Shuckers, also a raw bar, and The Black Duck. Space for transients is very limited, so plan far in advance. Woods Hole also manages moorings in Great Harbor and may have some available. The nearby 4 mile Shining Sea Bike Path runs from Woods Hole to Falmouth along an old railroad bed. Harbormaster: 457-2550. All medical services are in Falmouth.

Notable -- Woods Hole is a world-class center of oceanographic research. There are 5 marine science facilities right here -- 3 of them are open to the public, and all are fascinating: The MBL, Marine Biological Labs, established in 1888, offers tours Mon-Sat, 10am-4pm, free, reservations mandatory, 2-weeks min. 548-3705. Woods Hole Oceanographic Institutes' Exhibit Center (largest private marine research center in the world), Mon-Sat 10am-4:30pm, Sun 12-4:30pm. $2/free 289-2252. Northeast Fisheries Science Center's Woods Hole Science Aquarium Mon-Fri 10am-4pm 495-2001. Woods Hole Historical Museum Tue-Sat 10am-4pm, walking tour of town Tuesday 4pm. Woods Hole Film Festival End of July. Illumination Weekend early June.

PHOTOS ON CD-ROM: 9

Navigational Information

Lat: 41°32.655' **Long:** 070°39.113' **Tide:** 5 ft. **Current:** 0.25 kt. **Chart:** 1322
Rep. Depths (*MLW*): Entry 9 ft. **Fuel Dock** 16 ft. **Max Slip/Moor** -/25 ft.
Access: 1 mi. NE of Woods Hole Passage; look for entrance flasher R2

Marina Facilities *(In Season/Off Season)*

Fuel: No
Slips: 1 Total, 0 Transient **Max LOA:** 70 ft. **Max Beam:** n/a
Rate *(per ft.)*: **Day** n/a **Week** n/a **Month** n/a
Power: 30 amp n/a, **50 amp** n/a, **100 amp** n/a, **200 amp** n/a
Cable TV: No **Dockside Phone:** No
Dock Type: n/a
Moorings: 25 Total, 12 Transient **Launch:** No, Dinghy Dock (Free)
Rate: Day $25 **Week** $175 **Month** Inq.
Heads: 1 Toilet(s)
Laundry: None **Pay Phones:** Yes
Pump-Out: OnCall, Full Service, 1 Port **Fee:** Free **Closed Heads:** No

Marina Operations

Owner/Manager: Weatherly Barnard Dorris **Dockmaster:** Rick Dorris
In-Season: Jun-Aug, 8am-6pm **Off-Season:** Sep-May, 9am-4:30pm
After-Hours Arrival: Pick up a mooring marked "QBY" in the outer harbor
Reservations: No **Credit Cards:** Cash or check only
Discounts: None
Pets: Welcome **Handicap Access:** No

Quissett Harbor Boatyard

PO Box 46; 36 Quissett Harbor Road; Falmouth, MA 02541

Tel: (508) 548-0506 **VHF: Monitor** n/a **Talk** n/a
Fax: (508) 540-8991 **Alternate Tel:** n/a
Email: n/a **Web:** n/a
Nearest Town: Woods Hole *(1.25 mi.)* **Tourist Info:** (508) 487-3424

Marina Services and Boat Supplies

Services - Trash Pick-Up **Communication -** FedEx, UPS, Express Mail **Supplies - OnSite:** Ice *(Block, Cube)* **1-3 mi:** Ships' Store, West Marine, Bait/Tackle, Propane

Boatyard Services

OnSite: Railway *(10T)*, Engine mechanic *(gas, diesel)*, Brightwork, Divers, Propeller Repairs, Woodworking, Yacht Broker *(Weatherly Dorris)* **1-3 mi:** Electrical Repairs, Electronic Sales, Rigger, Sail Loft, Canvas Work, Bottom Cleaning, Compound, Wash & Wax, Interior Cleaning. **Dealer for:** Dyer dinghy. **Yard Rates:** $50/hr., Haul & Launch $2, Power Wash $50, Bottom Paint $50/ft. **Storage:** On-Land $6/ft./mo.

Restaurants and Accommodations

OnCall: Pizzeria *(Steve's 547-9454)* **Near:** Inn/B&B *(Woods Hole Passage B&B 548-9575, $100-165)* **Under 1 mi:** Motel *(Nautilus Motor Inn 548-1525, $65-165)* **1-3 mi:** Restaurant *(Landfall 548-1758, L $6-9, D $11-20)*, *(Capt Kidd 548-8563, L $7-16, D $16-25)*, *(Fishmonger 540-5376, L $6-13, D $8-22)*, *(Dome 548-0800, D $9-21)*, *(Shuckers 548-3850, L $6-9, D $10-20)*, Seafood Shack *(Clam Shack)*, Snack Bar *(Pie in the Sky 540-5475, B $3, L $7)*, Hotel *(Ramada Inn 457-0606, $80-500)*

Recreation and Entertainment

OnSite: Beach, Jogging Paths **Near:** Roller Blade/Bike Paths, Sightseeing *(Carey Bird Sanctuary)* **Under 1 mi:** Special Events *(Falmouth Road Race, 2nd week in Aug)* **1-3 mi:** Picnic Area, Grills, Playground, Tennis Courts, Golf Course *(Woodbriar Golf Club 495-5500)*, Fitness Center, Boat Rentals, Bowling, Fishing Charter, Movie Theater *(Falmouth Mall Cinema 540-2169)*, Video Rental, Video Arcade, Park, Museum *(NEFSC Aquarium 495-2001, Falmouth Woods Hole Historical Society)*, Cultural Attract *(Marine Biological Laboratory 548-3705, Woods Hole Oceanographic Institute)*

Provisioning and General Services

1-3 mi: Supermarket *(Stop & Shop 548-4033, Windfall Market)*, Gourmet Shop *(Windfall Market 548-0099)*, Delicatessen, Health Food *(Amber Waves)*, Wine/Beer *(Windfall Market)*, Liquor Store *(Kappy's, John's)*, Bakery, Green Grocer, Fishmonger *(Clam Man)*, Lobster Pound, Meat Market, Bank/ATM, Post Office, Catholic Church, Protestant Church, Library, Beauty Salon, Barber Shop, Dry Cleaners, Laundry, Bookstore *(Booksmith 540-6064)*, Pharmacy *(Woods Hole Pharmacy 548-0741)*, Newsstand, Hardware Store *(Wood Lumber 548-3154)*, Florist, Retail Shops, Department Store *(Puritans Clothing, Falmouth)*, Copies Etc. **3+ mi:** Synagogue *(6 mi.)*

Transportation

OnCall: Rental Car *(Enterprise 540-7784)*, Taxi *(Falmouth Taxi 548-3100)* **Near:** Local Bus *(WHOOSH Trolley to Falmouth-Woods Hole)* **1-3 mi:** Bikes *(Corner Cycle 540-4195)*, InterCity Bus *(Bonanza)*, Ferry Service *(SSA-Martha's Vineyard, Island Queen-Martha's Vineyard)* **Airport:** Barnstable *(28 mi.)*

Medical Services

911 Service **OnCall:** Ambulance **1-3 mi:** Doctor, Dentist, Holistic Services **Hospital:** Falmouth 457-1200 *(5 mi.)*

Setting -- Beautiful Quissett Harbor is quiet, residential and unspoiled. Its lovely shoreside is populated with beautiful old summer houses and conservation lands. The Boatyard consists of transient moorings, minimal landside facilities and some boatyard services -- in a classically beautiful and charming setting.

Marina Notes -- A small, friendly, old-time boatyard, owned by the Barnard family, it has been the only business on the harbor for more than four decades. Encourages Yacht Club Cruises; it's a nice gathering spot -- but reservations are not taken under any circumstances. There is one head, a modest boatyard facility (that specializes in wooden boats and can haul up to 40 ft.), a dinghy dock, and one very short-term slip for work or water. Good hurricane hole. The Quissett Yacht Club 457-1055 is on the west side of the inner harbor. There is a pump-out boat that serves the harbor.

Notable -- It's easy to be inspired by the walk out to "The Knob", in the Cornelia L. Carey Bird Sanctuary (on the northwest end of the harbor) with its magnificent views of Buzzards Bay and spectacular seaside sunsets. Hiking trails wind through 13 acres of this protected bird sanctuary. Entrance to The Shining Sea Bikeway is a couple of miles away; this paved four mile pathway weaves across an ancient coastal plain which passes sandy beaches, ocean harbors, saltwater marshes, kettle hole ponds and quiet woodlands on the way to the quaint, but bustling village of Woods Hole. There are no services or dining options nearby; everything is about 1.5-2 miles south in Woods Hole or in Falmouth Village. The very convenient WHOOSH trolley is a short walk away, runs every 1/2 hour in season, and provides transportation to Woods Hole and Falmouth -- for shopping, restaurants, entertainment, etc.

PHOTOS ON CD-ROM: 4

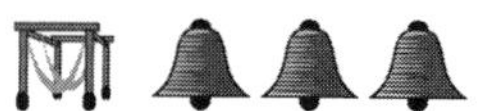

Brewer Fiddler's Cove Marina

27 Fiddlers Cove Road; North Falmouth, MA 02556

Tel: (508) 564-6327 **VHF: Monitor** 9 **Talk** 10
Fax: (508) 564-6724 **Alternate Tel:** n/a
Email: brewerfcm@aol.com **Web:** www.byy.com
Nearest Town: Falmouth *(5 mi.)* **Tourist Info:** (508) 548-8500

Navigational Information

Lat: 41°38.808' **Long:** 070°38.160' **Tide:** 3 ft. **Current:** n/a **Chart:** 13236
Rep. Depths (*MLW*): Entry 7 ft. **Fuel Dock** 7 ft. **Max Slip/Moor** 9 ft./-
Access: Megansett Harbor to R6 to Fiddler's Cove

Marina Facilities *(In Season/Off Season)*

Fuel: Gasoline, Diesel
Slips: 135 Total, 8 Transient **Max LOA:** 55 ft. **Max Beam:** n/a
Rate *(per ft.)*: **Day** $2.50/Inq. **Week** Inq. **Month** Inq.
Power: 30 amp $3.75, **50 amp** $5.75, **100 amp** n/a, **200 amp** n/a
Cable TV: Yes **Dockside Phone:** No
Dock Type: Long Fingers, Floating, Composition
Moorings: 0 Total, 0 Transient **Launch:** n/a
Rate: Day n/a **Week** n/a **Month** n/a
Heads: 9 Toilet(s), 9 Shower(s) *(with dressing rooms)*
Laundry: 2 Washer(s), 2 Dryer(s) **Pay Phones:** Yes
Pump-Out: OnSite, Full Service, 1 Central **Fee:** n/a **Closed Heads:** No

Marina Operations

Owner/Manager: Al Doppke **Dockmaster:** n/a
In-Season: Apr-Nov, 8am-6pm **Off-Season:** Dec-Mar, 8am-5pm
After-Hours Arrival: Call in advance
Reservations: Yes **Credit Cards:** Visa/MC, Dscvr, Amex
Discounts: None
Pets: Welcome **Handicap Access:** Yes, Heads, Docks

Marina Services and Boat Supplies

Services - Docking Assistance, Boaters' Lounge, Trash Pick-Up, Dock Carts **Communication -** Data Ports *(Office)*, FedEx, AirBorne, UPS, Express Mail **Supplies - OnSite:** Ice *(Block, Cube)*, Ships' Store **OnCall:** Marine Discount Store *(Stem To Stern Mobile Marine Service 563-6553)* **Near:** Propane **3+ mi:** West Marine *(457-6500, 8 mi.)*

Boatyard Services

OnSite: Travelift *(35T)*, Railway, Forklift, Crane, Engine mechanic *(gas, diesel)*, Hull Repairs, Rigger, Bottom Cleaning, Compound, Wash & Wax, Interior Cleaning, Woodworking, Inflatable Repairs, Painting **OnCall:** Electronic Sales, Electronics Repairs, Air Conditioning, Refrigeration, Divers, Propeller Repairs, Upholstery, Yacht Interiors **Member:** ABYC

Restaurants and Accommodations

OnCall: Pizzeria *(House Of Pizza 563-9879)* **Under 1 mi:** Restaurant *(Jillians 564-5029, L $12-15, D $12-20)*, Motel *(Ideal Spot 548-2257, $65-115)* **1-3 mi:** Restaurant *(Silver Lounge 564-4355, L $4-11, D $11-15)*, *(Courtyard Rest & Pub 563-1818)*, *(Chapoquoit Grill 540-7794, D $7-18)*, *(Sea Crest 540-9400, B: 7-10:30am, D 5:30-11pm)*, Motel *(Cataumet 563-6133)*, *(Sjoholm Inn 540-5706, $90-125)*, Hotel *(Sea Crest Resort $160-240)* **3+ mi:** Hotel *(7-8 mi., many in downtown Falmouth)*

Recreation and Entertainment

OnSite: Picnic Area, Playground **Near:** Jogging Paths **Under 1 mi:** Horseback Riding *(Haland Stables 540-2552)* **1-3 mi:** Beach *(Old Silver Beach)*, Golf Course *(Ballymeade Country Club 540-4005)*, Video Rental *(Video Shoppe of No. Falmouth 563-7877)* **3+ mi:** Roller Blade/Bike Paths *(Shining Trail Bike Path, 4 mi.)*, Bowling *(Ryan Family Amusement Co. 759-9892, 7 mi.)*, Movie Theater *(Hoyts Nickelodeon 563-6510, 4 mi.)*, Park *(4 mi.)*, Cultural Attract *(4 mi.)*, Sightseeing *(Bourne Farm 548-8484, 4 mi.)*

Provisioning and General Services

Near: Convenience Store, Catholic Church, Beauty Salon, Dry Cleaners, Newsstand **Under 1 mi:** Bank/ATM, Post Office, Library *(Falmouth 563-2922)*, Florist **1-3 mi:** Supermarket *(Village Pantry 563-6942)*, Liquor Store *(No. Falmouth Liquors 563-3331)*, Green Grocer *(Village Fresh Pond Farm Stand)*, Barber Shop, Pharmacy *(No. Falmouth Pharmacy 563-9250)*, Hardware Store *(No. Falmouth Hardware & Marine Supply 564-6160)*, Copies Etc. *(Gallagher Graphics 563-3399)* **3+ mi:** Gourmet Shop *(West Falmouth Market 548-1139, 4 mi.)*, Farmers' Market *(4 mi.)*

Transportation

OnCall: Rental Car *(Thrifty 540-9942, Enterprise 540-7784)* **Under 1 mi:** Taxi *(Cape Cod Livery 563-5669)* **1-3 mi:** Bikes *(Art's Bike Shop 563-7379)*, InterCity Bus *(Bonanza 888-751-8800)* **3+ mi:** Ferry Service *(Edgartown & Oak Bluffs, 7 mi.)* **Airport:** Barnstable/Falmouth 548-9617 *(24 mi./8 mi.)*

Medical Services

911 Service **OnCall:** Ambulance **Under 1 mi:** Chiropractor *(Falmouth Chiro Center 457-0440)*, Holistic Services *(Massey Massage 540-4975)* **1-3 mi:** Doctor, Dentist **Hospital:** Falmouth 457-1200 *(7 mi.)*

Setting -- Just off Megansett Harbor, tucked away in a well-protected, man-made cove, this beautifully landscaped and carefully maintained facility offers extensive dockage surrounded by eel grass, bayberry and rosa rugosa. Overlooking the marina is a large "Cape Cod contemporary" turreted, decked, gray-shingled clubhouse. The dredged entrance channel is marked with private buoys.

Marina Notes -- This full service boatyard is well situated, keeping its service building and 35 ton travelift out of the sightlines of the slips. The clubhouse is convenient to the docks and contains a spacious, very nicely appointed room with sofas, reading areas, several card tables, and a pool table plus kitchen, laundry, data ports, and private bathrooms. This is available to all marina guests. Onsite, full-service pump-out. Moorings may also be available from Megansett Yacht Club 563-9812.

Notable -- This is a very quiet part of the Cape -- perfect for exploring by bike, dinghy, or on foot. Dinghy south around Nyes Neck and down to Wild Harbor to Old Silver Beach, one of the nicest -- and warmest -- on the western shore. Or north to the Megansett Town Wharf. Spectacular sunsets. 34 acre Bourne Farm is a restored 1775 working farm on Crocker's Pond (548-8484). Old Silver Beach is a dinghy ride away - a long, sandy beach with tidal pools, a life guard, snack bar and bath house. Bonanza Bus line runs along Route 28 - south to Woods Hole and north to Plymouth, TF Green, Boston/Logan and NY City.

Navigational Information

Lat: 41°40.368' **Long:** 070°37.063' **Tide:** 2 ft. **Current:** n/a **Chart:** 13236
Rep. Depths (*MLW*): Entry 6 ft. **Fuel Dock** 7 ft. **Max Slip/Moor** 7 ft./8 ft.
Access: East of Wings Neck traffic light near entrance to Cape Cod Canal

Marina Facilities *(In Season/Off Season)*

Fuel: Gasoline, Diesel
Slips: 9 Total, 1 Transient **Max LOA:** 40 ft. **Max Beam:** n/a
Rate *(per ft.)*: **Day** $1.50/$1.50 **Week** $10.50 **Month** $45
Power: 30 amp Incl., **50 amp** n/a, **100 amp** n/a, **200 amp** n/a
Cable TV: No **Dockside Phone:** No
Dock Type: Wood, Long Fingers
Moorings: 130 Total, 6+ Transient **Launch:** Yes (Free), Dinghy Dock
Rate: Day $35/25 **Week** Inq. **Month** Inq.
Heads: 2 Toilet(s), 2 Shower(s)
Laundry: None, Book Exchange **Pay Phones:** No
Pump-Out: OnSite, Full Service, 1 Central **Fee:** Free **Closed Heads:** No

Marina Operations

Owner/Manager: Bruce Parker **Dockmaster:** n/a
In-Season: Jun-Aug, 8am-8pm **Off-Season:** Sep-May, 8am-5pm
After-Hours Arrival: n/a
Reservations: Yes, Preferred **Credit Cards:** Visa/MC
Discounts: None
Pets: Welcome, Dog Walk Area **Handicap Access:** No

Parker's Boat Yard

PO Box 38; 68 Red Brook Harbor Road; Cataumet, MA 02534

Tel: (508) 563-9366 **VHF: Monitor** 69 **Talk** n/a
Fax: (508) 563-3899 **Alternate Tel:** n/a
Email: pbparker@capecod.net **Web:** www.parkersboatyard.com
Nearest Town: Falmouth *(10 mi.)* **Tourist Info:** (508) 759-6000

Marina Services and Boat Supplies

Services - Docking Assistance, Boaters' Lounge, Trash Pick-Up, Dock Carts **Communication -** Mail & Package Hold, Phone Messages, Data Ports *(Office)*, FedEx, AirBorne, UPS, Express Mail **Supplies - OnSite:** Ice *(Block, Cube)*, Ships' Store, CNG **1-3 mi:** Live Bait, Propane **3+ mi:** West Marine *(457-6500, 9 mi.)*, Bait/Tackle *(Sealure 759-7848, 5 mi.)*

Boatyard Services

OnSite: Travelift *(35T)*, Crane, Engine mechanic *(gas, diesel)*, Electrical Repairs, Electronic Sales, Hull Repairs, Rigger, Bottom Cleaning, Brightwork, Compound, Wash & Wax, Interior Cleaning, Woodworking, Metal Fabrication, Painting, Awlgrip **OnCall:** Electronics Repairs, Air Conditioning, Refrigeration, Divers, Propeller Repairs, Inflatable Repairs, Life Raft Service **Near:** Launching Ramp. **Under 1 mi:** Sail Loft. **1-3 mi:** Upholstery, Yacht Interiors. **Member:** ABBRA, ABYC - 4 Certified Tech(s) **Yard Rates:** $64/hr., Haul & Launch $11/ft., Power Wash $2.50/tf., Bottom Paint $11/ft. **Storage:** On-Land $40/ft.

Restaurants and Accommodations

OnCall: Pizzeria *(Graziella's 563-5541, L $4-9, D $4-9, or by dinghy, pizza, pasta, grinders, seafood)* **Near:** Restaurant *(Chart Room 563-5350, L $3-16, D $6-22, at Kingman Yacht Center)*, Inn/B&B *(Cataumet Depot 564-4824)*, *(Wood Duck Inn 564-6404, $80-115, 3 rooms)*, *(Red Brook 564-5215)* **Under 1 mi:** Restaurant *(Courtyard 563-1818, L $4-11, D 411-17)*, *(Parrot 563-6464, L $5-8, D $7-17)* **1-3 mi:** Hotel *(Sea Crest Resort 540-9400, $125-285)*

Recreation and Entertainment

OnSite: Beach *(dinghy to Bassett's Island)*, Picnic Area, Grills, Jogging Paths **Near:** Boat Rentals *(Kayaks)*, Park *(Nivling-Alexander Reserve)* **Under 1 mi:** Playground, Tennis Courts **1-3 mi:** Golf Course *(Ballymeade 540-4005)*, Horseback Riding *(Haland Stables 540-2552)*, Roller Blade/Bike Paths, Video Rental *(Video Shoppe of No. Falmouth 563-7877)* **3+ mi:** Movie Theater *(Hoyts 563-6510, 5 mi.)*, Museum *(Aptucxet Trading Post Museum 759-9487, 6 mi.)*

Provisioning and General Services

Near: Delicatessen **Under 1 mi:** Fishmonger, Lobster Pound, Post Office, Protestant Church *(Methodist)*, Laundry **1-3 mi:** Convenience Store, Supermarket *(Village Pantry 563-6942, A&P 759-5957- 5 mi., Pocasset Country Market)*, Wine/Beer, Liquor Store *(No. Falmouth Liquors 563-3331)*, Bakery, Farmers' Market, Meat Market, Bank/ATM, Catholic Church, Library *(Falmouth 563-2922)*, Barber Shop, Dry Cleaners, Pharmacy *(No. Falmouth 563-9250)*, Newsstand, Hardware Store *(No. Falmouth Hardware & Marine 564-6160)*, Florist, Copies Etc.

Transportation

OnSite: Courtesy Car/Van, Bikes **OnCall:** Rental Car *(Enterprise, 7 mi. 759-2299, Budget, Hertz)*, Taxi *(White Tie 563-9773 / No. Falmouth 548-2900)* **3+ mi:** InterCity Bus *(Bonanza 759-7715, 6 mi.)*, Ferry Service *(To MV & Nantucket, 8 mi.)* **Airport:** Barnstable/Falmouth *(28 mi./8 mi.)*

Medical Services

911 Service **Near:** Dentist **1-3 mi:** Doctor, Chiropractor **Hospital:** Falmouth 457-1200 *(8 mi.)*

Setting -- This quintessential Cape Cod boatyard, with its charming weathered shingled buildings, looks out over quiet, protected, mooring-filled Red Hook Harbor, on to Bassett's Island. It also has views of nearby Kingman Yacht Center. The surrounding community is rural and residential, inviting nature walks.

Marina Notes -- Family-owned since 1948, Parker's is a full-service yacht yard, with a knowledgeable, professional staff. Focus is on sailboats. The prevailing attitude is friendly, helpful and service-oriented. Dealer for Volvo, Yanmar, Universal, Westerbeke. A courtesy car and onsite bicycles make provisioning, restauranting, and sightseeing easier. Some discounting is offered on a per job basis. Good onsite chandlery. Bourne Pumpout Boat VHF Ch.9.

Notable -- Kingman Yacht Center, with all its services and supplies, is a short hike or dinghy ride away. Dinghy a little farther to Barlows Landing in Pocassett Harbor with 2 eateries -- Graziella's & Corner Café, Pocasset Hardware, Larry's Market & Cumberland Farms about 0.25 mile inland. A half mile farther, on Rte 28 is a bank and many services & shops. 40 acre Nivling-Alexander Reserve offers wooded land trails overlooking cranberry bogs and Red Brook Pond. Bonanza Bus is 5 miles away with 1.5 hr. service to either Boston or Providence (connecting to NY). There are three taxi services and a limo service that will provide interim transportation. Tedeschi Food Market is at the bus stop. Only 6 land miles to the Bourne Bridge, 7 nautical miles to the Cape Cod Canal.

PHOTOS ON CD-ROM: 9

Kingman Yacht Center

PO Box 408; 1 Shipyard Lane; Cataumet, MA 02534

Tel: (508) 563-7136 **VHF: Monitor** 9 **Talk** 71
Fax: (508) 563-6493 **Alternate Tel:** n/a
Email: harbormaster@kingmanyachtcenter.com **Web:** kingmanyachtcenter.
Nearest Town: Pocasset *(1 mi.)* **Tourist Info:** (508) 759-3122

Navigational Information

Lat: 41°40.595' **Long:** 070°36.954' **Tide:** 4 ft. **Current:** n/a **Chart:** 13236
Rep. Depths (*MLW*): Entry 6 ft. **Fuel Dock** 10 ft. **Max Slip/Moor** 10 ft./12 ft.
Access: Buzzards Bay - East End to Pocasset Habor to Red Brook

Marina Facilities *(In Season/Off Season)*

Fuel: Gasoline, Diesel
Slips: 235 Total, 30 Transient **Max LOA:** 100 ft. **Max Beam:** n/a
Rate *(per ft.)*: **Day** $3.00* **Week** n/a **Month** n/a
Power: 30 amp Incl., **50 amp** Incl., **100 amp** n/a, **200 amp** n/a
Cable TV: No **Dockside Phone:** No
Dock Type: Wood, Long Fingers, Short Fingers, Pilings, Floating
Moorings: 135 Total, 0 Transient **Launch:** Yes (Free), Dinghy Dock
Rate: Day $45 **Week** $315 **Month** 1/6 of seasonal
Heads: 12 Toilet(s), 8 Shower(s)
Laundry: 3 Washer(s), 3 Dryer(s) **Pay Phones:** Yes, 2
Pump-Out: OnSite, Self Service, 1 Central **Fee:** Free **Closed Heads:** No

Marina Operations

Owner/Manager: John Burman **Dockmaster:** Todd Steele
In-Season: June-Sep, 8am-8pm **Off-Season:** Sep-June, 8am-5pm
After-Hours Arrival: Call in advance and check-in in the morning
Reservations: Yes, Preferred **Credit Cards:** Visa/MC, Dscvr
Discounts: None
Pets: Welcome, Dog Walk Area **Handicap Access:** No

Marina Services and Boat Supplies

Services - Docking Assistance, Dock Carts **Communication -** Mail & Package Hold, Phone Messages, Fax in/out *($1)*, Data Ports *(Office)*, FedEx, AirBorne, UPS, Express Mail *(Sat Del)* **Supplies - OnSite:** Ice *(Block, Cube)*, Ships' Store *(Boater's Essentials 563-7136, Ch.71, 7 days)* **1-3 mi:** Propane *(Majors RV or Taylor 563-1960)* **3+ mi:** West Marine *(457-6500, 9 mi.)*, Bait/Tackle *(Sealure 759-7848, 5 mi.)*

Boatyard Services

OnSite: Travelift *(60T)*, Engine mechanic *(gas, diesel)*, Electrical Repairs, Electronic Sales, Electronics Repairs, Hull Repairs, Rigger, Bottom Cleaning, Brightwork, Compound, Wash & Wax, Interior Cleaning, Woodworking, Upholstery, Yacht Interiors, Metal Fabrication, Painting, Awlgrip, Total Refits **OnCall:** Air Conditioning, Refrigeration, Divers, Propeller Repairs, Inflatable Repairs, Life Raft Service **Under 1 mi:** Launching Ramp. **1-3 mi:** Sail Loft. **Dealer for:** Osmotic Blister Repair, Alerion, FinnGulf. **Member:** ABBRA, ABYC **Yard Rates:** $80/hr., Haul & Launch $11/ft. *(blocking incl.)*, Power Wash $1.50/ft., Bottom Paint $8-10/ft. **Storage:** In-Water $21/ft., On-Land $28/ft. Inside $6.50/sq.ft.

Restaurants and Accommodations

OnSite: Restaurant *(Chart Room 563-5350, L $3-16, D $6-22)* **OnCall:** Pizzeria *(Graziella's 563-5541, L $4-9, D $4-9, or by dinghy, also seafood)* **Under 1 mi:** Restaurant *(Courtyard 563-1818, L $6-11, D $11-17)*, Coffee Shop *(Corner Café 563-6944, by dinghy)*, Motel *(Cataumet 563-6133)*, Inn/B&B *(Wood Duck Inn 564-6404, $80-115)* **1-3 mi:** Restaurant *(Jillian's 564-5029, L $12-15, D $12-20)*, Inn/B&B *(Somewhere Among My Flowers 563-5028)* **3+ mi:** Hotel *(Sea Crest 540-9400, $125-285, 5 mi.)*

Recreation and Entertainment

OnSite: Picnic Area, Grills **Near:** Beach *(Bassetts Island Beach, a short dinghy ride away.)*, Jogging Paths, Sightseeing *(Nivling-Alexander Reserve, 40 acres of wooded hiking trails overlooking cranberry bogs and Red Brook Pond)* **Under 1 mi:** Park **1-3 mi:** Golf Course *(Ballymeade Country Club 540-4005)*, Horseback Riding *(Haland Stables 540-2552)*, Video Rental *(Video Shoppe 563-7877)* **3+ mi:** Museum *(Aptucxet Trading Post Museum 759-9487, Briggs McDermott House 759-6120, 6 mi.)*

Provisioning and General Services

OnSite: Convenience Store, Newsstand **OnCall:** Liquor Store *(Bay State $200 min 564-6505)* **Under 1 mi:** Market *(Pocasset Country Market 564-4258 delivers)*, Bakery, Green Grocer, Catholic Church, Barber Shop, Hardware Store *(Pocasset 563-6042 by dinghy + No. Falmouth 564-6160 3 mi.)*, Florist **1-3 mi:** Delicatessen *(Larry's Market)*, Wine/Beer *(No. Falmouth Liquors 563-3331)*, Fishmonger *(Cataumet Fish)*, Lobster Pound, Bank/ATM, Post Office, Library *(Town of Falmouth 563-2922)*, Beauty Salon, Dry Cleaners, Bookstore, Pharmacy *(No. Falmouth 563-9250)*, Copies Etc. *(Gallagher's 563-3399)* **3+ mi:** Supermarket *(A&P 759-5957, 6 mi.)*

Transportation

OnCall: Rental Car *(Enterprise 759-2299)*, Taxi *(White Tie Limo 563-9773/ Canal Cab 548-2900)* **1-3 mi:** Bikes *(Art's Bike 563-7379)*, InterCity Bus *(Bonanza to TF Green & Boston)* **3+ mi:** Ferry Service *(Martha's Vineyard & Nantucket, 15 mi.)* **Airport:** Barnstable/Logan *(28 mi./70 mi.)*

Medical Services

911 Service **1-3 mi:** Doctor **Hospital:** Falmouth 548-5300 *(8 mi.)*

PHOTOS ON CD-ROM: 9

Setting -- The largest marina and boatyard facility in the Cape Cod area, bustling Kingman is tucked into pristine Red Brook Harbor - just 7 miles south of the CC Canal -- and protected by Bassett's Island. Entry is through either the North (deeper) or South Channels around the island. The facility sits on a peninsula surrounded by docks. An enclosed basin "behind" the marina holds one network of docks; the open harborside, the other. Chart Room Restaurant creates a festive atmosphere with lounge chairs perched on the small point overlooking the docks and harbor.

Marina Notes -- Founded 1932. Comprehensive Service and Repair Facility with haul out up to 60 tons. Courtesy dinghy and loading docks. For longer stays, dockside phone and cable TV available direct from vendors. Two sets of heads, one with laundry, both new 2001. Pump-out at Fuel dock - both 8am-7:30pm (also Bourne Pump-out Boat Ch.9). Dock & Launch crew 8am-9pm, Ch.71 (reduced service shoulder season). Most moorings 8,000 lbs. Limited number of hurricane moorings. Boater's Essentials store onsite, 7 days. Dealer for most major electronics and engine manufacturers. Emergency towing.

Notable -- Chart Room Restaurant & Piano Bar offers casual dining overlooking the harbor (complimentary dining docking) - Lunch/Dinner 7 days 11:30am-10pm, mid-Jun-LabDay. Weekends only MemDay-mid-Jun, LabDay-ColDay. Reservations critical. Crews Ltd. opens at 6:30am in season for breakfast, newspapers and general "convenience" items 564-7559. Periwinkles Gifts has souvenirs, shirts, toys, etc. Bassett's Island, a mile-long white sand beach is just a short dinghy ride away. Or dinghy to Barlows Landing in Pocasset Harbor for 2 casual restaurants, hardware store, convenience store and small market.

Navigational Information
Lat: 41°42.862' **Long:** 070°36.938' **Tide:** n/a **Current:** 3 kt. **Chart:** 13236
Rep. Depths (*MLW*): Entry 40 ft. **Fuel Dock** 6 ft. **Max Slip/Moor** 8 ft./30 ft.
Access: West of Wings Neck to Phinney's Harbor

Marina Facilities *(In Season/Off Season)*
Fuel: *93* - Gasoline, High-Speed Pumps
Slips: 60 Total, 3 Transient **Max LOA:** 50 ft. **Max Beam:** 13 ft.
Rate *(per ft.)*: **Day** $1.50/Inq. **Week** Inq. **Month** n/a
Power: 30 amp Incl., **50 amp** n/a, **100 amp** n/a, **200 amp** n/a
Cable TV: No **Dockside Phone:** No
Dock Type: Wood, Floating, Vinyl
Moorings: 35 Total, 1 Transient **Launch:** n/a, Dinghy Dock
Rate: Day $21.25 **Week** n/a **Month** n/a
Heads: 2 Toilet(s)
Laundry: None **Pay Phones:** Yes, 1
Pump-Out: OnCall, Full Service, 1 Port **Fee:** Free **Closed Heads:** No

Marina Operations
Owner/Manager: Timothy Mullen **Dockmaster:** Michael Gratis
In-Season: May-Oct, 8 am-5 pm **Off-Season:** Nov-Apr, Closed
After-Hours Arrival: Tie up and see attendant at 8 am the next day
Reservations: Yes **Credit Cards:** Visa/MC
Discounts: None
Pets: Welcome **Handicap Access:** Yes, Heads, Docks

Monument Beach Marina

24 Emmons Road; Monument Beach, MA 02553

Tel: (508) 759-3105 **VHF: Monitor** 9 **Talk** 11
Fax: n/a **Alternate Tel:** n/a
Email: n/a **Web:** www.townofbourne.com
Nearest Town: Bourne *(3 mi.)* **Tourist Info:** (508) 759-6000

Marina Services and Boat Supplies
Services - Docking Assistance, Dock Carts **Communication -** FedEx, AirBorne, UPS, Express Mail **Supplies - Near:** Ice *(Block, Cube)*, Bait/Tackle **3+ mi:** Ships' Store *(15 mi.)*, Propane *(AmeriGas 295-6399, 7 mi.)*, CNG *(Parker's Boat Yard, 4 mi.)*

Boatyard Services
OnSite: Launching Ramp **3+ mi:** Travelift *(4 mi.)*, Engine mechanic *(gas, diesel)*, Electrical Repairs *(4 mi.)*, Electronic Sales *(4 mi.)*, Electronics Repairs *(4 mi.)*, Hull Repairs *(4 mi.)*, Rigger *(4 mi.)*, Sail Loft *(4 mi.)*, Canvas Work *(4 mi.)*, Bottom Cleaning *(4 mi.)*, Brightwork *(4 mi.)*, Air Conditioning *(4 mi.)*, Refrigeration *(4 mi.)*, Divers *(4 mi.)*, Compound, Wash & Wax *(4 mi.)*, Interior Cleaning *(4 mi.)*, Propeller Repairs *(4 mi.)*, Woodworking *(6 mi.)*, Inflatable Repairs *(4 mi.)*, Life Raft Service *(6 mi.)*, Painting *(4 mi.)*, Awlgrip *(4 mi.)*, Yacht Building *(4 mi.)*, Total Refits *(4 mi.)*. **Nearest Yard:** Parker's Boatyard (508) 563-9366

Restaurants and Accommodations
OnSite: Snack Bar *(B $2-3, L $3-7)* **OnCall:** Pizzeria *(Elio's 564-5954)* **Under 1 mi:** Restaurant *(Holllyberry's 759-8955, delivery)*, *(Lobster Trap 759-3992, L $5-15, D $5-15, Kids' menu, BYO)* **1-3 mi:** Restaurant *(Trowbridge Tavern 759-1776, L $5-8, D $5-12)*, *(Chartroom 563-5350, L $3-16, D $6-22)*, Motel *(Eastern Inn 759-2711, $60-120)*, *(Best Western Bridge 759-0800, $70-170)*, *(Trowbridge Inn 759-0006, $60-100)*, Inn/B&B *(Buttermilk Bay Inn 743-0800)*, *(Cape Cod Canalside B&B 759-6564)*

Recreation and Entertainment
OnSite: Beach **Near:** Video Rental **Under 1 mi:** Playground, Dive Shop, Tennis Courts, Boat Rentals *(Paddler's Shop at Rivendell Marine 759-0330)*, Bowling *(Ryan Family Amusement Co. 759-9892)*, Park **1-3 mi:** Golf Course *(Brookside Golf Club 743-4653)*, Museum *(Aptucxet Trading Post Museum 759-9487)* **3+ mi:** Jogging Paths *(4 mi.)*, Fishing Charter *(5 mi.)*, Sightseeing *(Canal Tours, 6 mi.)*

Provisioning and General Services
Near: Convenience Store *(Cumberland Farms)*, Fishmonger, Post Office **Under 1 mi:** Supermarket *(A&P 759-5957)*, Delicatessen *(Tedeschi 759-6671)*, Wine/Beer, Liquor Store *(Gray Gables)*, Pharmacy *(Bourne Pharm 759-3050)*, Copies Etc. **1-3 mi:** Bank/ATM, Catholic Church, Other, Library, Newsstand, Hardware Store, Florist **3+ mi:** Department Store *(Wal-Mart 295-8890, 4 mi.)*

Transportation
OnCall: Rental Car *(Enterprise 759-2299)*, Taxi *(Roadrunner Taxi 759-2337)* **Near:** Bikes *(Village Cycles 759-6773)* **Under 1 mi:** Local Bus **1-3 mi:** InterCity Bus *(P&B 771-6191; Bonanza 888-751-8800 to Boston, TF Green, Hyannis)* **3+ mi:** Ferry Service *(Steamship Authority - Woods Hole, 10 mi.)* **Airport:** Barnstable *(20 mi.)*

Medical Services
911 Service **OnCall:** Ambulance **Under 1 mi:** Doctor *(Buzzards Bay Health Care 759-5731)* **Hospital:** Falmouth 833-4950 *(9 mi.)*

Setting -- Set in the corner of Phinney's Harbor, 3+ miles up Phinney's Harbor Channel, which starts just south of the Cape Cod Canal, this rustic "down home" municipal facility promises a beautiful location, busy, yet quiet, harbor, and a lovely, wide, real sand beach. A perfect place for a respite before or after traversing the canal.

Marina Notes -- Maximum of 42 feet at docks and 50 feet on moorings. Very accommodating and helpful seasonal staff, and lifeguards at beach. 30 amp power. Dinghy dock. Beachside snack bar offers 4 breakfast entrées and an unexpected variety of sandwiches to take-out. Heads are standard municipal cinderblock. Gas, but not diesel, available. Pump-out boat VHF Channel 9/13.

Notable -- There is another nice beach on Hog Island Causeway, accessible only by boat. A couple of restaurants, a convenience store and recreational facilities are within a 0.8 mile walk. About 2 miles is Apucxet Trading Post Museum, a reproduction of a 1627 trading post with Native American, Pilgrim and early Phoenician relics. The site also has an herb garden, saltworks, Grover Cleveland's RR station, and a picnic area - Mon-Sat 10am-5pm, Sun 2-5pm $3.50/150. Scusset Beach State Reservation.

PHOTOS ON CD-ROM: 5

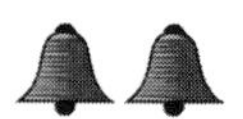

Bourne Marina

1 Academy Drive; Buzzards Bay, MA 02532

Tel: (508) 759-2512 **VHF: Monitor** 9 **Talk** 9
Fax: (508) 759-0725 **Alternate Tel:** n/a
Email: TMcKenzie@mma.mass.edu **Web:** n/a
Nearest Town: Buzzards Bay *(0.1 mi.)* **Tourist Info:** (508) 759-6000

Navigational Information

Lat: 41°44.700' **Long:** 070°37.200' **Tide:** 4 ft. **Current:** 4 kt. **Chart:** 13230
Rep. Depths (*MLW*): Entry 8 ft. **Fuel Dock** 8 ft. **Max Slip/Moor** 10 ft./-
Access: Turn NW into Channel at G25 of Cape Cod Canal

Marina Facilities *(In Season/Off Season)*

Fuel: *Citgo* - Gasoline, Diesel, High-Speed Pumps
Slips: 150 Total, 5 Transient **Max LOA:** 50 ft. **Max Beam:** 15 ft.
Rate *(per ft.)*: **Day** $2.50/$2.50 **Week** $15 **Month** $60
Power: 30 amp $0.17/ft., **50 amp** $0.17/ft., **100 amp** n/a, **200 amp** n/a
Cable TV: Yes Only 80 docks **Dockside Phone:** Yes
Dock Type: Long Fingers, Concrete, Alongside, Floating, Aluminum
Moorings: 0 Total, 0 Transient **Launch:** n/a
Rate: Day n/a **Week** n/a **Month** n/a
Heads: 11 Toilet(s), 7 Shower(s) *(with dressing rooms)*, Lockers
Laundry: None **Pay Phones:** No
Pump-Out: Full Service, 1 Central, 2 Port **Fee:** n/a **Closed Heads:** Yes

Marina Operations

Owner/Manager: Thomas McKenzie **Dockmaster:** Kristopher Davis
In-Season: Jun-Sep 1, 5 am-9 pm **Off-Season:** Sep 1-Jun 1, 6 am-6 pm
After-Hours Arrival: Call ahead
Reservations: No **Credit Cards:** Visa/MC, Dscvr, Citgo
Discounts: Frequent Fueler **Dockage:** n/a **Fuel:** Yes **Repair:** n/a
Pets: Welcome, Dog Walk Area **Handicap Access:** Yes, Heads, Docks

Marina Services and Boat Supplies

Services - Docking Assistance, Boaters' Lounge, Security *(24 hrs., Campus police)*, Dock Carts **Communication -** Mail & Package Hold, Phone Messages, FedEx, AirBorne, UPS, Express Mail *(Sat Del)* **Supplies - OnSite:** Ice *(Block, Cube)*, Ships' Store **Near:** Bait/Tackle *(Budd's 759-6600)* **Under 1 mi:** Propane

Boatyard Services

OnSite: Launching Ramp **OnCall:** Canvas Work, Bottom Cleaning, Divers **Under 1 mi:** Engine mechanic *(gas, diesel)*, Electrical Repairs, Electronic Sales, Electronics Repairs, Hull Repairs, Rigger, Brightwork, Compound, Wash & Wax, Interior Cleaning, Propeller Repairs, Woodworking, Inflatable Repairs, Life Raft Service, Upholstery, Yacht Interiors, Metal Fabrication, Painting, Awlgrip. **1-3 mi:** Air Conditioning, Refrigeration. **Nearest Yard:** Onset Bay Marina (508) 273-0357

Restaurants and Accommodations

OnCall: Restaurant *(Way Ho Szechuan & Mandarin 759-3886, 10% disc)*, Pizzeria *(Mark Anthony's 295-5956)* **Near:** Restaurant *(Beachmoor 759-7522, D $13-28, Wed-Sat 5:30on, Sun noon-8pm)*, *(Penner's Place 735-3335, B, L, D, kids' menu, 10% disc)*, Snack Bar *(Hungry Buzzard Deli 759-1188)*, Inn/B&B *(Beachmoor Inn & Rest 759-7522, $85-125)* **Under 1 mi:** Restaurant *(Mezza Luna 759-4667, L $5-12, D $13-20, 15% disc, kids' menu)*, Seafood Shack *(East Wind Lobster 759-1857)*, Snack Bar *(Leo's Breakfast 759-7557, B $5, L $7, D $7)*, Motel *(Bay Motor Inn 759-3989, $45-110)*, *(Buttermilk Bay Inn 743-0800)* **1-3 mi:** Restaurant *(Trowbridge Tavern 759-1776, L $5-8, D $5-13, no lunch Mon-Tue)*, Motel *(Best Western 759-0800, $70-170)*, Inn/B&B *(Cape Cod Canalside B&B 759-6564)*

Recreation and Entertainment

OnSite: Picnic Area, Grills **Near:** Dive Shop, Boat Rentals, Roller Blade/Bike Paths, Movie Theater, Video Rental *(Royal Video 759-4889)*, Park, Sightseeing **Under 1 mi:** Pool *(Bourne Scenic Park's tidal swimming pool)*, Beach *(Scusset Beach State Reservation)*, Playground, Tennis Courts, Bowling *(Ryan Amusements 759-9892)*, Video Arcade **1-3 mi:** Golf Course *(Brookside 743-4653)*, Fitness Center *(Old Iron 291-7479)*, Horseback Riding *(Irish Charm 743-9122)*, Museum *(Aptucxet Trading Post 759-9487)*

Provisioning and General Services

Near: Delicatessen *(Hunrgy Buzzard)*, Farmers' Market *(CofC Fri 10am-2pm)*, Catholic Church, Protestant Church, Library *(Hurley at MMA 8am-4pm)*, Beauty Salon, Bookstore *(MMA Mon-Fri 10am-3pm)*, Pharmacy *(Bourne 759-3050)*, Florist **Under 1 mi:** Liquor Store *(Liberty 759-5120)*, Fishmonger, Bank/ATM, Post Office, Dry Cleaners, Laundry, Retail Shops, Department Store *(Wal-Mart)* **1-3 mi:** Supermarket *(A&P 759-5957/Stop & Shop)*, Gourmet Shop *(Tedeschi 759-6671)*, Bakery

Transportation

OnCall: Rental Car *(Enterprise 759-2299)*, Taxi *(Road Runner 759-2337)* **Near:** Bikes *(P&M Cycles 759-2830)*, Local Bus, InterCity Bus *(P&B 771-6191; Bonanza, 888-751-8800 Wareham to Boston, TF Green, Hyannis)* **3+ mi:** Ferry Service *(Cape Cod to Martha's Vineyard and Nantucket, 20 mi.)* **Airport:** Barnstable 775-2020 *(24 mi.)*

Medical Services

911 Service **OnCall:** Ambulance **Near:** Doctor **1-3 mi:** Chiropractor **Hospital:** Tobey 295-0880 *(8 mi.)*

PHOTOS ON CD-ROM: 5

Setting -- Snugged into a well protected basin, literally filled with docks, this professional operation sits on the other side of Taylor Point from the Cape Cod Canal. It is on the southwest side of Cohasset Narrows, just before the bascule bridge. Landside it's at the entrance to the Massachusetts Maritime Academy and just off Main Street in the small Cape Cod town of Buzzards Bay.

Marina Notes -- This municipal facility provides one of the training opportunities for MMA cadets. It's operated, under supervision, by MMA students. Service is a staff priority. The floating docks are of fairly recent vintage. Very active launch ramp at the head of the basin. Fairly good heads and showers with separate dressing rooms. Built in 1983, it was designed to handle extreme tide and hurricane conditions.

Notable -- Within an easy walk are antiques and collectible shops, a video store, music shop, the Hungry Buzzard Deli and the Chamber of Commerce. Penner's Place Restaurant and Raw Bar overlooks the marina, 7 days, 7am-Mid, Fri-Sat, 'til 3am. Provisioning is a bit farther afield. A short walk across the point is the Cape Cod Canal Park which has bicycle paths on both sides. Across the canal, via the Bourne Bridge, is the Aptucxet Trading Post (759-9487), a reproduction of the original, built on that site in 1627 - includes an herb garden, saltworks, a RR station built for Grover Cleveland, and a picnic area overlooking the Canal. The Ryan Family Amusement Co. offers discounts for marina guests - ask for "summer fun" coupons. Sippican Historical Society 748-1116.

Navigational Information
Lat: 41°44.385' **Long:** 070°38.818' **Tide:** 4 ft. **Current:** n/a **Chart:** 13236
Rep. Depths (*MLW*): Entry 6 ft. **Fuel Dock** 10 ft. **Max Slip/Moor** 10 ft./9 ft.
Access: West end of Cape Cod Canal; turn NW into Channel at G21

Marina Facilities *(In Season/Off Season)*
Fuel: *Citgo* - Gasoline, Diesel
Slips: 120 Total, 8 Transient **Max LOA:** 110 ft. **Max Beam:** n/a
Rate *(per ft.)*: **Day** $2.50/$1.50* **Week** Inq. **Month** Inq.
Power: 30 amp Incl., **50 amp** Incl., **100 amp** n/a, **200 amp** n/a
Cable TV: Yes Incl. **Dockside Phone:** No
Dock Type: Wood, Long Fingers, Floating
Moorings: 34 Total, 10 Transient **Launch:** None, Dinghy Dock
Rate: Day $20 **Week** $100 **Month** n/a
Heads: 2 Toilet(s)
Laundry: 1 Washer(s), 1 Dryer(s) **Pay Phones:** Yes
Pump-Out: OnSite, Full Service, 1 Central **Fee:** Free **Closed Heads:** Yes

Marina Operations
Owner/Manager: Greg Glavin **Dockmaster:** Don Pesaturo
In-Season: May-Oct, 7am-6pm **Off-Season:** Nov-Apr, 8am-4:30pm
After-Hours Arrival: Call in advance
Reservations: Yes, Preferred **Credit Cards:** Visa/MC, Amex
Discounts: Safe/Sea **Dockage:** 25% **Fuel:** n/a **Repair:** n/a
Pets: Welcome **Handicap Access:** No

Onset Bay Marina

PO Box 780; RFD #3 Green Street; Buzzards Bay, MA 02532

Tel: (508) 295-0338 **VHF: Monitor** 9 **Talk** n/a
Fax: (508) 295-8873 **Alternate Tel:** n/a
Email: info@onsetbay.com **Web:** www.onsetbay.com
Nearest Town: Village of Onset *(1 mi.)* **Tourist Info:** (508) 295-7072

Marina Services and Boat Supplies
Services - Docking Assistance, Security, Dock Carts **Communication -** FedEx, AirBorne, UPS, Express Mail **Supplies - OnSite:** Ice *(Block, Cube, Shaved)* **Near:** Bait/Tackle *(Macos 759-9836)* **1-3 mi:** Marine Discount Store *(Stem To Stern Mobile Marine Service 563-6553)*, Propane *(Roby's 295-3737)*

Boatyard Services
OnSite: Forklift, Engine mechanic *(gas, diesel)*, Launching Ramp, Electrical Repairs, Electronic Sales, Electronics Repairs, Hull Repairs, Rigger, Bottom Cleaning, Brightwork, Air Conditioning, Compound, Wash & Wax, Interior Cleaning, Propeller Repairs, Woodworking, Inflatable Repairs, Upholstery, Yacht Interiors, Metal Fabrication, Painting, Awlgrip, Yacht Design, Yacht Broker *(Ron Cahoon)*, Yacht Building, Total Refits **OnCall:** Divers **Yard Rates:** $65/hr., Haul & Launch $10/ft., Power Wash $2/ft.

Restaurants and Accommodations
Under 1 mi: Restaurant *(Lindsey's Seafood 295-5544, L $5-10, D $8-20)*, *(Mermaid Inn)*, Seafood Shack *(Pier View 295-5968, B only 6am-noon, lounge 11am-1am DJ weekends)*, Snack Bar *(Kenny's 295-8828)*, Coffee Shop *(Dunkin Donuts)*, Pizzeria *(Mark Anthony's 295-5956)*, Inn/B&B *(Bridge View 295-0511, $85-195)*, *(Hollyhurst Cottage 291-2200, $50-150)*, *(Onset Pointe 295-8100)*, *(Mermaid Inn 295-4600)*, *(Reynold's House 291-4036, $60-150)*

Recreation and Entertainment
OnSite: Beach *(larger, much more inviting beach in village)*, Picnic Area, Grills **Near:** Jogging Paths **Under 1 mi:** Playground, Boat Rentals *(Onset Kayak 274-6612)*, Fishing Charter *(Neat Lady 295-9402, Onset Chief 759-7100 both at Town Pier)*, Video Rental *(Blockbuster 295-9151)*, Park *(Prospect Park)*, Cultural Attract *(The O-n-i-set Wigwam Historic Spritualist Summer Camp 291-0073)*, Sightseeing *(Cape Cod Canal Cruises 295-3883 depart from Town Pier)*, Special Events *(Band concerts at Prospect Park Fridays 7pm, mid July Cape Verdean Festival, early August Blues Festival)* **1-3 mi:** Golf Course *(Brookside 743-4653)*, Movie Theater *(Hoyts 759-3212)*, Museum *(Sippican Historical Society 748-1116 Plymouth Park)*

Provisioning and General Services
Under 1 mi: Convenience Store *(Friends Marketplace 428-7835)*, Supermarket *(Village Market 291-1440 will deliver, $50 min., or A&P 759-5957 3 mi.)*, Wine/Beer *(Onset General Store 291-8419)*, Liquor Store, Bakery, Farmers' Market, Fishmonger *(Shell Point Seafood)*, Pharmacy *(Bridgeview 295-1675)*, Copies Etc. *(Round Printing 759-3231)* **1-3 mi:** Lobster Pound *(East Wind 759-1857)*, Bank/ATM *(ATM at Village Market)*, Hardware Store *(Anchor Hardware 295-9190)*

Transportation
OnCall: Taxi *(Cel's 295-0947)* **Under 1 mi:** Rental Car *(Thrifty 291-3200, Enterprise 759-2299)*, Local Bus *(OWL Trolley from Onset Village to Wareham Center 295-7072 Mon-Fri 7am-8:30pm, Sat 8:30am-6:30pm $0.75)* **1-3 mi:** InterCity Bus *(P&B Bus between Wareham & Boston 746-0378)* **Airport:** Barnstable 775-2020 *(25 mi.)*

Medical Services
911 Service **OnCall:** Ambulance **3+ mi:** Doctor *(Bourne Bridge Medical 759-5731, 3 mi.)* **Hospital:** Tobey 295-0880 *(11 mi.)*

Setting -- This protected full-service facility provides a welcome, quiet respite before or after a trip through the Canal. It is a professional, well-regarded operation within walking distance of delightfully quirky and evolving Onset Village.

Marina Notes -- *Rates $2.50/ft. per day, with a $35 minimum. Heads, showers, fuel, pump-out, laundry are all onsite. Active dry stack storage operation as well. Awlgrip applications, hull extensions, repowering. Some major refits have been handled here in recent years. Emergency hauling of boats up to 70 ft. Caters to sport fishing boats. Note: The turn into the channel to Onset Bay can be tricky if the current is swift.

Notable -- Less than a mile walk is charming Victorian Onset Village. It boasts inviting beaches and parks, all with a picturesque, if a bit ragged, 19thC ambiance mixed with some contemporary honky tonk. The views from Onset Bluffs are truly spectacular. The town is benefitting from a major, decade-long restoration effort. Quite a number of 19thC gingerbread houses have been lovingly renovated into B&Bs -- some with restaurants. The "restaurant scene" seems continually in transition - call first. Right downtown, the Onset Town Pier maintains 7 slips for boats up to 35 ft. (no power) $1/ft. and 3 moorings for boats up to 40 ft. $12/nt. which includes dinghy dockage at the main pier. Call 295-8160. They welcome transients when other facilities are full; they also permit temporary tie-ups to provide another method of getting into town.

PHOTOS ON CD-ROM: 8

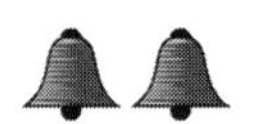

Point Independence Yacht Club

PO Box 367; 15-17 Independence Lane; Onset, MA 02558

Tel: (508) 295-3972 **VHF: Monitor** 9 **Talk** 10
Fax: n/a **Alternate Tel:** n/a
Email: n/a **Web:** n/a
Nearest Town: Onset *(1 mi.)* **Tourist Info:** (508) 295-7072

Navigational Information

Lat: 41°44.440' **Long:** 070°38.937' **Tide:** 4 ft. **Current:** n/a **Chart:** 13236
Rep. Depths (*MLW*): Entry 14 ft. **Fuel Dock** 6 ft. **Max Slip/Moor** 6 ft./7 ft.
Access: West end of Cape Cod Canal; turn NW into Channel at G21

Marina Facilities *(In Season/Off Season)*

Fuel: Gasoline, Diesel
Slips: 100 Total, 8 Transient **Max LOA:** 50 ft. **Max Beam:** n/a
Rate *(per ft.)*: **Day** $2.00/Inq. **Week** Inq. **Month** Inq.
Power: 30 amp $7, **50 amp** $14, **100 amp** n/a, **200 amp** n/a
Cable TV: Yes Included **Dockside Phone:** No
Dock Type: Wood, Short Fingers, Pilings, Floating, Fixed
Moorings: 30 Total, 30 Transient **Launch:** None, Dinghy Dock
Rate: Day $20 **Week** $100 **Month** Inq.
Heads: 6 Toilet(s), 4 Shower(s)
Laundry: 2 Washer(s), 3 Dryer(s), Book Exchange **Pay Phones:** Yes, 1
Pump-Out: OnSite, OnCall, 1 Central, 1 Port **Fee:** Free **Closed Heads:** Yes

Marina Operations

Owner/Manager: David Derosier **Dockmaster:** n/a
In-Season: May1-Oct 31 **Off-Season:** n/a
After-Hours Arrival: Make prior arrangements
Reservations: Yes, Preferred **Credit Cards:** n/a
Discounts: None **Dockage:** n/a **Fuel:** Fuel, **Repair:** n/a
Pets: Welcome, Dog Walk Area **Handicap Access:** Yes, Heads, Docks

Marina Services and Boat Supplies

Services - Docking Assistance, Dock Carts **Communication -** FedEx, AirBorne, UPS, Express Mail **Supplies - OnSite:** Ice *(Block, Cube)* **Near:** Bait/Tackle *(Macos 759-9836)* **1-3 mi:** Propane *(AmeriGas 295-6399)* **3+ mi:** West Marine *(Plymouth 830-3150, 10 mi.)*

Boatyard Services

OnSite: Launching Ramp **Nearest Yard:** Onset Bay Marina (508) 295-0338

Restaurants and Accommodations

Under 1 mi: Restaurant *(Pier View 295-5968)*, *(Ninety Nine 295-9909)*, *(Onset Harbor Inn & Boat Club 295-4600)*, Snack Bar *(Cup of the Bay 295-3527)*, *(Kenny's 295-8828)*, Fast Food, Lite Fare *(Cappulina's Sandwich Shop 295-5026)*, Pizzeria *(Francas II 759-6662)*, *(Mark Anthony's 295-5956)*, Motel *(Silver Lake 295-1266)*, Inn/B&B *(Bridge View 295-0511, $85-195)*, *(Hollyhurst Cottage 291-2200, $50-150)*, *(Onset Pointe 295-8100)*, *(Harborview Inn 295-4123)* **1-3 mi:** Restaurant *(Lindsey's Seafood 759-5544, L $5-10, D $8-20)*, *(Barnacle Bills 759-1822)*

Recreation and Entertainment

OnSite: Beach, Picnic Area, Grills **Under 1 mi:** Boat Rentals *(Onset Kayak 274-6612)*, Fishing Charter *(Neat Lady 295-9402, Onset Chief 759-7100 both at Town Pier)*, Video Rental *(Blockbuster 295-9151)*, Park *(Prospect Park)*, Cultural Attract *(The O-n-i-set Wigwam Historic Spritualist Summer Camp 291-0073)*, Sightseeing *(Cape Cod Canal Cruises 295-3883 depart from Town Pier)*, Special Events *(Band concerts at Prospect Park Fridays 7pm, mid July Cape Verdean Festival, early August Blues Festival)* **1-3 mi:** Fitness Center *(Old Iron Gym 291-7479)*, Movie Theater *(Hoyts 759-3212)*, Museum *(Sippican Historical Society 748-1116 Plymouth Park)* **3+ mi:** Tennis Courts *(Marion Indoor Tennis Club 748-2889, 7 mi.)*, Golf Course *(Brookside Golf Club 743-4653, 6 mi.)*

Provisioning and General Services

Near: Fishmonger *(Shell Point Seafood)* **Under 1 mi:** Convenience Store *(Friends Marketplace 428-7835)*, Supermarket *(Village Market 291-1440 will deliver, $50 min., or A&P 759-5957 3 mi.)*, Wine/Beer *(Onset General Store 291-8419)*, Liquor Store, Bakery, Farmers' Market, Pharmacy *(Bridgeview 295-1675)*, Copies Etc. *(Round Printing 759-3231)* **1-3 mi:** Lobster Pound *(East Wind 759-1857)*, Bank/ATM *(ATM at Village Market)*, Hardware Store *(Anchor Hardware 295-9190)* **3+ mi:** Library *(Wareham 295-2343, 5 mi.)*

Transportation

OnCall: Taxi *(Cel's 295-0947)*, Airport Limo *(A Touch of Class 295-5459)* **Under 1 mi:** Rental Car *(Thrifty 291-3200, Enterprise 759-2299)*, Local Bus *(OWL Trolley 295-7072 - Onset Village to Wareham Center Mon-Fri 7am-8:30pm, Sat 8:30am-6:30pm $0.75)* **Airport:** Barnstable 775-2020 *(25 mi.)*

Medical Services

911 Service **OnCall:** Ambulance **3+ mi:** Doctor *(Wareham Medical Center 295-1200, 4 mi.)*, Chiropractor *(Gateway Chiropractic 295-1173, 4 mi.)*
Hospital: Tobey 295-0880 *(11 mi.)*

Setting -- After entering Onset Bay, Point Independence Yacht Club is the second facility to starboard, easily identified by its large network of docks. A modest, but attractive two story clubhouse, with pyramid-shaped roof, sits at the head of a long pier - docks fan out from either side. A single-story pavilion sits between the pier and the clubhouse, and a fuel dock house is at the Bay end. On the far side of the pier is a crescent-shaped sandy beach and dinghy dock.

Marina Notes -- Founded in 1903 by Bostonians who vacationed in Onset, then a very popular resort served by both the railway and large steamers. The transient dockage and moorings are available to all visiting boaters and do not require yacht club reciprocity. Good docks and moorings - dinghy dock, but no launch service. Tile heads with separate showers and an inviting laundry room. Friday night is the weekly Seafood Fry - open to all. Additional moorings and dockage are available in town at the Onset Town Pier -- if the marinas are full -- 7 slips for boats up to 35 ft. (at $1/ft., no power) - 13 ft. depth - and 3 moorings for boats to 40 ft. ($12/night). Contact the Harbormaster 295-8160 or Ch.9/16. Best used for temporary tie-up for shopping or to take on water.

Notable -- It's less than a mile walk to the gradually gentrifying village of Onset. The neon is slowly giving way to some wonderful Victorian and turn-of-last-century building restorations. This valuable housing stock is being turned into inns, B&Bs and restaurants. "Downtown" Onset is basically one street - Onset Avenue - which runs along the hill above the Town Pier. There are a few eateries, a laundromat, pharmacy, hardware store, and farther, a supermarket. Pick up a copy of "Tour the Historic Victorian Village of Onset" to help the discovery process, or take the Onset-Wareham Trolley to historic Wareham.

PHOTOS ON CD-ROM: 5

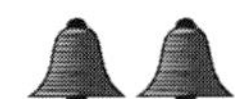

Navigational Information

Lat: 41°45.566' **Long:** 070°42.558' **Tide:** 4 ft. **Current:** 3 kt. **Chart:** 13236
Rep. Depths (*MLW*): Entry 6 ft. **Fuel Dock** 6 ft. **Max Slip/Moor** 6 ft./7 ft.
Access: Buzzards Bay to Wareham River

Marina Facilities *(In Season/Off Season)*

Fuel: *Texaco* - Gasoline, Diesel, High-Speed Pumps
Slips: 120 Total, 10 Transient **Max LOA:** 50 ft. **Max Beam:** 17 ft.
Rate *(per ft.)*: **Day** $2.00 **Week** $12 **Month** $40
Power: 30 amp Incl., **50 amp** n/a, **100 amp** n/a, **200 amp** n/a
Cable TV: No **Dockside Phone:** No
Dock Type: Wood, Long Fingers, Short Fingers, Pilings, Fixed
Moorings: 60 Total, 2 Transient **Launch:** None, Dinghy Dock
Rate: Day $10 **Week** n/a **Month** n/a
Heads: 4 Toilet(s), 2 Shower(s) *(with dressing rooms)*
Laundry: None **Pay Phones:** Yes
Pump-Out: Full Service, 1 Central, 1 Port **Fee:** Free **Closed Heads:** Yes

Marina Operations

Owner/Manager: Tony Zecco **Dockmaster:** Frank Oliver
In-Season: Year-Round, 8am-4:30pm **Off-Season:** n/a
After-Hours Arrival: Call fuel dock
Reservations: Preferred **Credit Cards:** Visa/MC, Dscvr, Din, Amex, Tex
Discounts: Commercial **Dockage:** n/a **Fuel:** n/a **Repair:** n/a
Pets: Welcome, Dog Walk Area **Handicap Access:** Yes, Heads, Docks

Warr's Marina

2 Warr Avenue; Wareham, MA 02571

Tel: (508) 295-0022 **VHF: Monitor** 9 **Talk** 9
Fax: (508) 295-5361 **Alternate Tel:** n/a
Email: n/a **Web:** www.zeccomarine.com
Nearest Town: Wareham *(0.3 mi.)* **Tourist Info:** (508) 295-7072

Marina Services and Boat Supplies

Services - Docking Assistance, Room Service to the Boat, Security *(12 Hrs.)*, Trash Pick-Up, Dock Carts **Communication -** Mail & Package Hold, Phone Messages, Fax in/out, Data Ports, FedEx, AirBorne, UPS, Express Mail *(Sat Del)* **Supplies - OnSite:** Ice *(Block, Cube)*, Ships' Store **Near:** Bait/Tackle *(M&D 291-0820)*, CNG *(Kents)* **1-3 mi:** Propane *(Kents or AmeriGas 295-6399)*

Boatyard Services

OnSite: Travelift *(35T)*, Railway, Forklift, Crane, Engine mechanic *(gas, diesel)*, Launching Ramp, Electrical Repairs, Electronics Repairs, Hull Repairs, Rigger, Sail Loft, Bottom Cleaning, Brightwork, Air Conditioning, Refrigeration, Compound, Wash & Wax, Interior Cleaning, Propeller Repairs, Woodworking, Metal Fabrication, Painting, Awlgrip, Total Refits **OnCall:** Electronic Sales, Divers, Inflatable Repairs, Life Raft Service, Upholstery, Yacht Interiors, Yacht Design, Yacht Broker *(Dick's Marine Service)* **Dealer for:** Proline Boats, OMC, Mercruiser, Volvo Penta. **Member:** ABBRA, ABYC - 4 Certified Tech(s), Other Certifications: Puffin Dinghies, Evinrude & Johnson, Mercruiser, OMC Cobra, Volvo Penta **Yard Rates:** $59/hr., Haul & Launch $8/ft. *(blocking incl.)*, Power Wash $2.50/ft.

Restaurants and Accommodations

OnCall: Pizzeria *(Papa Gino's 295-7474)* **Near:** Restaurant *(Narrows Crossing 295-9345)*, *(Somebody's Mom 291-4941)*, *(Woh Lun 295-3122)*, Snack Bar *(Merchants Way Café & Bakery 295-3624)*, Pizzeria *(Minerva 295-3909)*, Motel *(Briarwood Beach 295-2766)*, *(Starlight 295-0216)*, Inn/B&B *(Cranberry Gardens 295-9475)* **Under 1 mi:** Inn/B&B *(Rosemary Inn 295-5369)*, *(Mulberry B&B 295-0684, $55-75)*

Recreation and Entertainment

OnSite: Beach, Picnic Area, Grills, Playground, Jogging Paths, Roller Blade/Bike Paths **Under 1 mi:** Dive Shop, Horseback Riding, Park, Museum *(Capt. Kendrick's House, 1690 Fearing Tavern, Tremont Nail Co. 295-0038)* **1-3 mi:** Heated Pool, Golf Course *(Bay Pointe Country Club 759-8802)*, Boat Rentals, Group Fishing Boat, Other *(Water Wizz Water Park 295-3255)*, Cultural Attract, Sightseeing *(Cranberry bogs)*, Special Events **3+ mi:** Video Rental *(Blockbuster 295-9151, 4 mi.)*

Provisioning and General Services

OnSite: Newsstand, Copies Etc. **Near:** Convenience Store *(Cumberland)*, Wine/Beer, Liquor Store *(Jug Shop 295-7449)*, Bakery, Farmers' Market, Bank/ATM, Post Office, Catholic Church, Protestant Church, Synagogue, Beauty Salon, Dry Cleaners, Bookstore *(Castle Books 291-4377)*, Pharmacy *(Brooks/CVS 295-5772)*, Florist, Retail Shops **Under 1 mi:** Supermarket *(First National 295-4887 or IGA)*, Delicatessen *(Deli Two 295-9853)*, Fishmonger *(Main St. Seafood 291-2220 - also prepared take-out)*, Lobster Pound, Library *(295-2343)*, Laundry *(295-9833)*, Hardware Store *(Aubuchon 295-2123)* **1-3 mi:** Meat Market, Buying Club

Transportation

OnCall: Rental Car *(Enterprise 295-1414)*, Taxi *(Del's 295-0974)* **Near:** Local Bus, InterCity Bus *(Bonanza 295-3665 at Deca's Variety)*, Rail **3+ mi:** Ferry Service *(10 mi.)* **Airport:** Barnstable 775-2020 *(30 mi.)*

Medical Services

911 Service **OnCall:** Ambulance **Near:** Dentist **Under 1 mi:** Doctor, Chiropractor, Holistic Services **Hospital:** Tobey 295-0880 *(1 mi.)*

Setting -- This expansive 15 acre facility is located on the Wareham River, about 5 miles from the Cape Cod Canal Channel. The marina's extensive dockage is on the west side. Its attractive gray buildings, with brick red trim, are easy to spot. The docks are strung out opposite the parking lot, separated by a large swath of grass. The small city of Wareham, one of the cranberry capitals of the world, is a short walk up river.

Marina Notes -- Established in 1939, this family owned and run facility is part of Zecco Marine Company. An inland part of the operation is at Dick's Marine Service, which provides many of the boatyard services (759-3753). Warr's offers complete boatyard services and has 4 ABYC certified technicians on staff. First Federal no discharge harbor. Complimentary pump-out onsite. Additional dockage and moorings at Wareham Town Pier 295-8160, Ch.9

Notable -- Wareham provides most of the services, provisioning resources, restaurants, and lodgings that cruisers might require. The town begins at the railroad bridge, about a half mile north. It's an easy, pleasant walk through town and Main Street has many 18th & 19thC houses to keep it interesting. At the bridge end of town is the Kendrick Maritime Museum (tours Jul & Aug), and at the north end are 18thC Fearing Tavern and the Tremont Nail Company (call the Historical Society 295-6839). There is nearby bus and rental car service, coupled with a protected harbor and good security -- this might be a good place to "leave the boat". Wareham Gatemen, semi-pro baseball (295-3956), and Minot Forest Nature Walk (295-7070) are within 3 miles. Wareham is home ot Cape Cod Shipbuilding - small sailboats.

PHOTOS ON CD-ROM: 7

Barden's Boat Yard

Barden's Boat Yard

PO Box 577; 2 Island Wharf; Marion, MA 02738

Tel: (508) 748-0250 **VHF: Monitor** 68 **Talk** n/a
Fax: (508) 748-2478 **Alternate Tel:** n/a
Email: n/a **Web:** n/a
Nearest Town: Marion *(0 mi.)* **Tourist Info:** (508) 259-7072

Navigational Information

Lat: 41°42.286' **Long:** 070°45.668' **Tide:** 4 ft. **Current:** n/a **Chart:** 13236
Rep. Depths (*MLW*): Entry 14 ft. **Fuel Dock** n/a **Max Slip/Moor** -/13 ft.
Access: Sippican Harbor, past Ram Island, second facility to port

Marina Facilities *(In Season/Off Season)*

Fuel: No
Slips: 0 Total, 0 Transient **Max LOA:** 60 ft. **Max Beam:** 16 ft.
Rate *(per ft.)*: **Day** n/a **Week** n/a **Month** n/a
Power: 30 amp n/a, **50 amp** n/a, **100 amp** n/a, **200 amp** n/a
Cable TV: No **Dockside Phone:** No
Dock Type: n/a
Moorings: 90 Total, 10 Transient **Launch:** Yes (Free)
Rate: Day $30 **Week** $125 **Month** n/a
Heads: 2 Toilet(s), 2 Shower(s)
Laundry: None **Pay Phones:** No
Pump-Out: OnCall, Full Service, 1 Port **Fee:** Free **Closed Heads:** Yes

Marina Operations

Owner/Manager: Fred Coulson **Dockmaster:** n/a
In-Season: MemDay-LabDay, 8am-6pm* **Off-Season:** n/a
After-Hours Arrival: Call ahead for instructions
Reservations: No **Credit Cards:** Visa/MC, Dscvr
Discounts: None
Pets: Welcome **Handicap Access:** No

Marina Services and Boat Supplies

Services - Dock Carts **Communication -** FedEx, UPS, Express Mail **Supplies - OnSite:** Ice *(Block, Cube)* **OnCall:** Ships' Store **Near:** Propane *(Hiller Fuels 748-0020)* **1-3 mi:** CNG *(Wareham)* **3+ mi:** West Marine *(994-1122, 12 mi.)*, Boat/US *(992-8484, 10 mi.)*, Bait/Tackle *(M&D 291-0820, 5 mi.)*

Boatyard Services

OnSite: Travelift *(35T)*, Forklift, Crane, Engine mechanic *(gas, diesel)*, Electronic Sales, Hull Repairs, Rigger, Bottom Cleaning, Brightwork, Compound, Wash & Wax, Woodworking, Painting **OnCall:** Electrical Repairs, Electronics Repairs, Sail Loft, Air Conditioning, Refrigeration, Divers, Interior Cleaning, Propeller Repairs, Inflatable Repairs, Life Raft Service, Upholstery, Yacht Interiors, Metal Fabrication, Total Refits **Near:** Launching Ramp *(Town ramp)*. **Dealer for:** Yanmar, Johnson Outboards. **Yard Rates:** $65/hr., Haul & Launch $12/ft., Power Wash $3/ft., Bottom Paint $12/ft. *(paint included)* **Storage:** On-Land Outside $18/ft.

Restaurants and Accommodations

Near: Snack Bar *(Sugar Shack 748-9992)* **Under 1 mi:** Restaurant *(Moonfish 748-9956)*, *(Wave 748-2986, B $5, L $7-15, D $11-20, seafood & pizza)*, Coffee Shop *(Uncle Jon's 748-0063)*, Pizzeria *(Santoro's 748-9599)* **1-3 mi:** Restaurant *(Frigate Steak House 748-0970)*, *(Gildas Stone Rooster 748-9700)*, Inn/B&B *(Hideaway Haven Guests 748-3666)*, *(Pineywood Farm B&B 748-3925)*

Recreation and Entertainment

Near: Playground, Tennis Courts *(Elementary school)*, Jogging Paths, Park, Museum *(Sippican Historical Society & Marion Natural History Museum 748-2098, Whaling Museum, New Bedford)*, Cultural Attract *(Marion Art Center, the Music Hall)*, Sightseeing *(Village of Marion and Tabor Academy)*, Special Events *(July 4, Marion to Bermuda Race)* **Under 1 mi:** Beach, Golf Course *(Marion Golf Club 748-0199)* **1-3 mi:** Movie Theater **3+ mi:** Bowling *(Bowlmor Lanes 758-6783, 5 mi.)*

Provisioning and General Services

Near: Convenience Store *(Marion General Store)*, Delicatessen, Wine/Beer *(Spirits 748-0004)*, Liquor Store *(Marion Country Package 748-2319)*, Fishmonger *(Seahorse 748-3870)*, Post Office, Catholic Church, Bookstore *(Bookstall 748-1041)* **Under 1 mi:** Supermarket *(Christy's of Cape Cod 748-2382 or IGA 295-4887 4 mi.)*, Gourmet Shop, Bakery, Bank/ATM, Library *(748-1252)*, Barber Shop, Dry Cleaners, Laundry, Newsstand, Hardware Store *(Sippican Hardware)*, Florist, Clothing Store **1-3 mi:** Lobster Pound, Meat Market, Beauty Salon, Retail Shops **3+ mi:** Pharmacy *(CVS 291-6289, 4 mi.)*

Transportation

OnCall: Rental Car *(Enterprise 295-1414)*, Taxi *(Elite Transportation 990-0017, New Bedford, Wareham 295-0947)* **1-3 mi:** Local Bus *(Greyhound, Wareham)* **Airport:** New Bedford 991-6161/Plymouth 746-2020/Falmouth 548-9617 *(12-20 mi.)*

Medical Services

911 Service **OnCall:** Ambulance **Under 1 mi:** Doctor *(Khoury 748-3000)*, Holistic Services *(Stillwaters 508-748-0228)* **1-3 mi:** Chiropractor *(Crabbe 748-6632)* **Hospital:** Tobey 295-0880 *(5 mi.)*

Setting -- A three-sided basin, Sippican Harbor is one of the best all-around harbors on Buzzards Bay. Its shores are lined with beautiful homes interspersed with a couple of interesting islands and some beautiful marsh areas. Barden's manages 90 of the 750 moorings that dot this primarily sailboat haven. Its attractive, welcoming, and nicely landscaped shoreside boatyard facility lies between the Beverly Yacht Club and the Municipal Wharf.

Marina Notes -- *Office open year 'round. Yard hours 7:30am-4pm Mon-Fri. Family business since 1927. This is a boatyard with a mooring field, there are no transient slips. Very nice, seasonal launch is included in the mooring fee - MemDay-LabDay 8am-6pm Mon-Thu, 8am-9:30pm weekends. It lands at a dedicated pier at Barden's park-like waterfront. 35 ton travelift, along with a forklift and crane, support this active and long-respected boatyard. Closed heads. For pump-out (and water), go to the town dock or hail the Harbormaster on Ch.9/748-3535. Heads and showers are part of the public town facility. Town pier also has restaurants, showers, dumpsters. Homeport for Tabor Boy, Tabor Academy's black hulled 2-masted training ship.

Notable -- Marion, a quintessential New England village, is worth a detour. Just strolling the attractive lanes is a delightful way to spend an afternoon. Most services are within a couple of blocks. There are a number of historic architectural gems (the Marion Art Center has a brief, suggested walking tour) and some lovely homes. Monday night concerts at the town pier. Nearby New Bedford has much to offer, including the Whaling Museum (997-0046) which offers special events and lectures in season, and the Museum of Madeiran Heritage (994-2573) open Sun 10am- 4pm.

PHOTOS ON CD-ROM: 5

Navigational Information
Lat: 41°42.790' **Long:** 070°45.926' **Tide:** 4 ft. **Current:** n/a **Chart:** 13236
Rep. Depths (*MLW*): Entry 6 ft. **Fuel Dock** 6 ft. **Max Slip/Moor** 6 ft./8 ft.
Access: Buzzards Bay to the head of Sippican Harbor

Marina Facilities *(In Season/Off Season)*
Fuel: *Texaco* - Gasoline, Diesel
Slips: 30 Total, 2 Transient **Max LOA:** 70 ft. **Max Beam:** 18 ft.
Rate *(per ft.)*: **Day** $1.50/Inq. **Week** 7.50 **Month** Inq.
Power: 30 amp n/a, **50 amp** Incl., **100 amp** Incl., **200 amp** n/a
Cable TV: No **Dockside Phone:** No
Dock Type: Concrete, Floating
Moorings: 100 Total, 10 Transient **Launch:** Yes (Free), Dinghy Dock
Rate: Day $30 **Week** $150 **Month** n/a
Heads: 2 Toilet(s), 2 Shower(s)
Laundry: None **Pay Phones:** Yes, 1
Pump-Out: OnCall, Full Service **Fee:** Free **Closed Heads:** Yes

Marina Operations
Owner/Manager: Dennis Joaquin **Dockmaster:** Carl Arruda
In-Season: Year-Round, 8am-4:30pm **Off-Season:** n/a
After-Hours Arrival: Fri, Sat, Sun open 'til 8pm
Reservations: No **Credit Cards:** Visa/MC, Amex
Discounts: None
Pets: Welcome **Handicap Access:** No

Burr Bros. Boats, Inc.

309 Front Street; Marion, MA 02738

Tel: (508) 748-0541 **VHF: Monitor** 68 **Talk** n/a
Fax: (508) 748-0963 **Alternate Tel:** n/a
Email: burrbros@burrbros.com **Web:** www.burrbros.com
Nearest Town: Marion *(0 mi.)* **Tourist Info:** (508) 296-7072

Marina Services and Boat Supplies
Services - Docking Assistance, Security, Trash Pick-Up, Dock Carts **Communication -** Mail & Package Hold, Phone Messages, Fax in/out, FedEx, UPS, Express Mail *(Sat Del)* **Supplies - OnSite:** Ice *(Block, Cube)*, Ships' Store, Propane, CNG **3+ mi:** Boat/US *(992-8484, 10 mi.)*, Bait/Tackle *(M&D 291-0820, 6 mi.)*

Boatyard Services
OnSite: Travelift *(55T)*, Forklift, Crane, Engine mechanic *(gas, diesel)*, Launching Ramp, Electrical Repairs, Electronic Sales, Electronics Repairs, Hull Repairs, Rigger, Bottom Cleaning, Brightwork, Air Conditioning, Refrigeration, Divers, Compound, Wash & Wax, Interior Cleaning, Propeller Repairs, Woodworking, Inflatable Repairs, Metal Fabrication, Painting, Awlgrip, Yacht Design, Yacht Building, Total Refits **OnCall:** Sail Loft, Life Raft Service, Upholstery, Yacht Interiors, Yacht Broker **Dealer for:** Yanmar, Mercury, Yamaha, OMC, Lazer, Sunfish. **Member:** ABBRA, ABYC, Other Certifications: Honda, Vacuflush **Yard Rates:** $68/hr., Haul & Launch Time & Equipment

Restaurants and Accommodations
Near: Restaurant *(Wave Restaurant 748-2986, B $5, L $7-15, D $11-20, pizza, too)*, *(Santoro's Pizza & More 748-9599)*, *(Sippican Café 748-0176)*, Snack Bar *(Uncle Jon's Coffee 748-0063, B $2)* **Under 1 mi:** Restaurant *(Andrew's 748-9956, L $8, D $15)*, *(Moonfish 748-9956, Tue-Sat, L 11:30am-2:30pm, D 5-9pm, Sun D only)*, Lite Fare *(Continental Deli House 748-2658)* **1-3 mi:** Restaurant *(Frigate Steak House 748-0970)*, *(Gildas Stone Rooster 748-9700)*, Inn/B&B *(Pineywood Farm B&B 748-3925)*, *(Village Landing 748-0350)*, *(Hideaway Haven 748-3336)*

Recreation and Entertainment
Near: Picnic Area, Cultural Attract *(Marion Art Center Main & Pleasant Sts.)*, Sightseeing *(the streets of Marion)* **Under 1 mi:** Golf Course *(Marion Golf Club 748-0199)*, Museum *(Marion Natural History Museum 748-2098)* **1-3 mi:** Beach, Playground, Tennis Courts, Fitness Center, Jogging Paths, Roller Blade/Bike Paths **3+ mi:** Bowling *(Bowlmor Lanes 758-6783, 5 mi.)*

Provisioning and General Services
Near: Supermarket *(Christy's Of Cape Cod 748-2382)*, Delicatessen, Bakery *(Village Bakery 748-0434)*, Farmers' Market, Green Grocer, Fishmonger *(Seahorse Seafoods 748-3870)*, Lobster Pound, Meat Market, Bank/ATM, Post Office, Barber Shop, Dry Cleaners, Laundry, Newsstand, Hardware Store *(Sippican Hardware 748-6700)*, Florist, Retail Shops **Under 1 mi:** Convenience Store *(Cumberland 748-3699)*, Wine/Beer *(Spirits 748-0004)*, Liquor Store *(Marion Country Package 748-2319)*, Catholic Church, Protestant Church, Library *(Marion 748-1252)*, Beauty Salon, Bookstore *(Bookstall 748-1041)* **3+ mi:** Pharmacy *(CVS 291-6289, 4 mi.)*

Transportation
OnCall: Rental Car *(Enterprise 295-1414)*, Taxi *(Rochester Trans 763-8716)* **3+ mi:** InterCity Bus *(New Bedford to Boston to Fall River, 15 mi.)*, Ferry Service *(MV, 15 mi.)* **Airport:** New Bedford 991-6161 *(15 mi.)*

Medical Services
911 Service **OnCall:** Ambulance **Near:** Doctor **Under 1 mi:** Dentist *(Marion Dental 748-0744)*, Chiropractor *(Marion Chiro 748-6632)*, Veterinarian *(Marion Animal Hosp 748-1203)* **Hospital:** Wareham Medical 295-1200 *(4 mi.)*

Setting -- Tucked way up at the head of beautiful Sippican Harbor, this unassuming facility is actually a full-service marina and sophisticated boatyard --a fact testified to by the many immaculately tended vessels at its docks and in its mooring field. Its large, gray shed with brick red doors is hard to miss. It has the added advantages of being in one of the loveliest villages in the area. Note: the mooring field is closer to town than the boatyard.

Marina Notes -- Schedule: MidMay - MidJun Mon-Thu 8am-6pm, Fri-Sun 8am-8pm; MemDay-LabDay Mon-Thu & Sat 8am-8pm, Fri & Sun 8am-9pm. Holidays = Fri Schedule. MemDay-ColDay Mon-Thu 8am-4:30pm, Fri-Sun 8am-6pm. There is "club-quality" launch service to the mooring field. Established in 1946, this family run, service-oriented facility has been providing distinctive and high-end boatyard services to a wide variety of vessels. The boatyard has again been significantly upgraded with three large new buildings (2 on a new inland site), a 55 ton travelift, a dedicated awlgrip facility, and inside storage. Updated pedestals. Heads on second floor of building near street; separate shower rooms. Pump-out and water available at the town dock, or hail the Harbormaster on Ch.9, 748-3535. Beverly Yacht Club offers moorings to members of reciprocal clubs Ch.68 8am-9pm.

Notable -- Take a walking tour of this charming, picturesque village; see Town Hall, the Library/Museum, General Store, Marion Art Center, the Music Hall, lovely homes, and well-known Tabor Academy. The Marion Art Center offers amateur theatrical events, 2 art galleries and children's classes. Tue-Fri 1-5pm, Sat 10am-2pm. Great July 4th parade & fireworks. The Marion to Bermuda Race is hosted by nearby Beverly Yacht Club.

PHOTOS ON CD-ROM: 9

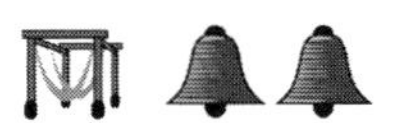

Mattapoisett Boatyard

PO Box 1030; 32 Ned's Point Road; Mattapoisett, MA 02739

Tel: (508) 758-3812 **VHF: Monitor** 68 **Talk** 68
Fax: (508) 758-2527 **Alternate Tel:** n/a
Email: info@mattapoisettboatyard.com **Web:** mattapoisettboatyard.com
Nearest Town: Mattapoisett *(1 mi.)* **Tourist Info:** (508) 999-5231

Navigational Information

Lat: 41°39.150' **Long:** 070°47.900' **Tide:** 3 ft. **Current:** n/a **Chart:** 13230
Rep. Depths (*MLW*): Entry 12 ft. **Fuel Dock** 6 ft. **Max Slip/Moor** 12 ft./19 ft.
Access: Buzzard's Bay, past Ned's Point Light, first facility to starboard

Marina Facilities *(In Season/Off Season)*

Fuel: *Texaco* - Gasoline, Diesel
Slips: 6 Total, 2 Transient **Max LOA:** 50 ft. **Max Beam:** n/a
Rate *(per ft.)*: **Day** $1.00/Inq. **Week** Inq. **Month** Inq.
Power: 30 amp Incl., **50 amp** n/a, **100 amp** n/a, **200 amp** n/a
Cable TV: No **Dockside Phone:** No
Dock Type: Fixed
Moorings: 200 Total, 15 Transient **Launch:** Yes (Free)
Rate: Day $20 **Week** $125 **Month** $400
Heads: 2 Toilet(s), 1 Shower(s)
Laundry: None **Pay Phones:** Yes, 2
Pump-Out: OnSite, Full Service, 1 Central **Fee:** Free **Closed Heads:** No

Marina Operations

Owner/Manager: Arthur W. McLean **Dockmaster:** Same
In-Season: Year-Round, 8am-8pm **Off-Season:** n/a, 8am-5pm
After-Hours Arrival: Call ahead
Reservations: Yes **Credit Cards:** Visa/MC, Dscvr, Din, Amex, Tex
Discounts: None
Pets: Welcome **Handicap Access:** No

Marina Services and Boat Supplies

Services - Docking Assistance, Trash Pick-Up, Dock Carts **Communication -** Mail & Package Hold, Phone Messages, Fax in/out, FedEx, AirBorne, UPS, Express Mail *(Sat Del)* **Supplies - OnSite:** Ice *(Block, Cube)*, Ships' Store **1-3 mi:** Propane *(Sea Gas 758-4338)* **3+ mi:** West Marine *(994-1122, 9 mi.)*, Boat/US *(992-8484, 6 mi.)*

Boatyard Services

OnSite: Travelift *(35T)*, Electrical Repairs, Electronics Repairs, Hull Repairs, Rigger, Bottom Cleaning, Brightwork, Refrigeration

Restaurants and Accommodations

Near: Snack Bar *(Oxford Creamery 758-3847)* **Under 1 mi:** Restaurant *(Tokyo 758-3400)*, *(Nest Diner 758-3600)*, *(Mattapoisett Inn 758-4922, L $6-10, D $6-25, across from town dock, 7 days, 11am-10pm, Sun Brunch)*, Seafood Shack *(Turks Seafood 758-3117)*, Motel *(Hillside Motel 758-2989)*, Inn/B&B *(23 Water Street B&B 758-9733)*, *(Mattapoisett Inn 758-4922, $90-110, 3 rooms)* **1-3 mi:** Restaurant *(Mattapoisett Chowder House 758-2333)*, Pizzeria *(Nick's 758-2277)*

Recreation and Entertainment

Near: Beach *(Ned's Point)*, Park *(Ned's Point)* **Under 1 mi:** Picnic Area, Tennis Courts *(Hammond St. Public courts)*, Museum *(Mattapoisett Historical Society 758-2844)*, Cultural Attract *(Shipyard Park - band concerts Wed nights, square dancing Sat nights)*, Sightseeing *(Walk the streets of historic Mattapoisett)*, Special Events *(Harbor Days, July 4th Road Race)* **1-3 mi:** Bowling *(Bowlmor Lanes 758-6783)* **3+ mi:** Golf Course *(Marion Golf Club 748-0199, 5 mi.)*, Horseback Riding *(Ashland Stables 758-6672, 4 mi.)*

Provisioning and General Services

Under 1 mi: Wine/Beer *(Freddie's 758-3821)*, Fishmonger *(Turks 758-3113)*, Library *(Mattapoisett PL 758-4171)*, Pharmacy *(Seaport Pharmacy 758-6904)* **1-3 mi:** Convenience Store, Gourmet Shop *(Cerullis Gourmet 758-6111)*, Delicatessen, Liquor Store *(Village Package 758-4334)*, Bakery, Meat Market, Bank/ATM, Post Office, Catholic Church, Beauty Salon, Dry Cleaners, Laundry, Hardware Store *(Mahoney True Value 758-6800)*, Clothing Store, Retail Shops **3+ mi:** Supermarket *(Fairhaven Stop & Shop 990-4500, 4 mi.)*

Transportation

OnCall: Rental Car *(Enterprise 994-8289)*, Taxi *(Elite Transportation 990-0017)*, Local Bus *(SRTA 999-5211)* **3+ mi:** Rail *(Middleboro, 23 mi.)*
Airport: TF Green *(45 mi.)*

Medical Services

911 Service **OnCall:** Ambulance **Under 1 mi:** Doctor *(Pellegrino 758-9700)*, Dentist *(Tavares 758-2571)*, Veterinarian *(Mattapoisett Animal Hospital 758-6400)* **1-3 mi:** Chiropractor *(Wagner 758-6124)* **Hospital:** Tobey 295-0800 *(9 mi.)*

Setting -- Just inside wide-open, unspoiled Mattapoisett Harbor, on the starboard side, are the docks and work sheds of Mattapoisett Boatyard. Located about a mile from Mattapoisett, a picturesque New England town with deep roots as a center of the whaling ship industry. Old, restored houses from that era line the streets and make a perfect destination for strolling.

Marina Notes -- Founded in 1962 by the present operating family. Well-stocked parts department. Launch serves both the boatyard's own dock and Long Wharf town dock, and operates during daylight hours. There are approximately 800 moorings spread throughout the harbor and the outlying beach areas; 200 of these belong to the Mattapoisett Boatyard. In addition to the launch, there are also dinghy docks at the Boatyard, Long Wharf, and the town beach.

Notable -- A short walk up the road is Veterans Park at Ned's Point, a wide open grassy park with spectacular views of Buzzard's Bay; it's a popular windsurfing destination and the home of the 160 year old landmark Ned's Point Light. Shopping is out on the main road, a walkable distance from Long Wharf. Don't be surprised if a resident, or even a patrol car, offers you a ride when laden with packages. Mattapoisett Historical Society Museum (758-2844) includes early carriages and other 19th century artifacts. At Shipyard Park near Long Wharf are: Band concerts on Wednesday nights, Square Dances on Saturday nights, Teen Dances Thursday nights. Harbor Days are the 3rd weekend in July. The Mattapoisett Yacht Club makes its home here.

PHOTOS ON CD-ROM: 9

Navigational Information
Lat: 41°39.330' **Long:** 070°48.859' **Tide:** 4 ft. **Current:** n/a **Chart:** 13230
Rep. Depths (*MLW*): Entry 17 ft. **Fuel Dock** 6 ft. **Max Slip/Moor** -/15 ft.
Access: Buzzards Bay, past Ned's Point Light, to the head of the harbor

Marina Facilities *(In Season/Off Season)*
Fuel: Slip-Side Fueling, Gasoline, Diesel, On Call Delivery
Slips: 2 Total, 0 Transient **Max LOA:** n/a **Max Beam:** n/a
Rate *(per ft.)*: **Day** n/a **Week** n/a **Month** n/a
Power: 30 amp n/a, **50 amp** n/a, **100 amp** n/a, **200 amp** n/a
Cable TV: No **Dockside Phone:** No
Dock Type: Floating, Fixed
Moorings: 16 Total, 14 Transient **Launch:** None, Dinghy Dock
Rate: Day $0 **Week** Inq. **Month** n/a
Heads: 2 Toilet(s)
Laundry: None **Pay Phones:** Yes, 1
Pump-Out: Self Service, 1 Central **Fee:** Free **Closed Heads:** Yes

Marina Operations
Owner/Manager: Jay Parker **Dockmaster:** n/a
In-Season: Year-Round, 8am-4pm **Off-Season:** n/a
After-Hours Arrival: Find an empty mooring and take it
Reservations: No **Credit Cards:** Cash or check
Discounts: None
Pets: Welcome **Handicap Access:** Yes, Docks

Brownell Boatyard

PO Box 0744; 1 Park Street; Mattapoisett, MA 02739

Tel: (508) 758-3671; (800) 533-8433 **VHF: Monitor** 16 **Talk** 68
Fax: (508) 758-3574 **Alternate Tel:** n/a
Email: Sales@BrownellBoatYard.com **Web:** www.boatstands.com
Nearest Town: Mattapoisett *(0.1 mi.)* **Tourist Info:** (508) 999-5231

Marina Services and Boat Supplies
Supplies - Under 1 mi: Ice *(Block, Cube)*, Ships' Store, Propane *(Sea Gas 758-4338)* **3+ mi:** West Marine *(994-1122, 7 mi.)*, Boat/US *(992-8484, 5 mi.)*

Boatyard Services
OnSite: Travelift *(60T)*, Engine mechanic *(gas, diesel)*, Launching Ramp, Electrical Repairs, Bottom Cleaning, Divers, Compound, Wash & Wax, Interior Cleaning **Under 1 mi:** Hull Repairs, Rigger, Sail Loft, Brightwork, Woodworking, Painting, Awlgrip, Yacht Building, Total Refits. **3+ mi:** Electronic Sales *(6 mi.)*, Propeller Repairs *(5 mi.)*, Inflatable Repairs *(5 mi.)*, Life Raft Service *(5 mi.)*, Upholstery *(6 mi.)*, Metal Fabrication *(5 mi.)*. **Yard Rates:** $60/hr., Haul & Launch $6/ft., Power Wash $2.50/ft.

Restaurants and Accommodations
Near: Restaurant *(Mattapoisett Inn 758-4922, L $6-10, D $6-25, 7 days until 10pm, inside and outside. Sun brunch, entertainment, and open bar until 1am)*, Inn/B&B *(23 Water St. B&B 758-9733)*, *(Mattapoisett Inn 758-4922, $90-110, across from town dock, has three guest rooms)* **Under 1 mi:** Restaurant *(Parma 758-4000)*, Snack Bar *(Seaport)* **1-3 mi:** Restaurant *(Mike's 996-9810)*, *(Leeward 758-9939)*, Seafood Shack *(Mattapoisett Chowder House 758-2333)*, Pizzeria *(Nick's 758-2277)*, Motel *(Hillside Motel 758-3396)*

Recreation and Entertainment
OnSite: Picnic Area, Park, Cultural Attract *(Wed Shipyard Park Band Concerts)* **Near:** Beach *(Town Beach)*, Playground, Tennis Courts *(Hammond St. Courts)*, Jogging Paths, Sightseeing *(Stroll the streets of Mattapoisett)*, Special Events *(Harbor Days, July 4th Road Race)* **Under 1 mi:** Bowling *(Bowlmor Lanes 758-6783)*, Museum *(Mattapoisett Museum & Carriage House 758-2844)* **3+ mi:** Golf Course *(Rochester Golf Club 763-5155, 6 mi.)*, Group Fishing Boat *(5 mi.)*, Video Rental *(Lancaster Video 997-4499, 5 mi.)*

Provisioning and General Services
Near: Barber Shop, Pharmacy *(Seaport Pharmacy 758-6904)* **Under 1 mi:** Convenience Store, Gourmet Shop *(Cerullis Gourmet 758-6111)*, Delicatessen, Health Food, Liquor Store *(Village Package 758-4334)*, Fishmonger *(Turks 758-3113)*, Bank/ATM, Post Office, Catholic Church, Protestant Church, Beauty Salon, Dry Cleaners, Laundry *(Pearl Street)*, Florist **1-3 mi:** Wine/Beer *(Freddie's 758-3821)*, Bakery, Hardware Store *(Mahoney True Value 758-6800)*, Retail Shops *(The Rope Walk)* **3+ mi:** Supermarket *(Stop & Shop 990-4500, Shaw's, 5 mi.)*, Farmers' Market *(5 mi.)*, Library *(Marion 748-1252, 6 mi.)*, Department Store *(Wal-Mart, 5 mi.)*

Transportation
OnCall: Taxi *(Elite Transportation 990-0017)* **Near:** Local Bus *(SRTA 999-5211)* **3+ mi:** Bikes *(Village Peddler 997-2453, 5 mi.)*, Rental Car *(Alamo 991-4220, Enterprise 994-8289, 5 mi.)*, Rail *(Middleboro, 23 mi.)* **Airport:** New Bedford *(8 mi.)*

Medical Services
911 Service **Under 1 mi:** Doctor *(Hopewell Associates 758-3200)* **1-3 mi:** Dentist, Chiropractor *(Mattapoisett Chiropractic 758-3666)*, Holistic Services, Ambulance **Hospital:** St. Lukes 979-5100 *(9 mi.)*

Setting -- Almost to the Harbor's head, Brownell's waterfront access is actually Long Wharf, the Mattapoisett Municipal Dock, which is quite convenient to the quiet, well-appointed town. There Brownell dispenses fuel, and the town provides a dinghy dock for Brownell's complimentary moorings. The boatyard facility is not on the water, but about a half mile inland.

Marina Notes -- 14 moorings are available for transient use. They are free of charge, and are available on a first-come, first-served basis. The moorings are located in the middle of Mattapoisett Harbor, set in two rows in a Northeast to Southwest direction. Identify them by their cone shaped buoys with blue and yellow stripes (each is equipped with a one-inch nylon pennant and a pick-up buoy). Brownell's delivers gasoline and diesel to the Mattapoisett Town Wharf Mon-Fri, 8am-4pm. Please call 758-3671 in advance to ensure a timely delivery. The town maintains heads on the wharf, as well as pump-out. Brownell is located on 36 tree-lined "high and dry" acres, 1.5 mi. from the harbor. It hauls boats to the yard there for work and winter storage. Beware of SE storms.

Notable -- Across the street from the Municipal Long Wharf is charming 1799 Mattapoisett Inn, the oldest seaside inn in the country. Onsite is Shipyard Park, home to Wednesday night band concerts and Saturday night square dances; a short walk is the town beach. Long Wharf piers are the original granite ones built to accommodate the whaling and tall ships. The mizzen mast of the "Wanderer", the last whaling ship built in Mattapoisett in 1878, is the flag pole in Shipyard Park at the Town Wharf. Route 6, the main drag, is about 5 blocks from the water, but most restaurants and services tend to be about a 1-1.5 mile walk.

PHOTOS ON CD-ROM: 4

Fairhaven Shipyard & Marina

50 Fort Street; Fairhaven, MA 02719

Tel: (508) 996-8591 **VHF: Monitor** 9 **Talk** 10
Fax: (508) 992-1326 **Alternate Tel:** n/a
Email: fhvnship@aol.com **Web:** www.fairhavenship.com
Nearest Town: New Bedford *(3 mi.)* **Tourist Info:** (508) 970-4085

Navigational Information

Lat: 41°37.782' **Long:** 070°54.229' **Tide:** 4 ft. **Current:** n/a **Chart:** 13230
Rep. Depths (*MLW*): Entry 23 ft. **Fuel Dock** 17 ft. **Max Slip/Moor** 15 ft./-
Access: Buzzards Bay to Acushnet River, through huricane barrier

Marina Facilities *(In Season/Off Season)*

Fuel: *Valvtect* - Gasoline, Diesel, High-Speed Pumps
Slips: 165 Total, 20 Transient **Max LOA:** 150 ft. **Max Beam:** n/a
Rate *(per ft.)*: **Day** $1.50/$0.50 **Week** $8.75 **Month** $18/150
Power: 30 amp $5/cord, **50 amp** $10/cord, **100 amp** $20/cord, **200 amp** n/a
Cable TV: No **Dockside Phone:** No
Dock Type: Wood, Long Fingers, Concrete, Alongside, Floating, Fixed
Moorings: 0 Total, 0 Transient **Launch:** n/a, Dinghy Dock
Rate: Day n/a **Week** n/a **Month** n/a
Heads: 4 Toilet(s), 4 Shower(s)
Laundry: 1 Washer(s), 1 Dryer(s), Book Exchange **Pay Phones:** Yes, 2
Pump-Out: OnCall, Full Service, 1 Port **Fee:** Free **Closed Heads:** Yes

Marina Operations

Owner/Manager: Roger Judge **Dockmaster:** Same
In-Season: May-Oct, 7:30am-7pm **Off-Season:** Nov-Apr, 7:30am-4pm
After-Hours Arrival: Pull alongside Valvtect fuel dock
Reservations: Preferred **Credit Cards:** Visa/MC, Dscvr, Amex
Discounts: None
Pets: Welcome, Dog Walk Area **Handicap Access:** Yes, Heads, Docks

Marina Services and Boat Supplies

Services - Docking Assistance, Security *(24 Hrs., Watchmen)*, Trash Pick-Up, Dock Carts, Megayacht Facilities **Communication -** Fax in/out *($1.25)*, FedEx, AirBorne, UPS, Express Mail **Supplies - OnSite:** Ice *(Block, Cube)*, Ships' Store **OnCall:** Propane **1-3 mi:** West Marine *(994-1122)*, Boat/US *(992-8484)* **3+ mi:** Bait/Tackle *(Goin' Fishin' 993-1559, 4 mi.)*

Boatyard Services

OnSite: Travelift *(330T & 35T)*, Forklift, Crane, Engine mechanic *(gas, diesel)*, Electrical Repairs, Electronic Sales, Hull Repairs, Rigger, Sail Loft, Bottom Cleaning, Brightwork, Air Conditioning, Compound, Wash & Wax, Interior Cleaning, Propeller Repairs, Woodworking, Metal Fabrication, Painting, Awlgrip, Total Refits **OnCall:** Divers, Inflatable Repairs, Yacht Interiors **Under 1 mi:** Launching Ramp. **Member:** ABBRA, ABYC **Yard Rates:** $54/hr., Haul & Launch $12/ft., Power Wash $4/ft. **Storage:** In-Water $22/ft., On-Land Inside $5/sq.ft., Outside $24/ft.

Restaurants and Accommodations

OnCall: Pizzeria *(Minerva's 997-5120, L $3-7, D $3-7)* **Near:** Restaurant *(Margarets 992-9942, B $4, L $7, D $12+)*, *(Pumpernickles 990-2026)*, *(Wah May 992-8668)*, Inn/B&B *(Fairhaven Harborside 990-7760, $100-145)* **Under 1 mi:** Snack Bar *(Morgan's 997-4443, B $4, L $6)*, Inn/B&B *(Holiday Inn 997-1281, $100-130)* **1-3 mi:** Restaurant *(99 Restaurant L $7, D $8-15)*, Seafood Shack *(Fairhaven 996-4100)*, Hotel *(Hampton Inn 990-8500, $110-150)*, Inn/B&B *(Edgewater B&B 995-5512, $70-110)*

Recreation and Entertainment

OnSite: Picnic Area, Grills **Near:** Beach, Tennis Courts *(Fort Phoenix)*, Jogging Paths, Roller Blade/Bike Paths **Under 1 mi:** Cultural Attract *(Zeiterion Theater 994-2900)* **1-3 mi:** Playground, Dive Shop, Boat Rentals *(Buzzards Bay Kayak School 996-8885)*, Movie Theater *(Bijou 990-8616)*, Video Arcade, Park *(New Bedford Whaling Nat'l. Park)*, Museum *(Whaling Museum 997-0046)* **3+ mi:** Golf Course *(New Bedford Whaling City 996-9393, 5 mi.)*, Bowling *(Wonder Bowl 993-1746, 4 mi.)*

Provisioning and General Services

Near: Retail Shops **Under 1 mi:** Convenience Store *(Cumberland Farms)*, Gourmet Shop *(Gourmet Outlet 999-3665)*, Post Office, Protestant Church, Library *(992-5342)*, Hardware Store *(Fairhaven 997-3307)* **1-3 mi:** Supermarket *(Shaw's, Stop & Shop 990-4500)*, Delicatessen, Health Food *(Natural Food Mkt 997-9117)*, Wine/Beer *(Douglas Wine & Spirits 997-0311)*, Liquor Store *(Moriarty 984-0490)*, Bakery, Farmers' Market, Green Grocer, Fishmonger, Meat Market, Bank/ATM, Catholic Church, Beauty Salon, Barber Shop, Dry Cleaners, Laundry, Pharmacy *(Fairhaven 997-0006)*, Newsstand, Florist, Clothing Store, Copies Etc. *(Hiller 990-2701)*

Transportation

OnCall: Water Taxi, Rental Car *(Enterprise 994-8289, Alamo 991-4220)*, Taxi *(Whaling City 984-4979)* **1-3 mi:** Local Bus *(SAF T Cab 999-5213)*, InterCity Bus *(American Eagle 993-5040 to Boston South; Bonanza to Providence, NYC)*, Ferry Service *(Schamonchi to MV, Alert II to Cuttyhunk)* **Airport:** TF Green/New Bedford *(30 mi./3 mi.)*

Medical Services

911 Service **OnCall:** Ambulance **Under 1 mi:** Dentist, Chiropractor **1-3 mi:** Doctor **Hospital:** St. Lukes 979-5100 *(2 mi.)*

Setting -- The first set of docks to starboard just inside the New Bedford Hurricane Barrier, this shipyard and marina has managed to create an attractive, inviting facility. A 330 ton travelift looms over the carefully tended patches of grass and abundant pots of flowers. Great care has been taken to make the marina part feel less like a shipyard.

Marina Notes -- In operation since 1879. Services commerical and recreational vessels up to 150 ft. in its 6 acre yard. The largest travelift in U.S., also a 35 ton for smaller jobs. Hurricane barrier promises protected dockage. Floating docks up to 120 ft., fixed pier up to 200 ft. Pier 1 is now available for megayachts. Concrete floating docks with 100 amp power. Fuel dock 7am-7:30pm. 24 hr. emergency haul-out and repair. Sandblasting and spray painting, authorized awlgrip applicator. Crane service, spars up to 150'.

Notable -- There is much to see in both Fairhaven and the nearby whaling capital of New Bedford: The Fairhaven waterfront was built to handle whaling ships. A short walk is the Fort Phoenix State Beach & Reservation with views of the harbor entrance. In the 1890's, Capt. Joshua Slocum rebuilt an oyster sloop to sail solo around the world. Standard Oil tycoon Henry Huttleson Rogers donated many beautiful public buildings to Fairhaven, most considered true architectural gems -- join a free walking tour (979 -4085). Also bike paths and Moby Dick walking trails. Across the harbor are the New Bedford Whaling Museum $6/4 997-0046 and its attendant parks. Special events include Homecoming Fair, Portuguese Feast.

PHOTOS ON CD-ROM: 9

Navigational Information

Lat: 41°38.182' **Long:** 070°54.421' **Tide:** 4.5 ft. **Current:** n/a **Chart:** 13229
Rep. Depths (*MLW*): Entry 20 ft. **Fuel Dock** 15 ft. **Max Slip/Moor** 15 ft./-
Access: Buzzards Bay to New Bedford Harbor to Fairhaven side

Marina Facilities *(In Season/Off Season)*

Fuel: Slip-Side Fueling, Diesel, On Call Delivery
Slips: 30 Total, 5 Transient **Max LOA:** 250 ft. **Max Beam:** 45 ft.
Rate *(per ft.)*: **Day** $1.50/$1.00 **Week** Inq. **Month** Inq.
Power: 30 amp $5, **50 amp** $10, **100 amp** $20, **200 amp** $30
Cable TV: No **Dockside Phone:** No
Dock Type: Wood, Long Fingers, Short Fingers, Alongside, Fixed
Moorings: 0 Total, 0 Transient **Launch:** n/a, Dinghy Dock
Rate: Day n/a **Week** n/a **Month** n/a
Heads: 3 Toilet(s), 4 Shower(s) *(with dressing rooms)*
Laundry: None **Pay Phones:** Yes
Pump-Out: OnSite, Full Service, 20 InSlip **Fee:** n/a **Closed Heads:** Yes

Marina Operations

Owner/Manager: David N. Kelley **Dockmaster:** Kevin McLaughlin
In-Season: Year-Round, 7am-5pm **Off-Season:** n/a
After-Hours Arrival: Call ahead
Reservations: Preferred **Credit Cards:** Visa/MC, Amex
Discounts: None
Pets: Welcome **Handicap Access:** No

D.N. Kelley & Son Shipyard

PO Box 191; 32 Water Street; Fairhaven, MA 02719

Tel: (508) 999-6266 **VHF: Monitor** 16 **Talk** n/a
Fax: (508) 999-2513 **Alternate Tel:** n/a
Email: DNKHawl@aol.com **Web:** www.DNKelley.com
Nearest Town: Fairhaven *(0 mi.)* **Tourist Info:** (508) 979-4085

Marina Services and Boat Supplies

Services - Docking Assistance, Security *(24 Hrs., Watchman)*, Dock Carts, Megayacht Facilities **Communication -** Mail & Package Hold, Phone Messages, Fax in/out, Data Ports *(Main Office)*, FedEx, AirBorne, UPS, Express Mail *(Sat Del)* **Supplies - OnSite:** Ships' Store **OnCall:** Propane, CNG **Near:** Ice *(Block, Cube, Shaved)*, Live Bait **Under 1 mi:** West Marine *(994-1122)*, Marine Discount Store **1-3 mi:** Boat/US *(992-8484)* **3+ mi:** Bait/Tackle *(Goin' Fishin' 993-1559, 4 mi.)*

Boatyard Services

OnSite: Travelift *(160T)*, Railway, Forklift, Crane, Engine mechanic *(diesel)*, Electrical Repairs, Electronic Sales, Electronics Repairs, Hull Repairs, Bottom Cleaning, Brightwork, Divers, Compound, Wash & Wax, Interior Cleaning, Woodworking, Metal Fabrication, Painting, Awlgrip, Total Refits **OnCall:** Rigger, Sail Loft, Air Conditioning, Refrigeration, Propeller Repairs, Inflatable Repairs, Life Raft Service, Upholstery, Yacht Design, Yacht Building **Near:** Launching Ramp, Yacht Interiors. **Dealer for:** Detroit Diesel, Volvo. **Member:** ABBRA **Yard Rates:** $55/hr., Haul & Launch $6-10/ft., Power Wash $3/ft., Bottom Paint $10/ft. **Storage:** In-Water $30/ft., On-Land Inside $50/ft., Outside $30/ft.

Restaurants and Accommodations

OnCall: Pizzeria *(Minerva's 997-5120, L $4-7, D $4-7)* **Near:** Restaurant *(Margaret's 992-9942, B $8, L $8, D $12)*, *(Pumpernickles 990-2026, B $6, L $8, D $10)*, *(Huttleston House 999-1791, L $8-15, D $14-23)*, Seafood Shack *(Crawdaddys 999-1112)*, Inn/B&B *(Fairhaven Harborside Inn 990-7760, $100-140)* **Under 1 mi:** Motel *(Days Inn 996-4400)*, Hotel *(Hampton Inn 990-8500, $110-150)*, *(Holiday Inn Express 997-1281, $100-130)*

Recreation and Entertainment

Near: Pool, Picnic Area, Grills, Playground, Dive Shop, Jogging Paths, Roller Blade/Bike Paths, Fishing Charter, Group Fishing Boat, Sightseeing **Under 1 mi:** Beach *(Fort Phoenix)*, Movie Theater *(Bijou 990-8616)*, Video Arcade, Park *(Fort Phoenix)*, Museum, Cultural Attract *(Zeiterion Theater 994-2900)* **1-3 mi:** Tennis Courts, Fitness Center, Bowling *(Wonder Bowl 993-1746)*, Video Rental *(Knapp 999-2990)* **3+ mi:** Golf Course *(New Bedford Whaling City 996-9393, 5 mi.)*

Provisioning and General Services

Near: Convenience Store, Lobster Pound, Meat Market, Bank/ATM, Post Office, Catholic Church, Protestant Church, Synagogue, Beauty Salon **Under 1 mi:** Supermarket *(Stop & Shop 990-4500)*, Delicatessen, Green Grocer, Library *(Millicent 992-5342)*, Dry Cleaners, Laundry, Pharmacy *(Fairhaven Pharm 997-0006)*, Hardware Store *(Fairhaven 997-3307)*, Florist, Retail Shops, Department Store **1-3 mi:** Gourmet Shop *(Gourmet Outlet 999-3665)*, Health Food *(Natural Food 997-9117)*, Liquor Store *(Moriarty 984-0490)*, Bookstore *(Heritage House 984-4300)*, Buying Club *(BJ's)*

Transportation

OnSite: InterCity Bus *(Bonanza & American Eagle 993-5040)* **OnCall:** Rental Car *(Enterprise 999-5400)*, Taxi *(Yellow Cab 999-5213)* **1-3 mi:** Bikes *(Village Peddler 997-2453)*, Ferry Service **3+ mi:** Rail *(Providence, 20 mi.)* **Airport:** TF Green/New Bedford *(30mi/3mi.)*

Medical Services

911 Service **OnCall:** Dentist, Ambulance **Under 1 mi:** Chiropractor, Holistic Services **1-3 mi:** Doctor **Hospital:** St. Lukes 979-5100 *(2 mi.)*

Setting -- On the east (starboard) side of New Bedford Harbor just north of Fairhaven Shipyard, is this historic facility. Streetside is a picturesque town with lovely colonial homes and buildings, all in a pleasant harbor setting. Inside, the atmosphere is pure shipyard, with large recreational and commercial vessels in various stages of repair and maintenance. Many boaters will find a close-up view of this operation, and the vessels it serves, truly fascinating.

Marina Notes -- Five generations have run this mega shipyard -- 135 years of continuous family operation. Two sets of docks are for transient recreational vessels. Recent acquisition of Norlantic added over 4 acres for a total of more than 10 acres on the Fairhaven waterfront. The 4 Railways and 160 ton travelift can now accommodate boats to 900 tons and 180' in length. There's little this yard can't accommodate or deliver. Dealer for Northern Lights, Volvo, Awlgrip, Detroit Diesel, Lugger, ZF Gears. Nearby Holiday Inn Express has 12 docks; Fairhaven Harborside Inn also has 10 moorings.

Notable -- Fairhaven has more than 60 restaurants and offers some interesting diversions. Standard Oil tycoon Henry Huttleson Rogers donated many beautiful public buildings to Fairhaven, most considered true architectural gems - join a free walking tour or pick up a descriptive booklet from 43 Center St. (979-4085). Also Phoenix Bike Trail and Moby Dick walking paths. Across the bridge is the New Bedford Whaling Museum $6/4 997-0046 and its attendant parks. Buttonwood Park Zoo 991-4556 is a bit farther. Easy access to Boston, NY, Providence by train or bus -- i.e. American Eagle makes 16 trips daily to Boston. Nearby ferry or plane service to Nantucket Island, Block Island or the Vineyard. Ferry to Cuttyhunk.

PHOTOS ON CD-ROM: 9

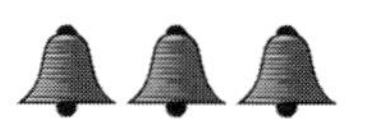

Pope's Island Marina

102 Pope's Island; New Bedford, MA 02740

Tel: (508) 979-1456 **VHF: Monitor** 74 **Talk** 9
Fax: (508) 979-1469 **Alternate Tel:** (508) 979-1469
Email: mandmpim@aol.com **Web:** n/a
Nearest Town: Fairhaven *(0.1 mi.)* **Tourist Info:** (508) 997-1250

Navigational Information

Lat: 41°38.375' **Long:** 070°54.945' **Tide:** 3 ft. **Current:** 1.5 kt. **Chart:** 13229
Rep. Depths (*MLW*): Entry 9 ft. **Fuel Dock** n/a **Max Slip/Moor** 11 ft./-
Access: Buzzards Bay to New Bedford Harbor to Pope's Island

Marina Facilities *(In Season/Off Season)*

Fuel: No
Slips: 198 Total, 12 Transient **Max LOA:** 150 ft. **Max Beam:** 40 ft.
Rate *(per ft.)*: **Day** $1.50/Inq. **Week** n/a **Month** n/a
Power: 30 amp Incl., **50 amp** Incl., **100 amp** n/a, **200 amp** n/a
Cable TV: No **Dockside Phone:** No
Dock Type: Concrete, Floating
Moorings: 0 Total, 0 Transient **Launch:** n/a
Rate: Day n/a **Week** n/a **Month** n/a
Heads: 8 Toilet(s), 8 Shower(s)
Laundry: 4 Washer(s), 4 Dryer(s), Book Exchange **Pay Phones:** Yes, 2
Pump-Out: OnSite, Full Service, 1 Central **Fee:** Free **Closed Heads:** Yes

Marina Operations

Owner/Manager: Martin Manley **Dockmaster:** 3 seasonal
In-Season: Apr-Oct, 8am-8pm **Off-Season:** Nov-Mar, Closed
After-Hours Arrival: VHF Channel 74 or 9
Reservations: Yes, Required **Credit Cards:** Visa/MC, Dscvr, Amex
Discounts: None
Pets: Welcome, Dog Walk Area **Handicap Access:** Yes, Heads, Docks

Marina Services and Boat Supplies

Services - Docking Assistance, Security *(24 Hrs., Elec. magnetic entry gate)*, Trash Pick-Up, Dock Carts **Communication -** Mail & Package Hold, Phone Messages, Fax in/out, FedEx, AirBorne, UPS, Express Mail **Supplies - OnSite:** Ice *(Block, Cube)* **Near:** West Marine *(994-1122)* **Under 1 mi:** Ships' Store, Propane *(Boc Gases 997-9457)* **1-3 mi:** Boat/US *(992-8484)*, Bait/Tackle *(Goin' Fishin' 993-1559)*

Boatyard Services

OnCall: Engine mechanic *(gas)*, Divers, Compound, Wash & Wax, Interior Cleaning, Woodworking, Inflatable Repairs, Life Raft Service, Upholstery **Near:** Launching Ramp, Electrical Repairs, Electronics Repairs, Hull Repairs, Sail Loft, Bottom Cleaning, Brightwork, Air Conditioning, Refrigeration, Propeller Repairs, Metal Fabrication. **Under 1 mi:** Travelift, Rigger. **Nearest Yard:** Kelley & Son (508) 999-6266

Restaurants and Accommodations

OnCall: Pizzeria *(Minerva 997-5120, L $4-7, D $4-7)* **Near:** Restaurant *(Ground Round 999-1112), (Pumpernickles 990-2026, B $6, L $8, D $10)* **Under 1 mi:** Restaurant *(Candleworks 997-1294), (Margaret's 992-9942, B $8, L $8, D $12), (Freestone's City Grill 993-7477, L $5-8, D $5-18)*, Motel *(Harbor View 627-7000), (Holiday Inn Express 997-1281, $110-130)* **1-3 mi:** Motel *(Huttleson House 997-7655)*, Hotel *(Hampton Inn 990-8550, $100-150)*, Inn/B&B *(Edgewater B&B 997-5512, $80-125)*

Recreation and Entertainment

OnSite: Picnic Area, Grills, Playground **Near:** Dive Shop, Jogging Paths, Roller Blade/Bike Paths *(Phoenix Bike Trail)*, Fishing Charter **Under 1 mi:** Movie Theater *(Bijou 990-8616)*, Park, Museum *(Whaling Museum 997-0046)*, Cultural Attract *(Zeiterion Theater 994-2900)*, Sightseeing *(Seamen's Bethel & New Bedford Whaling Nat'l. Park 996-4095)*, Special Events *(Summerfest, 1st week-end in July)* **1-3 mi:** Beach *(Fort Phoenix State Beach)*, Tennis Courts *(Ft. Phoenix)*, Bowling *(Wonder Bowl 993-1746)*, Video Rental *(Knapp 999-2990)* **3+ mi:** Golf Course *(New Bedford Whaling City 996-9393, 5 mi.)*

Provisioning and General Services

Near: Hardware Store *(Fairhaven 997-3307)*, Florist **Under 1 mi:** Convenience Store, Liquor Store *(Moriarty 984-0490)*, Bakery, Farmers' Market, Bank/ATM, Post Office, Catholic Church, Protestant Church, Library *(992-5342)*, Beauty Salon, Dry Cleaners, Laundry, Bookstore *(Heritage House 984-4300)*, Pharmacy *(Fairhaven 997-0006)*, Newsstand, Copies Etc. *(Hiller Printing 990-2701)* **1-3 mi:** Supermarket *(Stop & Shop 990-4500)*, Gourmet Shop *(Gourmet Outlet 999-3665)*, Delicatessen, Health Food *(Natural Food Market 997-9117)*, Fishmonger, Meat Market

Transportation

OnCall: Rental Car *(Avis 999-6900, Enterprise 994-8289)*, Taxi *(Checker 999-4545)* **Near:** Water Taxi **Under 1 mi:** Bikes *(Village Peddler 997-2453)*, InterCity Bus *(Bonanza 990-3366, American Eagle 993-5040)* **1-3 mi:** Ferry Service *(MV, Cuttyhunk)* **Airport:** New Bedford/TF Green *(3 mi./28mi.)*

Medical Services

911 Service **OnCall:** Ambulance **Near:** Dentist **Under 1 mi:** Doctor, Chiropractor **Hospital:** St. Lukes 979-5100 *(2 mi.)*

Setting -- On Pope's Island in the center of New Bedford Harbor -- equidistant to New Bedford and Fairhaven -- this municipal facility is the most convenient marina to the historic whaling town's extensive attractions and historic district. It is set in the middle of the city's Marine Park with wide expanses of green on either side and views straight down the harbor to the hurricane barrier. Out its "back door" is busy and convenient Route 6.

Marina Notes -- Tucked safely well behind the hurricane barrier, this is the largest marina in New Bedford. Very service-oriented with good security including a 24 hr. electronic gate and a single entrance that requires passing the dockmaster's office. Onsite pump-out as well as the city pump-out boat. Across the street is West Marine and True Value Hardware. Heads, showers and pleasant laundry room. Note: all dogs must be leashed. Additional dockage at nearby Holiday Inn and moorings at Fairhaven Harborside Inn. Free shuttle throughout New Bedford Mon-Fri 7:30am-6:30pm, Sat 10am-6pm.

Notable -- Less than a mile walk or cab ride is the 34 acre New Bedford Whaling Nat'l. Historical Park (Visitors' Center 33 William St.) daily 9am-4pm 996-4095, free guided tours. Adjacent is the Whaling Museum, daily 9am-5pm, 997-0046 $6/4. Films, interactive exhibits, history of Moby Dick, half scale, boardable replica of an 89 ft. whaling bark and a fully-equipped whaleboat. Across the way is the 1832 Seamen's Bethel, a non-denominational chapel described in Moby Dick, daily 10am-4pm, 992-3295. Also follow the Moby Dick Trail. Art museum. Buttonwood Zoo. Watch for the new $85 million, world-class Oceanarium project in the former harbor front COM/Electric power plant - 2003/4. Free Summer Night Concerts every Sat 991-6295, Thurs. nights in the Whaling Park 996-4095.

PHOTOS ON CD-ROM: 9

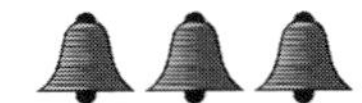

Navigational Information

Lat: 41°35.098' **Long:** 070°56.622' **Tide:** 3.5 ft. **Current:** n/a **Chart:** 13229
Rep. Depths (*MLW*): Entry 18 ft. **Fuel Dock** 6 ft. **Max Slip/Moor** 9 ft./18 ft.
Access: North of Dumpling Rocks to Apponagansett Bay to R12

Marina Facilities *(In Season/Off Season)*

Fuel: *Texaco* - Gasoline, Diesel
Slips: 100 Total, 5 Transient **Max LOA:** 60 ft. **Max Beam:** n/a
Rate *(per ft.)*: **Day** $1.50 **Week** n/a **Month** n/a
Power: 30 amp n/a, **50 amp** n/a, **100 amp** n/a, **200 amp** n/a
Cable TV: No **Dockside Phone:** No
Dock Type: Wood, Floating, Fixed
Moorings: 100 Total, 20 Transient **Launch:** Yes, Dinghy Dock
Rate: Day $40 **Week** n/a **Month** n/a
Heads: 6 Toilet(s), 6 Shower(s) *(with dressing rooms)*, Hair Dryers
Laundry: None, Book Exchange **Pay Phones:** Yes
Pump-Out: OnCall, Full Service, 1 Port **Fee:** Free **Closed Heads:** Yes

Marina Operations

Owner/Manager: Stephen Downes **Dockmaster:** Joe Cosme
In-Season: Jun 15-LabDay, 8am-10pm **Off-Season:** LabDay-Sep 30, 8-7
After-Hours Arrival: Mid Jun-LabDay open 'til 10pm
Reservations: No **Credit Cards:** Visa/MC
Discounts: None
Pets: Welcome, Dog Walk Area **Handicap Access:** No

New Bedford Yacht Club

PO Box 4; 208 Elm Street; South Dartmouth, MA 02748

Tel: (508) 992-0762 **VHF: Monitor** 68 **Talk** n/a
Fax: (508) 992-1299 **Alternate Tel:** n/a
Email: info@nbyc.com **Web:** www.nbyc.com
Nearest Town: Dartmouth *(0.1 mi.)* **Tourist Info:** (508) 999-5231

Marina Services and Boat Supplies

Services - Docking Assistance, Concierge, Boaters' Lounge, Security *(Overnight)*, Trash Pick-Up, Dock Carts **Communication -** Mail & Package Hold, Phone Messages, Fax in/out *($1)*, Data Ports *(Lounge)*, FedEx, AirBorne, UPS, Express Mail **Supplies - OnSite:** Ice *(Block, Cube)* **Near:** Ships' Store, Bait/Tackle *(Buzzard's Bay Tackle 999-5066)* **1-3 mi:** Propane *(Boc Gases 997-9457)* **3+ mi:** West Marine *(994-1122, 5 mi.)*, Boat/US *(992-8484, 7 mi.)*

Boatyard Services

Near: Travelift, Launching Ramp, Electrical Repairs, Sail Loft *(Doyle Manchester)*. **Nearest Yard:** Concordia Yachts (508) 996-2365

Restaurants and Accommodations

OnSite: Restaurant *(New Bedford YC Dining Room 997-0762, D $8-22, L Tue-Fri, Wed family buffet, Thu prime rib, Sun sundaes)*, Snack Bar *(NBYC Snack Bar Lunch only, 7 days)* **Near:** Restaurant *(Village Kitchen/Galley 992-4432, B $5, L $6, D $10)*, *(Riverhouse Grille 999-6975)*, *(Tattoo Turtle Café 993-5000, B $4, L $6, D $10)*, *(Bridge St. Café)*, Lite Fare *(Cecily's Café 994-1162, B $3, L $5, D $6)*, Inn/B&B *(Saltworks B&B 991-5491)* **1-3 mi:** Restaurant *(Ma Raffa's 992-8467, L $6, D $10)*, Pizzeria *(Friendly Pizza 996-5511)*, Inn/B&B *(The Orchard Street Manor 984-3475)*, *(Bedford Hill Inn 991-7400)* **3+ mi:** Hotel *(Holiday Inn 997-1281, $100-130, 5 mi.)*

Recreation and Entertainment

Near: Playground, Jogging Paths, Fishing Charter *(Buzzard's Bay Tackle)*, Sightseeing *(Natural Resources Trust Walking Tours 991-2289)* **Under 1 mi:** Fitness Center *(Escape To Fitness 998-7933)*, Video Arcade **1-3 mi:** Beach, Tennis Courts, Golf Course *(New Bedford Whaling 996-9393)*, Bowling *(Wonder Bowl 993-1746)*, Video Rental *(Knapp Videos 999-2990)* **3+ mi:** Horseback Riding *(Cedarwood Farms 998-3305, 5 mi.)*, Park *(Demarest Lloyd State Park 636-8816, 4 mi.)*, Museum *(New Bedford Whaling Museum, 4 mi.)*

Provisioning and General Services

Near: Convenience Store *(D&S Mini Market 997-7037)*, Delicatessen *(Tattoo Turtle 993-5000)*, Liquor Store *(Biltmore Package 992-2535)*, Bookstore *(Navigator 997-8816, extensive maritime collection)*, Newsstand, Florist *(Flora 996-2332)*, Retail Shops *(The Packet 994-0759 sport clothing, charts, post)* **Under 1 mi:** Bank/ATM, Post Office, Catholic Church, Protestant Church, Library *(Millicent 992-5342)*, Beauty Salon, Barber Shop, Dry Cleaners *(Delken)*, Laundry *(Delken 992-9423)*, Copies Etc. *(Bristol County Blueprint 993-4770)* **1-3 mi:** Gourmet Shop *(Gourmet Outlet 999-3665)*, Health Food *(Natural Food 997-9117)*, Bakery, Fishmonger *(Cape Quality 996-6724)*, Synagogue, Pharmacy *(CVS 991-7934)*, Hardware Store *(Marvin Grain 993-7672)* **3+ mi:** Supermarket *(4 mi.)*

Transportation

OnCall: Rental Car *(Enterprise 998-7200)*, Taxi *(Checker 999-4545)* **1-3 mi:** Bikes *(Vandals Cyclery 992-9772)*, Ferry Service *(Schamonchi - Martha's Vineyard; Alert II Cuttyhunk)* **Airport:** New Bedford/TF Green *(3 mi./35 mi.)*

Medical Services

No 911 Service **Near:** Chiropractor *(Chiropractic Wellness 994-9660)*
1-3 mi: Doctor, Dentist, Ambulance **Hospital:** St. Lukes 979-5100 *(3 mi.)*

Setting -- In Apponagansett, to starboard, is the Club's extensive network of docks and large mooring field. Founded in 1877, this private, hospitable club boasts a lovely 100 year-old clubhouse, with spectacular harbor views from its dining room and deck. Grassy knolls with comfortable chairs provide additional outlooks. A couple of blocks' walk is the charming village of So. Dartmouth/Padanaram with shops, restaurants and modest provisioning.

Marina Notes -- Private club but welcomes all boaters. After reaching R12, hail launch driver on Ch.68 for instructions. Note: After Sep 30, launch service 8am-4pm weekdays only. Fresh water, fuel, block ice and oil at the Gas Shack on the North Pier. Twenty-minute tie-up limit strictly enforced. Launch attendant and office also have block & bagged ice. The lovely club lounge has a telephone for local calls and Internet access. Showers, open 24 hrs., are on the south side of the Clubhouse. Upper Deck cocktail lounge, Tue-Sun 4:30pm-10pm. Snack Bar open for lunch MidJun-Late Aug, Mon-Fri 11:30am- 2pm. MemDay-LabDay Dinner is served Wed-Sun 5:30pm-9pm (Reservations requested). Pump-out service available from Dartmouth Harbormaster, Ch.9, 999-7579. Padanaram Harbormaster is Arthur Dias 999-0759. FYI: Concordia and Davis & Tripp no longer have transient facilities, but it's always worth a call.

Notable -- Dartmouth Natural Resources Trust 991-2289, in the village, offers a book of walking trails. 55 acre Lloyd Center for Environmental Studies 990-0505 is about 4 mi. and has five walking trails with views of Buzzards Bay, Demarest Lloyd State Park, Mishaum Pt, and the islands. Renowned marine photographer Norman Fortier has a studio nearby. Concordia Yachts, famous for their yachts and Beetle Cats, is next door - an interesting stop.

PHOTOS ON CD-ROM: 6

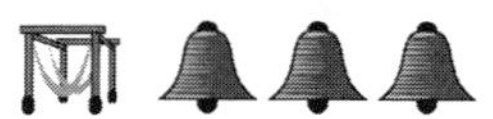

F. L. Tripp & Sons, Inc.

F. L. Tripp & Sons, Inc.

PO Box 23; 211 Cherry and Webb Rd.; Westport Point, MA 02791

Tel: (508) 636-4058 **VHF: Monitor** 9 **Talk** 8
Fax: (508) 636-4178 **Alternate Tel:** (508) 636-4058
Email: carl@fltripp.com **Web:** www.fltripp.com
Nearest Town: Westport *(6 mi.)* **Tourist Info:** (508) 999-5231

Navigational Information
Lat: 41°30.801' **Long:** 071°04.618' **Tide:** 3 ft. **Current:** 3 kt. **Chart:** 13218
Rep. Depths (*MLW*): Entry 10 ft. **Fuel Dock** 15 ft. **Max Slip/Moor** 20 ft./20 ft.
Access: Westport Harbor, 1st docks to starboard

Marina Facilities *(In Season/Off Season)*
Fuel: *Texaco* - Gasoline, Diesel
Slips: 160 Total, 5 Transient **Max LOA:** 65 ft. **Max Beam:** 15 ft.
Rate *(per ft.)*: **Day** $1.75 **Week** n/a **Month** n/a
Power: 30 amp Incl., **50 amp** Incl., **100 amp** n/a, **200 amp** n/a
Cable TV: No **Dockside Phone:** No
Dock Type: Wood, Short Fingers, Pilings, Fixed
Moorings: 230 Total, 6 Transient **Launch:** Yes ($1/pp), Dinghy Dock
Rate: Day $25 **Week** $145 **Month** $465
Heads: 5 Toilet(s), 5 Shower(s) *(with dressing rooms)*, outside shower
Laundry: 2 Washer(s), 2 Dryer(s), Book Exchange **Pay Phones:** Yes, 1
Pump-Out: OnCall, 1 Central, 1 Port **Fee:** Free **Closed Heads:** Yes

Marina Operations
Owner/Manager: The Tripp Family **Dockmaster:** Seasonal
In-Season: Year-Round, 7am-5pm* **Off-Season:** n/a
After-Hours Arrival: Call ahead
Reservations: Preferred **Credit Cards:** Visa/MC, Dscvr, Amex, Tex
Discounts: None
Pets: Welcome, Dog Walk Area **Handicap Access:** Yes, Heads, Docks

Marina Services and Boat Supplies
Services - Docking Assistance, Boaters' Lounge, Security *(8 hrs., Night watch)*, Dock Carts **Communication -** Mail & Package Hold, Phone Messages, Fax in/out, Data Ports *(Boaters' Lounge)*, FedEx, UPS, Express Mail **Supplies - OnSite:** Ice *(Block, Cube)*, Ships' Store **1-3 mi:** Bait/Tackle *(Marine Specialties 636-8100)* **3+ mi:** Propane *(10 mi.)*

Boatyard Services
OnSite: Crane *(18T)*, Engine mechanic *(gas, diesel)*, Electrical Repairs, Electronic Sales, Electronics Repairs, Hull Repairs, Rigger, Bottom Cleaning, Brightwork, Air Conditioning, Refrigeration, Divers, Compound, Wash & Wax, Interior Cleaning, Propeller Repairs, Woodworking, Metal Fabrication, Painting, Yacht Broker *(Tripp's Marine Brokerage)* **Near:** Launching Ramp. **3+ mi:** Inflatable Repairs *(25 mi.)*, Life Raft Service *(25 mi.)*, Upholstery *(20 mi.)*, Yacht Design *(25 mi.)*. **Yard Rates:** $60/hr., Haul & Launch $5/ft., Power Wash $2.25/ft. **Storage:** In-Water $20/ft., On-Land nside $44/ft., Outside $32/ft.

Restaurants and Accommodations
Near: Restaurant *(Back Eddy 636-6500, L $7-15, D $7-26, Mon-Wed 5-10pm, Thu-Sun Noon-10pm)*, Coffee Shop *(Paquachuck Inn B $1-5, L $1-5, by dinghy or launch 7am-2pm, 7 days)*, Inn/B&B *(Paquachuck Inn 636-4398, $100-130, 8 rooms, dock, ice, waterside deck)* **1-3 mi:** Inn/B&B *(Harbor Inn 636-5915)* **3+ mi:** Restaurant *(Priscilla Room at White's L $5-10, D $8-15, 5 mi.)*, Fast Food *(4 mi.)*, Inn/B&B *(Whites of Westport 675-8500, 5 mi.)*

Recreation and Entertainment
OnSite: Picnic Area, Grills, Fishing Charter **Near:** Beach *(Horseneck Beach)*, Jogging Paths, Museum *(Historic Westport Point)*, Sightseeing *(Cherry & Webb Conservation Area's well marked trails)* **Under 1 mi:** Tennis Courts *(Dartmouth Indoor Tennis 993-4811)* **1-3 mi:** Video Rental *(Video Excapade & Magazine Center 324-1211)*, Special Events *(River Day Celebrations Late June)* **3+ mi:** Golf Course *(New Bedford Whaling City 996-9393, 6 mi.)*, Horseback Riding *(Driftway Meadows 636-8864, 4 mi.)*, Bowling *(Durfee Bowling Lanes 675-2220, 5 mi.)*

Provisioning and General Services
OnSite: Copies Etc. *(at Tripp's Office)* **Near:** Fishmonger *(Lee's)*, Lobster Pound *(Lee's Wharf Lobster 636-6161)* **Under 1 mi:** Post Office, Pharmacy *(CVS 224-3312)* **1-3 mi:** Farmers' Market *(The Farmstand & Paradise Hill Farm 636-6228)* **3+ mi:** Convenience Store *(Partners Village Store 636-2572 books, gifts, and deli, 3 mi.)*, Supermarket *(Lee's Supermarket 636-3348, 4 mi., take a taxi)*, Health Food *(Gooseberry Natural Foods 636-2241, 4 mi.)*, Liquor Store *(Westport Beer & Wine, Old Westport 636-3892, 4 mi.)*, Bank/ATM *(6 mi.)*

Transportation
OnCall: Rental Car *(Enterprise 999-9400)* **Near:** Bikes *(Scottees Westport 636-1266)*, Taxi *(Westport 636-6910)* **3+ mi:** InterCity Bus *(Reliable Bus 992-3042, 8 mi.)* **Airport:** Taunton Municipal/TF Green *(25 mi./30 mi.)*

Medical Services
911 Service **OnCall:** Ambulance **1-3 mi:** Chiropractor **Hospital:** St. Lukes 979-5100 *(9 mi.)*

Setting -- This extensive, full-service facility is located just inside the mouth of Westport River on the backside of the 3 mi. stretch of Horseneck Beach. The docks and mooring field are strung out along the starboard side. Pristine views out to the mouth of the river and of unspoiled, undeveloped Westport Harbor.

Marina Notes -- *Closed Sun Oct 15-Apr. Third generation family business is over 70 years old. Transient moorings are usually in the west end of the field, marked with a small yellow float. Occasionally, a closer, seasonal one might be available. Lengths up to 65' at the dock and 45' on a mooring. Launch MemDay-LabDay, Sun-Thu 8am- 8pm, Fri & Sat 8am-10pm, $1/pp. Also service to/from Westport Harbor, Point and to the Back Eddy Restaurant. F.L. Tripp manages the restaurant's docks - three large transient slips. Tripp has two picinic areas, with grills, along the docks, and a small harbor beach. Fiberglass showerstalls. Laundry room next to a comfortable boaters' lounge with data ports -- both with views of the dock. Tripp Anglers Boats are built here. Additional moorings from Town of Westport Harbormaster 363-1105, Leach & Son 636-2093, or Westport Yacht Club 636-8885 (reciprocal only). Complimentary pump-out on Ch.9.

Notable -- Across the road is the access trail to spectacular Horseneck Beach. Dinghy or launch across to historic Westport Point - public dinghy dock. Lee's Wharf for lobster and very fresh fish. Back on the marina side, walk or launch to superb Back Eddy - eat inside, on the covered porch, or the floating decks - features local growers & purveyors. Dinghy 3 miles north up the East Branch, dock at Hix Bridge for Paradise Hill Farm, Westport Rivers Vineyard - tastings daily 11am-5pm, tours Sat & Sun (636-3423); Food/Wine Courses at Long Acre House. Buzzards Bay Brewing tours/tastings Sat 11am-5pm (636-2288).

PHOTOS ON CD-ROM: 9

X. Rhode Island: Newport & Narragansett Bay

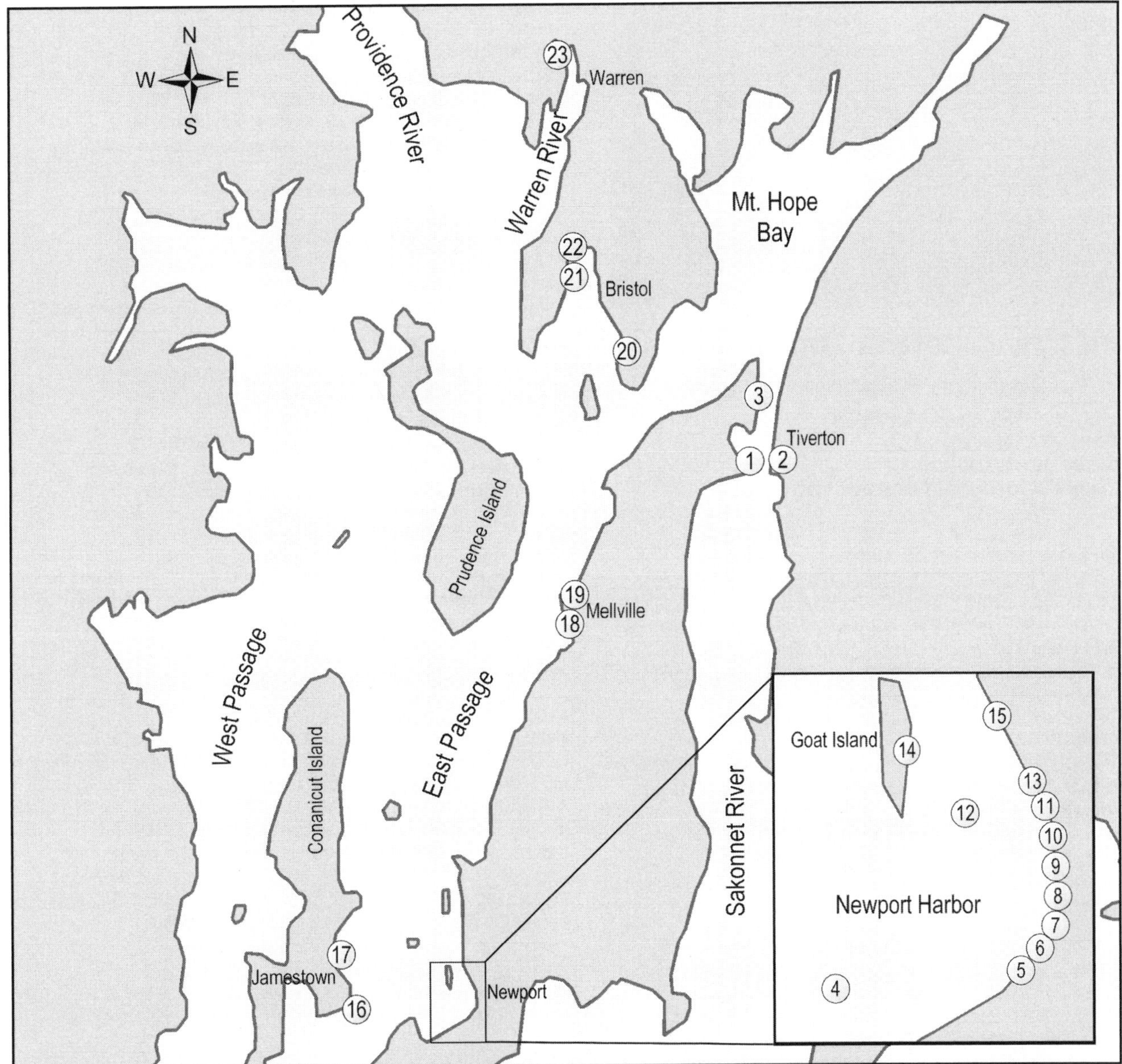

MAP	MARINA	HARBOR	PAGE
1	**Pirate Cove Marina**	*Sakonnet River*	*214*
2	**Standish Boat Yard**	*Sakonnet River*	*215*
3	**Brewer Sakonnet Marina**	*Sakonnet River*	*216*
4	**Newport, Brenton Cove & White Cloud**	*Newport Harbor*	*217*
5	**West Wind Marina**	*Newport Harbor*	*218*
6	**Casey's Marina**	*Newport Harbor*	*219*
7	**Brown & Howard Wharf Marina**	*Newport Harbor*	*220*
8	**Newport Marina**	*Newport Harbor*	*221*
9	**Christie's Marina**	*Newport Harbor*	*222*
10	**Newport Yachting Center**	*Newport Harbor*	*223*
11	**Bannister's Wharf**	*Newport Harbor*	*224*
12	**Oldport Marine Services Moorings**	*Newport Harbor*	*225*
13	**Newport Harbor Hotel & Marina**	*Newport Harbor*	*226*
14	**Goat Island Marina**	*Newport Harbor*	*227*
15	**The Newport Shipyard**	*Newport Harbor*	*228*
16	**Jamestown Boat Yard**	*East Passage*	*229*
17	**Conanicut Marina**	*East Passage*	*230*
18	**Hinckley Yacht Services**	*East Passage*	*231*
19	**East Passage Yachting Center**	*East Passage*	*232*
20	**Herreshoff Marine Museum**	*Bristol Harbor*	*233*
21	**Bristol Yacht Club**	*Bristol Harbor*	*234*
22	**Bristol Marine Co.**	*Bristol Harbor*	*235*
23	**Barrington Yacht Club**	*Warren River*	*236*

Pirate Cove Marina

109 Point Road; Portsmouth, RI 02871

Tel: (401) 683-3030 **VHF: Monitor** 9 **Talk** n/a
Fax: (401) 683-6914 **Alternate Tel:** n/a
Email: DKidd3030@aol.com **Web:** n/a
Nearest Town: Newport *(8 mi.)* **Tourist Info:** (401) 466-2982

Navigational Information

Lat: 41°37.707' **Long:** 071°13.111' **Tide:** 3 ft. **Current:** 2 kt. **Chart:** 13226
Rep. Depths (*MLW*): Entry 8 ft. **Fuel Dock** 10 ft. **Max Slip/Moor** 18 ft./65 ft.
Access: 10 mi. north of Sakonnet River mouth; 2 mi. south of Mt. Hope Bay

Marina Facilities *(In Season/Off Season)*

Fuel: *Gulf* - Gasoline, Diesel
Slips: 92 Total, 20 Transient **Max LOA:** 80 ft. **Max Beam:** 22 ft.
Rate *(per ft.)*: **Day** $1.50/$1.50 **Week** $10.50 **Month** $45
Power: 30 amp Incl, **50 amp** Incl, **100 amp** n/a, **200 amp** n/a
Cable TV: No **Dockside Phone:** No
Dock Type: Wood, Alongside, Floating, Fixed
Moorings: 36 Total, 15 Transient **Launch:** None, Dinghy Dock
Rate: Day $25 **Week** $140 **Month** $600
Heads: 2 Toilet(s), 2 Shower(s) *(with dressing rooms)*
Laundry: None **Pay Phones:** No
Pump-Out: OnSite, Full Service, 1 Central **Fee:** $6 **Closed Heads:** Yes

Marina Operations

Owner/Manager: Donald R. Kidd **Dockmaster:** Brandon E. Kidd
In-Season: May-Oct, 8am-5pm **Off-Season:** n/a
After-Hours Arrival: Call prior to arrival
Reservations: Yes, Preferred **Credit Cards:** Visa/MC, Dscvr
Discounts: Safe/Sea **Dockage:** 25% **Fuel:** n/a **Repair:** n/a
Pets: Welcome, Dog Walk Area **Handicap Access:** Yes, Heads

Marina Services and Boat Supplies

Services - Docking Assistance, Security *(Local Police Patrol)*, Trash Pick-Up, Dock Carts **Communication -** Mail & Package Hold, Phone Messages, FedEx, AirBorne, UPS, Express Mail **Supplies - OnSite:** Ice *(Block, Cube)*, Ships' Store **Under 1 mi:** Marine Discount Store *(Ocean Options 624-7334)*, Bait/Tackle *(Riverside Marine 625-5181)*, Live Bait, Propane *(Agway; Humphrey)* **3+ mi:** West Marine *(841-9880, 10 mi.)*

Boatyard Services

OnSite: Travelift *(40T)*, Crane, Engine mechanic *(gas, diesel)*, Hull Repairs, Rigger, Bottom Cleaning, Brightwork, Compound, Wash & Wax, Propeller Repairs, Woodworking, Painting, Awlgrip **OnCall:** Divers, Interior Cleaning, Inflatable Repairs **Near:** Launching Ramp. **Under 1 mi:** Life Raft Service. **1-3 mi:** Sail Loft, Upholstery, Yacht Interiors. **Yard Rates:** $50/hr., Haul & Launch $5-8/ft. *(blocking $35-40)*, Power Wash $2/ft., Bottom Paint $2.50/ft. **Storage:** In-Water $74/ft., On-Land $23/ft.

Restaurants and Accommodations

OnCall: Pizzeria *(No. End Pizza 683-6633)* **Near:** Restaurant *(15 Point Road 683-3138, D $12-22)*, *(Tremblay's 683-9999, L $3-8, D $8-14)*, Seafood Shack *(Flo's Clam Shack)*, *(Sakonnet Fish Co 683-1180)* **1-3 mi:** Motel *(Founders Brook 368-1244, $40-160)*, *(Best Western Bay Point 683-3600, $60-120)*, Hotel *(Roger Williams University Conference Center 683-6300)*

Recreation and Entertainment

OnSite: Picnic Area, Grills **Near:** Beach *(Island Park)*, Playground *(Island Park)* **1-3 mi:** Pool, Golf Course *(Montaup Country Club 683-0955; Pocasset Country Club 683-7300)*, Video Rental *(Briggs Video Etc. 683-5440)* **3+ mi:** Dive Shop *(4 mi.)*, Tennis Courts *(4 mi.)*, Horseback Riding *(Sakonnet Equestrian Center 625-1458, 4 mi.)*, Fishing Charter *(4 mi.)*, Movie Theater *(5 mi.)*, Park *(Blithewold Mansion & Gardens 253-2707, Green Animals Topiary Gardens 683-1267, 4-5 mi.)*, Sightseeing *(Newport Mansions, beaches, 6 mi.)*

Provisioning and General Services

Near: Fishmonger *(Stonebridge Seafoods 683-3805)*, Lobster Pound, Catholic Church, Protestant Church *(Episcopal; Methodist; A/G)* **Under 1 mi:** Convenience Store *(Cumberland Farms)*, Wine/Beer *(Moriarty's 683-4441)*, Liquor Store, Green Grocer, Post Office, Library *(683-9457, Internet access)*, Florist, Copies Etc. *(Hamilton Printing 683-2100)* **1-3 mi:** Delicatessen *(Little Corner)*, Bank/ATM, Beauty Salon, Barber Shop, Dry Cleaners, Pharmacy *(Brooks 624-8411)*, Newsstand, Hardware Store *(Humphrey's 624-8800)* **3+ mi:** Supermarket *(Shaw's 508-674-8445, 5 mi.)*, Synagogue *(Temple Shalom; Touro Synagogues, 5-6 mi.)*

Transportation

OnCall: Rental Car *(Enterprise 672-1988)*, Taxi *(Rainbow Cabs 849-1333)* **3+ mi:** Rail *(Amtrak, 30 mi.)* **Airport:** TF Green 737-8222 *(33 mi.)*

Medical Services

911 Service **OnCall:** Ambulance **1-3 mi:** Doctor *(McMahon 683-2290)*, Dentist *(Dess 683-4335)*, Chiropractor *(Chiropractic Center Of Tiverton 624-4111)*, Holistic Services *(Positive Works 683-2013)* **Hospital:** Saint Annes 508-235-5000 *(7 mi.)*

Setting -- In the Tiverton Basin, near the entrance to The Cove, Pirate Cove Marina's docks are fully protected from the river by a large L-shaped breakwater - an earth and rock berm. The surrounding area, the northern part of Aquideck Island, is as quiet and tranquil as the marina itself.

Marina Notes -- Built in 1967 by Thomas Kidd, Jr, it has been family owned & operated ever since. Today the second and third generations manage the facility. Personal customer service is a hallmark; staff is onsite 7 days, year-round. Slips are single loaded - a rarity these days. Most slip holders are long-term seasonal, three-quarters of them for more than five years. Most basic boatyard services are available onsite. Winter in-water storage. Larger boatyards in Portsmouth are a short sail south. Marina Hours: Mon-Fri 9am-5pm, Sat-Sun 8am-5pm. Fuel Dock Hours: Daily 8am-5pm. Service Department Hours: Mon-Fri 8am-4:30pm.

Notable -- Within walking distance are five restaurants -- white table cloth "15 Point Road", two seafood shacks, and two casual restaurants. A public beach is nearby and it's 1.3 miles to semi-private Montaup Country Club's 18 hole course. It's five miles to the nearest serious grocery. The environs are quite rural and afford an opportunity for a good hike. Just under the 25 foot bridge, next to the Marina, is The Cove -- a good destination for smaller boat, shallow-draft gunk holing (charted at 3-4 ft.) or dinghy exploration. Reportedly clamming is very good here; check with the marina office for local knowledge.

PHOTOS ON CD-ROM: 6

Navigational Information
Lat: 41°37.768' **Long:** 071°12.720' **Tide:** 4 ft. **Current:** 2 kt. **Chart:** 13226
Rep. Depths (*MLW*): Entry 35 ft. **Fuel Dock** 10 ft. **Max Slip/Moor** 20 ft./65 ft.
Access: 10 mi. north of Sakonnet River mouth; 2 mi. south of Mt. Hope Bay

Marina Facilities *(In Season/Off Season)*
Fuel: Gasoline, Diesel
Slips: 25 Total, 2 Transient **Max LOA:** 65 ft. **Max Beam:** 16 ft.
Rate *(per ft.)*: **Day** $1.50/Inq. **Week** $10.50 **Month** $45
Power: 30 amp $5, **50 amp** n/a, **100 amp** n/a, **200 amp** n/a
Cable TV: No **Dockside Phone:** No
Dock Type: Wood, Alongside, Floating, Fixed
Moorings: 65 Total, 15 Transient **Launch:** None, Dinghy Dock
Rate: Day $20 **Week** Inq. **Month** Inq.
Heads: 2 Toilet(s)
Laundry: None **Pay Phones:** No
Pump-Out: Full Service, 1 Central, 1 Port **Fee:** $5 **Closed Heads:** Yes

Marina Operations
Owner/Manager: Ken Hilton & Jack Brimicomb **Dockmaster:** Same
In-Season: Year-Round, 8am-5pm **Off-Season:** Closed Sun
After-Hours Arrival: Gas dock or white mooring ball
Reservations: Preferred **Credit Cards:** Visa/MC
Discounts: Safe/Sea **Dockage:** 25% **Fuel:** n/a **Repair:** n/a
Pets: Welcome **Handicap Access:** No

Standish Boat Yard

RI - NEWPORT & NARRAGANSETT BAY

Standish Boat Yard

1697 Main Road; Tiverton, RI 02878

Tel: (401) 624-4075 **VHF: Monitor** 16 **Talk** 69
Fax: (401) 624-3438 **Alternate Tel:** n/a
Email: n/a **Web:** n/a
Nearest Town: Tiverton *(3 mi.)* **Tourist Info:** (401) 466-2892

Marina Services and Boat Supplies
Services - Docking Assistance, Dock Carts **Communication -** Phone Messages, Fax in/out, FedEx, AirBorne, UPS, Express Mail *(Sat Del)* **Supplies - OnSite:** Ice *(Block, Cube)*, Ships' Store, CNG **Near:** Marine Discount Store *(Ocean Options 624-7334)* **Under 1 mi:** Bait/Tackle *(Riverside Marine 625-5181)* **1-3 mi:** Propane *(Ferrellgas 624-8013)* **3+ mi:** West Marine *(841-9880, 12 mi.)*

Boatyard Services
OnSite: Railway, Crane, Engine mechanic *(gas, diesel)*, Electrical Repairs, Electronic Sales, Hull Repairs, Rigger, Bottom Cleaning, Brightwork, Air Conditioning, Refrigeration, Divers, Compound, Wash & Wax, Interior Cleaning, Woodworking, Painting, Awlgrip, Yacht Broker *(Standish Boat Yard Inc.)*, Total Refits **Near:** Launching Ramp, Inflatable Repairs. **1-3 mi:** Life Raft Service. **3+ mi:** Propeller Repairs *(15 mi.)*. **Dealer for:** Albin Manufacturing 27'-36'. **Yard Rates:** $50/hr., Haul & Launch $8/ft. *(blocking $2/ft.)*, Power Wash $3/ft., Bottom Paint $3/ft. **Storage:** In-Water $17/ft.

Restaurants and Accommodations
OnCall: Pizzeria *(Famous 624-8900)* **Near:** Restaurant *(Stone Bridge 625-5780, L $10-12, D $13-20)* **Under 1 mi:** Restaurant *(Moulin Rouge 624-4320)* **1-3 mi:** Seafood Shack *(Evelyn's Nanaquaket Drive-In 624-3100, 1.5 mi. or by dinghy)*, Motel *(Founders Brook 683-1244, $40-140)*, Hotel *(Best Western Bay Point 683-3600, $60-120)* **3+ mi:** Motel *(Bristol Motor Lodge 253-7600, 5 mi.)*, Inn/B&B *(William's Grant 253-4222, $80-130, 5 mi.)*

Recreation and Entertainment
OnSite: Picnic Area, Grills **Near:** Dive Shop, Park *(Fort Barton - 3 miles of trails)*, Museum *(Fort Barton 625-6700 sunrise-sunset)* **Under 1 mi:** Beach *(Grinnel Beach, south of Old Stone Bridge)* **1-3 mi:** Tennis Courts, Golf Course *(Montaup Country Club 683-0955)*, Jogging Paths, Video Rental *(Briggs Video Etc. 683-5440)* **3+ mi:** Fitness Center *(Tiverton Health & Fitness 624-3440, 4 mi.)*, Sightseeing *(Blithewold Mansion & Gardens 253-2707, Green Animals Topiary Gardens 683-1267, 5 mi.)*

Provisioning and General Services
Near: Convenience Store, Delicatessen, Bank/ATM, Catholic Church, Protestant Church, Beauty Salon, Newsstand, Florist **Under 1 mi:** Wine/Beer, Liquor Store *(Moriarty's 683-4441)*, Fishmonger, Lobster Pound, Barber Shop **1-3 mi:** Bakery, Green Grocer *(Grand Central Market 624-9914)*, Meat Market, Post Office, Library *(Tiverton 625-6796)*, Dry Cleaners, Laundry, Pharmacy *(Brooks 624-8411)*, Hardware Store *(Humphrey's 624-8800)*, Retail Shops **3+ mi:** Supermarket *(Shaw's 508-674-8445, 5 mi.)*, Synagogue *(4 mi.)*, Bookstore *(Books From 4 Corners 624-4311, 5 mi.)*

Transportation
OnCall: Rental Car *(Enterprise 508-672-1988)*, Taxi *(B&E Taxi 624-7100)*, Airport Limo *(Fantasy Limo 508-683-6677)* **3+ mi:** InterCity Bus *(Fall River, 10 mi.)*, Rail *(Providence, 25 mi.)* **Airport:** TF Green 737-8222 *(20 mi.)*

Medical Services
911 Service **OnCall:** Ambulance **Near:** Doctor *(Family Physicians 624-1400)*, Dentist *(Jenkins 624-2375)* **1-3 mi:** Chiropractor *(Chiro Center of Tiverton 624-4111)*, Holistic Services *(Coastal Massage 624-7500)*, Veterinarian *(Sakonnet Vet 624-6624)* **Hospital:** Saint Annes 508-235-5000 *(6 mi.)*

Setting -- About a half mile north of the remains of the Old Stone Bridge, on the east side of the Sakonnet River, Standish Boat Yard's red, white and blue "Gas-Diesel" sign beckons. The facility appears to be built into the side of the steep river bank, snuggled in between the river and the road. The atmosphere is strictly boatyard, but the down-home friendliness obviously appeals to the owners of some very good looking yachts.

Marina Notes -- Season mooring rate - $850 April 1st. through Nov, plus $125 for use of dinghy dock. Closed Sun in Off-Season and Christmas through New Year's. Very deep water, limited slips, 65 moorings stretch along the river. Substantial current runs through cut of the Old Bridge. Originally built in 1933; the current owners took over in 1969. They are still active, and now the second generation of sons has joined the team. Sales and Brokerage for new and used Albins, plus other power and sail vessels. Well equipped marine store, including parts for inboard Mercruisers. Heads, but no showers. No launch. Ocean Options is up the street 624-7534. The nearby Tiverton Yacht Club (625-5311) may also have a mooring available for members of other clubs.

Notable -- Walk up the short, steep driveway to Main Road and the area becomes quite rural and quiet. 1778 Fort Barton, an original redoubt built during the American Revolution as the staging area for the invasion of Aquidneck Island (and the Battle of Rhode Island), is an easy 0.3 miles walk. It has 3 miles of walking trails and a 30 ft. observation tower. The little town of Tiverton is 3 miles away. Directly across the river is The Cove, a good dinghy destination. Another might be Nanaquaket Pond; Evelyn's Dock & Dine is there. And south, just below the Old Stone Bridge jetties, is Grinnel Beach - a quarter mile crescent.

PHOTOS ON CD-ROM: 5

Brewer Sakonnet Marina

222 Narragansett Boulevard; Portsmouth, RI 02871

Tel: (401) 683-3551 **VHF: Monitor** 9 **Talk** 72
Fax: (401) 683-9188 **Alternate Tel:** n/a
Email: bsm@byy.com **Web:** www.byy.com/portsmouth
Nearest Town: Newport *(18 mi.)* **Tourist Info:** (401) 466-2982

Navigational Information

Lat: 41°38.754' **Long:** 071°13.105' **Tide:** 4 ft. **Current:** 2 kt. **Chart:** 13226
Rep. Depths (*MLW*): Entry 6 ft. **Fuel Dock** 8 ft. **Max Slip/Moor** 10 ft./-
Access: Sakonnet River or Mt. Hope Bay to top of Aquidneck Island

Marina Facilities *(In Season/Off Season)*

Fuel: Gasoline, Diesel
Slips: 320 Total, 10 Transient **Max LOA:** 60 ft. **Max Beam:** n/a
Rate *(per ft.)*: **Day** $1.50 **Week** Inq. **Month** Inq.
Power: 30 amp Inq., **50 amp** Inq., **100 amp** n/a, **200 amp** n/a
Cable TV: Yes **Dockside Phone:** Yes
Dock Type: Wood, Long Fingers, Pilings, Floating, Vinyl
Moorings: 0 Total, 0 Transient **Launch:** n/a
Rate: Day n/a **Week** n/a **Month** n/a
Heads: 7 Toilet(s), 5 Shower(s)
Laundry: 2 Washer(s), 2 Dryer(s) **Pay Phones:** Yes, 4
Pump-Out: OnSite, Full Service, 1 Central **Fee:** $5 **Closed Heads:** Yes

Marina Operations

Owner/Manager: Jay Burns **Dockmaster:** n/a
In-Season: Summer, 8am-8pm **Off-Season:** n/a, 7:30am-5pm
After-Hours Arrival: Call ahead for instructions
Reservations: Yes **Credit Cards:** Visa/MC, Dscvr, Amex
Discounts: Safe/Sea **Dockage:** 25% **Fuel:** n/a **Repair:** n/a
Pets: Welcome, Dog Walk Area **Handicap Access:** No

Marina Services and Boat Supplies

Services - Docking Assistance, Security *(Evenings, 7 days)*, Dock Carts **Communication -** Mail & Package Hold, Phone Messages, Fax in/out, FedEx, AirBorne, UPS, Express Mail *(Sat Del)* **Supplies - OnSite:** Ice *(Block, Cube)* **OnCall:** Propane **Under 1 mi:** Ships' Store, Bait/Tackle **1-3 mi:** CNG **3+ mi:** West Marine *(10 mi.)*

Boatyard Services

OnSite: Travelift *(35T)*, Forklift, Crane, Engine mechanic *(gas, diesel)*, Launching Ramp, Electrical Repairs, Electronics Repairs, Hull Repairs, Rigger, Bottom Cleaning, Brightwork, Air Conditioning, Refrigeration, Compound, Wash & Wax, Woodworking, Painting, Awlgrip, Yacht Broker, Total Refits **OnCall:** Divers **Near:** Interior Cleaning. **Under 1 mi:** Metal Fabrication, Yacht Design. **1-3 mi:** Sail Loft, Inflatable Repairs, Life Raft Service, Yacht Building. **Dealer for:** Awlgrip, Yanmar, Koehler Generators, Westerbeke. **Member:** ABBRA, ABYC - 3 Certified Tech(s), Other Certifications: Mercruiser, A/C **Yard Rates:** $48-50/hr., Haul & Launch $6/ft. *(blocking incl.)*, Power Wash $2/ft., Bottom Paint $10/ft.

Restaurants and Accommodations

OnSite: Snack Bar **1-3 mi:** Restaurant *(15 Point Road 683-3138, D $12-22, 5-9pm, Fri-Sat 'til 10pm, Sun 4-9pm)*, *(Tremblay's 683-9899, L $3-8, D $8-14)*, *(Stone Bridge 625-5780, L $10-12, D $13-20)*, *(Sea Fare Inn 683-2910, D $14-24, Tue-Sat 5-9pm)*, *(Sakonnet Fish Co. 683-1180)*, *(501 Park Avenue 683-0750)*, Motel *(Best Western Bay Point 683-3600, $60-120)*, Inn/B&B *(Founders Brook 683-1244, $40-160)* **3+ mi:** Motel *(Bristol Motor Lodge 253-7600, 4 mi.)*, Inn/B&B *(William's Grant 253-4222, $80-135, 4 mi.)*

Recreation and Entertainment

OnSite: Pool, Spa, Picnic Area, Grills, Playground, Volleyball **Near:** Beach *(Island Park)*, Dive Shop, Jogging Paths **Under 1 mi:** Golf Course *(Montaup Country Club 683-0955, Pocasset C.C. 683-7300 3 mi.)* **1-3 mi:** Video Rental *(Briggs Video Etc. 683-5440)* **3+ mi:** Horseback Riding *(Sakonnet Equestrian Center 625-1458, 5 mi)*, Museum *(6 mi.)*

Provisioning and General Services

Near: Delicatessen **1-3 mi:** Wine/Beer, Liquor Store *(Moriarty's Liquor Locker 683-4441)*, Green Grocer *(Grand Central Market 624-9914)*, Fishmonger *(Stonebridge 683-3805)*, Bank/ATM, Post Office, Library *(683-9457, Internet access)*, Beauty Salon, Dry Cleaners, Pharmacy *(Brooks 683-5270)*, Hardware Store, Florist, Retail Shops, Copies Etc. **3+ mi:** Supermarket *(Clements Market 683-0180, 5 mi.)*

Transportation

OnSite: Bikes **OnCall:** Rental Car *(Enterprise 672-1988)*, Taxi *(Rainbow Cabs 849-1333)*, Airport Limo *(Fantasy Limo 683-6677)* **3+ mi:** Rail *(Providence Amtrak, 30 mi.)* **Airport:** TF Green 732-3621 *(33 mi.)*

Medical Services

911 Service **Near:** Ambulance **1-3 mi:** Doctor *(Miesner/Cummings 625-1001)*, Dentist *(Van Regenmorter/Marks 624-9177)*, Holistic Services *(Positive Works 683-2013)*, Veterinarian *(Sakonnet Vet. Hosp 624-6624)*
Hospital: Saint Annes 508-235-5000 *(6 mi.)*

PHOTOS ON CD-ROM: 7

Setting -- Located at the northern end of Aquidneck Island, where Narragansett Bay, Mt. Hope Bay and the Sakonnet River converge, this impeccably landscaped and maintained boatyard/marina is truly a refuge of peace and quiet. Lush displays of flowers, underscored by swaths of green grass, amplify that perception. There are two separate dock areas: Sakonnet South is a bit roomier but directly on the River. Sakonnet North is tucked into completely sheltered Cedar Island Pond, which is accessed by a small inlet from the River.

Marina Notes -- Sakonnet South has 189 slips, as well as rack storage. Sakonnet North has 140 slips. A nice air conditioned boaters' lounge boasts a big screen TV and microwave. In North Yard, the pool and its erratically open snackbar overlook the Sakonnet River and bridge. Volleyball court & playground are in South Yard. Both yards have very nice heads, showers & laundry (including a large wash tub). The Brewer Customer Club Card offers free dockage and discounts. The recent installation of a new whaler provides more wave protection to the South Yard, particularly from the northeast.

Notable -- The surrounding area offers very little to do except enjoy the lovely, peaceful setting - particularly spectacular in the Fall. But, onsite are good recreation facilities including a pool, with Jacuzzi, playground, basketball and volleyball courts. Semi-private Montaup Country Club is a mile away and several restaurants are within a 1.5-2.5 mile hike. 15 Point Road offers upscale fine dining, the others are more casual. The Cove is an interesting dinghy-ride destination and is reportedly a good clamming spot. Or consider exploring the Kickamuit River's gunk holes and inlets.

Navigational Information
Lat: 41°28.583' **Long:** 071°19.821' **Tide:** 4 ft. **Current:** n/a **Chart:** 13223
Rep. Depths (*MLW*): Entry 30 ft. **Fuel Dock** n/a **Max Slip/Moor** -/18 ft.
Access: Newport Harbor; Main, Spindle or Brenton Cove Mooring Fields

Marina Facilities *(In Season/Off Season)*
Fuel: No
Slips: 0 Total, 0 Transient **Max LOA:** 70 ft. **Max Beam:** n/a
Rate *(per ft.)*: **Day** n/a **Week** n/a **Month** n/a
Power: 30 amp n/a, **50 amp** n/a, **100 amp** n/a, **200 amp** n/a
Cable TV: No **Dockside Phone:** No
Dock Type: n/a
Moorings: 60 Total, 40 Transient **Launch:** Ch.68 ($2/1-way), Dinghy Dock
Rate: Day $40* **Week** Less 10% **Month** Less 20%
Heads: None
Laundry: None **Pay Phones:** No
Pump-Out: OnCall, Full Service, 2 Port **Fee:** $15** **Closed Heads:** Yes

Marina Operations
Owner/Manager: Carl Bolender, Niel Gray, Bill Thoad **Dockmaster:** n/a
In-Season: May 15-Oct 15, 8am-10pm **Off-Season:** Closed, but at phone
After-Hours Arrival: Always call first
Reservations: Yes **Credit Cards:** Check or Cash
Discounts: None
Pets: Welcome, Dog Walk Area **Handicap Access:** No

Newport Mooring Fields

Newport, RI 02840

Tel: (401) 846-7535 **VHF: Monitor** 9 **Talk** 12
Fax: n/a **Alternate Tel:** (401) 849-2210
Email: n/a **Web:** n/a
Nearest Town: Newport *(0 mi.)* **Tourist Info:** (401) 845-9123

Marina Services and Boat Supplies
Communication - Data Ports *(Seamen's Institute)* **Supplies - Near:** Ice *(Block, Cube)*, Ships' Store *(JT's 846-7256)*, CNG *(Oldport 847-9109)* **Under 1 mi:** West Marine, Bait/Tackle *(Saltwater Edge 842-0062)* **1-3 mi:** Live Bait, Propane *(BOC 846-3706)*

Boatyard Services
OnCall: Engine mechanic *(gas, diesel)*, Electrical Repairs, Electronics Repairs, Rigger, Sail Loft, Bottom Cleaning, Brightwork, Divers **Near:** Travelift, Railway, Electronic Sales, Hull Repairs, Propeller Repairs, Inflatable Repairs, Life Raft Service, Yacht Interiors, Metal Fabrication, Awlgrip. **Nearest Yard:** Newport Shipyard (401) 846-6000

Restaurants and Accommodations
OnCall: Raw Bar *(Ch.66)*, Snack Bar *(Harbor Java 846-5402, Ch.72)* **Near:** Restaurant *(Salas' Upstairs 846-8772, D $6-20)*, *(Puerini's 847-5506, D $10-22)*, *(The Pier 849-3100, L $6-12, D $14-26)*, *(Christie's 847-5400, L $6-12, D $18-29)*, Pizzeria *(Pizza Hollywood 846-1470)*, Inn/B&B *(Spring St. Inn 847-4767, $120-280)*, *(Francis Malbone House 846-0392, $300-425)* **Under 1 mi:** Hotel *(Hyatt Regency Hotel & Spa 851-1234, $200-400)*, *(Newport Harbor Hotel & Marina 847-9000, $100-675)*

Recreation and Entertainment
Near: Fitness Center *(Waterfront Fitness 846-3720)*, Boat Rentals, Group Fishing Boat, Movie Theater, Video Arcade, Park, Museum *(Int'l. Tennis Hall of Fame 849-3990 $8/4; Museum of Yachting 847-1018 $4/3)*, Cultural Attract *(Fort Adams 841-0707)*, Special Events *(Folk, Jazz Fest - early Aug; Boat Show Mid Sep)* **Under 1 mi:** Spa, Tennis Courts *(Nat'l. Tennis Club 849-6672)*, Fishing Charter, Video Rental *(Broadway Joes 848-5859)*, Sightseeing *(The Mansions - 5 $29/10)* **1-3 mi:** Heated Pool, Beach, Dive Shop, Golf Course, Bowling *(Hi Way Bowl/Mini Golf 849-9990)*

Provisioning and General Services
Near: Provisioning Service, Convenience Store, Delicatessen *(Morning Glory 842-0520)*, Liquor Store *(Wellington Square 846-9463)*, Bakery, Fishmonger, Lobster Pound *(Aquidneck 846-0106)*, Meat Market, Bank/ATM, Post Office, Catholic Church, Protestant Church, Synagogue, Beauty Salon, Barber Shop, Dry Cleaners, Laundry *(Micki's 847-5972)*, Bookstore *(Armchair Sailor 847-4252)*, Pharmacy *(CVS 846-4990)*, Newsstand, Hardware Store *(One Stop 847-8460)*, Clothing Store, Retail Shops, Copies Etc. *(Printing & Copying 849-3820)* **Under 1 mi:** Supermarket *(Stop & Shop 848-7200)*, Gourmet Shop *(Market on the Boulevard 848-2600)*, Health Food, Farmers' Market *(behind Salvation Café Wed 2-6pm, Sat 9am-1pm 849-7359)*, Library *(847-8720)*, Florist

Transportation
Near: Water Taxi, Taxi, Local Bus *(RIPTA 781-9400)*, InterCity Bus *(Greyhound 846-1820)*, Ferry Service *(Newport-Providence $8/4)* **Under 1 mi:** Bikes *(Ten Speed Spokes 847-5609)*, Rental Car *(Cartemps 846-4458, Enterprise 849-3939)* **3+ mi:** Rail *(Amtrak Kingston, RIPTA Rt. 64 bus, 17 mi.)* **Airport:** TF Green *(20 mi.)*

Medical Services
911 Service **OnCall:** Ambulance **Near:** Doctor *(Defreitas 847-1040)* **Under 1 mi:** Dentist, Chiropractor *(Newport C.C. 847-4224)*, Holistic Services *(Bessette 849-5560)* **Hospital:** Newport 783-9718 *(1 mi.)*

Setting -- These three independent vendors manage moorings in most of the mooring fields in Newport Harbor. They have a few "front row center" in the Main mooring field across from Bannister's Wharf, a couple at the Point, but most are in the Spindle and Brenton Cove mooring fields.

Marina Notes -- *Rates: $30-$55 depending on service and size of vessel: up to 39' $35, 40-49' $40, 50-59' $50, 60-69' $55. Brenton Cove is $40 up to 60'. Direct numbers: Newport Mooring - Niel Gray 846-7535 (reservations for 2 weeks). Brenton Cove - Carl Bolender 849-2210. White Cloud Mooring - Bill Thoad 527-2754 9-10pm only. All monitor Ch.9. No private landside services. Public dinghy docks (which also have heads): Bowen's Wharf (849-2234, Ch.78), Anne Street Pier $1/hr., $6/day (847-1069, Ch.78), King Park (trash facility); Sail Newport, Ft. Adams State Park (short term only - has showers). Additional dinghy docks being built at Elm St. Pier & Ferry Terminal. Nice public restrooms at Harbormaster's Office (Tim Mills 848-6492, Ch.16, 14.) in Perrotti Park - also a dog walk park. Restrooms, showers, self-service laundry, Internet access, Aloha Café, & library at Seamen's Institute (847-4260). **Harbor Sanitation (part of Brenton Cove Moorings) has 2 pump-out boats, 7 days, 8am-7pm, cell # 474-3044, Ch.9, $15 first 30 gals, $5 each add'l 30 gals.

Notable -- Gateway Info Center next to Perrotti Park (Ferry dinghy dock) is a good 1st stop. From King Park dinghy dock, The Elms is an easy walk. Then walk or trolley (Yellow rte. #67) to the other mansions ($29/10 comb ticket to 5) or to south end of Cliff Walk, a spectacular 3 mi. trail adjoining many of the "cottages". The Orange #61 bus meets its North End ($1.25 1-way, $5 all-day, $10 family). Hail Harbor Java on Ch.72 for coffee, pastries, wraps, newspapers.

PHOTOS ON CD-ROM: 6

West Wind Marina

Waite's Wharf; Newport, RI 02840

Tel: (401) 849-4300 **VHF: Monitor** 9 **Talk** n/a
Fax: (401) 847-0862 **Alternate Tel:** n/a
Email: westwindri@aol.com **Web:** n/a
Nearest Town: Newport *(0 mi.)* **Tourist Info:** (401) 849-8048

Navigational Information

Lat: 41°28.797' **Long:** 071°19.013' **Tide:** 4 ft. **Current:** n/a **Chart:** 13223
Rep. Depths (*MLW*): **Entry** 18 ft. **Fuel Dock** n/a **Max Slip/Moor** 13 ft./-
Access: Narragansett Bay, past Ft. Adams, past Little Rock, Ida Lewis

Marina Facilities *(In Season/Off Season)*

Fuel: Slip-Side Fueling, On Call Delivery
Slips: 60 Total, 50 Transient **Max LOA:** 200 ft. **Max Beam:** n/a
Rate *(per ft.)*: **Day** $3.50/Inq. **Week** Inq. **Month** Inq.
Power: 30 amp Inq., **50 amp** Inq., **100 amp** Inq., **200 amp** n/a
Cable TV: No **Dockside Phone:** No
Dock Type: Wood, Long Fingers, Floating, Fixed
Moorings: 0 Total, 0 Transient **Launch:** n/a, Dinghy Dock
Rate: Day n/a **Week** n/a **Month** n/a
Heads: 4 Toilet(s), 4 Shower(s) *(with dressing rooms)*
Laundry: 2 Washer(s), 2 Dryer(s) **Pay Phones:** Yes
Pump-Out: OnCall, Full Service, 2 Port **Fee:** $15+ **Closed Heads:** Yes

Marina Operations

Owner/Manager: Abruzese Family **Dockmaster:** James McCarthy
In-Season: Apr-Nov, 7am-8pm **Off-Season:** Closed
After-Hours Arrival: Call in advance
Reservations: Yes, preferred **Credit Cards:** Visa/MC, Amex, Check
Discounts: None
Pets: Welcome **Handicap Access:** Yes, Heads

Marina Services and Boat Supplies

Services - Docking Assistance, Concierge, Security, Trash Pick-Up, Dock Carts, Megayacht Facilities, 3 Phase **Communication -** Mail & Package Hold, Phone Messages, Fax in/out, FedEx, AirBorne, UPS, Express Mail *(Sat Del)* **Supplies - OnSite:** Ice *(Block)* **Near:** Ships' Store *(JT's Chandlery 846-7356)*, CNG *(Oldport 847-9109)* **Under 1 mi:** Bait/Tackle *(Saltwater Edge 842-0062)* **1-3 mi:** West Marine *(841-9880)*, Propane *(U-Haul 847-3219)*

Boatyard Services

OnSite: Compound, Wash & Wax, Interior Cleaning **OnCall:** Engine mechanic *(diesel)* **Nearest Yard:** The Newport Shipyard (401) 846-6000

Restaurants and Accommodations

OnSite: Restaurant *(West Deck 847-3610, D $15-35)*, Lite Fare *(The Deck L&D $5-18)* **Near:** Restaurant *(Bouchard 846-0123, D $60, 3 courses)*, *(Scales & Shells 846-3474, D $10-42)*, *(Café Zelda 849-4002, D $10-20)*, *(Mamma Luisa 848-5257, D $12-23)*, Lite Fare *(Gary's 847-9480, B $2-6, L $2-6)*, Inn/B&B *(Ivy Lodge 849-6865, $135-190)*, *(Adm. Fitzroy 848-8000, $85-230)*, *(Francis Malbone 846-0392, $150-290)*

Recreation and Entertainment

OnSite: Fishing Charter *(Mayflower 846-7225)* **Near:** Beach *(King Park)*, Picnic Area, Playground, Jogging Paths, Boat Rentals, Movie Theater *(Jane Pickens 846-5252)*, Video Arcade *(Ryan's 846-5774)*, Park *(King)* **Under 1 mi:** Tennis Courts *(City of Newport free courts)*, Fitness Center *(Waterfront Fitness 846-3720)*, Museum *(R.I. Fisherman & Whale 849-1340 $2.50/1.50; Hammersmith Farm is about 1.5 mi. 846-0420)*, Cultural Attract *(The Mansions - The Elms is nearest $10/4 847-1000)*, Sightseeing *(Gateway Center: Trolley Tours 849-8005 or Viking Tours 847-6921)* **1-3 mi:** Horseback Riding *(Surprise Valley Farm 847-2660)* **3+ mi:** Golf Course *(Jamestown G.C. 423-9930, 5 mi.)*, Bowling *(Hi Way Bowl/Mini Golf, 4 mi.)*

Provisioning and General Services

Near: Provisioning Service, Convenience Store, Gourmet Shop *(Market on the Blvd. 848-2600)*, Delicatessen *(Sandwich Board 849-5358)*, Health Food, Wine/Beer *(Thames Street 847-0017)*, Liquor Store *(Wellington 846-9463)*, Fishmonger, Lobster Pound *(Aquidneck 846-0106)*, Bank/ATM, Post Office, Catholic Church, Protestant Church, Synagogue *(Touro 847-4794 oldest in North America)*, Beauty Salon, Dry Cleaners, Laundry, Bookstore *(Armchair Sailor 847-4252)*, Newsstand, Hardware Store *(One Stop 847-8460)*, Retail Shops, Copies Etc. **Under 1 mi:** Supermarket *(Stop & Shop 848-7200)*, Library *(847-8720)*, Pharmacy *(CVS 846-4990)* **1-3 mi:** Farmers' Market *(M. Wheatland Blvd. Sat 9am-1pm & Wed 2-6pm 849-7359)*

Transportation

OnCall: Taxi *(Cozy 846-2500)* **Near:** Bikes *(Newport Wheels 849-4400)*, Water Taxi, Rental Car *(Hertz 846-1645)*, Local Bus *(Trolley)* **Under 1 mi:** InterCity Bus *(Bonanza, P&B)*, Ferry Service *(to Providence)* **3+ mi:** Airport Limo *(Amtrak at Kingston, 17 mi.)* **Airport:** TF Green *(20 mi.)*

Medical Services

911 Service **OnSite:** Ambulance **Near:** Doctor *(Newport Internal Med & Cardiology 846-3800)*, Dentist **Under 1 mi:** Chiropractor *(Aquidneck Health Center 849-7011)*, Holistic Services *(Wave Lengths 849-4427)* **Hospital:** Newport 783-9718 *(1 mi.)*

Setting -- The southernmost marina, West Wind's "C" shaped facility is a bit on the edge of downtown Newport, but convenient to everything. This relatively new and nicely maintained facility is easily identified by the large number of megayachts that cluster around its outer docks. The Boat Dockside -- a large, aging, three level ship that houses occasional entertainment -- dominates the landside views.

Marina Notes -- Family owned and operated. Protected dockage for smaller vessels inside the "C". Service-oriented staff caters to transients and encourages large megayachts to 200 ft. Boats docked within the "C" are more protected. Those on the 350 feet of dockage that reaches out into the harbor will find it more exposed -- but much quieter. 100 amp, 3 phase. 24 hr, security and concierge service will arrange limos, taxis, reservations. Lovely heads, showers, laundromat, plus 3 bars and a highly rated restaurant. Readily available dock hands. Dealers for Cranchi boats from Italy. Off-season the outer docks are used for cruise ships. A main site for Newport International Boat Show in September.

Notable -- The West Deck restaurant offers several options: The Dining Room has white tablecloths and a warm, cozy atmosphere -- dining tables and an open bar surround the kitchen -(Wed-Sun, 6-10pm). Outside, The Deck is a tented area with a big bar and umbrellaed tables overlooking the marina, 7 days, (12 noon-10pm, Jun 20- LabDay). The West Deck Bar is well populated and has live jazz several nights a week. Onsite disco on weekends. Short walk to the nearest mansions; take the Yellow Trolley line to the more distant ones as well as to the southern end of the Cliff Walk.

PHOTOS ON CD-ROM: 8

Navigational Information

Lat: 41°28.831' **Long:** 071°19.010' **Tide:** 4 ft. **Current:** n/a **Chart:** 13223
Rep. Depths (*MLW*): Entry 22 ft. **Fuel Dock** n/a **Max Slip/Moor** 14 ft./-
Access: Fort Adams to starboard, then straight ahead

Marina Facilities *(In Season/Off Season)*

Fuel: No
Slips: 30 Total, 20 Transient **Max LOA:** 185 ft. **Max Beam:** n/a
Rate *(per ft.)*: **Day** $4.00/Inq. **Week** Inq. **Month** Inq.
Power: 30 amp Incl., **50 amp** Incl., **100 amp** Incl., **200 amp** n/a
Cable TV: No **Dockside Phone:** Yes, a total of 7 lines for all boats
Dock Type: Wood, Alongside, Fixed
Moorings: 0 Total, 0 Transient **Launch:** n/a
Rate: Day n/a **Week** n/a **Month** n/a
Heads: 2 Toilet(s), 2 Shower(s)
Laundry: None **Pay Phones:** No
Pump-Out: OnCall, 2 Port **Fee:** $15 **Closed Heads:** Yes

Marina Operations

Owner/Manager: Bill McGinn **Dockmaster:** Same
In-Season: May-Oct, 8am-8pm **Off-Season:** Nov-Apr, Closed
After-Hours Arrival: Call Ahead
Reservations: Yes **Credit Cards:** Visa/MC, Cash or Checks
Discounts: None
Pets: Welcome **Handicap Access:** No

Casey's Marina

PO Box 187; Spring Wharf; Newport, RI 02840

Tel: (401) 848-5945 **VHF: Monitor** 9 **Talk** 68
Fax: (401) 849-9209 **Alternate Tel:** n/a
Email: n/a **Web:** n/a
Nearest Town: Newport *(0 mi.)* **Tourist Info:** (401) 849-8048

Marina Services and Boat Supplies

Services - Docking Assistance, Trash Pick-Up, Megayacht Facilities, 3 Phase **Communication -** Mail & Package Hold, Phone Messages, Data Ports *(phone lines dockside)*, FedEx, AirBorne, UPS, Express Mail *(Sat Del)* **Supplies - OnSite:** Ice *(Block, Cube)* **Near:** Ships' Store *(JT's Chandlery 846-7256, Newport Nautical 847-3933)*, Bait/Tackle *(Saltwater Edge 842-0062)*, CNG *(Oldport 847-9109)* **1-3 mi:** West Marine *(841-9880)*, Propane *(U-Haul 847-3219)*

Boatyard Services

OnSite: Crane **Nearest Yard:** The Newport Shipyard (401) 846-6000

Restaurants and Accommodations

Near: Restaurant *(Scales & Shells 846-3474, D $10-42)*, *(Café Zelda 849-4082, D $10-20)*, *(The West Deck 847-3610, D $15-35)*, Lite Fare *(Gary's 847-9480, B $2-6, L $2-6)*, *(The Deck L $5-18, D $5-18)*, Inn/B&B *(Admiral Fitzroy 848-8000, $85-230)* **Under 1 mi:** Inn/B&B *(Cliffside Inn 847-1811, $235-550)*, *(Castle Hill Inn 849-3800, $255-600)*

Recreation and Entertainment

Near: Fitness Center *(Waterfront 846-3720)*, Jogging Paths, Roller Blade/Bike Paths, Video Arcade *(Ryan Family 846-5774)*, Park *(Aquidneck)*, Sightseeing *(Newport Historical Society Walking Tours 846-0813 $7 - or follow the signs on Historic Hill)*, Special Events *(Jazz & Folk Festivals at Ft. Adams - dinghy)* **Under 1 mi:** Beach *(King Park)*, Picnic Area, Grills, Playground, Tennis Courts *(Casino at Int'l. Tennis Hall of Fame $35/1.5 hr. 846-4567 or Newport's free courts)*, Movie Theater *(3 screen Opera House 847-3456)*, Video Rental *(Bellevue 847-9330)*, Cultural Attract *(Historic Homes and Mansions)*, Galleries *(Bellevue Ave. galleries)* **1-3 mi:** Horseback Riding *(Surprise Valley Farm 847-2660)*, Museum *(Ft. Adams - Museum of Yachting 847-1018 $3)* **3+ mi:** Golf Course *(Jamestown 423-9930, 5 mi.)*, Bowling *(Hi Way 849-9990, 4 mi.)*

Provisioning and General Services

Near: Convenience Store, Gourmet Shop *(Market on the Blvd. 848-2600)*, Delicatessen *(Sandwich Board 849-5358)*, Health Food, Wine/Beer *(Wellington Sq. 846-9463)*, Liquor Store *(Thames St. 847-0017)*, Bakery, Fishmonger, Lobster Pound *(Aquidneck 846-0106)*, Bank/ATM, Post Office, Catholic Church, Protestant Church, Synagogue *(Touro - oldest in North America)*, Library, Beauty Salon, Barber Shop, Dry Cleaners, Laundry, Bookstore *(Armchair Sailor 847-5242)*, Newsstand, Retail Shops, Copies Etc. **Under 1 mi:** Supermarket *(Stop & Shop 848-7200)*, Farmers' Market *(Marcus Wheatland Blvd. 849-7359 Wed 2-6pm, Sat 9am-1pm)*, Pharmacy *(CVS 849-8058)*, Hardware Store *(Newport 847-7224)*

Transportation

OnCall: Taxi *(Cozy Cab 846-2500)* **Near:** Bikes *(Newport Wheels 849-4400)*, Water Taxi, Rental Car *(Hertz 846-1645)*, Local Bus *(Trolley)* **Under 1 mi:** InterCity Bus *(Bonanza, P&B, Greyhound)*, Ferry Service *(to Providence, Goat Island and Jamestown)* **3+ mi:** Rail *(Amtrak in Kingston - bus to station, 17 mi.)* **Airport:** TF Green *(20 mi.)*

Medical Services

911 Service **OnCall:** Ambulance **Near:** Doctor, Dentist, Holistic Services **Under 1 mi:** Chiropractor **Hospital:** Newport 783-9718 *(1 mi.)*

Setting -- Casey's Marina, just north of West Wind, is the temporary home to some of the largest megayachts visiting Newport. From the outermost docks, the views are of the harbor, chock-ablock with a wide variety of vessels. From the inner docks, views are of other very large, mostly impeccable yachts. Landside there is very little to see and virtually no facilities.

Marina Notes -- Because it was designed and built with transient megayachts in mind, there are very few actual slips -- most of the dockage is "alongside". The owners also recognized that most large yachts are usually set up as self-contained worlds. Consequently, Casey's has very limited physical facilities, but it does offer some concierge-type services. A storeroom holds advance mail and packages. They take messages and focus on the needs of yacht crews. There are 7 phone lines to be shared among the yachts. There are some smaller, interior slips which are seasonal only. Same management as Brown and Howard's Wharf.

Notable -- This end of Newport is a bit quieter and quite convenient to a couple of the mansions. The others are accessible via the Yellow #67 Trolley. The "action" part of town is an easy walk. Nearby West Wind has an onsite restaurant and the well-reviewed and very pricey classic French restaurant, Bouchard is within walking distance. The International Yacht Restoration School is close by (848-5777) - watch shipwrights restore classic sail and power vessels, tour the 1885 schooner Coronet. Or take a trolley out to Fort Adams and tour the Museum of Yachting (847-1018) 7 days 10am-5pm, $4/3/6 families.

PHOTOS ON CD-ROM: 5

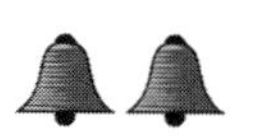

Brown & Howard Wharf Marina

21 Brown & Howard Wharf, 411 Thames St.; Newport, RI 02840

Tel: (401) 846-5100 **VHF: Monitor** 9 **Talk** 68
Fax: (401) 751-7088 **Alternate Tel:** (401) 274-6611
Email: info@paolinoproperties.com **Web:** www.paolinoproperties.com
Nearest Town: Newport *(0 mi.)* **Tourist Info:** (401) 521-5000

Navigational Information

Lat: 41°28.844' **Long:** 071°18.969' **Tide:** 4 ft. **Current:** n/a **Chart:** 13223
Rep. Depths (*MLW*): Entry 22 ft. **Fuel Dock** 20 ft. **Max Slip/Moor** 20 ft./-
Access: Ft. Adams to starboard, straight ahead to 3rd set of docks heading N

Marina Facilities *(In Season/Off Season)*

Fuel: Diesel
Slips: 20 Total, 20 Transient **Max LOA:** 250 ft. **Max Beam:** n/a
Rate *(per ft.)*: **Day** $3.75/Inq. **Week** Inq. **Month** Inq.
Power: 30 amp $15, **50 amp** $25, **100 amp** $40, **200 amp** n/a
Cable TV: Yes, Incl. **Dockside Phone:** Yes, Incl.
Dock Type: Floating, Fixed
Moorings: 0 Total, 0 Transient **Launch:** n/a
Rate: Day n/a **Week** n/a **Month** n/a
Heads: None
Laundry: None **Pay Phones:** Yes
Pump-Out: OnCall, Full Service, 2 Port **Fee:** n/a **Closed Heads:** Yes

Marina Operations

Owner/Manager: Joseph R. Paolino, Jr. **Dockmaster:** Same
In-Season: May-Oct 31, 8am-8pm **Off-Season:** Nov 1-Apr 30, Closed
After-Hours Arrival: Call in advance
Reservations: Preferred **Credit Cards:** Visa/MC, Dscvr, Cash or Check
Discounts: None
Pets: No **Handicap Access:** Yes, Docks

Marina Services and Boat Supplies

Services - Docking Assistance, Trash Pick-Up, Megayacht Facilities, 3 Phase **Communication -** Mail & Package Hold, Data Ports *(Tel Dockside)*, FedEx, AirBorne, UPS, Express Mail *(Sat Del)* **Supplies - OnSite:** Ice *(Block, Cube)* **Near:** Ships' Store *(Newport Nautical 847-3933)*, Bait/Tackle *(Saltwater Edge 842-0062)*, CNG *(Oldport 847-9109)* **Under 1 mi:** Propane *(U-Haul 847-3219)* **1-3 mi:** West Marine *(841-9880)*

Boatyard Services

OnCall: Electrical Repairs, Electronics Repairs, Rigger, Sail Loft, Air Conditioning, Refrigeration **Under 1 mi:** Travelift, Railway, Engine mechanic *(diesel)*, Hull Repairs, Propeller Repairs, Inflatable Repairs. **Nearest Yard:** Newport Shipyard (401) 846-6000

Restaurants and Accommodations

OnSite: Restaurant *(Amici Trattoria 847-6070)* **Near:** Restaurant *(White Horse Tavern 849-3600, L $7-15, D $25-35)*, *(The Mooring 846-2260, L $7-15, D $15-30)*, *(Seafare's American 849-9188, L $6-12, D $11-19)*, *(Elizabeth's 846-6862, across the street)*, *(Red Parrot 487-3800, L $5-15, D $10-24)*, Seafood Shack *(Rhode Island Quahog 848-2330)*, Pizzeria *(Via Via 846-4075, delivers)*, Hotel *(Newport Bay Club 849-8600)*, Inn/B&B *(Admiral Fitzroy Inn 848-8018)*, *(Vanderbilt Hall 846-6200, $100-450)*

Recreation and Entertainment

OnSite: Boat Rentals *(Newport Kayaks 849-4400)* **Near:** Fitness Center *(Waterfront Fitness 846-3720)*, Jogging Paths, Movie Theater *(Jane Pickens)*, Video Rental *(Bellevue 847-9330)*, Video Arcade, Park, Museum *(Breakers 847-1000 & Chateau-Sur-Mer)*, Cultural Attract, Special Events *(Jazz & Folk Festivals)*, Galleries **Under 1 mi:** Dive Shop *(Northeast Diving 841-0446)*, Tennis Courts *(Nat'l Tennis Club 849-6672)*, Sightseeing *(Cliff Walk)* **1-3 mi:** Bowling *(Hi-Way Bowl & Mini Golf 849-9990)* **3+ mi:** Golf Course *(Jamestown G.C. 423-9930, 5 mi.)*

Provisioning and General Services

Near: Provisioning Service, Convenience Store, Gourmet Shop *(Market On the Blvd 848-2600)*, Delicatessen *(Sandwich Board 849-5358)*, Health Food, Wine/Beer *(Spring Street 846-0959)*, Liquor Store *(Aidinoffs 846-7001)*, Bakery, Green Grocer, Fishmonger, Lobster Pound *(Aquidneck 846-0106)*, Bank/ATM, Post Office, Catholic Church, Protestant Church, Synagogue, Library *(847-8720)*, Beauty Salon, Barber Shop, Dry Cleaners, Laundry, Bookstore *(Thames Street Books 849-5589)*, Newsstand, Hardware Store *(Newport 847-7224)*, Florist, Clothing Store, Retail Shops, Copies Etc. *(849-3820)* **Under 1 mi:** Supermarket *(Stop & Shop 848-7200)*, Farmers' Market *(behind Salvation Café Wed 2-6pm, Sat 9am-1pm 849-7359)*, Pharmacy *(CVS 849-8058)*

Transportation

OnCall: Taxi *(Cozy Cab 846-2500)* **Near:** Bikes *(Newport Wheels 849-4400 8:30am-6:30pm)*, Water Taxi, Rental Car *(Hertz 846-1645)*, Local Bus *(Trolley)*, InterCity Bus *(Bonanza, P&B)*, Ferry Service *(Providence)* **3+ mi:** Rail *(Kingston, 17 mi.)* **Airport:** TF Green *(20 mi.)*

Medical Services

911 Service **OnCall:** Ambulance **Near:** Doctor *(Aquidneck Medical 847-2290)*, Dentist, Holistic Services *(Body Central 848-5885)* **Under 1 mi:** Chiropractor *(Aquidneck 849-7011)* **Hospital:** Newport 783-9718 *(1 mi.)*

Setting -- This big boat marina is conveniently located at the southern end of the harbor, the third set of docks heading north. It is clearly recognizable by the large number of megayachts hanging off its very well maintained docks -- which surround a large cement wharf. The facility is clean, neat and attractive, with a Newport rarity - lots of parking. Landside, just steps from the wharf is one of Newport's main thorofares - Thames Street.

Marina Notes -- Marina caters to 50-250 ft yachts. Its docks can handle boats this size and there is adequate power (100 AMP/3 phase, 20V power) dockside to meet their requirements. In addition find telephone, cable, water, ice, diesel fuel, boat hauling, and winter storage. There is little else here except dockage, the assumption being that larger yachts don't need outside facilities. Dockmaster's direct line is 640-4458. Nov-Apr Management address: 76 Dorrance Street, Providence, RI 02903 Tel: 401 274-6611, Fax: 401 751-7088.

Notable -- All of Newport is very, very convenient. Amici Trattoria is right on the wharf (Contemporary Italian cuisine, dinner only Mon Thu Sun 5-9pm, Fri & Sat 5-10pm), along with Gelati per Tutti, an ice-cream shop, and Newport Wheels -- which rents bikes ($5/hr., $20/day, $70/wk.), scooters ($35/hr., $150/day) and kayaks ($30-40/half-day, $45-50/day). Elizabeth's Diningroom is across the street (family style - entrées easily serve two), and within minutes are dozens of restaurants, historic sites, pubs, water sports, great provisioning, and tons of retail shops. Most crews love Newport, and Brown & Howard puts them right in the thick of things -- for restocking, supplies, parts or services, or just some R&R.

PHOTOS ON CD-ROM: 9

Navigational Information
Lat: 41°28.889' **Long:** 071°18.955' **Tide:** 4 ft. **Current:** n/a **Chart:** 13223
Rep. Depths (*MLW*): Entry 18 ft. **Fuel Dock** n/a **Max Slip/Moor** 10 ft./-
Access: Fourth set of docks in Newport Harbor, east shore

Marina Facilities *(In Season/Off Season)*
Fuel: No
Slips: 45 Total, 8 Transient **Max LOA:** 125 ft. **Max Beam:** n/a
Rate *(per ft.)*: **Day** $3.00/Inq. **Week** Inq. **Month** Inq.
Power: 30 amp $6, **50 amp** $10, **100 amp** n/a, **200 amp** n/a
Cable TV: No **Dockside Phone:** No
Dock Type: Wood, Pilings, Alongside, Floating, Fixed
Moorings: 0 Total, 0 Transient **Launch:** n/a, Dinghy Dock
Rate: Day n/a **Week** n/a **Month** n/a
Heads: 4 Toilet(s), 4 Shower(s)
Laundry: 1 Washer(s), 1 Dryer(s) **Pay Phones:** Yes
Pump-Out: OnCall, 2 Port **Fee:** $15* **Closed Heads:** Yes

Marina Operations
Owner/Manager: Doreen Halliwell **Dockmaster:** n/a
In-Season: May-Oct, 8am-8pm **Off-Season:** Oct 20-Apr 30, Closed
After-Hours Arrival: Call ahead
Reservations: Yes **Credit Cards:** Visa/MC, Amex
Discounts: None
Pets: Welcome, Dog Walk Area **Handicap Access:** No

Newport Marina

Lee's Wharf; Newport, RI 02840

Tel: (401) 849-2293 **VHF: Monitor** 9 **Talk** 72
Fax: n/a **Alternate Tel:** (401) 849-2293
Email: n/a **Web:** n/a
Nearest Town: Newport *(0 mi.)* **Tourist Info:** (401) 849-8048

Marina Services and Boat Supplies
Services - Docking Assistance, Trash Pick-Up, Dock Carts, Megayacht Facilities **Communication -** FedEx, AirBorne, UPS, Express Mail **Supplies - OnSite:** Ice *(Block, Cube)* **Near:** Ships' Store *(JT's 846-7356)*, CNG *(Oldport 847-9109)* **Under 1 mi:** Bait/Tackle *(Saltwater Edge 842-0062)* **1-3 mi:** West Marine *(841-9880)*, Propane *(U Haul 847-3219)*

Boatyard Services
OnSite: Compound, Wash & Wax **OnCall:** Rigger, Brightwork, Air Conditioning, Refrigeration, Divers, Interior Cleaning, Woodworking, Inflatable Repairs **Near:** Crane, Engine mechanic *(diesel)*, Launching Ramp, Electronic Sales, Electronics Repairs, Hull Repairs, Bottom Cleaning, Upholstery, Yacht Interiors. **Nearest Yard:** Newport Shipyard (401) 846-6000

Restaurants and Accommodations
OnSite: Restaurant *(Vincent's on the Pier 847-3645, L $8-19, D $16-29, Lounge $8-12, Sunset Specials $11-14)* **Near:** Restaurant *(Salas 846-8772, D $6-22), (Bouchards 846-0123), (Scales & Shells 846-3474, D $10-42, Upper price range at Upscales upstairs)*, Seafood Shack *(West Deck 847-3610)*, Pizzeria *(Firehouse 946-1199)*, Inn/B&B *(Spring Street 847-4767, $120-280), (Banister John 846-0059)* **Under 1 mi:** Restaurant *(Yesterdays 847-0116)*, Snack Bar *(Gary's)*, Hotel *(Marriott 849-1000, $275-500), (Newport Harbor 847-9000, $120-680)*

Recreation and Entertainment
OnSite: Pool, Picnic Area, Grills **Near:** Beach *(King Park)*, Playground, Jogging Paths, Boat Rentals, Fishing Charter, Movie Theater *(Jane Pickens 846-5252)*, Video Arcade, Park, Museum *(Naval War College Museum 848-8306)*, Cultural Attract *(Newport Playhouse 848-7529)*, Special Events **Under 1 mi:** Tennis Courts *(Nat'l Tennis Club 849-6672)*, Fitness Center *(Waterfront Fitness 846-3720)*, Video Rental *(Bellevue 847-9330)* **1-3 mi:** Sightseeing *(Fort Adams)* **3+ mi:** Golf Course *(Jamestown 423-9930, 5 mi.)*, Bowling *(Hi Way Bowl/Mini Golf 849-9990, 4 mi.)*

Provisioning and General Services
Near: Convenience Store, Delicatessen *(Sandwich Board 849-5358)*, Health Food, Wine/Beer, Liquor Store *(Thames St. 847-0017)*, Bakery, Green Grocer, Bank/ATM, Post Office, Catholic Church, Protestant Church, Synagogue, Library *(847-8720)*, Beauty Salon, Barber Shop, Dry Cleaners, Laundry, Bookstore *(Thames Street Books 849-5589)*, Florist, Clothing Store, Retail Shops, Department Store, Copies Etc. *(Printing & Copying 849-3820)* **Under 1 mi:** Supermarket *(Stop & Shop 848-7200)*, Gourmet Shop, Farmers' Market *(behind Salvation Café Wed 2-6pm, Sat 9am-1pm 849-7359)*, Fishmonger, Lobster Pound *(Aquidneck 846-0106)*, Pharmacy *(CVS 846-4990)*, Hardware Store *(Newport 849-9442)*

Transportation
OnCall: Rental Car *(Enterprise 849-3939)*, Taxi *(Yellow Cab 846-1500)* **Near:** Ferry Service *(Providence)* **Under 1 mi:** Bikes *(Ten Speed 847-5609)*, InterCity Bus *(Greyhound 846-1820)* **3+ mi:** Rail *(Kingston, 17 mi.)* **Airport:** TF Green *(20 mi)*

Medical Services
911 Service **OnCall:** Ambulance **Near:** Doctor, Dentist, Holistic Services **Under 1 mi:** Chiropractor **Hospital:** Newport 783-9718 *(1 mi.)*

Setting -- The fourth set of docks, heading north along the eastern Newport shore, this facility offers considerable convenience while being a bit out of the madding crowd. Look for the bright red tops on the pilings. On one pier, an inviting pool overlooks the clean, well maintained docks, enlivened by the occasional flower pot. An adjacent pier offers deck dining at umbrellaed tables -- part of the onsite restaurant. And a blue and white awning shelters a dockside bar.

Marina Notes -- A small picnic area with table, umbrella and grill sits at the back of the property. Entertainment on weekends. Only outside dockside pool in Newport. Heads with showers and separate dressing rooms. Stationary pump-out available at Goat Island Marina, Newport Shipyard, Long Wharf, Newport Yachting Center, Newport Y.C., Ida Lewis Y.C. *Harbor Sanitation has two pump-out boats, 7 days, 8am-7pm, cell # 474-3044, Ch.9, $15 first 30 gals, $5 each additional 30 gals. Harbormaster Tim Mills is at 401 848-6492, Ch.16 & 14.

Notable -- Landside, Newport Marina is just off Lower (South) Thames Street - lined with shops, restaurants and history. Yellow Trolley line makes the mansions easily accessible - the Astors' Beechwood 846-3772, the Vanderbilts' Belcourt Castle 846-0669, 10am-4pm $10/8 and The Breakers 10am-5pm $15/4 847-1000. Comb. tickets available. Rough Point, Doris Duke's dramatic ocean estate, is now open as well -- Tue-Sat 849-7300. Limited tickets at Gateway Center 845-9130. Or take a trolley or ferry to Ft. Adams Park which sports a small, clean beach, an historic fort, the Museum of Yachting (847-1018) $3, $6 family, and great views of Newport. Fort Adams is the site of the famous music, folk and jazz festivals.

PHOTOS ON CD-ROM: 6

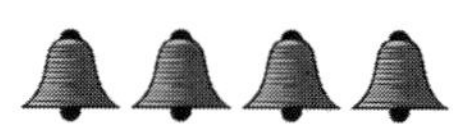

Christie's Marina

RI - NEWPORT & NARRAGANSETT BAY

Christie's Marina

Off 351 Thames Street; Newport, RI 02840

Tel: (401) 848-7950 **VHF: Monitor** 9 **Talk** 9
Fax: (401) 847-4970 **Alternate Tel:** (401) 847-5400
Email: info@christiesofnewport.com **Web:** www.christiesofnewport.com
Nearest Town: Newport *(0 mi.)* **Tourist Info:** (401) 845-9123

Navigational Information

Lat: 41°29.039' **Long:** 071°18.985' **Tide:** 4 ft. **Current:** n/a **Chart:** 13223
Rep. Depths (*MLW*): Entry 10 ft. **Fuel Dock** n/a **Max Slip/Moor** 14 ft./-
Access: Straight into Newport Harbor, watch for Christie's sign

Marina Facilities *(In Season/Off Season)*

Fuel: No
Slips: 25 Total, 25 Transient **Max LOA:** 200 ft. **Max Beam:** n/a
Rate *(per ft.)*: **Day** $2.00/Inq. **Week** $14 **Month** Inq.
Power: 30 amp $5, **50 amp** $5, **100 amp** $10, **200 amp** n/a
Cable TV: No **Dockside Phone:** No
Dock Type: Wood, Long Fingers, Pilings, Alongside, Fixed
Moorings: 0 Total, 0 Transient **Launch:** n/a
Rate: Day n/a **Week** n/a **Month** n/a
Heads: 13 Toilet(s), 3 Shower(s)
Laundry: None **Pay Phones:** Yes
Pump-Out: OnCall, 2 Port **Fee:** $15 **Closed Heads:** Yes

Marina Operations

Owner/Manager: Mary O'Donohoe **Dockmaster:** Chris Connerton
In-Season: May-Oct, 8am-10pm **Off-Season:** Oct-May, Closed
After-Hours Arrival: Call in advance
Reservations: Yes **Credit Cards:** Visa/MC, Dscvr, Din, Amex
Discounts: None
Pets: Welcome **Handicap Access:** No

Marina Services and Boat Supplies

Services - Docking Assistance, Concierge, Security *(Yes)*, Dock Carts, Megayacht Facilities **Communication -** Mail & Package Hold, Phone Messages, Fax in/out, Data Ports, FedEx, AirBorne, UPS, Express Mail **Supplies - OnSite:** Ice *(Block)* **Near:** Ships' Store *(JT's 846-7356)*, CNG *(Oldport 847-9109)* **1-3 mi:** West Marine *(841-9880)*, Bait/Tackle *(Saltwater Edge 842-0062)*, Propane *(U Haul 847-3219)*

Boatyard Services

OnSite: Divers, Compound, Wash & Wax, Interior Cleaning **Near:** Travelift, Engine mechanic *(gas, diesel)*, Electrical Repairs, Electronics Repairs, Rigger, Sail Loft. **Nearest Yard:** American Shipyard (401) 846-6000

Restaurants and Accommodations

OnSite: Restaurant *(Christie's 847-5400, L $5-13, D $19-28, Pub $6-13, Kids' menu)*, *(Sabina Doyle's Irish Pub 849-4466, L $6-8, D $14-18)*, Raw Bar *(Christie's On Dock L $6-13)*, Inn/B&B *(Inn on the Harbor 849-6789, $150-250)*, *(Harborside Inn 846-6600)* **Near:** Restaurant *(Cheeky Monkey 845-9494)*, *(Alva Restaurant D $19-30, in Vanderbilt Hall)*, *(Canfield House 847-0416, D $15-25)*, *(Percy's Bistro 849-7895, D $16-33)*, Pizzeria *(Via Via 846-4075, delivers)*, Inn/B&B *(Vanderbilt Hall 846-6200, $220-800)*, *(Mill Street 849-5500, $75-325)*, *(Spring Street 847-4767, $120-280)*

Recreation and Entertainment

Near: Playground, Fitness Center, Boat Rentals *(Newport Boat Rentals 842-0297)*, Fishing Charter, Movie Theater, Video Arcade, Park, Museum *(Brick Market Museum Of Newport History 841-8770)*, Cultural Attract *(Newport Repertory Theater 847-8412)*, Sightseeing *(The Mansions 847-1000, Cliff Walk)*, Special Events *(Music festivals)*, Galleries **Under 1 mi:** Video Rental *(Broadway Joes 848-5859)* **1-3 mi:** Beach *(Easton's 848-6491)*, Tennis Courts *(Nat'l Tennis Club 849-6672)*, Bowling *(Hi Way Bowl/Mini Golf 849-9990)* **3+ mi:** Golf Course *(Jamestown G.C. 423-9930, 4 mi.)*

Provisioning and General Services

OnSite: Newsstand **OnCall:** Dry Cleaners, Laundry **Near:** Convenience Store, Delicatessen *(Sandwich Board 849-5358)*, Health Food, Wine/Beer, Liquor Store *(Fifth Ward 849-5690)*, Bakery, Fishmonger, Lobster Pound *(Aquidneck 846-0106)*, Bank/ATM, Catholic Church, Protestant Church, Synagogue *(Touro 847-4794)*, Library *(847-8720)*, Beauty Salon, Bookstore *(Thames Street 849-5589, Armchair Sailor 847-1219)*, Hardware Store *(One Stop 847-8460)*, Retail Shops, Department Store *(Cherry Web)*, Copies Etc. *(Printing & Copying 849-3820)* **Under 1 mi:** Supermarket *(Stop & Shop 848-7200)*, Gourmet Shop *(Market On The Boulevard 848-2600)*, Farmers' Market *(M. Wheatland Blvd. Sat 9am-1pm, Wed 2-6pm 849-7359)*, Pharmacy *(CVS 846-4990)* **1-3 mi:** Buying Club *(BJ's)*

Transportation

OnCall: Rental Car *(Enterprise 849-3939)*, Taxi *(Yellow Cab 846-1500)*, Airport Limo *(Als Classic Limo 846-5562)* **Near:** Bikes *(Newport Wheels 849-4400)*, Local Bus *(NRTA)*, InterCity Bus *(Greyhound 846-1820)* **3+ mi:** Rail *(Kingston Amtrak, 18 mi.)* **Airport:** TF Green *(20 mi.)*

Medical Services

911 Service **OnCall:** Ambulance **Near:** Holistic Services *(Wave Lengths 849-4427)* **Under 1 mi:** Doctor *(Newport Family 849-6852)*, Dentist, Chiropractor, Veterinarian **Hospital:** Newport 783-9718 *(1-3 mi)*

Setting -- The large "Christie's" sign on the side of the original waterside building, along with the blue and white striped pavilions and gaggle of megayachts, clearly mark this marina. Christies of Newport is a charming complex, including a hotel, inn, six dining areas, three bars and a marina, sprawling from wharf's edge to the street. The atmosphere is festive, noisy, and perpetual party.

Marina Notes -- Handles at least 5 megayachts on the outside and "T" head with slip dockage for slightly smaller vessels on the inside. Established in 1945, Christie's is Newport's oldest waterfront restaurant. The Yachtsmen's Lounge (lunch and pub food) and waterside dock have been the site of many America's Cup celebrations. Live music for listening/dancing year 'round, 7 nights 6pm-1am. Lunch outside on deck and inside in pub 11:30am-3:30pm. Dinner outside on deck and inside in the main, white tablecloth restaurant 3:30-10pm. Raw bar on porch overlooking the harbor activity. Can accommodate large group events; tour/group/banquet menus $17-35. Three attractive full bathrooms have been set aside exclusively for marina guests.

Notable -- Across the Harbor are the Jazz, Irish, and Folk Festivals. Across the road is famous JT's Chandlery 846-7256. Anne Street Pier and public dinghy dock is the next wharf south, along with Newport Boat Rentals - boats and kayaks. Mansions are easily accessible by foot, Yellow trolley, or cab. International Yacht Restoration School 848-5777 is down the street. Black Ships Festival on Bellevue Ave. in July. Or stroll three-mile Cliff Walk to Bailey's Beach.

PHOTOS ON CD-ROM: 8

Navigational Information
Lat: 41°29.108' **Long:** 071°19.059' **Tide:** 4 ft. **Current:** n/a **Chart:** 13223
Rep. Depths (*MLW*): Entry 22 ft. **Fuel Dock** 17 ft. **Max Slip/Moor** 17 ft./-
Access: Narragansett Bay to Newport Harbor; look for large white water tank

Marina Facilities *(In Season/Off Season)*
Fuel: *Texaco* - Gasoline, Diesel, High-Speed Pumps
Slips: 100 Total, 60 Transient **Max LOA:** 180 ft. **Max Beam:** n/a
Rate *(per ft.)*: **Day** $3.50/$2.50 **Week** Inq. **Month** Inq.
Power: 30 amp $8, **50 amp** $16, **100 amp** $45, **200 amp** n/a
Cable TV: No **Dockside Phone:** No
Dock Type: Wood, Long Fingers, Alongside, Floating
Moorings: 0 Total, 0 Transient **Launch:** n/a
Rate: Day n/a **Week** n/a **Month** n/a
Heads: 8 Toilet(s), 8 Shower(s) *(with dressing rooms)*
Laundry: 2 Washer(s), 2 Dryer(s) **Pay Phones:** Yes, 2
Pump-Out: OnSite, Full Service, 1 Central **Fee:** n/a **Closed Heads:** Yes

Marina Operations
Owner/Manager: n/a **Dockmaster:** Chuck Moffitt
In-Season: MidMay-MidOct, 8am-8pm **Off-Season:** LateOct-May, 9am-5pm
After-Hours Arrival: Call in advance
Reservations: Yes **Credit Cards:** Visa/MC, Dscvr, Amex, Tex
Discounts: Boat/US; Restrictions **Dockage:** 25% **Fuel:** $.10g **Repair:** n/a
Pets: Welcome, Dog Walk Area **Handicap Access:** No

Newport Yachting Center

PO Box 550; Commercial Wharf; Newport, RI 02840

Tel: (800) 653-3625 **VHF: Monitor** 9 **Talk** n/a
Fax: (401) 847-9262 **Alternate Tel:** (401) 846-1600
Email: info@newportyachtingcenter.com **Web:** newportyachtingcenter.com
Nearest Town: Newport *(0 mi.)* **Tourist Info:** (401) 845-9123

Marina Services and Boat Supplies
Services - Docking Assistance, Concierge, Trash Pick-Up, Dock Carts, Megayacht Facilities, 3 Phase **Communication -** Mail & Package Hold, Phone Messages, Fax in/out, FedEx, AirBorne, UPS, Express Mail *(Sat Del)* **Supplies - OnSite:** Ice *(Block, Cube)*, CNG *(Oldport 847-9109)* **Near:** Ships' Store *(JT's Chandlery 846-7256)* **Under 1 mi:** Bait/Tackle *(Saltwater 842-0062)* **1-3 mi:** West Marine *(841-9880)*, Propane *(U Haul 847-3219)*

Boatyard Services
OnCall: Electrical Repairs, Electronics Repairs, Rigger, Brightwork, Refrigeration **Under 1 mi:** Hull Repairs, Bottom Cleaning. **Nearest Yard:** Newport Shipyard (401) 846-6000

Restaurants and Accommodations
OnSite: Restaurant *(The Mooring 846-2260, L $8-28, D $16-40, no res. Sat)*, *(Smokehouse Café 848-9800, L $6-16, D $6-16)*, *(22 Bowen's Wine Bar & Grille 841-8844, L $5-14, D $24-35, Raw Bar $10-15)* **Near:** Restaurant *(Salas 846-8772, D $7-20)*, *(Le Bistro 849-7778, L $6-16, D $10-28)*, Pizzeria *(Via Via 846-4075, delivers)*, Hotel *(Marriott 849-1000, $275-500)*, Inn/B&B *(Mill Street 849-9500, $75-325)*, *(Harborside Inn 846-6600)* **Under 1 mi:** Hotel *(Viking 847-3300, $100-400)* **3+ mi:** Restaurant *(Castle Hill Inn L $10-18, D $25-39, 4 mi.)*, Inn/B&B *(Castle Hill $100-250, 3.5 mi.)*

Recreation and Entertainment
Near: Pool *(at Marriott)*, Playground, Fitness Center *(Marriott)*, Jogging Paths, Boat Rentals, Movie Theater, Park, Cultural Attract *(Newport Playhouse 848-7529)*, Special Events *(Int'l Boat Show, Used Boat Show, Great Chowder Cook-Off, Oktoberfest)* **Under 1 mi:** Tennis Courts *(Nat'l Tennis Club 849-6672)*, Video Rental *(Bellevue 847-9330)* **1-3 mi:** Beach, Museum *(Naval War College 848-8306)*, Sightseeing *(Fort Adams)* **3+ mi:** Golf Course *(Jamestown G.C. 423-9930, 4 mi.)*, Bowling *(Hi Way Bowl/Mini Golf 849-9990, 3.5 mi.)*

Provisioning and General Services
Near: Convenience Store *(JD 842-0545)*, Gourmet Shop, Delicatessen *(Sandwich Board 849-5358)*, Wine/Beer, Liquor Store *(Spring Street 846-0959)*, Fishmonger, Lobster Pound *(Aquidneck 846-0106)*, Bank/ATM, Post Office, Catholic Church, Synagogue *(Touro 847-4794)*, Library *(847-8720)*, Beauty Salon **Under 1 mi:** Supermarket *(Stop & Shop 848-7200)*, Bakery, Farmers' Market *(Salvation Café Wed 2-6pm, Sat 9am-1pm 849-7359)*, Meat Market, Dry Cleaners, Laundry, Bookstore *(Mind's Eye 849-7333, Armchair Sailor 847-1219)*, Pharmacy *(CVS 846-4990)*, Newsstand, Hardware Store *(Newport 849-9442)*, Department Store *(Wal-Mart 848-8341)*, Copies Etc. *(Printing & Copying 849-3820)* **1-3 mi:** Buying Club *(BJ's 848-9242)*

Transportation
OnSite: Bikes **OnCall:** Rental Car *(Cartemps USA 846-4458, Enterprise 849-3939)*, Taxi *(Yellow Cab 846-1500)* **Near:** Local Bus *(NRTA 781-9400 www.ripta.com)*, InterCity Bus *(Greyhound 846-1820)*, Ferry Service *(Providence, Jamestown)* **3+ mi:** Rail *(Kingston Amtrak, 18 mi.)* **Airport:** TF Green *(20 mi.)*

Medical Services
911 Service **OnCall:** Ambulance **Under 1 mi:** Doctor *(Newport Fam 849-6852)*, Chiropractor *(Aquidneck 849-7011)*, Veterinarian *(Newport 849-3401)* **1-3 mi:** Dentist **Hospital:** Newport 783-9718 *(1 mi.)*

Setting -- The fifth set of docks heading north, centrally located N.Y.C. is the largest facility in Newport. Its protected docks fan out from a main wharf, which has an easily accessed fuel dock on its outer end. The expansive complex runs almost to America's Cup Avenue and includes two large permanent blue & white striped tents, an occasional additional one or two white ones, extensive parking, restaurants and an easily spotted large white water tank.

Marina Notes -- Guest-oriented, attentive staff offers concierge services and event planning. Complimentary passes to Newport Marriott Hotel's indoor and outdoor pools, sauna, and health club - 0.3 miles walk. Hosts many club cruises and rendezvous - boats are either racked (stern-to, gunwale to gunwale) or rafted (alongside, 2-3 deep), depending on space requirements (this explains its nickname -- "The Newport Parking Lot"). Three restaurants onsite (the Mooring's front deck has great views). Inviting heads, showers and laundry. Three-phase electric. Recycling receptacles. Largest dry storage facility in Newport. Extensive car parking $8/day marina guests, $16 others. Affiliated with Castle Hill Inn on Ocean Drive.

Notable -- The onsite Adirondack II, a 78-foot classically designed schooner built in 1999 offers day sails and accommodates 60, $23-30 call 846-3018. Onsite Mooring Restaurant's earlier incarnation was as N.Y. Yacht Club Station #6; it's open Mon-Fri 11:30am-9pm, Sat noon-10pm, Sun noon-9pm. Within a short walk, retail shops abound. RIPTA Red #62 and Orange #61 buses stop near gate, headed to Fort Adams, Cliff Walk North End and Easton's and Second Beaches. Some mansions are walkable; then pick up Yellow #67 trolley (which also goes to Cliff Walk South).

PHOTOS ON CD-ROM: 9

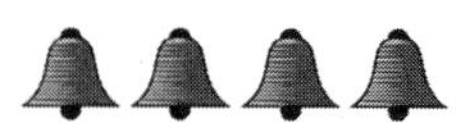

Bannister's Wharf

Bannister's Wharf; Newport, RI 02840

Tel: (401) 846-4500 **VHF: Monitor** 9 **Talk** 11
Fax: (401) 849-8750 **Alternate Tel:** (401) 846-4556
Email: bannisterswharf@msn.com **Web:** www.bannisterswharf.net
Nearest Town: Newport *(0 mi.)* **Tourist Info:** (401) 845-9123

Navigational Information

Lat: 41°29.180' **Long:** 071°19.023' **Tide:** 5 ft. **Current:** n/a **Chart:** 13223
Rep. Depths (*MLW*): Entry 16 ft. **Fuel Dock** 16 ft. **Max Slip/Moor** 16 ft./-
Access: Narragansett Bay to Newport, look for Bannister's Wharf sign

Marina Facilities *(In Season/Off Season)*

Fuel: *Various* - Slip-Side Fueling, Gasoline, Diesel, High-Speed Pumps
Slips: 30 Total, 30 Transient **Max LOA:** 245 ft. **Max Beam:** 28 ft.
Rate *(per ft.)*: **Day** $3.25/Inq.* **Week** Inq. **Month** Inq.
Power: 30 amp $8, **50 amp** $15, **100 amp** $30, **200 amp** n/a
Cable TV: No **Dockside Phone:** Yes, $5, 3 line(s) per day
Dock Type: Wood, Long Fingers, Short Fingers, Alongside, Floating, Fixed
Moorings: 0 Total, 0 Transient **Launch:** n/a
Rate: Day n/a **Week** n/a **Month** n/a
Heads: 2 Toilet(s), 2 Shower(s) *(with dressing rooms)*
Laundry: 1 Washer(s), 1 Dryer(s), Iron, Iron Board **Pay Phones:** Yes, 2
Pump-Out: OnCall, 2 Port **Fee:** $15 **Closed Heads:** Yes

Marina Operations

Owner/Manager: n/a **Dockmaster:** Jan Buchner
In-Season: June-Oct, 8am-8pm **Off-Season:** Nov-May, 9am-5pm
After-Hours Arrival: Find a berth and see office in the morning
Reservations: Yes, Required **Credit Cards:** Visa/MC, Dscvr, Din, Amex
Discounts: Negotiated Individually **Dockage:** n/a **Fuel:** Yes **Repair:** n/a
Pets: Welcome **Handicap Access:** No

Marina Services and Boat Supplies

Services - Docking Assistance, Room Service to the Boat, Security *(10pm - 5am)*, Trash Pick-Up, Dock Carts, Megayacht Facilities, European Voltage **Communication -** Mail & Package Hold, Phone Messages, Fax in/out, Data Ports *(Dock Office)*, FedEx, AirBorne, UPS, Express Mail *(Sat Del)* **Supplies - OnSite:** Ice *(Block, Cube)* **Near:** CNG *(Oldport)* **Under 1 mi:** Ships' Store *(JT's 846-7256)* **1-3 mi:** West Marine *(841-9880)*, Bait/Tackle *(Saltwater Edge 842-0062)*, Propane *(U Haul 847-3219)*

Boatyard Services

OnCall: Engine mechanic *(gas, diesel)*, Electrical Repairs, Electronics Repairs, Rigger, Sail Loft, Bottom Cleaning, Brightwork, Air Conditioning, Refrigeration, Divers, Compound, Wash & Wax, Interior Cleaning **Nearest Yard:** The Newport Shipyard (401) 846-6000

Restaurants and Accommodations

OnSite: Restaurant *(Clarke Cooke House 849-2900, D $27-40)*, *(Candy Store L $2-25, D $16-26, casual dining, raw bar)*, *(LeBistro 849-7778, L $8-17, D $19-29)*, *(Black Pearl Tavern 846-5264, L $7-20, D $15-24, Commodore's Room $20-30)*, Lite Fare *(Black Pearl Patio)*, Inn/B&B *(Bannister's Wharf Guest Rooms $150 weeknights, $245 weekends)* **Near:** Restaurant *(Wharf Pub 846-9233, L $6-8, D $11-17)*, *(22 Bowens 841-8884, L $14-26, D $22-37)*, Motel *(Admiral Fitzroy Inn 848-8018)*, *(Harborside Inn 846-6600)*, Hotel *(Marriott 849-1000)*

Recreation and Entertainment

OnSite: Group Fishing Boat **Near:** Boat Rentals, Movie Theater, Video Arcade, Park, Museum *(Museum of Yachting 847-1018)*, Sightseeing *(Fort Adams, via ferry)*, Galleries **Under 1 mi:** Dive Shop, Fitness Center, Fishing Charter, Video Rental *(Broadway Joes 848-5859)* **1-3 mi:** Beach *(2nd 846-6273)*, Playground, Tennis Courts *(Nat'l Tennis Club 849-6672)*, Golf Course *(Jamestown)*, Bowling *(Hi Way Mini Golf 849-9990)*

Provisioning and General Services

OnSite: Retail Shops **Near:** Delicatessen *(Morning Glory 842-0520)*, Wine/Beer, Liquor Store *(JD)*, Bakery *(Cookie Jar)*, Fishmonger, Lobster Pound *(Aquidneck 846-0106)*, Bank/ATM, Post Office, Catholic Church, Protestant Church, Synagogue, Library *(847-8720)*, Beauty Salon, Barber Shop, Dry Cleaners, Laundry, Bookstore *(Armchair Sailor 847-1219)*, Newsstand **Under 1 mi:** Convenience Store *(JD 842-0545)*, Supermarket *(Stop & Shop 848-7200)*, Gourmet Shop, Health Food, Farmers' Market *(M. Wheatland Blvd. Sat 9am-1pm, Wed 2-6pm 849-7359)*, Pharmacy *(CVS 846-4990)*, Hardware Store *(One Stop 847-8460)*, Florist, Department Store *(Wal-Mart 848-8341)* **1-3 mi:** Buying Club *(BJ's 848-9242)*

Transportation

OnCall: Water Taxi, Rental Car *(Thrifty 846-3200)*, Taxi *(Yellow Cab 846-1500)* **Near:** Local Bus *(Trolley)*, Ferry Service *(Goat Isl. & Jamestown)* **Under 1 mi:** Bikes *(Ten Speed 847-5609)*, InterCity Bus *(Greyhound 846-1820)* **3+ mi:** Rail *(Kingstown, 20 mi.)* **Airport:** TF Green *(20 mi.)*

Medical Services

911 Service **Near:** Holistic Services *(Wave Lengths 849-4427)* **Under 1 mi:** Doctor *(Community Health Center 848-2160)*, Dentist, Chiropractor *(Newport C.C. 847-4224)*, Ambulance, Veterinarian *(Newport 849-3401)*
Hospital: Newport 783-9718 *(1 mi.)*

Setting -- The sixth major set of docks heading north, Bannister's Wharf is one of the most centrally located marinas in the harbor. It is a hub of waterfront activity, with an easly accessed fuel dock, lovely guest rooms, four onsite restaurants, 20 upscale shops, and most basic yachting services.

Marina Notes -- Founded in 1742 by John Bannister, as one of many wharfs built to support trade between Europe, the Colonies and the West Indies, Bannister's Wharf was intended to function as a tie between the commercial and social lives of Newport. Its modern incarnation, which dates to the late 1800s, is as a busy marina on an historic street lined with exclusive shops and eclectic eateries. Four restaurants are onsite, including the charming and romantic Clarke Cooke House (upstairs the roofed deck has great views of the harbor).For lunch, the Black Pearl Patio offers chili, chowder, and a raw bar. Quantity discounts on fuel. Ten 50-foot slips. 1200 feet of dockage. CNG available from nearby Oldport Marine (847-9019).

Notable -- Bowens' Wharf, next door, is home to many more retail shops (20), galleries (5), restaurants (7), services, and the Aquidneck Lobster Co. The famous Newport mansions are a trolley ride away (a package rate offers admission to 5 mansions for $29); Chateau Sur Mer, Hunter House, Kingscote, Marble House and The Breakers are worth the trip. Across the street is the Newport Blues Café (841-5510) with live music in the summer, and the Post Office. Another trolley will take you to the beaches, 1st (Easton) is full service but a little "gray"; 2nd Beach (Sachuest) may be prettier and more enticing, and 3rd Beach is the calmest. The International Yacht Restoration School is close; watch students restoring classic yachts or tour the 1885 grand yacht Coronet.

PHOTOS ON CD-ROM: 9

Navigational Information
Lat: 41°29.117' **Long:** 071°19.283' **Tide:** 6 ft. **Current:** n/a **Chart:** 13223
Rep. Depths (*MLW*): Entry 18 ft. **Fuel Dock** n/a **Max Slip/Moor** -/18 ft.
Access: Narragansett Bay; head east at Fort Adams to central mooring field

Marina Facilities *(In Season/Off Season)*
Fuel: No
Slips: 0 Total, 0 Transient **Max LOA:** n/a **Max Beam:** n/a
Rate *(per ft.)*: **Day** n/a **Week** n/a **Month** n/a
Power: 30 amp n/a, **50 amp** n/a, **100 amp** n/a, **200 amp** n/a
Cable TV: No **Dockside Phone:** No
Dock Type: n/a
Moorings: 115 Total, 17 Transient **Launch:** Yes ($2), Dinghy Dock
Rate: Day $35-50/$20-35* **Week** n/a **Month** $830-1200
Heads: None
Laundry: None **Pay Phones:** No
Pump-Out: OnCall, Full Service, 2 Port **Fee:** $15 **Closed Heads:** Yes

Marina Operations
Owner/Manager: Matt Gineo **Dockmaster:** Same
In-Season: May-Oct, 8am-5pm **Off-Season:** Oct-May, 8am-5pm weekdays
After-Hours Arrival: Pick up cone-shaped buoy marked "Rental"
Reservations: No **Credit Cards:** Visa/MC
Discounts: None
Pets: Welcome, Dog Walk Area **Handicap Access:** No

Oldport Marine Services

PO Box 141; Sayers Wharf; Newport, RI 02840

Tel: (401) 847-9109 **VHF: Monitor** 68 **Talk** 68
Fax: (401) 846-5599 **Alternate Tel:** n/a
Email: Oldportmar@aol.com **Web:** www.Oldportmarine.com

Nearest Town: Newport *(0 mi.)* **Tourist Info:** (401) 845-9123

Marina Services and Boat Supplies
Communication - Mail & Package Hold, Fax in/out, FedEx, UPS **Supplies - OnSite:** Ice *(Block, Cube)*, CNG *($18/20)* **Near:** Ships' Store *(JT's Chandlery 846-7256)* **Under 1 mi:** Bait/Tackle *(Saltwater Edge 842-0062)* **1-3 mi:** West Marine *(841-9880)*, Live Bait, Propane *(U Haul 847-3219)*

Boatyard Services
OnSite: Engine mechanic *(gas, diesel)*, Electrical Repairs, Hull Repairs, Compound, Wash & Wax **OnCall:** Sail Loft, Bottom Cleaning, Brightwork, Divers, Interior Cleaning **Near:** Travelift, Electronic Sales, Electronics Repairs, Rigger, Air Conditioning, Refrigeration. **Under 1 mi:** Launching Ramp. **Nearest Yard:** American Shipyard (401) 846-6000

Restaurants and Accommodations
OnSite: Restaurant *(Smokehouse 848-9800, L $6-16, D $6-16)* **Near:** Restaurant *(The Mooring 846-2260, L $8-28, D $16-40)*, *(The Wharf 846-9233, L $6-15, D $7-$17)*, *(LeBistro 849-7778, L $8-17, D $19-29)*, *(Black Pearl Tavern 846-5264, L $7-20, D $15-24, also raw bar)*, *(Landing 847-4514)*, *(Café di Mare 847-2962)*, Pizzeria *(Via Via 846-4075, delivers)*, Hotel *(The Newport 847-9000, $100-400)*, Inn/B&B *(Vanderbilt Hall 846-6200, $100-460)* **Under 1 mi:** Hotel *(Marriott 498-1000)*

Recreation and Entertainment
OnSite: Sightseeing *(Amazing Grace, 99 passenger 1-hr. tours noon-sunset, $9/5.50)* **Near:** Fitness Center, Fishing Charter, Movie Theater, Video Arcade, Park *(Fort Adams State Park)* **Under 1 mi:** Dive Shop, Boat Rentals, Video Rental *(Broadway Joes 848-5859)*, Museum *(Yachting Museum 847-1018, Naval War College 848-8306)*, Cultural Attract *(The Mansions)* **1-3 mi:** Beach *(1st & 2nd Beaches)*, Tennis Courts *(Nat'l Tennis Club 849-6672)*, Golf Course **3+ mi:** Horseback Riding *(Newport Equestrian 848-5440, 5 mi.)*, Bowling *(Hi Way Bowl/Mini Golf 849-9990, 3.5 mi.)*

Provisioning and General Services
OnSite: Bank/ATM **OnCall:** Dry Cleaners, Laundry **Near:** Convenience Store *(JD Convenience and Liquor)*, Delicatessen *(Morning Glory 842-0520)*, Health Food, Wine/Beer *(Wellington Square 846-9463)*, Bakery, Lobster Pound *(Aquidneck 846-0106)*, Post Office, Catholic Church, Protestant Church, Synagogue, Barber Shop, Bookstore *(Mind's Eye 849-7333, Armchair Sailor 847-1219)*, Hardware Store *(One Stop 847-8460)*, Retail Shops **Under 1 mi:** Provisioning Service, Supermarket *(Stop & Shop 848-7200)*, Gourmet Shop *(Market on the Boulevard 848-2600)*, Farmers' Market *(behind Salvation Café Wed 2-6pm, Sat 9am-1pm 849-7359)*, Fishmonger, Library *(847-8720)*, Beauty Salon, Pharmacy *(CVS 846-4990)*, Florist, Department Store *(Wal-Mart 848-8341)*, Copies Etc. *(Printing & Copying 849-3820)* **1-3 mi:** Buying Club *(BJ's 848-9242)*

Transportation
OnSite: Water Taxi *($2)* **OnCall:** Rental Car *(Enterprise 849-3939)*, Taxi *(Cozy Cab 846-2500)* **Near:** Local Bus *(Trolley)* **Under 1 mi:** Bikes *(Ten Speed 847-5609)*, InterCity Bus *(Greyhound 846-1820)* **3+ mi:** Rail *(No Kingstown Amtrak, 16 mi.)* **Airport:** TF Green *(20 mi.)*

Medical Services
911 Service **Near:** Dentist *(Violet 847-3497)* **Under 1 mi:** Doctor *(Community Health 848-2160)*, Chiropractor *(Newport C. 847-4224)*, Holistic Services *(Body Central 848-5885)* **Hospital:** Newport 783-9718 *(1 mi.)*

Setting -- The majority of the transient moorings in the Main (central) mooring field are owned and managed by Oldport Launch which maintains a landside facility just north of the Newport Yachting Center on Sayers Wharf. Look for an attractive, green-trimmed, shingled building with gambrelled roof. Their launches service all mooring fields and anchorages throughout Newport Harbor and land at their very convenient, centrally located dock (also next to NYC).

Marina Notes -- *Mooring rates: up to 39' $35, 40-49' $40, 50'+ $50. Rafting $15 for 2nd boat. Launch $2/pp each way. Hours: Mid-May to Mid-Jun Mon-Fri 8am-8pm, Sat-Sun 8am-Mid; Mid-Jun to LabDay 7 days 7am-1am. LabDay to MidSep 8am-10pm, to 1am weekends. MidSep-MidOct 8am-6pm, to 10pm weekends. "Alert" Ferry to Goat Island $2/pp each way. CNG onsite. Water float in harbor. Add'l water plus trash receptacles on Oldport's dock. Repairs/sells diesel engines (largest Yanmar dealer), transmissions, generators, engine parts, fuel/oil filters, batteries, alternators, propellers. Builders of Oldport Launches.

Notable -- Crewed day sails on the 37 ft. Patriot, Sally Forth and Amazing Grace. Bowen's Wharf is very near with shopping, galleries, and more restaurants. Public dinghy docks (which also have heads): Bowen's Wharf (849-2234, Ch.78), Anne Street Pier $1/hr., $6/day (847-1069, Ch.78), King Park (a public trash facility). Nice heads at Perrotti Park Harbormaster's Office (also dog walk park). Restrooms, showers, laundry, internet access, café, & library at Seamen's Institute (847-4260). Pump-out boats from Harbor Sanitation, 7 days, 8am-7pm, cell 474-3044, Ch.9, $15 first 30 gals, $5 each add'l 30 gals, trash $1/bag.

PHOTOS ON CD-ROM: 7

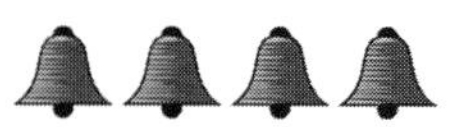

Newport Harbor Hotel & Marina

49 America's Cup Avenue; Newport, RI 02840

Tel: (401) 847-9000 **VHF: Monitor** 9 **Talk** n/a
Fax: (401) 849-6380 **Alternate Tel:** (800) 955-2558
Email: dockmaster@newporthotel.com **Web:** www.newporthotel.com
Nearest Town: Newport *(0 mi.)* **Tourist Info:** (401) 845-9123

Navigational Information

Lat: 41°29.259' **Long:** 071°19.009' **Tide:** 4 ft. **Current:** n/a **Chart:** 13223
Rep. Depths (*MLW*): Entry 17 ft. **Fuel Dock** n/a **Max Slip/Moor** 8 ft./-
Access: NE Corner of Newport Harbor off Narragansett Bay

Marina Facilities *(In Season/Off Season)*

Fuel: No
Slips: 65 Total, 65 Transient **Max LOA:** 150 ft. **Max Beam:** n/a
Rate *(per ft.)*: **Day** $3.50/$3.50 **Week** Same **Month** Same
Power: 30 amp $5, **50 amp** $10, **100 amp** n/a, **200 amp** n/a
Cable TV: Yes **Dockside Phone:** Yes
Dock Type: Floating
Moorings: 0 Total, 0 Transient **Launch:** n/a
Rate: Day n/a **Week** n/a **Month** n/a
Heads: 2 Toilet(s), 2 Shower(s)
Laundry: 2 Washer(s), 2 Dryer(s) **Pay Phones:** Yes
Pump-Out: No **Fee:** n/a **Closed Heads:** Yes

Marina Operations

Owner/Manager: n/a **Dockmaster:** Mark Holden
In-Season: Year-Round, 7am-7pm **Off-Season:** n/a
After-Hours Arrival: n/a
Reservations: Yes **Credit Cards:** Visa/MC, Dscvr, Din, Amex
Discounts: None
Pets: No **Handicap Access:** No

Marina Services and Boat Supplies

Services - Docking Assistance, Concierge, Trash Pick-Up, Dock Carts, Megayacht Facilities **Communication -** Mail & Package Hold, Phone Messages, Fax in/out, FedEx, AirBorne, UPS, Express Mail *(Sat Del)* **Supplies - OnSite:** Ice *(Cube)* **Near:** Ice *(Block, Shaved)*, Ships' Store *(JT's 846-7256)*, Bait/Tackle *(Saltwater Edge 842-0062)*, CNG *(Oldport 847-9109)* **1-3 mi:** Boat/US *(841-9880)*, Propane *(U Haul 847-3219)*

Boatyard Services

OnSite: Electrical Repairs, Brightwork **OnCall:** Electronics Repairs, Bottom Cleaning **Near:** Yacht Broker. **Under 1 mi:** Engine mechanic *(gas, diesel)*, Launching Ramp, Hull Repairs, Rigger, Refrigeration, Divers. **Nearest Yard:** The Newport Shipyard (401) 846-6000

Restaurants and Accommodations

OnSite: Restaurant *(Waverly's 847-9000, L $7-15, D $7-15, reasonably priced steamers & lobster boil)*, Snack Bar, Hotel *(Newport Harbor 847-9000, $120-280)* **OnCall:** Pizzeria *(Mama Leone's 847-7272)* **Near:** Restaurant *(Brick Alley Pub 849-6334, L $5-14, D $12-23)*, *(Lucia Italian 846-4477, L $6-13, D $12-20)*, *(Landing 847-4514)*, *(22 Bowens 841-8884, L $14-26, D $22-37)*, *(Panini Grill 847-7784)*, *(American Café 849-9188)*, Fast Food, Motel *(Harbor Base Motel 847-2600)*, Hotel *(Marriott 849-1000)*, Inn/B&B *(Inntowne Inn 846-9200)*, *(Queen Anne Inn 846-5676)*

Recreation and Entertainment

OnSite: Heated Pool, Picnic Area **OnCall:** Fishing Charter, Group Fishing Boat **Near:** Grills, Playground, Dive Shop, Volleyball, Fitness Center *(Waterfront Fitness 846-3720)*, Jogging Paths, Boat Rentals, Roller Blade/Bike Paths, Movie Theater, Video Rental, Video Arcade, Park, Cultural Attract, Sightseeing **Under 1 mi:** Beach, Tennis Courts *(Nat'l Tennis Club 849-6672)* **1-3 mi:** Bowling *(Hi Way Mini Golf 849-9990)*, Museum *(Naval War College 848-8306)* **3+ mi:** Golf Course *(Jamestown 423-9930, 4 mi.)*

Provisioning and General Services

OnCall: Dry Cleaners, Laundry **Near:** Convenience Store *(JD)*, Gourmet Shop, Delicatessen *(Blue Water Wraps 849-9995)*, Wine/Beer, Liquor Store *(Spring Street 846-0959)*, Bakery, Fishmonger, Lobster Pound *(Aquidneck 846-0106)*, Bank/ATM, Post Office, Catholic Church, Protestant Church, Synagogue, Beauty Salon, Bookstore *(Mind's Eye 849-7333)*, Newsstand, Retail Shops **Under 1 mi:** Supermarket *(Stop & Shop 848-7200)*, Farmers' Market *(M. Wheatland Blvd. Sat 9am-1pm, Wed 2-6pm 849-7359)*, Meat Market, Library *(Newport 847-8720)*, Pharmacy *(CVS 846-4990)*, Hardware Store *(Newport 849-9442)*, Florist, Copies Etc. *(Printing & Copying 849-3820)* **1-3 mi:** Department Store *(Wal-Mart 848-8341)*, Buying Club *(BJ's)*

Transportation

OnCall: Rental Car *(Cartemps USA 846-4458, Enterprise 849-3939)*, Taxi *(Yellow Cab 846-1500)* **Near:** Courtesy Car/Van, Bikes *(Ten Speed Spokes 847-5609)*, Local Bus, InterCity Bus *(Greyhound 846-1820)* **3+ mi:** Rail *(Providence, 18 mi.)* **Airport:** TF Green *(20 mi.)*

Medical Services

911 Service **OnCall:** Ambulance **Near:** Doctor *(Newport Fam 849-6852)*, Dentist *(Carlson 846-9770)*, Holistic Services *(Body Central 848-5885)* **Under 1 mi:** Chiropractor *(Aquidneck 849-7011)*, Veterinarian *(Newport 849-3401)* **Hospital:** Newport 783-9718 *(1 mi.)*

PHOTOS ON CD-ROM: 8

Setting -- Located toward the northern end of Newport's Main Harbor, at the edge of the downtown district, the Hotel & Marina are a short walk to shopping and restaurants. The museums and historic mansions are a five minute cab or trolley ride. The outer slips afford lovely harbor views (unless a megayacht takes a T-head). The tall ship HMS Rose sits adjacent to the docks and is lit at night adding to the festive atmosphere.

Marina Notes -- Reservations a must. Marina is owned and operated by Shaner Hotel Group as part of the hotel facility. Built in 1971, it was acquired in 1996. A guest of the marina is effectively a guest of the hotel - with full resort privileges, indoor pool, sauna, heads & showers adjacent to the pool, laundromat, etc. No cable TV. Phones/data ports on some pedestals (inquire if important). Docks recently refurbished. Onsite parking for marina guests - $10/night.

Notable -- From May-Oct, the Marina is the "exclusive" home to the legendary America's Cup Yachts. Six 12-meter class yachts available for charter. Onsite Waverly's Restaurant offers fine dining indoors or outside overlooking the docks, plus live entertainment (also lawn parties/clam boils for up to 250). Lighter fare at the seasonal Terrace Café. More restaurants located next door at Bowen's Wharf along with a deli, upscale boutiques, art galleries and ferries to Ft. Adams, Jamestown and Providence. Two major shopping districts nearby. 30 shops at Brick Marketplace across the street, as is the village green. Newport sightseeing tours, tourist office, Perrotti Park, Harbormaster's office and bus depot are a couple of blocks north. Farmers' Market is at 73 Drive & Marcus Wheatland Blvd., Stop & Shop and Wal-Mart about one mile away, and BJ's Wholesale (848-9242) is 3 miles away.

Navigational Information

Lat: 41°29.226' **Long:** 071°19.592' **Tide:** 4 ft. **Current:** .3 kt. **Chart:** 13223
Rep. Depths (*MLW*): Entry 19 ft. **Fuel Dock** 17 ft. **Max Slip/Moor** 17 ft./-
Access: Narragansett Bay; E Shore of Goat Island in Newport Harbor

Marina Facilities *(In Season/Off Season)*

Fuel: *Mobil* - Gasoline, Diesel, High-Speed Pumps
Slips: 175 Total, 20 Transient **Max LOA:** 200 ft. **Max Beam:** n/a
Rate *(per ft.)*: **Day** $3.50* **Week** n/a **Month** n/a
Power: 30 amp $15, **50 amp** $30, **100 amp** $40, **200 amp** n/a
Cable TV: Yes Free **Dockside Phone:** Yes, $1
Dock Type: Wood, Long Fingers, Pilings, Alongside, Floating, Fixed
Moorings: 0 Total, 0 Transient **Launch:** n/a, Dinghy Dock
Rate: Day n/a **Week** n/a **Month** n/a
Heads: 6 Toilet(s), 6 Shower(s)
Laundry: 6 Washer(s), 6 Dryer(s) **Pay Phones:** Yes, 4
Pump-Out: Self Service **Fee:** $10 **Closed Heads:** Yes

Marina Operations

Owner/Manager: n/a **Dockmaster:** Mike Sweeney
In-Season: May 15-Oct 31, 8am-Dusk **Off-Season:** Nov - May15, 8am-4pm*
After-Hours Arrival: Call ahead
Reservations: Yes **Credit Cards:** Visa/MC, Amex, Mobil
Discounts: Safe/Sea **Dockage:** 25% **Fuel:** n/a **Repair:** n/a
Pets: Welcome, Dog Walk Area **Handicap Access:** No

Goat Island Marina

5 Marina Plaza; Goat Island, RI 02840

Tel: (401) 849-5655 **VHF: Monitor** 9 **Talk** 11
Fax: (401) 848-7144 **Alternate Tel:** (401) 849-2600
Email: n/a **Web:** www.newportexperience.com
Nearest Town: Newport *(0.5 mi.)* **Tourist Info:** (401) 845-9123

Marina Services and Boat Supplies

Services - Docking Assistance, Concierge, Security *(24 Hrs.)*, Trash Pick-Up, Dock Carts **Communication -** Mail & Package Hold, Phone Messages, Fax in/out, Data Ports *(Main dock phone booth , $1)*, FedEx, AirBorne, UPS, Express Mail *(Sat Del)* **Supplies - OnSite:** Ice *(Block, Cube)*, Ships' Store **Under 1 mi:** Bait/Tackle, CNG *(Oldport Marine 847-9109 by water taxi)* **1-3 mi:** West Marine *(841-9880)*, Propane *(U-Haul 847-3219)*

Boatyard Services

Near: Travelift, Railway, Forklift, Crane, Engine mechanic *(gas, diesel)*, Electrical Repairs, Hull Repairs, Rigger, Bottom Cleaning. **1-3 mi:** Life Raft Service. **Nearest Yard:** American Shipyard 1/4 mile (401) 846-6000

Restaurants and Accommodations

OnSite: Restaurant *(Marina Grille 841-0999, L $6.50-20, D $6.50-20)* **Near:** Restaurant *(The Windward Grille 851-1234, B,L,D)*, Lite Fare *(Pineapples Entertainment Fri-Mon)*, Hotel *(Hyatt Regency 851-1234, $130-385, on Goat Island)* **Under 1 mi:** Restaurant *(Rhumb Line 849-6950)*, *(Long Wharf Steakhouse 847-7800)*, *(Dinner Train 841-7800, dinner & tours aboard restored train cars)*, Seafood Shack *(JWS Sea Grill & Oyster Bar 849-7788)*, Hotel *(Marriott 849-1000)*, *(The Fairfield Resort)*, Inn/B&B *(Mariner House 847-6938)*, *(Corner House Inn 847-8888)* **1-3 mi:** Pizzeria *(Via Via 846-4075, delivers)*, Motel *(Inn at Newport Beach 846-0310)*

Recreation and Entertainment

OnSite: Pool, Picnic Area, Playground, Tennis Courts, Fishing Charter *(Fishin' Off 683-5777)* **Near:** Fitness Center *(Stillwater Spa 851-3225)*, Other *(Viking Boat Tours 847-6921)*, Video Rental **Under 1 mi:** Movie Theater, Video Arcade, Museum *(Museum Of Newport History 841-8770, Museum Of Yachting 847-1018)* **1-3 mi:** Dive Shop, Bowling *(Hi Way Bowl & Mini Golf 849-9990)*, Sightseeing *(Mansions, harbor tours, Fort Adams)*

Provisioning and General Services

OnSite: Wine/Beer, Liquor Store, Laundry **OnCall:** Supermarket *(Stop & Shop, 2 mi. 848-7200)* **Near:** Convenience Store *(Rum Runner Spirits and Provisions)*, Bank/ATM, Post Office, Catholic Church, Protestant Church, Synagogue, Beauty Salon *(Stillwater)*, Newsstand **Under 1 mi:** Barber Shop, Dry Cleaners, Bookstore *(Mind's Eye 849-7333)* **1-3 mi:** Gourmet Shop *(Market On The Boulevard 848-2600)*, Delicatessen *(Blue Water Wraps 849-9995)*, Farmers' Market *(Salvation Café Sat 9am-1pm, Wed 2-6pm 849-7359)*, Library *(847-8720)*, Pharmacy *(CVS 849-8058)*, Hardware Store *(Newport Hware 847-7224)*, Department Store *(Wal-Mart 848-8341)*, Buying Club *(BJ's 848-9242)*, Copies Etc. *(Printing & Copying 849-3820)*

Transportation

OnSite: Bikes, Water Taxi *(to Oldport Marine's dock in Newport)*, Ferry Service *(Jamestown, Ft. Adams 423-9900)* **OnCall:** Rental Car, Taxi *(Cozy Cab 846-2500)*, Airport Limo *(Al's Classic Limo 846-5562)* **1-3 mi:** InterCity Bus *(Greyhound 846-1820)* **3+ mi:** Rail *(Providence/Kingstown Amtrak Stations, 40 min.)* **Airport:** TF Green *(20 mi.)*

Medical Services

911 Service **OnCall:** Ambulance *(Medevac)* **Near:** Holistic Services *(Stillwater)* **Under 1 mi:** Doctor *(Newport Fam 849-6852)*, Veterinarian *(Newport 849-3401)* **1-3 mi:** Chiropractor *(Newport Center 847-4224)* **Hospital:** Newport 783-9718 *(1.5 mi.)*

Setting -- Located in a quiet residential community, Goat Island is the only marina on the west side of Newport Harbor. Its extensive network of well maintained docks and mooring fields sprawls along the shoreline and offers spectacular views of Newport, especially at night. Nearby nature trails and a low-key ambiance are unique for Newport and offer an interesting alternative.

Marina Notes -- *$3.75 for 80' and up. Largest marina in Newport Harbor. Ample parking. 10 minute water shuttle to Newport's "downtown" leaves every half hour and stops at Bowen's Wharf . Cable TV & telephone (data ports $1 flat rate). Laundromat and laundry pick-up. Daily trash collection. Pump-out onsite. Newport Sailing School onsite. Please note: dockage no longer includes complimentary use of the Hyatt Regency's health club, pool and spa facilities. Hyatt's Stillwater Spa charges $20/day for use of health club, including indoor & outdoor pools.

Notable -- Onsite Marina Grille 11:30am-10pm has both a cozy, tableclothed dining room and canopied patio overlooking the Harbor. It also offers lobster bakes. 101 foot, 80 passenger schooner Aurora is at the docks and available for charter. All of Newport's many special events (folk and jazz festivals, boat show, etc.) are an easy water shuttle away. On Goat Island are tennis courts, a liquor and convenience store, the Hyatt Hotel's Windward Grill, Auld Mug Lounge, and al fresco Pineapples on the Bay restaurants. Additional services and supplies are a 0.3 mile/20 minute walk across the bridge or a short water shuttle ride. Jamestown Ferry (423-9900) will stop at Goat Island and at Fort Adams on request.

The Newport Shipyard

1 Washington Street; Newport, RI 02840

Tel: (401) 846-6000 **VHF: Monitor** 9 **Talk** 8
Fax: (401) 846-6001 **Alternate Tel:** n/a
Email: info@americanshipyard.com **Web:** www.americanshipyard.com
Nearest Town: Newport *(0 mi.)* **Tourist Info:** (401) 845-9123

Navigational Information

Lat: 41°29.420' **Long:** 071°19.365' **Tide:** 4 ft.. **Current:** n/a **Chart:** 13223
Rep. Depths (*MLW*): Entry 21 ft. **Fuel Dock** n/a **Max Slip/Moor** 21 ft./-
Access: Narragansett Bay, turn right before bridge in Newport Harbor

Marina Facilities *(In Season/Off Season)*

Fuel: No
Slips: 24 Total, 24 Transient **Max LOA:** 300 ft. **Max Beam:** n/a
Rate *(per ft.)*: **Day** $3.50/Inq. **Week** Inq. **Month** Inq.
Power: 30 amp $8, **50 amp** $15, **100 amp** $30, **200 amp** $60
Cable TV: Yes, $5 **Dockside Phone:** Yes, $0
Dock Type: Wood, Long Fingers, Alongside, Floating
Moorings: 0 Total, 0 Transient **Launch:** n/a
Rate: Day n/a **Week** n/a **Month** n/a
Heads: 4 Toilet(s), 5 Shower(s)
Laundry: 2 Washer(s), 2 Dryer(s) **Pay Phones:** Yes, 2
Pump-Out: OnCall, Full Service, 2 Port **Fee:** $15 plus **Closed Heads:** Yes

Marina Operations

Owner/Manager: Jan Buchner **Dockmaster:** Same
In-Season: May-Oct, 7:30am-7:30pm **Off-Season:** Oct-May, 9am-5pm
After-Hours Arrival: Call security on Ch.9
Reservations: Yes, Preferred **Credit Cards:** Visa/MC, Dscvr, Amex
Discounts: None
Pets: Welcome, Dog Walk Area **Handicap Access:** Yes, Heads, Docks

Marina Services and Boat Supplies

Services - Docking Assistance, Concierge, Boaters' Lounge, Crew Lounge, Security *(24 Hrs.)*, Dock Carts, Megayacht Facilities, 300 amps, 3 Phase **Communication -** Mail & Package Hold, Phone Messages, Fax in/out *(Free)*, Data Ports *(Lounge, Wireless, too)*, FedEx, AirBorne, UPS, Express Mail *(Sat Del)* **Supplies - OnSite:** Ice *(Block, Cube)* **Under 1 mi:** Ships' Store *(JT's 846-7256)*, Bait/Tackle *(Saltwater Edge 842-0062)* **1-3 mi:** West Marine *(841-9880)*, Propane *(Newport County Bottled Gas 847-6878)*, CNG *(East Passage Yachting 683-4000)*

Boatyard Services

OnSite: Travelift *(330T, 70T)*, Railway *(2000T)*, Engine mechanic *(gas, diesel)*, Electrical Repairs, Hull Repairs, Rigger, Bottom Cleaning, Brightwork, Air Conditioning, Refrigeration, Divers, Compound, Wash & Wax, Propeller Repairs, Woodworking, Metal Fabrication, Painting, Awlgrip, Yacht Design, Total Refits **OnCall:** Sail Loft, Interior Cleaning, Inflatable Repairs, Life Raft Service, Upholstery, Yacht Interiors **Dealer for:** Hinckley, Bertram, Brackshoff. **Yard Rates:** $60/hr., Haul & Launch $14/ft.

Restaurants and Accommodations

OnSite: Restaurant *(Belle's B&L)* **OnCall:** Pizzeria *(Via Via 846-4075)* **Near:** Restaurant *(Grappa 849-0011)*, *(Celtica Pub 847-4770)*, *(Brick Alley Pub 849-6334)*, *(Long Wharf Steakhouse 847-7800)*, *(Iguana's 843-8300)*, *(Dinner Train 841-7800, dinner tour aboard restored train cars)*, *(La Petite Auberge 849-6669, L $13-17, D $21-33)*, Seafood Shack *(JWS Sea Grill & Oyster Bar 849-7788)*, Hotel *(Newport Bay Club 849-8600, $130-350)*, *(Marriott 849-1000, $150-600)*, *(Newport Harbor 849-9000, $140-650)*, *(Inn on Long Wharf 847-7800, $180-250)*

Recreation and Entertainment

OnSite: Movie Theater **Near:** Pool, Fitness Center *(Waterfront 846-3720)*, Boat Rentals *(Adventure Sports 849-4820 kayaks)*, Video Arcade, Park, Museum *(Museum Of Newport History, Brick Market 841-8770)* **1-3 mi:** Beach *(Easton's 848-6491, Sachuest 846-6273)*, Tennis Courts *(Int'l Tennis 849-6672)*, Bowling *(Hi Way Bowl/Mini Golf 849-9990)*, Video Rental *(Broadway Joes 848-5859)*

Provisioning and General Services

OnSite: Bank/ATM **OnCall:** Dry Cleaners, Laundry **Near:** Convenience Store *(JD 842-0545)*, Liquor Store *(Fifth Ward 849-5690)*, Farmers' Market *(Salvation Café Wed 2-6pm, Sat 9am-1pm 849-7359)*, Post Office, Beauty Salon, Newsstand, Copies Etc. *(849-3820)* **Under 1 mi:** Supermarket *(Stop & Shop 848-7200)*, Gourmet Shop *(Market On The Blvd 848-2600)*, Health Food, Bakery, Lobster Pound *(Aquidneck 846-0106)*, Library *(847-8720)*, Barber Shop, Bookstore *(Mind's Eye 849-7333)*, Pharmacy *(CVS 846-4990)*, Hardware Store *(Newport 847-7224)*

Transportation

OnSite: Bikes *(Mopeds, too)* **OnCall:** Water Taxi *(Oldport)*, Rental Car *(Hertz)*, Taxi *(Rainbow 849-8294)*, Airport Limo *(Al's 846-5562)* **Near:** Local Bus *(Trolley)*, InterCity Bus *(Greyhound 846-1820)*, Ferry Service *(Providence)* **3+ mi:** Rail *(Kingston, 16mi.)* **Airport:** TF Green *(20 mi.)*

Medical Services

911 Service **OnCall:** Ambulance **Near:** Doctor *(Newport Fam 849-6852)*, Dentist, Holistic Services *(Body Central 48-5885)* **Under 1 mi:** Chiropractor, Veterinarian **Hospital:** Newport 783-9718 *(1 mi.)*

Setting -- The last facility on the east side of Newport Harbor, just before the Goat Island Bridge, this all-transient marina sits just north of its mega shipyard parent. The recreational docks are nestled in a protected basin, just past the working boats. A clear attempt has been made to create a pleasant and productive experience -- from the immaculate shipyard grounds to the extensive crew services and facilities -- and it has been successful!

Marina Notes -- Formerly known as the Marina at American Shipyard, the Newport Shipyard, completely renovated in 2002, specializes in vessels over 80 feet, (recreational and working), but welcomes all. Length to 300 ft., power to 480 3-phase. 2000T dry dock. Fairly recent docks are state-of-the-art. A small "picnic area" sits on the wharf at the head of the basin. Heads, showers, laundry, and a surround-sound movie theater are all upstairs in the main building. Crew Lounge has phones, meeting area, computer station, laptop data ports with high-speed connections, plus marina-wide Wi-Fi. ATM at the gate. Launch Service. Airport pickup/delivery. Box lunches and catering. Private office with reservation. Onsite Belle's Restaurant offers al fresco dining for breakfast and lunch.

Notable -- "Downtown" Newport is a short ten minute walk south. The information center and transportation hub are a block away - intercity buses (including those to Kingston Amtrak and Providence) and local trolleys make it easy to get just about anywhere. Take the Yellow line to the mansions or south end of Cliff Walk, the Orange to the north end of Cliff Walk or the beaches, the Red to lower downtown or on to Fort Adams for the festivals or The Museum Of Yachting 847-1018, ($1.25, all-day pass $5, families $10). A block farther is Long Wharf, Perrotti Park, the Providence ferry dock and the Brick Marketplace.

PHOTOS ON CD-ROM: 9

Navigational Information

Lat: 41°28.927' **Long:** 071°21.610' **Tide:** 4 ft. **Current:** 1 kt. **Chart:** 13223
Rep. Depths (*MLW*): Entry 12 ft. **Fuel Dock** n/a **Max Slip/Moor** -/50 ft.
Access: Narragansett Bay, East Passage, left after G11 (The Dumplings)

Marina Facilities *(In Season/Off Season)*

Fuel: No
Slips: 4 Total, 0 Transient **Max LOA:** 75 ft. **Max Beam:** n/a
Rate *(per ft.)*: **Day** $1.00/$0.50* **Week** n/a **Month** n/a
Power: 30 amp n/a, **50 amp** Incl., **100 amp** n/a, **200 amp** n/a
Cable TV: No **Dockside Phone:** No
Dock Type: Floating, Fixed
Moorings: 60 Total, 2 Transient **Launch:** Yes (Free)
Rate: Day $35-50 **Week** n/a **Month** $900-1200
Heads: Toilet(s)
Laundry: None **Pay Phones:** Yes
Pump-Out: No **Fee:** n/a **Closed Heads:** Yes

Marina Operations

Owner/Manager: Jim Archibald **Dockmaster:** Same
In-Season: May-Oct, 7am-3:30pm **Off-Season:** Oct-May, 7am-3:30pm
After-Hours Arrival: n/a
Reservations: No **Credit Cards:** Visa/MC, Dscvr, Amex
Discounts: None
Pets: Welcome **Handicap Access:** Yes, Heads, Docks

Jamestown Boat Yard

PO Box 347; Racquet Road; Jamestown, RI 02835

Tel: (401) 423-0600 **VHF: Monitor** 72 **Talk** 72
Fax: (401) 423-0060 **Alternate Tel:** n/a
Email: jby@ids.net **Web:** www.jby.com
Nearest Town: Newport *(1 mi.)* **Tourist Info:** (401) 423-3650

Marina Services and Boat Supplies

Services - Docking Assistance, Dock Carts **Communication -** Mail & Package Hold, Phone Messages, Fax in/out, FedEx **Supplies - OnSite:** Ice *(Block)*, Ships' Store **1-3 mi:** Bait/Tackle *(Zeeks Creek Bait & Tackle 423-1170)* **3+ mi:** West Marine *(841-9880, 4 mi.)*, Marine Discount Store *(Newport Nautical 847-3933, 4 mi.)*, Propane *(U Haul 847-3219, 4 mi.)*

Boatyard Services

OnSite: Railway *(150T)*, Engine mechanic *(gas, diesel)*, Electrical Repairs, Electronic Sales *(Jamestown Electronics 423-2253)*, Electronics Repairs, Hull Repairs, Rigger, Bottom Cleaning, Brightwork, Air Conditioning, Refrigeration, Divers, Compound, Wash & Wax, Interior Cleaning **OnCall:** Sail Loft **Dealer for:** Perkins, Volvo Penta, Westerbeke, Universal Marine Air, Grunert-Cruisair, Sea Frost, Espar, Raytheon, Max Prop, Nanni. **Yard Rates:** $58/hr., Haul & Launch $7-10 *(blocking $1.50-2.50/ft.)*, Power Wash $2.50/ft. **Storage:** On-Land Inside $7.25 sq.ft. Outside $27.50-$34.50/ft**

Restaurants and Accommodations

Near: Motel *(Newport Overlook 423-1886)* **Under 1 mi:** Restaurant *(Oyster Bar & Grille 423-3380, L $5, D $20)*, *(Theater Family 423-0907)*, *(Chopmist Charlies 423-1020, L $7-13, D $7-19)*, *(Tricia's Tropigrille 423-1490)*, Pizzeria *(House of Pizza 423-3060)*, Inn/B&B *(Bay Voyage 423-2100, $90-300, 1-bed suites)* **1-3 mi:** Restaurant *(Trattoria Simpatico L $10, D $25)*, Inn/B&B *(Chestnut Inn 847-6949)* **3+ mi:** Hotel *(Marriott 849-1000, 5 mi.)*

Recreation and Entertainment

OnSite: Beach *(plus Mackerel Cove w/in walking distance)* **Under 1 mi:** Park *(Ft. Getty)* **1-3 mi:** Picnic Area *(Ft. Wetherill State Park)*, Golf Course *(Jamestown G.C. 423-9930)*, Video Rental *(Video Showcase 423-2194)*, Museum *(Sydney L. Wright Museum 423-7280, has Indian and Colonial artifacts; Jamestown Museum 423-0784 Tue-Sat 1-4pm)*, Sightseeing *(Jamestown Windmill 423-1798, Beavertail Lighthouse 423-9941)* **3+ mi:** Tennis Courts *(Nat'l Tennis Club 849-6672, 4.5 mi.)*, Bowling *(Hi Way Bowl/Mini Golf 849-9990, 6 mi)*

Provisioning and General Services

Under 1 mi: Convenience Store, Supermarket *(McQuade 423-0873)*, Wine/Beer, Liquor Store *(Jamestown Liquors 423-0415)*, Bakery, Farmers' Market, Green Grocer, Fishmonger, Lobster Pound, Bank/ATM, Post Office, Catholic Church, Beauty Salon, Barber Shop, Dry Cleaners, Laundry, Pharmacy *(Bakers Pharmacy 423-2800)*, Newsstand, Hardware Store *(Jamestown True Value 423-0490)*, Florist, Clothing Store, Retail Shops **1-3 mi:** Gourmet Shop, Delicatessen *(East Ferry Market & Deli 423-1592)*, Library *(Philomenian Library 423-7280)*

Transportation

OnSite: Courtesy Car/Van **OnCall:** Rental Car *(Enterprise 849-3939)*, Taxi *(Yellow Cab 846-1500)* **Near:** Ferry Service *(at Conanicut Marina to Newport & Ft. Adams)* **3+ mi:** InterCity Bus *(Greyhound 846-1820, 5 mi.)*, Rail *(Kingstown Amtrak, 15 mi.)* **Airport:** TF Green 732-3621 *(20 mi.)*

Medical Services

911 Service **OnCall:** Ambulance **Under 1 mi:** Doctor *(Jamestown Fam 423-2616)*, Dentist *(Bush 423-2110)*, Veterinarian *(Jamestown Clinic 423-2288)* **1-3 mi:** Chiropractor *(Newport Center 847-4224)* **Hospital:** Newport 783-9718 *(5 mi.)*

Setting -- This lovely, tranquil, picturesque mooring field has front porch views of all the yachting activity along the East Passage. Spectacular views of Fort Adams and the Newport Bridge. It is well protected, except from the north and northeast. Landside is a true working boatyard in a rural setting; this spot has been the home of shipwrights for over 100 years.

Marina Notes -- * Moorings: $35/night up to 50', $50 over 50'. Monthly $900 up to 50', $1200 over 50'. Dockage: $50/night up to 50', $75/night over 50'. **Outside Storage: $27.50 ft. with rig removed, $34.50/ft. with rig in. Extremely service-oriented. Launch runs 7am-9pm MemDay-LabDay, 7am-7pm May & Oct. Dinghy storage also available. Specializes in providing a broad array of maintenance and refit services to Nautor Swans. Repair/Maintenance services include: mechanical, carpentry, paint & glass, electronics, storage & hauling, plus a full-service rigging shop. Noted for paint and bottom stripping. 9000 sq. ft. permanent inside storage. Fiberglass and Osmo repair shop. Lots of onsite parking. Small boaters' lounge with phones and data ports.

Notable -- Small, private onsite beach. Free customer pick-up service from Kingston Amtrak, Newport Transport Hub (Visitors' Center), New London Ferry and TF Green Airport -- first come, first served. Crew pick-up from western L.I., NYC area, and western Connecticut, $150 - 3 days' notice. Great walking and hiking in this delightful area: nearby Fort Wetherill State Park (423-1771) - a picnic destination since the 1800s - has stone cliffs and a small cove for swimming. 280 acre Watson Farm (423-0005) offers agrarian educational programs and 2 miles of trails with breathtaking vistas along the southwestern shore.

Conanicut Marina

One Ferry Wharf; Jamestown, RI 02835

Tel: (401) 423-1556 **VHF: Monitor** 71 **Talk** 71
Fax: (401) 423-7152 **Alternate Tel:** (401) 423-7158
Email: info@conanicutmarina.com **Web:** www.conanicutmarina.com
Nearest Town: Jamestown *(0 mi.)* **Tourist Info:** (401) 423-3650

Navigational Information
Lat: 41°29.782' **Long:** 071°21.970' **Tide:** 4 ft. **Current:** 1 kt. **Chart:** 13221
Rep. Depths (*MLW*): Entry 35 ft. **Fuel Dock** 15 ft. **Max Slip/Moor** 22 ft./60 ft.
Access: Narragansett Bay, East Passage, left at G11

Marina Facilities *(In Season/Off Season)*
Fuel: *Texaco* - Gasoline, Diesel, High-Speed Pumps
Slips: 100 Total, 10 Transient **Max LOA:** 175 ft. **Max Beam:** 50 ft.
Rate *(per ft.)*: **Day** $2.85/$1.00 **Week** $16.50/5.00 **Month** $66/20
Power: 30 amp $6, **50 amp** $12, **100 amp** $24, **200 amp** n/a
Cable TV: No **Dockside Phone:** No
Dock Type: Wood, Long Fingers, Alongside, Floating, Fixed
Moorings: 205 Total, 30 Transient **Launch:** 8am-9pm* (Free), Dinghy Dock
Rate: Day $41/31 **Week** $38/21 **Month** $35/$21
Heads: 6 Toilet(s), 2 Shower(s) *(with dressing rooms)*
Laundry: 4 Washer(s), 4 Dryer(s) **Pay Phones:** Yes, 2
Pump-Out: OnSite, 2 Port, 6 InSlip **Fee:** n/a **Closed Heads:** Yes

Marina Operations
Owner/Manager: William Munger **Dockmaster:** Steve Munger
In-Season: Jun-Sep 1, 8am-9pm **Off-Season:** Sep 1-May 30, 8am-5pm
After-Hours Arrival: Contact fuel dock on Ch. 71 or 401-423-7157
Reservations: Preferred **Credit Cards:** Visa/MC
Discounts: Extended stays **Dockage:** n/a **Fuel:** Volum **Repair:** n/a
Pets: Welcome, Dog Walk Area **Handicap Access:** No

Marina Services and Boat Supplies
Services - Docking Assistance, Security *(10 Hrs., nights)*, Dock Carts, Megayacht Facilities, 3 Phase **Communication -** Mail & Package Hold, Phone Messages, Fax in/out, FedEx, AirBorne, UPS, Express Mail *(Sat Del)* **Supplies - OnSite:** Ice *(Block, Cube)*, Ships' Store *(Extensive parts & supplies)*, CNG **Under 1 mi:** Bait/Tackle *(Zeeks Creek 423-1170)* **3+ mi:** West Marine *(841-9880, 5 mi.)*, Propane *(Suburban 847-6878, 5 mi.)*

Boatyard Services
OnSite: Railway *(200T)*, Crane, Engine mechanic *(gas, diesel)*, Launching Ramp, Electrical Repairs, Electronic Sales, Electronics Repairs, Hull Repairs, Rigger, Bottom Cleaning, Brightwork, Divers, Propeller Repairs, Woodworking, Inflatable Repairs, Metal Fabrication, Painting, Awlgrip, Total Refits **OnCall:** Sail Loft, Air Conditioning, Refrigeration, Life Raft Service, Upholstery, Yacht Interiors **Dealer for:** Honda, Westerbeke, Yanmar, Johnson, Avon, Evinrude, Universal. **Member:** ABBRA, ABYC - 4 Certified Tech(s), Other Certifications: OMC, Honda, IMI, Volvo **Yard Rates:** $65/hr., Haul & Launch $13/ft. *(blocking incl.)*, Power Wash $1.90/ft., Bottom Paint $12/ft. **Storage:** On-Land $7/ft./mo.

Restaurants and Accommodations
OnSite: Lite Fare *(Spinnaker's Café 423-3077)*, *(East Ferry Deli 423-1592, B&L)*, Condo/Cottage *(Marina 423-1556)* **OnCall:** Pizzeria *(House of Pizza 423-3060)* **Near:** Restaurant *(Theater Family 423-0907, B,L&D)*, *(Portuguese American 423-9909)*, *(Trattoria Simpatico 423-3731, D $19-26, L Fri-Sun)*, *(Chopmist Charlie's 423-3500, L $7-13, D $7-19)*, *(Bay Voyage 423-2100, D $22-34)*, *(Jamestown Oyster Bar 423-3380)*, Hotel *(Bay Voyage 423-2100)*, Inn/B&B *(East Bay 423-2715)*, *(Jamestown B&B 423-1338)*

Recreation and Entertainment
OnSite: Beach, Picnic Area, Grills, Special Events *(Fools Rules Regatta)* **Near:** Jogging Paths, Roller Blade/Bike Paths, Museum *(Sydney L. Wright Museum 423-7280, has Indian and Colonial artifacts; Ferry Museum)*, Cultural Attract *(Jamestown Community Concerts)* **Under 1 mi:** Playground, Dive Shop, Golf Course *(Jamestown G.C. 423-9930)* **1-3 mi:** Movie Theater, Video Rental *(Video Showcase 423-2194)*, Sightseeing *(Jamestown Windmill 423-1798, Beavertail Lighthouse 423-9941)*

Provisioning and General Services
OnSite: Delicatessen *(East Ferry Market & Deli 423-1592)*, Wine/Beer, Bakery, Lobster Pound, Bank/ATM, Newsstand, Clothing Store **Near:** Convenience Store *(Cumberland)*, Supermarket *(McQuades 423-0873)*, Gourmet Shop *(Truffles by the Bay 423-9869)*, Post Office, Catholic Church, Protestant Church, Library *(423-7280)*, Beauty Salon, Dry Cleaners, Laundry, Bookstore, Pharmacy *(Bakers 423-2800)*, Hardware Store *(True Value 423-0490, Ace 423-2824)*, Florist, Retail Shops, Copies Etc. **Under 1 mi:** Liquor Store *(Pages 423-0100)*, Fishmonger *(Zeeks Creek 423-1170)*

Transportation
OnSite: Bikes, Water Taxi, InterCity Bus *(RIPTA- Newport/Kingston)*, Ferry Service *(Newport 423-9900)* **OnCall:** Rental Car *(Enterpr 849-3939)*, Taxi *(Yellow 846-1500)* **3+ mi:** Rail *(Kingston)* **Airport:** TF Green *(20 mi.)*

Medical Services
911 Service **OnCall:** Ambulance **Near:** Doctor *(Jamestown Fam 423-2616)*, Dentist *(Bush 423-2110)*, Veterinarian *(Jamestown Clinic 423-2288)* **Hospital:** Newport 783-9718 *(5 mi.)*

Setting -- A large mooring field buffers the network of well-maintained docks; little shops and eateries bind two sides of the boat basin and line Narragansett Ave. as it heads up the hill. Together all of the elements create a picturesque, welcoming village atmosphere. Jamestown is a quieter alternative to the bustle of Newport, with almost everything within walking distance. Views from the docks and moorings are of the bridge and Newport in the distance.

Marina Notes -- Very professional operation with personal service. Launch 8am-9pm, 8am-10pm Fri & Sat in July-Aug. Host to many club cruises, rendezvous and regattas. Founded and operated by the Mungers 1974-today. Major renovation 1995-6. New dock office, reception and large, well-equipped ships' store in 2001. Spruced-up heads. Full service boatyards: Round House & Taylor Point. 10 acres of inside and outside storage. Boat transport. Extended stay and fuel discounts, maintenance packages, wood boat restorations. Self-serve pump-out dock and pump-out boat (Mon-Fri only). Courtesy van to off-site parking lot and boatyard, which is next door to McQuade's supermarket, pizzeria, liquor/hardware combo & laundromat.

Notable -- Onsite are: Spinnaker's Café for breakfast, lunch & snacks, East Ferry Market Deli (cheeses, baked goods, gourmet items), and an ice cream shop. Within a very short walk are 13 eateries from coffee shops to high-end restaurants, including Chopmist Charlie's (casual with late night entertainment) and Bay Voyage Inn, jacket & tie (RI Mag's Best Sun Brunch for 11 years) 10am-2pm & the Navigator Lounge. Ferry to Newport (Bowen's Landing), Ft. Adams, Rose Island, and Goat Island, every 90 min, $7each way. Bus to Newport and Kingston Amtrak. Great biking. Weekly concerts and other special events.

PHOTOS ON CD-ROM: 9

Navigational Information

Lat: 41°35.090' **Long:** 071°17.225' **Tide:** 4 ft. **Current:** n/a **Chart:** 13221
Rep. Depths (*MLW*): Entry 20 ft. **Fuel Dock** 15 ft. **Max Slip/Moor** 15 ft./-
Access: East Passage, 6 miles north of Newport Bridge in Melville

Marina Facilities *(In Season/Off Season)*

Fuel: Diesel
Slips: 100 Total, 50 Transient **Max LOA:** 120 ft. **Max Beam:** n/a
Rate *(per ft.)*: **Day** $2.00 **Week** $30 **Month** $95
Power: 30 amp Incl., **50 amp** n/a, **100 amp** n/a, **200 amp** n/a
Cable TV: No **Dockside Phone:** Yes
Dock Type: n/a
Moorings: 0 Total, 0 Transient **Launch:** n/a
Rate: Day n/a **Week** n/a **Month** n/a
Heads: 1 Toilet(s), 1 Shower(s)
Laundry: 2 Washer(s), 2 Dryer(s) **Pay Phones:** Yes
Pump-Out: OnSite, Full Service **Fee:** n/a **Closed Heads:** Yes

Marina Operations

Owner/Manager: Bain, Willard & Co. **Dockmaster:** John Cawley
In-Season: Year-Round, 8am-5pm* **Off-Season:** n/a
After-Hours Arrival: Call for security clearance
Reservations: Preferred **Credit Cards:** Visa/MC, Amex
Discounts: Boat/US; Safe/Sea **Dockage:** 25% **Fuel:** n/a **Repair:** n/a
Pets: Welcome, Dog Walk Area **Handicap Access:** No

Hinckley Yacht Services

One Little Harbor Landing; Portsmouth, RI 02871

Tel: (401) 683-7100 **VHF: Monitor** 9 **Talk** n/a
Fax: (401) 683-7118 **Alternate Tel:** n/a
Email: inquiries@thco.com **Web:** hinckleyyachtservices.com/rhode_island/
Nearest Town: Newport *(6 mi.)* **Tourist Info:** (401) 847-1600

Marina Services and Boat Supplies

Services - Docking Assistance, Concierge, Trash Pick-Up, Dock Carts **Communication -** Mail & Package Hold, Phone Messages, Fax in/out, Data Ports *(In marina)*, FedEx, UPS, Express Mail **Supplies - OnSite:** Ice *(Block, Cube)*, Ships' Store, Propane **Under 1 mi:** Bait/Tackle **1-3 mi:** CNG **3+ mi:** West Marine *(Newport, 841-9880, 8 mi.)*

Boatyard Services

OnSite: Travelift *(35, 40 & 180T, 15' draft)*, Forklift *(20T hydraulic trailer)*, Engine mechanic *(diesel)*, Electrical Repairs, Electronic Sales, Electronics Repairs, Hull Repairs, Rigger, Sail Loft, Bottom Cleaning, Brightwork, Air Conditioning, Refrigeration, Divers, Compound, Wash & Wax, Interior Cleaning, Propeller Repairs, Woodworking, Metal Fabrication, Painting, Awlgrip, Yacht Design, Yacht Building, Total Refits **Near:** Inflatable Repairs, Life Raft Service. **Yard Rates:** $67.50-80/hr., Haul & Launch $8/ft. *(blocking $2.50/ft.)*, Power Wash $2.50/ft., Bottom Paint $62.50/hr. **Storage:** On-Land Outside $40/ft. Inside $110/ft. Heated $140/ft.

Restaurants and Accommodations

Near: Restaurant *(Schooners 683-2380, L $5-19, D $5-19)* **1-3 mi:** Restaurant *(Reidys Family Restaurant 683-0892)*, Lite Fare *(Claires Roadside Café 683-5134)*, Pizzeria *(West Main Pizza 683-1498)*, Motel *(Founders Brook Motel 683-1244)*, Inn/B&B *(Brown's Bay View Guest House 683-0155)* **3+ mi:** Motel *(Best Western Bay Point 683-3600, 4 mi.)*, *(Quality Inn 846-7600, 4 mi.)*, Hotel *(Newport Marriott 849-8000, 6 mi.)*

Recreation and Entertainment

1-3 mi: Golf Course *(Green Valley Country Club 847-9543)*, Fitness Center *(YMCA 847-9200)*, Video Rental *(Tortoise Video 466-8990)*, Museum *(Green Animals Topiary Gardens 683-1267)*

Provisioning and General Services

OnCall: Liquor Store *(Gleesons 683-0108, Vickers 847-0123)*, Dry Cleaners *(Plaza Cleaners 847-0500)*, Laundry *(Shop & Wash 846-8845)* **Near:** Convenience Store *(Extra Mart 683-2067)*, Pharmacy *(Brooks 683-1270, Walgreens 847-8510)* **Under 1 mi:** Green Grocer *(DeCastro 683-4688)*, Library *(Portsmouth 683-9457)*, Copies Etc. *(J & M 683-0988)* **1-3 mi:** Fishmonger *(Anthony's 846-9620)*, Meat Market *(Aquidneck 847-6982)* **3+ mi:** Supermarket *(Shaw's 848-7560, 5 mi.)*, Delicatessen *(Fatullis Bakery/Deli 847-5166, 4 mi.)*, Farmers' Market *(Aquidneck Market 848-0099 Sat 9am-1pm, 6 mi.)*, Hardware Store *(Rocky's Ace 846-9088, 5 mi.)*

Transportation

OnSite: Courtesy Car/Van *(for provisioning/airport runs)* **OnCall:** Rental Car *(Enterprise 849-3939; International 847-4600)*, Taxi *(Rainbow Cab 849-1333)*, Airport Limo *(TF Green Airport Shuttle 846-1500)* **Near:** Local Bus *(RIPTA to Newport)* **3+ mi:** InterCity Bus *(Greyhound/Bonanza 846-1820, 6 mi.)*, Rail *(Amtrak - Kingston/Providence, 30 min)*, Ferry Service *(Newport-Block Island, Bristol-Prudence Is., 6 mi.)* **Airport:** TF Green *(18 mi.)*

Medical Services

911 Service **OnCall:** Ambulance **1-3 mi:** Dentist *(Swanson 683-0112)*, Veterinarian *(Portsmouth Clinic 683-0803)* **3+ mi:** Doctor *(Aquidneck Medical 683-2290, 3.5 mi.)*, Chiropractor *(Knapp 849-6469, 4 mi.)*, Holistic Services *(January Body Works 683-7733, 4 mi.)* **Hospital:** Newport 847-9592 *(7 mi.)*

Setting -- This 14-acre service yard and 100 slip marina is tucked behind a large wave barrier. On shore are multi-story worksheds that are about as attractive as can be reasonably expected. The docks themselves are state-of-the-art and home to some of the world's most beautiful vessels. Ted Hood designed the comprehensive complex to "accommodate and improve the lives of cruising boaters"; he seems to have succeeded.

Marina Notes -- Little Harbor Marine was acquired in 2001 by Bain, Willard Companies, which bought The Hinckley Co. in 1997 - and has now integrated the two superstars. First-class, full-service boatyard (3 travelifts up to 160T) with an unusual and complete array of on-site marina suppliers and services, including yacht designers, yacht brokers, wet and dry storage, repair/refit facilities, a sailing school and yacht charters. Specializes in complete re-fits - over 20 per year. Facilities, which had begun to show some age, are no doubt seeing immediate upgrade and maintenance. Dockhands on duty 7 days. Telephone, postal, fax, courier services plus a crew lounge, heads, showers and laundry. One acre inside storage, 5 acres outside. 27-page booklet details the amenities.

Notable -- If your pleasure is being surrounded by beautiful vessels in various stages of dress, then this could be your fantasy stop. A convenience store, liquor store, chandlery, and Schooners-on-the-Bay restaurant (11am-10pm, lounge to 1am, 7 days) are a 7-minute walk at East Passage Yachting Center. Newport is 6 miles via rental car, taxi or local bus. Green Animals (847-1000), a topiary garden with over 80 sculpted trees, a Victoriana collection, plant shop and a picnic grove, is a little over a mile, 10am-5pm, $9. Old Colony & Newport RR (624-6951) makes 3 hr. RT with an hour stop at gardens, $6.

PHOTOS ON CD-ROM: 5

East Passage Yachting Center

One Lagoon Road; Portsmouth, RI 02871

Tel: (401) 683-4000 **VHF: Monitor** 9 **Talk** n/a
Fax: (401) 683-6774 **Alternate Tel:** n/a
Email: info@neboatworks.com **Web:** www.neboatworks.com
Nearest Town: Newport *(6 mi.)* **Tourist Info:** (401) 847-1600

Navigational Information

Lat: 41°35.400' **Long:** 071°17.010' **Tide:** 4 ft. **Current:** n/a **Chart:** 13223
Rep. Depths (*MLW*): Entry 15 ft. **Fuel Dock** 15 ft. **Max Slip/Moor** 15 ft./-
Access: East Passage, 6 miles north of Newport Bridge

Marina Facilities *(In Season/Off Season)*

Fuel: Gasoline, Diesel
Slips: 380 Total, 10 Transient **Max LOA:** 110 ft. **Max Beam:** 22 ft.
Rate *(per ft.)*: **Day** $3.00/$1.50 **Week** $17/8.50 **Month** $50/25
Power: 30 amp Incl., **50 amp** Incl., **100 amp** Incl., **200 amp** n/a
Cable TV: No **Dockside Phone:** Yes
Dock Type: Wood, Long Fingers, Pilings, Floating
Moorings: 0 Total, 0 Transient **Launch:** n/a
Rate: Day n/a **Week** n/a **Month** n/a
Heads: 8 Toilet(s), 8 Shower(s) *(with dressing rooms)*
Laundry: 3 Washer(s), 3 Dryer(s), Book Exchange **Pay Phones:** Yes, 5
Pump-Out: OnSite, Full Service, 1 Central **Fee:** $5 **Closed Heads:** Yes

Marina Operations

Owner/Manager: n/a **Dockmaster:** Stan Piszcz III
In-Season: MemDay-LabDay, 7:30-6:30 **Off-Season:** Sep-May, 8:30-3:30
After-Hours Arrival: Call ahead for instructions
Reservations: Recommended **Credit Cards:** Visa/MC, Amex
Discounts: None
Pets: Welcome, Dog Walk Area **Handicap Access:** No

Marina Services and Boat Supplies

Services - Docking Assistance, Security *(24 Hrs., Guards)*, Trash Pick-Up, Dock Carts, Megayacht Facilities **Communication -** Mail & Package Hold, Phone Messages, Fax in/out, FedEx, UPS **Supplies - OnSite:** Ice *(Block, Cube)*, Ships' Store, Propane, CNG **1-3 mi:** Bait/Tackle *(Riverside 625-5181)*, Live Bait **3+ mi:** West Marine *(841-9880, 8 mi.)*

Boatyard Services

OnSite: Travelift *(70T/50T)*, Forklift, Crane, Engine mechanic *(gas, diesel)*, Electrical Repairs, Electronic Sales, Electronics Repairs, Hull Repairs, Rigger, Bottom Cleaning, Brightwork, Air Conditioning, Refrigeration, Compound, Wash & Wax, Woodworking, Metal Fabrication, Painting, Awlgrip, Yacht Broker, Yacht Building, Total Refits **OnCall:** Divers, Interior Cleaning, Propeller Repairs, Inflatable Repairs **Near:** Launching Ramp, Sail Loft, Life Raft Service, Upholstery, Yacht Interiors. **Yard Rates:** $56/hr., Haul & Launch $12/ft. *(blocking incl.)*, Power Wash Incl., Bottom Paint $11/ft. **Storage:** In-Water $25/ft., On-Land $32/ft.

Restaurants and Accommodations

OnSite: Restaurant *(Schooner's 683-2380, L $5-19, D $5-19)* **OnCall:** Pizzeria *(West Main Pizza 683-1498)* **1-3 mi:** Restaurant *(Chris's Diner 683-9814)*, *(Claire's Roadside Café 683-5134)*, Inn/B&B *(Shamrock Farm 851-1240)*, *(Founders Brook Motel 683-1244, $40-140)* **3+ mi:** Restaurant *(Sea Fare Inn 683-0577, 4 mi., D Tue-Sat)*, Motel *(Roger Williams U. Conf. Ctr. 683-3600, 4 mi.)*, Hotel *(Royal Plaza 846-3555, $120-200, 4 mi.)*

Recreation and Entertainment

OnSite: Heated Pool, Picnic Area, Grills, Playground, Volleyball **Near:** Park **Under 1 mi:** Golf Course *(Montaup Country Club 683-0955)*, Fitness Center *(Island Fitness 683-6033)*, Jogging Paths, Museum *(Green Animals Topiary Gardens 683-1267)* **1-3 mi:** Dive Shop **3+ mi:** Bowling *(Hi Way Bowl/Mini Golf 849-9990, 6 mi.)*, Movie Theater *(6 mi.)*, Video Rental *(Tortoise Video 466-8990, 6 mi.)*

Provisioning and General Services

OnCall: Provisioning Service, Liquor Store *(Gleesons 683-0108)*, Dry Cleaners *(Plaza Cleaners 847-0500)*, Laundry *(Shop & Wash 846-8845)* **Near:** Wine/Beer **Under 1 mi:** Convenience Store *(Extra Mart 683-2067)*, Bakery, Green Grocer *(De Castro 683-4688)*, Bank/ATM, Post Office, Catholic Church, Protestant Church, Library *(Portsmouth 683-9457)*, Beauty Salon, Barber Shop, Pharmacy *(Brooks 683-1270; Walgreens 847-8510)*, Newsstand, Hardware Store, Florist, Retail Shops **1-3 mi:** Supermarket *(Clements Market 683-0180; Shaw's 848-7560 5 mi.)*, Fishmonger, Meat Market, Bookstore, Clothing Store **3+ mi:** Farmers' Market *(Aquidneck Growers Market 848-0099 Sat 9am-1pm in Middletown, 6 mi.)*, Buying Club *(BJ's, 5 mi.)*

Transportation

OnCall: Rental Car *(Enterprise 849-3939)*, Taxi *(Rainbow 849-1333)* **Near:** Local Bus *(RIPTA)* **3+ mi:** InterCity Bus *(Greyhound 846-1820, 10 mi.)*, Rail *(Providence, 40 min.)* **Airport:** TF Green 732-3621 *(18 mi.)*

Medical Services

911 Service **OnCall:** Ambulance **1-3 mi:** Doctor *(Amundson/Bond/Wolf son/Deleo 683-4817)* **3+ mi:** Dentist *(Portsmouth Dent. 683-9724, 4 mi.)*, Chiropractor *(Knapp 849-6469, 4 mi.)* **Hospital:** Newport 847-9592 *(7 mi.)*

Setting -- Just south of Coggeshall Point and just north of Hinckley-Little Harbor, the East Passage Yachting Center is sheltered in a hurricane-safe harbor almost totally enclosed by an earth berm. Originally created to train World War II PT boat crews, the basin now houses the largest marina on Narragansett Bay. Its 380 slips line nine parallel piers that open onto a spacious, quiet and exceptionally well maintained full service facility punctuated by welcome spots of floral displays and greenery.

Marina Notes -- 30, 50, and 100 amp electrical service, potable water, telephone hook-up. 50T and 70Tmarine Travelifts. 55,000 square feet of heated, covered workshops. Diesel repair, yacht brokerage, marine electronics, ships' store, rigging shop and a Restaurant & Lounge. The amenities at EPYC include a laundry, shower and toilets, an inviting swimming pool (overlooking the docks), picnic and BBQ area (under a large canopy) and a volleyball court. Wet and dry storage. Limited (4 slips) megayacht dockage but full shipyard/repair/WOD facilities. Owned and operated by New England Boatworks.

Notable -- On site is Schooners on the Bay restaurant, open 7 days from 11am-10pm, the Lounge until 1am offers inside and deck dining. Tuesday night sailboat races and regular monthly social and cookout or clam boil. A mile away is Green Animals Topiary Gardens (847-1000); kids of all ages -- and horticulturists -- will love it. More than 80 century-old trees have been scissored into a wildly whimsical display of animals and objects - antique toy collection, too, 10am-5pm, $9. NRTA bus to Newport stops nearby, also taxis and rental cars at hand.

PHOTOS ON CD-ROM: 9

Navigational Information

Lat: 41°39.410' **Long:** 071°16.150' **Tide:** 4 ft. **Current:** n/a **Chart:** 13221
Rep. Depths (*MLW*): Entry 12 ft. **Fuel Dock** n/a **Max Slip/Moor** 12 ft./12 ft.
Access: East Side of Harbor - under 107' (Red, White & Blue) flagpole

Marina Facilities *(In Season/Off Season)*

Fuel: No
Slips: 10 Total, 10 Transient **Max LOA:** 180 ft. **Max Beam:** n/a
Rate *(per ft.)*: **Day** $2.50/$2.50* **Week** Inq. **Month** Inq.
Power: 30 amp Incl., **50 amp** Incl., **100 amp** n/a, **200 amp** n/a
Cable TV: No **Dockside Phone:** No
Dock Type: Wood, Pilings, Alongside, Floating
Moorings: 14 Total, 14 Transient **Launch:** Yes (Free), Dinghy Dock
Rate: Day $30 **Week** n/a **Month** n/a
Heads: 2 Toilet(s), 2 Shower(s) *(with dressing rooms)*
Laundry: None **Pay Phones:** No
Pump-Out: 1 Port **Fee:** $5 **Closed Heads:** Yes

Marina Operations

Owner/Manager: Bill Knowles **Dockmaster:** Charles White
In-Season: Apr-Dec 31, 7:30am-6pm **Off-Season:** Closed
After-Hours Arrival: Pick up mooring and check in next morning
Reservations: Preferred **Credit Cards:** Visa/MC, Amex
Discounts: Museum Membership **Dockage:** n/a **Fuel:** n/a **Repair:** n/a
Pets: Welcome **Handicap Access:** Yes, Heads, Docks

Herreshoff Marine Museum

PO Box 450; 1 Burnside Street; Bristol, RI 02809

Tel: (401) 253-5000 **VHF: Monitor** 68 **Talk** 68
Fax: (401) 253-6222 **Alternate Tel:** (401) 253-5035
Email: b.knowles@herreshoff.org **Web:** ww.herreshoff.org
Nearest Town: Bristol *(0.5 mi.)* **Tourist Info:** (401) 245-0750

Marina Services and Boat Supplies

Services - Docking Assistance, Trash Pick-Up, Dock Carts, Megayacht Facilities **Supplies - Near:** Ice *(Cube)*, Ships' Store **Under 1 mi:** Ice *(Block)* **1-3 mi:** Boat/US, Bait/Tackle *(Neves Bait Tackle & Marine 253-5358)*, Propane *(Bristol True Value 253-8180)* **3+ mi:** West Marine *(15 mi.)*

Boatyard Services

Near: Launching Ramp. **Under 1 mi:** Travelift. **Nearest Yard:** Bristol Marine (401) 253-2200

Restaurants and Accommodations

Near: Restaurant *(Lobster Pot 253-9100, L $5-14, D $8-25, moorings/dinghy dock)*, *(Hotpoint 254-7474)*, *(Roberto's 254-9732)*, Lite Fare *(Aidan's Pub & Grub 254-1940)*, Inn/B&B *(William's Grant Inn 253-0040, $80-135)* **Under 1 mi:** Restaurant *(S.S. Dion 253-2884, D $12-26)*, Seafood Shack *(Quito's 253-4500, L $9-22, D $9-22, take-out 'til 5pm)*, Snack Bar *(Bristol Bagel 254-1390)*, Coffee Shop *(Café La France L, snacks)*, Pizzeria *(Sam's 253-7949)*, Inn/B&B *(Bradford-Dimond-Norris House 253-6338, $90-130)*, *(Rockwell House Inn 253-4222, $100-175)* **1-3 mi:** Motel *(Bristol Motor Lodge 253-7600)*, Inn/B&B *(Reynolds House Inn 254-0230)*

Recreation and Entertainment

OnSite: Museum **Near:** Roller Blade/Bike Paths *(Access to East Bay Bike Path to Providence)*, Sightseeing *(Bristol's streets)*, Special Events *(Oldest July Fourth Celebraton in the U.S.)* **Under 1 mi:** Movie Theater *(Bristol Cinema 253-4312)*, Cultural Attract *(Blithewold Mansion & Arboretum 253-2707 and Ship owner George deWolfe's 1810 Linden Place 253-0390)* **1-3 mi:** Golf Course *(Pocasset Country Club 683-7300)*, Boat Rentals *(Kayaks from Bristol Marine)*, Video Rental *(Videozone 253-4456)*, Park *(Colt State Park & Coggeshall Farm Museum)* **3+ mi:** Fitness Center *(East Bay Fitness 247-7440, 4 mi.)*, Bowling *(Dudek Bowling Alleys 245-9471, 5 mi.)*

Provisioning and General Services

OnSite: Bookstore, Clothing Store **Near:** Bank/ATM, Protestant Church, Newsstand **Under 1 mi:** Delicatessen *(Café La France)*, Wine/Beer *(Violas 253-8094)*, Liquor Store *(Bristol Bagel Works 254-1390)*, Bakery, Meat Market *(Azorians Butcher Shop 253-7724)*, Post Office, Catholic Church, Beauty Salon, Barber Shop, Dry Cleaners, Laundry, Pharmacy *(Compagna's 253-8808; CVS 253-2050)*, Hardware Store *(Hope Hdwre 253-9777)*, Florist **1-3 mi:** Convenience Store *(Goglia's 253-9876)*, Supermarket *(Stop & Shop 254-2525; Hi Lo Market 254-0644)*, Farmers' Market *(Colt State Park 222-2781 Fri 9am-1pm)*, Library *(Rogers 253-6948)*

Transportation

OnCall: Water Taxi *(Bristol Marine "Olivia")*, Rental Car *(Carefree 254-2900, Enterprise 253-0233)*, Taxi *(A Taxi 245-6684)* **Under 1 mi:** Ferry Service *(Prudence & Hog Islands 253-9808)* **1-3 mi:** Bikes *(Bristol Marine)*, InterCity Bus *(New England Coach 253-9566)* **3+ mi:** Rail *(Providence Amtrak, 40 mi.)* **Airport:** TF Green *(45 mi.)*

Medical Services

911 Service **OnCall:** Ambulance **Under 1 mi:** Veterinarian *(Bristol Clinic 253-1810)* **1-3 mi:** Doctor *(Bristol County Medical Center 253-8900)*, Dentist, Chiropractor *(East Bay 253-7475)* **Hospital:** Saint Annes 235-5312 *(9 mi.)*

Setting -- Situated on the eastern shore at the mouth of protected (except from the S & SW) and pristine Bristol Harbor, the exceptionally well-executed Herreshoff Marine Museum is a must for anyone with a passion for messing about in boats -- especially since it's also within walking distance of the historic village of Bristol. The attractive new wharves and floating docks are part of the recently restored waterfront park, an integral part of the Museum.

Marina Notes -- *Slips: Members 1st night free, consecutive nights $2/ft. Moorings: Members 1st night free, consecutive nights $20. Memberships begin at $35. Slip count approximate; alongside dockage (stationary and floating) and three moorings. Dockage fees include museum entrance. An increasingly favorite stop for club cruises and rendezvous; a tent is usually erected along the water for events (rafting permits accommodation of more boats). Museum open May-Oct, 10am-5pm, 7 days, reg. admission $5/2. Heads/showers are on the main floor; an additional men's on the third. The major waterfront renovation continues and includes new heads/showers on the waterfront. Town Rockwell Park Marina may also have smaller boat dockage; Harbormaster: 253-1700 Ch.16.

Notable -- The Herreshoff Marine Museum is a complex of buildings and open air exhibits across the road from the docks. It is home to the America's Cup Hall of Fame (8 winners were Herreshoff designs) and also to more than 60 sailing and power vessels that were designed and built by Herreshoff Manufacturing from 1859 to 1914. Highlights are Sprite (1859) and Aria (1914), considered by some the most beautiful hull form ever built. The main museum building is thoughtfully constructed with an overhead walk-way to permit "top-down" viewing of most of the yachts.

PHOTOS ON CD-ROM: 8

Bristol Yacht Club

Bristol Yacht Club

PO Box 180; 101 Poppasquash Road; Bristol, RI 02809

Tel: (401) 253-2922 **VHF: Monitor** 68 **Talk** 68
Fax: (401) 253-3283 **Alternate Tel:** n/a
Email: bristolyc@ids.net **Web:** www.bristolyc.com
Nearest Town: Bristol *(1.5 mi.)* **Tourist Info:** (401) 245-0750

Navigational Information

Lat: 41°40.560' **Long:** 071°17.334' **Tide:** 4 ft. **Current:** 1 kt. **Chart:** 13223
Rep. Depths (*MLW*): Entry 9 ft. **Fuel Dock** n/a **Max Slip/Moor** -/8 ft.
Access: Bristol Harbor Western Shore - East side of Poppasquash Point

Marina Facilities *(In Season/Off Season)*

Fuel: No
Slips: 0 Total, 0 Transient **Max LOA:** n/a **Max Beam:** n/a
Rate *(per ft.)*: **Day** n/a **Week** n/a **Month** n/a
Power: 30 amp n/a, **50 amp** n/a, **100 amp** n/a, **200 amp** n/a
Cable TV: No **Dockside Phone:** No
Dock Type: Floating
Moorings: 50 Total, 20 Transient **Launch:** Yes (Free)
Rate: Day $30 **Week** n/a **Month** n/a
Heads: 4 Toilet(s), 4 Shower(s)
Laundry: None **Pay Phones:** Yes
Pump-Out: OnCall, 1 Port **Fee:** $5 **Closed Heads:** Yes

Marina Operations

Owner/Manager: Christopher Healey **Dockmaster:** n/a
In-Season: May 6-Oct 15, 8am-9pm **Off-Season:** Closed
After-Hours Arrival: Call in advance
Reservations: Yes, Preferred **Credit Cards:** Visa/MC, Dscvr, Amex
Discounts: None
Pets: Welcome **Handicap Access:** No

Marina Services and Boat Supplies

Services - Security *(Two Bristol town police boats patrol the harbor)*, Dock Carts **Communication -** FedEx, AirBorne, UPS, Express Mail **Supplies - OnSite:** Ice *(Block, Cube, Shaved)* **1-3 mi:** Propane *(Bristol True Value 253-8180)* **3+ mi:** Ships' Store *(Boat Locker 683-0400, 6 mi.)*, West Marine *(508-336-5004, 10 mi.)*, Marine Discount Store *(Boater's World 508-336-0417, 10 mi.)*

Boatyard Services

Nearest Yard: Bristol Marine (401) 253-2200

Restaurants and Accommodations

OnCall: Pizzeria *(Caldo 253-2866)* **1-3 mi:** Restaurant *(Sandbar 253-5485)*, *(Redlefsen's Rotisserie & Grill 254-1188, L $3-11, D $4-19)*, *(Hope Diner 253-1759)*, *(Hotpoint 254-7474)*, *(Roberto's 254-9732)*, *(Lobster Pot 253-9100, L $5-14, D $8-25, Moorings & dinghy dock)*, *(S.S. Dion 253-2884)*, Seafood Shack *(Quito's 243-4500, L $9-22, D $9-22, Take-out 'til 5pm)*, Lite Fare *(Papa Joe's Wrap Shack 253-9911)*, *(The Sandbar 253-5485, L&D)*, Inn/B&B *(Reynolds House 254-0230)*, *(Point Pleasant Inn 253-0627)*, *(Hearth House 253-1404)*, *(Rockwell House 253-0040, $100-175)*

Recreation and Entertainment

OnSite: Picnic Area, Grills, Playground **Near:** Beach *(Bristol Town Beach)*, Boat Rentals *(Ocean State Kayaks 254-4000)*, Roller Blade/Bike Paths *(connect to East Bay Bike Path to Providence)*, Park *(Colt State Park)*, Museum *(Coggeshall Farm 243-9062 Tue-Sun)*, Special Events *(Country's oldest 4th of July parade)* **1-3 mi:** Golf Course *(Bristol Golf Club 254-1282)*, Movie Theater *(Bristol Cinema 253-4312)*, Video Rental *(Blockbuster 254-6940)*, Cultural Attract *(Roger Williams University Dance Theater 254-3624 and Performing Arts Center 254-3626)*, Galleries *(Bristol Art Gallery 253-0672)* **3+ mi:** Fitness Center *(East Bay Fitness 247-7440, 5 mi.)*, Bowling *(Dudek Bowling 245-9471, 3 mi.)*, Fishing Charter *(Striper Marina 245-6121, 4 mi.)*

Provisioning and General Services

Near: Farmers' Market *(Colt State Park 222-2781 Fri 9am-1pm)* **Under 1 mi:** Post Office **1-3 mi:** Convenience Store, Supermarket *(Stop & Shop 254-2525; Hi Lo Market 254-0644)*, Liquor Store *(Mt. Hope 253-2291)*, Bakery *(Steph's Pastry & Coffee 253-6032)*, Fishmonger, Lobster Pound, Bank/ATM, Catholic Church, Protestant Church, Library *(Rogers 253-6948)*, Beauty Salon, Barber Shop, Laundry *(King's Coin Laundry 253-1613)*, Bookstore *(Good Books 254-0390)*, Pharmacy *(CVS 253-2052)*, Newsstand, Hardware Store *(Hope Hardware 253-9777)*, Retail Shops **3+ mi:** Delicatessen *(Hall's Deli 247-2066, 4 mi.)*

Transportation

OnSite: Rental Car *(Enterprise 253-0233, Sensible 253-3433)* **OnCall:** Taxi *(A Taxi 245-6684)* **Near:** Water Taxi **Under 1 mi:** Ferry Service *(Prudence & Hog Islands 253-9808)* **1-3 mi:** InterCity Bus **Airport:** TF Green *(45 mi.)*

Medical Services

911 Service **OnCall:** Ambulance **Under 1 mi:** Chiropractor *(East Bay Chiropractic 253-7475)*, Holistic Services *(Massage Therapy 935-5656)* **1-3 mi:** Doctor *(Bristol County Medical Center 253-8900)*, Dentist *(Lukasiewicz 253-9613)*, Veterinarian *(Bristol Vet Clinic 253-1810)* **Hospital:** St. Annes 508-235-5285 *(9 mi.)*

Setting -- The gracious Bristol Yacht Club commands the first set of docks to port almost to the head of Bristol Harbor. It is located on the quiet side on beautiful, residential Poppasquash Point -- half of which is 460 acre Colt State Park. The attractive mansard roofed, two-story gray shingled clubhouse, and the small fuel dock pavilion, make this an easy place to find. The views from the mooring field are of unspoiled shoreline interspersed with handsome homes, on one side, and an historic New England village on the other. The clubhouse's deep front deck is populated with inviting tables and chairs.

Marina Notes -- Two launches service the mooring field from 8am-9pm. Some limited dockside tie-up, 6 feet of water. Ample dinghy dockage and dinghy storage space. Launch will take groups across to the town by pre-arrangement. Open to all boaters. All club facilities available to mooring guests -- bar, lounge, deck, and four cinder-block full baths. Harbor open to the southwest; can be rolly. Dinghy landings in town at Town Pier or Bristol Harbor Inn.

Notable -- Almost adjacent is Colt State Park with a beach, picnicking, fishing and hiking. Also home to the Coggeshall Farm Museum, an 18thC working farm with oxen, crafts, herb/vegetable gardens and many special events (e.g. animal blessing in Aug, sheep shearing in May). Across the harbor, Herreshoff Marine Museum (253-5000) $5/2, has a dinghy dock. Close at hand are several interesting attractions: 2.5 mi. is 1908, 45-room, Blithewold Mansion and Arboretum (253-2707) $7.50 - (or dinghy to Herreshoff and walk); 1.4 mile, in town, is extraordinary 1810 Linden Place (253-0390), the pinnacle of Bristol's "fair houses", $4. Farther afield, 500 acre Brown U. Haffenreffer Museum of Anthropology is devoted to Native American artifacts (253-8388).

PHOTOS ON CD-ROM: 6

Navigational Information

Lat: 41°40.609' **Long:** 071°17.311' **Tide:** 4 ft. **Current:** n/a **Chart:** 13223
Rep. Depths (*MLW*): Entry 12 ft. **Fuel Dock** n/a **Max Slip/Moor** 7 ft./8 ft.
Access: NW corner of Bristol Harbor. East side of Poppasquash Point

Marina Facilities *(In Season/Off Season)*

Fuel: No
Slips: 25 Total, 5 Transient **Max LOA:** 70 ft. **Max Beam:** n/a
Rate *(per ft.)*: **Day** $2.00/$2.00 **Week** $10.50 **Month** n/a
Power: 30 amp Yes, **50 amp** Yes, **100 amp** n/a, **200 amp** n/a
Cable TV: No **Dockside Phone:** No
Dock Type: Wood, Floating
Moorings: 60 Total, 5 Transient **Launch:** Yes ($3), Dinghy Dock
Rate: Day $250/$25 **Week** $21/$21 **Month** $16/$16
Heads: 1 Toilet(s), 1 Shower(s) *(with dressing rooms)*
Laundry: None, Book Exchange **Pay Phones:** No
Pump-Out: OnSite, Full Service, 1 Central **Fee:** $5 **Closed Heads:** Yes

Marina Operations

Owner/Manager: Andy Tysca **Dockmaster:** Patrick O'Connell
In-Season: Year-Round, 6am-5pm* **Off-Season:** n/a
After-Hours Arrival: Call ahead
Reservations: Preferred **Credit Cards:** Visa/MC, Dscvr, Amex
Discounts: Boat/US **Dockage:** 25% **Fuel:** n/a **Repair:** n/a
Pets: Welcome, Dog Walk Area **Handicap Access:** No

Bristol Marine Co.

99 Poppasquash Road; Bristol, RI 02809

Tel: (401) 253-2200 **VHF: Monitor** 69 **Talk** 69
Fax: (401) 253-0007 **Alternate Tel:** n/a
Email: mail@bristolmarine.com **Web:** www.bristolmarine.com
Nearest Town: Bristol *(1.6 mi.)* **Tourist Info:** (401) 245-0750

Marina Services and Boat Supplies

Services - Docking Assistance, Dock Carts **Supplies - OnSite:** Ice *(Block, Cube)* **1-3 mi:** Bait/Tackle *(Neves Bait Tackle & Marine 253-5358)*, Propane *(Bristol Ace True Value 253-8180)*

Boatyard Services

OnSite: Travelift *(50T)*, Forklift, Crane, Engine mechanic *(gas, diesel)*, Electrical Repairs, Hull Repairs, Rigger, Brightwork, Air Conditioning, Refrigeration, Divers, Compound, Wash & Wax, Interior Cleaning, Propeller Repairs, Woodworking, Upholstery, Yacht Interiors, Painting, Awlgrip, Yacht Design, Yacht Building, Total Refits **Member:** ABBRA, ABYC **Yard Rates:** $58/hr., Haul & Launch $6/ft., Power Wash $2/ft., Bottom Paint $9/ft. **Storage:** On-Land $60/ft.

Restaurants and Accommodations

OnCall: Pizzeria *(House of Pizza 253-2550)* **Near:** Inn/B&B *(Hearth House B&B 253-1404)* **1-3 mi:** Restaurant *(Lobster Pot 253-9100, L $5-14, D $8-25, moorings/dinghy dock)*, *(Sandbar 253-5485)*, *(Hope Diner 253-1759)*, *(Redlefsens Rotisserie & Grill 254-1188, L $3-11, D $4-19)*, *(Café La France 253-0360)*, Seafood Shack *(Quito's 253-4500, L $7-22, D $10-22, also take-out 'til 5pm)*, Motel *(King Philip 253-7600, $40-90)*, Hotel *(Bristol Harbor 254-1444)*, Inn/B&B *(Willliam's Grant 253-4222, $80-130)*, *(Bradford-Dimond-Norris House 253-6338, $90-125)*, *(Rockwell House 253-0040, $100-145)*, *(Point Pleasant 253-0627, $175-350)*, *(Reynolds House 254-0230)*

Recreation and Entertainment

OnSite: Picnic Area, Boat Rentals *(Ocean State Kayaks 254-4000)*, Fishing Charter **Near:** Beach *(Bristol Town Beach)*, Jogging Paths, Roller Blade/Bike Paths *(Connects to East Bay Bike Path)*, Park *(Colt State Park)*, Museum *(Coggeshall Farm 243-9062)* **Under 1 mi:** Playground **1-3 mi:** Golf Course *(Bristol 253-9844)*, Video Rental *(Videozone 253-4456)*, Cultural Attract *(Barn Summer Theater & Bristol Theater at Roger Williams U. 254-3626, Also Blithewold Mansion 253-2707, Linden Place 253-0390, Haffenreffer Museum of Anthropology 253-8388)*

Provisioning and General Services

OnCall: Dry Cleaners, Laundry **Near:** Farmers' Market *(Colt State Park 222-2781 Fri 9-1)* **1-3 mi:** Convenience Store *(Hi-Lo Supermarkets 254-0644)*, Supermarket *(Stop & Shop 254-2525)*, Wine/Beer, Liquor Store *(Mt. Hope 253-2291)*, Bakery, Fishmonger, Lobster Pound, Meat Market, Bank/ATM, Post Office, Catholic Church, Protestant Church, Library *(Rogers 253-6948)*, Beauty Salon, Barber Shop, Bookstore *(Good Books 254-0390)*, Pharmacy *(Barrington 245-8855)*, Newsstand, Hardware Store *(Pansa 253-7616)*, Florist **3+ mi:** Delicatessen *(Hall's 247-2066, 4 mi.)*

Transportation

OnSite: Bikes **OnCall:** Rental Car *(Enterprise 253-0233, Sensible 253-3433)*, Taxi *(A Taxi 245-6684)* **Near:** Water Taxi *($3.00)* **Under 1 mi:** Local Bus *(RIPTA)*, InterCity Bus *(New England Coach 253-9566)* **1-3 mi:** Ferry Service *(Prudence & Hog Islands 253-9808)* **3+ mi:** Rail *(Amtrak, Providence, 40 mi.)* **Airport:** TF Green *(45 mi.)*

Medical Services

911 Service **OnCall:** Ambulance **1-3 mi:** Doctor *(Bristol County Medical Center 253-8900)*, Dentist *(Allen 253-9636)*, Chiropractor *(East Bay 253-7475)* **Hospital:** St. Annes 508-235-5285 *(9 mi.)*

Setting -- Located on Poppasquash Point, a mile and a half around the harbor from the historic village of Bristol, Bristol Marine is a recent iteration of the facility that was once home to the venerable boat builder, Bristol Yachts. The docks and mooring field are tucked well into the harbor with expansive views.

Marina Notes -- *Closed Sat & Sun. Launch & water taxi service provided by 26 passenger, club-quality "Olivia" - one-trip, ten-trip, seasonal passes (starting at $3 pp, 1-way, $20 10-trip). In 1998, a new ownership team took over this boatyard. Subsequently there have been significant facility upgrades, including a new travelift. They purchased the original molds from Bristol Yachts (which ceased production in 1997 after 30 years) and are re-commencing production with a Bristol 48.8. There are 16,000 sq.ft of heated indoor storage. 3 RI state guest moorings at harbor's head. Harbormaster: 253-1700.

Notable -- The launch service will deliver guests to Bristol Marine's docks, the Herreshoff Museum (253-5000), or to "downtown" Bristol -- at the centrally-located town dock. Dinghies and boats under 30 feet can find transient dockage at the town dock and Bristol Harbor Inn -- located in the center of Thames Street Landing, a boardwalk-style complex of 9 historic buildings integrated with retail shops and pedestrian walkways. Don't miss Hope Street's famous colonial houses! More than 250,000 people participate in Bristol's July 4th celebration, held every year since 1785 -- the oldest celebration in the U.S. Bristol Marine is adjacent to the 460-acre Colt State Park,which features fitness trails & exercise stations, the Chapel-by-the-Sea and Coggeshall Farm Museum, a working 18-19thC farm with craft demos (Tue-Sun 243-9062, Harvest Fair in Mid-Sep). A 13-mile shoreside bike path to Providence begins nearby.

PHOTOS ON CD-ROM: 6

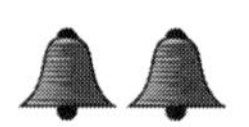

Barrington Yacht Club

25 Barton Avenue; Barrington, RI 02806

Tel: (401) 245-1181 **VHF: Monitor** 68 **Talk** 68
Fax: (401) 245-0275 **Alternate Tel:** n/a
Email: nelson@barringtonyc.com **Web:** www.barringtonyc.com
Nearest Town: Barrington *(1.4 mi.)* **Tourist Info:** (401) 245-0750

Navigational Information

Lat: 41°44.052' **Long:** 071°17.057' **Tide:** n/a **Current:** 4 kt. **Chart:** 13221
Rep. Depths (*MLW*): Entry 10 ft. **Fuel Dock** n/a **Max Slip/Moor** 6 ft./10 ft.
Access: Warren River channel to G3, left into Barrington River

Marina Facilities *(In Season/Off Season)*

Fuel: Gasoline, Diesel
Slips: 0 Total, 0 Transient **Max LOA:** 42 ft. **Max Beam:** n/a
Rate *(per ft.)*: **Day** n/a **Week** n/a **Month** n/a
Power: 30 amp n/a, **50 amp** n/a, **100 amp** n/a, **200 amp** n/a
Cable TV: No **Dockside Phone:** No
Dock Type: n/a
Moorings: 30 Total, 10 Transient **Launch:** Yes (Included)
Rate: Day $20 **Week** Inq. **Month** Inq.
Heads: 6 Toilet(s), 4 Shower(s)
Laundry: None **Pay Phones:** No
Pump-Out: OnSite, Full Service, 1 Central **Fee:** n/a **Closed Heads:** Yes

Marina Operations

Owner/Manager: Nelson Hawkins **Dockmaster:** Varies
In-Season: May-Oct, 8am-Sunset **Off-Season:** Nov-Apr, Closed
After-Hours Arrival: Call ahead - must pre-arrange
Reservations: Varies, Call **Credit Cards:** Visa/MC, Dscvr
Discounts: Reciprocal only **Dockage:** n/a **Fuel:** n/a **Repair:** n/a
Pets: Welcome, Dog Walk Area **Handicap Access:** No

Marina Services and Boat Supplies

Services - Docking Assistance, Boaters' Lounge, Trash Pick-Up, Dock Carts **Communication -** Phone Messages, Data Ports *(At the Library)*, FedEx, AirBorne, UPS, Express Mail *(Sat Del)* **Supplies - OnSite:** Ice *(Block, Cube)* **Under 1 mi:** Propane *(Bristol County Bottled Gas 245-4862)* **1-3 mi:** Bait/Tackle *(Lucky's 247-2223)* **3+ mi:** West Marine *(336-5004, 6 mi.)*, Boat/US *(5 mi.)*

Boatyard Services

Nearest Yard: Stanley's Boat Yard (401) 245-5090

Restaurants and Accommodations

OnSite: Restaurant *(Tyler Point Grille 247-0017, D $8-20)* **Under 1 mi:** Restaurant *(TaVino 245-0231)*, *(Golden Bowl 247-1800)*, *(Bulllock's 245-6502)*, *(Nathaniel Porter 245-6622, D $13-22)*, *(Wharf Tavern 245-5043)*, Coffee Shop *(D'Angelo's Sandwich 247-0102)*, Pizzeria *(Chicago Pizza 247-2202)*, Inn/B&B *(Nathaniel Porter L&D, restored 1795 sea captain's home - innkeeper is a descendant)*, *(Candlewick Inn 247-2425)*

Recreation and Entertainment

Near: Jogging Paths, Roller Blade/Bike Paths *(Access to 14 mi. paved East Bay Bicycle Path - Providence to Bristol)*, Park *(30 acre Osamequin River Nature Trail & Walker Farm in Hundred Acre Cove)*, Sightseeing *(1702 Tyler Point Cemetery, a mile farther is 1710 Barrington Congregational Church & 1887 Town Hall)* **Under 1 mi:** Picnic Area *(Veterans' Park)*, Playground, Tennis Courts *(Barrington YMCA & Barrington H.S.)*, Fitness Center *(Body Natural 245-0022)*, Video Rental *(Movie Gallery 245-8567)*, Museum *(Warren's Firemen's Museum 245-7600 by app't)*, Special Events *(Warren is the "Clambake Capital" with events many summer weekends, reservations critical $20, 245-1977)* **1-3 mi:** Beach *(Barrington Town Beach)*, Golf Course *(Windmill GC 245-1463)*, Bowling *(Dudek 245-9471)*

Provisioning and General Services

Near: Bank/ATM, Beauty Salon *(Salon Elite 245-7609)*, Newsstand, Retail Shops **Under 1 mi:** Supermarket *(Center 245-4900, Shaw's 245-5882)*, Delicatessen *(Hall's 247-2066)*, Liquor Store *(1776 Barrington 245-1776)*, Fishmonger, Post Office, Catholic Church, Protestant Church, Synagogue, Library *(Barrington PL 247-1920 - Internet access)*, Dry Cleaners *(Grandpa's 245-9288)*, Laundry *(Launder 'n Luxury 245-8060)*, Bookstore *(Barrington Books 245-7925)*, Hardware Store *(Mercier's 245-8964)*, Copies Etc. *(East Bay 245-9060)* **1-3 mi:** Pharmacy *(Brooks 245-9079)* **3+ mi:** Buying Club *(Sam's Club 336-8262, 5 mi.)*

Transportation

OnCall: Rental Car *(Enterprise 336-1118)*, Taxi *(A Taxi 245-6684)*, Airport Limo *(Starlight 245-0575)* **Near:** Local Bus *(RIPTA 781-9400 $1.25/zone Bike racks, too)* **3+ mi:** Rail *(Amtrak 727-7382, 12 mi.)* **Airport:** TF Green *(19 mi.)*

Medical Services

911 Service **OnCall:** Ambulance **Near:** Doctor *(Capizzo 247-0130)* **Under 1 mi:** Dentist, Chiropractor *(Barrington Chiro 245-7010)*, Veterinarian *(Barrington Vet 245-9226)* **1-3 mi:** Holistic Services *(Massageworks 254-9675)* **Hospital:** Rhode Island 274-1122 *(12 mi.)*

Setting -- This low-key, gracious, family yacht club sits on Tyler Point, between the Warren and Barrington Rivers. Rocking chairs line the broad front porch that overlooks the docks, river and homes on the far bank. A short way up river, a fixed bridge ends big boat navigation creating the sense of a basin.

Marina Notes -- Established in 1908. Two moored floating docks accommodate boats on both sides and are likely homes for transient boats. All visiting yachtspeople welcomed. Pool is for use of members only. Launch 8am-9pm. One of the largest fleets of Optimists and 420s on the Bay. Pump-out station open Tue-Thu 4-7pm. Pump-out boat will not call to transient boats unless pre-paid. Beware the ledge near the main dock; call for local knowledge. Stanley's Boat Yard next door may have an open slip for smaller boats. Tyler Point Grille is virtually onsite and also offers take-out Sun-Thu 4:30-10pm, Fri & Sat 4:30-11pm.

Notable -- Historic Barrington village, first settled in 1632, is now a pretty, prosperous Providence suburb, with deep roots and beautiful old homes. A walk along Rumstick & Mathewson Roads will yield some of the best. One block to Rte 114 and RIPTA bus to Providence and Newport. Samsonite factory nearby mars the landscape but has a factory outlet. A small shopping plaza is about 0.6 mile with Center Market and a couple of eateries (Golden Bowl, Chicago Pizza Express, D'Angelo's). Shaw's supermarket is 0.1 mile farther. It's a 0.7 mile dinghy ride (or mile walk) to the funky Warren waterfront -- 8 area restaurants (Wharf & TaVino are "dock & dine"), Firemen's Museum, antique shops, fish market, hardware, laundry & liquor store. Next to Wharf Tavern is the home of the Dyer dink. The area between the River (Water Street) and Rte 114 is worth a stroll for its wide range of 18th & 19thC structures.

XI. Rhode Island: Western Narragansett Bay

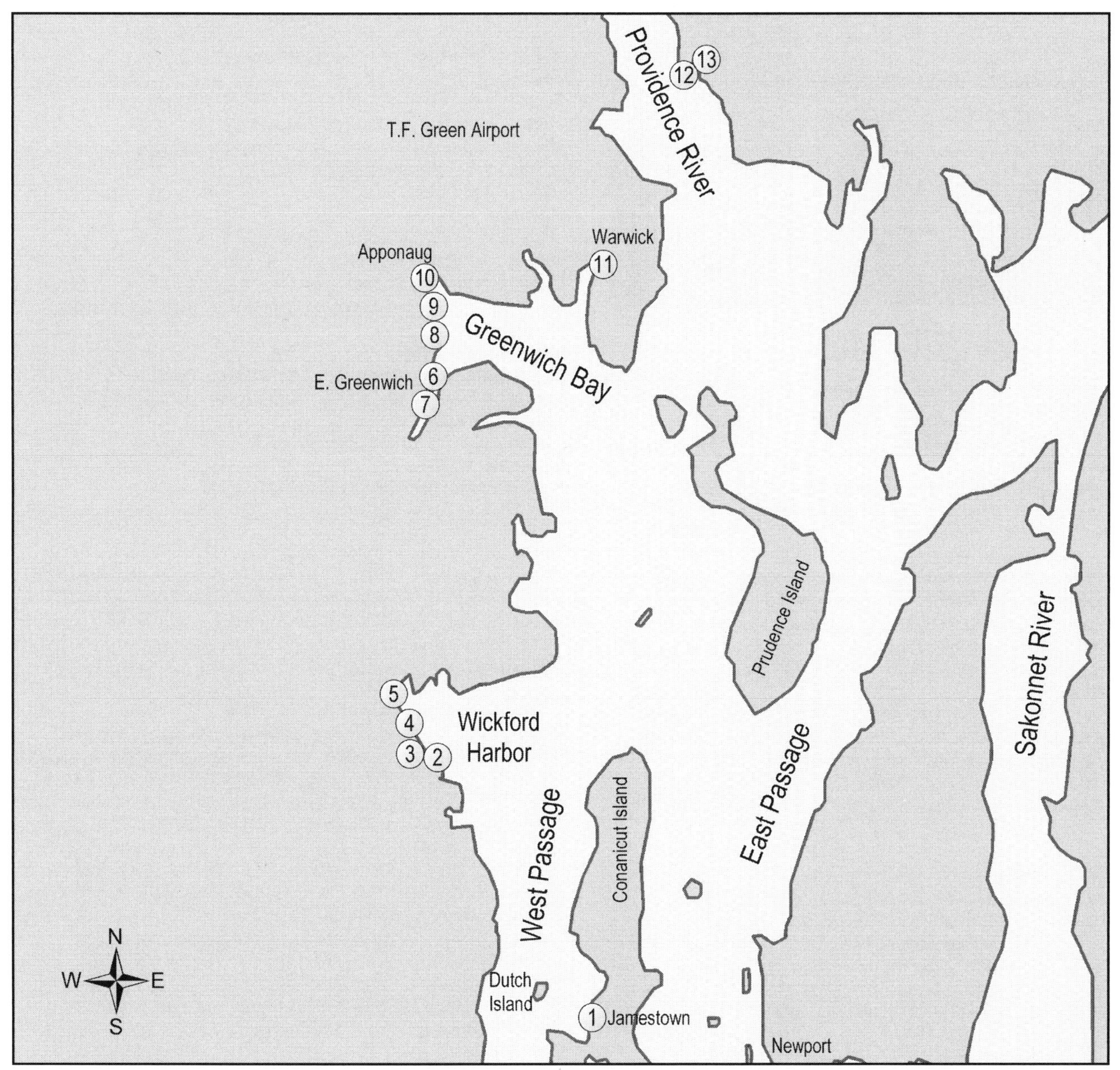

MAP	MARINA	HARBOR	PAGE	MAP	MARINA	HARBOR	PAGE
1	**Dutch Harbor Boatyard**	*Dutch Island Harbor*	238	8	**Brewer Yacht Yard Cowesett**	*Greenwich Bay*	245
2	**Wickford Shipyard, Inc.**	*Wickford Cove*	239	9	**Greenwich Bay Marinas**	*Greenwich Bay*	246
3	**Brewer Wickford Cove Marina**	*Wickford Cove*	240	10	**Apponaug Harbor Marina**	*Greenwich Bay*	247
4	**Pleasant Street Wharf**	*Wickford Cove*	241	11	**Bay Marina, Inc.**	*Greenwich Bay*	248
5	**Wickford Marina**	*Wickford Cove*	242	12	**Bullock Cove Marine**	*Bullock Cove*	249
6	**Norton's Shipyard & Marina**	*Greenwich Bay*	243	13	**Brewer Cove Haven Marina**	*Bullock Cove*	250
7	**Milt's Marina/Twenty Water Street**	*Greenwich Bay*	244				

Dutch Harbor Boatyard

PO Box 175; 252 Narragansett Avenue; Jamestown, RI 02835

Tel: (401) 423-0630 **VHF: Monitor** 68 **Talk** n/a
Fax: (401) 423-3834 **Alternate Tel:** n/a
Email: n/a **Web:** n/a
Nearest Town: Jamestown *(0.7 mi.)* **Tourist Info:** (401) 423-3650

Navigational Information
Lat: 41°30.000' **Long:** 071°23.060' **Tide:** n/a **Current:** n/a **Chart:** 13221
Rep. Depths (*MLW*): Entry 15 ft. **Fuel Dock** 12 ft. **Max Slip/Moor** -/15 ft.
Access: West Passage to Dutch Island Harbor past steel pier

Marina Facilities *(In Season/Off Season)*
Fuel: No
Slips: 0 Total, 0 Transient **Max LOA:** 50 ft. **Max Beam:** 18 ft.
Rate *(per ft.)*: **Day** n/a **Week** n/a **Month** n/a
Power: 30 amp n/a, **50 amp** n/a, **100 amp** n/a, **200 amp** n/a
Cable TV: No **Dockside Phone:** No
Dock Type: Floating
Moorings: 108 Total, 8-10 Transient **Launch:** Yes (Free)
Rate: Day $35.00 **Week** n/a **Month** n/a
Heads: 2 Toilet(s), 2 Shower(s)
Laundry: None **Pay Phones:** Yes
Pump-Out: OnSite, Self Service, 1 Central **Fee:** n/a **Closed Heads:** Yes

Marina Operations
Owner/Manager: Brad Lorensen **Dockmaster:** Same
In-Season: May-Oct 12, 8am-8pm **Off-Season:** Oct 13-Apr, Closed
After-Hours Arrival: n/a
Reservations: No **Credit Cards:** Visa/MC
Discounts: None
Pets: Welcome **Handicap Access:** No

Marina Services and Boat Supplies
Services - Dock Carts **Communication -** FedEx, AirBorne, UPS, Express Mail **Supplies - OnSite:** Ice *(Block, Cube)* **Under 1 mi:** Ships' Store, Bait/Tackle *(Zeeks Creek 423-1170)* **1-3 mi:** Propane *(Suburban 847-6878)* **3+ mi:** West Marine *(841-9880, 5 mi.)*

Boatyard Services
OnSite: Railway *(30T)*, Engine mechanic *(gas, diesel)*, Electrical Repairs, Hull Repairs, Rigger, Bottom Cleaning, Brightwork, Compound, Wash & Wax, Interior Cleaning, Woodworking, Painting, Awlgrip **OnCall:** Air Conditioning, Refrigeration, Divers, Propeller Repairs, Inflatable Repairs, Upholstery, Yacht Interiors, Metal Fabrication, Total Refits **Member:** ABBRA

Restaurants and Accommodations
Under 1 mi: Restaurant *(Portuguese American 423-9909)*, *(Theater Family 423-0907, B,L&D)*, *(Chopmist Charlies 423-1020, L $7-10, D $7-19)*, *(Tricia's Tropigrille 423-1490)*, *(Trattoria Simpatico 423-3731, D $19-26, L Fri-Sun)*, Seafood Shack *(Jamestown Oyster Bar 423-3380)*, Lite Fare *(East Ferry Deli 423-1592, B&L)*, *(Spinnaker's Café 423-3077)*, Pizzeria *(House of Pizza 423-3060)*, Inn/B&B *(East Bay 423-2715)*, *(Jamestown B&B 423-1338)* **1-3 mi:** Restaurant *(Bay Voyage 423-2100, D $22-34, Coat & Tie)*, Motel *(Newport Overlook 423-1886)*, Hotel *(Bay Voyage 423-2100)*

Recreation and Entertainment
Near: Beach *(Mackerel Cove)*, Picnic Area *(Ft. Getty Recreation Area)* **Under 1 mi:** Playground *(Jamestown Community Playground, North Rd.)*, Dive Shop, Special Events *(Fools' Rules Regatta - Aug)* **1-3 mi:** Golf Course *(Jamestown Golf Course 423-9930)*, Video Rental *(Video Showcase 423-2194)*, Museum *(The Jamestown Museum Tue-Sat, 1-4pm, Sydney L. Wright Museum 423-7280)*, Sightseeing *(Beavertail Lighthouse 423-9941, Jamestown Windmill 423-1798)* **3+ mi:** Fitness Center *(Steves Gym 789-7256, 4 mi.)*, Bowling *(Hi Way Bowl/Mini Golf 849-9990, 5 mi.)*

Provisioning and General Services
Under 1 mi: Convenience Store *(Cumberland Farms)*, Supermarket *(McQuades 423-0873)*, Gourmet Shop, Delicatessen *(East Ferry Mkt & Deli 423-1592)*, Wine/Beer *(Pages Wines & Spirits 423-0100)*, Liquor Store *(Jamestown 423-0415)*, Bakery, Fishmonger, Lobster Pound *(Zeeks Creek 423-1170)*, Bank/ATM, Post Office, Catholic Church, Protestant Church, Library *(Philomenian Library 423-7280)*, Beauty Salon, Barber Shop, Dry Cleaners, Laundry, Pharmacy *(Bakers Pharmacy 423-2800)*, Hardware Store *(Pages Hardware 423-0300)*, Florist, Clothing Store, Retail Shops **3+ mi:** Copies Etc. *(Pro Printing 846-6550, 5 mi.)*

Transportation
OnCall: Rental Car *(Enterprise 849-3939)*, Taxi *(Cozy Cabs 846-2500)*, Airport Limo *(Airport Car 841-8778)* **Under 1 mi:** Ferry Service *(to Newport)* **3+ mi:** InterCity Bus *(Greyhound 846-1820, 5 mi.)* **Airport:** TF Green *(18 mi.)*

Medical Services
911 Service **OnCall:** Ambulance **Under 1 mi:** Doctor *(Jamestown Family Practice 423-2616)*, Dentist *(Bush 423-2110)*, Veterinarian *(Jamestown Animal Clinic 423-2288)* **Hospital:** Newport Hospital 253-4063 *(6 mi.)*

Setting -- Located on the western side of Conanicut Island, Dutch Harbor has the best of both worlds -- the services of Jamestown within a mile and the uncrowded, comparatively unspoiled ambiance of the West Passage. West Ferry is a quiet neighborhood -- it's surrounded by farms, conservancy land and Dutch Island which is part of the State of Rhode Island Park System.

Marina Notes -- A low-key, down-home boatyard with moorings, DHBY offers a considerable array of services in its yard -- including launch service to its moorings. Dutch Harbor Marina is built on the site of the landing for the old ferry that traversed the West Passage from Saunderstown, on the mainland, to Conanicut Island. There are also 6 free State of Rhode Island Guest Moorings at the south end of Dutch Harbor - white balls with blue stripes.

Notable -- Just south of the marina is Sheffield Cove, noted for its oysters, and just north of the marina, is Dutch Island Harbor, where mussels are reported to be bountiful. If hunting and gathering does not appeal, it's a short 3/4 mile walk along Narragansett Avenue to the other side of the Island and the many restaurants and services of Jamestown. 31-acre Ft. Getty park is at the south end of the harbor. Consider a dinghy trip to 81-acre Dutch Island, part of the Bay Islands Park System and a wildlife refuge. Hike to the south end to the lighthouse or take a swim. Ft. Getty Recreation Area - with picnic areas, beaches, fishing dock and rest rooms is a short hike or dinghy ride. The Town Beach, Mackerel Cove, is also within striking distance.

Navigational Information
Lat: 41°34.233' **Long:** 071°26.679' **Tide:** 3 ft. **Current:** .5 kt. **Chart:** 13223
Rep. Depths (*MLW*): Entry 9 ft. **Fuel Dock** 9 ft. **Max Slip/Moor** 7 ft./-
Access: Wickford Harbor, left at G7, first facility to port

Marina Facilities *(In Season/Off Season)*
Fuel: *Texaco* - Gasoline, Diesel
Slips: 135 Total, 10 Transient **Max LOA:** 60 ft. **Max Beam:** 18 ft.
Rate *(per ft.)*: **Day** $1.50 **Week** n/a **Month** n/a
Power: 30 amp Inq., **50 amp** Inq., **100 amp** n/a, **200 amp** n/a
Cable TV: No **Dockside Phone:** No
Dock Type: Wood, Long Fingers, Floating, Fixed
Moorings: 0 Total, 0 Transient **Launch:** n/a
Rate: Day n/a **Week** n/a **Month** n/a
Heads: 2 Toilet(s), 2 Shower(s)
Laundry: 3 Washer(s), 4 Dryer(s) **Pay Phones:** Yes
Pump-Out: No **Fee:** n/a **Closed Heads:** Yes

Marina Operations
Owner/Manager: Don Fraser **Dockmaster:** n/a
In-Season: May 25-Sep 5, 8am-6pm **Off-Season:** Sep 6-May 24, 8am-4:30pm
After-Hours Arrival: Tie up at gas dock
Reservations: No **Credit Cards:** Visa/MC, Dscvr, Amex, Tex
Discounts: None
Pets: Welcome, Dog Walk Area **Handicap Access:** No

Wickford Shipyard, Inc.

125 Steamboat Avenue; North Kingstown, RI 02852

Tel: (401) 884-1725 **VHF: Monitor** n/a **Talk** n/a
Fax: (401) 294-7736 **Alternate Tel:** n/a
Email: n/a **Web:** n/a
Nearest Town: Wickford *(0.4 mi.)* **Tourist Info:** (401) 295-5566

Wickford Shipyard, Inc.

RI - WESTERN NARRAGANSETT BAY

Marina Services and Boat Supplies
Services - Docking Assistance **Communication -** Mail & Package Hold, Phone Messages, Fax in/out *($1)*, FedEx, AirBorne, UPS, Express Mail *(Sat Del)* **Supplies - OnSite:** Ice *(Block, Cube)*, Ships' Store **Near:** Marine Discount Store *(Newport Nautical 294-8504)* **Under 1 mi:** Bait/Tackle *(Robin Hollow 267-0102)* **1-3 mi:** Boat/US, Propane *(Star Gas 294-9547)*

Boatyard Services
OnSite: Forklift, Crane, Engine mechanic *(gas)*, Launching Ramp, Hull Repairs, Bottom Cleaning, Brightwork, Compound, Wash & Wax, Metal Fabrication, Awlgrip, Total Refits **OnCall:** Air Conditioning, Refrigeration, Divers, Interior Cleaning, Propeller Repairs, Inflatable Repairs, Life Raft Service **Near:** Rigger, Sail Loft. **Under 1 mi:** Woodworking. **Member:** ABBRA **Yard Rates:** $50/hr., Haul & Launch $2.50, Power Wash $1.50

Restaurants and Accommodations
OnCall: Restaurant *(HoofFinFeathers Carriage Inn 294-2727, D $7-23, lunch week-ends - provides transport)*, Pizzeria *(Chicago 295-1550)*, *(Place 294-0800)* **Near:** Lite Fare *(Harborside Grill 295-0444, B&L)* **Under 1 mi:** Restaurant *(Seaport Tavern 294-0771, L $5-13, D $12-23)*, *(Waterfront Grille 294-1150)*, Seafood Shack *(Champlin's 295-4600, or dinghy)*, Motel *(Hamilton Village Inn 295-0700, $70-110)* **1-3 mi:** Seafood Shack *(Duffy's 294-3733, L $4-14, D $6-14, Lobster 12-33 Kids Menu)*, Fast Food *(Burger King)*, Motel *(Budget Inn 294-4888)*, *(Wickford Motor Inn 294-4852)*

Recreation and Entertainment
OnSite: Pool **Near:** Beach, Picnic Area, Grills, Playground **Under 1 mi:** Tennis Courts *(Wilson Park)*, Boat Rentals *(Kayaks 295-4400)*, Park, Sightseeing *(Historic district)* **1-3 mi:** Golf Course *(No.Kingstown Mun. 294-0684)*, Fitness Center *(Physical Pursuit 295-2996)*, Horseback Riding *(Little Bit Stables 884-2360)*, Bowling *(Wickford Lanes 295-5304)*, Fishing Charter, Movie Theater, Video Rental *(Blockbuster 294-6340)*, Museum *(Smith's Castle 294-3521 $3)*

Provisioning and General Services
OnSite: Laundry **Near:** Supermarket *(Ryan's 294-9571 or Dave's Marketplace 268-3991 1 mi.)*, Delicatessen, Health Food, Liquor Store *(Colonial 294-4623)*, Bakery, Fishmonger, Meat Market, Bank/ATM, Catholic Church, Dry Cleaners, Bookstore *(Book Garden 294-3285)*, Newsstand, Clothing Store, Retail Shops **Under 1 mi:** Gourmet Shop *(Wickford Gourmet 295-8190)*, Lobster Pound *(Champlin's)*, Post Office, Protestant Church, Hardware Store *(Mancini 294-4288)*, Florist **1-3 mi:** Green Grocer, Synagogue, Library *(294-3306)*, Beauty Salon, Barber Shop, Pharmacy *(Wickford Pharm. 294-3662)*, Copies Etc. *(Wickford Printing 295-0129)*

Transportation
OnCall: Rental Car *(Enterprise 885-7558)*, Taxi *(Bay Taxi 461-0780)*, Airport Limo *(Airport Taxi 737-2868)* **Under 1 mi:** InterCity Bus *(RIPTA Providence)* **1-3 mi:** Bikes *(Rons Bicycle 294-2238)* **3+ mi:** Rail *(W. Kingston, 15 mi.)* **Airport:** TF Green *(20 mi.)*

Medical Services
911 Service **OnCall:** Ambulance **Under 1 mi:** Doctor *(Wickford Intern. 295-3120)*, Dentist *(Wickford 295-8806)*, Chiropractor *(Brunelle 295-2527)* **1-3 mi:** Holistic Services *(Therapeutic Massage 294-3838)*, Veterinarian *(Wickford 295-9739)* **Hospital:** So. County 294-3393 *(12 mi.)*

Setting -- On entering Wickford Cove, the massive 2-story white structure that is part of Wickford Shipyard, dominates the landscape. In short, it's the first facility to port and you can't miss it. Wickford Cove is very narrow and filled with docks and "stem to stern" moorings lined up along the channel.

Marina Notes -- The shipyard's convenient fuel dock sits at the head of harbor. Nicely constructed wood docks make user-friendly single berth slips in a well sheltered harbor. Fuel dock attendant is usually the only service. In the center of the main building is an aging pool surrounded by a chain-link and barbed-wire fence; it is open part-time. Next to it is a natural wood foliaged trellis of undetermined purpose. Locked heads, showers and laundry. A small chandlery but few other amenities. Maintenance could use a boost. Note: Marine Consignment of Wickford has moved.

Notable -- Located within walking distance (about a half mile) of picturesque, historic downtown Wickford. The village is truly that fantasy New England harborside town - it really exists. A mile-long hike would be to literally circle the Cove: walk along Steamboat Ave, a right on Beach St., another onto Boston Neck Rd - then cut over to the water -- window shopping -- then back onto Boston Neck and across the bridge onto Rte 1A and then to Washington St. You'll be in the charming, 1.5 square mile Historic District with dozens of lovingly cared-for 18th & 19thC houses and Old St. Paul's Narragansett Church (1707). It's another mile back. Another hike is 1.5 mi. to Smith's Castle, C 1678, one of the oldest plantation houses in the U.S., May-Sep Fri-Sun, Jul-Aug Thu-Mon noon-4pm. Wickford Arts Festival is the 2nd week July. Int'l Quahog Festival 294-9606 late Aug. The Town Dock permits 2-hour tie-ups.

PHOTOS ON CD-ROM: 9

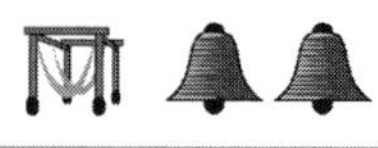

Brewer Wickford Cove Marina

65 Reynolds Street; North Kingstown, RI 02852

Tel: (401) 884-7014 **VHF: Monitor** 9 **Talk** 10
Fax: (401) 294-1541 **Alternate Tel:** n/a
Email: brewerwickford@juno.com **Web:** www.byy.com/wickford
Nearest Town: Wickford *(0.25 mi.)* **Tourist Info:** (401) 295-5566

Navigational Information

Lat: 41°34.091' **Long:** 071°26.873' **Tide:** 3 ft. **Current:** 1 kt. **Chart:** 13221
Rep. Depths (*MLW*): Entry 10 ft. **Fuel Dock** 9 ft. **Max Slip/Moor** 9 ft./-
Access: Wickford Harbor, then 2nd facility to port in Wickford Cove

Marina Facilities *(In Season/Off Season)*

Fuel: Gasoline, Diesel
Slips: 171 Total, 10 Transient **Max LOA:** 80 ft. **Max Beam:** n/a
Rate *(per ft.)*: **Day** $2.25 **Week** Inq. **Month** Inq.
Power: 30 amp Incl., **50 amp** Incl., **100 amp** n/a, **200 amp** n/a
Cable TV: No **Dockside Phone:** No
Dock Type: Wood, Long Fingers, Floating
Moorings: 37 Total, 3 - 5 Transient **Launch:** Yes (Free), Dinghy Dock
Rate: Day $1.00/ft. **Week** Inq. **Month** n/a
Heads: 4 Toilet(s), 4 Shower(s) *(with dressing rooms)*
Laundry: 1 Washer(s), 1 Dryer(s), Book Exchange **Pay Phones:** Yes
Pump-Out: OnSite, 1 Central **Fee:** $5 **Closed Heads:** Yes

Marina Operations

Owner/Manager: George Varga **Dockmaster:** Same
In-Season: May-Oct, 7am-6pm **Off-Season:** Nov-Apr, 7:30am-5pm
After-Hours Arrival: Call ahead
Reservations: Yes, Required **Credit Cards:** Visa/MC, Dscvr, Amex
Discounts: Brewer Customer Club **Dockage:** n/a **Fuel:** n/a **Repair:** n/a
Pets: Welcome, Dog Walk Area **Handicap Access:** Yes, Heads, Docks

Marina Services and Boat Supplies

Services - Docking Assistance, Dock Carts **Communication -** Mail & Package Hold, Phone Messages, Fax in/out *($3)*, Data Ports *(Office)*, FedEx, AirBorne, UPS, Express Mail **Supplies - OnSite:** Ice *(Block, Cube)*, Ships' Store *(Newport Nautical Supply 294-8504)*, CNG **OnCall:** Propane *(Star Gas 294-9547)* **Under 1 mi:** Bait/Tackle *(Robin Hollow Outfitters 267-0102)*, Live Bait **3+ mi:** West Marine *(884-0900, 5 mi.)*

Boatyard Services

OnSite: Travelift *(70T)*, Forklift, Crane, Engine mechanic *(gas, diesel)*, Electrical Repairs, Hull Repairs, Rigger, Bottom Cleaning, Brightwork, Refrigeration, Compound, Wash & Wax, Interior Cleaning, Woodworking, Yacht Interiors, Painting, Awlgrip, Yacht Broker, Total Refits **OnCall:** Electronic Sales, Electronics Repairs, Sail Loft, Air Conditioning, Divers, Propeller Repairs, Inflatable Repairs, Life Raft Service, Upholstery, Metal Fabrication **1-3 mi:** Launching Ramp. **Member:** ABBRA, ABYC **Yard Rates:** $52/hr., Haul & Launch $10-12/ft. hwb *(blocking incl.)*, Power Wash $2/ft., Bottom Paint $10/ft. **Storage:** In-Water $25/ft., On-Land $2.85/sq.ft.

Restaurants and Accommodations

OnCall: Restaurant *(HoofFinFeathers Carriage Inn 294-2727, D $7-23, provides transport both ways, lunch weekends)*, Pizzeria *(Chicago 295-1550)*, *(Place 294-0800)* **Near:** Restaurant *(Waterfront Grille 294-1150)*, Inn/B&B *(Haddie Pierce House 294-7674)* **Under 1 mi:** Restaurant *(Duffys 294-3733, L $4-14, D $6-33, $12-33 lobsters, Kids' Menu)*, Seafood Shack *(Champlin's 295-4600)*, Lite Fare *(Harborside Grille B&L)* **1-3 mi:** Restaurant *(Gils Place 294-6010)*, *(E&J 295-0420)*, Fast Food *(Burger King)*, Motel *(Wickford Motor Inn 294-4852)*

Recreation and Entertainment

OnSite: Picnic Area, Grills, Fishing Charter **Near:** Beach, Playground, Boat Rentals *(Kayaks 295-4400)*, Park, Galleries **Under 1 mi:** Tennis Courts *(Wilson Park)* **1-3 mi:** Golf Course *(No. Kingstown Mun.294-0684)*, Fitness Center *(Physical Pursuit 295-2996)*, Horseback Riding *(Little Bit Stables 884-2360)*, Bowling *(Wickford Lanes 295-5304)*, Movie Theater, Video Rental *(Blockbuster 294-6340)*, Cultural Attract *(Smith's Castle 294-3521 $3)*

Provisioning and General Services

OnCall: Provisioning Service **Near:** Supermarket *(Ryan's Market 294-9571 or Dave's Marketplace 268-3991 1 mi.)*, Delicatessen, Bakery, Fishmonger, Bank/ATM, Post Office, Catholic Church, Beauty Salon, Dry Cleaners, Bookstore *(Book Garden 294-3285)*, Florist **Under 1 mi:** Gourmet Shop *(Wickford Gourmet 295-8190)*, Liquor Store *(Colonial 294-4623)*, Lobster Pound *(Champlin's)*, Protestant Church, Hardware Store *(Mancini 294-4288)* **1-3 mi:** Library *(294-3306)*, Barber Shop, Pharmacy *(Wickford 294-3662)*, Copies Etc. *(Wickford Print 295-0129)*

Transportation

OnCall: Rental Car *(Enterprise 885-7558)*, Taxi *(Bay 461-0780)*, Airport Limo *(J J F 294-6380)* **Under 1 mi:** InterCity Bus *(RIPTA Providence)* **3+ mi:** Rail *(Amtrak So Kingston, 12 mi.)* **Airport:** TF Green *(15 mi.)*

Medical Services

911 Service **OnCall:** Ambulance **Under 1 mi:** Doctor *(Wickford Internists 295-3120)*, Dentist *(Wickford 295-8806)*, Chiropractor *(Therapeutic Massage 294-3838)* **1-3 mi:** Holistic Services, Veterinarian *(Wickford Vet 295-9739)*
Hospital: South County 789-1410 *(12 mi.)*

Setting -- Comfortably tucked into well protected Wickford Cove, Brewers is the second facility to port after you pass their long line of tie-fore-and-aft-system moorings. It is easy to spot their sea green shed. A casual brick patio with green/white striped awnings offers a nice "front porch" place to sit and an attractive wooden walkway runs the width of the matrix of docks. The occasional pot of flowers softens the boatyard ambiance.

Marina Notes -- Wet & dry storage. Boatyard labor rate ranges from $52-56/hr. Brewers Preferred Customer Card Program good at all northeast Brewer Boat Yards and offers free dockage and chandlery discounts. Exceptionally nice full, individual, tiled bathrooms. A fish cleaning table with running water is available. The marina's tie-fore-and-aft mooring system works well for boats up to 80 feet in 10-foot water and is serviced by an attractive "club-quality" launch. Wickford Cove is one of the best hurricane holes in the area. The marina sponsors the Block Island Sleigh Ride, an October sailing race to Block Island.

Notable -- A short walk, or shorter dinghy ride, to town nets some interesting provisioning options, great stores, galleries and antique shops -- some unchanged for decades -- a nice selection of casual restaurants, and, farther, an active and varied business section. On the waterfront is the town dock with 2 hour free tie-up for big boats or dinghies. The cross roads of Brown and West Main have two 19thC business sectors - the redbrick Avis Block and the brick and stone Gregory Block that house many services. Farther along is a 1.5 square mile historic homes district - most dating to the 18th & 19thC and Narragansett Episcopal Church built in 1707. The well-known Wickford Arts Fair is usually the second weekend in July. Int'l. Quahog Festival 294-9606 is in late Aug.

Navigational Information
Lat: 41°34.628' **Long:** 071°26.887' **Tide:** 4 ft. **Current:** 2 kt. **Chart:** 13221
Rep. Depths (*MLW*): Entry 13 ft. **Fuel Dock** 13 ft. **Max Slip/Moor** 13 ft./10 ft.
Access: Wickford Harbor, starboard to R10 & entrance to Mill Cove

Marina Facilities *(In Season/Off Season)*
Fuel: Gasoline, Diesel
Slips: 50 Total, 2 Transient **Max LOA:** 40 ft. **Max Beam:** 13 ft.
Rate *(per ft.)*: **Day** $1.50/$1.50 **Week** $10.50 **Month** $45
Power: 30 amp n/a, **50 amp** n/a, **100 amp** n/a, **200 amp** n/a
Cable TV: No **Dockside Phone:** No
Dock Type: Wood, Floating
Moorings: 10 Total, 1 Transient **Launch:** Yes, Dinghy Dock
Rate: Day $25 **Week** n/a **Month** n/a
Heads: 1 Toilet(s)
Laundry: None, Book Exchange **Pay Phones:** No
Pump-Out: No **Fee:** n/a **Closed Heads:** Yes

Marina Operations
Owner/Manager: Eric Collins **Dockmaster:** Rob Collins
In-Season: Mem-LabDay, 8am-8pm **Off-Season:** Sep-May, 8am-2pm
After-Hours Arrival: Call in advance
Reservations: No **Credit Cards:** Visa/MC
Discounts: None
Pets: Welcome **Handicap Access:** No

Pleasant Street Wharf

160 Pleasant Street; North Kingstown, RI 02852

Tel: (401) 294-2791 **VHF: Monitor** n/a **Talk** n/a
Fax: (401) 295-8032 **Alternate Tel:** n/a
Email: n/a **Web:** n/a
Nearest Town: Wickford *(0.25 mi.)* **Tourist Info:** (401) 295-5566

Marina Services and Boat Supplies
Services - Boaters' Lounge, Trash Pick-Up **Communication -** FedEx, AirBorne, UPS **Supplies - OnSite:** Ice *(Block, Cube)* **Under 1 mi:** Marine Discount Store *(Newport Nautical Supply 294-8504)*, Live Bait *(Robin Hollow Outfitters 267-0102)* **1-3 mi:** Ships' Store, Bait/Tackle, Propane *(Star Gas Service 294-9547)* **3+ mi:** West Marine *(884-0900, 8 mi.)*

Boatyard Services
OnSite: Travelift *(15T)*, Engine mechanic *(gas, diesel)*, Hull Repairs, Propeller Repairs **OnCall:** Rigger, Sail Loft, Canvas Work, Bottom Cleaning, Brightwork, Air Conditioning, Refrigeration, Divers, Compound, Wash & Wax

Restaurants and Accommodations
OnCall: Restaurant *(HoofFinFeathers Carriage Inn 294-2727, D $7-24, lunch weekends - picks up)*, Pizzeria *(Place 294-0800)* **Near:** Restaurant *(Seaport Tavern 294-0771, L $5-13, D $12-23)*, Seafood Shack *(Champlin's 295-4600, fresh off their own boats, 11am-9pm)*, Lite Fare *(Harborside Grill 295-0444, B&L)* **Under 1 mi:** Restaurant *(Waterfront Grille 294-1150)*, Fast Food *(Burger King 789-7479)*, Inn/B&B *(Haddie Pierce House 294-7674)* **1-3 mi:** Restaurant *(Gils Place Family Restaurant 294-6010)*, *(E&J 295-0420)*, Pizzeria *(Chicago 295-1550)*, Motel *(Budget Inn Of North Kingston 294-4888)*, *(Wickford Motor Inn 294-4852)*, *(Hamilton Village Inn 295-0700, $70-110)*, Hotel *(Best Western 884-5080)*

Recreation and Entertainment
Near: Tennis Courts *(Wilson Park)*, Sightseeing *(Wickford Historic District)*, Galleries **Under 1 mi:** Beach, Boat Rentals *(Kayaks 295-4400)* **1-3 mi:** Golf Course *(No. Kingstown Mun. 294-0684)*, Fitness Center *(Physical Pursuit 295-2996)*, Horseback Riding *(Little Bit Stables 884-2360)*, Bowling *(Wickford Lanes 295-5304)*, Video Rental *(Blockbuster 294-6340)* **3+ mi:** Movie Theater *(So. Kingston Cinemas 792-8008, 5 mi.)*

Provisioning and General Services
Near: Supermarket *(Ryan's Market 294-9571, Dave's Marketplace 268-3991 1 mi.)*, Gourmet Shop *(Wickford Gourmet 295-8190)*, Health Food, Wine/Beer *(Wickford Package 294-4681)*, Lobster Pound *(Champlin's)* **Under 1 mi:** Liquor Store *(Colonial Liquor 294-4623)*, Fishmonger *(Ryan's)*, Library *(North Kingstown 294-3306)*, Bookstore *(Book Garden 294-3285)*, Pharmacy *(Wickford Pharmacy 294-3662)* **1-3 mi:** Convenience Store *(Wickford Mini Mart 295-2080)*, Hardware Store *(Mancini True Value 294-4288)*, Copies Etc. *(Wickford Printing 295-0129)*

Transportation
OnCall: Rental Car *(Enterprise 885-7558, Thrifty 885-0400 - 2 mi.)*, Taxi *(Bay Taxi 461-0780)*, Airport Limo *(Airport Taxi 737-2868)* **Under 1 mi:** InterCity Bus *(RIPTA Providence)* **1-3 mi:** Bikes *(Rons Bicycle Shop 294-2238)* **3+ mi:** Rail *(Amtrak W. Kingstown, 12 mi.)* **Airport:** TF Green *(20 mi.)*

Medical Services
911 Service **Under 1 mi:** Doctor *(No. Kingstown Med Cntr. 294-3393)*, Dentist *(Wickford Dental 295-8806)*, Chiropractor *(Dunphy 294-4313)* **1-3 mi:** Holistic Services *(Therapeutic Massage 294-3838)*, Veterinarian *(Wickford Vet 295-9739)* **Hospital:** South County 789-1410 *(12 mi.)*

Setting -- Near the entrance to Mill Cove, in the northwest corner of the Wickford's Outer Harbor, is Pleasant Street Wharf - a delightful, carefully maintained old-time boatyard, with docks and moorings. It's perfectly situated in the middle of the historic district and a quarter mile walk to Wickford village. The atmosphere, while mainly "boatyard", is very convivial and one frequently finds a gathering on the docks.

Marina Notes -- Basic, limited services. No pump-out, no electricity. Fuel, ice, a small travelift, and some onsite storage. There is, occasionally, a stocked lobster pound (call first). Three free RI State moorings are in the outer harbor - white with a blue lateral stripe marked "State of Rhode Island Guest Mooring" - good for 24 hrs. (weight of the ground tackle is clearly marked). Additional moorings may be available from Wickford Harbormaster 294-3311, Ch.12.

Notable -- The outer harbor is beautiful and peaceful with extraordinary views. Easy access to Cornelius Island (with a sandy beach, marsh and woods) and Rabbit Island (mostly marsh) -- both have public rights of way. Walk through the streets surrounding Pleasant Wharf for a trip back to the 18th and 19thC. Every street and byway is lined with impeccably preserved private houses (some restored and some just always well maintained). Stop by "Old" St. Paul's Church; built in 1707, it is one of the oldest Episcopal churches in America, July-Aug, Fri-Sat, 11am-4pm. At "New" St. Paul's (294-4357) Sun Services 8am, 9:30am. Champlin's Seafood (with 25 lobster boats) is 0.3 mile - eat in/take out for freshest seafood at reasonable prices. Wickford Arts Festival - 2nd week July; Int'l. Quahog Festival 294-9606 Late Aug.

PHOTOS ON CD-ROM: 6

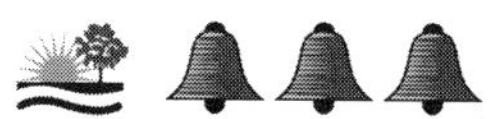

Wickford Marina

PO Box 1402; 67 Esmond Avenue; North Kingstown, RI 02852

Tel: (401) 294-8160 **VHF: Monitor** 10 **Talk** 10
Fax: (401) 294-6063 **Alternate Tel:** (401) 294-6063
Email: wickfordmarina@edgenet.net **Web:** www.wickfordmarina.com
Nearest Town: Wickford *(0.4 mi.)* **Tourist Info:** (401) 295-5566

Navigational Information

Lat: 41°34.600' **Long:** 071°26.960' **Tide:** 4 ft. **Current:** .2 kt. **Chart:** 13221
Rep. Depths (*MLW*): Entry 12 ft. **Fuel Dock** n/a **Max Slip/Moor** 10 ft./-
Access: Wickford Breakwater to R10 through cut to Mill Cove

Marina Facilities *(In Season/Off Season)*

Fuel: No
Slips: 70 Total, 6 Transient **Max LOA:** 100 ft. **Max Beam:** 18 ft.
Rate *(per ft.)*: **Day** $2.15/$1.75 **Week** Inq. **Month** Inq.
Power: 30 amp $7, **50 amp** $10, **100 amp** n/a, **200 amp** n/a
Cable TV: No **Dockside Phone:** No
Dock Type: Wood, Long Fingers, Floating, Fixed
Moorings: 0 Total, 0 Transient **Launch:** n/a, Dinghy Dock
Rate: Day n/a **Week** n/a **Month** n/a
Heads: 2 Toilet(s), 2 Shower(s) *(with dressing rooms)*
Laundry: 1 Washer(s), 1 Dryer(s), Book Exchange **Pay Phones:** Yes, 1
Pump-Out: OnSite, Self Service, 1 Central **Fee:** $5 **Closed Heads:** Yes

Marina Operations

Owner/Manager: Paul Galego **Dockmaster:** Same
In-Season: Jun-Oct 15, 8am-5pm **Off-Season:** Oct 15-May, 8am-10am
After-Hours Arrival: Tie up to the pump-out station
Reservations: Yes, Required **Credit Cards:** Visa/MC
Discounts: None
Pets: Welcome, Dog Walk Area **Handicap Access:** Yes, Docks

Marina Services and Boat Supplies

Services - Docking Assistance, Boaters' Lounge, Dock Carts, Megayacht Facilities **Communication -** Mail & Package Hold, Phone Messages, Fax in/out *($2)*, Data Ports *(Office)*, FedEx, AirBorne, UPS, Express Mail *(Sat Del)* **Supplies - OnSite:** Ice *(Block, Cube)* **OnCall:** Ships' Store, Propane *(Star Gas 294-9547)* **Under 1 mi:** Marine Discount Store *(Newport Nautical Supply 294-8504)*, Bait/Tackle *(Robin Hollow Outfitters 267-0102)*

Boatyard Services

OnSite: Bottom Cleaning, Brightwork, Divers, Compound, Wash & Wax, Interior Cleaning, Woodworking **OnCall:** Engine mechanic *(gas, diesel)*, Electrical Repairs, Hull Repairs, Rigger, Sail Loft, Air Conditioning, Refrigeration, Propeller Repairs, Inflatable Repairs, Life Raft Service, Upholstery, Yacht Interiors, Metal Fabrication **Near:** Travelift, Railway, Forklift, Crane, Launching Ramp. **Yard Rates:** $50/hr., Haul & Launch $10/ft. *(blocking $2/ft.)*, Power Wash $2/ft., Bottom Paint $8/ft. **Storage:** In-Water $500/winter, On-Land $500/winter

Restaurants and Accommodations

OnCall: Restaurant *(HoofFinFeathers Carriage Inn 294-2727, B $5, D $7-23, will transport both ways)*, Pizzeria *(The Place 294-0800)* **Near:** Restaurant *(Harborside Grill 295-0444)*, Inn/B&B *(John Updike House 294-4905)* **Under 1 mi:** Restaurant *(Seaport Tavern L $14, D $24)*, Snack Bar *(Treats of Wickford, ice cream)*, Lite Fare *(Harborside B $5, breakfast & lunch)*, Motel *(Budget Inn 294-4888)*, Inn/B&B *(Haddie Pierce House 294-7674, $95)* **1-3 mi:** Restaurant *(Duffy's Tavern 294-3733, L $4-14, D $6-33, seafood, raw bar, lobsters $12-33, Kids' menu)*, Motel *(Wickford Motor Inn 294-4852)*, Hotel *(Hamilton House 295-2500, $50)*

Recreation and Entertainment

OnSite: Spa, Picnic Area, Grills, Boat Rentals *(Canoes)* **Near:** Beach, Tennis Courts *(Wilson Park)*, Sightseeing *(Old Narragansett/St. Paul's Churches)* **1-3 mi:** Golf Course *(North Kingstown Municipal 294-0684)*, Horseback Riding *(Little Bit Stables 884-2360)*, Bowling *(Wickford Lanes 295-5304)*, Video Rental *(Blockbuster 294-6340)*

Provisioning and General Services

Near: Protestant Church, Beauty Salon, Bookstore *(Book Garden 294-3285)* **Under 1 mi:** Supermarket *(Ryan's 294-9571, Dave's Marketplace 268-3991)*, Gourmet Shop *(Wickford 295-8190)*, Wine/Beer *(Wickford Package 294-4681)*, Liquor Store *(Colonial 294-4623)*, Bakery *(Pastry Gourmet)*, Fishmonger *(Champlain's 294-4600)*, Bank/ATM *(BankBoston)*, Library *(No. Kingstown 294-3306)*, Dry Cleaners, Pharmacy *(Wickford Pharm. 294-3662, Earnshaw Drug)*, Newsstand, Florist, Retail Shops, Copies Etc. *(Wickford Print 295-0129)* **1-3 mi:** Post Office, Catholic Church, Hardware Store *(Mancini 294-4288)*, Department Store *(Wal-Mart)*

Transportation

OnCall: Rental Car *(Enterprise, 3 mi. 885-7558,)*, Taxi *(Bay 461-0780)* **Under 1 mi:** InterCity Bus *(RIPTA Providence)* **1-3 mi:** Bikes *(Rons 294-2238)* **3+ mi:** Rail *(Amtrak, 12 mi.)* **Airport:** TF Green *(20 mi.)*

Medical Services

911 Service **OnCall:** Ambulance **Under 1 mi:** Doctor *(Wickford Intern. 295-3120)*, Dentist *(Wickford 295-8806)*, Chiropractor *(Brunelle 295-2527)* **1-3 mi:** Holistic Services *(Therapeutic Mass. 294-3838)*, Veterinarian *(Wickford 295-9739)* **Hospital:** South County 789-1410 *(12 mi.)*

Setting -- In the northwest corner of Wickford Harbor is the entrance to peaceful, pristine, relatively shallow Mill Cove. It's bounded by a 60-acre wildlife preserve containing Conanicus/Cornelius Island and Rabbit Island. Wickford Marina is quickly recognized by the red-roofed cupola on top of the main building.

Marina Notes -- Family owned and operated; very service-oriented. A pretty, elevated, 3,000 sq. ft. patio deck, with an al fresco "restaurant feel", overlooks the docks - tables with umbrellas surround a large, gloriously colorful raised flower bed. An impressive outdoor grill kitchen includes setups - everything from plates to BBQ sauce - just bring your own food. The heated Jacuzzi sits several steps up from the deck and has spectacular views across the Cove. Continental breakfast on weekends/holidays in summer. Hosts groups of up to 20 boats on weekends. Built in 1997 on the site of century old Wickford Shellfish Co.

Notable -- The tented pavilion on the dock, known as the "Island," is the place to watch the sunset. Pre-ordered, prepared Italian casserole meals available onsite. For exploring Mill Cove, there are canoe rentals (marina guests only) -- take a picnic to one of the islands. Airport pick-up or drop-off for marina guests: $20 each way. 4/10th mile walk to the historic village of Wickford - the quintessential New England harbor town. John Updike modeled the village in his novel, "The Witches of Eastwick", on Wickford. The historic district is 1.5 square miles of densely packed, lovingly restored 18th & 19thC houses. Also see the perfectly preserved "Old" St. Paul's Narragansett Church, built in 1701, moved here in 1800; it's open weekends. Sunday services held at "New" 1847 St. Paul's Episcopal and at The 1816 Baptist Church - transport to both provided by the marina. Int'l Quahog Festival 294-9606 late August.

PHOTOS ON CD-ROM: 7

Navigational Information

Lat: 41°39.995' **Long:** 071°26.767' **Tide:** 3 ft. **Current:** 1 kt. **Chart:** 13224
Rep. Depths (*MLW*): Entry 10 ft. **Fuel Dock** n/a **Max Slip/Moor** 15 ft./15 ft.
Access: West Passage to Greenwich Bay to G7 at Greenwich Cove

Marina Facilities *(In Season/Off Season)*

Fuel: No
Slips: 180 Total, 20 Transient **Max LOA:** 200 ft. **Max Beam:** 20 ft.
Rate *(per ft.)*: **Day** $2.00/Inq. **Week** Inq. **Month** Inq.
Power: 30 amp Incl., **50 amp** Incl., **100 amp** n/a, **200 amp** n/a
Cable TV: No **Dockside Phone:** No
Dock Type: Wood, Long Fingers, Floating, Fixed
Moorings: 100 Total, 5 Transient **Launch:** Yes (Free)
Rate: Day $2.50/ft. **Week** n/a **Month** n/a
Heads: 3 Toilet(s), 3 Shower(s)
Laundry: None **Pay Phones:** Yes
Pump-Out: No **Fee:** n/a **Closed Heads:** Yes

Marina Operations

Owner/Manager: Pat Norton **Dockmaster:** n/a
In-Season: Apr-Oct, 8am-6pm **Off-Season:** n/a
After-Hours Arrival: Call ahead
Reservations: Yes, Preferred **Credit Cards:** Visa/MC, Dscvr
Discounts: Safe/Sea **Dockage:** 25% **Fuel:** n/a **Repair:** n/a
Pets: Welcome, Dog Walk Area **Handicap Access:** No

Norton's Shipyard & Marina

PO Box 106; Foot of Division Street; East Greenwich, RI 02818

Tel: (401) 884-8828 **VHF: Monitor** 9 **Talk** n/a
Fax: (401) 884-3163 **Alternate Tel:** n/a
Email: n/a **Web:** www.nortonsmarina.com
Nearest Town: East Greenwich *(0.5 mi.)* **Tourist Info:** (401) 885-0020

Norton's Shipyard & Marina

RI - WESTERN NARRAGANSETT BAY

Marina Services and Boat Supplies

Services - Docking Assistance, Dock Carts **Communication -** Mail & Package Hold, Fax in/out *($1/pg)*, FedEx, AirBorne, UPS, Express Mail *(Sat Del)* **Supplies - OnSite:** Ice *(Block, Cube)*, Ships' Store, CNG **1-3 mi:** West Marine *(884-0900)*, Boat/US *(886-6790)*, Bait/Tackle *(John's 885-3761)*, Propane *(Arlington RV 884-7550)*

Boatyard Services

OnSite: Travelift *(35T)*, Crane, Engine mechanic *(gas, diesel)*, Electrical Repairs, Electronic Sales, Electronics Repairs, Hull Repairs, Rigger, Bottom Cleaning, Brightwork, Divers, Compound, Wash & Wax, Interior Cleaning, Metal Fabrication, Awlgrip **OnCall:** Sail Loft, Air Conditioning, Refrigeration, Propeller Repairs, Inflatable Repairs **Near:** Launching Ramp. **Dealer for:** Yanmar, Volvo, Mercruiser. **Yard Rates:** $50/hr., Haul & Launch $9.50/ft. *(blocking $25)*, Power Wash $1/ft., Bottom Paint $10/ft. **Storage:** In-Water $25/ft., On-Land $38/ft.

Restaurants and Accommodations

OnSite: Coffee Shop *(Meritime 884-7760, B $4-6, L $5-8, weekends only)* **OnCall:** Pizzeria *(Roberto's Pizza & Restaurant 884-3796)* **Near:** Restaurant *(Harborside/Lobstermania 884-6363, L $20, D $20)*, *(20 Water St. 885-3700, L $6-19, D $15-24)*, *(Pals 884-9701, L $7, D $12)*, *(Blue Parrot Café 884-2002, L $7-8, D $9-20)* **Under 1 mi:** Inn/B&B *(1873 House 884-9955)*, *(Vincent House 885-2864)* **1-3 mi:** Motel *(Open Gate 884-4490, $50-70)* **3+ mi:** Hotel *(Holiday Inn 732-6000, 4 mi.)*

Recreation and Entertainment

Near: Beach *(Goddard State Park 884-2010 via dinghy)*, Picnic Area, Playground, Fishing Charter, Museum *(Varnum House Museum 884-1776, New England Wireless & Steam Museum 885-0545 5 mi.)* **Under 1 mi:** Golf Course *(Goddard Park G.C. 884-2010, or East Greenwich G.C. 884-5656 5 mi.)*, Fitness Center *(Body Language 886-7411)*, Video Rental *(Videofair 885-4910)*, Cultural Attract *(The Odeum 885-9119)* **1-3 mi:** Tennis Courts *(Tennis R.I. 828-4450)*, Bowling *(Kingstown Bowl 884-4450)*

Provisioning and General Services

OnCall: Provisioning Service *(Butcher Block 884-0530)* **Near:** Library *(East Greenwich 884-9510)*, Pharmacy *(CVS 884-7044)*, Newsstand, Florist, Clothing Store, Retail Shops **Under 1 mi:** Convenience Store *(E. Greenwich Farm 886-4811)*, Supermarket *(Dave's Marketplace 885-7966 or Shaw's 823-1820 3 mi.)*, Gourmet Shop *(Greenwich Bay 541-9190)*, Delicatessen *(Pick Pockets 884-0488)*, Wine/Beer *(Thorpe's Wines 885-4485)*, Bakery, Farmers' Market *(Goddard Park Fri 9am-1pm 222-2781-dinghy)*, Bank/ATM, Post Office, Catholic Church, Protestant Church *(Methodist, Episcopial)*, Beauty Salon, Dry Cleaners *(Waterford Laundry & Drycleaning 884-9772)*, Laundry, Copies Etc. *(Pegasus Printing 884-7733)*

Transportation

OnCall: Rental Car *(Enterprise 885-7558)*, Taxi *(Bay Taxi 461-0780)*, Airport Limo *(Bellevue Limousine 884-5754)* **Near:** Local Bus **3+ mi:** Bikes *(Casters Bicycle Center 739-0393, 4 mi.)*, InterCity Bus *(Pawtuxet Valley Bus Lines 821-3834, 6 mi.)* **Airport:** TF Green *(5 mi.)*

Medical Services

911 Service **OnCall:** Ambulance **Near:** Dentist, Chiropractor **Under 1 mi:** Doctor *(Fallon & Horan 884-2476)* **Hospital:** Kent 736-1988 *(4 mi.)*

Setting -- Norton's is the first facility to starboard ,just at the mouth of Greenwich Cove. The docks have views of the boat basin, Goddard State Park, Long Point to the east, and the wide expanse of Greenwich Bay. Landside one sees a well-maintained, very comfortable "boatyard".

Marina Notes -- Norton's is a family owned and operated marina that works at maintaining a friendly, family atmosphere. 180 slips ranging from 26' to 300' plus 100 moorings for smaller boats up to 30'. It was founded in Newport in 1945, moved to E. Greenwich in 1966. Full service boatyard. Onsite discount retail and catalog marine store. Also on the premises: Dockside Maid Service, Bessette Marine Finishes, West Bay Yacht Club, Accurate Marine Engine Repair, Meritime Restaurant, Nor'East Gypsy Charters and Aluminum Marine Fabricators plus New England Yacht Rigging around the corner. Fuel & pump-out is next door at very lovely East Greenwich Yacht Club Ch.9, which also offers slips, moorings, launch, showers, and laundry to members of other clubs (884-7700).

Notable -- A short dinghy ride nets a beach, swimming, hiking, and picnicking at Goddard Memorial State Park (plus a farmers' market on Friday mornings). Its 18-hole golf course will require land transport. This 400 acre forest, once a sand dune, was privately planted by Henry Russell starting in the1870's, continued by William Goddard and given to RI in 1927. Several restaurants (including Twenty Water Street, Harborside/Lobstermania) are up the Cove from Norton's, and the center of town of East Greenwich -- with many specialty shops, liquor, drug and convenience stores -- is an easy walk. TF Green Airport is about a 10 minute drive. The West Bay Yacht Club is a small, family-oriented yacht club with Monday night races, summer cruises and other activities.

PHOTOS ON CD-ROM: 6

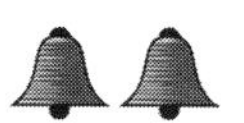

Milt's Marina

PO Box 760; 20 Water Street; East Greenwich, RI 02818

Tel: (401) 885-3700 **VHF: Monitor** n/a **Talk** n/a
Fax: (401) 885-2501 **Alternate Tel:** n/a
Email: n/a **Web:** n/a
Nearest Town: East Greenwich *(0.5 mi.)* **Tourist Info:** (401) 885-0020

Navigational Information

Lat: 41°39.820' **Long:** 071°26.700' **Tide:** 3 ft. **Current:** 1 kt. **Chart:** 13221
Rep. Depths (*MLW*): Entry 10 ft. **Fuel Dock** n/a **Max Slip/Moor** 8 ft./-
Access: West Passage to Greenwich Bay to C7 at Greenwich Cove

Marina Facilities *(In Season/Off Season)*

Fuel: No
Slips: 30 Total, 6 Transient **Max LOA:** 75 ft. **Max Beam:** n/a
Rate *(per ft.)*: **Day** $1.25/$1.25 **Week** n/a **Month** n/a
Power: 30 amp Incl., **50 amp** Incl., **100 amp** n/a, **200 amp** n/a
Cable TV: Yes **Dockside Phone:** No
Dock Type: Wood, Long Fingers, Floating
Moorings: 0 Total, 0 Transient **Launch:** n/a
Rate: Day n/a **Week** n/a **Month** n/a
Heads: 2 Toilet(s)
Laundry: None **Pay Phones:** Yes
Pump-Out: No **Fee:** n/a **Closed Heads:** Yes

Marina Operations

Owner/Manager: Milt Tanner **Dockmaster:** Kristin McCabe
In-Season: Year-Round, 9am-8pm **Off-Season:** n/a
After-Hours Arrival: Call ahead and inquire
Reservations: No **Credit Cards:** Visa/MC, Dscvr, Amex
Discounts: None
Pets: Welcome **Handicap Access:** No

Marina Services and Boat Supplies

Supplies - Near: Ice *(Block, Cube)*, Ships' Store **Under 1 mi:** Boat/US *(886-6790)* **1-3 mi:** West Marine *(884-0900)*, Bait/Tackle *(Rays 738-7878)* **3+ mi:** Propane *(Boc Gas 884-0486, 4 mi.)*

Boatyard Services

Nearest Yard: Norton's Shipyard (401) 854-8828

Restaurants and Accommodations

OnSite: Restaurant *(20 Water Street 885-3700, L $6-19, D $15-24, Mon-Sat 6pm-?, Sun 4pm-?, Deck opens noon weekends, $7-16. Take-Out Menu, too)* **OnCall:** Pizzeria *(Sandonna's 886-4429)* **Near:** Restaurant *(Blue Parrot 884-2002, L $7-8, D $9-20)*, *(Pals 884-9701)*, *(Jiggers Diner 884-5388)*, *(The Grille 885-2200)*, *(Eds Roost 885-3358)*, *(Harborside-Lobstermania 884-6363, L $7-14, D $12-20)*, Coffee Shop *(Meritime 884-7760, B $4-6, L $5-8, weekends only)*, Lite Fare *(The Third Rail snacks, desserts Thu 5-9pm, Fri & Sat 7am-9pm. Sun 7am-5pm)* **Under 1 mi:** Motel *(Harmony Lodge 5 885-1795)*, Inn/B&B *(1873 House 884-9955)* **1-3 mi:** Restaurant *(The Outrigger 541-9100, L $6-12, D $6-12, at Brewer Yacht Yard)*, Inn/B&B *(Vincent House 885-2860)* **3+ mi:** Hotel *(Crowne Plaza Hotel 732-6000, $180-280, 4 mi.)*

Recreation and Entertainment

Near: Beach *(Goddard State Park by dinghy)*, Picnic Area, Grills, Playground, Golf Course *(Goddard Park G.C. by dinghy 884-2010 or East Greenwich G. C. 884-5656 5 mi.)*, Park *(Goddard)*, Museum *(Varnum House Museum 884-1776)* **Under 1 mi:** Fitness Center *(Flex Appeal 886-7411)*, Video Rental *(Videofair 885-4910, Blockbuster 885-6670)* **1-3 mi:** Horseback Riding, Bowling *(Kingstown Bowl 884-4450)* **3+ mi:** Movie Theater *(Showcase Cinemas 885-1621, 4 mi.)*

Provisioning and General Services

Near: Convenience Store *(E. Greenwich Farm 886-4811)*, Gourmet Shop *(Greenwich Bay 541-9190)*, Delicatessen *(Pick Pockets 884-0488)*, Bakery *(J&K Kreations 886-0778)*, Farmers' Market *(Goddard State Park, Fri 9am-1pm 222-2781 - by dinghy)* **Under 1 mi:** Supermarket *(Dave's Marketplace 885-7966, or Shaw's 823-1820, 3 mi.)*, Wine/Beer, Liquor Store *(Thorpe's Wines & Spirits 885-4485)*, Meat Market, Post Office, Catholic Church, Protestant Church, Library *(East Greenwich 884-9510)*, Beauty Salon, Barber Shop, Dry Cleaners *(Waterford Laundry & Drycleaning 884-9772)*, Laundry, Pharmacy *(CVS 884-7044)*, Florist **3+ mi:** Hardware Store *(Salk's Hardware & Marine 739-1027 , 5 mi.)*

Transportation

OnCall: Rental Car *(Enterprise 732-5261/ Hertz 738-7500)*, Taxi *(Apponaug Cab 737-6400)*, Airport Limo *(Airport Taxi 737-2868)* **3+ mi:** Rail *(Providence/Kingston, 12 mi.)* **Airport:** TF Green *(4.5 mi.)*

Medical Services

911 Service **OnCall:** Ambulance **Near:** Dentist *(East Greenwich Dental 884-6262)*, Chiropractor *(Frye Family 886-4255)*, Holistic Services *(All's Well Massage 884-0410)*, Veterinarian *(Pancholi 885-2221)* **1-3 mi:** Doctor *(Fallon & Horan 884-2476)* **Hospital:** Kent 734-9596 *(4 mi.)*

Setting -- Greenwich Cove's third facility to starboard, just past East Greenwich Yacht Club, is Milt's Marina. The impeccable docks lie at the foot of the Twenty Water Street Restaurant complex, with views across the mooring field to Goddard State Park, which occupies all of the opposite shore. Landside is dominated by the sleek, multi-level eatery with its brightly colored umbrellas and creatively divided spaces -- all housed in a renovated 19thC warehouse.

Marina Notes -- No reservations, no marina services, no showers. Heads are shared with the restaurant. Limited transient dockage, mostly on the T-heads and bulkheads. The well maintained docks are edged in vinyl and have relatively recent full-service pedestals. Established in May 1982. Private East Greenwich Yacht Club (884-7700) on the north side usually has transient slips for members of reciprocating yacht clubs (attractively landscaped, great clubhouse with rocking chair porch, full-bath heads/showers, no reservations there, either). To the south, East Greenwich Marina/Blue Parrot Café (885-2991) usually has a transient berth or two and offers dock hands, radio monitoring, aging docks, restaurant heads, and no showers. Rating reflects the lack of cruiser amenities.

Notable -- Twenty Water Street offers a casual fine dining white tablecloth restaurant, a tavern, and cozy dining decks; there's live entertainment Wed-Sun eves. All the dining spaces share the same great view as does the large, glass walled second floor banquet room - the Sky Room. Easy walking distance to several other restaurants (including Blue Parrot, Harborside Lobstermania, The Third Rail), and to the village of East Greenwich - with even more restaurants. 400 acre Goddard Memorial Park across the cove has a sandy swimming beach, a 9-hole gof course, bridle paths, walking trails, concerts, and picnic areas.

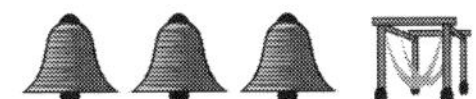

Navigational Information
Lat: 41°40.910' **Long:** 071°26.930' **Tide:** 4 ft. **Current:** n/a **Chart:** 13221
Rep. Depths (*MLW*): Entry 8 ft. **Fuel Dock** n/a **Max Slip/Moor** 10 ft./10 ft.
Access: Western part of Narragansett Bay to Greenwich Cove

Marina Facilities *(In Season/Off Season)*
Fuel: No
Slips: 240 Total, 5-6 Transient **Max LOA:** 60 ft. **Max Beam:** 16 ft.
Rate *(per ft.)*: **Day** $2.00 **Week** Inq. **Month** Inq.
Power: 30 amp Incl., **50 amp** Incl., **100 amp** n/a, **200 amp** n/a
Cable TV: Yes **Dockside Phone:** Yes
Dock Type: Long Fingers, Concrete, Pilings, Floating
Moorings: 14 Total, 5 Transient **Launch:** None
Rate: Day $32 **Week** n/a **Month** n/a
Heads: 4 Toilet(s), 4 Shower(s)
Laundry: None **Pay Phones:** Yes, 2
Pump-Out: OnSite, Self Service **Fee:** n/a **Closed Heads:** Yes

Marina Operations
Owner/Manager: Chris Ruhling **Dockmaster:** Ron Webster
In-Season: May-Oct, 8am-5pm* **Off-Season:** Nov-Apr, 8am-5pm Mon-Fri*
After-Hours Arrival: Call in advance and pre-arrange
Reservations: Yes **Credit Cards:** Visa/MC, Dscvr, Amex
Discounts: Safe/Sea **Dockage:** 25% **Fuel:** n/a **Repair:** n/a
Pets: Welcome, Dog Walk Area **Handicap Access:** No

Brewer Yacht Yard Cowesett

100 Folly Landing; Warwick, RI 02886

Tel: (401) 884-0544 **VHF: Monitor** 9 **Talk** 72
Fax: (401) 885-5620 **Alternate Tel:** n/a
Email: cow@byy.com **Web:** www.byy.com/Warwick
Nearest Town: East Greenwich *(1.5 mi.)* **Tourist Info:** (401) 732-1100

Marina Services and Boat Supplies
Services - Docking Assistance, Trash Pick-Up, Dock Carts **Communication -** Mail & Package Hold, Phone Messages, Fax in/out, Data Ports, FedEx, AirBorne, UPS, Express Mail *(Sat Del)* **Supplies - OnSite:** Ice *(Block, Cube)*, Ships' Store, CNG **Near:** Live Bait **1-3 mi:** Boat/US *(886-6790)*, Bait/Tackle *(Ericksons Bait & Tackle 739-7437)*, Propane *(Boc Gas 884-0486)* **3+ mi:** West Marine *(884-0900, 4 mi.)*

Boatyard Services
OnSite: Travelift *(35T)*, Forklift *(3T)*, Crane *(7T)*, Engine mechanic *(gas, diesel)*, Electrical Repairs, Electronics Repairs, Hull Repairs, Rigger, Bottom Cleaning, Brightwork, Divers, Compound, Wash & Wax, Interior Cleaning, Propeller Repairs, Woodworking, Painting, Awlgrip, Yacht Broker, Total Refits **OnCall:** Air Conditioning, Refrigeration, Metal Fabrication **Near:** Inflatable Repairs, Life Raft Service, Upholstery, Yacht Interiors, Yacht Building. **Under 1 mi:** Launching Ramp. **1-3 mi:** Sail Loft. **Dealer for:** Kohler, Westerbeke. **Member:** ABBRA, ABYC - 3 Certified Tech(s) **Yard Rates:** $62/hr., Haul & Launch $10/ft. *(blocking $2/ft.)*, Power Wash $2, Bottom Paint $7.50/ft. **Storage:** In-Water $22/ft., On-Land $26/ft.

Restaurants and Accommodations
OnSite: Restaurant *(Outrigger 541-9100, L $6-12, D $6-12)* **Near:** Restaurant *(Chelos Waterfront 884-3000, L $4-9, D $6-13)*, *(Ward's Publick House 884-7008)*, Fast Food *(MacD's)*, Lite Fare *(The Third Rail)*, Pizzeria *(Frank & John's 884-9751)* **1-3 mi:** Restaurant *(Crows Nest 732-6575, L $5-15, D $5-15, delivers, too)*, Motel *(Econolodge 737-7400)*, *(Best Western 884-8000)*, *(Holiday Inn 732-6000)*, Hotel *(Crowne Plaza 732-6000)*, Inn/B&B *(1873 House 884-9955)*

Recreation and Entertainment
OnSite: Pool, Spa, Beach, Picnic Area, Grills **Near:** Playground, Dive Shop, Jogging Paths, Horseback Riding, Roller Blade/Bike Paths, Fishing Charter, Group Fishing Boat, Sightseeing **1-3 mi:** Fitness Center *(Golds Gym 739-9408)*, Video Rental *(Video Junction 781-5440)*, Park, Museum *(Warwick Art 737-0010)* **3+ mi:** Golf Course *(Seaview 739-6311, 5 mi.)*, Bowling *(Meadowbrook 737-5402, 4 mi.)*, Movie Theater *(792-8008 , 5 mi.)*

Provisioning and General Services
Near: Convenience Store *(7-Eleven)*, Farmers' Market *(Goddard Park Fri 9am-1pm 222-2781)* **Under 1 mi:** Pharmacy *(CVS 737-2305)* **1-3 mi:** Gourmet Shop, Delicatessen *(Martinelli's 738-5474)*, Health Food, Liquor Store *(Peoples 737-0900)*, Bakery, Fishmonger *(Captain's Catch 738-6762)*, Bank/ATM, Post Office, Catholic Church, Protestant Church, Library *(Warwick 739-5440)*, Dry Cleaners, Laundry, Bookstore *(Barnes & Noble 828-7900)*, Florist, Copies Etc. *(Copy World 739-7400)* **3+ mi:** Supermarket *(Shaw's 823-1820, 4 mi.)*, Hardware Store *(Salks 739-1027, 4 mi.)*

Transportation
OnSite: Courtesy Car/Van **OnCall:** Rental Car *(Enterprise 732-5261)* **Near:** Local Bus *(RIPTA)* **Under 1 mi:** Bikes *(Casters 739-0393)* **3+ mi:** Rail *(Providence/Kingston, 10 mi.)* **Airport:** TF Green *(1 mi.)*

Medical Services
911 Service **OnCall:** Ambulance **Near:** Dentist, Veterinarian *(East Greenwich 885-2221)* **Under 1 mi:** Chiropractor *(Frye Family 886-4255)* **1-3 mi:** Doctor *(Davis/Schulman 737-2280)*, Holistic Services *(All's Well 884-0410)* **Hospital:** Kent County 737-7000 *(2.5 mi.)*

Setting -- Mature plantings, a two-story waterfront restaurant and open views of Greenwich Bay are highlights of this thoughtfully landscaped, full-service boatyard/marina. A picnic area sits at the water's edge and a private, inviting pool area looks out onto the breakwater and Greenwich Bay beyond. Its slips are filled with big, classic sailboats and the grounds and docks reflect a caring hand. The nearby streets are lined with nicely restored houses.

Marina Notes -- * Office closes at 5pm, ships' store at 4:30. Off-season 8am-5pm Mon-Fri, 'til 4pm Sat & Sun. The well protected docks are literally surrounded by a curved Rip-Rapped jetty and wave fence. The breakwater dramatically minimizes the impact of wakes but also cuts the breeze. Fairly recent, very nice heads and showers with separate dressing rooms. Full-service boatyard, good docks with current pedestals. Originally this was the Providence Coal Company; Brewer acquired it in 1981 and has been renovating and upgrading ever since. Discounts and packages for Brewer's members.

Notable -- The onsite Outrigger restaurant offers inside & outside dining options -- all with views of the marina and the Bay - and entertainment Thu-Sun. A modest beach is directly adjacent to the marina, and a 300 yard dinghy ride takes you to Goddard Park - with roller blading and bicycling paths, a good beach, picnic area, hiking paths and a concession stand. 3 miles to Pontiac Mills, a restored textile mill that houses about 80 artisans and shops. Very close to TF Green Airport & in its landing pattern -- as are almost all the marinas located on Warwick's 39 miles of coastline. Varnum House and Wireless & Steam Museum are good rainy day options.

PHOTOS ON CD-ROM: 8

Greenwich Bay Marinas

Greenwich Bay Marinas

1 Masthead Drive; Warwick, RI 02886

Tel: (401) 884-1810 **VHF: Monitor** 9 **Talk** 10
Fax: (401) 884-4751 **Alternate Tel:** (401) 478-0368
Email: info@greenwichbay.com **Web:** www.greenwichbay.com
Nearest Town: E. Greenwich *(2 mi.)* **Tourist Info:** (401) 732-1100

Navigational Information

Lat: 41°41.126' **Long:** 071°26.972' **Tide:** 4 ft. **Current:** 2 kt. **Chart:** 13221
Rep. Depths (*MLW*): Entry 9 ft. **Fuel Dock** 5 ft. **Max Slip/Moor** 8 ft./-
Access: Narragansett Bay to Greenwich Bay

Marina Facilities *(In Season/Off Season)*

Fuel: Gasoline, Diesel
Slips: 500 Total, 40 Transient **Max LOA:** 125 ft. **Max Beam:** 19 ft.
Rate *(per ft.)*: **Day** $2.00 **Week** $8.00 **Month** $22
Power: 30 amp $7.50, **50 amp** $10, **100 amp** n/a, **200 amp** n/a
Cable TV: Yes **Dockside Phone:** Yes
Dock Type: Concrete, Floating
Moorings: 0 Total, 0 Transient **Launch:** n/a, Dinghy Dock
Rate: Day n/a **Week** n/a **Month** n/a
Heads: 4 Toilet(s), 4 Shower(s) *(with dressing rooms)*, Hair Dryers
Laundry: 2 Washer(s), 2 Dryer(s) **Pay Phones:** Yes, 1
Pump-Out: Full Service, 1 Central, 1 Port **Fee:** $5 **Closed Heads:** Yes

Marina Operations

Owner/Manager: John McGovern **Dockmaster:** Same
In-Season: Year-Round, 8am-5pm **Off-Season:** n/a
After-Hours Arrival: Call pager (401-4339-5100) and tie to fuel dock
Reservations: Yes, Required **Credit Cards:** Visa/MC
Discounts: Safe/Sea **Dockage:** 25% **Fuel:** n/a **Repair:** n/a
Pets: Welcome **Handicap Access:** Yes, Heads, Docks

Marina Services and Boat Supplies

Services - Docking Assistance, Dock Carts **Communication -** Mail & Package Hold, Phone Messages, FedEx, AirBorne, UPS, Express Mail **Supplies - OnSite:** Ice *(Block, Cube)*, Ships' Store **Under 1 mi:** Live Bait **1-3 mi:** Boat/US *(886-6790)*, Marine Discount Store, Bait/Tackle *(Ericksons 739-7437)*, Propane *(Boc Gas 884-0486)* **3+ mi:** West Marine *(884-0900, 4 mi.)*

Boatyard Services

OnSite: Travelift *(55T)*, Forklift, Crane, Engine mechanic *(gas, diesel)*, Electrical Repairs, Electronics Repairs, Hull Repairs, Rigger, Bottom Cleaning, Brightwork, Divers, Compound, Wash & Wax, Propeller Repairs *(ZF Marine)*, Woodworking, Inflatable Repairs, Upholstery, Yacht Interiors, Painting, Yacht Broker *(Bassett Sea Ray)* **OnCall:** Air Conditioning, Refrigeration, Interior Cleaning, Life Raft Service, Metal Fabrication **Under 1 mi:** Launching Ramp, Electronic Sales. **1-3 mi:** Sail Loft. **3+ mi:** Yacht Design, Total Refits. **Member:** ABBRA, ABYC - 1 Certified Tech(s) **Yard Rates:** $67.50/hr., Haul & Launch $3/ft. *(blocking $2/ft.)*, Power Wash $2.50, Bottom Paint $9/ft.+ /ft.up to 95'

Restaurants and Accommodations

OnSite: Restaurant *(Chelo's 884-3000, D $8)* **OnCall:** Pizzeria *(Excellent Pizza 884-5858)* **Near:** Restaurant *(Ward's 884-7008, L $5, D $7-15)*, *(Outrigger 541-9100)*, Lite Fare *(The Third Rail D $3-5)* **Under 1 mi:** Restaurant *(Harborside Lobstermania 884-6363, L $5, D $10-25)* **1-3 mi:** Restaurant *(Crow's Nest 632-6575)*, Fast Food *(Burger King)*, Motel *(Comfort Inn 732-0470, $100-230)*, *(Best Western 884-8000)*, Hotel *(Crowne Plaza 732-6000, $180-275)*, *(Marriott Residence Inn 437-7100, $170-240)*

Recreation and Entertainment

OnSite: Pool, Picnic Area, Grills, Playground **Under 1 mi:** Sightseeing *(Apponaug Village)* **1-3 mi:** Beach *(Goddard - dinghy)*, Tennis Courts *(Tennis R.I. 828-4450)*, Fitness Center *(Golds 739-9408)*, Fishing Charter, Movie Theater, Video Rental *(Video Junction 781-5440)*, Park, Museum *(Warwick Art 737-0010)* **3+ mi:** Golf Course *(Seaview 739-6311, 5 mi.)*

Provisioning and General Services

Under 1 mi: Convenience Store *(7-Eleven)*, Farmers' Market *(Goddard Park)*, Catholic Church, Protestant Church *(Episcopal)*, Pharmacy *(CVS 737-2305)* **1-3 mi:** Delicatessen *(Sweet Temptations 732-2516)*, Wine/Beer *(Peoples 737-0900)*, Liquor Store, Bakery *(Sweet Temptations)*, Fishmonger *(Captain's Catch 738-6762)*, Meat Market *(Butcher's Block)*, Bank/ATM, Post Office, Library *(739-5440)*, Beauty Salon, Barber Shop, Dry Cleaners, Laundry, Florist *(Blossom)*, Retail Shops *(Pontiac Mills 737-2700)*, Copies Etc. *(Copy World 739-7400)* **3+ mi:** Supermarket *(Shaw's, 4 mi.)*, Green Grocer *(Morris Farms, 4 mi.)*, Hardware Store *(Salks 739-1027, 4 mi.)*

Transportation

OnCall: Rental Car *(Thrifty 732-2000/Enterprise 732-5261)*, Taxi *(Apponaug 737-6400)* **Near:** Local Bus **Under 1 mi:** Bikes *(Casters 739-0393)* **3+ mi:** Rail *(Providence/Kingston, 8 mi.)* **Airport:** TF Green *(2.5 mi.)*

Medical Services

911 Service **OnCall:** Ambulance **Near:** Veterinarian *(East Greenwich 885-2221)* **Under 1 mi:** Dentist, Chiropractor *(Frye Family 886-4255)* **1-3 mi:** Doctor *(Davis/Schulman 737-2280)*, Holistic Services *(All's Well 884-0410)* **Hospital:** Kent 737-7000 *(2.5 mi.)*

Setting -- This large, beautifully landscaped marina sits just south of the mouth of Apponaug Harbor, on the main part of Greenwich Bay. It sports an expansive lawn, dotted with umbrellaed tables, and a bandstand at the water's edge that encourages a lively, party atmosphere. Overlooking the lawn and docks is a popular restaurant. All aspects of mostly power-boat Greenwich Bay Marina - docks to pool - are well attended and reflect an attention to detail.

Marina Notes -- Fuel dock open 8am-7pm. Inviting pool also overlooks the marina. Heads are behind the restaurant but are for the exclusive use of marina guests and residents. Note: Only 40 of the slips have cable and dockside phone - request if this is important. Formerly Masthead Marina, established in 1963, then bought by current owner in 1989 and extensively renovated and upgraded. Mostly a dockominium but some seasonal and almost always transient slips. Does not have a full dock staff but does have a staffed full-service boatyard.

Notable -- The onsite restaurant Chelo's offers inside and deck dining - on two levels - plus lawn dining -- all with views of the marina and Bay. There is entertainment seven nights a week right on the lawn in front of the docks. A 7-11 and The Outrigger Restaurant are both a short walk as is The Third Rail for light meals & dessert Thurs 5-9pm, Fri-Sat 7-9pm, Sun 7-5pm. Just a little over a mile to Historic Apponaug Village with 30 historic and architecturally interesting buildings. Three miles away is the 1863 Historic Pontiac Mills, now home to some eighty shops and artisans, with an outdoor market on Sat & Sun. Goddard State Park is a dinghy ride across the bay and has beaches, picnic areas, trails, a snack bar and, on Fridays, a Farmers' Market 9am-1pm 222-2781.

PHOTOS ON CD-ROM: 7

Navigational Information
Lat: 41°41.422' **Long:** 071°26.805' **Tide:** 5 ft. **Current:** 2 kt. **Chart:** 13221
Rep. Depths (*MLW*): Entry 6 ft. **Fuel Dock** n/a **Max Slip/Moor** 7 ft./6 ft.
Access: Narragansett Bay to Greenwich Bay to Apponaug Cove

Marina Facilities *(In Season/Off Season)*
Fuel: No
Slips: 218 Total, 10 Transient **Max LOA:** 40 ft. **Max Beam:** 12 ft.
Rate *(per ft.)*: **Day** $1.00* **Week** n/a **Month** n/a
Power: 30 amp Inq., **50 amp** n/a, **100 amp** n/a, **200 amp** n/a
Cable TV: No **Dockside Phone:** No
Dock Type: Floating
Moorings: 30 Total, 2 Transient **Launch:** n/a, Dinghy Dock
Rate: Day $25 **Week** n/a **Month** n/a
Heads: 2 Toilet(s), 2 Shower(s)
Laundry: None **Pay Phones:** Yes, 1
Pump-Out: Self Service, 1 Central **Fee:** Free **Closed Heads:** Yes

Marina Operations
Owner/Manager: John Dickerson **Dockmaster:** n/a
In-Season: n/a, 8:30am-5pm **Off-Season:** n/a, 8:30am-5pm
After-Hours Arrival: Anchor outside
Reservations: Yes, Required **Credit Cards:** Visa/MC
Discounts: Safe/Sea **Dockage:** 25% **Fuel:** n/a **Repair:** n/a
Pets: Welcome, Dog Walk Area **Handicap Access:** No

Apponaug Harbor Marina

Rear 17 Arnolds Neck Drive; Warwick, RI 02886

Tel: (401) 739-5005 **VHF: Monitor** n/a **Talk** n/a
Fax: (401) 738-4459 **Alternate Tel:** n/a
Email: capjak@ids.net **Web:** www.apponaugmarina.com
Nearest Town: Apponaug *(1 mi.)* **Tourist Info:** (401) 732-1100

Marina Services and Boat Supplies
Supplies - Near: Propane *(Boc Gases 884-0486)* **Under 1 mi:** Ice *(Block, Cube, Shaved)*, Bait/Tackle *(Ericksons Bait & Tackle 739-7437)* **1-3 mi:** Ships' Store *(Jatco Marine 828-5590)*, Boat/US **3+ mi:** West Marine *(884-0900, 5 mi.)*

Boatyard Services
OnSite: Travelift *(25T)*, Crane **OnCall:** Engine mechanic *(gas, diesel)*, Electronic Sales, Electronics Repairs, Hull Repairs, Rigger, Sail Loft, Canvas Work, Bottom Cleaning, Divers, Propeller Repairs, Yacht Broker **Near:** Painting, Awlgrip. **Dealer for:** Universal Motors. **Member:** ABBRA **Yard Rates:** $59/hr., Haul & Launch $28/ft., Power Wash $1.50/ft. **Storage:** In-Water $15/ft. season, On-Land $8/ft./mo.

Restaurants and Accommodations
OnCall: Pizzeria *(Papa Gino's 826-0661)* **Near:** Restaurant *(Crow's Nest 732-6575, L $5-15, D $5-15, delivers, too)*, *(Chelos Waterfront 884-3000, L $4-9, D $6-13)* **Under 1 mi:** Restaurant *(Remington 736-8388, L $10, D $16)*, *(Outrigger 541-9100, L $6-12, D $6-12)*, *(Good Fortune Chinese 738-6162)*, *(Ward's Publick House 884-7008)*, Snack Bar *(Dee's New York System 732-9733)* **1-3 mi:** Restaurant *(Contes 739-8998)*, *(Cappellis 737-9758)*, Motel *(Comfort Inn 732-0470)*, Hotel *(Radisson 739-3000)*, *(Holiday Inn 736-5000)*, *(Crowne Plaza 732-6000)*, Inn/B&B *(1873 House 884-9955)*

Recreation and Entertainment
Near: Beach, Video Rental *(Video Junction 781-5440)*, Cultural Attract *(Historic Apponaug Village)* **Under 1 mi:** Museum *(Warwick Museum Of Art 737-0010)* **1-3 mi:** Tennis Courts *(Tennis Rhode Island 828-4450)*, Fitness Center *(Golds Gym 739-9408)* **3+ mi:** Golf Course *(Midville CC 828-9215, 5 mi.)*

Provisioning and General Services
Under 1 mi: Convenience Store *(Dairy Mart Convenience 738-6190)*, Delicatessen *(Martinelli's 738-5474)*, Wine/Beer, Liquor Store *(Peoples Liquor Warehouse 737-0900)*, Lobster Pound *(Captain's Catch 738-6762)*, Bank/ATM, Post Office, Protestant Church, Library *(Warwick 739-5440)*, Beauty Salon, Barber Shop, Laundry, Pharmacy *(Walgreens 737-1905)*, Copies Etc. *(Copy World 739-7400)* **1-3 mi:** Supermarket *(IGA736-0383/Shaw's 823-1820)*, Florist *(Peter PT's)*, Buying Club *(Sam's)* **3+ mi:** Farmers' Market *(Goddard State Park Fri 9am-1pm 222-2781, 4 mi. or dinghy across Greenwich Bay)*, Bookstore *(Barnes & Noble 828-7900, 4 mi.)*, Hardware Store *(Salks Hardware & Marine 739-1027, 4 mi.)*

Transportation
OnCall: Rental Car *(Avis 736-7500/Enterprise 732-5261)*, Taxi **Under 1 mi:** Bikes *(Casters Bicycle 739-0393)*, Local Bus *(RI PTA 781-9400)* **3+ mi:** Rail *(Providence/Kingston, 10 mi.)* **Airport:** TF Green *(3 mi.)*

Medical Services
911 Service **OnCall:** Ambulance **Under 1 mi:** Veterinarian *(Cowesett Animal Hospital 732-4050)* **1-3 mi:** Doctor *(Bansal/Dimarco/Martin 732-0880)*, Dentist, Chiropractor *(Apponaug Chiropractic Cntr. 738-9611)*, Holistic Services *(Ahhhhhhh Massage 738-3752)* **Hospital:** Kent County 737-7000 *(2 mi.)*

Setting -- Conveniently located right off the northwest corner of Greenwich Bay in Apponaug Cove, this reasonably large facility provides very protected dockage in a quiet, rural, residential environment -- somewhat unusual for busy Greenwich Bay. There are lovely views from the docks -- of the open Bay and the surrounding area -- and there's a cool southwest breeze most of the summer.

Marina Notes -- * Seasonal rate $60-64/ft. for slips, $29/ft for moorings. Closed Sundays and holidays. Formal name is Dickerson's Marina, Inc. Quite nice heads with showers. Family owned and managed - second generation now involved. Second oldest floating docks in Rhode Island - dating from the 1950's. Most of the docks are plywood with the exception of those nearest the Bay and the walkways which are now floating cement. A Do-It-Yourself boatyard that only provides haul, launch and storage. Apponaug Harbor Marina was originally Universal Engine's East Coast Warehouse and Distributor prior to that company's sale to Westerbeke. As a result, they still have a tremendous inventory of Atomic 4 (gas) and Universal Diesel parts.

Notable -- Within ten minutes of TF Green Airport and twenty minutes of Providence, making this a good place to leave the boat. Rhode Island Public Transit's local bus stops nearby. The onsite Apponaug Harbor Yacht Club was founded in 1968 and has a very active schedule of racing and social events. Nearby is Historic Apponaug Village which is comprised of more than 30 buildings stretched along Post Road between Greenwich Ave. and West Shore Rd.

PHOTOS ON CD-ROM: 6

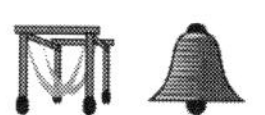

Bay Marina

1800 West Shore Road; Warwick, RI 02889

Tel: (401) 739-6435 **VHF: Monitor** n/a **Talk** n/a
Fax: (401) 732-3436 **Alternate Tel:** n/a
Email: baymarina@aol.com **Web:** n/a
Nearest Town: Warwick *(4 mi.)* **Tourist Info:** (401) 732-1100

Navigational Information

Lat: 41°41.878' **Long:** 071°23.331' **Tide:** 5 ft. **Current:** n/a **Chart:** 13221
Rep. Depths (*MLW*): Entry 6 ft. **Fuel Dock** n/a **Max Slip/Moor** 7 ft./-
Access: Greenwich Bay to the head of Warwick Cove

Marina Facilities *(In Season/Off Season)*

Fuel: No
Slips: 200 Total, 10 Transient **Max LOA:** 50 ft. **Max Beam:** 16 ft.
Rate *(per ft.)*: **Day** $1.00/Inq. **Week** Inq. **Month** Inq.
Power: 30 amp $5, **50 amp** $10, **100 amp** n/a, **200 amp** n/a
Cable TV: No **Dockside Phone:** No
Dock Type: Wood, Long Fingers, Floating
Moorings: 4 Total, 0 Transient **Launch:** n/a, Dinghy Dock
Rate: Day n/a **Week** n/a **Month** n/a
Heads: 2 Toilet(s), 2 Shower(s)
Laundry: None **Pay Phones:** Yes, 1
Pump-Out: OnSite, Self Service, 1 Central **Fee:** n/a **Closed Heads:** Yes

Marina Operations

Owner/Manager: Kristin Cataldi **Dockmaster:** Same
In-Season: Year-Round, 8am-4:30pm **Off-Season:** n/a
After-Hours Arrival: Call ahead
Reservations: Required **Credit Cards:** Visa/MC
Discounts: Sea Tow **Dockage:** n/a **Fuel:** n/a **Repair:** n/a
Pets: Welcome, Dog Walk Area **Handicap Access:** No

Marina Services and Boat Supplies

Services - Dock Carts **Communication -** Mail & Package Hold, Fax in/out *($1)* **Supplies - OnSite:** Ships' Store **Near:** Ice *(Block)* **1-3 mi:** Bait/Tackle *(Caseys Bait & Tackle 732-4734)*, Propane *(U-Haul/Rhode Island Rentals 738-3855)* **3+ mi:** West Marine *(884-0900, 8 mi.)*

Boatyard Services

OnSite: Travelift *(20T)*, Crane, Engine mechanic *(gas, diesel)*, Hull Repairs, Bottom Cleaning, Brightwork, Compound, Wash & Wax, Propeller Repairs, Painting **OnCall:** Air Conditioning, Inflatable Repairs, Life Raft Service, Upholstery, Metal Fabrication **Near:** Launching Ramp. **Under 1 mi:** Electronic Sales. **Dealer for:** Crusader Marine Engines, Onan generators, Cummins Engines. **Yard Rates:** $60/hr., Haul & Launch $6/ft. *(blocking $1.50/ft.)*, Power Wash $1.5, Bottom Paint $7/ft. **Storage:** On-Land $24/ft. (Winter only)

Restaurants and Accommodations

OnCall: Pizzeria *(Dominos 732-2940)*, *(Ronzio Pizza 737-8800)* **Under 1 mi:** Restaurant *(One Bay Ave 738-4777)*, *(The Inn 737-6073)*, Snack Bar *(Meadowbrook Lanes 739-4753)*, Pizzeria *(Papa John's 732-7077)* **1-3 mi:** Restaurant *(Peter's 738-8567)*, *(The Islander 738-9875)*, *(Ocean Bar & Grill 739-4636)*, *(Cherrystones 732-2532, L $3-11, D $6-17, on Oakland Beach)*, *(Peter's Coney Island System 732-6499)*, *(Nonna Cherubina 738-5221)*, Seafood Shack *(Iggy's Doughboys & Chowder House 737-9459, L $2-9, D $2-9)*, Motel *(Best Western 884-8000)* **3+ mi:** Motel *(Comfort Inn 732-0470, 4 mi.)*, Hotel *(Sheraton 738-4000, 4 mi.)*, *(Hampton Inn 739-1550, 4 mi.)*, Inn/B&B *(Henry Johnson House 781-4387, 5 mi.)*, *(Edgewood Manor 781-0099, 4 mi.)*

Recreation and Entertainment

OnSite: Picnic Area, Grills **Near:** Beach **Under 1 mi:** Golf Course *(Seaview Country Club 739-6311)*, Bowling *(Meadowbrook Lanes 737-5402)*, Fishing Charter, Movie Theater, Video Rental *(Blockbuster 732-2080)* **3+ mi:** Museum *(Warwick Museum Of Art 737-0010, 6 mi.)*

Provisioning and General Services

Near: Convenience Store *(Cumberland Farms 736-6950)*, Delicatessen *(Michael's Deli & Sandwich 739-7299)*, Green Grocer **Under 1 mi:** Supermarket *(Stop & Shop 732-4616)*, Wine/Beer, Liquor Store *(Haxtons West Bay 737-6737)*, Bakery, Meat Market, Bank/ATM, Beauty Salon, Barber Shop, Laundry, Pharmacy *(Walgreens 737-3540, Stop & Shop 732-4060)*, Florist **1-3 mi:** Post Office, Catholic Church, Protestant Church, Library *(Warwick 739-5440)*, Hardware Store *(Salks Hardware & Marine 739-1027)*

Transportation

OnCall: Rental Car *(Enterprise 732-3795/Hertz 739-5012)*, Taxi *(Best Taxi 781-0706)*, Airport Limo *(After Five Limousine 737-2226)* **3+ mi:** Rail *(Amtrak 800-USA-RAIL, 10 mi.)* **Airport:** TF Green *(4 mi.)*

Medical Services

911 Service **OnCall:** Ambulance **1-3 mi:** Veterinarian *(West Shore Clinic 785-2222)* **3+ mi:** Doctor *(Warwick Medical Walk-In 785-9333, 3.5 mi.)*, Chiropractor *(Brodeur Center 463-9520, 3.5 mi.)* **Hospital:** Kent County 737-7000 *(6 mi.)*

Setting -- This nicely maintained facility is the last marina to port at the head of crowded, busy Warwick Cove. It is well protected, quiet, offers a family-oriented environment -- and is far enough off the Bay and up the Cove to be out of the hustle and bustle of activity.

Marina Notes -- Full boatyard services onsite. Dealer for Crusader Marine Engines, Onan generators, Cummins Engines. A certified Crusader service center. Comfortable picnic patio with grills sits dockside. Basic heads. Transient moorings may be available from the Harbormaster - 738-2000 - they are sprinkled throughout the Cove beginning at Harbor Light Marina.

Notable -- There isn't much right near by - but if you are willing to hike a bit there are twelve restaurants within 1.5 miles. Oakland Beach, on Horse Neck, is about 1.25 miles. This is an "official" beach with lifeguards, activities, concessions and even one of the restaurants - "Cherrystones" 732-2532. Bay Marina's proximity to TF Green Airport gives it potential as a good place to leave the boat.

PHOTOS ON CD-ROM: 3

Navigational Information

Lat: 41°44.794' **Long:** 071°21.354' **Tide:** 4 ft. **Current:** 0.25 kt. **Chart:** 1322
Rep. Depths (*MLW*): Entry 6 ft. **Fuel Dock** n/a **Max Slip/Moor** 8 ft./-
Access: From G1, channel into Bullock Cove, 1st facility immediately to port

Marina Facilities *(In Season/Off Season)*

Fuel: No
Slips: 50 Total, 2 Transient **Max LOA:** 45 ft. **Max Beam:** 14 ft.
Rate *(per ft.)*: **Day** $1.00 **Week** Inq. **Month** Inq.
Power: 30 amp Incl., **50 amp** Incl., **100 amp** n/a, **200 amp** n/a
Cable TV: No **Dockside Phone:** No
Dock Type: Wood, Pilings, Floating
Moorings: 0 Total, 0 Transient **Launch:** n/a
Rate: Day n/a **Week** n/a **Month** n/a
Heads: 2 Toilet(s), 2 Shower(s)
Laundry: None **Pay Phones:** No
Pump-Out: No **Fee:** n/a **Closed Heads:** Yes

Marina Operations

Owner/Manager: Kennard.G. Gregory **Dockmaster:** Same
In-Season: May-Nov, 8am-5pm **Off-Season:** n/a
After-Hours Arrival: Call in advance
Reservations: Required **Credit Cards:** Visa/MC
Discounts: None
Pets: Welcome **Handicap Access:** No

Bullock Cove Marine

254 Riverside Drive; Riverside, RI 02915

Tel: (401) 433-3010 **VHF: Monitor** n/a **Talk** n/a
Fax: (401) 433-3128 **Alternate Tel:** n/a
Email: kggregory@bullockcovemarine.com **Web:** www.bullockcove.com
Nearest Town: Riverside *(2 mi.)* **Tourist Info:** (401) 438-1212

Marina Services and Boat Supplies

Services - Trash Pick-Up, Dock Carts **Communication -** FedEx, AirBorne, UPS, Express Mail **Supplies - OnSite:** Ships' Store **1-3 mi:** Ice *(Block)*, Bait/Tackle *(Gameday Products 437-1884)* **3+ mi:** West Marine *(508-336-5004, 5 mi.)*, Marine Discount Store *(Boaters World 508-336-0417, 5 mi.)*, Propane *(Corp Brothers 331-8020, 7 mi.)*, CNG *(Corp Brothers, 7 mi.)*

Boatyard Services

OnSite: Travelift *(35T)*, Crane *(40T)*, Launching Ramp, Electrical Repairs, Hull Repairs, Rigger, Bottom Cleaning, Brightwork, Compound, Wash & Wax, Interior Cleaning, Woodworking, Painting, Awlgrip **3+ mi:** Sail Loft *(8 mi.)*. **Member:** ABYC **Yard Rates:** $45/hr., Haul & Launch $5/ft., Power Wash $1.50, Bottom Paint $9/ft. **Storage:** In-Water $25/ft., On-Land $25/ft.

Restaurants and Accommodations

OnCall: Pizzeria *(Hollywood 437-0707)* **Under 1 mi:** Restaurant *(Rooster's Grill 433-0023)* **1-3 mi:** Restaurant *(Lee's Chinese 433-4312)*, *(Riverside Grille 433-9825)*, *(Siam Square 433-0123, L $5-7, D $8-14)*, *(Rickshaw Inn Restaurant 433-0700)*, Snack Bar *(Riverside Kitchen New York System 433-0395, B,L,D)*, Fast Food *(One River Street 437-9333)*, Pizzeria *(Town Pizza and Family Restaurant 433-0300)*, Inn/B&B *(Henry L Johnson House 781-4387)* **3+ mi:** Motel *(Best Western 884-8000, 6 mi.)*, *(Motel 6 467-9800, 6 mi.)*, Hotel *(Sheraton Providence Airport 738-4000, 6 mi.)*, Inn/B&B *(Edgewood Manor B&B 781-0099, 4 mi.)*

Recreation and Entertainment

Under 1 mi: Park *(Bullock Point)*, Cultural Attract *(Crescent Park Carousel)* **1-3 mi:** Tennis Courts *(Centre Court Tennis Club 437-1210)*, Golf Course *(Silver Spring Golf 434-9697)*, Fitness Center *(Art Of Fitness 437-0900)*, Video Rental *(Five Star Video 433-3337)* **3+ mi:** Movie Theater *(7 mi.)*, Museum *(Museum Of Natural History 785-9457, Warren Fire Museum 245-3790, 6 mi.)*

Provisioning and General Services

Under 1 mi: Copies Etc. **1-3 mi:** Supermarket *(Shaw's 433-3180)*, Delicatessen *(Riverside Depot Deli 433-2647)*, Health Food *(Village Natural 941-8028)*, Wine/Beer, Liquor Store *(Haxtons 433-0900)*, Bakery *(Crown Sweet Shoppes 437-1555)*, Bank/ATM, Post Office, Catholic Church, Library *(433-4877)*, Dry Cleaners, Laundry *(Abs Laundromat 433-2830)*, Pharmacy *(CVS 433-0233)*, Newsstand, Hardware Store *(Barrington Lumber & Supplies 246-0550)*, Clothing Store

Transportation

OnCall: Rental Car *(Enterprise 732-3795)*, Taxi *(Best Taxi 781-0706)*, Airport Limo *(Airport Taxi 737-2868)* **Under 1 mi:** Local Bus *(RIPTA 32 to Providence 781-9400)* **1-3 mi:** Bikes *(Your Bike Shop 433-4491)* **3+ mi:** Rail *(Amtrak 800-USA-RAIL, 8mi.)* **Airport:** TF Green *(4 mi.)*

Medical Services

911 Service **OnCall:** Ambulance **1-3 mi:** Doctor *(Bianco 433-0600)*, Chiropractor *(Riverside Chiropractic Center 433-5559)*, Veterinarian *(Riverside Animal Hosp 433-2070)* **Hospital:** Rhode Island 444-4000 *(6 mi.)*

Setting -- Bullock Cove Marine is a small rustic boatyard located at the East End of Bullock Neck -- a point of land with the Providence River on its west side and Bullock Cove on its east side. It is the first facility to port just inside the entrance to the well protected cove and offers basic services to transient boaters. The Peninsula is called Narragansett Terrace and is largely a residential neighborhood.

Marina Notes -- Bullock Cove Marine was originally two boatyards that had been built prior to World War II. In 1988, the yards were purchased and combined into one facility. Personal attention and a close relationship between customers and craftspeople. Do-it-yourself or full-service. Specializes in finish varnishing, fiberglass repair, Awlgrip, marine carpentry, painting, plus inboard/outboard gas and Diesel engine installation and repair.

Notable -- The Crescent Park Carousel and Park on Bullock Point are less than a mile away. The 19thC medieval-style Barrington Town Hall (247-1900) on SR114 is another interesting destination - Mon-Fri, 8:30am-4:30pm. About 8 miles away is downtown Providence. Head up river for a look at a city in the throes of physical and cultural gentrification and renovation. The now-famous Water Fire Providence begins just beyond the hurricane gate and continues along the River to Waterpark Place. About ten times, from May to Oct, a string of 100 bonfires blaze in the middle of the three Providence rivers, accompanied by all manner of music and theater. During the day, gondolas ply the river. The new Providence is exciting, romantic and chock-a-block with creative restaurants and history. Visit Benefit Street, the city's "mile of history" or the 40 acre Roger Williams Park & Zoo - decreed by the Boston Globe as best in New England.

PHOTOS ON CD-ROM: 4

Brewer Cove Haven Marina

101 Narragansett Avenue; Barrington, RI 02806

Tel: (401) 246-1600 **VHF: Monitor** 16 **Talk** 9
Fax: (401) 246-0731 **Alternate Tel:** n/a
Email: chc@byy.com **Web:** www.byy.com/barrington
Nearest Town: Providence *(7 mi.)* **Tourist Info:** (401) 438-1212

Navigational Information

Lat: 41°45.057' **Long:** 071°21.064' **Tide:** 5 ft. **Current:** n/a **Chart:** 13221
Rep. Depths (*MLW*): Entry 10 ft. **Fuel Dock** 8 ft. **Max Slip/Moor** 8 ft./-
Access: Narragansett Bay to Providence River to Bullock Cove

Marina Facilities *(In Season/Off Season)*

Fuel: Gasoline, Diesel, On Call Delivery
Slips: 210 Total, 5 Transient **Max LOA:** 60 ft. **Max Beam:** n/a
Rate *(per ft.)*: **Day** $1.00/Inq. **Week** Inq. **Month** n/a
Power: 30 amp Inq., **50 amp** Inq., **100 amp** n/a, **200 amp** n/a
Cable TV: No **Dockside Phone:** Yes
Dock Type: Long Fingers, Pilings, Floating
Moorings: 0 Total, 0 Transient **Launch:** n/a
Rate: Day n/a **Week** n/a **Month** n/a
Heads: 6 Toilet(s), 8 Shower(s)
Laundry: None **Pay Phones:** No
Pump-Out: OnSite, Self Service, 2 Central **Fee:** n/a **Closed Heads:** Yes

Marina Operations

Owner/Manager: J. Michael Keyworth **Dockmaster:** Same
In-Season: Year-Round, M-F 7:30am-4:30pm, S 8am-12 **Off-Season:** n/a
After-Hours Arrival: Call ahead
Reservations: Yes **Credit Cards:** Visa/MC, Dscvr, Amex
Discounts: Safe/Sea **Dockage:** 25% **Fuel:** n/a **Repair:** n/a
Pets: Welcome **Handicap Access:** No

Marina Services and Boat Supplies

Services - Docking Assistance, Security, Trash Pick-Up, Dock Carts **Communication -** Mail & Package Hold, Phone Messages, Fax in/out *($3)*, FedEx, AirBorne, UPS, Express Mail *(Sat Del)* **Supplies - OnSite:** Ice *(Cube)*, Ships' Store **Under 1 mi:** Propane *(Lumber 246-0550)* **1-3 mi:** Bait/Tackle *(Gameday 437-1884)* **3+ mi:** West Marine *(336-5004, 4 mi.)*

Boatyard Services

OnSite: Travelift *(150T)*, Forklift, Crane, Engine mechanic *(gas, diesel)*, Electrical Repairs, Electronics Repairs, Hull Repairs, Rigger, Bottom Cleaning, Brightwork, Refrigeration, Compound, Wash & Wax, Woodworking, Upholstery, Metal Fabrication, Awlgrip, Yacht Broker **OnCall:** Divers, Propeller Repairs, Inflatable Repairs **Dealer for:** Yanmar, Westerbeke, Kohler, Edson, Spectra Watermakers, Spurs, Sealand, Marine Air, Cruisair, Webasto, Universal, Ocean Marine, Heart Interface-Xantrex, Village Watermakers, Sea Recovery, Sea Frost, Wacco Adler/Barbour, Hatteras. **Member:** ABBRA, ABYC **Yard Rates:** $68/hr., Haul & Launch $7/ft. -60', $10/ft. 60'+ *(blocking $2-3/ft.)*, Power Wash $2-3/ft., Bottom Paint $9.50/ft. **Storage:** In-Water $40/ft., On-Land Out $3.10/sq.ft. In $9/sq.ft.

Restaurants and Accommodations

OnCall: Pizzeria *(Town 433-0300)*, *(Hollywood 433-0707)* **Under 1 mi:** Restaurant *(Siam Square 433-0123, take-out, too)*, *(Rooster's Grill 433-0023)*, Coffee Shop *(Dunkin Donuts)* **1-3 mi:** Restaurant *(One River Street 497-9333)*, *(Riverside Grille 433-9825)*, Motel *(Neptune House 466-2988)* **3+ mi:** Restaurant *(Tyler Point Grille 247-0017, D $8-20, 4 mi.)*, Hotel *(Ramada 508-336-7300, $70-95, 4 mi.)*, *(Johnson & Wales 508-336-8700, $85-150, 5 mi.)*, Inn/B&B *(Edgewood Manor 781-0099, 4 mi)*

Recreation and Entertainment

OnSite: Pool, Picnic Area, Grills **Near:** Playground, Jogging Paths, Roller Blade/Bike Paths, Park, Cultural Attract **Under 1 mi:** Video Rental *(Five Star Video 433-3337)* **1-3 mi:** Tennis Courts *(Centre Court 437-1210)*, Fitness Center *(Art Of Fitness 437-0900)*, Sightseeing *(Medieval-style Town Hall built by area farmers on SR114 - 247-1900, Mon-Fri, 8:30am-4:30pm)* **3+ mi:** Bowling *(Meadowbrook 737-5402, 5 mi.)*, Movie Theater *(5 mi.)*

Provisioning and General Services

OnCall: Hardware Store, Florist **Near:** Barber Shop **Under 1 mi:** Convenience Store, Supermarket *(Shaw's 433-3180)*, Wine/Beer *(Christy's 433-4223)*, Liquor Store *(Haxton's 433-0900)*, Bank/ATM, Catholic Church, Beauty Salon, Dry Cleaners, Bookstore *(Barrington Books 245-7925)*, Pharmacy *(CVS 433-1120, Brooks 433-5710)* **1-3 mi:** Delicatessen *(Riverside Depot 433-2647)*, Bakery, Fishmonger, Meat Market, Post Office, Library *(Barrington PL 247-1920)*, Laundry **3+ mi:** Buying Club *(Sam's Club 336-8262, 5 mi.)*

Transportation

OnSite: Courtesy Car/Van, Bikes **OnCall:** Rental Car *(Thrifty 435-3300, Enterprise 438-8550)*, Taxi *(Best Taxi 781-0706, East Providence 434-2000)* **Near:** Local Bus *(RIPTA 32 to Providence 781-9400)* **3+ mi:** Rail *(Amtrak 800-USA-RAIL, 8 mi.)* **Airport:** TF Green *(10 mi.)*

Medical Services

911 Service **Under 1 mi:** Doctor *(Thomas 246-1010)*, Veterinarian *(Creature Comforts 246-1105)* **1-3 mi:** Dentist, Ambulance **Hospital:** Rhode Island 444-4000 *(6 mi.)*

Setting -- At the head of Narragansett Bay, just off the east side of the Providence River, Brewer Cove Haven is tucked into Bullock's Cove -- 2nd facility to starboard. The well-protected harbor is home to a variety of vessels, including some America's Cup boats maintained by the boatyard. This seasonal marina and boatyard offers good slips and a pool to the occasional transient boater. The slips' views are dominated by two large travelifts and a row of boat sheds.

Marina Notes -- Open 8am-12noon on Sat. The boatyard is known for its work with 12 Meters, J-Boats, and other high-performance racing machines. Recently renovated docks have new electric boxes with 30/50 Amp, 125/240 Volt outlet options, telephone and cable outlets, and two water faucets per pedestal. Pool is at the rear of the property. Recently purchased adjacent property on the south side for expansion. Onsite are: Custom Navigation Systems, Marine Metal Fabricators, Ken's Canvas, Twin City Yacht Sales, Anchor Yacht Sales. Brewer's Preferred Customer program.

Notable -- Right next door, the hundred acre Haines State Park offers wonderful picnic and walking possibilities -- including 33 treed "picnic sites" with grills overlooking the cove. This is an access point for the 14.5 mile East Providence-to-Bristol paved East Bay Bike Path built on an old railway bed -- joggers, walkers and roller bladers welcome, too. Don't miss the Crescent Park Carousel and Park on Bullock Point (1 mile); small shopping center is adjacent. About 3 miles away is the center of the upscale Providence bedroom community of Barrington - with its lovely 19thC riverfront homes. It's a 7 mile cab ride to phoenix-like Providence, home to an extraordinary number of historic sites -- Benefit Street and up College Hill to Brown University.

PHOTOS ON CD-ROM: 9

XII. Rhode Island: Block Island Sound

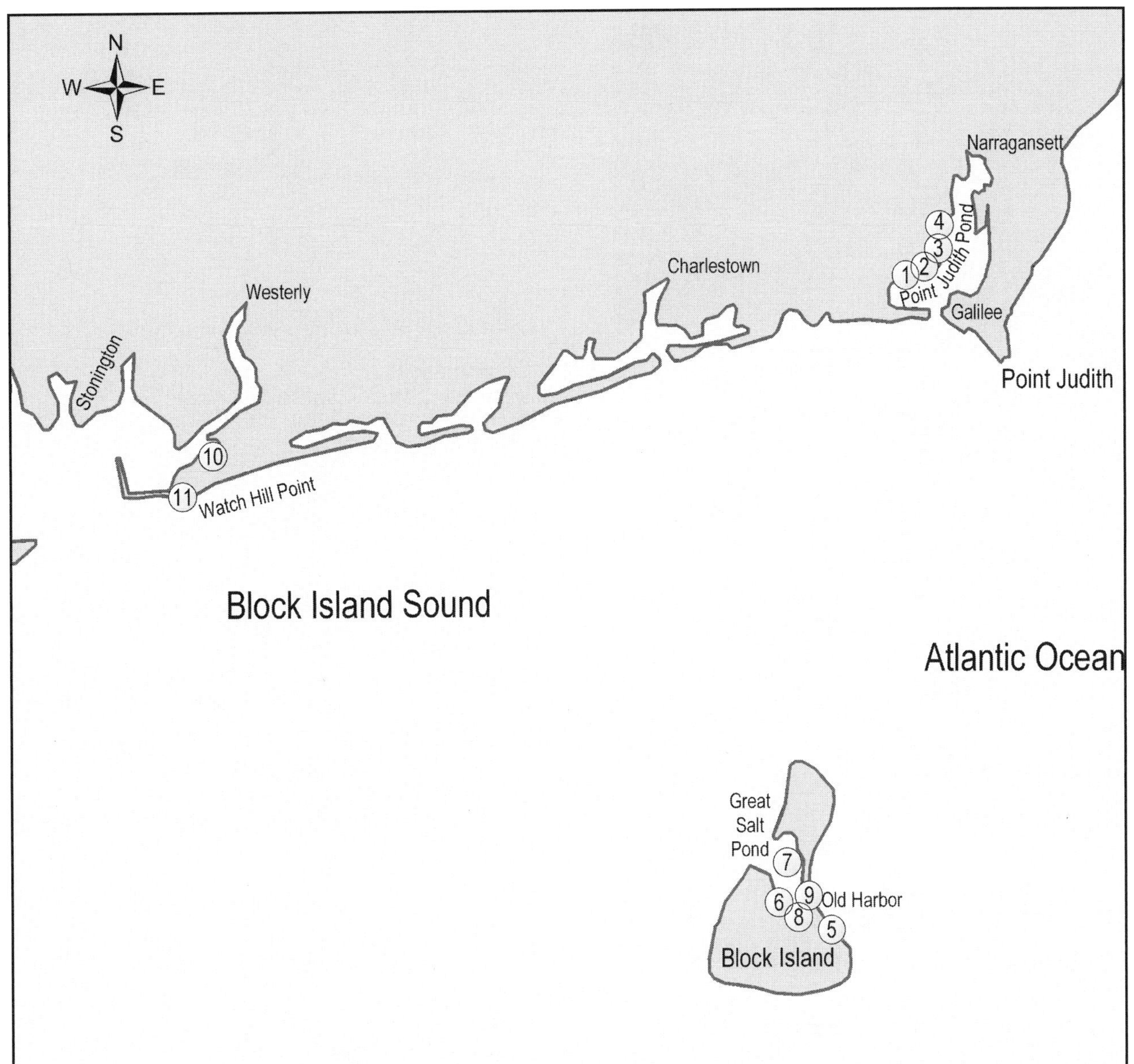

MAP	MARINA	HARBOR	PAGE
1	**Snug Harbor Marina**	*Point Judith Pond*	252
2	**Southern View Yachting Center**	*Point Judith Pond*	253
3	**Point Judith Marina**	*Point Judith Pond*	254
4	**Point View Marina**	*Point Judith Pond*	255
5	**Old Harbor Dock**	*Old Harbor*	256
6	**Champlin's Marina**	*Great Salt Pond*	257
7	**New Harbor Moorings**	*Great Salt Pond*	258
8	**Block Island Boat Basin**	*Great Salt Pond*	259
9	**Payne's New Harbor Dock**	*Great Salt Pond*	260
10	**Watch Hill Boatyard**	*Pawcatuck River*	261
11	**Watch Hill Docks**	*Watch Hill Cove*	262

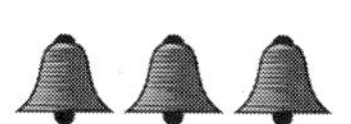

Snug Harbor Marina

410 Gooseberry Road; Wakefield, RI 02879

Tel: (401) 783-7766 **VHF: Monitor** 66 **Talk** n/a
Fax: (401) 782-9040 **Alternate Tel:** n/a
Email: shmfishing@netsense.net **Web:** www.snugharbormarina.com
Nearest Town: Wakefield *(5 mi.)* **Tourist Info:** (401) 783-2801

Navigational Information

Lat: 41°23.179' **Long:** 071°31.089' **Tide:** 4 ft. **Current:** 4 kt. **Chart:** 13219
Rep. Depths (*MLW*): Entry 8 ft. **Fuel Dock** 6 ft. **Max Slip/Moor** 6 ft./-
Access: Pt. Judith HOR through Breachway 0.5 nm north to G7

Marina Facilities *(In Season/Off Season)*

Fuel: *Mobil* - Slip-Side Fueling, Gasoline, Diesel, High-Speed Pumps
Slips: 11 Total, 1-2 Transient **Max LOA:** 86 ft. **Max Beam:** n/a
Rate *(per ft.)*: **Day** $1.50 **Week** n/a **Month** n/a
Power: 30 amp Incl., **50 amp** Incl., **100 amp** n/a, **200 amp** n/a
Cable TV: No **Dockside Phone:** No
Dock Type: Wood, Fixed
Moorings: 0 Total, 0 Transient **Launch:** n/a
Rate: Day n/a **Week** n/a **Month** n/a
Heads: 2 Toilet(s)
Laundry: None, Book Exchange **Pay Phones:** No
Pump-Out: No **Fee:** n/a **Closed Heads:** Yes

Marina Operations

Owner/Manager: Elisa Jackman **Dockmaster:** Matthew Conti
In-Season: Jul-LabDay, 5am-9pm **Off-Season:** Apr-Jun/Sep-Nov, 6am-5pm
After-Hours Arrival: Call in advance
Reservations: Yes **Credit Cards:** Visa/MC, Dscvr, Amex, Mobil
Discounts: Boat/US; Safe/Sea **Dockage:** 25% **Fuel:** $0.10 **Repair:** n/a
Pets: Welcome **Handicap Access:** No

Marina Services and Boat Supplies

Services - Docking Assistance, Dock Carts **Communication -** Fax in/out, FedEx, UPS, Express Mail **Supplies - OnSite:** Ice *(Block, Cube)*, Ships' Store, Bait/Tackle, Live Bait *(Herring, butterfish, mackerel, eels, sandworms, crabs, chum, seaclams)* **3+ mi:** Propane *(Columbia Propane 783-3357, 5 mi.)*

Boatyard Services

OnSite: Divers **Near:** Travelift, Engine mechanic *(gas, diesel)*, Launching Ramp. **Nearest Yard:** Point Judith (401) 789-7189

Restaurants and Accommodations

OnSite: Snack Bar *(Snug Harbor Snack Bar 783-3427, B $4, L $4)* **Under 1 mi:** Restaurant *(Captain Jack's 789-4556, D $16)*, *(Fish Stories 789-2864)*, *(Jim's Dock 783-2050)* **3+ mi:** Restaurant *(Sea Horse Grill 789-2422, 5 mi., on the grounds of Theater-by-the-Sea)*, Seafood Shack *(Main Street Fish Market 782-2366, 5 mi.)*, Inn/B&B *(Larchwood Inn 783-5454, $35-150, 5 mi., 12 rooms + Holly House)*, *(Admiral Dewey 783-2090, 4.5 mi.)*

Recreation and Entertainment

OnSite: Fishing Charter *(40 boats 26'-50' - half-day to 30' $275, 31-40' $350. Inshore full-day - to 30' $350, 31-40' $425, Offshore full-day to 35' $650, 36-50' $850.)*, Sightseeing *(Night Heron Nature Cruise - check for availability, may be out of service)*, Special Events *(Four Tournament Series, held on weekends in June, July, August, October)* **1-3 mi:** Beach, Playground, Tennis Courts **3+ mi:** Golf Course *(Rose Hill Golf Club 788-1088, 9 mi.)*, Fitness Center *(River Bend Athletic 789-9585, 6 mi.)*, Bowling *(Amscot 783-5511, 6 mi.)*, Video Rental *(Blockbuster 782-4950, 6 mi.)*, Museum *(Museum Of Primitive Culture 783-5711, South County Museum 783-5400, 5 mi.)*

Provisioning and General Services

OnSite: Delicatessen, Fishmonger, Lobster Pound **3+ mi:** Convenience Store *(Seaview Marketplace 788-9000, 6 mi.)*, Supermarket *(Shaw's 792-9888, 6 mi.)*, Liquor Store *(Patsy's 783-5043, 6 mi.)*, Farmers' Market *(789-1388 Marina Park Tue 3-6pm, U.R.I. Flagg Rd. Sat 9am-Noon, 5 mi.)*, Green Grocer *(Carpenter's Farm Stand 783-7550, 5 mi.)*, Post Office *(783-7215, 5 mi.)*, Library *(South Kingston 789-1555, 6 mi.)*, Laundry *(Pier Cleaners 783-2030, 6 mi.)*, Bookstore *(Bears' Book Den 782-6660, 6 mi.)*, Pharmacy *(CVS 783-9396, 6 mi.)*, Hardware Store *(Damons Hardware 783-4851, 6 mi.)*, Copies Etc. *(Printing Express 782-2278, 6 mi.)*

Transportation

OnSite: Courtesy Car/Van *(Owners' car to local restaurant)* **OnCall:** Rental Car *(Enterprise 792-0185)*, Taxi *(Wakefield Cab 788-0007)* **3+ mi:** Bikes *(Stedman 789-8664, 4.5 mi.)*, Rail *(Amtrak Kingston, 10 mi.)*, Ferry Service *(Block Island, 10 mi.)* **Airport:** TF Green *(25 mi.)*

Medical Services

911 Service **Near:** Holistic Services *(Snug Harbor Massage Therapy 792-8656)* **3+ mi:** Chiropractor *(Center For Health 789-5008, 4.5 mi.)*, Veterinarian *(Kingston Kennel 783-4020, 7 mi.)* **Hospital:** South County 782-8010 *(5 mi.)*

PHOTOS ON CD-ROM: 3

Setting -- Through the Breachway, past the State Piers to green can "7", is a cluster of marinas that cater mostly to sport fishing boats. The first facility immediately to port is Snug Harbor. It's easy to spot, with its name emblazoned on the roof. The facility is small, but its services and reputation are great.

Marina Notes -- For more than 20 years, Snug Harbor has been one of Pt. Judith's main sport fishing centers. Onsite you'll find what may well be Rhode Island's most complete inshore/offshore bait and tackle store - with extensive stocks of live bait, as well. It is truly remarkable and well worth a visit. The store also sells groceries, deli items, staples, ice cream, snacks, dairy, charts, gifts and clothing. Ice is available packaged or bulk. The onsite seafood market offers local, line-caught, fresh-off-the-boat fish and live lobsters -- yellow fin tuna, albacore, fluke, striped bass, cod, bluefish (call or check their website for daily specials). Prices are quite reasonable; large quantities (like a whole tuna) are even more reasonable. Fuel: Both No. 2 and Marine diesel.

Notable -- The onsite restaurant opens 5am daily for full breakfasts, lunches, seafood specials, box lunches, and snacks. Snug Harbor is the booking agent for more than 40 Coast Guard approved charter vessels ranging from 26' to 50' - staffed by licensed captains and knowledgeable fishing guides. Vessels available range from: JC, Topaz, Harris, Bertram. Sponsors the Four Tournament Series; held on weekends in June, July, August and October, it attracts hundreds of anglers and spectators annually (783-7766). There are three casual restaurants and a massage therapist nearby, but very little else. Most services, major provisioning, lodgings, fine dining restaurants, transportation options and medical care are 5-6 miles away in Wakefield.

Navigational Information
Lat: 41°23.220' **Long:** 071°31.041' **Tide:** 4 ft. **Current:** 4 kt. **Chart:** 13219
Rep. Depths (*MLW*): Entry 10 ft. **Fuel Dock** n/a **Max Slip/Moor** 13 ft./-
Access: 0.5 miles into Point Judith Pond past Snug Harbor

Marina Facilities *(In Season/Off Season)*
Fuel: *Tex/Mobil* - Gasoline, Diesel
Slips: 74 Total, 6 Transient **Max LOA:** 110 ft. **Max Beam:** n/a
Rate *(per ft.)*: **Day** $2.50/$1.75 **Week** Inq. **Month** Inq.
Power: 30 amp $5, **50 amp** $7, **100 amp** $10, **200 amp** n/a
Cable TV: Yes, $5 Some slips **Dockside Phone:** Yes
Dock Type: Short Fingers, Concrete, Pilings, Alongside, Floating
Moorings: 0 Total, 0 Transient **Launch:** n/a
Rate: Day n/a **Week** n/a **Month** n/a
Heads: 6 Toilet(s), 4 Shower(s)
Laundry: 2 Washer(s), 2 Dryer(s) **Pay Phones:** Yes, 1
Pump-Out: OnSite, Full Service, 1 Central **Fee:** $15 **Closed Heads:** Yes

Marina Operations
Owner/Manager: Lisa Bears **Dockmaster:** Same
In-Season: Jun-Sep 1, 8am-7pm **Off-Season:** Sep 1-Jun 1, 9am-5pm
After-Hours Arrival: Use open areas at the end of docks or channel
Reservations: Preferred **Credit Cards:** Visa/MC, Amex
Discounts: Safe/Sea **Dockage:** 25% **Fuel:** n/a **Repair:** n/a
Pets: Welcome **Handicap Access:** Yes, Heads, Docks

Southern View Yachting Center

392-D Gooseberry Road; Wakefield, RI 02879

Tel: (401) 782-8899 **VHF: Monitor** 9 **Talk** 10
Fax: (401) 788-0136 **Alternate Tel:** n/a
Email: info@southernviewmarina.com **Web:** southernviewmarina.com
Nearest Town: Wakefield *(5 mi.)* **Tourist Info:** (401) 783-2801

Marina Services and Boat Supplies
Services - Docking Assistance, Concierge, Trash Pick-Up, Dock Carts **Communication -** Mail & Package Hold, Phone Messages, Fax in/out *($1)*, Data Ports *(Office)*, FedEx, UPS, Express Mail **Supplies - OnSite:** Ice *(Block, Cube)* **OnCall:** Bait/Tackle *(Snug Harbor)* **Near:** Ships' Store *(Snug Harbor)*, Live Bait *(eels, clams, etc.)* **3+ mi:** Propane *(Liberty 789-7332, 6 mi.)*

Boatyard Services
OnSite: Travelift *(55T)*, Forklift, Engine mechanic *(gas, diesel)*, Electrical Repairs, Hull Repairs, Bottom Cleaning, Divers, Compound, Wash & Wax **OnCall:** Brightwork, Air Conditioning, Refrigeration, Interior Cleaning, Propeller Repairs, Woodworking, Inflatable Repairs, Life Raft Service, Upholstery, Yacht Interiors **Near:** Launching Ramp. **1-3 mi:** Electronic Sales, Electronics Repairs.

Restaurants and Accommodations
OnCall: Pizzeria *(Snug Harbor 788-9441)* **Near:** Snack Bar *(Snug Harbor B $4, L $4)* **Under 1 mi:** Restaurant *(Jim's Dock 783-2050)*, *(Captain Jacks 789-4556, D $16)*, *(Fish Stories 789-2864)* **3+ mi:** Restaurant *(Sea Horse Grille 789-2422, 5 mi., at Theater-by-the-Sea)*, Motel *(Coachman Motor Inn 783-2516, 6 mi.)*, Inn/B&B *(Larchwood Inn 783-5454, $35-150, 5 mi., 12 rooms)*, *(Admiral Dewey 783-2090, 4.5 mi.)*

Recreation and Entertainment
OnSite: Heated Pool, Spa, Picnic Area, Grills **Near:** Boat Rentals, Fishing Charter **Under 1 mi:** Group Fishing Boat **1-3 mi:** Beach *(East Matunuck)*, Playground, Dive Shop, Tennis Courts, Park **3+ mi:** Golf Course *(Rose Hill Golf Club 788-1088, 9 mi.)*, Fitness Center *(River Bend Athletic Club 789-9585, 6 mi.)*, Horseback Riding *(Smithbridge Stable 783-0741, 7 mi.)*, Bowling *(Amscot 783-5511, 6 mi.)*, Video Rental *(Blockbuster 782-4950, 6 mi.)*, Museum *(Primitive Culture 783-5711, 6 mi.)*, Cultural Attract *(Theater by the Sea 782-8587, 5 mi.)*

Provisioning and General Services
Near: Delicatessen *(Snug Harbor)*, Fishmonger, Lobster Pound, Newsstand **1-3 mi:** Bank/ATM **3+ mi:** Convenience Store *(Seaview 788-9000, 6 mi.)*, Supermarket *(Shaw's 792-9888, 6 mi.)*, Health Food *(Alternative Food 789-2240, 6 mi.)*, Liquor Store *(Patsy's 783-5043, 6 mi.)*, Farmers' Market *(789-1388 Marina Park Tue 3-6pm, U.R.I. Flagg Rd. Sat 9am-Noon, 5 mi.)*, Green Grocer *(Carpenter's 783-7550, 5 mi.)*, Post Office *(783-7215, 6 mi.)*, Library *(South Kingston 789-1555, 6 mi.)*, Laundry *(Pier Cleaners 783-2030, 6 mi.)*, Bookstore *(Bears' Book Den 782-6660, 6 mi.)*, Pharmacy *(CVS 783-9396, 6 mi.)*, Hardware Store *(Damons 783-4851, 6 mi.)*, Retail Shops *(6 mi.)*

Transportation
OnSite: Courtesy Car/Van, Bikes **OnCall:** Rental Car *(Enterprise 792-0185)*, Taxi *(Wakefield Cab 788-0007)*, Airport Limo *(All Occasion Limo 782-2612)* **3+ mi:** Rail *(Amtrak Kingston, 8 mi.)*, Ferry Service *(Block Island, 10 mi.)* **Airport:** TF Green *(25 mi.)*

Medical Services
911 Service **OnCall:** Ambulance **Near:** Holistic Services *(Snug Harbor Massage 792-8656)* **1-3 mi:** Chiropractor *(Center For Health 789-5008)* **3+ mi:** Dentist *(4 mi.)*, Veterinarian *(Kingston Kennel 783-4020, 7 mi.)* **Hospital:** South County 782-8010 *(5 mi.)*

Setting -- The second set of docks to port, just past green can "7", this very comfortable marina and boatyard provides a luxurious, well protected berth after the rigors of offshore fishing or sailing. The two story contemporary main office and the pavilion out on the dock make this easy to spot.

Marina Notes -- Built in 1999, the entire facility still feels fresh, new, and well maintained. A lovely heated pool with spa overlooks the marina and Point Judith Pond. Inviting heads, showers, and laundry. Customer-oriented staff offers concierge services. Fresh or frozen bait delivery. Dockside telephone and cable at some of the slips - inquire if this is important. Marina provides land transport and bicycles- very, very useful with so little within walking distance.

Notable -- The pavilion on the Southern View docks is a great place to relax and watch the boats go by and monitor the day's catch. Great local beaches. Snug Harbor Marina, down the road, manages more than 40 charter fishing boats, has a huge bait and tackle inventory, convenience store, snack bar, and fresh fish and lobster for sale. Kayaks on Pt Judith Pond & Succotash Salt Marsh available for rent. Five miles away Theater-by-the-Sea has been providing Broadway's best in a "National Register" historic theater for more than six decades.

PHOTOS ON CD-ROM: 6

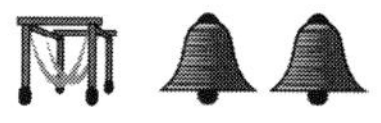

Point Judith Marina

PO Box 129; 360 Gooseberry Road; Wakefield, RI 02879

Tel: (401) 789-7189 **VHF: Monitor** 9 **Talk** 68
Fax: (401) 783-5350 **Alternate Tel:** (401) 783-5350
Email: ptjd7189@aol.com **Web:** n/a
Nearest Town: Wakefield *(5 mi.)* **Tourist Info:** (401) 783-2801

Navigational Information

Lat: 41°23.260' **Long:** 071°31.035' **Tide:** 4 ft. **Current:** 4 kt. **Chart:** 13219
Rep. Depths (*MLW*): Entry 10 ft. **Fuel Dock** 8 ft. **Max Slip/Moor** 8 ft./-
Access: 0.5 nm into Point Judith, past G7, on left

Marina Facilities *(In Season/Off Season)*

Fuel: *Texaco* - Gasoline, Diesel
Slips: 40 Total, 4 Transient **Max LOA:** 55 ft. **Max Beam:** 17 ft.
Rate *(per ft.)*: **Day** $1.50/$1.00 **Week** Inq. **Month** Inq.
Power: 30 amp Incl., **50 amp** Incl., **100 amp** n/a, **200 amp** n/a
Cable TV: No **Dockside Phone:** No
Dock Type: Wood, Short Fingers, Pilings, Floating
Moorings: 0 Total, 0 Transient **Launch:** n/a
Rate: Day n/a **Week** n/a **Month** n/a
Heads: 3 Toilet(s), 2 Shower(s) *(with dressing rooms)*
Laundry: None **Pay Phones:** No
Pump-Out: No **Fee:** n/a **Closed Heads:** Yes

Marina Operations

Owner/Manager: Don Vivenzio **Dockmaster:** Same
In-Season: May-Sep 15, 6am-8pm **Off-Season:** Sep 15-May 1, 8am-4pm
After-Hours Arrival: Tie up at Fuel Dock
Reservations: No **Credit Cards:** Visa/MC, Dscvr, Din, Amex, Tex
Discounts: Boat/US; Safe/Sea **Dockage:** 25% **Fuel:** 5% **Repair:** n/a
Pets: Welcome **Handicap Access:** No

Marina Services and Boat Supplies

Services - Docking Assistance, Dock Carts **Communication -** FedEx, UPS, Express Mail **Supplies - OnSite:** Ice *(Block, Cube)*, Ships' Store **OnCall:** Bait/Tackle *(Snug Harbor Marina 783-7766)* **Near:** Live Bait *(Snug Harbor Marina)*, Propane

Boatyard Services

OnSite: Travelift *(50T)*, Forklift, Engine mechanic *(gas, diesel)*, Electrical Repairs, Hull Repairs, Rigger, Bottom Cleaning, Compound, Wash & Wax, Woodworking **OnCall:** Air Conditioning, Refrigeration, Divers, Propeller Repairs, Life Raft Service, Upholstery, Yacht Interiors **Under 1 mi:** Launching Ramp. **Dealer for:** Cummins, Volvo, Yanmar. **Member:** ABBRA, Other Certifications: Cummins, Volvo **Yard Rates:** $65/hr., Haul & Launch $8/ft., Power Wash $2/ft.

Restaurants and Accommodations

OnCall: Pizzeria *(Harbor Pizza 788-9441)* **Near:** Snack Bar *(Snug Harbor 783-7766, B $3, L $4)* **Under 1 mi:** Restaurant *(Capt. Jacks 789-4556, L $5, D $8), (Jim's Dock 783-2050)*, Seafood Shack *(Fish Stories 789-2864)* **3+ mi:** Restaurant *(Sea Horse Grill 789-2424, 5 mi., on the grounds of Theater-by-the-Sea), (Cassidy's by the Beach 782-2697, 5 mi.)*, Inn/B&B *(Larchwood Inn 784-5454, 5 mi.), (Admiral Dewey Inn 783-2090, 4.5 mi.)*

Recreation and Entertainment

OnSite: Picnic Area, Grills, Boat Rentals *(Capt. Kelly Smith 364-9774)*, Fishing Charter **Near:** Special Events *(Fishing Tournaments)* **Under 1 mi:** Playground **1-3 mi:** Beach, Tennis Courts **3+ mi:** Golf Course *(Rose Hill Golf Club 788-1088, 9 mi.)*, Fitness Center *(River Bend Athletic Club 789-9585, 6 mi.)*, Bowling *(Amscot 783-5711, 6 mi.)*, Video Rental *(Blockbuster 782-4950, 6 mi.)*, Museum *(South County Museum 783-5400, 5 mi.)*, Cultural Attract *(Theater-by-the-Sea 782-8587, 5 mi.)*

Provisioning and General Services

Near: Delicatessen *(Snug Harbor 783-7766)*, Fishmonger *(Snug Harbor)*, Lobster Pound **3+ mi:** Convenience Store *(Seaview Marketplace 788-9000, 6 mi.)*, Supermarket *(Shaw's 792-9888, 6 mi.)*, Health Food *(Alt. Food 789-2240, 6 mi.)*, Liquor Store *(Patsy's 783-5043, 6 mi.)*, Farmers' Market *(789-1388 Marina Park Tue 3-6pm, U.R.I. Flagg Rd. Sat 9am-Noon, 5 mi.)*, Green Grocer *(Carpenter's Farm Stand 783-7550, 5 mi.)*, Bank/ATM *(6 mi.)*, Post Office *(783-7215, 6 mi.)*, Catholic Church *(6 mi.)*, Protestant Church *(6 mi.)*, Library *(South Kingston 789-1555, 6 mi.)*, Dry Cleaners *(6 mi.)*, Laundry *(Pier Cleaners 783-2030, 6 mi.)*, Bookstore *(Bears' Book Den 782-6660, 6 mi.)*, Pharmacy *(Brooks 783-4250, 6 mi.)*, Hardware Store *(Damons 783-4851, 6 mi.)*, Retail Shops *(6 mi.)*, Copies Etc. *(Printing Express 782-2278, 6 mi.)*

Transportation

OnCall: Rental Car *(Enterprise 792-0185)*, Taxi *(Wakefield Cab 783-0007)* **3+ mi:** Rail *(Amtrak Kingston, 10 mi.)*, Ferry Service *(Block Island, 10 mi.)* **Airport:** TF Green *(25 mi.)*

Medical Services

911 Service **OnCall:** Ambulance **Near:** Holistic Services *(Snug Harbor Massage 792-8656)* **3+ mi:** Doctor *(5 mi.)*, Dentist *(5 mi.)*, Chiropractor *(Center for Health 789-5008, 5 mi.)*, Veterinarian *(Kingston Kennel 783-4020, 7 mi.)* **Hospital:** South County 782-8010 *(5 mi.)*

Setting -- Third facility to port -- after green can "7" -- Point Judith is a full-service working marina catering largely to sport fishing boats. The landside services are limited - here it's all about the docks and the fishing.

Marina Notes -- Closed weekends Nov 15-May 15. Gas & diesel mechanic, and most boatyard services generally available for emergency same-day transit repairs. Easily accessible fuel dock. Founded in 1978. 85% sport fishing boats, 15% cruising and sail boats. Factory authorized engine parts and service for: Cummins, Detroit, Volvo, Ford, Westerbeke, Yanmar, MAN and Marine Power. Well-stocked parts department. Home to Safe/Sea towing.

Notable -- Capt. Kelly Smith 364-9774, 32 ft. C-Devil II (4-6 passengers) Sportfishing: 4 hr. Inshore $350-450, 6 hr. Twilight $500-575, 8 hr. Inshore $500-575, 10 hr. Offshore $600-800, 12 hr. Offshore $700-900; 18 ft. Lil Devil Fly-fishing: $200 for 4 hrs, $300 for 6 hrs for up to two (2) passengers. Dinghy north to Plato Island, reportedly excellent clamming there. Or take the dinghy or big boat north another few miles through the pond to Ram Point Marina (783-4353) or Hanson's Landing Pub & Deck (782-0210) - which offers dock'n'dine.

Point View Marina

11 Sherman Road; Wakefield, RI 02879

Tel: (401) 789-7660 **VHF:** **Monitor** 68 **Talk** 68
Fax: (401) 789-4675 **Alternate Tel:** n/a
Email: n/a **Web:** n/a
Nearest Town: Wakefield *(3 mi.)* **Tourist Info:** (401) 783-2801

Navigational Information

Lat: 41°23.304' **Long:** 071°31.031' **Tide:** 3 ft. **Current:** 4 kt. **Chart:** 13219
Rep. Depths (*MLW*): Entry 10 ft. **Fuel Dock** n/a **Max Slip/Moor** 10 ft./-
Access: Breachway to Point Judith Pond - west of R8

Marina Facilities *(In Season/Off Season)*

Fuel: No
Slips: 60 Total, 5 Transient **Max LOA:** 90 ft. **Max Beam:** 36 ft.
Rate *(per ft.)*: **Day** $1.00 **Week** $5.00 **Month** $20
Power: 30 amp $5, **50 amp** $10, **100 amp** Inq., **200 amp** n/a
Cable TV: No **Dockside Phone:** No
Dock Type: Wood, Floating
Moorings: 0 Total, 0 Transient **Launch:** n/a
Rate: Day n/a **Week** n/a **Month** n/a
Heads: 4 Toilet(s), 2 Shower(s) *(with dressing rooms)*
Laundry: None **Pay Phones:** Yes, 1
Pump-Out: No **Fee:** n/a **Closed Heads:** Yes

Marina Operations

Owner/Manager: Roger Kroha **Dockmaster:** Same
In-Season: Year-Round, 8am-5pm **Off-Season:** n/a
After-Hours Arrival: n/a
Reservations: Preferred **Credit Cards:** Visa/MC
Discounts: None
Pets: Welcome, Dog Walk Area **Handicap Access:** Yes, Heads, Docks

Marina Services and Boat Supplies

Services - Docking Assistance, Security *(Surveillance cameras)*, Dock Carts **Communication -** Fax in/out *(Free)*, FedEx, UPS, Express Mail **Supplies - Near:** Ice *(Cube)*, Ships' Store, Bait/Tackle *(Snug Harbor 783-7766)*, Live Bait *(Snug Harbor)*, Propane **1-3 mi:** West Marine *(788-9977)*

Boatyard Services

OnSite: Travelift *(38T)*, Engine mechanic *(gas, diesel)*, Electrical Repairs, Hull Repairs, Bottom Cleaning, Brightwork, Compound, Wash & Wax, Woodworking, Painting, Awlgrip **OnCall:** Electronic Sales, Electronics Repairs, Rigger, Air Conditioning, Refrigeration, Divers, Interior Cleaning, Propeller Repairs, Inflatable Repairs, Life Raft Service, Upholstery, Yacht Interiors, Metal Fabrication **Near:** Launching Ramp. **Yard Rates:** $65/hr., Haul & Launch $8/ft., Power Wash $2/ft., Bottom Paint $5/ft. **Storage:** In-Water $20/ft., On-Land $10/ft.

Restaurants and Accommodations

OnCall: Pizzeria *(Harbor Pizza 788-9441)* **Near:** Seafood Shack *(Snug Harbor Marina 783-7766, B $4-, L $4-)* **Under 1 mi:** Restaurant *(Capt. Jacks 789-4556, L $5-8, D $8-16)*, *(Fish Stories 789-2864)* **3+ mi:** Restaurant *(Larchwood Inn Dining Room B $2-7, L $4-10, D $10-16, 5 mi., Reservations suggested. Fresh seafood and choice prime rib.)*, *(Sea Horse Grill 789-2424, 5 mi., on grounds of Theater-by-the-Sea)*, *(Cassidy's by the Beach 782-2697, 5 mi.)*, Inn/B&B *(Larchwood Inn $35-150, 5 mi.)*, *(Brookside Manor 788-3527, $195-250, 6 mi., 17thC Colonial home with 8 acres of landscaped gardens and a brook)*, *(Admiral Dewey Inn 783-2090, 4.5 mi.)*

Recreation and Entertainment

OnSite: Picnic Area, Grills, Fishing Charter **1-3 mi:** Beach, Playground, Tennis Courts, Jogging Paths, Park, Sightseeing *(Pt. Judith Lighthouse)* **3+ mi:** Golf Course *(Rose Hill 788-1088, 9 mi.)*, Fitness Center *(River Bend 789-9585, 5 mi.)*, Bowling *(Amscot 783-5711, 5 mi.)*, Museum *(Primitive Culture 783-5711; South County Museum 783-5400, 5 mi.)*, Cultural Attract *(Theater-by-the-Sea 782-8587, 5 mi.)*

Provisioning and General Services

OnCall: Provisioning Service, Convenience Store *(Seaview 788-9000)* **Near:** Delicatessen *(Snug Harbor 783-7766)*, Fishmonger *(Snug Harbor)*, Lobster Pound **Under 1 mi:** Bank/ATM **1-3 mi:** Newsstand **3+ mi:** Supermarket *(Shaw's 792-9888, 6 mi.)*, Health Food *(Alt. Food 789-2240, 5 mi.)*, Liquor Store *(Patsy's 783-5043, 5 mi.)*, Farmers' Market *(789-1388 Marina Park Tue 3-6pm, U.R.I. Flagg Rd. Sat 9-Noon, 5 mi.)*, Green Grocer *(Carpenter's 783-7550, 4 mi.)*, Post Office *(5 mi.)*, Library *(South Kingston 789-1555, 5 mi.)*, Bookstore *(Bears' Book Den 782-6660, 5 mi.)*, Pharmacy *(Brooks 783-4250, 5 mi.)*, Hardware Store *(Damons 783-4851, 5 mi.)*

Transportation

OnCall: Rental Car *(Enterprise 792-0185)*, Taxi *(Wakefield Cab 783-0007)* **3+ mi:** Rail *(Kingstown, 10mi.)*, Ferry Service *(Galilee-Pt Judith Ferry to Block Island, 12 mi.)* **Airport:** TF Green *(25mi.)*

Medical Services

911 Service **OnCall:** Ambulance **Near:** Holistic Services *(Snug Harbor Massage 792-8656)* **1-3 mi:** Doctor **3+ mi:** Chiropractor *(Center for Health 789-5008, 4.5 mi.)* **Hospital:** South County 782-8010 *(5 mi.)*

Setting -- Just past Point Judith Marina, which is the fourth facility to port, is this relatively recent addition to the sport fishing world. Its impeccable docks are filled with high end sport fishing boats and its boatyard services are capable of maintaining them. Three-quarters of a mile from the Breachway, it has views of the marsh and the Pt. Judith Pond Islands.

Marina Notes -- A recent recreational boats installation that was formerly part of the commercially-oriented Salt Pond Marine Railway. Awlgripping, fiberglass work, engine repairs and custom installs are specialties of the on-site boatyard. Anything they can't handle will be available next door at Point Judith Marina. An active sport fishing facility with good staff support; a number of charter boats make their home here. The channel is very active; expect some roll.

Notable -- The Point Judith Pond is the largest saltwater pond in Rhode Island and home to eleven very different islands. A dinghy cruise can be a good way to see them, with, perhaps, a break for some quahogging (which is reportedly quite good). Alternatively, consider the relatively long dinghy ride south to the commercial port of Galilee - contact the Harbormaster in advance for permission to tie up. But watch out for the ferries! Galilee is home to may seafood shacks and slightly higher-end seafood restaurants -- most with views of the very active commercial harbor. Consider the well known Portside Restaurant & Chowder House, Top of the Dock, Champlin's ($4-16), and George's ($4-11) -- take-out, too. Five miles south is Matunuck Beach on the ocean with Cassidy's by the Beach restaurants.

PHOTOS ON CD-ROM: 4

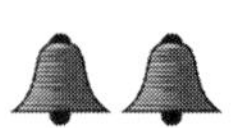

Old Harbor Dock

PO Box 220; Water Street; Block Island, RI 02807

Tel: (401) 466-3235 **VHF: Monitor** 12 **Talk** 12
Fax: (401) 466-3219 **Alternate Tel:** (401) 466-3204
Email: n/a **Web:** n/a
Nearest Town: Old Harbor *(0 mi.)* **Tourist Info:** (401) 466-2982

Navigational Information

Lat: 41°10.353' **Long:** 071°33.330' **Tide:** n/a **Current:** n/a **Chart:** 13215
Rep. Depths (*MLW*): Entry 15 ft. **Fuel Dock** n/a **Max Slip/Moor** 15 ft./-
Access: East side of Block Island, through breakwater at G3

Marina Facilities *(In Season/Off Season)*

Fuel: No
Slips: 60 Total, 60 Transient **Max LOA:** 100 ft. **Max Beam:** n/a
Rate *(per ft.)*: **Day** $2.00/Inq. **Week** Inq. **Month** Inq.
Power: 30 amp Inc., **50 amp** Inc., **100 amp** n/a, **200 amp** n/a
Cable TV: No **Dockside Phone:** No
Dock Type: Wood, Fixed
Moorings: 0 Total, 0 Transient **Launch:** n/a
Rate: Day n/a **Week** n/a **Month** n/a
Heads: 2 Toilet(s), 2 Shower(s) *(with dressing rooms)*
Laundry: None **Pay Phones:** No
Pump-Out: OnSite, 1 Port **Fee:** Free **Closed Heads:** Yes

Marina Operations

Owner/Manager: Larry Constantine **Dockmaster:** John Calhoun
In-Season: May 15-Oct 15, 7am-9pm **Off-Season:** n/a
After-Hours Arrival: Find a spot
Reservations: No **Credit Cards:** Cash / check
Discounts: None
Pets: Welcome, Dog Walk Area **Handicap Access:** No

Marina Services and Boat Supplies

Services - Docking Assistance **Supplies - Near:** Ice *(Cube)* **Under 1 mi:** Ships' Store, Bait/Tackle *(Orvis 466-5131)*, Live Bait *(Twin Maples 466-5547)*, Propane

Boatyard Services

OnCall: Engine mechanic *(gas, diesel)*, Electrical Repairs, Rigger, Sail Loft, Divers, Propeller Repairs **Under 1 mi:** Travelift, Forklift, Launching Ramp. **Nearest Yard:** A.H. Edwards Marine (401) 466-2655

Restaurants and Accommodations

OnSite: Restaurant *(Ballard's Main Room L $7-9, D $10-25)*, Raw Bar *(Ballard's 11am-10pm, Sushi 2pm on)*, Lite Fare *(Beachfront Café B, L, D)*, Inn/B&B *(Ballard's Inn 466-2231, $90-195)* **Near:** Restaurant *(Finns Seafood 466-2473, L $5-35, D $5-35)*, *(Hotel Manisses Dining Room 466-2836, D $16-35)*, *(Harborside D.R. L $10-20, D $20-30, L&D, B on weekends)*, *(Gatsby Room 466-2836, D $14-29)*, *(National Tap & Grille 466-2901, steak house)*, *(Mohegan Café 466-5911, L $4-10, D $9-19)*, Pizzeria *(Capizzanos 466-2829)*, Hotel *(National 466-2901, $80-250)*, Inn/B&B *(Gothic 466-2918, $35-160)*, *(Blue Dory Inn 466-5891, $65-295)*, *(The 1661 Inn/Hotel Manisses 466-2421, $145-370)*, Condo/Cottage *(Harborside Inn 466-5504, $70-210)* **Under 1 mi:** Restaurant *(Atlantic Inn 466-5883, D $42, 4-Course Prix fixe)*, Inn/B&B *(Atlantic Inn 466-5883, $100-210)*

Recreation and Entertainment

OnSite: Picnic Area, Grills, Fishing Charter *(28' Harris Cuttyhunk, G. Willie Makit 466-5151)* **Near:** Beach *(Ballard's Beach)*, Dive Shop *(Island Outfitters 466-5502)*, Boat Rentals *(Oceans & Ponds Kayaking 466-5131)*, Movie Theater *(Empire 466-2555)*, Video Rental, Museum *(BI Historical Society 466-2481 10am-5pm)* **Under 1 mi:** Playground, Jogging Paths, Roller Blade/Bike Paths, Park, Cultural Attract, Sightseeing *(Animal farm - Spring & High Sts.)* **1-3 mi:** Horseback Riding *(Rustic Rides 466-5060)*

Provisioning and General Services

OnSite: Lobster Pound *(John Grant 466-2997 4-6pm)* **Near:** Supermarket *(Seaside Market 466-5876)*, Gourmet Shop *(Daily Market 466-9908)*, Delicatessen, Health Food *(BI Depot 466-2403)*, Wine/Beer, Liquor Store *(Red Bird Pkg. 466-2441)*, Bakery, Farmers' Market *(Manisses Corner Wed 9-11am, Negus Park Sat 9-11am 466-2875)*, Fishmonger *(Finn's 466-2102)*, Meat Market, Bank/ATM, Post Office, Catholic Church, Protestant Church, Library *(466-3233 Dodge St.)*, Beauty Salon, Laundry, Bookstore *(Book Nook 466-2993, Ship to Shore 466-5193)*, Pharmacy *(Block Island Health 466-5825)*, Clothing Store, Retail Shops **Under 1 mi:** Hardware Store *(Island Hardware & Supply 466-5831)*, Florist, Copies Etc.

Transportation

OnSite: Ferry Service *(Pt. Judith, New London, Providence, Newport 783-4613)* **OnCall:** Taxi *(Minuteman 466-3131, Ladybird 466-3133)* **Near:** Bikes *(Old Harbor Bikes 466-2029, Island Bike & Moped 466-2700)*, Rental Car *(Old Harbor Bike 466-2029)* **3+ mi:** InterCity Bus *(Adventure East to New York meets Ferry 847-8751, 20 mi.)* **Airport:** Block Island *(1 mi.)*

Medical Services

911 Service **OnCall:** Ambulance **Under 1 mi:** Doctor *(BI Medical Center 466-2974)* **Hospital:** South County 782-8010 *(20 mi.)*

Setting -- Set on the east side of Block Island, Old Harbor is a compact, man-made basin surrounded by rocks and reefs. The city has created a small transient marina for pleasure boats as well as for its seasonal working boats. Landside, it is also surrounded by BI's main "downtown" area. Virtually onsite is Ballard's "beach club" complex. Up the hill are most of BI's restaurants, shops and wonderful old inns.

Marina Notes -- Note: No Reservations. All med-style, stern-to or alongside dockage (no finger piers). Home to the Block Island Ferry to both Pt. Judith and New London -- so there is a lot of traffic and serious wakes coming and going. Shoreside are municipal heads and showers. Harbormaster's office is right on site. A $0.50 per head landing fee is assessed to support the development of better facilities. All of Block Island is "closed head" territory. A free pump-out service makes this very easy.

Notable -- There are at least 18 eateries -- from fine dining to casual restaurants, raw bars, and seafood shacks -- and 7 lovely inns or B&B's, all within easy walking distance. Ferries come from Pt. Judith (Galilee $8.50 1/way), New London ($15/1-way), and from Montauk (to New Shoreham - $20 1-way). Adventure East buses ($90 RT) go directly from New York City to Galilee docks, Westerly Airport or Newport -schedules timed to meet ferries. Greyhound Terminal in New London is next to the BI ferry dock, as is the Amtrak station. New England Air flies from Westerly airport to BI Airport ($75 RT). Taxis from TF Green airport to BI Ferry are approx $50 1/way - Best 800-231-2222. BI Seafood Festival & Chowder Cook-off 466-2982 3rd weekend in June.

Navigational Information
Lat: 41°11.000' **Long:** 071°34.958' **Tide:** 3 ft. **Current:** n/a **Chart:** 13215
Rep. Depths (*MLW*): Entry 18 ft. **Fuel Dock** 18 ft. **Max Slip/Moor** 18 ft./-
Access: Block Island Sound to Great Salt Pond

Marina Facilities *(In Season/Off Season)*
Fuel: Gasoline, Diesel, High-Speed Pumps
Slips: 240 Total, 200 Transient **Max LOA:** 195 ft. **Max Beam:** n/a
Rate *(per ft.)*: **Day** $2.25* **Week** Less 10% **Month** Less 15%
Power: 30 amp Incl., **50 amp** Incl., **100 amp** n/a, **200 amp** n/a
Cable TV: No **Dockside Phone:** No
Dock Type: Floating, Fixed
Moorings: 0 Total, 0 Transient **Launch:** n/a, Dinghy Dock
Rate: Day n/a **Week** n/a **Month** n/a
Heads: 1 Toilet(s), 1 Shower(s)
Laundry: 15 Washer(s), 15 Dryer(s) **Pay Phones:** Yes
Pump-Out: OnSite, OnCall **Fee:** Free **Closed Heads:** Yes

Marina Operations
Owner/Manager: Joe Grillo **Dockmaster:** Seasonal
In-Season: May 15-ColDay, 7am-9pm **Off-Season:** ColDay-May 14, Closed
After-Hours Arrival: Call in advance
Reservations: Required for weekends **Credit Cards:** Visa/MC, Amex
Discounts: None
Pets: Welcome **Handicap Access:** No

Champlin's Marina

P.O. Drawer J; Block Island, RI 02807

Tel: (401) 466-7777; (800) 762-4541 **VHF: Monitor** 68 **Talk** 68
Fax: (401) 466-2638 **Alternate Tel:** n/a
Email: n/a **Web:** www.champlinsresort.com
Nearest Town: New Harbor **Tourist Info:** (401) 466-2982

Marina Services and Boat Supplies
Services - Docking Assistance, Concierge, Dock Carts **Communication -** Mail & Package Hold, Phone Messages, Fax in/out, FedEx, Express Mail **Supplies - OnSite:** Ice *(Block, Cube, Shaved)*, Ships' Store, Bait/Tackle

Boatyard Services
OnSite: Compound, Wash & Wax **OnCall:** Engine mechanic *(gas, diesel)*, Electrical Repairs, Electronics Repairs, Hull Repairs **Nearest Yard:** A.H. Edwards (401) 466-2655

Restaurants and Accommodations
OnSite: Restaurant *(Dockside Restaurant, Pier 76 D B $4-7, L $6-9, D $6-25, 7am on)*, Raw Bar, Hotel *(Champlin's Hotel 466-7777, $150-295, BI's only air conditioned hotel)* **Near:** Restaurant *(Finns Seafood 466-2473)*, *(The Oar 466-8820, B $2-7, L $3-12.50, D $5-14, 6:30am-1am, raw bar, too)*, *(Dead Eye Dicks 466-2654, D $16-22, lunch Sat & Sun)*, *(Narragansett Inn)*, *(Samuel Peckham Tavern 466-5458)*, Snack Bar *(7am-midnight)*, Pizzeria *(Capizzanos 466-2829)*, Hotel *(Samuel Peckham 466-2231, $75-175)*, Inn/B&B *(Sullivan House 466-5020, $135-195)*, *(Hygeia House 466-9616, $65-235, a '99 total restoration of one of the Champlin family homesteads)* **Under 1 mi:** Restaurant *(1661 Inn 466-2421, D $15-25, Al fresco Brunch on the hill overlooking the ocean)*, Hotel *(National 466-2901, $80-220)*

Recreation and Entertainment
OnSite: Pool, Beach, Picnic Area, Grills, Playground *(New 2002)*, Volleyball, Tennis Courts, Fitness Center, Jogging Paths, Boat Rentals *(Aldo's at Champlin's Marina 466-5811 kayaks, bumper boats, paddle boats, pontoon boats, zodiaks)*, Movie Theater *(240 seat Ocean West 466-2971)*, Video Rental, Video Arcade *(9am-11pm)*, Sightseeing **OnCall:** Horseback Riding *(Rustic Rides 466-5060)*, Fishing Charter **Near:** Park **1-3 mi:** Museum *(North Light Maritime Museum)*

Provisioning and General Services
OnSite: Convenience Store *(Lighthouse Variety)*, Bakery *(& ice cream parlor, too 7am-11pm)*, Laundry *(wash & fold service)*, Newsstand, Copies Etc. **OnCall:** Hardware Store *(Island Hardware & Supply 466-5831)* **Near:** Delicatessen, Wine/Beer, Liquor Store *(Red Bird 466-2441)*, Lobster Pound, Bank/ATM, Pharmacy *(BI Health 466-5825)*, Florist **Under 1 mi:** Supermarket *(BI Grocery 466-2949, Seaside Market 466-5876)*, Gourmet Shop *(The Daily Market 466-2949)*, Health Food *(BI Depot 466-2403)*, Farmers' Market *(Manisses Corner Wed 9-11am, Negus Park Sat 9-11am 466-2875)*, Fishmonger, Post Office, Catholic Church, Protestant Church, Synagogue, Library *(466-3233 Dodge St.)*, Beauty Salon, Barber Shop, Bookstore *(Book Nook 466-2993, Ship to Shore 466-5193)*, Clothing Store, Retail Shops

Transportation
OnSite: Courtesy Car/Van, Ferry Service *(Viking to Montauk 631-668-5700 $40/20RT)* **OnCall:** Taxi *(Minuteman Taxi 466-3131)*, Airport Limo *(Regal Limousine 596-6570 on the mainland)* **Near:** Bikes *(Block Island Bike & Car Rental 466-2297 & mopeds, too)*, Rental Car *(Boat Basin Car & Rental 466-5811)* **Airport:** Block Island *(1 mi.)*

Medical Services
911 Service **OnCall:** Ambulance **Under 1 mi:** Doctor *(Block Island Medical Center 466-2974)* **Hospital:** South County 782-8010 *(20 mi.)*

Setting -- The Great Salt Pond's first facility to starboard is Champlin's, a complete resort with extensive facilities -- a self-contained, full-service destination for cruising families. The atmosphere is very lively, particularly on weekends. Its 5000 feet of dockage fans out from the shore like a candelabra, and it's frequently crowded with revelers.

Marina Notes -- *up to 30', $2.75/ft., 31-40' $3.00, 46-60' $3.25, 61-75' $3.50, 76-90' $3.75, over 90' $4.00/ft. 10% off for more than 7 days. 15% off for more than 30 days. Rafting at the discretion of the dockmaster. Dockage rate includes shower facilities and pool. Bicycle & moped rentals are available. Future reservations taken at any time. Only place for gas/diesel. Pump-out available to all boats. Note: Deposit required with reservation. Cancellations 14 days prior to arrival date receive a full refund, less $35 administration fee. Cancellations less than 14 days forfeit half the deposit, no-shows forfeit all. Many boats spend the season and their living quarters tend to "overflow" onto the docks. The Montauk Ferry lands here - expect arriving/departing crowds at 10:45am & 4:30pm.

Notable -- Onsite are: an Olympic size fresh water pool (with Tiki bar), tennis, volleyball, video game room, gift shop, a movie theater with 1st run features every night and kids' matinées, brand new playground, a couple of eateries and a motel with air-conditioned rooms, suites, cable and views of the Great Salt Pond and beyond. Dockside Restaurant, featuring Cajun cuisine, is open for B, L & D and also has a raw bar and great views across the Pond. The 19th century North Light(house) is now a maritime museum (466-2982). House & Garden Tour 466-2982 every August.

PHOTOS ON CD-ROM: 9

New Harbor Moorings

P.O. Drawer 220; Block Island, RI 02807

Tel: (401) 466-3204 **VHF: Monitor** 9 **Talk** 12
Fax: (401) 466-3219 **Alternate Tel:** n/a
Email: n/a **Web:** n/a
Nearest Town: New Harbor **Tourist Info:** (401) 466-2982

Navigational Information

Lat: 41°11.091' **Long:** 071°34.776' **Tide:** 3 ft. **Current:** n/a **Chart:** 13215
Rep. Depths (*MLW*): Entry 14 ft. **Fuel Dock** n/a **Max Slip/Moor** -/50 ft.
Access: Block Island Sound to Great Salt Pond

Marina Facilities *(In Season/Off Season)*

Fuel: No
Slips: 0 Total, 0 Transient **Max LOA:** n/a **Max Beam:** n/a
Rate *(per ft.)*: **Day** n/a **Week** n/a **Month** n/a
Power: 30 amp n/a, **50 amp** n/a, **100 amp** n/a, **200 amp** n/a
Cable TV: No **Dockside Phone:** No
Dock Type: n/a
Moorings: 90 Total, 90 Transient **Launch:** Yes*, Dinghy Dock
Rate: Day $30/20 **Week** Inq. **Month** Inq.
Heads: 1 Toilet(s), 1 Shower(s)
Laundry: 1 Washer(s), 1 Dryer(s) **Pay Phones:** Yes, 1
Pump-Out: OnCall, Full Service, 2 Port **Fee:** Free **Closed Heads:** Yes

Marina Operations

Owner/Manager: Larry Constantine (Harbormaster) **Dockmaster:** Same
In-Season: Year-Round, 7am-9pm **Off-Season:** n/a
After-Hours Arrival: Call in advance
Reservations: Not Accepted **Credit Cards:** Cash or check
Discounts: None
Pets: Welcome, Dog Walk Area **Handicap Access:** No

Marina Services and Boat Supplies

Services - Docking Assistance, Dock Carts **Supplies - OnCall:** Ice *(Block, Cube)* **Near:** Ships' Store, Bait/Tackle *(Orvis 466-5131)*, Live Bait, Propane

Boatyard Services

OnCall: Divers, Propeller Repairs, Woodworking **Near:** Travelift, Engine mechanic *(gas, diesel)*, Launching Ramp, Electrical Repairs, Electronic Sales, Rigger, Sail Loft, Bottom Cleaning. **Nearest Yard:** BI Marine (401) 466-2028

Restaurants and Accommodations

Near: Restaurant *(Samuel Peckham 466-5458)*, *(The Oar 466-8820, L $3-13, D $8-26, at B.I. Boat Basin)*, *(Dead Eye Dick's 466-2473, D $16-22, lunch Sat&Sun)*, *(Dockside 466-7777, B $4-7, L $6-9, D $6-25, at Champlin's, opens 7am)*, Pizzeria *(Capizzanos 466-2829)*, Hotel *(Samuel Peckham's Inn 466-2439, $75-175)*, *(Champlin's 466-7777, $150-295)*, *(The Narrangansett 466-2626, $95-125)*, Inn/B&B *(Hygeia House 466-9616, $65-235)* **Under 1 mi:** Restaurant *(Harborside 466-5504, L $10-20, D $20-30)*, *(Winfield's 466-5856, D $15-30)*, *(Hotel Manisses 466-2421, D $16-34)*, Hotel *(The National 466-2901, $80-220)*, Inn/B&B *(The Gothic 466-2918, $50-165)*

Recreation and Entertainment

OnCall: Fishing Charter **Near:** Beach *(Charlestown, Fred Benson)*, Picnic Area, Grills, Playground, Tennis Courts, Jogging Paths, Movie Theater *(Oceanwest at Champlin's 466-2971)*, Video Arcade *(Champlin's)*, Special Events *(Block Island Race Week)* **Under 1 mi:** Dive Shop *(Island Outfitters 466-5502)*, Horseback Riding *(Rustic Rides 466-5060)*, Boat Rentals *(Oceans & Ponds Kayaks 466-5131)* **1-3 mi:** Museum *(North Light Maritime Museum 466-2982)*, Sightseeing *(Mohegan Bluffs)*

Provisioning and General Services

OnCall: Bakery *(Aldo's, Ch.68 or listen for "Andiamo", his boat plies the harbor with pastries and baked goods; store within walking distance)*, Florist **Near:** Convenience Store *(Champlin's)*, Delicatessen, Lobster Pound, Meat Market, Bank/ATM, Post Office, Catholic Church, Library *(466-3233 Dodge St.)*, Hardware Store *(Island Hardware & Supply 466-5831)* **Under 1 mi:** Supermarket *(BI Grocery 466-2949, 466-5876, Seaside Market 466-9908 - in Old Harbor)*, Gourmet Shop *(The Daily Market 466-2949)*, Health Food *(BI Depot 466-2403)*, Wine/Beer *(Red Bird 466-2441)*, Liquor Store, Farmers' Market *(Manisses Corner Wed 9-11am, Negus Park Sat 9-11am 466-2875)*, Fishmonger, Bookstore *(Book Nook 466-2993, Ship to Shore 466-5193)*, Pharmacy *(BI Health 466-5825)*, Newsstand, Clothing Store, Retail Shops

Transportation

OnCall: Rental Car *(Boat Basin Car & Rental 466-5811)*, Taxi *(O.J. 741-0050)* **Near:** Bikes *(Block Island Bike & Car Rental 466-2297)*, Ferry Service *(to Montauk)* **Airport:** Block Island *(1 mi.)*

Medical Services

911 Service **OnCall:** Ambulance **Under 1 mi:** Doctor *(Block Island Medical Center 466-2974)* **Hospital:** South County 782-8010 *(20 mi.)*

Setting -- The Great Salt Pond, home to the Town of New Shoreham Mooring Field, provides a completely protected harbor surrounded by the simple beauty of Block Island's hills and beaches. The mooring field sits directly in front of two of the Pond's three transient marinas: Champlin's & the BI Boat Basin.

Marina Notes -- Mooring Balls are lime green (500 lbs. - up to 39') and orange (800 lbs. "H" - over 40'). Radio before taking an orange one. Weekends, moorings are generally taken by 10am. There's an anchorage on west side of channel (18-50' water). Stay within white buoys or gendarmes will call. Dinghies zip around mooring field from 8-11am looking for an opening. 2-boat maximum raft-up ($30 each). No limit on days. Can leave boat unoccupied if paid in advance. To save your mooring, leave dink or request official orange "Occupied" buoy. Check-out noon. Major turnover Sat & Sun. Harbormaster will stop by or pay at office at BI Boat Basin (pick up a Harbor Guide). *Launch service from Old Port Launch or Champlin's Launch - both Ch.68 - or dinghy to BI Boat Basin (trash and recycling bins there, too). Efficient, high-speed pump-out - 2 boats monitor Ch.73. Free to moored boats (tips appreciated); small charge to anchored boats.

Notable -- Ice Deliveries Ch.72 8-10am daily, also 3-5pm weekends - cubes $4, block $3. Several restaurants, inns and a growing roster of services are in nearby New Shoreham; most of the island's shops and eateries are about a mile overland in Old Harbor. Dinghy dock is at BI Boat Basin, but the heads and showers are available ONLY to their dockage customers. $0.50 per person landing fee assessed by town to improve BI facilities.

Navigational Information

Lat: 41°10.932' **Long:** 071°34.655' **Tide:** 3 ft. **Current:** n/a **Chart:** 13217
Rep. Depths (*MLW*): Entry 14 ft. **Fuel Dock** 10 ft. **Max Slip/Moor** 10 ft./-
Access: Block Island Sound to Great Salt Pond

Marina Facilities *(In Season/Off Season)*

Fuel: No
Slips: 100 Total, 85 Transient **Max LOA:** 110 ft. **Max Beam:** 24 ft.
Rate *(per ft.)*: **Day** $2.50/Inq.* **Week** 7th night free **Month** Inq.
Power: 30 amp Yes, **50 amp** Yes, **100 amp** n/a, **200 amp** n/a
Cable TV: No **Dockside Phone:** No
Dock Type: Floating
Moorings: 0 Total, 0 Transient **Launch:** Old Port Marine, VHF 68
Rate: Day n/a **Week** n/a **Month** n/a
Heads: 6 Toilet(s), 8 Shower(s)
Laundry: None **Pay Phones:** Yes, 4
Pump-Out: OnSite, 1 Central **Fee:** Free **Closed Heads:** Yes

Marina Operations

Owner/Manager: Rally Migliaccio **Dockmaster:** Justin Lewis, Ben Edwards
In-Season: MemDay-LabDay, 7am-7pm **Off-Season:** n/a
After-Hours Arrival: n/a
Reservations: Suggested in Jul & Aug **Credit Cards:** Visa/MC
Discounts: None
Pets: Welcome, Dog Walk Area **Handicap Access:** No

Block Island Boat Basin

PO Box 369; West Side Road; Block Island, RI 02807

Tel: (401) 466-2631 **VHF: Monitor** 9 **Talk** n/a
Fax: (401) 466-5120 **Alternate Tel:** (401) 446-2632
Email: n/a **Web:** n/a
Nearest Town: New Harbor *(1 mi.)* **Tourist Info:** (401) 466-2982

Marina Services and Boat Supplies

Services - Docking Assistance, Trash Pick-Up, Dock Carts **Communication -** Mail & Package Hold, Phone Messages, FedEx, AirBorne, UPS, Express Mail **Supplies - OnSite:** Ice *(Block, Cube)*, Ships' Store **Near:** Propane **Under 1 mi:** Bait/Tackle *(Twin Maples 466-5547)* **1-3 mi:** Live Bait

Boatyard Services

OnSite: Engine mechanic *(gas, diesel)*, Electrical Repairs **OnCall:** Rigger, Sail Loft *(Block Island Sail & Canvas 466-8981)*, Bottom Cleaning, Refrigeration **Nearest Yard:** A.H. Edwards Marine Repair (401) 466-2655

Restaurants and Accommodations

OnSite: Restaurant *(The Oar 466-8820, B $2-7, L $3-12.50, D $5-14, 6:30am-1am, raw bar, too)*, Snack Bar **Near:** Restaurant *(Narragansett Inn 466-2626, B $8, L $5-8, D $8-16, Breakfast buffet 7 days $8/4)*, *(Smuggler's Cove 466-7961)*, *(Aldo's 466-5871)*, Hotel *(Champlin's Hotel 466-7777, $150-295)*, *(The Narranganstt 466-2626, $95-125)*, *(Samuel Peckham 466-2231, $75-175)* **Under 1 mi:** Restaurant *(Finns Seafood 466-2473)*, *(Samuel Peckham Tavern 466-5458)*, *(Moneghan Café 466-5911, D $8-20)*, *(Winfield's 466-5856, D $15-30)*, Hotel *(National 466-2901, $80-220)*, Inn/B&B *(Blue Dory and Adrian Inns 466-5891, $85-365)* **1-3 mi:** Hotel *(Atlantic Inn 466-5883, $99-210)*

Recreation and Entertainment

OnSite: Picnic Area, Grills **OnCall:** Boat Rentals *(Oceans & Ponds 466-5131)*, Fishing Charter **Near:** Playground *(Lion's Playground)*, Roller Blade/Bike Paths, Movie Theater *(Oceanwest at Champlin's 466-2971)*, Video Rental, Video Arcade **Under 1 mi:** Beach *(Mosquito Beach on the Pond, Crescent Beach on RI Sound)*, Dive Shop, Jogging Paths **1-3 mi:** Tennis Courts, Horseback Riding *(Rustic Rides 466-5060)*, Museum *(Block Island's 1867 North Light 466-2982)*

Provisioning and General Services

OnSite: Convenience Store, Bank/ATM **OnCall:** Bakery *(Listen for Aldo's "Andiamo" - Champlin's also near)* **Near:** Hardware Store *(Island Hardware & Supply 466-5831)* **Under 1 mi:** Gourmet Shop *(The Daily Market 466-9908)*, Health Food *(BI Depot 466-2403)*, Farmers' Market *(Manisses Corner Wed 9-11am, Negus Park Sat 9-11am 466-2875)*, Post Office, Catholic Church, Library *(466-3233 Dodge St.)*, Beauty Salon, Barber Shop **1-3 mi:** Supermarket *(BI Grocery 466-2949, Seaside Market 466-9908 - in Old Harbor)*, Wine/Beer *(Red Bird 466-2441)*, Liquor Store, Fishmonger, Lobster Pound, Protestant Church, Synagogue, Laundry, Bookstore *(Book Nook 466-2993, Ship to Shore 466-5193)*, Pharmacy *(BI Health 466-5825)*, Newsstand, Clothing Store, Retail Shops

Transportation

OnSite: Rental Car *(Boat Basin Rental 466-5811)* **OnCall:** Water Taxi *(Oldport Launch)*, Taxi *(O.J. 466-2872)* **Near:** Bikes *(Aldo's 466-5871)*, Ferry Service *(to Montauk, & at Old Harbor to Pt. Judith and New London - about 1.3 mi. walk)* **Airport:** Block Island *(1 mi.)*

Medical Services

911 Service **OnCall:** Ambulance **Under 1 mi:** Doctor *(Block Island Medical Center 466-2974)* **Hospital:** South County 782-8010 *(20 mi.)*

Setting -- The second - or middle - marina to starboard in the Great Salt Pond is the Block Island Boat Basin. It sits just a little to the right of the main channel and its docks form a wide double crossed "T" providing great views of the whole Pond. It's home to Oldport Launch and provides a dinghy dock for moored or anchored boats.

Marina Notes -- * $2.75' for 50' and over. Six nights dockage, 7th night free. Individual slips - no rafting. Old Port Marine Launch, Ch.68 runs from the dock to boats anchored in the Pond. BI Boat Basin also hosts the dinghy dock for tenders (note showers are for marina guests only). Moped and bike rentals onsite. Note: Reservations are necessary and require a deposit (accepted after Jan 1 for coming season). Cancellations: up to 14 days in advance, full refund; 2-13 days 50%, 2 days or less, forfeiture of deposit. Beware of the many local ordinances regarding trash removal and sewage pump-out - no used oil storage.

Notable -- Onsite Oar Restaurant (decorated with hundreds of oars of all sizes and shapes) serves breakfast, lunch, raw bar and dinner - inside or out -- all tables have great views. It's an easy mile walk to the shops and eateries of Old Harbor (marina has list of nearby restaurants). BI's east coast has two miles of spectacular beaches which are well worth a bike or dinghy ride -- the first heading north (off Corn Neck Road) is Crescent, then Scotch, then Mansion. Followed by the Clay Head Nature Trail. At the northernmost tip of the Island is Sandy Point and the 19thC North Light (house), now a museum. (An alternate approach is to beach your dinghy at Salt Pond's Mosquito Beach and walk across to Crescent Beach.) Heading south toward Old Harbor is more crowded Benson Beach.

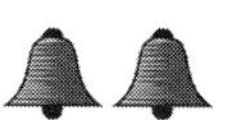

Payne's New Harbor Dock

PO Box 646; Ocean Avenue; Block Island, RI 02807

Tel: (401) 466-5572 **VHF: Monitor** n/a **Talk** n/a
Fax: n/a **Alternate Tel:** (401) 466-5572
Email: n/a **Web:** n/a
Nearest Town: Block Island *(1 mi.)* **Tourist Info:** (401) 466-2982

Navigational Information

Lat: 41°10.936' **Long:** 071°34.493' **Tide:** 3 ft. **Current:** n/a **Chart:** 13215
Rep. Depths (*MLW*): Entry 12 ft. **Fuel Dock** n/a **Max Slip/Moor** 21 ft./-
Access: Blck Is. Sound to bell 23, into Great Salt Pond, then straight across

Marina Facilities *(In Season/Off Season)*

Fuel: Slip-Side Fueling, Gasoline, Diesel, High-Speed Pumps
Slips: 100 Total, 100l Transient **Max LOA:** 300 ft. **Max Beam:** n/a
Rate *(per ft.)*: **Day** $2.00/lnq. **Week** $2.00 **Month** $2.00
Power: 30 amp Incl., **50 amp** Incl., **100 amp** n/a, **200 amp** n/a
Cable TV: No **Dockside Phone:** No
Dock Type: Floating, Fixed
Moorings: 0 Total, 0 Transient **Launch:** n/a
Rate: Day n/a **Week** n/a **Month** n/a
Heads: 8 Toilet(s), 8 Shower(s) *(with dressing rooms)*
Laundry: None **Pay Phones:** Yes, 3
Pump-Out: OnCall, Self Service, 1 Port **Fee:** Free **Closed Heads:** Yes

Marina Operations

Owner/Manager: Cliff Payne **Dockmaster:** Sands Payne
In-Season: Year-Round, 7am-1am **Off-Season:** n/a
After-Hours Arrival: Tie up anywhere
Reservations: No **Credit Cards:** Visa/MC
Discounts: None
Pets: Welcome, Dog Walk Area **Handicap Access:** Yes, Heads, Docks

Marina Services and Boat Supplies

Services - Docking Assistance, Boaters' Lounge, Trash Pick-Up, Dock Carts, Megayacht Facilities **Communication -** Mail & Package Hold, Phone Messages, FedEx, UPS *(Sat Del)* **Supplies - OnSite:** Ice *(Cube)* **Near:** Ships' Store *(Block Island Marine Repair 466-2028)*, Bait/Tackle **Under 1 mi:** Propane

Boatyard Services

Nearest Yard: Point Judith Marina

Restaurants and Accommodations

OnSite: Snack Bar *(B $2-6.50, L $2-6.50, D $2-6.50)* **OnCall:** Pizzeria *(Pizza Plus 466-9939)* **Near:** Restaurant *(The Oar 466-8820, B $2-7, L $3-12.50, D $5-14, at BI Boat Basin)*, *(Dockside B $4-7, L $6-9, D $6-25, at Champlin's)*, *(Narragansett Inn 466-2626, B $8/4, D $8-16, adjacent to Payne's, can land your dinghy on their beach)*, *(Samuel Peckham Tavern 466-5458)*, *(Dead Eye Dicks 466-2654, D $16-22, lunch Sat & Sun)*, Lite Fare *(Smuggler's Cove)*, Hotel *(Champlin's 466-7777, $150-395)*, *(The Narragansett 466-2626, $65-295)* **Under 1 mi:** Restaurant *(Finns Seafood 466-2473)*, *(Aldo's Place 466-5871)*, *(Hotel Manisses 466-2421, D $16-35)*, *(1661 Inn 466-2421, D $15-30, Sun Brunch on lawn)*, Hotel *(National 466-2901, $80-220)*, *(Harborside Inn 644-5504, $70-200)*, Inn/B&B *(Blue Dory and Adrian Inns 466-5891, $85-365)*

Recreation and Entertainment

OnSite: Picnic Area, Grills, Fitness Center, Boat Rentals, Fishing Charter **Near:** Jogging Paths, Roller Blade/Bike Paths *(On the Island)* **Under 1 mi:** Movie Theater *(Champlin's)*, Video Rental, Video Arcade, Park, Sightseeing **1-3 mi:** Beach *(small one is onsite, Mosquito is on Salt Pond, Crescent on RI Sound)*, Horseback Riding *(Rustic Rides 466-5060)*, Museum *(North Light Maritime)*

Provisioning and General Services

Near: Bakery *(Champlin's and Aldo's boat)*, Fishmonger, Clothing Store **Under 1 mi:** Convenience Store *(Block Island Depot 466-2403)*, Supermarket *(BI Grocery 466-2949, Seaside Market 466-9908 - in Old Harbor)*, Gourmet Shop *(Daily Market 466-9908)*, Health Food *(Natural Grocery; Block Island Depot 466-2403)*, Wine/Beer, Liquor Store *(Red Bird Liquor 466-2441)*, Farmers' Market *(Manisses Corner 466-2875 Wed & Sat 9-11am)*, Lobster Pound *(at Old Harbor direct from boat)*, Meat Market, Bank/ATM, Post Office, Catholic Church, Protestant Church, Synagogue, Other, Library *(466-3233 Dodge St.)*, Beauty Salon, Barber Shop, Dry Cleaners, Bookstore *(Book Nook 466-2993, Ship to Shore 466-5193)*, Newsstand, Hardware Store *(Island Hardware & Supply 466-5831)*, Retail Shops **1-3 mi:** Pharmacy *(Block Island Health 466-5825)*

Transportation

OnCall: Taxi *(Rose 741-5598)* **Near:** Bikes *(Block Island Bike & Car Rental 466-2297)*, Water Taxi, Rental Car *(Block Island Bike & Car Rental)*, Ferry Service *(to Montauk, 1 mi. to Old Harbor for New London & Pt. Judith)* **Airport:** Block Island 466-5511 *(1 mi.)*

Medical Services

911 Service **OnCall:** Ambulance **Near:** Holistic Services **Under 1 mi:** Doctor *(Block Island Medical Center 466-2974)*, Chiropractor **Hospital:** South County 782-8010 *(20 mi.)*

Setting -- Payne's New Harbor Dock is the last transient facility in the Great Salt Pond, the least gentrified, and the closest to the restaurants, shops and services of Old Harbor. Amenities are quite limited, but there is a very basic, yet appealing, rustic, down-home atmosphere -- one that is becoming more and more difficult to find. The views of the moored boats and the green arms of the Pond are wonderful.

Marina Notes -- Note: boats are docked stern-to, directly next to each other (almost rafted) and literally bow-to-bow -- there are no finger piers. If this is a problem, then the inside "ends" are the only solution. Watching the dockmaster maneuver a new load of boats into these quarters is an amazingly creative and instructive experience. The onsite snack bar (7am-6pm), souvenir, and marine supplies shop offers, among other things, clam cakes, chowder, lobster rolls, hot dogs, drinks, and taffy.

Notable -- The porches and rooms of the classic, beachy Narragansett Inn overlook Payne's docks. This quintessential BI Victorian Inn offers a lovely "all-you-can eat" breakfast buffet every morning ($7.95, $3.95 for kids), dinner Fri & Sat, a turkey dinner on Sunday, and clean, airy rooms - some with shared bath others with private. Narragansett's veranda is the perfect place for a quiet drink; land your dinghy on its sandy beach. Other restaurants, classic inns, and services are a reasonable one mile walk to Old Harbor. A wonderful bike ride is southwest to 100 acre Rodman's Hollow Wildlife Preserve (off Cherry Road), then a picnic at Vail Beach, ending at Southeast Light atop 200 foot Monhegan Bluffs, which stand guard over the Atlantic.

PHOTOS ON CD-ROM: 8

Navigational Information
Lat: 41°19.458' **Long:** 071°50.712' **Tide:** n/a **Current:** n/a **Chart:** 12372
Rep. Depths (*MLW*): Entry 6 ft. **Fuel Dock** n/a **Max Slip/Moor** 5 ft./6 ft.
Access: Fishers Island Sound to Sandy Point, follow channel

Marina Facilities *(In Season/Off Season)*
Fuel: No
Slips: 55 Total, 2 Transient **Max LOA:** 40 ft. **Max Beam:** n/a
Rate *(per ft.)*: **Day** $1.50/Inq. **Week** Inq. **Month** Inq.
Power: 30 amp Incl., **50 amp** n/a, **100 amp** n/a, **200 amp** n/a
Cable TV: No **Dockside Phone:** No
Dock Type: Wood, Floating, Fixed
Moorings: 24 Total, 3 Transient **Launch:** None, Dinghy Dock
Rate: Day $1.00/ft. **Week** n/a **Month** n/a
Heads: 2 Toilet(s), 1 Shower(s)
Laundry: None **Pay Phones:** No
Pump-Out: OnCall, 1 Port **Fee:** n/a **Closed Heads:** Yes

Marina Operations
Owner/Manager: James E. Long **Dockmaster:** Same
In-Season: May 15-Oct 15, 8am-4:30pm **Off-Season:** Oct 15-May 14, same
After-Hours Arrival: Call ahead
Reservations: Yes **Credit Cards:** Cash only, No credit cards
Discounts: None
Pets: Welcome, Dog Walk Area **Handicap Access:** No

Watch Hill Boatyard

21 Pasadena Avenue; Watch Hill, RI 02891

Tel: (401) 348-8148 **VHF: Monitor** 9 **Talk** 8
Fax: (401) 596-4711 **Alternate Tel:** n/a
Email: n/a **Web:** www.watchhillboatyard.com
Nearest Town: Westerly *(3 mi.)* **Tourist Info:** (401) 596-7761

Marina Services and Boat Supplies
Services - Trash Pick-Up, Dock Carts **Communication -** Mail & Package Hold, FedEx, AirBorne, UPS, Express Mail **Supplies - OnSite:** Ice *(Block, Cube)* **Near:** Live Bait **1-3 mi:** Ships' Store *(Hall's Marine Supply 348-9530)* **3+ mi:** West Marine *(860-536-1455, 6 mi.)*, Boat/US *(10 mi.)*, Bait/Tackle *(Covedge Bait & Tackle 348-8888, 4 mi.)*, Propane *(Spicer Gas 596-6531, 4 mi.)*

Boatyard Services
OnSite: Crane, Launching Ramp, Rigger, Bottom Cleaning, Divers **OnCall:** Electronic Sales, Electronics Repairs, Sail Loft, Propeller Repairs, Inflatable Repairs, Upholstery, Yacht Interiors

Restaurants and Accommodations
1-3 mi: Restaurant *(Maria's Seaside Café 596-6886, D $13-29, on the ocean)*, *(Olympia Tea Room 348-8211, L $10-12, D $20-28)*, *(Windjammer 322-9283)*, *(Seaside Grille 348-6333, L $8-17, D $18-30, inside or Veranda Deck or Patio at Watch Hill Inn)*, Motel *(Breezeway Resort 348-8953, $70-230)*, *(Andrea 348-8788)*, Inn/B&B *(Pleasant View Inn 348-6300)*, *(Narragansett Inn)*, *(Watch Hill Inn 348-8200, $100-500)*

Recreation and Entertainment
1-3 mi: Beach *(Watch Hill Beach)*, Movie Theater, Video Arcade, Park, Museum *(Lighthouse Museum 860-535-1440, Marine Museum, 10 mi. 860-572-0711)*, Cultural Attract *(Flying Horse Carousel 348-6007)* **3+ mi:** Dive Shop *(Aqua Shop 348-8957, 4 mi.)*, Tennis Courts *(Pond View Racquet Club 322-1100, 4 mi.)*, Golf Course *(Elmridge Golf Course 860-599-2248, 4 mi.)*, Fitness Center *(New Attitude Fitness 348-6288, 5 mi.)*, Horseback Riding *(Rainbow Stables 860-535-3411, 5 mi.)*, Bowling *(Alley Katz 596-7474, 4 mi.)*, Video Rental *(Visual Concepts 596-9555, 3.5 mi.)*

Provisioning and General Services
Under 1 mi: Catholic Church, Protestant Church **1-3 mi:** Convenience Store *(Linda's Landing 348-8144 snacks, coffee, ATM)*, Gourmet Shop *(Fras Italian Gourmet 596-2888)*, Delicatessen *(Bay St. Deli 596-6606)*, Health Food, Bakery, Green Grocer, Fishmonger, Bank/ATM, Post Office, Beauty Salon, Dry Cleaners, Laundry, Bookstore *(Mo Books N Art 348-0940)*, Florist, Clothing Store, Retail Shops **3+ mi:** Supermarket *(Ritaccos Mkt 596-1835, 5 mi.)*, Wine/Beer *(Cove Ledge Package 599-4844, 4 mi.)*, Liquor Store *(Warehouse Beer Wine Liquor 596-6160, 4 mi.)*, Library *(Westerly 596-2877, 4 mi.)*, Pharmacy *(Brooks 596-2901, 4 mi.)*, Hardware Store *(Big M Home Center 596-0302, 4 mi.)*, Copies Etc. *(Agjo Printing 599-3143, 4 mi.)*

Transportation
OnCall: Rental Car *(Enterprise 596-7847, Thrifty 596-3441, Avis)*, Taxi *(Eagle Cab 596-7300)*, Airport Limo *(King Charles Limousine 364-9999)* **3+ mi:** InterCity Bus *(Greyhound 860-447-3841, 19 mi.)* **Airport:** Westerly/Groton New London 860-445-2824 *(5 mi/20 mi.)*

Medical Services
911 Service **OnCall:** Ambulance **1-3 mi:** Doctor *(Giancaspro 596-2230)* **3+ mi:** Dentist *(Stadelmann & Gulino 596-0337, 4 mi.)*, Chiropractor *(Antonino Clinic 860-599-5551, 4 mi.)*, Veterinarian *(Westerly Animal Hospital 596-2865, 4 mi.)* **Hospital:** Westerly 348-3346 *(3 mi.)*

Setting -- Past the entrance to Watch Hill Cove to the mouth of the Pawcatuck River (just past Green 3), Watch Hill Boatyard dominates nicely protected, small, rural Colonel Willie Cove. The views waterside are pastoral; landside they are of a well maintained boatyard.

Marina Notes -- 81 slips for boats to 50'; 27 moorings for sailboats to 40'. Full service boatyard and marina. Closest full-service boatyard to Napatree Point and the reefs off Watch Hill. Most services and provisioning resources are in either Westerly to the north or Stonington to the west. The facility is nicely maintained, very quiet and family-oriented. Staff is focused on customer service. There is plenty of parking. Enterprise and several other auto rental agencies are nearby.

Notable -- The fishing right outside the river is reportedly great - especially for flounder, fluke, bass, and blues. It's about a 1.25 mile walk to the charming little village of Watch Hill. Antique shops, upscale clothing stores, gift shops, and eateries line the main street of this affluent, storied community. The town is famous as an exclusive summer colony and for its beautiful, classic early 20thC shingle-style "cottages". Right next to the town dock is the famous Flying Horse Carousel, and beyond that is Watch Hill Beach. Walk a little bit farther to arrive at the beautifully preserved Napatree and Sandy Point Beaches with great bathing, surfing, and fishing.

PHOTOS ON CD-ROM: 5

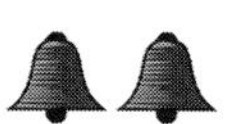

Watch Hill Docks

Bay Street; Westerly, RI 02891

Tel: (401) 596-7807 **VHF: Monitor** 16 **Talk** 9
Fax: (401) 348-6090 **Alternate Tel:** (401) 348-8005
Email: n/a **Web:** n/a
Nearest Town: Watch Hill *(0 mi.)* **Tourist Info:** (401) 596-7761

Navigational Information

Lat: 41°18.616' **Long:** 071°51.499' **Tide:** n/a **Current:** n/a **Chart:** 12372
Rep. Depths (*MLW*): Entry 7.5 ft. **Fuel Dock** n/a **Max Slip/Moor** 8 ft./-
Access: Fishers Island Sound to Sandy Point, follow Channel

Marina Facilities *(In Season/Off Season)*

Fuel: Gasoline, Diesel
Slips: 20 Total, 5 Transient **Max LOA:** 100 ft. **Max Beam:** n/a
Rate *(per ft.)*: **Day** $2.00 **Week** $14 **Month** No Discount
Power: 30 amp Incl., **50 amp** Incl., **100 amp** n/a, **200 amp** n/a
Cable TV: No **Dockside Phone:** No
Dock Type: Wood, Short Fingers, Pilings, Fixed
Moorings: 0 Total, 0 Transient **Launch:** n/a, Dinghy Dock
Rate: Day n/a **Week** n/a **Month** n/a
Heads: None
Laundry: None **Pay Phones:** Yes, 1
Pump-Out: OnCall, 1 Port **Fee:** n/a **Closed Heads:** Yes

Marina Operations

Owner/Manager: Frank Hall Boatyard **Dockmaster:** Seasonal
In-Season: MemDay-LabDay, 8am-8pm **Off-Season:** LabDay-Nov 15
After-Hours Arrival: Call in advance
Reservations: Yes **Credit Cards:** Visa/MC, Dscvr, Amex
Discounts: None
Pets: Welcome **Handicap Access:** No

Marina Services and Boat Supplies

Services - Docking Assistance, Trash Pick-Up **Communication -** FedEx, AirBorne, UPS, Express Mail **Supplies - Near:** Ice *(Cube)*, Ships' Store *(Hall's Marine Supply 348-9530)*, Bait/Tackle *(Watch Hill Fly Fishing 596-1914)* **3+ mi:** Propane *(Spicer Plus 596-6531, 6 mi.)*

Boatyard Services

OnCall: Electronic Sales, Electronics Repairs, Sail Loft, Propeller Repairs, Inflatable Repairs, Upholstery, Yacht Interiors **Under 1 mi:** Crane, Launching Ramp, Rigger, Bottom Cleaning, Divers. **Nearest Yard:** Watch Hill Boat Yard (401) 348-8148

Restaurants and Accommodations

OnCall: Pizzeria *(Watch Hill Pizza 596-3663)* **Near:** Restaurant *(Seaside Grille 348-6300, L $8-17, D $18-30, Part of Watch Hill Inn)*, *(Olympia Tea Room 348-8212, L $10-12, D $20-28, B, L, D)*, Snack Bar *(Bay Street Deli 596-6606, L $5-8)*, Coffee Shop *(St. Claire Annex 348-8407, B, L 8am-10pm ice cream)*, Lite Fare *(Café Espresso II 348-0103)*, Hotel *(Ocean House 348-8461, $125-260, Commanding Yellow Structure on the cliff as you approach)*, Inn/B&B *(Watch Hill Court 348-8273, $70-250)*, *(Watch Hill Inn 348-8200, $85-220)*

Recreation and Entertainment

OnSite: Beach *(Watch Hill Beach - right behind the carousel and Ocean House Beach, in front of Ocean House Hotel - right of way off Bluff Avenue)*, Cultural Attract *(Flying Horse Carousel 348-6007 $1 children only)* **Near:** Jogging Paths, Boat Rentals, Fishing Charter, Park, Museum *(Watch Hill Lighthouse Museum Tue & Thu, 1-3pm, Jul-Aug)* **1-3 mi:** Tennis Courts *(Pond View Racquet Club 322-1100)* **3+ mi:** Dive Shop *(Aqua Shop 348-8957, 4 mi.)*, Golf Course *(Weekapaug Golf Club 322-7870 , 5 mi.)*, Horseback Riding *(Manatuck Stables 860-535-3199, 5 mi.)*

Provisioning and General Services

Near: Convenience Store *(The Galley 348-8998, Linda's Landing 348-8144 snacks, coffee, ATM)*, Delicatessen *(Bay Street Deli 596-6606)*, Clothing Store, Retail Shops **Under 1 mi:** Bookstore *(Book & Tackle Shop 596-0700, note no tackle! Mo Books N Art 348-0940)* **3+ mi:** Supermarket *(Stop & Shop 599-2433, 6 mi.)*, Health Food *(Nutrition Connection 596-0117, 5 mi.)*, Liquor Store *(Warehouse-Beer Wine Liquor 596-6160, 5 mi.)*, Fishmonger *(McQuades 596-3474, 5 mi.)*, Catholic Church *(5 mi.)*, Protestant Church *(5 mi.)*, Library *(Westerly 596-2877, 4 mi.)*, Pharmacy *(CVS 348-2070 , 5 mi.)*, Hardware Store *(McQuade's Ace Home Center 596-0302, 5 mi.)*

Transportation

OnCall: Rental Car *(Enterprise 596-7847)*, Taxi *(Eagle Cab 596-7300 from Westerly)* **Airport:** Westerly State Airport 596-2357 *(5 mi.)*

Medical Services

911 Service **OnCall:** Ambulance **3+ mi:** Doctor *(Seaside Internal Medicine 596-0328, 5 mi.)*, Chiropractor *(Antonino Clinic 860-599-5551 , 5 mi.)*
Hospital: Westerly Hospital 348-3346 *(5 mi.)*

Setting -- Just past Watch Hill Yacht Club, this town facility is tucked into small, protected Watch Hill Cove -- in the heart of this pretty, Victorian, very affluent resort community. The cove is filled with classic yachts and vintage, beautifully restored sailboats along with more contemporary vessels. Ashore, the lanes are lined with large, impeccably maintained 19thC shingle-style and Queen Anne summer "cottages". Major services are in either Stonington or Westerly.

Marina Notes -- Deposit required with reservation. No landside services to speak of -- except, of course, charming Watch Hill. The town dinghy dock is available, free, to anchored boats. The Watch Hill Yacht Club, also in Watch Hill Cove, has several transient moorings available to members of reciprocating yacht clubs 596-4986, Ch.10. The street side of their floats is available for dinghy tie-up by transients using Club moorings.

Notable -- Watch Hill is quite small and very accessible; the main street is about 4/10 mile long and lined with some interesting clothing shops, boutiques, antique shops, galleries, and eateries. Virtually onsite is the famous Flying Horse Carousel; each horse, hand carved from a single block of wood, is beautifully embellished with a leather saddle, a horse-hair mane and agate eyes. Jun15-LabDay, 1-9pm. children only. The Watch Hill Inn, built in 1845, is a block's walk. Its restaurant has 3 dining options - Main Inside Dining room plus, overlooking the Harbor, the Veranda & the Patio Deck. The Watch Hill Lighthouse, at the east entrance to Fisher's Island Sound, was originally built in 1808, then replaced in 1856 with the white brick and granite tower. Spectacularly beautiful Napatree Beach is an easy walk or dinghy ride (absolutely no dogs!). At the Point is Fort Mansfield, built for the Spanish American War.

Recommended Reading List

SPECIFIC REGIONAL CRUISING GUIDES

Cruising Guide to the New England Coast: Including the Hudson River, L. I. Sound, & the Coast of New Brunswick — 12th Edition by Robert C. Duncan, W. Wallace Fenn, Paul W. Fenn, Roger S. Duncan
The original cruising guide to New England — written by four generations of cruisers over half a century — just updated again. An uncompromising, highly detailed, very complete editorial work, it integrates a bit of maritime history into every harbor description. An absolute must-have.

Northern Waterway Guide by Waterway Publishing
Comprehensive coverage — New Jersey through the Canadian Maritimes, extremely thorough and complete, updated annually — just keeps getting bigger and better — contains extensive advertisements.

A Cruising Guide to the Maine Coast — 4th Edition, by Hank Taft, Jan B. Taft, Curtis Rindlaub — www.mainecoastguides.com
The best and most complete cruising guide to Maine, updated again by its new co-author. An objective, thorough, advertising-free editorial work that delivers the critical information and also captures the essence of the experience. If you're headed Downeast, don't leave home without it.

Maptech's Embassy Guide — Maine Coast — 1st Edition
Helpful and useful with a double-page for every harbor with well-done charts and good harbor info — includes advertisements.

Cruising Guides to Maine: Kittery to Rockland by Don Johnson
Cruising Guides to Maine: Rockport to Eastport by Don Johnson
Both excellent editorial books that cover every harbor in depth (1994).

Maptech's Embassy Guide to Massachusetts, Rhode Island and New Hampshire — 8th Edition
Comprehensive, detailed and very useful with a multi-page spread for every harbor with nicely executed charts — includes advertisements.

A Cruising Guide to Narragansett Bay and the South Coast of Massachusetts: Including Buzzards Bay, Nantucket, Martha's Vineyard, and Block Island by Lynda Morris Childress &Tina Martin
Complete and very helpful editorial work circa 1995 that covers the Narragansett Bay region with more detail than any other guide.

GENERAL CRUISING GUIDES

Voyaging Under Power by Robert Beebe
A little dated, but it's still filled with important and useful information.

Nigel Calder's Cruising Handbook by Nigel Calder
From the basics for a coastal cruise to readying for an off shore passage, this is a good place to start.

Stapleton's Powerboat Bible: The Complete Guide to Selection, Seamanship, and Cruising by Sid Stapleton
Comprehensive and current, it's written for larger, cruising powerboats.

Cruising for Cowards — 2nd Edition by Liza & Andy Copeland
A terrific "how-to" guide to cruising applicable to any destination - 'round the world or 'round the bay; it's funny and filled with details and great information. ***Just Cruising*** *and* ***Still Cruising*** *continue the adventure.*

Voyager's Handbook: the Essential Guide to Blue Water Cruising by Beth Leonard
Lots of really useful information even for planning a coastal cruise.

Comfortable Cruising Around North & Central America by Liza Copeland
A cruising guide to destinations that don't require ocean crossings; the sections on the North American seaboard will be of particular interest.

Sail Book of Common Sense Cruising by Patience Wales
A collection of interesting articles from Sail Magazine.

The Perfect First Mate by Joy Smith
Provisioning and organizing for comfort afloat

PROVISIONING GUIDES

All wonderful and full of great ideas — you can't have too many cookbooks — at home or afloat ...

The Cruising Chef Cookbook by Michael Greenwald
Thorough and practical for a weeklong cruise or an ocean voyage.

Cruising Cuisine: Fresh Food from the Galley by Kay Pastorius
Lots of really good recipes.

Dining on Deck: Fine Foods for Sailing & Boating by Linda Vail
Encourages a little style and panache at anchor.

Feasts Afloat: 150 Recipes for Great Meals from Small Spaces by Jennifer Trainer Thompson, Elizabeth Wheeler
An earlier version was called ***The Yachting Cookbook*** *and it was a long-time favorite of many cruisers.*

The Care and Feeding of Sailing Crew by Lin Pardey, Larry Pardey
A true classic — a comprehensive guide to preparing and managing a "cruising galley" — there's lots that we'd never think of on our own.

Cooking Under Pressure by Lorna J. Sass
Teaches the basics and the sophisticated possibilities of pressure cooking — one of the best methods of cooking under way.

Guilt Free Gourmet by megayacht chef Sam Miles
Over 1200 low-fat recipes in one easily stowable volume — get the ***70 Days of Menus*** *companion pamphlet, too. Tons of easy, creative ideas.*

USEFUL NEW ENGLAND TRAVEL GUIDES

The Coast of New England: A Pictorial Tour from Connecticut to Maine by Stan Patey

Smithsonian's Northern New England — 4th Edition by Vance Muse, Paul Rocheleau, Donald Young

Lonely Planet — New England — 3rd Edition by Randall, Peffer, Kim Grant, Andrew Rebold, John Spelman
A very good general guide to all of New England. A favorite.

Insight Guide / New England — 7th Edition by Susan Gordon

The Rough Guide to New England — 2nd Edition by David Tarr

Mobil's New England - Eastern Canada by Exxon Mobil Travel
A quick annual overview with emphasis on restaurants & lodgings.

Where Should We Take the Kids? — 3rd Edition by Elin McCoy
Northeast, activity-centered reviews of kid friendly places that intrigue and capture imaginations – many along the coast are easily reachable.

Great Outdoor Guide to Southern New England by Peter Oliver

Smithsonian Southern New England by Henry Wiencek

Moon Handbooks Coastal Maine by Kathleen M. Brandes
The best and most complete travel guide to the Maine coast.

The Rockbound Coast: Travels in Maine by Christopher Little
Spectacular photographs that compel a Downeast cruise.

Maine off the Beaten Path — 5th Edition by Wayne Curtis

Longstreet Highroad Guide to Maine Coast by Elizabeth Edwardsen

Frommer's Portable Maine Coast by Wayne Curtis

The Coast of Maine Book: A Complete Guide — 4th Edition by Rick Ackermann, Kathryn Buxton

Maine Lighthouses: A Pictorial Guide by Courtney Thompson

Maine Lighthouses Map & Guide by Robert Hartnett, Peter Dow Bachelder

Compass American Guides: Maine by Charles C. Calhoun, Patricia Harris, David Lyon, Thomas Mark Szelog

Maine: An Explorer's Guide — 10th Edition by Christina Tree, Elizabeth Roundy Richards, Kimberly Grant

Massachusetts: Off the Beaten Path — 4th Edition by Barbara Radcliffe Rogers & Stillman Rogers

Travellers Boston and New England (Thomas Cook) by Robert Holmes

Lonely Planet Boston: Condensed by Tom Given

Insight Guide to Boston by Christopher Kenneally, Natasha Babaian

National Geographic Traveler Boston & Environs: With Cape, Providence & Newport by Paul Wade, Kathy Arnold

Cape Cod, Martha's Vineyard & Nantucket by Kim Grant
A very detailed tome with good coverage and a little personality.

Short Bike Rides in Cape Cod, Nantucket & the Vineyard — 7th Edition by Edwin Mullen, Jane Griffith

Land's End: A Walk Through Provincetown by Michael Cunningham

Guide to Martha's Vineyard by Polly Burroughs

Rhode Island: An Explorer's Guide — 3rd Edition by Phyllis Meras, Tom Gannon

The Rhode Island Guide by Barbara Radcliffe Rogers, Stillman D. Rogers

A Guide To Newport's Cliff Walk by Ed Morris

NEW ENGLAND HISTORY and CULTURAL PERSPECTIVES

For rainy days and long passages ...

Writing New England: An Anthology from the Puritans to the Present by Andrew Delbanco

Coastal Maine: A Maritime History by Roger F. Duncan
A wonderful introduction to Maine from a nautical perspective.

The Great New England Sea Serpent: An Account of Unknown Creatures Sighted by Many Respectable Persons Between 1638 and the Present Day by J. P. O'Neill

Ducktrap: Chronicles of a Maine Village by Diane Roesing O'Brien
Covers the Islesboro, Lincolnville, Camden area.

The Maine Reader: The Down East Experience, 1614 to the Present by Charles Shain, Samuella Shain

Maine: Where America Really Began by Bill Caldwell

Islands of the Mid-Maine Coast: Penobscot Bay by Charles B. McLane, Carol Evarts McLane

Islands in Time: A Natural and Cultural History of the Islands of the Gulf of Maine by Philip W. Conkling

The Lobster Chronicles: Life on a Very Small Island by Linda Greenlaw
An inspiring essay and interesting follow-up to The Hungry Ocean — especially if Isle au Haut is on your itinerary.

The Perfect Storm by Sebastian Junger
Stop in Gloucester for the "Perfect Storm" walking tour.

Salem-Village Witchcraft: A Documentary Record of Local Conflict in Colonial New England by Paul Boyer, Stephen Nissenbaum

My World Is an Island by Elisabeth Ogilvie

Cape Cod by Henry David Thoreau

The Enduring Shore: A History of Cape Cod, Martha's Vineyard, and Nantucket by Paul Schneider

The Outermost House: A Year of Life on the Great Beach of Cape Cod by Henry Beston

Gift from the Sea by Anne Morrow Lindbergh

CHILDREN'S BOOKS — PRE-SCHOOL

Boats by Jan Pienkowski

Boo and Baa at Sea by Olof Landstrom, Lena Landstrom

Counting Our Way to Maine by Maggie Smith

L is for Lobster — A Maine Alphabet by Cynthia Furlong Reynolds, Jeannie Brett (Illustrator)

Little Toot and the Lighthouse by Linda Gramatky-Smith

One Little, Two Little, Three Little Pilgrims by B. G. Hennessy

CHILDREN'S BOOKS — AGES 4 – 8

The Boat Alphabet Book by Jerry Pallotta

Nellie the Lighthouse Dog by Jane Scarpino Robert Ensor, Jane Weinberger

Mabel Takes a Sail by Emily Chetkowski

Newberry: The Life and Times of a Maine Clam by Marie Litterer, Vincent G. Dethier

One Morning in Maine by Robert McCloskey
If you're planning to stop at Bucks Harbor Marine in Brooksville, Maine — you can take the kids to see the places McCloskey wrote about.

Keep the Lights Burning, Abbie by Connie Roop, Peter Geiger Roop

Birdie's Lighthouse by Deborah Hopkinson

Rebecca of Sunnybrook Farm by Kate Douglas Smith Wiggin

Journey Around Boston From A to Z by Martha Day Zschock

Witch Hunt: It Happened in Salem Village by Stephen Krensky

Boston Tea Party by Pamela Duncan Edwards

Journey Around Boston From A to Z by Martha Day Zschock

The Orphan Seal by Fran Hodgkins
A wonderful true story centered at the Boston Aquarium.

Nickommoh : A Thanksgiving Celebration by Jackie French Koller

Three Young Pilgrims by Cheryl Harness

On the Mayflower: Voyage of the Ship's Apprentice and a Passenger Girl by Kate Waters

The Rhode Island Colony by Bob Italia

The Big Rhode Island Reproducible Activity Book by Carole Marsh, Kathy Zimmer

CHILDREN'S BOOKS — AGES 9 – 12

Boat — an Eyewitness Book by Eric Kentley

Into the Wind: Sailboats Then and Now by Steven Otfinoski

Schooner by Pat Lowery Collins

The Call of the Running Tide: A Portrait of an Island Family by Nancy Price Graff
An engaging introduction to Swan's Island, ME and Burnt Coat Harbor.

Maine: A Year of Wicked Good Poetry by Robert Pottle

Lobsters: Gangsters of the Sea by Jeffrey L. Rotman, Mary M. Cerullo

Bigfoot Stalks the Coast of Maine and other Twisted Downeast Tales by Thomas A. Easton

A Seal Called Andre by Harry Goodridge, Lew Dietz
A true and touching story by a former Rockport, ME harbormaster.

Mystery in Massachusetts by Bob Schaller

The Witchcraft of Salem Village by Shirley Jackson

A Break with Charity: the Salem Witch Trials by Ann Rinaldi

Casey and the Boston Freedom Trail by Jane Sarah Staffier

The Big Dig: Reshaping an American City by Peter Vanderwarker

The Trouble with Tea by Jeanette E. Alsheimer, Patricia J. Friedle

Daily Life in the Pilgrim Colony 1636 by Paul Erickson

N.C. Wyeth's Pilgrims by Robert D. San Souci

The Journal of Jasper Jonathan Pierce: Pilgrim Boy by Ann Rinaldi

Roger Williams by Amy Allison

Rhode Island Facts and Factivities by Carole Marsh

Little Maid of Narragansett Bay by Alice Turner Curtis

The Scrimshaw Ring by William Jaspersohn

Pump-Out

Each state, and its communities, continues to grapple with the issues of harbor clean-up, no discharge zones, and pump-out services. Some states are underwriting the construction of pump-out facilities and then requiring that these be made available to all comers at affordable rates. Other states are simply creating no discharge zones and leaving it up to the marina operators to provide the required mechanisms. This leads to a wide variety of services, facilities and rates. In committed communities, pump-out boats ply the waters and the services are usually free (tip appreciated!). In areas where facilities have been underwritten, the services are frequently land-based, the charges are nominal, often $5, and "self-service" is the rule. In areas where it's left up to the marinas, the quality and costs vary widely. Ecologically committed facilities will often charge very modest fees, take responsibility for the proper functioning of their systems, and will graciously assist with full-service pump-out. Others will charge outrageous fees — sometimes well over $25, their hours will be inconvenient, and their systems will be frequently "out of order."

We have tried to be as specific as possible on this point, but beware! Call ahead to confirm the rate, the operating hours and the current "availability" of the pump-out system. If it isn't working or the hours are ridiculous or the rate is exorbitant, perhaps you might consider another facility and let both marina managers know why you have made that choice. To be honest, pump-out is "nasty." No one wants to do it, neither the marinas nor the cruisers. But it is very important, especially in crowded harbors. The only way that it will become standard operating procedure for everyone is to make it easily available, relatively simple and inexpensive.

- **Federal Law:** According to the Environmental Protection Agency, a "'No Discharge Area' is a designated body of water that prohibits the discharge of treated and untreated boat sewage. Federal Law prohibits the discharge of untreated sewage from vessels within all navigable waters of the U.S., which include territorial seas within three miles of shore. Boats with Type I and Type II Marine Sanitation Devices may discharge treated effluent in coastal waters UNLESS they are in a 'No Discharge Area.'" For more information, contact the EPA (617) 918-1538.
- **Maine:** As of this publication date, the state of Maine does not have any "No Discharge Areas." However, individual towns and harbors have made local determinations. ACC has attempted to alert cruisers to those particular harbors that are very concerned about discharge and have listed facilities in those areas as "Closed Heads." Those harbor towns are also the most progressive in providing pump-out boats and facilities.
- **New Hampshire:** As of this publication date, the state of New Hampshire has designated only fresh water in-land lakes as "No Discharge Areas." Coastal towns and facilities are making these decisions on their own.
- **Massachusetts:** As of this publication date, the state of Massachusetts has designated the following areas "No Discharge": Buzzards Bay (from Gosnold in the east to Westport in the west), Waquoit Bay (Falmouth), Barnstable, Westport Harbor, Wareham Harbor, Harwich, Chatham (Stage Harbor Complex), Wellfleet and Nantucket.
- **Rhode Island:** As of 1998, the state of Rhode Island designated all of its marine waters as "No Discharge Areas." According to the EPA, as of the date of this publication, RI has 43 pump-out facilities, with more on the way.

Wi-Fi Wireless Broadband Network Services

The ability to access both the web and email, while cruising, has become increasingly important to many boaters. Marinas, and their surrounding communities, are providing a variety of solutions — some more useful than others. As noted earlier, each Marina Report details the existence and location of dataports — either at the marina or its environs, and also notes the availability of Wi-Fi — potentially the most useful solution to the access problem. Wi-Fi, or Wireless Fidelity, allows you to connect to the Internet from a bunk on your boat (or anywhere else). It's a wireless technology that can send and receive data indoors and out; anywhere within the range of a base station (called "hotspots"). It's fast, faster than most cable modem connections. And it doesn't require an expensive and cumbersome installation like a satellite dish.

To access a commercial Wi-Fi broadband system, one needs a portable, PC card or built-in wireless modem that operates on the chosen network, a computer (laptop, handheld, or PDA type device), and a subscription to the commercial wireless network that hosts the "hotspots" you've identified. Unfortunately, there are many providers, and they are not all working together — but cooperation is inevitable if the industry is to survive. LinkSys (recently acquired by Cisco) is the most popular PC-Card Wi-Fi modem brand; fortunately, unlike the providers, all Wi-Fi hardware is compatible.

Increasingly, larger marinas are installing Wi-Fi (currently 802.11) wireless systems. While this is a tremendous convenience and advantage, it's still quite new and marinas are handling delivery of the service in a variety of ways. Most are sub-contracting the installation to the subscription provider, which deals directly with the boater, while others are offering free system access. Log-on procedures vary widely, too. Some marinas, or their sub-contractor, even have Wi-Fi PC cards available for nightly rental for those who don't have either a PC card or internal card.

Since the requisite PC cards (or internal cards) are relatively inexpensive (under $50), buying your own, even if you don't have a wireless network elsewhere, could make sense. According to Business Week, in 2003, 35% of laptops are shipping Wi-Fi ready and by 2005 that will jump to 90%. (Currently all Dell laptops and 70% of HP laptops ship Wi-Fi ready.) Airports, hotels, coffee shops, like Starbucks, and other public spaces are also installing these systems. Maine, for instance, has recently contracted for the installation of free Wi-Fi access points in 40 libraries. And, if you travel with more than one computer onboard, a Wi-Fi base station on the boat is a simple and inexpensive way to create a private network to share files and Internet access. FYI: Windows XP makes Wi-Fi installation a breeze.

Beacon Wi-Fi Technologies (www.beaconwifi.com) and Telesea (www.teleseawireless.net) are leading providers of Wi-Fi hotspots to marinas on the East Coast. Marinas are notoriously slow adapters of new technologies — witness the remarkable number or marinas in this book with neither email addresses nor a website. In the Northeast, the Brewer chain is, once again, leading the pack and is planning a trial as we go to press; Beacon is installing the system. Beacon's rates are $39.95 for a 6 month seasonal contract, $29.95 for an annual contract or $19.95 for 3 days of access including a pc card rental. Right now, the majority of marinas with Wi-Fi access tend to be in Florida — but it is just beginning.

If the marina you've selected doesn't have a Wi-Fi system check out the local coffee houses and hotels. A search on www.80211hotspots.com, www.ezgoal.com/hotspots, or www.wifinder.com will help in locating Wi-Fi access points or use "Wi-Fi Sniffer" software to track down commercial, private or free networks in the area. There are currently several large commercial Wi-Fi networks, including Toshiba, Boingo, VoiceStream, and Cometa. T-Mobile is one of the largest hot-spot providers with almost 2500 Starbucks and airport lounges at press time. Their rates are $29.99/month on a yearly basis; or monthly ($39.99) and pay-as-you-go ($2.99 for the first 15 minutes, then $.10 cents for each additional minute). Hotels are another source; Wayport has wired over 500 hotspots (options include $7/session, prepaid cards $25/3 sessions, or $30-50/mo.) and Boingo has wired over 1,200 (at $8/day, $25/mo. for 10 days, or $50/mo. unlimited use). Even McDonald's promises Wi-Fi for $3 an hour and Borders is wiring 400 stores. Everyone's numbers are growing daily and rates are constantly adjusting to market pressures.

Deciphering the Marine Industry Alphabets and Certifications

There are a number of trade organizations that assist the professional boating industry. They each serve a variety of purposes — some of greater interest to the boating services consumer than others. But knowledge is power, so we have listed the most prevalent ones — preceded by the initials by which each is known.

In addition to the certifications provided by the manufacturers, there are several marine industry certifications. They are listed below as part of the description of their sponsoring organization. Facilities' memberships in these organizations, as well as the number of on-site employees which have been certified by each, is included under "Boatyard Services" in the Marina Reports — if we are aware of them. We have focused more specifically on ABBRA and ABYC as these relate directly to technicians who may work on your boat. It is, however, quite possible that a facility may hold these, or other, certifications but did not, for a variety of reasons, relay that information to ACC. Exactly what is required to achieve each of these certifications is generally disclosed on the organization's website. In a number of cases, certification programs are offered jointly by two of these organizations. If such certifications are a deciding factor in choosing a marina or boatyard, it might be helpful to inquire.

- **ABBRA** is the American Boat Builders & Repairers Association located in Warren, Rhode Island — 401-247-0318 www.abbra.org. ABBRA is a 250-member network of boatyards, repairers and associated industries that, among other functions, trains its members' management and employee craftsmen. It offers a series of Technician certificate programs (fiberglass, bottom paint, basic and advanced diesel repair) and management training programs.

- **ABYC** is the American Boat and Yacht Council in Edgewater, Maryland — 410-956-1050 www.abycinc.org. ABYC develops the consensus safety standards for the design, construction, equipage, maintenance, and repair of small craft. It offers a variety of workshops, seminars and a Marine Technician Certification program.

- **IMI** is the International Marina Institute in Jupiter, Florida — 561-741-0626 www.imimarina.org. IMI is a non-profit membership marine trade organization which offers management training, education and information about research, legislation and environmental issues affecting the marina industry. It offers a variety of workshops, training and certifications in marina management and equipment operations — particularly the Certified Marina Manager Program.

- **NMMA** is the National Marine Manufacturers' Association in Chicago, Illinois — 312-946-6200 www.nmma.org. NMMA is the primary trade organization for producers of products used by recreational boaters. It devotes its resources to public policy advocacy, promoting boating as a lifestyle, enhancing the consumer experience, education and training, and building partnerships and strategic alliances. To serve the needs of its 1400 members, NMMA provides a variety of programs and services related to technical expertise (some include certification), standards monitoring, government relations avocation, and industry statistics. They also produce recreational boat shows in key North American markets and two trade shows, BoatBuilding and Marine Aftermarket Accessories. NMMA certifications that would be of most interest are the Yacht and Boat Certification Programs (based on ABYC guidelines) that help manufacturers comply with established standards and safety regulations. (To obtain a Yacht Certification, all components used must be on the NMMA "Type Accepted" list.)

- **MOAA** is the Marina Operators' Association of America in Washington, DC — 866-367-6622 www.moaa.com. MOAA is the national trade association of the marina industry. It represents over 950 marinas, boatyards, yacht clubs, and public/private moorage basins across the United States. These companies provide slip space for over 240,000 recreational watercraft and employment for over 13,000 marine tradesmen and women. Suppliers of equipment and services to this industry complete MOAA's membership. Their mission is to provide critical legislative and regulatory support, serve as a communication base and to offer practical, money saving programs.

Alphabetical Listing of Marinas, Harbors and Cities

About the Authors: Beth and Richard Smith

Richard and Beth have been "messing about in boats" at various times throughout their lives, individually and together. The last two decades have seen a move up to "big boats." Coastal cruises have included numerous trips up and down the Eastern seaboard including the ICW — where they've perfected the art of "achievable cruising" — a one or two week cruise, leave the boat, go home, and come back two weeks or a month or two later. Other cruising adventures have taken them to Bermuda, the Bahamas, the Caribbean, the South Pacific and the Mediterranean. They have shared many of these experiences with three superb crewmembers — their now-grown children, Jason and Amanda, and their sea-dog, Molly. They are firm believers in "going" even if it means taking the office along. Technology has made that not only possible, but amazingly easy. Even their boat is networked. They are also committed to wonderful food along the way — on board and ashore. Provisioning, they've discovered, may be the most entertaining and useful of all cruising skills (bested, perhaps, only by sail trim, engine mechanics and a clear understanding of navigation) and they seek out the best resources at every landfall. Along the way, they've also visited more than 1500 marinas on the East coast as both cruisers and authors.

ELIZABETH ADAMS SMITH

Elizabeth Adams Smith, Ed.D., is Editor-in-Chief of Jerawyn Publishing, Inc. (JPI) and one of the primary writer/photographers of the *Guides to Marinas*. She is also a new media designer/producer focused on developing electronic methods of delivering large quantities of unique information in ways that are readily understood and manipulated.

In addition to her marine-oriented publishing work (nurturing the growth of the *Atlantic Cruising Club's Guides to Marinas* and incubating the Coastal Communities and Wandering Mariner series), she has produced video documentaries and multiple media projects in the areas of complementary and integrative medicine, holistic living, ecology, peace-making, technology, and food and health (including the award-winning "Children of War," the Mellon-funded "Students at Work," and "EarthFriends"). She created and developed the first, and largest, full-text and image database on complementary medicine, "Alt-HealthWatch," and is an advisor/consultant to firms focused on healthy living and integrative medicine.

Beth received a Doctorate from Columbia University in Educational Technology and New Media, Masters degrees in both Health Education (with a Nutrition focus) and Ed Tech from Columbia, and a B.S. in Broadcast Journalism from Boston University. She is a Certified Health Education Specialist and a graduate of James Gordon's Advanced Mind-Body Professional Training Program and the Natural Gourmet Institute for Food and Health. She is also Past President of the Board of Trustees of Wainwright House, an educational institution focusing on the integration of body, mind and spirit, a former Trustee of the Rye Free Reading Room, a Director of the International Tibetan Medical Association and is a member of the International Food, Wine and Travel Writers Association and Boating Writers International.

RICHARD Y. SMITH

Richard Y. Smith is Publisher of Jerawyn Publishing Inc. and President of Evergreen Capital Partners Inc. JPI is an umbrella company for the Atlantic Cruising Club and other publishing imprints. In addition to marine facilities, JPI focuses on coastal lifestyles, maritime-oriented travel and holistic living. JPI's activities involve data collection and publication using Datastract™, a proprietary data input and publishing program that permits the creation, maintenance, and direct publication of extensive databases of both factual and editorial information.

Evergreen Capital Partners Inc. undertakes merchant banking and private capital transactions both as an advisor and as a principal. As an advisor, the firm offers private financing, merger, acquisition, and divestiture advice to managements, directors, private investors, and institutional funds. As a principal, Evergreen Capital invests its own funds, often in conjunction with other individual or institutional private equity investors.

Prior to establishing Evergreen Capital in 1993, Richard was a Managing Director of Chemical Bank (now JP Morgan Chase) with responsibility for several investment and merchant banking groups. He was also a Senior Vice President of Rothschild Inc., an investment banking, venture capital, and money management firm. Richard received a B. A. degree from Wesleyan University and an M.B.A. from Harvard Business School. He has also been awarded the Chartered Financial Analyst (CFA) designation. When not reviewing marinas, editing books, attempting to close private equity deals, or out sailing, Richard is active in a number of not-for-profit activities including service as a former Chair of the Rye Arts Center, Inc., Past Chair of the Wesleyan (University) Annual Fund, current Fleet Captain of the American Yacht Club, and, occasionally, bass player in the venerable 60's rock 'n' roll band, "Gary and the Wombats."

Order Form

Please ask for the *Guides* at your local book store or order directly.

☐ **Please register me as a member of the Atlantic Cruising Club**

☐ **Please send me the following 7th Edition *Atlantic Cruising Club's Guides to Marinas — as soon each is available.***
Each Book, with bound-in CD-ROM, is US $24.95 (CN $34.95*)*

***Quantity Discounts Available** *(Titles may be mixed for maximum discount)*
For orders of 2 books or more, deduct 10% — 4 books or more, deduct 17% — 6 books or more, deduct 25%. *For larger quantities, please contact ACC*

____ ***Atlantic Cruising Club's Guide to New England Marinas***
Bar Harbor, ME to Block Island, RI *(Including Buzzards Bay, Narragansett Bay, Martha's Vineyard and Nantucket)*

____ ***Atlantic Cruising Club's Guide to Long Island Sound Marinas***
Block Island, RI to Cape May, NJ *(Including Connecticut River, New York Harbor and New Jersey Shore)*

____ ***Atlantic Cruising Club's Guide to Chesapeake Bay Marinas***
Cape May, NJ to Hampton Roads, VA *(Including C&D Canal and the Delmarva Peninsula)*

____ ***Atlantic Cruising Club's Guide to Mid-Atlantic Marinas***
Hampton Roads, VA to St. Mary's GA *(Including the Virginia Coast, the ICW, Bermuda and the North Carolina Sounds)*

____ ***Atlantic Cruising Club's Guide to Florida East Coast Marinas***
Fernandina, FL to Key West FL *(Including St. John's River and the Florida Keys)*

____ ***Atlantic Cruising Club's Guide to Gulf Coast Marinas***
Key West, FL to Padre Island, TX *(Including the West Coast ICW and Mobile Bay)*

______ *Sub-Total x US $24.95 (CN $34.95)*
______ *Quantity Discount Percentage (see above)**
______ *Tax (New York State Residents only add 6.75%)*
______ *Shipping & Handling (USPS — add $4.00 for first book and $2.00 for each subsequent book)*

Final Total *Note: Credit cards will not be charged until books are shipped.*

Please Charge the following Credit Card: Amex ☐ MasterCard ☐ Visa ☐ Discover ☐ Check Enclosed ☐

Number: ______ *Amex Four-Digit Number:* ______
Expiration Date: ______ *Signature:* ______

Name: ______ *Email:* ______
Address: ______ *City:* ______ *State or Province:* ______ *Zip:* ______
Home Phone: ______ *Office Phone:* ______ *Fax:* ______

Boat Name: ______ *Length:* ______ *Manufacturer:* ______
Boat Type: Sail Mono-Hull ☐ Sail Multi-Hull ☐ Power ☐ Trawler ☐ Megayacht ☐
Home Port: ______ *Cruising Grounds:* ______

Please mail, fax. email, or call-in your order to:
Atlantic Cruising Club at Jerawyn Publishing, Inc.
PO Box 978; Rye, New York 10580
Tel: 914-967-0994 or 888-967-0994; Fax: 914-967-5504
Email: Orders@AtlanticCruisingClub.com